Contemporary Authors®

Contemporary Authors
was named an
"Outstanding
Reference Source" *by*
the American Library
Association Reference
and Adult Services
Division after its 1962
inception.
In 1985 it was listed by
the same organization
as one of the
twenty-five most
distinguished reference
titles published in the
past twenty-five years.

Contemporary Authors®

A Bio-Bibliographical Guide to
Current Writers in Fiction, General Nonfiction,
Poetry, Journalism, Drama, Motion Pictures,
Television, and Other Fields

DONNA OLENDORF
Editor

volume **140**

 Gale Research Inc. • DETROIT • WASHINGTON, D.C. • LONDON

STAFF

Donna Olendorf, *Editor, Original Volumes*

Joanna Brod, Kathleen J. Edgar, Marie Ellavich, David M. Galens, Denise E. Kasinec, Mark F. Mikula,
Michelle M. Motowski, and Polly A. Vedder, *Associate Editors*

Michele Emerick, Jeff Hill, Jane M. Kelly, Scot Peacock, Aarti D. Stephens, Linda Tidrick,
and Roger M. Valade III, *Assistant Editors*

Arlene True, *Sketchwriter*
Jean W. Ross, *Interviewer*

Sonia Benson, Debra G. Darnell, Pamela S. Dear, Susan M. Reicha, Mary K. Ruby, Bryan Ryan,
Les Stone, and Elizabeth Wenning, *Contributing Editors*

Thomas Wiloch, *Index Coordinator*

James G. Lesniak, *Senior Editor, Contemporary Authors*

Victoria B. Cariappa, *Research Manager*
Mary Rose Bonk, *Research Supervisor*
Reginald A. Carlton, Clare Collins, Andrew Guy Malonis, and Norma Sawaya, *Editorial Associates*
Rachel A. Dixon, Eva Marie Felts, Shirley Gates, and Sharon McGilvray, *Editorial Assistants*

Arthur Chartow, *Art Director*
C. J. Jonik, *Keyliner*

∞ ™ The paper used in this publication meets the minimum requirements of
American National Standard for Information Sciences—Permanence
Paper for Printed Library Materials, ANSI Z39.48-1984.

Library of Congress Catalog Card Number 62-52046
ISBN 0-8103-1971-3
ISSN 0010-7468

Printed in the United States of America.

Published simultaneously in the United Kingdom
by Gale Research International Limited
(An affiliated company of Gale Research Inc.)

I(T)P™

The trademark **ITP** is used under license.
10 9 8 7 6 5 4 3 2 1

Contents

Indexing note: All *Contemporary Authors* entries are indexed in the *Contemporary Authors* cumulative index, which is published separately and distributed with even-numbered *Contemporary Authors* original volumes and odd-numbered *Contemporary Authors New Revision Series* volumes.

As always, the most recent *Contemporary Authors* cumulative index continues to be the user's guide to the location of an individual author's listing.

Preface

Contemporary Authors (*CA*) provides information on more than 96,000 writers in a wide range of media, including:

- Current writers of fiction, nonfiction, poetry, and drama whose works have been issued by commercial, risk publishers, or university presses (authors whose books have been published only by known vanity or author-subsidized firms are ordinarily not included)

- Prominent print and broadcast journalists, editors, photojournalists, syndicated cartoonists, screenwriters, television scriptwriters, and other media people

- Authors who write in languages other than English, provided their works have been published in the United States or translated into English

- Literary greats of the early twentieth century whose works are popular in today's high school and college curriculums and continue to elicit critical attention

A *CA* listing entails no charge or obligation. Authors are included on the basis of the above criteria and their interest to *CA* users. Sources of potential listees include trade periodicals, publisher's catalogs, librarians, and other users.

How to Get the Most out of *CA*: Use the Index

The key to locating an author's entry is the *CA* cumulative index. It provides access to *all* entries in *CA* and *Contemporary Authors New Revision Series* (*CANR*), which contains completely updated versions of only those *CA* sketches requiring significant change. The index is published separately and distributed with even-numbered *CA* volumes and odd-numbered *CANR* volumes. Always consult the latest index to find an author's most recent entry.

For the convenience of users, the *CA* cumulative index also includes references to all entries in these Gale literary series: *Authors and Artists for Young Adults, Authors in the News, Bestsellers, Black Literature Criticism, Black Writers, Children's Literature Review, Classical and Medieval Literature Criticism, Concise Dictionary of American Literary Biography, Concise Dictionary of British Literary Biography, Contemporary Authors Autobiography Series, Contemporary Authors Bibliographical Series, Contemporary Literary Criticism, Dictionary of Literary Biography, Drama Criticism, Hispanic Writers, Literature Criticism from 1400 to 1800, Major Authors and Illustrators for Children and Young Adults, Major 20th-Century Writers, Nineteenth-Century Literature Criticism, Poetry Criticism, Short Story Criticism, Something about the Author, Something about the Author Autobiography Series, Twentieth-Century Literary Criticism, World Literature Criticism,* and *Yesterday's Authors of Books for Children.*

A Sample Index Entry:

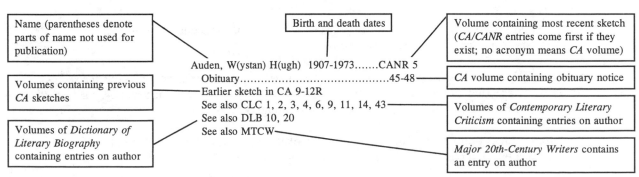

Note: Some index entries contain "Brief Entry" citations. These refer to a short *CA* entry (now discontinued) typically containing birth information, a prose summary that highlights an author's career and writings, and often a few sources where additional information may be found.

How Are Entries Compiled?

Authors' responses to our questionnaires and query letters provide most of the information featured in *CA*. For deceased writers, or those who fail to reply to requests for data, we consult other reliable biographical sources, such as those indexed in Gale's *Biography and Genealogy Master Index,* and bibliographical sources, such as *National Union Catalog,* LC MARC, and *British National Bibliography*. Further details come from published interviews, feature stories, and book reviews, and often the authors' publishers supply material.

An * at the end of a sketch indicates that a listing has been compiled from secondary sources believed to be reliable but has not been personally verified for this edition by the author sketched.

What Kinds of Information Does an Entry Provide?

Sketches in *CA* provide in-depth information in a format designed for ease of use. A typical sketch contains the following:

- **Entry heading:** the most complete form of the author's name, plus any pseudonyms or name variations used for writing

- **Personal information:** author's date and place of birth, family data, educational background, political and religious affiliations, and hobbies and leisure interests

- **Addresses:** author's home, office, or agent's addresses as available

- **Career summary:** name of employer, position, and dates held for each career post; resume of other vocational achievements; military service

- **Awards and honors:** military and civic citations, major prizes and nominations, fellowships, grants, and honorary degrees

- **Membership information:** professional, civic, and other association memberships and any official posts held

- **Writings:** a comprehensive, chronological list of titles, publishers, dates of original publication and revised editions, and production information for plays, television scripts, and screenplays

- **Adaptations:** a list of films, plays, and other media which have been adapted from the author's work

- **Work in progress:** current or planned projects, with dates of completion and/or publication, and expected publisher, when known

- **Sidelights:** a biographical portrait of the author's development; information about the critical reception of the author's works; revealing comments, often by the author, on personal interests, aspirations, motivations, and thoughts on writing

- **Biographical and critical sources:** a list of books and periodicals in which additional information on an author's life and/or writings appears

Some sketches also feature in-depth interviews that provide exclusive, primary information on writers of special interest. Prepared specifically for *CA,* the never-before-published conversations give users the opportunity to learn authors' thoughts, in detail, about their craft.

Obituary Notices in *CA* provide date and place of birth and death information about authors whose full-length sketches appeared in the series before their deaths. These entries also summarize the authors' careers and writings and list other sources of biographical and death information.

Related Titles in the *CA* Series

Contemporary Authors Autobiography Series complements *CA* original and revised volumes with specially commissioned autobiographical essays by important current authors, illustrated with personal photographs they provide. Common topics include their motivations for writing, the people and experiences that shaped their careers, the rewards they derive from their work, and their impressions of the current literary scene.

Contemporary Authors Bibliographical Series surveys writings by and about important American authors since World War II. Each volume concentrates on a specific genre and features approximately ten writers; entries list works written by and about the author and contain a bibliographical essay discussing the merits and deficiencies of major critical and scholarly studies in detail.

Suggestions Are Welcome

The editors welcome comments and suggestions from users on any aspect of the *CA* series. If readers would like to recommend authors whose entries should appear in future volumes of the series, they are cordially invited to write: The Editors, *Contemporary Authors,* 835 Penobscot Bldg., Detroit, MI 48226-4094; call toll-free at 1-800-347-GALE; or fax to 1-313-961-6599.

CA Numbering System and Volume Update Chart

Occasionally questions arise about the *CA* numbering system and which volumes, if any, can be discarded. Despite numbers like "29-32R," "97-100" and "140," the entire *CA* series consists of only 104 physical volumes with the publication of *CA* Volume 140. The following charts note changes in the numbering system and cover design, and indicate which volumes are essential for the most complete, up-to-date coverage.

CA **First Revision**
- 1-4R through 41-44R (11 books)
  Cover: Brown with black and gold trim.
  There will be no further First Revision volumes because revised entries are now being handled exclusively through the more efficient *New Revision Series* mentioned below.

CA **Original Volumes**
- 45-48 through 97-100 (14 books)
  Cover: Brown with black and gold trim.
- 101 through 140 (40 books)
  Cover: Blue and black with orange bands.
  The same as previous *CA* original volumes but with a new, simplified numbering system and new cover design.

CA **Permanent Series**
- *CAP*-1 and *CAP*-2 (2 books)
  Cover: Brown with red and gold trim.
  There will be no further *Permanent Series* volumes because revised entries are now being handled exclusively through the more efficient *New Revision Series* mentioned below.

CA **New Revision Series**
- *CANR*-1 through *CANR*-40 (40 books)
  Cover: Blue and black with green bands.
  Includes only sketches requiring extensive changes; **sketches are taken from any previously published *CA*, *CAP*, or *CANR* volume.**

If You Have:	You May Discard:
CA First Revision Volumes 1-4R through 41-44R **and** *CA* Permanent Series Volumes 1 and 2	*CA* Original Volumes 1, 2, 3, 4 Volumes 5-6 through 23-24 Volumes 25-28 through 41-44
CA Original Volumes 45-48 through 97-100 and 101 through 140	NONE: These volumes will not be superseded by corresponding revised volumes. Individual entries from these and all other volumes appearing in the left column of this chart may be revised and included in the various volumes of the *New Revision Series*.
CA New Revision Series Volumes *CANR*-1 through *CANR*-40	NONE: The *New Revision Series* does not replace any single volume of *CA*. Instead, volumes of *CANR* include entries from many previous *CA* series volumes. All *New Revision Series* volumes must be retained for full coverage.

A Sampling of Authors and Media People
Featured in This Volume

Mitch Albom
Albom has won numerous awards for his insightful, often humorous sports and feature columns, many of which have been collected in *The Live Albom: The Best of Mitch Albom, Live Albom II,* and *Live Albom III: Gone to the Dogs.*

Dorothy E. Allison
Allison earned a 1992 National Book Award nomination for her first novel, *Bastard out of Carolina,* which depicts the life of a poor Southern girl and her family.

Frank Bidart
Noted for dramatic monologues narrated by troubled characters, Bidart has established a reputation for introspective poetry included in such volumes as *The Sacrifice* and *The Book of the Body.*

Michael Blake
Blake garnered top honors, including an Academy Award, for scripting the widely acclaimed 1990 film *Dances with Wolves,* based on his own novel of the same title.

Karel Capek
Capek, a prolific and well-respected Czech writer, penned such acclaimed works as *The War with the Newts,* a sci-fi novel, and *Hordubal, Meteor,* and *An Ordinary Life,* a trilogy that explores facets of reality and truth.

Jean-Claude Carriere
Carriere's collaborative screenwriting has produced exceptional films such as *The Unbearable Lightness of Being* and *The Return of Martin Guerre.* He earned an Academy Award for *The Tin Drum* in 1980.

Gretel Ehrlich
Ehrlich received critical recognition for *The Solace of Open Spaces,* a book of naturalistic essays that evoke the landscape of Wyoming. She returned to the West for the setting of her first novel, *Heart Mountain.*

Gary Geddes
A leading Canadian political poet, Geddes depicts injured figures and examines human relations throughout his works, which include the long poems *War and Other Measures* and *The Terracotta Army.*

Reidar Joensson
Swedish-born Joensson earned a Golden Globe Award and an Academy Award nomination for *Mitt liv som hund,* a screenplay adaptation of his coming-of-age novel, known to English-speaking audiences as *My Life as a Dog.*

Terry McMillan
Author of the novels *Mama, Disappearing Acts,* and 1992's *Waiting to Exhale,* McMillan has reaped accolades from readers and critics alike for her portrayals of strong African American women.

Roger Morris
A nonfiction writer and former member of the National Security Council, Morris garnered a National Book Award Silver Medal for his 1990 biography *Richard Milhous Nixon: The Rise of an American Politician.*

Jeff Moss
Moss is the Emmy Award-winning original head writer for the children's television series *Sesame Street.* His witty, rhymed poems in *The Butterfly Jar* and *The Other Side of the Door* examine everyday life from a child's perspective.

Whitney Otto
Otto received widespread praise for her debut novel, *How to Make an American Quilt,* which focuses on the members of a sewing circle in California. The book achieved best-seller status after its 1991 release.

Camille Paglia
Paglia's unconventional brand of feminism, outlined in her 1990 work, *Sexual Personae,* spawned heated debate in both the media and academia. She later published a collection of lectures and essays titled *Sex, Art, and American Culture.*

Julia Phillips
The first female producer to receive an Academy Award for best picture, Phillips depicts her turbulent Hollywood career in her best-selling memoir *You'll Never Eat Lunch in This Town Again.*

Christopher Reid
One of the prominent figures in the innovative "Martian School" of English poetry, Reid has produced several acclaimed volumes of verse, including *Arcadia, Katerina Brac,* and *In the Echoey Tunnel.*

Jerry Seinfeld
Seinfeld is a stand-up comedian who is also the driving force behind the popular comedy series *Seinfeld,* acting as coproducer, cowriter, and star of the program.

Contemporary Authors®

ABE, Kobo 1924-1993

OBITUARY NOTICE—See index for *CA* sketch: Born March 7, 1924, in Tokyo, Japan; died of heart failure, January 22, 1993, in Tokyo. Novelist and playwright. An immensely popular writer in his native country, Abe achieved worldwide recognition for surrealistic works that emphasized the loss of identity in modern society. As a child, Abe lived in Manchuria, China, where his father taught at a medical college. He returned to Japan in 1940 and studied medicine at the University of Tokyo. After graduating in 1948, he concentrated on writing and soon established his reputation by winning the Akutagawa Prize in 1951. Critics have often noted the influence of Western writers on Abe; he read the works of American Edgar Allan Poe and Russian novelist Fyodor Dostoyevsky in his youth, and Abe's work has been frequently compared to that of Czech writer Franz Kafka. One of Abe's best-known works, the 1962 novel *Suna no onna* (*The Woman in the Dunes*), presents an allegorical tale that explores the themes of identity and alienation, subjects which underlie many of the author's works. English translations of Abe's writing include the novels *The Face of Another, The Ruined Map,* and *Secret Rendezvous,* and the plays *Friends* and *The Man Who Turned into a Stick.*

OBITUARIES AND OTHER SOURCES:

BOOKS

Contemporary Literary Criticism, Volume 53, Gale, 1989.
Who's Who in the World, 11th edition, Marquis, 1991.

PERIODICALS

Chicago Tribune, January 24, 1993, section 2, p. 6.
Los Angeles Times, January 23, 1993, p. A22.
Times (London), January 25, 1993, p. 19.
Washington Post, January 23, 1993, p. C4.

ABRAMS, Elliott 1948-

PERSONAL: Born January 24, 1948, in New York, NY; son of Joseph (a lawyer) and Mildred (a teacher; maiden name, Kauder) Abrams; married Rachel Decter (a homemaker), March 9, 1980; children: Jacob, Sarah, Joseph. *Education:* Harvard University, A.B., 1969; London School of Economics and Political Science, M.Sc.Econ., 1970; Harvard University, J.D., 1973. *Politics:* Republican. *Religion:* Jewish.

ADDRESSES: Home—Washington, DC. *Office*—Hudson Institute, 1015 Eighteenth St. NW, Washington, DC 20036.

CAREER: United States Department of State, Washington, DC, assistant secretary of state for international organization affairs, 1981, assistant secretary of state for human rights and humanitarian affairs, 1981-85, assistant secretary of state for inter-American affairs, 1981-89; Hudson Institute, Washington, senior fellow, 1990—; writer. Trustee of Caribbean/Latin American Action and Francisco Marroquin Foundation, 1989—. Member of Council on Foreign Relations, 1983—, and board of trustees of Center for Security Policy, 1989—.

AWARDS, HONORS: Distinguished Service Award, Secretary of State, 1988.

WRITINGS:

Undue Process: A Story of How Political Differences Are Turned into Crimes (memoir), Free Press, 1992.

Contributor to periodicals, including *Commentary* and *National Review.*

WORK IN PROGRESS: Shield and Sword, a book on post-Cold War U.S. foreign policy, publication expected in 1994.

SIDELIGHTS: Elliott Abrams served as U.S. assistant secretary of state during much of President Ronald Reagan's two terms in office. Abrams ran afoul of the U.S. judicial system after he was implicated in the Iran-Contra scandal. Special prosecutor Lawrence E. Walsh was appointed to conduct an investigation of the affair, in which various officials within the Reagan administration engineered weapons sales to Iran and then used the profits to fund Nicaraguan rebels. Abrams was called before Congress and during his testimony he deliberately withheld information about some government activities. In 1991 Abrams pleaded guilty to two counts of withholding information and received a sentence of two years probation (later reduced to one year) and one hundred hours of community service. "Abrams maintains that he was singled out, even scapegoated, for doing something that has been done in Washington since at least the time of President James K. Polk," wrote Joseph Finder in the *New York Times Book Review.* On Christmas Day, 1992, President George Bush officially pardoned Abrams.

In 1992 Abrams published *Undue Process: A Story of How Political Differences Are Turned into Crimes,* which he described to *CA* as "the story of my prosecution by Iran-Contra special prosecutor Lawrence Walsh." He added: "The book is a memoir of a political trial, and its purpose is to prevent a recurrence—to influence the 1993 Congressional reconsideration of the current law. It's a very personal account of how such a 'special' prosecution affects a man, a marriage, and a family, and as such the level of emotion, passion, pain, and humor is high." Finder assessed *Undue Process* similarly, writing in the *New York Times Book Review* that "Abrams's narrative of his misfortune is told in often febrile and melodramatic prose." The reviewer added, though, that "as a legal and political brief in [Abrams's] own defense, [*Undue Process*] is less heated and more persuasive." *Wall Street Journal* reviewer Theodore B. Olson proclaimed *Undue Process* a "Kafkaesque saga" and deemed it "the stuff of nightmares for anyone daring enough to consider an executive-branch position, especially if the opposition party controls Congress." Michael Ledeen affirmed in *American Spectator* that *Undue Process* "is a gripping account of what it is like to be in the jaws of the Special Prosecutor," and regarded the volume "a very important book, one that should be given to anyone thinking of a career in 'public service.'"

Abrams told *CA:* "I do not expect to write a book similar to *Undue Process,* and *Shield and Sword,* the foreign policy book I am working on now, manages to go 250 pages without using the word 'I.'"

BIOGRAPHICAL/CRITICAL SOURCES:

PERIODICALS

American Spectator, November, 1992, pp. 66-68.

Legal Times, January 4, 1993, p. 46.
National Review, November 30, 1992, p. 46.
New York Times Book Review, November 15, 1992, p. 7.
Wall Street Journal, November 13, 1992, p. A13.
Washingtonian, January, 1993, p. 37.
Washington Times, November 24, 1992, p. F4.

*   *   *

ABURDENE, Patricia   1947(?)-

PERSONAL: Born c. 1947; married John Naisbitt (a lecturer and writer). *Education:* Received B.A. from Newton College of the Sacred Heart and M.A. from Catholic University of America.

ADDRESSES: Home—Telluride, CO, and Cambridge, MA. *Office*—Megatrends, Ltd., 1901 Pennsylvania Ave., N.W., Suite 500, Washington, DC. 20006.

CAREER: Lecturer and writer. Worked as a researcher and reporter for *Forbes.* Member of board of directors of Search for Common Ground and Telluride Institute.

AWARDS, HONORS: Medal of Italy from Senate of Italy, 1990. Has received several honorary doctorates.

WRITINGS:

WITH HUSBAND, JOHN NAISBITT

Reinventing the Corporation: Transforming Your Job and Your Company for the New Information Society, Warner Books, 1985.
Megatrends 2000: Ten New Directions for the 1990s, Morrow, 1990.
Megatrends for Women, Random House, 1992.

SIDELIGHTS: Patricia Aburdene earned recognition as a collaborator with her husband, John Naisbitt, on the popular prognostic volumes *Reinventing the Corporation: Transforming Your Job and Your Company for the New Information Society* and *Megatrends 2000: Ten New Directions for the 1990s,* both of which became best-sellers. In 1982 Naisbitt gained considerable attention as the author of *Megatrends,* in which he speculated on changes in American society and business. The American economy, Naisbitt predicted, would eventually shift in emphasis from heavy industry to information. He also anticipated major changes in the American work force, which he envisioned as becoming more creative and less hierarchical.

Aburdene and Naisbitt first teamed as cowriters on *Reinventing the Corporation,* which continues the speculative nature of Naisbitt's earlier *Megatrends.* In *Reinventing the Corporation* the authors foresee the development of a more collaborative management strategy in the American work force. In addition, they anticipate that businesses will become involved in the education system by sponsoring specific schools and that corporate day-care facilities will become increasingly available. Such developments, Aburdene and Naisbitt contend, will enable America to remain competitive in the ever-evolving global market.

Although *Reinventing the Corporation* sold numerous copies, some critics complained that the authors merely recycled the obvious and were, furthermore, naive and simplistic. Naisbitt dismisses such appraisals as mere jealousy. "Here's how the mentality goes," he told *People*. "[The critic says to himself,] 'They have written a book that is greatly inferior to what I can do if I were going to do it . . . and they are making money!' "

After the considerable popular success of *Reinventing the Corporation*, Aburdene and Naisbitt produced *Megatrends 2000*, where they once again offer predictions on American business and social development. For the authors, the twenty-first century will be a time of unmatched opportunity for global economic practices and workplace equality. In addition, they foresee a revival of cultural concerns, with regional arts playing a more significant role in society. Even social programs will undergo drastic change, Aburdene and Naisbitt contend, with the privatization of welfare being one of many possible changes.

With *Megatrends 2000* Aburdene and Naisbitt again found both favor with book buyers and disfavor with critics, many of whom renewed allegations that the authors were simply reiterating news of rather obvious developments. But Aburdene and Naisbitt themselves appear undaunted by such criticism. "People are always saying 'I sort of knew that' about our books," Aburdene conceded to *People*. "We just make it clearer and, by doing so, we empower readers in their lives." And to the *Los Angeles Times* she said: "All we do is notice what is happening. It's the world around us we are reflecting in these trends."

Aburdene and Naisbitt, who consider themselves "social forecasters," have also met with great success on the lecture circuit and in their presentations to various businesses and groups. Bill Leigh, whose agency handles the couple's speaking engagements, considers their appearances unique successes. "I've never seen another program out there where this joint-play really works," Leigh told the *Los Angeles Times*. "It's very much their relationship—something they have evolved together."

BIOGRAPHICAL/CRITICAL SOURCES:

BOOKS

Bestsellers 90, Issue 3, Gale, 1990.

PERIODICALS

Atlantic Monthly, July, 1990, pp. 97-100.

Business Week, September 9, 1985, pp. 10-11; January 22, 1990, p. 14.
Los Angeles Times, January 17, 1990.
New Republic, April 28, 1986, pp. 30-32.
New York Times Book Review, October 20, 1985, p. 52; January 7, 1990, p. 20.
People, July 30, 1990, pp. 57-61.
Time, January 8, 1990, p. 72.
Washington Post Book World, October 20, 1985, p. 11.

* * *

ABURISH, Said K. 1935-

PERSONAL: Born May 1, 1935, in Jerusalem, Palestine (now Israel); son of Abu Said (a journalist) and Surrya (Shahine) Aburish; married Cathryn Louise Beck, 1982 (divorced, 1984); children: Charla Josephine. *Education:* University of Chicago, B.A., 1957. *Religion:* Quaker.

ADDRESSES: Home—23 Drayton Ct., Drayton Gardens, London, England. *Agent*—Vardy and Brunton, 325 Moore Park Rd., London, England.

CAREER: Writer. Worked in advertising and as a reporter for Radio Free Europe.

WRITINGS:

Payoff: Wheeling and Dealing in the Arab World, Deutsch, 1985.
Children of Bethany: The Story of a Palestinian Family, Tauris, 1988, Indiana University Press, 1989.
Bar al-San Jurj: wakr al jawasis fi Bayrut (title means "Day in the Life of St. George Hotel Bar"), Riad El Rayyes, 1989, published in the United States as *The St. George Hotel Bar,* Trafalgar Square, 1991.
One Day I Will Tell You, Prion, 1990.
Cry Palestine: Inside the West Bank, Bloomsbury, 1991.

Also contributed to periodicals, including *Independent, Washington Post,* and *Liberation*.

WORK IN PROGRESS: Writing *Memoirs of A Cultural Schizoid;* researching the Christians of the Holy Land.

SIDELIGHTS: In *Children of Bethany: The Story of a Palestinian Family,* author Said K. Aburish relates the true three-generation saga of the Aburish clan, beginning with and centering on the author's grandfather. Once a poor orphan, Khalil Aburish became an entrepreneur in the 1890s after discovering the alleged tomb of the biblical figure Lazarus on his property in Bethany, Palestine. He charged tourists to see the historic burial place and further supplemented his income by buying and selling plots of land to churches of religious denominations other than Muslim. Aburish's book then discusses the changing times of Palestine and its people. He chronicles such events as World War I and the new British rule, the war between Arabs and Jews in 1948, and the country's divided land and eventual rule by Jordan. The author parallels these changes with those of his own family—the death of his grandfather, his father's flight for Beirut, and his divided family and westernized way of living. *New York Times Book Review* contributor Inea Bushnaq commented that "he probes into the past with clear-eyed thoroughness . . . Some of the truths he reveals make unhappy reading, but ultimately it is his book's brusque frankness that gives it value." She further stated that *"Children of Bethany* is a welcome and articulate addition to the documentation of the Palestinian experience since World War I."

Aburish told *CA:* "My books constitute footnotes to the history of the modern Middle East, essentially a revisionist history. My purpose is to correct certain impressions before it becomes too late."

BIOGRAPHICAL/CRITICAL SOURCES:

PERIODICALS

Globe and Mail (Toronto), May 5, 1990.
New York Times Book Review, February 11, 1990, p. 25.
Washington Post, January 8, 1990.

*   *   *

ADAMS, Bronte (Jane) 1963-

PERSONAL: Born February 21, 1963, in Perth, Western Australia; daughter of Geoffrey Hugh Southey (in business) and Kathleen Marie (a nurse; maiden name, Brebner) Adams. *Education:* Attended University of Western Australia, 1984; Balliol College, Oxford, D.Phil., 1991. *Politics:* "Left of center."

ADDRESSES: Home—15/22 New Beach Rd., Darling Point, New South Wales 2027, Australia.

CAREER: Worked variously as a secretary and research officer, 1985-86; University of Western Australia, Perth, tutor/lecturer, 1986; Virago Press, London, England, reader, 1987-90; Oxford University, Oxford, England, tutor, 1989-91; McKinsey & Co., consultant, 1991—; writer.

MEMBER: International Federation of University Women, Amnesty International, Rhodes Scholars Against Apartheid, National Trust of Australia.

AWARDS, HONORS: First prize in school division, Young Writers' Competition, 1979; Rhodes Scholarship for Western Australia, 1986; grant from Rhodes Trustees, 1988; Audrey Jorss-Freida Freeman Fellowship, Australian Federation of University Women, 1989; grant from

Australian Federation of University Women, 1989, for *That Kind of Woman.*

WRITINGS:

(Editor with Trudi Tate) *That Kind of Woman: Stories from the Left Bank and Beyond,* Virago, 1991.
Brought to Book (mystery novel), Virago, 1992.

Author of afterword for *Wandering Girl,* by Glenys Ward, Virago, 1988. Coauthor and director of a play, adapted from the novel *Wide Sargasso Sea* by Jean Rhys, produced at Oxford University, 1989. Contributor to *The Oxford Companion to Twentieth-Century Literature,* edited by Margaret Drabble for Oxford University Press.

SIDELIGHTS: Bronte Adams is the author of *Brought to Book,* a mystery about an editor who finds herself suspected in the slaying of her boss. Although the editor, Aphra Colqhoun, is fearful that her curious past may be exposed, she nonetheless perseveres to clear herself in the murder case. Teaming with a journalist, a lawyer, and two roommates, Colqhoun determines to discover the actual killer.

Adams told *CA:* "I'm interested in voice. How do we speak? How do we come to articulate ourselves? What means and motives of articulation are available to us, and how do they determine how we speak? These questions are central to feminism, and I think they are a lot more complex and double-edged than much popular commentary allows.

"Before writing *Brought to Book* I asked myself, 'Why do people commit murder—for love or money?' I wanted to incorporate both possibilities into the book, along with the development of a central character that isn't usually characteristic of crime fiction. I didn't want Aphra Colqhoun to be a professional detective, and I didn't want a 'feminized' version of the tough, hard-hitting, hard-drinking male detective. What appealed to me was someone more vulnerable, without a clear sense of mission, with a sense of self-doubt and self-irony that could at times verge on the debilitating. Crime would be something that happened to her, that she didn't seek out. Colqhoun resorts to a community of friends rather than male stereotypes of force and single-mindedness. Her complexity is not supposed to be the mushy center beneath the tough shell but the way she has to redefine herself and her relations with the world and its inhabitants."

*   *   *

AGER, Derek Victor 1923-1993

OBITUARY NOTICE—See index for *CA* sketch: Born April 21, 1923, in Harrow, England; died February 8,

1993. Geologist, educator, and writer. Ager's books received acclaim for analyzing geological processes in an entertaining and readable manner, making the science more accessible to nonexperts. After serving with the Royal Tank Regiment in World War II, Ager studied geology at Chelsea College. His first teaching position was at London University's Imperial College of Science and Technology beginning in 1951. Ager then moved to the University College of Swansea in 1969, acting as professor and head of the geology department until his retirement in 1989. He was also a visiting professor at numerous universities around the world and served as editor-in-chief of *Palaeogeography, Palaeoclimatology, Palaeoecology.* Ager began his publishing career with *Introducing Geology* in 1961, and two years later he produced *Principles of Palaeoecology,* the first English textbook on the subject. In 1973 he published *The Nature of the Stratigraphical Record,* an influential text that the author cited as one of his proudest accomplishments, according to the obituary in the London *Times.* Shortly before his death, Ager wrote *The New Catastrophism,* a sequel to *The Nature of the Stratigraphical Record,* though he did not live to see the book in print.

OBITUARIES AND OTHER SOURCES:

BOOKS

The Writers Directory: 1992-1994, St. James Press, 1991.

PERIODICALS

Times (London), February 24, 1993, p. 19.

*   *   *

AHMED, Leila 1940-

PERSONAL: Born May 29, 1940, in Cairo, Egypt; daughter of Abdel Aziz and Iqbal (Radi) Ahmed. *Education:* Cambridge University, B.A. (with honors), 1961, M.A., 1966, Ph.D., 1971. *Religion:* Muslim.

ADDRESSES: Office—208 Bartlett Hall, University of Massachusetts at Amherst, Amherst, MA 01002.

CAREER: University of Massachusetts at Amherst, professor, 1980—.

WRITINGS:

E. W. Lare and British Ideas of the Middle East, Longman, 1978.
Women and Gender in Islam: Historical Roots of a Modern Debate, Yale University Press, 1992.

WORK IN PROGRESS: An autobiography.

ALALI, A. Odasuo 1957-

PERSONAL: Born November 17, 1957, in Port Harcourt, Nigeria; son of Andrew and Unice (Oleh) Alali. *Education:* Alabama Agricultural & Mechanical University, B.A., 1980; Murray State University, M.A., 1981; Howard University, Ph.D., 1985. *Politics:* Independent. *Religion:* "Undeclared."

ADDRESSES: Home—Bakersfield, CA. *Office*—Department of English and Communication Studies, California State University, 9001 Stockdale Hwy., Bakersfield, CA 93311.

CAREER: Bowie State University, Bowie, MD, assistant professor of journalism, 1984-86; California State University, Bakersfield, associate professor of communications, 1986-87 and 1989—; California State University, Dominguez Hills, assistant professor of communications, 1987-89; California Lutheran University, Thousand Oaks, assistant professor of communications, 1988—. College Media Advisors, member of non-daily newspaper committee, 1987-88; Los Angeles Trade and Technical College, member of journalism advisory board, 1988.

MEMBER: American Heart Association (Kern County Chapter; member of board of communications).

AWARDS, HONORS: Named an outstanding young man of America in 1983; "An Enemy among Us" research scholarship, Center of Population Options, 1988.

WRITINGS:

(With Kenoye K. Eke) *Media Coverage of Terrorism: Methods of Diffusion,* Sage Publications, 1991.
Mass Media Sex and Adolescent Values: An Annotated Bibliography and Directory of Organizations, McFarland & Co., 1991.
Mass Media and Development in Nigeria: A Primer for Policymakers, Peter Lang, 1991.

Contributor to numerous newspapers and journals.

WORK IN PROGRESS: Perspectives on HIV/AIDS in Public Schools, for State University of New York Press; research on music videos and children and on the human immunodeficiency virus and children.

SIDELIGHTS: A. Odasuo Alali told *CA:* "Those of us who are members of the professorate are told to 'publish or perish.' It has always been the job of the senior faculty to condition the junior faculty to believing that teaching and research are inescapably compatible. They would often say that one can develop new teaching strategies if one is enmeshed in culture-dominated research. This was not new to me because my education at Howard University was designed to prepare me to contribute to my profession and society through research. In fact, because my professors were active researchers, the Howard culture influenced my professional orientation. It was at Howard that I decided to be part of a research culture that will stimulate my intellect and help me contribute to debate in society. So when I hear some of my colleagues who have never published talk about 'publish or perish,' it bothers me because I see some hypocrisy in their mind-set. It is a sort of lip service.

"My first edited work, with Dr. Kenoye Eke, was *Media Coverage of Terrorism.* Dr. Eke has been a friend since childhood, and I am happy that we have been positive influences on each other. He is an essential part of my development. There is also a connection between my intellectual growth and the guidance of my undergraduate professor, James Powell, Jr., who persistently demanded that I be all I can be. Also, without the love and patience of my parents, Andrew and Unice, I would not have accomplished so much in such a short time.

"I began writing *Mass Media Sex and Adolescent Values* when I received the 'An Enemy among Us' research scholarship from the Center of Population Options in 1988. The book is designed to illuminate the dark alleys that people walk into when trying to understand complex phenomena such as the media. The positive reviews it has received are gratifying."

* * *

ALBERT, Fred 1957-

PERSONAL: Born March 30, 1957, in Boston, MA; son of Leonard I. Albert (an electrical engineer and owner of a car rental franchise) and Corinne Geist (a secretary and partner in the car rental franchise; maiden name, Simkin). *Education:* Yale University, B.A., 1979. *Religion:* Jewish. *Avocational interests:* Photography, attending theater, art museums, and galleries.

ADDRESSES: Home—Seattle, WA. *Office—Pacific* magazine, *Seattle Times,* P.O. Box 70, Seattle, WA 98111; and *Pacific Northwest,* 701 Dexter Ave. N., Suite 101, Seattle, WA 98109.

CAREER: John Graham and Co., Seattle, WA, assistant in architectural design department, 1979-80; Seattle Children's Theatre, Seattle, public relations director, 1981-83; *Herald,* Everett, WA, author of column "Design Notebook," 1981-85; *Seattle Times,* Seattle, writer for *Pacific,* 1985—. *Pacific Northwest,* contributing editor, 1990—; *Greater Seattle* (now *Seattle*), contributing editor, 1990—. Seattle Repertory Theatre, publications manager, 1983-90. Volunteer fundraiser for Northwest AIDS Foundation.

WRITINGS:

(With Linda Humphrey) *American Design: The Northwest,* Bantam, 1989.

Contributor to periodicals, including *Home* and *Decorating Remodeling.* Editor of *Prologue,* Seattle Repertory Theatre, 1983-90.

SIDELIGHTS: Fred Albert told *CA:* "I began writing about houses by chance although, unconsciously, I'd been preparing for the assignment my whole life. An enthusiastic journalist in high school, I filled my college years with courses in architecture, decorative arts, fine art, and design. After graduation, when a journalist friend suggested I approach her paper for a job, the editor surprised me by offering me a column on home design.

"Nowadays, I visit hundreds of houses each year. Time and again, the people I visit will say to me, 'You have the greatest job in the world!' I have to laugh at first. They are not thinking about the perpetual deadlines, the struggle to capture a home's unique appeal in a fresh, new way, week after week. They only see a guy who goes around and looks at beautiful houses all day long.

"When I think about what I do, however, I have to admit I *am* pretty lucky. That is not just because I get to peer into the closets and baths of the sort-of-rich-and-semi-famous, but because of the people I meet. They are fascinating individuals, from all walks of life, who share their experiences, knowledge, talents, and insights. In addition, someone pays me to listen to them. Now *that* is a great job!

"I want my articles to educate and inspire, to show readers things they may not have seen before, and give them ideas that they can apply to their own surroundings. While good design is paramount, character is nearly as important. The house should be so rich in atmosphere and originality that you feel transformed when you step inside. It doesn't matter whether the style is contemporary or traditional, the furnishings from Roche Bobois or the Salvation Army. If a house reflects the personality and vision of its creators, it will usually make a good story.

"I've been writing about houses since 1981. Naturally, a person can get jaded after a while. The look that made your toes tingle three years ago may barely register today. Every now and then, however, you walk through someone's door and feel the excitement surge through your body. More than anything else, you want to put that sensation into print. It's a pleasure you never outgrow."

ALBOM, Mitch (David) 1958-

PERSONAL: Born May 23, 1958, in Passaic, NJ; son of Ira and Rhoda Albom. *Education:* Brandeis University, B.A., 1979; Columbia University, M.J., 1981, M.B.A., 1982.

ADDRESSES: Home—Farmington Hills, MI. *Office*—Detroit Free Press, 321 West Lafayette, Detroit, MI 48231.

CAREER: Queens Tribune, Flushing, NY, editor, 1981-82; contributing writer for *Sport, Philadelphia Inquirer,* and *Geo,* 1982-83; *Fort Lauderdale News and Sun Sentinel,* Fort Lauderdale, FL, sports columnist, 1983-85; *Detroit Free Press,* Detroit, MI, sports columnist, 1985—; WLLZ-radio, Farmington Hills, MI, sports director, 1985—, cohost of sports talk show, "Sunday Sports Albom," 1988—; WDIV-TV, Detroit, broadcaster and commentator, 1987—. Piano player; composer of a song for the television movie *Christmas in Connecticut,* 1992.

MEMBER: Baseball Writers of America, Football Writers of America, Tennis Writers of America.

AWARDS, HONORS: Award for best sports news story in the United States, 1985; named number one sports columnist in Michigan, Associated Press (AP) and United Press International (UPI), 1985, 1986, 1987, and 1988; named number one sports columnist in the United States by AP Sports Editors, 1987, 1988, 1989, 1990, 1991, 1992, and 1993; named number one sports columnist in Michigan, National Association of Sportswriters and Broadcasters, 1988 and 1989; number two outstanding writer, National Headliners Award, 1989; award for best feature writing, AP Sports Editors, 1993, for article on University of Michigan basketball player Juwan Howard.

WRITINGS:

The Live Albom: The Best of Mitch Albom, Detroit Free Press, 1988.
(With Bo Schembechler) *Bo,* Warner Books, 1989.
Live Albom II, foreword by Ernie Harwell, *Detroit Free Press,* 1990.
Live Albom III: Gone to the Dogs, Detroit Free Press, 1992.

Contributor to periodicals, including *Gentlemen's Quarterly, Sports Illustrated,* and *Sport.*

SIDELIGHTS: Mitch Albom, a Michigan journalist, has earned national attention and awards for his sports columns distinguished by insight, humor, and empathy. These writings have been collected in *The Live Albom: The Best of Mitch Albom, Live Albom II,* and *Live Albom III: Gone to the Dogs.* Disdaining the questionable ethical conduct, drug problems, and over-inflated egos often found in the sports world, Albom highlights instances of athletic courage and determination while providing honest commentary on a team's performance. After stints in New York and Florida, Albom arrived in Detroit, Michigan, in 1985 as a staff member of the *Detroit Free Press.* Introducing himself to his new audience in his first column, he explained that readers could expect "some opinion, some heart, some frankness. Some laughs. Some out of the ordinary." Albom also made a good first impression with area sports fans by rejecting the negative stereotype—a crime-ridden and dying city—that Detroit held for the nation. He added, "Some people apparently look at a new job in Detroit as something to be endured or tolerated. . . . I, for one, am thrilled to be here. For sports, they don't make towns any better than this one."

One of Albom's most distinguished traits as a columnist is his sympathy with disappointed fans when local professional teams struggled unsuccessfully for championships. He commiserated with area readers in 1988 when Detroit's basketball team, the Pistons, battled to the National Basketball Association (NBA) finals and pushed Los Angeles to a full seven-game series, only to lose the last game by three points. He reasoned, "They went further than any Pistons team before them. They came onto the stage as brutes and left with an entire nation's respect—for their courage, for their determination, for their talent. . . . They took on all comers. . . . They could beat any team in the league. They just couldn't beat them all." A year earlier, when the underdog Red Wings reached the National Hockey League (NHL) semifinals but lost, Albom reported how, on the long flight home, the players dealt with this defeat. Upon learning that a devoted fan—who was riding the team's charter plane home—had flown to Edmonton to watch the game, Detroit players chipped in to reimburse him for his ticket. They also joined in on a chorus of that fan's favorite cheer. Witnessing this, Albom wrote, "Amazing. Here were these bruising, scarred, often toothless men, on the night of a season-ending loss, singing a high school cheer. Simply because it made an old guy happy. Many people will remember goals and saves and slap shots from this season. I hope I never forget that cheer."

With columns such as these, Albom earned a loyal following and a reputation as a blue-collar sports fan. His success in print carried over to other media, including radio and television. He joined the staff of rock station WLLZ in 1985, initially serving as sports director. In 1988 he and cohost Mike Stone began a weekly program, "The Sunday Sports Albom." Guests included both local and national sports figures and the program's format allowed calls by listeners. His stellar guest list was evidence of the comfortable rapport Albom shared with many area athletes and coaches. This accord extended beyond interviews; in 1987 he was even a good luck charm for Detroit's NHL team, the Red Wings. As he explained in a column reprinted in *The Live Albom,* "I am not sure when my car and the fortunes of the Red Wings actually became intertwined. I do know [coach] Jacques Demers and I have now driven to five playoff games together and Detroit has won all five, and now even Demers, who is not superstitious, is asking me what time we're leaving."

Albom's relationship with another state sports figure, former University of Michigan football coach Bo Schembechler, led to a collaboration on Schembechler's autobiography, *Bo.* Respected as a top college coach for his Big Ten championships and frequent bowl appearances, Schembechler reputedly had a quick temper and churlish personality. In *Bo,* Albom presents Schembechler as a sincere family man whose demeanor was a deliberate act and who inspired love and respect from his football players. Albom credits Schembechler with turning the Michigan football program around. When he began as coach, Michigan was a perennial runner-up to Ohio State. Bo promised championships, and he delivered without ever suffering through a losing season. Albom notes a greater accomplishment, however, is that Schembechler ran a program free from rules violations and saw his athletes graduate. A reviewer for the *New York Times Book Review* concluded that while *Bo* did not offer much new information about Schembechler, the work strengthened Schembechler's position as a role model for college athletes.

While Albom has reigned as the darling of the Detroit sports scene, he has also been involved with his share of controversy. He raised the ire of a Detroit Tigers' pitcher with a column and, eleven months later, had a bucket of ice water dumped over his head in the Tigers' clubhouse (the pitcher blamed his disintegrating effectiveness on Albom's commentary). Albom also broke the 1988 story of the after-curfew bar visits of several Red Wings players. He reported that, when confronted with the news, the coach "looked as if he was going to cry." Albom added that this black mark on the team's accomplishments was "not the story I wanted to write. Not the one you wanted to read."

In these instances, a prediction Albom made in his first column came true: "I try to be honest. . . . This is not always a pretty job. Sometimes you have to write that the good guys lost, or that somebody's favorite baseball hero in the whole world just checked into the rehab clinic. Still, sports are the only show in town where no matter how many times you go back, you never know the ending. That's special."

BIOGRAPHICAL/CRITICAL SOURCES:

BOOKS

Albom, Mitch, *The Live Albom, Detroit Free Press,* 1988, pp. 12, 208, 218.

Albom, *Live Albom II, Detroit Free Press,* 1990, pp. 33, 35, 44.

PERIODICALS

Detroit Free Press, March 30, 1993, p. 1C.
New York Times Book Review, November 19, 1989, p. 44.*

—*Sketch by Mary K. Ruby*

*   *   *

al-KHALIL, Samir [a pseudonym]

CAREER: Writer.

WRITINGS:

Republic of Fear: The Inside Story of Saddam's Iraq, University of California Press, 1989.
The Monument: Art, Vulgarity, and Responsibility in Iraq, University of California Press, 1991.

SIDELIGHTS: Samir al-Khalil is a pseudonymous Iraqi exile who has published works on various aspects of life in Iraq under dictator Saddam Hussein. Fearing that the information he has dispersed concerning Hussein has put his life in danger, he writes under the pseudonym. Al-Khalil's first book, *Republic of Fear: The Inside Story of Saddam's Iraq,* is a detailed account of the Baathist political party's violent ascent to power following Israel's 1967 defeat of the Arab states, a war in which Iraq participated. Here al-Khalil recounts the proliferation of show trials and public executions that served to unite, and ultimately terrorize into submission, the Iraqi citizenry. He contends that violence is inherent in Hussein's Baathist party and that fear has been Hussein's principle means of repression since he assumed ultimate authority in Iraq.

Republic of Fear, as Adrienne Edgar reported in the *New York Times Book Review,* "met with a resounding silence" when it first appeared in 1989. But the book was reprinted after Hussein authorized the Iraqi invasion of neighboring Kuwait in 1990, and upon reprinting it received recognition as a dramatic and incisive account. Patrick Tyler, writing in the *Washington Post,* declared that in *Republic of Fear* al-Khalil "assembles and discusses with clarity a formidable history of Baathist development from which the reader can learn much about Saddam [Hussein] and the culture of violence over which he presides." Another reviewer, James Yuenger, wrote in *Tribune Books* that al-Khalil "picks through Baathism's contradictions . . . with an analytical fervor so scathing that it's evident why . . . he still feels the need to operate under a pseudonym." And Edgar deemed *Republic of Fear* "required reading for anyone with a serious interest in Iraq or in the political dynamics of dictatorship."

Al-Khalil followed *Republic of Fear* with *The Monument: Art, Vulgarity, and Responsibility in Iraq,* a provocative political, cultural, and psychological analysis of Baghdad's Victory Arch, a massive monument comprised of two arms (replicas of Saddam Hussein's own limbs) holding crossed sabres. Malise Ruthven, in a review for *New Statesman and Society,* described *The Monument* as "a meditation on art and kitsch" and declared that the volume "attests to the spiritual cost exacted by a regime that not only rules by terror, but forces its subjects to participate in its fantasy world of grandiosity and paranoia."

BIOGRAPHICAL/CRITICAL SOURCES:

PERIODICALS

Current History, January, 1991, p. 33.
Economist, April 27, 1991, p. 94.
Foreign Affairs, summer, 1991, p. 179.
New Statesman and Society, April 20, 1991, pp. 29-30.
New York Times, September 7, 1990, p. 3.
New York Times Book Review, October 21, 1990, pp. 13-14.
Tribune Books (Chicago), October 28, 1990, p. 3.
Washington Post, October 16, 1990.*

*   *   *

ALLISON, Dorothy E. 1949-

PERSONAL: Born April 11, 1949, in Greenville, SC; daughter of Ruth Gibson Allison (a waitress and cook); companion of Alix Layman (a printer); children: Wolf Michael. *Education:* Florida Presbyterian College (now Eckerd College), B.A., 1971; received M.A. from New School for Social Research.

ADDRESSES: Home—Box 112, Monte Rio, CA 95462. *Agent*—Frances Goldin, 305 East Eleventh St., New York, NY 10003.

CAREER: Writer.

MEMBER: PEN, Authors Guild, Writers Union.

AWARDS, HONORS: Lambda Literary awards, best small press book and best lesbian book, both 1989, for *Trash;* National Book Award finalist, 1992, for *Bastard out of Carolina.*

WRITINGS:

The Women Who Hate Me (poems), Long Haul Press, 1983.
Trash (stories), Firebrand Books, 1988.
The Women Who Hate Me: Poetry, 1980-1990, Firebrand Books, 1991.
Bastard out of Carolina (novel), Dutton, 1992.
Skin (essays), Firebrand Books, 1993.

Cavedweller (novel), Dutton, in press.

SIDELIGHTS: Dorothy E. Allison became a recognized poet and short story writer in the 1980s with her collections *The Women Who Hate Me* and *Trash.* In 1992, she earned high critical praise as a novelist for *Bastard out of Carolina,* a portrayal of a young girl's life in a poor Southern family. Ruth Anne Boatwright, the protagonist, relates how she earned her nickname, "Bone," when she was prematurely born—the size of a knucklebone—after her mother was in a car accident. Allison admitted in an interview with Lynn Karpen in *New York Times Book Review* that these introductory details are largely autobiographical. The author further commented, "A lot of the novel is based on real experience, but not the entire thing. The characters are modeled on members of my family and on stories I heard when I was growing up."

Bone's illegitimacy, her plain looks, and her lack of talent for gospel singing make her an outcast among her peers, but she finds shelter among the women of her family. She particularly admires her Aunt Raylene, an ex-carnival worker who once had a love affair with another woman. Bone's mother, Anney, attempts to establish a more traditional home for herself and her daughter by marrying the son of a wealthy local family. Daddy Glen, Anney's new groom, is kind to his wife, but takes out his frustrations by physically and sexually assaulting Bone. Anney refuses to acknowledge these acts until a brutal confrontation occurs, which leaves Bone feeling, at the age of thirteen, that her life is over. A *Booklist* reviewer noted, however, that at this turning point of adolescence, Bone, like Mark Twain's Huckleberry Finn, realizes that in order to live her life she must move on to new territory.

Reviewers of *Bastard out of Carolina* praised Allison for her realistic, unsentimental, and often humorous portrayal of her eccentric characters, and in 1992 the novel was nominated for a National Book Award. In *Publishers Weekly,* a reviewer of *Bastard out of Carolina* stated that Allison "doesn't condescend to her 'white trash' characters; she portrays them with understanding and love." A *Washington Post Book World* contributor complained that *Bastard out of Carolina* "has a tendency to bog down in its own heat, speech and atmosphere," but also acknowledged that "Allison has a superb ear for the specific dialogue of her characters." George Garrett, writing in the *New York Times Book Review,* described the novel as being "as richly various, with its stories and memories and dreams, as a well-made quilt." Garrett further declared that Allison's "technical skill in both large things and details, so gracefully executed as to be always at the service of the story and its characters and thus almost invisible, is simply stunning."

BIOGRAPHICAL/CRITICAL SOURCES:

PERIODICALS

Booklist, June 15, 1992, p. 1814.
Library Journal, March 1, 1992, p. 116.
New York Times Book Review, July 5, 1992, p. 3.
Publishers Weekly, November 18, 1988, p. 74; March 22, 1991, p. 77; January 27, 1992, p. 88.
Times Literary Supplement, March 8, 1991, p. 18.
Washington Post Book World, May 3, 1992, p. 11.

* * *

ALNASRAWI, Abbas

PERSONAL: Education: Received B.A. from University of Baghdad; Harvard University, Ph.D., 1965.

ADDRESSES: Office—Department of Economics, University of Vermont, Burlington, VT 05405-0001.

CAREER: Held staff positions with the Iraq Ministry of Finance, Central Bank of Iraq, and the Grain Board, Baghdad, Iraq; University of Vermont, Burlington, 1963—, currently professor of economics, associate dean of College of Arts and Sciences, 1972-77. Consultant to the Organization of Petroleum Exporting Countries (OPEC), the United Nations Educational, Scientific, and Cultural Organization (UNESCO), and the United Nations Development Programme (UNDP).

MEMBER: Middle East Economic Association (president, 1990-91), Arab Society for Economics Research, American Economic Association, Middle East Studies Association, Association of Arab-American University Graduates (president, 1984).

WRITINGS:

Financing Economic Development in Iraq, Praeger, 1967.
Arab Oil and United States Energy Requirements, Association of Arab-American University Graduates, 1982.
OPEC in a Changing World Economy, Johns Hopkins University Press, 1985.
(Editor with Cheryl Rubenberg) *The Consistency of U.S. Foreign Policy: The Gulf War and the Iran-Contra Affair,* Association of Arab-American University Graduates, 1989.
Arab Nationalism, Oil, and the Political Economy of Dependency, Greenwood Press, 1991.

Contributor to economic and Middle East studies journals, including *American Economic Review, Journal of World Trade Law,* and *Middle East Journal.*

ALSTON, Philip 1950-

PERSONAL: Born January 23, 1950; children: two. *Education:* Received LL.B. (with honors), B. Comm., and LL.M. from University of Melbourne; received LL.M. and J.S.D. from University of California, Berkeley; received diploma from International Institute of Human Rights, Strasbourg, France.

ADDRESSES: Office—Department of Law, Australian National University, GPO 4, Canberra, Australian Capital Territory 495111.

CAREER: University of Melbourne, Parkville, Australia, research associate and tutor in law, 1973-74; Australian Government, senior adviser to the minister for the Capital Territory, 1974-75; United Nations Centre for Human Rights, Geneva, Switzerland, legal officer, 1978-84; Tufts University, Fletcher School of Law and Diplomacy, Boston, MA, associate professor of international law, 1985-89; Australian National University, Canberra, professor of law and director of Centre for International and Public Law, 1989—. Harvard University, lecturer, 1984-89, visiting professor, 1989, 1993. Australian Capital Territory, discrimination commissioner. United Nations Children's Fund (UNICEF), senior legal adviser on children's rights, 1984—; member of board of directors of American Committee for Human Rights, 1986-88, Physicians for Human Rights, 1987-89, and International League for Human Rights, 1989—; Human Rights Internet, member of board of directors and editorial committee, 1987-90; United Nations Institute for Training and Research, member of Human Rights Advisory Committee, 1987—; Commission on Human Rights, chair of Task Force on Computerization, 1989-90; United Nations Committee on Economic, Social, and Cultural Rights, chair, 1991—; consultant to UNESCO and Australian Human Rights Commission.

MEMBER: International Law Association.

AWARDS, HONORS: Ford Foundation fellow in Geneva, 1977.

WRITINGS:

Development and the Rule of Law, International Commission of Jurists, 1981.
(Editor of English edition, and contributor) *The International Dimensions of Human Rights,* two volumes, UNESCO, 1982.
(Editor with K. Tomasevski, and contributor) *The Right to Food,* Nijhoff, 1984.
(Editor with Bustelo, and contributor) *Whose New World Order: What Role for the United Nations?* Federation Press (Sydney), 1991.
(Editor with Brennan, and contributor) *The United Nations Children's Convention and Australia,* Australian

Human Rights and Equal Opportunity Commission, 1991.

(Editor with Parker and Seymour, and contributor) *Children, Rights, and the Law,* Clarendon Press, 1992.

(Editor and contributor) *The United Nations and Human Rights: A Critical Appraisal,* Clarendon Press, 1992.

Commentary on the Convention on the Rights of the Child, UNICEF and United Nations Centre for Human Rights, 1992.

Work represented in anthologies, including *United Nations Assistance for Human Rights,* Radda Barnen and Swedish Section, International Commission of Jurists, 1988; *Human Rights in a Pluralist World: Individuals and Collectivities,* edited by Berting and others, Meckler, 1990; and *The Future of Human Rights Protection in a Changing World,* Norwegian University Press, 1991. Contributor of more than eighty articles and reviews to professional journals. Editor, *Australian Yearbook of International Law,* 1992; guest coeditor, *Bulletin of Peace Proposals,* 1980, and *Development: Journal of the Society for International Development,* 1984.

*   *   *

AMES, Gerald   1906-1993

OBITUARY NOTICE—See index for *CA* sketch: Born Gerald Otto, October 17, 1906, in Rochester, NY; died January 2, 1993, in Manhattan, NY. Painter and author. Ames cowrote over fifty science and magic books for children with his wife, Rose Wyler. Trained in biology and geology, Ames explained complex scientific terms and theories using clear, simple language. He also contributed frequently to scientific journals. Ames had his paintings exhibited with Arts Interaction in New York and the Port Clyde Arts and Crafts Society in Port Clyde, Maine. Among his works were *The Giant Golden Book of Biology, First Days of the World, Magic Secrets,* and *Secrets in Stone.*

OBITUARIES AND OTHER SOURCES:

BOOKS

Authors of Books for Young People, 3rd edition, Scarecrow, 1990.

PERIODICALS

New York Times, January 15, 1993, p. A21.

*   *   *

ANDERSON, Elijah   1943-

PERSONAL: Born in 1943 in Hermandale, MO; son of Vernel (a blue-collar worker) and Carrie (a domestic, grocer, and seamstress; maiden name, Byrd) Anderson; married December 26, 1976; wife's name, Nancy; children: E. Luke, Caitlin. *Education:* Indiana University, B.A., 1969; University of Chicago, M.A., 1972; Northwestern University, Ph.D., 1976.

ADDRESSES: Office—University of Pennsylvania, Department of Sociology, 3718 Locust Walk, Philadelphia, PA 19104.

CAREER: Swarthmore College, Swarthmore, PA, assistant professor of sociology, 1973-75; University of Pennsylvania, Philadelphia, assistant professor, 1975-80, associate professor, 1981-88, professor of sociology, 1988—, Max and Heidi Berry Term Professor in the Social Sciences, 1988-90, Charles and William Day Professor of the Social Sciences, 1990—.

WRITINGS:

A Place on the Corner, University of Chicago Press, 1978.
Streetwise: Race, Class, and Change in an Urban Community, University of Chicago Press, 1990.

Contributor to periodicals, including *Annals of the American Academy of Political and Social Science* and *Public Interest.*

WORK IN PROGRESS: Researching both urban inequality and the ethnography of the African American experience.

SIDELIGHTS: Elijah Anderson is an ethnographer and sociologist well known for his studies of urban life and culture. He is the author of *A Place on the Corner* and *Streetwise,* books that chronicle the social climates of inner cities. In the former work, Anderson told *CA,* he "presents the concept of the extended primary group and centers on how people create and re-create a social stratification system within their own setting." He began his research for *A Place on the Corner* while attending graduate school at the University of Chicago. Focusing on a single gathering place on Chicago's South Side, Anderson sought to define a microcosm of life in one of America's largest cities. The "place" named in the book's title is Jelly's, a liquor store that sits in the center of one of Chicago's worst neighborhoods. Because they are a favored target of armed robbers, liquor stores are often considered the most dangerous small business operation in America. Anderson's book provides a portrait of Jelly's that goes beyond this common perception. He concedes that Jelly's is a place where violent crime could occur at any moment, yet he also defines the store as a gathering place essential to its neighborhood's social strata. Anderson discovered that Jelly's patrons classify themselves as belonging to three separate groups: "regulars," "wineheads," and "hoodlums." The "regulars" consider themselves above the other customers, and they respect order, steady work, and honestly earned possessions. The "wineheads" are mostly out to get drunk and have fun, often hanging out in front of the store and pestering other customers for wine money. Anderson describes the "hoodlums" as younger men obsessed with money and image; this group frequently admires or actively participates in the drug trade. Analyzing these groups, Anderson concluded in his book that Jelly's acts as a "special hangout for the urban poor and working-class people, serving somewhat as more formal social clubs or domestic circles do for the middle or upper classes."

Critical reaction to *A Place on the Corner* was favorable, with many commenting on Anderson's clearly drawn characterizations. While finding Anderson's day-to-day accounts repetitious at times, a reviewer for the *Library Journal* did offer praise for the book's "interesting, intimate recollections." Peter Kovler, a contributor to the *Nation,* appraised that Anderson "makes these characters come to life, an extraordinary accomplishment considering most of the muck produced by his profession." In summarizing his review, Kovler complained of a lack of indignation from the author regarding the horrible condition of many urban centers, but overall he concluded that "Anderson's book is enlightening."

In his next book, *Streetwise,* Anderson compares two neighborhoods in Philadelphia, Pennsylvania. One is the upper middle-class suburb that the author and his family moved into in 1975, when he began teaching at the University of Pennsylvania; the other is a lower-class ghetto only a few blocks away. Anderson began to frequent the ghetto, studying the social structure and conducting numerous interviews with the community's inhabitants. What he found, and relates in the book, is a neighborhood crippled by crime, drug abuse, apathy, and despair. Contrasted with the portrayal of his nice, upwardly mobile, and integrated suburb, the ghetto is a predominantly African American enclave that is fraught with violent crime and rampant drug abuse. The denizens consist of young men eager to prove their manhood through acts of violence, women who will do just about anything for a drug fix, and older members of the community who are terrified to go beyond the confines of their homes. Anderson asserts that the ghetto has degenerated from a place where the working class were once respected role models to an anarchic society where predatory skills reign and drugs are king. He points to a lack of dignified jobs with decent wages and an erosion of traditional values as the major factors in the neighborhood's decline. In his final assessment, Anderson places the blame on an economic system that has provided favorable "breaks" for upscale communities, such as the one he resided in, and virtually ignored, and thus stifled and damned, the lower-class neighborhoods.

As with *A Place on the Corner,* reviewers were impressed with Anderson's attention to detail and his clear descriptions in *Streetwise.* Michael Di Leonardo wrote in the *Nation,* "What Anderson does very well is both to lay out how these urban residents negotiate their public lives—the 'ballet' of interactions among strangers in public—and to apprehend the ways in which differing groups define themselves vis-a-vis others." Anderson's book was also repeatedly lauded for dealing with an important and interesting topic. A review of *Streetwise* in the *Los Angeles Times* called the book "astute" and "compelling." While some reviewers found Anderson's presentation too clinical despite the highly interesting material, critic Tamar Jacoby felt otherwise. Writing in the *New York Times Book Review,* Jacoby said of Anderson and his book: "The sharpness of his observations and the simple clarity of his prose recommend his book far beyond an academic audience. Vivid, unflinching, finely observed, *Streetwise* is a powerful and intensely frightening picture of the inner city."

BIOGRAPHICAL/CRITICAL SOURCES:

BOOKS

Anderson, Elijah, *A Place on the Corner,* University of Chicago Press, 1978.

PERIODICALS

Annals of the American Academy of Political and Social Science, January, 1989, p. 59.
Nation, August 17-24, 1992, pp. 183-85.
New Republic, December 16, 1978. pp. 31-32.
New York Times Book Review, December 9, 1990, p. 1.
Philadelphia Magazine, May, 1991, p. 18.
Washington Post, April 30, 1991, p. B3.

　　　　　　　　　　　　　　　　　—Sketch by David M. Galens

*　　　*　　　*

ANDERSON, Janet A.　1934-

PERSONAL: Born March 29, 1934, in Washington, DC; daughter of John Kenneth (a publisher and real estate broker) and Alice (a business adviser and piano teacher; maiden name, Morgan) Anderson. *Education:* Pennsylvania State University, B.A., 1956, M.A., 1958; University of Michigan, Ph.D., 1970. *Politics:* "Middle of the road." *Religion:* Christian. *Avocational interests:* Drawing, painting, gardening, breeding Arabian horses.

ADDRESSES: Home—N7750 Engel Rd., Route 3, Whitewater, WI 53190. *Office*—Department of Art, Center of the Arts, University of Wisconsin—Whitewater, Whitewater, WI 53190.

CAREER: Penn Hall Junior College, Chambersburg, PA, instructor in art and art history, 1958-65; University of Wisconsin—Whitewater, professor of art history, 1969—. Anderson House Publishers, co-owner.

MEMBER: National Museum of Women in the Arts, Smithsonian Institution.

AWARDS, HONORS: Grants from National Endowment for the Humanities, 1976 and 1979.

WRITINGS:

Women in the Fine Arts: A Bibliography and Illustration Guide, McFarland and Co., 1991.

Work represented in books, including *On the Threshold of a Dream,* National Library of Poetry, 1991.

WORK IN PROGRESS: Pedro de Mena: Spanish Sculptor; A University Handbook of Multidisciplinary Fine Arts Materials; a photographic album of women's art; research on the seventeenth-century Spanish sculptors Andrea and Claudia de Mena.

SIDELIGHTS: Janet A. Anderson told *CA:* "Born and brought up in Washington, D.C., daughter of a book publisher and a piano teacher, I experienced stimulating contact with museums, concert halls, theatres, and political forums. Saturday mornings were devoted to private art lessons, a prologue to further university training and my vocation.

"In my mind, education—both my own and that of my students—has always been paramount. I have always thought of arts culture as a great canvas of human experience and expression, often the source of vital strokes for tomorrow. I have never tired of searching its fractured pieces for truth to share with others, or of traveling, or of touching and photographing works of art themselves. From the travels came the research for my book on the Spanish sculptor Pedro de Mena. My book on women in the fine arts came from a request from the women's studies department for a course on beleaguered, often forgotten women artists. The book is designed to serve scholars on various levels of research and to guide them to illustrations of individual works for visual study.

"To give librarians a respite from my frequent demands and satisfy my need for atmosphere beyond university walls, I grow a small organic garden. To indulge my passion for beauty and elegance, I raise Arabian horses on my twenty-one-acre farm. In addition, I am a partner with my brother in a private publishing business."

ANDERSON, Kirk 1965-

PERSONAL: Born June 25, 1965, in Kalamazoo, MI; son of Roger Raymond (a manufacturing representative) and Andree (a homemaker; maiden name, Gallaudet) Anderson; married Virginia Navarro (a travel agent), May 25, 1991. *Education:* Kenyon College, B.A., 1987; Harvard University, M.A., 1989.

ADDRESSES: Home—8 Custer St., No. 1, Jamaica Plain, MA 02130.

CAREER: Independent translator, 1990—.

WRITINGS:

TRANSLATOR

Pedro Almodovar, *Patty Diphusa and Other Writings,* Faber & Faber, 1992.
Monica Zak, *Save My Jungle* (children's book), Harcourt, 1992.

WORK IN PROGRESS: A translation of *Little Red Riding Hood in Manhattan,* by Carmen Martin Gaite, to be published in 1994.

SIDELIGHTS: Kirk Anderson told *CA:* "I got into translation by accident, but I quickly discovered that it was my true calling. I started translating contemporary Chinese short stories, then fell in love with a Spaniard and Spanish literature. As a result, much of my work focuses on contemporary Spain."

*   *   *

ANDRE, Judith 1941-

PERSONAL: Born April 21, 1941, in Spokane, WA; daughter of Louis Armand Andre and Margaret Anita White. *Education:* Viterbo College, B.A. (cum laude), 1967; Michigan State University, M.A., 1970, Ph.D., 1979.

ADDRESSES: Home—650 Pine Forest Dr., No. 203, East Lansing, MI 48823. *Office*—Center for Ethics and Humanities in the Life Sciences, C-201 East Fee Hall, Michigan State University, East Lansing, MI 48824-1316.

CAREER: Elementary teacher for sixth, seventh, and eighth grades in Wisconsin, 1963-66; Mercy College of Detroit, Detroit, MI, adjunct professor of philosophy, 1973-76; Wayne County Community College, Detroit, adjunct professor of philosophy, 1973-76; Bowling Green State University, Bowling Green, OH, adjunct instructor, 1976-77; Washburn University of Topeka, Topeka, KS, visiting instructor, 1977-78; Loyola Marymount University, Los Angeles, CA, visiting instructor and adjunct instructor, 1978-80; Old Dominion University, Norfolk,

VA, assistant professor, 1980-85, associate professor of philosophy, 1986-91, associate professor of women's studies, 1990-91, director of Institute of Applied Ethics, 1985-88; Michigan State University, East Lansing, associate professor of philosophy, 1991—. Lecturer at colleges and universities, including Lander College, University of Texas Medical Branch at Galveston, Darton College, Virginia Polytechnic Institute and State University, Mary Washington College, and Southwestern University. Consultant on women's issues to film producers.

MEMBER: American Philosophical Association, Society for Health and Human Values, American Association of University Professors (president, 1987-88), Society for Women in Philosophy, National Women's Studies Association, Hastings Center.

AWARDS, HONORS: Fellow of National Endowment for the Humanities, 1981, 1984, and 1987; Griffith Award, Southern Society for Philosophy and Psychology, 1983; Virginia Foundation for the Humanities and Public Policy, grants, 1986 and 1987, fellowship, 1989; grant from Matchette Foundation, 1987; fellow of Program in Ethics and the Professions, Harvard University, 1988-89; Rockefeller fellow, Institute of Medical Humanities, University of Texas Medical Branch, 1990.

WRITINGS:

(Editor with William Brenner, and contributor) *Essays in Introduction to Philosophy,* Ginn, 1985.
(Editor with David James) *Rethinking College Athletics,* Temple University Press, 1991.

Work represented in anthologies, including *Racism and Sexism in a Changing America,* edited by Paulta Rothenberg, St. Martin's, 1987. Contributor of articles and reviews to academic journals.

WORK IN PROGRESS: What Should Be for Sale? The Values at Stake in Commodification, dealing with the issues underlying the sale of blood, organs, and babies; "Respect for Bodies," to be included in *The Good Body,* edited by Mary Winkler and Letha Cole.

*   *   *

ANNE (Elizabeth Alice Louise Windsor), Princess 1950-

PERSONAL: Born August 15, 1950, in London, England; daughter of Philip Mountbatten (prince consort and duke of Edinburgh) and Elizabeth Alexandra Mary Windsor (queen of England); married Mark Anthony Peter Phillips (a farmer and equestrian), November 14, 1973 (divorced in June, 1992); children: Peter Mark Andrew, Zara Anne Elizabeth. *Education:* Benenden School, graduate, 1968.

Avocational interests: Equestrian sports, tennis, sailing, swimming, skiing, listening to music, reading.

ADDRESSES: Home—Buckingham Palace, London S.W.1, England; Gatcombe Park, Minchinhampton, Stroud, Gloucestershire GL6 9AT, England.

CAREER: Royal representative of the United Kingdom, equestrian, and writer. Commandant in chief of St. John Ambulance and Nursing Cadets and Women's Transport Service; colonel in chief of Royal Corps of Signals, Royal Scots, Worcester and Sherwood Foresters' Regiment, 14th/20th King's Hussars, 8th Canadian Hussars, Royal Regina Rifles, Canadian Armed Forces Communications and Electronics Branch, Royal Australian Corps of Signals, Royal New Zealand Corps of Signals, Royal New Zealand Nursing Corps, and Grey and Simcoe Foresters Militia; chief commandant of Women's Royal Naval Service; honorary air commodore for Royal Air Force, Lyneham. President of Benevolent Trust, Save the Children Fund, Royal School for Daughters of Officers of Royal Navy and Royal Marines, British Academy of Film and Television Arts, Council for National Academy Awards, British Olympic Association, Hunters' Improvement and Light Horse Breeding Society, and Windsor Horse Trials; patron of numerous organizations, including British School of Osteopathy, Royal Corps of Signals Association, Royal Corps of Signals Institute, Communications and Electronics Branch Institute, Missions to Seamen, Association of Wrens, Gloucestershire and North Avon Federation of Young Farmers' Clubs, Home Farm Trust, Jersey Wild Life Preservation Trust, Royal Port Moresby Society for the Prevention of Cruelty to Animals, British Knitting and Clothing Export Council, Riding for the Disabled Association, All England Women's Lacrosse Association, Royal Lymington Yacht Club, Royal Tournament, Army and Royal Artillery Hunter Trials, Horse of the Year Ball, and Benenden Ball; vice-patron of British Show Jumping Association; member of International Olympic Committee. Freeman of City of London and Fishmongers Company; master warden of Farriers Company; master and honorary liveryman of Carmen's Company; honorary liveryman of Farriers Company; honorary freeman of Farmers Company and Loriners Company; yeoman of Saddlers Company; honorary member of Lloyds of London. Chancellor of University of London, 1981—; visitor of Felixstowe College.

MEMBER: Royal British Legion Women's Section (life member), Royal Naval Volunteer Reserve Officers Association (honorary life member), International Equestrian Foundation (president, 1986—), British Equine Veterinary Association (honorary member), Royal Naval Saddle Club (life member), Royal Yacht Squadron (honorary member), Royal Thames Yacht Club (honorary member),

Island Sailing Club, Minchinhampton Golf Club (honorary member).

AWARDS, HONORS: Dame, Order of St. John of Jerusalem; Grand Gold Cross, Order of Merit of Austria; six first prizes in equestrian competitions, 1969; Raleigh Trophy, Individual European Three-Day Event, was named Sportswoman of the Year by Sports Writers' Association, *Daily Express,* and *World Sport,* and was named British Broadcasting Corporation Sports Personality, all 1971; Silver Medal, Individual European Three-Day Event, 1975; named Princess Royal by Queen Elizabeth II, 1986; Humanitarian Award, Variety Clubs International, 1986; Nobel Peace Prize nomination, 1990.

WRITINGS:

(With Mark Phillips) *Princess Anne and Mark Phillips Talking about Horses with Genevieve Murphy,* Paul, 1976.
(With Ivor Herbert) *Riding through My Life,* Pelham Books, 1991.
What Is Punishment For and How Does It Relate to the Concept of Community?, Cambridge University Press, 1991.

SIDELIGHTS: Widely known as the daughter of England's Queen Elizabeth II, Princess Anne has earned her own personal renown for her wide-ranging involvement in equestrian sports and humanitarian causes. Her dedication to organizations such as Save the Children, of which she is president, so far exceeded the service expected from British royalty that she became known as "the hardest-working royal." In 1984 alone she made more than five hundred public appearances. Anne has also won recognition independent of her social position. An accomplished horsewoman, she has competed in steeplechasing, flat racing, and eventing, a three-day affair during which a horse and rider tackle challenging show jumping and cross-country courses as well as elegant dressage routines. In 1976 she rode for England's Olympic team in Montreal, Quebec. Anne's long-standing love of horses also provided the occasion for her 1991 book *Riding through My Life.*

Anne was born in London a few years before her mother became queen. Energetic and bold from an early age, she liked to run, sail, and ride horses, and she reportedly outshone her older brother, Charles, in many such pursuits. She received the private tutoring given to royal children, but she was also allowed to socialize with other girls in the Girl Guides, an organization akin to America's Girl Scouts. At thirteen Anne entered a girls' school; the move countered the royal tradition of at-home education, but followed Charles's precedent of attending private school. Although her performance in academic subjects such as history was less than impressive, she excelled in sports and reveled in her ongoing equestrian training.

In adulthood, Anne's boldness and self-will drew mixed public reactions. As a young woman, she earned a reputation for spontaneity and a frankness unexpected in British high society. She gave informal teas and late-night parties, earned a number of speeding tickets, and gamely tried her hand at all manner of activities, from driving a bus to joining the dancing actors onstage during a musical. Her hands-on style surprised and pleased Britons accustomed to more staid royal behavior. Later she alienated some with what seemed a "dour" manner, exemplified by her unsentimental remarks about motherhood and her reserved attitude toward her much-touted sister-in-law Diana, Charles's wife. And outspoken Anne did not hesitate to give intrusive journalists a crisp rebuff. The princess once admitted, "I just didn't fit the image the media thought I ought to have—a Princess coming from a fairy story," reported Jonathan Cooper in a 1987 *People* article. Gradually, however, Anne's increasing commitment to public works began to improve her image. She won respect for her dedication, down-to-earth approach, and willingness to visit war-torn, impoverished areas on behalf of the needy. In 1986 she received a Humanitarian Award for her efforts.

BIOGRAPHICAL/CRITICAL SOURCES:

BOOKS

Anne, Princess, and Ivor Herbert, *Riding through My Life,* Pelham Books, 1991.
Hoey, Brian, *Anne: The Princess Royal—Her Life and Work,* Chivers Press, 1990.
Parker, John, *The Princess Royal,* Hamish Hamilton, 1990.

PERIODICALS

Christian Science Monitor, July 14, 1970.
Good Housekeeping, May, 1965, p. 20; July, 1970, p. 44.
Life, August 20, 1971.
Look, July 28, 1970, p. 28.
McCall's, May, 1972, p. 91.
Newsweek, March 17, 1969, p. 66; July 27, 1970, p. 12; June 11, 1973, p. 44; November 5, 1973, p. 78; November 26, 1973, p. 50; April 1, 1974, pp. 34 and 36.
New York Post, July 18, 1970, p. 17; June 2, 1973, p. 21.
New York Times, September 1, 1989, p. 11.
People, September 6, 1982, p. 78; March 30, 1987; October 26, 1987; April 24, 1989, p. 66; September 18, 1989, p. 114.
Seventeen, June, 1970, p. 122.
Time, July 20, 1970, p. 11; July 27, 1970, p. 10; February 22, 1971, p. 27; June 11, 1973, p. 35; November 19, 1973, p. 54; November 26, 1973, p. 50; April 1, 1974, p. 35.
Washington Post, August 10, 1971, p. 3.*

ANTAR, Johanna 1953-

PERSONAL: Born December 17, 1953, in New York, NY; daughter of John F. (a police officer) and Ida M. (a telephone operator; maiden name, Vallone) Goosmann; married Mitchell Green, August 13, 1977 (divorced, 1983); married Eddie Antar (a computer consultant), October 2, 1988; children: Matthew Irwin. *Education:* College of Mount St. Vincent, B.A., 1975. *Politics:* Independent. *Religion:* Buddhist.

ADDRESSES: Home and office—Class M Systems, 730 West 183rd St., New York, NY 10033. *Agent*—Carol Mann, Carol Mann Agency, 55 Fifth Ave., New York, NY 10003.

CAREER: General Motors Corp., New York City, senior programmer, 1975-80; CBS, Inc., New York City, project manager for CBS Records, 1980-83; Morgan Guaranty Trust Co., New York City, senior systems analyst, 1983-84; American Society of Composers, Authors, and Publishers, New York City, senior systems analyst and manager of information center, 1984-87; independent consultant, 1987-91; Class M Systems, New York City, co-founder, 1991, owner, 1991—. Actress and playwright in New York City, 1983-88.

MEMBER: National Association of Professional Organizers.

WRITINGS:

(With Louise Edeiken) *Now That You're Pregnant,* Collier Books, 1992.

SIDELIGHTS: Johanna Antar told *CA:* "I believe that we all have spiritual helping hands (guardian angels) who guide us through life, if we are open enough to listen to and be guided by them. My helping hands have been very busy promoting my writing career while I was trying to make a living in another field. Although I have always been involved in the computer industry, I have always been presented with opportunities to write. My earliest efforts were in the theater. In November of 1987, I was suddenly diagnosed with an illness which required immediate surgery and quite a bit of recuperative time. This made me physically unable to pursue the acting end of my theater work, but I was invited to try my hand at writing one-acts for my theater group. Much to my surprise (and sometimes to my great dismay), my writing was received much more favorably than my acting ever was, and actors sought me out to write specifically for them. I started to think that, perhaps, I was on to something.

"My current book was also an act of my helping hands. During my pregnancy in 1989 and 1990, I found that my natural inclination toward research helped me very much to accumulate the information that I needed to make edu-cated choices and decisions. I also found that my natural inclination for schmoozing helped me disseminate this information to other pregnant women. Then one day, my very pregnant friend told me that I should help pregnant women for a living. I immediately saw a book in my head, but thought that it would be too big an undertaking for me. That is when I met my coauthor, Louise Edeiken, a woman with a vast amount of knowledge, creative drive, energy to spare, and a friend who happens to be a book agent. Call it karma, call it *kismet,* but we suddenly had a contract and a manuscript deadline.

"I've been asked what advice I could give to aspiring writers. The best I can tell you is open yourself up and let life come in and visit. Every event in your life, every person you meet, every illness you have, every birth, and every death have a blessing attached. Write something because you think it might help, entertain, move, teach somebody—or even yourself. Write because you have to. I had to write my book. I was compelled to give information to other women. I needed to write my book because I had been so badly treated during my son's birth that writing the book was my only way to make my experience better. I needed to save just one woman from the awful birth and postpartum treatment I received. My inspiration comes from reading and listening to writers whose style I admire: that means my husband, [rock 'n' roll singer] Bruce Springsteen, and [American author] Tom Robbins. It's an odd mix at best, but my husband taught me about listening to life, Bruce taught me about expressing it, and Tom taught me about making fun of it.

"Do I feel my life is blessed? Well, I'm amazed . . . I was born, raised, and still live in Manhattan—and lived to tell the tale. I had a strict Catholic education from kindergarten through college—and survived. I had an early first marriage that ended in an ugly divorce—and I still managed to find the best partner in the world. I was told by my doctor that I may never have children—and I have a beautiful son. I think blessed is an understatement."

*   *   *

APPIAH, (K.) Anthony 1954-

PERSONAL: Born May 8, 1954, in London, England; son of Joseph Emmanuel (a lawyer, diplomat, and politician) and Enid Margaret (an art historian and writer; maiden name, Cripps) Appiah. *Education:* Clare College, Cambridge, B.A., 1975, M.A., 1980, Ph.D., 1982. *Politics:* "Complicated." *Religion:* None. *Avocational interests:* Music, reading.

ADDRESSES: Home—Boston, MA. *Office*—Department of African-American Studies, Harvard University, 1430

Massachusetts Ave., Cambridge, MA 02138. *Agent*—Carl D. Brandt, Brandt & Brandt, 1501 Broadway, New York, NY 10036.

CAREER: University of Ghana, Legon, teaching assistant, 1975-76; Yale University, New Haven, CT, visiting fellow, 1979, assistant professor, became associate professor of philosophy, 1981-86; Cornell University, Ithaca, NY, associate professor, 1986-89, professor of philosophy, 1989; Duke University, Durham, NC, professor of philosophy and literature, 1990-91; Harvard University, Cambridge, MA, professor of Afro-American studies, 1991—. Cambridge University, visiting fellow of Clare College, 1983-84. Social Science Research Council and American Council of Learned Societies, chair of Joint Committee on African Studies, 1991—. Boston Algebra in the Middle Schools, member of community board; Facing History, member of advisory board; consultant to International Labor Organization.

MEMBER: Society for African Philosophy in North America (founding member; president, 1991-92), African Literature Association, American Philosophical Association, Aristotelian Society, Modern Language Association of America, English Institute.

AWARDS, HONORS: Morse fellow, 1983-84; Woodrow Wilson fellow at Florida A & M University, 1989, and Dillard University, 1991; Andrew W. Mellon fellow, National Humanities Center, 1990-91; honorary degree, Harvard University, 1991.

WRITINGS:

Assertion and Conditionals, Cambridge University Press, 1985.

For Truth in Semantics, Basil Blackwell, 1986.

Necessary Questions: An Introduction to Philosophy, Prentice-Hall, 1989.

(Editor and author of introduction) *Early African-American Classics,* Bantam, 1990.

Avenging Angel (novel), Constable, 1990, St. Martin's, 1991.

In My Father's House: Africa in the Philosophy of Culture, Oxford University Press, 1992.

Contributor to periodicals. Guest co-editor, *Critical Inquiry,* Volume XVIII, number 4; assistant editor, *Theoria to Theory,* 1974-79; associate editor, *Philosophical Review,* 1987-89; editor, *Transition,* 1991—. Member of editorial board, *Universitas,* 1976, *Perspectives in Auditing and Information Systems,* 1986—, *Diacritics,* 1987—, *Common Knowledge,* 1990—, and *GLQ: A Journal of Lesbian and Gay Studies,* 1992—; member of editorial collective, *Public Culture,* 1989—; member of editorial advisory board, *Callaloo,* 1990—.

WORK IN PROGRESS: The Oxford Book of African Literature, for Oxford University Press; *A Dictionary of Global Literacy,* with H. L. Gates, Knopf; editing and writing introductions to volumes on Langston Hughes, Zora Neale Hurston, Toni Morrison, Gloria Naylor, Alice Walker, and Richard Wright, with H. L. Gates, Jr., for the series "Amistad Critical Studies in African-American Literature," Warner Books; *Bu Me Be: The Proverbs of the Akan,* with mother Enid Margaret Appiah and others; *Tolerable Falsehoods: Idealization and Human Understanding; Nobody Loves Letitia: A Patrick Scott Mystery;* research on multiculturalism, the significance of race, idealization in the social sciences, and the African novel.

SIDELIGHTS: Anthony Appiah told *CA:* "In the preface to *In My Father's House,* I wrote: 'My first memories are of a place called Mbrom, a small neighborhood in Kumasi, capital of Asante, as that kingdom turned from being part of the British Gold Coast colony to being a region of the Republic of Ghana . . . We went from time to time to my mother's native country, to England, to stay with my grandmother in the rural West Country . . . and the life there . . . seems, at least now, to have been mostly not too different.' Later I took degrees in philosophy at Cambridge and came to the United States in the early eighties to teach philosophy and African-American studies.

"All of this is relevant because, though I write—and enjoy writing—about many things, most of my publications have grown out of my philosophical training, my upbringing in Europe and in Africa, my explorations of African-American culture and history, and my love of reading. (Professors of literature these days are supposed to hide their enjoyment of fiction. I'm a philosopher, so I don't have to be coy.)

"My first publications, outside school magazines and newspapers, were poems, published privately in the 1970s by my mother, in a volume of family poetry for my grandmother. I was in my early twenties, and I was thrilled. Then came a long hiatus, in which I published only reviews and set about the life of a graduate student. (It is an axiom of graduate student life that one avoids writing at all costs.) Only with the pressure created by the imminence of my first 'proper' job and the refusal of my graduate adviser to grant me more extensions, did I finally settle down to write a dissertation.

"I've now published my first novel, a mystery set at Cambridge University, titled *Avenging Angel.* Another, set this time on a Scottish island, rather like one I used to visit, is on the way. The mystery is a wonderful genre for an academic dabbler."

B

BABER, Asa 1936-

PERSONAL: Name pronounced "aye-*sa bay*-burr"; born June 19, 1936, in Chicago, IL; son of Jim (an executive) and Dorothy (a journalist; maiden name, Mercer) Baber; divorced; children: James Lawrence, Brendan Patrick. *Education:* Princeton University, B.A., 1958; Northwestern University, M.A., 1963; University of Iowa, M.F.A., 1969.

ADDRESSES: Home—Chicago, IL. *Office*—*Playboy,* 680 North Lake Shore Dr., Chicago, IL 60611. *Agent*—Candice Fuhrman, 30 Ramona Rd., Box F, Forest Knolls, CA 94933.

CAREER: Robert College, Istanbul, Turkey, teacher of English and theatre, 1963-66; University of Hawaii, Honolulu, tenured assistant professor of English, 1969-74; *Playboy,* Chicago, IL, contributing editor, 1978—; writer. Has been interviewed on numerous radio and television programs, including *The Oprah Winfrey Show* and *The Today Show. Military service:* U.S. Marine Corps (active duty), 1958-61.

MEMBER: PEN, Authors Guild, Vietnam Veterans of America, Illinois Vietnam Veterans Leadership Program.

AWARDS, HONORS: Shubert fellowship, University of Illinois, 1966-67; Felton fellowship, University of Iowa, 1967-68; teaching and writing fellowship, University of Iowa, 1968; Danforth fellowship, University of Hawaii, 1970-74; Best Article of the Year award, *Playboy,* 1977, for "The Commodities Markets," and 1979, for "The Condo Conspiracy"; Lisagor Award, Sigma Delta Chi, for outstanding investigative reporting, 1979 and 1983; Best Short Story of the Year award, *Playboy,* 1980, for "Papageno," and 1981, for "The French Lesson"; H. L. Mencken Award, Free Press Association, 1984; Vietnam Veterans of America Award, 1987, for "contributions to American culture"; citation, Coalition of Free Men, 1988.

WRITINGS:

The Land of a Million Elephants (novel), Morrow, 1970.
Goslings (musical), produced at Eastern Illinois University, 1977.
Tranquility Base and Other Stories, Fiction International, 1979.
Naked at Gender Gap: A Man's View of the War between the Sexes (collected columns), Birch Lane, 1992.
Papageno and Other Stories, Academy Press, 1993.

Author of "Men" column, *Playboy,* 1982—. Contributor to periodicals, including *American Way, Chicago,* and *Illinois Issues.*

WORK IN PROGRESS: A book about men's issues.

SIDELIGHTS: Asa Baber is an accomplished writer who is probably best known for his various contributions to *Playboy.* Among his writings for the magazine is "Men," a column that Baber originated and has been producing since 1982. In this column Baber provides a male perspective on a wide range of subjects. In addition, he has championed men's liberation. "The aggressive male who is being roundly mocked and put down today is absolutely necessary to a successful society," he contended to Bill Brashler in the *Chicago Tribune Magazine.* "It is a part of the male makeup." Monte Williams, writing in the *New York Daily News,* proclaimed Baber "one of the men's movement's most vocal proponents." Williams added that "many minds [perceive Baber] as an unadulterated sexist," but Baber countered that he supports "equal rights for men and women." And he told *USA Today* that women are starting to accord greater understanding to his work. "I think there are a lot of women out there now ready to hear men tell their story," he related.

Although Baber is most recognized for his *Playboy* columns, which have been collected as *Naked at Gender Gap: A Man's View of the War between the Sexes,* he has also published a novel, *The Land of a Million Elephants,* and two short story collections, *Tranquility Base and Other Stories* and *Papageno and Other Stories.* In addition, he wrote a musical, *Goslings,* which was staged at Eastern Illinois University in 1977.

BIOGRAPHICAL/CRITICAL SOURCES:

PERIODICALS

Chicago Tribune Magazine, June 30, 1991.
New York Daily News, May 14, 1992.
USA Today, April 15, 1992.

*   *   *

BAKER, Richard A(llan)   1940-

PERSONAL: Born March 18, 1940, in Stoneham, MA; son of H. Allan and Eleanor Baker; married Patricia Stec (a social worker), July 6, 1963; children: Christopher Allan, David Richard. *Education:* University of Massachusetts at Amherst, B.A., 1962; Michigan State University, M.A., 1965; Columbia University, M.S., 1968; University of Maryland at College Park, Ph.D., 1982.

ADDRESSES: Office—Historical Office, U.S. Senate, Washington, DC 20510.

CAREER: Holy Apostles College, Cromwell, CT, assistant professor of history, 1965-67; Library of Congress, Washington, DC, specialist in American history for Legislative Reference Service, 1968-69; U.S. Senate, Washington, DC, acting curator, 1969-70; Government Research Corp., Washington, DC, director of research, 1970-75; U.S. Senate, director of Historical Office, 1975—. University of Maryland at College Park, adjunct instructor, 1983-84; University of Texas at Arlington, Walter Prescott Webb Lecturer, 1984; Cornell University, adjunct professor in Cornell in Washington Program, 1987-90, 1992. University of Oklahoma, member of board of directors of Carl Albert Congressional Studies Center, 1980—; Everett Dirksen Congressional Leadership Research Center, member of board of directors, 1988—; American University, member of board of directors of Center for Presidential and Congressional Studies, 1988—; U.S. General Accounting Office, member of history advisory board, 1989—; Federal Judicial Center, member of historical advisory committee, 1989-93; U.S. Environmental Protection Agency, member of historical advisory committee, 1991—. National Bicentennial Competition on the Constitution and Bill of Rights, member of national advisory

committee, 1987—; Advisory Committee on the Records of Congress, member, 1991—.

MEMBER: Society for History in the Federal Government (chairperson of Committee on Federal Historical Programs, 1981-82; member of executive council, 1982-85; president, 1985-87), American Historical Association, Organization of American Historians, Western History Association, Phi Kappa Phi, Beta Phi Mu.

AWARDS, HONORS: Ralph W. Hidy Award, Forest History Society, 1985, for the article "The Conservation Congress of Anderson and Aspinall"; Henry Adams Prize, Society for History in the Federal Government, 1988, for his contribution to *The Senate.*

WRITINGS:

The United States Senate: A Historical Bibliography, U.S. Government Printing Office, 1977.
(Editor) *Proceedings: Conference on Research Use and Disposition of Senators' Papers,* U.S. Government Printing Office, 1979.
Conservation Politics: The Senate Career of Clinton P. Anderson, University of New Mexico Press, 1985.
The Senate of the United States: A Bicentennial History, Robert E. Krieger, 1988.
(Editor with Bob Dole, and contributor) *Historical Almanac of the United States Senate,* U.S. Government Printing Office, 1989.
(Editor with Roger H. Davidson) *First among Equals: Senate Leaders of the Twentieth Century,* Congressional Quarterly, 1991.

Work represented in anthologies, including *The Senate, 1789-1989: Addresses on the History of the United States Senate,* edited by Robert C. Byrd, U.S. Government Printing Office, Volume I, 1988, Volume II, 1991. Contributor of articles and reviews to academic journals. Editor, *Senate History,* 1978—; contributing editor, *Cobblestone,* 1984.

WORK IN PROGRESS: A social history of the U.S. Senate from 1841 to 1859, completion expected in 1996.

*   *   *

BALES, Kevin   1952-

PERSONAL: Born February 9, 1952, in Tulsa, OK; son of Jack (a special agent of the Federal Bureau of Investigation) and Mary (a homemaker; maiden name, Still) Bales; married Virginia Baumann (a charity worker), July 18, 1992. *Education:* University of Oklahoma, B.A., 1974; University of Mississippi, M.A. (sociology), 1977; attended Vanderbilt University, 1978-82; London School of Economics and Political Science, M.Sc. (economic history), 1983, Ph.D., 1993. *Politics:* Labour. *Religion:* Society of Friends (Quakers).

ADDRESSES: Home and office—32 Wells St., London W1P 3FG, England.

CAREER: Researcher for the U.S. Department of Labor, 1975, and the U.S. Department of Public Health in Mississippi, 1976; University of Mississippi, instructor, 1976-77, research associate at the Institute of Urban Research, 1979, acting assistant professor of sociology, 1979-80; Ganier & Associates, Nashville, TN, director of research and personnel, 1977; University of Tennessee, instructor in sociology at Turney Prison, 1977-78; Vanderbilt University, Nashville, teaching fellow, 1977-78, research assistant for National Institute of Mental Health employment study, 1980-81; Southern Coalition on Jails and Prisons, Nashville, director of Lyndhurst Sentencing Project, 1980-82; Volunteer State Community College, TN, instructor, 1981-82; Booth Archive Project, director, 1982-87; Booth Archive Collection, editor of research publications, 1988—; University of Westminster, London, England, codesigner of master's program in applied social research and senior lecturer in social research, 1988—. Visiting lecturer at the University of London, 1983-84, and London School of Economics and Political Science, 1991-93; chief research officer for Great Britain's Economic and Social Research Council Data Archive, 1985-86; visiting professor of sociology, Moscow University, 1992-93. SHELTER, research methods consultant and expert witness, 1990—.

WRITINGS:

(Editor with Martin Bulmer and Kathryn K. Sklar) *The Social Survey in Historical Perspective,* Cambridge University Press, 1992.
Man in the Middle: The Life and Work of Charles Booth, Routledge, in press.

Contributor to books, including *Sociological Theory,* edited by Randall Collins, Jossey-Bass, 1984; and, with V. Baumann, *The World's Prisons,* Howard League, 1991. Also author of the booklet *British Crime Survey for Schools,* 1989. Contributor to periodicals, including *Southern Journal of Educational Research, Journal of the National Academy of Recording Arts and Sciences, American Naturalist,* and *Sociological Spectrum.*

WORK IN PROGRESS: A study of slavery in the modern world.

*   *   *

BAREHAM, Lindsey   1948-

PERSONAL: Born September 18, 1948; divorced; children: Ben John, Zachary, Henry John.

ADDRESSES: Home—23 Fraser St., London W4 2DA, England. *Agent*—Bruce Hunter, David Higham, 5-8 Lower John St., Golden Sq., London W1R 4HA, England.

CAREER: Writer and food critic. *Sell Out* (consumer section of *Time Out* magazine), editor, 1970-85; LBC-Radio, weekly broadcast on restaurants and cookbooks on *First Edition,* 1992—.

WRITINGS:

The Time Out Guide to Shopping in London, Hamblyn, 1983.
In Praise of the Potato: Recipes from around the World, Michael Joseph, 1989, Overlook Press, 1990.
Pauper's London, Pan, 1990.
A Celebration of Soup, Michael Joseph, 1993.

Also author of *A Guide to London's Ethnic Restaurants* and *Mood Food.* Contributing editor to *The Time Out Book of London,* NEL, 1983, *A Time Out Guide to Shopping in London,* Time Out Publications, 1986—, and to Fodor travel guides on Great Britain. Consumer columnist for the *Observer* magazine, 1977-79, London *Times,* 1983-84, and *London Daily News,* 1987. Contributor to periodicals, including *Good Housekeeping, Cosmopolitan, Design, Evening Standard,* and the *Sunday Times.*

WORK IN PROGRESS: How to Cook A Chicken and other Stories, with Simon Hopkinson, for Jill Norman/Random Century.

*   *   *

BARKER, Garry   1943-

PERSONAL: Born November 26, 1943, in Otway, OH; son of James H. (a carpenter) and Loval (Cox) Barker; married Anita Hurst (a counselor), June 29, 1973; children: Gregory Thomas, Elizabeth Carole. *Education:* Berea College, B.A., 1965; graduate study at Morehead State University. *Avocational interests:* "Basketball, beer, guns, pickup trucks, country music, baseball caps."

ADDRESSES: Home—110 Holly St., Berea, KY 40403. *Office*—C.P.O. 2347, Berea, KY 40404.

CAREER: Southern Highland Handicraft Guild, Asheville, NC, assistant director, 1965-70; Kentucky Guild of Artists and Craftsmen, Berea, director, 1971-80; Morehead State University, Morehead, KY, in communications at Appalachian Development Center, 1984-85; Berea College, Berea, assistant director and marketing manager of student crafts program and instructor in Appalachian literature, 1985—. Berea Craft Enterprises, Inc., vice-president, 1982-87.

MEMBER: Poets and Writers, Appalachian Studies Association (chair of program committee, 1991), Appalachian Writers Association (executive secretary, 1985-91), Southern Highland Handicraft Guild (life member; member of board of trustees).

AWARDS, HONORS: Best Short Story Award, Catholic Press Association, 1985, for a story published in *Mountain Spirit;* Fiction Award, *Inscape,* 1985; award from Kentucky State Poetry Society, 1985; Professional Assistance Award, Kentucky Arts Council, 1990-91.

WRITINGS:

Fire on the Mountain (stories), Kentucke Imprints, 1983.
Copperhead Summer (novel), Kentucke Imprints, 1985.
Mountain Passage and Other Stories, Kentucke Imprints, 1986.
All Night Dog (stories), Kentucke Imprints, 1988.
The Handcraft Revival in Southern Appalachia, 1930-1990, University of Tennessee Press, 1991.
Mitchell Tolle: American Artist, Painted Treasures, 1992.
Notes From a Native Son, University of Tennessee Press, in press.

Work represented in anthologies, including *Groundwater,* Lexington Press, 1992. Author of a monthly humor column in *Salt River Arcadian,* "Head of the Holler," a biweekly column in *Richmond Register,* and a weekly column in *Lewis County Herald.* Contributor of articles, stories, and poems to magazines, including *Mountain Ways, Ceramics Monthly, Heirloom, Appalachian Heritage, Cavalier,* and *Uneven Ground.* Editor, *Appalachian Studies Journal,* 1992.

WORK IN PROGRESS: Kentucky Rain, a mystery novel.

SIDELIGHTS: Garry Barker told *CA:* "I am an Appalachian writer with no regrets about the label or the subject matter. I am also a crafts marketing administrator, a sometimes teacher of Appalachian literature and creative writing, and an advocate of mountain culture, crafts, literature, lifestyle, and basic values."

*   *   *

BARON, Naomi S(usan) 1946-

PERSONAL: Born September 27, 1946, in New York, NY; daughter of Leonard and Ruth Joan (Josephson) Baron; married; children: Aneil. *Education:* Brandeis University, B.A. (magna cum laude), 1968; Stanford University, Ph.D., 1972.

ADDRESSES: Office—College of Arts and Sciences, American University, Washington, DC 20016.

CAREER: Brown University, Providence, RI, assistant professor, 1972-78, associate professor of linguistics,

1978-85, associate dean of the college, 1981-83; American University, Washington, DC, professor of language and foreign studies, 1987—, associate dean for undergraduate affairs, 1987-92, associate dean for curriculum and faculty development, 1992—. Rhode Island School of Design, visiting faculty member, 1982-83; Emory University, visiting National Endowment for the Humanities chair, 1983-84; University of Texas at Austin, visiting scholar, 1984-85; Southwestern University, Brown Visiting Chair, 1985-87.

MEMBER: Linguistic Society of America, Semiotic Society of America (vice president, 1985-86; president, 1986-87), Phi Beta Kappa.

AWARDS, HONORS: Grants from Bureau of Education for the Handicapped, 1976-84, American Council of Learned Societies, 1977, and National Endowment for the Humanities, 1979-81; Guggenheim fellow, 1984-85; *Computer Languages* was selected by *Library Journal* as one of the best one hundred science and technology books of 1986.

WRITINGS:

Language Acquisition and Historical Change, Horth-Holland, 1977.
Speech, Writing, and Sign, Indiana University Press, 1981.
Computer Languages: A Guide for the Perplexed, Doubleday, 1986.
Pigeon-Birds and Rhyming Words: The Role of Parents in Language Learning, Prentice-Hall, 1990.
Growing Up with Language: How Children Learn to Talk, Addision-Wesley, 1992.

Contributor to *Encyclopedia of Language and Linguistics* and *Encyclopedic Dictionary of Semiotics.* Contributor to periodicals, including *Semiotica, Liberal Education, Computers and Translation,* and *Journal of Creole Studies.* Co-editor, *Semiotica,* Volume XXVI, numbers 3-4, 1979; member of editorial board, *Visible Language.*

SIDELIGHTS: Naomi S. Baron told *CA:* "Computers, language acquisition, language in social context, writing systems, the history and future of higher education—all of these threads make up my field of inquiry. The threads often interconnect in my work, as when I look at the effects of computers on written and spoken language, and when I study how new disciplines (including linguistics) find their way into the academy.

"My next project is to learn Japanese. The relationship between language structure and the social web is radically different in Japan than in societies speaking Indo-European languages. I also want to understand how the intricate writing system in Japan affects the development of literacy."

BARRY, P(atricia) S(teepee) 1926-

PERSONAL: Born October 12, 1926, in East Liverpool, OH; daughter of Linton T. (in sales) and Zola (a teacher; maiden name, Hepburn) Steepee; married Thomas W. Barry (a research scientist), 1948; children: Samuel J. Education: University of Rochester, B.A., 1948; University of Alberta, M.A., 1969, Ph.D., 1974.

ADDRESSES: Home—14322 Ravine Dr., Edmonton, Alberta, Canada T5N 3M3.

CAREER: Rochester Democrat and Chronicle, Rochester, NY, journalist, 1943-53; Cornell University, Ithaca, NY, research assistant at School of Industrial and Labor Relations; conducted biological field research in the western Canadian Arctic, 1959-69; University of Alberta, Edmonton, instructor in English, 1968-69 and 1974-75; free-lance writer, editor, and researcher. Province of Alberta, registered historian, Historical Resources and Site Services; Alberta Historical Resources Foundation, member. Public speaker on drama, art, and scientific topics.

MEMBER: Petroleum History Society (Calgary).

AWARDS, HONORS: Mystical Themes in Milk River Rock Art was chosen for a touring book show, Association of American University Presses, 1992.

WRITINGS:

The King in Tudor Drama, University of Salzburg, 1977.
The Canol Project: An Adventure of the U.S. War Department in Canada's Northwest, privately printed, 1985.
Snow Geese of the Western Arctic, 1958-1983, Canadian Wildlife Service, 1985.
Mystical Themes in Milk River Rock Art (self-illustrated), University of Alberta Press, 1991.

Contributor of articles, stories, poems, songs, and drawings to periodicals, including Arctic, Dalhousie Review, Wascana Review, and Edge.

WORK IN PROGRESS: Culture Delivered, a study of sources and the control of Canadian culture; The Banquet Scene in Tudor Drama; Chapman's Political Allegory in Ovid's Banquet.

SIDELIGHTS: P. S. Barry told CA: "I have been a Canadian citizen since 1965. I have lived in Edmonton, Alberta, since 1957, except for six years in Inuvik, Northwest Territories, from 1963 to 1969.

"I like to give short, succinct talks based on historical research, such as symbolism in art. I experiment with writing styles and with making lino-prints. I write, illustrate, and bind (in 'editions' of one) books on symbolism and mythology, as well as volumes of poems. My drawings in colored ink of Milk River rock art images are for sale in the Provincial Museum and at Vik Gallery, Edmonton."

BARTLETT, Sarah 1955-

PERSONAL: Born April 28, 1955, in Buffalo, NY; daughter of Arthur (a car dealer) and Margaret (a homemaker; maiden name, Hildebrand) Bartlett; married John Petrarca (an architect), September 8, 1989; children: Emilia. Education: University of Sussex, B.A., 1977, M.Phil., 1979.

ADDRESSES: Office—Business Week, 1221 Avenue of the Americas, New York, NY 10020. Agent—John Hawkins, 71 West Twenty-third St., New York, NY 10010.

CAREER: Fortune, New York City, reporter, 1981-83; Business Week, New York City, editor, 1983-88; New York Times, New York City, reporter, 1988-92; Business Week, assistant managing editor, 1992—.

AWARDS, HONORS: Award from Overseas Press Club, 1984, for Business Week cover story on Mexico.

WRITINGS:

The Money Machine: How KKR Manufactured Power and Profits (nonfiction), Warner Books, 1991.

Contributor to periodicals.

SIDELIGHTS: Sarah Bartlett is a prominent financial writer who has reported for such periodicals as Fortune, the New York Times, and Business Week, where she is assistant managing editor. In 1991 Bartlett released The Money Machine: How KKR Manufactured Power and Profits, in which she charts the success of Kohlberg, Kravis, Roberts, and Company (KKR). This investment firm, which began in 1976 with $120,000, came to realize extraordinary profits through leveraged buyouts, a technique that enabled KKR to obtain many major corporations by buying out public stockholders with borrowed money. In 1986, for instance, the firm obtained Beatrice for $5.6 billion, and the following year they acquired RJR Nabisco for $26 billion. Bartlett alleges that such maneuvers may derive, at least in part, from lapses in business ethics, with KKR reportedly involved in several questionable, though not illegal, activities. As Newsweek reviewer Larry Reibstein noted, The Money Machine "contends that KKR built its empire by showering largesse on the right people," making the company the epitome of the greed-driven 1980s. Reibstein added that Bartlett's book "alleges—not always convincingly—that KKR may have given some public-pension-fund administrators sweetheart deals and large campaign contributions while allowing certain lawyers ethically questionable opportunities to invest in lucrative deals."

Speaking about the information she uncovered while writing The Money Machine, Bartlett told Publishers Weekly: "Who had power in the 1980s had a lot to do with who had money and who was willing to dispense that money.

KKR really was a money machine. The fees it generated were very influential on Wall Street, with pension funds, law firms, with all sorts of institutions. And I was shocked by their extremely close relationship with the press. I found that deeply troubling, and as a result I think their recent purchase of the Murdoch magazines raises many disturbing questions."

Reviewers of *The Money Machine,* even those who found it somewhat less than convincing in its entirety, acknowledged its merits. Max Holland wrote in the *Washington Post Book World* that Bartlett effectively advances "understanding of the 1980s by showing how KKR raised the huge pool of capital necessary to leverage corporate America." And Gordon Williams, in his assessment of *The Money Machine* for the *New York Times Book Review,* declared that Bartlett's book provides "insights into the making of those who made the deals."

BIOGRAPHICAL/CRITICAL SOURCES:

PERIODICALS

Economist, June 29, 1991.
Newsweek, May 27, 1991, p. 42.
New York Times Book Review, June 2, 1991, pp. 9, 11.
Publishers Weekly, May 17, 1991, pp. 35-36.
Washington Post Book World, July 14, 1991, p. 4.

*   *   *

BATES, Craig D.   1952-

PERSONAL: Born August 2, 1952, in Oakland, CA; son of Dana Raymond (a factory manager) and June (a homemaker; maiden name, Robinson) Bates; married Jennifer Dawn Bernido (an owner of an art gallery), May 12, 1973; children: Carson Dana. *Education:* Attended Columbia Junior College, 1970-72.

ADDRESSES: Home—P.O. Box 218, Yosemite National Park, CA 95389. *Office*—Yosemite Museum, National Park Service, P.O. Box 577, Yosemite National Park, CA 95389.

CAREER: National Park Service, Yosemite National Park, CA, park technician in Division of Interpretation, 1973-76, Indian cultural specialist, 1976-80, assistant curator, 1980-82, curator of ethnography, 1982—. Merced Community College, instructor, 1974; California Department of Parks and Recreation, instructor, 1977-84; Point Reyes Field Seminars, instructor, 1978-88; Humboldt State University, instructor, 1980; Santa Barbara Museum of Natural History, research associate, 1983—; Miwok Archaeological Preserve of Marin, instructor at Coast Miwok/Pomo Dance Regalia Workshop, 1990. National Park Service, member of Grandee Task Force, 1979,

member of Ethnographic Steering Committee, Curatorial Services Division, 1982-83; Oakland Museum, guest curator, 1984-85; consultant to museums.

WRITINGS:

(With Frank La Pena) *Legends of the Yosemite Miwok,* Yosemite Natural History Association, 1981.
The Indian Cultural Museum: A Guide to the Exhibits, Yosemite Natural History Association, 1985, revised edition (with Martha J. Lee), Yosemite Association, 1987.
(With Martha J. Lee) *Tradition and Innovation: A Basket History of the Indians of the Yosemite-Mono Lake Area,* Yosemite Association, 1990.
(With Travis Hudson) *People From the Water: Indian Art and Culture from Russian California,* Ballena, 1993.

Work represented in anthologies, including *Pleasing the Spirits: A Catalogue of a Collection of American Indian Art,* edited by Douglas C. Ewing, Ghylen Press, 1982; *Native American Basketry of Central California,* edited by Christopher L. Moser, Riverside Museum Press, 1986; and *California Indian Shamanism,* edited by Lowell John Bean, Ballena, 1992. Contributor to periodicals, including *Pacific Historian, Yosemite, Moccasin Tracks, National Parks,* and *American Indian Art.* Member of editorial advisory board, *American Indian Basketry,* 1982-85.

*   *   *

BEE, Ronald J.   1955-

PERSONAL: Born February 22, 1955, in Oakland, CA; son of Keith Willard (a music teacher) and Virginia Cecelia (a homemaker; maiden name, Rakowski) Bee. *Education:* University of California, San Diego, B.A., 1978; Johns Hopkins University, M.A., 1981.

ADDRESSES: Home—P.O. Box 18551, Washington, DC 20036.

CAREER: International Atomic Energy Agency, Vienna, Austria, public information assistant, 1981; Congressional Research Service, Washington, DC, foreign-affairs analyst, 1982; Palomar Corp., Washington, DC, special assistant for national security affairs, 1982-87; international affairs researcher and advisor in West Germany, 1987—; writer. Consultant to System Planning Corp., 1987-89, and Urban Institute, 1988-89.

AWARDS, HONORS: Semi-finalist for Rhodes Scholarship competition in California, 1977; scholarship from Johns Hopkins University, 1980-81; Robert Bosch fellowship, 1987-88; *Looking the Tiger in the Eye* received a Christopher Award and was named a notable book by the *New York Times,* a best nonfiction book of the year by

Publishers Weekly, a best book for young adults by the American Library Association, and an "editor's choice" by *Booklist,* all 1988.

WRITINGS:

(Editor with Sanford Lakeoff, Jeffrey Leifer, and Eric Markusen) *Science and Ethical Responsibility: Proceedings of the U.S. Student Pugwash Conference,* Addison-Wesley, 1980.

(With Carl B. Feldbaum) *Looking the Tiger in the Eye: Confronting the Nuclear Threat* (for young adults), Harper, 1988.

Contributor to periodicals, including *Bulletin of Atomic Scientists, Christian Science Monitor,* and *McGill Law Journal.*

WORK IN PROGRESS: A history of postwar Berlin; a history of the Urban Institute, a nonprofit organization "that investigates the social and economic problems confronting the United States."

SIDELIGHTS: Ronald J. Bee is an international relations expert specializing in military affairs, notably nuclear weaponry. With Carl B. Feldbaum, Bee wrote *Looking the Tiger in the Eye: Confronting the Nuclear Threat,* a history of nuclear weapons. This volume, intended for young-adult readers, recounts the testing, application, and continued development of nuclear weaponry from the first atomic bomb to more advanced, and more lethal, explosives, from World War II through the Cold War and beyond. Ina Navazelskis, writing in the *Philadelphia Inquirer,* proclaimed *Looking the Tiger in the Eye* "fascinating" and declared, "Adults should buy this book for their teenagers—and read it themselves." She added that Bee and Feldbaum "maneuver through the complexities of sophisticated nuclear weapons systems to tell us what they are." And Thomas Powers, in his assessment for the *New York Times Book Review,* noted the book's "fairness, its attention to detail [and] its usefulness as a careful introductory history of the 'nuclear threat.'" Powers concluded, "If you have children, or teach children, and worry about the bomb, [*Looking the Tiger in the Eye*] is a fine way to tell them what you're worried about."

Bee told *CA:* "Young adults and adults need to understand the background and context of nuclear weapons history in order to fulfill their democratic responsibility as citizens. I wrote *Looking the Tiger in the Eye* with this in mind, that objective treatment of this subject matter was possible to present in a way that is both approachable and interesting. Voters and those approaching voting age need nothing less, if their judgment is to be informed."

BIOGRAPHICAL/CRITICAL SOURCES:

PERIODICALS

New York Times Book Review, November 13, 1988, p. 10.
Philadelphia Inquirer, January 15, 1989.

*   *   *

BEERS, Mark H. 1954-

PERSONAL: Born April 21, 1954, in Brooklyn, NY. *Education:* Tufts University, B.S., 1978; University of Vermont, M.D., 1982.

ADDRESSES: Home—1903 Walnut St., No. 535, Philadelphia, PA 19103. *Office*—Merck and Co., Inc., BLA-22, P.O. Box 4, West Point, PA 19486-0004. *Agent*—Mel Berger, William Morris Agency, 1350 Avenue of the Americas, New York, NY 10019.

CAREER: Massachusetts General Hospital, Boston, research assistant in developmental biology, 1975-77; New England Medical Center, Boston, intern, 1982-83, assistant in medicine, 1982-84; junior assistant resident, 1983-84; Mount Sinai Hospital, New York City, senior assistant resident and assistant in medicine, 1984-85; Beth Israel Hospital, Boston, clinical fellow, 1985-87; University of California, Los Angeles, assistant professor of medicine and medical director of Inpatient Geriatric Unit at university Medical Center, 1987-92, medical adviser to Department of Coordinated Care and Discharge Planning, 1988-92, codirector of Geriatric Review Course, 1990-92, medical director of Home Care Program, 1991-92; Merck and Co., Inc., West Point, PA, associate editor, 1992—. Harvard University, Medical School, clinical fellow in geriatric medicine and fellow of Program for the Analysis of Clinical Strategies, Division on Aging, 1985-87; Brigham and Women's Hospital, clinical fellow, 1985-87; Hebrew Rehabilitation Center for the Aged (Boston), clinical fellow, 1985-87; Jewish Memorial Hospital (Boston), attending physician, 1985-86; RAND Corp., senior natural scientist, 1989-92; California Department of Health, member of Aging Program advisory board, 1989—.

MEMBER: American Geriatric Society, Gerontological Society of America (fellow), American College of Physicians (fellow), American Academy of Home Care Physicians, American Society for Clinical Pharmacology and Therapeutics, Massachusetts Medical Society, Alpha Omega Alpha.

AWARDS, HONORS: Charles A. Dana fellow, 1988-89, advanced fellow, 1989-90; grant from National Institute on Aging, 1990-92; National Quality Scholars Competition Award, 1991.

WRITINGS:

(With I. M. Rollingher) *A Guide to Medications for Older Persons,* University of California, Los Angeles, 1991.
(With S. K. Urice) *Aging in Good Health: A Complete, Essential Medical Guide for Older Men and Women and Their Families,* Pocket Books, 1992.

Work represented in anthologies, including *The Practice of Geriatrics,* edited by E. Calkins, A. B. Ford, and P. R. Katz, Saunders, 1992. Contributor of articles and reviews to medical journals. Member of editorial board, *UCLA Health Insights,* 1988-90, and *Journal of the American Geriatric Society,* 1989—.

* * *

BEGLEY, Louis   1933-

PERSONAL: Born October 6, 1933, in Stryj, Poland; immigrated to United States, 1948; naturalized U.S. citizen, 1953; son of Edward David (a physician) and Frances (Hauser) Begley; married Sally Higginson, February 11, 1956 (divorced May, 1970); married Anne Muhlstein Dujarric dela Riviere (a writer), March 30, 1974; children: (first marriage) Peter, Amey B., Adam C. *Education:* Harvard University, A.B. (summa cum laude), 1954; LL.B. (magna cum laude), 1959. *Politics:* Democrat.

ADDRESSES: Home—925 Park Ave., New York, NY 10022. *Office*—Debevoise & Plimpton, 875 Third Ave., New York, NY 10022. *Agent*—Georges Borchardt, 136 East 57th St., New York, NY 10022.

CAREER: Admitted to the Bar of New York State, 1961; Debevoise & Plimpton (law firm), New York City, associate, 1959-67, partner, 1968—; writer; lecturer. Senior visiting lecturer at University of Pennsylvania, 1985 and 1986. *Military service:* U.S. Army, 1954-56.

MEMBER: Association Bar of City of New York, Union Internationale des Avocats, Council on Foreign Relations, Century Association.

AWARDS, HONORS: Irish Times-Aer Lingus International Fiction Prize, 1991; National Book Award nomination, 1991; National Book Critics' Circle Award nomination, 1991; *Los Angeles Times* Book Prize nomination, 1991; PEN/Ernest Hemingway First Fiction Award, 1992; Prix Medicis Etranger, 1992.

WRITINGS:

Wartime Lies (novel), Knopf, 1991.
The Man Who Was Late: A Novel, Knopf, 1993.

Contributor to periodicals, including *New York Times Book Review.*

WORK IN PROGRESS: A novel.

SIDELIGHTS: Louis Begley, a prominent attorney specializing in international corporate law, won substantial acclaim with his literary debut, *Wartime Lies.* This novel recounts the experiences of a six-year-old orphan, Maciek, and his hearty aunt, Tania, as they struggle to survive in war-torn Poland during World War II. Maciek and Tania adopt false identities, using these "wartime lies" to avoid persecution as Jews. Recalling his childhood decades later, Maciek likens his memories to the very lies he promoted to survive during that time. As Judith Grossman noted in the *New York Times Book Review,* "The final perspective on little Maciek is given to the man in mid-life, who . . . speaks an epitaph consigning his childhood self to the realm of *vanitas*—the emptiness of lies." She added that this resolution remains "faithful to the dark ironies of Maciek's fate, which it is Louis Begley's great achievement to have confronted and sustained."

Wartime Lies won praise as an incisive, compelling account of suffering and survival. Grossman, for example, wrote in the *New York Times Book Review* that Begley's novel is "masterly." *Newsweek* reviewer James N. Baker described the book as "melancholy" and added that it "shows us that survival can have too high a price." And *Times Literary Supplement* reviewer Bryan Cheyette, who perceived *Wartime Lies* as Begley's "bid to recapture his lost childhood," noted that the novel "is as much about the psychological consequences of this loss as anything else."

Although critics such as Cheyette have explicitly linked Begley's life with that of Maciek in *Wartime Lies,* Begley himself has been less precise on the subject. "It is no secret," he acknowledged in the *New York Times Book Review,* "that I am a Jew, that I was born in Poland in the same year as Maciek, that I lived in Poland during the war and that the name I bear is not the one that was written in my first birth certificate." But he noted that any memoir he might produce would prove much less dramatic than his novel. "I can only trust my recollection of feelings I had, and of the general tone of those years," he wrote in the same *New York Times Book Review* piece. "Any memoir I wrote would have to be scrupulously truthful. I would have written a very short and—in all likelihood—a rather boring book." And to the *New York Times* he explained: "Reality is really not very interesting, except colossal events or if you have a special interest. If there's no intrinsic interest you have to rework it so there's a structure, and then your imagination gets involved."

Begley's 1993 novel, *The Man Who Was Late,* is the story of Ben, a fiercely self-made man, as told by his closest friend, Jack. Jack pieces the facts of Ben's life together from his own memory and from the personal papers that come into his possession as executor of Ben's will. One prominent element of the narrative is the revealing of

Ben's tumultuous love affair with Jack's cousin Veronique, a woman whose dazzling beauty masks darkness and disquiet. In recounting the story, Jack comes to understand why Ben believed himself to be "late in the major matters of existence." R. Z. Shepard, in his *Time* assessment of *The Man Who Was Late,* called Begley "a fine technician," praising the author's ability to "reveal the hidden flaws in an outwardly flawless character." *Washington Post Book World* contributor Paul Buttenwieser lauded the narrative's "urbanity and wit and filigree elegance." "With *The Man Who Was Late* the organization is as sophisticated as the content," declared Gabriele Annan in *New York Review of Books.* The reviewer concluded: "It is a very elegant, and readable novel, and very serious as well."

BIOGRAPHICAL/CRITICAL SOURCES:

PERIODICALS

Boston Globe, March 16, 1993, p. 1.
Los Angeles Times, January 24, 1993, p. 3.
Newsweek, July 29, 1991, p. 51.
New York Review of Books, June 13, 1991, p. 16; January 28, 1993.
New York Times, October 6, 1991, section LI, p. 10; January 15, 1993, p. 25.
New York Times Book Review, May 5, 1991, pp. 1, 27; August 16, 1992, p. 1, 22-23.
Sunday Times (London) January 17, 1993.
Time, May 27, 1991, p. 69; February 1, 1993, p. 70.
Times Literary Supplement, August 16, 1991, p. 23.
Vanity Fair, February, 1993.
Washington Post Book World, January 10, 1993, p. 1.

*   *   *

BELKAOUI, Ahmed R.
See RIAHI-BELKAOUI, Ahmed

*   *   *

BELLMON, Patricia   1948-
(Pat Copeland)

PERSONAL: Born March 11, 1948, in Enid, OK; daughter of Henry Louis (a farmer and politician) and Shirley Lee (a manufacturer; maiden name, Osborn) Bellmon; married Larry Lewis, May, 1969 (divorced, 1972); married Richard Copeland, March, 1976 (divorced March, 1992); married Jim Hoerth (an anesthetist), May 29, 1993; children: (second marriage) Will Casey. *Education:* Oklahoma State University, B.S., 1970. *Avocational interests:* Music.

ADDRESSES: Home—Enid, OK. *Office*—Northern Oklahoma College, 106 Central Hall, Tonkawa, OK

74653. *Agent*—Fran Collin, 110 West Fortieth St., New York, NY 10018.

CAREER: Washington Star, Washington, DC, writer, 1970-81; Phillips University, Enid, OK, instructor in journalism, 1985-87; Northern Oklahoma College, Tonkawa, OK, instructor in journalism, 1991—. Kaleidoscope (artists' organization), vice president, 1984-85; Youth Services of Northern Oklahoma, member of board of directors, 1986-87.

AWARDS, HONORS: Oklahoma Book Award for nonfiction, Oklahoma Center for the Book, 1993, for *The Life and Times of Henry Bellmon.*

WRITINGS:

NONFICTION; UNDER NAME PAT COPELAND

Oklahoma Cooks, Oklahoma Folklife Council, 1987.
(With Henry Bellmon) *Farmer, Governor, Statesman: The Life and Times of Henry Bellmon,* Council Oak Books, 1992.

Contributor to *The Culture of Oklahoma,* edited by Howard Stein and William Hill, University of Oklahoma Press, 1993. Contributor to newspapers, including the *Tulsa Tribune.*

WORK IN PROGRESS: Short stories; children's stories; essays; researching the music traditions of early Oklahomans.

SIDELIGHTS: Patricia Bellmon told *CA:* "I'm not sure why I started writing; I always have. I suspect I became a journalist because the first time I heard my father cuss, he was chewing out a reporter. Then it became a matter of trying to communicate how people handled their lives. After that, I think I wrote because I was looking for some answers for myself. Now I see my writing changing again, because I'm willing to accept that there aren't answers for everything. Instead of explaining some people's answers-for-the-moment in a concrete, journalistic way, I want to write narratives, stories that give the reader some pleasure, some challenge, and a sense that life is a worthwhile mystery."

*   *   *

BENEDICT, Helen   1952-

PERSONAL: Born November 5, 1952, in London, England; daughter of Burton (a professor of anthropology) and Marion (a writer; maiden name, Steuber) Benedict; married Stephen O'Connor (a writer and teacher), May 10, 1980; children: Simon, Emma. *Education:* University of Sussex, B.A., 1975; University of California, Berkeley, M.A., 1979.

ADDRESSES: Home—New York, NY. *Office*—Graduate School of Journalism, Columbia University, New York, NY 10027. *Agent*—Molly Friedrich, Aaron Priest Literary Agency, 708 Third Ave., New York, NY 10017.

CAREER: New Wings, Novato, CA, managing editor, 1979; *Independent and Gazette,* Richmond, CA, reporter and feature writer, 1980-81; Columbia University, New York City, assistant professor of journalism, 1986—; writer. Director of Delacorte Center's Magazine Career Institute, 1986; visiting lecturer at University of California, Berkeley, 1991.

MEMBER: PEN, Society for Professional Journalists, Association for Education in Journalism and Mass Communication.

AWARDS, HONORS: Fellowships from Virginia Center for the Creative Arts, 1986, MacDowell Colony for Writers and Artists, 1987, and Cummington Community and School of the Arts, 1988, 1989, and 1990; awards for "best book of the year for teenagers" from New York Library and for "best book for young adults" from American Library Association, both 1988, and citation as one of "best books of the decade" from *Booklist,* 1989, all for *Safe, Strong, and Streetwise;* special mention in *Pushcart Prize,* 1988-89, for story "A World Like This"; grants from Columbia Graduate School of Journalism, 1989, and Gannett Foundation's National Research and Publications Program for Journalists in Education, 1989.

WRITINGS:

NONFICTION

(With others) *Women Making History: Conversations with Fifteen New Yorkers,* New York City Commission on the Status of Women, 1985.
Recovery: How to Survive Sexual Assault, Doubleday, 1985.
Safe, Strong, and Streetwise (for young adults), Little, Brown, 1987.
Portraits in Print, Columbia University Press, 1991.
Virgin or Vamp: How the Press Covers Sex Crimes, Oxford University Press, 1992.

OTHER

A World Like This (novel), Dutton, 1990.

Work represented in anthologies, including *Fiction Writer's Market,* Writer's Digest Books, 1984; and *Conversations with Bernard Malamud,* edited by Lawrence Lasher, University of Mississippi Press, 1991. Contributor to periodicals, including *Antioch Review, Columbia Journalism Review, Fordham Law Review, Glamour, Ms., New York Times Book Review, New York Woman, Ontario Review, San Francisco Examiner, San Francisco Review of Books,* *Soho News, Washington Post Book World, Working Woman,* and *Writer's Digest.*

WORK IN PROGRESS: A novel; more nonfiction.

SIDELIGHTS: Helen Benedict is a distinguished journalist who has received attention for her writings on rape and sex crimes. Among her earliest works is the book *Recovery: How to Survive Sexual Assault,* which she derived from extensive interviews with rape victims. Benedict told *CA* that she still "receives letters in reaction to this book to this day." She followed *Recovery* with *Safe, Strong, and Streetwise,* in which she advises young adults on safety and well-being. In 1990 she produced a novel, *A World Like This,* which she described to *CA* as the story of "a teenager in prison and what happens to her upon her release." Benedict next published *Portraits in Print,* which includes profiles on such writers as Joseph Brodsky, Bernard Malamud, and Susan Sontag. Accompanying these profiles, which appeared earlier in various magazines, are discussions of what Benedict considers "the ethical dilemmas inherent in interviewing people about their private lives."

Benedict is also author of *Virgin or Vamp: How the Press Covers Sex Crimes.* In this work she exposes the sexism that she perceives as inherent in coverage accorded sex crimes in which women are victims. Furthermore, she denotes the manner in which female victims are seemingly cast as either unrealistically innocent or sexually reckless. Benedict reported to *CA* that *Virgin or Vamp* "has broken new ground: no other book has been written about how the press covers sex crimes, even though these crimes are such popular fodder for the press." A critic for the *New York Times Book Review* proclaimed that *Virgin or Vamp* "makes a powerful case for reform in the way the daily press approaches its coverage of sex crimes."

Benedict told *CA:* "I came to my current specialization as a press critic on a path that is natural to journalists. Unlike academic scholars, journalists tend not to specialize early in their career but to generalize until their experience and research lead them to particular subjects. I thus began my career writing about almost anything, but soon developed two main focuses: crime victims, particularly women; and literature.

"My interest in victims began, in a sense, as early as my childhood. I lived for several years in Mauritius and the Seychelles, islands full of poverty and disease. On returning home to England, where I grew up, I was much affected by the contrast between the haves and the have-nots and developed an early, passionate intolerance of injustice. This same passion later drove me to choose journalism as a career.

"My interest in literature, meanwhile, was almost a birthright. I grew up in the midst of London's literary world, wrote a 'novel' at the age of eight, a book about how to raise children at age nine, and another 'novel' at eleven. Journalism seemed the perfect career to combine my love of writing with my passion for justice.

"Once I reached college I majored in developmental psychology and, as part of my training, went to work as a volunteer in a prison for minor girls. Being only twenty-one and more interested in the downtrodden than the authorities, I befriended and studied the inmates and was appalled to discover that seventy percent of them had been raped by relatives. The tragedy of their plight led to my lifelong interest in rape and its victims, to my decision to become a journalist, and to my books on related subjects.

"At the University of California, Berkeley, I continued my interest in rape by interviewing victims about whether they should be named by the press. I also published magazine and newspaper pieces about rape.

"In 1979 I went to work as a feature writer for the *Independent and Gazette* in California, where I was able to write dozens of articles on rape, battered women, child prostitutes, and related subjects, as well as many pieces on authors and the literary world.

"Finally deciding I was more suited to long-form journalism than to newspaper writing, I left the *Gazette* and moved to New York City to free-lance. After five years of writing on the subject of rape, I wrote *Recovery.* My next book, *Safe, Strong, and Streetwise,* appeared shortly after I was hired at Columbia University to teach magazine journalism. Teaching gave me the freedom to think more and write for money less, and thus I was able to finally combine my literary bent with my work in the prison and my interviews with rape victims by writing the novel *A World Like This.* A year later I published *Portraits in Print.*

"As my experience teaching journalism grew, my two fields of specialization—literature and sex crimes—began to fuse. I found myself increasingly using a literary approach to journalism in the way I edited and analyzed newspaper and magazine stories with my students. I also found myself increasingly interested in the language used about sex crimes. I thus conceived of *Virgin or Vamp.*"

BIOGRAPHICAL/CRITICAL SOURCES:

PERIODICALS

Columbia Journalism Review, October 15, 1992.
New York Times Book Review, November 22, 1992.

BENJAMIN, Kathleen Kelly
See KELLY-BENJAMIN, Kathleen

*   *   *

BENNETT, Carl D(ouglas)   1917-

PERSONAL: Born July 22, 1917, in Waycross, GA; son of George A. and Tiffie (Spell) Bennett; married Margaret Kate Weir, April 10, 1942; children: Katharine Bennett Gregg, Susan Bennett Tucker, Patty Bennett Uffelman. *Education:* Emory University, A.B. (with honors), 1940, M.A., 1945, Ph.D., 1962. *Politics:* Democrat. *Religion:* Baptist.

ADDRESSES: Home—380 Sycamore Lane, Laurinburg, NC 28352. *Office*—Department of English, St. Andrews Presbyterian College, Laurinburg, NC 28352.

CAREER: West Georgia College, Carrollton, instructor in English, 1941-42; Wesleyan College, Macon, GA, 1944-59, began as assistant professor, became associate professor of English; St. Andrews Presbyterian College, Laurinburg, NC, professor of English, 1959-82, distinguished professor, 1982—, past department head and chair of Humanities and Fine Arts Division. Seinan Gakuin University, visiting professor, 1980-81; Mercer University, visiting professor; lecturer at Kansai Gaidai, English Center, Kyoto, Japan, and Hiroshima Jogakuin College. Southern Regional Council, researcher, 1949. Scotland Arts Council, member of board of directors; member of board of directors of local Literacy Council; Red Cross first aid instructor.

MEMBER: Modern Language Association of America, Asian Studies Association, American Association of University Professors (past chapter chair), Danforth Association (past regional chair), South Atlantic Modern Language Association, South Atlantic States Association for Asian and African Studies, Southern Historical Association.

AWARDS, HONORS: Fulbright fellow in India, 1964; fellow in England, Piedmont University Center, 1972-73; Lilly scholar, Duke University, 1977, 1978; grant from National Endowment for the Humanities, 1978; Carnegie grants; grants from Southern Fellowship Fund.

WRITINGS:

Joseph Conrad, Continuum, 1991.

Work represented in anthologies, including *Humane Learning in a Changing Age,* 1971. Contributor of articles and reviews to scholarly journals.

SIDELIGHTS: Carl D. Bennett told *CA:* "The germ of the Conrad book can be traced back to graduate years in

Emory University's Institute of the Liberal Arts. There we students, together with a team of professors, explored ancient Greek dramas, with their accent on human confrontation with the tragic dilemmas of life. On my own, I discovered German philosopher Georg Wilhelm Friedrich Hegel's analysis of such choices, not as we often construe them—as a forced choice between two evils, the painful pressure to choose the lesser of the two—but rather as a tragic choice between two goods, saving one good at the cost of losing the other. I then discovered Karl Jaspers's concept of awareness beyond ability. For my dissertation, Joseph Conrad became the inevitable paradigm. After several articles on Conrad, and massive surgery on an expanded version of the dissertation, the task was done, and my book was published in 1991."

* * *

BERKEY, Jonathan P. 1959-

PERSONAL: Born December 5, 1959, in Northampton, MA; son of Robert F. Berkey (a college professor) and Carolyn Berkey (a director of alumnae relations; maiden name, Miller); married Vivien E. Dietz (a college professor), September, 1988. *Education:* Attended University College, London, 1979-80; Williams College, B.A., 1981; attended Harvard University, 1981-83; Princeton University, M.A., 1986, Ph.D., 1989.

ADDRESSES: Home—P.O. Box 1923, Davidson, NC 28036. *Office*—Department of History, Davidson College, Davidson, NC 28036.

CAREER: Princeton University, Princeton, NJ, lecturer in history, 1988-90; Mount Holyoke College, South Hadley, MA, assistant professor of religion, 1990-93; Davidson College, Davidson, NC, assistant professor of history, 1993—.

MEMBER: American Historical Association, Middle East Studies Association of North America.

WRITINGS:

The Transmission of Knowledge in Medieval Cairo: A Social History of Islamic Education, Princeton University Press, 1992.

WORK IN PROGRESS: "Research on popular culture in medieval Cairo."

* * *

BERLE, Gustav 1920-

PERSONAL: Born March 4, 1920, in Germany; married Esther Pinto (a teacher); children: Ellen Berle Matlins, Jonathan B. *Education:* Received Ph.D. *Avocational interests:* Jazz music, crossword puzzles.

ADDRESSES: Home—801 South Ocean Dr., No. 502, Hollywood Beach, FL 33019-2143; and P.O. Box 756, Silver Spring, MD 20918-0756. *Agent*—Bert Holtje, James Peter Associates, Inc., P.O. Box 772, Tenafly, NJ 07670.

CAREER: In advertising in Baltimore, MD, 1952-58; in public relations in Baltimore, 1958-66; publisher in Baltimore, 1966-82; writer. University of Baltimore, instructor, 1949-67; Florida International University, instructor, 1991-93. Small Business Administration, national marketing director, Service Corps of Retired Executives (SCORE), 1987-89. *Military service:* U.S. Army, agent in Counter Intelligence Corps, 1944-46; served in European theater.

MEMBER: Mensa.

WRITINGS:

The PUNdit's Dictionary, Pundit Press, 1986.
Do-It-Yourself Business Book, Wiley, 1988.
(With William M. Alarid) *Free Help From Uncle Sam to Start Your Own Business, or Expand the One You Have,* Puma Publishing, 1989, 3rd edition, 1993.
Raising Start-Up Capital for Your Firm, Wiley, 1990.
Planning and Forming Your Company, Wiley, 1990.
The Small Business Information Handbook, Wiley, 1990.
(With William M. Alarid) *Money Sources for Small Business: How You Can Find Private, State, Federal, and Corporate Financing,* Puma Publishing, 1991.
The Green Entrepreneur: Business Opportunities That Can Save the Earth and Make You Money, TAB Books, 1991.
Business Information Sourcebook, Wiley, 1991.
The SBA Hot Line Answer Book, Wiley, 1992.
The Complete Book of Small Business Forms and Agreements, Prentice-Hall, 1992.
Retiring to Your Own Business: How You Can Launch a Satisfying, Productive, and Prosperous Second Career, Puma Publishing, 1993.
Instant Business Plans, Puma Publishing, 1993.
On the American Hero Trail, Preservation Press, 1993.
NTHP Junior Encyclopedia of American History, Preservation Press, in press.

SIDELIGHTS: Gustav Berle told *CA:* "My retirement in 1986 confirmed the fact that man is not fit for retirement. Ergo, I started planning and writing books, and published fourteen in the first seven years of untimed living. This resulted in occasional travel, speeches, extensive correspondence, consulting, renewed teaching activities, completion of academic work for a belated Ph.D., a condominium with an ocean view, and enough book ideas to last me until I am a hundred-twenty. Writing is much recommended, as an exercise that maintains the brain's elasticity. It can even serve, if consistently pursued, as a guaranty for longevity and for keeping off the government's and family's dole."

* * *

BERNSTEIN, Blanche 1912-1993

OBITUARY NOTICE—See index for *CA* sketch: Born October 6, 1912, in New York, NY; died of lung cancer, January 27, 1993, in New York, NY. Economist, government official, educator, and writer. Bernstein's *Politics of Welfare: The New York City Experience* presented her views on the American welfare system and recounted her experiences as a welfare administrator. Bernstein began her career in public service as an economist with the War Production Board during World War II. She served with various departments in the federal government until 1969, when she became the director of research on urban social problems at the New School for Social Research. In 1975 she joined the New York Department of Social Services, and three years later she was appointed head of New York City's Human Resources Administration, directing the largest local welfare agency in the United States. *The Politics of Welfare* detailed the obstacles Bernstein confronted on the job and presented her belief that the existing welfare system fostered dependency rather than allowing welfare recipients to improve their situation. After leaving her post with the Human Resources Administration, Bernstein returned to the New School for Social Research where she stayed until her retirement.

OBITUARIES AND OTHER SOURCES:

PERIODICALS

New York Times, January 28, 1993, p. B7.

* * *

BIDART, Frank 1939-

PERSONAL: Born in 1939; father was a farmer. *Education:* Graduated from University of California, Riverside; attended Harvard University.

ADDRESSES: Office—Department of English, Wellesley College, Wellesley, MA 02181.

CAREER: Poet. Affiliated with Wellesley College, Wellesley, MA.

WRITINGS:

POETRY COLLECTIONS

Golden State, Braziller, 1973.

The Book of the Body, Farrar, Straus, 1977.
The Sacrifice, Random House, 1983.
In the Western Night: Collected Poems, 1965-90, Farrar, Straus, 1990.

SIDELIGHTS: Frank Bidart first gained the attention of critics with *Golden State* and *The Book of the Body,* introspective verse collections that were published during the 1970s. On the basis of Bidart's early work, David Lehman, in a *Newsweek* assessment, called him "a poet of uncommon intelligence and uncompromising originality." In the early 1980s Bidart wrote *The Sacrifice,* which furthered his reputation as a prominent voice in American poetry. Much of Bidart's work, critics suggest, focuses on the origins and consequences of guilt. Among his most notable pieces are dramatic monologues presented through such characters as Herbert White, a child-murderer, and Ellen West, an anorexic woman. "Part of his effectiveness comes simply from his ability as a storyteller," commented Michael Dirda in *Washington Post Book World.* "You long to discover what happens to his poor, doomed people."

Bidart grew up in California, where he developed a love for the cinema. He entertained thoughts of becoming an actor when he was young and later, at the time he enrolled in college, considered becoming a film director. His plans began to change, however, when he was introduced to literature at the University of California at Riverside. While an undergraduate, he was introduced to such critical works as *The Liberal Imagination* by Lionel Trilling and *The Idea of a Theater* by Francis Fergusson—both of which exerted a strong influence on his early attitudes toward literary expression. He also became familiar with the work of notable twentieth-century poets T. S. Eliot and Ezra Pound. In a 1983 interview with Mark Halliday, which is included in Bidart's *In the Western Night: Collected Poems, 1965-90,* the poet spoke of how reading Pound's cantos, long works which were first released in 1917, introduced him to the potential of poetry to encompass a wide range of subjects: "They were tremendously liberating in the way that they say that anything can be gotten into a poem, that it doesn't have to change its essential identity to enter the poem—if you can create a structure that is large enough or strong enough, *anything* can retain its own identity and find its place there."

After graduating from the University of California at Riverside, Bidart continued his education at Harvard University. He was not, however, certain of where his course of study would lead him. Bidart related in his interview with Halliday: "I took classes with half my will—often finishing the work for them months after they were over; and was scared, miserable, hopeful. I wrote a great deal. I wrote lugubrious plays that I couldn't see had characters with no character. More and more, I wrote poems." Bidart's first attempts at poetry were, by his own admission, failures. "They were terrible; no good at all," he continued in his interview. "I was doing what many people start out by doing, trying to be 'universal' by making the entire poem out of assertions and generalization about the world—with a very thin sense of a complicated, surprising, opaque world outside myself that resisted the patterns I was asserting. These generalizations, shorn of much experience, were pretty simple-minded and banal."

After honing his craft, Bidart submitted his work to Richard Howard, who was then editor of a poetry series at Braziller. Howard decided to publish Bidart's poetry in a volume entitled *Golden State,* which was released in 1973. In the title poem to Bidart's debut collection, a son and father vainly attempt to understand and accept one another. The poem, presented as an address to the father, is divided into ten separate sections. Critics remarked on the autobiographical nature of the piece and on the sparse quality of the language that Bidart employs throughout the work. Other poems in the collection also touch upon the relationship between parent and child. In his interview Bidart discussed how he came upon the theme of family that enters into some of the poems in *Golden State:* "When I first faced the central importance of 'subject matter,' I knew what I would have to begin by writing about. In the baldest terms, I was someone who had grown up obsessed with my parents. The drama of their lives dominated what, at the deepest level, *I* thought about."

Also included in *Golden State* is "Herbert White," a poem which is presented through the voice of a psychopathic child-murderer and necrophiliac. In his interview Bidart stated that his intent in writing the piece was to present "someone who was 'all that I was not,' whose way of 'solving problems' was the *opposite* of that of the son in the middle of the book. The son's way . . . involves trying to 'analyze' and 'order' the past, in order to reach 'insight'; Herbert White's is to give himself a violent pattern growing out of the dramas of his past, a pattern that consoles him as long as he can feel that someone *else* has acted within it." According to several reviewers, the dramatic monologue, which opens the collection, is the most notable work in the book. Sharon Mayer Libera, in her *Parnassus: Poetry in Review* assessment, stated that "Bidart's achievement, even a *tour de force,* is to have made [Herbert White] human. The narrator's gruesome adventures become the least important aspect of the monologue— what is significant is his reaching out, in a language both awkward and alive, for the reasons he seeks power over his experience in peculiar and violent ways."

In Bidart's second collection, *The Book of the Body,* he includes several poems which feature characters who are struggling to overcome both physical and emotional adversity. The book opens with "The Arc," in which the author presents the musings of an amputee, who at the be-

ginning of the poem provides instructions on how to care for his stump. Bidart also gives voice to Ellen West, a woman with anorexia, a condition which causes her to starve herself continuously because she is dissatisfied with the appearance of her body. Based on a case study by noted psychiatrist Ludwig Binswanger, "Ellen West" was regarded by Edmund White in *Washington Post Book World* as "a work that displays Bidart's talents at their most exacting, their most insistent."

In the opinion of several reviewers, Bidart's work gains strength by disregarding the conventions of poetry. In an appraisal of *The Book of the Body,* Helen Vendler of the *Yale Review* stated that "Bidart's method is not narrative; unlike the seamless dramatic monologues we are used to, his are spliced together, as harrowing bits of speech, an anecdote, a reminiscence, a doctor's journal notes, a letter, an analogy, follow each other in a cinematic progression." Reviewers have also often drawn attention to liberties that Bidart takes when spacing his words and lines in his poetry and when punctuating and capitalizing the English. In his interview with Halliday Bidart explained that "the only way I can sufficiently . . . express the relative weight and importance of the parts of a sentence—so that the reader knows where he or she is and the 'weight' the speaker is placing on the various elements that are being laid out—is [through] punctuation. . . . Punctuation allows me to 'lay out' the *bones* of a sentence visually, spatially, so that the reader can see the pauses, emphases, urgencies and languors in the voice."

The Sacrifice, released in 1983, received widespread praise from reviewers for its insightful poems, many of which focus on guilt. Central to the volume is a thirty-page work entitled "The War of Vaslav Nijinsky." The title character in the poem is a dancer who pays witness to World War I and eventually loses his sanity. Feeling responsible for the injustices inflicted upon humanity during the conflict, Nijinsky offers penance by performing a dance in which he enacts his own suicide. As with most of his poetry, "The War of Vaslav Nijinsky" went through a series of revisions with Bidart experimenting with language and punctuation throughout its development. "The Nijinsky poem was a nightmare," he remarked in his interview. "There is a passage early in it that I got stuck on, and didn't solve for two years. Undoubtedly there were a number of reasons for this; the poem scared me. Both the fact that I thought it was the best thing I had done, and Nijinsky's ferocity, the extent to which his mind is *radical,* scared me. But the problem was also that the movement of his voice is so mercurial, and paradoxical: many simple declarative sentences, then a long, self-loathing, twisted-against-itself sentence. The *volume* of the voice (from very quiet to extremely loud) was new; I found that many words and phrases had to be not only entirely capitalized, but in italics." In reviewing the poem, Lehman of *Newsweek* offered praise for Bidart's technique of alternating portions of the dancer's monologue with prose sections on Nijinsky's life. According to Lehman, "the result combines a documentary effect with an intensity rare in contemporary poetry." Also included in Bidart's third collection is "Confessional," in which he presents the musings of a person who places himself in the role of a patient undergoing psychotherapy. The piece was regarded by Don Bogen of *Nation* as "one of the most intelligent and moving poems on family relations" to be published at the time.

Although he has written in a variety of forms, Bidart is best known for his dramatic monologues of troubled characters like Herbert White, Ellen West, and Vaslav Nijinsky. In his interview Bidart discussed how he is able to write dramatic monologues through voices different from his own: "Once I finally get the typed page to the point where it does seem 'right'—where it does seem to reproduce the voice I hear—something very odd happens: the '*being*' of the poem suddenly becomes the poem on paper, and no longer the 'voice' in my head. The poem on paper suddenly seems a truer embodiment of the poem's voice than what I still hear in my head. I've learned to trust this when it happens—at that point, the entire process is finished." Later in the interview he commented on his approach toward expression through language as a whole, remarking that "again and again, insight is dramatized by showing the conflict between what is ordinarily seen, ordinarily understood, and what now is experienced as real. Cracking the shell of the world; or finding that the shell is cracking under you."

BIOGRAPHICAL/CRITICAL SOURCES:

BOOKS

Bidart, Frank, *In the Western Night: Collected Poems, 1965-90,* Farrar, Straus, 1990.

PERIODICALS

American Poetry Review, September, 1985, p. 14.
Nation, December 10, 1983, pp. 610-11; August 13, 1990, pp. 170-73.
Newsweek, January 30, 1984, pp. 71-72.
New York Times Book Review, November 27, 1983, p. 13.
Parnassus: Poetry in Review, spring/summer, 1975, pp. 259-69.
Tribune Books (Chicago), August 5, 1990, p. 3.
Washington Post Book World, November 20, 1977, p. E5; October 9, 1983, p. 8; March 3, 1991, p. 6.
Yale Review, autumn, 1977, pp. 78-79.*

—*Sketch by Mark F. Mikula*

BIESEL, David B. 1931-

PERSONAL: Born September 12, 1931, in Chicago, IL; son of William James Trimble (a newspaper reporter) and Aileen Louise (a secretary and newspaper reporter; maiden name, Jacquith) Biesel; married Donna Louise Scoggan, May 20, 1957 (marriage ended, May 6, 1976); married Diane Jane Stephens (a school media specialist), September 25, 1982; children: Deborah Louise Biesel Brugger, William Warren. *Education:* Attended University of Maryland at College Park, Columbia University, and Rutgers University. *Politics:* Independent. *Religion:* Episcopalian.

ADDRESSES: Home and office—St. Johann Press, 315 Schraalenburgh Rd., Haworth, NJ 07641.

CAREER: Worked as a sports writer in Washington, DC; American Institute of Physics, New York City, manager of editorial department, 1962-69; R. R. Bowker (Xerox), New York City, began as managing editor, became editor of reference books, 1969-73; Macmillan Publishing Co., Inc., New York City, senior editor in Professional and Reference Book Division, 1973-82; Elsevier Science Publishing Co., New York City, senior editor, 1982-84; R. R. Bowker (Xerox), editor in chief of Book Division, 1984-86; M. E. Sharpe, Inc., Armonk, NY, vice-president and editorial director, 1986-88; St. Johann Press (book packagers and publishing consultants), Haworth, NJ, president, 1988—. Scarecrow Press, Inc., director of Association Publishing Program, 1991—. *Military service:* U.S. Marine Corps, 1953-57; became sergeant.

MEMBER: North American Society for Sport History, American Library Association, Society for American Baseball Research, Professional Football Research Association.

AWARDS, HONORS: In 1991 *Can You Name That Team?* was included among the best reference books of the year by *Library Journal.*

WRITINGS:

Can You Name That Team? A Guide to Professional Baseball, Football, Soccer, Hockey, and Basketball Teams and Leagues, Scarecrow, 1991.

WORK IN PROGRESS: Professional Sports in New Jersey; A History of Women's Professional Basketball; History of the Saddlery Industry in America; revising *Can You Name That Team?*

*   *   *

BILGRAMI, Akeel 1950-

PERSONAL: Born February 28, 1950, in India; son of Syed Taki (a judge) and Asghari (Jaffrey) Bilgrami. *Edu-*

cation: Received B.A. and M.A. from Oxford University; attended University of Chicago.

ADDRESSES: Home—110 Morningside Dr., No. 58, New York, NY 10027. *Office*—719 Philosophy Hall, Columbia University, New York, NY 10027.

CAREER: Columbia University, New York City, associate professor of philosophy, 1985—.

AWARDS, HONORS: Rhodes scholar, Oxford University, 1971-74; Society of Fellows, Columbia University, 1983-85; Whitney humanities fellow, 1992-93.

WRITINGS:

Belief and Meaning: The Unity and Locality of Mental Content, Basil Blackwell, 1992.

Editor, *Journal of Philosophy.*

WORK IN PROGRESS: The Politics of Contemporary Islamic Identity, publication expected in 1994; *Self-Knowledge,* publication expected in 1996.

*   *   *

BINA, Cyrus 1946-

PERSONAL: Born March 21, 1946; son of Jalile (a civil servant) and Homa (a homemaker) Bina; married, wife's name Shanaz, October 9, 1969; children: Babak, Roxanna. *Education:* Institute of Advanced Accounting, Tehran, Iran, B.Sc., 1968, Chartered Accountant, 1969; Ball State University, M.A. (management), 1972, M.A. (economics), 1975; American University, Ph.D., 1982.

ADDRESSES: Office—Center for Middle Eastern Studies, Harvard University, Cambridge, MA 02138.

CAREER: Teacher of mathematics, social sciences, and English at a high school in Tehran, Iran, 1965-66; Iranian Treasury Department, Plan and Budget Organization, Tehran, foreign exchange analyst, 1966-68; Division of Social Security and Insurance, Tehran, chief auditor, 1969-71; Ball State University, Muncie, IN, instructor in economics, 1972-74; American University, Washington, DC, instructor in economics, 1977-79; Towson State University, Towson, MD, instructor in economics, 1979-80; EMAY Corp., McLean, VA, senior economist, 1980-81; Washington International College, Washington, DC, associate professor of economics and statistics, 1981-82; American University, instructor at Center for Technology and Administration, summer, 1982; Olivet College, Olivet, MI, professor of economics and director of Economics Program, 1982-87; Providence College, Providence, RI, professor of economics, 1987-90; Harvard University, Cambridge, MA, faculty associate and visiting scholar at

Center for Middle Eastern Studies, 1989-91, research associate, 1991—, member of Dudley House, 1992—. Globalenergy, Inc., president; Congress of Political Economists International, founding member, 1989; member of Center for Iranian Research and Analysis. New Hampshire College, member of board of advisers, International Business Program, 1991—. Guest on television and radio programs.

MEMBER: International Economic Association, International Association for Energy Economics, Middle East Studies Association of North America, American Economic Association, Association for Social Economics, Middle East Economic Association (member of board of directors, 1988-92), Eastern Economic Association, Kress Society of History of Economic Thought (Harvard University).

AWARDS, HONORS: Faculty Enrichment Award, Center for Near Eastern and North African Studies, University of Michigan, 1985.

WRITINGS:

Accounting Handbook for Community Development, EMAY Corp., 1980.
The Economics of the Oil Crisis, St. Martin's, 1985.
(Editor with Hamid Zangeneh, and contributor) *Modern Capitalism and Islamic Ideology in Iran,* St. Martin's, 1992.
(Editor) *Theories of Rent Since Adam Smith,* JAI Press, 1993.

Work represented in anthologies, including *Readings in Introductory Macroeconomics,* edited by Peter D. McClelland, McGraw, 1991; *Mobilizing Democracy: Changing the U.S. Role in the Middle East,* edited by Greg Bates, Common Courage Press, 1991; and *The Labor Process and Control of Labor: The Changing Nature of Work Relations in the Late Twentieth Century,* edited by B. Berberoglu, Praeger, 1993. Contributor of articles and reviews to economic, political studies, and sociology journals. Member of editorial board, *Journal of Iranian Research and Analysis* and *Journal of Economic Democracy,* 1989—.

WORK IN PROGRESS: The Economics of Energy Sources: Price Formation, Crisis, and Competition in the International Energy Industry; Toward a New Global Order: U.S. Hegemony at Bay; editing *Beyond Survival: Wage-Labor and Capital in the Late Twentieth Century,* with C. Davis and L. Clements.

*   *   *

BING, Leon 1950-

PERSONAL: Born in 1950.

ADDRESSES: Agent—Eric Ashworth, Donadio & Ashworth Literary Representatives, 231 West 22nd St., New York, NY 10011.

CAREER: Fashion model; free-lance journalist; writer.

WRITINGS:

Do or Die, HarperCollins, 1991.

Contributor to periodicals, including *L.A. Weekly. Do or Die* has been excerpted in *Harper's* and *Rolling Stone.*

SIDELIGHTS: In the nonfiction work *Do or Die* Leon Bing allows members of the Bloods and the Crips, rival gangs in Los Angeles, to speak about their experiences in the impoverished neighborhoods in which they live and operate. A one-time fashion model and now a free-lance journalist, Bing became curious about the thought processes of gang members after hearing accounts of drive-by shootings in Los Angeles. For four years she reported on gang activities for *L.A. Weekly* and used her experiences to inform *Do or Die.* Upon its publication, a reviewer for *Publishers Weekly* regarded the account as "a book that should be read by everyone professionally involved or personally concerned with the future of urban America."

By spending time with many gang members, Bing learns of the nature of the violent acts that the Bloods and the Crips commit. She reveals that many gang members believe that it is justifiable to shoot another person for wearing the colors of an enemy gang, for giving a menacing look, or for defacing a piece of property with the symbol or the initials of a known rival. In situations in which an offender is not immediately available for retribution, a substitute member of the adversarial gang might be clipped in a drive-by shooting. At times, innocent bystanders are wounded or murdered in gunfire between the two groups. Bing chronicles one occasion during which a gang member misread the address of a targeted family and ultimately killed four guiltless people on a city street, believing that he was carrying out his responsibility to the Crips.

Several reviewers noted that despite Bing's background—as a member of a rich family and a resident of Pasadena—she is able to gain the trust of gang members who lack the same opportunities available to her. In a Chicago *Tribune Books* assessment, Sylvester Monroe praised Bing for her ability to access information from both the Bloods and the Crips. "A middle-aged, white, female former model is not the most likely person to gain the trust of hard-core gang members," acknowledged Monroe. "But somehow Bing manages to do just that; and with a good ear, an engaging narrative style and a rare objectivity, she presents a seldom-seen human side of a deadly group of adolescents with names like 'G-Roc,' 'Faro,' and 'Sidewinder.' " (Bing altered the names of the people who

agreed to speak with her in order to provide them with a sense of comfort during interviews.)

When Janice Castro in *Time* asked the author how she first accessed members of the gangs, Bing spoke of a gathering of the Bloods that she attended. When she approached the gang members with her plan to provide them with an opportunity to be heard. Bing attributes their willingness to eventually speak with her to her "lack of fear. . . . They dissed me at first, but I told them they were wasting my time, and I started to leave. One of the kids followed me and said he would talk to me. And then the word got around about this strange white lady who wanted to talk to them, who wasn't afraid."

In *Do or Die* Bing enters the neighborhoods and homes of gang members. She witnesses their interactions with one another, visits them in correctional facilities, and speaks to their friends and family members. In the hope of reuniting with Hart—a member of the Crips whom Bing met at a detention camp a few months before—the author speaks with his half-sister Bijou, who is pregnant with a third child. After the author and Bijou find Hart, Bing witnesses the two siblings get into an altercation that erupts into a fist fight. Hart is humiliated by his half-sister in front of a handful of spectators and resists the urge to disfigure Bijou with a broken bottle that he has picked up during the skirmish.

Although gang members in *Do or Die* pledge their loyalty to the Bloods or the Crips, Bing shows how individual gang members follow personal codes of honor. Some advocate murder but decry rape; others disparage stealing from the elderly. One of her interviewees, Sidewinder, after witnessing a mugging, returns to the victim some money that was amassed through drug dealing. Several reviewers noted that Bing provided an important service in humanizing members of the Bloods and the Crips. "For those willing to try to close the gap, to see gang members the way they see themselves and to try to understand how they see the rest of the world, 'Do or Die' is a book worth reading," accorded Monroe in Chicago *Tribune Books.* In the *New York Times Book Review,* Mike Davis remarked that " 'Do or Die,' a poignant, sometimes chilling record of conversations with hard-core gang members in south central Los Angeles, constantly reminds us, these are our own appalling, damaged and lost children." And Walter Dean Myers, in the *Los Angeles Times Book Review,* commented: Bing "has given a brutally honest portrait of a growing phenomenon in American society, young people whose ethics are steeped in mass violence. It's up to the rest of us whether we will ever give the young men and women alternatives that we can live with."

In her interview with *Time* Bing stated that some of the gang members who helped her with the book "are among my best friends." Remarking on the American tendency to stereotype gang members and treat them as less than human, Bing said in the interview that "these are American kids. Nobody cares about them. We are so obsessed with the rights of the unborn, but we don't care about these kids after they are born. They are not just social aberrations. They are children, and they are being ground into dust."

BIOGRAPHICAL/CRITICAL SOURCES:

PERIODICALS

Los Angeles Times Book Review, August 11, 1991, p. 1.
New York Times Book Review, August 11, 1991, p. 6.
People, September 23, 1991, p. 31.
Publishers Weekly, July 5, 1991, p. 50.
Rolling Stone, July 11, 1991, p. 72.
Time, March 16, 1992, p. 12.
Tribune Books (Chicago), August 25, 1991, p. 4.*

—*Sketch by Mark F. Mikula*

*   *   *

BISHOP, Claire Huchet   1899(?)-1993

OBITUARY NOTICE—See index for *CA* sketch: Born c. 1899, in Geneva, Switzerland (one source says Brittany, France); died of an aortal hemorrhage, March 11, 1993, in Paris, France. Political activist, librarian, and author. Bishop, whose early career was spent as a storyteller in Paris and New York City, created prize-winning books that have been translated into numerous languages. In 1924, Bishop helped open France's first children's library, L'Heure Joyeuse, and she later worked at the New York Public Library. A fable she told to youngsters at that library became her first book, *The Five Chinese Brothers.* In her serious works, like *Twenty and Ten* and *Yeshu, Called Jesus,* Bishop examined war and religion. A leading opponent of anti-Semitism, Bishop served as the president of both the Jewish-Christian Fellowship of France, from 1968 to 1981, and the International Council of Christians and Jews, from 1975 to 1977. Her crusade against racial and religious prejudice led to several significant changes, including the omission of anti-Semitic language in the Catholic catechism. Among Bishop's most popular works are *Pancakes Paris, All Alone,* and *How Catholics Look at Jews.*

OBITUARIES AND OTHER SOURCES:

BOOKS

The Writers Directory: 1990-1992, St. James Press, 1990.

PERIODICALS

New York Times, March 14, 1993, p. 42.

BISSINGER, H(arry) G(erard III)   1954-

PERSONAL: Born November 1, 1954, in New York, NY; son of Harry Gerard II and Eleanor (Lebenthal) Bissinger; married (divorced, 1986); married Sarah Macdonald; children: (twins) Harry Gerard IV, Zachary Stone. *Education:* University of Pennsylvania, B.A., 1976.

ADDRESSES: Office—Chicago Tribune, 435 North Michigan Ave., Chicago, IL 60611.

CAREER: Ledger-Star, Norfolk, VA, reporter, 1976-78; *St. Paul Pioneer Press Dispatch,* St. Paul, MN, reporter, 1978-81; *Philadelphia Inquirer,* Philadelphia, PA, reporter, beginning in 1981, editor, ending in 1988; *Chicago Tribune,* Chicago, IL, investigative reporter. Nieman Fellow, Harvard University, 1985-86.

MEMBER: Society of Professional Journalists, New Jersey Press Association.

AWARDS, HONORS: Frank Premack Memorial Award, 1982; Livingston Young Journalists' Award, Mollie Parniss Livingston Foundation, 1983; National Headliner Award, 1987; Pulitzer Prize corecipent, Columbia University Graduate School of Journalism, 1987, for series on the Philadelphia court system.

WRITINGS:

Friday Night Lights: A Town, a Team, and a Dream, Addison-Wesley, 1990.

SIDELIGHTS: In his best-selling nonfiction work *Friday Night Lights: A Town, a Team, and a Dream,* journalist H. G. Bissinger attempts to explain the mystique surrounding high school football in Texas and its effect on the towns that house the teams. Bissinger's project was inspired by a *Sports Illustrated* feature on a Texas quarterback that he read when he was a teenager. The author told *Sports Illustrated* publisher Donald Barr, "The story just stuck in the recesses of my brain, and I never forgot it. . . . I became fascinated by high school football as the glue that keeps a small town together." After a careful selection process in which he surveyed teams in Pennsylvania, Ohio, and Texas, Bissinger took a leave of absence and moved to Odessa, Texas, the home of the Permian High School Panthers, to follow the team during the 1988-89 school year. The Permian team, nicknamed Mojo, reigns as one of the most successful high school football programs in Texas, having made eight trips to the state finals and having won five state championships since 1965. Permian's accomplishments on the gridiron have attracted a throng of faithful fans; the team regularly draws crowds of more than ten thousand and plays in a stadium—able to hold more than nineteen thousand people—that cost $5.6 million to build in 1982.

Bissinger presents football as a redeeming quality for this seemingly uninviting western Texas town. The city is noted for both its barren landscape and the smell of oil which permeates the area. Odessa's economy depends largely on the volatile oil market, and residents have weathered both booms and recessions. Their love of football, however, has remained constant. One retired citizen explained to Bissinger, "Mojo football, it helps you survive all this sand, the wind, the heat. I wouldn't live any other place." Noting the community's lack of a university, art museum, or similar drawing card, a former football booster club president stated, "There are so few other things we can look at with pride." He added, "When somebody talks about West Texas, they talk about football. There is nothing to replace it. It's an integral part of what made the community strong. You take it away and it's almost like you strip the identity of the people."

While Bissinger acknowledges the pride that the football team brings to the community, he feels that the residents' priorities are sometimes skewed by the attention paid to the sport. He charges that football players are afforded special privileges in the classroom and are not held to the same expectations as other students. One team member remarked, "All I do in class is show up. They should make these classes fifteen minutes long." A teacher complained, "This community doesn't want academic excellence. It wants a gladiatorial spectacle on a Friday night." Using a preseason party with standing-room only as an example, Bissinger shows that because football is a cornerstone of the town's life, young men gain status for merely being part of the team. The author alleges that the majority of young males at Permian are not outstanding athletes, but the athletes' work ethic and the quality of coaching combine to create excellent teams. Players often reach a caliber of play that they will be unable to match later on in life, leaving their high school accomplishments as the epitome of their athletic careers. The wife of a former player stated, "We all feel that our husbands have been unhappier with everything after they got out of [football]. You see your name up in lights and people follow you and they put your name in the newspaper and then all of a sudden the season is over."

Another problem Bissinger examines in *Friday Night Lights* is Odessa residents' racial attitudes, which he believes are distorted by football. The author observes that racial intolerance is suspended on the gridiron but, unfortunately, returns when the game is over. He notes that the school system was not desegregated until 1982, partly due to a fear that the football program would collapse. When officials closed the high school on the city's south side (which was overwhelmingly black and Hispanic), residents began to see a bright side to desegregation. Since the infusion of black student athletes would help the football

team, the two local high schools initiated a fight over school district boundaries. Yet even after desegregation, attitudes concerning minorities remained entrenched in the past. After considering a star black player's worth without football, a coach remarked that he would be just "a big ol' dumb nigger." A black coach at Permian told Bissinger, "We fit as athletes, but we really don't fit as a part of society. . . . We know that we're separate, until we get on the field. We know that we're equal as athletes. But once we get off the field we're not equal. When it comes times to play the game we are a part of it. But after the game, we are not a part of it." A Permian fan echoed this sentiment: "We don't have to have any contact with them, except on the Permian football team. It's the only place in Odessa where people interact at all with blacks."

Bissinger weaves his commentary about social issues together with game summaries and follows the Permian drive to the state playoffs. In another statistically successful year, Coach Gary Gaines's 1989 team won eight games and lost two (by a total of two points). A playoff bid was at stake, though, because three teams were tied for first place in the league. This unfamiliar situation raised the ire of fans who blamed Gaines for the failure. Gaines found "for sale" signs in his front yard and was confronted with public criticism. An irate resident wrote a letter to the editor of a local paper berating Gaines for having stated, "It doesn't matter if you win or lose if two good teams are playing." The writer responded, "Never in the history of sports has anything been more ludicrously said. He talks like a coach, he acts like a coach, but he is not a football coach." This tense situation was defused when officials decided that a coin toss would determine which two teams would make the playoffs. Some critics retracted their harsh words when Permian won the toss and a trip to the playoffs. After winning three games to reach the semifinals, the Mojo team lost to the eventual state champions from Carter High School.

Critics noted that in *Friday Night Lights,* Bissinger presents a balanced portrait of the team and community, but gets caught up in the whirlwind of the state championship drive. *New York Times Book Review* contributor Michael Swindle assessed that Bissinger's work "offers a biting indictment of the sports craziness" of Odessa but also includes "a moving evocation of its powerful allure." A reviewer for *Washington Post Book World* observed, "The affection he feels for all of these people permeates the book, and in a most attractive way; even as Bissinger recognizes the flaws of the system in which Texas football thrives, he acknowledges and celebrates the humanity of those who work and play within that system. *Friday Night Lights* is a decent, good-spirited book." Despite his sometimes negative observations about the importance placed on football, the author admitted to caring for his subjects, especially the players. He wrote in his volume, "I remember the first time I saw them in the field house, with no idea of what they would be like and how they would take to me, or for that matter, how I would take to them. And I remember how I thought of them at the end, as kids that I adored."

When *Friday Night Lights* was published, some people in Odessa accused Bissinger of slanting his story to present the town in a negative light. The controversy escalated when the football coach of crosstown rival Odessa High School charged that Permian High had conducted supervised workouts before the official start of practice. The University Interscholastic League found Permian guilty and prohibited the team from appearing in the state playoffs in 1990. Bissinger believes that because he brought national attention to Permian High School with *Friday Night Lights,* he was made to be the scapegoat. He canceled promotional stops at two Odessa bookstores after those stores received calls threatening him. The owner of one shop commented in *Sports Illustrated:* "People here took the book as an attack on their values." In a *Sports Illustrated* editorial Bissinger acknowledged, "There are many decent, right-thinking people in Odessa, but there are many others who have built their lives around Permian football and who have lost all perspective on what a game should be."

BIOGRAPHICAL/CRITICAL SOURCES:

BOOKS

Bissinger, H. G., *Friday Night Lights: A Town, a Team, and a Dream,* HarperCollins, 1991.

PERIODICALS

Chicago Tribune, October 10, 1990.
Los Angeles Times Book Review, October 21, 1990, p. 5.
New York Times Book Review, October 7, 1990.
Sports Illustrated, September 17, 1990, pp. 3, 82-96; October 8, 1990, p. 132.
Washington Post Book World, September 16, 1990, p. 3.*

—*Sketch by Mary K. Ruby*

*   *   *

BLACKWELL, James
See Blackwell, James A., Jr.

*   *   *

BLACKWELL, James A., Jr.
(James Blackwell)

PERSONAL: Education: Tufts University, Ph.D., 1985.

ADDRESSES: Office—Center for Strategic and International Studies, 1800 K St. N.W., Washington, DC 20006.

CAREER: Has worked as a division operations officer for the U.S. Army, an instructor at the U.S. Military Academy, and as director of political-military studies, a senior fellow, and cochair of the Project on Persian Gulf War Military Lessons Learned, all at the Center for Strategic and International Studies; writer. Member of board of directors of Dupuy Institute; member of Council on Foreign Relations. Has appeared on worldwide television and radio as a military expert. Has testified before the U.S. Senate Armed Services Subcommittee on Defense Industry and Technology, the House Banking Subcommittee on Economic Stabilization, and the House Armed Services Committee.

WRITINGS:

(Editor with Barry M. Blechman) *Making Defense Reform Work,* foreword by Harold Brown and James Schlesinger, Brassey's, 1990.
(As James Blackwell) *Thunder in the Desert: The Strategy and Tactics of the Persian Gulf War,* Bantam, c. 1991.

Contributor of articles and editorials to periodicals, including *Parameters, Military Technology, National Defense, Washington Post, San Diego Union,* and *Chicago Tribune.*

*   *   *

BLADES, John (D.) 1936-

PERSONAL: Born December 21, 1936, in Springfield, IL; son of Gilbert (a state government administrator) and Margaret (a state legislative clerk; maiden name, Stokes) Blades; married Barbara Herlt (an artist and teacher), April 28, 1962; children: Elizabeth, Patrick, Michael, William. *Education:* Washington University, B.A., 1959; graduate study at University of Illinois at Urbana-Champaign, 1959-60. *Politics:* "Apolitical." *Religion:* "Areligious."

ADDRESSES: Home—2111 Maple, Evanston, IL 60201. *Office*—*Chicago Tribune,* 435 North Michigan Ave., Chicago, IL 60611. *Agent*—David Black, 220 Fifth Ave., Suite 1400, New York, NY 10001.

CAREER: Illinois State Register, reporter, 1959; *Miami Herald,* Miami, FL, reporter, 1961-64; *Chicago Sun-Times,* Chicago, IL, copy editor of *Midwest* magazine, 1964-65, managing editor, 1965-69; *Chicago Tribune,* Chicago, daily book editor, 1969-71, staff writer and articles editor for *Sunday* magazine, 1969-77, book editor, 1977-85, book critic, 1985-88, staff writer for "Tempo" section, 1988—.

MEMBER: National Book Critics Circle (past vice president and member of board of directors).

AWARDS, HONORS: James Friend Memorial Award for Criticism, 1989; writing award from *Chicago Tribune*, 1990.

WRITINGS:

Small Game (novel), Henry Holt, 1992.

Also author of *Body Politic*, a play produced at Hull House Playwrights Center. Contributor of articles and short fiction to periodicals, including *Chicago, Focus Midwest, Film Heritage,* and *The Quarterly.*

WORK IN PROGRESS: A Free Agent, a novel, completion expected in 1995.

*   *   *

BLAKE, Michael   1945-

PERSONAL: Born July 5, 1945; son of a telephone company executive and a homemaker (maiden name, Blake). *Education:* Attended University of New Mexico, 1970.

ADDRESSES: Office—2918 Gilmerton Ave., Los Angeles, CA 90064. *Agent*—(books) Marcy Posner, William Morris Agency, 1350 Avenue of the Americas, New York, NY 10019; (films) Daniel Ostroff, 9200 Sunset Blvd., Suite 402, Los Angeles, CA 90069.

CAREER: Writer. *Military service:* U.S. Air Force, 1964-68.

MEMBER: Academy of Motion Picture Arts and Sciences.

AWARDS, HONORS: Academy Award for best adapted screenplay, Academy of Motion Picture Arts and Sciences, Golden Globe Award for best screenplay, Hollywood Foreign Press Association, Writers Guild Award for best adapted screenplay, Writers Guild of America, and Western Writers of America Award, all 1991, for *Dances with Wolves.*

WRITINGS:

Stacy's Knights (screenplay), Crown International Pictures, 1983.
Dances with Wolves (novel), Fawcett, 1988.
Dances with Wolves (screenplay), Orion, 1990.
(With Kevin Costner and Jim Wilson) *Dances with Wolves: The Illustrated Story of the Epic Film,* edited by Diana Landau, photographs by Ben Glass, Newmarket Press, 1990.
Airman Mortensen (novel), Seven Wolves, 1991.

Blake recorded *Dances with Wolves* and *Airman Mortensen* on audiocassette, both Seven Wolves, 1991.

WORK IN PROGRESS: Screenplays *Airman Mortensen,* for Columbia, and *The Unwanted,* for Universal.

SIDELIGHTS: After years of virtually fruitless struggle, Michael Blake finally made a name for himself as a screenwriter in 1990 with his second produced script, the celebrated *Dances with Wolves.* Set during the Civil War, it centers on the interaction between a Union soldier, newly transferred from a battleground to a remote frontier outpost, and the Plains Indians whose survival is increasingly threatened by the encroaching white civilization. Hailed by reviewers—and native Americans—as the most accurate cinematic presentation of Plains culture to date, the film was a box-office hit as well as a critical success, earning millions of dollars and garnering for Blake the most prestigious awards in the industry.

Dances with Wolves had begun for Blake in the mid-1980s as yet another film idea in a long string of unproduced screenplays. Knowing Blake had not had a screenplay filmed since 1983's *Stacy's Knights,* the writer's actor friend Kevin Costner persuaded him that he would have a better chance of reaching his audience in print instead. Blake was living in his car and his friends' houses by the time the novel version was done, and then he struggled to get it published. It took over a year and numerous rejections before the manuscript found a home with Fawcett, which issued just thirty thousand copies in 1988. By then Costner was eager to do a film version, so Blake penned the script at last. Filming brought its own difficulties. The production exceeded its schedule and budget, creating particular concern among financial backers over its use of Indian language and subtitles. Costner, who coproduced, directed, and starred in the film, stuck to his guns nonetheless, deferring his own salary to finish the picture. Perseverance paid off: The resulting film grossed more than seven times its eighteen-million-dollar cost and drew widespread acclaim, winning several of the industry's highest writing honors, including the prized Academy Award.

At the film's heart is Lieutenant John Dunbar, a Union officer who chooses a post on the western frontier as his reward for heroics on a Civil War battlefield. When his new garrison proves to be deserted, Dunbar dutifully settles in anyway, chronicling his days in a journal and befriending first a curious lone wolf and then, gradually, several Lakota Indians. The more he sees of the Indians, the more fascinated by their life he becomes. Dunbar even leaves his post to live with the tribe for a time, taking part in their activities, learning their language, and falling in love with a woman among them, a white adopted by the Lakotas as a young orphan. Ultimately he makes a painful choice between white society, which has come to disgust him, and an Indian culture facing extinction.

Deemed "the best Western since John Ford left us" by *Los Angeles Times* arts editor Charles Champlin, *Dances with Wolves* won accolades from many critics. Michael Kilian of the *Chicago Tribune*, for example, commended the movie's authenticity, objectivity, and sympathy for the Indian perspective, and *Washington Post* writer Hal Hinson judged it "one of the year's most satisfying and audaciously entertaining films." Some reviewers, on the other hand, found fault with its naive tone and Dunbar's openness to the foreign culture, which they judged out of place for his time period. Writing in *Newsweek,* David Ansen acknowledged that the film "is vulnerable both to charges of sentimentality and anachronism. . . . But if one's mind sometimes balks, one's heart embraces the movie's fine, wide-open spirit, its genuine respect for a culture we destroyed without a second thought." In Ansen's opinion, *Dances with Wolves* "has a true epic reach and a romantic generosity of spirit that one is happy to succumb to."

The film's sensitivity to the Indian way of life reflects Blake's long-standing preoccupation with the subject. In a *Detroit Free Press* article, he commented: "I was interested in knowing more about the Indians from the time I was a little boy. . . . I picked up every book I could find, and every one broke my heart. Among all the Indian groups, there was a spirituality that was transcendent and a way of life that was marvelous. 'Dances with Wolves' is about my devastation to think that way of life is gone and we had no chance to learn from it." Blake felt that his script touched a widespread American guilt over how the Indians, the wildlife, and even the land itself have been treated. Discussing the film with *New York Times* writer Mervyn Rothstein, Blake remarked that "in a certain way, 'Dances with Wolves' is a very contemporary movie. Because we are still treating certain people as if they're just in the way."

Blake's success with *Dances with Wolves* opened the door to a brighter future. He bought a house, began writing scripts for the Universal and Orion studios, and saw the paperback printing of the *Wolves* novel reach eight hundred thousand copies and the book about the film's production sell sixty-five thousand copies. He founded his own audio book company to publish a best-selling, unabridged audiocassette version of the novel. Through his company, Seven Wolves, Blake also worked to help other artists meet and get their work noticed. One of his projects was to bring Seven Wolves into book publishing to issue poetry, novels, and out-of-print reference works. As Kevin Costner observed in a *People* article about Blake, "He's always known what he's wanted to do with success—and that's to share it."

BIOGRAPHICAL/CRITICAL SOURCES:

PERIODICALS

Chicago Tribune, October 30, 1990; November 9, 1990; October 18, 1991, section 2C, p. 1.
Detroit Free Press, November 25, 1990, pp. 1Q and 7Q.
Film Comment, November-December, 1991, p. 62.
Los Angeles Times, November 22, 1990, pp. F1 and F11; February 2, 1991, pp. F1 and F6-7; October 7, 1991, p. E5.
Newsweek, November 19, 1990, pp. 67-68.
New York, November 19, 1990, p. 107.
New Yorker, December 17, 1990, pp. 115-16.
New York Times, March 25, 1991, pp. C13 and C18.
People, March 25, 1991, pp. 57-58.
Premiere, October, 1990, p. 57.
Washington Post, November 9, 1990, pp. C1 and C9; March 24, 1991, p. G1.

—*Sketch by Polly A. Vedder*

*   *   *

BLASI, Anthony J(oseph) 1946-

PERSONAL: Born April 3, 1946, in Dayton, OH; son of Emmanuel Anthony (an aerospace scientist) and Mary Ella (Marshall) Blasi. *Education:* St. Edward's University, B.A., 1968; University of Notre Dame, M.A., 1971, Ph.D., 1974; University of St. Michael's College, M.A., 1984; Regis College, Toronto, Ontario, S.T.L., 1985.

ADDRESSES: Office—Department of Sociology, Muskingum College, 52 East Main St., New Concord, OH 43762.

CAREER: University of Louisville, Louisville, KY, assistant professor of sociology, 1976-78; Daemen College, Amherst, NY, associate professor of sociology and chairperson of department, 1978-80; University of Hawaii at Hilo, assistant professor of sociology, 1986-90; Muskingum College, New Concord, OH, associate professor of sociology, 1990—.

MEMBER: Association for the Sociology of Religion, American Sociological Association, Society for the Scientific Study of Religion, Religious Research Association.

WRITINGS:

A Phenomenological Transformation of the Social Scientific Study of Religion, Peter Lang, 1985.
Moral Conflict and Christian Religion, Peter Lang, 1988.
Early Christianity as a Social Movement, Peter Lang, 1989.
Making Charisma: The Social Construction of Paul's Public Image, Transaction Books, 1991.

WORK IN PROGRESS: A monograph on the sociology of Johannine Christianity; a study of the German Catholic community of Zanesville, Ohio; a study of the state-wide Ohio Ninth-Grade Proficiency Test results.

SIDELIGHTS: Anthony J. Blasi told *CA:* "I have generally worked as a sociologist who specializes in social theory, and who does research on religion and other cultural phenomena. At one juncture, I thought it necessary to learn more about the religion I had studied sociologically, and I proceeded on course work that led toward a second doctorate. *Making Charisma* is a work in which I interpret the posthumous charisma of Saint Paul in terms of a tradition in sociological theory called 'sociology of knowledge.' It entailed my exploring charisma from the perspective of a phenomenologically informed sociology of knowledge, and as such might be seen as a continuation of my earlier work, as reflected in *A Phenomenological Transformation of the Social Scientific Study of Religion.* It also entailed the techniques of literary criticism common to biblical scholars; and, as a work in the sociology of early Christianity, it might be seen as a sequel to my *Early Christianity as a Social Movement.*"

*　　*　　*

BLOCH, Dan 1943-

PERSONAL: Born in New York, NY, 1943.

ADDRESSES: Home— Amsterdam, Holland.

CAREER: Writer.

WRITINGS:

NOVELS

Double Take, Gollancz, 1979.
The Modern Common Wind, Heinemann, 1985.
Passing Through, Heinemann, 1987.
Face Value, New Amsterdam Books, 1989.

SIDELIGHTS: Dan Bloch has been celebrated, particularly in England, as a humanitarian writer with a quirky style. He first gained recognition for *The Modern Common Wind,* his 1985 novel about three generations of inhabitants at a Kenyan leper colony. Though full of gruesome episodes—including one in which a leper's toes are gnawed by a rat, then sliced off—the novel offers a perspective that is compassionate rather than sensationalist, and charming instead of discomforting. The style itself is somewhat unconventional, as if it were being told by someone for whom English was a second language. This technique, as Jim Crace noted in the *Times Literary Supplement,* enables Bloch to maintain a position "between the mawkish and the grotesque with unerring self-confidence." Crace, who described the novel's prose as a "clever mimicry of Kenyan sugarcane English," deemed *The Modern Common Wind* "an optimistic and heartening portrayal of lepers."

Passing Through, Bloch's next novel, is a three-part account of two volunteer workers and their experiences in underdeveloped regions. In one episode, Eric, who serves as the narrator, and Koert Jan try to practice egalitarianism while contending with amiably self-subordinating inhabitants of remote Indonesia. Eric is frustrated by the seeming futility of the entire enterprise, and he comes to question his own humanitarian motivations. Eric and Koert Jan also travel to Yemen and Kenya, where they continue to aid the needy despite occasional bouts of doubt and despair. Neville Shack, writing in the *Times Literary Supplement,* proclaimed *Passing Through* "a candid tour of the imagination," and he noted the book's "great authenticity."

Bloch is also author of the novel *Face Value,* in which a prominent Boston surgeon, Jasper Whiting, forsakes professional and domestic complacency for life in a squalid ghetto. There he meets an assortment of endearing oddballs, including Luigi, a one-legged homosexual photographer who becomes a star model; Sloan Glintz, a mentally retarded person; and Rhoda Massler, a vivacious teacher of handicapped children. Jasper and Rhoda, who become lovers, find themselves embroiled in controversy when several of Rhoda's mute charges kill a policeman attempting rape at a rally. To the consternation of the Boston public, cripples throughout the city show their support for the mute children by becoming a more visible and vocal presence. In his *New Statesman* assessment, Boyd Tonkin called *Face Value* a "curiously nervous performance." Tonkin speculated that in fashioning his humanitarian novel "Bloch just tries too hard," and he added, "Bloch should have trusted the tools of his craft more often; they work when he lets them." In a more positive review, a *Publishers Weekly* contributor described *Face Value* as "distinctive" calling it a "rare book" that successfully transposes an issue into a much larger context. The reviewer summarized Bloch's novel as "compelling."

BIOGRAPHICAL/CRITICAL SOURCES:

PERIODICALS

London Review of Books, May 23, 1985, p. 22.
New Statesman, May 24, 1985, pp. 29-30; November 26, 1986; July 17, 1987, pp. 29-30.
Publishers Weekly, June 2, 1989, p. 67.
Times Literary Supplement, June 7, 1985, p. 627; January 9, 1987, p. 42.

BODE, Carl 1911-1993

OBITUARY NOTICE—See index for *CA* sketch: Born March 14, 1911, in Milwaukee, WI; died January 5, 1993, in Chestertown, MD. Educator, diplomat, and writer. Bode published and edited numerous books related to various facets of American culture. His biography of H. L. Mencken was considered an early and influential study of the journalist, and Bode also edited a number of books related to American writers Henry David Thoreau and Ralph Waldo Emerson. Bode began his academic career at the University of California at Los Angeles following service in World War II. In 1947 he joined the faculty of the University of Maryland where he taught for the rest of his career. Bode also served as the cultural attache at the American embassy in London from 1957 to 1959, and he was the founder of numerous academic and cultural organizations, including the American Studies Association and the Mencken Society. In addition to the biography *Mencken*, Bode's books include *The Anatomy of American Popular Culture, 1840-1861* and several collections of his own poetry, including *The Sacred Seasons* and *Practical Magic*. Bode was the editor of *The Portable Thoreau*, *Ralph Waldo Emerson: A Profile*, and *The Editor, the Bluenose, and the Prostitute: H. L. Mencken's History of the "Hatrack" Censorship Case.*

OBITUARIES AND OTHER SOURCES:

BOOKS

The Writers Directory: 1992-1994, St. James Press, 1991.

PERIODICALS

Chicago Tribune, January 8, 1993, p. I11
New York Times, January 7, 1993, p. A21.

*　　*　　*

BOFFA, Giuseppe 1923-

PERSONAL: Born July 23, 1923, in Milan, Italy; son of Potito and Cesarina (Mazzi) Boffa; married Iris Laura Zoffoli; children: Massimo, Sandro. *Education:* Attended University of Milan, 1942-47. *Politics:* "Left: Democratic Party."

ADDRESSES: Home—Via Masina 5/B, 00153 Rome, Italy. *Office*—Center for Studies on International Politics, Via della Vite 13, 00189 Rome, Italy.

CAREER: L'Unita, Rome and Milan, Italy, worked as foreign editor, foreign and special correspondent, and columnist, 1946-87; Center for Studies on International Politics (CESPI), Rome, president, 1982-92. Senator of the Italian Republic, 1987-92. *Military service:* Served in World War II, 1943-45.

MEMBER: Associazione della Stampa, Associazione degli Ex-Parlamentari, Ordine dei giornalisti.

AWARDS, HONORS: Premio Viareggio, 1959 and 1979; Premio Acqui-Storia, 1976; Premio Napoli, 1989.

WRITINGS:

La grande svolta, Editori Riuniti, 1959.
Dopo Krusciov, Einaudi, 1965.
Storia dell'Unione Sovietica, Mondadori, Volume I, 1976, Volume II, 1979.
(With Gilles Martinet) *Dialogo sullo Stalinismo*, Laterza, 1976.
Il fenomeno Stalin nella storia del XX secolo, Laterza, 1982.
The Stalin Phenomenon, Cornell University Press, 1992.

Contributor to periodicals.

Boffa's works have been published in England, France, Germany, Russia, Japan, Mexico, Brazil, Slovenia, Serbia, and Croatia.

WORK IN PROGRESS: From the U.S.S.R. to Russia; research on Eastern European history and international politics.

*　　*　　*

BOGEN, Hyman 1924-

PERSONAL: Born February 6, 1924, in Manhattan, NY; son of Samuel (a carpenter) and Annie (a homemaker; maiden name, Kerstein) Bogen; married Nancy Warshaw, May 30, 1965 (divorced, 1971); married Thelma Finestone, April 15, 1972 (died April 26, 1991); children: (stepsons from second marriage) Bernard M. Carreno, Mark J. Carreno. *Education:* New York University, Washington Square College, B.A., 1951; Adelphi University, M.S.W., 1969. *Politics:* Liberal. *Religion:* Jewish. *Avocational interests:* Photography, folk dancing, theater.

ADDRESSES: Home—80 Knolls Cres., Bronx, NY 10463.

CAREER: Assistant to press agent Bernard Simon, New York City, 1952; Human Resources Administration, New York City, staff member, 1954-73, director of Division of Family Homes for Adults, 1973-84; retired, 1984. Knolls Cooperative Association, president, 1987-89. *Military service:* U.S. Army, 1943-46, served in Ordnance Department; became private first class.

MEMBER: HOA Association (president, 1987—).

WRITINGS:

The Luckiest Orphans: A History of the Hebrew Orphan Asylum of New York, University of Illinois Press, 1992.

Work represented in collections, including *Readings in Adult Foster Care,* New York State Department of Social Services. Contributor to periodicals. Editor, *Rising Bell;* member of editorial board, *Adult Residential Care Journal.*

SIDELIGHTS: Hyman Bogen told *CA:* "*The Luckiest Orphans: A History of the Hebrew Orphan Asylum of New York,* is the only book I have ever wanted to write. Since I am now sixty-nine, I don't know how many other books I can hope to complete, but if a good idea comes along, I might try it. Chances are it wouldn't be fiction. My advice to aspiring writers is that you need a lot of stamina and faith in your project to keep going. It took me five years to write *The Luckiest Orphans* and sixteen years to get it published. My research on the book started in 1957. A previous version, written in the late 1960s, was abandoned. I had an agent for the current version, who stuck with the book for fourteen years until she died in 1985."

BIOGRAPHICAL/CRITICAL SOURCES:

PERIODICALS

Jewish Week, December 18, 1992.

* * *

BONGARD, David L(awrence) 1959-

PERSONAL: Born June 19, 1959, in Summit, NJ; son of Charles Bernard and Marilyn Louise (Rudiger) Bongard. *Education:* Ohio University, B.A. (with honors; history), 1980, B.A. (with honors; political science), 1981; University of Maryland at College Park, M.A., 1985.

ADDRESSES: Home—7912 Towerbell Court, Annandale, VA 22003-1410. *Office*—Dupuy Institute, 1324 Kurtz Rd., McLean, VA 22101.

CAREER: National Archives and Records Administration, Washington, DC, archives aide, 1983-85; DMSI/HERO (research and consulting firm), Fairfax, VA, research associate, 1986-89, researcher, 1989-90; TNDA (research and consulting firm), McLean, VA, staff associate, 1990-92; Dupuy Institute, McLean, corporate secretary, researcher, and writer, 1992—.

MEMBER: Phi Alpha Theta.

AWARDS, HONORS: Outstanding Performance Citation, General Services Administration and National Archives and Records Service, 1983-84.

WRITINGS:

(With T. N. Dupuy, Curt Johnson, and Arnold C. Dupuy) *How to Defeat Saddam Hussein,* Warner Books, 1991.
(With T. N. Dupuy and Curt Johnson) *The Harper Encyclopedia of Military Biography,* HarperCollins, 1992.
(Associate managing editor and contributor) *International Military and Defense Encyclopedia,* Brassey's, 1993.
(With T. N. Dupuy and Richard C. Anderson) *The Battle of the Bulge,* HarperCollins, in press.

Work represented in anthologies, including *Future Wars,* by T. N. Dupuy, Warner Books, 1993; and *The Harper-Collins Encyclopedia of Military History,* 4th edition, edited by R. E. Dupuy and T. N. Dupuy, HarperCollins, 1993.

SIDELIGHTS: David Bongard told *CA:* "I have spent my professional career as a military historian and consultant on military affairs and national security. As a registered Democrat and sometimes political liberal, this has led to some interesting situations; many of my colleagues, and most of the people I encounter professionally, have political views rather different than mine.

"The occasional sense of being a voice crying in the wilderness, at least until President Clinton's election, has been heightened by the generally low regard with which historical analysis is viewed in the United States, especially within the national security community. Very few professional analysts will admit to anything other than a paraphrase of Henry Ford's comment that 'History is bunk!' On the other hand, it is clear that, after the events of 1989-1991, we have entered a new age of international politics, although it may be some time before that essential fact has sunk into the political consciousness of the United States.

"As a cautionary tale, I report a conversation with a co-worker from early spring, 1990. We were discussing the shape of a post-Cold War U.S. Army. I said something to the effect that we would do well to retain half-a-dozen or so 'heavy' (mechanized or armored) divisions. To this my co-worker replied: 'Who do we have to worry about that we need more than two or three heavy divisions?' 'Well,' I replied, 'there's always Iraq. They have several thousand tanks.' My co-worker snorted in disbelief. 'How likely is it that we'll ever fight them?' he asked. Less than six months later, the United States was at war with Iraq."

* * *

BORNEMAN, John 1952-

PERSONAL: Born May 3, 1952, in Antigo, WI; son of Edward (a dairy farmer) and Marjorie (a dairy farmer;

maiden name, Smith) Borneman. *Education:* University of Wisconsin—Madison, B.A., 1973; University of Washington, Seattle, M.A. (political science), 1983; Harvard University, M.A. (anthropology), 1985, Ph.D., 1989; attended Humboldt University, 1986-87, and Free University of Berlin, 1987-89. *Politics:* "Critical left."

ADDRESSES: Home—1310 East State St., Ithaca, NY 14850. *Office*—Department of Anthropology, Cornell University, Ithaca, NY 14853.

CAREER: Harvard University, Cambridge, MA, lecturer in social studies, 1989-90; University of California, San Diego, La Jolla, assistant professor of anthropology and political science, 1990-91; Cornell University, Ithaca, NY, assistant professor of anthropology, 1991—. Guest lecturer at University of Rochester, Johns Hopkins University, University of Heidelberg, Humboldt University, and Free University of Berlin. Conducted field research in East and West Berlin, beginning in 1984.

MEMBER: American Anthropological Association, American Ethnological Society, Society for the Anthropology of Europe, German Studies Association.

AWARDS, HONORS: Grants from Deutscher Akademischer Austauschdienst (German Academic Exchange Service), 1983, Social Science Research Council, 1984-89, International Research and Exchange Board, 1986-87 and 1989, German Marshall Fund and Spencer Foundation, both 1990, MacArthur Foundation, 1991, and National Council for Soviet and East European Research, 1992-94; Fulbright-Hays grant, 1986-87.

WRITINGS:

After the Wall: East Meets West in the New Berlin, Basic Books, 1991.
(Editor and author of introduction) *Gay Voices from East Germany,* Indiana University Press, 1991.
Belonging in the Two Berlins: Kin, State, Nation, Cambridge University Press, 1991.

Contributor to books, including *AIDS: Cultural Activism/Cultural Analysis,* edited by Douglas Crimp, MIT Press, 1988; *Culture, Power, Place: Explorations in Critical Anthropology,* edited by Roger Rouse, J. Ferguson, and A. Gupta, Westview, 1992; and *Altered States: A Reader in the New World Order,* Interlink Publishing Group, 1993. Contributor of articles and reviews to periodicals, including *Journal of Popular Culture* and *American Ethnologist.*

WORK IN PROGRESS: Returned: Postwar Life Reconstructions of German Jews in the Two Berlins, with Jeffrey Peck; research on the restructuring of justice in the former East Germany.

BIOGRAPHICAL/CRITICAL SOURCES:

PERIODICALS

New York Times Book Review, July 14, 1991, p. 15.

*   *   *

BORSTEN, Rick 1955-

PERSONAL: Born May 13, 1955, in West Palm Beach, FL; son of Larry (a hotel manager) and Lily (a homemaker; maiden name, Crosby) Borsten; married Kim Crane (a teacher, caterer, and homemaker), August 2, 1980; children: Sarah Rebecca, Lukas Michael. *Education:* University of North Carolina at Chapel Hill, B.A., 1977. *Politics:* "Rainbow/Green Democrat." *Religion:* Unitarian. *Avocational interests:* Gardening, hiking, environmental protection, peace activism.

ADDRESSES: Home—Corvallis, OR.

CAREER: Chamberlin House, Albany, OR, direct care worker, 1980-84; Linn County Department of Mental Health, Albany, community skills trainer, 1984-86; writer. Worked variously as a waiter and dishwasher.

MEMBER: Phi Beta Kappa.

WRITINGS:

The Great Equalizer, Permanent Press, 1986.
Rainbow Rhapsody, Breitenbush Books, 1989.

WORK IN PROGRESS: Insane for the Light, "a historical novel set in a sequoia grove in mid-nineteenth-century California, concerning a man with a logging heritage and a woman who is part Native American."

SIDELIGHTS: In his first novel, *The Great Equalizer,* Rick Borsten depicts a young man's struggle to find meaning in life. Protagonist Benny Horowitz drops out of college shortly before graduating and sits alone in his bedroom, worrying about the deterioration of the environment and the possibility of nuclear holocaust. Benny, who refers to death as the Great Equalizer, is afraid of becoming caught up in the monotony of work and duty without having time to discover the purpose of living. Subsequently, he disdains his mother for her regimented, proper behavior. Benny's mother chides him out of a fear that he will end up like his father, an unemployed and antisocial man. To appease his mother, Benny takes a job on the weekend shift at a halfway house for mentally retarded adults. Borsten chronicles Benny's budding admiration for the vivacious approach to life that the residents show and his infatuation with one of the residents, Nadia, a beautiful sculptress whose only subject is trees. Critics praised both the author's presentation of his retarded characters without condescension and his ability to make his plot believable. Carolyn See concluded in her *Los Angeles Times* review that *The Great Equalizer* is "an earnest, brave, interesting novel."

Borsten told *CA:* "On my way to a probable career as a teacher, I broke my larynx in a basketball game the term before my graduation. I lost my voice—in fact, nearly lost my life. Unable to speak (one vocal cord had been paralyzed and the other twisted out of place), but delighted to have survived the accident, I poured my energy into writing. My voice returned unexpectedly after three months, but by that time I was determined to attempt a career as a novelist."

BIOGRAPHICAL/CRITICAL SOURCES:

PERIODICALS

Albany Democrat-Herald, July 12, 1989, p. 17.
Los Angeles Times, December 8, 1986.
Spectator, August 16, 1989.

*   *   *

BOSTON, Jonathan   1957-

PERSONAL: Born January 21, 1957, in Birmingham, England; son of George Herbert (a medical practitioner) and Phyllis Eva May (a nurse; maiden name, Russell) Boston; married Mary Louise Hutchinson (a medical practitioner), December 9, 1989; children: Jessie Alice. *Education:* Received B.A. and M.A. (with honors) from University of Canterbury, and D.Phil. from Oxford University. *Politics:* Social Democrat. *Religion:* Christian.

ADDRESSES: Home—47 Wright St., Mount Cook, Wellington, New Zealand. *Office*—Public Policy Group, Victoria University of Wellington, P.O. Box 600, Wellington, New Zealand.

CAREER: New Zealand Treasury, Wellington, investigating officer, 1984; University of Canterbury, Christchurch, New Zealand, lecturer, 1985-87; Victoria University of Wellington, senior lecturer, 1987—. Institute of Policy Studies (Wellington), research fellow, 1984, then executive. Anglican Church, New Zealand Province, member of public affairs unit.

AWARDS, HONORS: Crisp Medal, Australasian Political Studies Association, 1989.

WRITINGS:

Incomes Policy in New Zealand, Victoria University of Wellington, 1984.
(Coeditor) *The Fourth Labour Government,* Oxford University Press, 1987.

The Future of New Zealand Universities, Victoria University of Wellington, 1988.
(Coeditor) *Reshaping the State,* Oxford University Press, 1991.

WORK IN PROGRESS: Coediting *The Decent Society* (tentative title), publication by Oxford University Press expected in 1999; research on the role of the state and on ethics in the public sector.

*   *   *

BOTTOMORE, T(homas) B(urton)   1920-1992

OBITUARY NOTICE—See index for *CA* sketch: Born April 8, 1920, in Nottingham, England; died December 9, 1992. Sociologist, educator, editor, and writer. Bottomore was considered an influential sociologist whose work concentrated on Marxist social theory. He began his academic career at the London School of Economics and Political Science in 1952 and three years later published his first book, *Classes in Modern Society.* Bottomore's next book project, *Karl Marx: Selected Writings in Sociology and Social Philosophy,* began his scholarly involvement with the work of Marx, and he would go on to edit numerous other texts involving the famed political philosopher. In 1965 Bottomore came to Canada to head the department of political science, sociology, and anthropology at Simon Fraser University in Vancouver. Two years later he returned to England and taught at the University of Sussex, completing his teaching responsibilities in 1985. Bottomore produced numerous publications throughout his career, including *Elites and Society, Marxist Sociology,* and *Theories of Modern Capitalism.* Collaborating with William Outhwaite, he edited a dictionary on twentieth-century social thought shortly before his death.

OBITUARIES AND OTHER SOURCES:

PERIODICALS

Times (London), December 18, 1992, p. 17.

*   *   *

BOULDING, Kenneth E(wart)   1910-1993

OBITUARY NOTICE—See index for *CA* sketch: Born January 18, 1910, in Liverpool, England; died of cancer, March 18 (one source says March 19), 1993, in Boulder, CO. Economist, social scientist, peace activist, and writer. Boulding's diverse interests and experience allowed him to blend various disciplines, transcending the normal boundaries of economics to consider a variety of social and philosophical concerns. He was highly respected in several fields, becoming president of the American Economic Association and receiving Nobel Prize nominations for both economics and peace. Boulding taught in Scotland before coming to the United States in 1937. He held positions at a variety of universities in the U.S. and Canada in the 1940s and 1950s and was an economist with the League of Nations before his opposition to World War II ended his involvement with the organization. A Quaker, Boulding refused to serve in the U.S. army during the war and was vocal peace activist throughout his life. Boulding taught at the University of Michigan from 1948 to 1968, becoming director of the university's Center for Research on Conflict Resolution. He was a professor of economics at the University of Colorado from 1968 to 1980, continuing his involvement with the university's Institute of Behavioral Sciences after retiring from teaching. A prolific author, Boulding's works addressed his many fields of interest. His economic texts include *Economic Analysis, The Economics of Peace,* and *Economics as a Science.* He was the author of numerous books on the social sciences and other topics, including *The Impact of the Social Sciences, Stable Peace,* and *The World as a Total System.* He also published several collections of poetry, including *Sonnets for Elise* and *Sonnets from the Interior Life and Other Autobiographical Verse.*

OBITUARIES AND OTHER SOURCES:

BOOKS

The Writers Directory: 1992-1994, St. James Press, 1991.

PERIODICALS

Chicago Tribune, March 21, 1993, section 2, p. 8.
New York Times, March 20, 1993, p. 10.
Washington Post, March 20, 1993, p. B6.

* * *

BOURNE, Kenneth   1930-1992

OBITUARY NOTICE—See index for *CA* sketch: Born March 17, 1930, in Wickford, Essex, England; died December 13, 1992. Historian, educator, writer, and editor. Bourne specialized in the history of British foreign policy in the 1800s, producing a number of well-received studies on the subject. Bourne joined the faculty at the London School of Economics and Political Science in 1957 and remained at the institution throughout his career. In 1967 he published *Britain and the Balance of Power in North America, 1815-1908,* which was awarded the Albert B. Corey Prize from the British and American Historical Associations. His next work, *The Foreign Policy of Victorian England, 1830-1902,* earned the author further acclaim, becoming a standard text in English universities. Much of

Bourne's scholarly work concerned the life of Lord Palmerston, the nineteenth-century British politician who served as prime minister and foreign secretary. Bourne edited *The Letters of the Third Viscount Palmerston to Laurence and Elizabeth Sulivan, 1804-1863* and followed with *Palmerston: The Early Years, 1784-1841,* the first of a planned multivolume biography. He was at work on the sequel at the time of his death.

OBITUARIES AND OTHER SOURCES:

BOOKS

The Writers Directory: 1992-1994, St. James Press, 1991.

PERIODICALS

Times (London), December 17, 1992, p. 17.

* * *

BOWMAN, David   1957-

PERSONAL: Born December 8, 1957; son of an industrial writer and a homemaker; married Chloe Wing (a photographer), August 25, 1989. *Education:* Attended a private high school in Interlochen, MI. *Politics:* None. *Religion:* "Jehovah better watch out."

ADDRESSES: Home—39 Garden Pl., Edgewater, NJ 07020.

CAREER: Strand Bookstore, New York City, staff member, 1976-78; free-lance writer, 1978—. Ear Inn, bartender.

MEMBER: Editorial Freelancers Association, Herman Melville Society.

AWARDS, HONORS: Elmer H. Bobst Emerging Writer Award, New York University, 1992, for *Let the Dog Drive.*

WRITINGS:

Let the Dog Drive (novel), New York University Press, 1993.

WORK IN PROGRESS: Cold Trail: The Life of Black Mask Writer Paul Cain, a biography; *Crickets Duponte,* a novel.

SIDELIGHTS: David Bowman told *CA:* "My publisher is a university house and, therefore, doesn't offer bound pre-publication proofs to reviewers (which, as you know, is the only way a book can be reviewed in a big-league periodical). I didn't get into a funk about being denied this opportunity. Instead I duplicated my proofs myself, and then paid to have them velum-bound. Finally, I hand-delivered each one to periodicals like *Publishers Weekly* and the *New York Times.* Four months later (three months after the bound book became available) I received a wonderful review from the *New York Times*. I phoned the reviewer and learned that he had never seen the bound book. He had read the proofs I had provided.

"I think this is an inspiring story. If ever you feel your publisher is neglecting or unable to promote your work, do it yourself. My life didn't change because I had a novel published; my life changed because my published novel was reviewed. This is the way things work.

"My second story is not so inspiring. On January 4, 1989, while walking across a frozen beach in Montauk, New York, I was struck by a pickup truck. The driver reported that he had been driving into the sun and didn't see anything. He told a reporter: 'I thought I hit a seagull.' For him I became a seagull and lay in a coma for a month. The doctors told my wife that, if and when I woke up, it was unlikely I would be able to dress myself, let alone write again. Four years later, my novel was published.

"My wife Chloe pointed out that ever since my accident I've been on the warpath against Jehovah, blaming Him for getting run over. 'If the truck was His fault,' she says, 'then the *Times* review came from Him, too. You should be on your knees thanking Him.' I thought about this. I give Jehovah a nod, but continue to watch him with a cold eye."

BIOGRAPHICAL/CRITICAL SOURCES:

PERIODICALS

Los Angeles Times, March 2, 1993, p. E4.
New York Times Book Review, February 7, 1993, p. 11.

*   *   *

BOYLE, Kay   1902-1992

OBITUARY NOTICE—See index for *CA* sketch: Born February 19, 1902, in St. Paul, MN; died December 27, 1992, in Mill Valley, CA. Educator and writer. Boyle's long literary career saw her emerge from the community of expatriate American writers in Europe in the 1920s and achieve critical acclaim, especially as a writer of short stories. Boyle moved to France with her first husband in 1923, and also lived in England and Austria throughout the 1920s and 1930s. In 1929 she published her first collection of short stories and two years later issued *Plagued by the Nightingale,* the first of her many novels. In the 1930s Boyle's stories began to be published in *Harper's, The New Yorker,* and other prominent periodicals, and she claimed the first of two O. Henry awards for her stories in 1934. Throughout her life, Boyle was involved with political and social causes; she opposed the anti-Communist actions led by Senator Joseph McCarthy in the 1950s and was also a vocal opponent of American involvement in Vietnam. From 1963 to 1979 she taught creative writing at San Francisco State University. Boyle published essays, non-fiction, poetry, and children's books in addition to her novels and short stories. Her titles include *The White Horses of Vienna and Other Stories, The Underground Woman, Fifty Stories,* and *Words that Must Somehow Be Said: Selected Essays of Kay Boyle, 1927-1984.*

OBITUARIES AND OTHER SOURCES:

BOOKS

Contemporary Literary Criticism, Volume 58, Gale, 1990.
Dictionary of Literary Biography, Volume 86: *American Short Story Writers, 1910-1945, First Series,* Gale, 1989.
Short Story Criticism, Volume 5, Gale, 1990.
The Writers Directory: 1992-1994, St. James Press, 1991.

PERIODICALS

New York Times, December 29, 1992, p. A13.
Washington Post, December 30, 1992, p. B6.

*   *   *

BOYLE, Nicholas   1946-

PERSONAL: Born June 18, 1946, in London, England; son of Hugh and Faith (Hopkins) Boyle; married Rosemary Devlin, 1983; children: Mary Rose, Michael, Doran. *Education:* Attended King's School, Worcester, and Magdalene College, Cambridge. *Politics:* "Skeptical." *Religion:* Roman Catholic. *Avocational interests:* "Thinking about the future."

ADDRESSES: Office—Magdalene College, Cambridge University, Cambridge CB3 OAG, England.

CAREER: Cambridge University, Cambridge, England, fellow at Magdalene College, fellow, 1968—, reader in German literary and intellectual history, 1993—; writer.

MEMBER: PEN International, Internationale Goethegesellschaft.

AWARDS, HONORS: W. H. Heinemann Prize, Royal Society of Literature, 1992.

WRITINGS:

(Editor with Martin Swales) *Realism in European Literature: Essays in Honor of J. P. Stern,* Cambridge University Press, 1986.
Goethe, Faust, Part One, Cambridge University Press, 1987.
Goethe, the Poet and the Age, Volume 1: *The Poetry of Desire (1749-1790),* Oxford University Press, 1991.

WORK IN PROGRESS: Goethe, the Poet and the Age,
Volume 2: *The Age of Renunciation.*

SIDELIGHTS: Nicholas Boyle is an authority on eighteenth-century culture and the author of the biography
Goethe, the Poet and the Age. In the first volume, *The Poetry of Desire (1749-1790),* Boyle recounts the early life
and times of Johann Wolfgang von Goethe, the master
German writer who also distinguished himself as an artist,
philosopher, statesman, and scientist. In this lengthy
work, Boyle details Goethe's early studies as a lawyer and
recounts the poet's travels across Europe. In addition,
Boyle provides considerable detail regarding many of the
various personages whom Goethe encountered and the
places he visited during the first forty-one years of his life.
As Christoph Schweitzer related in the *New York Times
Book Review,* "The reader is given superb character
sketches of all the major and many of the minor people
with whom the poet came into contact." *Times Literary
Supplement* reviewer Theodore Ziolkowski affirmed that
the book "is punctuated . . . by sharp, lively characterizations of the figures who surrounded Goethe and the books
that shaped his mind."

Since its appearance in 1991, the first volume of *Goethe,
the Poet and the Age* has won recognition as a commanding portrait of the great German figure. Schweitzer, in his
New York Times Book Review appraisal, hailed the book
as "a study replete with penetrating insights and unsur-
passed in thoroughness." He added that the biographical
volume "is crammed with reliable and up-to-date information" and declared that "many will refer to it again and
again for information on Goethe's life and work." *Los Angeles Times Book Review* contributor Elisabeth Wehr-
mann acknowledged the first volume as "a work of dili-
gence." And Ziolkowski praised Boyle's "sovereign command of the biographical and socio-cultural material" and
commended the author for his "lucid and often witty
prose." Ziolkowski added that Boyle's biography of Goethe is "one of the finest in any language."

The Age of Renunciation, the second, concluding volume
of *Goethe, the Poet and the Age,* is forthcoming.

Boyle told *CA:* "I think German philosophy and culture
have had a much greater influence on the English-
speaking world than most people realize. I want to explain
that influence to the ordinary reader and bring to life the
extraordinary character of the man who wrote *Faust*—in
my view the greatest long poem of the modern age."

BIOGRAPHICAL/CRITICAL SOURCES:

PERIODICALS

American Spectator, December, 1991, p. 39.
Atlantic Monthly, April, 1991, p. 102.
Christian Science Monitor, June 12, 1991, p. 13.

Economist, June 8, 1991, p. 87.
Los Angeles Times Book Review, June 9, 1991, p. 4.
New Statesman and Society, October 14, 1988, p. 27.
New Yorker, September 23, 1991, p. 110.
New York Review of Books, October 24, 1991, p. 3.
New York Times, June 25, 1991, section C, p. 15.
New York Times Book Review, July 28, 1991, pp. 3, 25.
Times Literary Supplement, January 16, 1987, p. 65; May
   10, 1991, p. 3; April 17, 1987, p. 419.
Wall Street Journal, May 16, 1991, section A, p. 14.

*   *   *

BOYLES, Denis 1946-

PERSONAL: Born August 15, 1946, in Texas; son of D.
W. and Marilyn Boyles; married; wife's name, April.

ADDRESSES: Home—Baltimore, MD.

CAREER: Writer and editor. Has worked as a staff editor
for *Crawdaddy, New York Times Magazine,* and *National
Lampoon;* has worked as a lecturer and assistant professor
in Baltimore, MD; London, England; and Dublin, Ireland.

AWARDS, HONORS: Three-Art Award for poetry, 1969.

WRITINGS:

Trashing Ladies (poetry), IMC Press, 1971.
Maxine's Flattery (poetry), Dryad, 1976.
Design Poetics (criticism), Assembling Press, 1976.
(With Alan Rose and Alan Wellikoff) *The Modern Man's
   Guide to Life,* Harper, 1987.
*African Lives: White Lies, Tropical Truth, Darkest Gossip,
   and Rumblings of Rumor—from Chinese Gordon to
   Beryl Markham, and Beyond,* Weidenfeld & Nicol-
   son, 1988.
*Man Eaters Motel and Other Stops on the Railway to No-
   where: An East African Traveller's Nightbook, Includ-
   ing a Summary History of Zanzibar and an Account
   of the Slaughter at Tsavo: Together with a Sketch of
   Life in Nairobi and at Lake Victoria, a Brief and Worried Visit to the Ugandan Border, and a Survey of Angling in the Aberdares,* Ticknor & Fields, 1991.

Also contributing editor of *Playboy.*

*WORK IN PROGRESS: Mariner: Tony Cornero and the
Fleet of Chance,* a biography, for Grove.

SIDELIGHTS: In his 1987 work *The Modern Man's
Guide to Life,* Denis Boyles, with coauthors Alan Wellikoff and Alan Rose, creates a how-to source on a wide
range of subjects for men. Arranged as an encyclopedia,
this book "aims to give advice and information about everything from making pasta to wearing the right clothes,"

according to *Washington Post* staff writer David Streitfeld. Other topics include aftershaves, haircuts, and women (a subject that appears often in the book's three thousand entries). More than five hundred men contributed their helpful hints to Boyles for use in the guide. According to the coauthor, not all of the information will be new to its readers, but it contains "little tidbits of wisdom that men don't usually share unless they're intimate friends."

In *Man Eaters Motel and Other Stops on the Railway to Nowhere: An East African Traveller's Nightbook, Including a Summary History of Zanzibar and an Account of the Slaughter at Tsavo: Together with a Sketch of Life in Nairobi and at Lake Victoria, a Brief and Worried Visit to the Ugandan Border, and a Survey of Angling in the Aberdares,* published in 1991, Boyles chronicles his journey by train through East Africa. The author admitted in an interview for the *New York Times Book Review* that he used this train trip as "a device for threading together a few good stories and a lot of personal observations." Beginning in Zanzibar and continuing through parts of Kenya, Nairobi, and Uganda, Boyles relates tales of the people and cultures he finds as he travels through different landscapes. The title story focuses on the Man Eaters Motel in Tsavo, the name of a now-abandoned location where, in 1898, a group of Indian railroad workers were attacked by man-eating lions. More than one hundred of the workers were killed. Other episodes in *Man Eaters Motel* encompass a confrontation at the Ugandan border and a fishing trip in the Aberdare Mountains. The author also analyzes white European tourists, dwelling on them "with delicious cruelty, noting how they . . . scurry over the Kenya savannah in their zebra-striped vans," a *New York Times Book Review* contributor commented. *Washington Post Book World* reviewer Judith Chettle reported that Boyles "combines this narrative with clear-eyed commentary on the way it is now and the way it was," and has "done it with wit, honesty, and a rare good humor."

BIOGRAPHICAL/CRITICAL SOURCES:

PERIODICALS

New York Times Book Review, December 25, 1988, p. 7; June 9, 1991, p. 48.
Washington Post, January 15, 1988.
Washington Post Book World, July 14, 1991, p. 9.

*   *   *

BRADBURY, Jim 1937-

PERSONAL: Born February 27, 1937, in London, England; son of George James (a furniture designer) and Sarah Helena (a homemaker; maiden name, Joel) Bradbury; married Patricia Ann Hooper (a secretary), 1958; children: Stephen James, Jane Louise. *Education:* King's College, London, B.A., 1958, M.A., 1976; attended Institute of Education, London, 1958-59. *Politics:* Labour Party. *Religion:* "None—atheist." *Avocational interests:* Art, music, playing the cornet, horse racing, travel.

ADDRESSES: Home—27 East St., Selsey, West Sussex PO20 0BN, England.

CAREER: Shoreditch Comprehensive School, London, England, school teacher, 1959-61; Manhood Secondary School, school teacher, 1961-69; Borough Road College, West London, England, history lecturer, 1969-89, part-time lecturer, 1989—; writer.

WRITINGS:

Shakespeare and His Theatre (for children), Longman, 1975.
The Medieval Archer, St. Martin's, 1985.
The Medieval Siege, Boydell, 1992.

Contributor to books, including *Castles: A History and Guide,* published by Blandford. Contributor of articles to journals.

WORK IN PROGRESS: Philip Augustus, an undergraduate biography of Philip II, King of France, for Longman.

SIDELIGHTS: Jim Bradbury told *CA:* "I had always wanted to write; as a teenager, it was poetry, as a young man, novels—I finished four which are all now filed away, the last never even seen by a publisher. Family and work seemed to take over. When I moved from school teaching to higher education, I began to give occasional public lectures, at first on teaching history, later on medieval history. On one such occasion, I gave a talk on medieval archers. Another speaker that day was Richard Beuber, author and publisher with Boydell. He suggested that it might be worthwhile to write a book about the subject. I had already written a children's book on Shakespeare out of one piece of uncompleted academic research. I decided to abandon a Ph.D. and concentrate on a book. It has changed my life, maybe not for the better financially, but certainly in terms of satisfaction. I write largely for pleasure. I do not write for academic historians, but to try to inform and entertain the ordinary, intelligent reader with an interest in history."

*   *   *

BRADFORD, M(elvin) E(ustace) 1934-1993

OBITUARY NOTICE—See index for *CA* sketch: Born May 8, 1934, in Fort Worth, TX; died of complications following heart surgery, March 3, 1993, in Midland, TX. Educator and writer. After establishing his scholarly reputation with numerous historical and literary studies of the southern United States, Bradford gained public attention in the 1980s when he was nominated by President Ronald Reagan to head the National Endowment for the Humanities (NEH). Bradford taught at the U.S. Naval Academy and a number of universities in the southern United States before settling at the University of Dallas in 1967. He roused controversy in works that espoused his conservative views of U.S. history, including his criticism of Abraham Lincoln's belief in equality. Analysts believe that it was these ideas, in part, that kept Bradford from being awarded the NEH position. His books include *The Reactionary Imperative: Essays Literary and Political, Original Intentions: On the Making and Ratification of the U.S. Constitution, A Resolute Persistence: Reflections on Familiar Themes,* and *Against the Barbarians and Other Reflections.*

OBITUARIES AND OTHER SOURCES:

BOOKS

The Writers Directory: 1992-1994, St. James Press, 1991.

PERIODICALS

New York Times, March 9, 1993.

*   *   *

BRANT, Marley   1950-

PERSONAL: Born July 26, 1950, in Syracuse, NY; daughter of Herbert (a master printer) and Gladys (a secretary; maiden name, Wall) Olmstead; married David Bruegger (a financial manager); children: Timothy Zane Bruegger. *Education:* Attended Lee Strasberg Theater Institute; received B.A. from California State University, Northridge. *Religion:* Christian. *Avocational interests:* History, travel, and people.

ADDRESSES: Office—P.O. Box 5175, Marietta, GA 30061.

CAREER: Chrysalis Records, Beverly Hills, CA, staff member in artist development, 1976-78; Paramount Television, Hollywood, CA, publicist, 1980-81; ICPR Public Relations, Los Angeles, CA, account executive, 1981-83; Sierra Records, Pasadena, CA, producer, 1983-91; freelance writer, 1986—. President of Friends of the James Farm; member of board of directors, Friends of the Youngers.

MEMBER: National Academy of Recording Arts and Sciences, Publicists Guild of America, Western Writers of America, Country Music Association, Association of Outlaw and Lawmen History.

AWARDS, HONORS: Grammy Award nominee; honorary Kentucky colonel.

WRITINGS:

The Outlaw Youngers: A Confederate Brotherhood, Madison Books, 1992.

Contributor of articles to periodicals, including *James Farm Journal, True West Old West,* and country music magazines; writer of music trivia booklets.

WORK IN PROGRESS: Evolution of the American Outlaw, publication expected in 1994.

SIDELIGHTS: Marley Brant told *CA:* "Everyone is fascinated by outlaws. I am intrigued by questions of who the outlaws really were and why they continue to have such a huge influence on modern day America and on the media. I travel all over the country in search of the next outlaw story and have met hundreds of captivating personalities."

*   *   *

BRAUN, Lilian Jackson   1916(?)-

PERSONAL: Born c. 1916.

ADDRESSES: Home—Bad Axe, MI. *Agent*—Blanche C. Gregory, Inc., 2 Tudor Place, New York, NY 10017.

CAREER: Detroit Free Press, Detroit, MI, editor until 1978; writer.

AWARDS, HONORS: Edgar Award nomination, Mystery Writers of America, 1986, for *The Cat Who Saw Red.*

WRITINGS:

THE "CAT" SERIES; MYSTERY NOVELS, UNLESS OTHERWISE NOTED

The Cat Who Could Read Backwards, Dutton, 1966.
The Cat Who Ate Danish Modern, Dutton, 1967.
The Cat Who Turned On and Off, Dutton, 1968.
The Cat Who Saw Red, Jove, 1986.
The Cat Who Played Brahms, Jove, 1987.
The Cat Who Played Post Office, Jove, 1987.
The Cat Who Knew Shakespeare, Jove, 1988.
The Cat Who Had Fourteen Tales (stories), Jove, 1988.
The Cat Who Sniffed Glue, Putnam, 1988.
The Cat Who Went Underground, Putnam, 1989.
The Cat Who Talked to Ghosts, Putnam, 1990.
The Cat Who Lived High, Putnam, 1990.
The Cat Who Knew a Cardinal, Putnam, 1991.
The Cat Who Wasn't There, Putnam, 1992.
The Cat Who Moved a Mountain, Putnam, 1992.

Work represented in anthologies, including *Mystery Cats: Feline Felonies by Modern Masters of Mystery,* Dutton, 1991.

SIDELIGHTS: Lilian Jackson Braun is author of the "Cat" mystery series featuring amateur sleuth Jim Qwilleran and the Siamese cats Koko and Yum Yum. Braun began the series in 1966 with *The Cat Who Could Read Backwards,* in which Qwilleran, a respected journalist, investigates treachery and murder within the art community of a Midwest town. Of particular assistance to Qwilleran is the enterprising Koko, a Siamese cat whose seemingly psychic abilities often help the reporter as he attempts to solve the mystery.

The Cat Who Could Read Backwards won Braun recognition as an important new mystery writer. She followed with two more mysteries, *The Cat Who Ate Danish Modern* and *The Cat Who Turned On and Off,* but then abandoned literary work to continue her career as an editor at the *Detroit Free Press.* She left the paper in 1978, the year she turned sixty-two. Eight years later, she revived her once-popular mystery series with *The Cat Who Saw Red.* Here Qwilleran, who has become a restaurant reviewer, comes to suspect that a former lover has met with foul play. As the amateur sleuth once again tries to uncover the truth, he suspects that someone is trying to poison Koko and Yum Yum. The popularity of *The Cat Who Saw Red* proved that Braun's work had lost none of its appeal, and the novel earned an Edgar Award nomination from the Mystery Writers of America in 1986.

In the ensuing years Braun has produced more works in the series. In 1988 she published *The Cat Who Knew Shakespeare,* in which Qwilleran, who has inherited a substantial fortune and moved to a mansion, investigates the mysterious suicide of a newspaper publisher. As is usual in the series, the profoundly intuitive Koko proves of considerable use to Qwilleran in his sleuthing. *The Cat Who Went Underground,* the tenth entry in Braun's series, finds Qwilleran and his cats immersed in considerable intrigue when their vacation is disrupted by the suspicious disappearance of a handyman.

The succeeding mystery, *The Cat Who Talked to Ghosts,* involves peculiar circumstances at a historical museum in Qwilleran's isolated hometown. The action begins when the institution's curator informs Qwilleran of supernatural events at the museum. Her death soon afterward serves as further motivation for Qwilleran to investigate, and he soon uncovers secrets about one of the town's prominent families. *The Cat Who Lived High* concerns Qwilleran's efforts to help a friend spare an old building from demolition. Attempting to determine the structure's usefulness, Qwilleran decides to live there for the winter, and is soon investigating the murder of a previous tenant. He is as-

sisted by Koko, who uses a board game to help catch the killer.

In the 1990s Braun has found topical mysteries to challenge the trio. In *The Cat Who Moved a Mountain,* published in 1992, Qwilleran and his cats are confronted the demise of a land developer whose murder has been attributed to environmentalists. Though they are ostensibly on vacation, Qwilleran, Koko, and Yum Yum trade relaxation for suspense in order to find the killer.

Braun began her writing career after a tragedy involving her own cat—also named Koko—who fell from a window in her high-rise apartment. "I was heartbroken," Braun was quoted as saying in *Publishers Weekly.* "I began to have nightmares about friends and relatives falling from tenth-floor windows. . . . I realized that to get rid of these feelings I'd have to write about it." She began with short stories, but later hit upon the idea for the "Cat" novels. Nearly three decades after her first book was published, Braun continues to create her distinctive tales of human intrigue and feline resourcefulness.

BIOGRAPHICAL/CRITICAL SOURCES:

PERIODICALS

Globe & Mail (Toronto), December 17, 1988.
New York Times Book Review, March 6, 1966, p. 38; June 18, 1967, p. 37; January 12, 1969, p. 43; April 2, 1989, p. 33; May 19, 1991, p. 45.
Observer, July 16, 1967, p. 21; March 16, 1968, p. 29; March 24, 1968, p. 29; July 27, 1969, p. 25.
Publishers Weekly, July 8, 1988, p. 29.
Saturday Review, March 26, 1966, p. 35.
Times Literary Supplement, September 21, 1967, p. 844; June 6, 1968, p. 603; September 18, 1969, p. 1018.
Tribune Books (Chicago), October 19, 1986, p. 5; January 7, 1990, p. 6.*

*   *   *

BRAXTON, Joanne M(argaret) 1950-
(Jodi Braxton)

PERSONAL: Born May 25, 1950, in Washington, DC; daughter of Harry McHenry (a machinist and civic leader) and Mary Ellen (a homemaker and civil service worker; maiden name, Weems) Braxton. *Education:* Sarah Lawrence College, B.A., 1972; Yale University, M.A., 1974, Ph.D., 1984.

ADDRESSES: Office—American Studies Program, College of William and Mary, Williamsburg, VA 23185.

CAREER: University of Michigan, Ann Arbor, Michigan Society of Fellows, 1976-79; College of William and Mary,

Williamsburg, VA, assistant professor, 1980-86, associate professor, 1986-89, Frances L. and Edwin L. Cummings Professor of American Studies and English, and professor of English, 1989—.

MEMBER: Modern Language Association, American Studies Association, College Language Association.

AWARDS, HONORS: National Endowment of the Humanities fellow, 1984; American Council of Learned Societies fellow, 1986; Thomas Jefferson Teaching Award, College of William and Mary, 1986; received grant from National Endowment of the Humanities, 1986; fellow, College of William and Mary Society of the Alumni, 1988; *Wild Women in the Whirlwind: Afra-American Culture and the Contemporary Literary Renaissance* received the Koppleman Book Award in 1990; Outstanding Faculty Award, State Council of Higher Education in Virginia, 1992.

WRITINGS:

(As Jodi Braxton) *Sometimes I Think of Maryland,* Sunbury Press, 1977.

Black Women Writing Autobiography: A Tradition within a Tradition, Temple University Press, 1989.

(Editor with Andree N. McLaughlin) *Wild Women in the Whirlwind: Afra-American Culture and the Contemporary Literary Renaissance* (anthology), Rutgers University Press, 1990.

(Editor) *The Collected Poetry of Paul Laurence Dunbar,* University Press of Virginia, 1993.

Contributor of essays to books, including *The Private Self: Theory and Practice in Women's Autobiographical Writings,* edited by Shari Benstock, University of North Carolina Press, 1988; and *Modern American Women Writers,* edited by Elaine Showalter, A. Walton Litz, and Lea Baechler, Scribner's, 1990. Also contributor of poetry to anthologies, including *Equal-Time,* Equal Time Press, 1972; *Drum,* University of Massachusetts, 1975; *We Become New,* Bantam, 1975; *Synergy,* Energy Black South, 1976; *Celebrations,* Follet, 1977; and *Woman Poet: The South,* Women in Literature Press, 1988. Author of introduction to *The Work of the Afro-American Woman,* Oxford University Press, 1988. Member of editorial advisory boards, *African-American Review,* 1990—, *Autobiography Studies,* 1991—, and *Legacy,* 1992—. Contributor to periodicals, including *Massachusetts Review, Women's Review of Books, New Republic, Journal of Black Poetry, Encore, Black Creation, Presence Africaine.*

WORK IN PROGRESS: Writing "*Songs of the Southern Slave, 1755-1865,* a documentary collection of Afro-American music."

SIDELIGHTS: Joanne M. Braxton is a poet and author who explores themes of black folklore and tradition, as well as loss and personal experience. Family and relationships also figure prominently in her written word. Born in 1950 in Washington, D.C., Braxton grew up in the small Maryland town of Lakeland and was influenced by her tight-knit family, including her parents, three brothers, and two grandmothers. As the author relates in a biographical note in her first book, *Sometimes I Think of Maryland:* "My grandmothers taught me family history and genealogy, and told me stories they had heard about slavery; tales of horror and strength. This oral tradition constitutes the source of my artistic consciousness and my personal strength."

In *Sometimes I Think of Maryland,* Braxton reflects on topics ranging from her childhood home and love, to her late grandmother. Of the latter she writes, "No straight lines but drooping shoulders / And old hands chewed a red-brick brown / Hands that healed my bee stings / With three different kinds of leaves and loves / Offset by two skinny yellow bowed legs / Knotted with brown spots." Other verse, such as the three poems that constitute "Conversion," delves into mythological themes. The collection, written under the name Jodi Braxton, was met with praise from both critics and the public alike.

Braxton pursued her interest in black folklore and literary history in her second book, published in 1989. Titled *Black Women Writing Autobiography: A Tradition within a Tradition,* the volume was inspired by stories of the poet's ancestry. In the work's introduction Braxton explains that her "consciousness was ready shaped for the study of the slave narrative. I had learned to *listen.*" The end result is a book delineating a tradition of black women's autobiographical writing, including its various subgenres like modern autobiography, slave narrative, reminiscence, travelogue, and historical memoir. The volume, according to Braxton, "views the autobiography of black American women . . . as a form of symbolic memory that evokes the black woman's deepest consciousness" and as "an occasion for viewing the individual in relation to those with whom she shares emotional, philosophical, and spiritual affinities, as well as political realities."

In 1990 Braxton returned her attention to the literature of black American women writers by coediting *Wild Women in the Whirlwind: Afra-American Culture and the Contemporary Literary Renaissance.* This collection contains essays covering the contemporary renaissance, which *New York Times Book Review*'s Eric J. Sundquist explained "includes not just the Caribbean (as a crucial part of black America) but also Africa, the Pacific Islands, or anywhere that black women have made writing an instrument of liberation." Articles explore the work of specific individuals, such as Zora Neale Hurston, Gwendolyn Brooks, Alice Walker, and Paule Marshall, and treat various aspects of black feminist literary theory as well as political topics.

BIOGRAPHICAL/CRITICAL SOURCES:

BOOKS

Braxton, Joanne M., *Black Women Writing Autobiography: A Tradition within a Tradition,* Temple University Press, 1989.
Braxton, Jodi, *Sometimes I Think of Maryland,* Sunbury Press, 1977.
Dictionary of Literary Biography, Volume 41: *Afro-American Poets since 1955,* edited by Trudier Harris and Thadious M. Davis, Gale, 1985, pp. 42-47.

PERIODICALS

New York Times Book Review, February 25, 1990, p. 11.

*   *   *

BRAXTON, Jodi
See BRAXTON, Joanne M(argaret)

*   *   *

BREZNITZ, Shlomo   1936-

PERSONAL: Born August 3, 1936, in Bratislava, Slovakia; son of Joseph (an engineer) and Janka (Klein) Breznitz; married Zvia Gerstein (a psychologist), November 16, 1971; children: Dan, Ruth, Nurit. *Education:* Hebrew University of Jerusalem, Ph.D., 1965. *Religion:* Jewish. *Avocational interests:* Chess, travel, Africa.

ADDRESSES: *Home*—19 Hakhsharat Hayishuv, Haifa 34985, Israel. *Office*—Department of Psychology, University of Haifa, Mount Carmel, Haifa 31905, Israel.

CAREER: University of Haifa, Haifa, Israel, professor of psychology, 1974—, rector, 1975-77, director of R. D. Wolfe Center for the Study of Psychological Stress, 1979—. New School for Social Research, professor, 1985—. *Military service:* Israel Defense Forces, 1954-57.

WRITINGS:

(Editor with L. Goldberger) *Handbook of Stress,* Free Press, 1982, 2nd edition, 1993.
Stress in Israel, Van Nostrand, 1982.
Denial of Stress, International Universities Press, 1983.
Cry Wolf: The Psychology of False Alarms, LEA, 1984.
Memory Fields, Knopf, 1993.

BRINT, Michael (E.)   1955-

PERSONAL: Born September 9, 1955; son of Harold L. (a computer scientist) and Shirl (Grayson) Brint; married Camille A. Collett; children: Case Tyler. *Education:* University of California, Santa Cruz, B.A., 1976; Balliol College, Oxford, D.Phil., 1983.

ADDRESSES: *Home*—P.O. Box 832, Gambier, OH 43022. *Office*—Timberlake House, Kenyon College, Gambier, OH 43022.

CAREER: University of Virginia, Charlottesville, assistant professor, 1986-93, associate professor of humanities, 1992—, director of Integrated Program in Humane Studies, 1992—; Cambridge University, Cambridge, England, Thomas Jefferson Professor, 1989-90.

AWARDS, HONORS: Outstanding Faculty Award, Z Society, 1990.

WRITINGS:

A Genealogy of Political Culture, Westview, 1991.
Tragedy and Denial: The Politics of Difference in Western Political Thought, Westview, 1991.
(Editor with William Weaver) *Pragmatism in Law and Society,* Westview, 1991.
A Scientific Journey: From the Evolution of Physical Laws to the Physical Laws of Evolution, IPHS, 1993.

WORK IN PROGRESS: *Rousseau's Political Theater,* completion expected in 1995.

*   *   *

BRONNER, Ethan (Samuel)   1954-

PERSONAL: Born November 26, 1954, in New York, NY; son of Felix (a biology professor) and Leah (a public health educator; maiden name, Horowitz) Bronner; married Naomi Kehati (a psychology researcher), June 27, 1985; children: Eli, Gabriel. *Education:* Wesleyan University, B.A., 1976; Columbia University, M.S.J., 1980. *Religion:* Jewish.

ADDRESSES: *Office*—*Boston Globe,* 37 Hillel St., Jerusalem, Israel. *Agent*—Mildred Marmur, 310 Madison Ave., New York, NY 10017.

CAREER: Reuters America Inc. (news service), correspondent in London, England, 1980-81, Madrid, Spain, 1981-82, and Jerusalem, Israel, 1983-85; *Boston Globe,* Boston, MA, staff reporter, 1985-89, correspondent in Washington, DC, 1989-91, Middle East bureau chief, 1991—.

AWARDS, HONORS: Washingtonian Book Award and citation as one of twenty-five outstanding books by the

New York Public Library, both 1989, and American Bar Association Silver Gavel, 1990, all for *Battle for Justice: How the Bork Nomination Shook America.*

WRITINGS:

Battle for Justice: How the Bork Nomination Shook America, Norton, 1989.

WORK IN PROGRESS: Researching Israel and the Middle East.

SIDELIGHTS: In his book, *Battle for Justice: How the Bork Nomination Shook America,* Ethan Bronner recounts the controversy surrounding the nomination of Circuit Judge Robert H. Bork to the U.S. Supreme Court in 1987. As the author points out, Bork—a former law professor at Yale University who became a highly regarded federal judge—was originally considered an exemplary candidate. His confirmation hearing, which ended in his rejection by the Senate Judiciary Committee and the Senate, was therefore a surprise to both his advocates and opposing forces. Bronner's book delves into the many elements—political, legal, and personal—that led to the Senate's decision to reject the judge.

Had he been appointed, Bork would have given the Supreme Court a conservative majority. In the hearings, liberal committee members interrogated him about his ultra-conservative interpretation of the law in various cases, including some involving civil rights for blacks, women, and homosexuals. A poll taken after the hearings indicated that the Amcrican public would not welcome a candidate for Supreme Court whose strict interpretation of the Constitution did not seem to encompass contemporary interpretations of civil rights or the right to privacy. Bronner points out that, in addition to Bork's positions on constitutional rights, his unemotional and erudite manner at the hearings weighed heavily against him.

In Bronner's view, these legal issues served as fuel for the fire in an all-out campaign waged against Bork. The author states in his book that "the most striking thing about the campaign was its move away from classic left-wing tactics into a world dominated by the right—marketing." The anti-Bork "marketing," led by senators Edward Kennedy and Joseph Biden, Jr., and liberal or left-wing groups, was picked up by the media, creating a prevailing image of Bork as a conservative extremist that was, according to Bronner, not a full picture of the judge.

Several reviewers praised *Battle for Justice* for getting beyond this image. Chicago *Tribune Books* contributor Stanley I. Kutler asserted that Bronner "ably reported both the public and less visible sides of the fight over the Bork nomination." Christopher Lehmann-Haupt commented in his *New York Times* review that "Bronner tries to be as even-handed as possible . . . he shows us Robert H. Bork's . . .

courage in following the intricate trail of his convictions, his personal integrity. On the other hand, he makes clear how the jurist lent himself philosophically to distortion and misunderstanding." Carol E. Rinzler in her *Washington Post Book World* review, however, maintained that although Bronner "is a splendid reporter," the author "swallowed the judicial smear pretty much whole." Nevertheless, *Battle for Justice* has elicited widespread praise for its insight into the controversial event. Garry Wills concluded in the *New York Times Book Review* that Bronner's "strength is in the personal details of the story, expertly elicited and sympathetically conveyed."

BIOGRAPHICAL/CRITICAL SOURCES:

BOOKS

Bronner, Ethan, *Battle for Justice: How the Bork Nomination Shook America,* Norton, 1989.

PERIODICALS

Los Angeles Times Book Review, September 17, 1989, p. 14.
New York Times, September 7, 1989.
New York Times Book Review, September 10, 1989, p. 7.
Tribune Books (Chicago), October 22, 1989, p. 5.
Washington Post Book World, September 24, 1989, pp. 1 and 10.

*   *   *

BROOK, Timothy (James) 1951-

PERSONAL: Born in January, 1951, in Toronto, Ontario, Canada; son of John Frederick (a university administrator) and Barbara Ada (MacLatchy) Brook; married Margaret Taylor, June 9, 1979 (divorced April 25, 1991); companion, Fay Sims (a refugee coordinator); children: Vanessa, Katherine, Taylor, Jonah. *Education:* University of Toronto, B.A., 1973; attended Beijing University, 1974-75, and Fudan University, 1975-76; Harvard University, A.M., 1977, Ph.D., 1984; attended University of Tokyo, 1979-81. *Avocational interests:* Poetry, music.

ADDRESSES: Home—647 Carlaw Ave., Toronto, Ontario M4K 3K6, Canada. *Office*—Department of History, University of Toronto, Toronto, Ontario M5S 1A1, Canada. *Agent*—Beverley Slopen, Beverley Slopen Literary Agency, 131 Bloor St. W., Suite 711, Toronto, Ontario M5S 1S3, Canada.

CAREER: University of Alberta, Edmonton, Alberta, Canada, MacTaggart fellow, 1984-86; University of Toronto, Toronto, Ontario, Canada, associate professor of history, 1986—. Needham Research Institute, research associate, 1978—; University of Toronto/York University

Joint Centre for Asia Pacific Studies, director of China Documentation Project, 1989—; consultant on Chinese human rights issues.

MEMBER: Association for Asian Studies, Canadian Asian Studies Association, Amnesty International.

WRITINGS:

Geographical Sources of Ming-Qing History, Center for Chinese Studies, University of Michigan, 1988.

(Editor) *The Asiatic Mode of Production in China,* M. E. Sharpe, 1989.

(Editor with Philip A. Kuhn) Min Tu-ki, *National Polity and Local Power: The Transformation of Late Imperial China,* Council on East Asian Studies, Harvard University, 1989.

Quelling the People: The Military Suppression of the Beijing Democracy Movement, Oxford University Press, 1992.

Praying for Power: Buddhism and the Formation of Gentry Society in Late-Ming China, Council on East Asian Studies, Harvard University, 1993.

(Editor with Kenneth Robinson) Joseph Needham, *Science and Civilisation in China,* Volume VII, Part 1: *The Social and Economic Background,* Cambridge University Press, 1993.

Work represented in books, including *The Encyclopedia of China Today,* edited by Frederic Kaplan and others, Harper, 1979; *Chinese Local Elites and Patterns of Dominance,* edited by Joseph Esherick and Mary Rankin, University of California Press, 1990; and *Christianity and China: Essays in Religion and Social Change,* edited by Daniel Hays, 1993. Contributor of articles and reviews to periodicals, including *Commonweal.*

WORK IN PROGRESS: Moving China: The Mobility of People, Things, and Ideas in the Ming Dynasty; "Mobility," to be included in *The Cambridge History of China,* Volume VIII, for Cambridge University Press; "The Chinese Sense of History," to be included in Joseph Needham's *Science and Civilisation in China,* Volume VII, Part 4; research on Chinese collaboration with the Japanese during Japan's occupation of central China before and during the regime of Liang Hongzhi, 1937-41.

SIDELIGHTS: Timothy Brook told *CA:* "Although I had long dreamed of pursuing a career in writing, I became sidetracked, as many are, by the academic world. What I thought would be a career in English literature collapsed in my fourth year at university, when my advisor encouraged me to pursue an interest in Chinese studies. That interest had germinated out of a fascination with Buddhism and, although I never became a Buddhologist, I have directed much of my research toward understanding the place of religion in Chinese society.

"Two years as an exchange student in China, first in Beijing and subsequently in Shanghai, established both my fluency in the Chinese language and my abiding concern with the problems facing contemporary China. Although I have continued to follow current affairs out of personal interest, I chose to specialize in the social history of the Ming dynasty (1368-1644). The research for my dissertation led me to Japan, where I spent two years at the University of Tokyo.

"The violent measures the Communist government took against student protesters gathered in Tiananmen Square on June 4, 1989, jolted every student of China, myself included. Rather than let the event pass as something tragic for those involved but as no concern of mine, I decided to put my academic research on hold and commit my energies to figuring out what happened in Beijing. I interviewed dozens of eyewitnesses, acquired underground publications smuggled out of China, and combed the Chinese and foreign press for information that would help me understand the events of June 4. Although the subject was much written about early on, what was lacking was an objective account of precisely what happened. I decided that would be my contribution.

"The result was *Quelling the People: The Military Suppression of the Beijing Democracy Movement.* Unlike the other books I have written and edited, which were intended solely for scholarly audiences, *Quelling the People* was written to tell both the nonspecialist and the China expert what happened at Tiananmen Square.

"The experience of writing for the general reader has brought me back to the sort of writing I originally wanted to do. I enjoy producing scholarly publications, but I also intend to continue writing books of interest to nonspecialists. My two current research projects—on the mobility of people, things, and ideas in the Ming dynasty, and on the collaboration during the first four years of Japan's occupation of China in World War II—will result in something for both audiences."

BIOGRAPHICAL/CRITICAL SOURCES:

PERIODICALS

Globe and Mail (Toronto), October 3, 1992, p. C18.
Manchester Guardian Weekly, February 28, 1993.
Toronto Star, December 12, 1992.

*   *   *

BROOKE, John L.   1953-

PERSONAL: Born May 19, 1953, in Pittsfield, MA. *Education:* Cornell University, B.A., 1976; University of

Pennsylvania, M.A., 1977, Ph.D., 1982. *Politics:* Democrat.

ADDRESSES: Office—Department of History, Tufts University, Medford, MA 02155.

CAREER: Amherst College, Amherst, MA, visiting assistant professor of history, 1982-83; Tufts University, Medford, MA, assistant professor, 1983-89, associate professor of history, 1989—.

MEMBER: American Historical Association, Organization of American Historians, American Association of University Professors.

AWARDS, HONORS: S. F. Haven fellow, American Antiquarian Society, 1982; Charles Warren fellow, Harvard University, 1986-87; junior fellow, National Endowment for the Humanities, 1986-87; award from National Society of Daughters of the Colonial Wars, 1989, for an article in *William and Mary Quarterly;* E. Harold Hugo Memorial Book Prize, Old Sturbridge Village Research Library, 1989, Book Prize for American History, National Historical Society, 1991, and Merle Curti Award for Intellectual History, Organization of American Historians, 1991, all for *The Heart of the Commonwealth;* Commonwealth Center senior fellow in early American history, Institute of Early American History and Culture, 1990-91; fellow, American Council of Learned Societies, 1990-91.

WRITINGS:

The Heart of the Commonwealth: Society and Political Culture in Worcester County, Massachusetts, 1713-1861, Cambridge University Press, 1989.

Contributor to professional journals.

WORK IN PROGRESS: The Refiner's Fire: The Hermetic Tradition and the Origins of Mormon Cosmology, 1644-1844, for Cambridge University Press.

*   *   *

BROOKS, David (Gordon) 1953-

PERSONAL: Born January 12, 1953, in Canberra, Australian Capital Territory, Australia; son of (Harland) Gordon (a civil servant) and Norma Margaret (Jeffrey) Brooks; married Alison Summers, 1975 (divorced, 1983); married Nicolette Stasko (a writer); children: Jessica Lane Stasko Brooks. *Education:* Australian National University, B.A. (with honors), 1974; University of Toronto, M.A., 1976, Ph.D., 1981.

ADDRESSES: Home—9 Henry St., Five Dock, New South Wales 2046, Australia. *Office*—University of Sydney, Sydney, New South Wales 2006, Australia. *Agent*—

Tim Curnow, Curtis Brown, P.O. Box 19, Paddington, New South Wales 2021, Australia.

CAREER: University of Toronto, Toronto, Ontario, Canada, instructor in bibliography and operation of hand press, 1976-78, teaching assistant of twentieth-century literature, 1978-79; University of New South Wales, Canberra, Australian Capital Territory, Australia, lecturer, 1981; University of Western Australia, Perth, Western Australia, Australia, senior tutor, 1982-85; Australian National University, Canberra, lecturer in English literature, 1986-91; University of Sydney, Sydney, New South Wales, Australia, lecturer in Australian literature, 1991—. *Canberra Poetry,* photographer and member of editorial board, 1973-75; Open Door Press, founder, editor, and printer, 1974-77; *New Poetry,* overseas and associate editor, 1976-82; *Helix* magazine, corresponding editor, 1977-78, began as guest editor, became general editor, 1983-86; *Phoenix Review,* founder and editor, 1987—.

AWARDS, HONORS: Fellow, University of Toronto, 1975-80; E. J. Pratt Medal and Prize for Poetry, University of Toronto, 1978; Anne Gelder Award for Poetry, National Book Council, Australia, 1983, National Book Award (Australia), for best first book of poetry, 1984, and short-listed, New South Wales Premier's Prize, 1984, all for *The Cold Front.*

WRITINGS:

(Editor) *New South: Australian Poetry of the Late 1970s,* Dreadnaught, 1980.
Five Poems, Flying Fox, 1981.
The Cold Front (poems), Hale and Iremonger (Sydney, Australia), 1983.
The Book of Sei and Other Stories (includes "The Family of the Minister" and "The Lost Wedding"), Hale and Iremonger, 1986, revised edition, Faber & Faber, 1988.
(Editor with Brenda Walker) *Poetry and Gender: Statements and Essays on Australian Women Poets,* International Specialized Book Services, 1989.
Sheep and the Diva (stories; includes "The Garden" and "Nadia's Lover"), McPhee Gribble, 1990.
The Necessary Jungle: Literature and Excess (essays), McPhee Gribble, 1990.

Works represented in anthologies, including *Transgressions: Australian Writing Now,* edited by Don Anderson, Penguin, 1986; *The Faber Book of Contemporary Australian Short Stories,* edited by Murray Bail, Faber & Faber, 1988; and *The State of the Art,* Penguin. Contributor of essays and reviews to periodicals, including *American Poetry Review, New England Review, Canberra Times,* and *Australian Book Review.* Member of the editorial boards of Logbridge-Rhodes Foundation, 1980-85, and *Westerly,* 1983-85.

The Book of Sei has been translated into Japanese.

WORK IN PROGRESS: Beyond Tomis, "collection of essays on postcolonial critique in the deep structure and poetics of Australian literature"; *The House of Balthus* (a novel); editing *A. D. Hope,* for the *Studies in Australian Literature* series, and *Selected Poems of R. F. Brissenden;* translating *Les deliquescences d'Adore Floupette (1885/1911),* with Graham Halligan and John A. Scott.

SIDELIGHTS: According to *National Times* critic Don Anderson, Australian writer David Brooks established himself as a reputable poet with the award-winning 1983 collection of his work titled *The Cold Front.* Brooks is now gaining the same reputation as an author of short stories. Anderson reported that Brooks's first story collection, *The Book of Sei and Other Stories,* is "the most exciting short-fiction debut in Australia since Peter Carey's *The Fat Man in History,*" and deemed it "pure imagination." The author's second collection of stories, *Sheep and the Diva,* also met with critical approval. *Australian National University Reporter* columnist Stephen Hyde concluded that the stories "reveal an extraordinary intellectual imagination." Reviewers of these works have suggested that Brooks's writing style is reminiscent of the fiction created by the Argentine author Jorge Luis Borges and the Italian writer Italo Calvino.

Critic's note that the fiction forms used in Brooks's *The Book of Sei and Other Stories* are unrestrained by the boundaries of the typical short story. The author combines imagination with understated prose to relate tales of science fantasy, erotic symbolism, and magic realism. Anna Vaux of the *Times Literary Supplement* labeled much of the fiction surreal and stated that "the everyday world is not much in evidence in the twenty-three stories. . . . When it does appear, it tends to disappoint, or at least, to seem 'dull and confusing.' " Evidence of this can be found in "The Family of the Minister," in which nature takes its revenge on a man who wants to restrain it by invading the bodies of his wife and children. The title story depicts a Chinese traveller in a passionate encounter, and "The Lost Wedding" focuses on an aging woman who imagines that marriage was proposed to her long ago. Anderson responded to *The Book of Sei and Other Stories* by naming Brooks "the leading edge of the new Australian writing."

Brooks's second book of short fiction, *Sheep and the Diva,* is a collection of stories "whose brevity belies the depth of imagination and thought within," according to Hyde. Brooks again brings an element of science fiction to his works and combines it with mythology and spirituality. The stories—often related in a first-person point of view—revolve around such characters as a girl with the mental power to change cows into trees and an opera star who drives her audience to suicide with an emotional performance. "The Garden," which *Age* contributor Brian Matthews called "a knockout," tells the story of a man whose flowers only bloom at the saddest points in his life—their most bountiful time coming at his death. Matthews further stated that *Sheep and the Diva* "confirms earlier judgements of [Brooks] as a writer of considerable elegance, inventiveness and daring."

Brooks told *CA:* "I have lived in Australia, the United States, Canada, and when very young, in Greece and Yugoslavia. I experienced a significant formative period in North America from 1975 to 1980, when I worked with such poets as Galway Kinnell and Mark Strand. My stories are frequently compared to those of Borges, Calvino, and in my own country, to those of Peter Carey."

BIOGRAPHICAL/CRITICAL SOURCES:

PERIODICALS

Age, May 26, 1990.
Australian National University Reporter, August 10, 1990, p. 6; November 23, 1990, p. 3.
National Times, April 4, 1986, p. 32.
Sunday Times, March 27, 1988.
Times Literary Supplement, May 13, 1988, p. 534.

* * *

BROWN, H. Jackson, Jr. 1940-

PERSONAL: Born March 14, 1940, in Nashville, TN; son of Horace J. (in sales) and Sarah C. (a homemaker; maiden name, Crowell) Brown; married Rosemary Carleton (a homemaker, seminar leader, and writer), November 1, 1969; children: Adam C. *Education:* Emory University, B.A., 1963.

ADDRESSES: Home—3307 Wimbledon Rd., Nashville, TN 37215. *Office*—END, Inc., 607 West Iris Dr., Nashville, TN 37204.

CAREER: END, Inc. (advertising and marketing firm), Nashville, TN, president and creative director, 1974-92; writer.

MEMBER: Writers Alliance (member of board, 1991-93).

AWARDS, HONORS: Abbey Honor Book Award, 1992.

WRITINGS:

A Father's Box of Wisdom, Rutledge Press, 1989.
P. S. I Love You, Rutledge Press, 1990.
Life's Little Instruction Book, Rutledge Press, 1991.
Live and Learn and Pass It On, Rutledge Press, 1991.

Life's Little Instruction Book has been translated into fifteen languages.

WORK IN PROGRESS: Life's Little Instruction Book II.

*   *   *

BROWN, Howard Mayer   1930-1993

OBITUARY NOTICE—See index for *CA* sketch: Born April 13, 1930, in Los Angeles, CA; died of a heart attack, February 20 (one source says February 21), 1993, in Venice, Italy. Musician, musicologist, educator, and writer. A specialist in the music of the Renaissance, Brown produced a number of influential works on the subject. He taught at Harvard University and Wellesley College before joining the faculty at the University of Chicago in 1960. Brown remained with the university until the time of his death, though he was the King Edward Professor of Music at London's Kings College from 1972 to 1974. He was named the Ferdinand Schevill Distinguished Service Professor of Music at the University of Chicago in 1976. His books include *Music in the French Secular Theater, 1400-1550, Music in the Renaissance,* and the two-volume work *A Florentine Chansonnier from the Time of Lorenzo the Magnificent.*

OBITUARIES AND OTHER SOURCES:

BOOKS

The Writers Directory: 1992-1994, St. James Press, 1991.

PERIODICALS

Chicago Tribune, February 23, 1993, section 3, p. 11.
New York Times, February 24, 1993, p. B6.

*   *   *

BROWN, Lyn Mikel

PERSONAL: Education: Ottawa University (Ottawa, KS), B.A., 1979; Harvard University, Ed.D., 1989.

ADDRESSES: Home—R.R.3, Box 5250, Winslow, ME 04901. *Office*—Program in Education and Human Development, Colby College, Waterville, ME 04901.

CAREER: CETA Program, Calais, ME, preschool teacher and coordinator, 1979-81; Connection, Inc., Middletown, CT, substance abuse counselor, 1981-83; Harvard University, Cambridge, MA, director of Laurel-Harvard Project, 1986-89, lecturer in education, 1989-90, research associate in human development psychology, 1989—. Colby College, assistant professor and co-chair of education and human development program, 1991—; Shakespeare, Women, and Girls Project, project scholar; workshop presenter; consultant to Ms. Foundation and National Girls' Initiative.

MEMBER: American Educational Research Association, Association for Women in Psychology, Modern Language Association of America, National Women's Studies Association, Society for Research on Adolescence, American Association of University Women (member of Gender Equity Roundtable, 1992).

WRITINGS:

(With C. Gilligan) *Meeting at the Crossroads: The Psychology of Women and the Development of Girls,* Harvard University Press, 1992.

Work represented in anthologies, including *The Role of Values in Psychology and Human Development,* edited by M. Azmitia, W. Kurtines, and J. Gewirtz, Wiley, 1992; *Adolescents, Schooling, and Social Policy,* edited by F. Miller, State University of New York Press, 1992; and *Moral Behavior and Development: An Introduction,* edited by W. Kurtines and J. Gewirtz, McGraw, 1992. Contributor to periodicals. Coeditor, *Women's Studies Quarterly,* spring/summer, 1991.

*   *   *

BRUCK, Connie   1946-

PERSONAL: Born May 22, 1946, in North Arlington, NJ; daughter of Carl (a realtor) and Edith (a teacher; maiden name, Bornstein) Bruck; married Ben Schlossberg, 1970 (divorced, 1978); children: Ari. *Education:* Attended Wellesley College, 1964-66; Barnard College, B.A., 1968; Columbia University, M.S., 1969. *Politics:* Democrat. *Religion:* Jewish.

ADDRESSES: Office—*New Yorker,* 20 West Forty-third St., New York, NY 10036. *Agent*—Amanda Urban, International Creative Management, 40 West 57th St., New York, NY 10019.

CAREER: Free-lance journalist, 1970-79; *American Lawyer* (magazine), staff reporter, 1979—1989; *New Yorker,* staff writer, 1989—.

AWARDS, HONORS: Hancock Award for excellence in business and financial journalism, John Hancock Mutual Life Insurance Company, 1985, for an article on Ivan Boesky in *Atlantic Monthly;* Front Page Award, 1990, National Magazine Award for reporting, 1991, and Gerald Loeb Award for excellence in business reporting, 1991, all for the article "Deal of the Year" in the *New Yorker.*

WRITINGS:

The Predators' Ball: The Junk Bond Raiders and the Man Who Staked Them, Simon & Schuster, 1988, revised edition, Penguin, 1989.

Contributor to periodicals, including *Atlantic Monthly, New York Times,* and *Washington Post.*

WORK IN PROGRESS: A book about Steven J. Ross for Simon & Schuster.

SIDELIGHTS: Journalist Connie Bruck earned national attention and the ire of Wall Street investment firm Drexel Burnham Lambert with the publication of *The Predators' Ball: The Junk Bond Raiders and the Man Who Staked Them.* In this work the author claims that the powerful company gained clients by intimidating competitors and ignored star employee Michael Milken's engagement in activities that constituted a conflict of interest. Bruck did not initially conceive *The Predators' Ball* as an indictment of Drexel's methods. In 1985 Drexel reigned as the most profitable of Wall Street's investment houses, and Bruck arranged interviews with several Drexel executives—including Milken—to chronicle the firm's meteoric rise. After learning more about the tactics employed for such success, however, Bruck became convinced that Drexel had violated securities laws and her book turned into an expose.

In *The Predators' Ball,* Bruck explains that Drexel Burnham Lambert owed a significant portion of its success to Milken's theory that substantial financial rewards existed in trading junk bonds. Kurt Eichenwald, writing in the *New York Times,* explained that "junk bonds are securities issued by companies that do not qualify for an 'investment grade' rating by the country's leading rating agencies. As a result, the bonds pay a higher return, but are considered riskier." Milken first traded those bonds and then persuaded customers to buy them. When large profits were realized with junk bonds, desire for them increased. Milken invested in these bonds, issued them for companies that could not raise money through conventional debt, and eventually used them to raise billions of dollars for corporate raiders seeking to take over companies. Milken had a personal network of lenders who helped him finance takeovers. This financial base allowed Drexel a virtual monopoly and, Bruck charges, weakened the nation's corporate climate because businesses fearing takeovers focused on short-term goals and defense rather than methods for long-term growth.

Bruck relates that as the junk-bond market flourished, Milken gained a religious following. The Predator's Ball of the title refers to an annual spring party Milken hosted in Beverly Hills, California, where clients and corporate raiders would pay tribute to Milken. Wall Street insiders also touted Milken as a financial wizard, but the author paints a portrait of Milken as a controlling, power-hungry man obsessed with secrecy. Milken's star began to fade, however, after coworker and merger specialist Dennis Levine was caught in an insider trading scandal that led to

the imprisonment of stock speculator and Drexel client Ivan Boesky in 1986. Beginning that same year, Drexel and Milken were under investigation by the Securities and Exchange Commission.

Bruck's book ends before the investigation's conclusion and some reviewers suggested that the volume would have had greater impact had the author waited to publish her work. In his *Los Angeles Times Book Review* appraisal, however, Douglas Frantz commented that with her disclosures about Milken, Bruck has produced "a vivid, rich account of one of the most controversial figures in American finance." *Chicago Tribune* contributor William Neikirk judged, "Bruck has written a fine book that makes a significant contribution to the history of modern American business." While acknowledging that Bruck wrote on a timely subject, some critics faulted the author for having insufficient evidence for her claims. Nonetheless, Bruck's allegations proved prophetic. In April of 1990, Milken pled guilty to six securities-related charges and agreed to pay a fine of $600 million. Milken's employer, Drexel Burnham Lambert, was forced to file for bankruptcy.

BIOGRAPHICAL/CRITICAL SOURCES:

PERIODICALS

Chicago Tribune, June 30, 1988; June 11, 1989.
Los Angeles Times Book Review, June 26, 1988, p. 8.
New York Times, May 20, 1988; June 16, 1988; April 21, 1990; April 25 1990, pp. A1, A29, D1, D14, D28; October 11, 1990, pp. D1, D6; November 22, 1990, pp. A1, D4, D5.
New York Times Book Review, July 10, 1988, p. 20.

* * *

BUCKLEY, Kevin 1941(?)-

PERSONAL: Born c. 1941; married Gail Lumet. *Education:* Received degree from Yale University, 1962.

ADDRESSES: *Home*—New York, NY. *Office*—c/o *Playboy,* 747 Third Ave., New York, NY 10017.

CAREER: *Playboy,* Chicago, IL, executive editor based in New York City, 1992—; free-lance journalist and writer. Affiliated with *Newsweek,* beginning in 1963, worked as correspondent in Vietnam, bureau chief in Vietnam, 1970-72; has worked in editorial capacities for *New Times,* 1978, *Look,* 1979, *Lear's,* 1986-87, and *Geo;* has taught at the Columbia School of Journalism, Boston University, and Hampshire College.

AWARDS, HONORS: Nieman fellow, Harvard University.

WRITINGS:

Panama: The Whole Story, Simon & Schuster, 1991.

Contributor of articles and reviews to newspapers and magazines, including *Nation, New Republic, New York Times Magazine, New York Times Book Review,* and *Washington Post.*

SIDELIGHTS: As a correspondent in Vietnam in the late 1960s and early 1970s, Kevin Buckley established his journalistic reputation by reporting on a very well-publicized war. Twenty years later, his *Panama: The Whole Story* has cast him in a different role. The book won Buckley acclaim for analyzing an event that many critics feel has been inadequately covered by the press—the United States' invasion of Panama in 1989. "This book is an extraordinary account of a largely untold, dramatically underreported, and often unbelievable story," wrote Jorge G. Castaneda in the *New York Times Book Review.* This praise was echoed by Henry Raymont in *Washington Post Book World.* "If you are interested in the background of Panama," Raymont wrote, "and the kinds of elements that prompt President [George] Bush to resort to force in international relations, the book to get is Kevin Buckley's *Panama: The Whole Story.*"

The man at the center of Buckley's account is General Manuel Noriega, the Panamanian leader who was indicted by a Florida district attorney on drug trafficking charges in 1988. Thereafter, Presidents [Ronald] Reagan and Bush considered Noriega "the ugly symbol of reigning evil," according to Buckley, and they attempted to remove the general from power. After other means failed—including an economic blockade and a rebellion by elements of the Panamanian army—the United States invaded in December, 1989, eventually arresting Noriega.

"But," as Castaneda notes, "the story [in *Panama*] is rightfully centered on the role the United States played in the entire episode." The book explores Noriega's history prior to the drug indictment and details the numerous ties between the military leader and members of the United States government. The Central Intelligence Agency is alleged to be a onetime ally of Noriega, and Buckley also chronicles the general's contacts with Colonel Oliver North and other members of the Reagan administration. North and his cohorts were seeking arms and training for the Contra rebels who were battling the Sandinista government of nearby Nicaragua. As a result, they courted Noriega's favor at the same time that other U.S. officials were chastising the general for drug trafficking and corruption. Given this contradictory treatment, Castaneda remarks, "Mr. Noriega never really understood what the United States wanted of him."

Critics registered some minor complaints about Buckley's reporting in *Panama*. Raymont found that the author "left some critical Panamanian aspects of the story unexplored," while Christopher Caldwell, writing in *National Review,* noted that Buckley "adds no shocking revelations" to previous accounts of Noriega and the invasion. This criticism aside, Caldwell declared that Buckley has "given us an important new history, the first full chronicle of the Noriega fiasco." Castaneda was equally enthusiastic about Buckley's "masterly" handling of his material. "He shows what happens," the critic wrote, "when the United States latches onto an unsavory but useful foreign leader for reasons of *realpolitik* or ideological affinity, and then must go to great lengths . . . to divest itself of a no-longer manageable ally."

BIOGRAPHICAL/CRITICAL SOURCES:

BOOKS

Buckley, Kevin, *Panama: The Whole Story,* Simon & Schuster, 1991.

PERIODICALS

Business Week, June 10, 1991, p. 12.
National Review, July 29, 1991, p. 43.
New York Times Book Review, June 16, 1991, p. 10.
Washington Post Book World, July 28, 1991, p. 9.

* * *

BUNGERT, D. Edward 1957-

PERSONAL: Born June 1, 1957, in New York, NY; son of Edward Bungert and Elizabeth (Banaghan) Bungert; married Katherine Santulli, March 31, 1979; children: Adam, Zachariah. *Education:* Attended Baruch Business College. *Politics:* "Whatever works." *Religion:* "Whatever works."

ADDRESSES: Home—5-25 First St., Fairlawn, NJ 07410. *Office*—World-Wide Business Centres, 575 Madison Ave., New York, NY 10022. *Agent*—John Hawkins, John Hawkins Associates, 71 West Twenty-third St., New York, NY 10011.

CAREER: World-Wide Business Centres, New York City, 1977—, began working in the mailroom, became vice-president, 1988—.

MEMBER: International Association of Crime Writers.

WRITINGS:

Deep Cover, NAL/Dutton, 1993.
Strangle Hold, NAL/Dutton, in press.

WORK IN PROGRESS: Researching "the third Martin Walsh Federal Bureau of Investigation (FBI) assignment, which deals with kidnapping and devil cults"; also researching religion and witchcraft.

SIDELIGHTS: D. Edward Bungert told *CA:* "To me there is always more than meets the eye. From outlaw bikers to professional wrestlers, we are a society of subcultures each with its own morals and codes of behavior. My inspiration for the Martin Walsh Federal Bureau of Investigation (FBI) novels is the discovery of these worlds within worlds that exist all around us. I want to treat the reader to an intimate experience of these groups, which is normally unavailable through traditional sources like the news media, etc."

* * *

BURFORD, Eleanor
See HIBBERT, Eleanor Alice Burford

* * *

BURKETT, Larry 1939-

PERSONAL: Born March 3, 1939, in Winter Park, FL; son of Warren Levi (an electrician) and Nuna (a homemaker; maiden name, Boatwright) Burkett; married; wife's name, Judy (a manager); children: Allen, Dan, Todd, Kim. *Education:* Received B.S. and M.S. (summa cum laude) from Rollins College. *Religion:* Christian. *Avocational interests:* Rebuilding antique autos.

ADDRESSES: Home—3647 Tradition Dr., Gainsville, GA 30506. *Office*—Christian Financial Concepts, 601 Broad St. SE, Gainsville, GA 30501.

CAREER: General Electric, Cape Canaveral, FL, manager, 1961-68; Testline, Inc., Titusville, FL, manager, 1968-71; Campus Crusade for Christ, Arrowhead, CA, manager, 1971-73; Christian Financial Concepts, Gainsville, GA, manager, 1973—; radio broadcaster and writer.

AWARDS, HONORS: Author of the year, Christian Booksellers Association; radio programmer of the year, National Religious Broadcasters.

WRITINGS:

NONFICTION

How to Manage Your Money, Moody, 1975.
What Husbands Wish Their Wives Knew about Money, Victor, 1977.
The Financial Planning Workbook, Moody, 1979.
Your Finances in Changing Times, Moody, 1982.
(With William Proctor) *How to Prosper in the Underground Economy: A Completely Legal Guide to the*

Hidden, Multi-Billion-Dollar Cash Economy, Morrow, 1982.
Using Your Money Wisely: Guidelines from Scripture, Moody, 1986.
Answers to Your Family's Financial Questions, Tyndale, 1987.
What the Bible Says about Money, Wolgemuth & Hyatt, 1989.
Debt-Free Living, Moody, 1989.
The Complete Financial Guide for Young Couples, Victory, 1989.
Business by the Book: The Complete Guide of Biblical Principles for Business Men and Women, Nelson, 1990.
The Coming Economic Earthquake, Moody, 1991.
The Complete Financial Guide for Single Parents, Victor, 1991.
Investing for the Future, Victor, 1992.

Also author of audio and video materials, study guides, instructional manuals, and radio commentaries. Contributor to periodicals, including *Christian Herald.*

OTHER

The Illuminati (novel), Nelson, 1991.

WORK IN PROGRESS: The Last American Dream and *Career Pathways,* nonfiction; *70 Hours* and *Solar Flare,* fiction; research on "the economic and social decline of America."

SIDELIGHTS: Larry Burkett specializes in books which provide a Christian perspective on various financial and economic issues. He told *CA:* "I am a Christian teacher of biblical principles of finances. My primary mediums are two daily radio broadcasts—aired on approximately one-thousand stations—and books on family finances. I also published my first fiction work, *The Illuminati,* in 1991. I try to address every issue I write about from a biblical perspective, and this influence is felt strongly in every publication."

BIOGRAPHICAL/CRITICAL SOURCES:

PERIODICALS

Christian Herald, March-April, 1992.
Christianity Today, February 10, 1992.
Los Angeles Times, May 14, 1982.

* * *

BURROUGH, Bryan 1961-

PERSONAL: Born in 1961, in Temple, TX; son of John and Mary Burrough; married Marla Dorman (an editor). *Education:* University of Missouri—Columbia, B.A., 1983.

ADDRESSES: Office—*Wall Street Journal,* 200 Liberty St., New York, NY 10281-1099.

CAREER: Journalist and author. *Wall Street Journal,* New York City, worked in Dallas, TX, bureau while in college, reporter assigned to Houston, TX, bureau, 1983-85, assigned to Pittsburgh, PA, bureau, 1986-87, reporter on mergers and acquisitions, 1987—. Has also worked as a reporter for *Columbia Missourian* and *Waco Tribune-Herald.*

AWARDS, HONORS: Missouri College Newspaper Award, 1981, for newswriting, and 1982, for editorial writing; John Hancock Award for Excellence in Business and Financial Journalism, 1987, for an article on a chronic embezzler; Gerald Loeb Award in Distinguished Business and Financial Journalism for deadline writing, with John Helyar, 1989, for a series of articles on the leveraged buy out of RJR Nabisco, Inc.

WRITINGS:

(With John Helyar) *Barbarians at the Gate: The Fall of RJR Nabisco,* Harper, 1990.
Vendetta: American Express and the Smearing of Edmond Safra, Harper, 1992.

Contributor to periodicals, including *New York.* Served as editor-in-chief of college student newspaper.

ADAPTATIONS: Barbarians at the Gate was filmed by HBO and broadcast in 1993.

SIDELIGHTS: Journalist Bryan Burrough has been reporting business news for the *Wall Street Journal* since his college days in the early 1980s. In 1987 he won the John Hancock Award for Excellence in Business and Financial Journalism for his article on a chronic embezzler; then he teamed with fellow *Wall Street Journal* reporter John Helyar for a series of articles on the leveraged buy out of RJR Nabisco, Inc. These articles garnered Burrough and Helyar a Gerald Loeb Award in Distinguished Business and Financial Journalism in 1989, and the pair decided to turn the articles into a book. The result, *Barbarians at the Gate: The Fall of RJR Nabisco,* reached number one on the *New York Times* best-seller list in 1990. Burrough followed up his first book success with a solo effort, *Vendetta: American Express and the Smearing of Edmond Safra.*

Burrough was born in Temple, Texas, but he studied journalism at the University of Missouri—Columbia. While there, he served as editor-in-chief of the university's student newspaper and won awards for his efforts both as a reporter and as an editorialist. Burrough also managed to get a reporting job at the local city newspaper while still a student, and he returned to Texas to do his internships at the *Waco Tribune-Herald* and the Dallas bureau of the *Wall Street Journal.* After graduation, he worked for the *Journal* at various locations until finally being employed at its bureau in New York City.

When Burrough and Helyar turned their award-winning series of articles into *Barbarians at the Gate* in 1990, they covered the buy out in greater detail. The book, as Michael Massing explained in the *Times Literary Supplement,* "offers a blow-by-blow account of the 'deal of the century'—the takeover battle for RJR Nabisco. . . . Burrough and . . . Helyar . . . nimbly recount the manic clash of wills and ambitions that, even by Wall Street standards, reached lunatic proportions. Admirably, the writers managed to interview all of the key players—executives, lawyers, bankers and brokers. And virtually everyone seems to have behaved badly." The takeover started in the mind of RJR Nabisco's own chief executive, F. Ross Johnson, who secretly began plotting a leveraged buy out in 1988. When negotiations with Henry Kravis of Kohlberg Kravis Roberts & Co. ended, Kravis began making his own bids for the corporation, and a bidding war ensued, with RJR Nabisco finally going to Kravis's company.

Barbarians at the Gate has been widely praised by critics, though Nancy Goldstone, reviewing in *Washington Post Book World,* complained that the book is "too detailed, too all-encompassing to be comprehensible." *Business Week* contributor Judith H. Dobrzynski, however, asserted that the volume "becomes a page-turner. It puts readers smack in the middle of the action [and] sketches marvelous portraits of the major characters." A critic in *Economist* noted that while "accounts of individual takeover battles . . . do not usually make good books," Burrough and Helyar's "effort is a mostly honourable exception. . . . They tell a good story without getting bogged down in analysis." Patricia O'Toole, writing in the *New York Times Book Review,* was similarly impressed, noting that the authors "chronicle the fight with verve and relish, giving *Barbarians at the Gate* all the suspense of a first-rate thriller."

Harper, the publisher of *Barbarians at the Gate,* was pleased with the success of the book and offered Burrough one million dollars for his next book project. Burrough confided to John Greenwald in *Time:* "I was absolutely stunned. To me, the money is not a real thing. It's kind of like it's happening to someone else." The project in question turned out to be *Vendetta: American Express and the Smearing of Edmond Safra.* Concerned with the American Express executives who spread rumors of money laundering and other illegal activities against a competing banker, the book has met with favorable critical response. For example, Leah Nathans Spiro wrote in *Business Week:* "What the author proves most successfully is that he can deliver another good read, a fly-on-the-wall account of the twists and turns in this bitter feud."

One of the things Burrough had set out to prove in *Vendetta,* however, was the involvement of American Express chief executive James D. Robinson III, and, as Spiro noted, "Burrough convinces us only that Robinson probably knew." Concerning the issue, Spiro quoted Burrough, who asserted that Robinson either "knew and approved of what his aides were doing, or he knew he didn't want to know. It's hard to say which is worse." Robinson has denied knowledge of the smear campaign, and one of Burrough's sources, Harry Freeman, sued Burrough for libel, claiming, as Esther B. Fein reported in the *New York Times,* that Burrough "recklessly disregarded and distorted the truth in the [*Wall Street Journal*] article" that preceded *Vendetta.* But Burrough is unperturbed and has been the subject of lawsuits before for his reporting. He told Fein: "Big lawsuits and threats are very popular these days . . . but I'm not going to let that threat stand in the way of getting at the truth."

BIOGRAPHICAL/CRITICAL SOURCES:

BOOKS

Bestsellers 90, Issue 3, Gale, 1990, pp. 7-9.
Burrough, Bryan, *Vendetta: American Express and the Smearing of Edmond Safra,* Harper, 1992.

PERIODICALS

Business Week, January 29, 1990, p. 16; June 1, 1992, p. 14.
Economist, January 20, 1990.
Los Angeles Times Book Review, January 28, 1990, pp. 1, 13.
Newsweek, May 11, 1992, p. 78.
New York Times, May 4, 1992.
New York Times Book Review, January 21, 1990.
Time, February 19, 1990, p. 71; October 22, 1990, p. 50.
Times Literary Supplement, August 10, 1990, p. 846.
Washington Post Book World, January 14, 1990.*

—Sketch by Elizabeth Wenning

C

CAHN, Sammy 1913-1993

OBITUARY NOTICE—See index for *CA* sketch: Born January 18, 1913, in Manhattan, NY; died of congestive heart failure, January 15, 1993, in Los Angeles, CA. Lyricist, performer, and writer. In his long and successful career, Cahn wrote lyrics for numerous hit songs, some of which were featured in motion pictures and stage productions. His autobiography, *I Should Care: The Sammy Cahn Story,* recounted his career, including his attempts to become a vaudeville violinist and his more successful endeavors in songwriting. Cahn and his early partner Saul Chaplin penned several hits for performers such as Louis Armstrong and the Andrews Sisters while living in New York City in the 1930s. Cahn then went to Hollywood where he wrote songs for motion pictures such as *Anchors Away* and *Romance on the High Seas.* Beginning in the 1940s, Cahn wrote the lyrics for many Frank Sinatra recordings, producing the hits "I Walk Alone," "The Tender Trap," "Love and Marriage," and "Come Fly With Me." In writing for stage musicals, Cahn teamed with Jule Styne on the 1947 Broadway hit *High Button Shoes* and worked with frequent collaborator Jimmy Van Heusen on several other productions. He also appeared in a successful retrospective show of his songs entitled *Words and Music.* Other popular hits written by Cahn include "My Kind of Town," "Let It Snow! Let it Snow! Let it Snow!," and "Three Coins in the Fountain." For his songwriting efforts, Cahn received four Academy awards and was named to the Songwriters Hall of Fame.

OBITUARIES AND OTHER SOURCES:

BOOKS

Who's Who, 144th edition, St. Martin's, 1992.
Who's Who in the Theatre: A Biographical Record of the Contemporary Stage, 17th edition, Gale, 1981.

PERIODICALS

Chicago Tribune, January 17, 1993, section 2, p. 6.
Los Angeles Times, January 16, 1993, p. A2.
New York Times, January 16, 1993.
Times (London), January 18, 1993, p. 17.

* * *

CAIL, Carol 1937-
(Kara Galloway)

PERSONAL: Born March 18, 1937, in Richmond, IN; daughter of Lester W. (a florist) and June (a florist; maiden name, Stephens) Peters; married Norman Cail (an owner of a retail office supply company), July 8, 1956; children: Matthew, Todd. *Education:* University of Arkansas, B.Ed. (with honors), 1961; University of Kentucky, M.Ed., 1964. *Avocational interests:* Reading, cooking, hiking, listening to music.

ADDRESSES: Home and office—4 Colgate Court, Longmont, CO 80503.

CAREER: Teacher of American history at a junior high school in Fayetteville, AR, 1965-67; Daily Office Supply, Longmont, CO, co-owner and operator, 1978-89; full-time writer, 1989—. Adult education teacher in Boulder, CO, 1991—. Longmont Landmark Designation Commission, commissioner, 1990—.

MEMBER: Mystery Writers of America, American Crime Writers League, National Writers Club, Romance Writers of America, Sisters in Crime.

WRITINGS:

(Under pseudonym Kara Galloway) *Sleight of Heart* (romantic suspense novel), Harlequin, 1990.

(Under pseudonym Kara Galloway) *Love at Second Sight* (romantic suspense novel), Harlequin, 1991.

Ivory Lies (romantic suspense novel), Meteor Publishing, 1992.

Private Lies (mystery novel), Harper, 1993.

Road Games (romantic suspense novel), Meteor Publishing, in press.

Author of a monthly book review column in *Home Cooking,* 1976—. Contributor of poems, stories, articles, and reviews to magazines and newspapers, including *Alfred Hitchcock's Mystery, Creative Computing, Hawaii Review, Pinehurst Journal,* and *True West* magazine.

WORK IN PROGRESS: Two mystery novels; research on the southwest corner of Utah, with a novel expected to result.

SIDELIGHTS: Carol Cail told *CA:* "My tombstone should read 'Born to Write.' I wrote poetry before I learned to print, thanks to my mother taking dictation. In public school, I wrote stories for and about my friends.

"I graduated from Eaton High School, in Ohio, in 1955, and opened a flower shop in nearby Brookville. One year was enough of that. I got married, left my parents to make the shop a big success, and settled with my husband Norm in West Lafayette, Indiana, where he was an engineering student at Purdue University. I became a service representative (read that as complaint department) for Public Service.

"Next, we moved to Fayetteville, Arkansas, where Norm taught at the University of Arkansas, and I enrolled in the College of Education and discovered I could earn all A's now that I didn't have to worry about boys and where my next date was coming from. Degree in hand, I found a position teaching American history. It was as much fun as writing.

"Since this was before women's lib, there was never any question that I would give up this job and tag along with Norm on his next career move, to International Business Machines (IBM) in Lexington, Kentucky. No problem. I found something else I liked—giving birth to two sons and staying home to keep them from killing one another. Still a spare-time writer, I sold a poem at last, to a newspaper in Oregon, and shortly after that, a story to *Ellery Queen's Mystery* magazine.

"The publication log jam broken, I began to sell other poems and stories. IBM relocated Norm to Boulder, Colorado, and when Norm decided he'd rather work overtime for his own company, we purchased Daily Office Supply, and I helped him work those self-employed overtime hours. Writing time was scarce, but I kept my hand in. Too soon, our sons grew up, finished college, and moved away.

"I continued to sell various writings, until I could claim I'd sold as many poems as I was years old. In 1989, with patron Norm to pay my bills, I stepped off an imaginary bungee cord platform to the ups and downs of a full-time writing career. Then I wrote my first novel. Having read somewhere that romances account for forty percent of all mass market paperbacks sold, I knew that was where I should begin, even though I preferred to write a mystery. Five novel sales later—sure enough, four romances to one mystery—I'm having the time of my life. Norm is thinking about retirement. I'm never retiring—not until I'm too old to remember the words."

*　　*　　*

CAIRNS, David   1904-1992

OBITUARY NOTICE—See index for *CA* sketch: Born June 11, 1904, in Ayton, Berwickshire, Scotland; died in 1992. Minister, theologian, educator, and writer. A longtime professor at Christ's College in Aberdeen, Scotland, and a prolific author, Cairns attained a prominent position in the field of theological study. After serving as a minister, an army chaplin, and as the secretary of the Student Christian Movement at Oxford University, Cairns joined the faculty at Christ's College in 1948. His writings include *The Image of God in Man, God up There? A Study in Divine Transcendence,* and *Worship Now: A Collection of Services and Prayers for Public Worship.* He was also the editor and compiler of *A System of Christian Doctrine.*

OBITUARIES AND OTHER SOURCES:

BOOKS

The Writers Directory: 1990-1992, St. James Press, 1990.

PERIODICALS

Times (London), December 9, 1992, p. 19.

*　　*　　*

CALLAHAN, David   1965(?)-

PERSONAL: Born c. 1965. *Education:* Attended Hampshire College. *Politics:* Liberal.

ADDRESSES: Office—*American Prospect,* P.O. Box 7645, Princeton, NJ 08543.

CAREER: American Prospect, Princeton, NJ, currently managing editor; writer.

WRITINGS:

Dangerous Capabilities: Paul Nitze and the Cold War (nonfiction), HarperCollins, 1990.

Contributor to periodicals, including *Commonweal, New York Times Book Review,* and *Technology Review.*

SIDELIGHTS: David Callahan is author of *Dangerous Capabilities: Paul Nitze and the Cold War,* which recounts longtime bureaucrat Paul Nitze's role in shaping America's cold war policies. Nitze served under five U.S. presidents—John F. Kennedy, Lyndon Johnson, Richard Nixon, Gerald Ford, and Ronald Reagan—and, in various capacities, proved influential in U.S.-Soviet relations. A protege of Dean Acheson, who served as secretary of state during the presidency of Harry S. Truman, Nitze was named assistant secretary of defense during Kennedy's administration, and he became defense secretary under Johnson. Nitze, though a self-avowed Democrat, was also a steadfast bipartisan figure, and so he remained a key governmental figure under Republican leaders Nixon, Ford, and Reagan. Throughout his career, Nitze was known for approaching relations with the Soviets by inevitably considering the worst likely outcome of any military or diplomatic maneuvers. Joseph S. Nye, Jr., writing in the *New York Times Book Review,* noted Nitze's "systematic pessimism" and his faith in nuclear superiority as a deterrent to armed conflict. Nye pronounced Nitze "a fascinating individual" and deemed Callahan's *Dangerous Capabilities* "an immensely readable account."

Despite the extensive detail on Nitze's life and career that Callahan provides in *Dangerous Capabilities,* the author only interviewed his subject twice and mainly restricted his questions to those of a biographical nature. Callahan stated in the *New York Times Book Review* that Nitze's "former friends and colleagues provided me with all the ammunition I needed to make my attack anyway." As a lifelong liberal, Callahan harbored inherent opposition to many of Nitze's policies and ideologies, but, as he related in the same article, he was impressed with his subject: "He is a marvelous man who is intellectually much more thorough and thoughtful than many of the people who have served in Government with him."

BIOGRAPHICAL/CRITICAL SOURCES:

PERIODICALS

Foreign Affairs, spring, 1991.
Journal of American History, September, 1991.
New York Times Book Review, September 9, 1990, pp. 22-23.*

*   *   *

CAMPBELL, Georgia Arianna Ziadie 1949-
(Lady Colin Campbell)

PERSONAL: Born August 17, 1949, in St. Andrew, Jamaica, West Indies; daughter of Michael George (in busi-

ness) and Gloria Dey (Smedmore) Ziadie; married Lord Colin Campbell, March 23, 1974 (divorced May, 1975). *Education:* Attended St. George's College, 1960-67; Fashion Institute of Technology, associate degree, 1970. *Politics:* Independent. *Religion:* Roman Catholic.

ADDRESSES: Home—Lochmore House, East Bury St., London SW1W 9JX, England. *Agent*—Sara Fisher, A.M. Heath and Co., Ltd., 79 St. Martin's Ln., London WC1, England.

CAREER: Writer.

WRITINGS:

UNDER NAME LADY COLIN CAMPBELL

Guide to Being a Modern Lady, Heterodox, 1986.
Diana in Private: The Princess Nobody Knows, St. Martin's, 1992.

WORK IN PROGRESS: A book on Britain's Royal Family.

*   *   *

CAMPBELL, Lady Colin
See CAMPBELL, Georgia Arianna Ziadie

*   *   *

CANDY, Philip C(arne) 1950-

PERSONAL: Born October 14, 1950, in Melbourne, Victoria, Australia; son of John Carne (a real estate agent) and Helen Emilie (Millar) Candy; married Mary-Anne Janet Ley (a high school teacher), January 19, 1973; children: Janet Heather, Stuart Gordon Carne, Fiona Elizabeth. *Education:* University of Melbourne, B. Com., 1972, B.A., 1977; University of Adelaide, graduate diploma in education, 1977; University of Manchester, M. Ed., 1979; University of New England (Australia), graduate diploma in continuing education, 1981; University of British Columbia, Ed. D., 1987. *Religion:* Anglican. *Avocational interests:* History, travel.

ADDRESSES: Home—Sherwood, Queensland, Australia. *Office*—Queensland University of Technology, 2 George St., Brisbane, Queensland, Australia 4000.

CAREER: Australian Consolidated Industries, Melbourne, Victoria, graduate trainee, 1972-73; Australian Consolidated Industries, Adelaide, South Australia, assistant management accountant, 1974; South Australian Department of Further Education, Adelaide, lecturer and training specialist, 1974-79; South Australian College of Advanced Education, Armidale, lecturer in adult education, 1979-87; University of New England, Adelaide, lecturer in higher education, 1987-89; Queensland University of Technology, Brisbane, associate professor and director of academic staff development, 1989—. Consultant for UNESCO, Colombo Plan Staff College, Australian International Development Assistance Bureau, and Commonwealth Fund for Technical Cooperation. *Military service:* Citizen's Military Forces, 1974-79, served as specialist instructor; became lieutenant.

MEMBER: Higher Education Research and Development Society of Australia (executive member, 1989—), American Association for Adult and Continuing Education, American Education Research Association.

AWARDS, HONORS: Coolie Verner Memorial Prize, University of British Colombia, 1985; Cyril Houle World Award for Literature in Adult Education, American Association for Adult and Continuing Education, 1991.

WRITINGS:

Mirrors of the Mind, Department of Adult Education, University of Manchester, 1981.
Self-direction for Lifelong Learning: A Comprehensive Guide to Theory and Practice, Jossey-Bass, 1991.

WORK IN PROGRESS: Editing, with J. Laurent, of *Pioneering Culture: Mechanics' Institutes and Schools of Arts in Australia,* 1993.

SIDELIGHTS: Philip C. Candy told *CA:* "For some reason, academic writers—unless their field is in the humanities and especially in English literature—tend not to think of themselves as authors. In my experience, writing itself is not greatly discussed in most disciplines, except at a mechanical level, and elegance of style often takes second place to rigour in research. I became aware of myself as an author during the editing of my book *Self-direction for Lifelong Learning.* I was flattered by the very careful attention that the copy editor bestowed on my manuscript, and I deliberately sought to achieve some literary as well as scholarly merit in the final product. I enjoy words and admire people who use them well. I strive to express myself lucidly and economically, and when time permits, I edit for pleasing—not simply technically correct—usage.

"I enjoy reading for pleasure, though my professional responsibilities do not permit me as much time for reading as I would like. I read history and travel and works of imaginative fiction; in many of these I find the use of language more inspired and inspirational than the majority of theses and articles in scholarly journals. This, of course, need not necessarily be the case. I am considerably persuaded by William Zinsser's thesis, articulated in his book *Writing to Learn,* that good clear expository writing in the disciplines is not only edifying for the writer but can make most subjects both interesting and accessible to non-specialist readers.

"Long interested in history, I strive to provide a historical dimension to my writing wherever appropriate. Sometimes this takes the form of tracing the antecedents of current events and ideas, and sometimes I highlight parallels derived from other eras. In either case, my intention is to emphasize the fact that contemporary debates and events have historical roots and, very often, historical precedents as well.

"I appreciate and enjoy writing which is recursive or symmetrical rather than strictly linear and which works at a symbolic as well as a literal level. I do seek in my own writing to deal with several themes simultaneously, as I believe that attentive readers enjoy the structure as well as the content of a piece of writing.

"Since the publication of my book in 1991, I have read several books and articles on writing. I feel privileged to belong to the great company of authors, and believe that academics can, and indeed should, strive for the highest standards of written expression. Whether writing research reports, journal articles, or monographs, they should see the craft of writing as important. Academics should be encouraged to discuss with others not just what, but how and why they write."

*   *   *

CANTLUPE, Joe 1951-

PERSONAL: Surname is pronounced "*cant*-loop"; born November 27, 1951, in Newark, NJ; son of Joseph J. (an engineer) and Ann (a bookkeeper; maiden name, Galante) Cantlupe; married Rachelle DePalma, June 13, 1976 (divorced January, 1980); married Michele Molnar (a writer), May 16, 1981; children: Benjamin, Max. *Education:* Received B.A. from Seton Hall University; attended New School for Social Research. *Politics:* Independent. *Religion:* "Lapsed Roman Catholic."

ADDRESSES: Home—8237 Hillandale Dr., San Diego, CA 92120. *Office—San Diego Union Tribune,* 350 Camino de la Rena, San Diego, CA 92112.

CAREER: Currently affiliated with *San Diego Union Tribune,* San Diego, CA.

WRITINGS:

(With Lisa Petrillo) *Badge of Betrayal: The Devastating True Story of a Rogue Cop Turned Murderer,* Avon, 1991.

CANTWELL, Mary

PERSONAL: Born in Providence, RI; daughter of I. Leo (a production manager) and Mary G. (a teacher; maiden name, Lonergan) Cantwell; married Robert Lescher, December 19, 1953 (divorced); children: Katherine, Margaret. *Education:* Connecticut College, B.A., 1953.

ADDRESSES: Office—*New York Times,* 229 West 43rd St., New York, NY 10036. *Agent*—Lynn Nesbit, Janklow-Nesbit Associates, 598 Madison Ave., New York, NY 10022.

CAREER: Mademoiselle magazine, New York City, copywriter, 1953-58, chief copywriter, 1962-67, managing and features editor, 1968-77, senior features editor, 1978-80; *New York Times,* New York City, member of editorial board, 1980—, columnist, 1988-90; writer.

AWARDS, HONORS: Connecticut College Medal, 1983; Walker Stone Award, Scripps Howard Foundation, 1986.

WRITINGS:

St. Patrick's Day (juvenile; part of "Crowell Holiday" series), illustrated by Ursula Arndt, Crowell, 1967.
American Girl: Scenes from a Small Town Childhood, Random House, 1992.

Contributor of articles and fiction to magazines.

WORK IN PROGRESS: "A memoir of New York from the mid-1950s to the end of the 1960s, publication expected in 1995 (unless I finish it earlier)."

SIDELIGHTS: Mary Cantwell relates her experiences as an Irish American Catholic growing up in Protestant territory in *American Girl: Scenes from a Small Town Childhood.* Her personal history and coming-of-age are not marked by prejudice, anguish, or torment, though. Instead Cantwell recounts for readers the story of a safe, clean, quiet childhood in a simple, happy place.

Throughout the book, Cantwell recalls with affection and sensitivity the people and place that gave her a sense of community in Bristol, Rhode Island, during the 1930s and 1940s. In *American Girl* Cantwell paints kind but realistic portraits of her neighbors and family, including the bully who cracked her head on the sidewalk, a demoralizing music teacher, her socially correct grandmother who occasionally gambles through her equally formal bookie, and her hero—her dad. Susan Dodd, writing in *Washington Post Book World,* noted that Cantwell's townspeople "are spitting images of folk we all know—or would wish to."

Cantwell also offers a loving view of Bristol. She warmly describes her house on Hope Street—the home of her family for three generations. She recalls Bristol's harbor and remembers local haunts and rituals, such as skiing down sloping streets in winter and stopping by the soda fountain at Buffington's Drugstore after the movies on Friday nights. Cantwell recreates the lore and legend of her hometown, such as the incident of George Washington walking down the main street.

More than one reviewer of *American Girl* noticed Cantwell's nostalgia and commended her for effectively preserving an ended era. "What Ms. Cantwell is nostalgic for," explained David Plante in *New York Times Book Review,* "is the middle-class Protestant light—the pure glow—that once unified the whole of America, which she belonged to. Her book is a kind of hymn to that America."

Cantwell told *CA:* "My second book, like my first, is a memoir. But I don't think of myself as a memoirist—assuming there's such a word—but as a kind of historian. I'm trying to record what certain American places were like at a certain time—albeit through a certain filter."

BIOGRAPHICAL/CRITICAL SOURCES:

PERIODICALS

Kirkus Reviews, January 15, 1967, p. 59.
Library Journal, March 15, 1967, p. 1309; April 1, 1992, p. 126.
New York Times Book Review, June 14, 1992, p. 9.
People, August 17, 1992, p. 41.
Publishers Weekly, April 6, 1992, p. 44.
Washington Post Book World, June 21, 1992, pp. 5, 12.

* * *

CAPEK, Karel   1890-1938

PERSONAL: Born January 9, 1890, in Male Svatonovice, Bohemia (now part of Czechoslovakia); died of pneumonia, December 25, 1938, in Prague, Czechoslovakia; son of Antonin (a doctor) and Bozena Capek; married Olga Scheinplugova (an actress and novelist), 1935. *Education:* Attended University of Prague; educated in Berlin, c. 1910, and Paris; received doctorate from Charles University, 1915. *Avocational interests:* Gardening, raising dogs and cats, photography, collecting oriental carpets and exotic phonograph records, traveling.

CAREER: Playwright, novelist, short story author, and travel writer. *Narodni listy,* Prague, Czechoslovakia, staff writer, c. 1919-23; Prague Municipal Theater, director of plays, including *The Cenci,* 1921-23; *Lidove noviny* (newspaper), Brno, Czechoslovakia, staff writer, beginning c. 1923. "Friday Circle," founder, 1924.

MEMBER: Czech P.E.N. Club (president, beginning in 1925), P.E.N. Club in Slovakia (cofounder).

WRITINGS:

INDIVIDUAL WORKS

(With brother Josef Capek) *Zarive hlubiny* (short stories; title means "The Luminous Depths"; includes the verse play *Lasky hra osudna,* title means "The Fateful Game of Love"), [Prague], 1916.

Bozi muka (title means "Wayside Crosses"; includes "Slepej," title means "The Imprint"; "Ztracena cesta," title means "The Lost Way"; "Hora," title means "The Mountain"; and "Pomoc!" title means "Help!"), [Prague], 1917.

Pragmatismus cili Filosofie practickeho zivota, [Prague], 1918.

(With Josef Capek) *Krakonosova zahrada* (title means "The Garden of Krakonos"), [Prague], 1918.

(Translator) *Francouzska poezie nove doby* (French poetry), [Prague], 1920.

Loupeznik (drama; title means "The Outlaw"; produced in Prague at the National Theater, March 2, 1920), [Prague], 1920.

R.U.R.: Rossum's Universal Robots (drama; produced in Prague at the National Theater, January 25, 1921), [Prague], 1920.

Kritika slov (title means "A Critique of Words"), [Prague], 1920.

Trapne povidky (short stories; includes "Kosile," title means "The Shirts"), [Prague], 1921, translation by F. P. Marchant, published as *Money and Other Stories,* [London], 1929.

(With Josef Capek) *Ze zivota hmyzu* (drama; also known as *The Insect Play;* produced in Prague at the National Theater, March 8, 1922), [Prague], 1921, translation by Paul Selver, published as *The World We Live In,* [London], 1923, and *And So ad Infinitum,* [New York], 1923.

Lasky hra osudna (drama), [Prague], c. 1922.

Tovarna na absolutno (novel; originally appeared in the newspaper *Lidove noviny*), [Prague], 1922, translated as *The Absolute at Large,* [New York], 1927.

Vec Makropulos (drama; produced in Prague at the National Theater, November 21, 1922), [Prague], 1922, translation by Selver, published as *The Macropulos Secret,* [Boston], 1925.

Italske listy (travel sketches), self-illustrated, [Prague], 1923, translation by Marchant, published as *Letters from Italy,* [London], 1929.

Krakatit (novel), [Prague], 1924, translation by Lawrence Hyde, published as *Krakatit,* [New York], 1925.

Anglicke listy (travel sketches), self-illustrated, [Prague], 1924, translation by Selver published as *Letters from England,* [London], 1925.

O nejblizsich vecech, [Prague], 1925, translation by Dora Round published as *Intimate Things,* [New York], 1931.

(With Josef Capek) *Adam Stvoritel* (drama; produced in Prague at the National Theater, 1927), [Prague], 1927, translation by Round published as *Adam the Creator,* [London], c. 1929.

Hovory s T. G. Masarykem, three volumes, [Prague], 1928-35, translation by Round published as *President Masaryk Tells His Story,* [London], 1934.

Povidky z jedne kapsky (short stories; title means "Tales from One Pocket"; also see below), [Prague], 1929.

Povidky z druhe kapsky (short stories; title means "Tales from the Other Pocket"; includes "Zavrat," title means "Vertigo"; "Balado o Juraji Cupovi," title means "The Epic Exploit of Juraj Cup"; and "Soud pana Havleny," title means "Mr. Havlena's Verdict"), [Prague], 1929.

Zahradnikuv rok (sketches), illustrated by Josef Capek, [Prague], 1929, translation by M. and R. Weatherall published as *The Gardener's Year,* [London], 1931.

Vylet do Spanel (travel sketches), self-illustrated, [Prague], 1930, translation by Selver published as *Letters from Spain,* [London], 1931.

Marsyas cili na okraj literatury (essays), [Prague], 1931, translation by M. and R. Weatherall published as *In Praise of Newspapers,* [London], 1950, [New York], 1951.

Tales from Two Pockets (abridged version of *Povidky z jedne kapsky* and *Povidky z druhe kapsky*), translated by Selver, [London], 1932.

Apokryfy, [Prague], 1932, translation by Round published as *Apocryphal Stories,* [New York], 1939.

Devatero pohadek, [Prague], 1932, translation by M. and R. Weatherall published as *Fairy Tales,* [London], 1934.

O vecech obecnych cili Zoon politikon (articles; title means "On Political Matters, or Zoon Politikon"; includes "Proc nejsem kominista," title means "Why I Am Not a Communist"; "Betlem," title means "Bethlehem"; and "Male pomery," title means "On a Small Scale"), [Prague], 1932.

Obrazky z Holandska (travel sketches), self-illustrated, [Prague], 1932, translation by Selver published as *Letters from Holland,* [London], 1933.

Dasenka cili Zivot stenete, [Prague], 1933, translation by M. and R. Weatherall published as *Dashenka, or The Life of a Puppy,* [London], 1933.

Hordubal (novel), [Prague], 1933.

Povetron (novel; also published as *Meteor,* 1935), [Prague], c. 1934.

Obycejny zivot (novel; also published as *An Ordinary Life,* 1936), [Prague], 1934.

Valka s mloky (novel; originally appeared in the newspaper *Lidove noviny*), [Prague], 1936, translation by M. and R. Weatherall published as *The War with the Newts,* [New York], 1937.

Cesta na sever (travel sketches), self-illustrated, [Prague], 1936, translation by M. and R. Weatherall published as *Travels in the North,* [London], 1939.

Prvni parta (novel), [Prague], 1937, translation by M. and R. Weatherall, published as *The First Rescue Party,* [London], 1939.

Bila nemoc (drama), [Prague], 1937, translation by Selver published as *Power and Glory,* [London], 1938, also published as *The White Plague,* 1988.

Matka (drama), [Prague], 1938, translation by Selver published as *The Mother,* [London], c. 1938.

Mel jsem psa a kocku, [Prague], 1939, translation by M. and R. Weatherall published as *I Had a Dog and a Cat,* [New York], 1941.

Zivot a dilo skladatele Foltyna (unfinished novel), [Prague], 1939, translation by M. and R. Weatherall published as *The Cheat,* [London], 1941.

Bajky a podpovidky (title means *Fables and Would-Be Tales*), [Prague], 1946.

Three Novels: Hordubal, Meteor, An Ordinary Life, translation by M. and R. Weatherall, [London], 1948.

Also author of the essay "Miceni s T. G. M." (title means "Silence with T. G. M."), 1935. The story "Slepej" (title means "The Imprint") appears in *The Best Continental Short Stories, 1923-24,* edited by Richard Eaton, Boston, 1924; and the story "Pomoc!" (title means "Help!") appears in *Czech Prose: An Anthology,* edited and translated by William E. Harkins, Ann Arbor, 1983.

R.U.R. has been translated into numerous languages and performed throughout the world; one version has been translated by Claudia Novack-Jones and published in *Toward the Radical Center: A Karel Capek Reader* (includes six previously untranslated stories), edited by Peter Kussi, Highland Park, 1990.

COLLECTED WORKS

Spisy bratri Capku, [Prague], 1929-47.
Dilo bratri Capku, [Prague], 1955-60.
Spisy, [Prague], 1981—.

OTHER

Karel Capek and his brother Josef made their literary debut with *Navrat vestce Hermotina* (title means *The Return of the Prophet Hermotinos*), which appeared in the newspaper *Lidove noviny,* 1908. Contributor of stories, causeries, feuilletons, and book and art reviews to periodicals, including *Narodni listy* and *Lidove noviny,* beginning in 1908.

SIDELIGHTS: Czech author Karel Capek is well-respected the world over as a playwright, novelist, essayist, short story artist, and travel writer. He is perhaps best remembered for his 1920 stage play *R. U. R.: Rossum's Universal Robots,* which introduced the word "robot" into many languages. Critics, however, maintain that Capek did his best work in the novel genre, citing his satiric science fiction book, 1937's *The War of the Newts,* as being superior to *R. U. R.,* and assert that his novel trilogy, *Hordubal, Meteor,* and *An Ordinary Life,* in which he expounds his ideas on the relativity of truth and the virtues of democracy, is his true masterpiece.

Capek was born January 9, 1890, in Male Svatonovice, Bohemia—now a part of Czechoslovakia. He was frail and sickly as a child (and also as an adult), but he was looked after by his older brother Josef, who also grew up to be a writer and often collaborated with Karel. The two Capek brothers also had a sister, Helena, who became a writer as well.

Karel and Josef Capek began contributing stories and articles to newspapers in 1908, before they had completed their educations. Their first publication was the philosophical fable "The Return of the Prophet Hermotinos" in the newspaper *Lidove noviny.* Afterward, they steadily published in this newspaper and other periodicals. Both brothers, Josef in particular, were knowledgeable about the visual arts as well and also penned art and book reviews.

Some two years after he and his brother were first published, Karel Capek went to Berlin to study. He also studied briefly in Paris before returning to Prague to enroll in Charles University, from which he obtained a doctorate in 1915. The following year, the Capek brothers published their first collection of writings, *Zarive hlubiny,* which means "The Luminous Depths." The title story concerns a survivor of the *Titanic* shipwreck; the volume also includes a verse play entitled *Lasky hra osudna,* or "The Fateful Game of Love," which pokes fun at eroticism and is considered a commedia del l'arte, an Italian comedy form that draws upon a standardized set of character types and situations.

Because of his physical problems, which included calcified spinal vertebrae, Karel Capek was not able to serve in the military during World War I. Instead, he spent the war years as a tutor to a count's son in western Bohemia. Capek also managed to write his next volume of tales during this period, *Bozi muka* or "Wayside Crosses." The stories had a strong metaphysical bent to them and are generally considered pessimistic. "Slepej," or "The Imprint" depicts the reactions of two men who find a single footprint in new-fallen snow; "Pomoc!" or "Help!" tells of a man awakened by a woman's cry for aid but unable to find her. As Rene Wellek explained in an article for *The Slavonic Review,* "Wayside Crosses" is "a collection of 'detective stories.' But they are very unusual detective or rather mystery stories, without any solution for the mysteries. The very disappointment of our expectation is their main point: just the most important part of the event told remains behind the scene. The justification of this interesting technical device is, of course, in the view of life the stories are meant to convey. . . . The world appears as a whirlwind of chance and contingencies without deeper coherence."

As demonstrated in most of his fictitious works, Capek was deeply concerned with philosophy, and 1918 saw the publication of his *Pragmatismus cili Filosofie practickeho zivota,* a sympathetic discussion of the pragmatic philosophies of William James and Henri-Louis Bergson. He also worked on a translation of modern French poetry, which came out in 1920. But the same year saw the beginning of a major trend in Capek's creativity; his first stage play, *Loupeznik* (or "The Outlaw"), was produced at Prague's National Theater. At about this time, he also became acquainted with Olga Scheinplugova, a young actress who would perform in many of his plays and would later become his wife.

"The Outlaw," which centers on a woman trying to choose between her love for a rebellious young man and the values of her staunchly conservative parents, was successful enough that the National Theater agreed to produce Capek's next play, *R.U.R.: Rossum's Universal Robots.* Despite the many flaws in the work pointed out by drama critics, *R.U.R.* proved extremely popular, catching the imagination of audiences not only in Czechoslovakia but the world over—the play was rapidly translated into many languages for performances abroad. The narrative is concerned with robots, created to relieve mankind from toil, revolting and seizing control of the world from humans who have become both dehumanized and incapable of sexual reproduction. William E. Harkins asserted in his book, *Karel Capek,* that "what is new in Capek's play is the complex meaning of the symbol of the robot, which represents not only the machine and its power to free man from toil but, at the same time, symbolizes man himself, dehumanized by his own technology. . . . dehumanized by the very freedom from toil which the machine assures him; gone are the struggle of life and the challenge to man's spirit." Harkins added, "In *R.U.R.* man loses even his ability to reproduce, the last thing which distinguishes him from the robot. The complexity of the robot symbol must be realized for a proper understanding of Capek's play. He was too honest a writer to create a superficial melodrama about man-like machines which revolt against man—though this is obviously the aspect of the play which made it so popular."

Critic Ashley Dukes, discussing *R.U.R.* in his *The Youngest Drama: Studies of Fifty Dramatists* two years after its first production, argued that "the play is not a piece of dramatic literature; it is scarcely even a deep or thoughtful work. It is a piece of brilliant journalism of the stage, a work of temperamental power that 'carries' as actors say, because the author believes in it, and believes in his audience, and is interested in their reaction to what he has to say. . . ." The commentator concluded, "But Capek goes farther than belief. He has a natural understanding of crowds and crowd psychology. Europe of to-day is his stage and the world his audience, not because we feel his plays to be immortal, but because we feel them to be inevitable." Though *R.U.R.* continues to be the best-known work of Capek's oeuvre, the author reportedly cited it as his least favorite.

The success of *R.U.R.* was followed by another popular Capek play, this time in collaboration with his brother Josef. *Ze zivota hmyzu,* also known as *The Insect Play,* was produced at the National Theater in Prague early in 1922. It is an allegorical work, comparing different elements of human society with the behavior of various insects. William A. Drake declared the play "an ironical fantasy of human egoism and weakness" in his *Contemporary European Writers,* but George Jean Nathan, reviewing a revival of the work in *The Theatre Book of the Year, 1948-1949: A Record and an Interpretation,* noted that while "there is some ingenuity in the treatment" he generally disliked the method of using animals or insects as representatives of human behavior. While *The Insect Play* was being staged, Karel Capek had been given the position of stage director at the Prague Municipal Theater. In the period ranging from 1921 to 1923, he directed approximately thirteen plays, including a version of the rarely staged verse play *The Cenci,* by English romantic poet Percy Bysshe Shelley.

Another of Capek's better-known plays is *The Macropulos Secret,* first produced late in 1922. The central character is Elena Macropulos, the daughter of a Greek scientist who discovered the secret of eternal life and bestowed it upon her. In more than three hundred years of living, she has taken on various identities, the latest as singer Emilia Marty. She eventually decides, however, to discontinue using her father's secret, and the paper containing it is burned by a young girl.

Critics at first felt that *The Macropulos Secret* was a response to George Bernard Shaw's play *Back to Methuselah,* in which a much more positive view of long-life spans is presented, but Capek spoke both to this question and to accusations of pessimism in the play's preface: "I make these statements because Bernard Shaw's new play . . . which I have seen in synopsis only, appeared this winter. . . . The likeness in theme is entirely accidental. . . .

Mr. Shaw believes that it is possible for an ideal community of people to live several hundred years in a sort of paradise. As the play-goer perceives, long life in my play is treated quite differently; I think that such a condition is neither ideal or desirable. . . . Whether I am called an optimist or a pessimist, will make me neither happier nor sadder; yet, 'to be a pessimist' implies, it would seem, a silent rebuke from the world for bad behavior. In this comedy I have striven to present something delightful and optimistic. Does the optimist believe that it is bad to live sixty years but good to live three hundred? I merely think that when I proclaim a life of the ordinary span of sixty years as good enough in this world, I am not guilty of criminal pessimism." Drake, however, labeled the play "a satirical demonstration of the worthlessness of human life."

Capek's last play of the 1920s, *Adam the Creator,* written in collaboration with Josef, was produced in 1927. But he had already largely abandoned the form in favor of the novel. Earlier in 1922, Capek was intrigued with the possibilities of science fiction for a time and penned *The Absolute at Large,* a book dealing with the consequences of splitting the atom—still a fictional concept at that time. In *The Absolute at Large,* the energy released by splitting the atom causes a sort of religious mania to influence all the people, causing wars and other kinds of conflict. Eventually, however, the effects wear off and life returns to normal. Capek explored another consequence of nuclear fission in his 1924 novel *Krakatit,* in which an inventor discovers the explosive power created from the division of atoms.

Capek's best-known and most acclaimed science fiction novel, however, is *The War with the Newts.* Not published in book form until 1936, it was printed in serial form in the newspaper *Lidove noviny.* In *The War with the Newts,* a race of intelligent salamanders is discovered and enslaved by man, but they eventually revolt and take over the world. Though similar in theme to *R.U.R.,* the novel is considered by many critics to be superior to the play in terms of depth and quality of satire. George A. Test asserted in an article for *Studies in Contemporary Satire* that "*War with the Newts* presents a more terrifying fantasy world than either [Aldous Huxley's] *Brave New World* or [George Orwell's] *1984.*" Test went on to explain that "even as a satire, *War with the Newts* is unconventional. Episodic in extreme, without a central hero, a grab bag of satiric techniques, Capek's work will not satisfy readers and critics who come to the book with conventional novelistic expectations. To call it episodic is in fact generous. A major portion of the novel is really a mock-historical narrative interspersed with various kinds of documents exhibited in mock-scholarly style. Although *War with the Newts* has several richly realized characters, the scope of Capek's satire would have been undesirably restricted by the convention of a novelistic hero."

One of the major objects of Capek's satire in *War with the Newts* was German fuehrer Adolf Hitler and the rise of Nazism. As Darko Suvin pointed out in his book *Metamorphoses of Science Fiction: On the Poetics and History of a Literary Genre,* while watching "the rise of Hitler, Capek reconsidered the role of the intellect which he satirized earlier. . . . Now he wrote sharply against an intellect that is giving up its rights 'in favor of irrationalism and daimonism, be it the cult of will, of the land, of the subconscious, of the mass instincts, or of the violence of the powerful—that is a decadent intellect because it tends toward its own downfall.' A limit was found beyond which the pseudo-human became clearly evil; that limit is reached when the new creatures in *War with the Newts* grow into an analogy to the Nazi aggressors. That is why in his final [science fiction] novel Capek's satire is most clearly focused, the envelopment of the novum most consistent, and there is no conciliatory happy ending."

Before the publication of *The War with the Newts,* however, Capek had completed work on one of the major achievements of his later career, the novel trilogy of *Hordubal, Meteor,* and *An Ordinary Life.* All three explore Capek's philosophy of the relativism of truth: *Hordubal* is told first from the point of view of the title character, a man who continues to love his wife even though she cheats on him. The second half of the novel, however, is an objective, clinical account of the events surrounding Hordubal's murder by his wife and her lover. In *Meteor,* a stranger wrecks his plane in a village, and three separate people postulate theories about who he is and what his life was like. Though the views are all different, a synthesis of them does tell some basic truths about the unfortunate stranger. *An Ordinary Life* focuses on a man who has decided to record his own life story because he is convinced he is completely ordinary. In the process of writing he discovers he in fact possesses several unique personalities. William E. Harkins declared in a *Slavic and East European Journal* article that "there is little doubt that Karel Capek's trilogy of novels . . . represents his crowning achievement, perhaps that of modern Czech literature. . . . [The] three novels . . . represent serious attempts to develop new forms for the modern novel. In them Capek comes to grips with the philosophical problem of truth and reality, as well as the esthetic problem of the representation of reality in the novel."

Capek was still working on *The Cheat,* a novel about a man masquerading as a great musical talent, when he died of pneumonia on Christmas Day, 1938, in Prague. When the Nazis invaded the city the following year, they came to arrest Capek because of what they felt were seditious writings, not realizing he had already died. They did, however, arrest his brother Josef, who died in a concentration camp in 1945. Commenting on Capek's brief life and writing career, Harkins summarized in *The Czechoslovak Contribution to World Culture:* "His premature death cut short the philosophical and creative development of a great writer, a profound thinker, and a great human spirit."

BIOGRAPHICAL/CRITICAL SOURCES:

BOOKS

Capek, Karel, *The Macropulos Secret,* translated by Paul Selver, Boston, 1925.
Drake, William A., *Contemporary European Writers,* John Day, 1928.
Dukes, Ashley, *The Youngest Drama: Studies of Fifty Dramatists,* Ernest Benn, Ltd., 1923.
Harkins, William E., *Karel Capek,* Columbia University Press, 1962.
Nathan, George Jean, *The Theatre Book of the Year, 1948-1949: A Record and an Interpretation,* Knopf, 1949.
Rechcigl, Miloslav Jr., editor, *The Czechoslovak Contribution to World Culture,* Mouton & Co., 1964.
Suvin, Darko, *Metamorphoses of Science Fiction: On the Poetics and History of a Literary Genre,* Yale University Press, 1979.
Twentieth-Century Literary Criticism, Gale, Volume 6, 1982, Volume 37, 1990.

PERIODICALS

Slavic and East European Journal, summer, 1957, pp. 92-100.
Slavonic Review, July, 1936.
Studies in Contemporary Satire, spring, 1974, pp. 1-10.*

—*Sketch by Elizabeth Wenning*

*   *   *

CARCATERRA, Lorenzo 1954-

PERSONAL: Born October 16, 1954, in New York, NY; son of Mario (a butcher) and Raffaela (a homemaker) Carcaterra; married Susan J. Toepfer (a magazine editor), May 16, 1981; children: Katherine, Nicholas. *Education:* St. John's University, B.S., 1976. *Politics:* "Moderate." *Religion:* Catholic.

ADDRESSES: Home—498 Manor Ln., Pelham Manor, NY 10803. *Office*—1600 Broadway, Suite 701, New York, NY 10020. *Agent*—Loretta Fidel, Weingel-Fidel Agency, 310 East 46th St., New York, NY 10017.

CAREER: New York Daily News, New York City, reporter and editor, 1976-83; *TV-Cable Week,* staff writer, 1983; free-lance writer, 1983—; Columbia Broadcasting

System, Inc., New York City, managing editor of *Top Cops,* 1990—.

MEMBER: International Association of Crime Writers, Authors Guild.

WRITINGS:

A Safe Place: The True Story of a Father, a Son, a Murder, Villard Books, 1993.

Also author of a script, *Street Boys,* Boardwalk Entertainment. Contributor to periodicals, including *People, Life, Us,* and *Cop Talk.*

WORK IN PROGRESS: Sleepers, a Hell's Kitchen saga, publication by Villard expected in 1995.

SIDELIGHTS: Lorenzo Carcaterra told *CA:* "I was raised in a violent world, but one which I found great comfort in. I didn't own a book until I was twenty, though I always thought of writing. Since then it's been one lesson after another, all learned in the hopes of making myself a better writer. Some of the lessons were enjoyable (such as my years spent as a reporter for the *New York Daily News,* a tabloid that proved to be a great place for a young writer to grow up), while some of the lessons were stark and difficult (a number of lean free-lance years, for example). I have written for all types of magazines, some well-known (*People, Life*), and others less so. Then, in 1990, I got lucky when a producer put me in charge of *Top Cops,* a television show that found an audience.

"That same year I decided to write about my life. My first book, *A Safe Place: The True Story of a Father, a Son, a Murder,* is a memoir about my father and our life together. My second, *Sleepers,* is about four childhood friends embroiled in a murder. Both books share a return to that violent world I knew, understood, and took comfort in for so many years—a world I've decided to open and share."

*   *   *

CARLSON, Laurie 1952-

PERSONAL: Born January 27, 1952, in Sonora, CA; daughter of Ed (a mechanic and farmer) and Juanita (a library technician) Winn; married Terry Carlson, May 19, 1973; children: Ed, John. *Education:* University of Idaho, B.S., 1975; Arizona State University, M.Ed., 1991. *Politics:* Democrat. *Religion:* Roman Catholic. *Avocational interests:* Drawing, gardening, history, fishing.

ADDRESSES: Home—2903 Fernan Terrace Dr., Coeur d'Alene, ID 83814. *Agent*—Lyle Steele, 511 East 73rd St., Suite 7, New York, NY 10021.

CAREER: High school home economics teacher in Deary, ID, 1976-77; artist and sculptor, with art work and sculptured dolls exhibited in galleries, 1977-86; elementary schoolteacher in Mesa, AZ, 1988-92.

MEMBER: Society of Children's Book Writers and Illustrators, Idaho Writers League.

WRITINGS:

Home Study Opportunities: A Complete Guide to Going to School by Mail, Betterway, 1989.
Kids Create! (juvenile), Williamson Publishing, 1990.
Eco Art! Earth-Friendly Art and Craft Experiences for Three-to-Nine-Year-Olds, Williamson Publishing, 1993.
More Than Bows and Arrows, Chicago Review Press, in press.
Huzzah! Medieval Make and Do, Chicago Review Press, in press.

Contributor to periodicals, including *Crafts Report, Doll Reader, National Doll World, Successful Farming, Instructor,* and *Learning 93.*

*   *   *

CARNER, Gary 1955-

PERSONAL: Born September 24, 1955, in New York; son of Richard (in construction) and Barbara (Goot) Carner; married Nancy Thorne (a psychologist), September 28, 1985; children: Erin Maya Carner. *Education:* Private study of guitar and Renaissance lute with John Varner, 1979-85; Fairleigh Dickinson University, B.A., 1982; City College of the City University of New York, M.A. (English), 1985; Tufts University, M.A. (musicology), 1989.

CAREER: Longy School of Music, Cambridge, MA, instructor, 1987; Assumption College, Worcester, MA, lecturer, 1987-88; Quinsigamond Community College, Worcester, lecturer, 1988; Mannes College of Music, New York City, lecturer in jazz, 1992—; writer. WMFO-FM, announcer for "Jazz Variations," 1986-87; Lexington Community Education Program, instructor, 1987; Newton Adult Education Program, instructor in jazz, 1987. Producer of recordings and musical concerts and symposia; conductor of workshops; guest speaker on radio shows.

MEMBER: International Association of Jazz Record Collectors, Jazz Worcester Society (historian), Sonneck Society, Duke Ellington Society.

AWARDS, HONORS: Travel grants from National Endowment for the Humanities and Massachusetts Arts Lottery Council, both 1988; grants from Billy Strayhorn Symposium, 1989, and New Jersey Historical Commission.

WRITINGS:

Jazz Performers: An Annotated Bibliography of Biographical Materials, Greenwood Press, 1990.
(Editor with Evrard Deckers) *Jazz Discography Series, Volume 1,* G. K. Hall, 1993.

Contributor to *New Grove Dictionary of Jazz,* Macmillan, 1988; contributor of articles and reviews to periodicals, including *Cadence* and *Annual Review of Jazz Studies. Black American Literature Forum,* contributing editor, 1986, editor of special issue on jazz literature, 1991.

WORK IN PROGRESS: Billy Strayhorn: Man, Music, and Influence, a collection of musicological articles about Strayhorn, Duke Ellington's chief collaborator; *Jazz Discography Series* (volumes 2-17), to be published by G. K. Hall; *In Love with Night: The Authorized Biography of Pepper Adams,* a "jazz biography," publication by Smithsonian Institution Press expected in 1996.

*   *   *

CARR, Philippa
See HIBBERT, Eleanor Alice Burford

*   *   *

CARRIERE, Jean-Claude 1931-

PERSONAL: Born September 17, 1931, in Languedoc, France; son of Felix and Alice Carriere; married December 27, 1952; wife's name, Nicole (a painter and interior decorator); children: Iris.

ADDRESSES: Home—5 rue Victor Massi, Paris 75009, France. *Agent*—c/o Writers Guild of America, East, 555 West Fifty-seventh St., New York, NY 10019.

CAREER: Screenwriter. Director, with Pierre Etaix, of *Rupture,* 1961, and *Happy Anniversary,* 1962, and of the short film *La pince a ongles (The Nail Clippers),* 1968. Actor in films, including *Diary of a Chambermaid,* 1964, and *L'Alliance,* 1971. Head of the French film school FEMIS, 1986—; conductor of writing and directing workshops.

AWARDS, HONORS: Academy Award for best short film, 1962, for *Happy Anniversary,* and for best foreign film, 1972, for *The Discreet Charm of the Bourgeoisie,* and 1980, for *The Tin Drum;* best picture prize, Venice International Film Festival, 1967, for *Belle de jour;* British Academy of Film and Television Arts awards, best original screenplay, 1973, for *The Discreet Charm of the Bourgeoisie,* and best adapted screenplay, 1988, for *The Unbearable Lightness of Being;* cowinner of the best picture prize, Cannes Film Festival, 1979, for *The Tin Drum.*

WRITINGS:

SCREENPLAYS; WITH LUIS BUNUEL

The Diary of a Chambermaid (adapted from Octave Mirbeau's novel; released in France as *Le Journal d'une femme de chambre;* Speva, 1964), Seuil, 1971.

Belle de jour (adapted from Joseph Kessel's novel; Allied Artists, 1968), translated from the unpublished French manuscript by Robert Adkinson, Simon & Schuster, 1971.

The Milky Way (also released as *La Voie lactee*), United Artists, 1969.

The Discreet Charm of the Bourgeoisie (released in France as *Le Charme discret de la bourgeoisie*), Twentieth Century-Fox, 1972.

The Phantom of Liberty (released in France as *Le Fantome de la liberte*), Greenwich Productions, 1974.

That Obscure Object of Desire (adapted from Pierre Louys's novel *La Femme et le pantin;* released in France as *Cet Obscur Objet du desir*), First Artists, 1977.

OTHER SCREENPLAYS

(With Pierre Etaix) *The Suitor* (released in France as *Le Soupirant*), CAPAC, 1963.

(With Louis Malle) *Viva Maria!,* United Artists, 1965.

(With Jesus Franco) *The Diabolical Dr. Z* (adapted from a novel by David Kuhne; also released as *Dans le griffes du maniaque* and *Miss Muette*), U.S. Films, 1966.

(With Peter Glenville) *Hotel Paradiso* (adapted from Georges Feydeau and Maurice Desvallieres's play *L'Hotel du libre echange*), Metro-Goldwyn-Mayer (MGM), 1966.

(With Malle) *The Thief of Paris* (based on the story by Georges Darien; released in France as *Le Voleur*), Lopert, 1967.

(With Etaix) *Yoyo,* CAPAC, 1967.

(With Jacques Deray) *Borsalino,* Paramount, 1970.

(With Christian De Chalonge) *L'Alliance* (adapted from a book by Carriere; also see below), CAPAC, 1970.

(With Milos Forman, John Guare, and John Klein) *Taking Off,* Universal, 1971.

(With Francoise Xenakis, Jean Bolvary, and Eric Le Hung) *Le Droit d'aimer* (title means "The Right to Love"; adapted from a book by Xenakis), Twentieth Century-Fox/Lira Films, 1972.

(With Marco Ferreri) *Liza* (adapted from Ennio Flaiano's novel), Lira Films, 1972.

(With Deray and Ian McLellan Hunter) *The Outside Man* (released in France as *Un Homme est mort*), United Artists, 1973.

(With Juan Bunuel, Philippe Nuridzany, Pierre Maintigneux, and Clement Biddle Wood) *Leonor* (adapted from a story by Ludwig Tieck), New Line, 1977.

(With Tonino Guerra) *A Butterfly on the Shoulder* (also released as *Un Papillon sur l'epaule*), Gaumont, 1978.

(With Claude Pinoteau and Charles Israel) *The Angry Man* (released in France as *L'Homme en colere*), United Artists, 1979.

(With Franz Seitz and Volker Schlondorff) *The Tin Drum* (adapted from Gunter Grass's novel; released in Germany as *Die Blechtrommel*), New World, 1979.

(With Anne-Marie Mieville and Jean-Luc Godard) *Every Man for Himself* (released in France as *Sauve qui peut la vie*), New Yorker Films, 1980.

(With Schlondorff, Margarethe von Trotta, and Kai Hermann) *Circle of Deceit* (adapted from a novel by Nicolas Born; released in Germany as *Die Faelschung*), United Artists Classics, 1982.

(With Rene Gainville) *The Associate,* Quartet, 1982.

(With Daniel Vigne) *The Return of Martin Guerre,* European International, 1983.

(With Andrzej Wajda and others) *Danton* (adapted from Stanislawa Przybyszewska's play *The Danton Affair*), Triumph, 1983.

(With Peter Brook and Marie-Helene Estienne) *Swann in Love* (adapted from portions of Marcel Proust's novel *A la recherche du temps perdu*), Orion Classics, 1984.

La Jeune Fille et l'enfer, Orphee Arts, 1985.

(With Jerome Diamant-Berger and Olivier Assayas) *L'Unique* (title means "The One and Only"), Revcom, 1986.

(With Nagisa Oshima) *Max mon amour* (title means "Max My Love"), Greenwich Films, 1986.

(With Peter Fleischmann) *Les Exploits d'un jeune Don Juan* (adapted from Guillaume Apollinaire's novel; title means "The Exploits of a Young Don Juan"), AAA, 1987.

(With Philip Kaufman) *The Unbearable Lightness of Being* (adapted from Milan Kundera's novel), Orion, 1988.

(With Nicolas Klotz) *The Bengali Night* (adapted from Mircea Eliade's novel *La Nuit Bengali*), Gaumont, 1988.

(With Holland, Wajda, and Edward Zebrowski) *Les Possedes* (adapted from Fyodor Dostoyevsky's novel *The Possessed*), Gaumont, 1988.

(With Fleischmann) *Hard to Be a God* (adapted from a novel by Arkadii Strugatskii and Boris Strugatskii; released in Germany as *Es ist nicht leicht ein gott zu sein*), 1988.

Valmont (adapted from Choderlos de Laclos's novel *Les Liaisons dangereuses*), Orion, 1989.

(With Jean-Paul Rappeneau) *Cyrano de Bergerac* (adapted from Edmond Rostand's play; released by Orion Classics, 1990), Ramsay (Paris), c. 1990.

(With Brook and Estienne) *The Mahabharata* (adapted from the Sanskrit epic; also see below), Reiner Moritz, 1990.

(With Malle) *May Fools* (released in France as *Milou en mai*), Orion Classics, 1990, published as *Milou in May*, Faber & Faber, 1990.

(With Hector Babenco) *At Play in the Fields of the Lord* (adapted from Peter Matthiessen's novel), Saul Zaentz, 1991.

Also author, with Pierre Etaix, of *Rupture*, 1961, and *Happy Anniversary*, 1962. Author of *La Piscine* (title means "The Swimming Pool"), 1969. Author, with Joel Santoni, of *Ils sont grands ces petits*, 1979.

STAGE PRODUCTIONS

L'Aide-Memoire (play; produced in Paris, 1968, produced on Broadway as *The Little Black Book*, 1972), translation by Jerome Kilty, Samuel French, c. 1973.

Le Client (two-act play; title means "The Customer"), produced in Paris, 1971.

The Conference of the Birds, Dramatic Publishing (Chicago), c. 1982.

(With Peter Brook and Marius Constant) *La Tragedie de Carmen* (opera; abridgement of Georges Bizet's opera *Carmen;* produced on Broadway, 1983), Centre International de Creations Theatrales (Paris), c. 1981.

(With Bernard Slade) *La fille sur la banquette arriere*, L'Avant Scene, 1983.

(With Brook) *The Mahabharata* (play; adapted from the Sanskrit epic; produced at Brooklyn Academy of Music's New Wave Festival, 1987), Harper, c. 1987.

Also author, with Colin Higgins, of *Harold and Maude*, 1971. Author of adaptations of plays, including Anton Chekhov's *The Cherry Orchard* and William Shakespeare's *Timon of Athens, Measure for Measure*, and *The Tempest*.

OTHER

Lezard, R. Laffont, 1956.

L'Alliance, R. Laffont, 1963.

(With Guy Bechtel) *Dictionnaire de la betise et des erreurs de jugement*, R. Laffont, c. 1965.

Le pari, R. Laffont, 1973.

Les petits mots inconvenants, Balland, c. 1981.

(With Natalie Zemon Davis) *Le retour de Martin Guerre*, R. Laffont, c. 1982.

Credo, Balland, c. 1983.

(With Jean Audouze and Michel Casse) *Conversations sur l'invisible*, Le Pre aux clercs, 1987.

Anthologie de l'humour 1900, Editions 1900, c. 1988.

La paix des braves, Le Pre aux clercs, 1988.

La controverse de Valladolid, Le Pre aux clercs, 1992.

SIDELIGHTS: Known for his intelligent, witty productions, Jean-Claude Carriere is an acclaimed writer who has collaborated with some of the most distinguished artists of the stage and screen. His frequent coauthor status led Joe Morgenstern to call him "the unsung dramatist of our time" in *New York Times Magazine*. Although he has shown his versatility and talent by working with a range of filmmakers from throughout the world, he is probably best known for his several French collaborations with Spanish surrealist director Luis Bunuel. Carriere first teamed with the director in 1964 to write *Diary of a Chambermaid*, a reworking of the Octave Mirbeau novel that earlier inspired Jean Renoir's film of the same title. Carriere and Bunuel collaborated again in 1968 with *Belle de jour*, an eccentric production about a bored homemaker who begins working as a prostitute. The woman soon meets a variety of unusual clients, including a young gangster sporting metal dentures. The film is usually ranked among the best works of both Bunuel and lead actress Catherine Deneuve.

"With Bunuel," Carriere told Morgenstern, "the writing always came last. Every day, we'd begin by acting out a given scene: What's happening in it? Who enters? What does he do, what does he say? I'd bring a few pieces of paper with me, but I'd have to hide them while we worked. Then he'd go to sleep at eight or nine o'clock, and I'd stay up alone, trying to write the scene we'd acted out. We'd spend weeks together doing this, though not more than four or five weeks at a time, because we were two men cooped up in a hotel room without women, after all. We ate together more than 2,000 times. Like an old married couple."

Carriere and Bunuel next worked together on films that are largely episodic, a structure that allowed for greater expression of Bunuel's surrealist perspective. *The Milky Way*, the duo's 1969 venture, recounts the exploits of two men on a religious pilgrimage. During their travels the two pilgrims meet various eccentrics, and also come upon a pagan ritual. In *The Discreet Charm of the Bourgeoisie*, an Academy Award-winning film written by Carriere and Bunuel, a band of hapless rich people wander through restaurants and homes in a vain effort to enjoy a meal. On one occasion, their dining experience is disturbed by the presence of a corpse. Another time, a woman among the party is regaled by a soldier who insists that he once dreamt of her. The film's mocking of bourgeois behavior and conventions found favor with many filmgoers and reviewers. *New York Times* critic Vincent Canby called *The Discreet Charm of the Bourgeoisie* "brilliant," and "extraordinarily funny."

Carriere and Bunuel collaborated again in 1977 with *That Obscure Object of Desire*, a comedy about one man's sexual obsession for a young woman. In an attempt to show the protagonist's singleminded ignorance, Carriere and Bunuel alternated two different actresses as the pursued woman, with the hero never noticing the difference. While some viewers were confused by the dual casting of the female lead, many more found it yet another example of director Bunuel's unconventional filmmaking talent. The film marked Carriere's final venture with Bunuel, who died in 1983. In his memoir, *My Last Sigh,* Bunuel referred to Carriere as his most intimate collaborator. "The writer closest to me," he declared, ". . . is undoubtedly Carriere."

Although he is frequently lauded for his collaborations with Bunuel in the 1960s and 1970s, Carriere also worked on many other popular, if not critically acclaimed, films during those years. In 1965, for instance, he teamed with filmmaker Louis Malle on *Viva Maria!,* a musical comedy-adventure pairing celebrated French actresses Brigitte Bardot and Jeanne Moreau as revolutionaries in Mexico. Carriere rejoined Malle in writing *The Thief of Paris,* which featured popular French actor Jean-Paul Belmondo as an accomplished jewel thief. Carriere also collaborated on the script of *Borsalino,* in which Belmondo is cast with matinee idol Alain Delon as a gangster in 1930s Marseilles.

In the late 1970s, after Bunuel began concentrating on his memoirs, Carriere began to establish himself as a leading screenwriter independent of the renowned Spanish filmmaker. In 1979 he worked on director Volker Schlondorff's adaptation of Gunter Grass's novel *The Tin Drum,* which tells the story of a young boy who stops growing in order to protest the wartime horrors of the adult world. The next year Carriere contributed to Jean-Luc Godard's *Every Man for Himself,* and in 1983 he collaborated with Andrzej Wajda and others on *Danton.* The film—which focused on the final days of the title character, a French Revolution hero who was executed by his former ally—was lauded by *Time*'s Richard Schickel as "a film of high dramatic power." *The Tin Drum, Every Man for Himself,* and *Danton* all enjoyed considerable prominence on the international-film circuit, thus gaining greater recognition for Carriere.

Throughout the ensuing years Carriere continued to prove himself a versatile writer. In 1983, for example, he teamed with filmmaker Daniel Vigne in writing *The Return of Martin Guerre,* a popular historical drama about a man who claims to be the long-lost resident of an impoverished village. He moves in with the wife of the missing man and becomes both a model husband and a prominent figure in the community. When he demands a share of the profits from his family's land, however, new suspicions arise about his identity, and a court case ensues. *Newsweek*'s David Ansen noted that *The Return of Martin Guerre*

"has as many twists and ambiguities and surprises as a good suspenseful thriller."

Among Carriere's other significant works from the 1980s is *The Unbearable Lightness of Being,* director Philip Kaufman's rendering of Milan Kundera's non-linear philosophical novel. Set in Czechoslovakia around the time of the 1968 Soviet invasion, the film concerns Tomas, an arrogant yet charming brain surgeon and womanizer, and his relationships with Tereza, his sweet, small-town wife, and Sabina, his sophisticated lover. This production, though largely acknowledged for its eroticism, also received attention for showing uncommon subtlety in its considerations of love, sex, freedom, commitment, and politics.

Aside from his screenwriting ventures, which also include *Valmont, Cyrano de Bergerac, May Fools,* and 1991's *At Play in the Fields of the Lord,* Carriere has collaborated with celebrated stage director Peter Brook. Brook has impressed many—and alienated others—with his unconventional renderings of such classics as William Shakespeare's *Measure for Measure* and Georges Bizet's opera *The Tragedy of Carmen.* Carriere collaborated with Brook on the latter work, which significantly scaled-down Bizet's original conception and transformed the opera into a gripping, fast-paced expression of love and death. *Newsweek*'s Alan Rich was among the production's many enthusiasts, deeming it "a dazzling piece of theater craft." Carriere also teamed with Brook on *The Mahabharata,* an ambitious stage adaptation of India's Sanskrit epic, a complex work that is roughly comparable to the Christian Bible. This staging, which ran approximately ten hours, was recognized by *Newsweek*'s Jack Kroll as "a triumph of sustained inspiration and high intelligence." A film version of significantly reduced length was released in 1990.

Carriere described his working relationship with Brook to Margaret Croyden in the *New York Times Magazine:* "Peter changed my life. He showed me a new way of working. I never had such a luxury, to have such access to a director. I call him, he comes; I read him my work on the telephone, he listens. He is totally there. But that does not mean that he is not hard to please." Carriere noted that in contrast to working in film, where, as Croyden described it, scenes are "carefully planned and immediately set," working with Brook in the theater involves constant revision of material. "From the very beginning, Peter gives criticism and proposes changes. Then, all of a sudden, some actors come; they unroll a carpet and try some of the text which is not even totally finished. Slowly, the direction starts and I'm still there writing until the very last moment, at least until 15 performances after the opening." Brook also had Carriere audition with the actors, reading each part. "The purpose," Carriere explained to Croyden, "was to understand what I had written. If I couldn't do it, I was obliged to admit that the scene did not work. It was devilish of Peter, but extremely helpful."

Speaking of his collaborator in an interview with Morgenstern, Brook commented that "there's a strong connection between the quality of the work and the quality of the person. [Carriere's] a very passionate person, a Renaissance man with a passion for life in all its forms. At the same time, he's very disciplined, highly organized, with an encyclopedic mind—he's working on a book about nuclear physics, and he just brought out a book of pornographic limericks. So you have a man who does an enormous amount, who travels a lot and lives a very vivid life."

In addition to his work on screenplays and stage productions, Carriere is the author of several books in French. Storytellers, the author explained to Morgenstern, are essential to any society, "just like bakers, workers, peasants—no more, but no less. There's a beautiful phrase in *The Mahabharata* where Vyasa, the legendary author, says: 'You must listen to stories. It's pleasant, and sometimes it makes you feel better.'" Morgenstern assessed that "there are screenwriters, who write movies, and real writers, who write books. Carriere is both, an intellectual who knows how to entertain."

BIOGRAPHICAL/CRITICAL SOURCES:

BOOKS

Bunuel, Luis, *My Last Sigh,* translated by Abigail Israel, Knopf, 1983.

PERIODICALS

Nation, December 11, 1989, p. 727-28.
New Republic, October 17, 1983, pp. 24-26; November 30, 1987, pp. 26-28; February 29, 1988, pp. 26-28; December 11, 1989, pp. 24-25, 28; May 7, 1990, pp. 28-29; July 9, 1990, pp. 32-33.
New Statesman and Society, April 27, 1988; May 25, 1990.
Newsweek, June 27, 1983, p. 80; November 21, 1983, p. 105; August 19, 1985, p. 65; September 21, 1987, pp. 74-75; December 16, 1991, p. 77.
New York, May 23, 1983, pp. 132-33.
New Yorker, October 31, 1983; November 28, 1983, p. 168; November 2, 1987, pp. 146-48; July 16, 1990, pp. 73-75; December 16, 1991, pp. 118-19.
New York Times Magazine, October 4, 1987; April 17, 1988.
Time, September 26, 1983, p. 76; October 15, 1984.

*   *   *

CASS, James (Michael) 1915-1992

OBITUARY NOTICE—See index for CA sketch: Born November 19, 1915, in Saranac Lake, NY; died of heart failure, December 4, 1992, in New Paltz, NY. Research director, editor, and writer. Cass was the coauthor, with Max Birnbaum, of *Comparative Guide to American Colleges,* an acclaimed resource for prospective students since 1964. After working as a schools-related research director, Cass became an education editor for the *Saturday Review* in 1964. He remained at the magazine until 1978, when he became a full-time writer. Cass coauthored several other books related to the original college guide, among them *Comparative Guide to Science and Engineering Programs, Directory of Facilities for the Learning Disabled and Handicapped,* and *Comparative Guide to Two-Year Colleges and Career Programs.*

OBITUARIES AND OTHER SOURCES:

PERIODICALS

New York Times, December 15, 1992, p. B15.

*   *   *

CASSIDY, David C(harles) 1945-

PERSONAL: Born August 10, 1945, in Richmond, VA; son of Charles W. (an executive) and Meline (a librarian; maiden name, Shamlian) Cassidy; married Janet Hardy (a teacher). *Education:* Rutgers University, B.A., 1967, M.S., 1970; Purdue University, Ph.D., 1976. *Avocational interests:* Armenian studies, German literature.

ADDRESSES: Office—Natural Science Program, Hofstra University, Hempstead, NY 11550.

CAREER: University of California, Berkeley, postdoctoral research fellow, 1976-77; University of Stuttgart, Stuttgart, Germany, fellow, 1977-80; University of Regensburg, Regensburg, Germany, assistant professor, 1980-83; Boston University, Boston, MA, associate editor of "Albert Einstein Papers," 1983-90; Hofstra University, Hempstead, NY, associate professor of natural science, 1990—.

MEMBER: History of Science Society, American Physical Society (fellow), Deutsche Gesellschaft fuer Geschichte der Naturwissenschaften, New York Academy of Sciences.

AWARDS, HONORS: Humboldt Foundation fellow, 1977-80; Science Writing Award, American Institute of Physics, 1992, for *Uncertainty.*

WRITINGS:

(Associate editor) *The Collected Papers of Albert Einstein,* Princeton University Press, Volume I, 1987, Volume II, 1989.
Uncertainty: The Life and Science of Werner Heisenberg, W. H. Freeman, 1992.

Contributor to German- and English-language history of science journals.

WORK IN PROGRESS: A book on Einstein for undergraduates; research on the impact of the Allied and U.S. occupation on German science after World War II.

* * *

CENTOLELLA, Thomas Carmen 1952-

PERSONAL: Born August 27, 1952, in Ithaca, NY; son of Thomas Louis and Carmella (Acey) Centolella. *Education:* Syracuse University, B.A., 1974; State University of New York at Buffalo, M.A.H., 1977.

ADDRESSES: Office—College of Marin, Community Education, Kentfield, CA 94904.

CAREER: Jowonio Free School, teacher of language arts, 1973-74; Senior Center of San Francisco, San Francisco, CA, teacher of poetry, 1979; Unitarian Center of San Francisco, San Francisco, teacher of poetry, 1980; Seniors Teaching Educational Programs (STEP) Project, San Francisco, 1984-85; California Poets in the Schools, poetry instructor at various schools, San Francisco, 1985—; College of Marin, Kentfield, CA, lecturer in creative writing, 1987—; University of California, San Francisco, instructor in recent American literature and twentieth-century American novels, 1989—; San Francisco State University, San Francisco, lecturer in contemporary world poetry, 1993. Brandon School, guest lecturer, 1974-75; San Francisco Institute on Aging (ART-WORKS), guest artist, 1989-90; writer-in-residence, Headlands Center for the Arts, 1990.

AWARDS, HONORS: Leonard Brown Prize for poetry, Syracuse University, 1973; Academy of American Poets Prize, State University of New York at Buffalo, 1976; certificate of merit, Senior Center of San Francisco, 1980; Wallace Stegner Fellowship in creative writing, Stanford University, 1986-87; finalist, Dewar's Young Artists Achievement Awards, 1989; National Poetry Series Winner, 1989, first prize in Poetry division, American Society on Aging, 1990, Bay Area Book Reviewers Association Award, 1991, and American Book Award, Before Columbus Foundation, 1991, all for *Terra Firma;* Lannan literary fellowship, 1992.

WRITINGS:

Terra Firma, Copper Canyon Press, 1990.

Contributor of poetry to periodicals, including *New England Review, American Poetry Review, Ironwood, Blue Buildings,* and *The Practical Mystic;* contributor of articles to *California Living* and *Convention Daily.*

WORK IN PROGRESS: Lights and Mysteries and *Two-Part Inventions and One Long Suite;* researching theater, film, and songwriting.

SIDELIGHTS: Thomas Centolella told *CA:* "My poetry has such a strong narrative thrust that I often think of myself as a frustrated filmmaker—though writing poems goes a long way to relieving that frustration. Sometimes my poems can seem prescriptive, reminders not merely of what is but of what could be or should be (an idea I derive from Polanyi via William S. Wilson: Writing is 'a systematic course in teaching myself to hold my own beliefs'). More than anything, my poems aspire to what Tomas Transtroemer has called 'meeting places for souls.' The souls, in my case, would include the writer, the characters in the poem (which often includes the writer), and the reader of the poem: the self and the world engaged in social discourse, in an illuminating dialogue that continually defines each in terms of the other."

* * *

CHAMBERS, Leland H. 1928-

PERSONAL: Born March 11, 1928, in Los Angeles, CA; son of William L. (a high school printing teacher) and Ida T. (a homemaker) Chambers; divorced, June, 1979; partner of Sieglinde Lug (a professor of German and comparative literature); children: Vanessa Chambers Thompson, Sydney, Benjamin, Basim Kadhim (stepson). *Education:* University of Southern California, B.A., 1953; Indiana University—Bloomington, M.A., 1957; University of Michigan, Ph.D., 1962. *Politics:* "Despair." *Religion:* "Hope."

ADDRESSES: Home—2884 South Raleigh, Denver, CO 80236.

CAREER: Central Michigan University, Mount Pleasant, began as instructor, became assistant professor of English, 1958-63; University of Denver, Denver, CO, began as assistant professor, became professor of English and comparative literature, 1963-92; retired, 1992.

MEMBER: American Literary Translators Association.

WRITINGS:

(Translator) Ezequiel Martinez Estrada, *Holy Saturday and Other Stories,* Latin American Literary Review Press, 1988.

(Translator) Julieta Campos, *She Has Reddish Hair and Her Name Is Sabina* (novel), University of Georgia Press, 1993.

(Translator) Julieta Campos, *The Fear of Losing Eurydice* (novel), Dalkey Archive Press, 1993.

(Editor with Enrique Jaramillo, and contributor of translations) *To Tell the Story: Fifty-One Short Stories from*

Central America, 1963-1988, University of Texas Press, 1993.

Editor, *Denver Quarterly,* 1977-83.

WORK IN PROGRESS: Translating short fiction by Spanish author Juan Benet and Mexican author Maria Luisa Puga; translating novels of the Spanish writer Francisco Umbral and the novels of several Latin American writers.

SIDELIGHTS: Leland H. Chambers told *CA:* "I am a translator of contemporary prose fiction in Spanish, working with both Latin American and peninsular Spanish authors. The kind of work that interests me most is one that uses language interestingly, focuses on unfamiliar ideas or points of view, and manages to realize a considerable artistic achievement. The writer has sought to put together a fascinating verbal shape that occupies a well-defined space and is capable, perhaps, of fully overwhelming its readers. My translation seeks to create a parallel effect, something equally shapely, equally invasive. Being successful at this means something more than merely being 'faithful to the text.' It means getting inside the original text and calling up parallel language that incites the imagination of the reader, pushing it in the same directions the original writer had in mind.

"Carlos Fuentes insisted that the novelist's task is not to inform but to imagine, and to assist the reader in imagining, what the world we actually live in could be like. Perhaps literary translators should consider this a legitimate goal for their translations as well."

*   *   *

CHANDLER, Marilyn R(uth)   1949-

PERSONAL: Born May 19, 1949, in Kolar, Mysore State, India; daughter of Thomas LeGare (an antiquarian book dealer) and Mary (a teacher; maiden name, Wellcome) Chandler; married Frederick A. Teichert, 1969 (divorced, 1982); children: Mary Therese, Elizabeth Francisca, Margaret Rose. *Education:* Pomona College, B.A., 1970; graduate study at University of Salzburg, 1970-73; University of California, Davis, M.A., 1980; Princeton University, Ph.D., 1984. *Politics:* Democrat. *Religion:* Protestant. *Avocational interests:* Writing personal essays, tennis, swimming, church-related activities.

ADDRESSES: Office—Department of English, Mills College, 5000 MacArthur Blvd., Oakland, CA 94613-1301.

CAREER: Schoolteacher in Monterey, CA, 1974-77; Mills College, Oakland, CA, assistant professor, 1984-90, associate professor of English, 1990—, and chair of department.

MEMBER: International Arts-Medicine Association, Modern Language Association of America, National Council of Teachers of English, Society for Literature and Science.

AWARDS, HONORS: Arnold Graves Award, American Council of Learned Societies, 1988; grants from National Endowment for the Humanities, 1988 and 1989; Outstanding Teaching Award, Phi Beta Kappa of Northern California, 1989.

WRITINGS:

A Healing Art: Regeneration through Autobiography, Garland Publishing, 1990.
Dwelling in the Text: Houses in American Fiction, University of California Press, 1991.

Contributor to books, including *Essays on Southern Autobiography,* University of Georgia Press, 1988; *Approaches to Teaching T. S. Eliot,* Modern Language Association of America, 1988; and *Suburbia Re-Examined,* Greenwood Press, 1988. Contributor of more than twenty articles and reviews to periodicals, including *Academic Medicine, Northwest Review, Auto/Biography Studies, Perspectives in Biology and Medicine, Pharos,* and *Studies in Jewish American Literature.*

WORK IN PROGRESS: Editing and writing a contribution to *Illness and the Imagination: Exploring the Work of Writers with Chronic Illness; Encounters with the Earth: Nature and Character in American Fiction,* completion expected in 1994; *Charting the Moral Wilderness: A Theological Guide to "The Scarlet Letter,"* with John McEntyre, 1995.

SIDELIGHTS: Marilyn R. Chandler told *CA:* "My favorite way of thinking about literary criticism and commentary is, in Sandra Gilbert's phrase, as 'the great conversation.' My two books and various articles are efforts to join that conversation, to raise questions that address, not only the craft of writing and historical contexts, but also the moral imagination. I am most deeply interested in why and how stories and poetry come to matter to us—why we need them.

"My first book, *A Healing Art,* was written about the kind of need that drives people to write their own stories and how the process of writing addresses that need. Focusing on autobiographies written out of periods of life crisis, I tried to discern what are some of the questions and issues that must be confronted to assume authorship over one's own life. The relation of story to experience is never simple. For that reason, neither are the acts of writing and reading. So, it seems to me that the primary task of a literary critic is to model a way of reading, to hold up some lens through which we can see something about a text that we didn't see before. It also seems to me crucially important that a good reader be pluralistic: that a particular way of reading texts not become an orthodoxy, but be put in relation to other readings so that the interpretive possibilities and generative power of the text are maximized.

"In my second book, *Dwelling in the Text,* I took on another kind of question that continues to interest me, namely how the symbolic imagination works upon the ordinary elements of life to invest them with significance. Bachelard, in *The Poetics of Space,* maintains that there is no such thing as neutral space: that all the spaces we occupy are rife with significance and assigned meaning. It is this process of assigning meaning that engages my curiosity and brings together literary, psychological, social, and theological questions. Those various dimensions of reading, and of life, are, after all, never fully separable."

*   *   *

CHAPPELL, Audrey 1954-

PERSONAL: Born January 31, 1954, in Norwich, Norfolk, England; daughter of James Stanley (a teacher) and Margaret Saunders (a teacher) Chappell. *Education:* Attended Norwich City College; Furzedown College of Education, education certificate, 1975.

ADDRESSES: Home—"The Old Forge," Berghapton, Mill Rd., Norwich NR15 1BQ, England; 54 Fisher House, Copenhagen St., London N1 0JE, England.

CAREER: Islington school, London, preschool teacher, 1976-83; Haringey school, London, preschool teacher, 1984-91.

WRITINGS:

A Surprise for Oliver, Blackie Children's Books, 1989.
An Outing for Oliver, Blackie Children's Books, 1990.

SIDELIGHTS: Audrey Chappell commented: "I've always enjoyed writing, and love reading and books generally. Working with young children provides many incidents worthy of inclusion in a story, and with an illustrator as a friend I have been lucky enough to create two so far. Children love being read these stories and so many others, and I love reading to them."

*   *   *

CHESLER, Ellen 1947-

PERSONAL: Born April 26, 1947, in Cleveland, OH; daughter of Howard and Celia (Sloban) Chesler; married Matthew (a lawyer), December 30, 1973; children: Jona-

than, Elizabeth. *Education:* Vassar College, A.B., 1969; Columbia University, M.A., 1972, Ph.D., 1990.

ADDRESSES: Home—New York, NY. *Office*—Twentieth Century Fund, 41 East 70th St., New York, NY 10021.

CAREER: Writer. Campaign manager and chief of staff to New York City Council President Carol Bellamy, 1977-83; presently affiliated with Barnard College as an adjunct assistant professor and with Twentieth Century Fund.

WRITINGS:

Woman of Valor: Margaret Sanger and the Birth Control Movement in America, Simon & Schuster, 1992.

Contributor to periodicals, including *New York Times Book Review.*

SIDELIGHTS: Ellen Chesler is the author of *Women of Valor: Margaret Sanger and the Birth Control Movement in America.* The book recounts the career of radical activist Sanger, who spearheaded birth-control advocacy in the United States. Sanger, who lived from 1879 to 1966, devoted much of her life to the birth-control cause. In 1914, for instance, she published pamphlets on contraception and the prevention of venereal disease, and in the early 1920s she organized the American Birth Control League, which is now known as the Planned Parenthood Federation. Later, in the 1950s, she organized funding for the research and development of the birth-control pill.

Chesler's *Woman of Valor* is considered an incisive account of Sanger's life and work by many critics. Diane Cole, in her review for Chicago *Tribune Books,* described *Woman of Valor* as an "absorbing, comprehensive biography," which demonstrates that Sanger's "complex legacy will remain with us for some time to come." Ruth Brandon, writing in *Washington Post Book World,* expressed a reservation about the book, noting that "at times, . . . the detail is such that the story gets swamped." Despite this drawback, Brandon praised the biography. The book's "chief virtue," she reported, "is a sweeping and authoritative grasp not only of Sanger's life but of the political detail and maneuvering behind it." And Daniel J. Kevles wrote in the *New York Times Book Review* that *Woman of Valor* "brilliantly reveals and revitalizes Margaret Sanger in the context of the tempestuous public battles for birth control that she waged through the first half of the century."

BIOGRAPHICAL/CRITICAL SOURCES:

PERIODICALS

Los Angeles Times Book Review, June 28, 1992, p. 4.
National Review, August 17, 1992, pp. 42-43.
Newsweek, July 6, 1992.

New York, June 22, 1992, p. 62.
New Yorker, August 10, 1992.
New York Times, June 17, 1992, p. C16.
New York Times Book Review, June 28, 1992, pp. 1, 34.
Tribune Books (Chicago), June 6, 1992, p. 5.
Washington Post Book World, July 5, 1992, p. 1.

*   *   *

CHIRONIS, Nicholas P. 1921-

PERSONAL: Born October 9, 1921, in New York; son of Paul and Antigone (Dafniotis) Chironis; married Evelyn Abbrancati (a senior library clerk), April 30, 1949; children: Thea, Philip. *Education:* Received B.A. and M.A. from Polytechnic University.

ADDRESSES: Home—37 Farm Rd., St. James, NY 11780.

CAREER: Worked as a design engineer for several companies, including IBM and Mergenthaler Linotype; McGraw-Hill, group editor of product engineering magazine, beginning in 1954, senior editor of mining publication; writer. Instructor at Cooper Union School of Engineering. *Military service:* Served in infantry in World War II as a machine gunner with Patton's Third Army; wounded twice.

WRITINGS:

Mechanisms and Mechanical Devices Sourcebook, McGraw, 1991.

Also author of *Machine Devices and Instrumentation, Gear Design and Application,* and *Spring Design and Application.* Contributor to books, including *Operating Handbook of Surface Mining,* and *Operating Handbook of Underground Mining.* Contributing editor to several publications, beginning in 1988.

SIDELIGHTS: Nicholas P. Chironis told *CA:* "Since my first job with IBM as an engineer after graduation from Polytechnic University, I have been interested in how different mechanisms and mechanical motions for automated production lines function. Later, during my writing career, I met many designers, engineers, and inventors at their companies and technical society meetings who had developed ingenious designs to meet their needs. I would illustrate and write up these creations; recently I brought the best of them together in *Mechanisms and Mechanical Devices Sourcebook.*"

CHRISTIE, William 1960-

PERSONAL: Born May 21, 1960; son of William T. and Ruth E. Christie. *Education:* University of Pennsylvania, B.A., 1982.

ADDRESSES: Agent—Larry Gershel, Wieser & Wieser, Inc., 118 East Twenty-fifth St., New York, NY 10010.

CAREER: Writer, 1988—. *Military service:* U.S. Marine Corps, Infantry, 1984-87; became first lieutenant.

WRITINGS:

The Warriors of God, Presidio Press, 1992.

WORK IN PROGRESS: The Ceremony of Innocence, a novel.

*   *   *

CIEE, Grace 1961-

PERSONAL: Surname is pronounced "see"; born Grace Melecia Cornish, August 22, 1961, in Jamaica. *Education:* Hampshire College, B.A., 1982; attended New School for Social Research, 1990.

ADDRESSES: Home—New York, NY, and London, England. *Office*—c/o Fortune 27 Resources, 610 Fifth Ave., Box 4739, New York, NY 10185-0040. *Agent*—c/o Joan Ryder, CIEE Global Communications Group, 610 Fifth Ave., P.O. Box 4739, New York, NY 10185-0040.

CAREER: International image consultant for department stores and cosmetic companies, 1982—. Fashion designer and consultant to Jessica International and Captiva Couture, 1989.

AWARDS, HONORS: Certificate of Recognition for Black Women in Literature, International Public Relations Group, 1992, for *The Fortune of Being Yourself: You Can Have It All—Love, Beauty, Money, and Happiness.*

WRITINGS:

The Fortune of Being Yourself: You Can Have It All—Love, Beauty, Money, and Happiness, Fortune 27 Resources, 1991.
Think and Grow Beautiful: A Teenage Woman's Guide to Total Beauty, Fortune 27 Resources, 1992.
Radiant Women of Color: Embrace, Enhance and Enjoy the Beauty of Your Natural Coloring, Kola Publishing, 1993.

The Fortune of Being Yourself: You Can Have It All—Love, Beauty, Money, and Happiness was translated into Spanish.

SIDELIGHTS: Grace Ciee told *CA:* "Although it is true that when you look good, you feel good, it is more important that when you think good about yourself, you'll look and feel even better. This makes you happy, and happiness is the birthright of every person on Earth."

* * *

CLAIBORNE, Sybil   1923-1992

OBITUARY NOTICE—See index for *CA* sketch: Born November 1, 1923, in Liverpool, England; died of lung cancer, December 16, 1992. Activist and writer. Though Claiborne did not begin writing until she was nearly fifty years old, she published a variety of works, including novels, plays, and a short story collection. She was also active in antiwar efforts, opposing the Vietnam War and the nuclear arms buildup. Her last book, *In the Garden of the Dead Cars,* to be published posthumously, also concerns the topic of war and the danger of oppressive leaders. Her other works include the story collection *Loose Connections,* the novel *A Craving for Women,* and the one-act plays *Merging* and *An Incurable Malady.*

OBITUARIES AND OTHER SOURCES:

BOOKS

Directory of American Poets and Fiction Writers, 1991-1992 edition, Poets & Writers, 1991.

PERIODICALS

New York Times, December 19, 1992, p. 11.

* * *

CLAYSON, (S.) Hollis   1946-

PERSONAL: Born December 26, 1946, in Chicago, IL. *Education:* Wellesley College, B.A. (with distinction), 1968; University of California, Los Angeles, M.A., 1975, Ph.D., 1984.

ADDRESSES: Home—2439 Ridgeway Ave., Evanston, IL 60201-1857. *Office*—Department of Art History, 254 Kresge Hall, Northwestern University, 1859 Sheridan Rd., Evanston, IL 60208.

CAREER: Pierce College, Athens, Greece, adviser on student affairs, 1968-69; California Institute of the Arts, Valencia, instructor in complementary studies, 1974-76; Schiller College, Strasbourg, France, instructor in English and art history, 1977-78; Wichita State University, Wichita, KS, assistant professor of art history, 1978-82; Northwestern University, Evanston, IL, visiting assistant professor of art history, 1982-84; University of Illinois at Chicago Circle, Chicago, assistant professor of the history of architecture and art, 1984-85; Northwestern University,

assistant professor, 1985-91, associate professor of art history, 1991—, director of Andrew W. Mellon Program in the History of Art Objects, 1989-90 and 1992-93, faculty associate of Chapin Humanities Residential College, 1985-87 and 1989-91, co-chairperson of Organization of Women Faculty, 1992-94. Chicago Art History Colloquia, organizer, 1985-86.

MEMBER: College Art Association, Society for French Historical Studies, Society for Interdisciplinary Nineteenth-Century Studies, Berkshire Conference of Women Historians, Association of Art Historians (England), Midwest Art History Society, Midwest Victorian Studies Association.

AWARDS, HONORS: Grant from Lilly Endowment, 1985-86; Distinguished Teaching of Art History Award, College Art Association, 1990; fellow of American Council of Learned Societies, 1990-91; grant from Hewlett Fund for Curricular Innovation, 1992-93.

WRITINGS:

Painted Love: Prostitution in French Art of the Impressionist Era, Yale University Press, 1991.

Contributor of articles and reviews to art journals.

WORK IN PROGRESS: Women and Representation in the Terrible Year (1870-1871), a study of the practice of art during the Siege of Paris and the Commune; an exhibition on the art of the Siege of Paris, for Musee de l'Art de la ville de Saint-Denis, France.

* * *

CLEARY, Edward L.   1929-

PERSONAL: Born August 4, 1929, in Chicago, IL; son of Emmet and Mary V. C. Cleary. *Education:* Attended Marquette University; Aquinas Institute, B.A. (magna cum laude), 1953, M.A., 1954; University of Chicago, Ph.D., 1975. *Religion:* Roman Catholic. *Avocational interests:* Mountain trekking, music.

ADDRESSES: Office—Providence College, Providence, RI 02918.

CAREER: University of Pittsburgh, Pittsburgh, PA, assistant director of Latin American studies; Aquinas Institute, St. Louis, MO, academic dean and vice-president; Pontifical College Josephinum, Columbus, OH, professor and director of Hispanic studies, 1985-93; Providence College, Providence, RI, professor of Latin American studies, 1993—. Visiting professor at University of Pittsburgh, New York University, and Florida International University. Bolivian Institute of Social Study, president; Ohio Commission on Spanish-Speaking Affairs, member.

MEMBER: American Sociological Association, American Anthropological Association, Latin American Studies Association, American Academy of Religion, Association for the Sociology of Religion.

WRITINGS:

(Editor) *Shaping a New World: An Orientation to Latin America,* Orbis Books, 1971.

Crisis and Change: The Church in Latin America Today, Orbis Books, 1985.

(Editor) *Path from Puebla: Significant Documents of the Latin American Bishops since 1979,* U.S. Catholic Conference, 1989.

(Editor) *Born of the Poor: The Latin American Church since Medellin,* University of Notre Dame Press, 1990.

(Coeditor and contributor) *Conflict and Competition: The Latin American Church in a Changing Environment,* Lynne Rienner Publications, 1992.

Author of a book on religion in Latin America, Orbis Books, in press. Work represented in anthologies, including *The Latin American and Caribbean Contemporary Record,* Holmes & Meier, Volume VII, 1990, Volume VIII, 1993. Contributor to sociology and Latin American studies journals. *Estudios Andinos,* cofounder, 1970, editor, 1970-76, member of advisory board, 1976-83.

WORK IN PROGRESS: Editing a book on Pentecostal Christians in Latin America.

SIDELIGHTS: Edward L. Cleary told *CA:* "After years of editing other people's writings, I spent a two-year writing sabbatical at Columbia University and the Research Institute for the Study of Man in New York City, 1980-82. Since that time I have been writing consistently in various settings, but living in Manhattan for two years gave me a great beginning."

* * *

CLEVELAND, Harold van B(uren)   1916-1993

OBITUARY NOTICE—See index for *CA* sketch: Born May 12, 1916, in Cincinnati, OH; died after suffering a cerebral stroke, March 11, 1993, in Paris, France. Economist, lawyer, and author. A 1942 graduate of Harvard University's law school, Cleveland served in the foreign affairs and economic divisions of the U.S. Department of State until 1956, and was coauthor with Ben T. Moore of a plan outlining the economic recovery of war-torn Europe after World War II. This plan, along with another state department program, was submitted to U.S. Secretary of State General George C. Marshall, who used it to form the Marshall Plan in 1947. Cleveland later joined the

John Hancock Mutual Life Insurance Company as legal counsel and then served as director of Atlantic policy studies for New York City's Council on Foreign Relations from 1963 to 1965. In 1965 he joined First National City Bank (now Citibank) to become vice president for international economics. He retired in 1985. In addition to writing the economic revival plan with Moore, Cleveland authored numerous books on international finance and economy, including *Strains in International Finance and Trade, Money and the Coming World Order,* and, with W. H. Bruce Brittain, *The Great Inflation: A Monetarist View.*

OBITUARIES AND OTHER SOURCES:

PERIODICALS

Chicago Tribune, March 14, 1993, section 2, p. 6.
New York Times, March 13, 1993.

* * *

CLIFFORD, Clark (McAdams)   1906-

PERSONAL: Born December 25, 1906, in Fort Scott, KS; son of Frank Andrew (a railroad official) and Georgia (a writer; maiden name, McAdams) Clifford; married Margery Pepperell Kimball, October 3, 1931; children: Margery Pepperell Clifford Lanagan, Joyce Carter Clifford Burland, Randall Clifford Wight. *Education:* Washington University, St. Louis, MO, LL.B., 1928.

ADDRESSES: Home—9421 Rockville Pike, Bethesda, MD 20814. *Office*—815 Connecticut Ave., Washington, DC 20006.

CAREER: Lawyer. Called to the bar in Missouri, 1928; Holland, Lashly, and Donnell (became Holland, Lashly, and Lashly), St. Louis, MO, associate, 1928-37; Lashly, Lashly, Miller, and Clifford, St. Louis, partner, 1938-43; special counsel to President Harry S Truman, 1946-50; Clifford and Miller, Washington, DC, senior partner, 1950-68; U.S. Secretary of Defense, 1968-69; Clifford and Warnke, Washington, DC, senior partner, 1969-91. Member of Committee on the Defense Establishment, 1960, and Foreign Intelligence Advisory Board, 1961. Chair of Foreign Intelligence Advisory Board, 1962-68, and First American Bankshares, 1982-91. Director of Phillips Petroleum Co., 1960-79, and Knight-Ridder Newspapers, 1969-92. Trustee of Washington University (St. Louis), 1967-77. *Military service:* U.S. Naval Reserve, 1944-46, served as naval aide to U.S. president, 1946; became captain.

MEMBER: American Bar Association, Missouri Bar Association, D.C. Bar Association, St. Louis Bar Association, Burning Tree, Metropolitan, Chevy Chase, Kappa Alpha.

AWARDS, HONORS: Medal of Freedom from U.S. President Harry S Truman, 1969; Harry S Truman Public Service Award from city of Independence, MO, 1980.

WRITINGS:

(With Richard Holbrooke) *Counsel to the President* (memoir), Random House, 1991.

SIDELIGHTS: Clark Clifford is a key government figure who has long held considerable influence in the American political forum. He began his career as a lawyer in a St. Louis firm in the late 1920s, and he stayed in law until 1944, when he volunteered and joined the U.S. Naval Reserve to serve in World War II. After the war Clifford was sent to Washington, D.C., where he became naval aide to President Harry S Truman. In 1946 Clifford was named special counsel to the president, and for the next four years he was involved in a range of government activities, including preparations for the development of an intelligence network. In addition, he helped develop American policy toward the Soviet Union, a country that was considered by some to be a threat to world peace. Clifford was also involved in the establishment of various government policies contributing to the development of the military-industrial complex, and he helped shape the administration's relations with Israel after that nation was established in 1948.

When Truman ran for the presidency in 1948, Clifford conceived a campaign strategy in which the incumbent leader would court both the working class and the intelligentsia. This strategy is credited with making a significant contribution to Truman's ultimately successful candidacy. But after Truman returned to the presidency, Clifford himself left the White House to assume private law practice, though the capitol remained his sphere of activity.

While ostensibly in private practice, Clifford remained active in American politics during the administration of President John F. Kennedy. In 1962, for instance, he assumed chair of the Foreign Intelligence Advisory Board, which held particular importance to the president, particularly after U.S. troops invaded Cuba in 1961 and were soundly defeated by Fidel Castro's troops at the Bay of Pigs.

Clifford's government involvement increased when Lyndon B. Johnson assumed the presidency after Kennedy's assassination in 1963. Under Johnson, Clifford assumed great importance in shaping America's foreign policy, particularly as it related to military activity in Vietnam.

In 1968 Clifford—who had earlier rejected various cabinet positions, including that of attorney general—accepted the role of secretary of defense, and he soon became a leading spokesperson for the administration on military policy in Vietnam. Clifford was initially supportive of the war effort in Vietnam, but he eventually became disillusioned with America's costly military involvement there. He encouraged President Johnson to cease the bombing of North Vietnam, and he urged the president to commence peace talks with the communists. Such activities, Warren I. Cohen noted in *Nation,* are "generally considered to be Clifford's finest hour."

When Johnson chose not to run for reelection in 1968, Clifford again returned to his private law practice in Washington. But he nonetheless maintained involvement in American politics. In 1972, for instance, he assisted Senator Edmund Muskie in his aborted bid for the Democratic Party's presidential nomination, and during the Jimmy Carter administration Clifford fulfilled various presidential assignments.

In 1982 Clifford, who had once again withdrawn from government activity, assumed the chair of the First American Bankshares. "I wanted a new challenge in life," he later told *Time.* Unfortunately for Clifford, the bank, years later, became implicated in a scandal involving Arab investors and the Bank of Credit and Commerce International (BCCI). As questions arose over possible ties between the BCCI, one of Clifford's clients, and the First American Bankshares, which he managed, Clifford himself became the subject of investigations. Allegations were made that Clifford had misled government regulators regarding BCCI's possible control of the First American Bankshares. Clifford, who resigned from the bank chair in 1991, maintained that he had been deceived and that he was innocent of any wrongdoing. "It's been an *un*attractive period for me," he told *Newsweek.*

Clifford is author of *Counsel to the President,* a memoir recounting his experiences in American government and politics. Roger Morris, writing in the *New York Times Book Review,* pronounced the volume "rich in portraits, scenes, savory anecdotes," and he lauded Clifford for his considerable achievements. "Altogether," declared Morris, "it is a career, and memoir, of extraordinary sweep, the experience of one man—discreetly one of the most influential men of the century—as a veritable metaphor for an American political epoch."

BIOGRAPHICAL/CRITICAL SOURCES:

BOOKS

Clifford, Clark, and Richard Holbrooke, *Counsel to the President,* Random House, 1991.

PERIODICALS

Business Week, August 12, 1991, p. 25.
Forbes, June 24, 1991, p. 10.
Foreign Affairs, winter, 1991, p. 190.
Fortune, May 6, 1991, p. 115.

Nation, October 5, 1992, pp. 354-356.
New Republic, July 8, 1991, pp. 32-36.
Newsweek, March 18, 1991, p. 54; May 20, 1991, pp. 52-53.
New York Times, May 17, 1988.
New York Times Book Review, May 19, 1991, pp. 1, 43-44.
Time, May 27, 1991, p. 66; June 23, 1991, p. 24; August 26, 1991, p. 40.
U.S. News and World Report, August 26, 1991, p. 20.

—*Sketch by Les Stone*

* * *

COHEN, Barbara 1932-1992

OBITUARY NOTICE—See index for *CA* sketch: Born March 15, 1932, in New Jersey; died of cancer, November 29, 1992, in Bridgewater, NJ. Educator and author. Cohen, an award-winning writer, penned more than thirty books for children and young adults. She taught in New Jersey from 1955 until 1972, when she published her first book, *The Carp in the Bathtub.* Cohen's best-known work, *Molly's Pilgrim,* tells the story of a Jewish immigrant girl who teaches her classmates the meaning of Thanksgiving; a movie version of that book won the 1986 Academy Award for best short subject. In 1991, Cohen was inducted into the New Jersey Literary Hall of Fame. She also authored such works as *Seven Daughters and Seven Sons, King of the Seventh Grade, Canterbury Tales, The Long Way Home,* and a sequel to *Molly's Pilgrim* entitled *Make a Wish Molly.* At the time of her death, Cohen had several new books slated for publication.

OBITUARIES AND OTHER SOURCES:

BOOKS

The Writers Directory: 1992-1994, St. James Press, 1992.

PERIODICALS

Detroit Free Press, December 2, 1992, p. 7B.
Los Angeles Times, December 5, 1992, p. A26.
New York Times, December 1, 1992, p. B13.
School Library Journal, January, 1993, p. 18.

* * *

COHEN, Richard 1952-

PERSONAL: Born March 22, 1952, in Bronx, NY; son of Nathan (a junior high school English teacher) and Jean (a psychiatric social worker; maiden name, Fiddle) Cohen; married May 19, 1973 (divorced); children: John, Christopher. *Education:* University of Michigan, B.A., 1973. Re-ligion: Jewish. *Avocational interests:* "Literature, my family, the usual self-improvement fads."

ADDRESSES: Home—Madison, WI. *Agent*—c/o Ellen Levine Literary Agency, Inc., 15 East 26th St., Suite 1801, New York, NY 10010.

CAREER: Manuscript reader for a literary agency, 1973-76 and 1977-79; homemaker, 1979-87; University of Wisconsin—Madison, lecturer in creative writing, 1988; free-lance writer, 1987—.

AWARDS, HONORS: Avery Hopwood Award for fiction, University of Michigan, 1973.

WRITINGS:

NOVELS

Domestic Tranquility, Seaview Books, 1981.
Don't Mention the Moon, Seaview/Putnam, 1983.
Say You Want Me, Soho, 1988.

Contributor of short stories to periodicals.

SIDELIGHTS: In the 1980s Richard Cohen earned recognition for *Domestic Tranquility* and *Say You Want Me,* fictional works featuring characters involved in strained relationships. His debut novel, *Domestic Tranquility,* focuses on Julie Wilcox, who struggles to rise above her situation as the member of a dysfunctional family. Her father suffers from lung cancer, and her mother loses her sanity after blaming herself for the death of Laura, Julie's baby sister, who dies shortly after being born with a spinal cord injury.

On her own, as a student in nursing school, Julie meets her eventual husband, Tom Crane, who works in the field of advertising. After marrying Tom, she gives birth to a daughter, Emily. When Julie discovers that her husband is an alcoholic, she tries—in vain—to preserve cordial relations among all family members. Tom is unreceptive to her efforts and also becomes distressed by his maturing daughter's growing perception of his substance-abuse problem. Tom ultimately commits suicide, and Emily blames Julie, in part, for his death. In her assessment for the *New York Times Book Review,* Sheila Weller praised Cohen for his ability to capture the emotions of his characters. She also remarked that *Domestic Tranquility* "is a beautiful first novel—built on observations so minutely and constantly intelligent that one feels as intellectually engaged by it as emotionally seized."

In 1988 Cohen released *Say You Want Me,* which features Brendan Beame, a free-lance artist who works at home and cares for his son while his wife Lila works as an executive in the oil industry. At the beginning of the novel, Brendan feels frustrated with his career and his married life. He has an affair with a woman that he meets in a park in Brooklyn, and his relationship with Lila disintegrates. Sybil Steinberg of *Publishers Weekly,* although she found a few of the elements in the story to be predictable, complimented Cohen for the authentic dialogue between the two main characters. She closed her review, stating that "the story is powerful and sad, the writing exhilarating." Joyce Slater of Chicago *Tribune Books* also praised the conversations among characters in the novel, comparing the dialogue to writings by notable fiction authors such as John Updike and John Cheever. She further remarked that Cohen "is a writer as intuitive as he is stylish. His scenes between Brendan and Jeff, especially, are marvels of warmth and control. The exchanges are sweet without being sappy, telling without being didactic." And *Los Angeles Times Book Review* contributor Jack Miles called *Say You Want Me* a "poignantly imagined, perfectly realized novel of two-career family life in the 1980s." He also remarked, "It is the book that I most regret not seeing reviewed in the *Los Angeles Times Book Review*" at the time of its publication.

Cohen told *CA:* "Allen Ginsberg once said, 'There should be no difference between what you write and what you really know.' My ambition is to achieve that state. Of course, it's particularly impressive if you actually *know* something. I'm working on that too."

He also commented: "I've made various false and true starts toward a fourth novel and now have a draft, tentatively called *So Close,* with which I'm pleased. More recently, however, I've concentrated on short stories. Contrary to the conventional wisdom, I find them easier to write than novels. You can see the whole project in your mind at once; you don't feel like you're just slogging along; you can work on more ideas in a given time period; and it doesn't hurt as much when an idea doesn't work."

BIOGRAPHICAL/CRITICAL SOURCES:

PERIODICALS

Los Angeles Times Book Review, January 1, 1989, p. 11.
New York Times Book Review, February 15, 1981, p. 12.
Publishers Weekly, May 13, 1988, p. 262.
Tribune Books (Chicago), July 31, 1988.

*   *   *

COLFAX, David (John) 1936-
(J. David Colfax)

PERSONAL: Born May 13, 1936, in Pittsburgh, PA; son of John D. (a government official) and Margaret E. (an accountant; maiden name, Pristas) Colfax; married Mary-Alice "Micki" Nash (a rancher), June 13, 1959; children: Grant, Drew, Reed, Garth. *Education:* Pennsylvania State University, B.S., 1958; University of Pittsburgh, M.A., 1960; University of Chicago, Ph.D., 1964.

ADDRESSES: Home and office—246 Redwood Ridge Rd., Boonville, CA 95415.

CAREER: University of Connecticut, Storrs, CT, associate professor, 1963-69; Washington University, St. Louis, MO, associate professor, 1969-72; Colfax Associates, Boonville, CA, partner, 1972—; National Center for Appropriate Technology (NCAT), Boonville, regional director, 1977-81; Mountain House Press, Philo, CA, publisher and editor, 1988—. "The David Colfax Show," KZYX-FM, Philo, host, 1991—. Policy Research Group, Winchester, MA, senior consultant, 1979-81. Mendocino County, Ukiah, CA, vice president of Democratic Central committee, 1983-87, vice president of Arts Council, 1983-87; Mendocino County Board of Education, president and trustee, 1986—; Mountain School, Boonville, member of board of directors; Black Fox Productions, Boonville, member of board of directors; Northern California Homeschooling Association, vice president and member of board of directors.

AWARDS, HONORS: Research fellow, London School of Economics and Political Science, 1960-61.

WRITINGS:

(With wife, Micki Colfax) *Homeschooling for Excellence,* Mountain House Press, 1987.
(Editor with M. Colfax) Joseph Crepin, *La Chevre,* translated by Will Culver and Don Lipmanson, Mountain House Press, 1990.
(With M. Colfax) *Hard Times in Paradise: An American Family's Struggle to Carve Out a Homestead in California's Redwood Mountains,* Warner Books, 1992.
101 Ways to Enhance Your Child's Education, Mountain House Press, 1993.

Contributor to various periodicals. Contributing editor, *Anderson Valley Advertiser,* 1983—; editor, *Goat Notes,* 1986—.

UNDER NAME J. DAVID COLFAX

The Big City Voter: A Study of Political Participation in Chicago, University of Chicago Library, 1964.
(With Irving L. Allen and Henry G. Stetler) *Metropolitan Connecticut: A Demographic Profile,* University of Connecticut, Institute of Urban Research, 1965.
(With Allen) *Urban Sample Survey Field Procedures: Materials and Strategies,* University of Connecticut, Institute of Urban Research, 1967.
(With Allen) *The Inner City in Crisis: The Case of Connecticut,* University of Connecticut, 1968.

(With Allen) *Urban Problems and Public Opinion in Four Connecticut Cities,* University of Connecticut, Institute of Urban Research, 1968.

(With Albert Kircidel Cohen and Maurice L. Farber) *A Panel Discussion of Urban Demonstrations,* University of Connecticut, Institute of Urban Research, 1968.

(Editor with Jack L. Roach) *Radical Sociology,* Basic Books, 1971.

SIDELIGHTS: In the 1992 nonfiction account *Hard Times in Paradise: An American Family's Struggle to Carve Out a Homestead in California's Redwood Mountains,* former university associate professor David Colfax chronicles his family's move in the early 1970s to an isolated homestead in the California wilderness. Colfax, prevented from teaching due to his civil rights and antiwar activism, details in the book the story of his family's pioneering efforts to tame the land, build shelters, and learn to survive without electricity, running water, roads, phone service, or schools. Amid the hardships and danger, the Colfaxes strove to homeschool their children and were so effective that all three boys subsequently were accepted at Harvard University. Called an "engaging story" by a *Publishers Weekly* reviewer, *Hard Times in Paradise* garnered praise from *Library Journal's* Cheryl Childress as well, who judged it "a well-told tale of what it takes truly to live off the land."

BIOGRAPHICAL/CRITICAL SOURCES:

PERIODICALS

Booklist, June 15, 1992, p. 1803.
Library Journal, July, 1992, p. 109.
Nation, September 18, 1972, pp. 213-15.
Publishers Weekly, May 25, 1992, pp. 45-46.

*   *   *

COLFAX, J. David
See COLFAX, David (John)

*   *   *

COLLINS, George R(oseborough)   1917-1993

OBITUARY NOTICE—See index for *CA* sketch: Born September 2, 1917, in Springfield, MA; died of Alzheimer's disease, January 5, 1993, in Falmouth, MA. Educator, historian, and author. A longtime professor of art history at Columbia University, Collins was well known for his expertise on the work of Spanish architect Antonio Gaudi. Collins began his teaching career as an instructor and became a professor. He also served as executive secretary of the university art program and director

of Amigos de Gaudi—U.S.A., a significant collection of the architect's work. Throughout his career Collins penned a number of articles and books on Gaudi, including *Antonio Gaudi,* the first book on the architect in the English language; *The Drawings of Antonio Gaudi;* and *A Bibliography of Antonio Gaudi and the Catalan Movement, 1870-1930.* In addition, in the mid-1960s Collins served as adviser on a film about Gaudi and in 1977 he organized an exhibition of recently recovered Gaudi drawings in New York that was considered one of the year's major architectural exhibitions. Collins was awarded fellowships from the Guggenheim and Rockefeller Foundations.

OBITUARIES AND OTHER SOURCES:

BOOKS

Who's Who in American Art, 1991-1992, 19th edition, Bowker, 1990.

PERIODICALS

New York Times, January 6, 1993, p. B6.

*   *   *

COLLINS, Stephen L.   1949-

PERSONAL: Born January 22, 1949, in London, England; son of David and Blanche Collins; married Diane Tyler; children: Morris. *Education:* University of Rochester, B.A., 1970; Emory University, M.A., 1975, Ph.D., 1979.

ADDRESSES: Home—128 Westchester, Jamaica Plain, MA 02130. *Office*—Department of History, Babson College, Babson Park, MA 02157.

CAREER: Shimer College, Mount Carroll, IL, member of humanities faculty, 1975-78; Boston University, Boston, MA, assistant professor of social science, 1978-83; Babson College, Babson Park, MA, assistant professor, 1983-88, associate professor of history, 1988—, William R. Dill Term Chair Holder in History and Society, 1992—.

WRITINGS:

From Divine Cosmos to Sovereign State: An Intellectual History of Consciousness and the Idea of Order in Renaissance England, Oxford University Press, 1989.

WORK IN PROGRESS: Self-Presentation, Theatricality, and Gender in Late Medieval England, publication expected in 1994; *Cultural History of the Self in Sixteenth- and Seventeenth-Century England,* completion expected in 1994.

BIOGRAPHICAL/CRITICAL SOURCES:

PERIODICALS

Times Literary Supplement, September 22-28, 1989, pg. 1036.

*   *   *

CONNELL, Jan
   See CONNELL, Janice T(imchak)

*   *   *

CONNELL, Janice T(imchak) 1939-
   (Jan Connell)

PERSONAL: Born March 30, 1939, in Johnstown, PA; daughter of Louis John and Edna Ann (Bonistall) Timchak; married Edward F. Connell, November 24, 1960; children: Elizabeth Ward, Edward F. III, William Troy. *Education:* Georgetown University, B.S.F.S., 1961; University of Pittsburgh, M.P.I.A., 1976; Duquesne University, J.D., 1979. *Avocational interests:* Boating, golfing, bridge.

ADDRESSES: Office—Two Gateway Center, Suite 720, Pittsburgh, PA 15222.

CAREER: Business executive, lawyer, arbitrator, and writer. Regency Advertising, Jacksonville, FL, and Pittsburgh, PA, president, 1968-74; Connell Leasing of Florida, Jacksonville and Pittsburgh, president, 1970-80; National Motor Leasing, Inc., Pittsburgh, vice president, 1980-86; International Motor Leasing, Inc., Pittsburgh, president, 1986—; Transportation Lease Consultants, Inc., Pittsburgh, vice president, 1986—; Power Sources, Inc., president and chief executive officer, 1986—. Admitted to the Bar of Pennsylvania, 1979, the Bar of U.S. District Court for the Western District of Pennsylvania, 1979, the Bar of U.S. Court of Appeals, Third Circuit, 1979, and the Bar of U.S. Supreme Court, 1983; U.S. District Court for the Western District of Pennsylvania, judicial law clerk, 1979; Connell & Connell, Pittsburgh, partner, 1980—. New York Stock Exchange, arbitrator, 1981—; National Association of Securities Dealers, arbitrator, 1983—; American Arbitration Association, arbitrator, 1985—. Duquesne University, member of women's advisory board, 1980—, founding director of the university's Institute for World Concern, 1981—; Pittsburgh Center for Peace, founder and president.

MEMBER: American Bar Association, Pennsylvania Bar Association, Allegheny Bar Association; Association of Junior Leagues, Inc. (member of board of directors for Wheeling, WV, and Pittsburgh chapters), Salvation Army, United Way, Young Women's Christian Association, Legal Aid Society of Pittsburgh, Marion Peace Center (member of board of directors), Parents Fundraising Committee of Phillips Academy; Allegheny Country Club, Twentieth Century Club.

WRITINGS:

(Under name Jan Connell) *Queen of the Cosmos,* Paraclete, 1990.
Visions of the Children: The Apparitions of the Blessed Mother at Medjugorje, St. Martin's, 1992.

Editor, *Queen of Peace* newsletter.

*   *   *

COPE, Wendy 1945-

PERSONAL: Born July 21, 1945, in Erith, Kent, England; daughter of Fred Stanley (a company director) and Alice Mary (a company director; maiden name, Hand) Cope. *Education:* St. Hilda's College, Oxford, B.A., 1966; Westminster College of Education, Oxford, diploma, 1967. *Avocational interests:* Music, playing piano and guitar.

ADDRESSES: Home—London, England. *Office*—c/o Faber & Faber, 3 Queen Sq., London WC1N 3AU, England. *Agent*—Pat Kavanagh, Peters, Fraser and Dunlop, 503/4 The Chambers, Chelsea Harbour, London SW10 0XF, England.

CAREER: Portway Junior School, London, England, teacher, 1967-69; Keyworth Junior School, London, teacher, 1969-73; Cobourg Junior School, London, teacher, 1973-81, deputy headmaster, 1980-81; *Contact* (a newspaper), arts and reviews editor, 1982-84; Brindishe Primary School, London, music teacher, 1984-86; freelance writer, 1986—; *Spectator,* London, columnist, until 1990.

AWARDS, HONORS: Cholmondeley Award for poetry, 1987; fellow of the Royal Society of Literature, 1992.

WRITINGS:

Shall I Call Thee Bard? A Portrait of Jason Strugnell (radio drama), British Broadcasting Corporation (BBC) Radio 3, 1982.
Making Cocoa for Kingsley Amis (poems), Faber & Faber, 1986.
Hope and the Forty-two, Other Branch Readings, c. 1987.
Poem from a Colour Chart of House Paints, Priapus, c. 1987.
Does She Like Word-Games? (poems), Anvil Press, 1988.
Men and Their Boring Arguments (poems), Wykeham Press, 1988.

Twiddling Your Thumbs (hand-rhymes for children), illustrated by Sally Kindberg, Faber & Faber, 1988.
The River Girl (poem), illustrations by Nicholas Garland, Faber & Faber, 1991.
(Editor) *Is That the New Moon?* (poems), illustrations by Christine Roche, Collins, c. 1991.
Serious Concerns (poems), Faber & Faber, 1992.
(Editor) *The Orchard Book of Funny Poems* (anthology for children), Orchard Books, 1993.

Author of a booklet, *Across the City,* Priapus Press, 1980. Contributor to *Poetry Introduction 5,* Faber & Faber, 1982; *Making for the Open,* Chatto & Windus; *The Faber Book of Twentieth Century Women's Poetry,* edited by Fleur Adcock, Faber & Faber; *Faber Book of Parodies;* and *The Penguin Book of Limericks.* Contributor of poems and book reviews to periodicals, including *Times Literary Supplement, Observer, New Statesman,* and *London Review of Books;* contributor of poems to radio programs, including *Poetry Now,* BBC Radio 3; *Rollercoaster,* BBC Radio 4; and *Pick of the Week,* BBC Radio 4.

SIDELIGHTS: British poet Wendy Cope is the author of *Making Cocoa for Kingsley Amis,* a collection of poems that includes several parodies and other literary jokes. The title is explained in the first poem, which reads: "It was a dream I had last week / And some kind of record seemed vital. I knew it wouldn't be much of a poem, / But I loved the title." In other pieces, Cope parodies such poets as T.S. Eliot, Philip Larkin, and Ted Hughes. Cope's imitations reveal an irreverent attitude toward modernist poetry, lightly veiled beneath the guise of good clean fun. The parodies are attributed to Jason Strugnell, a character created by Cope and introduced in a British Broadcasting Corporation (BBC) radio program in 1982. An ambitious but inferior poet, Strugnell continually finds himself imitating major contemporary voices, and the results are always entertaining. Other selections in the volume use traditional poetic forms, such as the sonnet and the villanelle, to express a view of love that is both sincere and satirical. Critical response to *Making Cocoa for Kingsley Amis* was generally favorable. Robert Nye, writing in the London *Times,* referred to Cope as "a writer of very stylish and clever light verse which is a great pleasure to read." Although London *Times Literary Supplement* contributor Bernard O'Donoghue found the quality of the writing somewhat lacking, he referred to the work as an "amusing book, which you can read from cover to cover, tum-ti-tum, in a very pleasant hour."

In 1991 Cope published *The River Girl,* an entirely different type of poetry from *Making Cocoa for Kingsley Amis.* A single long narrative poem, the work was commissioned by a marionette company, which eventually performed it on a theatre barge. The tale explores a love affair between a mortal and an immortal being. John Didde is a young poet who spends his time gazing out at the river. He encounters Isis, the daughter of the river king, Father Thames. Isis serves as John's muse; he immediately begins to spout glorious poetry, and he and Isis fall in love at first sight. Father Thames is distressed that his daughter has fallen in love with a poet, but he does not forbid her to associate with John. John and Isis marry, and John's book is accepted by a major publisher, Tite and Snobbo. He begins to attract a following, and his fans shower him with praise, which goes straight to his head. His egotism causes him to neglect his wife, who changes first into a bird and then into a fish as she leaves him to return to her father. George Szirtes, writing in the *Times Literary Supplement,* lauded the poem's "delicate balance between the affairs of this world and the world of under the river," and called the work "a well-written, entertaining story with a great deal of charm."

Cope's 1992 work, *Serious Concerns,* is a volume of poetry similar to *Making Cocoa for Kingsley Amis,* prompting London *Times Saturday Review* contributor Robert Nye to predict that it is "likely to please the same audience all over again." The book includes parodies by Jason Strugnell as well as poems that play directly on the lives of literary figures. Cope also includes a number of romantic pieces that mingle humor with the sadness of loss and rejection. Although the subject of *Serious Concerns* is men, Nye noted that the poet herself is usually the butt of the jokes.

Cope told *CA:* "I dislike the term 'light verse' because it is used as a way of dismissing poets who allow humor into their work. I believe that a humorous poem can also be 'serious'—i.e., deeply felt and saying something that matters.

"Although it includes a few happy poems, I think my second full-length collection, *Serious Concerns,* is a bleak book. A key poem is 'Some More Light Verse.' I see this as a poem about feeling suicidal, but managing to see the funny side, and therefore being able to carry on. I would like this poem, and the whole book, to be seen in the context of the high suicide rate of an earlier generation of poets. If we don't want to go down that road, poets of my generation have to find a different approach."

BIOGRAPHICAL/CRITICAL SOURCES:

BOOKS

Cope, Wendy, *Making Cocoa for Kingsley Amis,* Faber & Faber, 1986.

PERIODICALS

London Review of Books, April 17, 1986, pp. 20-22.
New Statesman, May 2, 1986, pp. 24-25.
Times (London), March 13, 1986.

Times Literary Supplement, June 6, 1986, p. 616; July 12, 1991, p. 21.
Times Saturday Review, March 14, 1992, p. 37.

*   *   *

COPELAND, Pat
See BELLMON, Patricia

*   *   *

COVENEY, Peter (Vivian) 1958-

PERSONAL: Born October 30, 1958, in London, England; son of James (a professor) and Patricia Yvonne (Townsend) Coveney; married Samia Nehme (a scientist), July 27, 1987. *Education:* Oxford University, B.A., 1981; Princeton University, M.A. and D.Phil., both 1985.

ADDRESSES: Home—11 Station Approach, Theydon Bois, Essex CM16 7HR, England. *Agent*—John Brockman Associates, 2307 Broadway, New York, NY 10024.

CAREER: Oxford University, Oxford, England, junior research fellow, 1984-87; University of Wales, Bangor, lecturer, 1987-90; Schlumberger Cambridge Research Laboratory, Cambridge, England, program leader, 1990—.

MEMBER: Royal Society of Chemistry, Institute of Physics, Society of Petroleum Engineers, American Institute of Physics.

WRITINGS:

(With Roger Highfield) *The Arrow of Time: A Voyage through Science to Solve Time's Greatest Mystery,* W. H. Allen, 1990, Fawcett Columbine, 1991.

WORK IN PROGRESS: Various projects in theoretical physics and chemistry.

BIOGRAPHICAL/CRITICAL SOURCES:

PERIODICALS

New York Times Book Review, June 23, 1991, p. 6.

*   *   *

COYLE, Harold (W.) 1952-

PERSONAL: Born in 1952.

ADDRESSES: Agent—Robert Gottlieb, William Morris Agency, 1350 Avenue of the Americas, New York, NY 10019.

CAREER: Affiliated with the United States Army; writer.

WRITINGS:

NOVELS

Team Yankee: A Novel of World War III, Presidio, 1987.
Sword Point, Simon & Schuster, 1988.
Bright Star, Simon & Schuster, 1990.
Trial by Fire, Simon & Schuster, 1992.

SIDELIGHTS: Harold Coyle is a U.S. Army officer who has also become known as the author of military thrillers. He began his literary career in 1987 with *Team Yankee: A Novel of World War III,* a sequel to General John Hackett's novel *The Third World War.* In *Team Yankee,* Coyle relates the hardships of an American squad fighting in West Germany. Here combat escalates and nuclear warfare between Americans and Soviets appears inevitable.

Coyle followed *Team Yankee* with *Sword Point,* a 1988 novel in which Americans and Soviets vie for military supremacy in Iran. The Iranian forces, fighting both the Americans and the Soviets, threaten to trigger atomic explosives. The Soviets, meanwhile, might be preparing to launch chemical warfare.

In 1990 Coyle released *Bright Star,* an account of Cold War tensions threatening to degenerate into armed combat. The conflict begins after American forces arrive in Egypt for a training operation. Confronted by the presence of American troops in the already volatile Middle East, the Soviets reinforce their own military in Libya. This escalation, in turn, serves to exacerbate existing tensions between the two super powers, and nuclear conflict soon threatens global stability.

Coyle's fourth novel, *Trial by Fire,* concerns a border conflict between American and Mexican armies. This confrontation is engineered by a Mexican drug dealer hoping to subvert his own government's forceful anti-drug activities. The ensuing conflict holds grave repercussions for both factions, and Coyle presents the unfolding battle with maps and numerous technical details.

BIOGRAPHICAL/CRITICAL SOURCES:

PERIODICALS

New York Times Book Review, November 27, 1988, p. 23; June 17, 1990, p. 19.*

*   *   *

COZZENS, Peter 1957-

PERSONAL: Born June 25, 1957, in Long Branch, NJ; son of James W. (an office manager) and Audrey (a secretary; maiden name, Heineman) Cozzens. *Education:*

Knox College, B.A. (summa cum laude), 1979; attended Chinese University of Hong Kong, 1977-78. *Politics:* "Democrat: liberal in domestic affairs, a bit conservative in foreign policy." *Religion:* "Protestant by upbringing, but I've always felt good works are good enough." *Avocational interests:* Weightlifting, running, collecting books of early twentieth-century American fiction, poetry, and literary biographies.

ADDRESSES: Home—c/o Audrey Cozzens, 209 South Hazelton, Wheaton, IL 60187. *Agent*—David Stewart Hull Literary Agency, 240 East 82nd St., New York, NY 10028.

CAREER: U.S. Department of State, Washington, DC, foreign service officer, 1983—, U.S. consul in Lima, Peru, 1993. *Military service:* U.S. Army, military intelligence officer, 1979-83; became captain.

MEMBER: American Foreign Service Association, National Parks and Conservation Association, Phi Beta Kappa.

WRITINGS:

No Better Place to Die: The Battle of Stones River (Book-of-the-Month Club selection), University of Illinois Press, 1990.
This Terrible Sound: The Battle of Chickamauga, University of Illinois Press, 1992.
The Shipwreck of Their Hopes: The Battles for Chattanooga, University of Illinois Press, in press.

Contributor to *Civil War Times Illustrated* and *Illinois Historical Journal.*

WORK IN PROGRESS: Research for a biography of nineteenth-century journalist and author Ambrose Bierce.

SIDELIGHTS: Peter Cozzens told *CA:* "With the current revival of interest in the Civil War, we too often forget that, for those who fought it, the war was anything but glorious. Rather, it was a long, mostly tedious ordeal punctuated by a few brief, horrific moments of combat. The courage of the common soldiers was equalled, if not exceeded, by the selfishness and egotism of their commanders. Battles were won by those who bungled the least.

"It is to convey the madness and misery of the war that I have written three campaign studies; not to glorify, but to remind Americans of the senseless brutality of a conflict that tore us apart. I try to weave the experiences of those who fought the war into my narrative, to portray these battles as human tragedies, rather than as the sterile, chessboard-like maneuvering of units that is too often conveyed in traditional histories. I am grateful that reviewers, and I hope the reading public, appreciate this perspective.

"Although my first three books have dealt with the Civil War, I don't think of myself as a Civil War historian, but rather as a writer who has developed a fascination with that epoch. Those writers who have most influenced my work are not historians, but novelists and those who fought the war and left behind their letters and memoirs. Far and away the most profound and direct influence has come from my reading of Joseph Pennell's all-but-forgotten 1942 novel *A History of Rome Hanks and Kindred Matters,* and of the short stories and autobiographical writings of Ambrose Bierce. Indeed, his writings have so moved me that my present project is a biography of Bierce. Of modern works, nothing continues to impress me so greatly as Carl Sandburg's biography of Abraham Lincoln.

"As a foreign service officer subject to extended periods of residence abroad, I have found that research and writing can be hard. I have developed rewarding friendships with archivists at a number of institutions, which has eased the difficulties of writing about American history from several thousand miles away, and with Civil War buffs who have generously shared materials from their private collections. I cannot stress to aspiring writers of nonfiction the utility—and rewards—of developing such relationships with the reader."

BIOGRAPHICAL/CRITICAL SOURCES:

PERIODICALS

New York Times, November 29, 1992.
Washington Times, November 28, 1992.

*   *   *

CRAIG, Robert H. 1942-

PERSONAL: Born February 7, 1942, in San Jose, CA; son of Robert Hugh and Marian Grace Craig; married Gail Peterson (a special education specialist), August 3, 1963; children: R. Andrew, Ian Thomas. *Education:* University of California, Santa Barbara, B.A., 1965; Union Theological Seminary, M.Div., 1968; Columbia University, Ph.D., 1975. *Politics:* Socialist. *Religion:* United Methodist.

ADDRESSES: Home—2410 Ridgewood Ave., Alliance, OH 44601. *Office*—Department of Religion and Philosophy, Mount Union College, 1972 Clark Ave., Alliance, OH 44601-3993.

CAREER: National University of Costa Rica, San Jose, professor of religion, 1978-82; Bucknell University, Lewisburg, PA, associate professor of religion and political science, 1983-86; College of the Holy Cross, Worcester, MA, assistant professor of social ethics, 1986-90; Mount Union College, Alliance, OH, associate professor of religious studies, 1990—. Latin American Biblical Seminary, professor, 1980-82.

MEMBER: American Academy of Religion, Society of Christian Ethics, Methodist Federation for Social Action (co-convenor of East Ohio chapter), National Association for the Advancement of Colored People (NAACP).

AWARDS, HONORS: Burma-Bucknell Award for Promoting International Understanding, 1986; Wye fellow, 1992.

WRITINGS:

(With Jose Miguez Bonino and Carmelo Alvarez) *Protestantismo y Liberalismo en America Latina,* 2nd edition, DEI/SBL, 1985.
Religion and Radical Politics: An Alternative Christian Tradition in the United States, Temple University Press, 1992.

WORK IN PROGRESS: Research on religion and criminology, on criminal justice, and on American religious history.

SIDELIGHTS: Robert H. Craig told *CA:* "Martin Duberman has emphasized how much 'a particular personality intersects with a particular subject.' In other words, there is a correlation between what we write and the material we select or ignore, who we are as individuals, and how we perceive the world. My perception of social reality has been influenced by the work of E. P. Thompson, Antonio Gramsci, and W. E. B. Du Bois. In addition, I grew up in a working-class community, and my understanding of myself and the world around me has been shaped by my experience with the Black church, involvement in the anti-war movement, and teaching in Central America.

"I have learned over the years that what is most unsettling to those who wield power over others, whether they are within the church or the society at large, is that ordinary people, who have been excluded on the basis of race, class, and gender, have clearly understood that the face of God is to be found in the struggle for justice. God is present where people seek to substitute solidarity for racial hatred, sexual equality for patriarchal domination, and democratic participation in the economic and political life of one's society for tunnel-visioned politics and the dictates of corporate profit-making.

"I am both a social historian and a social ethicist, who believes that sociohistorical analysis is an important ingredient in the development of a liberative approach to Christian ethics. As a writer, one of my constant fears is not always being able to find the right words or images that do complete justice to the life histories of individuals and social movements I have researched. At the same time, I am very much aware that it is only in and through human praxis, and not analysis, that history is altered.

"My writing has not only been influenced by the personal and political commitments I have made, but by my teaching. I have had appointments in political science, philosophy, and religious studies, and have tried to introduce students to the importance of a global perspective on their own culture and society. Working with students has forced me to try and clarify for myself and for them how the contradictions of a market economy affect human beings, and that how we structure our economic life has to do with the lack of control people exercise over the conditions that govern their lives. Just as important is the necessity of wrestling with issues of race and gender, and how central they are to the perception we have of ourselves and our society. Racism and sexism, I contend, are related, not only to questions of politics and economics, but to the distortions of human hopes, sensibilities, and aspirations."

* * *

CRAMER, Richard Ben 1950-

PERSONAL: Born June 12, 1950, in Rochester, NY; son of A. Robert and Blossom (Lackritz) Cramer. *Education:* Johns Hopkins University, B.A., 1971; Columbia University, M.S., 1972.

ADDRESSES: Agent—Sterling Lord Literistic, Inc., One Madison Ave., New York, NY 10010.

CAREER: Sun, Baltimore, MD, reporter, 1973-76; *Philadelphia Inquirer,* Philadelphia, PA, reporter, 1976-78, foreign correspondent in Europe, Africa, and the Middle East, beginning in 1978; free-lance journalist and writer. Has worked as a contributing editor for *Esquire.*

MEMBER: Pen and Pencil, Stampa Estere d'Italia.

AWARDS, HONORS: Pulitzer Prize for international reporting, 1979, for reports from the Middle East; Sigma Delta Chi award for foreign correspondence, 1980; Ernie Pyle Award, Scripps Howard News Service, 1980; Hal Boyle Award, Overseas Press Club of America, 1981, for coverage of Afghan guerrillas fighting the Russians; American Society of Newspaper Editors award for excellence in writing.

WRITINGS:

Ted Williams: The Season of the Kid, photo essays by John Thorn, Prentice-Hall, 1991.
What It Takes: The Way to the White House, Random House, 1992.

Contributor to newspapers and periodicals, including *New York Times, New York Times Book Review, Esquire,* and *Rolling Stone.*

SIDELIGHTS: During his award-winning career as a newspaper journalist, Richard Ben Cramer spent most of his time covering affairs outside the United States. As the *Philadelphia Inquirer*'s correspondent for Europe, Africa, and the Middle East, he spent many years overseas, reporting on both the civil war in Lebanon and on the fighting between Soviet troops and Afghan guerrillas. In the years since he left the *Inquirer,* however, Cramer has been concerned with uniquely American subjects. His 1992 book, *What It Takes: The Way To the White House,* presents a study of six of the 1988 presidential candidates. He has also focused on the sports world of his native country, producing *Ted Williams: The Season of the Kid* in 1991. Both books have been praised by critics for delivering an unusual glimpse of their prominent and powerful subjects.

In profiling baseball legend Williams, Cramer was faced with a man who was renowned for his exploits on the field but who was uncomfortable with his role as a superstar. As the last professional player to hold a season batting average of .400, Williams has been touted by many experts as the best hitter to ever play the game. His career was also marred by incidents in which he spit at fans and threw his bat into the crowd to silence hecklers. *Ted Williams: The Season of the Kid* opens with an account of Cramer's visit to the aging star in his Florida retirement home, then chronicles Williams's career and personal life. *Newsweek* reviewer Charles Leerhsen proclaimed the book "a timeless piece of journalism" that results in "a brilliantly crafted profile" of Williams, a man, Cramer writes, who "wanted fame . . . but could not stand celebrity."

The celebrities in *What It Takes,* Cramer's second book, are also involved in a competitive American pastime: politics. The author studies six of the candidates in the 1988 presidential campaign: Gary Hart, Joseph Biden, Richard Gephardt, Michael Dukakis, Bob Dole, and George Bush. Cramer was not content in writing a conventional political analysis of the race, however. "I wanted to know not about the campaign, but about the campaigners," the author notes in his introduction to the book. "Who are these guys. . . . What happened to their idea of themselves? What did *we do to them,* on the way to the White House?" In order to answer these questions Cramer worked on the book for a total of six years, before, during, and after 1988. He conducted over one thousand interviews with people involved in the campaign, including extensive discussions with each of the six candidates. The resulting book is over one thousand pages in length, providing an extensive study of the men who aspired to be president.

Douglas Bell, reviewing the book in the Toronto *Globe & Mail,* noted that "Cramer zeroes in and with surgical precision dissects layer upon layer of his subject's persona." These insights stem, in part, from the details the author relates about the candidates. The book pictures Biden as

he shops for real estate between political rallies, discusses Hart's choice of cocktails at a campaign stopover, and describes the mysterious tune that Bob Dole continually whistles and hums throughout the primaries. "Cramer has a particularly sensitive ear for dialogue," Bell continued, "capturing not just what the candidate said but the way he said it." In addition to documenting the behavior of the candidates, *What It Takes* also provides the author's assessment of the campaign's headline stories. Cramer defends the two candidates who withdrew from the race after allegations of impropriety—Biden, who plagiarized a campaign speech, and Hart, who was accused of having an extramarital affair. In both cases Cramer feels the candidates were the victims of an overzealous news media who were hungry for sensational stories.

The media are only one of many forces that impact the candidates in Cramer's account. The author also considers the so-called "handlers"—the group of analysts, pollsters, and image consultants that help manage each candidate's campaign. Jack Shafer, reviewing the book in *Washington Post Book World,* noted that "the subtext of *What It Takes* is that a candidate must maintain his vigilance lest the handlers (Cramer calls them 'the white men') take over." The author also describes the closed world that the candidates exist in, a claustrophobic environment created by their non-stop travel and carefully orchestrated appearances. This quality is made clear, according to *Time* reviewer Walter Shapiro, in the book's depiction of George Bush on the campaign trail. "Where Cramer excels," wrote Shapiro, "is in portraying Bush's sterile life inside the bubble—the Secret-Service-secure world of motorcades, advancemen, rope lines, and step-by-step schedules." Cramer argues that such elements created a campaign environment where Bush would "never see one person who was not a friend, or someone whose sole purpose it was to serve or protect him."

The epic length of *What It Takes* became an issue for critics reviewing the book. Some, such as *New Statesman & Society* reviewer Boyd Tonkin, found the book excessively detailed. "No one ever stopped to think that this project might have worked better at 300 pages than at *1046,*" Tonkin complained. "Few will finish it, and no skimmer can use its information, as it lacks an index." Shapiro conceded that "only the dust jacket is terse" in *What It Takes,* but he found that the length of the book was justified. "Despite its heft," Shapiro wrote, "the prose is a joyous journey" that results in an "artful reworking" of the campaign.

Cramer's writing style in the book—his use of numerous exclamation points and capitalized words, for instance—was singled out by many reviewers and compared to the writing of other experimental journalists such as Tom Wolfe and Hunter S. Thompson. *Newsweek*'s Joe Klein addressed another aspect of Cramer's technique, noting that the author doesn't cite his sources as is the normal journalistic practice. Because of this, Klein speculated that *What It Takes* "is bound to cause a fair amount of controversy among the political and media priesthoods, as it blithely skirts the boundaries of responsibility and good taste." Despite this danger, the critic felt that the book succeeded in its quest to explain the political candidates. "Even if only semi-journalistic," Klein wrote, "this is still great fun and . . . far more insightful about pols and political tradecraft than the common run of campaign effluvia."

In the end, the book suggests that "what it takes" to be president is a willingness to give all. Shapiro, summing up Cramer's views, wrote that the president must be "so driven in his pursuit of the White House that he jettisons family, friends, any semblance of privacy or normal human existence." And a similar question was addressed by the critics who reviewed Cramer's study: did the book have "what it takes" to be worthwhile reading? The *Globe & Mail*'s Bell was one of many who felt it did, citing the author's "deft mix of insight and breathtaking reportage." The critic went on to proclaim the book an important document of the campaign, declaring that "Cramer's delightfully unexpected insights capture the tenor and the timbre of his political times."

BIOGRAPHICAL/CRITICAL SOURCES:

BOOKS

Cramer, Richard Ben, *Ted Williams: The Season of the Kid,* Prentice Hall, 1991.
Cramer, *What It Takes: The Way to the White House,* Random House, 1992.

PERIODICALS

Globe & Mail (Toronto), July 11, 1992, p. C5.
New Statesman & Society, July 31, 1992, p. 37.
Newsweek, October 28, 1991, p. 62; July 6, 1992, p. 55.
Time, July 13, 1992, pp. 78-80.
Washington Post Book World, June 28, 1992, pp. 1, 10.*

—*Sketch by Jeff Hill*

*   *   *

CRANE, Stephen (Townley)   1871-1900
(Johnston Smith)

PERSONAL: Born November 1, 1871, in Newark, NJ; died of tuberculosis, June 5, 1900, in Badenweiler, Germany; buried at Hillside, NJ; son of Jonathan Townley (a minister) and Mary Helen (a religious writer; maiden name, Peck) Crane; lived with Cora Taylor. *Education:* Attended Lafayette College, 1890; attended Syracuse University, 1891.

CAREER: Journalist, poet, and author of short stories and novels. Affiliated with *New York Tribune, New York Herald,* and *New York Journal.*

WRITINGS:

(Under pseudonym Johnston Smith) *Maggie: A Girl of the Streets* (novella), privately printed, 1893; revised edition published under the name Stephen Crane, Appleton, 1896.
The Black Riders, and Other Lines (poetry), Copeland & Day, 1895.
The Red Badge of Courage: An Episode of the American Civil War (novella), Appleton, 1895.
George's Mother (novel), Edward Arnold, 1896.
The Little Regiment, and Other Episodes of the American Civil War (short stories; includes "The Veteran"), Appleton, 1896, published in England as *Pictures of War,* Heinemann, 1898.
The Third Violet (novel), Appleton, 1897.
The Open Boat, and Other Tales of Adventure (short stories; also contains "The Bride Comes to Yellow Sky," "A Man and Some Others," "One Dash," "Horses," "Flanagan," "The Wise Men," "Death and the Child," and "The Five White Mice"), Doubleday & McClure, 1898.
Active Service (novel), Stokes, 1899.
The Monster, and Other Stories (short stories; includes "The Blue Hotel" and "His New Mittens"), Harper, 1899.
War Is Kind (poetry), illustrated by Will Bradley, Stokes, 1899.
Whilomville Stories (short stories), illustrated by Peter Newell, Harper, 1900.
Wounds in the Rain: A Collection of Stories Relating to the Spanish-American War of 1898 (short stories), Stokes, 1900.
Great Battles of the World, illustrated by John Sloan, Lippincott, 1901.
Last Words (short stories; contains "The Reluctant Voyagers," "Spitzbergen Tales," "Wyoming Valley Tales," "London Impressions," "New York Sketches," "The Assassins in Modern Battles," "Irish Notes," and "Sullivan County Sketches"), Digby, Long, 1902.
(With Robert Barr) *The O'Ruddy* (novel), Stokes, 1903.
Men, Women and Boats (contains "Stephen Crane: An Estimate," "The Open Boat," "The Reluctant Voyagers," "The End of the Battle," "The Upturned Face," "An Episode of War," "An Experiment in Misery," "The Duel That Was Not Fought," "A Desertion," "A Dark-Brown Dog," "The Pace of Youth," "Sullivan County Sketches: A Tent in Agony, Four Men in

a Cave, The Mesmeric Mountain, The Snake, London Impressions, and The Scotch Express"), edited and introduced by Vincent Starrett, Boni and Liveright, 1921.

The Works of Stephen Crane, twelve volumes, edited by Wilson Follett, Knopf, 1925-26.

The Collected Poems of Stephen Crane (poetry), edited by Follett, Knopf, 1930.

A Battle in Greece (nonfiction), illustrated by Valenti Angelo, Peter Pauper Press, 1936.

The Sullivan County Sketches of Stephen Crane (sketches; originally serialized in *New York Tribune* and *The Cosmopolitan,* 1892), edited by Melvin Schoberlin, Syracuse University Press, 1949.

Stephen Crane: An Omnibus, edited and introduced with notes by R. W. Stallman, Knopf, 1952.

Love Letters to Nellie Crouse, edited and introduced by Edwin H. Cady and Lester G. Wells, Syracuse University Press, 1954.

Stephen Crane: Letters, edited by Stallman and Lillian Gilkes, New York University Press, 1960.

An Illusion in Red and White, edited by Don Honig, Avon, 1962.

The Complete Short Stories and Sketches, edited and introduced by Thomas A. Gullason, Doubleday, 1963.

Stephen Crane: Uncollected Writings, edited by Olov W. Fryckstedt, Studia Anglistica Upsaliensia, 1963.

Poems, edited by Gerald D. McDonald, illustrated by Nonny Hogrogian, Crowell, 1964.

The War Dispatches of Stephen Crane, edited by Stallman and E. R. Hagemann, New York University Press, 1966.

The New York City Sketches of Stephen Crane, and Related Pieces, edited by Stallman and Hagemann, New York University Press, 1966.

A Critical Edition, edited by Joseph Katz, Cooper Square Publishers, 1966.

The Complete Novels, edited and introduced by Gullason, Doubleday, 1967.

Sullivan County Tales and Sketches, edited with an introduction by Stallman, Iowa State University Press, 1968.

The Notebook of Stephen Crane, edited by Donald and Ellen Greiner, John Cook Wyllie Memorial Publication, 1969.

The Blue Hotel (contains criticism), edited by Katz, C. E. Merrill, 1969.

The Portable Stephen Crane, edited and introduced by Katz, Viking, 1969.

The Works of Stephen Crane, edited by Fredson Bowers, University Press of Virginia, Volume I: *Bowery Tales: Maggie [and] George's Mother,* 1969, Volume II: *The Red Badge of Courage,* 1975, Volume IV: *The O'Ruddy,* 1971, Volume V: *Tales of Adventure,* 1970, Volume VI: *Tales of War,* 1970, Volume VII: *Tales of Whilomville,* 1969, Volume VIII: *Tales, Sketches, and Reports,* 1973, Volume IX: *Reports of War,* 1971, Volume X: *Poems and Literary Remains,* 1975.

Stephen Crane in the West and Mexico, edited by Katz, Kent State University Press, 1970.

The Complete Poems of Stephen Crane, edited and introduced by Katz, Cornell University Press, 1972.

The Stephen Crane Reader, edited by Stallman, Scott, Foresman, 1972.

The Correspondence of Stephen Crane, edited by Paul Sorrentino and Stanley Wertheim, Columbia University Press, 1988.

Work also contained in *Stephen Crane: Prose and Poetry,* 1984.

ADAPTATIONS: The Red Badge of Courage was adapted for films of the same name by director John Huston for Metro-Goldwyn-Mayer, 1951, starring Audie Murphy and Bill Mauldin, and by Richard Slote for Universal Education and Visual Arts, 1970. The story was refilmed under its original title for a television movie, featuring Richard Thomas and Michael Brandon, airing on National Broadcasting Company (NBC-TV) in 1974. *The Red Badge of Courage* was also adapted for filmstrip by Brunswick Productions, 1967, Educational Dimensions Corp., 1968, Popular Science Publishing, 1968, and by Thomas S. Klise Co., 1973. Passages of *The Red Badge of Courage* were featured in the motion picture *Reading Out Loud: Jackie Robinson,* Westinghouse Broadcasting in association with the American Library Association.

"The Bride Comes to Yellow Sky" was adapted for dramatizations by Paul T. Nolan, Pioneer Drama Service, 1963, and by Frank Crocitto, Dramatists Play Service, 1970. "The Bride Comes to Yellow Sky" was used along with *The Secret Sharer* by Joseph Conrad as the basis for the film *Face to Face,* Theasquare Productions, 1952. *The Monster* was adapted for the motion picture *Face of Fire,* starring Cameron Mitchell and James Whitmore, Allied Artists, 1959. "The Upturned Face" was filmed under its original title for Changeling Productions, 1973. James Agee adapted "The Blue Hotel" into a screenplay.

Crane's work has also been used in other filmstrips, including: "The Civil War in Prose and Poetry" (includes *The Red Badge of Courage;* series of six filmstrips, color, silent), Miller-Brody Productions; "The Great Novel of the Civil War: The Red Badge of Courage" (seventeen minutes with sound cassette, color), Educational Dimensions Group; "The Vision of Stephen Crane" (two filmstrips, sound, record or cassette, color), Guidance Associates, 1972.

Recordings include: "The Red Badge of Courage," read by Edmond O'Brien (record or cassette), Caedmon; "Stephen Crane's The Red Badge of Courage," read by Jack Dahlby (five records or four cassettes, text), Miller-Brody Productions; "Stories of War," CMS Records.

SIDELIGHTS: Stephen Crane was one of the most important and influential American authors of the late 1800s. His 1895 novella of the American Civil War, *The Red Badge of Courage,* won him great critical praise in both the United States and England. He has been claimed by literary movements as diverse as the realistic, the impressionistic, and the symbolistic; and he has been compared with literary greats such as Leo Tolstoy and Joseph Conrad. Crane's poetry—primarily published in the two volumes *The Black Riders* and *War Is Kind*—was also an influence on imagist poets such as Amy Lowell. In addition to his poetry and the famous *Red Badge of Courage,* Crane wrote other novels, including *Maggie: A Girl of the Streets* and *George's Mother.* Many of his short stories continue to be revered, such as "The Open Boat," "The Blue Hotel," and "The Bride Comes to Yellow Sky."

Stephen Crane was born November 1, 1871, in Newark, New Jersey. His family was deeply religious; his father was a minister and his mother was a religious writer descended from many famous Methodist clergymen. Crane was the youngest of fourteen children, nine of whom survived to adulthood. His father died when he was only nine years old, and his mother moved the family to Asbury Park, New Jersey, a resort town then primarily patronized by Methodists. One of his older brothers operated a news agency there for the *New York Tribune,* and during his adolescence, Crane began helping his sibling with news and gossip for the column he wrote.

Crane's schooling was somewhat sketchy. He attended prep school before enrolling at Lafayette College, where he lasted one term before being advised to leave because he had not completed any of his classwork. He then went to Syracuse University, where he was known primarily for his athletic skill, particularly in baseball, but he enjoyed football as well. To support himself while at the university, he became increasingly involved with his brother's newspaper work, reporting on the Syracuse slums and its police court. At this time, he decided that he would become a writer, and left school—again with very little work completed—feeling that it was more important to study the lives of everyday people than the works of great masters.

After leaving Syracuse University, Crane took over his brother's newspaper column. He also became interested in the theories of realism in fiction propounded by Hamlin Garland and William Dean Howells, and was greatly influenced by English novelist Rudyard Kipling's *The Light That Failed,* about a realist painter living in poverty. One of the ideas expressed in the book was that to create great art, an artist must know hardship; Crane took this to heart

and began living on very little money in New York's Bowery area, hoping to improve his writing. Scholars believe that at this time he probably began working on his first novel, *Maggie: A Girl of the Streets,* in addition to writing sketches that appeared in the *New York Tribune.*

Crane kept revising *Maggie* every time he showed it to an editor—each of whom protested that the story was too harsh and cruel to publish. Eventually the author gave up and had the novel privately printed at his own expense, borrowing money to do so. Because of the negative reactions he had received from editors, he decided to publish the book under a pseudonym, Johnston Smith. As the title suggests, *Maggie* concerns a girl from the slums whose environment leads her to become a prostitute after being abused by her drunken parents and seduced by her brother's best friend. In the end, she is driven to suicide. *Maggie* attracted little attention when it was first published, but when Crane reissued it under his real name after the success of *The Red Badge of Courage,* the earlier work received some of the acclaim it deserved. Even at its first publication, however, the novel garnered some praise, particularly from Crane's mentor in realism, Hamlin Garland. In a review of the book for *Arena,* Garland called *Maggie* "a work of astonishingly good style. It deals with poverty and vice and crime also, but it does so, not out of curiosity, not out of salaciousness, but because of a distinct art impulse, the desire to utter in truthful phrase a certain rebellious cry." Garland also concluded that in the book Crane "has met and grappled with the actualities of the street in almost unequalled grace and strength."

Crane worked on *The Red Badge of Courage* and his first book of verse, *The Black Riders,* during the same period. He started writing poems after being exposed to the work of Emily Dickinson, and "more than half of the sixty-eight poems" which make up *The Black Riders,* according to James B. Colvert in volume twelve of *Dictionary of Literary Biography (DLB),* "are on religious themes." Crane was deeply troubled about religion, having come to abandon the strong beliefs of his parents, and the topics of his poems, Colvert asserted, included "the inscrutability of God, man's futile quest for God, God's wrath, the terrors of a Godless universe, and man's pride and impotence."

While the poems of *The Black Riders* were deeply personal to Crane, and his novel *Maggie* had been based on his personal observations of life in the slums, the author departed somewhat from a strict theory of realism in writing *The Red Badge of Courage.* Crane had never seen a battle when he wrote the novel, and he later said that he improvised the battle scenes in it from memories of his days on the football field in college. He also, however, studied the many published memoirs of Civil War veterans that were available at the time. Nevertheless, critics have continued to praise the novel's realism. *The Red*

Badge of Courage is the story of a young soldier, Henry Fleming, who enlists to fight on the Union side, thinking, because of all of the patriotic rhetoric that he has heard, that war will be a glorious adventure. Instead, he first experiences the boredom of waiting days on end for battle action, and then the fear of losing control and running when battle actually does occur. He does run, and seeks shelter in a pristine forest, only to discover the corpse of another soldier there. Fleming eventually returns to fight, and becomes as steady a veteran of battle as any of the older soldiers in his platoon.

The Red Badge of Courage became a huge popular success in the United States and Great Britain, and critics raved. George Wyndham, for instance, critiquing the work in the British *New Review,* enthusiastically praised the work's descriptive power: "the sights flashed indelibly on the retina of the eye; the sounds that after long silences suddenly cypher; the stenches that sicken in after-life at any chance allusion to decay; or, stirred by these, the storms of passions that force yells of defiance out of inarticulate clowns; the winds of fear that sweep by night along prostrate ranks, with the acceleration of trains and the noise as of a whole town waking from nightmare with stertorous, indrawn grasps—these colossal facts of the senses and the soul are the only [colors] in which the very image of war can be painted." The critic added, "Mr. Crane has composed his palette with these [colors], and has painted a picture that challenged comparison with the most vivid scenes of [Russian author Leo Tolstoy's *War and Peace*] or of [French author Emile Zola's] *La Debacle.*" Wyndham concluded further that Crane "is a great artist" and "in *The Red Badge of Courage* . . . has surely contrived a masterpiece." The book's reputation has continued to the present day, and is studied in American literature classes in many schools and universities.

While Crane was composing *The Red Badge of Courage* and *The Black Riders,* he was also at work on another realistic novel of the slums called *George's Mother.* This book centers on a young man growing up in the slums and turning gradually to a life of dissipation—to the dismay of his deeply religious mother, who dies of a broken heart at the end of the novel. For this effort, Crane not only drew on his knowledge of New York's Bowery, but on his relationship with his own mother, who had been saddened by Crane's turning from religion before her death. Published after the success of *The Red Badge of Courage,* and at the same time as a reissue of *Maggie: A Girl of the Streets, George's Mother* received some good reviews, including one from Crane's fellow novelist and acquaintance, Frank Norris. "*George's Mother* seems to me better than *Maggie,*" Norris judged in *Wave.* "For a short novel it is less pretentious, has fewer characters and more unity, conveying one distinct impression. . . . There is some-

thing about [the] death of 'the little old woman' that rings surprisingly true."

But fans and critics alike demanded that Crane return to war stories. Somewhat embarrassed, because readers preferred his writing on a subject he knew little about to that of his carefully studied slum stories, the author obliged, publishing a collection of short tales called *The Little Regiment* late in 1896. As Colvert asserted in *DLB,* "the general tendency in these stories . . . is toward a more conventional realism. Although they draw heavily on the characteristic metaphors and images of *The Red Badge of Courage,* they tend toward a more conventional description, picturing the world not as a projection of the hero's anxieties and fantasies, as in the earlier fiction, but as a world objectively described by a disinterested narrator." *The Little Regiment* includes a short story entitled "The Veteran," which depicts Henry Fleming of *The Red Badge of Courage* as an old man, attempting to save two colts from a burning barn. After *The Little Regiment,* Crane published a novel called *The Third Violet,* a love story about an impressionist painter; most critics discount its literary value.

Late in 1896, Crane was offered a position as a special correspondent covering Cuba's revolt against Spain. He jumped at the chance, perhaps because it was his first opportunity to cover actual military action. While in Jacksonville, Florida, on the way to Cuba, he met Cora Taylor, a woman who had deserted her husband. She would eventually become Crane's common-law wife.

From Florida, Crane boarded the *Commodore,* a ship carrying guns and ammunition to Cuba. Once out to sea, the ship sank, and Crane spent thirty hours with other survivors adrift in a small dinghy. These events were to inspire what most critics agree to be his finest short story, "The Open Boat," later published in a volume bearing the same title. Unfortunately, however, Crane's exposure to the elements also marked the beginning of the physical problems that eventually resulted in his death from tuberculosis at age twenty-eight.

After his rescue, Crane was nursed back to health by Cora Taylor, who went with him to Greece in 1897 for his next reporting assignment—this time covering the fighting between the Greeks and the Turks. There he finally witnessed some actual battles, and satisfied himself that his descriptions in *The Red Badge of Courage* had been adequate. He also garnered materials for more short stories because of this experience; "Death and the Child," considered to be among his better efforts, was one of them. When the fighting was over in Greece, Crane and Taylor went to live in London, England.

In London, Crane became friends with many of that country's literary giants, including Joseph Conrad and Ford

Madox Ford. He continued to write there, except for a brief return to Cuba to cover some of the Spanish-American War. While in Havana, he managed to write the collection of war stories *Wounds in the Rain,* and a novel, *Active Service*—a love story set against the backdrop of the Greek and Turkish fighting he had previously covered. Early in 1899, he finally returned to Taylor in England.

By this time, Crane was in very bad health, but he continued writing because, due to various debts, he needed money. Though he was hemorrhaging frequently due to tuberculosis during the spring of 1900, Crane started to work on a swashbuckling romance novel, *The O'Ruddy.* When he began to feel that he would never be well enough to finish it, he turned the first half and an outline of the last half over to his friend Robert Barr, who eventually completed the book for him. In the last few months of Crane's life, Cora Taylor was unwilling to give up on him, and took him first to Dover, and then to Badenweiler, Germany, in hopes that a change of climate would arrest his disease. This was not the case, however, and Crane died there in a sanitarium on June 5, 1900. He left many finished stories behind, and they were published posthumously in collections such as *Whilomville Stories.*

BIOGRAPHICAL/CRITICAL SOURCES:

BOOKS

Beer, Thomas, *Stephen Crane: A Study in American Letters,* Knopf, 1923.
Bergon, Frank, *Stephen Crane's Artistry,* Columbia University Press, 1975.
Berryman, John, *Stephen Crane,* Sloane, 1950.
Bloom, Harold, editor, *Modern Critical Views: Stephen Crane,* Chelsea House Publishers, 1987.
Cady, Edwin H., *Stephen Crane,* Twayne, 1980.
Dictionary of Literary Biography, Gale, Volume 12: *American Realists and Naturalists,* 1982, Volume 54: *American Poets, 1880-1945, Third Series,* 1987, Volume 78: *American Short Story Writers, 1880-1910,* 1989.
Gullason, Thomas A., editor, *Stephen Crane's Career: Perspectives and Evaluations,* New York University Press, 1972.
Hoffman, Daniel G., *The Poetry of Stephen Crane,* Columbia University Press, 1957.
Stallman, R. W., *Stephen Crane: A Biography,* Brazillier, 1968.
Twentieth-Century Literary Criticism, Gale, Volume 11, 1983, Volume 17, 1985, Volume 32, 1989.

PERIODICALS

Arena, June, 1893.
New Review, January, 1896, pp. 30-40.
Wave, July 4, 1896.*

—Sketch by Elizabeth Wenning

CRENSHAW, Charles A(ndrew) 1933-

PERSONAL: Born January 11, 1933, in Paris, TX; son of Andrew J. (a tractor agent) and Mary Leone (a homemaker; maiden name, Vorholzer) Crenshaw; married Susan Lea Light, October 24, 1979; children: Charles A. *Education:* Southern Methodist University, B.S., 1953; East Texas State University, M.S., 1955; conducted postgraduate research at Baylor University, 1955-57; University of Texas Southwestern Medical School at Dallas, M.D., 1960. *Politics:* Independent. *Religion:* Protestant.

ADDRESSES: Home—215 North Rivercrest Dr., Fort Worth, TX 76107. *Office*—1500 South Main, 303 OPC, Fort Worth, TX 76104. *Agent*—Tony Seidl, 360 East Fifty-seventh St., New York, NY 10022.

CAREER: Veteran's Administration Hospital, Dallas, TX, internist, 1960-61; University of Texas Southwestern Medical School, Dallas, research fellow in department of surgery, 1961-62, assistant clinical professor, 1969-73, associate clinical professor, 1974-77, clinical professor of surgery, 1977—; Parkland Memorial Hospital, Dallas, assistant resident, 1961-65, senior resident of surgery, 1965-66, member of junior attending staff, 1966—; John Peter Smith Hospital, Fort Worth, TX, director and chair of surgery department, 1966-92, chair emeritus of department of surgery, 1992—; St. Joseph Hospital, Fort Worth, member of attending staff, 1966—. Tarrant County Cancer Society, director, 1969-72; Department of Health, Education, and Welfare, Region VI for Emergency Medical Service, regional medical consultant in Texas, Arkansas, Louisiana, New Mexico, and Oklahoma, 1977-80. American Trauma Society, member of board of directors, 1987; Texas Southwestern Surgical Society, vice-councilor, 1987. Southwestern Surgical Congress, member, 1971—.

MEMBER: American College of Surgeons (national and North Texas chapters), American Trauma Society, American Burn Association, American Medical Association, Texas Surgical Society, Texas Historical Society, Texas Medical Society, Fort Worth Surgical Society, Tarrant County Medical Society, Tarrant County Academy of Science, Southern Medical Society, Beta Theta Phi, Phi Chi Medical Fraternity, Phi Alpha Theta, Sigma Alpha Iota, Delta Phi Alpha.

AWARDS, HONORS: National Institute of Health Research Fellow, 1964-65.

WRITINGS:

(With Jens Hansen and Gary J. Shaw) *JFK—Conspiracy of Silence,* introduced by John H. Davis, Penguin, 1992.

Contributor to medical journals, including *American Journal of Surgery, Clinical Research, Current Therapeu-*

tic Research, Southern Medical Journal, and *Surgical Forum.*

WORK IN PROGRESS: Researching the medical history of U.S. President John F. Kennedy.

SIDELIGHTS: Charles A. Crenshaw's *JFK—Conspiracy of Silence* provides a first-hand account of events associated with both the assassination of U.S. President John F. Kennedy by alleged assailant Lee Harvey Oswald, and the latter's subsequent murder by Jack Ruby. Crenshaw, who was working as a surgeon at Parkland Memorial Hospital in Dallas, Texas, at the time of the separate shootings, was part of the medical team that attempted to save both lives in November of 1963. In his book, coauthored with Jens Hansen and Gary J. Shaw, the doctor records his observations of what transpired in the trauma rooms where Kennedy and Oswald were treated, including information that contradicts the supposition that Oswald acted alone in slaying the president. In the thirty years following the incident, a number of theories have surfaced regarding a "conspiracy" to kill the president. Among those accused are officials of the Central Intelligence Agency, Cuban leader Fidel Castro, organized crime bosses, and the Soviet secret police, the KGB. Part of the reason for the mystery and confusion surrounding the incident, which some call the "Crime of the Century," concerns another conspiracy—the collusion of silence suggested in Crenshaw's book title.

JFK—Conspiracy of Silence claims that a governmental coverup did occur following the assassinations, including a quieting of the medical staff at Parkland Memorial Hospital. "Dr. Crenshaw tells us that he kept silent to protect his medical career," writes John II. Davis in the book's introduction. "Dr. Charles Baxter, director of the emergency room at Parkland, had issued an edict of secrecy just after President Kennedy was pronounced dead. No one who had attended the dying President would be permitted to talk about what he or she did or saw in Trauma Room 1." Some three decades later, however, Crenshaw does talk about what he witnessed. Most importantly, he asserts that Kennedy was not killed by two shots through the back of the head, as was claimed by the Warren Commission, the group of officials appointed by Kennedy's successor, President Lyndon Baines Johnson, to investigate the deaths and conspiracy theories. In opposition to the Commission's findings, Crenshaw announces in *JFK—Conspiracy of Silence* that he observed the president having four wounds—two in the front, one on the right side, and one in the neck. This long-awaited, eye-witness account contradicts the Commission's assertion that Oswald acted alone, shooting two bullets through the back of the president's head.

Crenshaw told *CA:* "The passage of the Boren Stokes Resolution will release all files pertaining to the assassination of President John F. Kennedy. I'm also asking for the release of KGB records from Russia."

BIOGRAPHICAL/CRITICAL SOURCES:

BOOKS

Crenshaw, Charles A., Jens Hansen, and Gary J. Shaw, *JFK—Conspiracy of Silence,* introduced by John H. Davis, Penguin, 1992.

*   *   *

CRICHTON, Robert   1925-1993

OBITUARY NOTICE—See index for *CA* sketch: Born January 29, 1925, in Albuquerque, NM; died of heart failure, March 23, 1993, in New Rochelle, NY. Writer. Crichton was perhaps best known for two best-selling novels that were made into films: *The Great Impostor,* his first novel, which was made into a 1961 movie starring Tony Curtis, and *The Secret of Santa Vittoria,* which was filmed in 1969 and starred Anthony Quinn. Crichton turned to writing after serving in World War II, for which he was awarded a Bronze Star, a Purple Heart, and a Presidential Unit Citation. He graduated from Harvard University in 1950 and undertook chicken farming for a time before becoming a full-time writer. Crichton also authored *The Camerons, The Rascal and the Road,* and *Memoirs of a Bad Soldier.*

OBITUARIES AND OTHER SOURCES:

BOOKS

The Writers Directory: 1990-1992, St. James Press, 1990.

PERIODICALS

Detroit Free Press, March 25, 1993, p. 6B.

*   *   *

CROW, Bill   1927-

PERSONAL: Born December 27, 1927, in Othello, WA; son of Harry Barnum (a sewage plant operator) and Lucile Viola (a singer and teacher; maiden name, Knepper) Crow; married Aileen Armstrong (a therapist), July 9, 1965; children: Daniel. *Education:* Attended University of Washington, 1945 and 1949.

ADDRESSES: Office—c/o Oxford University Press, 200 Madison Ave, New York, NY 10016.

CAREER: Jazz musician, 1945—; Broadway theater musician, New York City, 1975—; writer. Local 802 of the American Federation of Musicians of the United States and Canada, union official, 1983—. *Military service:* United States Army, 1946-49.

WRITINGS:

Jazz Anecdotes, Oxford University Press, 1990.
From Birdland to Broadway, Oxford University Press, 1992.

Author of column "The Band Room" in *Allegro,* 1983—. Contributor to periodicals, including *DownBeat, Jazzletter,* and *Jazz Review.* Contributor of liner notes for recordings.

SIDELIGHTS: Bill Crow has drawn on his background as a musician to produce lively accounts of the music world. His first publication, *Jazz Anecdotes,* was described by David Lancashire in the Toronto *Globe and Mail* as "the kind of book that stomp-their-feet jazz fans will eat up." The book contains quotes and stories related to many of the jazz world's luminaries, including Billie Holiday, Duke Ellington, and Miles Davis. While some of the anecdotes address serious issues such as racism, much of the book's material is humorous and has been perceived by reviewers as reflecting the buoyant nature of the musicians. Crow's second book, *From Birdland to Broadway,* is a personal memoir of his music career. The book includes humorous incidents from Crow's years as a young musician in New York City, and also recounts his contact with such notable names as Charlie Parker, Benny Goodman, and Stan Getz.

Reviewers have frequently praised Crow's work. Lancashire reported that *Jazz Anecdotes* is "full of verbal snapshots," adding that "exuberance comes through in just about every page of Crow's chronicle." Another reviewer, John Litweiler, wrote in the *Chicago Tribune* that *Jazz Anecdotes* "is certainly one for laughing out loud, something to cheer or intrigue the reader on a dark, boring day." A *Publishers Weekly* review of *From Birdland to Broadway* noted that Crow's story is "relayed with a musician's sure pacing." And Michael Horovitz, writing in the London *Times,* remarked that *Jazz Anecdotes* is "jam-packed with hundreds of . . . rattling good riffs and exhilarating laughs. Dig it!"

BIOGRAPHICAL/CRITICAL SOURCES:

PERIODICALS

Chicago Tribune, July 5, 1990.
Globe and Mail (Toronto), June 16, 1990.
Publishers Weekly, August 31, 1992, p. 61.
Times (London), January 11, 1992, pp. 32-33.
Washington Post Book World, June 10, 1990, p. 3.

CULLIFORD, Pierre 1928-1992
(Peyo)

OBITUARY NOTICE—See index for *CA* sketch: Born June 25, 1928, in Brussels, Belgium; died December 24, 1992, in Brussels. Cartoonist and author. Culliford, who worked under the name "Peyo," was the creator of the popular blue cartoon dwarfs known as the Smurfs. Culliford spent his early career as a cartoonist for a Brussels animation studio, then began a long association with *Spirou,* a weekly comic magazine, in 1954. The Smurfs first appeared as extras in Culliford's comic strip "Johan et Pirlouit," and by 1957 the cartoonist had created a separate strip starring the tiny trolls. Since then, the Smurfs have appeared in an animated feature film, a highly-rated television series, a number of television specials, and a series of recordings. The Smurfs are not only successful as entertainments but as marketable merchandise; their likeness adorns hundreds of products, including toys, games, and clothing. A Smurf theme park was even opened in France, although it closed due to financial difficulty. Among Culliford's other works are *Les Taxis Rouges, Pour faire une flute, The Smurfs and the Toyshop, The Wonderful World of Smurfs,* and *What Do Smurfs Do All Day?* His last work was a Smurfs recording titled *The Money Smurfs.*

OBITUARIES AND OTHER SOURCES:

PERIODICALS

Chicago Tribune, December 25, 1992, section 2, p. 10.
Los Angeles Times, December 25, 1992, p. A30.
New York Times, December 25, 1992, p. A29.
Times (London), January 2, 1993, p. 15.
Washington Post, December 25, 1992, p. D7.

*   *   *

CURREY, Dave 1953-

PERSONAL: Born March 10, 1953, in Bognor Regis, West Sussex, England; son of Allan (a Methodist minister) and Barbara (a homemaker; maiden name, Botham) Currey. *Education:* London University, B.A., 1976. *Politics:* "Green." *Religion:* None.

ADDRESSES: Office—Environmental Investigation Agency, 2 Pear Tree Ct., London EC1R 0DS, England. *Agent*—Doubleday UK, Transworld Publishing, 61-63 Uxbridge Rd., London W5 55A, England.

CAREER: Free-lance photographer, 1978—; lecturer on photography in London, England, and Essex, England, 1980-86; Environmental Investigation Agency, London, executive director, 1986—; writer. Work in film production for environmental documentaries, 1990—. Director of Ecodetectives Ltd.

AWARDS, HONORS: Schweitzer Medal from Animal Welfare Institute (Washington, DC), 1990.

WRITINGS:

(With Jennifer Lonsdale) *Pilot Whaling in the Faroe Islands,* Environmental Investigation Agency, Volume 1, 1985, Volume 2, 1986, Volume 3, 1987.
(With L. A. Carter) *Trade in Wildlife,* Environmental Investigation Agency, 1987.
(With Allan Thornton) *A System of Extinction,* Environmental Investigation Agency, 1989.
(With Thornton) *To Save an Elephant: The Undercover Investigation into the Illegal Ivory Trade,* Doubleday, 1991.
(With David Bowles, Peter Knights, and Ann Michels) *Flight to Extinction,* Environmental Investigation Agency, 1992.
(With Kathi Austin, Steve Galster, Ros Reeve, Thornton, and Susie Watts) *Under Fire: Elephants in the Frontline,* Environmental Investigation Agency, 1992.

WORK IN PROGRESS: Conducting environmental investigations of wild bird trade in West Africa, dolphin and whale meat smuggling in Japan, ivory and rhino horn poaching investigations, and other activities.

SIDELIGHTS: Dave Currey is a prominent environmental activist who has served as executive director of England's Environmental Investigation Agency since 1986. Among his writings is *To Save an Elephant: The Undercover Investigation into the Illegal Ivory Trade.* This work, which Currey wrote with Allan Thornton, exposes the billion-dollar, international trade in ivory. This illegal trade, which prompted the destruction of an estimated one million elephants in the 1980s alone, prospered within a sprawling network of illicit business dealers and corrupt political and religious figures. Currey and Thornton risked their lives to expose this illegal trade, and their achievement proved a contributing factor in the 1989 decision—made by the Convention of International Trade in Endangered Species—to impose what Robert Hunter, writing in the Toronto *Globe and Mail,* described as a "total ban" on the trafficking in ivory. In his review, Hunter lauded the endeavor of Currey and Thornton as "good work."

Currey told *CA:* "Writing comes as a natural part of my work as an environmental campaigner and photographer. Although I do not consider myself a writer of great literary merit, I hope to communicate important environmental issues to as wide an audience as possible. My skill comes in anticipating the needs of target audiences,

whether it be a film script for prime-time television or a book about a serious but exciting investigation, such as *To Save an Elephant.*

"Our role at the Environmental Investigation Agency has been aptly described as that of the Ecodetectives. Hardnosed and uncompromising investigations are followed by well-planned, forceful campaigning supported by the facts, film, and photos. It is through years of such work that you get involved in writing different types of literature almost daily and all are for the express purpose of communicating the issue and making others sit up and listen—and act."

BIOGRAPHICAL/CRITICAL SOURCES:

PERIODICALS

Globe and Mail (Toronto), October 19, 1991, p. C7.

*   *   *

CURTIS, Thomas Bradford   1911-1993

OBITUARY NOTICE—See index for *CA* sketch: Born May 14, 1911, in St. Louis, MO; died of congestive heart failure, January 10, 1993, in Allegan, MI. Lawyer, congressperson, presidential appointee, and author. A congressperson from Missouri for eighteen years, Curtis began his career in 1935 as a lawyer for the firm of Biggs, Curtis, Casserty & Barnes after graduating from Dartmouth College and Washington University in St. Louis. He was elected to Congress on the Republican ticket in 1951 and served on numerous committees, including the Ways and Means Committee, the Joint Economic Committee, and the National Republican Congressional Committee. Curtis ran for U.S. Senate in 1968 and 1974 but lost both elections. He became vice president and general counsel for *Encyclopaedia Britannica* in the late 1960s and the board chairman of Lafayette Federal Savings and Loan. In 1974 Curtis was a member of the Task Force on International Development and the Committee on All-Volunteer Armed Forces under President Richard Nixon. In 1975 he was appointed chair of the Federal Election Commission by President Gerald R. Ford. Curtis also served as chair of the Corporation for Public Broadcasting and as a trustee for several colleges, including Dartmouth, William Woods, Westminster, and Lincoln Institute. In the election years of 1976 and 1980, he was a principal writer of the Republican national platforms under presidential candidate Ronald Reagan. Curtis authored *Eighty-Seven Million Jobs: A Dynamic Program to End Unemployment* and *Decision Making in the U.S. Congress,* and wrote, with John Robert Vastine, Jr., *The Kennedy Round and the Future of American Trade.*

OBITUARIES AND OTHER SOURCES:

BOOKS

Who's Who in American Law, 7th edition, Marquis, 1992.

PERIODICALS

Chicago Tribune, January 17, 1993, p. 2-6.
Los Angeles Times, January 15, 1993, p. A30.

*   *   *

CZEKANOWSKA, Anna 1929-

PERSONAL: Born June 25, 1929, in Lwow, Poland; daughter of Jan (an anthropology professor) and Elzbieta (a neurologist) Czekanowski; married Antoni Kuklinski (an economist and professor); children: Jan Rafal Kuklinski. *Education:* University of Poznan, M.A., 1952; University of Warsaw, Ph.D., 1958.

ADDRESSES: Home—Warsaw 01 541, Czarnieckiego 76. Office—Institute of Musicology, University of Warsaw, Warsaw 93, Zwirki i Wigury.

CAREER: University of Warsaw, Warsaw, Poland, associate professor, 1976-86, professor, 1986—, director of the Institute of Musicology, 1976-1990, chair of department of ethnomusicology. Member of coordinating committee of European Seminar in Ethnomusicology.

MEMBER: International Musicological Society, Societe Internationale de Musique Contemporaine, International Council for Traditional Music (president of Polish national committee, 1975—), Polish Union of Composers.

AWARDS, HONORS: Ford Foundation grant, 1958-59; grant from Polish Ministry of High Education, 1962; prize of the Minister for Education, 1990.

WRITINGS:

Polish Folk Music: Slavonic Heritage, Polish Tradition, Contemporary Trends, Cambridge University Press, 1990.

Also author of a textbook and scholarly books in Polish.

WORK IN PROGRESS: A compact disc collection of Polish folk music for Atelier d'Ethnomusicologie; "On the Poetics of Folk Song," a chapter for *Cahiers de Musique Traditionelles,* edited by Laurent Aubert; preparing the lecture "Political Transformation and the Role of Musical Performance: The Case of Kazakhstan" for publication.

SIDELIGHTS: Anna Czekanowska told CA: "My interests and dedication have oscillated between the discipline of scientific thinking and art and its fugitive associations. It was rather a hard decision to leave poetry and writing to turn toward scholarship. Perhaps, under different circumstances—not being under the pressure of strong censorship—my passion could have developed differently. However, I have always had a feeling that I am not good enough for art.

"During my student years, I discovered the natural beauty of Polish folk song, both in its music and poetry. I was fascinated by this simple way of artistic transmission, its shortness, density, and richness of metaphors. This new experience to a certain extent filled the gap which existed after I left writing and the nostalgia I felt.

"My studies concentrate on Polish folk music, Slavonic music, and music of some republics of the former Soviet Union. I am in close cooperation with colleagues from the Ukraine and Belorussia. I also have had the opportunity to conduct field research in Kazakhstan, investigating among others the Uighur people in Alma-Ata. I am also deeply interested in teaching activities concentrating on preparation of university programs of ethnomusicology. Under my guidance, thirty-four students have earned M.A. degrees and six have received doctorates.

"My last book on Polish folk music is to be understood as a kind of return to my young years and to the excitement I found in the folk artifacts. It is probably difficult to discover the traces of personal engagement in the presented texts and in the methodological discussions and historical hypotheses. One needs to know the context which accompanied the situations and artifacts being collected. It is only a memory which still exists and may evoke the atmosphere of these performances and their actors reacting so spontaneously and transmitting their messages in so simple and authentic a way. I am going to remember the old women crying during presentations which reminded them of their weddings or of an orphan's fate.

"The standards of life have changed much in this time of rapid transformation—and so have the concepts, sensitivity, and aesthetic choices of contemporary people. The main dedication of *Polish Folk Music* is to create, as far as possible, the vision of that time which is over and to confront it with the reality of the contemporary world."

D

DAHL, Arlene (Carol) 1928-

PERSONAL: Born August 11, 1928, in Minneapolis, MN; daughter of Rudolph S. (an automotive executive) and Idelle (a homemaker; maiden name, Swan) Dahl; married Alexander Chrichlow Barber (divorced); married Fernando Lamas (divorced); married Christian R. Holmes III (divorced); married Alexis Lichine (divorced); married Rounsevelle W. Schaum (divorced); married Marc A. Rosen (a vice president in corporate design), July 30, 1984; children: (second marriage) Lorenzo Lamas; (third marriage) Carole Christine; (fifth marriage) Stephen Schaum. *Education:* Attended Minneapolis College of Music, 1940-45; University of Minnesota, summer courses, 1941-44; Minneapolis College of Business at the University of Minnesota; and Walker Art Gallery, summer courses, 1942-45.

ADDRESSES: Office—Dahlmark Productions, P.O. Box 116, Sparkill, NY 10976. *Agent*—Mitch Douglas, International Creative Management, 40 West 57th St., New York, NY 10019.

CAREER: Actress, designer, cosmetic executive, advertising executive, and author. Starred in children's radio show in Minneapolis at age eight; Broadway debut, *Mr. Strauss Goes to Boston,* 1946; other stage appearances include *Cyrano de Bergerac,* 1952, *The King and I, Life with Father, A Little Night Music, Blithe Spirit,* and *Applause,* 1972. Film debut, *My Wild Irish Rose,* Warner Brothers, 1947; other starring film roles include *The Bride Goes Wild,* 1948, *A Southern Yankee,* 1948, *Ambush,* 1949, *The Outriders,* 1950, *Three Little Words,* 1950, *Watch the Birdie,* 1950, *Inside Straight, Desert Legion,* 1953, *Here Come the Girls,* 1953, *Sangaree,* 1953, *Diamond Queen, Bengal Rifles, Woman's World, Slightly Scarlet,* 1956, *Journey to the Center of the Earth,* 1959, *Kisses for My President,* 1964, *Les Poneyettes, The Way to Katmandu, The Big Bankroll,*

The Land Raiders, Who Killed Max Thorne?, and *Midnight Warrior,* 1991. Television appearances include *Pepsi Cola Playhouse; Arlene Dahl's Beauty Spot,* 1965; *Arlene Dahl's Starscope,* 1980; *One Life to Live,* 1981-84; and *Arlene Dahl's Lovescopes,* 1982. Nightclub acts include performances at the Flamingo Hotel, Las Vegas, and the Latin Quarter, New York City.

Arlene Dahl Enterprises, president, 1951-75; A. N. Saab & Co., sleepwear designer, 1952-57; Kenyon & Eckhart Advertising Company, vice president, then president of Woman's World division, 1967-72; Sears, Roebuck & Co., national beauty director, 1970-75; O.M.A., fashion consultant, 1975-78; Dahlia Perfumes Inc., president, 1975-1980; Vogue Patterns, designer, 1978-85; president and chief executive officer, Dahlia Productions, 1978-81, and Dahlmark Productions, 1981—; Lasting Beauty Ltd., president and chair, 1986—. Honorary life member of Father Flannagan's Boys Town; International chair of Pearl Buck Foundation for Amerasian Children; Ambassador at Large for the City of Hope.

MEMBER: UNIFEM, Academy of Television Arts & Sciences (member of the board of governors), Academy of Motion Picture Arts & Sciences (member of New York screening committee), Le Commanderie des Bontemps du Medoc et Graves, International Platform Association, Sierra Club, National Trust Historical Preservation, Vesterheim Norwegian/American Foundation, The Film Society, Smithsonian Institute.

AWARDS, HONORS: Received eight Motion Picture Laurel awards, *Box Office* magazine, 1948-63; received Bronze Star on Hollywood's Walk of Fame, 1952; Heads of Fame awards, 1967-72 and 1980; named Woman of the Year, Advertising Club of New York City, 1969; named Best Coiffed, 1970-72; named Mother of the Year, 1979; named Today's Woman, New York Advertising Council,

1981; named One of the World's Most Elegant Women, 1982; Bronze Halo, California Motion Picture Council, 1983; Deauville Film Festival tribute, *Coup de Chapeau,* 1983; French Cinematique tribute, Paris, 1983.

WRITINGS:

Always Ask a Man, Prentice-Hall, 1965.
Your Beautyscope, twelve volumes, Pocket Books, 1969, revised, 1978.
Arlene Dahl's Secrets of Skin Care, Arlene Dahl Enterprises, 1971.
Arlene Dahl's Secrets of Hair Care, Bantam, 1978.
Beyond Beauty: A Three-Part Journey, Simon & Schuster, 1980.
Arlene Dahl's Lovescopes, Bobbs-Merrill, 1983.

Also author of internationally syndicated beauty column "Let's Be Beautiful," Chicago *Tribune*/New York News Syndicate, 1950-70. Author of "Arlene Dahl's Lucky Stars" column, Globe Communications, 1988-90, and "Arlene Dahl's Astrological Forecast." Contributing editor of magazines, including *Girl Talk, Family Circle, The Best,* and *Soap Opera Digest.*

WORK IN PROGRESS: The Corporate Body, a novel; *Lasting Beauty.*

SIDELIGHTS: Arlene Dahl told *CA:* "Heeding my father's advice, I trained for three careers: fashion design, acting, and voice. My writing career came as a surprise when the late Colonel Robert R. McCormick of the Chicago *Tribune* suggested I write a beauty column for him three times a week. I have lived abroad and speak French (and Norwegian, my native language). A woman's greatest beauty secret? Love: to love and be loved."

*   *   *

DANCE, Helen Oakley 1913-

PERSONAL: Born February 15, 1913, in Toronto, Ontario, Canada; immigrated to United States, 1933; naturalized U.S. citizen, 1943; daughter of John Peleg (in fashion) and Mary Winifred (an investor; maiden name, Simpson) Oakley; married Stanley Frank Dance (a writer), January 30, 1947; children: Terry, Rupert, Francis, Maria Lindley. *Education:* Attended Trinity College, Toronto, 1930, and Les Fougeres, Lausanne, Switzerland, 1931. *Politics:* Democrat. *Religion:* Roman Catholic.

ADDRESSES: Home and office—1745 Bittersweet Hill, Vista, CA 92084.

CAREER: Writer and entrepreneur. Free-lanced for *Chicago Herald American,* 1934-36; produced early jazz recordings for Okeh, 1935; founded Chicago Rhythm Club,

1935; worked in New York City for Mills, Inc., 1936-38, Gale, Inc., 1938, Duke Ellington, Inc., 1939, and Doubleday Literary Guild, 1939-42. Chair of Norwalk Catholic Interracial Council, 1965-75; vice-chair of Norwalk Human Relations Commission and Bridgeport Diocesan Human Relations Commission, 1970-75. *Military service:* Office of Strategic Services, 1943-45; operated with undercover agents in Algerian and Italian theaters.

WRITINGS:

Stormy Monday: The T-Bone Walker Story, Louisiana State University Press, 1987.

Contributor to a book series written by her husband, Stanley Dance. Contributor to periodicals, including *Downbeat, Tempo, Jazz Hot, Swing, JazzTimes,* and *Saturday Review.* Editor of *Dialog,* 1971-73.

WORK IN PROGRESS: Memoirs, completion expected in 1995.

SIDELIGHTS: Helen Oakley Dance is a authority on jazz and blues music. Her writings include the book *Stormy Monday: The T-Bone Walker Story,* in which she recounts the life of the prominent electric guitarist known for his contribution to and influence on electric blues. Walker was viewed as a pioneer of electric guitar music who, along with his good friend Charlie Christian, developed the instrument for popular music. While Christian lacked show business savvy and was thus labeled a jazz musician, Walker was a born showman who utilized his charisma to translate his music to a large audience. Songs such as "Call it Stormy Monday" and "T-Bone Shuffle" defined what came to be known as the Southwestern style of blues, and Walker's music greatly influenced future artists such as B. B. King, Elvis Presley, and the Allman Brothers, who would all expand upon the groundwork laid by T-Bone. Through the course of interviewing Walker for her book, Dance developed a close relationship with the legendary musician, and she brings their friendship to bear in her writing. Larry Kart, reviewing *Stormy Monday* for the *Chicago Tribune,* stated that "Walker was authentic . . . both as a musician and as a man. And Dance's biography, full of accurate social detail, not only brings him to life but also preserves . . . the sweet, richly complex friendship that developed between her and her subject." Kart also described the book as "warmhearted" and "shrewd."

Dance told *CA:* "My lifelong interest in jazz and blues inevitably led to involvement in the cause of interracial justice."

BIOGRAPHICAL/CRITICAL SOURCES:

PERIODICALS

Chicago Tribune, June 24, 1987.

DANESH, Abol Hassan 1952-

PERSONAL: Born May 14, 1952, in Gazvin, Iran; son of Abol Ghasem and Fatemeh (Hajsaidjavadi) Danesh; married Sholeh Ghedari, 1983; children: Shabnam Ayda, Sheida Anya. *Education:* Tehran University, B.A., 1974; California State University, Los Angeles, M.A., 1979; University of California, Riverside, M.A., 1981, Ph.D., 1985. *Religion:* "Monotheism (Islam)." *Avocational interests:* Mountain climbing, running, free wrestling, gardening.

ADDRESSES: Office—Sociology and Anthropology Department, University of Rhode Island, Kingston, RI 02881.

CAREER: University of California, Riverside, associate in sociology, 1981-84; Colby College, Waterville, ME, visiting assistant professor of sociology, 1985-89; University of Rhode Island, Kingston, assistant professor, 1989-92, associate professor of sociology, 1992—, member of sociology graduate program evaluation committee and urban affairs committee, both 1989—, and Community Revitalization and Economic Development Issue Group. Consultant to United Nations, 1992.

MEMBER: American Sociological Association, Eastern Sociological Society, Massachusetts Sociological Association.

WRITINGS:

Rural Exodus and Squatter Settlements in the Third World, University Press of America, 1987.
The Informal Economy: A Research Guide, Garland Publishing, 1991.
The Informal Economy and Informalization in Photography, University Press of America, 1994.

Also author of *An Introduction to a Theory of Irregular Rural-Urban Migration,* 1983. Contributor to periodicals, including *Urban Anthropology: Studies of Cultural Systems and World Economic Development, Research in Social Movements: Conflict and Change, Iranian Journal of International Affairs,* and *Research in Inequality and Social Conflict;* also contributor of articles in Farsi to *Roosena-meh-e Ete-la-at.*

WORK IN PROGRESS: The Informal Economy in Comparative Perspective, for Greenwood Press; research in informal economy, sociology, Islam, industrialization and marginalization, and development in developing countries.

SIDELIGHTS: Abol Hassan Danesh told *CA:* "I try to cling to the integrated spirit, which is general and omnipotent, in order to raise the beauty of my work from a chaotic, dim, and irrelevant activity to that of unity and comprehensiveness. Thus, I hope that by looking at the calm-ing horizon of the ocean my intellectual seasickness regenerates stability, confidence, and health in my mind and in my heart as well as in others."

*   *   *

DANNEN, Fredric 1955-

PERSONAL: Born November 13, 1955, in Manhattan, New York; son of Edwin (an educator) and Evelyn (an artist; maiden name, Lambert) Dannen. *Education:* Attended University of Paris, 1976-77; New York University, B.A., 1977. *Politics:* "Incorrect." *Religion:* "Mozart."

ADDRESSES: Home—Manhattan, NY. *Agent*—Eugene H. Winick, McIntosh & Otis, Inc., 310 Madison Ave., New York, NY 10017.

CAREER: McGraw-Hill Book Co., book editor, 1978-81; McGraw-Hill Publications Co., trainee, 1981-82; *Chemical Week,* staff writer, 1982-84; *Institutional Investor,* staff writer, 1984-86 and 1989-90; *Business Week,* copy editor, 1987; *Vanity Fair,* contributing editor, 1990-92; *New Yorker,* contributor, 1992—; free-lance writer.

MEMBER: Authors Guild.

WRITINGS:

Hit Men: Power Brokers and Fast Money inside the Music Business, Time Books/Random House, 1990.

Also contributor of articles to periodicals, including *New York Times, Rolling Stone, Barron's, Vanity Fair,* and *New Yorker.*

Hit Men has been translated into Japanese.

WORK IN PROGRESS: Nonfiction book about Chinese gangsters in America.

SIDELIGHTS: In Fredric Dannen's best-selling book, *Hit Men: Power Brokers and Fast Money inside the Music Business,* the term "hit men" describes the book's subjects—the men who are in the business of making rock and roll recordings into hits—while at the same time purposefully invoking the image of the hired guns of organized crime. The two connotations of the term indicate the prevailing perspective of the book, which leaves little doubt about the wide-spread corruption in the rock industry. "It is a system without redeeming qualities in a world without character or ethics," wrote a *Washington Post Book World* reviewer of *Hit Men.* "At the end of the story you feel as if you need a long bath, if not defumigation."

According to Dannen, the music industry's power brokers are men who understand the dollar very well, but have little or no interest in music. One of the pioneers of the rock industry, Morris Levy, founder of Birdland and Roulette

Records, was known to have connections with organized crime and was convicted in 1988 of conspiracy to commit extortion. Prior to his death in 1990, Levy talked to Dannen about the business side of rock music, providing the author with numerous anecdotes of shady dealings. Dannen also profiles some of the moguls of the next generation of music industry executives, including Walter Yetnikoff, president of CBS Records, Clive Davis, also of CBS Records, and Frank Dileo, a former bookie who was at one time Michael Jackson's manager. Although these contemporary industry leaders are not mobsters like Levy, "Dannen suggests that a man like Levy is still the real role model for the lean-and-hungry lawyers and MBAs who pick the hits nowadays," observed *Los Angeles Times Book Review* contributor Jonathan Kirsch. A *Washington Post Book World* reviewer remarked, "In a business heavily geared to young people and dependent on women and blacks both as artists and as consumers, these dealers are middle-aged and white and male. They know almost nothing about music . . . and are if anything contemptuous of those who make it; their sole interest is in the accumulation of wealth and power, and there seems precious little they won't do to acquire it."

But while profiling the men in charge, Dannen also demonstrates that the music industry's corrupt practices are due as much to thirty years of corporate evolution as to the personalities of industry leaders. In the 1950s smaller record labels competed freely with the large labels. At that time, record company representatives regularly bribed radio disc jockeys—who were then responsible for the selection of recordings to be given air time—to play their music. This system, called "payola," was available to large and small labels alike. When the practice of payola came into the public eye in 1960, disc jockeys were quickly relieved of their decision-making duties, and radio station program directors took over the selection of music to be aired.

Under the management of program directors, payola became a multi-million dollar business. The large record companies hired independent promoters to persuade radio stations to give air time to their recordings. Dannen notes that in 1982 alone CBS Records spent $10 million on promoters. Since the cost of high-powered independent promoters was too great for smaller record labels, the larger labels were able to take over the market. In turn, the independent promoters banded together in a bloc known as the Network. The Network had enough power to ensure that only the records it promoted would ever receive radio air time, and was thus able to procure more and more money from the large record companies. *Nation* critic Gene Santoro asserted that, with this system of institutionalized payola, the Network and the large record companies achieved almost complete control over the music heard by the American public. Without the influence of the musical interests and idiosyncracies of individual disc jockeys, musical trends were strictly determined in terms of financial gain. Santoro observed that "radio has become progressively stratified over the past two decades into narrow-band formats dictated by program directors and programming consultants, and . . . experimental, pioneering and even just-left-of-center sounds have largely disappeared." Dannen goes further in his indictment of the industry, suggesting that its record promotion tactics are often highly suspicious and frequently linked to organized crime. Kirsch summarized: "According to Dannen, the star-making machinery that has literally given us the soundtrack of our lives is brutal, exploitive, ruthless, venal and, at times, outrightly corrupt."

Critical reception to *Hit Men* was enthusiastic, particularly in regard to Dannen's anecdotal style of presenting his well-documented material. *New York Times Book Review* contributor Robert Christgau, although criticizing Dannen for some holes in his knowledge of rock and roll, praised the author's significant insight into the business world and his "knack for the telling quote and a healthy appetite for the juicy story." *New York Times* contributor Stephen Holden concluded, "*Hit Men* is written in a raw, punchy prose style that is entirely appropriate for describing such a tough, knockabout milieu. . . . Anyone with more than a passing interest in the inner workings of the industry will be enthralled by the juicy tales [Dannen] has to tell."

Dannen told *CA:* "I got into journalism by mistake. I think my real ambition is to be a playwright."

BIOGRAPHICAL/CRITICAL SOURCES:

PERIODICALS

Los Angeles Times Book Review, July 29, 1990, p. 1.
Nation, September 10, 1990, pp. 251-52.
New York Times, August 27, 1990.
New York Times Book Review, August 12, 1990, pp. 11-12.
Publishers Weekly, June 22, 1990, p. 40.
Washington Post Book World, July 22, 1990, p. 3.

—*Sketch by Sonia Benson*

* * *

D'ANTONIO, Michael 1955-

PERSONAL: Born May 11, 1955, in Portsmouth, NH; son of Albert (a construction executive) and Patricia (a homemaker; maiden name, Barr) D'Antonio; married Toni Raiten (a psychotherapist), June 3, 1978; children: Elizabeth Allyn, Amy Margaret. *Education:* University of

New Hampshire, B.A., 1977. *Politics:* Independent. *Religion:* Roman Catholic.

ADDRESSES: Home—Farmingville, NY. *Agent*—Philip Spitzer, 780 9th Ave., New York, NY 10019.

CAREER: Dover Democrat, Dover, NH, reporter, 1976-77; *Portland Press Herald,* Portland, ME, reporter, 1977-78, correspondent in Washington, DC, 1978-83; *Newsday,* New York City, writer, 1983-90.

AWARDS, HONORS: Pulitzer Prize for journalism (with others), 1984, for *Newsday*'s coverage of the Baby Jane Doe case; First Amendment Award, Sigma Delta Chi, 1986; Alicia Patterson Foundation fellowship, 1987.

WRITINGS:

Fall from Grace: The Failed Crusade of the Christian Right, Farrar, Straus, 1990.
Heaven on Earth: Dispatches from America's Spiritual Frontier, Crown, 1992.
Atomic Harvest, Crown, 1993.

Contributor to periodicals, including *Boston Globe Magazine, Boston Magazine, Christian Science Monitor, Esquire, Los Angeles Times Magazine,* and *Washington Post.* Contributing editor of *Child,* 1988—.

SIDELIGHTS: Michael D'Antonio is a former journalist who covered religion for *Newsday* before he began writing books full-time in 1990. His first work, *Fall from Grace: The Failed Crusade of the Christian Right,* documents the rise of Christian conservatism as a force in American politics. D'Antonio structures the book around an examination of television evangelist Pat Robertson's failed bid for the Republican party's presidential nomination in 1988. In addition to assessing the Robertson candidacy, D'Antonio provides an overview of Christian conservatism and its development, particularly as it occurred in the American South and Southwest. D'Antonio also charts the exploits of other noted, and notorious, television evangelists, including Jimmy Swaggart, a preacher who was photographed consorting with a prostitute, and Jim Bakker, a church leader who was accused of sexual misconduct and convicted of financial impropriety. In his *Washington Post* review of *Fall from Grace,* Edwin M. Yoder, Jr., contended that D'Antonio's skepticism sometimes prohibits profound reflection on the subject, but the reviewer added that the book is nonetheless "good reporting."

In his next book, *Heaven on Earth: Dispatches from America's Spiritual Frontier,* D'Antonio reflects on the ethics and values held by people involved in the New Age movement, which stresses unconventional means toward improved health and religious fulfillment. The volume includes accounts of D'Antonio's meetings with faith healers, clairvoyants, and self-professed spiritual business operators. Reviewers noted that some of the book's subjects appear to be mere opportunists and con artists. Nonetheless, John Doyle, writing in the Toronto *Globe and Mail,* found *Heaven on Earth* a useful "overview" of New Age culture. D'Antonio told *CA* that his third book, *Atomic Harvest,* is "an account of the disintegration of America's atomic weapons complex."

D'Antonio also commented: "I am interested in journalism as current history. Rather than focus on the famous, I prefer to illuminate the lives of everyday people who struggle with momentous issues. I am fascinated by the democratic process and inspired by citizens who become part of the process and affect events in meaningful ways. This may be traced to my childhood on a small island off the New Hampshire coast where six hundred residents used town meetings to come together and determine their own futures."

BIOGRAPHICAL/CRITICAL SOURCES:

PERIODICALS

Globe and Mail (Toronto), April 18, 1992, p. C6.
Washington Post, February 1, 1990.

*   *   *

DASCAL, Marcelo 1940-

PERSONAL: Born November 11, 1940, in Sao Paulo, Brazil; son of Adolfo (owner of a furniture shop) and Sarah Ita (a secretary; maiden name, Schwartz) Dascal; married Varda Ghilscher (a dance therapist), February, 1964; children: Hagit Weichendler-Dascal, Shlomit, Tamar. *Education:* Attended University of Sao Paulo, 1963-64; Universite de Provence, Certificat d'Etudes Superieures en Linguistique Generale, 1965; Hebrew University of Jerusalem, Ph.D., 1973. *Politics:* "Left." *Religion:* "I keep some Jewish traditions, non-observantly." *Avocational interests:* Music, skiing, politics, traveling.

ADDRESSES: Home—26 Hamaagal St., Kiryat Ono 55492, Israel. *Office*—Tel Aviv University, Department of Philosophy, 69978 Tel Aviv, Israel.

CAREER: University of Sao Paulo, Sao Paulo, Brazil, instructor, 1964; Hebrew University of Jerusalem, Jerusalem, Israel, researcher and lecturer, 1967-72; Ben Gurion University of the Negev, Beer-Sheva, Israel, 1967-76, began as lecturer, became senior lecturer, chair of the department of philosophy, 1969-73; Tel Aviv University, Tel Aviv, Israel, began as instructor, became professor of philosophy, 1967—; Universidade Estadual de Campinas, Campinas, Brazil, professor, 1974-85; Young Persons Institute for Arts and Sciences, Tel Aviv, teacher of logic, philosophy, and humor for gifted children, 1975-92; writer. University of Massachusetts, visiting lecturer, 1973-74; University of California at Berkeley, visiting associate professor of philosophy, 1980; researcher and educator at various institutions, including Technische University of Berlin, Universite de Provence, and Universidad Autonoma de Mexico. Member of the executive committee of Israel Philosophical Association, 1976-79; founding member and member of the executive committee of Sociedad de Filosofia Ibero Americana (SOFIA).

MEMBER: International Association of Semiotic Studies, International Pragmatics Association (member of the consultation board), International Society for the Study of Argumentation (representative for Israel), International Network for Economic Method (founding member), International Society for Humor Studies, The Jerusalem Philosophical Society, Cognitive Science Society, Society for Iberian and Latin American Thought, Leibniz Gesellschaft, Societe d'Histoire et Epistemologie des Sciences du Language (member of the international committee).

AWARDS, HONORS: Fellowships from French Government, 1964 and 1965, Indiana University, 1973, and Netherlands Institute for Advanced Studies, 1985 and 1986. Research grants from Hebrew University of Jerusalem, 1967, 1968, and 1979, Israel Academy of Sciences, 1972, 1976, and 1979, and Tel Aviv University, 1991 and 1992.

WRITINGS:

Filosofia das Ciencias (title means "Philosophy of Science"), Editora do Gremio da Faculdade de Filosofia da Universidade de Sao Paulo, 1964.

La Semiologie de Leibniz (title means "Leibniz's Semiotics"), Aubier Montaigne, 1978.

Pragmatics and the Philosophy of Mind, Volume 1: *Thought in Language,* John Benjamins, 1983.

Leibniz: Language, Signs, and Thought, John Benjamins, 1987.

EDITOR

(With A. Parush) *Harationali Vehairatzionali* (title means "The Rational and the Irrational"), Ben Gurion University of the Negev, 1975.

Fundamentos Metodologicos da Linguistica (title means "Methodological Foundations of Linguistics"), four volumes, Sao Paulo & Carupinas, 1978-82.

(With M. Brinker and D. Nesher) *Baruch de Spinoza: Kovetz ma'amarim al mishnato* (title means "Baruch de Sinoza: A Collection of Essays on His Thought"), University Publishing Projects, 1979.

(With J. Gracia, E. Rabossi, and E. Villanueva) *Philosophical Analysis in Latin America,* D. Reidel, 1984.

Dialogue: An Interdisciplinary Approach, John Benjamins, 1985.

(With the cooperation of Oscar Zimmermann) M. Buber, *Sobre Comunidade,* (title means "On Community"), Perspectiva, 1987.

(With O. Gruengard) *Knowledge and Politics: Case Studies in the Relationship between Epistemology and Political Philosophy,* Westview Press, 1989.

(With A. Cohen) *The Institution of Philosophy: A Discipline in Crisis?,* Open Court, 1989.

Conhecimento, Linguageui, Ideologia (title means "Knowledge, Language, Ideology"), Perspectiva, 1989.

Cultural Relativism and Philosophy: North and Latin American Perspectives, Brill, 1991.

(With D. Gerhardus, K. Lorenz, and G. Meggle) *Handbuch der Sprachphilosophie,* two volumes, De Gruyter, in press.

(With E. Yakira) *Leibniz and Adam,* University Publishing Projects, in press.

WORK IN PROGRESS: Pragmatics and the Philosophy of Mind, Volume 2: *Language in Thought,* to be published by John Benjamins; *From Bacon to the Ideologues: Language and Thought in the Classical Age,* two volumes of essays; *Interpretation and Understanding.* Researching philosophy of language, epistemology, history of ideas (seventeenth and eighteenth centuries), linguistics (pragmatics and semantics), cognitive science, philosophy of mind, and theory of argumentation.

SIDELIGHTS: Marcelo Dascal told *CA:* "Writing for me is a paradoxical enterprise for many reasons. Being a member of academia, I had to publish papers, books, etc., in order to ensure my promotions and prestige. Now that my career is more than ensured and I enjoy some international prestige, I find that I have to write (and publish) in order—how could I put it?—to express myself, to share with others those thoughts that seem to me important. Actually, it is much more than that: I am one of those who believes that thinking and expressing, reflecting and formulating, are not two separate things. Whenever I am unable to write down what I think, I have the strange feeling that I don't really think it. On one of my birthdays, I received a pencil with the inscription: 'I write, therefore I exist.' I guess this is quite true of me. I simply feel alive when I write, be it a scholarly paper, a scribbled note, a book, a letter, a page in my diary, a message in electronic mail. Without writing, experience is fleeting, for me. In writing it acquires a more durable quality, perhaps because it becomes referable. And yet—and here the paradox arises—I am aware that there is simply too much writing (and publishing) going on in the world. As a matter of justice, if I make demands upon others' time for reading my stuff, I feel I ought to be willing to read theirs as well. As everybody else at the present time, however, I am absolutely overwhelmed by the amount of publications that reach me, even without my actively seeking them. And I feel not only unjust in not reading all of it, but also frustrated, because my curiosity is boundless. Many years ago I bought the *Encyclopaedia Britannica,* with the definite intention of reading *all* of it. I earnestly began to do it, but finally gave up. I remember that when I was quite young I made a calculation of how many books I could read throughout my whole life. I assumed then that I could read about thirty books per year (no doubt an optimistic assumption, based on the amount of free time a youngster with no financial and professional obligations has), and reached the total amount of about two thousand books in my whole reading life. I am sure I did not keep the pace up to now, so I will fall short of that number. But does it really matter, given the enormous amount of material there is to read? If so, why to add to this? Why increase the frustration of other readers by writing more? Is it legitimate to do it just for 'expressing oneself'? These are questions that really trouble me. Perhaps they belong to a topic that should be called 'the ethics of writing.' I confess I am considering submitting a proposal to my university to change the academic evaluation procedure, so as not to encourage publishing as much as is done today. Perhaps people should receive prizes for refraining from publishing when they are not absolutely sure that what they write is new and inspiring. I also confess that, as an editor of two journals, I am applying ever more stringent criteria to accept papers; in fact, I am inclined to believe that a journal's evaluation depends perhaps more on the proportion of papers it rejects than on the quality of those it actually publishes.

"There is another paradoxical aspect in my life as a writer. It simply doesn't come easy to me. I suffer a lot when I write. It is as if I had to undergo the pain of child birth for every word, sentence, paragraph, paper. This suffering goes on for about three quarters of the text I am writing, i.e., until I begin to 'see the end.' At that point I get—from God knows where—new energies, which lead me through the end. And then the pleasure is really great, and all the suffering is immediately forgotten. The mind mysteriously clears up, and begins to think of the next project, as if it was eager to suffer again. Except for a few short stories, I have written so far mainly scholarly books and articles, none of which has yet 'made it' to become a best-seller or even a widely quoted book among scholars. As a scholar, I have still to write my magnum opus. And I will do it. But I am also interested in conveying whatever insights I may have gathered throughout my thinking life to a wider audience, and I think the novel is the way to achieve this. I had naively assumed that writing a novel would be much easier. Now that I have made the first steps into it, I realize it may even be more difficult. Never mind. It will be done."

DATES, Jannette L.

PERSONAL: Married to Victor Dates (an assistant professor). *Education:* Coppin State College, B.S.; Johns Hopkins University, M.Ed.; University of Maryland at College Park, Ph.D.

ADDRESSES: Home—2107 Carterdale Rd., Baltimore, MD 21209. *Office*—School of Communications, Howard University, Washington, DC 20059.

CAREER: Baltimore City Public School System, Baltimore, MD, classroom demonstration teacher, 1958-63, television demonstration teacher, 1964-69, producer and writer of elementary and secondary school telecourses, 1964-71; Goucher College, Baltimore, instructor in department of education, 1970-72; Morgan State University, Baltimore, instructor in department of education, 1970-72, instructor, 1972-77, assistant professor in department of communication and theater arts, 1977-80, coordinator of university television projects, 1973-80; Howard University, Washington, DC, assistant professor in department of radio, television, and film and sequence coordinator for broadcast management/policy, 1981-85; Coppin State College, Baltimore, associate professor in department of languages, literature, and journalism and director of video production service, 1985-87; Howard University, associate dean for educational affairs in school of communications, 1987-92, associate professor in department of radio, television and film, 1990—, member of numerous curriculum and executive committees; California State University, Dominguez Hills, Young, Gifted and Black Distinguished Resident Scholar, 1991. Executive producer of *North Star* (television series), 1971-73; Baltimore Cable Television Commission, commissioner and chairperson of education task force, 1979-81; Baltimore Cable Access Corporation, president, 1982-86, vice-president, 1986-88; Mayor's Cable Advisory Commission, member and chairperson of education task force, 1988-90; Mayor's Cable Communications Commission, member, 1990—. Speaker and panelist for numerous television programs, including *Square Off,* 1977-89; writer and narrator of various short documentaries; member of Baltimore City Cable Communication Commission.

MEMBER: National Communications Association, Speech Communications Association, Broadcast Education Association (chair, leadership challenge division, 1987-90; multicultural studies division, vice-chair, 1990-92, chair, 1992-93), Association for Education in Journalism and Mass Communication, National Black Media Coalition.

AWARDS, HONORS: Research grant, Maryland Committee for the Humanities, 1980; co-recipient, with William Barlow, of Gustavus Meyer National Award for best book written in the U.S. in the area of human rights, 1992, for *Split Image: African Americans in the Mass Media;* Freedom Forum Media Studies Center fellow, Columbia University, 1992-93.

WRITINGS:

(Editor with William Barlow, and contributor) *Split Image: African Americans in the Mass Media,* Howard University Press, 1990.

Contributor to books, including *Ethnic Images in American Film and Television,* edited by Randall Miller, Balch Institute, 1978; *Mass Media and Society,* edited by Alan Wells, D. C. Heath, 1987; *The Encyclopedia of African American History and Culture,* Macmillan, in press. Contributor to periodicals, including *Film History, Crisis, Philadelphia Inquirer, Journalism Quarterly, Journal of Communication,* and *Journal of Broadcasting.*

SIDELIGHTS: Jannette L. Dates and coeditor William Barlow received the Gustavus Meyer award for their book, *Split Image: African Americans in the Mass Media. Washington Post Book World* reviewer Salim Muwakkil considered this book the first comprehensive examination of the treatment of black Americans in the music, film, radio, television, news, and advertising industries. Dates and Barlow explain in the introduction that the book explores the media's stereotypical and discriminatory representation of black Americans and uses "the cultural prism of race in order to assess the development of the American mass media in the twentieth century." The book also traces the limited participation of black Americans in mainstream media and their response to the stereotypes perpetuated by it. Muwakkil called *Split Image* a "virtual treasure trove of historical jewels" and an indispensable source of information for students of American history and media.

BIOGRAPHICAL/CRITICAL SOURCES:

PERIODICALS

Washington Post Book World, July 29, 1990, pp. 1, 10.

* * *

DAVIS, Julia 1900(?)-1993
(F. Draco)

OBITUARY NOTICE—See index for *CA* sketch: Full name Julia Davis Adams, born July 23, 1900 (one source says 1904), in Clarkesburg, WV; died January 30, 1993, in Ranson, WV. Social worker, journalist, and author. Davis composed works that often focused on the history of West Virginia and her family's role in that history. In 1925, she began her career as a reporter for the Associated Press in New York City and later worked as an agent for New York's State Charities Aid Association. Davis also served as head of the adoption service of the Children's Aid Society from 1962 to 1965. Davis wrote *The Devil's Church* and *Cruise with Death* under the pseudonym F. Draco. Among her other books are *Sword of the Vikings, The Shenandoah,* and *A Valley and a Song.* Davis also wrote *The Anvil,* a play.

OBITUARIES AND OTHER SOURCES:

BOOKS

International Authors and Writers Who's Who, 12th edition, International Biographical Centre, 1991.

PERIODICALS

New York Times, February 2, 1993, p. A17.

* * *

DAWLEY, Alan 1943-

PERSONAL: Born December 18, 1943, in Milwaukee, WI; son of Clarence and Thelma Dawley; married Katherine Louise Wechsler, September 10, 1966; children: Aaron, Evan. *Education:* Attended University of Aix-en-Provence, 1962, and University of Wisconsin—Madison, 1964; Oberlin College, B.A. (cum laude), 1965; Harvard University, M.A., 1966, Ph.D., 1971.

ADDRESSES: Home—123 East Marshall Ave., Langhorne, PA 19047.

CAREER: Mississippi Free Press, Jackson, editor, 1963-64; Trenton State College, Trenton, NJ, assistant professor, 1970-78, associate professor, 1979-84, professor of history, 1984—. Pennsylvania State University, member of Union Leadership Academy, 1974; Trenton State College, director of Bicentennial Institute on the American Revolution, 1975; Worcester College of Higher Education, exchange professor, 1976-77; Princeton University, fellow of Davis Center, 1977-78, visiting professor, autumn, 1991, and autumn, 1992; University of Virginia, Jacobus Lecturer, 1979; University of Warwick, visiting senior lecturer at Centre for Social History, 1982-83; New York University, visiting member of graduate faculty, 1986; guest lecturer at Brown University, City University of New York, Columbia University, University of Pennsylvania, Rutgers University, State University of New York at Binghamton, McGill University, Concordia University, Oxford University, Cambridge University, University of Sussex, University of Birmingham, University of Manchester, and University of Bremen.

MEMBER: Organization of American Historians (chair of ABC-Clio Prize Committee, 1993-94), American Historical Association, Society for the Study of Labour History, Pennsylvania Labor History Society, Phi Beta Kappa, Phi Kappa Phi.

AWARDS, HONORS: Woodrow Wilson fellow, 1965-66; Bancroft Prize, 1977, for *Class and Community;* National Endowment for the Humanities, grant, 1980, fellow, 1986-87, 1993-94; Beveridge grant, American Historical Association, 1982; grant from Hagley Library, 1984; grants from Mellon Foundation and Murray Research Center, for Schlesinger Library, 1985, 1986; Distinguished Research Award, Trenton State College, 1987-89.

WRITINGS:

Class and Community: The Industrial Revolution in Lynn, Harvard University Press, 1976.
(Coeditor and contributor) *Working for Democracy: American Workers from the Revolution to the Present,* University of Illinois Press, 1985.
Struggles for Justice: Social Responsibility and the Liberal State, Harvard University Press, 1991.

Work represented in anthologies, including *American Working Class Culture,* edited by Milton Cantor, 1979. Contributor of articles and reviews to history journals. Member of editorial board, *Labor History,* 1979—.

WORK IN PROGRESS: American Democracy and World Affairs, 1918-1920, a study of the U.S. response to war, revolution, and social change.

*   *   *

DAY, Neil (Atherton) 1945-

PERSONAL: Born March 12, 1945, in Melbourne, Australia; son of Frank Melville (a manager) and Marjorie Myrtle (a homemaker) Day; married in 1969; wife's name, Janet Elizabeth (a farmer); children: Ellen Marjorie Alice, Katharine Elizabeth. *Education:* University of Melbourne, B.A. (with honors), 1968, Diploma of Education, 1969; University of Essex, M.A. (with first class honors), 1976, Diploma of Social Science Data Analysis, (with first class honors), 1979.

ADDRESSES: Home—"Ripley Vale," Balliang, Victoria 3340, Australia. *Office*—Centre for Programme Evaluation, University of Melbourne, Parkville, Victoria 3052, Australia.

CAREER: St. Margaret's School, Seria, Brunei, teacher, 1969; State College of Victoria at Melbourne (now Melbourne College of Advanced Education), Melbourne, Australia, lecturer, 1970-76, Research Associate Centre for Programme Evaluation, lecturer, 1980-83; University of Essex, Essex, England, research officer, 1977-80; University of Manchester, Manchester, England, research as-

sociate, 1983-87; University of Melbourne, Centre for Programme Evaluation, research associate and lecturer in political and computer sciences, 1987—. Conductor of workshops; worked as a consultant on various projects, including Institute for Policy Studies, London; Working Group on Education for Science and Technology, Victoria; Food Inquiry of the Regulation Review Unit, Department of Industry, Technology, and Resources, Government of Victoria; and 'Rural Health Better Health' projects, Lodden District Health Council and Commonwealth Department of Community Services and Health. Designer of research proposals and papers.

WRITINGS:

British Election Study, 1979: Survey Design, Sample and Fieldwork, University of Essex, 1981.
(With Clifford K. Malcolm) *Youth Employment and Unemployment in an Outer Suburban Area: A Survey of Employers,* Melbourne State College, 1982.
(With Malcolm) *Youth Employment and Unemployment: An Overview,* Melbourne State College, 1982.
(With Gerald R. Elsworth and others) *From School to Tertiary Study,* Australian Council for Educational Research, 1983.
(With John M. Owen) *Back to School: The Way Forward?,* Australian Government Publishing Service, 1984.
(With Elsworth and F. Naylor) *Careers Guidance and Counselling,* Australian Government Publishing Service, 1985.
(With D. C. Littlewood) *Evaluation of the Business License Centre,* Small Business Development Corporation, 1990.
(With G. Parry and G. Moyser) *Participation and Democracy in Britain,* Cambridge University Press, 1991.
(With Ivor M. Crewe and Anthony D. Fox) *The British Electorate, 1963-1987,* Cambridge University Press, 1991.

WORK IN PROGRESS: Researching health promotion evaluations.

SIDELIGHTS: Neil Day told *CA:* "My writing comes from involvement in research and evaluation. Involvement in research resulted from a series of happenings rather than any coherent career path. I've always been an unmitigated dilettante in interest: bees, politics, opera, cabinetmaking, church architecture, electric fences, tropical fish, collecting books, and ancient agricultural machinery just to mention a few. I usually lack the persistence and application to sustain these interests past the initial phase of wonderment and discovery.

"Music for instance: I always hoped there would be a musical instrument I could just pick up and play with an expressiveness flowing from innate sensibility, without enduring the tedium required for technical virtuosity. I fondly hoped that something elegant and simple, lacking any complex buttons, pistons, frets, or keys would fit the bill. Imagine my surprise when it turned out to be a DEC 10 computer rather than a trombone!

"About halfway through my career, I made the astonishing discovery that I could make computers (about which I previously knew nothing) do amazing things with surprisingly little effort or application. I was working as a politics lecturer then, so this discovery soon led to research into electoral behavior, surveys into political attitudes and the like. As I happened, at the time, to be in one of the few countries prepared to lavish sufficient funds on academics to let this type of research happen, I stayed on in England and worked on British Election Study.

"After returning to Australia, I started working in program evaluation, mainly as a result of a fortuitous lunchtime encounter. As far as I can work out, evaluation is the application of research techniques to all manner of different problems with the object of solving them rather than providing entertainment for academics. The range of issues is so inexhaustible and varied that it is just too tempting for an intellectual butterfly like me to resist.

"For example: why, at one stage, did so few students completing secondary education accept places in tertiary education? Answer: they had better things to do!

"The Australian government used to give money to adults who had left school early and wanted to return to secondary study. Should the program be continued since so many withdrew from the funding scheme? Answer: a trick question. Actually, most of them did succeed academically, it's just that many had to quit the program to do so!

"Can government programs help a small rural community devastated by falling commodity prices and escalating costs? Answer: yes, if the program development and delivery involves the extensive participation of local people, even at the cost of offending some outside experts.

"One final question: Am I really the sort of writer who deserves space in American reference books? Answer: if you're reading this, you won't have to ask!"

*   *   *

DeGRAZIA, Emilio   1941-

PERSONAL: Born February 16, 1941, in Dearborn, MI; son of Carmine (a factory worker) and Esterina (a homemaker; maiden name, Posa) DeGrazia; married Candace Rasmussen (divorced, 1978); married Monica Drealan (a writer), 1986; children: (first marriage) Emily; (second marriage) Leah Esterina. *Education:* Albion College,

B.A., 1963; Ohio State University, M.A., 1965, Ph.D., 1970. *Politics:* Liberal. *Religion:* Christian.

ADDRESSES: Home—211 West Wabasha, Winona, MN 55987. *Office*—Department of English, Winona State University, Winona, MN 55987.

CAREER: Winona State University, Winona, MN, assistant professor, 1969-79, associate professor, 1979-86, professor of English, 1986—; writer. Founder and codirector of Great River Conference at Winona State University, 1983-86. Writers-in-the-Schools program, member of advisory board, 1979-84. Wisconsin Literary Society Awards, judge, 1978; member of literature panels for Minnesota Arts Board, 1976-80 and 1986-87, Southeast Minnesota Regional Arts Council, 1989-92, and Ohio Arts Council, 1989.

MEMBER: Poets and Writers, The Loft.

AWARDS, HONORS: Fellowships from Minnesota State Arts Board, 1975 and 1992; honorable mention for fiction, *Kansas Quarterly,* 1980, for "Lanternlight," and 1989, for "Translations"; Loft-McKnight Award, The Loft, 1983, for fiction; named one of "best small press books of 1984," *Library Journal,* 1984, and Writer's Choice Award, 1985, both for *Enemy Country;* Lake Superior Contemporary Writers Award, The Depot (Duluth), 1985; Minnesota Voices Project award, 1991, and Minnesota Book Award nomination, New Rivers Press, 1992, both for *Billy Brazil.*

WRITINGS:

Enemy Country (short stories), New Rivers Press, 1984.
(With others) *Today's Gift* (prose meditations), Hazelden, 1985.
Billy Brazil (novel), New Rivers Press, 1991.
The Savior of America (novel), Guernica Editions, in press.

Also author of "Lanternlight" and "Translations." Work represented in anthologies, including *Twenty-five Minnesota Writers,* edited by Seymour Yesner, Nodin, 1979; *The Minnesota Experience,* edited by Jean Ervin, Adams, 1979; *Likely Stories,* edited by Bruce McPherson, Treacle, 1981; *Literature and Lore of the Sea,* edited by Patricia Anne Carlson, Amsterdam, 1985; and *A Perimeter of Light,* edited by Vivian Balfour, New Rivers Press, 1992.

Contributor to periodicals, including *Carleton Miscellany, Colorado Quarterly, Kansas Quarterly, Louisville Review, Madison Review, Northfield, North Dakota Review, Other Voices, Samizdat, Santa Clara Review, South Dakota Review, Tampa Bay Review, Touchstone,* and *Twin Tower Journal.* Editorial assistant for *North Country Anvil,* 1973-75; founding editor of *Great River Review,* 1977-80 and 1983-85.

WORK IN PROGRESS: The Witch of San Matteo, a novel; *Three Men: A Threnody,* a novel; *Seventeen Grams Worth of Soul,* short stories.

SIDELIGHTS: Emilio DeGrazia has won recognition as both a short story writer and novelist. In 1984 he released his first book, *Enemy Country,* which contains eleven stories related to the Vietnam War. Among the notable tales in the volume are "The Enemy," wherein a lone American soldier becomes involved in sex and violence; "The Mask," in which U.S. troops uncover evidence of an unsettling atrocity; "The Sniper," in which a soldier realizes a surprising measure of contentment while ensconced in a tree; and "Brothers of the Tiger," wherein an old Vietnamese man travels through the war-torn countryside to visit his brother near Saigon. Walter H. Howerton, Jr., writing in the *Minneapolis Star and Tribune,* described "Brothers of the Tiger" as "a tale of patience, endurance, beauty and struggle." He added that in *Enemy Country* DeGrazia "creates a series of fictions which respond to the dark privacy of the Vietnam experience, and it is in the powerful creation of dark, private spaces that the book succeeds." Another reviewer, David Hartung, reported in the *St. Paul Pioneer Press/Dispatch* that the tales in *Enemy Country* "vividly distill the images of Vietnam that so many of us bear today." Hartung hailed *Enemy Country* as a "magnificent" collection and concluded that the stories provide "masterful illuminations of what we have come to call the Vietnam Experience."

DeGrazia is also author of *Billy Brazil,* a novel about the bond that develops between an English professor and a schizophrenic student who longs to live in Brazil, a place where, he believes, he will finally gain knowledge and acceptance. The professor eventually realizes that his nine-year-old daughter has become the subject of the student's considerable scrutiny and interest. Although somewhat concerned for his daughter's well-being, the professor nonetheless maintains a relationship with the mentally-ill student. A *Bloomsbury Review* critic called *Billy Brazil* "a finely constructed first novel" and noted DeGrazia's literary "versatility," while *St. Paul Pioneer Press* reviewer Abigail Davis found *Billy Brazil* "compelling" and acknowledged DeGrazia's "masterful" execution in uncovering the student's illness. She added that the novel is "alive with suspense" and that it "touches the nerve endings, as well as the heart."

DeGrazia told *CA:* "I tend to be a persistent and disciplined writer who believes that writers of books should spend a lot of time reading and that teaching helps one discover what needs to be said. I'm driven by fairly old-fashioned ideas about the writing life: That one becomes a writer by discovering that one has something to 'say'— that the written result should be at once story, sermon, and song; that one should genuinely want to communicate, present a vision capable of evoking passionate response; that one serves an apprenticeship, goes through a long process of learning how structures and language make sense; that art results when passionate vision is married to expert craft; and that good art has one legitimate *raison d'etre,* the clarification of life for the purpose of enhancing it.

"Getting published is very difficult. I'm somewhat convinced that some of my very best work may never see publication. So why write? Because it is what I have been trained, perhaps doomed, to do; because I want to leave a record, pages toward a life and history of some sort, for at least a few. I am indeed one of the fortunate ones. I actually receive a salary for doing what I love and must do: read, teach, and write."

BIOGRAPHICAL/CRITICAL SOURCES:

PERIODICALS

Bloomsbury Review, April/May, 1992.
Minneapolis Star and Tribune, April 28, 1985.
St. Paul Pioneer Press, March 15, 1992.
St. Paul Pioneer Press/Dispatch, September 15, 1984.

*   *   *

DeLEON, Richard Edward 1942-

PERSONAL: Born August 18, 1942, in Long Beach, CA; son of John DeLeon (in the U.S. Army) and Bernice June (Shaw) Lyon; married Phyllis Ellen Hoos (marriage ended); married Arlene Petersen (an instructional assistant), June 26, 1982; children: Manya Lillian Miller, Deborah Rachel. *Education:* University of California, Berkeley, B.A., 1966; San Francisco State College, M.A., 1968; Washington University (St. Louis, MO), Ph.D., 1972. *Politics:* "Left-green." *Avocational interests:* Marlin fishing, chess, computers, poetry.

ADDRESSES: Office—Department of Political Science, San Francisco State University, 1600 Holloway Ave., San Francisco, CA 94132.

CAREER: San Francisco State University, San Francisco, CA, 1970—, currently professor of political science and urban studies, founder and director of Public Research Institute, 1984—. Associate editor of STATA Technical Bulletin. Consultant to San Francisco Bay area local governments, community groups, businesses, and nonprofit organizations on a range of urban problems and issues. *Military service:* U.S. Army, 1960-63; became specialist 5; received Army Commendation Medal.

MEMBER: Western Political Science Association, American Political Science Association, Midwest Political Science Association, California Commonwealth Club.

AWARDS, HONORS: Woodrow Wilson Dissertation Fellowship, 1969-70.

WRITINGS:

Left Coast City: Progressive Politics in San Francisco, 1975-1991, University of Kansas Publications, 1992.

WORK IN PROGRESS: "A book on exploratory data analysis with microcomputers; continuing study of San Francisco politics, urban politics generally, and the emergence of a left-progressive movement in U.S. politics."

SIDELIGHTS: Richard Edward DeLeon told *CA:* "After moving around a lot as a kid, I spent my teenage years in southern Texas. At the age of seventeen I joined the Army and served thirty-one months in Germany in a tank battalion. My Army experience civilized me and erased most of my racist attitudes. (The smartest people I worked with were black enlisted men.) I was dissuaded from reenlisting in the Army and encouraged to attend college by Lieutenant Colonel Crittenberger, who later was killed in battle in Vietnam. Lieutenant Hal C. Pattison also urged me on and gave me a taste of the arts. After discharge, I attended University of California, Berkeley, where I immediately became embroiled in the free speech movement and growing anti-war movement. The experience politicized and radicalized me—and also influenced my choice of political science as my major field of study. While still a freshman, I married my first wife, Phyllis, and worked full time at a grocery store to pay my way through. After graduating from University of California, I attended San Francisco State University and lived in San Francisco's Haight-Ashbury district. Although I looked like a hippie (long hair, bushy beard) and lived among them, at the time I despised the counterculture crowd as cowardly self-indulgent wimps who were afraid to oppose the war and to think and act politically. Only years later would I appreciate the unique political culture they had created in the Haight and draw upon that experience for insight and inspiration in writing *Left Coast City: Progressive Politics in San Francisco, 1975-1991.*

"While attending San Francisco State University, then department chair Jack Bunzel encouraged me to go on for the Ph.D., which I did. At Washington University, John Sprague and Bob Salisbury (among others) taught me the importance of asking the right questions, thinking rigorously, and writing gracefully. I have not attained their high standards but their works and exhortations continue to inspire me. I believe we are entering the most dangerous phase of a long-brewing national political crisis, especially in the cities, and that San Francisco activists are breaking one possible path to peace *and* justice in the twenty-first century. My book records some of their struggles over the period 1975-1991."

DENISON, Edward F(ulton) 1915-1992

OBITUARY NOTICE—See index for *CA* sketch: Born December 18, 1915, in Omaha, NE; died of heart ailments, October 23, 1992, in Washington, DC. Educator, economist, and author. A leading authority on national economic growth and productivity, Denison began his career as an instructor in economics at Brown University after receiving his doctorate. In 1941 he became an economist for the U.S. Department of Commerce and rose to assistant director of the Office of Business Economics, a post he held until 1956. Denison then worked for the Committee for Economic Development as a member of the research staff until 1962, when he became a senior fellow at the Brookings Institution in Washington, DC. He retired in 1978 but served as the director of the Bureau of Economic Analysis from 1979 to 1982. Denison translated economic articles into several languages, contributed to journals and professional publications, and wrote numerous books on economics, including *The Sources of Economic Growth in the United States and the Alternatives before Us, Trends in American Economic Growth, 1929-1982, Estimates of Productivity Change by Industry: An Evaluation and an Alternative,* and, with William K. Chung, *How Japan's Economy Grew So Fast.*

OBITUARIES AND OTHER SOURCES:

BOOKS

The Writers Directory: 1990-1992, St. James Press, 1990.

PERIODICALS

Washington Post, October 24, 1992, p. B4.

*   *   *

DENNEY, Robert (Eugene) 1929-

PERSONAL: Born September 26, 1929, in Shelby County, IN; son of Jess (a farmer, carpenter, and building contractor) and Martha V. (a waitress and homemaker; maiden name, Fox) Denney; married Frances Ann Taylor, December 6, 1952; children: Craig Alan, Paula Jo Jacques, Linda Ann Morgan, Bruce Eugene. *Education:* Strayer College, A.A. (with high honors), 1973, B.S. (with honors), 1974; American University, M.S. (with distinction), 1976. *Politics:* "Vote for issue or candidate, not a party voter. Last time voted for Harry Truman. Figured that dead, he could do a better job than either Bush or Clinton." *Religion:* "Practically none."

ADDRESSES: Home—6106 Cloud Dr., Springfield, VA 22150-1016.

CAREER: U.S. Marine Corps, 1947-50, served in China, then as squad leader and later platoon sergeant in Guam, beginning in 1948, stationed in Quantico, VA, until 1950; U.S. Army, 1950-67, drill instructor at Fort Knox, KY, 1950, staff sergeant, c. 1950, during Korean War served in intelligence unit operating in North Korea, 1951-52, first sergeant, 1953-54, sergeant major, 1954-55, warrant officer, 1956, chief warrant officer, mid-1950s, assistant operations officer in Hanau, Hesse, West Germany, 1957, deputy director, 1958-60, captain, signal corps, at Fort Huachuca, AZ, 1962, project officer at Fort Benning, GA, early 1960s, during Vietnam War served as project officer in Vietnam, 1966, operations officer and pilot for Chief of Staff of the Army at Fort Belvoir, VA, 1967, retired, 1967; worked in computer industry as project manager, systems designer, systems integrator, developer, and configuration management specialist, for twenty-two years; writer. Past president of Civil War Round Table of Washington, DC.

MEMBER: Lincoln Group of Washington, DC.

AWARDS, HONORS: Recipient of Purple Heart, Silver Star, and Bronze Star with 'V' device for service during Korean War; Army Commendation Medal for service in West Germany; Army Commendation Medal for service at Fort Huachuca, AZ; recipient of Distinguished Flying Cross, Bronze Star, and Purple Heart, c. 1966, for service during Vietnam War.

WRITINGS:

The Civil War Years: A Daily Account of the Life of a Nation, Sterling Pub., 1992.

Also author of a work on Civil War prisons, Sterling Pub., 1993.

WORK IN PROGRESS: Researching treatment of the wounded in the Civil War, Civil War spies, agents, and Copperheads, and women in the Civil War.

SIDELIGHTS: Robert Denney told *CA:* "I really didn't get into the writing of Civil War material until after I had decided to retire and let my wife support me in the manner in which I would like to become accustomed. It has been a lifelong joy of mine to read of the Civil War and that era of our history. Those four years shaped the destiny of the nation.

"Since childhood I have been an avid reader, spending much of my time alone in my own world of books and fantasy. I began work in a tomato canning factory at the age of thirteen during World War II, rising to be the straw boss of the cleanup crew in the evenings. At thirty-five cents an hour, ten and twelve hour days yielded a lot of money in 1944 and 1945.

"Never much of a joiner, I tended to do things that required only myself to compete with, or at least that is what I imagined. It was, however, not entirely true, since none of us are alone in this world. I felt, and still do to some extent, that my rather poor background required that I prove myself, if to no one else, then to myself. As a result, I usually attack any problem with cold analysis and develop a plan of action rather quickly. That trait saved my bacon more than once in Korea and Vietnam.

"Why did I want to write a Civil War book when more than ninety-five thousand had already been written? Well, I talked to my brother whose greatest literary achievement is to read Louis L'Amour's westerns. When I asked him one time why he didn't have an interest in the Civil War, he replied that he didn't understand what all those generals were talking about, and if he couldn't understand it, he wasn't going to read it. I thought about that for a while. Then I talked to some other people (not Civil War pundits or fans), and their reactions were much the same as my brother's. Huh. We must be doing something wrong here. If we cannot get the 'general' public to understand the books we write, who is going to buy them?

"*The Civil War Years* is an attempt to bring the war to the 'common' readers in language they can understand and that will be entertaining as well as informative. Results so far have been encouraging. The letters I get from these 'common' folk bear out my purpose.

"I sent a copy of the book to my brother as a gift. Several weeks later, during a telephone conversation, I asked how he liked the book. His reply was, 'I still don't like them generals. But when the others are talking, I can understand it.' Well said, brother. The diaries are the key to the problem as much as anything else. Why put words into the mouths of the protagonists when they speak so eloquently themselves?"

*   *   *

DICKENS, Monica (Enid) 1915-1992

OBITUARY NOTICE—See index for *CA* sketch: Born May 10, 1915, in London, England; died of cancer, December 25, 1992, in Reading, England. Humanitarian, columnist, and author. Dickens, a great-granddaughter of famous British novelist Charles Dickens (*Great Expectations, A Tale of Two Cities*), published over fifty books, many of them humorous novels that cast an eye on upper class British society. As a young woman, she rebelled against her cultured upbringing, refusing to become a debutante and instead going to work as a servant and a cook. Dickens later wrote for a local paper and had a column in *Woman's Own* for twenty years. In 1974, she opened the first American branch of The Samaritans, an organization that counsels the depressed and suicidal. Dickens's first book, *One Pair of Hands,* was a fictionalized account of her life as a domestic. She was also the author of *An Open*

Book, Enchantment, and One of the Family, among other titles.

OBITUARIES AND OTHER SOURCES:

BOOKS

The Writers Directory: 1990-1992, St. James Press, 1990.

PERIODICALS

Chicago Tribune, December 30, 1992, section 3, p. 11.
Los Angeles Times, December 28, 1992, p. A22.
New York Times, December 27, 1992, p. L41.
Times (London), December 28, 1992, p. 13.
Washington Post, December 28, 1992, p. B6.

*   *   *

DILLON, M(artin) C. 1938-

PERSONAL: Born December 7, 1938, in Los Angeles, CA; son of James Joseph and Retta (Walsmith) Dillon; first marriage ended; married Joanne Elizabeth Bubela, May 20, 1985; children: (first marriage) Kathleen, Elizabeth, Sarah. *Education:* University of Virginia, B.A. (with honors), 1960; University of California, Berkeley, M.A., 1964; Yale University, M.Phil., 1968, Ph.D., 1970.

ADDRESSES: Home—Ambremerine, Friendsville, PA 18818. *Office*—Department of Philosophy, State University of New York at Binghamton, Binghamton, NY 13902-6000.

CAREER: Washington and Lee University, Lexington, VA, instructor in philosophy, 1964-65; State University of New York at Binghamton, instructor, 1968-70, assistant professor, 1970-74, associate professor, 1974-88, professor of philosophy, 1988—, director of undergraduate studies in philosophy, 1978-90, acting chair of department, 1982, acting director of Law and Society Program, 1987-88. Yale University fellow, 1966-67 and 1967-68; International Business Machines (IBM), Inc., instructor, 1986—; lecturer at colleges and universities, including Salisbury State College, Colgate University, Duquesne University, and Vassar College. *Military service:* United States Navy, 1960-63. United States Naval Reserve, commanding officer of Surface Division, 1973-75, commanding officer of Military Sealift Command Office for the Central Mediterranean, 1979-81; became captain.

MEMBER: International Husserl and Phenomenological Research Society, International Association for Philosophy and Literature (member of executive committee, 1976-79; chairperson, 1978-79), American Philosophical Association, Society for Phenomenology and Existential Philosophy, Society for the Philosophy of Sex and Love, Merleau-Ponty Circle (general secretary, 1985—),

Human Science Research Conference, Canadian Society for Hermeneutics and Postmodern Thought, New York State Philosophical Association (Creighton Club).

AWARDS, HONORS: Woodrow Wilson fellow, 1963-64; Chancellor's Award for Excellence in Teaching, State University of New York at Binghamton, 1974; faculty research grants, State University of New York at Binghamton, 1971, 1973, 1978, 1980.

WRITINGS:

Merleau-Ponty's Ontology, Indiana University Press, 1988.
(Editor and contributor) *Merleau-Ponty Vivant,* State University of New York Press, 1991.

Work represented in anthologies, including *Merleau-Ponty, Hermeneutics, and Postmodernism,* edited by Busch and Gallagher, State University of New York Press, 1992; *Merleau-Ponty in Contemporary Perspective,* edited by Burke and Van der Veken, Kluwer, 1993; and *Philosophy and the Discourse of Desire,* edited by Silverman, Routledge, Chapman & Hall, 1993. Member of advisory board of the series "Continental Philosophy," Routledge, Chapman & Hall. Contributor of articles and reviews to philosophy journals.

WORK IN PROGRESS: Semiological Reductionism: A Critique of Derrida; Being and Love; The Powerjuice Agon, a novel.

*   *   *

DiMERCURIO, Michael 1958-

PERSONAL: Born April 9, 1958, in Denver, CO; son of Cyril (an executive and engineer) and Patricia Ruth (Wilson) DiMercurio; married; wife's name, Theresa; children: Matt, Marla. *Education:* U.S. Naval Academy, B.S.M.E., 1980; Massachusetts Institute of Technology, M.S.M.E., 1981.

ADDRESSES: Office—7201 Hamilton Blvd., Allentown, PA 18195. *Agent*—Natasha Kern, Box 2908, Portland, OR 97208-2908.

CAREER: Air Products and Chemicals Inc., Allentown, PA, project engineer, 1988—. *Military service:* U.S. Navy, 1980-88; became lieutenant.

WRITINGS:

Voyage of the Devilfish (novel), Donald I. Fine, 1992.
Attack of the Seawolf, Donald I. Fine, 1992.

WORK IN PROGRESS: Revenge of the Vortex, completion expected in 1994.

BIOGRAPHICAL/CRITICAL SOURCES:

PERIODICALS

Allentown Morning Call, August 30, 1992, p. F3.

*   *   *

DioGUARDI, Joseph J.   1940-

PERSONAL: Born September 20, 1940, in the Bronx, New York; son of Joseph DioGuardi (a store-owner) and Grace (Paparella) DioGuardi (a store-owner); married Carol Asselta (a homemaker), November 16, 1968; children: Kara, John. *Education:* Fordham University, B.S. (with honors), 1962. *Politics:* Republican-Conservative. *Religion:* Roman Catholic. *Avocational interests:* Traveling, writing, speaking, golf.

ADDRESSES: Home—50 Baraud Rd., Scarsdale, NY 10583. *Office*—Truth in Government, P.O. Box 97, Rye, NY 10580.

CAREER: Arthur Andersen & Co., New York City, certified public accountant, 1962-84, partner; U.S. House of Representatives, congressman from Westchester district, NY, 1985-89; Truth in Government, Rye, NY, chair, 1989—; writer, speaker, and human rights activist, 1989—. Phoenix House Foundation, board member, 1975-84, development fund board member, 1985-92; Albanian American Civil League, president, 1989—; founder and co-chair of Congressional Long Island Sound and Hudson River Caucuses. *Military service:* U.S. Army Reserves, 1963-68, active duty in Fort Dix, NJ, 1963.

MEMBER: American Institute of Certified Public Accountants, New York State Society of Certified Public Accountants, Ancient and Illustrious Order Knights of Malta, Winged Foot Golf Club.

AWARDS, HONORS: Man of the Year, Beta Gamma Sigma/Alpha Beta Psi.

WRITINGS:

House of Ill Repute, Princeton University Press, 1987.
Unaccountable Congress: It Doesn't Add Up, Regnery Gateway, 1992.

WORK IN PROGRESS: Sequel to *Unaccountable Congress,* Regnery Gateway.

SIDELIGHTS: Joseph J. DioGuardi was the first practicing certified public accountant elected to Congress. His tenure as congressman resulted in his book *Unaccountable Congress: It Doesn't Add Up,* an expose of congressional smoke-screen budgeting practices that, DioGuardi says, hide the real extent of the national deficit. The book traces DioGuardi's experiences and "education" as a congress-man and attempts to explain the crisis in the U.S. economy by tracing its beginnings in misleading accounting practices. DioGuardi terms the House of Representatives a "house of ill repute" and says that its members seem unaccountable to laws other Americans are required to uphold. *New York Post* reviewer Ray Kerrison classified the book as a "horror story." The critic said that the gold congressional credit card appearing on the book cover—"boasting an unlimited credit line, no expiration date and the bill to be sent to future generations"—tells the whole story. N. Zill in a *North County News* review recommended the book highly and asserted that DioGuardi "casts a discerning eye on the fiscal chicanery practiced in Congress." On a somber note, Kerrison concluded that the book makes "pretty scary reading."

DioGuardi told *CA:* "Having spent twenty-two years in the accounting profession, and then four years in Congress where I witnessed, firsthand, the outrageous accounting and budget gimmicks and financial sleight of hand used by our legislators to hide the real economic cost of government programs, I felt it was important for the public to know the *real cost of government* in simple everyday language.

"I hope that my writing will raise the public awareness level of the extraordinary lack of common sense, fiscal sanity, and public accountability in the federal government today. Someone once said, 'Information is the currency of democracy.'"

BIOGRAPHICAL/CRITICAL SOURCES:

PERIODICALS

New York Post, April 29, 1992.
North County News, August 12-18, 1992, p. 1.

*   *   *

DIONNE, E(ugene) J., Jr.   1952-

PERSONAL: Born in 1952, in Boston, MA. *Education:* Received Ph.D.

ADDRESSES: Office—c/o *Washington Post,* 1150 Fifteenth St. NW, Washington, DC 20071.

CAREER: Journalist and writer. Has worked as a reporter for *New York Times;* presently employed as a reporter for *Washington Post,* Washington, DC.

AWARDS, HONORS: Los Angeles Times Book Prize, current interest category, 1991, for *Why Americans Hate Politics.*

WRITINGS:

Why Americans Hate Politics: The Death of the Democratic Process (nonfiction), Simon & Schuster, 1991, revised edition, 1992.

Contributor to periodicals, including *Commonweal, New York Times Book Review,* and *Utne Reader.*

SIDELIGHTS: A political correspondent for the *Washington Post,* E. J. Dionne, Jr., is the author of *Why Americans Hate Politics: The Death of the Democratic Process.* The book gives a history of American political thought beginning in the 1960s and documents the public's growing disenchantment with government and divisive politics. According to Dionne, politicians—in order to woo powerful special interest groups—have increasingly concerned themselves with issues that America's centrist silent majority find irrelevant. Troubled by the economy, education, health care, and crime, the public, Dionne notes, is faced with politicians who debate symbolic issues such as gun control and the legality of burning the American flag. Both Democrats and Republicans, asserts Dionne, are guilty of concentrating on ideology instead of real problems, dividing voters in order to retain power.

Politicians, Dionne states in his book, pursue "a polarized politics that highlights symbolic issues, short-circuits genuine political debate, gives discontent few real outlets, allows money a paramount role in the electoral process, and leaves the country alarmed over whether it can maintain its standard of living. Is it any wonder that Americans have come to hate politics?" The solution, the author maintains, is to take the best elements from both liberal and conservative platforms to create a moderate, reasonable approach appealing to the centrist majority. And, "to restore popular faith in the possibilities of government," Dionne writes in his book, "government must be shown to work."

Though some critics were skeptical that idealogues of the left and right would be able to work toward common ground, several reviewers praised *Why Americans Hate Politics. Washington Post Book World* contributor George V. Higgins, for instance, called Dionne's book "a splendid and thoughtful piece of work." And writing in the *New York Time Book Review,* Norman J. Ornstein commented that "it would be hard to imagine a better chronicle of our recent intellectual ferment than *Why Americans Hate Politics.* It is knowledgeable and sympathetic to all viewpoints while comprehending and communicating intricate personality, policy and doctrinal disputes. Mr. Dionne writes with the sprightly facility of a good journalist, while displaying the intellectual depth of the Ph.D. historian he is."

BIOGRAPHICAL/CRITICAL SOURCES:

BOOKS

Dionne, E. J., Jr., *Why Americans Hate Politics,* Simon & Schuster, 1991.

PERIODICALS

Nation, July 20, 1992, pp. 110-14.
New Republic, June 3, 1991, pp. 35-38.
New York Times Book Review, May 19, 1991, p. 7.
Time, May 20, 1991, p. 60.
Washington Post Book World, May 19, 1991, p. 3.*

*   *   *

DIXON, George
See WILLIS, Ted

*   *   *

DONAGHY, Michael   1954-

PERSONAL: Born May 24, 1954, in New York, NY; son of Patrick (a machinist) and Eveline (Sheehy) Donaghy. *Education:* Fordham University, B.A., 1976; received M.A. from University of Chicago.

ADDRESSES: Home—London, England.

CAREER: University of London Birkbeck College, London, England, tutor, 1989—; poet. Has taught writing at the University of Chicago, the Arvon Foundation, City University, and the Poetry Society; musician. Has appeared on BBC radio broadcasts.

MEMBER: The Poetry Society.

AWARDS, HONORS: Second Prize, National Poetry Competition (United Kingdom), 1987, for poem "Shibboleth"; shortlisted for Arts Council Writer's Award, 1988, and Judith E. Wilson Writing Fellowship, University of Cambridge, 1989; Whitbread Award for poetry, 1989, and Geoffrey Faber Memorial Award, 1990, both for *Shibboleth.*

WRITINGS:

Slivers, Thompson Hill Press, 1985.
Machines, Circle Press, 1986.
Shibboleth, Oxford University Press, 1988.
Smith, Triangular Press, 1989.
Errata, Oxford University Press, 1993.

Contributor of poems and articles to periodicals, including *Paris Review, New Yorker, Times Literary Supplement,* and *Poetry.* Poetry editor of *Chicago Review,* 1979-85.

BIOGRAPHICAL/CRITICAL SOURCES:

PERIODICALS

New Statesman and Society, December 23, 1988, p. 36.
Times Literary Supplement, December 1, 1989, p. 1336.

*   *   *

DONALDSON, Loraine

PERSONAL: Born in Clearwater, FL; daughter of Lonnie Milton and Lois Lorene (Young) Donaldson. *Education:* University of Florida, B.S.B.A. (with high honors), 1960, M.A., 1961; Indiana University—Bloomington, D.B.A., 1965. *Avocational interests:* Art, tennis.

ADDRESSES: Home—1170 Pine Ridge Rd. N.E., Atlanta, GA 30324. *Office*—Department of Economics, Georgia State University, Atlanta, GA 30303.

CAREER: Georgia State University, Atlanta, assistant professor, 1964-66, associate professor, 1966-70, professor of economics, 1970—. Economic consultant. Pine Hills Civic Association, member of board of directors; Shepherd Spinal Center, member of auxiliary association; Scottish Rite Hospital, member of auxiliary association.

WRITINGS:

Development Planning in Ireland, Praeger, 1966.
Economic Development, West Publishing, 1984.
Fertility Transition, Basil Blackwell, 1991.

Contributor to economic and development journals.

WORK IN PROGRESS: Researching "differentials in black/white fertility rates."

SIDELIGHTS: Loraine Donaldson told *CA:* "I have devoted my career to understanding the causes of poverty and ways to lessen its repercussions."

*   *   *

DONOHUE, Gail
See STOREY, Gail Donohue

*   *   *

DOTSENKO, Paul 1894-1988

OBITUARY NOTICE—See index for *CA* sketch: Born November 19, 1894, in Chernigov, Russia; died in 1988. Historian, freedom fighter, and author. Dotsenko was exiled to Siberia in 1915 for his activities with the anti-Czarist Socialist-Revolutionary party. When the Communist party came to power in 1917, he was released and worked for a short time for the government until his democratic ideals again caused his arrest, this time by the Communist regime. He escaped, however, and became an organizer of a doomed revolt against the Communists in Siberia in 1918. Dotsenko immigrated to the United States in 1923 and later wrote about his experiences in *CA,* declaring, "I feel obligated to share my knowledge with people interested in Russian history." He authored *The Struggle for a Democracy in Siberia, 1917-1920: Eyewitness Account of a Contemporary.*

OBITUARIES AND OTHER SOURCES:

Date of death provided by daughter, Galena Dotsenko.

*   *   *

DRACO, F.
See DAVIS, Julia

*   *   *

DRANOW, John (Theodore) 1948-

PERSONAL: Born December 29, 1948, in Passaic, NJ; son of Nathan Dranow (a dancer) and Betty Jane Coleman McGregor; married Louise Glueck (a writer), January 1, 1977; children: Noah (adopted son). *Education:* Boston University, B.A., 1971; University of Iowa, M.A., 1972, M.F.A., 1974.

ADDRESSES: Home—R.D. 2, Box 1400, Plainfield, VT 05667. *Office*—New England Culinary Institute, 250 Main St., Montpelier, VT 05602. *Agent*—Phyllis Westberg, Harold Ober Associates, Inc., 425 Madison Ave., New York, NY 10017.

CAREER: University of Iowa, Iowa City, instructor, 1973-74; University of Missouri—Columbia, instructor, 1974-76; Radford University, Radford, VA, instructor, 1976-77; Goddard College, Plainfield, VT, instructor and director of summer writing program, 1977-79; New England Culinary Institute, Montpelier, VT, co-founder, 1979, chief operating officer, 1979—.

MEMBER: American Institute of Wine and Food.

AWARDS, HONORS: Grant from Vermont Council for the Arts, 1977-78; First Prize from Virginia Highlands Literary Festival, 1977; First Prize from a writer's contest sponsored by the Boston University Alumni Association, 1983; First Prize from the Small Press Book Fair at University of Cincinnati, 1988, for *Life in the Middle of the Century;* grant from National Endowment for the Arts, 1992-93.

WRITINGS:

Life in the Middle of the Century (contains the novellas "The Official and Final Version" and "Zone One"), Galileo Press, 1988.
The Magic Step (novel), Galileo Press, 1991.

Contributor of stories to periodicals, including *Kansas Quarterly, December,* and *New River Review.*

WORK IN PROGRESS: Seven Parents, a novel.

SIDELIGHTS: John Dranow told *CA:* "My parents ran an Arthur Murray Dance Studio. My father was a former vaudevillian, a Jewish man with a complicated past. He met my mother in the waning days of World War II. She was a German-Catholic, French, Scotch-Irish beauty queen from Wheeling, West Virginia, and he was the lead dancer in the morale troop. I grew up with a profound connection to all the major and several minor religions and a clear sense of multiple points of view.

"My sense of education was that each year got somewhat easier and better than the last. As influential to me as any course I ever had were the jobs I had while in school. Coffee breaks in the meat locker at the A & P, attempting to sell encyclopedias during the Newark riots of 1967, and working as a bank teller all taught me a great deal about aspiration, sadness, and love. While I had always read, became a literature major, and was a storyteller, the thought of becoming a writer did not come to me until I was a junior at Boston University, reading Philip Roth's *Letting Go* in a cool bank vault under the streets of Newark. I applied to the master's program in literature at the University of Iowa, took the undergraduate fiction writing course, wrote my first stories, and was accepted to the Writing Workshop.

"The Workshop, then under the direction of Jack Leggett, was exciting beyond my imagination. It was the first time in my life that I knew what I wanted to do, the first time I was ever in school with uniformly first-rate students, and the first time I ever had an opportunity to meet the gods of modern fiction. I loved everything about the place: the parties, the gossip, the intrigue. I studied with Gail Godwin, Fred Exley, William Price Fox, John Irving, Stanley Elkin, John Cheever, and many others. I went to school with Ron Hansen, Tom Boyle, Bob Hinck, and Charlie Phillips. I was also able to teach the undergraduate fiction course I had taken two years earlier, and discovered I loved to teach.

"After teaching at several colleges and universities, my career took a very interesting turn. My partner Francis Voigt and I decided that we needed to leave the struggling Goddard College. We also decided that we wanted to stay in Vermont, and we wanted to continue to work together. We got the idea to start a chef's school. We quit our jobs, invested our meager life savings, and were supported for the first two years by our wives. Today we have a school with more than four hundred students, a hundred-fifty employees, and we are fully accredited. We operate fourteen food services and work hard to be one of the best and most relevant hospitality schools in the country.

"While not everyone who wants to write has my interest in commerce, I would passionately advocate explorations outside teaching. People with our background have more abilities to succeed and create change than they might imagine, and the inside of a successful entity provides a unique vantage point for listening and learning.

"I married Louise Glueck, the poet, in 1977 and adopted her son Noah. The precision, rigor, and integrity of Louise's work has had a major effect on my own. Being a part of Noah's life has been a joy, pleasure, and honor. We live in northern Vermont, connected to the world through my satellite dish, on which I am able to see every Giants football game. We also have a large and demanding garden and cat."

BIOGRAPHICAL/CRITICAL SOURCES:

PERIODICALS

New York Times Book Review, March 8, 1992.

* * *

DRUETT, Joan 1939-

PERSONAL: Born April 11, 1939, in Nelson, New Zealand; married Ronald John Druett (a maritime artist), February 11, 1966; children: Lindsay John, Alastair Ronald. *Education:* Victoria University of Wellington, B.A.

ADDRESSES: Home—38 Pearsons Ave., Hamilton, New Zealand. *Agent*—Jennifer Kavanagh, 39 Camden Park Rd., London SW1 9AX, England.

CAREER: Teacher of biology and English literature until 1983; writer, 1983—. Member of Mystic Seaport Museum, New Bedford Whaling Museum, Kendall Whaling Museum, Wellington Maritime Museum, Auckland Maritime Museum, Huntingdon Library (San Marino, CA), Dixson Library of the State Library of New South Wales, and Alexander Turnbull Library of the National Library of New Zealand.

MEMBER: North American Society of Oceanic History, Sussex Archaeological Society (England), Dukes County Historical Society (Edgartown, MA).

AWARDS, HONORS: Award for best first prose book, International PEN, 1984; Fulbright Writer's Cultural Award, 1986.

WRITINGS:

Exotic Intruders: The Introduction of Plants and Animals to New Zealand, Heinemann (Auckland, New Zealand), 1983.

Fulbright in New Zealand, New Zealand-U.S. Educational Foundation, 1988.

Abigail: A Novel, Random House, 1988.

A Promise of Gold, Bantam, 1990.

Petticoat Whalers: Whaling Wives at Sea, 1820-1920, Harper Collins (Auckland), 1991, (New York), 1992.

(Editor) *"She Was a Sister Sailor": The Whaling Journals of Mary Brewster, 1845-1851,* Mystic Seaport Museum, 1991.

Murder at the Brian Boru, Harper Collins (Auckland), 1992.

Contributor to periodicals, including *Log of Mystic Seaport, Newport History, Field and Stream, New Zealand Outdoors,* and *Pacific Way.*

WORK IN PROGRESS: A "semi-fictional" book based on the journal of Eliza Underwood.

SIDELIGHTS: Joan Druett told *CA:* "I am writing a semi-fictional account of an Englishwoman, Eliza Underwood, who sailed on the London whaling ship *Kingsdown* to the South Seas in the years 1829 to 1831. The account is based on a partial journal which I found in the Dixson Library. Unearthing Mrs. Underwood's background is an all-consuming task. The journal is the penultimate one of several, the rest all lost. This partly explains why the account has to be semi-fictional. As well as that, the journal is quite wild, often hysterical, which, considering what life on shipboard in those particular seas was like at the time, is probably perfectly understandable.

"The journal begins in February, 1830, when Captain Underwood court-martials his wife 'for certain Crimes and Misdemeanors committed in the Ship *Kingsdown* on the High Seas in defiance of his Sovereign Majesty the King.' It ends during the journey home in September, 1831, with the words 'I hope I shall close my next book with a more pleasing reflection. Surely I shall, for the next will close in London, but yet I have much to dread.' "

Druett continued, "My engrossing interest in the history of women in whaling began in May, 1984, when I had an odd and prophetic experience on the tiny South Pacific island of Rarotonga. I came across a young Maori digging away in the noonday sun, scraping at a patch of waste ground. When I asked the reason for such a seemingly pointless task, I was told that he had a dream in which an ancestor came to him and told him to clear the land because it was a lost graveyard. The fact that I did not find this ridiculous says something for the ambience of the island of Rarotonga!

"Three days later the young man had gone, and so—of course—I investigated the heaps of weeds and broken stones, and ended up falling into a hole where a great tree had been uprooted during a recent storm. At the bottom of that hole, I found a coral rock grave with a headstone set into it like a door. The inscription was perfectly legible, uncovered for the first time in a hundred and thirty years—a memorial to a twenty-four-year-old American girl, Mary Ann Sherman, the wife of the captain of the American whaling ship *Harrison,* who had died January 5, 1850. A girl on a whaling ship? It seemed impossible! How had she lived . . . and died? This was the beginning of my quest, which has lasted for eight years and more than a million words of writing."

*   *   *

du BOIS, William (Sherman) Pene   1916-1993

OBITUARY NOTICE—See index for *CA* sketch: Born May 9, 1916, in Nutley, NJ; died following a stroke, February 5, 1993, in Nice, France. Illustrator, editor, and author. Du Bois, an award-winning author and illustrator of children's books, was known for his whimsical plotlines and imaginative drawings. Du Bois published his first children's book, *The Great Geppy,* at age nineteen, and his success convinced him to make children's literature his life's work. In 1948 he received the Newbery Medal for *The Twenty-One Balloons,* which recounts the remarkable travel adventures of a retired professor. Two other works, *Bear Party* and *Lion,* were named Caldecott honor books. In World War II du Bois edited and illustrated *Yank* and other military publications, and he later served as a founding editor of the *Paris Review.* Du Bois also illustrated *The Rabbit's Umbrella* and *The Owl and the Pussycat,* and he wrote and illustrated *Otto at Sea, Bear Circus,* and *Porko von Popbutton,* among other works.

OBITUARIES AND OTHER SOURCES:

BOOKS

The Writers Directory: 1990-1992, St. James Press, 1990.

PERIODICALS

Chicago Tribune, February 8, 1993, section 4, page 8.
New York Times, February, 1993.
School Library Journal, March, 1993, p. 108.

*   *   *

DURSCHMIED, Erik   1930-

PERSONAL: Born December 25, 1930, in Vienna, Austria; immigrated to Canada, naturalized Canadian citizen;

son of Carl and Helene Durschmied; married; wife's name, Annelise; children: Annemarie, Christina. *Education:* Attended McGill University. *Religion:* Roman Catholic.

ADDRESSES: Home—14 Rue Rambuteau, Paris 75003, France.

CAREER: Canadian Broadcasting Corp. (CBC-TV), Toronto, Ontario, camera operator, 1956-60; British Broadcasting Corp. (BBC-TV), London, England, camera operator for *Panorama,* 1960-72; independent film producer in Paris, France, 1973-80; Columbia Broadcasting System (CBS-TV), New York City, film director and camera operator, 1981-86; independent film producer in Paris and Los Angeles, CA, 1987—; filmmaker and writer. Lecturer at various institutions, including University of Western Ontario and West Point Academy.

AWARDS, HONORS: Two Cameraman of the Year awards for *Panorama;* Academy Award nomination, best documentary film, 1968, for *Hill 943.*

WRITINGS:

Don't Shoot the Yanqui: The Life of a War Cameraman (autobiography), Grafton (London), 1990, Pharos (New York), 1991.
Armee Rouge: Le dernier Combat, [Paris], 1991.

DOCUMENTARY SCREENPLAYS

Castro, CBC, 1958.
Guy Burgess: The Super Spy, BBC, 1959.
Algiers: A Day of Killing, BBC, 1961.
North Korea: Portrait of a Country, BBC, 1962.
Yemen Story, BBC, 1963.
The Seven Hundred Million: First-Ever Look at China, BBC, 1964.
Vietnam: Trilogy of Combat, BBC, 1964.
The Mills of the Gods, BBC, 1965.
Hill 943, CBS, 1968.
Army of the Holy Land, BBC, 1969.
Belfast Weekend: A Bomb and a Pub Crawl, BBC, 1969.
Dacca Massacre, BBC, 1971.
De Gaulle Funeral, BBC, 1971.
Aetna Eruption, BBC, 1972.
The France I Love, BBC, 1973.
Those Who Are Lost, BBC, 1974.
Dubai Army, BBC, 1975.
Day in the Life of an Oil Sheikh, BBC, 1975.
Dollars Like Sand, BBC, 1975.
A Short Street in Belfast, BBC, 1975.
Rhodesia White, BBC, 1976.
Help!! Cambodia's Killing Fields, CBS, 1980.
Vietnam: Bitter Victory, CBS, 1981.
Beirut (news reports), CBS, 1981.
Under the Soviet Gun—Afghanistan, CBS, 1983.

A Trial in Kabul: Dr. Augoyard, CBS, 1983.
Iraq: Portrait of a Country at War, CBS, 1984-86.
North Korea: A Portrait of Isolation, CBS, 1985.
Mystery of the Pyramid, CBS, 1988.

Also author, for National Geographic, of the documentary screenplays *Amazonian Indians,* 1969; *The Day the Reindeer Died,* 1986; and *The Storm,* 1987. Also author of the documentary screenplays *Tear for the Sea: Amoco Dadiz Oil Spill,* 1977; *Apartheid,* 1977; *Cobra and Co.,* 1978; *Defense of Europe,* 1979; *Battle of the Skies: Airbus versus Boeing,* 1980; and *Firebreak: World War III Rehearsal,* 1980.

WORK IN PROGRESS: A three-part novel, tentatively titled *The Mills of God,* about the Vietnam War from 1967 to 1977; *The Ivory Trail,* a novel.

SIDELIGHTS: Erik Durschmied is a prolific, highly regarded news cameraperson who has filmed many memorable events and people. *Newsweek* has called him "supremely gifted" and stated that he has "transformed" the medium of film reporting. Durschmied's experiences as a cameraperson are recounted in his 1990 autobiography, *Don't Shoot the Yanqui.* Durschmied first gained attention in 1958 by being the first to interview Fidel Castro when the future Cuban leader was still a rebel quartered in the Cuban hills. In the ensuing decades, Durschmied traveled throughout the war-torn world, covering combat in a variety of locations. Teamed with British Broadcasting Corporation reporter James Mossman, Durschmied filmed conflicts in Aden, Yemen, and Vietnam, where the team filmed the first American casualties in 1962. In 1968, the cameraperson shot footage for the Columbia Broadcasting System that he made into the highly regarded documentary *Hill 943.* Rather than take advantage of his civilian status and the comfort it afforded, Durschmied told *The Guardian*'s Anwar Bati, "What made Hill 943 special was that I stayed with them [the troops], and watched some of them die. I ate the same lousy food and took the same chances they took." In regard to combat filmmaking, Durschmied told Bati: "The rule is get in, get it and get out. Don't stay there." Durschmied added that filming in combat has profoundly changed him. "You can't take a picture without some of it rubbing off on you," he disclosed. "It's not only the person who gets hit—you also get hit." *Hill 943* was nominated for an Academy Award for its depiction of combat in Vietnam.

BIOGRAPHICAL/CRITICAL SOURCES:

BOOKS

Durschmied, Erik, *Don't Shoot the Yanqui: The Life of a War Cameraman,* Grafton, 1990.

PERIODICALS

Guardian, April 9, 1990.
Times Literary Supplement, June 1, 1990, p. 578.

*   *   *

DYER, Donald R(ay) 1918-

PERSONAL: Born September 29, 1918, in Mesa, CO; son of Ray (a commercial photographer) and Ethel (a homemaker; maiden name, Jaques) Dyer; married Marilyn Frost (a teacher), October 3, 1942; children: March Elizabeth Dyer Crooks, Meredith Claire. *Education:* Attended University of Kansas, 1936-37, Asbury College, 1938, and Mesa College, 1938-39; Stanford University, B.A., 1947; Northwestern University, Ph.D., 1950. *Politics:* "Left-of-center Democrat." *Religion:* Society of Friends (Quakers). *Avocational interests:* Music, sports.

ADDRESSES: Home—510 Caswell Rd., Chapel Hill, NC 27514.

CAREER: University of Florida, Gainesville, began as assistant professor, became associate professor, 1950-62; U.S. Department of State, Washington, DC, foreign service officer in Rio de Janeiro, Brazil, Mexico City, Mexico, and New Delhi, India, 1962-79. Visiting professor at Universidad de la Habana, 1953, and Universidad Nacional San Marcos, 1958-60. *Military service:* U.S. Navy, radio technician, 1942-45; became chief petty officer.

WRITINGS:

Lesser Antilles, Nelson Doubleday, 1959.
(Coauthor) *The Caribbean,* University of Florida Press, 1961.
(Coauthor) *Modern Brazil,* University of Florida Press, 1971.

Cross-Currents of Jungian Thought, Shambhala, 1991.

WORK IN PROGRESS: Research for *Jung and God* (tentative title), a study of Jung's writing on God and the image of God.

SIDELIGHTS: Donald R. Dyer told *CA:* "In 1973 I became interested in the depth psychology of C. G. Jung through a Quaker mentor, John Yungblut, whose 'triad' consisted of Teilhard de Chardin, Jung, and the Cosmic Christ. Following the founding, by my wife, Marilyn, of the C. G. Jung Society of the Triangle Area of North Carolina in 1983, I became interested in investigating the chronological development of Jung's writings published in English; later I expanded this to include all books in English written on Jungian subjects. I anticipated that there might be between two hundred and three hundred books but, as the search continued, I was amazed to find the total approaching eight hundred.

"My work was facilitated by the continued accession of many Jungian books by the Book Service of the Jung Society and by the availability of books at the very fine libraries at the University of North Carolina at Chapel Hill and Duke University. It was necessary, in some cases, to go to the Library of Congress for books not available at home and some books were obtained through inter-library loan. The largest amount of time was spent searching for book reviews of the titles included in my annotated bibliography, which I think will be of great value to those who want knowledge of something more than my descriptive annotation. More than four thousand book reviews were listed from more than five-hundred-seventy periodicals; I think this is a unique contribution to the field of annotated bibliographies."

E-F

EAGAN, Andrea Boroff 1943-1993

OBITUARY NOTICE—See index for *CA* sketch: Born July 26, 1943, in New York, NY; died of breast cancer, March 9, 1993, in Manhattan, NY. Educator, feminist advocate, editor, and writer. Eagan was perhaps best known for her activism in the areas of women's rights and health issues. A 1969 graduate of Columbia University, Eagan was the founding president of the National Writers Union, the editor of the National Women's Health Network Series, and an instructor at several local universities and colleges. Aside from her numerous contributions to pamphlets and periodicals, Eagan authored *Why Am I So Miserable, If These Are the Best Years of My Life?* and *The Newborn Mother: States of Her Growth.*

OBITUARIES AND OTHER SOURCES:

PERIODICALS

Los Angeles Times, March 13, 1993, p. A26.
New York Times, March 11, 1993, p. D23.

*   *   *

EASTERBROOK, Gregg 1953-

PERSONAL: Born March 2, 1953, in Buffalo, NY; son of George (a dentist) and Vimy (a teacher; maiden name, Hoover) Easterbrook; married Nan Kennelly (a diplomat), January 1, 1988; children: Grant, Mara Rose. *Education:* Colorado College, B.A., 1976; Northwestern University, M.S.J., 1977. *Religion:* Christian.

ADDRESSES: Home—Arlington, VA. *Office—Atlantic Monthly,* 745 Bolyston St., Boston, MA 02116. *Agent*—Michael Carlisle, William Morris Agency, 1350 Sixth Ave., New York, NY 10022.

CAREER: Writer, 1977—.

AWARDS, HONORS: Honorary doctorate, Colorado College, 1992.

WRITINGS:

This Magic Moment: A Love Story for People Who Want the World to Make Sense (novel), St. Martin's, 1987.
A Moment on the Earth (tentative title; nonfiction), Viking Penguin, in press.

Contributing editor to *Washington Monthly,* 1975—, *Atlantic Monthly,* 1980—, and *Newsweek,* 1986—.

WORK IN PROGRESS: A play, *Abide for Me Many Days;* a novel.

SIDELIGHTS: Gregg Easterbrook is the author of *This Magic Moment: A Love Story for People Who Want the World to Make Sense,* a novel about a well-meaning civil engineer who suffers a crisis of conscience when a dam that he helped design collapses and kills a worker. The engineer, Warren Gifford, is a man with a strict moral code and is disdainful of those that shirk life's responsibilities. Through his travels in the business world, Gifford has met many people seeking fame while dodging accountability. He has determined that those who do not face the minimum responsibility that life requires do not deserve that life. He then sets out to determine whether he is culpable for the dam accident—and if so end his own life—or if he is being set up as a scapegoat by his superiors. To complicate matters, Gifford has fallen in love with a woman, Nora Jocelyn. While Nora and Gifford are wildly passionate in their mutual love, there also arises a moral dilemma: Nora is married. As Gifford dejectedly wanders a museum, contemplating his sad affairs, he comes across a painting from the fifteenth century that resembles Nora and, right next to it, a piece from the same era that resembles him. In the coming days, Gifford receives mysterious newsletters from a New Age collective and eventually discovers that he and Nora were lovers in a previous life. As the novel reaches its conclusion, the lovers, their moral problems, themes of reincarnation and destiny, and the flawed perfection of God and the universe intertwine and resolve.

Upon publication in 1987, *This Magic Moment* gained a positive appraisal from many reviewers. Florence King, in her critique for the *Washington Post Book World,* expressed considerable enthusiasm. "To call this novel refreshing is an understatement," King declared, adding that "it is downright thrilling to find a so-called 'Love Story for the 80s' built upon the theme of honor." Gregory Blake Smith, writing in the *New York Times Book Review,* noted that *This Magic Moment* contains "more ideas per page than any piece of fiction in recent memory" and he noted Easterbrook's "witty, agile mind." Another enthusiast, Carolyn See, called Easterbrook's novel "wonderful" and affirmed in the *Los Angeles Times* that "If this book were a man or a woman. . . . you'd fall in love with it."

Easterbrook told *CA:* "As I think there are fewer serious novelists than serious journalists, I am attempting to learn fiction writing while continuing to write nonfiction. Having written a serious novel that sank without a trace, I am now attempting to make progress in one of the few writing arenas with less promise, the theater. Finding anyone interested in producing a play with a non-politically correct message (in this case, that life inconveniently does have meaning) appears to be even more frustrating than finding a publisher for a novel with the same unpopular core thought. Presumably if I fail at this I will have no choice but to attempt the least sensible writing form of all, poetry."

BIOGRAPHICAL/CRITICAL SOURCES:

PERIODICALS

Los Angeles Times, February 2, 1987.
New York Times Book Review, January 25, 1987, p. 12.
Washington Post Book World, January 18, 1987, p. 6.

*   *   *

EBEL, Roland H.   1928-

PERSONAL: Born October 11, 1928; son of Walter and Phoebe (Hinkley) Ebel; married Elaine Tonge (a teacher), December 22, 1955; children: James H., Daniel H. *Education:* Attended Gordon College, 1946-48; Wheaton College, B.A., 1950; Northwestern University, M.A., 1952; Michigan State University, Ph.D., 1960. *Religion:* Methodist. *Avocational interests:* Hiking, sailing, water skiing.

ADDRESSES: Home—8716 Tanglewild Pl., River Ridge, LA 70123. *Office*—Department of Political Science, Tulane University, New Orleans, LA 70118.

CAREER: Republican State Central Committee, Lansing, MI, assistant public director, 1956 and 1958; Western Michigan University, Kalamazoo, MI, assistant professor, 1960-64; Tulane University, New Orleans, LA, associate professor of political science, 1964—.

MEMBER: Latin American Studies Association, Southeast Conference of Latin American Studies, Pi Gamma Mu.

AWARDS, HONORS: Sturgis-Leavitt prize, 1990, for best article on Latin America.

WRITINGS:

(Editor) *Proceedings of the VI Inter-American University Seminar on Municipal Affairs,* Inter-American Municipal Organization, 1968.
Political Modernization in Three Guatemalan Indian Communities, Middle American Research Institute, 1969.
(Editor and contributor) *Cambio politico en tres comunidades indigenas de Guatemala,* Ministerio de Educacion, 1969.
(Editor and contributor) *Perspectives on the Energy Crisis,* Ponchartrain Press, 1976.
(With James D. Cochrane and Raymond Taras) *Political Culture and Foreign Policy in Latin America: Case Studies from the Circum-Caribbean,* State University of New York Press, 1991.

Work represented in books, including *Rift and Revolution: The Central American Imbroglio,* edited by Howard J. Wiarda, American Enterprise Institute, 1984; *Harvest of Violence: Guatemala's Indians in the Counterinsurgency War,* edited by Robert M. Carmack, University of Oklahoma Press, 1988; and *Latin American Politics and Development,* edited by Howard J. Wiarda and Harvey F. Kline, Westview Press, 1990. Contributor of articles to periodicals, including *Journal of Inter-American Studies, Journal of Interamerican Studies and World Affairs, Current History,* and *Human Mosaic.*

WORK IN PROGRESS: The Struggle to Succeed the Liberator: The Disputed Guatemalan Elections of 1957-1958, for New Mexico State University; *Between Tyrannies: Ydigoras Fuentes, A Political Profile.*

*   *   *

EDEIKEN, Louise   1956-

PERSONAL: Born June 23, 1956, in Philadelphia, PA; daughter of Stanley (a surgeon) and Evelyn (Rothfeld)

Edeiken; married Eliot Goldfinger (a sculptor and writer), October 17, 1982; children: Gary. *Education:* George Washington University, B.A., 1977.

ADDRESSES: Home and office—37 Rolling Way, New Rochelle, NY 10804. *Agent*—Carol Mann Agency, 55 Fifth Ave., New York, NY 10003.

CAREER: Actress, singer, professional organizer, and writer. Performer in numerous stage productions, including *Nine* on Broadway, *A Quiet Place* at Vienna State Opera, and *The Making of the Representatives of Planet 8* at Houston Grand Opera. Singer on recordings, including *A Quiet Place,* Deutsche Gramaphon, and *West Side Story,* Deutsche Gramaphon. Founder and professional organizer for Easily Done, 1990.

MEMBER: Actor's Equity Association, American Federation of Theatre and Radio Artists, Screen Actors Guild, National Association of Professional Organizers.

AWARDS, HONORS: George London grant and bronze medal from National Institute for Music Theatre, both 1985.

WRITINGS:

(With Johanna Antar) *Now That You're Pregnant,* Macmillan, 1992.

SIDELIGHTS: Louise Edeiken has enjoyed a multifaceted career as a singer, professional organizer, and writer. Her work as a performer encompasses both the stage and the recording studio, and her repertoire includes both opera and American musicals. She has especially distinguished herself in the company of conductor-composer Leonard Bernstein, whose works she has performed live and recorded. Among these works are *A Quiet Place,* in which Edeiken played at both the Vienna State Opera and Milan's equally prestigious La Scala. In addition Edeiken premiered Bernstein's last song cycle, *Arias and Barcarolles,* and sang a supporting part on the Deutsche Gramaphon recording of *West Side Story* conducted by Bernstein. Edeiken also appeared in the premiere of Philip Glass's opera *The Making of the Representatives of Planet Eight,* and she was a member of the original cast of the Broadway musical *Nine.* Edeiken told *CA:* "Recent solo concert work includes performances with Michael Tilson Thomas and the London Symphony Orchestra, John Mauceri at the Hollywood Bowl with the Los Angeles Philharmonic, and John Williams and the Boston Pops."

Aside from working in the performing arts, Edeiken has developed a successful business, Easily Done, which she described to *CA* as a venture that "specializes in clutter control, organizing the home office, and turning 'chaos into order.'" In addition Edeiken is coauthor of *Now That You're Pregnant,* a workbook designed to guide expectant mothers in decision making and organizing in the months prior to child birth.

*   *   *

EHRLICH, Gretel 1946-

PERSONAL: Born in 1946 in Santa Barbara, CA; married. *Education:* Attended Bennington College, University of California, Los Angeles Film School, and New School for Social Research.

ADDRESSES: Home—2051 Beaver Creek Rd., Shell, WY 82441.

CAREER: Writer, ranch hand, and sheepherder. Documentary filmmaker for Public Broadcasting System.

AWARDS, HONORS: Harold D. Vursell Memorial Award, American Academy and Institute of Arts and Letters, 1986, for *The Solace of Open Spaces;* Whiting Writer's Award, Mrs. Giles Whiting Foundation, 1987.

WRITINGS:

Geode/Rock Body (poems), Capricorn Press, 1970.
To Touch the Water (poems), edited by Tom Trusky, second edition published by Ahsahta, 1981.
The Solace of Open Spaces (essays; includes "About Men," "From a Sheepherder's Notebook," and "A Storm, the Cornfield, and Elk"), Viking, 1985.
Wyoming Stories (includes "Thursdays at Snuff 's"; bound with *City Tales,* by Edward Hoagland), Capra, 1986.
Heart Mountain (novel), Viking, 1988.
Drinking Dry Clouds: Stories from Wyoming (includes "Kai's Mother" and "Thursday's at Snuff 's"), Capra, 1991.
Islands, the Universe, Home (essays; includes "Architecture," "The Bridge to Heaven," "The Fasting Heart," "Home Is How Many Places," and "Summer"), Viking, 1991.
Arctic Heart: A Poem Cycle, imagery by David Buckland, Capra, 1992.

Work represented in anthologies, including *Legacy of Light,* edited by Constance Sullivan, introduction by Peter Schjeldahl, Knopf, 1987. Contributor of articles to periodicals, including *Harper's, Sierra,* and *Time. The Solace of Open Spaces* was recorded on audiocassette (consisting of six excerpts and three additional essays) and released by Audio Press, 1990.

SIDELIGHTS: Gretel Ehrlich, an acclaimed essayist and fiction writer, took five years to write her first work of nonfiction, *The Solace of Open Spaces,* which began as a series of journal entries but evolved into a collection of twelve essays. In 1976 Ehrlich travelled from New York to Wyoming to make a documentary film on sheepherders for the Public Broadcasting System. She was by herself because her coworker and lover, David, had just been informed that he was terminally ill. After she completed the film, Ehrlich learned that David had passed away, and in response to her anguish she began to travel. After two years of wandering, she found her way back to Shell, Wyoming, hoping to lose herself in solitude by learning the fine points of sheepherding. Ehrlich found a sense of contentedness in the landscape and was comforted by the manners of the people she found in the small community. "For the first time I was able to take up residence on earth with no alibis, no self-promoting schemes," she wrote in *The Solace of Open Spaces,* as quoted by *New York Times Book Review* contributor Judith Moore.

The essays, which won the Harold D. Vursell Memorial Award in 1986, evoke the beautiful Wyoming landscape and describe the isolation, forty-degrees-below-zero winters, and cabin fever experienced by the state's residents. Ehrlich details her life herding cattle and sheep; one essay argues against the American myth of rough, tough, silent cowboys. Critics praised Ehrlich's characterization of the people she finds in tiny Shell and her descriptions of the land itself. "She brings the long vistas into focus with the poise of an Ansel Adams, writing, 'At night, by moonlight, the land is whittled to slivers—a ridge, a river, a strip of grassland stretching to the mountains, then the huge sky,'" noted Moore. In the *Los Angeles Times Book Review,* Kristiana Gregory called the book "a tender, poetic salute to the West," and *National Review* contributor Paul Krza wrote, "*The Solace of Open Spaces* captures the essence of a huge, desolate, yet cozy place, where the notched-down and uncrowded pace of life easily compensates for the lack of nearness to the levers of power and the comfort of the urbanized landscape."

Ehrlich had written two volumes of poetry before *The Solace of Open Spaces,* and after its success she moved to prose fiction with the collection *Wyoming Stories.* The narratives in this volume serve as extended studies of the characters who later populate her first novel, *Heart Mountain,* published in 1988. *Heart Mountain* is set during World War II, a time when the United States organized camps to hold Japanese Americans, who were considered suspect because of their Japanese ancestry. The Heart Mountain Relocation Camp is constructed near fictional Luster, Wyoming, and becomes the home of nearly 11,000 Japanese Americans overnight. Ehrlich tells the story of individuals trying to maintain the guise of humanity in the face of questionable practices with a narrative that shifts among characters both inside and outside the camp. Linking the interned Japanese Americans and the Wyoming residents are two lovers: the painter Mariko Okubo, from the camp, and McKay Allison, a rancher. The lives of

both characters are difficult: Mariko, aside from the trauma the camp induces, suffers at the hands of an abusive husband who is also in the camp, and McKay experiences guilt because a leg injury renders him unable to serve in the war. Other relationships also pull on McKay: his housekeeper, Bobby Korematsu, is saddened because the country that is his home is now at war with the land of his ancestors; McKay's erratic love relationship with Madeleine Heaney, whose husband is being held as a prisoner of war, wearies him as he wavers between her and Mariko; and McKay's brother, who is unhappy with his brother's relationship with Mariko, goes off to fight in the war, further complicating their difficult relationship. The driving force of the narrative, however, remains the interaction between McKay and Mariko.

Heart Mountain received favorable reviews upon its publication. David Kishiyama, writing in the *Los Angeles Times Book Review,* called *Heart Mountain* "such a superb account of those dark war years it should be required reading for all Japanese-Americans." *Twentieth Century Western Writers* contributor Marian Blue noted: "Rarely has World War II literature successfully reached into the rural West and created a microcosm; Ehrlich had done so. She brings the world chaos into focus; by the conclusion, we understand that there are no winners of a war, but only survivors left in various stages of healing." "Ms. Ehrlich has novelistic skills, regional loyalty and expertise, and plenty of thematic courage in the manner of John Steinbeck or Ken Kesey," commented Garrett Hongo in the *New York Times Book Review.* He later continued: "*Heart Mountain* is a richly textured and grandly romantic work about individual alienation and sexual loneliness, a novel full of immense poetic feeling for the internal lives of its varied characters and the sublime high plains landscape that is its backdrop." In the *Chicago Tribune,* Charles R. Larson wrote: "The strength of the novel resides in the simplicity of [Ehrlich's] story: By concentrating always on the human element and by creating a panorama of believable characters, she has written a totally compelling narrative that never dominates her vision of life's unexpected mysteries."

Ehrlich returned to writing stories after her novelistic debut with the collection *Drinking Dry Clouds: Stories from Wyoming.* The volume combines the four stories that originally appeared in *Wyoming Stories* with an additional section, "After the War," which consists of ten new pieces. In "Thursdays at Snuff's," four people must take refuge in a bar during a power outage, and they tell each other their life stories to pass the time. "Kai's Mother," one of the new stories, relates a Japanese woman's struggle to reorganize her and her husband's life after having been held in an internment camp for four years. *New York Times Book Review* contributor Christopher Tilghman wrote:

"Together, the people in Ms. Ehrlich's stories seem compelled to bear witness to their times, to their land and the lives they have lived upon it. Thus, as a sort of testament, *Drinking Dry Clouds* achieves a mournful lyricism and a surprising weight."

Ehrlich's second collection of essays, *Islands, the Universe, Home,* is again set in the Wyoming of *The Solace of Open Spaces,* but in this volume the author also travels to the Channel Islands of California and to Japan. These islands and a third, a retreat in the middle of a small lake on Ehrlich's ranch, are the islands named in the title, and the last, which Ehrlich calls Alcatraz, is where she retreats to observe the seasons and to ponder. Her essays explore subjects as diverse as forestry management, the poetic works of Dante, Japanese folklore, geology, and loneliness. In the *Chicago Tribune,* Victoria Jenkins praised Ehrlich's prose, identifying it as "dense with metaphor and simile, rich in observed detail and recorded emotion," and concluded that the author "is at her best where she is most at home, and the most engaging of these essays are grounded in Wyoming—accounts of a heifer in trouble, training a horse, a wounded eagle, and always, the land and the weather in an infinity of permutations—subjects Ehrlich's eloquence and passion elevate to poetry."

BIOGRAPHICAL/CRITICAL SOURCES:

BOOKS

Twentieth Century Western Writers, St. James Press, 1991, pp. 205-206.

PERIODICALS

Boston Globe, November 29, 1985, p. 82; November 29, 1987, section A, p. 29; November 9, 1991, p. 51.
Los Angeles Times Book Review, January 5, 1986, p. 6; October 30, 1988, p. 6.
National Review, July 4, 1986, pp. 42-44.
New York Times Book Review, December 1, 1985, p. 41; December 6, 1987, p. 20; November 6, 1988, p. 31; May 26, 1991, p. 6.
Time, January 6, 1986, p. 92.
Tribune Books (Chicago), November 6, 1988, p. 1; November 3, 1991, p. 7.
Washington Post Book World, April 22, 1990, p. 12; September 29, 1991, p. 6.*

—*Sketch by Roger M. Valade III*

*   *   *

EISENMAN, Stephen F.   1956-

PERSONAL: Born February 22, 1956, in New York, NY; son of Bertram and Grace Eisenman. *Education:* Received B.A. from State University of New York at Albany, M.A.

from Williams College, and Ph.D. from Princeton University. *Politics:* "Left." *Religion:* Jewish.

ADDRESSES: Office—Department of Art History and the Visual Arts, Occidental College, 1600 Campus Rd., Los Angeles, CA 90041.

CAREER: Writer. Affiliated with Occidental College, Los Angeles, CA.

WRITINGS:

Le Fantastique Reel: Graphic Works by Odilon Redon, Katonah, 1990.
The Temptation of Saint Redon: Biography, Ideology, and Style in the Noirs of Odilon Redon, University of Chicago Press, 1992.

*   *   *

EISENSTADT, Jill   1963-

PERSONAL: Born June 15, 1963, in New York, NY. *Education:* Attended Bennington College.

ADDRESSES: Office—c/o Alfred A. Knopf, Inc., 201 East 50th St., New York, NY 10022.

CAREER: Writer. Worked previously in an advertising agency in New York City.

WRITINGS:

From Rockaway (novel), Knopf, 1988.
Kiss Out (novel), Knopf, 1991.

Contributor to periodicals, including *Glamour* and *New York Times Book Review.*

SIDELIGHTS: Novelist Jill Eisenstadt won attention with her literary debut, *From Rockaway,* a coming-of-age novel that concentrates on a group of working-class Irish Catholics. *From Rockaway*—the title refers to the blue-collar beach area of Queens, New York—traces the lives of four teenagers after they graduate from high school. Alex, who has left Rockaway to attend an exclusive New Hampshire college, emerges as the novel's protagonist, and a fair portion of the work depicts her somewhat trying adjustment to life at the prestigious institution. Her friends remain in Rockaway, working as lifeguards and hanging out. The novel closes with a beachside reunion of Alex and her friends, including the emotionally shattered boyfriend that she left behind.

When *From Rockaway* appeared in 1987, some critics compared it with other books by young, hip writers such as Bret Easton Ellis's *Less Than Zero* and Jay McInerney's *Bright Lights, Big City,* dismissing Eisenstadt as a literary "brat packer." But author Joe McGinniss, Eisenstadt's mentor at Bennington College, told *People* magazine that Eisenstadt "is terrific . . . and so different from those young writers brooding over their own metaphysical conditions. She doesn't have the jaded, self-absorbed, narcissistic, worn-out voice of alienated youth that's become so common. Jill is entirely different."

Reviewers were divided over the merits of *From Rockaway.* Some critics pointed to a lack of character development, while *Voice Literary Supplement* contributor Cynthia Cotts complained of "too many mundane details and no particular resolution." In Chicago *Tribune Books,* Sven Birkerts called *From Rockaway* "a slight, if engaging novel. Perhaps its true fate is to end up on celluloid. . . . The basic human conflicts are all there." A *Publishers Weekly* critic was more enthusiastic, calling the book a "finely tuned first novel" whose characters combine "innocence and experience, hope and hopelessness." *From Rockaway,* according to *Los Angeles Times Book Review* contributor Paul Rudnick, "is a sweet, wistful coming-of-age saga, a fragmentary view of teen-agers vibrating between high-school flings and adult responsibilities."

With the publication of *From Rockaway,* Eisenstadt realized a fair measure of celebrity status. The book was optioned for film by director and producer Sydney Pollack, and *Interview* magazine called Eisenstadt one of New York's "brightest literary young things." She was also profiled in *People,* where she lamented that critics were too quick to place her with other "brat pack" authors. "I wish I were older," she declared, "so I wouldn't be compared to a million other people." In the *Interview* piece, which paired her with former schoolmate and *Less Than Zero* author Ellis, Eisenstadt commented on the perceived autobiographical nature of *From Rockaway.* "The people who don't know me are going to think it's autobiographical," she observed, adding that "the people in Rockaway who know me are going to think I have no business writing about them since I grew up in another part of town. I write about an Irish community and I'm not Irish."

Eisenstadt followed *From Rockaway* with *Kiss Out,* which details the comic escapades of Sam, Oscar, and Fred, three Jewish friends from Queens. Sam is the lead singer of his family's rock and roll band (his 250-pound mother is the drummer), which performs at a variety of venues, including weddings and bar mitzvahs. Sam is engaged to rich, spoiled Claire Allswell, who informs her father that she's getting married because "nothing ever happens to me." Oscar is taking a correspondence course in ornithology while working as a pet-store manager, and his twin brother, Fred, is an aspiring street-corner juggler. A host of other eccentric characters are introduced in what Michael Cunningham called "an extended game of romantic musical chairs," in the *Los Angeles Times.* The reviewer

added that "there's no point in trying to describe the plot," in Eisenstadt's tightly packed second novel.

Critics generally found favor with *Kiss Out* when it was published in 1991. Stephen McCauley, writing in the *New York Times Book Review,* proclaimed the novel "a work of . . . extravagant wackiness, eccentricity and exuberance" and added that it is "very funny and colorful." He also lauded Eisenstadt as a novelist of "many admirable gifts. Foremost among them are a sharp eye for people, a playful love of language and, it's probably safe to assume, nearly boundless energy." Another enthusiast, Lisa Zeidner, noted the novel's "colorful, crisp feeling" and affirmed in her *Washington Post* appraisal that Eisenstadt manages "plenty of high-jinks." *Chicago Tribune* reviewer Douglas Seibold deemed *Kiss Out* "an episodic tale of willy-nilly comic misadventure, full of appropriately wacky characters and romantic complications," and he concluded that the "distinctively goofy flair" of Eisenstadt's writing "should keep her readers amused throughout."

BIOGRAPHICAL/CRITICAL SOURCES:

BOOKS

Contemporary Literary Criticism, Volume 50, Gale, 1988, pp. 38-42.

PERIODICALS

Antioch Review, winter, 1988, pp. 116-17.
Chicago Tribune, March 6, 1991.
Interview, October, 1987, pp. 102-06.
Los Angeles Times, March 24, 1991, pp. 2, 7.
Los Angeles Times Book Review, September 13, 1987, pp. 3, 16.
New York, August 31, 1987, p. 28.
New Yorker, October 5, 1987, p. 126.
New York Times, September 19, 1987, p. A17.
New York Times Book Review, October 4, 1987, p. 29; March 17, 1991, p. 10.
People, October 26, 1987.
Publishers Weekly, August 7, 1987, p. 434.
Tribune Books (Chicago), September 13, 1987, p. 10.
Voice Literary Supplement, September, 1987, p. 31.
Washington Post, March 25, 1991, p. C3.*

*   *   *

ELY, Melvin Patrick 1952-

PERSONAL: Born June 11, 1952, in Richmond, VA; son of Clarence Patrick (a public school principal) and Vivien (a teacher; maiden name, King) Ely; married Naama Zahavi (a computer systems analyst), September 14, 1983; children: Oren (son), Kinneret (daughter). *Education:*

Princeton University, A.B., 1973, received M.A. (history), Ph.D., 1985; University of Texas at Austin, M.A. (linguistics), 1979.

ADDRESSES: Home—219 Eramo Terr., Hawden, CT 06518. *Office*—Department of Afro-American Studies, Yale University, 3388 Yale Station, New Haven, CT 06520-3388. *Agent*—Balkin Agency, P.O. Box 222, Amherst, MA 01004.

CAREER: Huguenot High School, Richmond, VA, teacher, 1973-75; Granby High School, Granby, MA, teacher, 1975-76; University of Virginia, Charlottesville, postdoctoral fellow of Carter G. Woodson Institute, 1985-86; Yale University, New Haven, CT, assistant professor, 1986-1992, associate professor of history and Afro-American studies, 1986—.

WRITINGS:

The Adventures of Amos 'n' Andy: A Social History of an American Phenomenon, Free Press, 1991.

WORK IN PROGRESS: A history of Israel Hill, "a community of free African Americans created in about 1800 when a Virginia planter freed his slaves and granted them land on which to build new lives."

SIDELIGHTS: Melvin Patrick Ely is author of *The Adventures of Amos 'n' Andy: A Social History of an American Phenomenon,* which concerns the popular radio show that featured Caucasian actors Freeman Gosden and Charles Correll as a pair of endearing but often foolhardy blacks. Gosden and Correll had worked as directors of minstrel shows, a form of entertainment that originated before the Civil War. Minstrel performances often featured white entertainers with their faces painted black in a caricature of African Americans. In 1928, Gosden and Correll came up with the characters of hardworking Amos Jones and his lazy friend Andy Brown to create the radio equivalent of a comic strip. In its early years, the show told a daily, continuing story, becoming a forerunner of the radio soap opera as well as a comedy.

Ely shows that the program presented African Americans in a more complex light than previous entertainments had, but that it also helped perpetuate negative black stereotypes. Despite protests against the show as early as 1929, *Amos 'n' Andy* was immensely popular. In the 1950s the show was recast with black actors and adapted as a television comedy that enjoyed a temporary success in prime time and remained in syndication until 1966.

Mel Watkins, writing in the *New York Times Book Review,* reported that Ely's book "tracks the program from its debut as 'Sam 'n' Henry' in 1926, through its rise to national prominence during the early days of radio, and follows its continued success during the Depression and World War II, when the humor broadened." The book also charts the television show's rise and its eventual decline, caused partly by a protest from the National Association for the Advancement of Colored People (NAACP) in 1951.

Almost from its inception, the program had come under fire from some elements of the black community. The initial furor was directed at the fact that the program's stars were two white men mimicking and ridiculing black speech patterns and lifestyles. With the advent of the television show, the NAACP felt the problem was exacerbated due to television's potentially wide audience and its added visual factor.

Ely's book traces the history of these protests as well as that of the show itself. Watkins observed in the *New York Times Book Review* that *The Adventures of Amos 'n' Andy* "moves beyond a chronicle of the rise and fall of a black sitcom. Foremost this is a social history." And a *New Yorker* contributor wrote that Ely's "sensitive and scholarly work shows us why" *Amos 'n' Andy* became "both a national sensation and a subject of racial controversy."

Ely told *CA:* "I grew up in a white, Christian family in the South during the years of the Civil Rights movement, when neglecting to think about race, democracy, and justice became impossible. In my writing and teaching, I try to get beyond the cliches and the glib certainties that still pervade American thinking about race and class. *The Adventures of Amos 'n' Andy* is my effort to rediscover and understand a monument of American popular entertainment, which for years was hidden from view for fear that a second look would inflame emotions and upset our comfortable view of ourselves. It will be clear to those who read the book that, if emotional engagement with a subject disqualifies one from writing its history, then I have not been fit for this task. But I insist that good history requires both measured analysis and an emotional investment. The story of *Amos 'n' Andy* is a story of who we are as a nation. It has been my sometimes painful pleasure to try to tell it."

BIOGRAPHICAL/CRITICAL SOURCES:

PERIODICALS

Boston Globe, July 9, 1991, pp. 41, 46.
Chicago Tribune, July 5, 1991, section 5, p. 3.
Los Angeles Times Book Review, August 4, 1991, p. 6.
New Yorker, September 16, 1991, p. 96.
New York Times, August 9, 1991, p. C25.
New York Times Book Review, July 7, 1991, pp. 1, 24.
Washington Post, June 26, 1991, p. C2.

EMERSON, Steven A. 1954-

PERSONAL: Born June 6, 1954, in New York, NY; son of Michael and Elaine Emerson. *Education:* Brown University, B.A., 1976, M.A., 1977.

ADDRESSES: Home—3930 Connecticut Ave. N.W., Suite 202, Washington, DC 20008. *Agent*—Morton Janklow, Janklow & Nesbit, 598 Madison Ave., New York, NY 10022.

CAREER: U.S. Senate Foreign Relations Committee, Washington, DC, staff member, 1977-81; *U.S. News and World Report,* Washington, DC, senior editor, 1986-89; Cable News Network (CNN), contributing correspondent, 1990—.

AWARDS, HONORS: Has received three Investigative Reporters and Editors awards for best national investigative reporting.

WRITINGS:

NONFICTION

The American House of Saud: The Secret Petrodollar Connection, F. Watts, 1985.
Secret Warriors: Inside the Covert Military Operations of the Reagan Era, Putnam, 1988.
(With Brian Duffy) *The Fall of Pan Am 103: Inside the Lockerbie Investigation,* Putnam, 1990.
(With Cristina Del Sesto) *Terrorist: The Inside Story of the Highest-Ranking Iraqi Terrorist Ever to Defect to the West,* Random House, 1991.

Contributor to periodicals, including *American Journalism Review, Los Angeles Times, New Republic, New York Times, New York Times Magazine, Wall Street Journal,* and *Washington Post.*

WORK IN PROGRESS: Investigating conspiracy culture and American media.

SIDELIGHTS: Steven A. Emerson is a free-lance print and broadcast journalist who has gained considerable distinction with his probing, often controversial nonfiction investigations. In his first book, *The American House of Saud: The Secret Petrodollar Connection,* Emerson reveals that many American companies and businesses in various dealings—including arms sales—with the Saudis became, in effect, unofficial lobbyists acting on behalf of the Saudis in Washington, D.C. According to *New York Times* reviewer Bernard Gwertzman, *The American House of Saud* constitutes "a full-length compendium which lists, in elaborate detail, the financial stake of many prominent American corporations, law firms, public-relations outfits and educational institutions in Saudi Arabia." Hoyt Purvis, writing in the *New York Times Book Review,* reported that with *The American House of Saud* Emerson has "un-

earthed some inside intelligence," and J. B. Kelly, in his assessment for the *Los Angeles Times Book Review,* noted that Emerson "has done his research with commendable assiduity." Kelly added that the book is written "in lively, at times even gripping, fashion."

Emerson followed *The American House of Saud* with *Secret Warriors: Inside the Covert Military Operations of the Reagan Era.* Here he reports that the U.S. Department of Defense established its own undercover operation, distinct from the Central Intelligence Agency (CIA), after the failed attempt to rescue hostages from Iran in 1980. One such military operation, Emerson continues, involved CIA director William Casey, National Security Council staff member Oliver North, and former army general Richard Secord, all of whom were eventually implicated in an alleged agreement to provide the hostile Iranian government with weapons in exchange for the release of hostages. Thomas Powers, writing in the *New York Times Book Review,* described *Secret Warriors* as "a reporter's book, full of stories and colorful characters," and he proclaimed it a "fine book."

With his next volume, *The Fall of Pan Am 103: Inside the Lockerbie Investigation,* Emerson teamed with Brian Duffy to provide an insightful probe into the explosion that killed 270 people aboard a jumbo jet over Lockerbie, Scotland, in 1988. The explosion was traced to a Syrian-supported Palestinian organization operating in West Germany. In uncovering the terrorism behind the explosion, according to Emerson and Duffy, various European and American teams revealed considerable shortcomings—including corruption and incompetence—in their efforts to uncover and defeat terrorists. "What arises from reading [*The Fall of Pan Am 103*]," contended *Los Angeles Times* contributor Robert H. Kupperman, "is the specter of negligence and arrogance by governments before the tragedy, and a trail of cover-up and interstate competition during the subsequent mammoth international investigation." He added that the book is "worthwhile reading." *Washington Post Book World* reviewer Steven Luxenberg was disturbed by the book's indication that terrorists possess the necessary resources and conviction to continue triumphing over present preventative measures. "The lesson that emerges from [*The Fall of Pan Am 103*] is not that good or well-intentioned people sometimes screw up," contended Luxenberg. "The lesson is that bad people—terrorists—are smart enough and obsessed enough to get around some of the best security systems in the world."

Emerson is also author—with Cristina Del Sesto—of *Terrorist: The Inside Story of the Highest-Ranking Iraqi Terrorist Ever to Defect to the West.* The book's subject is Adnan Awad, who surrendered to American authorities in 1982. According to Emerson and Del Sesto, Awad subsequently cooperated with Justice Department investigators who were tracking another suspected terrorist, Mohammed Rashid. The department's efforts, however, were reportedly undermined by CIA and National Security Council operatives eager to maintain their own covert ties with terrorist sympathizers in Iraq. Adrienne Edgar, writing in the *New York Times Book Review,* noted that *Terrorist* "offers new evidence of the bankruptcy of United States foreign policy under Ronald Reagan" and she deemed the volume "a chilling indictment of the cynicism and shortsightedness of the Reagan foreign policy team."

BIOGRAPHICAL/CRITICAL SOURCES:

PERIODICALS

Commentary, September, 1985, pp. 68-70.
Globe and Mail (Toronto), April 7, 1990.
Los Angeles Times, August 7, 1990.
Los Angeles Times Book Review, May 19, 1985, p. 1.
Nation, August 13, 1988, p. 135.
New York Times, July 11, 1985; June 9, 1990.
New York Times Book Review, June 23, 1985, p. 14; June 26, 1988, p. 12; April 29, 1990, p. 12; May 19, 1991, p. 14.
Tribune Books (Chicago), May 6, 1990, p. 5.
Washington Post Book World, May 5, 1985, p. 4; May 6, 1990, pp. 1, 4.

*   *   *

EOYANG, Eugene Chen   1939-

PERSONAL: Surname is pronounced "Oh-yang"; born February 8, 1939, in Hong Kong; son of Thomas (an engineer) and Ellen (a homemaker) Eoyang; married Patricia Lee (a university administrator), March 10, 1962; children: Christopher, Gregory. *Education:* Harvard University, A.B. (magna cum laude), 1959; Columbia University, A.M. (with high distinction), 1960; Indiana University—Bloomington, Ph.D., 1971. *Politics:* Independent. *Avocational interests:* Tennis, bridge, travel.

ADDRESSES: Home—2230 Cape Cod Dr., Bloomington, IN 47401. *Office*—Department of Comparative Literature, 402 Ballantine, Indiana University—Bloomington, Bloomington, IN 47405-6606.

CAREER: Doubleday and Co., New York City, editorial trainee, 1960-61, editor of Anchor Books, 1961-66; Indiana University—Bloomington, lecturer, 1969-71, assistant professor, 1971-74, associate professor, 1974-78, professor of comparative literature, 1978—, associate dean of research and graduate development, 1977-80, chair of Department of East Asian Languages and Cultures, 1982-84, resident and founding director, East Asian Summer Language Institute, 1984-89, member of board of trustees of

Kinsey Institute for Research on Sex, Gender, and Reproduction, 1978—, member of board of trustees of Institute for Sex Research, 1980—. University of Illinois at Urbana-Champaign, visiting professor, 1987; lecturer at colleges and universities, including Seton Hall University, Trenton State College, Glassboro State College, University of Toledo, Chinese University of Hong Kong, and Jersey City State College; guest lecturer on the cruise ship *Song of Flower,* 1992. Member of Committee on Scholarly Communication with the People's Republic of China, 1989.

MEMBER: Society for the Comparative Study of Civilization, American Comparative Literature Association, Modern Language Association of America (member of executive committee, Asian Division, 1975-76; member of Texts and Translations Board, 1991—), Association for Asian Studies, American Literary Translators Association.

AWARDS, HONORS: Woodrow Wilson fellow, 1959-60; Fulbright fellow, 1968-69; Alfred Hodder fellow at Princeton University, 1974-75; fellow of Lilly Endowment, 1980-81; grants from National Endowment for the Humanities, 1982, and Japan Foundation, 1982 and 1985.

WRITINGS:

(Editor, translator, and author of introduction and notes) *Ai Qing: Selected Poems,* Foreign Languages Press, Indiana University—Bloomington, 1982.
The Transparent Eye: Translation, Chinese Literature, and Comparative Poetics, University of Hawaii Press, 1993.
(Regional editor for China) *HarperCollins World Reader,* HarperCollins, in press.

Work represented in anthologies, including *Sunflower Splendor: Three Thousand Years of Chinese Poetry,* edited by Wu-chi L. and Irving Lo, Anchor Press, 1975; *Comparative Literature East and West: Traditions and Trends,* edited by Cornelia N. Moore and Raymond Moody, East-West Center, University of Hawaii at Manoa; and *Reading World Literature,* edited by Sarah Lawall, University of Texas Press, in press. Contributor to literature and Asian studies journals and newspapers. Cofounder and coeditor, *Chinese Literature: Essays, Articles, Reviews,* 1979—; editor, *Research and Creative Activity,* 1977-80; member of board of editors, *China Review International: A Journal of Reviews of Scholarly Literature in Chinese Studies.*

WORK IN PROGRESS: The Coat of Many Colors: Occasional Essays on the Diversity in Us; "Seeing with Another I: Our Search for Other Worlds," to be included in *An Other Tongue: Essays on Bilingualism and Multiculturalism,* edited by Alfred Arteaga, for Duke University Press;

research on a theory of oral literature, comparative poetics, and Chinese-Western literary relations.

SIDELIGHTS: Eugene Chen Eoyang told *CA:* "In the first half of my life, I tried to become an American, having immigrated to the United States at the age of seven. In the second half of my life, I have tried to 'recuperate' the Chinese heritage which I had assiduously erased in my youth. Whereas I felt neither here nor there in the first part of my life, neither Chinese nor American, I now feel both Chinese and American, whether here or in China. What was seen as an inadequacy has now become a binocular or bifocal perspective. At my stage of life, I am beset by the ironic ailments of nearsightedness and farsightedness. While this creates a certain discomfort in my vision of things, it has the benefit of reminding me what it is like, and how precious it is, to see."

*　　*　　*

ERKKILA, Betsy 1944-

PERSONAL: Born September 17, 1944, in San Francisco, CA; daughter of Edwin Sulo and Jean (Troup) Erkkila; married Lawrence Stuelpnagel, August 19, 1978; children: Suli Elizabeth. *Education:* University of California, Berkeley, B.A., 1966, M.A., 1969, Ph.D., 1976; University of Grenoble, degree in French studies, 1967.

ADDRESSES: Office—Department of English, University of Pennsylvania, Philadelphia, PA 19104.

CAREER: University of Amiens, Amiens, France, Fulbright lecturer in American studies, 1972-74; University of Pennsylvania, Philadelphia, assistant professor, 1980-86, associate professor, 1986-90, professor of English, 1990—, director of Walt Whitman Conference, 1992. California State University, Chico, visiting assistant professor of English, 1974-80; California State University, director of London and Paris Travel-Study Program, 1977 and 1978; Columbia University, adjunct associate professor, 1988; Princeton University, adjunct professor, 1990.

MEMBER: Modern Language Association of America (member of executive committee on nineteenth-century American literature, 1986-91), Phi Beta Kappa.

AWARDS, HONORS: Grants from California State University, 1979, University of Pennsylvania, 1981 and 1982, American Council of Learned Societies, 1983-84, National Endowment for the Humanities, 1989-90, Pennsylvania Council on the Arts, 1991-92, and New Jersey Council of the Humanities, 1992; University Research Grant, 1988-89 and 1990-91; fellow, Woodrow Wilson International Center for Scholars, 1984.

WRITINGS:

Walt Whitman among the French: Poet and Myth, Princeton University Press, 1980.
Whitman the Political Poet, Oxford University Press, 1989.
The Wicked Sisters: Women Poets, Literary History, and Discord, Oxford University Press, 1992.
(Editor) *Ezra Pound: The Contemporary Reviews,* Cambridge University Press, 1992.

Work represented in anthologies, including *The Heath Anthology of American Literature,* Heath, 1989; *Approaches to Teaching "Leaves of Grass,"* edited by Donald Kummings, Modern Language Association of America, 1990; and *A Mixed Race: Ethnicity in Early America,* edited by Frank C. Shuffelton, Oxford University Press, 1992. Contributor of articles and reviews to periodicals, including *American Literary History* and *Walt Whitman Review.*

WORK IN PROGRESS: Writing the Revolution: Culture and Politics in the Early American Republic; editing, with Jay Grossman, *Whitman Breaking Bounds,* a collection of papers from the Centennial Symposium at the University of Pennsylvania.

BIOGRAPHICAL/CRITICAL SOURCES:

PERIODICALS

Times Literary Supplement, January 5, 1990, p. 3.

*　　*　　*

EROFEYEV, Victor 1947-

PERSONAL: Born September 19, 1947, in Moscow, U.S.S.R. (now Russia); son of Vladimir (an ambassador) and Galina (a translator; maiden name, Chechurin) Erofeyev; married Wieslawa Skora (a translator), June 20, 1969; children: Oleg. *Education:* Received D.Phil. from Moscow State University, D.Phil. *Politics:* Liberal. *Religion:* Christian.

ADDRESSES: Home—9 First Smolensky Lane, Moscow 121099, Russia. *Agent*—Michael Carlisle, William Morris Agency, 1350 Avenue of the Americas, New York, NY 10019.

CAREER: Gorky Institute of Literature, Moscow, Russia, researcher, until 1992; writer, 1992—.

WRITINGS:

Russian Beauty: A Novel, translated from the original Russian manuscript by Andrew Reynolds, Hamish Hamilton, 1990.

Author of a short story collection, *Life with an Idiot,* Hamish Hamilton; and a collection of literary essays, *The Labyrinth of the Damned Questions,* 1992; editor of essay collection *Metropol.*

WORK IN PROGRESS: Another novel.

BIOGRAPHICAL/CRITICAL SOURCES:

PERIODICALS

Moscow, January, 1991.
New York Times, February 15, 1990.
Times (London), August 22, 1992, p. 35.

*   *   *

ESTERHAZY, Peter   1950-

PERSONAL: Born April 1, 1950, in Budapest, Hungary; son of Matyas E. (a translator) and Lili (Manyoky) Esterhazy; married Gitti Reen (an artist), January 8, 1973; children: Dora, Marcell, Zsofia, Miklos. *Education:* University of Budapest, B.S. *Religion:* Roman Catholic.

ADDRESSES: Home—Emod 20, H-1031 Budapest, Hungary.

CAREER: Free-lance writer.

WRITINGS:

Helping Verbs of the Heart (novel; translated by Michael H. Heim), Grove Weidenfeld, 1991.

Also author of *Fancsiko es Pinta,* and *Papai vizeken ne kalozkodj,* 1977.

*   *   *

EVANS, Donald P(aul)   1930-1992

OBITUARY NOTICE—See index for *CA* sketch: Born December 11, 1930, in Rome, NY; died of heart failure, November 15, 1992, in Wilton, NY. Harness racing enthusiast, public relations executive, and writer. Evans was an award-winning author of articles and films about harness racing. He began his career as a reporter and sports editor for the *Rome Daily Sentinel.* In the mid-1960s he became publicity director for the Vernon Downs racetrack and later became president of a public relations agency. He was active in the North American Harness Publicists Association and in the U.S. Harness Writers Association. Evans's 1965 feature article, "The Byline Stable: Rags to Riches," was awarded the John Hervey Grand Prize by the Harness Racing Institute. Later, Evans received the CINE Golden Eagle Award and the Houston International Film Festival Gold Prize for *Queen*

Bea, a film about harness racing. Evans wrote several books, including *Hooked on Harness Racing, Hanover: The Greatest Name in Harness Racing,* and the semiautobiographical *Captain Slick: A Sports Novel.*

OBITUARIES AND OTHER SOURCES:

PERIODICALS

New York Times, November 11, 1992, p. D21.

*   *   *

EVANZZ, Karl   1953-

PERSONAL: Original name, Karl E. Anderson; born January 16, 1953, in St. Louis, MO; son of Adolphus and Bernice (Leake) Anderson; married Alexandra Jane Hamilton (a registered nurse), January 1, 1977; children: Aqila, Aaron, Kanaan, Arianna, Adrian. *Education:* Attended Forest Park Community College, 1970-71; Westminster College, Fulton, MO, B.A., 1975; studied law at American University, 1975-77. *Politics:* Independent. *Religion:* None. *Avocational interests:* Photography, mysticism, history.

ADDRESSES: Home—P.O. Box 296, Ashton, MD 20861. *Office*—*Washington Post,* 1150 Fifteenth St. N.W., Washington, DC 20071.

CAREER: Lowe, Mark & Moffett, Alexandria, VA, law clerk, 1976-77; law clerk to Harry T. Alexander, 1977-81; *Washington Post,* Washington, DC, on-line editor, 1980—. *St. Louis Argus,* Washington correspondent, 1981-83.

MEMBER: National Association of Black Journalists.

WRITINGS:

The Judas Factor: The Plot to Kill Malcolm X, Thunder's Mouth Press, 1992.

Contributor of articles and poems to periodicals, including *Southern Exposure, Black Film Review,* and *Big Red News.*

WORK IN PROGRESS: Malcolm's Son, an autobiographical novel, publication expected in 1996; *Elijah Muhammad,* a biography, publication expected in 1997.

SIDELIGHTS: Karl Evanzz told *CA:* "The books that secure the firmest lock on our imaginations all seem to have a common theme: man overcoming events so incredible that the truth sounds like fiction. Herman Melville mesmerized us on the high seas, while Mark Twain lured us into the caverns of Hannibal. Albert Camus baked our thoughts on the desert, and Ernest Hemingway took us on a safari. In my first novel, *Malcolm's Son,* I will take the reader deep into the asphalt jungle where I spent my youth—the St. Louis ghetto. People are often amazed when I recount events from my childhood, and frequently they ask me to retell the stories to their friends or co-workers. People are uniformly startled that I could have survived so many misadventures.

"*Malcolm's Son* is a story about a boy who imagines what life would be like if Malcolm X had been his father, and who then restructures his life as though the dream was true. I wanted to write a story about young black men, who are seldom the protagonists in today's literature. If African Americans can read, enjoy, and identify with autobiographical tales written by and about whites, there is no reason that a well-told story about African Americans should not appeal to whites.

"Although my first book, *The Judas Factor*, was generally well-received, I am terribly unhappy with it. There were several problems which should have been resolved before publication. For this reason, I plan to self-publish my next book. I am a bit of a perfectionist, and I doubt that I could find a publisher who cares more deeply than I about how a book looks and reads. In days gone by, books were regarded much like works of art. In addition to reading well, they looked good. I intend to have all of my books reflect this perspective.

"I don't know for certain when I decided to become a writer, but I was toying with the idea by the age of thirteen. If all goes well, I plan to publish at least ten more books before life bids me adieu. I want to leave a body of work which will inspire other African Americans to pursue the task of telling the history of African Americans. In doing so, we will be enhancing America's glorious culture and adding missing pieces to the human puzzle as well."

Evanzz added: "The publishing industry expects every writer to promote his own books nowadays; this is really impractical. A great many gifted writers (notably J. D. Salinger) are just that: writers, not hucksters. For this reason, most of today's bestsellers reflect the writer's and publisher's showmanship, rather than the quality of the book. In January of 1993, for example, most of the top twenty bestsellers were rubbish, pure and simple. Any time that Madonna and Rush Limbaugh produce the top-selling books in America, the publishing industry, and more importantly, American culture, are in serious trouble."

EVELYN, (John) Michael 1916-1992(?)
(Michael Underwood)

OBITUARY NOTICE—See index for *CA* sketch: Born June 2, 1916, in Worthing, Sussex, England; died c. 1992. Lawyer and author. Michael Evelyn had a distinguished legal career that spanned thirty years. He was, simultaneously, the immensely popular author of approximately fifty crime books under the pseudonym Michael Underwood. Evelyn graduated from Christ Church, Oxford, in 1938 and was called to the bar the following year at Grays Inn, London. Almost immediately, World War II broke out and Evelyn joined the British Army, serving for the next eight years and attaining the rank of major. In 1946, a civilian once more, he was appointed a member of the British Government legal service at the Department of Public Prosecutions and later became assistant director. It was during this time that Evelyn began writing under the pseudonym Michael Underwood; he published his first crime novel, *Murder on Trial,* in 1954. For the next thirty-eight years Evelyn published at least one book every year. In his crime writing, Evelyn used his own legal expertise—especially in the area of legal technicalities and procedures—to give his work a factual flavor while being totally fictional. Among Underwood's novels are *The Man Who Killed Too Soon, Silent Liars, The Uninvited Corpse, Dual Enigma, A Compelling Case, Rosa's Dilemma, The Seeds of Murder,* and his last book, *Guilty Conscience,* which was published in 1992.

OBITUARIES AND OTHER SOURCES:

BOOKS

Who's Who, 145th edition, St. Martin's, 1993.

PERIODICALS

Times (London), January 5, 1993, p. 15.

*   *   *

EYRE, Peter 1942-

PERSONAL: Born March 11, 1942, in New York City; son of Edward Joseph (a banker) and Dorothy Pelline (Acton) Eyre. *Education:* Studied at Portsmouth Priory, Portsmouth, RI, and Downside Abbey, Stratton-on-the-Fosse, Somerset, England. *Politics:* Democrat.

ADDRESSES: Home—12 South Terr., London SW7 2TD, England. *Agent*—Antony Harwood, Curtis Brown, 162-168 Regent St., London W1R 5TB, England.

CAREER: Professional actor, 1960—, and director. Worked with Royal Shakespeare Company at Old Vic Theatre; worked in regional theater, films, television, and radio.

MEMBER: International P.E.N., RAC, Groucho Club.

WRITINGS:

(Translator with Tania Alexander) Klaus Mann, *Siblings: The Children's Story,* Marion Boyars, 1992.

Contributor to periodicals, including *Vogue, Harpers and Queen, Vanity Fair,* and *Interview.*

SIDELIGHTS: Peter Eyre told *CA:* "My writing is minimal. I started by writing obituaries of friends and then a piece about a Greek island. More journalism followed, but it no longer interests me. It takes too long, is not well-enough rewarded, and I have little respect for the profession.

"I came to adapt a very obscure play by Klaus Mann because I wanted to try my wings as a director, and I didn't want to direct a play people knew. The production was successful, and the book came about as a result. I enjoyed the attempt to translate or adapt. I have a great respect for translators, as I do for all serious writers. I am hoping that the muse will one day pay me a visit."

* * *

FARRELL, Gillian B.

PERSONAL: Born in New York City; daughter of James Patrick (a bricklayer) and Genevieve (Gates) Murphy; married Larry Beinhart (a writer), February 29, 1988; children: Anna, James. *Education:* Attended Ladycliffe College, Northwestern University, Greenfield Community College, and University of Massachusetts at Amherst. *Politics:* Democrat. *Religion:* "Born Catholic."

ADDRESSES: Home—Woodstock, NY. *Agent*—Joy Harris, Robert Lantz-Joy Harris Literary Agency, 888 Seventh Ave., New York, NY 10106.

CAREER: Actress in Los Angeles, CA, and New York City, 1979—. Member of Maverick Theatre Company, Woodstock, NY; acting teacher; New York City detective.

MEMBER: Sisters in Crime, Actors' Equity Association, Screen Actors Guild.

WRITINGS:

Alibi for an Actress, Pocket Books, 1992.

WORK IN PROGRESS: Alibi or *Annie McGrogan, Book 2,* a sequel.

SIDELIGHTS: Gillian B. Farrell told *CA:* "I am and always will be an actor first. It is what motivates me, excites me, challenges me, and gives my life direction and purpose. It is an almost impossible task. To survive, I looked for work that pays, and discovered I was an excellent de-

tective when given an opportunity. The work provided an opportunity for extraordinary behind-the-scenes research for an actor whose job is to know and reflect human nature at its most fragile and frightening and everything in between. Conflict and drama are the actor's playing field; being a detective satisfied all the angles and approaches to understanding people in crisis.

"Afterward, I met a writer and married him, moved to the country, and began to tell the stories of my life in the city, both as an actress and as a detective. Writing is very cathartic. It is enjoyable to relive the cases, the stage and audition experiences, through someone like me, Annie McGrogan, yet someone who gets to say things I never dared, play roles I never got, and meet men who don't exist—not in my real world anyway. So now, I act, teach, write, and most importantly, have a life with my family and friends in a place where art and creativity matter and make a cultural difference."

* * *

FEIDEN, Karyn L. 1954-

PERSONAL: Born November 10, 1954, in Iowa; daughter of A. Barry Feiden (a publisher and labor negotiator) and Barbara Feiden (a social services administrator and writer; maiden name, Cole). *Education:* University of Massachusetts, B.A. (summa cum laude), 1976. *Politics:* "Left-leaning, like most writers with a conscience." *Avocational interests:* "Travelling to third-world countries."

ADDRESSES: Home—New York, New York. *Agent*—Barbara Lowenstein, Lowenstein Associates, 121 West 27th St., No. 601, New York, NY 10001.

CAREER: San Francisco Study Center, San Francisco, CA, production manager, 1978-81; Crown Publishers, New York City, development editor, 1982-85; free-lance writer and editor.

MEMBER: American Society of Journalists and Authors, National Writer's Union, National Women's Book Association.

AWARDS, HONORS: Book Award for Excellence in Family Issues, *Child,* 1991, for *Parent's Guide to Raising Responsible Kids.*

WRITINGS:

Job-Sharing Handbook, Ten Speed Press, 1985.
Parent's Guide to Raising Kids Who Love to Learn (part of "Children's Television Workshop" series), Prentice-Hall, 1989.
Cataract and Other Eye Surgery, Dell, 1990.
Hope and Help for Chronic Fatigue Syndrome, Prentice-Hall, 1990.

Indoor Pollution, Fawcett/Columbine, 1991.
Parent's Guide to Raising Responsible Kids (part of "Children's Television Workshop" series), Prentice-Hall, 1991.
Recovering from a Cesarean Section, HarperCollins, 1992.
(With Peter S. Arno) *Against the Odds: The Story of AIDS Drug Development, Politics and Profits,* HarperCollins, 1992.

Contributor to *Caring for the Elderly: Reshaping Health Policy,* Johns Hopkins University Press, 1988. Contributor to periodicals, including *Asiaweek, Legal Economics, New York Times* and *Newsday.*

WORK IN PROGRESS: Research on black history and on various Food and Drug Administration (FDA)-related topics, including gene therapy and clinical trial participation.

SIDELIGHTS: Karyn L. Feiden told *CA:* "After a brief career as an editor with a publishing house in Manhattan, I found my true calling in nonfiction writing. I see myself mostly as a distiller of information with an ability to turn complex concepts and arcane ideas into accessible and intriguing stories for the general public. By immersing myself into research and conducting in-depth interviews, I became an expert on topics from acquired immunodeficiency syndrome (AIDS) to eye surgery; indoor pollution to childrearing; chronic fatigue syndrome to cesarean sections; black history to gene therapy. I try to communicate what I have learned to inform, entertain, and help others."

*   *   *

FELDMAN, David Lewis 1951-

PERSONAL: Born June 1, 1951, in Cleveland, OH; son of George (a retired furniture retailer) and Ruth (a homemaker; maiden name, Frankel) Feldman; married Debbie Miller (a free-lance writer), December 16, 1973. *Education:* Kent State University, B.A., 1973; University of Missouri, M.A., 1975, Ph.D., 1979. *Religion:* Jewish. *Avocational interests:* Hiking, bicycling, collecting maps.

ADDRESSES: Home—1228 Chelsea Rd., Knoxville, TN 37922. *Office*—Oak Ridge National Laboratory, University of Tennessee, 327 South Stadium Hall, Knoxville, TN 37966.

CAREER: West Virginia State College, Institute, assistant professor, 1980-82; Moorhead State University, Moorhead, MN, associate professor and acting chair, 1982-88; Oak Ridge National Lab, Oak Ridge, TN, policy analyst, 1988—; University of Tennessee, Knoxville, senior editor of *Forum for Applied Research,* 1990   . Missouri Department of Natural Resources, resource planner, 1980. Coun-

cil member of East Tennessee American Society for Public Administration, 1992—.

MEMBER: American Political Science Association, American Society for Public Administration, Pi Sigma Alpha.

AWARDS, HONORS: Michael S. Corwin scholarship, University of Missouri, 1975; University of Missouri department of political science teaching awards, 1975 and 1977; finalist, Presidential Management Intern Program, Office of Personnel Management, 1979; listed in directory of American scholars, American Council of Learned Societies, 1982; grants from Moorhead State University, 1983 and 1986, and Oak Ridge Associated Universities, 1985-88; merit award for exceptional teaching and research, Moorhead State University, 1984; Oak Ridge Associated Universities fellow, 1986 and 1987.

WRITINGS:

Water Resources Management: In Search of an Environmental Ethic, Johns Hopkins University Press, 1991.

Contributor to books, including *Proceedings of the First New River Symposium,* Quality Printing Company, 1983; *The Decline of Military Regimes: The Civilian Influence,* edited by Constantine P. Danopoulos, Westview Press, 1988; *Environmental Politics and Public Policy in the West,* edited by Zachary Smith, 1992; and *International Organizations and Environmental Policy,* edited by Robert Bartlett, Macmillan, 1992. Contributor of articles to periodicals, including *Policy Sciences, Journal of Inter-American Studies and World Affairs, Political Psychology,* and *Society and Natural Resources.* Member of board of editors, *Policy Studies Journal,* 1992.

SIDELIGHTS: David Lewis Feldman comments in the introduction to his book, *Water Resources Management: In Search of an Environmental Ethic,* "My exposure to water policy came about quite accidentally while I was completing my doctoral dissertation at the University of Missouri. My name had been sent by way of the Presidential Management Internship Program to the director of the water resources planning program of the Missouri Department of Natural Resources. The director was dedicated to sound environmental management and the protection of his state against inappropriate encroachments by federal agencies.

"For me, the offer was particularly fortuitous. Although I had opportunities to apply for federal agency positions, this state position offered me the chance to continue to teach part time at a small liberal arts college while 'getting my feet wet' in government. Moreover, the director of the program enthusiastically supported his staff, its responsibilities, and my possible contribution. Finally, I was interested in environmental issues and the director was willing to overlook my relative lack of information about them.

"I began my work in 1980, the last year of Jimmy Carter's presidency. At that time, environmental policy was at the vortex of national controversy. Water issues prompted considerable discussion and study and at least some movement toward what was then too optimistically termed a national water policy. Almost all of my agency's efforts reflected this controversy. Squabbles over supplemental appropriations bills for the Water Resources Council, changes in principles and standards governing water resources projects, and almost daily discussion about the goals of water planning interfered with our work. To understate matters, it was an exciting time to be learning about, and working in, water policy.

"I was hired to help write a state plan to manage its water resources for recreation, agriculture, industry, utilities, municipalities, and navigation. The document, partially funded by Water Resources Council state planning grants (which, like the council itself, no longer exist), would elucidate strategies for achieving water conservation and control of nonpoint agricultural runoff. Most of all, it would tell citizens of Missouri how their state saw its most pressing water problems and what it expected to do about them with the help of upstream states and the federal government.

"In the several months I interned at this program, I also reviewed federal agency plans and environmental impact statements and helped to assess the policy implications of various river basin commission reports. Most challenging of all, I composed drafts of letters for the director of the council, which, in final iteration, represented the state policy on such matters as proposed Corps of Engineers' mitigation measures to prevent further fish kills at Harry S. Truman Dam on the Osage River. Once, I even prepared the state's formal request for Corps of Engineers' help for a resort owner on Table Rock Lake who wanted to move his fishing dock, which was caught high and dry (like his fishing business) when drought prompted a greater than normal reservoir drawdown for power and instream flow quality on the White River.

"I learned a great deal about the substance of water policy, its stakeholders and their concerns, the inner workings of state bureaucracy, and how governments use knowledge and information for making policy. It was frustrating to me that my detailed (and, I thought, well-conceived) reports were eventually reduced to the briefest of memoranda, stating recommendations without rationale.

"Most of all, I learned three lessons, which are reflected in [my writing]. First, most people who work in government are conscientious and dedicated. They may not always be able to define good public policy, but they have some intuitive sense of what it should be. For my colleagues at the Missouri Department of Natural Resources, such a policy would attempt to honestly, openly, and equitably accommodate the interests of a number of divergent stakeholders, and it would establish rules for water management that assured abundant, clean water for present and future Missourians. Civil servants may not often reflect on intergenerational justice, but they know that good policy entails long-term commitment to sound, scientific management supported by scrutable ethical justification. This commitment represents a promise by government that the implications of its decisions have been carefully studied. Our planning efforts were not only designed to meet a legislative mandate or deadline; they were elegant statements of the priorities valued by water resources professionals, articulating goals important to a just society.

"Second, natural resources issues spark contentious debate precisely because they strike at the core values of fairness, equity, and even aesthetics. Honest, fair-minded people can have honest, well-founded disagreements over priorities and programs. For example, when does government have the authority to order a family from its land? How does government assess a new dam that would attract significant tourism at the same time that it would inundate farms? Do the beauty and recreational quality of a white-water stream outweigh the benefits of improved navigation and additional electric power? To a greater degree than I realized, my colleagues were fighting battles in the trenches of American federal-state relations over economic development and environmental preservation. Policy makers' ethical justifications for their decisions are their weapons.

"Third and finally, I learned that political scientists trained in political theory have many important things to say about the two concerns expressed above. Some of the most cogent observations on the failings of natural resources management come from those who, like Lynton Caldwell, Theodore Lowi, [and] Grant McConnell, point out the shortcomings of the liberal state and its tenuous foundations of moral authority. These tenuous foundations explain, among other things, why established environmental policies pit region against region; resist centralized, rational management; are powerfully linked to conventional notions of private property; too often disregard the consequences of cavalier abuse of resources; and require a formal deontology of decision making—such as a procedure for assessing environmental impacts of proposed agency actions—in order to assure the accountability of government to its citizens.

"These observations and their basis in political theory extend far beyond water policy to a number of pressing environmental issues, including global climate change, transboundary air and water pollution, and deforestation and desertification. . . . [A]lthough our scientific understanding of the causes and consequences of environmental problems has steadily increased, the ways in which governments—local as well as national—react to these problems lag far behind our knowledge. I contend that the major reason for this lag is that this understanding challenges the positions of stakeholders, whose perceptions, interests, and goals hinge upon contending views of property, of our responsibility to protect and use nature, and even of our obligation to future generations."

BIOGRAPHICAL/CRITICAL SOURCES:

BOOKS

Feldman, David Lewis, *Water Resources Management: In Search of an Environmental Ethic,* Johns Hopkins University Press, 1991.

*   *   *

FERNANDEZ-SHAW, Carlos M(anuel) 1924-

PERSONAL: Born June 23, 1924, in Madrid, Spain; son of Guillermo (a playwright) and Maria Josefa (a homemaker; maiden name, Baldasano) Fernandez-Shaw; married Ilda Magda del Monico (a housewife), November 19, 1956; children: Maria Isabel, Maria Cristina, Carla Maria, Paloma Maria. *Education:* University of Madrid, L.L.M. and Ph.D.; Madrid Diplomatic School, graduated, 1948. *Religion:* Roman Catholic. *Avocational interests:* Golf.

ADDRESSES: Home and office—Claudio Coello 60, 28001 Madrid, Spain.

CAREER: Spanish Diplomatic Service, worked at Ministry of Foreign Affairs in Madrid, 1949-51, secretary of embassies in Copenhagen, Denmark, 1951-52, Stockholm, Sweden, 1952-53, and Asuncion, Paraguay, 1953-56, head of Department of Institutions and Publications, Cultural Relations Division, Madrid, 1956-58, consul in Montreal, Quebec, 1958-61, in charge of cultural affairs at embassies in Washington, DC, 1961-65, and Rome, Italy, 1965-70, assistant secretary of Cultural Affairs Division, Madrid, 1970-73, ambassador to Paraguay, 1973-77, Australia, 1977, New Zealand, 1978, Fiji and Papua New Guinea, both 1979, and Tonga and the Solomon Islands, both 1981, inspector general in Madrid, 1983-85, consul general in Miami, FL, 1986-89. University of Madrid, assistant lecturer in public international law, 1949-51; Institute of Spanish Culture, head of Department of Cultural Exchange, 1956-58. President of Border Commission With France and Portugal, 1985-86. *Military service:* Spanish Army, Infantry Reserve; became first lieutenant.

MEMBER: Asociacion Espanola de Amigos de los Castillos, Asamblea Amistosa Literaria (Cadiz), Club de Campo (Madrid).

AWARDS, HONORS: Decorated Knight Commander (with distinction), Order of Queen Isabella, 1966, and Order of King Alphonsus the Wise, 1970; Knight Commander, Order of Merit of Italy, 1970, and Order of Henry the Navigator, Portugal, 1971; Knight of the Grand Cross of Civil Merit, Spain, 1972; Knight Commander, Order of Andres Bello, Venezuela, 1973; Knight of Grand Merit, Paraguay, 1977.

WRITINGS:

Presencia Espanola en los Estados Unidos, Ediciones Cultura Hispanica (Madrid), 1972, 3rd edition, Facts on File, 1991, translation published as *The Hispanic Presence in North America From 1492 to Today,* Facts on File, 1991.

The Spanish Contributions to the Independence of the U.S.A., Interamerican Review of Bibliography, 1976.

Ventura y tribulaciones de un padre recien Estrenado (title means "The Joys and Anxieties of a Brand-New Father"), Studium Ediciones (Madrid), 1976.

Los Estados Independientes de Norteamerica (title means "The Independent States of North America"), Instituto de Estudios Politicos (Madrid), 1977.

El Primer Consul de Espana en Australia: Antonio Arrom (title means "The First Consul of Spain in Australia: Antonio Arrom"), M. Asuntos Exteriores (Madrid), 1988.

La Florida Contemporanea: Siglos XIX y XX (title means "Contemporary Florida: The Nineteenth and Twentieth Centuries"), Editorial Mapfre (Madrid), 1992.

El arpa en el contexto musical del Paraguay (title means "The Harp in the Musical Landscape of Paraguay"), ARLU (Madrid), 1992.

WORK IN PROGRESS: A book on Spanish-Australian relations throughout history.

SIDELIGHTS: Carlos M. Fernandez-Shaw told *CA:* "As a retired person, I am devoting myself to writing about topics related to my experience as a diplomat in the United States, Australia, the South Pacific, and so on. I will write history, and maybe a novel, too. I would also like to work in the field of theater, because that is the one in which my grandfather and father excelled, especially in the musical (*zarzuela*)."

*   *   *

FERRIGNO, Robert 1948(?)-

PERSONAL: Born c. 1948, in Florida; married, wife's name, Jody; children: Jake, Dani. *Education:* Received B.A.; Bowling Green State University, M.F.A., 1971.

ADDRESSES: Agent—Sandra Dijkstra, 1155 Camino del Mar, No. 515, Del Mar, CA 92014.

CAREER: Writer. Instructor in English and literature in Seattle, WA, 1971-73; feature writer for *Orange County Register,* until 1988; instructor in journalism at California State University, Fullerton.

WRITINGS:

The Horse Latitudes (novel), Morrow, 1990.
The Cheshire Moon (novel), Morrow, 1993.

Contributor to periodicals, including *California* and *Women's Sports and Fitness.*

SIDELIGHTS: Robert Ferrigno drew critical attention with the 1990 publication of his first novel, *The Horse Latitudes.* The author began the book after his wife survived a difficult pregnancy and gave birth to their son, Jake. "Even though they both pulled out of it, and they're both fine, it gave me a very powerful sense that life is fleeting," Ferrigno told Dennis McLellan in the *Los Angeles Times.* "It made me realize I had been talking and thinking about writing a book for a long time, but should probably not count on having the rest of my life to finish it." Ferrigno started *The Horse Latitudes* while working as a feature writer for the *Orange County Register,* rising at four each morning to write. But after about eighteen months his heavy schedule began to take its toll, and with his wife's encouragement, Ferrigno quit his job at the newspaper to work on his novel full-time.

Ferrigno's gamble proved to be a profitable one, as William Morrow and Company bought the rights to his unfinished novel for $150,000 in 1988. Set in southern California, *The Horse Latitudes* concerns Danny DiMedici, a former marijuana dealer who lost his taste for the outlaw life after killing a man. DiMedici's amoral wife Lauren, a corporate motivational psychologist, left him after he reformed, explaining that "God hates a coward." As the novel opens, DiMedici is attempting to come to terms with his recent divorce: "There were nights when Danny missed Lauren so bad that he wanted to take a fat man and throw him through a plate-glass window." He is soon visited by the police, who inform him that Lauren has disappeared and that her current lover, a scientist who has discovered a way to use fetal tissue to preserve youth, has been murdered at her beach house. A suspect in the killing, DiMedici searches for Lauren and is pursued himself by a pair of police officers and several other eccentric characters.

By turns darkly comic, erotic, and violent, Ferrigno's crime thriller generally found favor with reviewers, some of whom compared the author to Elmore Leonard and Raymond Chandler. Chicago *Tribune Books* contributor Gary Dretzka commented that "the chases, kidnappings, beatings, blackmail and extortion attempts that result after this crazy California salad is tossed are imaginatively

rendered and make for a quick, chilling, often humorous read." Though he found *The Horse Latitudes* to be unoriginal, Michael Dirda acknowledged in the *Washington Post* that "Ferrigno does possess some genuine storytelling skills. He can make you afraid, he can make you laugh, . . . and he can make you keep turning his pages." Like some other reviewers, Dirda also observed that *The Horse Latitudes* reads like a film script, "which may be fine if you were expecting a movie, but not so good if you were hoping for a novel." *Time* contributor Margaret Carlson was more enthusiastic, calling *The Horse Latitudes* "a work of *noir* literature that is the most memorable fiction debut of the season. With a magic all his own, [Ferrigno] has written an illuminating novel that never fails to entertain but also, surprisingly, makes us feel."

The seamy underworld Ferrigno depicts in *The Horse Latitudes* is similar to one the author experienced firsthand. Dissatisfied with the job teaching English and literature he had landed after graduate school, Ferrigno quit and spent the next six years playing poker for a living. He resided in a high-crime area of downtown Seattle, where one of his neighbors was a heroin dealer. Ferrigno turned to writing after taking a free-lance assignment for an alternative weekly newspaper. "There is an intensity in coming home at 4 in the morning and throwing a couple of thousand dollars on your bed and throwing it in the air [and saying], I won all of it!," he told McLellan. "But that wasn't even close to getting $10 for an article with your name on it."

Ferrigno followed *The Horse Latitudes* with *The Cheshire Moon,* which was published in 1993. In this novel a reporter, Quinn, and his photographer sidekick, Jen Takamura, pursue the murderer of Quinn's best friend Andy. Andy had witnessed a killing, and the murderer found it necessary to dispose of Andy as well, making his death appear a suicide. The killer is Emory Roy Liston, a "crazed rhinoceros of a former pro football player," according to Christopher Lehmann-Haupt in the *New York Times.* Liston, who attends night school, polishes his football trophies regularly, and is a frequent cable shopping channel customer, "provides the spice" of the novel, wrote Michael Anderson in the *New York Times Book Review.* "Despite the conventionality of its plot, Mr. Ferrigno develops the qualities he showed off with such promise in his first novel," commented Lehmann-Haupt, who particularly noted Ferrigno's "black wit embellished with images of violence." The reviewer concluded that *The Cheshire Moon* is "a lot of fun to read, and Mr. Ferrigno certainly knows how to lay contrasting colors on his canvas."

BIOGRAPHICAL/CRITICAL SOURCES:

BOOKS

Contemporary Literary Criticism, Volume 65, Gale, 1991, pp. 47-50.
Ferrigno, Robert, *The Horse Latitudes,* Morrow, 1990.

PERIODICALS

Los Angeles Times, March 2, 1990.
Los Angeles Times Book Review, April 8, 1990, pp. 2, 8.
New York Times, March 19, 1990, p. C20; February 25, 1993, p. B2.
New York Times Book Review, February 7, 1993, p. 22.
Time, March 26, 1990, p. 78.
Tribune Books (Chicago), March 11, 1990, pp. 6-7.
Village Voice, April 3, 1990, p. 76.
Wall Street Journal, March 9, 1990, p. A11.
Washington Post, March 16, 1990.

—Sketch by *Michelle M. Motowski*

* * *

FESHBACH, Murray 1929-

PERSONAL: Born August 8, 1929, in New York, NY; son of Benjamin and Lilly (Harfenist) Feshbach; married Muriel Joan Schreiner (a statistician), December 30, 1956; children: Michael L., David. *Education:* Syracuse University, A.B., 1950; Columbia University, M.A., 1951; American University, Ph.D., 1974. *Politics:* Democrat. *Religion:* Jewish. *Avocational interests:* Photography, stamp collecting, rock and mineral collecting, calligraphy.

ADDRESSES: Home—11403 Fairoak Dr., Silver Spring, MD 20902-3136. *Office*—Georgetown University, Department of Demography, Washington, DC 20057-1043.

CAREER: Affiliated with National Bureau of Economic Research, Inc., New York City, 1955-56; U.S. Bureau of the Census, Foreign Demographic Analysis Division, Washington, DC, analyst, 1957-67, chief of U.S.S.R. branch, 1967-68, chief of U.S.S.R./East Europe branch, 1969-78, chief of U.S.S.R. population, employment, and research and development branch, 1978-79; Georgetown University, Washington, DC, senior research scholar at the Center for Population Research and professional lecturer in demography, 1981-84, research professor of demography, 1984—. Columbia University, adjunct professor, 1983-85; North Atlantic Treaty Organization (NATO) Headquarters, Office of the Secretary General, Sovietologist-in-residence, 1986-87; lecturer at several universities and other institutions, including American University, George Washington University, Institute of East-West Security Studies, 1992, and Foreign Policy Research Institute, 1992. Consultant to the Rand Corp.,

Johnson & Johnson, U.S. Department of Defense, U.S. State Department, the World Bank, and other organizations. *Military service:* U.S. Army, 1951-55; became sergeant.

MEMBER: International Union for the Scientific Study of Population, Association for Comparative Economic Studies (vice president, 1983-84; president, 1984-85), American Association for the Advancement of Slavic Studies (Washington chapter secretary, 1962-74, president, 1974-78; national vice president, 1984-85, president, 1985-86), Population Association of America, British Association for Soviet and East European Studies, Omicron Delta Epsilon.

AWARDS, HONORS: Silver medal, U.S. Department of Commerce, 1979; fellow, Woodrow Wilson International Center for Scholars, Kennan Institute for Advanced Russian Studies, 1979-80.

WRITINGS:

(Editor) *National Security Issues in the U.S.S.R.,* Nijhoff (Dordrecht, Netherlands), 1987.
(With Alfred Friendly, Jr.) *Ecocide in the U.S.S.R.: Health and Nature under Siege,* Basic Books, 1992.

Contributor to *Cambridge Encyclopedia of Russia and the U.S.S.R.,* 1993. Work represented in anthologies, including *The Soviet Economy: Towards the Year 2000,* Allen & Unwin, 1983. Contributor to periodicals, including *Wilson Quarterly, Wall Street Journal, Washington Quarterly, Washington Post,* and *U.S. News & World Report.*

Ecocide in the U.S.S.R. has been translated into Russian and Spanish.

WORK IN PROGRESS: Researching ecology, health, and global security issues.

SIDELIGHTS: "Murray Feshbach, economist and demographer, would be well cast as the first victim in an espionage novel: the bespectacled, slightly awkward, utterly unsuspecting innocent killed because of something he found, something seemingly irrelevant," surmised Cullen Murphy in the *Atlantic Monthly.* As one of America's preeminent experts on the former Soviet Union, Feshbach is known for his ability to transform voluminous amounts of seemingly unrelated data into a general portrait of Soviet life. Feshbach frequently found his task challenging, as the Soviet government was secretive and, for example, rarely released complete census information. "He burrows in obscure and unlikely places," Murphy reported, "generating as a result large quantities of new information, preserving it all, and dispensing among his colleagues what he cannot use in his own studies of manpower, scientific training, health, mortality, population trends, ethnicity, the military, and industrial productivity."

An advisor to such organizations as the Rand Corporation, World Bank, and the U.S. State Department, Feshbach enlightens the general public in his 1992 book, *Ecocide in the U.S.S.R.: Health and Nature under Siege,* which he wrote with Alfred Friendly, Jr. *Ecocide in the U.S.S.R.* reveals how the Soviet government participated in the devastation of the nation's environment and disregarded the harmful effects of nuclear, industrial, and agricultural pollution on public health. Feshbach and Friendly's depiction of the former Soviet Union is one of a country whose "self-inflicted social and ecological wounds, compounding and compounded by its economic and political failures, sapped Soviet military strength and undermined Moscow's pretense to global influence," Douglas R. Weiner quoted in the *New York Times Book Review.* According to the authors, the former superpower is a "crippled giant" whose quality of life is in some areas comparable to the Third World.

Feshbach and Friendly report, for instance, that the average Soviet life expectancy is similar to that of Paraguay. The authors also reveal that in 1989 nearly three quarters of the country's surface water was considered polluted, that the widely publicized Chernobyl disaster contributed only a small portion of the nation's nuclear pollution, and that only a quarter of all Soviet schoolchildren are considered to be truly healthy. In Moscow pollution causes a fifth of all illnesses and in the city's finest maternity clinics eight out of ten babies born between late 1990 and mid-1991 had birth defects, were premature, or both. "No other great industrial civilization so systematically and [for] so long [has] poisoned its land, air, water, and people," W. Bruce Lincoln quoted *Ecocide in the U.S.S.R.* in Chicago *Tribune Books,* "and none, so loudly proclaiming its efforts to improve public health and protect nature, [has] so degraded both."

"For ghastly and depressing stories of wanton destruction of the human and natural resources of a great nation, nothing quite matches *Ecocide in the U.S.S.R.,*" assessed S. Frederick Starr in the *Washington Post Book World.* "To read it is to take a brisk walk through a chamber of horrors." Feshbach and Friendly impressed critics with the enormous amount of data they collected. And while some reviewers noted that *Ecocide in the U.S.S.R.* contains more of a cataloguing of the Soviet Union's environmental degradation than an analysis of its causes, Starr remarked that "this is a benchmark study nonetheless, a priceless compendium of information peppered with astute and commonsensical observations. Thanks to this fine study, other researchers will be able more readily to move the analysis to the next stage."

BIOGRAPHICAL/CRITICAL SOURCES:

BOOKS

Feshbach, Murray, and Alfred Friendly, Jr., *Ecocide in the U.S.S.R.: Health and Nature under Siege,* Basic Books, 1992.

PERIODICALS

Atlantic Monthly, February, 1983, pp. 33-52.
New York Times Book Review, June 7, 1992, p. 14.
Tribune Books (Chicago), April 26, 1992, p. 1.
Washington Post Book World, May 31, 1992, p. 1.

*   *   *

FIELDS, Debbi
 See FIELDS, Debra J.

*   *   *

FIELDS, Debra J.   1956-
 (Debbi Fields)

PERSONAL: Born September 18, 1956, in Oakland, CA; daughter of Edward Martin (a welder) and Mary Lucy (Casovia) Sivyer; married Randall Keith Fields (an economist and chair of the board and chief financial officer for Mrs. Fields Inc.), September 21, 1975; children: Jessica, Jenessa, Jennifer, Ashley, McKenzie. *Education:* Attended junior college.

ADDRESSES: Office—Mrs. Fields Cookies, 333 Main St., Park City, UT 84060.

CAREER: Owner and operator of Mrs. Fields Chocolate Chippery, Palo Alto, CA, beginning in 1977; Mrs. Fields Cookies Inc., Park City, UT, president and chief executive officer, 1980—. Member of board of trustees for Primary Children's Medical Center; foundation owner of Mrs. Fields Children's Health Foundation, 1986—.

MEMBER: Cystic Fibrosis Research Foundation (member of council for research and development).

WRITINGS:

(Under name Debbi Fields, with Alan Furst) *One Smart Cookie* (autobiography), Simon & Schuster, 1987.

SIDELIGHTS: In her book *One Smart Cookie,* written with Alan Furst, Debra J. Fields explains how she made the transition from homemaker to chief executive officer of a 160-million-dollar-a-year cookie business. Although her friends as well as financial institutions initially discouraged the idea, Fields opened Mrs. Fields Chocolate Chippery, a gourmet cookie shop, on August 18, 1977.

Fields now owns more than six hundred cookie stores and is hailed as the "cookie queen." Her famous cookies are made from a recipe that Fields began perfecting as a teenager—for recreational rather than business reasons—and they are now sold in seven countries. Industry leaders attribute the company's success to Fields's commitment to quality and her ability to obtain high productivity from her employees. In an interview for *Moxie* magazine, Fields shared her philosophy for success: "The main thing is—if you absolutely *know* what you're doing is good, it makes it very easy not to compromise and not to give up; because you *know* you're going to make this world a little bit better."

BIOGRAPHICAL/CRITICAL SOURCES:

PERIODICALS

Moxie, August, 1990.

*   *   *

FINCH, Roger   1937-

PERSONAL: Born April 17, 1937, in Pittsburgh, PA; son of Willard Grant (a laborer) and Phyllis Ivy (an artist; maiden name, Creek) Finch. *Education:* George Washington University, B.A., 1968; Harvard University, Ph.D., 1976. *Religion:* Shamanist. *Avocational interests:* Horticulture, music, traveling.

ADDRESSES: Home—0-AZA Kitagawa 176-6, Hanno, Saitama, Japan. *Office*—Surugadai University, Hanno, Saitama, Japan.

CAREER: Sophia University, Tokyo, Japan, lecturer in linguistics, 1979—; Surugadai University, Saitama, Japan, professor of English literature, 1990—. Advisor for Test of English for International Communication Committee.

MEMBER: Portsmouth Atheneum (Portsmouth, NH); Phi Beta Kappa.

WRITINGS:

What Is Written in the Wind, Sparrow Press, 1984.
According to Lilies (poetry), Carcanet, 1992.

Also Japan editor for the Asiatic Society of Japan.

WORK IN PROGRESS: Silk, a narrative poem; *Persistence of Memory,* a novel; research on the genetic relationship of circumpacific languages and reconstruction of vocabulary, morphology, and syntax.

SIDELIGHTS: Roger Finch told *CA:* "Like Gertrude Stein, I was born in Allegheny, Pennsylvania. Allegheny has long been the Northside of Pittsburgh, that part of Pittsburgh that spreads from the sill of the Ohio River up into the theatrical heights of the surrounding hills. But when I was a child, many of the books that I borrowed from the Northside Public Library proclaimed on their bookplates that they still belonged to the Carnegie Free Library of Allegheny, and those bookplates were my passport into another town that existed for me inside a city of foreigners.

"In the early 1940s, Pittsburgh was as brash and bleak as it had ever been, still recovering in some ways from the Depression but at the same time secretly stimulated by the Second World War. The frequent air-raid blackouts we experienced reminded us that we were the Duesseldorf and the Hiroshima of the United States. The day we dropped the atomic bomb on the Pittsburgh of Japan I was playing kick-the-can in front of our house. The announcement came out from the radio and frizzled me in my tracks, as though I were one of the shadows fixed forever into the glaze of a wall by that distant blast.

"My first exposure to the arts was not to literature but to painting and to music. My mother was an artist and, following her example, I learned to render real birds and flowers on paper before I ever learned to write the alphabet. My mother's mother sang as soloist in church, and at her house there was a piano and a harmonium where I spent hour after hour painting pictures in sound of natural phenomena—clouds and thunder and rain. These pictures may have been rather too vivid for any adult within earshot, but they undoubtedly foreshadowed my later interest in music.

"And yet, I was not unaware of language. Language was of two kinds: the flat, workaday language that the people of Pittsburgh spoke and the colorful and mysterious language the foreigners spoke. I would come home from school and listen to the Polish Hour and the Italian Hour and the Greek Hour, and though I did not understand what the words meant I understood the music of it. My own grandparents were foreigners; they were English. And my mother was Canadian. The English they spoke was not the English the people of Pittsburgh spoke but an English that the people of the other town might have spoken, so I used their greeting-card phrases and their nursery-rhyme accent.

"When I first began writing poetry at the age of fourteen, it was inevitable that my models were not American but European—models as diverse as Donne, Blake, Hopkins, Rilke, Gautier, and Verlaine. But I remained a Sunday poet. Architecture first, music theory second, linguistics third, I changed my majors until I settled into the last, believing in the heady atmosphere of the 1960s that a degree in linguistics would provide a surer path into the academic world than music theory would.

"But, unexpectedly, that path brought me to Japan. At some point in my life I would have had to experience the land of *ukiyo-e, ikebana,* and *noh,* for all my adolescent interests were urging me on in that direction, but I never expected that by now I should have spent nearly as many years here in exile as I spent in the city of my birth. Living abroad has had a tremendous impact on my development as a poet. Japan has not only been the primary source for totally different experiences in my life, it has also been the jumping-off place to all those exotic locales that have so appealed to me in my reading and are no longer exotic to me, but familiar. More importantly, the very fact of living abroad and being separated from my native land provoked in me a need to express my loneliness and to resist the assault on me of a culture much more alien, and alien in a far different way, than I expected. And so I turned again to poetry after a long silence, this time seriously. Even at this point my poetry might not have taken on the shape it has at present if I had not been asked to teach a course in American poetry, for it forced me to read much poetry I was unfamiliar with and poetry I had neglected. In the process I made great discoveries—Marianne Moore, Wallace Stevens, Richard Wilbur, James Merrill, Anthony Hecht—whose means of expression I feel such an affinity for and whose sense of structure has influenced my own style, in spite of the fact that the cultural milieu in which I now live might have inspired a far different art with a far different aesthetic."

BIOGRAPHICAL/CRITICAL SOURCES:

PERIODICALS

Times Literary Supplement, September 11, 1992, p. 25.

* * *

FINCHAM, Francis D. 1954-
(Frank D. Fincham)

PERSONAL: Born February 22, 1954; married Susan Kemp (a technical assistant), September 22, 1979; children: Alexander, Camilla. *Education:* University of Natal, B.A., 1974; University of the Witwatersrand, B.A. (honors), 1975, M.A. (with distinction), 1976; Oxford University, Ph.D., 1980; doctoral study at State University of New York at Stony Brook, 1980-81.

ADDRESSES: Office—Department of Psychology, University of Illinois at Urbana-Champaign, 603 East Daniel, Champaign, IL 61820.

CAREER: University of the Witwatersrand, Johannesburg, South Africa, junior lecturer in psychology, 1976-77; University of Illinois at Urbana-Champaign, assistant professor, 1982-88, associate professor of psychol-

ogy, 1988—, W. T. Grant faculty scholar, Program in Child Mental Health, 1986-91, fellow of Center for Advanced Study, 1987, clinical supervisor at Psychological Clinic, 1982—, associate director of clinical training, 1987-88. Johannesburg Crisis Clinic, crisis counselor, 1975-77; Johannesburg Children's Home, group therapist, 1976; State University of New York at Stony Brook, clinical psychology intern, 1981-82. Member of Martin Luther King Advocacy for Justice Committee, 1990—.

MEMBER: International Network on Personal Relationships, International Society for the Study of Personal Relationships, National Council for Family Relations, American Psychological Society (fellow), American Psychological Association (fellow), American Association of Applied and Preventive Psychology, Association for the Advancement of Behavior Therapy, Society for Research in Child Development, British Psychological Society, Midwestern Psychological Association.

AWARDS, HONORS: Rhodes scholar, Oxford University, 1977-80; named Young Social Psychologist of the Year, British Psychological Society, 1979; grants from National Institute of Mental Health, 1985-87, 1988-90, 1989-93, 1990-92, National Institute of Child Health and Human Development, 1985-87, W. T. Grant Foundation, 1986-91, and National Science Foundation, 1988-90; travel grant for Australia from American Psychological Association, 1988; Gerald R. Miller Award for Early Career Achievements, International Network on Personal Relationships, 1989; grant from Harry Frank Guggenheim Foundation, 1991-93; Berscheid-Hatfield Award, 1993.

WRITINGS:

(Editor with J. M. Jaspars and M. R. Hewstone, and contributor) *Attribution Theory and Research: Conceptual, Developmental, and Social Dimensions,* Academic Press, 1983.

(Editor with T. N. Bradbury, and contributor) *The Psychology of Marriage: Basic Issues and Applications,* Guilford, 1990.

(Editor with T. N. Bradbury, and contributor; under name Frank D. Fincham) *Cognition in Close Relationships,* Lawrence Erlbaum, 1991.

(With L. O. Fernandes and K. H. Humphreys) *Enhancing Communication in Personal Relationships: A Guide for Couples and Professionals,* Research Press (Champaign, IL), 1993.

Work represented in anthologies, including *Explaining One's Self to Others: Reason-Giving in a Social Context,* edited by M. L. McLaughlin, M. Cody, and J. S. Read, Lawrence Erlbaum, 1992; *Handbook of Developmental Family Psychology and Psychopathology,* edited by L. L'Abate, Wiley, 1993; and *Emotion in Marriage and Marital Ther-*

apy, edited by S. M. Johnson and L. S. Greenberg, Brunner Mazel, 1993. Contributor of about a hundred articles and reviews to psychology and social work journals. Guest editor, *Journal of Social and Clinical Psychology* and *Clinical Psychology Review;* associate editor, *Cognition and Emotion,* 1987—; member of editorial board, *Journal of Social and Clinical Psychology,* 1983—, *New Ideas in Psychology: An International Journal of Innovative Theory,* 1983—, *Cognitive Therapy and Research,* 1986—, *British Journal of Social Psychology,* 1986—, *Journal of Personality and Social Psychology,* 1990—, *Journal of Family Psychology,* 1991—, *Journal of Marriage and the Family,* 1991—, and *Topics in Family Psychology and Counseling,* 1992—.

* * *

FINCHAM, Frank D.
See FINCHAM, Francis D.

* * *

FINN, Susan C(alvert)

PERSONAL: Married; children: one son. *Education:* Bowling Green State University, B.S.; Case Western Reserve University, M.S.; Ohio State University, Ph.D.

ADDRESSES: Home—Worthington, OH. *Office*—Columbus, OH.

CAREER: Affiliated with Ross Laboratories, Columbus, OH, beginning 1974, currently director of nutrition and public affairs. Whittier College, assistant professor of nutrition; California State University, special lecturer; Ohio State University, clinical professor; Michigan State University, adviser to nutrition department. *Dietetic Currents,* editor, beginning mid-1970s. Speaker at Soviet Institute of Surgery, 1982, and Soviet Institute of Nutrition, 1986; guest on radio and television programs, including *The Today Show* and *Good Morning America.* Member of board of directors, Mount Carmel Hospital Foundation and Columbus Cancer Clinic.

MEMBER: American Dietetic Association (president, 1992-93).

AWARDS, HONORS: Distinguished Alumni Award, Ohio State University, 1984; Medallion Award, American Dietetic Association, 1988.

WRITINGS:

(With Linda S. Kass) *The Real Life Nutrition Book: Making the Right Choices without Changing Your Lifestyle,* Penguin, 1992.

Contributor of articles to periodicals, including *Journal of the American Dietetic Association, American Journal of Clinical Nutrition, American Baby, Family Circle, Mothers Today,* and *Working Parent.*

* * *

FISCHER, Dennis 1960-

PERSONAL: Born February 23, 1960, in Heidelberg, Germany; son of Heinz Fischer (a dean and professor) and Penella O'Kelly Smith/Zoern (a nurse); married Darleen Wingert (a clerk), July 28, 1985; children: Jared Kyle. *Education:* University of California, Los Angeles, B.A., 1981; California State University, Los Angeles, M.A., 1991. *Politics:* Liberal, independent. *Avocational interests:* Hiking, skiing, traveling, snorkeling, reading, filmgoing.

ADDRESSES: Home—6820 Alondra Blvd., Paramount, CA 90723.

CAREER: Spotlight Cable, assistant traffic controller, 1982-83; *Hollywood Reporter,* Hollywood, CA, assistant editor, 1984-85; high school teacher, Los Angeles, CA, 1985—.

MEMBER: National Geographic Society, United Teachers of Los Angeles, Los Angeles Science Fantasy Society, Paramount Film Society.

AWARDS, HONORS: Recipient of awards, including Byrant Holland scholarship, Viking Medal of Honor, and Spotlight Academy Award.

WRITINGS:

Horror Film Directors, 1931 to 1990, McFarland & Co., 1991.

Editor of *Westwind* (University of California, Los Angeles, literary journal), 1980-81; contributor to periodicals, including *Cinefantastique, SF Movieland, Starlog,* and *Enterprise Incidents.*

WORK IN PROGRESS: Science Fiction Films of the '80s; From Here to Paternity: A Handbook for New Fathers; and *New Crises in the Classroom.*

SIDELIGHTS: Dennis Fischer told *CA:* "Growing up I was one of those students who, when excited by a new subject, would haunt libraries looking for books which might fill me in on more details about whatever subject happened to catch my fancy. I always appreciated those writers who strove to write clearly rather than academically, who didn't want to waste the reader's time with excess verbiage, but presented the most solid information in the shortest amount of space, with a thoroughness and a love of the subject being explored.

"I have endeavored to retain some of these virtues in my own writing, seeking a middlebrow approach rather than high or low. I have also been fascinated by the creative process, by popular culture and its increasingly acknowledged effect and reflections on society, by the difficulties presented in bringing a creative work to fruition, and by the unlooked for assumptions and themes that might be buried below the surface of a seemingly simple piece of work.

"The world around us is full of things that arouse our thoughts, our passionate interest, our emotions. I'm stimulated by the works of various artists and wish to, in turn, stimulate other people and share ideas and information about the things I enjoy. One of the greatest joys in life is sharing, and one of the most important activities is passing the torch of knowledge—writing allows me to do both of these things at once. I regard the reader as a good friend and pupil who will be engaged by both my subject and the passion and enthusiasm I have for it. The dull and pedantic are sometimes highly regarded but little read. The best teachers and writers grapple with their subjects joyously and invite their audiences to participate likewise.

"I have had a lifelong passionate love affair with filmmaking and am endeavoring to write commercial screenplays, but whatever changes there have been in our technology, our culture, our society, reading still remains the fundamental form for storing and retrieving knowledge, and so I dedicate myself to the cause of furthering literacy."

*   *   *

FISCHMAN, Dennis 1958-

PERSONAL: Born March 13, 1958, in Pittsburgh, PA; son of Melvin Kenneth (a window display designer) and Florence Margaret (an office manager; maiden name, Chosky) Fischman; married Shulamit Hampton (divorced, 1985); married Rona Judith Stoloff (a realtor), June 25, 1989. *Education:* Yale University, B.A., 1980; University of Massachusetts at Amherst, Ph.D., 1988. *Politics:* Democrat. *Religion:* Jewish. *Avocational interests:* Mysteries, chess, writing poetry, walking.

ADDRESSES: Home—219-B School St., Somerville, MA 02145. *Office*—College of General Studies, Boston University, 871 Commonwealth Ave., Boston, MA 02215.

CAREER: Rosemont College, Rosemont, PA, assistant professor of political science, 1988-89; Boston University, Boston, MA, assistant professor of social science, 1989—. Member of New Jewish Agenda and Committee in Solidarity With the People of El Salvador.

MEMBER: American Political Science Association, American Association of University Professors.

WRITINGS:

Political Discourse in Exile: Karl Marx and the Jewish Question, University of Massachusetts Press, 1991.

Contributor to periodicals, including *Polity* and *Political Theory.* Member of editorial committee, *Somerville Community News.*

WORK IN PROGRESS: Ways of Knowing in Politics, completion expected in 1996; research on Aristotle and contemporary Aristotelians, feminist epistemology, coalition politics, multiculturalism, abortion, and Jews and political thought.

SIDELIGHTS: Dennis Fischman told *CA:* "I started graduate studies at the University of Massachusetts at Amherst in 1981, with one question in mind: Why is there no movement for revolution in the United States when the whole society cries out so compellingly for change? Being a working-class Jewish student from Pittsburgh at an elite institution—Yale, which was poised on the brink of an urban ghetto—had radicalized me before I was twenty years old. In graduate school, however, I began to realize something strange. Not everyone who saw the facts as I did drew the same (to me) inescapable conclusions. Very few shared my sense of urgency. Why, I wondered?

"At the same time, I began to notice that, on a deeper philosophical level, many of my fellow students and I seemed to live in different worlds. One of these classmates, for instance, came close to a nervous breakdown over Nietzsche. He felt he could not live in a world devoid of certainty. As a Jew in America, molded by two partially incompatible cultures, I always had.

"I began to detect a relation between the different ways other people and I responded to the state of American society, and how differently we conceived of the world as a whole, and of our places in it. Looking at politics from a Jewish standpoint seemed to make me a stranger in my own land. From this realization, from my personal crisis of meaning which followed the breakup of a youthful marriage, and from a scrap of poetry by Charles Reznikoff, my search for the meaning of exile was born. Now, just as Karl Marx had been a constant friend throughout college, so it was second nature to return to Marx, to use Marx's insights to flesh out the theme of exile, and to use the concept of exile to make new sense of Marx. *Political Discourse in Exile* is the result."

*   *   *

FISHER, Margery (Turner) 1913-1992

OBITUARY NOTICE—See index for *CA* sketch: Born March 21, 1913, in Camberwell, London; died December

24, 1992, in Northampton, England. Educator, lecturer, publisher, editor, critic, and author. An expert in the field of children's literature, Fisher wrote informative, analytic guides to children's fiction and nonfiction. She taught English from 1939 to 1945 in England and published her first work, the novel *Field Day,* in 1951. At that point, she turned her attention to children's books by other authors, becoming a prolific book reviewer, and, in 1962, she created her own reviewing journal, *Growing Point,* which she also edited and published. Fisher spoke about the state of children's book publishing at conferences, award ceremonies, and on radio. She was credited with creating books that addressed and examined neglected aspects of children's literature. Among Fisher's titles are *Intent upon Reading, Matters of Fact, Who's Who in Children's Literature,* and *The Bright Face of Danger.*

OBITUARIES AND OTHER SOURCES:

BOOKS

Who's Who, 145th edition, St. Martin's, 1993.

PERIODICALS

Junior Bookshelf, February, 1993, p. 8.
Times (London), January 4, 1993, p. 17.

* * *

FISK, Robert 1946(?)-

PERSONAL: Born c. 1946; married Lara Marlowe (a journalist). *Education:* Attended Trinity College.

ADDRESSES: Office—c/o *Western Sunday Independent,* Burrington Way, Plymouth, Devon P15 3LN, England.

CAREER: Correspondent in England and in Northern Ireland for the London *Times;* correspondent in Beirut for Plymouth, England's *Western Sunday Independent,* beginning in 1976; writer.

AWARDS, HONORS: Named reporter of the year by Granada Television, 1975; received journalism awards for articles about the Middle East in the London *Times.*

WRITINGS:

The Point of No Return: The Strike which Broke the British in Ulster, Deutsch, 1975.
In Time of War: Ireland, Ulster, and the Price of Neutrality, 1939-1945, University of Pennsylvania Press, 1983.
Pity the Nation: Lebanon at War, Deutsch, 1990, published as *Pity the Nation: The Abduction of Lebanon,* Atheneum, 1991.
(Contributor) Kjell Skjelsbaeck, editor, *The Multinational Force in Beirut: 1982-1984,* University Presses of Florida, 1991.

Contributor to periodicals, including *World Press Review.*

SIDELIGHTS: Robert Fisk is a British journalist who has distinguished himself with his coverage of events in Northern Ireland and Lebanon. In his first book, *The Point of No Return: The Strike which Broke the British in Ulster,* he relates the drastic consequences of a 1974 labor strike conducted by Protestants in the Ulster region of Northern Ireland. According to Fisk, the British-supported government in Northern Ireland substantially misunderstood the nature and intensity of the strike. That government, as a consequence, collapsed when the strike ended. *Listener* reviewer Don Anderson seconded that opinion, writing that "Fisk is correct when he says that the strike set the limits of British power in Ulster." John Morgan, in his *New Statesman* review, also expressed a degree of satisfaction with Fisk's perspective. In *The Point of No Return,* contended Morgan, Fisk "writes about the Protestant workers' strike . . . in great and convincing detail."

In his next book, *In Time of War,* Fisk reports on Ireland's controversial position of neutrality during World War II. Ireland's neutral stance, which allowed for the presence of German legation, drew the considerable ire of British and American officials. Negotiations actually ensued between Ireland and England in 1940, and Ireland's foremost condition—that the British would concede the union of Ireland and Northern Ireland after the conflict—was even accepted by Britain's prime minister, Winston Churchill. But Ireland's own leader, Eamon de Valera, ultimately rejected Churchill nonetheless, believing that the British leader would never really comply with the stipulation. David McKittrick, writing in *New Statesman,* hailed *In Time of War* as ample evidence of Fisk's considerable energy and resources. "This excellent book," McKittrick added, "is essential reading for serious students of the subject." Another reviewer, *Spectator* contributor Mary Kenny, deemed Fisk's book "rewarding," and she described him as "a painstaking journalist who methodically records each detail."

In 1990 Fisk saw publication of *Pity the Nation,* a lengthy chronicle of dangerous times in war-torn Lebanon. Fisk arrived in Beirut in 1976 when civil war was just underway. In the ensuing fifteen years he witnessed repeated bombings, ambushes, and shootouts between battling domestic factions—including Christians and Shiite Muslims—and foreign forces, notably the invading Israelis and Syrians as well as the homeless Palestine Liberation Organization (PLO). *Pity the Nation,* however, is more than mere reportage, for Fisk provides accounts of the war's effect on four families, including an Israeli clan and a Christian Palestinian one. David Lamb, writing in the *New York Times Book Review,* noted that Fisk depicts Lebanon as the place "where all the competing forces of the Middle East meld into a single catastrophe that has become symbolic of the region's volatility." *Pity the Nation,* Lamb added, "tells an important story—of the forces that led to a country's destruction." More praise came from the *Economist,* where a reviewer hailed Fisk as a "brilliant reporter," and from *Commonweal,* where commentator George Emile Irani called Fisk "a sharp and balanced observer." *Pity the Nation,* Irani affirmed, "is must reading for the lessons it contains for all those who are concerned with that vital region of the world."

Although journalists in Lebanon came under increasing risk of death or kidnapping in the late 1980s, Fisk resolved to continue reporting from the violent region. One of his fellow reporters, the *New York Times*'s Thomas Friedman, described him to *Washington Post*'s Elizabeth Kastor as someone "hooked on . . . adrenalin," and Kastor herself appraised Fisk as "a daring and eccentric character." Fisk, though, is less dramatic in explaining his desire to continue reporting from one of the world's most dangerous places. "The reason I wanted to stay," he told Kastor, "was I think Lebanon is a very important story."

BIOGRAPHICAL/CRITICAL SOURCES:

PERIODICALS

Commonweal, April 19, 1991, p. 267.
Economist, February 24, 1990, p. 89.
Listener, December 18, 1975, p. 837; June 2, 1983, p. 24.
London Review of Books, July 21, 1983, p. 8.
Los Angeles Times Book Review, December 9, 1990, p. 8.
New Statesman, November 14, 1975, p. 614; May 20, 1983, p. 20.
New York Times Book Review, December 16, 1990, p. 14.
Spectator, June 4, 1983, p. 31.
Times Literary Supplement, March 2, 1990, p. 219.
Washington Post, December 11, 1990, p. D1.
Washington Post Book World, January 27, 1991, p. 5.*

* * *

FITZPATRICK, Tony 1949-

PERSONAL: Born January 2, 1949, in Beardstown, IL; son of David P. (a postal worker) and Jayne L. (a secretary) Fitzpatrick; married February 5, 1972; wife's name, Sara R. (a free-lance illustrator); children: Ann Louise, James David. *Education:* University of Illinois, B.A., 1972; Bowling Green State University, M.F.A., 1975. *Politics:* Independent. *Religion:* "Same as politics." *Avocational interests:* Sports, history, nature, science, literature.

ADDRESSES: Home—354 Calvert Ave., St. Louis, MO 63119. *Office*—Washington University, 1 Brookings Dr., P.O. Box 1070, St. Louis, MO 63101.

CAREER: Writing teacher at junior high, high school, and college levels, 1972-83; University of Illinois, Urbana,

agriculture writer and editor, 1980-87; Washington University, St. Louis, MO, science editor, 1987—; writer.

MEMBER: National Association of Science Writers, Society of Environmental Journalists, American Association for the Advancement of Science.

AWARDS, HONORS: Award for science/technical writing, Council for the Advancement and Support of Education, 1991; Environmental Recognition Award, Garfield Farm Museum (LaFox, IL), 1993, for *Signals from the Heartland.*

WRITINGS:

Signals from the Heartland, Walker, 1993.

WORK IN PROGRESS: Researching sports, science, and midwestern historical topics.

SIDELIGHTS: A science editor at Washington University, Tony Fitzpatrick is the author of *Signals from the Heartland.* The book addresses the environmental degradation of the Midwest and profiles those who are committed to saving the natural resources of Illinois and Missouri, a region that Fitzpatrick considers to be the "heart" of the nation's Heartland. Those introduced in *Signals from the Heartland* include Peter Raven, director of the Missouri Botanical Garden; Robert Betz, a prairie restoration expert; Phoebe Snetsinger, a bird watcher who has sighted more than seven thousand species worldwide; farmer Earl Hesterberg; and Vicki O'Toole, who runs a wolf sanctuary in Missouri. "There is much to learn in these pages about the quiet practice of science and about Midwestern habitats, from the throttled Missouri River to some ancient Illinois swamps," commented Steve Paul in the *Kansas City Star.* Paul also observed that "Fitzpatrick balances his profiles with adequate helpings of natural history," and that the book "tells an inspired and inspiring story."

"I am a native Midwesterner—been here all my life—and I believe the region has been glossed over or misrepresented by most writers," Fitzpatrick told *CA.* "*Signals from the Heartland* is set entirely in the Midwest. While the book is a series of essays, they at times read like short stories. Part of the intent of writing the book was to show the broad cultural and historical diversity in my native region, as well as to show the deleterious impact humans have had on the environment. The region has undergone dramatic and disheartening change since the end of World War II. While I am from the Midwest, I consider my focus on people and why they do things to be universal.

"I have been writing since I was a teenager, intent on publishing and writing books, although success has taken a while. My early influences were the great fiction writers of the 1920s and 1930s—Ernest Hemingway, John Steinbeck, William Faulkner, and Erskine Caldwell. Later, I was taken by Jack Kerouac and Norman Mailer. Most of the influence has been from fiction writers, though poets Dylan Thomas, W. H. Auden, Walt Whitman, Emily Dickinson, and William Butler Yeats have also been influential. I've learned from John McPhee and Mailer in nonfiction, as well as George Orwell and E. B. White.

"I write best in the early mornings—on a word processor or with pen and paper, whatever is handy. Since I work full-time, my book writing is concentrated on one weekend day and whatever early-morning hours I can find. *Signals from the Heartland* was done on vacations, three-day weekends, holidays, and during early-morning hours. The book took about fifteen months to complete. I am working on another book about an obscure area of sports in St. Louis, and am developing other ideas—in science, rural Midwestern culture, and fiction—all the time."

BIOGRAPHICAL/CRITICAL SOURCES:

PERIODICALS

Farm Futures, March, 1993.
Kansas City Star, February 7, 1993, p. J11.
St. Louis Post-Dispatch, December 27, 1992.
Southern Illinoisan, January 3, 1993.
Washington Post Book World, February 7, 1993, p. 13.

*   *   *

FLINT, Kenneth C(ovey), Jr. 1947-
(Casey Flynn)

PERSONAL: Born June 23, 1947, in Omaha, NE; son of Kenneth Covey (an advertising executive) and Ruth (a housewife; maiden name, Bruhn) Flint; married Judith McCormick (a museum instructor and program developer), January 9, 1971; children: Devin McCormick, Gavin Donal. *Education:* University of Nebraska at Omaha, B.A., 1970, M.A., 1972, Certificate in English and Humanities, 1979. *Politics:* "Pro-environment, rapidly fluctuating at present." *Religion:* "Open, but humanities-based." *Avocational interests:* Family activities.

ADDRESSES: Home and office—11353 Jones St., Omaha, NE 68154. *Agent*—Russell Galen, Scott Meredith Literary Agency, Inc., 845 Third Ave., New York, NY 10022.

CAREER: University of Nebraska at Omaha, instructor in humanities, 1972-78; Plattsmouth Community Schools, Plattsmouth, NE, English teacher and department head, 1979-87; free-lance writer, 1987—. Gives writing seminars for schools and community groups. Omaha Western Heritage Museum, volunteer worker.

MEMBER: Nebraska Writers Guild, Irish American Cultural Institute.

WRITINGS:

A Storm upon Ulster, Bantam, 1981.
Riders of the Sidhe, Bantam, 1984.
Champions of the Sidhe, Bantam, 1985.
Master of the Sidhe, Bantam, 1985.
Challenge of the Clans, Bantam, 1986.
Storm Shield, Bantam, 1986.
Dark Druid, Bantam, 1987.
Isle of Destiny, Bantam, 1988.
Cromm, Doubleday, 1989.
Otherworld, Bantam, 1991.
(Under pseudonym Casey Flynn) *Most Ancient Song* (first in "Gods of Ireland" series), Bantam, 1991.
(Under Flynn pseudonym) *The Enchanted Isles* (second in "Gods of Ireland" series), Bantam, 1992.
Legends Reborn, Bantam, 1992.
Star Wars: The Heart of the Jedi, Bantam, 1993.

WORK IN PROGRESS: The Darkening Flood, a fantasy set in modern Ireland; research on Jules Verne and on the Scotland of Macbeth's period.

SIDELIGHTS: Kenneth C. Flint, Jr., told *CA:* "My writing career began in earnest when I got interested in Irish mythology. A chance college course in Celtic literature and a trip to Ireland with my wife got me started on my first published book, *A Storm upon Ulster.*

"I became aware of how much of the Celtic literature formed a basis for modern literature and of how much this fact had been ignored. I also became aware of how many writers of modern fantasy were ripping off Celtic elements of setting, character, and plot for their 'made-up' worlds. It seemed only fair and proper that the original stories should be presented in their own context. This I set out to do. It wasn't easy, as the old tales are often jumbled, inconsistent, and fragmentary. I saw my goal as putting these stories into a coherent form enjoyable to modern readers, while still retaining as much of the original plots, attitudes, and historical background of the originals as possible.

"Though I've gotten away from doing these stories in recent years, I always hope to go back to them one day. I want to write versions for all the wonderful myths and legends of Eire's three cycles of ancient bardic literature. There are, after all, more than forty million Americans who claim some Irish ancestry. My experience is that many of them are quite fascinated with their most ancient roots. I'd like to help make those roots more accessible."

FLYNN, Casey
See FLINT, Kenneth C(ovey), Jr.

* * *

FORD, Elbur
See HIBBERT, Eleanor Alice Burford

* * *

FORT, Ilene Susan 1949-

PERSONAL: Born March 18, 1949, in Philadelphia, PA; daughter of Irving N. and Bernice Goldstein; married Alvin Paul Fort (a physician; died January 17, 1979); married Gustavo D. Botvinikoff (an engineer), May 26, 1991. *Education:* Attended Philadelphia College of Art, 1958-66; Temple University, B.A. (magna cum laude), 1970; Columbia University, M.S.L.S., 1971; Queens College of the City University of New York, M.A., 1975; Graduate School and University Center of the City University of New York, M.Phil., 1986, Ph.D., 1990. *Religion:* Jewish. *Avocational interests:* Hiking, cooking, sewing.

ADDRESSES: Home—14947 Burbank Blvd., No. 204, Van Nuys, CA 91411. *Office*—Los Angeles County Museum of Art, 5905 Wilshire Blvd., Los Angeles, CA 90036.

CAREER: H. W. Wilson Co., Bronx, NY, indexer for *Reader's Guide to Periodical Literature,* 1971-73; Worldwide Books, Boston, MA, editor, 1975-79; consultant, 1979-83; Los Angeles County Museum of Art, Los Angeles, CA, assistant curator, 1983-87, associate curator, 1987—. Laguna Art Museum, panelist for California Light Symposium, 1990. Art Commission of the City of New York, director of mural survey, 1980-83.

MEMBER: American Association of Museums, American Studies Association, Association of Historians of American Art, College Art Association of America.

AWARDS, HONORS: Travel grant for France, Wyeth Foundation.

WRITINGS:

(Co-author) *American Art: A Catalogue of the Los Angeles County Museum of Art,* Los Angeles County Museum of Art, 1991.
Paintings of California, C. N. Potter, 1993.
Childe Hassam's New York, Pomegranate Publications, in press.

Work represented in anthologies, including *Dictionary of Art,* Macmillan, in press. Art critic, *Arts,* 1980-83. Contributor to art and antiques journals. Editor, *Worldwide Art Catalogue Bulletin,* 1975-79.

WORK IN PROGRESS: Egypt Through the Eyes of the Yankee, on American perceptions of ancient Egypt in the nineteenth and early twentieth centuries.

SIDELIGHTS: Ilene Susan Fort told *CA:* "I write about American art and am mainly interested in painting and sculpture created during the nineteenth century and twentieth century prior to World War II. I have several areas within that time frame that intrigue me most: American expatriates in Europe during the late nineteenth century, American modernism, murals and the federal art projects of the 1930s, and American surrealism. I am particularly concerned with the relationship between politics and art, and also with the impact of culture and society on the creation of art. Recently, I have also become fascinated with California painting and the development of its mythology. My book on Childe Hassam's paintings of flags was aimed at determining exactly what the iconography represented and meant to the artist in the context of the World War I period in which they were created. That publication, and also a book in progress, have enabled me to explore the history of New York, my favorite city. The little-explored field of American surrealism intrigues me because of the infinite potential for creativity the aesthetic offered artists."

* * *

FOSBURGH, Lacey 1942-1993

OBITUARY NOTICE—See index for *CA* sketch: Born October 3, 1942, in New York, NY; died of complications of breast cancer, January 11, 1993, in San Francisco, CA. Journalist, instructor, and writer. Fosburgh achieved success as a author, winning a Mystery Writers of America award for her first book, *Closing Time: The True Story of the 'Goodbar' Murder.* She was also the recipient of numerous publishers' prizes from the *New York Times.* Fosburgh graduated from Sarah Lawrence College in 1964 and spent the next two years in New Delhi, India, on a Fulbright study grant. Upon her return, she joined the staff of the *New York Herald Tribune* as a news assistant, then transferred to the *New York Times* as a staff correspondent, covering such notable events as the Sirhan Sirhan trial and the abduction of Patty Hearst. Fosburgh became a free-lance writer in 1974 and began teaching journalism at the University of California, Berkeley. Publications by Fosburgh include 1983's *Old Money,* a novel, and *India Gate,* released in 1991. She was working on an unfinished novel under contract to Simon & Schuster at the time of her death.

OBITUARIES AND OTHER SOURCES:

BOOKS

Who's Who in Writers, Editors, and Poets, 1989-1990, December Press, 1989.

PERIODICALS

Los Angeles Times, January 14, 1993, p. A26.
New York Times, January 13, 1993, p. A19.

*   *   *

FOSTER, Nora R(akestraw) 1947-

PERSONAL: Born October 2, 1947, in White Salmon, WA; daughter of Lawrence Rakestraw (a historian) and Mary (Watson) Rakestraw (a homemaker); married Frank Charles Foster, June 14, 1970; children: Louise Mary-Charlotte. *Education:* Attended Michigan Technological University, 1965-67; University of Alaska, B.S., 1969, M.S., 1979. *Politics:* Liberal. *Religion:* "Society of Friends (Quaker)." *Avocational interests:* Outdoor recreation, food and cooking, the arts.

ADDRESSES: Home—2998 Gold Hill Rd., Fairbanks, AK 99709. *Office*—University of Alaska Museum, 907 Yukon Dr., Fairbanks, AK 99775-1200.

CAREER: University of Alaska Museum, Fairbanks, AK, coordinator of aquatic collection, 1981—. Hidden Hill Friends Center, member of board of directors, 1984-90.

MEMBER: Western Society of Malacologists, American Malacological Union, Society for the Preservation of Natural History Collections, Association of Systematics Collections, Association for Women in Science.

WRITINGS:

Intertidal Bivalves: A Guide to the Common Marine Bivalves of Alaska, University of Alaska Press, 1991.

Also author of report *A Synopsis of the Marine Prosobranch Gastropod and Bivalve Mollusks in Alaskan Waters,* University of Alaska, Institute of Marine Science.

WORK IN PROGRESS: Research on history and status of mollusk (clam, oyster, and scallop) fisheries in Alaska and the ecology of mollusks in the Chukchi Sea.

*   *   *

FRANCE, David 1959-

PERSONAL: Born February 25, 1959, in Suffern, NY; son of Gerald (a packaging engineer) and Georgianne (an art supply wholesaler; maiden name, Beurket) France; partner of Doug Gould (an administrative assistant). *Education:* Kalamazoo College, B.A., 1982; attended New School for Social Research, 1982-83.

ADDRESSES: Agent—Nancy Love Literary Agency, 250 East 65th St., New York, NY 10021.

CAREER: Worked variously for *New York Native,* as senior editor for *Lear's,* and as a columnist for *Magazine Week,* all in New York City.

AWARDS, HONORS: Detroit Press Club Award, best magazine piece, 1988; Gay and Lesbian Press Club Award, best feature story, 1989.

WRITINGS:

Bag of Toys: A True Story of Sadomasochism and Murder in New York Society, Warner Books, 1992.

WORK IN PROGRESS: "I'm researching New York City in the 1930s and the rise of the mob for a possible biography of my father."

SIDELIGHTS: In *Bag of Toys: A True Story of Sadomasochism and Murder in New York Society,* which originally appeared in *Vanity Fair,* David France investigates the 1985 "death mask murder" of Eigil Dag Vesti, a Norwegian homosexual fashion design student. Eight years of undercover research by France disclosed a story of violence, drugs, and sadomasochism (S & M) involving well-known New York art dealer Andrew Crispo and his bodyguard, Bernard LeGeros. LeGeros was eventually prosecuted for the murder and was given the maximum penalty of a twenty-five years-to-life sentence. Vesti's torched and mutilated body—with two gunshot wounds to his head and a leather mask covering his face—was discovered on property belonging to LeGeros's father in Rockland County, New York. In *Bag of Toys* the author reveals the role that Crispo played in the execution-style killing of Vesti and relates in detail the violent world behind the closed doors of Crispo's limousines and in the back rooms of some homosexual night clubs.

France contends in *Bag of Toys* that Crispo was present at the murder and served as the driving force leading to the crime that LeGeros committed. After a night of violent sadomasochistic sex between the three men, Crispo, according to information given to the author at the Rockland County district attorney's office, and as quoted in Cynthia Robins's *San Francisco Examiner* article, "reportedly whispered a moment before LeGeros fired the fatal shots: 'He's ready now. He wants to die. Shoot him.' " High on cocaine, LeGeros responded to the order with two pulls of the trigger. Crispo, however, remains unprosecuted as an accomplice to murder, and because of this, France was determined to delve deeper into Crispo's world to discover, and hopefully prove, Crispo's guilt. In

Robins's article the author explained his reasons for pursuing the dangerous research for *Bag of Toys:* "My mission was to see it through. This was justice derailed. The truly grotesque part of the story isn't the drugs or the brutality or the criminality or the sexuality, but that Crispo was never charged. Never even indicted. Never a grand jury investigation. I really started to feel sick about the whole thing. That's what drove me to understand why." France gave up his previously quiet life for Crispo's world of art, cocaine, S & M, revenge, and threats of murder (including one aimed at himself). In return the author hopes his investigation will prompt the district attorney's office to reopen the case and indict Crispo. In an interview for *Outlines* with Owen Keehnen, France stated, "I just want the book to prove to the reader and maybe even to the prosecutors that Crispo was not only capable of being the architect of this murder, but that he did it beyond doubt."

In writing *Bag of Toys,* France didn't shy away from information that many felt was too graphic. Instead he captured the harshness of Crispo's environment by purposefully including descriptive detail of sadomasochistic ritual. At the same time, France wanted to prove that *this* S & M is not necessarily dangerous and that it is not found exclusively in a homosexual context. In Keehnen's interview, France commented that he "wanted to make sure this could not be interpreted as a story about the evils of homosexuality or sadomasochism." The author further admitted in Robins's article that he "wanted to show S & M in a way that was sexually exciting, that was dirty even, but not criminal. I felt like I had to really seduce a reader into it."

BIOGRAPHICAL/CRITICAL SOURCES:

PERIODICALS

Outlines, September, 1992, p. 32.
San Francisco Examiner, July 27, 1992.

* * *

FRANCK, Violet M. 1949-

PERSONAL: Born April 29, 1949, in North Bend, OR; daughter of a logger and lumber mill worker and a homemaker; married J. Philip Franck (a writer), December 22, 1990. *Education:* Oregon State University, B.A., 1978. *Religion:* "Eclectic, New Ageish." *Avocational interests:* Nature and the environment, personal growth, "helping others find their gifts."

ADDRESSES: Home and office—Elkton, OR. *Agent*—Eleanor Friede, Route 1, Box 175-V, Faber, VA 22938; and Barbara Bowen, 971 First Ave., Suite 4C, New York, NY 10022.

CAREER: Children's Services Division of Coos Bay, OR, counselor.

MEMBER: Phi Kappa Phi.

WRITINGS:

Hidden Victims: The Other Side of Murder, New Horizon Press, 1993.

WORK IN PROGRESS: No Matter What; a book about the fight against animal abuse, *Without It.*

SIDELIGHTS: Violet M. Franck told *CA:* "I believe that each individual is highly valuable. Each individual has a 'gift' that no other can give. The key to finding the gift is to look within. Then the individual must make the choice to follow where the gift leads, no matter what.

"Since this can require a great deal of courage, very few people find that gift and follow where it leads. This saddens me, because people are prevented from finding true happiness and fulfillment. It is my goal, through my writings, to inspire individuals to find and follow their dreams and to realize their own personal value. Love is the key, the most important ingredient that can be added to any endeavor."

* * *

FRATER, Alexander 1937-

PERSONAL: Born in 1937 in Paama, New Hebrides; immigrated to England; son of a doctor.

ADDRESSES: Office—Observer, 8 St. Andrews Hill, London EC4V 5JA, England.

CAREER: Observer, London, England, chief travel correspondent.

WRITINGS:

Stopping-train Britain: A Railway Odyssey, photographs by Alain Le Garsmeur, Hodder & Stoughton, 1983.
(Editor) *Great Rivers of the World,* photographs by Colin Jones, Little, Brown, 1984.
Beyond the Blue Horizon: On the Track of Imperial Airways, Scribner, c. 1986.
Chasing the Monsoon: A Modern Pilgrimage through India, Holt, 1990.

SIDELIGHTS: Alexander Frater, a columnist for *Observer* magazine in London, England, has recorded a number of travel experiences in his nonfiction books. Two of his works have focused on a particular means of travel as well as the places visited. *Stopping-train Britain: A Railway Odyssey* describes the historical significance and modern-day pleasures of the small rail lines of England, Scotland, and Wales. In *Beyond the Blue Horizon: On the Track of Imperial Airways,* Frater records his attempt to retrace the traditional route that the upper-class passengers of Imperial Airways followed on the voyage from London to Brisbane, Australia, in the 1930s.

Frater's 1990 book, *Chasing the Monsoon: A Modern Pilgrimage through India,* follows the author as he pursues a childhood dream inherited from his father: to visit the wettest place on earth, Cherrapunji, India, during the height of the monsoon. Beginning in the spring of 1987, Frater followed the path of the annual storm system, which brings the heavy rains necessary for successful crops, as it tracked across the subcontinent, culminating in the arrival of the rain at Cherrapunji. Starting at the southern tip of India at Kovalam Beach, and traveling up through cities such as Cochin, Goa, Bombay, and Calcutta as the rains reached each of these places, Frater encountered the many traditions and beliefs held by Indians regarding the monsoon. He notes the passion with which people await and receive the rains; in Cochin, he watched a group of business people run out of their offices and dance in the first downpour of the season. Frater also presents the way in which both old and new practices are used to insure a beneficial monsoon. In a land where a weather meteorologist is looked to for scientific predictions of the monsoon's path, there are also beliefs in the power of traditional rites and superstitions to appease the rain-gods.

Throughout the trip, from its beginning in southern India to its dream-dispelling finale in politically unstable Cherrapunji, Frater observes both the people and the bureaucracy of modern India, weaving these experiences together with images of the land and its climate. *Newsweek* reviewer Malcolm Jones, Jr., praised *Chasing the Monsoon,* stating that "Frater's deftly engaging account finds greatness in a neglected theme—the profound relationship among people, culture and climate." "In this annual meteorological event," observed Robert Potts in *Times Saturday Review,* "Mr. Frater locates both a potent metaphor for the capricious (and almost surreal) nature of Indian life, while simultaneously depicting a phenomenon that affects every aspect of the country: social, cultural, religious, medical and economic." M. J. McAteer, writing in the *Washington Post Book World,* also praised Frater's book, describing it as "part travelogue, part pilgrimage and part reminiscence, both meteorological and metaphysical." *New York Times Book Review* contributor Raleigh Trevelyan found *Chasing the Monsoon* to be "a delightful, witty and unusual travel book, full of humorous perceptions about modern India and its inescapable links with the past."

BIOGRAPHICAL/CRITICAL SOURCES:

PERIODICALS

Library Journal, September 15, 1984, p. 1757.
Los Angeles Times Book Review, October 7, 1984, p. 4; April 21, 1991, p. 6.
Newsweek, June 3, 1991, p. 61.
New Yorker, August 12, 1991, pp. 73-76.
New York Times Book Review, April 21, 1991, p. 13.
Observer (London), October 9, 1983, p. 33.
Publishers Weekly, July 13, 1984, p. 41.
Times Literary Supplement, January 16, 1987, p. 57.
Times Saturday Review, December 29, 1990, p. 19.
Washington Post Book World, May 12, 1991, p. 6.*

*   *   *

FREIDEL, Frank (Burt, Jr.) 1916-1993

OBITUARY NOTICE—See index for *CA* sketch: Born May 22, 1916, in Brooklyn, NY; died of pneumonia, January 25, 1993, in Cambridge, MA. Historian, educator, and author. A Harvard University instructor for twenty-six years, Freidel was best known for his comprehensive biography of U.S. President Franklin D. Roosevelt. *Franklin D. Roosevelt* consists of six volumes, each focused on a specific era of the president's life and career: *The Apprenticeship, The Ordeal, The Triumph, Launching the New Deal, F.D.R. and the South,* and *A Rendezvous With Destiny* (a seventh volume was left unfinished). Freidel earned his doctorate from the University of Wisconsin in 1942 and taught at several colleges—including Vassar and Stanford—before joining the staff at Harvard in 1955 as a professor of history. In 1981 Freidel transferred to the University of Washington in Seattle and taught there until he retired in 1986. During his career, Freidel was named Charles Warren Professor of American History, Harmsworth Professor of American History, and Bullitt Professor of History. Freidel coauthored *A History of the United States,* edited *The Golden Age of American History,* and wrote textbooks and history books, including *Splendid Little War* and *American History: A Survey.*

OBITUARIES AND OTHER SOURCES:

BOOKS

Who's Who in America, 47th edition, Marquis, 1992.

PERIODICALS

New York Times, January 26, 1993, p. B6.
Washington Post, January 30, 1993, p. B6.

FRIEDMAN, Josh(ua M.) 1941-

PERSONAL: Born December 22, 1941, in Roosevelt, NJ; son of Samuel Nathaniel (in business) and Charlotte (an art historian; maiden name, Safir) Friedman; married Carol Ash (an environmental official), September 12, 1976; children: Susannah. *Education:* Rutgers University, B.A., 1964; postgraduate study at University of Chicago, 1966-67; Columbia University, M.S., 1968.

ADDRESSES: Office—*Newsday,* 780 Third Ave., New York, NY 10017.

CAREER/WRITINGS: Texas Technological University Training Center, Lubbock, TX, instructor, 1966; Community News Service, New York City, assistant editor, 1970-72; *New York Post,* New York City, reporter and statehouse bureau chief, 1972-77; *Philadelphia Inquirer,* Philadelphia, PA, reporter, 1977-78; *Soho Weekly News,* New York City, editor-in-chief, 1979-c. 1980; *Newsday,* Long Island, NY, United Nations bureau chief, 1982—. Peace Corps, volunteer in Costa Rica, 1964-66; Rensselaerville Historical Society, trustee, 1984—; Committee to Protect Journalists, member of board of directors, 1985-86, chair, 1986-88.

AWARDS, HONORS: Keystone Press Award, Pennsylvania Newspaper Publishers' Association and Pennsylvania Society of Newspaper Editors, 1979; Public Service award, Associated Press Managing Editors Association, 1979; Thomas L. Stokes Award, Washington Journalism Center, 1979; Edward J. Meeman Conservation Reporting Award, Scripps Howard Foundation, 1979; Blue Pencil Award, Columbia University *Daily Spectator,* 1980; Pulitzer Prize for general reporting, Columbia University Graduate School of Journalism, 1980, shared with the staff of the *Philadelphia Inquirer* for a series on the Three-Mile Island nuclear reactor accident; Pulitzer Prize finalist for series on toxic waste, 1980; Page One Award for crusading journalism, Newspaper Guild of New York, 1985; Pulitzer Prize for international reporting, 1985, for reports with Dennis Bell and photographer Ozier Muhammad on the plight of victims of the 1984 African famine; First Place award for international reporting, National Association of Black Journalists, 1985.

CA INTERVIEW

CA interviewed Josh Friedman by telephone on April 10, 1989, in New York City.

CA: You won a 1985 Pulitzer Prize for international reporting for the 1984 Newsday *series "Africa: The Desperate Continent."* Newsday's *reports were the first to come from many of the famine areas. How did you and Dennis Bell and Ozier Muhammad happen to be the team doing the coverage?*

FRIEDMAN: I'd like to take credit for insight, but I'm not really sure where the idea to cover the drought in Africa came from. *Newsday* had run articles on hunger periodically. Long Island [New York, where the paper is published] is an extremely affluent area, and I think it was the feeling of Dave Laventhol, who was then the publisher, that the newspaper should do articles on that subject. In any case, in the summer of 1984 I was asked to do a series of articles on the drought in Africa. At that point there was already a famine, but it wasn't of the magnitude it later became.

As I got into the story in August and September, I encountered a lot of political difficulties, especially in Ethiopia, getting visas. As I later learned, the degree of political difficulty in getting into a place was directly related to the level of famine and probably had something to do with the fact that food wasn't getting there either. We worked from August until the middle of October trying to get visas to the important places. I had almost given up hope of being able to enter Ethiopia. Luckily I had pestered Ethiopian officials enough, calling them in the middle of the night so many times, that by the time the famine was getting worse and the government finally decided that they couldn't keep it a secret any longer, I was known to them. By then they trusted me enough to give us a visa.

CA: You never got into South Africa, did you?

FRIEDMAN: No. They refused to allow us visas, which is unfortunate because they had many problems with drought there too, and we never were really able to assess how they handled it.

CA: You reported on people like Pat Gorman, a nurse with an Irish relief agency, who were in the camps on a long-term basis to help the starving. What was morale like among those workers?

FRIEDMAN: Most of them were obviously extraordinary people in that they had volunteered to do that work. I don't think the famine demoralized them at first. They had their specific tasks to do, and they were doing them. I didn't encounter [volunteers suffering from] burnout. But, of course, I was there in the beginning. The famine started in earnest in September—in hindsight we know that. The camps didn't reach their full size, the big camps that were formed spontaneously, until the middle of October. The famine had been going for only a week or two before I got there. When I returned in March of 1985, I found more demoralization and despair among the relief workers. At first people were just in shock.

CA: U.S. efforts to help with famine relief came in for a lot of criticism, which often seems to be the case with U.S. aid. Was the American approach in Africa somehow misguided?

FRIEDMAN: Initially it was. At the beginning there was political reluctance on the part of [U.S. President Ronald] Reagan and his administration to help out in Ethiopia, because the country was a Soviet ally. We were deluging Kenya with supplies, which is closer to us politically, while neighboring Ethiopia needed aid and was not receiving it as readily. But fairly soon U.S. public opinion took over and made it politically untenable for the Reagan administration to stick to its policy. At that point they started being pretty forthcoming. We had a very large grain surplus in 1984, so it wasn't any great sacrifice for the U.S. to help out. I think we were the major donor.

The Reagan administration had politicized foreign aid tremendously, and many multilateral programs had become bilateral. There was some question about whether the U.S. was secretly supporting some of the rebel movements [which include guerrilla forces from the provinces of Eritrea and Tigre, who have engaged the Ethiopian government in an extended civil war]. One of the major problems of the relief operation was getting food aid to the areas held by the rebels and distributing it. The Ethiopian government insisted that supplies come through Addis Ababa [the capital city] while the U.S. government wanted to send it through Sudan, which at that time was reportedly a haven for some of the guerrilla groups. It went in both directions. Finally, after about six months or so, they signed an accord to get food to the marginal areas, which were like a no-man's land. That was always a big problem there, and politics was a big factor in aid relief.

CA: When you returned in the spring of 1985, you found "a fragile improvement," as you titled one of your stories. But the problems, you pointed out, go beyond immediate food supply: they threaten tribal identity, the nomadic way of life, even the basic unit of society—the family. Can you make any guesses about the future for those affected African countries?

FRIEDMAN: To start with, [in 1985] the Ethiopian central government was losing to the rebels in a way that it hadn't been for many years. In fact, some of the areas I visited, where the famine was hardest, have since fallen to the rebels. I don't know what role the famine played in weakening the central government. But, generally, the political face of Africa is changing—more, probably, because of [the policies of Soviet leader Mikhail] Gorbachev than any other factor. The Russians seem reluctant to continue sending unlimited arms to back up their allies in Africa. Much of the friction in African nations has been tribal, including the Ethiopian rebel movements, the struggle of the Polisario Front in Western Sahara [to create an independent republic and end Moroccan control], and the struggle [for liberation from South African rule] in Namibia [South-West Africa] where Cuban and South African

troops have been involved. All of these movements have been grinding down to some degree because of the improved relations between the East and West, the Soviet Union and the United States. All over the world, these tensions have been abating. But Africa is a special case; the standard of living is not improving, despite attempts of all sorts. The continent has a tremendous number of economic problems. They've had bad luck with nature. Now they have [cases of] acquired immunodeficiency syndrome (AIDS). It's a place that really has problems, with one of the biggest being population control. Maybe the AIDS scare will force people to use population control methods that weren't previously being used. But there are a lot of imponderables in Africa.

CA: Between graduation from Rutgers, where you majored in history, and postgraduate work at the University of Chicago, you spent two years in Costa Rica as a Peace Corps volunteer. Did that experience lead directly to your becoming a journalist?

FRIEDMAN: No, I had wanted to be a journalist anyway. But the Peace Corps did teach me a lot—much more than journalism school at Columbia University did—about how to be a good journalist. I learned a lot about not being put off by superficial differences, which made it easier to relate to people of other cultures and to feel comfortable with people [living] outside of capital cities. That's especially important in covering third world countries. I was vacillating between journalism and do-gooding, I guess you could call it. For a while, because of the Peace Corps, I was thinking more of the do-gooding part of it. But I finally opted for journalism. I guess you can argue that the information generated in journalism does do some good.

CA: Had you wanted from early on to be a journalist?

FRIEDMAN: As long as I can remember, since I was a little kid—to the great despair of my parents, especially my father. But he's very happy now. The major advantage of winning a Pulitzer Prize is that it makes your parents happy. After that, it's okay not to be rich.

CA: How did you and Newsday *get together?*

FRIEDMAN: I was looking for a job, and a friend of mine from the journalism school at Columbia University was one of the editors at *Newsday*. I had already been in touch with them and gotten to know the paper, because, when I was working for other papers, I had friends who worked there. I wrote them a letter and said I was looking for a job, and this man I knew responded very generously. I like the paper; it has the kind of approach that's good for the kind of journalism I do. I like to do big projects, not just the wire-service type of reporting. It's a visual paper also; I like the stories that are matched with photographs.

Newsday has become gigantic and so successful, that it's harder to do what was possible when it was a smaller paper, but it pioneered types of journalism that have become popular at other papers—big features, big investigations.

CA: Newspapers now are in the tough position of having to compete with television. What do you think papers can do better and at the same time keep a strong readership?

FRIEDMAN: I think [in preparing a paper's layout] newspaper writing and editing have to accept visual sophistication on the part of the readers. You have to match the writing with the pictures in a way that normally has not been happening. People in the pictures should be in the stories, and they should have names and be developed as persons. And the writing should be faster, because people have gotten accustomed to very rapid visual editing in television. If you watch old television sitcoms like "I Love Lucy," it's striking how long each scene goes without being cut, and you have old-fashioned set-piece scenes on the screen. If you look at new programs, you see the scenes move very fast. It's much more tightly cropped, and the eye accepts that because we've gotten used to it. You have to match that style in the newspaper article. Otherwise people get bored. They have a much shorter attention span now for reading a newspaper story. You have to make the paper more visual, with more visual anecdotes, and develop your story in the way a television news story would be developed—start out with sort of a visual small picture and get into the dryer stuff a little later.

CA: What newspapers and other periodicals do you rely on routinely for information and ideas and entertainment?

FRIEDMAN: Naturally I read the *New York Times,* but, frankly, I prefer the *Washington Post.* I read the *Financial Times,* sometimes the *Independent* of London, and the *Economist.* I read a huge number of magazines; the big problem is throwing them away at home! I read the *Smithsonian, Natural History, National Geographic,* the *New Yorker,* and sometimes the *Atlantic.* I'm more into nonfiction than fiction in my reading. *Consumer Reports* I love—I don't know why.

CA: You've been active, recently serving as chairman, on something called the Committee to Protect Journalists. What does that organization do?

FRIEDMAN: It's a very important organization which helps journalists, especially in third world countries, where the First Amendment [provision of the U.S. Constitution guaranteeing free speech] does not exist. If journalists do something to offend the powers that be, they're thrown into jail or their lives are threatened or somehow their work is curtailed. Our organization intervenes with

the authorities to let them know that we're scrutinizing the situation. We fact-find to see if it's true that journalists are being abused. We have an annual report on journalists under fire that lists how many have been killed in the line of duty: it's running about two dozen a year. We catalog those who are in prison and why. We have a number of prominent journalists on our board, like Walter Cronkite and Dan Rather, and when we contact governments about the case of a journalist in trouble, that seems to have an effect on them.

CA: So you feel you've been able to make a difference?

FRIEDMAN: Yes, I believe the organization has managed to save lives. We tend to be sort of naive about the First Amendment here in the U.S., to take it for granted. One of the things that I've learned from reporting overseas is that it's very risky to be a journalist in a lot of places, especially third world countries. The kind of intervention the Committee to Protect Journalists does is one of the things that we can contribute. It used to be fashionable not to want to export our cultural values overseas, but I think freedom of speech is one value we should export, and I have no shame about aggressively promoting it.

CA: Would you talk about your current work at the United Nations?

FRIEDMAN: Being a United Nations (UN) reporter enables me to work on the foreign desk and live in New York, and enables my wife to continue her job, which she likes very much. I can still take trips without being based overseas. I do a mixture of UN stories and larger projects overseas. The UN stories actually turned out to be much more frequent than anticipated because the UN itself has become much more active. I covered the first two months of the *intifada* [the Palestine Liberation Organization's uprising against Israeli military rule]. I'm supposed to do more projects like that but, because of the UN's recent activity in peacemaking, I've covered a lot of diplomatic efforts in that direction. I've done some work on chemical weapons and covered the chemical weapons conference in Paris. I've covered the Mideast-related peace initiatives both here and in Geneva and the efforts to end the Iran-Iraq War [the eight-year territorial conflict beginning in 1980 between the two southwest Asian republics].

Our newspaper doesn't try to match a paper like the *New York Times* in breaking news every day. We don't have as big a hole for foreign news anyway, so we try to present it in a different format—in a more feature-oriented way, and still get the same news across. We try to give the bigger picture of what's happening without reporting each incremental change. In a way, we're not as inhibited as the *Times;* their power is so massive that they have to be somewhat conservative in the way they present the news. I can be more informal, more visual, more feature oriented, and more anecdotal because of the difference between the two papers. The story still has to be accurate, but I can present the news in a little more relaxed fashion.

CA: You mentioned your wife's work. What does she do?

FRIEDMAN: She's an environmentalist; she's the New York State Environmental and Conservation Department's New York City regional director. It's quite a job, and I'm very proud of what she does. She's in a position where she's one of the few people really sticking up for the environment in New York City, and it's a thankless job, to some degree, because it has to be done with limited resources.

CA: And probably against many special interests.

FRIEDMAN: Yes. New York City is an area of vast wealth and power. If they could just pave over the rivers, just think how much more housing could be built there!

CA: And you have one daughter, I believe.

FRIEDMAN: Yes. My daughter is twelve, and just last week [in the spring of 1989] I took a trip to Costa Rica with her, to the village where I worked when I was in the Peace Corps. She's a great writer, but she doesn't want to be a writer! I grew up in a town where there are a lot of artists and writers, and I think it's pretty hard to be a writer or an artist if your father or mother was one. It probably doesn't make that much sense to do it. In fact, it's a stroke of luck to get into a position where you can do either job in an interesting way. I consider myself extraordinarily lucky that I fell into this niche, because for most journalists the job turns out to be sort of boring after a while. I just happened to luck out, to be in a place that values the kind of journalism that I like to do.

CA: Are there future plans or hopes you can mention?

FRIEDMAN: I'd like to do a book. That's the big transition for every journalist, from daily journalism to a book. I find the idea threatening, and I don't know why. I guess you get so used to the daily grind. For me, two or three thousand words is a big project, and that's why I feel stretched about as far as I can stretch in writing newspaper stories. I want to continue journalism, but I would like to see what I can do with a book.

CA: Is it too early to talk about a subject?

FRIEDMAN: I have a lot of ideas. I'm interested in the Third World, the Middle East—I have two or three ideas that I'm tossing around in my mind.

—*Interview by Jean W. Ross*

FRUIN, W. Mark 1943-

PERSONAL: Born October 22, 1943, in Chicago, IL; son of Richard Lawrence (a physician) and Gertrude (a nurse; maiden name, Winter) Fruin; children: Noah Glenn Wardrip, Nathan Mark Wardrip. *Education:* Stanford University, B.A., 1965, M.A., 1968, Ph.D., 1973.

ADDRESSES: Home—4060 Amaranta Ave., Palo Alto, CA 94306. *Office*—Asia Pacific Policy and Research Institute, University of British Columbia, Vancouver, British Columbia V6T 1Z2, Canada.

CAREER: European Institute of Business Administration, Fontainebleau, France, professor of strategy and management, 1988-92; University of British Columbia, Vancouver, Hong Kong Bank Professor of Asian Research and director of Asia Pacific Policy and Research Institute, 1992—. University of California, Los Angeles, visiting professor, 1991-92.

WRITINGS:

Kikkoman: Company, Clan, and Community, Harvard University Press, 1983.
The Japanese Enterprise System: Competitive Strategies and Cooperative Structures, Oxford University Press, 1992.
Knowledge Works, Oxford University Press, 1993.

*   *   *

FUKUYAMA, Francis 1952-

PERSONAL: Born October 27, 1952, in Chicago, IL; son of Yoshio (a Congregationalist minister and educator) and Toshiko (a potter; maiden name, Kawata) Fukuyama; married Laura Holmgren (a homemaker), September 8, 1986; children: Julia, David, John. *Education:* Cornell University, B.A., 1974; graduate studies at Yale University, 1974-75; Harvard University, Ph.D., 1981. *Religion:* Protestant.

ADDRESSES: Home—McLean, VA. *Office*—c/o RAND Corporation, 2100 M St. N.W., Washington, DC 20037. *Agent*—Esther Newberg, International Creative Management, 40 West 57th St., New York, NY 10019.

CAREER: Pan Heuristics, Inc., Los Angeles, CA, consultant, 1978-79; RAND Corporation, Santa Monica, CA, associate social scientist, 1979-81, senior staff member of political science department, 1983-89, consultant, 1990—; Policy Planning Staff, U.S. Department of State, Washington, DC, member of the U.S. Delegation to the Egyptian-Israeli talks on Palestinian autonomy, 1981-82, deputy director, 1989-90, consultant, 1990—. University of California, Los Angeles, visiting lecturer in political science, 1986 and 1989. Member of Council on Foreign Relations.

MEMBER: Sierra Club, American Association for the Advancement of Slavic Studies.

AWARDS, HONORS: Premio Capri International Award and *Los Angeles Times* Book Critics Award in current interest category, both 1992, for *The End of History and the Last Man.*

WRITINGS:

(Editor with Andrzej Korbonski) *The Soviet Union and the Third World: The Last Three Decades,* Cornell University Press, 1987.
A Look at "The End of History?," edited by Kenneth M. Jensen, United States Institute of Peace, 1990.
The End of History and the Last Man, Free Press, 1992.

Author of numerous documents for the RAND Corporation. Contributor to books, including *U.S. Strategic Interests in Southwest Asia,* edited by Shirin Tahir-Kheli, Praeger, 1982; *Hawks, Doves, and Owls,* edited by Graham Allison, Albert Carnesale, and Joseph Nye, Norton, 1985; and *The Future of the Soviet Empire,* edited by Henry Rowen and Charles Wolf, St. Martin's, 1987. Contributor to periodicals, including *American Spectator, Commentary, Current History, Foreign Affairs, Guardian, Journal of Democracy, Middle East Contemporary Survey, National Interest, New Republic, Orbis,* and *Political Science Quarterly.*

The End of History and the Last Man has also been published in Brazilian, Danish, Dutch, Finnish, French, German, Greek, Hebrew, Italian, Japanese, Korean, Portuguese, Spanish, and Swedish editions.

SIDELIGHTS: Following a stint as senior staff member of the political science department of the RAND Corporation, Francis Fukuyama captured attention worldwide in 1989 after penning an essay on the current state of history. Called "The End of History?," the sixteen-page article appeared in the foreign policy journal *National Interest* and became the topic of considerable debate. In his thesis, Fukuyama, who was then working as deputy director of the U.S. State Department's Policy Planning Staff, contended that history had evolved to its logical end—that of liberal democracy. Fukuyama's notion of "history," as explained by the Toronto *Globe and Mail*'s Jeffrey Simpson, is "the struggle for universal acceptance of the most effective and just organization of human society."

Based in part on the ideologies of German philosopher Georg Wilhelm Friedrich Hegel, the author's argument centers around the fact that one form of government will ultimately win out over all others. Fukuyama believes his assertion that liberal democracy has been victorious is wit-

nessed by the reunification of Germany and the collapse of communism. According to James Atlas in the *New York Times,* Fukuyama suggests that "history is a protracted struggle to realize the idea of freedom latent in human consciousness. In the 20th century, the forces of totalitarianism have been decisively conquered by the United States and its allies, which represent the final embodiment of this idea." The end result, predicts Fukuyama, will be "a very sad time" as people turn to solving technological troubles rather than fighting ideological battles.

Fukuyama's essay, which he later expanded into the 1992 book *The End of History and the Last Man,* continued to be the subject of much debate after publication in book form. While some commentators agreed with the author's delineations, others argued that liberal democracy certainly will be challenged by Third World countries and religious fundamentalists. Some critics pointed to the problems of drugs and poverty in American society as further evidence that liberal democracy may not be the key ideology. In response to such debate, Fukuyama told Atlas: "The last thing I want to be interpreted as saying is that our society is a utopia, or that there are no more problems." He added, "I simply don't see any competitors to modern democracy."

BIOGRAPHICAL/CRITICAL SOURCES:

PERIODICALS

Commonweal, June 19, 1992, pp. 25-26.
Globe and Mail (Toronto), April 4, 1992, p. C6.
National Review, November 24, 1989, p. 62.
New York Times, October 22, 1989, p. 38; January 24, 1990.
Time, September 4, 1989, p. 57.
Times (London), February 20, 1992, p. 4.

*   *   *

FUMERTON, Patricia

PERSONAL: Education: University of Toronto, B.A., 1975; Stanford University, Ph.D., 1981.

ADDRESSES: Home—941 West Campus Lane, Goleta, CA 93117. *Office*—Department of English, 2720 South Hall, University of California, Santa Barbara, CA 93106.

CAREER: Yale University, New Haven, CT, lecturer in English, 1981-82; University of Wisconsin—Madison, assistant professor of English, 1982-87; University of California, Santa Barbara, assistant professor, 1987-91, associate professor of English, 1991—, chair of Renaissance Studies Program. Presenter at academic conventions and conferences.

MEMBER: Spenser Society (member of executive committee, 1989-92).

AWARDS, HONORS: Summer stipend, National Endowment for the Humanities, 1983-84.

WRITINGS:

Cultural Aesthetics: Renaissance Literature and the Practice of Social Ornament, University of Chicago Press, 1991.

Work represented in anthologies, including *Representing the English Renaissance,* edited by Stephen Greenblatt, University of California Press, 1987. Contributor to academic journals.

WORK IN PROGRESS: Subdiscourse: Jonson Speaking Low.

G

GAARD, Greta 1960-

PERSONAL: Born February 29, 1960, in Hollywood, CA; daughter of Robert and Beverly Gaard. *Education:* Pepperdine University, B.A., 1979; Claremont Graduate School, M.A., 1980; University of Minnesota, Ph.D., 1989. *Politics:* Green Party. *Religion:* Woman Church. *Avocational interests:* Backpacking, rock climbing, knitting.

ADDRESSES: Home—Duluth, MN. *Office*—University of Minnesota, 420 Humanities Bldg., Duluth, MN 55812.

CAREER: University of Minnesota, Twin Cities, instructor in English and women's studies, 1980-89; University of Minnesota, Duluth, assistant professor of writing and women's studies, 1989—, chair of committee on teaching, 1991-93, co-chair of commission on lesbian, gay, bisexual, and diversity issues, 1991-92, member of various other faculty committees. Inver Hills Community College, instructor in English, 1985; Hamline University, instructor in introductory composition, 1986; Augsburg College, instructor in English, 1986-87. Commission on the Status of Women in the Profession, liaison representative, 1990-93; juror for Depot's Annual Lake Superior Writers' Contest, 1992; member of advisory board of Feminists for Animal Rights, 1993—.

MEMBER: National Council of Teachers of English, Modern Language Association (co-chair of Lesbian and Gay Caucus, 1990-92), Midwestern Modern Language Association (secretary of computer research section, 1992-94), Midwest Society of Women in Philosophy.

AWARDS, HONORS: Article of the year awards, *Minnesota English Journal,* 1990 and 1991; research grants, 1990-91 and 1992; CLA Research Committee, research grant, 1991, travel grants, 1991 and 1992.

WRITINGS:

(Editor and contributor) *Ecofeminism: Women, Animals, Nature,* Temple University Press, 1993.
(Editor) Helen Anderson, *Pity for Women,* Naiad Press, in press.

Contributor to books, including *Poets Who Haven't Moved to St. Paul,* Poetry Harbor, 1990; *Poets Who Haven't Moved to Minneapolis,* Poetry Harbor, 1990; *Word of Mouth,* Volume II, edited by Irene Zahava, Crossing Press, 1991; *Comparative/Feminist Criticism,* edited by Margaret Higonnet, Cornell University Press, 1993; and *Dancing in the Heart of Wonder: Women Exploring the Mind/Body Relationship,* edited by Arachne Stevens, 1993. Contributor to numerous journals, including *Society and Nature, Environmental Ethics, Journal of the Midwestern Modern Language Association, Minnesota Women's Press, Minnesota English Journal, APA Newsletter on Feminism and Philosophy, Women and Environments, Hurricane Alice, Minnesota Daily, Equal Time, North Coast Review, Creative Woman,* and *Collective Voice.* Editor, *Evergreen Chronicles: A Journal of Gay and Lesbian Writers,* 1991—.

WORK IN PROGRESS: Thinking Green, a documentary on the philosophies, activism, and politics of ecofeminists and other environmental activists; research on writing, women's studies, and twentieth-century multicultural literatures.

SIDELIGHTS: Greta Gaard told *CA:* "In our lifetimes, the survival of life on earth will be decided. This planet can no longer bear the burden of destructive technology, toxic waste, pollution, and massive deforestation. As writers, we have the power and the responsibility to communicate the imperative that we must act quickly if we are to bring about social and ecological justice."

GABRIEL, Kathryn (Ann) 1955-

PERSONAL: Born October 15, 1955, in Albuquerque, NM; daughter of Robert Eugene (a banker and accountant) and Alice Maria (a homemaker; maiden name, Oechsner) Gabriel; married John Miller Mead, 1976 (marriage ended, 1979); married David Anderson Loving (a technician in microprocessing industry), January 1, 1990; children: Andrew Cedric Robert. *Education:* University of New Mexico, B.U.S., 1979. *Politics:* "Hybrid."

ADDRESSES: Home and office—2521 Wheeler Peak Dr., Rio Rancho, NM 87124.

CAREER: Guymon Daily Herald, Guymon, OK, agriculture and energy editor, 1980; Golden Star Pub and Brewery, Norwich, England, in public relations, 1981; State Bar of New Mexico, Albuquerque, assistant to editor of *News and Views* newsletter, 1983-84; Cystic Fibrosis Foundation, Albuquerque, assistant director, 1984-85; United Way of Greater Albuquerque, Albuquerque, communications specialist, 1985-86; University of New Mexico, Albuquerque, media relations specialist, 1986-90; writer. Volunteer archivist in the Florence Hawley Ellis Archives.

MEMBER: Southwest Writers Workshop, Public Relations Society of America, Press Women of New Mexico.

WRITINGS:

Death Comes to the Archdirector (three-act play), produced in Albuquerque, NM, 1989.
Roads to Center Place: A Cultural Atlas to Chaco Canyon and the Anasazi, Johnson Books, 1991.
(Editor) *Marietta Wetherill: Reflections on Life with the Navajos in Chaco Canyon,* Johnson Books, 1992.

Contributor to periodicals, including *Albuquerque Living, Mirage, Albuquerque Journal Impact,* and *Quantum.*

FOR TELEVISION

Women Aware, KOB-TV, 1986.
(And producer) *Kids with Keys,* KOB-TV, 1986.
(And producer) *Our Town,* KOAT-TV, 1987.
(And producer) *Pueblo on the Mesa,* KNME-TV, 1988.
(And producer) *Second Century,* KNME-TV, 1989-90.

WORK IN PROGRESS: "Writing a screenplay about Marietta Wetherill and the murder of her husband, Richard, as well as fiction on the Chaco culture; researching early women anthropologists of the Southwest, including Florence Hawley Ellis. She was an early Chaco archaeologist—the first to use tree-ring dating—and also a Pueblo ethnologist."

SIDELIGHTS: Kathryn Gabriel is a prominent New Mexico writer whose first book, *Roads to Center Place: A Cultural Atlas to Chaco Canyon and the Anasazi,* merges archaeological research and folklore analysis to provide an incisive examination of the road system established more than one thousand years ago in northwestern New Mexico. Gabriel told *CA,* "I meant to fictionalize the thousand-year-old culture at Chaco, but during my research I found so much information not yet published that I decided to publish it myself." She added that *Roads to Center Place* "has been held up as an example for other interpretive books to emulate."

Gabriel followed *Roads to Center Place* with *Marietta Wetherill: Reflections on Life with the Navajos in Chaco Canyon,* which concerns Marietta Wetherill's experiences among the Chaco Navajo in the late nineteenth and early twentieth centuries. Wetherill provided her recollections in a series of interviews conducted a year before her death in 1954, and in her accounts, which Gabriel edited, she affords readers considerable insight into Navajo life. Margaret Carlin, writing in the *Rocky Mountain News,* noted that Wetherill "describes numerous details about medicine men, sand bathing, capturing eagles, healing feverish babies, the Indian reverence for the snake, sand paintings, chants, and much more." For Wetherill, life among the Navajos was hardly carefree. Sanitation, for instance, was quite crude, and socializing in general required considerable patience and occasional risk. Wetherill managed to gain a significant measure of acceptance from the Navajos, however, and was eventually invited into the tribe.

Less fortunate was Wetherill's husband, Richard, who is credited with having discovered the Anasazi cliffs of Colorado's Mesa Verde in the late 1880s. Richard Wetherill came to Chaco in 1896, and in the ensuing years he became increasingly preoccupied with excavation and the recovery of artifacts. In 1910 he was shot dead by one of the Navajos. Gabriel told *CA* that relations between Richard Wetherill and the Navajos were mutually exploitive, and that his killing "epitomizes the relationship between the Native Americans and the Euro-Americans." She added: "Throughout our history together, the atrocities one group committed against the other were reciprocated, as was the good will," and she deemed this history one of "cultural and personal forgiveness."

Marietta Wetherill won recognition as an accomplished achievement. Ray E. Jenkins proclaimed in the *Denver Westerners Roundup* that the book constitutes "a very significant contribution to the study of the Navajos." And Margaret Carlin reported in the *Rocky Mountain News* that Wetherill's "rambling memories . . . provide a vivid picture of day-to-day life in Chaco." Another reviewer, Susan Landon, noted in the *Albuquerque Journal* that *Marietta Wetherill* conveys "the flavor of a young woman's life at Chaco Canyon at the turn of the century." Landon added that Gabriel, in her editing and researching of Wetherill's recollections, "has done a first-rate job."

Gabriel told *CA:* "Most writers living in the Southwest must work in public relations or some such profession while writing the work in their spare time that eventually will allow them to go independent. This was the case for me. Apart from working for an Oklahoma daily as agriculture and energy editor, I've written radio advertising copy, edited fund-raising newsletters, produced public affairs programs for television, and peddled the dreaded press releases—all on a wide range of issues. But when I finally broke out on my own, it isn't any wonder I wrote about Southwestern antiquity.

"Probably the person most responsible for my subject matter is my father, a New Mexicophile. He moved to New Mexico from Illinois at age ten or so and later, while working as an accountant, took on the Navajo nation as a client. When I was an infant, I occasionally accompanied my parents to the headquarters at Window Rock, Arizona, where the Navajo women rubbed my blonde hair for luck or out of curiosity. Throughout my childhood, Sundays and vacations meant family excursions (including mother, one younger sister and two younger brothers) in a station wagon to Spanish missions and old Indian ruins, namely Chaco Canyon. The interest sustained itself through college where I filled up on courses in Southwestern history, anthropology, literature, politics, and ecology. This study was rounded out when I later worked at the same university as a writer in its public information office. The University built its reputation on becoming a laboratory of Southwestern culture and I took full advantage of it.

"The general American population's fascination with Native American culture motivated me to write *Marietta Wetherill.* (Although officially I edited this book, I consider myself to have written it, in the same way Studs Terkel wrote his oral histories, because of the extent of rewriting and ordering I had to do.) In her oral history, Marietta said she always wanted to live with the Indians. 'That was the thing, my life.' Marietta was the eldest daughter of a wealthy peripatetic family who travelled across the country in a horse-drawn Studebaker wagon from ruin to reservation to ranch 'giving entertainments.' Like my own father, Marietta's father was also from Illinois and considered himself an amateur archaeologist. He introduced Marietta to Chaco Canyon.

"Marietta's husband, Richard Wetherill, who discovered Mesa Verde, was obsessed with deciphering the buried clues of the Anasazi at Chaco Canyon, but Marietta was more interested in the Navajo, whom she dealt with on a day to day basis. While I can't identify with the trials and tribulations of a pioneer woman, I can appreciate her intense interest in the Navajo. It is the desire to learn about a culture which shares our origin, but whose evolution took a divergent path from our own. During the twelve

years of living in Chaco Canyon, Richard and Marietta employed the Navajos to work in the ruin, to weave rugs, and to herd sheep. The Navajos in turn used the Wetherill trading posts as an outlet for their own merchandise. At the end of twelve years, a Navajo murdered Richard. Was Richard wrong for encroaching on sacred lands and encouraging the Navajos to become dependent on him? Did he abuse them as was rumored? Did they take advantage of him as he claimed, stealing from him and refusing to pay off debt? I think it worked both ways.

"My advice to new writers: write. Writing is a lifetime practice. Learning to be a writer is like learning to be a doctor. You may have aptitude at birth, more than some, less than others, but it takes decades to learn the craft, the business of writing and the sound of your voice on paper. If you follow your desires with dedication and hard work, you will become that which you desire. It will seem like it was meant to be all along.

"We have many talented writers in New Mexico, partly because of the rich abundance of material, and partly because many are drawn to the mysterious pull of the Southwest. I, of course, had the foresight to have been born here."

BIOGRAPHICAL/CRITICAL SOURCES:

PERIODICALS

Albuquerque Journal, July 19, 1992.
Denver Westerners Roundup, July-August, 1992.
Rocky Mountain News, August 16, 1992, p. 16M.

*   *   *

GALLAGHER, Thomas (Michael)   1918-1992

OBITUARY NOTICE—See index for *CA* sketch: Born in 1918 in New York, NY; died of a heart attack, December 19, 1992, in Manhattan, NY. Writer. Gallagher was the award-winning author of *Fire at Sea: The Story of the Morro Castle,* an analysis of the cause of a fire that ravaged the luxury liner Morro Castle in 1934. In the book, Gallagher published the results of his painstaking investigation, which proved conclusively that the fire had been intentional. *Fire at Sea* won the Edgar Allan Poe Award for nonfiction in 1960. Among Gallagher's other well-known works are *The Gathering Darkness,* which was nominated for a National Book Award after being published in 1952; *The Monogamist,* which was adapted for television and produced by Time-Life; and his last book, 1982's *Paddy's Lament.*

OBITUARIES AND OTHER SOURCES:

BOOKS

International Authors and Writers Who's Who, 7th edition, Melrose, 1976.

PERIODICALS

New York Times, December 21, 1992, p. D13.

* * *

GALLOWAY, Kara
See CAIL, Carol

* * *

GARD, Robert Edward   1910-1992

OBITUARY NOTICE—See index for *CA* sketch: Born July 3, 1910, in Iola, KS; died December 7, 1992, in Madison, WI. Educator, folklorist, playwright, and author. Gard began his career as an instructor at several institutions, including Cornell University in Ithaca, New York, before becoming a professor at the University of Wisconsin at Madison, where he taught until his retirement. Active in the community, Gard was a member of several organizations including the Wisconsin Arts Foundation and Council and the Wisconsin Regional Writers Association. The author of more than forty books, Gard was interested in folklore and drama, writing such texts as *The Lake Guns of Seneca and Cayuga, and Eight Other Plays* and *Wisconsin Is My Doorstep: A Dramatists Yarn Book of Wisconsin Lore.* Gard also wrote for children, including *A Horse Named Joe* and *Scotty's Mare.* Among Gard's other publications are *The Big One, The Error of Sexton Jones, Innocence of Prairie,* and with Allen Crafton, *A Woman of No Importance.*

OBITUARIES AND OTHER SOURCES:

BOOKS

Authors of Books for Young People, 3rd edition, Scarecrow, 1990.

PERIODICALS

Chicago Tribune, December 8, 1992, sec. 1, p. 10.

* * *

GARRARD, Lancelot Austin   1904-1993

OBITUARY NOTICE—See index for *CA* sketch: Born May 31, 1904, in Skelbroke, Yorkshire, England; died January 7, 1993. Minister, educator, and writer. A longtime Unitarian minister and Bible scholar, Garrard worked variously as a tutor, a bursar, a librarian, and, from 1956 to 1965, the principal of Manchester College, Oxford. For the next seven years he taught philosophy and religion at Emerson College in Massachusetts, where he became professor emeritus in 1971. Garrard translated Albert Schweitzer's *The Kingdom of God and Primitive Christianity* in 1968. Among his other published works are *Duty and the Will of God, Athens or Jerusalem?: A Study in Christian Comprehension, The Interpreted Bible,* and *The Historical Jesus: Schweitzer's Quest and Ours after Fifty Years.*

OBITUARIES AND OTHER SOURCES:

BOOKS

The Writers Directory: 1990-1992, St. James Press, 1990.

PERIODICALS

Times (London), January 21, 1993, p. 19.

* * *

GATES, David   1947(?)-

PERSONAL: Born c. 1947; married Ann Beattie (a writer), 1972 (marriage ended); married second wife (separated). *Education:* Attended Bard College, mid-1960s; graduate study at University of Connecticut.

ADDRESSES: Home—New York, NY. *Office—Newsweek,* 444 Madison Ave., New York, NY 10022.

CAREER: Worked as a cab driver and worked for wholesale food distributor and electronics company; taught at University of Virginia and Harvard University; *Newsweek,* New York City, 1978—, began in correspondence department, became general editor; writer.

WRITINGS:

Jernigan (novel), Knopf, 1991.

Contributor to periodicals, including *Cosmopolitan, Esquire,* and *Rolling Stone.*

SIDELIGHTS: David Gates is a *Newsweek* writer specializing in books and popular music. In addition, he is author of *Jernigan,* an acclaimed novel about the tragic life of a pathetic, middle-aged alcoholic. When introduced, the book's protagonist, Peter Jernigan, is participating in a recovery program to help him quit drinking and regain control of his life. Narrating the book, Jernigan recalls his gloomy life. He reveals that his wife died after stripping at an outdoor party, vaulting into the family car, and speeding into the street only to be crushed by a passing van. Later, Jernigan finds himself paired with his son's girlfriend's mother, Martha, an astrology buff who raises, and slaughters, rabbits for personal consumption. After a blunt dismissal from his employer, Jernigan abruptly puts his home up for sale and moves in with Martha, where he wallows in drink. Matters culminate in violence when Martha's volatile ex-husband pays a Christmas-time visit. At this point, as *New York Times* reviewer Michiko Kakutani noted, "pent-up emotions explode, plunging Jernigan into a violent and furious despair that will have consequences for all their lives."

Upon publication in 1991, *Jernigan* won recognition as an impressive literary debut. Kakutani declared that with *Jernigan* Gates had immediately "established himself as a novelist of the very first order," and she added that the novel features "one of recent literature's most memorable anti-heroes." Another critic, Richard Eder, wrote in the *Los Angeles Times Book Review* of Gates's "considerable talent" and deemed his writing "always intelligent and sometimes powerful." And Sheila Ballantyne, writing in the *New York Times Book Review,* described *Jernigan* itself as "a profoundly sorrowful book, one that lingers . . . in the heart."

In a *New York Times* interview, Gates disclosed that his literary mentor is Samuel Beckett, author of such tragic-comic works as *Waiting for Godot* and *The Unnameable.* "Beckett writes so beautifully about such bleak things," Gates observed. "We're all going to die, and we all die alone." He also noted that *Jernigan,* unlike many first novels, is scarcely autobiographical. "The stuff that's taken from my life is really quite minimal," he observed. "It's the mood that's me."

BIOGRAPHICAL/CRITICAL SOURCES:

PERIODICALS

Los Angeles Times Book Review, June 2, 1991, p. 3.
New York Times, May 24, 1991, p. C29; June 18, 1991, p. C13.
New York Times Book Review, July 14, 1991, p. 18.*

*   *   *

GEANEY, Dennis J(oseph)   1914-1992

OBITUARY NOTICE—See index for *CA* sketch: Born August 2, 1914, in Boston, MA; died November 23, 1992, in Chicago, IL. Priest, educator, and author. A member of the Augustinian Order, Geaney was ordained a priest in 1942. He graduated with his master's degree from Catholic University of America in 1943 and began to teach at high schools in Chicago, IL; Rockford, IL; and Ft. Wayne, IN. During this time Geaney began his writing ca-

reer, publishing his first book, *You Are Not Your Own,* in 1954. His subsequent books include *You Shall Be Witnesses, Living with Your Conscience, Emerging Lay Ministries,* and *Full Church, Empty Rectory: Training Lay Ministers for Parishes without Priests.* In the 1965 Geaney became assistant pastor of St. Rita Church and, seven years later, prior of St. John Stone Priory. He was a founding member of the Chicago Association of Priests and edited two Catholic newsletters, *Upturn* and *ARCC LIGHT.* Geaney had recently celebrated his fiftieth anniversary as a priest.

OBITUARIES AND OTHER SOURCES:

BOOKS

American Catholic Who's Who, Volume 23: *1980-1981,* National Catholic News Service, 1979.

PERIODICALS

Chicago Tribune, November 25, 1992, section 3, p. 12.

*   *   *

GEDDES, Gary   1940-

PERSONAL: Born June 9, 1940, in Vancouver, British Columbia, Canada; son of Laurie James (a carpenter and shipwright) and Irene (Turner) Geddes; married Norma Joan Fugler (a nurse), 1963 (divorced, 1969); married Jan Macht (a publisher), May 2, 1973; children: (first marriage) Jennifer, (second marriage) Charlotte, Bronwen Claire. *Education:* University of British Columbia, B.A., 1962; University of Reading, diploma in education, 1964; University of Toronto, M.A., 1966, Ph.D., 1975.

ADDRESSES: Home—RR1, Dunvegan, Ontario, Canada K0C 1J0. *Office*—Department of English, Concordia University, 1455 de Maisonneuve Blvd W., Montreal, Quebec H3G 1M8, Canada.

CAREER: Affiliated with University of Toronto, Toronto, Ontario, Canada, 1965-70; York University, North York, Ontario, instructor in English, 1966-67; Ryerson Polytechnical Institute, Toronto, instructor in English, 1966-69; Trent University, Peterborough, Ontario, visiting lecturer in English, 1969; Carleton University, Ottawa, Ontario, visiting assistant professor in English, 1971-72; University of Victoria, Victoria, British Columbia, Canada, lecturer in English, 1972-74; British Columbia Institute of Technology, Vancouver, lecturer in English, 1974-76; University of Alberta, Edmonton, Canada, writer-in-residence, 1976, visiting assistant professor in English, 1977; Concordia University, Montreal, Quebec, Canada, associate professor of English, 1978-87, writer-in-residence, 1979, professor of English, 1987—; poet.

Founded three literary presses, including Quadrant Editions, 1981, and Cormorant Books, 1984; gives numerous worldwide poetry readings and public lectures.

MEMBER: League of Canadian Poets, Writers' Union of Canada, International PEN.

AWARDS, HONORS: Province of Ontario graduate fellowship, 1965-66; Imperial Oil graduate fellowship, 1968-70; Canada Council doctoral fellowship, 1968-70; Canada Council arts grants, 1971, 1974, 1977, 1979, 1981, 1987, and 1988; E. J. Pratt medal and prize, University of Toronto, 1970, for *Letter of the Master of Horse;* Ontario Arts Council Writers Reserve Grant, 1984-88; National Poetry Prize, Canadian Authors' Association, 1982, for *The Acid Test;* first prize in Americas division, British Airways Commonwealth Poetry Competition, 1985, for *The Terracotta Army;* National Magazine Gold Award, 1987, and Writers' Choice Award, 1988, both for play *Hong Kong;* Archibald Lampman Poetry Prize, 1990, for *No Easy Exit/Salida dificil;* runner-up silver medal from Milton Acorn Poetry Competition, 1991.

WRITINGS:

POETRY

Poems, Waterloo Lutheran Press, 1971.
Rivers Inlet, Talon Books, 1973.
Letter of the Master of Horse, Oberon Press, 1973.
Snakeroot, Talon Books, 1973.
War and Other Measures, House of Anansi, 1976.
The Acid Test, Turnstone Press, 1981.
The Terracotta Army, Oberon Press, 1984.
Changes of State, Coteau Books, 1986.
Hong Kong Poems (also see below), Oberon Press, 1987.
No Easy Exit/Salida dificil, Oolichan Books, 1989.
Light of Burning Towers: New and Selected Poems, Vehicule Press, 1990.

EDITOR

Twentieth-Century Poetry & Poetics, Oxford University Press, 1969.
Heart of Darkness and Other Stories by Joseph Conrad, Nelson, 1971.
Fifteen Canadian Poets, Oxford University Press, 1971.
Skookum Wawa: Writings of the Canadian Northwest, Oxford University Press, 1975.
Divided We Stand, Peter Martin Associates, 1977.
Chinada: Memoirs of the Gang of Seven, Quadrant Editions, 1983.
The Inner Ear, Quadrant Editions, 1983.
Vancouver: Soul of a City, Douglas & McIntyre, 1986.
(With Hugh Hazelton) *Companeros: An Anthology of Writings about Latin America,* Cormorant Books, 1990.

The Art of Short Fiction: An International Anthology, HarperCollins, 1992.

OTHER

(Cofounder with Hugo McPherson) *Studies in Canadian Literature,* fifteen volumes, Copp Clark Publishing, 1969-75, McGill-Queen's Press, 1975-79, Douglas & McIntyre, 1979-85.
Conrad's Later Novels, McGill-Queen's University Press, 1980.
Les Maudits Anglais (full-length play; produced in Montreal and Toronto by Theatre Passe Muraille, 1978), Playwrights Cooperative, 1984.
(Translator with George Liang) *I Didn't Notice the Mountain Growing Dark* (poems of Li Bai and Du Fu), Cormorant Books, 1986.
The Unsettling of the West (short stories), Oberon Press, 1986.
Hong Kong, (full-length play adaptation of Geddes's book *Hong Kong Poems*), produced in Winnipeg, 1986.
Letters from Managua: Meditations on Politics and Art, Quarry Press, 1990.

Contributor to periodicals, including *Edmonton Journal, Saturday Night, Globe and Mail, Ellipse, Fiddlehead, Ecrits du Canada Francais, Moosehead Review, Canadian Forum, Capilano Review, Best Canadian Stories, Canadian Literature, Books in Canada, Oxford Companion to Canadian Literature, Open Letter,* and *Lyric Paragraph.*

Geddes's work has been translated into French, Spanish, Dutch, and Chinese.

WORK IN PROGRESS: A new collection of poems tentatively titled *Afterbirth;* publication of a *Selected Poems* edition; two long-poem projects.

SIDELIGHTS: Gary Geddes—considered "Canada's best political poet" by *WQ Reviews* contributor George Woodcock—is distinguished for his political poetry that explores human relations. Describing the poet's work in a review of the 1990 collection *Light of Burning Towers, Vancouver Sun* reviewer John Moore stated: "His rigorous blend of instinct, insight and eloquence are the timeless qualities of greatness." In his verse Geddes stresses one's responsibility for other people and the need for compassion, and he displays his ethics through his dedicated promotion of Canadian writing. Geddes's poetry focuses on subjects, such as the relationship between art and politics, rather than language usage. In an interview with Alan Twigg in *Strong Voices: Conversations with Fifty Canadian Authors,* Geddes declared: "I am preoccupied with injured figures, figures caught in the machinery of society or politics or religion," which he said is possibly a result of harboring "a degree of violence that desperately needs capping." Geddes also revealed that he writes long poems because this type of presentation is the "most exciting form in my view" and that writing is "a way of getting in touch with my deepest feelings."

Geddes depicts an injured figure plagued by dreams and memories of war in his 1976 long poem *War and Other Measures*. Examining the agony and futility of war, the book focuses on a character similar to Paul Joseph Chartier, a man who died in May 1966 when a bomb he brought into the Canadian House of Commons [the lower house of the Canadian parliament] detonated. When journalists wrote that Chartier had bungled a terrorist attack, Geddes instead wondered if the man intended to kill himself solely to make a political statement without injuring other people. Such a death, according to Geddes, would have been an even more powerful statement. Geddes told Twigg that he found Chartier's suicide to be "a symbol for something tragic and deadly in our culture," which is how he portrays war in *War and Other Measures*. Geddes also maintains that Chartier, and subsequently the figure in his poem, had "no means of redressing injustices." Laurie Ricou, writing in *Dictionary of Literary Biography*, described Chartier as "an outcast Quebecois who must live life in a language other than his own," which is a prominent theme, Ricou proclaimed, in Geddes's works.

In 1984, some eight years after publishing *War and Other Measures*, Geddes produced another poem about war, politics, and art, called *The Terracotta Army*. Including twenty-five dramatic monologues, the book characterizes a select group of soldiers that potter Lao Bi sculpted for the first emperor of China, Ch'in Shi Huang, in the third century B.C. The emperor had the clay soldiers made in order to protect him in his afterlife. Geddes claims he was inspired to humanize the figures when he saw those that had been excavated from the emperor's grave in China between 1974 and 1980. His depictions of the soldiers interconnect art and politics; as Geddes explains, the politics of the soldiers are made immortal through his poetry. Revolving around Bi's sculpting, the monologues reveal political views, the soldiers' vain and selfish personalities, and the degradation of the State at the hands of the conceited, tyrannical emperor. The soldiers fear and respect Bi; he, in turn, is aware of his power and uses it to their mutual advantage. Instead of having a monologue of his own, the potter is described by the soldiers, who make contradictory observations about his character. John Cook, writing in *Queen's Quarterly*, observed that with *The Terracotta Army*, Geddes has "matured into an uncommonly good poet."

Geddes continued to delve into the subject of war and politics in his 1987 *Hong Kong Poems*. The volume takes the reader on a poetic journey into Canada's involvement in China during World War II. In 1941 Geddes's countrymen were sent ill-prepared into the British colony of Hong Kong to establish a Canadian presence there even though Canadian military leaders knew Japan could take over the island. Defeated by overwhelming odds, the surviving Canadian soldiers were incarcerated for three-and-a-half years, then returned from China only to find themselves denied their rights as veterans. In *Hong Kong Poems* Geddes calls for compassion from the Canadian people by writing about the soldiers' traumatic experiences in China and attempts to motivate his nation's citizens and government to take responsibility for their troops. A *Fiddlehead* review, called Geddes's interpretation of this emotionally volatile subject "masterfully restrained and controlled."

In 1989, Geddes went to Nicaragua and recorded his experiences with the country's politics and art in the form of letters. He made his journey during the tenth anniversary of the Sandinista revolution named for insurrectionist Augusto Cesar Sandino, which resulted in the Sandinistas seizing power in 1979 from the Somoza dictatorship. In his 1990 book, *Letters from Managua: Meditations on Politics and Art,* Geddes laments poetry's diminishing popularity in North American society, and rejoices over finding poets and poetry to be an important part of Nicaraguan society and politics. Ken McGoogan, writing in the *Calgary Herald,* commented that the author's work is a "call to action rarely seen in Canadian poetry," and added that "perhaps we would be better off if we ignored our empty-headed politicians and listened to poets like Gary Geddes." In *Canadian Literature,* Donald Stephens described Geddes as "not only a poet to watch but also a poet who will continually surprise and please."

Geddes told *CA:* "I have a sustained interest in poetics in general and the long poem in particular. The contemporary poem-sequence, at its best, includes the intensity of the lyric and the inclusiveness of the epic. I don't share the contemporary unease with narrative. Our lives are organized and enriched by narrative; we could not live without our capacity to explore, shape, and render meaningful our human experience. I also believe that writers have to take control of the promotion, distribution, and critical understanding of their own work, rather than leave it to chance and to commercial interests. In addition to doing my own writing, I review books widely, I have started three literary presses, and I have edited some forty books through publication. I continue to believe in art as a sign of the collective health of a society."

BIOGRAPHICAL/CRITICAL SOURCES:

BOOKS

Dictionary of Literary Biography, Volume 60: *Canadian Writers since 1960, Second Series,* Gale, 1987.

Twigg, Alan, editor, *Strong Voices: Conversations with Fifty Canadian Authors,* Harbour, 1988.

PERIODICALS

Calgary Herald, August 4, 1990.
Canadian Forum, December, 1985, p. 24.
Canadian Literature, no. 95 winter 1982, p. 150.
Globe and Mail (Toronto), August 18, 1990.
Journal of Canadian Poetry, Volume 6, 1991, pp. 60-62.
Queen's Quarterly, Volume 93, 1986, p. 2.
Vancouver Sun, September 20, 1990, p. D20.
WQ Reviews, Winter, 1982, p. 14.

—*Sketch by Jane M. Kelly*

*   *   *

GEIST, Bill
See GEIST, William E.

*   *   *

GEIST, William E. 1945(?)-
(Bill Geist)

PERSONAL: Born c. 1945; son of a teacher and Marjorie; married Jody (in real estate); children: Willie, Libby. *Education:* Graduated from University of Illinois; received journalism degree from University of Missouri.

ADDRESSES: Home—Ridgewood, NJ. *Office*—CBS News, 51 West 52nd St., New York, NY 10019-6165.

CAREER: Worked as photographer for U.S. Army in Vietnam; worked for *Chicago Tribune,* Chicago, IL, until 1980; *New York Times,* New York City, author of column "About New York," 1980-87; CBS News, New York City, commentator and feature reporter for shows such as *CBS Evening News* and *Sunday Morning with Charles Kuralt,* 1987—; writer.

WRITINGS:

Toward a Safe and Sane Halloween, and Other Tales of Suburbia (essays), Times Books, 1985, reprinted as *The Zucchini Plague, and Other Tales of Suburbia,* Simon & Schuster, 1987.
City Slickers (columns), Times Books, 1987.
About New York (columns), Times Books, 1987.
(Under name Bill Geist) *Little League Confidential: One Coach's Completely Unauthorized Tale of Survival* (nonfiction), Macmillan, 1992.

WORK IN PROGRESS: A novel about life in Ridgewood, NJ.

SIDELIGHTS: William E. Geist is popular humorist who has written for such publications as the *New York Times* and appeared on such television programs as *CBS Evening News* and *Sunday Morning with Charles Kuralt.* In addition, he has produced volumes of both humor collections and nonfiction. Early in his career he worked for the *Chicago Tribune,* then moved in 1980 to the *New York Times,* where he wrote the "About New York" column. In 1987 Geist joined CBS News as a commentator, and he has been prominently featured on several of the network's programs, including Kuralt's popular news and human interest show.

Among Geist's books are the essay collection *Toward a Safe and Sane Halloween, and Other Tales of Suburbia,* which was reprinted as *The Zucchini Plague, and Other Tales of Suburbia.* The book is a droll appraisal of life in suburban America, including such Middle American commonalities as Tupperware parties, polyester leisure suits, and plastic pink flamingos used as lawn decorations. Geist is also the author of *City Slickers,* a collection of his columns written for the *New York Times.* The humorous pieces featured in this book depict "a New York City seemingly created for Geist's amusement," according to Chicago *Tribune Books* reviewer Clarence Petersen. Among Geist's anecdotes of New York life are pieces on the hazards of golfing in the urban area of the Bronx and the chaotic backstage events at Radio City Music Hall's annual Christmas show. Petersen praised the book for conveying Geist's "childlike sense of wonder" and "his savvy sense of the absurd."

In addition, Geist has published *Little League Confidential: One Coach's Completely Unauthorized Tale of Survival.* Here Geist recounts his own experiences as coach of his children's baseball teams. Coaching children, Geist relates, is an exercise in futility. He notes, for instance, that affording all players equal opportunity inevitably draws the ire of parents, while affording better players greater opportunity inevitably draws the ire of parents too. Indeed, handling parents proves as difficult a task as the actual coaching of children. According to Geist, parents will even take legal action to guarantee sufficient playing time for their offspring. Considering why he even bothers to pursue such a frustrating endeavor, Geist concludes, "You come to realize that if *you* don't do it, some . . . *twit* . . . will."

Little League Confidential has been praised for its humorous insights into the world of children's sports. Elizabeth Gleick, writing in *People,* pronounced *Little League Confidential* a "laugh-filled" volume, and Larry Wallberg, in his appraisal for the *Los Angeles Times Book Review,* noted that Geist's book provides "amusing observations." *New York Times Book Review* contributor Diane Cole stated that Geist "has a gift for uncovering the quirky detail that makes the mundane humorous."

In a *People* profile, Geist noted that he does not explicitly conduct himself with intentions of deriving interesting material for his writing. "The opposite is true," he declared. "I'm making home movies that happen to be aired by CBS."

BIOGRAPHICAL/CRITICAL SOURCES:

PERIODICALS

Los Angeles Times Book Review, June 21, 1992, p. 1.
New York Times Book Review, November 1, 1987, p. 25; April 5, 1992, p. 21.
People, May 11, 1992; August 17, 1992.
Sporting News, May 11, 1992, p. 55.
Time, April 20, 1992, p. 101.
Tribune Books (Chicago), June 7, 1987, p. 4; January 8, 1989, p. 4.*

* * *

GERUSON, Richard J. 1957-

PERSONAL: Born September 30, 1957, in New York City; son of Richard Thomas (a professor) and Joan T. (a teacher; maiden name, Nicholas) Geruson; married Nanette Fondas (a professor), September, 1985. *Education:* La Salle University, B.A. (summa cum laude), 1979; Oxford University, Graduate Diploma in Economic Development, 1980, M.Phil., 1982, Ph.D., 1989; attended Harvard University, 1985. *Religion:* Roman Catholic.

ADDRESSES: Home—130 Windy Pointe, Orange, CA 92669. *Office*—Toshiba America Information Systems, 9740 Irvine Blvd., P.O. Box 19724, Irvine, CA 92713-9724.

CAREER: International Business Machines Co. (IBM), White Plains, NY, marketing representative assistant and planning analyst, 1981-85; McKinsey and Co., Boston, MA, engagement manager, 1985-89; Stratus Computer, Marlboro, MA, director of marketing, 1989-91; Toshiba America Information Systems, Irvine, CA, vice-president of marketing and director of corporate marketing, 1991—. Big Brother/Big Sister of South Middlesex, Inc., member of board of directors; Greater Marlboro Symphony Orchestra, member of board of directors and strategic planning committee.

AWARDS, HONORS: Rotary fellow; Finnegan fellow; United Kingdom Overseas Student Award.

WRITINGS:

A Theory of Market Strategy, Oxford University Press, 1992.

Work represented in anthologies, including *Winning Orations,* Tennessee Oratorical Society, 1976. Contributor to academic journals.

WORK IN PROGRESS: Research on strategy and on the computer industry.

* * *

GERZINA, Gretchen (Aletha) Holbrook 1950-

PERSONAL: Born September 6, 1950, in Ann Arbor, MI; daughter of Joseph Mathias (a factory worker) and Joyce Aletha (a social worker; maiden name, Grubaugh) Holbrook; married Anthony Gerzina (an account manager), February 9, 1973; children: Simon Alexander, Daniel Joseph. *Education:* Marlboro College, B.A., 1972; Simmons College, A.M., 1979; Stanford University, Ph.D., 1984. *Politics:* Democrat. *Religion:* None.

ADDRESSES: Home—Clifton Park, NY. *Office*—Department of English, Vassar College, Poughkeepsie, NY 12601. *Agent*—Lizzie Grossman, Sterling Lord Literistic, 1 Madison Ave., New York, NY 10010.

CAREER: Stanford University, Stanford, CA, assistant director of Center for Teaching and Learning, 1984-85; State University of New York at Albany, lecturer, 1985-86; Skidmore College, Saratoga Springs, NY, assistant professor of English, 1986-89; Princeton University, Princeton, NJ, humanities fellow, 1989-90; Vassar College, Poughkeepsie, NY, assistant professor of English, 1989—.

WRITINGS:

Carrington: A Life, Norton, 1989, published in England as *Carrington: A Life of Dora Carrington, 1893-1932,* John Murray, 1989.

WORK IN PROGRESS: Racial Fictions; Two American Families, a book about Gerzina's parents' interracial marriage in the 1940s.

SIDELIGHTS: In 1989, Gretchen Holbrook Gerzina published her study of Dora Carrington, a peripheral member of the famed Bloomsbury group of artists and literati in post-World War I England. While having achieved a certain amount of success as a painter, Carrington has remained best-known for her personal relationships and colorful correspondences with other important figures. The most notable of Carrington's numerous romantic involvements with both men and women was her approximately fifteen-year affair with homosexual writer Lytton Strachey, which ended with his death by cancer and her subsequent suicide in 1932. In their apparently platonic years together, the devoted Carrington kept house for Strachey, who gave her emotional and artistic support. Carrington's iconoclastic views on sexual freedom and emotional commitment have made her an important historical figure in some circles. In her review of *Carrington* for the London *Times,* Fiona MacCarthy noted that since the late 1960s, "Carrington has become a curious cult figure. Her negative views on marriage and motherhood have been seized on as prophetic pronouncements of women's liberation."

Reviewers of *Carrington* lauded Gerzina's scholarly approach and ability to avoid mythologizing her subject. MacCarthy deemed Gerzina's study to be "likably well-balanced." While disappointed in the author's prose style, Richard Shone acknowledged in his *Spectator* assessment that "Carrington emerges in all her siren-like complexity" in Gerzina's book. *New York Times Book Review* critic Andrea Barnet expressed concern that some of Gerzina's claims about Carrington's artistic importance were "exaggerated," but stated that "Carrington's interest as a character" would hold readers' attention. Evelyn Toynton in *Washington Post Book World* preferred the romantic aspects of *Carrington* to its academic analyses, declaring, "It is actually a very touching love story, and at times this biography reads like a novel, with two thoroughly engaging main characters."

Gerzina told *CA:* "I am most committed to contextualizing people's lives and literary works and to producing scholarship that is readable. No people lived and no literary works were produced in social and cultural vacuums. Hopefully I will continue to write books that bring sexual, social, and racial issues to mainstream as well as academic audiences."

BIOGRAPHICAL/CRITICAL SOURCES:

PERIODICALS

New York Times Book Review, October 22, 1989, p. 23.
Spectator, July 1, 1989.
Times (London), June 17, 1989.
Times Literary Supplement, June 9, 1989, p. 640.
Washington Post Book World, January 14, 1990, p. 7.

*   *   *

GETMAN, Julius (G.) 1931-

PERSONAL: Born August 21, 1931, in New York, NY; son of Samuel (a garment worker) and Charlotte (Shapiro) Getman; children: Dan, Mike, Poppy, Jason. *Education:* City College (now of the City University of New York), B.A., 1959; Harvard University, J.D., 1958, LL.M., 1963.

ADDRESSES: Home—606 East 46th St., Austin, TX 78751. *Office*—Law School, University of Texas at Austin, Austin, TX 78705.

CAREER: National Labor Relations Board, Washington, DC, attorney, 1959-61; Indiana University—Bloomington, assistant professor, 1963-67, professor of law, 1967-76; Stanford University, Stanford, CA, professor of law, 1976-77; Yale University, New Haven, CT, William K. Townsend Professor of Law, 1978-86; University of Texas at Austin, Earl E. Sheffield Regents Professor of Law, 1986—. Visiting professor at Benares Hindu University and Indian Law Institute, 1967-68, and University of Chicago, 1970-71; Boston College, Richard Huber Distinguished Visiting Professor, 1991-92. Arbitrator, 1963-86; Connecticut State Police Union, chief negotiator, 1978-82; mediator in the public and private sector; expert witness on labor cases. Government of Bermuda and Bermuda Federation of Unions, special instructor in negotiations.

MEMBER: American Association of University Professors (general counsel, 1980-83; president of Yale chapter, 1983-85; national president, 1986-88), National Academy of Arbitrators, Industrial Relations Research Association, American Bar Association (section of Labor and Employment Law).

WRITINGS:

(With Stephen B. Goldberg and Jeanne Brett Herman) *Union Representation Elections: Law and Reality,* Russell Sage Foundation, 1976.

Labor Relations: Law, Practice, and Policy, Foundation Press, 1978, 2nd edition (with John D. Blackburn), 1989.

(With Bertrand B. Pogrebin) *Labor Relations: The Basic Processes, Law and Practice,* Foundation Press, 1988.

(With William Gould, Cynthia Gramm, Ray Marshall, and others) *Employee Rights in a Changing Economy: The Issue of Replacement Workers,* Economic Policy Institute, 1991.

In the Company of Scholars: The Struggle for the Soul of Higher Education, University of Texas Press, 1992.

Co-author of *Casebook: Employment Discrimination BNA,* 1979. Contributor to law and labor relations journals.

WORK IN PROGRESS: The story of the strike by paper workers in Maine, 1986-87, publication expected in 1994; a mystery novel about the murder of a law professor.

SIDELIGHTS: Julius Getman told *CA:* "I am changing from a writer of academic articles and books to a writer about academic life, both fiction and non-fiction."

GILCHRIST, Andrew (Graham) 1910-1993

OBITUARY NOTICE—See index for *CA* sketch: Born April 19, 1910, in Lesmahagow, Scotland; died March 6, 1993. Ambassador, banker, and writer. A special agent during World War II, Gilchrist was especially well prepared for the political turmoil encountered in many of his Foreign Service assignments, including a firebombing of the embassy in Ireland and the stoning of his residence in Iceland. Gilchrist began his diplomatic career in the British Foreign Service, assigned to junior posts in Bangkok, Thailand; Paris, France; West Germany; and Singapore. He was promoted to ambassador and later held major posts in Iceland, Indonesia, and Ireland. Gilchrist wrote about many of his experiences, penning *Bangkok Top Secret: Being the Experiences of a British Officer in the Siam Country Section of Force 136* in 1970, *Cod Wars and How to Lose Them* in 1978, and *Malaya 1941: the fall of a fighting empire* in 1991. Upon his retirement from the Foreign office in 1970, he served as chair of the Scottish Highlands and Islands Development Board, a merchant banking enterprise serving rural business and trade in Scotland, for six years. He continued to write, adding fictional thrillers to historical memoirs, authoring such works as *The Watercress File, The Russian Professor, Ultimate Hostage,* and *Lafest.*

OBITUARIES AND OTHER SOURCES:

BOOKS

Who's Who, 144th edition, St. Martin's, 1992.

PERIODICALS

Times (London), March 11, 1993, p. 23.

* * *

GILLESPIE, Cynthia K. 1941-1993

OBITUARY NOTICE—See index for *CA* sketch: Born April 5, 1941, in Summit, NJ; died of breast cancer, January 29, 1993, in Seattle, WA. Lawyer and writer. Nationally known for her feminist activism, Gillespie's legal and writing career focused on family law and women's rights. Her 1989 book, *Justifiable Homicide: Battered Women, Self-Defense, and the Law,* was instrumental in decisions for clemency in twenty-six cases in Ohio and has been cited in numerous other legal trials across the nation. The volume was named Outstanding Academic Book of 1989 by *Choice* magazine and Outstanding Book in the Subject of Human Rights in the United States by the Gustavus Myers Center for the Study of Human Rights. Gillespie also contributed to *Representing Battered Women: The Role of Domestic Violence in Self-Defense, Custody, and Tort Cases.* In addition to her writing, Gillespie became cofounder of the Northwest Women's Law Center in Seattle, WA, where she assisted in a case leading to athletic programs for women being funded equally with those for men.

OBITUARIES AND OTHER SOURCES:

PERIODICALS

Chicago Tribune, February 3, 1993, section 3, p. 12.
New York Times, February 3, 1993, p. A21.

* * *

GISH, Lillian (Diana) 1893-1993

OBITUARY NOTICE—See index for *CA* sketch: Born Lillian Diana de Guiche, October 14, 1893, in Springfield, OH; died of heart failure, February 27, 1993, in Manhattan, NY. Actress, lecturer, and writer. Gish will be best remembered as a pioneer of the film industry and a legendary silent film star. An internationally famous performer who began acting on stage at age five and continued acting into her 90s, Gish found success as a leading lady in movies, starring in such silent film classics as *The Birth of a Nation, Broken Blossoms, Way Down East,* and *Intolerance.* She later made the transition to talking pictures, but after clashing with studio heads over contractual issues, Gish returned to the stage. She spent much of the rest of her career there, appearing in productions of *Uncle Vanya, Hamlet,* and *The Trip to Bountiful.* When she wasn't acting, Gish toured the world, lecturing and showing the films of legendary director D. W. Griffith, who gave Gish her most famous silent roles. Gish could also be seen on television in *The Autobiography of Grandma Moses* and *Arsenic and Old Lace.* In 1970, she received an honorary Academy Award for her contributions to film, and the American Film Institute honored her with its lifetime achievement award in 1984. Gish appeared in her last film, *The Whales of August,* in 1987. Her publications include *Lillian Gish: An Autobiography; Lillian Gish: The Movies, Mr. Griffith, and Me; Dorothy and Lillian Gish;* and *An Actor's Life for Me!*

OBITUARIES AND OTHER SOURCES:

PERIODICALS

Chicago Tribune, March 1, 1993, section 4, p. 9.
Los Angeles Times, March 1, 1993, p. A1.
New York Times, March 1, 1993, p. A1.
Times (London), March 1, 1993, p. 19.
Washington Post, March 1, 1993, p. D6.

GIVENS, Charles J. 1942(?)-

PERSONAL: Born c. 1942, in Decatur, IL; son of a private contractor; married Bonnie Lee Bond (an accountant), c. 1963 (marriage ended); remarried; wife's name, Adena; children: (first marriage) Charles III, Robert.

ADDRESSES: Home—Orlando, FL. *Office*—Givens Organization, 924 Douglas Ave., Altamonte Springs, FL 32714.

CAREER: Founded recording studio in Nashville, TN, 1963-66; systems analyst for Genesco, 1967-71; worked in "Dare to Be Great" promotional marketing with Glenn Turner, beginning in 1970; founder of Awareness Motivation Institute (biofeedback) and Givens Organization (brokerage). Also worked as a real estate broker.

WRITINGS:

Wealth without Risk: How to Develop a Personal Fortune without Going out on a Limb, Simon & Schuster, 1988, revised edition, 1991.
Money Strategies, Simon & Schuster, 1989.
Financial Self-Defense, Simon & Schuster, 1990.
More Wealth without Risk, Simon & Schuster, 1991.

SIDELIGHTS: Charles J. Givens, enormously popular as an investment advisor and lecturer, is the author of *Wealth without Risk: How to Develop a Personal Fortune without Going out on a Limb,* which was a mainstay on the *New York Times*'s bestseller list throughout 1989 and into 1990. *People* described *Wealth without Risk* as "a compendium of consumer strategies, tax tips and miscellaneous investment schemes all wrapped up in a psychological pep talk." The book is not without its detractors: *Forbes* reviewer Joe Queenan, for example, declared that "a lot of [Givens's] investing advice is flat-out wrong." And Givens—who owns several expensive cars, lives in a mansion, and employs domestic help—has been criticized as a self-serving opportunist. But the success of *Wealth without Risk* can itself be perceived as an example of Givens's applied optimism. "I always dreamed of being able to write a best-selling book," he told *People.* In that same profile he acknowledged his flashy reputation but cast it in a similarly favorable perspective. "I have a kind of *Entertainment Tonight* image out there in the financial world," he noted. "It helps me to get to people. And that's good marketing."

For Givens, success with *Wealth without Risk* came after many years of both prosperity and failure in a range of businesses. In the mid-1960s, for instance, he reportedly became a millionaire through his own recording studio in Nashville, and when he lost that investment following a fire (the studio was not insured), he allegedly recouped his wealth by playing the stock market. But he lost his second fortune when the stocks declined, whereupon he joined with Glenn Turner, promoter of "Dare to Be Great" courses. Givens later worked in real estate and even founded a biofeedback institute. In the early 1980s, though, he became increasingly active as a financial advisor. After appearing on a television show, he was contacted by a Simon & Schuster editor and urged to write a book. The result was *Wealth without Risk,* the work that established Givens as a popular, if not universally renowned, investments authority. Following the success of *Wealth without Risk,* Givens signed a multi-million-dollar contract to produce three more books. He has now completed those additional volumes: *Money Strategies, Financial Self-Defense,* and *More Wealth without Risk.* In addition, he has produced a revision of the original *Wealth without Risk.* This new edition was issued in 1991.

BIOGRAPHICAL/CRITICAL SOURCES:

PERIODICALS

Bestsellers 90, Number 3, 1990, pp. 16-17.
Forbes, November 27, 1989, p. 10.
Money, April, 1989, p. 15.
New Republic, October 29, 1990.
People, January 15, 1990.
Playboy, March, 1992, p. 30.
Venture, October, 1986.*

* * *

GLASSE, Robert Marshall 1929-1993

OBITUARY NOTICE—See index for *CA* sketch: Born April 3, 1929, in Brooklyn, NY; died of cancer, January 1, 1993, in Bronx, NY. Anthropologist, educator, and author. Glasse, who taught at Queens College of the City University of New York for twenty-five years, is remembered for his role in ending an epidemic among New Guinea tribesmen in the early 1960s. He visited the country several times between 1955 and 1969, documenting the customs of one tribe in his 1968 book, *Huli of Papua.* With M. J. Meggitt, Glasse edited *Pigs, Pearlshells, and Women: Marriage Arrangements in the New Guinea Highlands* in 1969. He began his tenure with Queens College in 1965 as an assistant professor, becoming professor of anthropology in 1971 and remaining for nearly twenty years.

OBITUARIES AND OTHER SOURCES:

PERIODICALS

New York Times, January 6, 1993, p. B6.

GODFREY, Donald G.

PERSONAL: Born in Cardston, Alberta, Canada; son of Floyd and Clarice (Card) Godfrey; married Christina Maria Kolibas, November 4, 1965; children: four. *Education:* Weber State College, B.S. (with honors); University of Oregon, M.S. (cum laude); University of Washington, Ph.D. (cum laude), 1975.

ADDRESSES: Home—1622 East Grove, Mesa, AZ 85204. *Office*—Walter Cronkite School of Journalism and Telecommunication, Arizona State University, Tempe, AZ 85287.

CAREER: University of Washington, Seattle, faculty associate, 1969-72, lecturer, 1972-75, assistant professor of communication, 1976-81; University of Arizona, Tucson, associate professor of radio and television studies, 1981-83; Southern Utah University, Cedar City, associate professor of communication and coordinator of telecommunications, 1983-86; Arizona State University, Tempe, assistant professor, 1988-91, associate professor of telecommunication, 1991—. KOET-Television, production director and local news anchor, 1966-68; KSVN-Radio, news director and news anchor, 1966-68; KEZI-Television, news reporter, 1968-69; KIRO-Television, production sound engineer, 1969-81; Philippine Imports, corporate communications director, 1986-87; media consultant to Corporate Communications.

MEMBER: National Academy of Television Arts and Sciences (member of Phoenix board of directors, 1989—), American Journalism Historians Association (co-chair of Radio-Television Committee, 1989—), Association for Education in Journalism and Mass Communications, Broadcast Education Association, Association for Canadian Studies in the United States.

AWARDS, HONORS: Grants from Saul Haas Foundation, 1974, and Canadian Embassy, 1978, 1987, 1990, and 1991; Historical Scholarship Award, National Broadcast Education Association, 1984, for *A Directory of Broadcast Archives;* Broadcast History Division first place award, National Broadcast Education Association, 1986, for a paper; Broadcast Production Division first place award, National Broadcast Education Association, 1992, for a training videotape.

WRITINGS:

(Editor) *A Directory of Broadcast Archives,* Broadcast Education Association, 1983.
Reruns on File: A Guide to Electronic Media Archives, Lawrence Erlbaum, 1992.
(Editor with B. Y. Card) *The Diaries of Charles Ora Card: The Canadian Years, 1886-1903,* University of Utah Press, 1993.

Member of editorial board, *American Journalism,* 1985—. Work represented in anthologies, including *Perspectives on Mass Communication History,* edited by David Sloan, Lawrence Erlbaum, 1991; *Teaching Mass Communication,* edited by Michael D. Murray and Anthony J. Ferri, Praeger, 1992; and *Media in America: A History,* edited by William David Sloan, Publishing Horizons, 1992. Contributor of articles and reviews to academic journals. Has produced training videotapes.

*   *   *

GOERLACH, Manfred   1937-

PERSONAL: Born July 12, 1937, in Berlin, Germany; son of Josef (an agricultural expert) and Elisabeth (Volk) Goerlach; married Mechthild G. Pohlmann, 1971; children: two sons. *Education:* Attended Universities of Berlin, Durham, and Heidelberg, and Oxford University, 1957-68; University of Heidelberg, Dr.Phil., 1970.

ADDRESSES: Home—Bertolt-Brecht-Strasse 116, D-5042 Ertstadt-Liblar, Germany. *Office*—English Seminar, University of Cologne, Albertus-Magnus-Platz, 5000 Cologne 41, Germany.

CAREER: University of Heidelberg, Heidelberg, Germany, lecturer in English, 1967-84; University of Cologne, Cologne, Germany, professor of English language and medieval studies, 1984—.

WRITINGS:

The South English Legendary, Gilte Legende and Golden Legend, Braunschweig, 1972.
The Textual Tradition of the South English Legendary, Leeds, 1974.
(Editor with R. W. Bailey) *English as a World Language,* University of Michigan Press, 1982.
(Editor) *Focus on Scotland,* Benjamins (Amsterdam), 1985.
(Editor) *Max and Moritz in English Dialects and Creoles,* Buske (Hamburg), 1986.
(Editor with John Holm) *Focus on the Caribbean,* Benjamins, 1987.
Introduction to Early Modern English, Cambridge University Press, 1991.

Contributor to periodicals.

IN GERMAN

Einfuehrung in die englische Sprachgeschichte, Quelle & Meyer, 1974, 2nd edition, 1982.
Maccus and Mauris: Largiedd on seofon fyttum, privately printed, 1977.
Einfuehrung ins Fruehneuenglische, Quelle & Meyer, 1978.

(Editor) *Max und Moritz in deutschen Dialekten, Mittel-hochdeutsch und Jiddisch,* Buske, 1982.

(Editor) *Max und Moritz polyglott,* [Muenchen], 1982, 4th edition, 1986.

(Editor) *Plisch und Plum in deutschen Dialekten,* [Muenchen], 1984.

(Editor) *Max und Moritz: Sieben Lausbubenstreiche in 21 deutschen Mundarten,* Van Acken, 1990.

* * *

GOLDBERGER, Avriel H. 1928-

PERSONAL: Born February 23, 1928, in Philadelphia, PA; daughter of Samuel and Sadie (Goldman) Horwitz; married Arnold Goldberger (a consultant engineer), June 11, 1950; children: Lee Alain, Ellen Margaret Goldberger Oppenheim. *Education:* University of Pennsylvania, B.A., 1949; Bryn Mawr College, M.A., 1951, Ph.D., 1960.

ADDRESSES: Home—120 Hampshire Rd., Great Neck, NY 11023. *Office*—Department of French, Hofstra University, Hempstead, NY 11550.

CAREER: Hofstra University, Hempstead, NY, professor of French, head of department, 1969-74 and 1986—. Director of international conferences.

MEMBER: Phi Beta Kappa.

AWARDS, HONORS: Fulbright scholar in Paris, 1952-53; fellow of National Endowment for the Humanities at Aston Magna, Baroque Music Academy, 1983; named Chevalier des Arts et des Lettres by French Ministry of Culture, 1988; grants from National Endowment for the Humanities, 1988 and 1991-92; *A Life of Her Own* was named to the New York Public Library's Annual Books to Remember List, the American Library Association's Notable Books List, the *New York Times*'s Notable Books of the Year List, and the London *Sunday Telegraph*'s Books of the Year List, all 1992.

WRITINGS:

Visions of a New Hero: The Heroic Life According to Andre Malraux and Earlier Advocates of Human Grandeur, Jean Minard, 1965.

(Translator and author of introduction and notes) Germaine de Stael, *Corinne; or, Italy,* Rutgers University Press, 1987.

(Editor) *Woman as Mediatrix: Essays on Nineteenth Century European Woman Writers,* Greenwood Press, 1987.

(Editor) *The Stendhal Bicentennial Papers,* Greenwood Press, 1987.

(Translator and author of introduction and afterword) Emilie Carles and Robert Destarque, *A Life of Her Own,* Rutgers University Press, 1991, also published as *A Wild Herb Soup,* Gollancz, 1991.

(Editor with M. Gutwirth and K. Szmurlo) *Germaine de Stael: Crossing the Borders,* Rutgers University Press, 1991.

Contributor to literature journals.

BIOGRAPHICAL/CRITICAL SOURCES:

PERIODICALS

New York Times Book Review, June 2, 1991, p. 1.

* * *

GOLDMAN, Ari L. 1949-

PERSONAL: Born in 1949. *Education:* Attended Yeshiva University and Harvard University. *Religion:* Orthodox Jew.

ADDRESSES: Office—New York Times, 229 West Forty-third St., New York, NY 10036.

CAREER: New York Times, New York City, began as reporter, became religion correspondent in 1984.

WRITINGS:

The Search for God at Harvard (nonfiction), Times Books/Random House, 1991.

Contributor to periodicals, including *New Leader.*

SIDELIGHTS: Ari L. Goldman is a religion correspondent for the *New York Times.* In 1985, after he was named to that position, he requested a year's paid sabbatical to Harvard University's Divinity School to gain a greater understanding of the world's various schools of faith. The *Times* complied, and for the next year Goldman, an Orthodox Jew, undertook studies in religion. He acquainted himself with Hinduism, Buddhism, Islam, Christianity, and various African religions and thus enabled himself—as Julius Lester observed in the *Washington Post Book World*—"to be open to the religious experiences of others without judgment."

In 1991 Goldman published *The Search for God at Harvard,* an account of both his year at Harvard and his own religious upbringing. Robert Ellsberg, writing in *Commonweal,* reported that Goldman's book provides both "an engaging portrait of life at an Ivy League seminary" and an "interesting" account of his upbringing as an Orthodox Jew. Ellsberg acknowledged the autobiographical portions as "the heart of the book." Another critic, David Tracy, described *The Search for God at Harvard* as "engaging" and affirmed, in his *New York Times Book Review* appraisal, that the book "gives us a plausible, often moving account of a new form of spiritual quest." And Lester, in his *Washington Post Book World* assessment, lauded Goldman's work as "a valuable and unique contribution to the growing literature of Jewish spiritual autobiography" and added, quoting Goldman's book, that it "speaks with the quiet confidence and security of one who believes 'there is a Supreme Being who delights in my efforts to live as a traditional Jew.'"

BIOGRAPHICAL/CRITICAL SOURCES:

PERIODICALS

Commonweal, August 9, 1991, p. 488.
Los Angeles Times Book Review, June 16, 1991, p. 6.
New York Times, July 5, 1991, p. C22.
New York Times Book Review, June 2, 1991, p. 14.
Washington Post Book World, July 7, 1991, p. 3.*

* * *

GOLDSTEIN, Imre 1938-

PERSONAL: Born July 6, 1938, in Budapest, Hungary; immigrated to United States, 1956; immigrated to Israel, 1974; son of Dezso (a grocer) and Ethel (a homemaker; maiden name, Klein) Goldstein; married Roberta Wohl (a vocational counselor), May 16, 1965; children: Lauren, Aviva. *Education:* Queen's College, B.A. (cum laude), 1971; City University of New York, Ph.D., 1975.

ADDRESSES: Home—7 Kaplan St., Apt. 10, Tel Aviv 64734, Israel. *Office*—Theatre Arts Department, Tel Aviv University, Tel Aviv 69978, Israel.

CAREER: Tel Aviv University, Tel Aviv, Israel, professor of theatre, 1974—; U.S. State Department, Washington, DC, escort and seminar interpreter (Hungarian and Hebrew), 1991—; director, translator, and writer. Hunter College, adjunct lecturer, 1972-74; University of North Carolina, visiting associate professor, 1990-91. *Military service:* U.S. Army, 1959-62; became specialist fourth class.

MEMBER: International Theatre Institute, American Translators Association, Israel Federation of Writers.

AWARDS, HONORS: John Gassner Award for poetry and drama, 1968; Peter Pauper Press Award for prose, 1968.

WRITINGS:

Triple Jump (poems), Eked Publishers (Tel Aviv), 1984.

Contributor of original poems and short stories in Hungarian, Hebrew, and English to periodicals, including *Voices, arc, Ravkol uj kelet, Shirim, Szivarvany,* and *uj latohatar.* Assistant editor, *ASSAPH: Studies in Theatre,* 1984.

TRANSLATOR

Uri Oren, *Loving Strangers* (from the Hebrew), Avon, 1975.

Frigyes Karinthy, *Three Short Plays* (from the Hungarian), produced in New York City, 1979.

Ahuva Artzi, *Godly Forces Revealed* (from the Hungarian), Traklin Publishers, 1981.

Gabriel Ben Simhon, *A Moroccan King* (play; from the Hebrew), produced by Habimak Theatre, 1982.

Yvette Biro, *Profane Mythology: The Savage Mind of the Cinema* (from the Hungarian), Indiana University Press, 1982.

Daniel Horowitz, *Uncle Arthur* (play; from the Hebrew), produced by Beit Lessin, 1982.

Daniel Horowitz, *Yossele Golem* (play; from the Hebrew), produced in New York City, 1982.

Ophelia Strahl, *Encounters in the Forest* (play; from the Hebrew), produced at Acre Theatre Festival, 1984.

Motti Lerner, *Kastner* (play; from the Hebrew; produced by Cameri Theatre, 1985), Modern International Drama, 1993.

Tibor Dery, *The Giant Baby* (play; from the Hungarian), Modern International Drama, 1986.

(And adapter and director) *The Dybbuk* (play), produced at North Carolina Shakespeare Festival, 1991.

Gyorgy Konrad, *A Feast in the Garden* (from the Hungarian), Harcourt, 1992.

(And adapter and director) *Oedipus Tyrannos* (play), produced at North Carolina Shakespeare Festival, 1992.

Also translator of *Ten Hungarian Plays* (from the Hungarian), 1974. Contributor of translations to periodicals, including *New Yorker* and *Paris Review.*

SIDELIGHTS: Imre Goldstein told *CA:* "Born in Hungary, moving to the United States at age eighteen (after the revolution of 1956), to Israel at age thirty-six, and unable to break with any of the three cultures, I find myself translating and interpreting one language into the other—with no particular order in mind—through words and theatre. I love to translate exciting works in any genre—from novels to plays and poetry. But as a director and teacher of theatre, writing for me serves primarily as an extension of my activities on the stage. Two of the latest and most successful efforts were the new translations and adaptations of *The Dybbuk* and *Oedipus Tyrannos,* both commissioned by the North Carolina Shakespeare Festival, where I also had the pleasure of directing these plays in 1991 and 1992, respectively.

"Just how fascinating and intriguing mixing theatre with translating and interpreting can be was most dramatically demonstrated for me in June of 1992. During a break in the rehearsals of *A Shayna Maidel* for the Hope Summer Repertory Theatre in Holland, Michigan, I was interpreting (over the telephone, from my kitchen) for U.S. President George Bush, who was calling from the White House to wish a speedy recovery to the ailing Prime Minister of Hungary in Budapest."

*   *   *

GOLLIN, Rita K.   1928-

PERSONAL: Born January 22, 1928, in Brooklyn, NY; daughter of Max (in business) and Sophie (in business; maiden name, Horowitz) Kaplan; married Richard M. Gollin (a professor of English), January 1, 1950; children: Kathryn Gollin Marshak, Michael, James. *Education:* Queens College (now of the City University of New York), B.A. (magna cum laude), 1949; University of Minnesota—Twin Cities, M.A., 1950, Ph.D., 1961.

ADDRESSES: Home—37 Glen Ellyn Way, Rochester, NY 14618. *Office*—Department of English, State University of New York College at Geneseo, Geneseo, NY 14454.

CAREER: University of Rochester, Rochester, NY, 1955-67, began as lecturer, became assistant professor of English; State University of New York at Geneseo, assistant professor, 1967-68, associate professor, 1968-75, professor of English, 1975—. Yale University, fellow at Institute on Reconstructing American Literature, 1982; organizer and chairperson of Concord Conference on Hawthorne's Last Years, 1980, and Thoreau Conference in Honor of Walter Harding, 1982.

MEMBER: Modern Language Association of America (chairperson of Nineteenth-Century American Literature Program, 1988), American Literature Association, Nathaniel Hawthorne Society (vice-president, 1978-80; president, 1980-93; member of executive board, 1975-77, 1987), Northeast Modern Language Association (member of executive council, 1975-77; vice-president, 1977-78; president, 1978-79), Phi Beta Kappa.

AWARDS, HONORS: Hawthorne Award, House of Seven Gables, 1984; fellow of Huntington Library, 1984, 1988; National Endowment for the Humanities, senior fellow, 1984-85, travel grant, 1988-89.

WRITINGS:

(Editor and author of introduction and bibliography) Charles Dudley Warner, *A Little Journey in the World,* Johnson, 1970.
(Editor and author of introduction and bibliography) Sarah Josepha Hale, *Northwood,* Johnson, 1972.
Nathaniel Hawthorne and the Truth of Dreams, Louisiana State University Press, 1979.
Portraits of Nathaniel Hawthorne: An Iconography, Northern Illinois University Press, 1983.

(Editor with James Scholes) *Thoreau Inter Alia: Essays in Honor of Walter Harding,* State University of New York College at Geneseo, 1985.
(With John L. Idol, Jr., and Sterling Eisiminger) *Prophetic Pictures: Hawthorne's Knowledge and Uses of the Visual Arts,* Greenwood Press, 1991.

Work represented in anthologies, including *Essays on "The Scarlet Letter,"* edited by David Kesterson, G. K. Hall, 1988; *New Essays on Hawthorne's Short Stories,* edited by Millicent Bell, Cambridge University Press, 1993; and *Women's Effect on Hawthorne and Hawthorne's Effect on Women,* edited by Melinda M. Ponder, John L. Idol, Jr., and others, University of Massachusetts Press, 1993. Contributor of about fifty articles and reviews to literature journals. Guest coeditor, *Essex Institute Historical Collection,* 1982; and *Studies in the Novel,* 1991; member of editorial board, *Nathaniel Hawthorne Review,* 1987—.

WORK IN PROGRESS: American Woman of Letters: Annie Adams Fields; The Shakers and American Writers.

*   *   *

GOLUBITSKY, Martin   1945-

PERSONAL: Born April 5, 1945, in Philadelphia, PA; son of Isaac Golubitsky (in dry cleaning) and Rose (Sarvetnick) Golubitsky (a homemaker); married Barbara Lee Keyfitz (a professor), May 30, 1976; children: Elizabeth, Alexander. *Education:* University of Pennsylvania, A.B., 1966, A.M., 1966; Massachusetts Institute of Technology, Ph.D., 1970. *Religion:* Jewish.

ADDRESSES: Home—6419 Sewanee, Houston, TX 77005. *Office*—Department of Mathematics, University of Houston, Houston, TX 77204-3476.

CAREER: University of California, Los Angeles, instructor in mathematics, 1970-71; Massachusetts Institute of Technology, Cambridge, instructor in mathematics, 1971-73; Queens College of City University of New York, New York, NY, 1973-79, began as assistant professor, became associate professor of mathematics; Arizona State University, Tempe, AZ, professor of mathematics, 1979-83; University of Houston, Houston, TX, professor of mathematics, 1983—, also Cullen Professor of Mathematics, 1989, and director of Institute for Theoretical and Engineering Science, 1988.

MEMBER: American Association for the Advancement of Science (fellow), American Mathematics Society, Society for Industrial and Applied Mathematics (council member, 1990-95).

AWARDS, HONORS: Research Award, Sigma Xi, 1991, for research in bifurcation theory.

WRITINGS:

(With V. Guilleanin) *Stable Mappings and Their Singularities,* Springer-Verlag, 1974.

(With D. G. Schaeffer) *Singularities and Groups in Bifurcation Theory I,* Springer-Verlag, 1984.

(With Ian Stewart and D. G. Schaeffer) *Singularities and Groups in Bifurcation Theory II,* Springer-Verlag, 1988.

(With Michael Field) *Symmetry in Chaos,* Oxford University Press, 1992.

(With Ian Stewart) *Fearful Symmetry,* Basil-Blackwell, 1992.

Member of editorial boards of *Texts in Applied Mathematics,* Springer-Verlag, *Archive Rational Mechanics and Analysis, Nonlinear Science, Bifurcation and Chaos, Dynamics and Differential Equations.*

WORK IN PROGRESS: Research on effects of symmetry on solutions to equations (including chaos) and how these effects can be seen in experiments and in nature.

SIDELIGHTS: Martin Golubitsky told *CA:* "At a conference at the University of Warwick in the summer of 1989 several of us were having tea and discussing—or lamenting—the fact that rather little popular material was being written about mathematics by mathematicians. There seemed little else to do about it except to try and write books aimed at a literate but uninformed audience ourselves.

"In any case, the decision to attempt two books—one concerning the ideas of symmetry breaking with Ian Stewart and one displaying the beautiful pictures of symmetric attractors with Michael Field—was made that day. Amazingly, both projects were carried through to completion and both books have received excellent reviews. Our purposes were to convey some of the excitement that we felt about our mathematical research and to discuss why the results of this research could be of interest to people who had no interest in the technical details."

*   *   *

GOODE, James (Arthur) 1924-1992

OBITUARY NOTICE—See index for *CA* sketch: Born January 22, 1924, in Indianapolis, IN; died of a heart attack, December 13, 1992, in Burbank, CA. Journalist and author. Known as editorial director of magazines such as *Penthouse* during the 1970s, Goode began his career as a correspondent for *Life* in 1952. He was the founder and publisher of *Earth* magazine and the founder of the related *Earth News* radio news service. He left those positions to begin his association with *Penthouse* in 1972. Goode's ca-

reer also encompassed a few years with *Playboy* and *Playgirl.* His writings include the book *The Story of "The Misfits"* and the screenplays *Tchaikovsky's Parrot* and *Silent Screen.*

OBITUARIES AND OTHER SOURCES:

PERIODICALS

Los Angeles Times, December 20, 1992, p. A41.

*   *   *

GORDIEVSKY, Oleg 1938-

PERSONAL: Born October 10, 1938, in Moscow, Russia; son of Anton (a teacher) and Olga (a homemaker; maiden name, Gornova) Gordievsky; married October 1, 1979; wife's name, Leila (a homemaker); children: Maria, Anna. *Education:* Moscow Institute of International Relations, B.A., 1962; attended KGB Intelligence School. *Avocational interests:* Philology.

ADDRESSES: Home—Surrey, England. *Agent*—William Hamilton, 79 St. Martin's Lane, London WC2N 4AA, England.

CAREER: KGB, member of first chief directorate (KGB's foreign intelligence service), 1962-85, deputy head of station in Copenhagen, Denmark, 1975-78, deputy head of station in London, England, 1982-85; writer. Lecturer on Russian affairs. *Military service:* Served in the military; became colonel.

WRITINGS:

WITH CHRISTOPHER ANDREW

KGB: The Inside Story, Hodder & Stoughton, 1989, HarperCollins, c. 1990.

Instructions from the Centre, Hodder & Stoughton, 1991.

More Instructions from the Centre, Frank Cass, 1992.

OTHER

Consulting editor on Russian and North European affairs for *Intelligence and National Security.*

WORK IN PROGRESS: KGB in Denmark.

SIDELIGHTS: As a member of the KGB, a secret Soviet police agency, from 1962 to 1985, Oleg Gordievsky grew familiar with the organization's history through a methodical study of its files. For nearly a dozen years toward the end of his association with the KGB, Gordievsky was additionally serving as a double agent, providing information to the British Secret Intelligence Services. After he was suspected by Russian officials of acting as a spy, he defected to the West in the mid-1980s. In *KGB: The Inside Story* Gordievsky and coauthor Christopher Andrew, a specialist in the study of intelligence operations, present an intensive look at the organization. Noting the bellwether nature of the book, Michael Howard of the *Washington Post Book World* predicted that the collaboration "will certainly open a new era for the growth industry of 'intelligence studies.'"

Gordievsky and Andrew trace the development of Soviet intelligence from 1917, when Lenin and the Bolsheviks came into power after the overthrow of the Russian imperialist administration. After setting up the first Soviet government, they established the Cheka, a precursor to the KGB that was designed to monitor anti-Bolshevik activities. The authors also chart the problems that have plagued Soviet intelligence operations throughout its history. In the opinion of Gordievsky and Andrew, Soviet adherence to Marxism, a political theory that warns against a possible revolution by the working class, contributed to overwhelming suspicion that other countries were intent on overthrowing the Soviet government. According to the authors, the KGB has also been hurt by power struggles and corruption within its own organization.

One of the primary concerns in *KGB* is the disclosure of the identity of the "Fifth Man," the high-ranking member of British intelligence who, along with four other double agents, provided the Soviets with classified information as a participant in the Cambridge spy ring of the 1930s. Gordievsky and Andrew name former member of the British Secret Intelligence Services John Cairncross as the Fifth Man. Shortly after the book's publication, Cairncross denied involvement in the Cambridge spy ring in an interview with a Parisian newspaper, but he later confirmed that he was recruited into the circle during World War II. Cairncross's revelation ended rampant speculation on the part of several other scholars who had proposed different theories on the identity of the Fifth Man.

Gordievsky and Andrew also offer insight on members of the United States government in *KGB*. The authors suggest that Harry L. Hopkins, who served as a personal adviser to U.S. President Franklin D. Roosevelt, often conferred with a Soviet agent during World War II and unknowingly provided the official with crucial information. Gordievsky and Andrew also discuss Operation Ryan, an exercise conducted by the Soviets to investigate what they perceived as suspicious American activity during the administration of President Ronald Reagan. At the time, the Soviets were concerned about the possibility of a nuclear attack from the United States. According to the *New York Times*, Andrew, in a news conference which occurred at the time of the book's release, regarded Operation Ryan as the consequence of "a combination of Soviet paranoia and American rhetoric."

When *KGB* was published, some reviewers expressed doubt concerning the reliability of some of its information. Howard of the *Washington Post Book World,* for instance, wondered how Gordievsky was able to accommodate the wealth of data that he had accessed if he defected wearing only a jogging suit. Others intimated that Gordievsky could not have had access to all of the material presented in the collaboration. Subsequent books written by Gordievsky and Andrew, such as *Instructions from the Centre* and *More Instructions from the Centre,* have, however, supported Gordievsky's credibility by presenting large blocks of material taken from confidential files held by the KGB. Speaking of Gordievsky and Andrew's accomplishment on their first collaboration, Noel Annan of the London *Times* called *KGB* "the most fascinating of all spy books. . . . It is a tale of remarkable organisation, brilliant operations abroad, labyrinthine conspiracy theories, and staggering brutality."

Gordievsky told *CA:* "As a Soviet intelligence officer, I spent nearly fifteen years in the West European countries. In the last eleven years of my career in the KGB, I was in touch with the British authorities, clandestinely working for the Western alliance. Such a background put me in a unique position from where I was able to observe the West with the eyes of a Soviet official and the East (i.e., the communist world) with the eyes of a Western person. I became a natural, and, I hope, an accurate interpreter of Soviet politics and thinking. And this role I tried to play first secretly for the Western governments, and after my dramatic escape from the hands of the KGB in 1985, in my writings and lectures.

"The Soviet communist legacy will stay in the minds and in the socio-political structures of Russia and of other former Soviet republics for a lifetime of one or two generations, and during that time the content of my writings will remain relevant."

BIOGRAPHICAL/CRITICAL SOURCES:

PERIODICALS

New York Times, May 16, 1990; September 23, 1991.
Times (London), October 20, 1990.
Washington Post, December 18, 1990.
Washington Post Book World, December 16, 1990, p. 1.

*   *   *

GORDON, George
See HASFORD, (Jerry) Gustav

GORDON, Jaimy 1944-

PERSONAL: Born July 4, 1944, in Baltimore, MD; daughter of David P. (an attorney) and Sonia (a potter; maiden name, Cohen-Wachovsky) Gordon; married Peter Blickle (a teacher and translator), 1988. *Education:* Antioch College, B.A., 1966; Brown University, M.A., 1972, D.A., 1975. *Politics:* Democrat. *Religion:* Jewish.

ADDRESSES: Home—930 Minor Ave., Kalamazoo, MI 49008. *Office*—Department of English, Western Michigan University, Kalamazoo, MI 49008. *Agent*—Geri Thoma, Elaine Markson Literary Agency, 44 Greenwich Ave., New York, NY 10011.

CAREER: Rhode Island State Council on the Arts, writer in residence, 1975-77; Stephens College, Columbia, MO, director of creative writing program, 1980-81; Western Michigan University, Kalamazoo, assistant professor, 1981-87, associate professor, 1987-92, professor of English, 1992—; writer.

MEMBER: Authors Guild.

AWARDS, HONORS: Creative writing fellowships from National Endowment for the Arts, 1979 and 1991; fellowship from Provincetown Fine Arts Work Center, 1979-80; creative writing grants from Michigan Council for the Arts and National Endowment for the Arts, both 1983; fellowship from Bunting Institute of Radcliffe College, 1984-85; creative writing grant from Michigan Council for the Arts, 1986; fiction award from American Academy and Institute of Arts and Letters, 1991, for the body of her work.

WRITINGS:

Shamp of the City-Solo (novel), Treacle Press, 1974.
The Bend, the Lip, the Kid (narrative poem), Sun, 1978.
Circumspections from an Equestrian Statue (novella), Burning Deck, 1979.
(Translator with husband, Peter Blickle) Maria Beig, *Lost Weddings* (novel), Persea Books, 1990.
She Drove without Stopping (novel), Algonquin Books of Chapel Hill, 1990.

Contributor to periodicals, including *Exquisite Corpse, Little Magazine, Missouri Review, Ploughshares, Shankpainter,* and *Sun.*

WORK IN PROGRESS: Bogeywoman, a novel; translations into English of German writings of Maria Beig.

SIDELIGHTS: Jaimy Gordon won acclaim in the 1990s with her picaresque feminist novel *She Drove without Stopping.* Gordon actually began her literary career in the mid-1970s with *Shamp of the City-Solo,* a novel that is regarded by some as an underground classic. In 1978 she produced another volume, *The Bend, the Lip, the Kid,* a narrative

poem that is a pastiche of the spoken language of prison and street corner, and in 1979 she released *Circumspections from an Equestrian Statue.* None of these works, however, won much attention from the mainstream media.

Eleven years passed before Gordon returned to the literary scene with *She Drove without Stopping,* a narrative about a headstrong young woman whose troubled relationship with her father spurs her to various escapades and adventures. The heroine, Jane, initially defies her father by leaving her college dormitory to share quarters with her boyfriend, a destitute artist. Jane's behavior is mistaken for sexual recklessness by an ignorant bully who consequently rapes her. Jane then departs for the West Coast, where she eventually finds work tending bar. More misadventures follow, whereupon Jane realizes that her anger toward her father has not provided her with the most suitable motivation for conducting her life.

Upon its publication in 1990, *She Drove without Stopping* was received as a compelling coming-of-age novel with a strong feminist perspective. Reading the novel, declared Elizabeth Hand in the *Washington Post Book World,* is somewhat like "re-living one's own youth, not the parts bathed in . . . nostalgia but the real stuff, the hilarious but hair-raising adventures you would never in a million years tell your parents." Hand appraised Gordon's prose as "unblinking feminist writing" and added that it is "witty and stylish." Similarly, *Chicago Tribune* reviewer Douglas Seibold noted Gordon's "distinctive narrative voice" and her success in bringing her heroine "to yearning, bristly, appealing life." Another critic, Marilyn Moss, wrote in the *Review of Contemporary Fiction* that *She Drove without Stopping* "is an extremely smart book," and Carolyn See, in her assessment for the *Los Angeles Times Book Review,* reported that Gordon has produced "a fine novel." Even more praise came from Baltimore *Sun* reviewer Ann G. Sjoerdsma, who described *She Drove without Stopping* as "a frenzied, quixotic, cross-country journey, rich in . . . passionate conflicts and strong, emotional language," while Muriel Spanier, in another *New York Times Book Review* appraisal, noted Gordon's "abundant gifts."

In 1990 Gordon also teamed with her husband, Peter Blickle, in releasing *Lost Weddings,* an English translation of Maria Beig's German novel *Hochzeitslose,* which concerns four women and their arduous social experiences in Europe during the decades that include two world wars. Ursula Hegi, writing in the *New York Times Book Review,* reported that though "Beig's prose is plain, choppy, stark—and extremely difficult to translate," Gordon and her husband succeed in rendering the characters of *Lost Weddings* "memorable—haunting even."

BIOGRAPHICAL/CRITICAL SOURCES:

PERIODICALS

Chicago Tribune, May 11, 1990.
Los Angeles Times Book Review, June 25, 1990.
New York Times Book Review, July 29, 1990, p. 26; August 19, 1990, p. 18.
Review of Contemporary Fiction, fall, 1990, p. 236.
Sun (Baltimore), May 1, 1990, p. 4C.
Washington Post Book World, June 10, 1990, p. 11.

*   *   *

GORLACH, Manfred
See GOERLACH, Manfred

*   *   *

GOROVITZ, Samuel 1938-

PERSONAL: Born November 23, 1938, in Boston, MA; son of Israel (a lawyer) and Della (a teacher; maiden name, London) Gorovitz; married Judith Baum (a clinical psychologist), July 3, 1960; children: Heidi L., Eric K. *Education:* Massachusetts Institute of Technology, B.S., 1960; Stanford University, Ph.D., 1963.

ADDRESSES: Home—5149 Peck Hill Rd., Jamesville, NY 13078. *Office*—300 Hall of Languages, College of Arts and Sciences, Syracuse University, Syracuse, NY 13244-1170.

CAREER: Wayne State University, Detroit, MI, instructor in philosophy, 1963-64; Case Western Reserve University, Cleveland, OH, assistant professor, 1964-68, associate professor of philosophy, 1968-73, director of Commission on Education at Mather and Adelbert Colleges, 1969-70, dean of Adelbert College, 1970-71, director of Moral Problems in Medicine Project, 1971-73; University of Maryland at College Park, professor of philosophy, 1973-84, distinguished scholar-teacher, 1984, chairperson of department, 1973-82, affiliate professor at School of Public Affairs, 1984-86; Syracuse University, Syracuse, NY, professor of philosophy and dean of College of Arts and Sciences, 1986—. Stanford University, visiting associate professor, summer, 1969. International Medical Benefit/Risk Foundation, member of board of overseers, 1991—; National Institutes of Health, member of Working Group on Human Gene Therapy, 1984-87; New York State Task Force on Life and the Law, member, 1988—; testified before President's Commission for the Study of Ethical Problems in Medicine and Biomedical and Behavioral Research, 1982, and U.S. House of Representatives committee on science and technology, 1982-84; consultant

to National Center for Health Care Technology, Woodrow Wilson Foundation, and World Health Organization. Lecturer in the United States and abroad, including England, Spain, Germany, Greece, and Norway; guest on television and radio programs, including the *Studs Terkel Show, All Things Considered,* and *The Larry King Show.*

MEMBER: American Philosophical Association (chairman of committee on freedom for Latin American philosophers, 1970-71; member of board of officers, 1986-90), Council for Philosophical Studies (executive secretary, 1972-78), Hastings Center (fellow), Phi Beta Kappa (honorary member), Phi Kappa Phi, Omicron Delta Kappa (honorary member), Golden Key National Honor Society (honorary member).

AWARDS, HONORS: Best of Show Award, color photography, Cultural Resources Council of Syracuse, 1968; senior scholar, National Center for Health Services Research, 1979-80; Dupont-Columbia Award for Broadcast Journalism, 1982, for the television series *Hard Choices;* visiting scholar, Beth Israel Hospital, Boston, MA, summer, 1985; grants from National Science Foundation, 1965, 1966, 1967, 1975-76, 1977-78, National Endowment for the Humanities, 1971-74, 1975-77, 1976-78, 1976-79, 1978-81, 1984, 1990, Exxon Education Foundation, 1972-74, Rockefeller Brothers Fund, 1974, 1977-78, and National Institutes of Health, Office for Protection From Research Risks, 1989.

WRITINGS:

(With R. G. Williams, D. Provence, and M. Provence) *Philosophical Analysis: An Introduction to Its Language and Techniques,* Random House, 1965, 3rd edition (with Williams, D. Provence, and M. Hintikka), 1979.
(Editor and author of introduction) *Freedom and Order in the University,* Western Reserve University Press, 1967.
(Editor and author of introduction) *Utilitarianism: Text and Commentary,* Bobbs-Merrill, 1971.
(With J. Kessler and others) *A Question of Values* (screenplay), released by Mental Development Center (Cleveland, OH), 1973.
(Senior editor and author of introduction) *Moral Problems in Medicine,* Prentice-Hall, 1976, 2nd edition, 1983.
Hard Choices (television series), Public Broadcasting System, 1981.
Doctors' Dilemmas: Moral Conflict and Medical Care, Macmillan, 1982.
Drawing the Line: Life, Death, and Ethical Choices in an American Hospital, Oxford University Press, 1991.

Work represented in anthologies, including *Improving Drug Safety: A Joint Responsibility,* edited by R. Dinkel, B. Horisberger, and K. Tolo, Springer-Verlag, 1991; *Fall-*

ing in Love With Wisdom, edited by D. Karnos and R. Shoemaker, Oxford University Press, 1992; and *The Ethics of Reproductive Technology,* edited by K. D. Alpern, Oxford University Press, 1992. General editor, "Series in Philosophy of Medicine," Prentice-Hall. Contributor of more than eighty articles and reviews to scholarly journals. Member of editorial advisory board, *Journal of Medicine and Philosophy* and *National Forum.*

*   *   *

GOULD, Steven (Charles) 1955-

PERSONAL: Born February 7, 1955, in Fort Huachuca, AZ; son of James Alan (an army officer) and Carita Louise (a watercolor artist; maiden name, Kee) Gould; married Laura Jean Mixon (a writer and environmental engineer), January 1, 1989; children: Emma Marie. *Education:* Attended Texas A & M University, 1973-78. *Politics:* Liberal Democrat. *Religion:* Agnostic. *Avocational interests:* Diving, sailing, wilderness survival, camping.

ADDRESSES: Home and office—New York City. *Agent*—Ralph M. Vicinanza Ltd., 111 Eighth Ave., Suite 1501, New York, NY 10011.

CAREER: Brazos Valley Community Action Agency, Bryan, TX, data processing manager, 1987-90; free-lance writer and computer professional, 1990—. Texas A & M University, guest instructor. Co-founder of Space City Writer's Ranch and Houston's Science Fiction and Fantasy Workshop.

MEMBER: Science Fiction and Fantasy Writers of America (director of south/central region, 1986-89).

AWARDS, HONORS: Hugo Award nomination, 1984, for the story "Rory"; Hugo Award and Nebula Award nominations, 1988, for the story "Peaches for Mad Molly."

WRITINGS:

Jumper (novel), Tor Books, 1992.
Wildside (science fiction novel), Tor Books, in press.
(With wife Laura J. Mixon) *Greenwar* (technical suspense novel), Tor Books, in press.

Work represented in anthologies, including *1989 World's Best Science Fiction,* edited by Donald A. Wolheim; *Cities in Space,* edited by Jerry Pournelle and John F. Carr, Ace Books, 1991; and *Isaac Asimov's Robots,* edited by Gardner Dozois and Sheila Williams, Ace Books, 1991. Contributor of stories and short novels to periodicals, including *Analog, Isaac Asimov's Science Fiction, Amazing,* and *New Destinies.*

SIDELIGHTS: Steven Gould told *CA:* "I'm an army brat who lived most of my childhood overseas. I attended col-

lege at Texas A & M University where, despite six years of intermittent study, I have not taken my degree in philosophy. I've worked as an appliance repairman, karate instructor, assistant manager of a cinema, youth room supervisor, salvage diver, oil tool expediter, book reviewer, and computer consultant. I have been writing and selling science fiction since 1979, when I was 'discovered' by the late Theodore Sturgeon in a writing workshop."

*   *   *

GOUMA-PETERSON, Thalia 1933-

PERSONAL: Born November 21, 1933, in Athens, Greece; U.S. citizen. *Education:* Pierce College, Athens, gymnasium diploma, 1951, junior college diploma, 1952; Mills College, A.B., 1954, M.A., 1957; University of Wisconsin—Madison, Ph.D., 1963.

ADDRESSES: Home—394 Edgemeer Pl., Oberlin, OH 44074. *Office*—Department of Art, College of Wooster, Wooster, OH 44691.

CAREER: University of Wisconsin—Madison, instructor in art history, 1958; Oberlin College, Oberlin, OH, lecturer, 1958-68, instructor, 1960-61; College of Wooster, Wooster, OH, assistant professor, 1968-74, associate professor, 1974-76, professor, 1976—, department chair, 1977-80 and 1984-87, museum director, 1984—. Wabash College, visiting scholar, 1986-87; Southern Methodist University, distinguished visiting professor, 1989-90. Oberlin College, member of Allen Art Museum purchase committee, 1965-84; Akron Art Museum, member of accessions committee, 1979-86. Great Lakes Colleges Association, member of women's studies committee, 1978-80; Women's Caucus for Art, member of national advisory board, 1978-80, chair of nominating committee, 1979, chair of national awards committee, 1980-82, national vice president, 1982-84, member of national advisory board, 1984-86; Byzantine Studies Conference, chair of organizing committee, 1981, member of governing board, 1985-89, member of program committee, 1987, chair of program committee, 1988, president, 1988-89; College Art Association of America, member of nominating committee, 1985-86, chair of nominating committee, 1986-87, member of board of directors, 1989-90, member of Porter Prize committee, 1989-90, member of museum committee, 1991, member of committee for the preservation of monuments, 1991. Organizer and curator of exhibitions at Wooster College, beginning in 1980. Organizer and chair of conferences and symposia, including "Middle Byzantine Art," University of Chicago, 1982, "Early Byzantine Iconography," Ohio State University, 1987, and "Women in Byzantium," Holy Cross Greek Orthodox School of Theology, 1991. Lecturer at colleges and universities, including Ohio State University, 1977, Miami International University, 1982, Wabash College, 1986, Southern Methodist University, 1989, Ohio University, 1990, and Miami University, 1991.

MEMBER: International Center of Medieval Art, National Women's Studies Association, National Committee for Byzantine Studies, Medieval Academy of America.

AWARDS, HONORS: Fulbright scholarship, 1952-54; University of Wisconsin fellowship, 1957-58; grants from American Council of Learned Societies, 1971, Ohio Arts Council, 1979-80 and 1982, and National Endowment for the Arts, 1980-81; Luce research grant, 1987-88; award from Women's Caucus for Art, 1987.

WRITINGS:

(Editor and coauthor) *Breaking the Rules: Audrey Flack, A Retrospective, 1950-1990,* Abrams, 1992.

Contributor to books, including *The Twilight of Byzantium: Aspects of Cultural and Religious History in the Late Byzantine Empire,* Princeton University Press, 1991, and *The Byzantine Tradition after the Fall of Constantinople,* edited by J. J. Viannias, University Press of Virginia, 1991. Contributor to periodicals and professional journals, including *Women's Review of Books, Arts Magazine, Art Bulletin, Greek Orthodox Theological Review,* and *Art Journal.* Consultant and reader for *Gesta* and *Art Bulletin,* 1986-87; guest editor of *Women's Studies Quarterly: Teaching about Women in the Visual Arts,* 1987.

*   *   *

GREEN, Bryan S(tuart) W(estmacott)   1901-1993

OBITUARY NOTICE—See index for *CA* sketch: Born January 14, 1901, in London, England; died March 6, 1993. Minister and author. Green established himself as a tireless evangelist, preaching Christianity for decades throughout the English-speaking world in annual journeys. His home base was Birmingham, England, where he served as honorary canon of the cathedral from 1950 to 1970 and as rector of the church of St. Martin's in the Bull Ring for twenty-two years. Green was ordained in the Church of England in 1924 and worked variously in churches, with a children's mission, and at Oxford University before moving to Birmingham. He was the author of the books *The Practice of Evangelism, Being and Believing,* and *Saints Alive!* and a regular contributor to the *Birmingham Post* and *Woman.*

OBITUARIES AND OTHER SOURCES:

BOOKS

Who's Who, 145th edition, St. Martin's, 1993, p. 756.

PERIODICALS

Times (London), March 10, 1993, p. 21.

*   *   *

GREEN, Jeffrey M.   1944-

PERSONAL: Born December 13, 1944, in New York, NY; son of Bernard A. (an attorney) and Florence S. (a homemaker) Green; married Judith Rubinstein (a classical archaeologist); children: Eden, Boaz, Asher, Hannah. *Education:* Princeton University, A.B. (summa cum laude), 1966; attended University of Poitiers, 1966-67; Harvard University, M.A., 1968, Ph.D., 1973. *Politics:* "Israeli Left." *Religion:* Jewish. *Avocational interests:* Saxophone.

ADDRESSES: Home—3 Avigayil St., 93551 Jerusalem, Israel.

CAREER: Writer and translator. Hebrew University of Jerusalem, presenter of a workshop in translation and literary criticism for School of Overseas Students; teacher of English to Israeli army officers. *Military service:* Served in Israel Army Reserve.

AWARDS, HONORS: Fulbright fellow, 1966-67.

WRITINGS:

(With Trudi Birger) *A Daughter's Gift of Love,* Jewish Publication Society, 1992.

Author of a weekly column on books published in Hebrew, *Jerusalem Post.* Contributor of stories, articles, and reviews to periodicals, including *Response, Midstream, Harper's, Forum, Ariel,* and *Modern Hebrew Literature.*

TRANSLATOR FROM HEBREW, EXCEPT WHERE INDICATED

(From French) Beatrice Leroy, *The Jews of Navarre in the Late Middle Ages,* Magnes Press (Jerusalem), 1985.
Aharon Appelfeld, *To the Land of the Cattails,* Weidenfeld & Nicolson, 1986.
Appelfeld, *The Immortal Bartfuss,* Weidenfeld & Nicolson, 1988.
Appelfeld, *For Every Sin,* Weidenfeld & Nicolson, 1989.
Gershon Shaked, *Shmuel Yosef Agnon: A Revolutionary Traditionalist,* New York University Press, 1989.
Appelfeld, *The Healer,* Grove Weidenfeld, 1990.
Appelfeld, *Katerina,* Random House, 1992.
Yizhar Hirschfeld, *Byzantine Monasteries of the Judean Desert,* Yale University Press, 1992.
Rachel Elior, *The Paradoxical Ascent to God: The Kabbalistic Theosophy of Habad Hasidism,* State University of New York Press, 1992.

Translator of articles and stories.

SIDELIGHTS: Jeffrey M. Green told *CA:* "I am currently working on writing in Hebrew. I believe a writer must have an organic connection with his readership, and I have been living in Israel for twenty years."

*   *   *

GREEN, Michelle 1953-

PERSONAL: Born December 10, 1953, in Atlanta, GA; daughter of Bobby and Georgia Green; married James Lyons (a journalist), January 18, 1992. *Education:* University of Georgia, B.A., 1975.

ADDRESSES: Home—New York, NY. *Office*—1271 Sixth Ave., Room 31-50, New York, NY 10020. *Agent*—Kristine Dahl, International Creative Management, 40 West Fifty-seventh St., New York, NY 10019.

CAREER: Free-lance writer, Atlanta, GA, 1978, and Los Angeles, CA, and Boston, MA, 1981-82; *Constitution,* Atlanta, feature writer, 1979-81; *People,* New York City, senior writer and associate editor, 1983—.

MEMBER: Authors Guild.

WRITINGS:

The Dream at the End of the World, HarperCollins, 1991.

SIDELIGHTS: In *The Dream at the End of the World,* Michelle Green depicts the liberated, although often decadent and debauched, life of expatriate European and American artists in post-World War II Tangier. The city of Tangier, a seaport in Morocco at the northwest tip of North Africa, was governed by a nine-nation consortium from 1945 until 1956. With its relaxed laws, Tangier became a haven for entrepreneurial criminals, trafficking in drugs, guns, and dirty money, and for alienated artists and intellectuals. It was, Victoria Glendinning wrote in her London *Times* review, "a free port and a free money market where the necessities of life, alcohol and hashish, were cheap. Tangier was the playground for war criminals, crooks, poseurs, drug addicts, misfits, eccentrics, nymphomaniacs and, above all, homosexuals."

In her book, Green, a senior writer for *People* magazine, recounts tales of "Tangerino" (the term for Western emigres in Tangier) life, focusing particularly on Paul and Jane Bowles, an American couple. From his home in Tangier, Paul Bowles, the author of the 1950 best-selling novel *The Sheltering Sky,* traveled extensively throughout the Arab world, discovering art, literature, and music—some of which was previously unknown to Western culture. He also pursued several affairs with young Arab men. Like her husband, Jane Bowles was a writer who devoted herself to homosexual affairs with Arabs. She did not thrive

on Tangier culture and landscape as her husband did, however, and eventually died in a mental hospital. Both of the Bowleses were, according to Roger Burford Mason in his Toronto *Globe and Mail* review, "the flame around which the moths flickered" in Tangerino life, a social world that included William Burroughs, Allen Ginsberg, Jack Kerouac, Barbara Hutton, Tennessee Williams, Truman Capote, and Timothy Leary. *New York Times Book Review* contributor John Lahr explained the allure of the Moroccan city to this notorious group: "For Mr. Bowles and the hordes of American literary renegades and high society low-riders who would bushwhack a path to his Tangier door . . . North Africa was an exercise in the unlearning of repression, a submersion in excess, a deliberate regression into a thrilling primitivism that was an antidote to the oppressive, button-down, consumer-durable conformity of postwar America."

Green was highly praised for her engaging narrative and her thorough research for *The Dream at the End of the World,* although the inherent sensationalism in this portrait disturbed some reviewers. Mason commented that the truth revealed in this nonfiction book—much racier and more shocking than anything a novelist would dare to write—"reads like a nightmare." The reviewer asserted, however, that "Green manages to make extraordinary events, and even more extraordinary people, convincing and understandable." Glendinning, observing that Green "pours out her potted biographies, spicy anecdotes and disconnected fragments of the rivalries, feuds, sexual extravaganzas, bad trips and fruity gossip of 1,001 nights in Tangier with untroubled, unanalytical exuberance," found the book's narrative "noisy." The critic added that "only occasionally, with Green, does discretion prevail." Lahr, however, calling *The Dream at the End of the World* a "well-researched and well-written book," was particularly impressed with Green's vivid depictions of Tangier. The critic summarized, "Green's narrative percolates with her enthusiasm for the sensual terrain she has so well researched."

BIOGRAPHICAL/CRITICAL SOURCES:

PERIODICALS

Globe and Mail (Toronto), August 31, 1991, p. C8.
New York Times Book Review, September 15, 1991, p. 14.
Times (London), February 15, 1992, p. 32.

*   *   *

GREEN, Vincent S(cott) 1953-

PERSONAL: Born December 16, 1953, in Wichita, KS; son of Edgar (a telephone company employee) and Peggy (Watkins) Green; married Mary C. Hutton (a professor of law), November 24, 1978; children: Molly, Maggie. *Education:* University of Michigan, B.G.S., 1975; Washburn University, J.D., 1978; University of Virginia, M.F.A., 1988.

ADDRESSES: Home—R.R.1, Box 290, Vermillion, SD 57069. *Agent*—Fran Collin, 110 West 40th St., New York, NY 10018.

CAREER: University of South Dakota, Vermillion, instructor in creative writing, 1988-89; South Dakota Supreme Court, Pierre, law clerk, 1989-90; Green's Legal Research, Vermillion, owner, 1990—. Member of South Dakota House of Representatives, 1993. *Military service:* U.S. Army, 1978-83, criminal trial lawyer in Germany and at Fort Leavenworth, KS; became captain; received Meritorious Service Medal and Army Commendation Medal.

AWARDS, HONORS: Grant from South Dakota Arts Council, 1991.

WRITINGS:

The Price of Victory, Walker & Co., 1992.

WORK IN PROGRESS: Extreme Justice, a "nonfiction novel" about German prisoners of war executed at the end of World War II.

SIDELIGHTS: Vincent S. Green told *CA:* "As a trial lawyer, I grew tired of reading novels where the trials were not believable. I set out to write a courtroom thriller where the legal action was accurate, yet the story was still a page-turner.

"People are often surprised that a lawyer can write an interesting story, since many people believe lawyers are dry and boring people. However, trial lawyers are different. What we do all the time in the profession is tell stories. We listen to witnesses, then shape their voices into a story that, hopefully, causes a jury to have reasonable doubt about a client's guilt. The whole process is very similar to that of writing novels."

*   *   *

GREENBERG, Cheryl Lynn 1958-

PERSONAL: Born August 13, 1958, in Massachusetts; daughter of Irwin (a professor of operations research) and Anita (Burland) Greenberg; married Dan Edward Lloyd (a professor of philosophy), June 10, 1990. *Education:* Princeton University, A.B. (summa cum laude), 1980; Columbia University, M.A., 1981, M.Phil., 1983, Ph.D., 1988.

ADDRESSES: Office—Department of History, Trinity College, Hartford, CT 06106.

CAREER: Trinity College, Hartford, CT, assistant professor, 1986-92, associate professor of African American and twentieth-century American history, 1992—. Hartford Humanities Alliance, member of planning committee, 1989—; member of board of directors of Trinity Hillel Foundation, 1991—, Greater Hartford Jewish Community Relations Council, 1992—, Connecticut State Anti-Defamation League, 1992—, and Hartford chapter of Anti-Discrimination League, 1992—.

MEMBER: American Historical Association, Organization of American Historians, American Studies Association, Social Science History Association, Coordinating Committee on Women in the Historical Profession, Society for the Scientific Study of Religion, Society for Values in Higher Education, Connecticut Jewish Historical Society (member of board of directors, 1989—), Phi Beta Kappa.

AWARDS, HONORS: Fellow of American Council of Learned Societies, 1990-91; fellow at Charles Warren Center for Studies in American History, Harvard University, 1993-94.

WRITINGS:

"Or Does It Explode?" Black Harlem in the Great Depression, Oxford University Press, 1991.

Work represented in anthologies, including *Women's History: Selected Reading Lists and Course Outlines,* edited by Annette Baxter and Louise Stevenson, Markus Wiener, 1987, 3rd edition published as *Women's History: Selected Course Outlines and Reading Lists,* edited by Stevenson, 1993; *Historical Dictionary of Civil Rights in the United States,* edited by Charles Lowery and John Marszalek, Greenwood Press, 1992; and *Encyclopedia of New York City,* edited by Kenneth Jackson, Yale University Press, 1993. Contributor of articles and reviews to periodicals, including *Journal of Urban History, Journal of American Ethnic History,* and *Jewish Currents.* Member of editorial board, *Connecticut Jewish History.*

WORK IN PROGRESS: A book on relationships between black and Jewish civil rights organizations from the 1930s through the 1950s, completion expected in 1995; research on responses of black and Jewish organizations to Japanese internment during World War II.

*   *   *

GREENBERG, Martin 1918-

PERSONAL: Born February 3, 1918, in Norfolk, VA; son of Joseph (in business) and Dora (a homemaker; maiden name, Brodwin) Greenberg; married Paula Fox (a writer),

June 9, 1962; children: David. *Education:* University of Michigan, B.A., 1938.

ADDRESSES: Home—306 Clinton St., Brooklyn, NY 11201.

CAREER: Schocken Books, New York City, editor, 1946-49; *Commentary* (magazine), New York City, editor, 1953-60; The New School, New York City, lecturer, 1961-67; C. W. Post College, Greenvale, NY, began as assistant professor, became professor of English literature, 1963-88. *Military service:* U.S. Army, 1941-45; became staff sergeant; received Bronze Star.

MEMBER: Academy of American Poets.

AWARDS, HONORS: Award for literature, American Academy and Institute of the Arts and Letters, 1989, for criticism and translation; Harold Morton Landon Translation Award, Academy of American Poets, 1989, for *Five Plays;* Guggenheim fellowship, 1963, for *The Terror of Art; Kafka and Modern Literature;* residency, Bellagio Center, Rockefeller Foundation, 1990.

WRITINGS:

The Terror of Art; Kafka and Modern Literature, Basic Books, 1968.
The Hamlet Vocation of Coleridge and Wordsworth, Iowa State University Press, 1986.

TRANSLATOR

The Diaries of Franz Kafka 1914-23, edited by Max Brod, Schocken, 1948-49.
Heinrich von Kleist, *The Marquise of O—, and Other Stories,* Criterion Press, 1960.
Heinrich von Kleist, *Five Plays,* Yale University Press, 1988.
J. W. von Goethe, *Faust, Part One,* Yale University Press, 1992.
J. W. von Goethe, *Faust, Part Two,* Yale University Press, in press.

*   *   *

GREENFELD, Josh(ua Joseph) 1928-

PERSONAL: Born February 27, 1928, in Malden, MA; son of Nathan Samuel (in business) and Kate (a homemaker; maiden name, Hellerman) Greenfeld; married Foumiko Kometani (a painter and writer), September 30, 1960; children: Karl Taro, Noah Jiro. *Education:* Attended Brooklyn College (now of the City University of New York), 1944-47; University of Michigan, B.A., 1949; Columbia University, M.A., 1953. *Religion:* "Jewish agnostic." *Avocational interests:* Assembling glockenspiels (a percussion instrument).

ADDRESSES: Home—14637 Bestor Blvd., Pacific Palisades, CA 90272. *Office*—15215 Sunset Blvd., Pacific Palisades, CA 90272. *Agent*—Lynn Nesbit, 598 Madison Ave., New York, NY 10022.

CAREER: Free-lance writer, 1956-60; *Newsweek,* New York City, book review editor, 1961-62; Hakuhodo Advertising, Osaka, Japan, copywriter, 1963-65; Doshisha University, Kyoto, Japan, professor of English, 1963-65; *Time,* New York City, book reviewer, 1966-70; writer. *Military service:* U.S. Army, 1953-55; became corporal.

MEMBER: PEN American Center, Dramatists Guild, Writers Guild of America, Academy of Motion Picture Arts and Sciences (member of Writers Branch Executive Committee, 1975-92).

AWARDS, HONORS: Ford Foundation grant, 1959; Guggenheim fellow, 1960; best article of the year, Society of Magazine Writers, 1970, for "A Child Called Noah"; Screen Award nomination, Writers Guild of America, and Academy Award nomination for best screenplay, Academy of Motion Picture Arts and Sciences, both 1974, for *Harry and Tonto;* Christopher Awards, Christophers, 1975, for *Harry and Tonto,* 1978, for *Lovey: Circle of Children, Part Two,* and 1979, for *A Place for Noah;* Harold U. Ribalow Prize nomination, Hadassah, 1984, for *The Return of Mr. Hollywood.*

WRITINGS:

NONFICTION

A Child Called Noah: A Family Journey, Holt, 1972.
A Place for Noah, Holt, 1978.
A Client Called Noah: A Family Journey Continued, Holt, 1986.

Contributor of article, "A Child Called Noah," to *Life;* contributor to periodicals, including *Time, New York Times Book Review, Newsweek, Chicago Tribune, Washington Post,* and *Los Angeles Times.*

NOVELS

O for a Master of Magic!, New American Library, 1968.
(With Paul Mazursky) *Harry and Tonto* (also see below), Saturday Review Press, 1974.
The Return of Mr. Hollywood, Doubleday, 1984.
What Happened Was This, Carroll & Graf, 1990.

SCREENPLAYS

(With Mazursky) *Harry and Tonto* (film; adapted from the novel of the same title), Twentieth Century-Fox, 1974.
Lovey: Circle of Children, Part Two (television movie), Columbia Broadcasting System, Inc. (CBS-TV), 1978.

(With Hal Goldman, Fred S. Fox, Seaman Jacobs, and
Melissa Miller) *Oh God! Book Two* (film; adapted
from a story by Greenfeld), Warner Bros., 1980.

STAGE PLAYS

Clandestine on the Morning Line: A Play in Three Acts
(produced in Washington, DC, at Arena Stage, 1959,
produced Off-Broadway, 1961), Dramatists Play Service, 1961.
I Have a Dream (adapted from the words of Martin Luther King, Jr.), produced in Washington, DC, at Ford
Theatre, 1976, produced on Broadway, 1976.

SIDELIGHTS: Josh Greenfeld, a novelist, playwright,
and screenwriter, received considerable critical recognition for his three autobiographical works about his severely brain-damaged son, Noah. The trilogy, consisting
of Greenfeld's daily journal entries, delves into Noah's
growth and describes the hardships of raising a mentally-
impaired child. The author believes that his introspective
books will help other families dealing with the same tragedy. He commented: "They know that they are not alone
and that they have nothing to be ashamed of. Their journey, actually, is a very common one. Indeed, I would venture to say that the developmentally disabled comprise
one of the single largest minorities in our country—and
also the one that is most discriminated against and
abused." In an appraisal of Greenfeld's second memoir,
A Place for Noah, New Republic contributor Helen Fea-
therstone judged that the book "is for everyone who wants
to learn about the bonds that tie people together in families, about crises, about anger, fear, grief, guilt, loneliness,
joy, pride, and love. About looking grim reality in the eye
and going on."

Greenfeld's first chronicle, 1972's *A Child Called Noah:
A Family Journey*, depicts aspects of Noah's life from the
time of his birth in 1966 to his fifth birthday. When Noah
was born, he appeared to be normal, remembers Greenfeld, but at the age of two, he began to regress in his development. He stopped talking and became preoccupied with
unusual activities, such as walking in circles, pulling
threads, catching lint, and laughing and crying for no apparent reason. Alarmed by Noah's condition, his parents
began consulting various medical professionals, hoping to
find a diagnosis. Most of the doctors who examined Noah
told Greenfeld and his wife Foumiko Kometani that their
son was suffering from autism, a disorder characterized by
introversion, repetitive behavior, and an inability to communicate properly.

As explained in *A Child Called Noah*, the Greenfelds decided to raise Noah themselves until they could find a reputable institution to provide full-time care for their son.
Taking responsibility for Noah's upbringing included visiting doctors, examining centers for brain-damaged chil-

dren, losing privacy and sleep, and slowing down the advancement of their personal careers. Greenfeld writes: "I
also know I must try not to feel more sorry for myself than
for Noah, but some days I forget." One of the author's primary aspirations for his memoir was to reveal his true
emotions. He asserts that other parents of mentally disturbed children who have published journals have not
achieved this goal in their writings. He states: "None of
them palpitated with truth for me. The parents didn't
burn with enough anger; they were too damned heroic for
me." In an interview with *New York Times Book Review*'s
Glenn Collins, Greenfeld proclaimed that *A Child Called
Noah* represents the "denial" stage of grief that he experienced when confronting his son's disability. Greenfeld's
first memoir met with good appraisals. *New York Times
Book Review*'s D. Keith Mano commented that among
comparable books, "it is certainly one of the best." A *Los
Angeles Times Book Review* contributor lauded, "Greenfeld's book is an extraordinary achievement, not only liter-
arily."

Greenfeld's next work in his autobiographical trilogy was
A Place for Noah. This award-winning volume contains
diary entries from 1971 to 1976. The daily accounts about
Noah's life elaborate on the difficulty of finding a decent
home for the boy and the strain his condition has put on
his parents' marriage. Greenfeld told Collins that while
writing his second memoir he felt "rage" about Noah's
condition. In the book's introduction, the author reveals
additional feelings: "What is my attitude toward Noah?
How do I view him? I think, put simply, I view him as a
responsibility, someone I have to take care of—almost like
a job that has to be done. Because if we don't do the job,
who will? It's our job by elimination. And I mean job, just
a job. I am no Job, and Noah is no great affliction and neither of us is part of any cosmic test-or otherworldly joke."
But Greenfeld did not lose his aspirations for Noah. He
points out, "If I were to say there is no hope for Noah I
would be saying there is no hope for any of us." And with
this hope, the Greenfelds opened a day-care center for
brain-damaged children, which Noah attended for a period of time. *A Place for Noah* fared well with the critics.
Time's R. Z. Sheppard proclaimed, "It is almost impossible to imagine readers of this book who would not make
a special place for Noah." Writing in *New York Times
Book Review*, Thomas Cottle called the volume "a moving
and exquisite diary."

The third memoir, *A Client Called Noah: A Family Journey Continued*, focuses on Noah's life from 1977 to 1986.
Within this time, Noah was admitted into a private residence and then into a group home. Greenfeld maintains
that his family became more productive after putting
Noah's care in the hands of professionals. "Noah has been
the central experience of all our lives," concludes Green-

feld. "And I would have traded it for anything." But he does admit, "There is simply the fact that, no matter how I slice it, no matter how incomplete he is, I love [Noah] with a wholeness I have never loved anyone or anything with since my childhood." And Greenfeld told Collins that while penning this final account he experienced "acceptance or resignation" for his son's disorder. The critics again elicited praise for Greenfeld's writing. Brigitte Weeks, a *Washington Post Book World* reviewer, maintained that "Noah's story through his father's eyes makes compulsive reading." Chicago *Tribune Books*'s Clarence Petersen commented, "I have never read a more affecting work."

During the course of writing books about Noah, Greenfeld won a Christopher Award for his television screenplay, *Lovey: Circle of Children, Part Two,* based on personal experiences with his son. The movie, a sequel to 1977's *A Circle of Children,* revolves around Jane Alexander, who is a teacher of mentally disturbed children. In the film, Alexander wrestles with decisions about her career and the futures of her students. In addition to *Lovey,* Greenfeld also allocated time for writing novels and other screenplays. He collaborated with Paul Mazursky on a book titled *Harry and Tonto,* published in 1974. They also adapted the story into a screenplay during the same year. The movie received a Christopher Award, a Screen Award nomination from Writers Guild of America, and an Academy Award nomination for best screenplay.

In the comic *Harry and Tonto,* seventy-two-year-old widower and retired college professor Harry Coombs is evicted from a New York apartment after it is designated to be demolished. He and his cat Tonto temporarily move in with his eldest son's family. Next he makes plans to visit his daughter in Chicago and then move to California where his youngest son resides. During his trek across the country, Harry discovers that his children have their own problems. He offers them some advice and condolences but eventually moves on to find happiness in his constantly changing life. Greenfeld and Mazursky received critical recognition for both the book and screenplay versions of *Harry and Tonto.* After reading the novel, Anatole Broyard of *New York Times* stated, "Josh Greenfeld and Paul Mazursky seem to know the elderly in a way that can only come through love." *New Yorker*'s Penelope Gilliatt described the cinematic production as "an affectionate and enlivening folktale view of New York." And a *Motion Picture Guide* reviewer called the film "a sweet, sentimental movie."

Greenfeld's next collaborative screenplay was for the 1980 motion picture *Oh God! Book II,* a sequel to Larry Gelbart's 1977 film titled *Oh God!* The second installment, penned by five writers, features a young girl named Tracy, who is singled out by God to steer mankind back in His direction. He chooses the child to lead the crusade, hoping to attract both children and adults. However, when Tracy begins a campaign for more believers, some people, including her separated parents, begin to wonder about her sanity. Soon a panel of psychiatrists is selected to interview the young girl to decide if she has a mental disorder. During the evaluation, God reveals himself to the members of the panel, and His appearance gives validity to Tracy's assertions. The motion picture concludes with the reconciliation of Tracy's parents. Critics were unimpressed with this cowritten screenplay, suggesting that the high number of writers may have spoiled the project.

Among Greenfeld's other notable works are his three novels *O for a Master of Magic!, The Return of Mr. Hollywood,* and *What Happened Was This.* Greenfeld's first novel, *O for a Master of Magic!* was published in 1968. Like the author, the book's protagonist is a Jewish man who grew up in Brooklyn, New York, moved to Japan, and married a Japanese painter. The story, written in diary form, focuses on the man's search for his identity. In an appraisal of the volume for *New York Times Book Review,* writer John Casey found the work's merit to be its "wry observation of life among American expatriates in Japan."

In 1984 Greenfeld saw publication of his *Return of Mr. Hollywood.* This story features Larry Lazar, a manipulative Hollywood director who has fostered his success in the film industry through various unethical means. In the midst of promoting a script for production, Lazar is told that his mother has died. Although he was not fond of his mother's overbearing ways, Lazar finds that he cannot get her out of his mind. When he returns to his childhood home in Brooklyn, New York, to attend the funeral, he is forced to confront his past. He encounters old friends and family, including his mother's ghost. And when he returns to Hollywood, he feels compelled to change his unscrupulous ways. *The Return of Mr. Hollywood* met with generally favorable reviews. *New York Times*'s Broyard commented, "Though I don't know anything about Hollywood, I think that what Larry says about it is interesting, convincing and a refreshing change from the familiar condescensions." Joy Fielding of the Toronto *Globe and Mail* contended, "The writing is crisp and the dialogue very real and plentiful." And *Washington Post Book World* contributor Faiga Levine called it "a mighty funny book."

What Happened Was This, like *The Return of Mr. Hollywood,* depicts the life of a Brooklyn-born film director. Published in 1990, the book features middle-aged protagonist Les Rose, who has prospered from his career but never reached fame with his accomplishments. One afternoon the filmmaker unexpectedly meets an old friend from Brooklyn, and the encounter triggers a number of memories from Rose's childhood. Through the reminiscing, the director reveals his life story. "*What Happened Was This* is tantalizingly good: every detail is sharply limned, the narrative moves at just the right pace and the characters are extraordinarily vivid," declared Frank Wilson of *New York Times Book Review.* Elaine Kendall, writing in *Los Angeles Times,* remarked that "if this deferred novel is a reward to [Greenfeld], he's earned it."

BIOGRAPHICAL/CRITICAL SOURCES:

BOOKS

Greenfeld, Josh, *A Child Called Noah: A Family Journey,* Holt, 1972.
Greenfeld, *A Place for Noah,* Holt, 1978.
Greenfeld, *A Client Called Noah: A Family Journey Continued,* Holt, 1986.
The Motion Picture Guide: 1927-1983, Volume VI, Cinebooks, 1986, pp. 1165, 2227.
Something about the Author, Volume 62, Gale, 1990.

PERIODICALS

Book World, September 1, 1968; May 21, 1972.
Globe and Mail (Toronto), September 29, 1984.
Los Angeles Times, September 28, 1990.
Los Angeles Times Book Review, January 29, 1989, p. 10.
New Republic, September 14, 1974, pp. 20, 33-34; July 8, 1978, p. 39.
Newsweek, September 2, 1974, pp. 60-61.
New York, September 2, 1974, pp. 66-67.
New Yorker, August 26, 1974, pp. 46, 48, 50.
New York Times, June 6, 1974, p. 35; October 3, 1980; May 26, 1984.
New York Times Book Review, November 24, 1968; June 11, 1972; April 23, 1978; February 15, 1987, pp. 1, 28-29; October 7, 1990, p. 40.
Time, September 9, 1974, pp. 4, 6; April 10, 1978; February 9, 1987, p. 65.
Tribune Books (Chicago), May 21, 1989, p. 4.
Washington Post Book World, May 19, 1984; February 22, 1987, pp. 5-6.

—*Sketch by Jane M. Kelly*

*   *   *

GREIF, Geoffrey L. 1949-

PERSONAL: Born April 13, 1949, in Baltimore, MD; son of Leonard L., Jr. (a photographer) and Ann (a volunteer worker; maiden name, Burgunder) Greif; married Maureen Lefton (a speech scientist), 1974; children: Jennifer, Alissa. *Education:* Ohio Wesleyan University, B.A., 1971; University of Pennsylvania, M.S.W., 1974; Philadelphia Child Guidance Clinic, certificate in family therapy, 1977; Long Island Society for Clinical Hypnosis, certificate in clinical hypnosis, 1979; Columbia University, D.S.W., 1983. *Religion:* "I rely on it increasingly."

ADDRESSES: Home—1917 Old Court Rd., Baltimore, MD 21204. *Office*—School of Social Work, University of Maryland at Baltimore, 525 West Redwood St., Baltimore, MD 21201. *Agent*—James Levine Communications, Inc., c/o FWI, 330 Seventh Ave., 14th floor, New York, NY 10001.

CAREER: School social worker in Camden, NJ, 1974-76; Drenk Memorial Guidance Center, Burlington, NJ, clinical social worker, 1976-79; University of Maryland at Baltimore, assistant professor, 1984-89, associate professor of social work, 1989—. Adjunct instructor at Philadelphia College of the Performing Arts, 1974-76, Widener University, 1982-84, and Cabrini College, 1983-84. Child Study Team (Camden), chairperson, 1974-76; social worker in private practice in Philadelphia, PA, 1975-77 and 1983-85; Community Counseling and Resource Center (Cockeysville, MD), clinical supervisor, 1985-90; Sinai Hospital (Baltimore), trainer and clinician for Drug Dependency Program, 1990—; Epoch House (Catonsville, MD), family therapy consultant, 1991—; Jewish Family Services (Baltimore), co-leader of divorce support group, 1991—; founder and co-leader of Baltimore area parent support group, "Help! My Kids Are Driving Me Crazy!," 1991—; National Victims Center, member of board of consultants, 1992-94; consultant to Juvenile Justice Resource Center. Parents Without Partners, member of international professional advisory board, 1984—; Parents Anonymous, member of board of directors, 1985—; Associated Jewish Charities, member of Task Force to Study the Jewish Family, 1986-87; Maryland Committee for Children, member of board of directors, 1987-88; Park School, member of board of directors, 1987—. Workshop presenter; public speaker; guest on television programs, including *Good Morning America, CBS Good Morning,* and *Donahue.*

MEMBER: Clinical Social Work Society of Maryland (member of board of directors, 1990-92), American Association of Marital and Family Therapy (clinical member), National Association of Social Workers, Academy of Certified Social Workers.

AWARDS, HONORS: Grant from Office of Juvenile Justice and Delinquency Prevention, 1992.

WRITINGS:

Single Fathers, Lexington Books, 1985.
(With M. S. Pabst) *Mothers without Custody,* Lexington Books, 1988.
The Daddy Track and the Single Father, Lexington Books, 1990.

(With R. L. Hegar) *When Parents Kidnap: The Families behind the Headlines,* Free Press, 1993.

(With Hegar) *Understanding Abducted Children,* U.S. Department of Justice, 1993.

(With Hegar) *Parents Who Abduct* (monograph), U.S. Department of Justice, in press.

Work represented in books, including *Clinical Social Work in the Eco-Systems Perspectives,* edited by Carol Meyer, Columbia University Press, 1983; *Equal Partnering: A Feminist Perspective,* edited by B. J. Brothers, Haworth Press, 1992; and *Men and Work,* edited by Jane Hood, Sage Books, 1993. Contributor of more than seventy articles and reviews to social work journals and popular magazines, including *Nurturing News, Single Dad's Lifestyle, Child Support Report, Family Therapy News, Healthwatch,* and *Men's Health.* Contributing editor, *Single Parent,* 1984—; member of editorial board, *Journal of Independent Social Work,* 1989-91, and *UMAB* magazine, 1991-92.

WORK IN PROGRESS: Parents Who Lose Contact with Their Children, completion expected in 1994.

*   *   *

GREY, J. David   1935-1993

OBITUARY NOTICE—See index for *CA* sketch: Born March 13, 1935, in Elizabeth, NJ; died of bone cancer, March 11, 1993, in Manhattan, NY. Educator and author. An expert on British novelist Jane Austen, Grey cofounded the Jane Austen Society of North America and wrote about her in *The Jane Austen Handbook.* He also edited the 1990 book *Jane Austen's Beginnings: The Juvenalia and "Lady Susan."* From 1958 to 1975 Grey supported himself by teaching in New York City schools, and he subsequently served as an assistant principal for nearly twenty years.

OBITUARIES AND OTHER SOURCES:

PERIODICALS

New York Times, March 15, 1993, p. B8.

*   *   *

GRIFFIN, P(auline) M.   1947-

PERSONAL: Born July 5, 1947, in Brooklyn, NY; daughter of Timothy Joseph (a bus driver) and Mary Christine (a homemaker; maiden name, Murphy) Griffin. *Politics:* "Conservative Democrat." *Religion:* Roman Catholic. *Avocational interests:* Writing, cats, reading, listening to music, needlework.

ADDRESSES: Office—McGraw-Hill, Sweet's, 1221 Avenue of the Americas, New York, NY 10020. *Agent*—Russell Galen, Scott Meredith Literary Agency, 845 Third Ave., New York, NY 10022.

CAREER: Sweet's, McGraw-Hill, New York City, became administrator for technical support, 1966—; writer.

MEMBER: Science Fiction Writers of America.

WRITINGS:

Star Commandos, Ace, 1986.
Star Commandos: Colony in Peril, Ace, 1987.
Star Commandos: Mission Underground, Ace, 1988.
Star Commandos: Death Planet, Ace, 1989.
Star Commandos: Mind Slaver, Ace, 1990.
Star Commandos: Return to War, Ace, 1990.
Star Commandos: Fire Planet, Ace, 1990.
Star Commandos: Jungle Assault, Ace, 1991.
Star Commandos: Call to Arms, Ace, 1991.
(With Andre Norton) *Storms of Victory,* Tor, 1991.
(With Norton and Mary H. Schaub) *Flight of Vengeance,* Tor, 1992.

Also author of *Redline the Stars,* 1993. Works represented in anthologies, including *Magic in Ithkar III,* edited by Andre Norton and Robert Adams, Tor, 1986; *Tales of the Witch World,* edited by Norton, Tor, Volume 1, 1987, Volume 3, 1990; *Catfantastic,* edited by Norton and Martin Greenberg, DAW, Volume 1, 1989, Volume 2, 1991, Volume 3, 1993.

WORK IN PROGRESS: A novel titled *Fire Hand.*

*   *   *

GRIGGS, Terry   1951-

PERSONAL: Born December 20, 1951, in Little Current, Manitoulin Island, Ontario, Canada; daughter of John Joseph (a tourist camp owner and operator) and Janet Marshall (a tourist camp owner and operator; maiden name, Scott) Griggs; married David Burr (a media specialist), November 17, 1978; children: Alexander Galen. *Education:* University of Western Ontario, B.A., 1977, M.A., 1979.

ADDRESSES: Home—27 Garfield Ave., London, Ontario, Canada N6C 2B4.

CAREER: Writer.

AWARDS, HONORS: Short-listed, Governor General's Award, 1991, for *Quickening.*

WRITINGS:

Harrier, Brick Books, 1982.
Quickening (short stories), Porcupine's Quill, 1990.

Contributor of short stories to *The New Press Anthology: Best Canadian Short Fiction,* General, 1984; *The Macmillan Anthology 1,* Macmillan, 1988; *The Journey Prize Anthology 2,* McClelland & Stewart, 1990; *Street Songs 1: New Voices in Fiction,* Longstreet Press, 1990; *The Third Macmillan Anthology,* Macmillan, 1990; *The New Story Writers,* Quarry Press, 1992.

WORK IN PROGRESS: A novel, publication expected in 1995.

SIDELIGHTS: Terry Griggs's short stories have received critical acclaim in Canada for their humor, imagination, structure, and language. They are also known for a certain quirkiness, since they are likely to unfold implausible events, to move without warning from the natural to the supernatural realm, to focus on odd or slightly disturbing everyday images, or to depict the world from unusual perspectives. Although they do not necessarily deliver a factual kind of truth, Griggs's stories have a way of getting to the heart of their subject matter. Griggs, initially calling her approach "poetic realism," refines the description of her work to "crazy" or "screwball realism." She explained these terms in an essay she wrote for the *New Quarterly:* "I need a narrative structure that is flexible, that can adapt to the kind of story being told, that can move like poetry, by indirection, circling, making (ideally) daredevil or unexpected leaps, landing with a concentrated force. And I want the stories to be *true,* embroidered truth perhaps, but not quite surrealism or magic realism, which can get awfully boring. So I'm interested in how far you can stretch the truth without losing it."

The truth that Griggs depicts is generally rooted in her experiences as a child growing up on the Manitoulin Island in Ontario, Canada, where her parents ran a tourist camp. Commenting in the *New Quarterly* that island life "has shaped my imagination, given me certain obsessions . . . and provides a rich source of material," Griggs concluded, "I can't foresee looking anywhere else for a story, though I may in time." But she does not consider her stories to be representative of the island and its people. "They're an idiosyncratic interpretation, island life refracted at strange angles through me."

In her first collection of short stories, *Quickening,* Griggs writes sixteen tales revolving around drownings, ghosts, husbands who may have been murdered by their wives, alcoholism, wife beating, and other dark and often eerie topics. Griggs blends these themes, however, with humor and lighter fare. "Her Toes," for example, written from the perspective of a baby, begins with a focus on his mother's toes: "*Yow!* The big ones knocked him flat every time. Sudden as eel faces poking out the dark holes at the end of her fuzzy pink slippers." During this baby's explorations, he encounters not only a wide and often disgusting variety of things to put in his mouth, but also the ghost of his dead father. The reader learns (via the thoughts of the dead man's dog) that the shooting death of the baby's father was not a hunting accident, as is publicly assumed.

Other topics and characters in *Quickening* have quirky aspects. In "Public Mischief," a hotel owner drinks himself to death, leaving his four hotels to his four daughters. Griggs launches a "hysterical and lyrical account," according to Eve Drobot in her Toronto *Globe and Mail* review, of the way that each of the hotels matches the personality traits of the daughter who inherits and then runs it. In "Man with the Axe," a dog digs up a wooden leg, which propels villagers to speculate about the leg's owner and about their own lives. Similarly, in "Visitation," when an old woman finds the body of a small devil on her floor, its smell invokes memories of her dead husband and years of abuse.

Critics maintained that Griggs's masterful handling of language adds humor and depth, as well as complexity, to her work. "Griggs is a whirling dervish with language," Drobot proclaimed. "Her ability to conjure up imagery is giddying, the inventiveness of her vocabulary can make you dizzy." *The New Story Writers* editor John Metcalf advised readers who were put off by the "downplaying of 'story' " in Griggs's work to "read with the care and attention one gives to poetry." Also noting the poetic nature of Griggs's work, *Canadian Book Review Annual* contributor Christy Conte remarked that the author's "skill is particularly dazzling in descriptions that are as original as they are musical." Several critics applauded the sheer joy—of words, notably, but also of life itself—within Griggs's work. "Everything here is words and names, all in a laughing tumble, and reality is blown up or miniaturized to envelop or map the roiling shanty towns of each story," Michael Kenyon commented in the *Malahat Review.* "The ride is as fun-filled as any fairground event, complete with the skilled barker's magician-evangelist spiel. Yet this is the surface, gleaming, noisy. Underneath, equal to the great love of language, is a love of people." A *Quill and Quire* contributor summarized: "Funny without irony or satire, poignant without pathos or melancholy, and smart without intellectual pretensions, *Quickening* is a whole lot of fun."

BIOGRAPHICAL/CRITICAL SOURCES:

BOOKS

Griggs, Terry, *Quickening,* Porcupine's Quill, 1990.
Metcalf, John, *The New Story Writers,* Quarry Press, 1992.

PERIODICALS

Books in Canada, January, 1991.
Canadian Book Review Annual, December, 1991.

Globe and Mail (Toronto), November 23, 1991.
London Free Press, December 22, 1990.
Malahat Review, Issue 98, 1991.
New Quarterly, winter, 1989, pp. 5-9.
Quill and Quire, December, 1990.

*   *   *

GRIMES, Tom 1954-

PERSONAL: Born September 30, 1954; son of John Grimes and Lillian Pellicane; married Mary Anne McKiernan, 1976 (divorced, 1982); married Joanne Murphy, August, 1992. *Education:* Queens College, B.A., 1976; University of Iowa Writers Workshop, M.F.A., 1991. *Politics:* "Occasionally. I waver between delusion and despair." *Religion:* "I'm with French writer Albert Camus when he said, 'Man is mortal. That may be; but let us die resisting; and if our lot is complete annihilation, let us not behave in such a way that it seems justice.' "

ADDRESSES: Agent—Donadio-Ashworth, Inc., 231 West Twenty-second St., New York, NY 10011.

CAREER: Private Papers, Inc., New York City, general manager, 1980-83; Wolfman-Gold & Good Co., New York City, general manager, 1983-86; Louie's Backyard, Key West, FL, waiter, 1986-89; University of Iowa, Iowa City, visiting professor, 1991-92; Southwest Texas State University, San Marcos, assistant professor of English/ M.F.A. program, 1992—.

MEMBER: PEN, Authors Guild, Dramatists Guild.

AWARDS, HONORS: PEN/Nelson Algren Award finalist, 1984, for manuscript *A Stone of the Heart; A Stone of the Heart* was named a notable book by the *New York Times,* 1990; Teaching-Writing fellowship, Iowa Writers Workshop, 1990; James Michener fellow, 1991, for *Season's End;* L.A. Dramalogue "Writing" Award, 1991, for *Spec.*

WRITINGS:

A Stone of the Heart (novel), Four Walls Eight Windows, 1990.
Spec (play), produced in Los Angeles, CA, 1991.
Season's End (novel), Little, Brown, 1992.

WORK IN PROGRESS: City of God (tentative title).

SIDELIGHTS: Tom Grimes is the author of *A Stone of the Heart* and *Season's End,* novels about troubled families that incorporate actual and fictionalized events from the history of baseball. He sets *A Stone of the Heart* in the borough of Queens, New York, during the 1961 baseball season when Roger Maris attempted to hit sixty-one home runs to break the single-season record of Babe Ruth. The narrator of the story is fourteen-year-old Michael, a baseball aficionado whose alcoholic father has, in the past, often left home for days at a time. At the story's beginning Michael's father, who has been sober for six weeks, has left home to attend a wake and has not come back.

Michael's father is not the only member of the McManus family with a problem. His mother must often lie to her husband's employers who often contact her to find out why he is absent from his job. Michael's six-year-old brother, Rudy, cannot speak. And the boys' grandfather, who lives with the family, lost all of his money after investing in an electronics corporation that went bankrupt and has had a history of heart failure. On a personal level, Michael must cope with a weight problem and the possibility that he might become an alcoholic like his father. For his characterization of Michael, Grimes was complimented by *New York Times Book Review* contributor Hilma Wolitzer, who wrote that "*A Stone of the Heart* renders the afflictions of adolescence in both unique and universal terms."

In one of the novel's most notable scenes, according to Christopher Zenowich of the *Chicago Tribune,* Michael uses the family's last few dollars to buy Yankees tickets for himself, his brother, and his grandfather. At the stadium, Michael gets drunk, while his grandfather tries to convince a vendor to sell him peanuts for worthless stock certificates. Zenowich regarded the novel as "an odd and compelling mixture of mystery, suspense and reminiscence." And Merle Rubin, in a review for the *Wall Street Journal,* called *A Stone of the Heart* "fast-paced, funny, dramatic and convincing."

Season's End, published in 1992, relates the story of Mike Williams, a young baseball prodigy who is called up to the major leagues to replace the star of a team who dies in midseason. The deceased player is buried in left field, the area that Williams covers as a defensive player. While playing his position, Williams is constantly aware of the presence of his predecessor. He remarks, "I felt I was going to fall into the earth, through the matter-packed and gravity-bound shell of the world, into the zone of the dead." Such reflections are typical of Williams, who, as Mitch Evich noted in the *Patriot Ledger,* occasionally "speaks with the diction and literary allusions of a cultural studies professor." While Evich questioned whether the voice of the narrator was true to character throughout the novel, he remarked that "Grimes is such an acrobatic stylist that it ultimately doesn't matter. He has an astonishing gift for imagery—successfully cramming multiple metaphors into a single sentence—and, like any aggressive hitter, he isn't afraid to look a little awkward now and then when he strikes out."

As a testament to his talent for the game, Williams is honored as rookie of the year during his first season as a player. His career is hampered by his exposure to three men, however: an uncaring father, a lackadaisical agent, and a scheming ball club owner who is confined to a wheelchair. Trouble begins in his second year in the major leagues during a disagreement over his contract. Both the media and his teammates turn on him, and Williams struggles to maintain his association with the ball club. His career eventually rights itself, however, and by the early 1980s Williams is earning substantial amounts of money and carrying a batting average of around .400. But although he prospers professionally, he experiences problems in his personal life. His relationship with his wife falters, he becomes addicted to amphetamines, and he worries that his daughter is becoming spoiled by the good life that he provides.

According to Terry McDermott of the *Seattle Times/ Seattle Post Intelligencer, Season's End* "is a more knowing, more complicated, messier and wiser take on the game than, say, the best-selling baseball fiction of W. P. Kinsella." Dave Paton, a writer for the *Virginian-Pilot/ Ledger Star,* also praised the novel, remarking that it is a "dense, well-wrought piece of serious fiction." And Evich of the *Patriot Ledger* noted that *Season's End* was "among the more powerful and provocative novels of recent years."

Grimes told *CA:* "I began writing fiction at age nineteen, but it wasn't really fiction. It was more like typed angst.

"In my twenties, I bounced around a bit. I worked as a waiter; worked in a fish-processing plant in Provincetown, Massachusetts; shaved my head, wore a diamond earring; and worked as a carpenter's apprentice. Then I returned to Manhattan and was lucky enough to find a job that taught me a lot about business. I eventually became general manager of the company, which made expensive, well-designed stationery.

"When I left in 1983 and began managing a retail business in Soho that sold expensive housewares (my education in wealth and social classes came through my jobs), I started to write seriously. I had mornings free and so wrote from ten till about one every day, six hours a day on weekends. It was then, while I was twenty-seven, that I wrote my first novel, *A Stone of the Heart.* I had been wrestling with it for years. Then, with a sudden and rare burst of determination, I finished it over a period of about four months. It was one of the few finalists for the 1984 PEN/Nelson Algren Award. And an editor at a trade house wanted to publish it, but the president of the company felt my next novel would be stronger. I was disappointed, but also already writing novel number two, a book called *Bones,*

which was about a mysterious virus that was fatal, and transmitted by information.

"Oddly, once I had the first book out of the way, work seemed to come pouring out. I wrote a few short stories that went on to be published in journals, a play, then started on *Bones.* I sent what I'd written of it off to that year's PEN/Algren competition, and to the editor who had liked my first book. She didn't like *Bones* at all. Crushed, I stopped the book in mid-sentence on page 230. A few months later, it was one of three finalists for another PEN/Algren Award, with a special note from the judges urging me to continue. At that young age, though, the least bit of discouragement can kill a work for a writer. I tried picking the book up, but could never regain the thread. It remains exactly where I left off in mid-sentence.

"I tried to write my way out of my disappointment. I began a book that seemed to be about baseball, though I had no clue why. I was simply searching for rhythms, trying to imitate F. Scott Fitzgerald's *The Great Gatsby,* and stumbled onto this particular voice. But after seventy-five pages, the work began falling apart. I put it away, then went on to yet another novel, *City of God,* which was about the end of the world. (I know, I have a light touch.) That was perhaps my most extreme vision—very dark, quite fantastic. Bits of sci-fi, World War II. It crashed and burned after three hundred pages. Or so I thought.

"At this point, my wife Jody and I left Manhattan and moved to Key West. I had published a few stories—I was thirty—but my work didn't seem to be coming together, despite writing for twenty-five hours a week, every week, for three years. In Key West I completed yet another novel shortly after arriving, a piece of work called *Notes from Downtown,* which was an updating of Fyodor Dostoyevsky's *Notes from Underground.* My version was a meditation on fame, told through the deranged perspective of an unpublished author living in downtown Manhattan in the mid-1980s. After completing that, I quit writing. Just quit. I waited tables, read.

"Then a lawyer friend got me involved with writing improbably bad screenplays for his production company. *Black Friday,* a biker movie that was never filmed, came out of the experience. Next came rewrites of a movie that was variously called *Sunstroke, American Heatwave,* and finally *Hot Splash,* the latest incarnation offered for viewing occasionally on the USA cable channel (though my name has graciously been removed from the credits, as requested.) After that, I wrote *Kiss of the Serpent,* also known as *Snake Island.* It was filmed on property owned by an old James Bond stuntperson, and the crew literally wrecked his house. I went back to waiting tables.

"I also began another play. It was about a naive, young literary writer who gets hustled into writing improbably bad screenplays by a slick lawyer. I'd get ten pages in, then stop. Every time a character with a conscience appeared, I'd come to an immediate roadblock. So the play sat there in the drawer, along with all the other unpublished, unfinished, unfathomable work.

"Then my father died.

"Now, *A Stone of the Heart* is a very autobiographical book. So much so that in the rush through galleys I added a page of new material and typed the name of the mother character in the book, whose name was Marie, as Lillian, which is my mother's name. When I returned from my father's funeral in New York, I drifted through time for a while. Then one day, I took the three hundred pages out of the drawer and began to read. Then edit. Then polish. When I was done I had a one-hundred-fifty page book.

"I had seen an article about a new house in New York called Four Walls Eight Windows. I thought they might like my *Notes from Downtown;* it seemed compatible with other things on their list. I sent the manuscript and received an encouraging note in return. But I couldn't revise the book, or expand it, or anything. I trimmed it to a novella and sent it to them, along with *A Stone of the Heart* and some other stories.

"I also decided that I couldn't wait tables any longer. My wife, disapproving of my plans to go to law school, suggested I apply to M.F.A. programs. I agreed, reluctantly. (Fear is a motivator, but it leads to no end of procrastination too.) I applied to Iowa and three other places—for some reason submitting the beginning of the baseball novel, even though I had other work which had been published, hence a better bet for being admitted to a program. Then I went back to waiting tables; also to scribbling the dialogue for the play I had begun on the back of guest checks and time cards while I was at work. Three months later, Frank Conroy called and told me to come finish the novel in Iowa. I finished the play first, leaving it behind with a local theater director.

"In late August of 1989 I began work on the baseball novel, the book that was to become *Season's End.* I wrote from three to six hours a day, seven days a week, until I ran out of gas, which happened about every eight weeks. The pace at which I was writing is, in retrospect, quite amazing to me. I imagine it had something to do with the book having been in the back of my mind for three years. Also something to do with the flood of adrenaline that being at a place like Iowa—where people actually talked about your work, about writing—brought on. I keep a log of hours worked when I write, this keeps me honest about putting the time in, and I was putting in nearly twenty-eight hours a week.

"By November I had the first half of the book finished. Two other interesting developments had also come along. Four Walls Eight Windows had decided to publish my first novel, *A Stone of the Heart,* on its own, not accompanied by any of the other material, and the play I had left with the Key West director was given a slot in his theater's upcoming season.

"After publication, *A Stone of the Heart* was included on the *New York Times*'s 'Summer Reading List.' It was also optioned for a movie version of the story, a script for which is currently in the works. From New York I went to Key West for the rehearsals and the opening of the play, which was now called *Spec.* The night before opening, I noticed someone familiar in the audience, though I couldn't place him. Then I remembered him from a Sam Shepard play I had seen in New York. I went over during intermission to tell him how much I had admired his work, and he told me he liked *Spec.* We agreed to have lunch, and at lunch he said he wanted to try to take *Spec* to Los Angeles. I said fine, but didn't really expect to ever hear from him again. But in October of that year, he called to say he wanted to option the play. We agreed on that, just as I was finishing, after fourteen months of work, *Season's End.*

"I had been given the opportunity to travel with the New York Mets during the spring in order to research *Season's End.* In 1990, I went to spring training, then on to New York with the team in June. I traveled with the Mets for several weeks. They were all very kind and very helpful. The technical information I picked up from them worked its way into the book; in other cases it simply confirmed what I hoped I was correct in imagining. Basically, what traveling with them did was remind me that baseball on television is not baseball. The game is quite beautiful. The players often practice ballet exercises, as that's the medium their movements most closely imitate. But it's really beautiful, especially in spring training when the game is being 'played.' At that time, with nothing on the line and the sun shining, it's possible to believe in God. That's why the game retains its power.

"Other than that, I read a lot of American novels written in the first person. Ralph Ellison said the hardest thing to do is write a good first-person novel. So I read, and taught, *Invisible Man, The Great Gatsby,* and other novels to help me along, technically. One other book that was important was *The Puritan Origin of the American Self* by Sacvan Bercovitch.

"*Season's End* was taken on by an agent and sold at auction in January of 1991. Five days later, I was told that *Spec* would open the MET Theatre in Los Angeles that May. I finished my stint at Iowa, revised the novel with my editor, then went to Los Angeles for rehearsals.

"The rehearsal stage of a play can be frustrating and maddening, but also exhilarating. After months of solitude at a desk, it's the perfect antidote to writing. Working with a cast and crew is great, and I revise throughout the rehearsal period, taking suggestions from actors whenever they seem appropriate.

"*Spec* opened and the usual Los Angeles scene of power lunches and breakfasts occurred. It's all terrific, as long as it's kept in perspective—mainly, don't expect anything to happen. I had one agency call after reading the *Los Angeles Times* review, saying they wanted to represent me. They hadn't seen the play, hadn't read *A Stone of the Heart,* didn't know the first thing about me. So why call? I was the new kid in town, for ten minutes. When my ten minutes was up, I went back to Iowa, back into my room, back to my blank pages.

"There is nothing more sobering in the craft of writing than confronting the blank page. Bad reviews make it worse, good reviews don't help. Nothing anyone has ever told you about your work does you any good when the sheet is empty and needs to be filled. You're on your own, alone. Except for two things—the work you've put behind you, good and bad; and the work you've read.

"In writing, no work is ever wasted. It all needs to be done. Writing is a very inefficient process. The good work comes out of the failed work. We simply distill what we have to say over a very long, often frustrating period of time. What sustains us? All of literature. That's behind each of us when we sit down and take on the blank page one more time. That and our own character. Frank Conroy told me once, 'Writing is more a test of character than of talent.' And over the long haul it is.

"I don't believe I have a necessarily 'characteristic' style, though people have told me when multiple qualifying clauses, dash marks, unending sentences, and the word zeitgeist start popping up, they know its me. But I try to allow the voice of the book dictate the style, and the voice in this new one is omniscient, and quite different from either *Season's End* or *A Stone of the Heart.*

"I generally begin a novel when I don't understand something consciously. If something—a voice, an image—is mysterious to me, and becomes more layered and mysterious as I begin to pursue what's behind it, then I know I've begun a novel. I believe we write in order to decode a part of the world for ourselves. So, the more resonant the mystery, the more range and thrust in the book. (Hopefully. Hopefully, one is not just incredibly stupid, something I always suspect in my case.)

"I tend not to conceptualize the form and shape of a book in advance. That's something I prefer to let emerge and define itself. If a book is any good, it usually demands its own shape and structure. The story will need to be told in a certain way, if you're to get the story and simply not the idea of the story. A reader, I believe, reacts to the design of a given book in a quieter, but almost deeper, way than to things like plot. There's a certain music each book must have, and that music is the book's structure. It's a synthesis of voice, which is the element that binds the world within the book, and dramatic action, its melodic system. A book is written in a certain key, with corresponding sharps and flats. So I begin to understand the music and structure of the book as I go. Discovering them is the same process as discovering the story as you go.

"I research my novels quite a bit, so I'm not reading fiction all that often, outside of what I teach. But when I do read contemporary writers, it's Don DeLillo, Thomas Pynchon, Thomas McGuane, Gabriel Garcia-Marquez, Salman Rushdie, Martin Amis, Robert Stone—guys (too many, I embarrassingly have to admit) with 'global,' rather hyperactive imaginations.

"My first reader is always my wife, Jody, who is quite astute and always (even when I hate to admit it) on the money about my work. Frank Conroy read all of *Season's End* as I was writing it. I'd give him big chunks, we'd talk, then I'd go back to the book. I think it would have been impossible to write without him. That's why I dedicated it to him. Otherwise, my agent reads my new book as it goes along.

"Who do I write for? I honestly don't know. I know I have one extremely sweet and dedicated fan living in New Rochelle, New York. He has all my work, even galleys that he found at the Strand, a bookstore in Manhattan, and sends them all to me for autographing. But outside of a few friends—some of whom are ex-students that I've come to be close with—I don't know. Italo Calvino talks of an 'imaginary bookshelf,' a place where you imagine your books fitting in among others you admire. I guess I write for that bookshelf—and to explain to myself what I don't understand. I guess I write to touch what is mysterious to me, and if I'm any good at it, others will find their way to it because it will have been mysterious to them as well.

"What do I hope to achieve through my work? I need my work to make the world comprehensible to me. I figure out the world, and myself, as I write. If I do it well enough, and am honest and compassionate enough in the work, then my work will find its way to others, and they in turn will take what they want or need from it and, in that it has informed their lives ever so slightly, pass that along to others—hopefully all for the better.

"As for my contemporaries: I admire any writer who sits down and tries to write a good and honest book. I wish more people would read them. And when you read your friends' work, write them and say, 'Thanks, bravo, good job.' There is no room in the writing life for jealousy. If we go forward, in terms of continuing to make literature, we go forward together.

"So now I'm facing blank pages again, mostly every day, in a room by myself—the same as any aspiring writer, to whom I offer the only word I can offer myself: Faith."

BIOGRAPHICAL/CRITICAL SOURCES:

BOOKS

Grimes, Tom, *Season's End,* Little, Brown, 1992.

PERIODICALS

Chicago Tribune, June 25, 1990, sec. 5, p. 3.
Flint Journal, May 3, 1992.
Los Angeles Times, May 17, 1991.
New York Times Book Review, May 20, 1990.
Patriot Ledger (Quincy, MA), April 17, 1992.
People, April 27, 1992.
Seattle Times/Seattle Post Intelligencer, April 12, 1992.
Virginian-Pilot/Ledger Star, April 26, 1992.
Wall Street Journal, July 11, 1990.

—Sketch by Mark F. Mikula

*   *   *

GROSS, David   1940-

PERSONAL: Born November 5, 1940, in Kankakee, IL. *Education:* St. Ambrose College, B.A., 1962; University of Wisconsin—Madison, M.A., 1964, Ph.D., 1969.

ADDRESSES: Home—Boulder, CO. *Office*—Department of History, Box 234, University of Colorado at Boulder, Boulder, CO 80309-0234.

CAREER: University of Wisconsin—Madison, instructor in history, 1968-69; University of Colorado at Boulder, assistant professor, 1969-73, associate professor, 1973-81, professor of history, 1981—. University of California, Irvine, visiting associate professor, 1979.

AWARDS, HONORS: Knapp grant for Germany, 1968; grant from American Philosophical Society, 1970; Jacob Van Ek Teaching Mentor Award, 1973; National Endowment for the Humanities, fellowship, 1974, grant, 1976-77; grant from Council on Research and Creative Work, 1985; Center for Theory in the Humanities fellow, 1985.

WRITINGS:

The Writer and Society: Heinrich Mann and Literary Politics in Germany, 1890-1940, Humanities, 1980.
The Past in Ruins: Tradition and the Critique of Modernity, University of Massachusetts Press, 1992.

Work represented in anthologies, including *Culture and Society in Twentieth Century Germany,* edited by Gary

Stark and Stanley Palmer, Texas A&M University Press, 1982; *Political Symbolism in Modern Europe: Essays in Honor of George L. Mosse,* edited by Seymour Drescher, David Sabean, and Allan Sharlin, Transaction Books, 1982; and *Race, Politics, and Culture: Critical Essays on the Radicalism of the 1960s,* edited by Adolph Reed, Jr., Greenwood Press, 1986. Contributor of about sixty articles and reviews to academic journals, including *Radical America, Humanities in Society, Minnesota Review, Science and Society, Continuum,* and *Journal of Contemporary History.* Associate editor, *Telos,* 1971—; contributing editor, *New German Critique,* 1973-76.

WORK IN PROGRESS: Remembering and Forgetting in Modern Culture.

*   *   *

GRUMBINE, R. Edward   1953-

PERSONAL: Born December 23, 1953, in Valdez, AK; son of Robert (a minister) and Fern Ray (a teacher) Grumbine. *Education:* Antioch College, B.A., 1976; University of Montana, M.S., 1982; Union Institute, Cincinnati, OH, Ph.D., 1991. *Politics:* "Green." *Religion:* "Earth-centered." *Avocational interests:* Walking, gardening, natural history, music, observing moonrises.

ADDRESSES: Home—1001 Smith Grade, Santa Cruz, CA 95060. *Office*—Sierra Institute, University of California Extension, 740 Front St., Suite 155, Santa Cruz, CA 95060.

CAREER: Antioch College, Yellow Springs, OH, instructor in environmental studies, 1975 and 1977; Evergreen State College, Olympia, WA, instructor in environmental studies, 1979; University of Montana, Missoula, administrative assistant at Wilderness Institute, 1979-80, instructor, 1981; University of California Extension, Santa Cruz, instructor in environmental studies and director of Sierra Institute, 1982—. U.S. Forest Service, research intern in fire ecology at Sequoia National Forest, 1974, fire fighter at Mount Baker-Snoqualmie National Forest, 1977; National Park Service, interpretive naturalist at Sitka National Historical Park, 1976, backcountry ranger at Olympic National Park, 1978, and North Cascades National Park, 1982. North Cascades Institute, member of advisory council, 1987—; Ecoforestry Institute, member of advisory council, 1991—.

MEMBER: International Society for Environmental Ethics, Society for Conservation Biology, Natural Areas Association, Fund for Wild Nature (president of board of directors, 1986—).

WRITINGS:

Ghost Bears: Exploring the Biodiversity Crisis, Island Press (Washington, DC), 1992.

Work represented in anthologies, including *Clearcut,* edited by B. Devall, Earth Island Press, 1992. Contributor of articles to periodicals, including *Forest Watch, Environmental Management, Natural Areas Journal, Conservation Biology, Earth First!,* and *High Country News.*

SIDELIGHTS: R. Edward Grumbine told *CA:* "I don't consider myself to be a writer by profession, though I have written for money and spend much of my time engaged in putting words on paper. Much of what I write is politically motivated by the ongoing destruction of Earth that can be summarized by the phrase 'environmental crisis.' If humans' relationship with the planet were more healthy, I would probably write less, garden more, and sleep peacefully at night.

"I write as an advocate, a teacher, and a lover of what [American author Henry David] Thoreau described as 'all things wild and free.' An advocate takes what he or she sees as a necessary stand; in my case, I'd like to contribute to a more sustainable lifeway in partnership with the ecosystems on which human life depends. A teacher loves to draw out learners so that they might challenge their most cherished ideas; almost all of my writing aims at respectful engagement, with education in mind. A lover of wildness wants to share the experiences that make clean air so special, clear water a joy to drink and swim in, and a long backpack hike a gate to mystery and understanding. At the close of the twentieth century, these experiences are increasingly hard to find. I have been exploring, through my writing, the many scientific, historical, philosophical, and practical reasons that make this true for citizens of industrial societies.

"Even as I grapple with untangling a subject so complex as the biodiversity crisis—the subject of my first book and much of my academic writing—I have found many pleasures. There is a great strength in the wild places that still remain: the fragments of old-growth forest, sections of undeveloped California coastline, the power and silence of high mountains, a town without homogeneous suburbs surrounding it, or a child who wants to learn about butterflies. The people who are working for a healthier world also give me strength, from tireless grassroots activists to congressional representatives working on environmental legislation in Washington, D.C. I have always felt the need to tell the positive stories that are part of working for social change.

"No single person is responsible for my interest in writing. In fact, my major literary influences are *places:* the blue and green islands of southeast Alaska where I grew up, the pastoral farm fields of central Maryland where I first learned about edible plants and forest succession, and the ice mountains of the Pacific Northwest where I began my apprenticeship to wildness. Certain forms of writing have also provided much freedom and information. Classic Chinese and Japanese 'nature' poetry has taught me the value of spareness in prose. Taxonomic keys from formal botany have helped me pursue logic and precision. Clouds have taught me about playfulness and change.

"It is an honor to write, to have something to share, and to have readers who want to engage your work."

*   *   *

GRUNDY, Pamela C. 1962-

PERSONAL: Born February 20, 1962, in Houston, TX; daughter of Scott M. (a professor of internal medicine) and Lois P. (a language therapist) Grundy. *Education:* Yale University, B.A., 1984; graduate study at University of North Carolina at Chapel Hill, 1988—.

ADDRESSES: Home—Campus Box 3195, Hamilton Hall, University of North Carolina at Chapel Hill, Chapel Hill, NC 27599.

CAREER: Star, Anniston, AL, reporter, 1986-87; Museum of the New South, Charlotte, NC, guest curator, 1992—.

WRITINGS:

You Always Think of Home: A Portrait of Clay County, Alabama, University of Georgia Press, 1992.

WORK IN PROGRESS: Researching the history of high school football in Clay County, Alabama, and the history of community basketball in Charlotte, North Carolina, and the central Piedmont.

*   *   *

GUBERNICK, Lisa Rebecca 1955-

PERSONAL: Born June 28, 1955, in Los Angeles, CA; daughter of Reuben and Grace (Israel) Gubernick; married Paul Fishleder, September 18, 1983. *Education:* Received B.A. from Bryn Mawr College.

ADDRESSES: Office—Forbes, 60 Fifth Ave., New York, NY 10011.

CAREER: Forbes, New York City, senior editor, 1989—; writer.

WRITINGS:

Squandered Fortune: The Life and Times of Huntington Hartford, Putnam, 1991.

WORK IN PROGRESS: Get Hot or Go Home: Trisha Yearwood, The Making of a Nashville Star.

SIDELIGHTS: Lisa Rebecca Gubernick is a senior editor for the business magazine *Forbes,* for which she has written on subjects ranging from the motion-picture industry to perfume manufacturers. In 1991 she saw publication of *Squandered Fortune: The Life and Times of Huntington Hartford,* which relates the dramatic life of the heir to the Great Atlantic and Pacific Tea Company (which became the A & P grocery chain). She reports that Hartford was dismissed from the family business in 1934 after he attended a college football game instead of reporting for work. This dismissal, in turn, left the wealthy Hartford to prove his own business acumen. But in the ensuing years he managed only a series of bad ventures and several disastrous investments. During one seven-year period, he reduced his fortune from thirty million dollars to less than two million. His personal life was also trying. He married four times and fathered four children, including one with a mistress who later killed herself. The child from that union also committed suicide. When Gubernick visited Hartford in 1989, she found him destitute and in squalor. In his *New York Times Book Review* assessment of *Squandered Fortune,* Michael Lewis commented that Gubernick "writes well and handles her subject with the touch of a natural storyteller." And *Publishers Weekly* contributor Genevieve Stuttaford called *Squandered Fortune* "a comprehensive, irresistible albeit disturbing biography."

BIOGRAPHICAL/CRITICAL SOURCES:

PERIODICALS

Los Angeles Times Book Review, January 13, 1991, p. 6.
New York Times Book Review, February 3, 1991, p. 12.
Publishers Weekly, November 23, 1990, p. 52.
Tribune Books (Chicago), February 24, 1991, p. 5.
Wall Street Journal, January 2, 1991, p. A5.
Washington Post, December 26, 1990, p. C2.*

*   *   *

GUNNING, Sally (Carlson) 1951-

PERSONAL: Born February 14, 1951, in Quincy, MA; daughter of Leonard (an administrator) and Nancy (a homemaker; maiden name, Abbott) Carlson; married Thomas M. Gunning (a clinical social worker), September 13, 1975. *Education:* University of Rhode Island, B.A., 1973.

ADDRESSES: Home—Brewster, MA. *Agent*—Andrea Cirillo, Jane Rotrosen Agency, 318 East Fifty-first St., New York, NY 10022.

CAREER: Writer. Worked as a museum tour guide, 1969-72, a cruise ship stewardess, 1973, and a bank accountant, 1974-79; office manager for a general practitioner, 1979—.

MEMBER: Mystery Writers of America (member of board of directors), Sisters in Crime.

WRITINGS:

MYSTERY NOVELS; "PETER BARTHOLOMEW" SERIES

Hot Water, Pocket Books, 1990.
Under Water, Pocket Books, 1992.
Ice Water, Pocket Books, 1993.
Troubled Water, Pocket Books, 1993.

OTHER

Contributor of the story "Water" to the *Malice Domestic* anthology and of the story "Wiggins Wags His Tale" to *Armchair Detective.*

WORK IN PROGRESS: The fifth Peter Bartholomew mystery, featuring a death on a whale-watching cruise, publication expected in 1994; the sixth Peter Bartholomew mystery, publication expected in 1995.

SIDELIGHTS: Sally Gunning told *CA:* "I live on Cape Cod, where my family's roots go back many generations. The Peter Bartholomew mystery series is set on the fictional island of Nashtoba, a mix of Cape Cod past and present. The series features Peter Bartholomew, owner of an odd-job company called Factotum, who can't quite bring himself to avoid dead bodies (or his ex-wife)."

BIOGRAPHICAL/CRITICAL SOURCES:

PERIODICALS

Cape Cod Times, December 20, 1992.

*   *   *

GUREVICH, David 1951-

PERSONAL: Born August 19, 1951, in Kharkov, Ukrainian Soviet Socialist Republic (now part of Commonwealth of Independent States); immigrated to the United States, 1976; naturalized citizen; son of Lev (in the military) and Gisya (a doctor; maiden name, Khaikin) Gurevich; married; wife's name, Natasha (marriage ended); children: Ilya (son). *Education:* Moscow Institute of Foreign Languages, B.A., 1973; Columbia University, M.F.A., 1991.

ADDRESSES: Home—175 West 73rd St., No. 6A, New York, NY 10023.

CAREER: Writer, interpreter, and free-lance book reviewer. Commentator for National Public Radio, 1991-92.

WRITINGS:

UNPUBLISHED PLAYS

Bargain Basement, performed as a staged reading in New York City at New York University, 1982.
Halfway House, performed as a staged reading in New York City at Playwrights Horizons, 1982.

BOOKS

Travels with Dubinsky and Clive (novel), Viking, 1987.
From Lenin to Lennon: A Memoir of Russia in the Sixties (autobiography), Harcourt, 1991.
(Translator from Russian) Vladimir Solovyov and Elena Klepikova, *Yeltsin: A Political Biography,* Putnam, 1992.

OTHER

Contributor to periodicals, including *American Spectator, Vox,* and *Avenue.*

WORK IN PROGRESS: Yankee, Go Home, a novel.

SIDELIGHTS: Jewish-Ukrainian author David Gurevich has received critical recognition for his writings, including *Travels with Dubinsky and Clive* and *From Lenin to Lennon: A Memoir of Russia in the Sixties.* Both books depict their protagonists' lives before and after emigrating from the communist Soviet Union to the democratic United States of America.

In the comic novel *Travels with Dubinsky and Clive,* Oleg Dubinsky, a Russian Jew, obtains a respectable position in the Soviet State Department despite widespread anti-Semitism in his country. He works in the African People's Republic of Pizdo affairs department until he is dismissed following an American takeover of Pizdo. Thereafter, he indulges in a gluttonous lifestyle, and soon his friends suggest that he defect to the United States. Taking their advice, he concocts an incredible scheme to secure him passage overseas without Soviet officials suspecting his subversive intentions. Later Dubinsky's friend, Clive, joins him in America, and the two men become embroiled in a commodities scam—fixing prices on the goods entering Pizdo, the same African republic with which Dubinsky worked in Moscow. With the money, the former Muscovites delve into drinking and debauchery. But the conspiracy does not last long. A Pizdoan official is caught facilitating the illegal activity, and to protect himself, he exposes Clive as the mastermind behind the project. Clive is arrested and jailed. Finding himself on his own, Dubinsky moves to Seattle and settles down with a woman that he meets at a bank. Gurevich's first novel elicited praise from many critics. A *Publisher's Weekly* reviewer called it "a brilliant spoof." And *New York Times Book Review* contributor Josh Greenfeld commented: "We need good comic novelists too, and in his debut the Russian-born David Gurevich shows great promise." He concluded, "I look forward to . . . Gurevich's next effort."

Gurevich's following achievement was *From Lenin to Lennon,* an account of the author's real-life experiences in the Soviet Union and later in America. In the book he states that he was raised in a small, decrepit town called Syzran, situated on the right bank of the Volga River. At the town school, Gurevich was taught politics at an early age. He explains that before reaching their teens, the students would often decide whether they wanted to be leaders or followers in the Russian regime. Not concerned with engaging in either role for his country, Gurevich partook in illicit and unhealthy activities. He drank often and read books that were banned from society by the government. These writings included Alexander Isayevich Solzhenitsyn's *Gulag Archipelago,* George Orwell's *Nineteen Eighty-Four,* and J. D. Salinger's *Catcher in the Rye.* In a *New York Times Book Review* article, Gurevich writes, "I could not haul books from the library fast enough—thrillers, sci-fi, adventures—anything that took place in another time and place." He also listened to albums and watched movies from America that were outlawed in Russia. After being exposed to Western entertainment, Gurevich opines in his autobiography, "it was easy to accept the reality of convertibles and swimming pools and other signs of economic prosperity; it was so much harder to accept the reality of so much freedom."

As outlined in *From Lenin to Lennon,* Gurevich continued to engage in underground activities throughout his college career. However, due to a lack of privacy, the author found it difficult to elude the informants who were rampant on campus. He also maintains that while attending Moscow Institute of Foreign Languages, he was exposed to Jewish discrimination and Russia's pursuit for military secrecy. After graduating from the institute in 1973, he worked as a translator. Three years later, under a Jewish quota, Gurevich was granted permission to leave his country; he chose to move to America. Not only was he leaving his homeland, but he was separating himself from a failed marriage and a young son. However, in his new home Gurevich experienced the freedom that he states in his book is "worth all the stumbling on your way to it." He compares the differences and similarities between Soviet and American life, and concludes his memoir by examining what he considers to be a bleak state of affairs in 1989 Russia. Cathy Young, a *Washington Post Book World* contributor, described *From Lenin to Lennon* as "highly entertaining, engaging, [and] thoughtful." Writing in *New York Times Book Review,* Terry Teachout reported that Gurevich's "dryly witty account of everyday life in the workers' paradise is one of the most revealing books ever written about the Soviet Union."

After the publication of his life story, Gurevich translated from Russian a biography about the president of the Russian Federation, Boris Yeltsin. This volume, titled *Yeltsin: A Political Biography,* was lauded by *Los Angeles Times Book Review*'s Martin Walker as "a splendid read." A reviewer for *Publishers Weekly* called the book a "vigorous, smoothly translated biography."

BIOGRAPHICAL/CRITICAL SOURCES:

BOOKS

Gurevich, David, *From Lenin to Lennon: A Memoir of Russia in the Sixties,* Harcourt, 1991.

PERIODICALS

Los Angeles Times Book Review, March 22, 1992, pp. 3, 9.
New York Times Book Review, October 25, 1987, p. 24; March 11, 1990; June 2, 1991, p. 9.
Publishers Weekly, May 22, 1987, p. 68; February 24, 1992, p. 41.
Washington Post Book World, June 16, 1991.

—*Sketch by Jane M. Kelly*

*   *   *

GYOHTEN, Toyoo 1931-

PERSONAL: Born January 2, 1931, in Yokohama, Japan; son of Ryoichi and Toshiko Gyohten; married Reiko Tauchi, April 13, 1958; children Kazuo (son), Keiko (daughter). *Education:* Tokyo University, B.A., 1955; attended Princeton University, 1956-58. *Avocational interests:* Pastel drawing, writing traditional Japanese poems.

ADDRESSES: Home—1-33-24 Sakuragaoka, Hodogaya-ku, Yokohama-shi, Kanagawa 240, Japan. *Office*—3-2 Nihombashi Hongokucho 1-chome, Chuo-ku, Tokyo 103, Japan.

CAREER: Ministry of Finance, Tokyo, Japan, worked in tax bureau, beginning in 1955; International Monetary Fund, Washington, DC, trainee, 1960-61, worked at Japan desk, 1964-66; Morioka Tax Office, Iwate, Japan, director, 1962-63; Asian Development Bank, Manila, Philippines, special assistant to the president, 1966-69; Tokyo International Airport, customs commissioner, 1972-73; Ministry of Finance, Tokyo, director of public loan and investment department, finance bureau, 1975-77, deputy director general of international finance bureau, 1980-83, deputy director general of banking bureau, 1983-84, director general of international finance bureau, 1984-86, vice minister of finance for international affairs, 1986-89, special adviser, 1989-90; Bank of Tokyo, Tokyo, adviser to board of directors, 1991, chair of board of direc-

tors, 1992—. Visiting professor at Harvard University, 1990, Princeton University, 1990-91, and University of St. Gallen, 1991. Member of various advisory groups, committees, and commissions.

WRITINGS:

(With Paul Volcker) *Changing Fortunes: The World's Money and the Threat to American Leadership,* Times Books, 1992.
(Editor with Makoto Kuroda) *One Hundred Key Words to Understand U.S.-Japan Economic Relations,* Yuhikaku, 1992.
Nihon Keizai no Shiza, Kappa Books, 1993.

SIDELIGHTS: After a long career in Japan's Ministry of Finance, Toyoo Gyohten collaborated with former U.S. Federal Reserve chair Paul Volcker to write *Changing Fortunes: The World's Money and the Threat to American Leadership.* Published in 1992, the book chronicles the changes in the international monetary system that have occurred since the 1950s, when the U.S. was an economic mentor to Japan, which was rebuilding after the destruction of World War II. Since then, the U.S. economy, while still powerful on a global scale, has grown relatively weaker while the phenomenal growth of Japan's economy has made the country a major international power. "Clearly, Japan is having as much trouble defining and accepting a larger global role as the U.S. has in acknowledging it is already playing a lesser one," commented Hobart Rowen in *Washington Post Book World.* "What emerges from this engaging book is that even Volcker and Gyohten, dedicated to preserving the alliance, don't know how to take the next necessary step."

Changing Fortunes, which consists of alternating chapters by Gyohten and Volcker adapted from seminar lectures they gave at Princeton University, was praised by critics as an accessible, informative volume. *New York Times Book Review* contributor Benjamin J. Cohen observed that "the book may be read at several levels: as personal memoir, as institutional history and as policy analysis." Though disappointed with the authors' policy analysis, Cohen noted that the book is successful as institutional history and that "each of the authors has fascinating inside stories to tell that are by turns amusing and hairraising." Rowen wrote in *Washington Post Book World,* "Replete with anecdotes and revealing insights into what motivates presidents and prime ministers when they must make momentous economic decisions, [Gyohten and Volcker's] book will be a gold mine for future historians."

BIOGRAPHICAL/CRITICAL SOURCES:

PERIODICALS

Economist, August 15, 1992, p. 78.
New York Times Book Review, June 7, 1992, p. 3.

Wall Street Journal, June 23, 1992, p. A18.
Washington Post Book World, July 19, 1992, pp. 4-5.

H

HAGEMAN, Howard G(arberich) 1921-1992

OBITUARY NOTICE—See index for *CA* sketch: Born April 19, 1921, in Lynn, MA; died of esophageal cancer, December 20, 1992, in Albany, NY. Minister, educator, and author. Hageman became a leading member of the Reformed Church in America, serving terms both as vice president and president of the church's general synod in the late 1950s. He began his ministry in 1945 with a twenty-five year stay at a parish in Newark, New Jersey. In 1973 he became president of the New Brunswick Seminary, where he served until retiring in 1985. In addition to his clerical work, Hageman contributed to Dutch-American relations as a founder of the Friends of New Netherlands, a translation society, and was named a Knight Commander of the Netherlands' Order of Orange-Nassau. Among Hageman's writings are the books *Lily among the Thorns, We Call This Friday Good, That the World May Know, Celebrating the Word, Two Centuries Plus,* and *Reformed Spirituality.* He also wrote a column for the *Church Herald.*

OBITUARIES AND OTHER SOURCES:

BOOKS

Who's Who in Religion, 4th edition, Marquis, 1992.

PERIODICALS

New York Times, December 24, 1992, p. B6.

* * *

HAILEY, Oliver 1932-1993

OBITUARY NOTICE—See index for *CA* sketch: Born July 7, 1932, in Pampa, TX; died of liver cancer, January 23, 1993, in Studio City (one source says Los Angeles),

CA. Television executive, journalist, screenwriter, and playwright. Hailey, an accomplished regional playwright, worked as a reporter for the *Dallas Morning News* from 1957 to 1959, then devoted himself full-time to writing for the stage and television. A graduate of the Yale School of Drama, Hailey cast a comic spin on life's realities in plays like *Hey You, Light Man,* the autobiographical *Who's Happy Now,* and *Father's Day.* In the early seventies, Hailey moved into television, writing for such series as *McMillan and Wife* and *Mary Hartman, Mary Hartman.* His screenplay for the 1981 television movie *Sidney Shorr,* on which the show *Love, Sidney* was based, earned him an Emmy nomination and a Writers Guild award. Hailey also served as a creative consultant for *Mary Hartman, Mary Hartman* and coproducer for the CBS series *Another Day.* Hailey was also the author of the movie screenplay *Just You and Me Kid* and contributed to the nonfiction works *Three Plays from the Yale School of Drama* and *New Theatre for Now.*

OBITUARIES AND OTHER SOURCES:

BOOKS

Who's Who in Entertainment, Marquis, 1992.
The Writers Directory: 1992-1994, St. James Press, 1992.

PERIODICALS

Los Angeles Times, January 25, 1993, p. A20.
New York Times, January 24, 1993, p. 34; January 25, 1993, p. B7.
Washington Post, January 26, 1993, p. D8.

* * *

HALE, Douglas 1929-

PERSONAL: Born October 2, 1929, in Jacksonville, TX; son of Douglas D., Sr. (an oil field worker), and Effie (a homemaker; maiden name, Musselwhite) Hale; married Betty Bishop, June 6, 1955 (divorced July 24, 1974); married Lou Moore (a sculptor), June 8, 1985; children: Charles Steven, Ellen Douglas. *Education:* Rice University, B.A., 1952; University of Missouri—Columbia, M.A., 1957; University of Texas at Austin, Ph.D., 1961. *Politics:* Democrat. *Religion:* Protestant. *Avocational interests:* Running, bicycling, hiking, music.

ADDRESSES: Home and office—P.O. Box 1051, Stillwater, OK 74076.

CAREER: University of North Carolina at Chapel Hill, assistant professor of history, 1961-63; Oklahoma State University, Stillwater, professor of history, 1963-82. *Military service:* U.S. Army, Counter Intelligence Corps, 1953-56; became sergeant.

AWARDS, HONORS: Grant from Swedish Cultural Foundation, 1952; Fulbright fellow, 1959; grant from American Philosophical Society, 1969.

WRITINGS:

The Germans from Russia in Oklahoma, University of Oklahoma Press, 1980.
The Third Texas Cavalry in the Civil War, University of Oklahoma Press, 1993.

Work represented in anthologies, including *Oklahoma: New Views of the Forty-Sixth State,* University of Oklahoma Press, 1982.

WORK IN PROGRESS: Wanderers between Two Worlds: German Revolutionaries in the American West, completion expected in 1994.

SIDELIGHTS: Douglas Hale told *CA:* "History ought to have a wider readership because it is an ennobling discipline. In at least five ways, it provides a practical, utilitarian approach to the pursuit of a purposeful life of fulfillment. In the first place, it places the cultural monuments of civilization in a context that permits us to enjoy them more. History gives us a perspective by which we may distinguish the ephemeral and transitory from the significant and abiding manifestations of any age. Through history, we learn to be more critical of ourselves and more tolerant of the feeble efforts of other generations to master their problems. In its pageant of tragedy, nobility, folly, and comedy, history provides first-rate entertainment. Finally, history is in large part the story of ourselves; we achieve self-knowledge from its study.

"By inclination and training, therefore, I attempt to combine in my writing new techniques of historical inquiry with an accessible and lively style of narrative, in order to bring serious themes and issues to the attention of a broad, non-professional audience. I have avoided narrow specialization in my work, but I range over a wide spectrum of interests. I have explored topics in modern German history, the history of the American West, immigration history, and the Civil War. In my research and writing, I am drawn to those topics which have hitherto been ignored or neglected, yet which involve significant historical developments and dramatic experiences by interesting men and women. I expend every effort to achieve accuracy in my research and eschew speculation and conjecture in what I write. I believe, furthermore, that it is the historian's responsibility to render judgment on the past, and I attempt to tell my story in clear, coherent prose that the intelligent adult reader can understand."

*　　*　　*

HALL, Blaine H(ill)   1932-

PERSONAL: Born December 12, 1932, in Wellsville, UT; son of James O. (a farmer) and Agnes Effie (an army depot worker; maiden name, Hill) Hall; married Carol Blanche Stokes (a teacher), June 5, 1959; children: Suzanne Hall Wilson, Cheryl, Derek Blaine. *Education:* Attended Utah State University, 1951-52, 1955; Brigham Young University, B.A., 1960, M.A., 1965, M.L.S., 1971. *Religion:* Church of Jesus Christ of Latter-day Saints.

ADDRESSES: Home—230 East 1910 S., Orem, UT 84058. *Office*—5220 HBLL, Brigham Young University, Provo, UT 84602.

CAREER: High school English teacher in Clearfield, UT, 1960-61; Brigham Young University, Provo, UT, instructor in English, 1963-72, senior English and American literature librarian at Harold B. Lee Library, 1972—. Utah advisory committee on library and information services, chairperson, 1983-90; Utah Governor's Conference on Library and Information Services, official delegate, 1991; Utah State Library, member of bibliographic access and resource-sharing committee; Orem Public Library, member of board of trustees, 1977-84; member of Orem Media Review Commission, 1984-86; member of Freedom to Read Foundation.

MEMBER: American Library Association (member of council, Utah chapter, 1988-92), Association of College and Research Libraries, Mountain Plains Library Association (member of executive board, 1978-83), Utah Library Association (president, 1980-81; managing editor, 1986-88; chairperson of committees on intellectual freedom, publications, public relations, and bylaws), Utah Academy of Sciences, Arts, and Letters, Phi Kappa Phi.

AWARDS, HONORS: Periodical Award, American Library Association, 1976, for *Utah Libraries;* Mountain Plains Library Association grants, 1979, 1988, Distinguished Service Award, 1991; Distinguished Service

Award, Utah Library Association, 1989; Marcia and Louis Posner Bibliography Award, Association of Jewish Libraries, 1992, for *Jewish American Fiction Writers.*

WRITINGS:

(With Charles Bradshaw and Marvin Wiggins) *Using the Library: The Card Catalog,* Brigham Young University Press, 1971.

Collection Assessment Manual for College and University Libraries, Oryx, 1985.

(With Gloria Cronin) *Saul Bellow: An Annotated Bibliography,* 2nd edition, Garland Publishing, 1987.

(With Cronin) *Jerzy Kosinski: An Annotated Bibliography,* Greenwood Press, 1991.

(With Cronin and Connie Lamb) *Jewish American Fiction Writers: An Annotated Bibliography,* Garland Publishing, 1991.

Work represented in anthologies, including *Saul Bellow and the Struggle at the Center,* edited by Eugene Hollahan, Greenwood Press, 1992. Contributor of more than seventy articles and reviews to library journals and other magazines, including *Saul Bellow Journal* and *Horsefeathers.* Editor, *Utah Libraries,* 1972-77, and *MPLA Newsletter,* 1978-83.

* * *

HALL, David C. 1943-

PERSONAL: Born May 27, 1943, in Madison, WI; son of Herbert Warren (a journalist) and Eileen (a department store sales clerk; maiden name, Sylvester) Hall. *Politics:* "Left." *Religion:* None. *Avocational interests:* Movies, wine, politics.

ADDRESSES: Home—Avenida Virgen de Montserrat 18, Sant Cugat del Valles, 08190 Barcelona, Spain.

CAREER: Self-employed English teacher in Barcelona, Spain, 1974-75; Summit School of English, Barcelona, teacher, 1975-79; English Three, Barcelona, teacher, 1980—; writer. Worked variously as a janitor, laborer in a frozen food plant, mail handler, forest service crew member, farm laborer, cook, bartender, library clerk, railroad clerk, and book warehouse clerk.

MEMBER: Spanish Crime Writers Association (member of governing committee), Comisiones Obreras (trade union).

AWARDS, HONORS: Winner of Semana Negra short story competition, 1991.

WRITINGS:

CRIME NOVELS

Cuatro dias (title means "Four Days"), Editorial Planeta, 1984.

No quiero hablar de Bolivia (title means "The Real Thing"), Ediciones Jucar, 1988.

Billete de vuelta, Ediciones B, 1990, translation published as *Return Trip Ticket,* St. Martin's, 1992.

Work represented in books, including *Negro como la noche,* Ediciones Jucar, 1991. Contributor of stories and reviews to magazines in Spain and the United States, including *Ellery Queen's Mystery Magazine.*

WORK IN PROGRESS: "A novel about a poet writing an apocalypse in post-nuclear-war Europe, a sort of black comedy."

SIDELIGHTS: David C. Hall told *CA:* "Like a lot of people, I started writing fiction before I had finished high school. I thought I was pretty good, and more or less assumed that I would be a published, professional writer at least by the age of twenty-five. That didn't happen. In the course of a rather vagrant existence, I left manuscripts in suitcases and boxes in a variety of places across the United States. I don't know whatever happened to all that stuff, but I hope that, in time, it has been reasonably disposed of.

"At thirty I came to Europe with not much money and no very clear idea of what I was intending to do. For a person who has always felt a bit out of place, there is perhaps nothing better than being a foreigner; the out of place feeling is both inevitable and obvious, and so ceases to be very important. As I was approaching forty, I came to the conclusion that it was time to publish something or forget it. Over the years I had read quite a number of crime novels without thinking much about them. I decided to try to write one myself. Barcelona, where I had then been living for seven or eight years, seemed like a good setting—both romantic and sinister.

"In July of that year, big forest fires broke out in the hills near the city; smoke clouds could be seen from the city center and sickening bits of ash fell in the streets. Newspaper accounts suggested arson, carried stories of two or three cars racing around the hills, men seen setting fires, empty gas cans found; but after a few days the official line was that the fires had been started accidentally. I had once worked for a few months for the U.S. Forest Service, so I knew a little about forest fires. I had a starting place for a story.

"Since I had always been a slow, hesitant writer, much given to rewriting, starting over again, and giving up, what I was most concerned with was just getting enough pages written before I got bogged down. I was determined, on vacation in the month of August, to write a minimum of five pages a day, moving forward no matter what, with the idea that, at the end of the month, I would have 150 pages and would have gone too far to turn back. I could rewrite later. That is more or less the way it happened. I have never been able to write a book straight out like that again, but I suspect that if I had not done the first book that way, I would not have been able to do any of the others."

* * *

HALL, David Locke 1955-

PERSONAL: Born August 28, 1955, in San Francisco, CA; son of Richard E. and Patricia (Meek) Hall; married Jennifer Krendel; children: Elizabeth, Richard, Rebecca. *Education:* Dartmouth College, A.B., 1978; Yale University, M.P.P.M., 1982; University of Pennsylvania, M.A., J.D., 1985.

ADDRESSES: *Agent*—c/o Westview Press, Inc., 5500 Central Ave., Boulder, CO 80301.

CAREER: Department of Justice, Philadelphia, PA, assistant U.S. attorney. *Military service:* U.S. Naval Reserve, intelligence officer.

WRITINGS:

The Reagan Wars: A Constitutional Perspective on War Powers and the Presidency, Westview, 1991.

Contributor to law and political studies journals and to *Naval War College Review.*

* * *

HALLIDAY, Nigel Vaux 1956-

PERSONAL: Born October 11, 1956, in Bexley, Kent, England; son of Bill Halliday (a bank manager) and Yvette (Noakes) Halliday (a homemaker); married Susan Vaux (a lecturer), April 12, 1980; children: Daniel, Emily, Joel. *Education:* Emmanuel College, Cambridge, B.A. (with honors), 1978; Courtauld Institute of Art, London, M.A., 1979, Ph.D., 1987. *Politics:* Liberal Democrat. *Religion:* Evangelical Christian.

ADDRESSES: *Home*—71 Marksbury Ave., Kew, Surrey TW9 4JE, England.

CAREER: Full-time father; writer. Pastor of independent Baptist church; elected local councillor.

WRITINGS:

More Than a Bookshop: Zwemmers and Art in the Twentieth Century, Philip Wilson Publishers Ltd., 1991.

HALTER, Marek 1936-

PERSONAL: Born January 27, 1936, in Warsaw, Poland; immigrated to France, 1950; son of Salomon (a printer) and Perl (a poet) Halter; married; wife's name, Clara. *Education:* Attended L'Ecole des Beaux-Arts in Paris, France. *Religion:* Jewish.

ADDRESSES: *Home*—Paris, France. *Office*—c/o Foundation Europeene des Sciences, Arts et Culture, 19 rue de Pris. Wilson, Paris F-75016, France.

CAREER: Artist, human rights activist, editor, and author. Worked as a mime for two years in Paris, France; paintings shown in exhibitions in locations including Buenos Aires, Argentina, Tel Aviv, Israel, and New York City. Involved for many years in informal peace negotiations between the Palestinians and Israel; involved in human rights protests including one criticizing the Soviet Union's invasion of Afghanistan. Founding editor of *Elements,* a magazine about the possibilities of peace in the Middle East.

WRITINGS:

Le fou et les rois (autobiography), A. Michel, c. 1976, translation by Lowell Bair published as *The Jester and the Kings: A Political Autobiography,* Little, Brown, 1989.
La vie incertaine de Marco Mahler (title means "The Uncertain Life of Marco Mahler"), A. Michel, c. 1979.
Le memoire d'Abraham, R. Laffont, c. 1983, translation by Bair published as *The Book of Abraham,* Holt, 1986.
The Children of Abraham, translation by Bair, Arcade, 1990.
Un homme, un cri (title means "One Man, One Cry"), R. Laffont, 1991.

ILLUSTRATOR

Edgar Morin, *Mais,* Nouvelles Editions Oswald, c. 1978.

SIDELIGHTS: Artist and human rights activist Marek Halter had already made a name for himself as a painter, showing his work in several different countries around the world, when he began his writing career with the autobiography *The Jester and the Kings,* which was published in his adopted home country of France in the late 1970s. But this work was not translated and published in the United States until after his novel, *The Book of Abraham,* made its debut in that country in 1986 and was lavishly praised by reviewers. *The Book of Abraham* traced a single Jewish family over two millennia and was often compared to Alex Haley's classic of black literature, *Roots,* and to the works of James Michener. Halter has penned other novels as well, including a 1990 sequel to *The Book of Abraham* entitled *The Children of Abraham.*

Halter was born in 1936 in Warsaw, Poland. He spent his early childhood in the Jewish ghetto there, but he and his family—a long line of printers and publishers—escaped the Holocaust as they were helped to flee before the Nazis occupied the area. Halter grew up in the Soviet Union and Poland, entertaining his friends by telling stories for them, until he and his family were allowed to immigrate to France in 1950. It took him a while to learn French, but as revealed in a *Publishers Weekly* interview with Shirley Ann Grau, "he got a job in pantomime and spent two years with make-up on his face and not much need to use words." But already he had decided to become an artist, and he enrolled in the L'Ecole des Beaux-Arts in Paris.

Halter was successful as an artist, showing his paintings in exotic locations such as Tel Aviv, Israel, Buenos Aires, Argentina, and New York City, but beginning in the late 1960s he began devoting much of his time to working on the possibilities of peace in the Middle East. After the 1967 Arab-Israeli war, he and his wife began discussing peace with other French intellectuals, and, as Grau notes, "they knocked on doors in Cairo [Egypt] as well as Jerusalem [Israel], bringing Arabs and Jews together to talk about their differences." Halter's experiences in this effort are recorded in detail in his book, *The Jester and the Kings,* and reviewers Roger Friedland and Richard Hecht in the *Los Angeles Times Book Review* explained that "Halter's account makes sad reading, for it reveals just how much the situation has changed" since the late 1960s and 1970s "and how the premises that might have brought peace even a decade ago no longer seem to have the capacity to persuade."

The Book of Abraham, Halter's most noteworthy work of fiction, was published in France during the early 1980s. He had worked on it for several years, researching his own family history, which he managed to trace back past the advent of Johann Gutenberg's printing press in the fifteenth century. He based the latter part of the novel on this family history, and for the earlier portion of the book—which begins in Jerusalem, A.D. 70—Halter used historical facts to construct a plausible past for the family it chronicles. Thus, *The Book of Abraham* traces a history of Jewish persecution, migration, and survival that spans two millennia. Some critics felt that the huge scope of the book made it impossible for Halter to develop his characters fully; Lothar Kahn in *World Literature Today,* for instance, lamented that "no sooner do we become intrigued with any one of the many Abrahams, Itzhaks and Josephs who populate the novel than he dies and we rush on to another locale, another historical episode, another birth and another death." Kahn admitted, nevertheless, that in spite of this, *The Book of Abraham* is "surprisingly good." Fellow historical novelist Irving Stone, reviewing *The Book of Abraham* in the *Los Angeles Times Book Review,* had

much more glowing praise for Halter, declaring that "the novel is so entirely credible and moving that the reader comes out at the end of the 700-page epoch feeling that he may have encountered a classic in the tradition of [Leo] Tolstoy's *War and Peace* or Halidor Laxness' *Independent People.*" Frederic Morton in the *New York Times Book Review* called the work "spectacular," and noted that "the author's ethical instincts help unify the book, drawing together parts that in the hands of another writer would be disparate. . . . Only an imagination as learned, as indomitable as Mr. Halter's could have even conceived *The Book of Abraham.*"

In 1990, Halter published a sequel to *The Book of Abraham* entitled *The Children of Abraham.* Again based on the lineage of his own family, this book has a much smaller scope, beginning in the 1960s and ending in the 1980s. Reviewers categorize the novel as a thriller, because it concerns the murder of one of Halter's cousins near Jerusalem in 1961. Halter's relatives from all over the world feature as characters, "showing up in the most exciting places," according to a *Los Angeles Times Book Review* critic.

BIOGRAPHICAL/CRITICAL SOURCES:

BOOKS

Halter, Marek, *The Jester and the Kings: A Political Autobiography,* Little, Brown, 1989.

PERIODICALS

Chicago Tribune, April 20, section 14, p. 41.
Los Angeles Times Book Review, April 13, 1986, pp. 1, 7; September 3, 1989, pp. 2, 10; December 23, 1990.
New York Times, April 3, 1986; December 27, 1990.
New York Times Book Review, April 6, 1986, p. 9.
Publishers Weekly, April 4, 1986, pp. 46-47.
Time, May 5, 1986, pp. 74-75.
Washington Post Book World, April 6, 1986, pp. 4-5.
World Literature Today, Spring, 1984, pp. 233-34.*

—*Sketch by Elizabeth Wenning*

*   *   *

HAMMOND, Herb(ert L.) 1945-

PERSONAL: Born January 5, 1945, in Medford, OR; son of Herb and Helen (Miller) Hammond; married Susan Amen (an administrator), December 27, 1967; children: Jody Lynne, Shannon Lee. *Education:* Oregon State University, B.S., 1967; University of Washington, Seattle, M.Forestry, 1969.

ADDRESSES: Home—R.R.1, Winlaw, British Columbia, Canada V0G 2J0. *Office*—Silva Ecosystem Consultants Ltd., R.R.1, Winlaw, British Columbia, Canada V0G 2J0.

CAREER: Hammond Builders Supply, Corvallis, OR, retail salesperson and builder of custom cabinets, part-time and summers, 1960-67; U.S. Forest Service, Union Creek, OR, cruiser checker in white pine blister rust control, 1964; Weyerhaeuser Co., North Bend, OR, field research assistant for the Coos Bay area, 1966; University of Washington, Seattle, graduate research assistant in forest resources, 1972-73; Crown Zellerbach Corp., Courtenay Division, Courtenay, British Columbia, forester, 1973-74; Silva Ecosystem Consultants Ltd., Winlaw, British Columbia, president, 1976—. Registered Professional Forester, Province of British Columbia. Selkirk College, instructor in forest ecology and silviculture, 1974-82, chair, Department of Forest Resources, 1979-81, forestry extension coordinator, 1981-82. Southern Interior Silviculture Committee, vice chair, 1976-77, chair, 1977-78; Slocan Valley Watershed Alliance, co-chair, 1982—; British Columbia Watershed Protection Alliance, chair, 1984-88; public speaker; consultant to Nisga'a Tribal Council, Siksika Nation, and Cortes Island Forest Committee. *Military service:* U.S. Coast Guard, maritime water pollution control officer and chief of Port Safety Section, 1969-72.

MEMBER: Society of American Foresters, Association of British Columbia Professional Foresters, Xi Sigma Pi, Blue Key.

WRITINGS:

Reforestation Syllabus, Silva Ecosystem Consultants, 1982, revised edition, 1984.

British Columbia Watershed Protection Alliance Handbook, British Columbia Watershed Protection Alliance, 1988.

Seeing the Forest among the Trees: The Case for Wholistic Forest Use, Polestar Press, 1991.

(With S. Hammond) *Community Guide to the Forest: Ecology, Planning, and Use,* Slocan Valley Watershed Alliance, 1992.

SIDELIGHTS: Herb Hammond told *CA:* "The concept of wholistic forest use means protection and wise use of the *whole* forest. To implement wholistic forest use, we must adopt a new way of thinking about and relating to forests, if we are to ensure their well-being as well as our own. Forests sustain us; we do not sustain forests. The rights of all parts of a forest and all forest users must be recognized, respected, and protected through new cooperative, community-based organizations responsible for forest protection and use. Wholistic forest use recognizes that healthy forests are the basis of our economy and society, indeed of our very survival. Maintaining a diverse forest landscape and carrying out diverse, balanced forest uses is a key part of attaining the objectives of wholistic forest use.

"Communities, where all interests are accommodated and decision-making power is shared, will be the places where wholistic forest use is implemented. This grass-roots human sharing and respect for our forests and for each other will permanently change the face of our forest activities and our relationships with each other."

BIOGRAPHICAL/CRITICAL SOURCES:

PERIODICALS

Globe and Mail (Toronto), June 6, 1992, p. C9.

*   *   *

HAMMOND, Thomas T(aylor)   1920-1993

OBITUARY NOTICE—See index for *CA* sketch: Born September 15, 1920, in Atlanta, GA; died after a stroke, February 11, 1993, in Charlottesville, VA. Educator, editor, and author. For more than forty years Hammond taught history at the University of Virginia, specializing in Russian and Eastern European history as well as the foreign policy of the Soviet Union. He also founded a Center for Russian and East European Studies at the university and served as its director in the mid-1960s. In 1976 he won a Phi Beta Kappa Prize for *The Anatomy of Communist Takeovers,* which he edited. His other writings include *Yugoslavia between East and West, Lenin on Trade Unions and Revolution,* and *Red Star over Afghanistan: The Soviet Invasion of Afghanistan and Its Consequences.* Hammond was also the editor of *Soviet Foreign Relations and World Communism: A Selected, Annotated Bibliography of 7,000 Books in 30 Languages and Witnesses to the Origins of the Cold War.*

OBITUARIES AND OTHER SOURCES:

BOOKS

Directory of American Scholars, Volume 1: *History,* 8th edition, Bowker, 1982, p. 306.

PERIODICALS

Washington Post, February 15, 1993, p. B4.

*   *   *

HAMOVITCH, Mitzi Berger   1924-1992

OBITUARY NOTICE—See index for *CA* sketch: Born December 22, 1924, in Montreal, Quebec, Canada; immigrated to United States, 1946, naturalized citizen, 1953; died after heart surgery, December 31, 1992, in Roslyn, NY. Educator and editor. Hamovitch launched a teaching career spanning more than thirty-five years in 1952, when she became an adjunct lecturer in English at Queens College. She advanced to adjunct assistant professor and, in 1982, to assistant professor, retiring in 1989. In 1982 she also edited a book, *The Hound and Horn Letters,* drawing on the correspondence between the editors of *Hound and Horn* magazine and its contributors, who included such noted authors as T. S. Eliot, Katherine Anne Porter, Ezra Pound, and William Carlos Williams. Hamovitch's other writings included contributions to periodicals such as *American Scholar, Centennial Review, Southern Review,* and *Women's Studies.*

OBITUARIES AND OTHER SOURCES:

PERIODICALS

New York Times, January 4, 1993, p. B14.

*   *   *

HANCOCK, Malcolm Cyril   1936-1993
(Mal)

OBITUARY NOTICE—See index for *CA* sketch: Born May 20, 1936, in Erie, CO; died of cancer, February 16, 1993, in Great Falls, MT. Cartoonist and author. Hancock's comic strips, which were signed simply "Mal" and included "Fantastic Foster Fenwick" and "The Lumpits," were syndicated across the United States. His cartoons appeared in magazines such as *Changing Times, Cosmopolitan, National Review, New Yorker, Saturday Review,* and *TV Guide,* as well as newspapers such as the *New York Times.* Among his books are *Welcome to the Hospital, The Giraffe Wouldn't Laugh,* and the cartoon collections *How Can You Stand It out There* and *The Name of the Game.*

OBITUARIES AND OTHER SOURCES:

BOOKS

World Encyclopedia of Cartoons, Chelsea House, 1980.

PERIODICALS

Los Angeles Times, February 19, 1993, p. A24.

*   *   *

HARRISON, James (Ernest)   1927-

PERSONAL: Born January 15, 1927, in Tricomalee, Ceylon (now Sri Lanka); son of George William (a Methodist minister) and Jane Elizabeth (a teacher; maiden name, Bell) Harrison; married Jean Eileen Back (died June 6, 1983); married Vivienne Kathleen Denton (a law librarian), January 19, 1990; children: Adam James, Simon Francis, Katharine Lucy, Naomi Rachel. *Education:* Uni-

versity of Durham, B.A., 1951, Diploma in Education, 1952, M.Litt., 1968. *Politics:* New Democrat. *Religion:* "Lapsed Anglican."

ADDRESSES: Home—18 Wolfrey Ave., Toronto, Ontario, Canada M4K 1K8.

CAREER: Worcester College for the Blind, Worcester, England, teacher of English, 1952-56; Bournemouth Technical College, Bournemouth, England, lecturer in English, 1956-59; Shenstone College of Education, Bromgrove, England, lecturer, 1959-62, senior lecturer, 1962-65, principal lecturer and department head, 1965-69; University of Guelph, Guelph, Ontario, assistant professor, 1969-72, associate professor, 1972-82, professor of English, 1982-92, professor emeritus, 1993—. Gives poetry readings at Canadian universities and high schools. *Military service:* British Army, 1945-48; became sergeant.

AWARDS, HONORS: Fellow of Social Science and Humanities Research Council of Canada, 1979-80; First Prize from Olympics Poster Poem Contest, 1976, for "Flying Dutchmen"; grant from Canada Council, 1976.

WRITINGS:

Catchment Area (poems), Oxford University Press, 1958.
(Editor) *Scientists as Writers,* MIT Press, 1965.
Rudyard Kipling, Twayne, 1982.
Flying Dutchmen (poems), Sono Nis, 1983.
Salman Rushdie, Twayne, 1992.

Work represented in anthologies, including *The Norton Introduction to Literature,* 4th edition, Norton, 1986; and *The Norton Book of Light Verse,* Norton, 1987. Contributor of articles, poems, and reviews to magazines, including *Canadian Forum, Journal of the History of Ideas, Dalhousie Review, Canadian Children's Literature, Fiddlehead,* and *Prism International.*

WORK IN PROGRESS: J. M. Coetzee; research on postcolonial literature from India and Africa.

SIDELIGHTS: James Harrison told *CA:* "No one, no matter how much of it he publishes, earns a living by writing poetry. I am not a prolific poet, but I have been writing the stuff since age seven, and I find it fits well with an academic career. Writing poetry gives me all kinds of insight into the creative process.

"My critical writing took off when I moved from high school and college teaching in England to university teaching in Canada. The theory is that one's research enriches one's teaching; I find the reverse is more often the case. Many of my best ideas come from interaction with my students—whether by working out what led some of them to such a strange reading, successfully defending my reading against a concerted attack, or being forced to admit that their reading is at least as good as mine and finding a way to incorporate both into a more complex one.

"My area of specialization used to be British Victorian. That, plus teaching children's literature, plus my being born in Ceylon and going to school in South India, led to a book on English writer Rudyard Kipling. That led in turn to courses on novels about India by English and Indian authors, and to my discovery of Indian author Salman Rushdie, my correspondence with him, and my article on *Midnight's Children* and *Shame*. When *The Satanic Verses* hit the fan, therefore, I naturally wrote a book about Rushdie.

"I have also read, taught, and/or written about such African writers as Chinua Achebe, Ngugi Wa Thiong'o, Andre Brink, and Nadine Gordimer. I am presently girding my loins for a book on the work of J. M. Coetzee—a brilliant, challenging, and somewhat intimidating novelist."

*   *   *

HARRISON, Roy M(ichael) 1948-

PERSONAL: Born October 14, 1948, in Reading, England; son of Wilfred (a schoolteacher) and Rosa (a schoolteacher; maiden name, Cotton) Harrison; married wife, Susan (a schoolteacher), December 22, 1989; children: Tom, Polly, Edmund. *Education:* University of Birmingham, B.Sc. (with first class honors), 1969, Ph.D., 1972, D.Sc., 1989. *Religion:* Church of England. *Avocational interests:* "Countryside pursuits."

ADDRESSES: Office—School of Biological Sciences, University of Birmingham, Edgbaston, Birmingham B15 2TT, England.

CAREER: Imperial Chemical Industries Ltd., laboratory technician, 1966; University of London, London, England, postdoctoral research assistant in public health engineering, 1972-74; University of Lancaster, Lancaster, England, lecturer in department of environmental sciences, 1974-84; University of Essex, Colchester, England, reader in department of chemistry and biological chemistry, 1984-91, director of Institute of Aerosol Science, 1985-91; University of Birmingham, Edgbaston, England, Queen Elizabeth II Birmingham Centenary Professor of Environmental Health, 1991—, deputy director of Institute of Public and Environmental Health, 1991—. Environmental health and pollution control consultant to numerous organizations, including World Health Organization, U.S. Environmental Protection Agency, Proctor and Gamble Ltd., and McDonald's Hamburgers Ltd.; member of numerous government committees on issues in environmental health and research; co-chair of international symposiums on pollution in England, 1986, Portugal, 1987, Germany, 1989, and Spain, 1992; member of technical program committees for numerous international conferences.

MEMBER: Royal Society of Chemistry (fellow and chartered chemist), Royal Meteorological Society (fellow), Royal Society of Health (fellow).

AWARDS, HONORS: Eric H. Vick Award, Institution of Public Health Engineers, 1976, for "General Trends in Air Pollution and Some Aspects of its Relation to Water Pollution Control," published in *Public Health Engineer;* various research grants and studentships.

WRITINGS:

(With D. P. H. Laxen) *Lead Pollution: Causes and Control,* Chapman and Hall, 1981.

(Editor) *Pollution: Causes, Effects and Control,* Royal Society of Chemistry Special Publications, 1983, second edition, Royal Society of Chemistry, 1990.

(Editor with R. Perry) *Handbook of Air Pollution Analysis,* second edition, Chapman and Hall, 1986.

(Editor with J. N. B. Bell, J. N. Lester, and R. Perry, and contributor) *Acid Rain: Scientific and Technical Advances,* Selper Ltd., 1987.

(Editor with S. Rapsomanikis, and contributor) *Environmental Analysis Using Chromatography Interfaced with Atomic Spectroscopy,* Ellis Horwood, 1989.

(With W. R. Johnston, S. Rapsomanikis, and S. J. de Mora) *Introductory Chemistry for the Environmental Sciences,* Cambridge University Press, 1991.

(Editor with R. S. Hamilton, and contributor) *Highway Pollution,* Elsevier, 1991.

(With L. Butterwick and Q. Merritt) *Handbook for Urban Air Improvement,* Commission of the European Communities, 1992.

(Editor) *Understanding Our Environment: An Introduction to Environmental Chemistry and Pollution,* Royal Society of Chemistry, 1992.

(Editor with M. Radojevic) *Atmospheric Acidity: Sources, Consequences and Abatement,* Elsevier Applied Science, 1992.

(With others) *Urban Air Quality in the United Kingdom,* Quality of Urban Air Review Group, 1993.

(Editor with F. E. Warner) *Radioecology after Chernobyl: Biogeochemical Pathways of Artificial Radionuclides,* Wiley, in press.

Contributor to books, including *Hazard Assessment of Chemicals: Current Developments,* Volume 3, edited by J. I. Saxena, Academic Press, 1984; *Organometallic Compounds in the Environment,* edited by P. J. Craig, 1986; *Understanding Our Environment,* edited by R. E. Hester, Royal Society of Chemistry, 1986; *Indoor Air Quality and Ventilation,* edited by F. Lunau and G. L. Reynolds, Selper, 1990; and *Environmental Particles,* edited by J. Buffle and H. P. van Leeuwen, Lewis, 1992. Coeditor of "Environmental Chemistry" series, Cambridge University Press and "Environmental Management" series, Elsevier. Contributor of article, "General Trends in Air Pollution and Some Aspects of its Relation to Water Pollution Control" to *Public Health Engineer;* contributor to journals, including *Chemistry in Britain, Nature, Journal of Air Pollution Control Association, Tellus, Experientia, Journal of Aerosol Science,* and *Journal of Environmental Analytical Chemistry. Environmental Technology,* joint executive editor, 1980—; *Atmospheric Environment,* associate editor; member of the editorial advisory board of *Environmental Science and Technology,* 1986-88, and of the editorial boards of *Science of the Total Environment* and *Applied Organometallic Chemistry.*

WORK IN PROGRESS: Editing a new book series titled "Issues in Environmental Science and Technology" with R. E. Hester, for the Royal Society of Chemistry.

SIDELIGHTS: Roy M. Harrison is an environmental scientist with specialized interests in environmental chemistry and environmental health. He has authored, coauthored, or edited a wide range of titles in environmental chemistry and health. He writes and edits at both the teaching and research levels; examples of the latter include his books on lead pollution and atmospheric acidity. His most successful publication ventures have been *Introductory Chemistry for the Environmental Sciences, Understanding Our Environment: An Introduction to Environmental Chemistry and Pollution,* and *Pollution: Causes, Effects and Control,* which are teaching books in environmental health and environmental chemistry.

*   *   *

HART, H(erbert) L(ionel) A(dolphus)   1907-1992

OBITUARY NOTICE—See index for *CA* sketch: Born July 18, 1907 (one source cites July 8, 1907), in Harrogate, England; died December 19, 1992. Educator, lawyer, and author. Hart, who combined legal training with an avid interest in philosophy, earned a reputation as one of the best teachers of philosophy in England. He began his legal career in 1932 in London and accepted his first academic post, as fellow and tutor in philosophy at Oxford University, in the mid-1940s. Affiliated with the university for more than thirty years, he worked variously in philosophy and jurisprudence. Hart received the rare distinction of being elected president of the Aristotelian Society while working as a law professor, and in 1962 he became a fellow of the British Academy. He was the author of books such as *The Concept of Law, Punishment and Responsibility: Essays in the Philosophy of Law, Essays on Bentham: Juris-*

prudence and Political Theory, and Essays in Jurisprudence and Philosophy. Hart also edited Horace William Brindley Joseph's *Knowledge and the Good in Plato's Republic* and works by jurist-philosopher Jeremy Bentham, including *Of Laws in General.*

OBITUARIES AND OTHER SOURCES:

BOOKS

The Writers Directory: 1992-1994, St. James Press, 1992, p. 425.

PERIODICALS

Times (London), December 24, 1992, p. 13.

*   *   *

HARTE, (Francis) Bret(t)   1836-1902

PERSONAL: Born August 25, 1836, in Albany, NY; died of throat cancer, May 5, 1902, in Camberley, Surrey, England; son of Henry (a teacher) and Elizabeth Rebecca (Ostrander) Harte; married Anna Griswold, August 11, 1862; children: Griswold, Francis King, Jessamy (Mrs. Henry Steel), Ethel. *Education:* Attended school until age thirteen.

CAREER: Short story writer, poet, playwright, editor, critic, and novelist. Held a variety of jobs during his early years. Worked in a lawyer's office and a counting house, Brooklyn, NY, until 1854; worked in a mine and a drug store, taught school, served as a pony express guard, a stage driver, a printer, a clerk, and a typesetter, San Francisco, CA, 1854-64; secretary of the California Mint, 1864-67. Assistant editor of *Northern California* and, in 1868, first editor of *Overland Monthly.* U.S. Consul in Crefeld, Germany, 1878-80, and Glasgow, Scotland, 1880-85.

WRITINGS:

SHORT STORIES

The Luck of Roaring Camp, and Other Sketches (includes "The Outcasts of Poker Flat," "Tennessee's Partner," and "M'liss"), Houghton, 1869, reissued, Jamestown, 1976; other editions illustrated by Valenti Angelo, Peter Pauper Press, 1943; Mallette Dean, Ransohoffs, 1948; Howard Mueller, Fountain Press, 1949.
Stories of the Sierras, and Other Sketches, J. C. Hotten, 1872.
Mrs. Skagg's Husbands, and Other Sketches, J. C. Hotten, 1972, J. R. Osgood, 1873.
An Episode of Fiddletown, and Other Sketches, Routledge, 1873.
M'liss: An Idyl of Red Mountain, DeWitt, 1873.
Tales of the Argonauts, and Other Sketches, J. R. Osgood, 1875, reprinted, Books for Libraries, 1971.

Thankful Blossom, and Other Tales, Routledge, 1877, reprinted, Books for Libraries, 1972.

The Twins of Table Mountain, and Other Stories, Houghton, 1879.

Flip and Found at Blazing Star, Houghton, 1882.

In the Carquinez Woods, Longmans, Green, 1883, Houghton, 1884.

The Queen of the Pirate Isle, illustrated by Kate Greenaway, Chatto & Windus, 1886.

A Millionaire of Rough-and-Ready, and Devil's Ford, Houghton, 1887.

Captain Jim's Friend, and The Argonauts of North Liberty, B. Tauchnitz, 1889.

Cressy, Houghton, 1889, reprinted, Books for Libraries, 1973.

A Sappho of Green Springs, and Other Tales, Houghton, 1891.

Colonel Starbottle's Client, and Some Other People, Houghton, 1892.

Susy: A Story of the Plains, Houghton, 1893.

A Bell-Ringer of Angel's, and Other Stories, Houghton, 1894, reprinted, Books for Libraries, 1973.

A Protegee of Jack Hamlin's, and Other Stories, Houghton, 1894.

Tales of Trail and Town, Houghton, 1898, reprinted, Books for Libraries, 1970.

From Sand Hill to Pine, Houghton, 1900, reprinted, Books for Libraries, 1970.

Trent's Trust, and Other Tales, Houghton, 1903.

Her Letter, His Answer, and Her Last Letter, illustrated by Arthur I. Keller, Houghton, 1905.

Tennessee's Partner, P. Elder, 1907.

Salomy Jane, illustrated by Keller, Houghton, 1910.

The Story of Enriquez: Chu Chu, The Devotion of Enriquez, The Passing of Enriquez, Grabhorn, 1924.

(With Mark Twain) *Sketches of the Sixties,* J. Howell, 1926, reprinted, Scholarly Press, 1970.

Contributor of short stories to periodicals, including *Atlantic Monthly.*

POETRY

The Lost Galleon, and Other Tales, Towne & Bacon, 1867, reprinted, Aeonian Press, 1976.

The Heathen Chinee; or, Plain Language from Truthful James, illustrated by Joseph Hull, Western News, 1870; other editions illustrated by Sol Eytinge, Jr., J. R. Osgood, 1871; Phil Little, Book Club of California, 1934.

Poems, Fields, Osgood, 1871.

East and West: Poems, J. R. Osgood, 1872.

The Poetical Works of Bret Harte, J. R. Osgood, 1872.

OTHER WRITINGS

Gabriel Conroy (novel), American Publishing, 1876, reissued, Literature House, 1970.

Two Men of Sandy Bar (four-act play), J. R. Osgood, 1876.

(With Mark Twain) *Ah Sin* (play), first produced in Washington, DC, May 5, 1877.

Also author of satirical parodies of famous contemporary authors, *Condensed Novels,* 1867, and *Condensed Novels, Second Series,* 1899-1902.

SELECTIONS

Bret Harte's Stories of the Old West, illustrated by Paul Brown, edited by Wilhelmina Harper and Aimee M. Penters, Houghton, 1940.

Tales of the Gold Rush, illustrated by Fletcher Martin, Limited Editions, 1944, reprinted, Heritage Press, 1967.

Outcasts of Poker Flat, Luck of Roaring Camp, and Other Stories, simplified and adapted by Robert J. Dixson, Regents Publishing, 1954.

The Luck of Roaring Camp, and Three Other Stories, illustrated by Leonard Everett Fisher, F. Watts, 1968.

COLLECTIONS

The Writings of Bret Harte, Standard Library Edition, 19 volumes, Houghton, 1896-1903, reprinted, AMS Press, 1966.

The Letters of Bret Harte, edited by Geoffrey Bret Harte, Houghton, 1926, reprinted, AMS Press, 1973.

Harte's Complete Works, California Edition, 10 volumes, Riverside Press, 1929.

ADAPTATIONS:

MOVIES AND FILMSTRIPS

Salomy Jane (motion pictures; adaptations of "Salomy Jane's Kiss"), California Motion Picture Corp., 1914, Famous Players-Lasky Corp., 1923.

M'liss (motion pictures), World Film Corp., 1915, Artcraft Pictures Corp., 1918, RKO-Radio Pictures, 1936.

The Lily of Poverty Flat (motion picture; adaptation of *Her Letter, His Answer, and Her Last Letter*), California Motion Pictures Corp., 1915.

Two Men of Sandy Bar (motion picture), Universal Films, 1916.

The Luck of Roaring Camp (filmstrip), Encyclopaedia Britannica Films, 1956.

Tongues of Flame (motion pictures; adaptations of *In the Carquinez Woods,* Bluebird Photoplays, 1918, Famous Players-Lasky Corp., 1924.

The Dawn of Understanding (motion picture; adaptation of *The Judgement of Bolinas Plains*), Viagraph, 1918.

The Outcasts of Poker Flat (motion picture), Universal Films, 1919, RKO-Radio Pictures, 1937, Twentieth Century-Fox, 1952.

The Luck of Roaring Camp (motion pictures), Thomas A. Edison, 1917, Monogram Pictures, 1937.

Fighting Cressy (motion picture), Jesse D. Hampton, 1920.

The Girl Who Ran Wild (motion picture; adaptation of "M'liss"), Universal Films, 1922.

The Flaming Forties (motion picture; adaptation of *Tennessee's Partner*), Stellar Productions, 1924.

The Golden Princess (motion picture), Famous Players-Lasky Corp., 1925.

The Man from Red Gulch (motion picture; adaptation of "The Idyl of Red Gulch") Cinema Corp. of America, 1925.

Wild Girl (motion picture; adaptation of "Colonel Starbottle's Client"), Realm Television, 1949.

The Post Mistress of Laurel Run (motion picture), General Television Enterprises, 1950.

Tennessee's Partner (motion picture), RKO-Radio Pictures, 1955.

Reading out Loud: Richard Boone (motion picture; a reading of "How Santa Claus Came to Simpson's Bar") Westinghouse Broadcasting, 1960.

The Outcasts of Poker Flat (filmstrip with captions), Brunswick Productions, 1973, filmstrip with cassette, Listening Library, 1977.

Salomy Jane's Kiss (filmstrip with cassette), Prentice-Hall Media, 1977.

PLAYS

Charles George, *M'liss* (three-act), Samuel French, 1939.

Robert Gene Bander, librettist, *The Outcasts of Poker Flat* (opera; music by Jonathan Elkus), 1959.

Robert Brome, *An Ingenue of the Sierras,* Eldridge, 1964.

Perry Edwards, *The Outcasts of Poker Flat* (one-act), Dramatic Publishing, 1968.

RECORDINGS

The Best of Bret Harte: The Outcasts of Poker Flat, The Luck of Roaring Camp, read by Ralph Bell, Listening Library, 1973.

SIDELIGHTS: Bret Harte's short stories greatly influenced the realism school of literature, and his tales of California life continued to be popular throughout his long and prolific career. Despite his popularity in the 1800s, he is now best remembered for only four of his stories—"M'liss," "The Luck of Roaring Camp," "The Outcasts of Poker Flat," and "Tennessee's Partner." Harte's power lasted beyond the printed page, however, and several of his works were immortalized on film during the early days of the motion picture industry; the more popular tales continued to be remade as films grew more advanced. Even in western films not directly based on Harte's stories, the types he created—prostitutes and gamblers with hearts of gold—became stock features. In addition to penning short stories, Harte also edited newspapers, wrote plays and novels, and critiqued the work of other authors.

Bret Harte was born Francis Brett Harte on August 25, 1836, in Albany, New York. His father was an unsuccessful school teacher who died when Harte was nine years old, putting the family into even deeper financial trouble. Harte himself was a frail and sickly child, and the combination of these factors led to his having attended at least eight different schools by the time his formal education ended at the age of thirteen. Nevertheless, perhaps because of his frailty, he spent a lot of time reading during his childhood; one of his favorite books was Alexandre Dumas's *The Count of Monte Cristo.* Harte also read the works of William Shakespeare at an early age, and enjoyed the novels of Charles Dickens.

Harte dreamed of becoming a writer while still very young. He had his first taste of literary success at the age of eleven, when his poem, "Autumn Musings," was published in New York's *Sunday Morning Atlas.* Harte did, however, have to turn to other means of making money after he left school, and he worked in a lawyer's office for a time, then a counting house.

In 1854, Harte's mother remarried. Her new husband, Andrew Williams, was a California businessman who would later become the mayor of Oakland, and he took his wife back to the San Francisco Bay area to live. Harte and one of his sisters followed later that year, and, once in California, he began to explore the nearby areas that would eventually figure so prominently in his fiction. He worked various jobs to support himself at this time, including teaching school, driving a stage, and working in a mine. By 1956, however, Harte announced to his family that he would make a serious attempt to become a writer, using the works of Charles Dickens as his guide. As a stepping-stone on the way to this goal, he became an apprentice printer on a newspaper entitled the *Northern Californian.*

Harte rose quickly at the periodical, soon contributing news stories to the paper and running it whenever the editor was out of town. But during one such occasion, a group of nearby peaceful Indians were slaughtered by local whites, and Harte's reportage of the incident was irate. He also wrote a strong editorial against the crime, and this made him so unpopular with the local readers that within a month he had left the *Northern Californian.*

He next took a job at the San Francisco literary magazine the *Golden Era,* first as a printer, then as a contributor of stories and sketches. It was in this paper, in 1860, that he published the first version of what would later become one of his important stories. Originally titled "The Work on

Red Mountain," it eventually became "M'liss." The title character is Melissa Smith, the daughter of an impoverished prospector who is revealed to have been rich after his death. M'liss is implicated in her father's death, but the mystery is never solved. Meanwhile, she competes for the affections of the local schoolmaster with another young girl and an older woman who may or may not be her mother. Harte eventually became well known for his ability to create mysterious, sensuous female characters. As Henry C. Merwin explained in the *Atlantic Monthly*, "Bret Harte's heroines have a strong family resemblance to those of both Ivan Turgenev and Thomas Hardy. In each case the women obey the instinct of love as unreservedly as men of an archaic type obey the instinct of fighting. There is no question with them of material advantage, of wealth, position, or even reputation. . . . They love as nature prompts, and having once given their love, they give themselves and everything that they have along with it."

At about time he became a printer for the *Golden Era*, Harte met Anna Griswold, a woman four years his senior who was living with her married sister in San Francisco. When Harte began to entertain thoughts of marrying Miss Griswold, he left the *Golden Era* for a steadier job as a clerk in the Surveyor General's office, but he continued to contribute material to the periodical. He married Griswold on August 11, 1962. By this time, through his wife and through his writings, Harte became acquainted with the literary and social circles of the San Francisco Bay area. Writers such as Charles Warren Stoddard, Robert Newell, and eventually Samuel Clemens (Mark Twain), became his friends. As the 1860s progressed, Harte had his work published in other periodicals, including the *Californian*, and edited an anthology of poetry.

In 1867 Harte published a book of parodies titled *Condensed Novels*, in which he playfully imitated the works of such great contemporary novelists as Charlotte Bronte, James Fenimore Cooper, Alexandre Dumas, and Charles Dickens. *Condensed Novels* was well received; British essayist G. K. Chesterton was particularly impressed. In the *Pall Mall Magazine* he announced: "The supreme proof of the fact that Bret Harte had the instinct of reverence may be found in the fact that he was a really great parodist. . . . Mere derision, mere contempt, never produced or could produce parody. A man who simply despises Paderewski for having long hair is not necessarily fitted to give an admirable imitation of his particular touch on the piano. If a man wishes to parody Paderewski's style of execution, he must emphatically go through one process first; he must admire it, and even reverence it. Bret Harte had a real power of imitating great authors, as in his parodies on Dumas, on Victor Hugo, on Charlotte Bronte. This means, and can only mean, that he had perceived the real beauty, the real ambition of Dumas and Victor Hugo and

Charlotte Bronte." Harte issued a second group of parodies later in his career.

Harte was selected in 1868 to edit a new magazine, the *Overland Monthly*. The periodical's publisher, Anton Roman, intended for the periodical to be a celebration of things Californian but hoped that it would attract a nationwide audience. It did just that in its second issue, which featured one of Harte's best-known short stories, "The Luck of Roaring Camp." "The Luck" of the title refers to the nickname of an Indian prostitute's baby, who is taken in by the entire mining town of Roaring Camp when his mother dies during childbirth. Having a baby to rear reforms the town and leads to incredible civic improvements, but the tale ends sadly when the baby and one of his primary caretakers dies in a flash flood. Ben Merchant Vorpahl revealed in the *Dictionary of Literary Biography* that "at a single stroke, the story fulfilled the *Overland Monthly*'s aspirations for a national audience. It also brought Harte instant fame as a master storyteller. Some San Francisco readers were dubious at first—suspecting, perhaps, that the tale made fun of them—but the *Atlantic Monthly* wrote to Harte from Boston requesting a story like 'The Luck of Roaring Camp' for its own pages as soon as possible. Some eastern critics even hailed Harte as an American Dickens."

Harte followed the success of "The Luck of Roaring Camp" with one of 1869's contributions to the *Overland Monthly*, "The Outcasts of Poker Flat." That story concerned a minor character from the previous tale, gambler John Oakhurst. He, along with two prostitutes and a drunk, are kicked out of the town of Poker Flat, in what Harte describes as a "spasm of virtuous reaction quite as lawless and ungovernable as any of the acts that provoked it." On their way to the next town, where they hope to be accepted, they meet a young couple on their way to settle in Poker Flat. All concerned are trapped in a blizzard—except for the drunk, Uncle Billy, who steals their mules, then leaves. But the rest perform various acts of kindness and heroism for each other before their eventual deaths, bearing witness to Harte's favorite theme—that even the outcasts of society can be revealed as worthy human beings.

"The Luck of Roaring Camp" and "The Outcasts of Poker Flat" were reprinted in Harte's first book of collected short stories in 1869. Also included in this collection was another of the author's better-known works, "Tennessee's Partner." This tale centers on a gambler named Tennessee, suspected of theft, who runs away with his partner's wife. When Tennessee is apprehended and tried, his partner tries to buy the gambler's freedom but this only serves to make the court indignant, and the accused is sentenced to be hanged. After the execution, Tennessee's partner provides the deceased with a touching and eloquent funeral. "Tennessee's Partner" was translated to film more than once; one of the later versions starred Ronald Reagan and Rhonda Fleming.

Harte also continued to write poetry. His best-known work in this genre was entitled *The Heathen Chinee; or, Plain Language from Truthful James,* published in 1870. Written in dialect verse, the poem concerns a pair of white card sharks outwitted by the Chinese man they attempted to cheat at euchre. As Vorpahl opined, *The Heathen Chinee* "caught on immediately, nearly everywhere," and "was pirated, recited, quoted, dramatized, and set to music until it seemed that everyone in the country knew it by rote." Unfortunately, for a man like Harte who hated prejudice, the poem was also used by whites in racist attacks on Asian immigrants.

By 1871 Harte's fame had grown to the point where he was offered and accepted a contract with *Atlantic Monthly* to contribute at least twelve stories to the magazine a year. He left California for New York but was unable to produce more than nine stories for the magazine—these of a lesser quality than expected. Thus his contract was not renewed, and his career and reputation as a writer began to decline. He continued to write, however, and tried his hand at a novel and some plays—one a collaboration with Mark Twain which caused the end of their long friendship—in addition to lecturing. Critics generally agree that by this time Harte no longer grew in his fiction but rather continued to rehash the same themes, characters, and style that had made him popular.

In 1878, Harte received an appointment from U.S. President Rutherford B. Hayes' administration to become the U.S. Consul at Crefeld, Germany. He sailed for Europe, never to return to the United States. His wife, Anna, remained at home until 1898; in the meantime, Harte is believed to have had a scandalous relationship with Marguerite Van de Veldes, the wife of a Belgian diplomat. In 1880, Harte managed to transfer his consulship to Glasgow, Scotland, but when Grover Cleveland, a Democrat, became president in 1885, Harte lost his government position. He stayed abroad, however, moving to England where his short stories were gaining considerable popularity. To the British, his tales of the Old West were still exotic and interesting. Although significantly decreased, his American popularity did not completely die out, and he continued writing prolifically, putting out story collections until his death from throat cancer in 1902. According to Vorpahl, "the problem" with Harte's later work "is in Harte's own reluctance to probe the depths of his vision as [Samuel] Clemens and [William Dean] Howells did. He merely rearranged the parts of his initial vision in different combinations. . . . Jack Hamlin, Colonel Starbottle, John Oakhurst, and other characters from the early tales, turn up repeatedly in later works—usually unchanged.

While Harte's later works satisfied the tastes of readers who liked knowing what to expect, they neither invite nor bear sustained critical attention."

BIOGRAPHICAL/CRITICAL SOURCES:

BOOKS

Barnett, Linda D., *Bret Harte: A Reference Guide,* G. K. Hall, 1980.
Boyton, Henry W., *Bret Harte,* McClure, Phillips, 1968.
Branham, Janet, *Bret Harte: Young Storyteller,* Bobbs-Merrill, 1969.
Dictionary of Literary Biography, Gale, Volume 12: *American Realists and Naturalists,* 1982, Volume 64: *American Literary Critics and Scholars, 1850-1880,* 1988.
Duckett, Margaret, *Mark Twain and Bret Harte,* University of Oklahoma Press, 1964.
Gaer, Joseph, editor, *Bret Harte: Bibliography and Biographical Data,* Burt Franklin, 1968.
Harte, Bret, *The Luck of Roaring Camp, and Other Sketches,* Houghton, 1869.
Merwin, Henry Childs, *The Life of Bret Harte,* Houghton Mifflin, 1911.
Morrow, Patrick D., *Bret Harte, Literary Critic,* Bowling Green University Popular Press, 1979.
O'Connor, Richard, *Bret Harte: A Biography,* Little, Brown, 1966.
Stewart, George R., *Bret Harte: Argonaut and Exile,* Houghton Mifflin, 1931.
Twentieth-Century Literary Criticism, Volume 25, Gale, 1988.
Walker, Franklin, *San Francisco's Literary Frontier,* Knopf, 1939.

PERIODICALS

Atlantic Monthly, September, 1908, pp. 297-307.
Pall Mall Magazine, July, 1902, pp. 428-32.*

—Sketch by Elizabeth Wenning

*   *   *

HARVEY, Stephen   1949-1993

OBITUARY NOTICE—See index for *CA* sketch: Born December 24, 1949, in New York, NY; died of complications of acquired immunodeficiency syndrome, January 1, 1993. Museum curator and author. An associate curator of film for the Museum of Modern Art, Harvey wrote *Directed by Vincente Minnelli,* a book widely regarded as a definitive study of the filmmaker. He began his work with the museum in 1972, after earning a bachelor's degree from Stanford University. During his tenure as a curator Harvey mounted retrospectives on a number of prominent film artists, notably Minnelli, Ida Lupino, Joseph Mankiewicz, and Vittorio de Sica. He contributed essays and criticism to periodicals including *Film Comment, Inquiry,* and *Nation.* In 1985, France recognized his writings by naming him a chevalier of its Order of Arts and Letters.

OBITUARIES AND OTHER SOURCES:

PERIODICALS

New York Times, January 5, 1993, p. A12.

*   *   *

HARVEY-JONES, John (Henry) 1924-

PERSONAL: Born April 16, 1924, in London, England; son of Mervyn and Eileen Harvey-Jones; married Mary Evelyn Atcheson, 1947; children: one daughter. *Education:* Attended Royal Naval Academy. *Avocational interests:* Sailing, swimming, cooking, contemporary literature, countryside travel, sleeping.

ADDRESSES: Office—Parallax Enterprises Ltd., P.O. Box 18, Ross-on-Wye, Herefordshire, HR9 7TL, England. *Agent*—Celebrity Speakers, Studio 230 Canalot, 222 Kensal Rd., London W10 5BN, England.

CAREER: Imperial Chemical Industries (ICI), London, England, work study officer, 1956, executive in Heavy Organic Chemicals Division, 1956-67, deputy chair of Heavy Organic Chemical Division, 1968, chair of Petrochemicals Division, 1970-73, member of main board, 1973, director of ICI Americas, 1975-76, deputy chair, 1978-82, chair, 1982-87; writer. Chair of Phillips-Imperial Petroleum, 1973-75, Burns Anderson, 1987-90, Trendroute, 1988—, *Economist,* 1989—, and Didacticus Video Productions, 1989—; deputy chair of Grand Metropolitan PLC, 1987—, and GPA, 1989—. Director of Fiber Industries, 1975-78, and Carrington Viyella, 1981-82; non-executive director of Reed International PLC, 1975-84; vice chair of PSI and BIM, both 1980-85; vice president of CEFIC, 1982-84; president of CBI, 1984-86. Honorary vice president of Institute of Marketing, 1982-89. Non-executive chair of board committee of Business International, 1988—; chair of Wider Share Ownership Council, 1988—.

Member of Tees and Hartlepool Port Authority, 1970-73, NE Development Board, 1971-73, Chemical Industries Association Ltd., 1980-82, Court of British Shippers' Council, 1982-87, Youth Enterprise Scheme, 1984-86, Foundation Board of International Management Institute and International Council of European Institute of Business Administration, both 1984-87, Advance Council of Prince's Youth Business Trust, 1986—, and Welsh Development International, 1989. Senior Industries Fellow at Leicester Polytechnic, 1990. Chancellor at Bradford University, 1986—. Chair of council of St. James's and the

Abbey School, Malvern, 1987—. Numerous community services and trusteeships, academic posts, and honorary positions. *Military service:* Royal Navy, 1937-56; became lieutenant commander.

MEMBER: National Canine Defense League, Industries Participation Association (vice president, 1983—), Wales Foundation, the Athenaeum club, the Groucho Club, Friends of Brecon Jazz.

AWARDS, HONORS: Commander of Order of British Empire and Gold Medal from BIM, both 1985; J. O. Hambro British Businessman of the Year Award and Centenary Medal from SCI, both 1986; Excellence in Communication Award from International Association of Business Communicators and Radar Man of the Year Award, both 1987; numerous honorary degrees, including L.L.D. from universities of Manchester, 1986, Liverpool, 1986, and London and Cambridge, both 1987; and D.B.A. from International Management Center, 1990.

WRITINGS:

Making It Happen: Reflections on Leadership, Collins, 1988.
(With Anthea Masey) *Troubleshooter,* BBC Books, 1990.
Getting It Together: Memoirs of a Troubleshooter, Heinemann, 1991.
Troubleshooter Two, BBC Books, 1992.
Managing to Survive: A Guide to Management through the Nineties, Heinemann, 1993.

Member of advisory editorial board of *New European,* 1987—.

ADAPTATIONS: Harvey-Jones's *Troubleshooter* books have been adapted to television by the British Broadcasting Corporation (BBC), Channel Two.

SIDELIGHTS: John Harvey-Jones is a prominent British business executive who served as chairman of Imperial Chemical Industries (ICI) from 1982 to 1987. During 1986, Harvey-Jones's last full year at ICI, the company recorded pre-tax profits of approximately $1.5 billion. The *Economist* reported that "much of the credit for the company's success must go to [Harvey-Jones]," who implemented a five-year plan where both the company's board and business sectors were reorganized and greater cross-company communication was emphasized. Iain Carson, who noted in the *Economist* that ICI reported only "meagre profits in the early 1980s," credited Harvey-Jones with "getting a whole organization to work smarter as well as harder."

In 1988 Harvey-Jones published *Making It Happen: Reflections on Leadership,* in which he stressed his priorities for successful business management. Carson described Harvey-Jones's book as "a refreshing breath of fresh air in a subject that needs it." Harvey-Jones is also author of an autobiography, *Getting It Together: Memoirs of a Troubleshooter.* Here he recounts not only his career at ICI but his childhood in India and his nearly twenty years in the Royal Navy, which he left in 1956 as lieutenant commander. A *Times Literary Supplement* reviewer considered *Getting It Together* a "beguiling memoir."

BIOGRAPHICAL/CRITICAL SOURCES:

BOOKS

Harvey-Jones, John, *Getting It Together: Memoirs of a Troubleshooter,* Heinemann, 1991.

PERIODICALS

Christian Science Monitor, June 7, 1990.
Economist, February 26, 1987, p. 79; February 6, 1988, p. 88.
Times Literary Supplement, June 21, 1991, p. 25.

* * *

HASFORD, (Jerry) Gustav 1947-1993
(George Gordon)

OBITUARY NOTICE—See index for *CA* sketch: Born November 28, 1947, in Haleyville, AL; died of complications from diabetes, January 29, 1993, in Greece. Writer. Hasford's critically acclaimed 1979 novel, *The Short-Timers,* was the basis for director Stanley Kubrick's 1987 Vietnam War film *Full Metal Jacket,* for which he shared an Academy Award nomination as coscreenwriter. The novel and film draw on the author's own experiences as a combat correspondent with the U.S. Marine Corps during the war. Hasford also wrote the books *The Phantom Blooper,* a sequel to *The Short-Timers,* and *A Gypsy Good Time.* In 1988 he added a measure of infamy to his reputation when police charged him with grand theft for taking more than seven hundred books from American and English libraries; Hasford was ultimately convicted of a lesser charge, possessing stolen property.

OBITUARIES AND OTHER SOURCES:

BOOKS

Directory of American Poets and Fiction Writers, 1991-1993 edition, Poets & Writers, 1991, p. 17.

PERIODICALS

Los Angeles Times, February 3, 1993, p. A12.

HASLUCK, Paul (Meernaa Caedwalla) 1905-1993

OBITUARY NOTICE—See index for *CA* sketch: Born April 1, 1905, in Fremantle, Western Australia, Australia; died January 9, 1993, in Perth, Western Australia, Australia. Statesman, journalist, poet, and author. Widely respected for his moral convictions and intellect, Hasluck was prominent in Australian government for more than thirty years. He served variously in the areas of defense, external affairs, and United Nations concerns, was a twenty-year member of Parliament, and from 1969 to 1974 was governor-general of Australia. As minister for territories during the 1950s and early 1960s he was credited with facilitating Papua New Guinea's transition from a tribal territory to an independent nation. Hasluck began his career with a sixteen-year stay on the editorial staff of the *West Australian,* and he continued his involvement with writing after entering politics. He published books of poetry such as *Into the Desert* and *Dark Cottage* as well as career-related works such as *Black Australians: A Survey of Native Policy in Western Australia, 1829-1897, The Government and the People,* and *Shades of Darkness: Aboriginal Affairs, 1925-65.* His autobiography, *Mucking About,* appeared in 1977.

OBITUARIES AND OTHER SOURCES:

BOOKS

The Writers Directory: 1992-1994, St. James Press, 1992, p. 428.

PERIODICALS

Times (London), January 12, 1993, p. 19.

* * *

HAUGHT, James A(lbert, Jr.) 1932-

PERSONAL: Born February 20, 1932, in Reader, WV; son of James Albert (a postmaster) and Beulah (a teacher; maiden name, Fish) Haught; married Nancy Carolyn Brady (a sanitarian), April 22, 1958; children: Joel, Jacob, Jeb, Cassie. *Education:* Attended University of Charleston and Morris Harvey College; also attended West Virginia State College, 1952-53 and 1960-63. *Politics:* Democrat. *Religion:* Unitarian.

ADDRESSES: Home—15 K.H. Lake Shore Dr., Charleston, WV 25313. *Office*—*Gazette,* 1001 Virginia St. E., Charleston, WV 25301.

CAREER: Daily Mail, Charleston, WV, apprentice printer, 1951-53; *Gazette,* Charleston, reporter, 1953—, full-time investigator, 1970-82, associate editor, 1983-92, editor, 1993—. Press aide to Senator Robert C. Byrd of West Virginia, 1959.

MEMBER: American Society of Newspaper Editors.

AWARDS, HONORS: Recipient of fifteen national writing awards, including National Headliner Award, 1971, for an expose on the operation of a pyramid-sales scam; consumer writing prizes from the National Press Club, 1973, 1979, and 1983; Uniroyal Highway Safety Journalism Award, and National Foundation for Highway Safety Award, both 1975, for articles concerning the lax prosecution of drunk drivers; Merit Award, American Bar Association, and First Amendment Award, Sigma Delta Chi, both 1977; Religion Newswriters Association special award, 1980; Health Journalism awards, American Chiropractic Association, 1981 and 1983; named best newspaper opinion commentary, People for the American Way, 1985, for articles in defense of the separation of church and state; work named best educational opinion writing, Education Writers Association, 1988; Hugh M. Hefner First Amendment Award, newspaper editorial/opinion category, Playboy Foundation, 1989, for articles concerning the matter of separation of church and state; and Benjamin Fine Award, education reporting, National Association of Secondary School Principals, 1990.

WRITINGS:

Holy Horrors: An Illustrated History of Religious Murder and Madness, Prometheus Books, 1990.
Science in a Nanosecond: Illustrated Answers to 100 Basic Science Questions (for children), Prometheus Books, 1990.
The Art of Lovemaking: An Illustrated Tribute, Prometheus Books, 1992.

Also contributor of articles to numerous magazines.

SIDELIGHTS: During his long association with the Charleston, West Virginia, *Gazette,* James A. Haught has won numerous awards for his writing on such issues as the separation of church and state, consumer fraud, and government corruption. Haught began his newspaper career as a trainee in the print shop of the Charleston *Daily Mail.* On the days when he was not required to work, Haught assisted in the newsroom—for no pay—with the intention of learning news reporting. In 1953 he was hired by the *Gazette.* Over the course of nearly forty years, he ascended in rank, and in 1993 succeeded Don Marsh as the paper's editor. In addition to serving on the staff of the *Gazette,* Haught is the author of several nonfiction books on such topics as religion, sex, and science.

In 1990, Haught published *Holy Horrors: An Illustrated History of Religious Murder and Madness,* which chronicles injustices committed by various religious groups throughout the centuries. "It's profoundly depressing that

religion—supposedly the cure for human cruelty—often is just another basis for murder and madness," Haught writes. Included in the book are discussions of persecution conducted by the Aztecs, who sacrificed more than twenty thousand people a year by some accounts; by Christians, who have in the past tortured members of the Jewish faith with the approval of the church; and by both Hindus and Moslems who have fought one another in India. Haught also examines American acts of sabotage such as the bombing of abortion clinics and hate crimes conducted against homosexuals in the name of religion. Lee Beard in the Charleston *Sunday Gazette-Mail* remarked that " 'Holy Horrors' is an important book because it chronicles what can happen when self-righteous people presume to exclusively know the mind of God and become intent upon imposing their belief upon others, whatever the price."

In 1990 Haught's *Science in a Nanosecond: Illustrated Answers to 100 Basic Science Questions* was also published. Inspired by both his own curiosity of the subject and the questions that he fielded from his four children while raising them, Haught began producing material for the book in 1987. After the publication of *Holy Horrors,* Prometheus Books agreed to release *Science in a Nanosecond.* In the book Haught employs drawings, diagrams, and cartoons to answer questions on such matters as the existence of the seasons, the speed of the earth's rotation, and the color of the sky. Haught published a third book, *The Art of Lovemaking: An Illustrated Tribute,* in 1992.

BIOGRAPHICAL/CRITICAL SOURCES:

BOOKS

Haught, James A., *Holy Horrors: An Illustrated History of Religious Murder and Madness,* Prometheus Books, 1990.

PERIODICALS

Sunday Gazette-Mail (Charleston), March 4, 1990.

*   *   *

HAURY, Emil W(alter)   1904-1992

*OBITUARY NOTICE—*See index for *CA* sketch: Born May 2, 1904, in Newton, KS; died of a heart ailment, December 5, 1992, in Tucson, AZ. Archaeologist, anthropologist, educator, and author. Haury, an expert on the American southwest, is remembered for helping identify and define several ancient Indian cultures, particularly those of the Mogollon and Hohokam peoples in what is now Arizona and New Mexico. His career began in 1928 at the University of Arizona, where he spent more than forty years, becoming the Fred A. Riecker Distinguished

Professor of Anthropology in 1970 and professor emeritus in 1980. In the 1930s he spent several years away from the university as assistant director of the Gila Pueblo. Haury was director of the Arizona State Museum from 1938 to 1964, and for many years he worked with federal agencies such as the Bureau of Land Management and National Park Service to help preserve archaeological remains. His numerous writings in his field include *Recently Dated Pueblo Ruins in Arizona,* which he wrote with Lyndon L. Hargrave; *Excavations in the Forestdale Valley, East-Central Arizona; The Hohokam, Desert Farmers and Craftsmen: Excavations at Snaketown, 1964-1965; Emil W. Haury's Prehistory of the American Southwest;* and *Point of Pines, Arizona: A History of the University of Arizona, Archaeological Field School.*

OBITUARIES AND OTHER SOURCES:

BOOKS

The International Who's Who, 55th edition, Europa, 1991, p. 674.

PERIODICALS

Los Angeles Times, December 12, 1992, p. A32.
New York Times, December 8, 1992, p. D22.

*　　　*　　　*

HAUXWELL, Hannah   1926-

PERSONAL: Born in 1926, in Baldersdale, Yorkshire, England.

ADDRESSES: Agent—c/o Century Hutchinson Ltd., Brookmount House, 62-65 Chandon Place, London WC2N 4NW, England.

CAREER: Farmer in Yorkshire, England, until 1988; writer.

WRITINGS:

AUTOBIOGRAPHIES; WITH BARRY COCKCROFT

Seasons of My Life: The Story of a Solitary Daleswoman, photographs by Mostafa Hammuri, Century Hutchinson, 1989.
Daughter of the Dales: The World of Hannah Hauxwell, Century Hutchinson, 1990.
Innocent Abroad: The Travels of Miss Hannah Hauxwell, Century Hutchinson, 1991.
Hannah: The Complete Story, Century Hutchinson, 1991.

SIDELIGHTS: Hannah Hauxwell worked as a farmer in England's Yorkshire Dales until 1988. She is the subject of the television show *Too Long a Winter,* which depicts her difficult life on the farm.

BIOGRAPHICAL/CRITICAL SOURCES:

BOOKS

Hauxwell, Hannah, and Barry Cockcroft, *Seasons of My Life: The Story of a Solitary Daleswoman,* Century Hutchinson, 1989.
Hauxwell and Cockcroft, *Innocent Abroad: The Travels of Miss Hannah Hauxwell,* Century Hutchinson, 1991.
Hauxwell and Cockcroft, *Hannah: The Complete Story,* Century Hutchinson, 1991.*

*　　　*　　　*

HAWLEY, T. M.   1953-

PERSONAL: Born March 8, 1953, in Oconto, WI; son of Thomas J. (a high school teacher) and Bernice (a registered nurse; maiden name, Vomastic) Hawley; married Elizabeth Johnson (a biochemist), April 9, 1988; children: Padraic, Kevin, Benedict. *Education:* Lawrence University of Wisconsin, B.A., 1975; graduate study at University of Wisconsin—Madison. *Politics:* "Human beings are more valuable than personal property, and the earth is more valuable than human beings." *Religion:* Roman Catholic. *Avocational interests:* Sacred choral music, Gregorian chant, mountaineering.

ADDRESSES: Home—9 Stedman St., Apt. 2, Jamaica Plain, MA 02130. *Agent*—Laura J. Blake, Curtis Brown, Ltd., 10 Astor Pl., New York, NY 10003.

CAREER: Writer. Grant and script writer for Interlock Media Associates, Cambridge, MA.

MEMBER: International Science Writers Association, Authors Guild, National Association of Science Writers, Society of Environmental Journalists, Association of Church Musicians.

WRITINGS:

(Editor) *America's Energy Choices,* Union of Concerned Scientists, 1991.
Against the Fires of Hell, Harcourt, 1992.

Editor, *Oceanus,* 1987-91.

WORK IN PROGRESS: Environmentalism in Central and Eastern Europe; The Legacy of the Cold War in the United States; Virgin Wasteland, to be completed in 1995; researching global environmental networks of indigenous peoples.

*　　　*　　　*

HAYES, Helen   1900-1993

OBITUARY NOTICE—See index for *CA* sketch: Name originally Helen Hayes Brown; born October 10, 1900, in

Washington, DC; died of heart failure, March 17, 1993, in Nyack, NY. Actress and author. In a career that spanned most of the twentieth century, Hayes became known to theatergoers as the First Lady of American Theater for her acting talent, appealing character, and professionalism. She received the Academy Award, Tony Award, and Emmy Award at least once each as well as numerous awards for lifetime achievement, notably the Presidential Medal of Freedom and Kennedy Center Honors. Her most acclaimed performances were in the plays *Victoria Regina, Happy Birthday,* and *Harriet* and the film *The Sin of Madelon Claudet,* for which she won an Academy Award for best actress. Hayes's career also led to leadership positions with professional organizations such as the American National Theater and Academy and the American Theater Wing. She also devoted her time to humanitarian groups such as the March of Dimes. She was the author or coauthor of the autobiographical books *A Gift of Joy, On Reflection: An Autobiography,* and *My Life in Three Acts,* and the novels *Star on Her Forehead* and *Where the Truth Lies: A Novel of Glamour and Murder in Hollywood.* She also wrote a historical guidebook, *Twice over Lightly: New York Then and Now.*

OBITUARIES AND OTHER SOURCES:

PERIODICALS

New York Times, March 18, 1993, p. B1.
Times (London), March 19, 1993, p. 21.
Washington Post, March 18, 1993, p. D1.

*   *   *

HEALY, Timothy S(tafford)   1923-1992

OBITUARY NOTICE—See index for *CA* sketch: Born April 25, 1923, in Manhattan, NY; died of a heart attack, December 30, 1992, in Newark, NJ. Minister, educator, editor, and author. Recognized as a talented administrator, Healy lived a controversial mix of secular and spiritual lives. He joined the Jesuit order in 1940 and became a priest in 1953, but he combined daily mass and the moral convictions of his faith with a succession of posts in education and librarianship. He began teaching in the 1940s, and, between 1956 and 1969, he advanced from instructor to executive vice president at Fordham University. Healy also enjoyed leadership positions at the City University of New York and Georgetown University. His thirteen-year presidency at Georgetown, however, was marred by at least one clash between the two sides of his life, when he battled with gay student groups over recognition and funding. He was more successful with Georgetown's financial concerns and increased endowments to six times their prior level. He also had fiscal success as president of

the New York Public Library, of which he became president in 1989. Healy was author of *Georgetown: A Meditation on a Bicentennial* and editor of John Donne's *Ignatius His Conclave* and, with Helen Gardner, *John Donne: Selected Prose.*

OBITUARIES AND OTHER SOURCES:

BOOKS

Newsmakers 90, Cumulation, Gale, 1990, pp. 214-17.
Who's Who in Entertainment, second edition, Marquis, 1992, p. 279.

PERIODICALS

Chicago Tribune, January 1, 1993, section 1, p. 11.
New York Times, January 1, 1993, p. A21.
Times (London), January 2, 1993, p. 15.

*   *   *

HELLEINER, Gerald K(arl)   1936-

PERSONAL: Born October 9, 1936, in St. Poelten, Austria; Canadian citizen; son of Karl Ferdinand (a professor) and Grethe (Deutsch) Helleiner; married Georgia Meda Stirrett (a teacher and community worker), August 16, 1958; children: Jane Leslie, Eric Noel, Peter David. *Education:* University of Toronto, B.A., 1958; Yale University, Ph.D., 1962.

ADDRESSES: Home—53 Wanda Rd., Toronto, Ontario, Canada M6P 1C7. *Office*—Department of Economics, University of Toronto, 150 St. George St., Toronto, Ontario, Canada M5S 1A1.

CAREER: Yale University, New Haven, CT, began as instructor, became assistant professor, 1961-65; University of Toronto, Toronto, Ontario, Canada, associate professor, 1965-71, professor, 1971—, director of the East African development and training program, 1968-71. University College, Dar es Salaam, Tanzania, director of the Economic Research Bureau, 1966-68; Economic Society of Tanzania, vice-president, 1967-69; International Development Research Center, senior fellow, 1975-76, member of board of governors and executive committee, 1985-91; Group of Twenty-four, researcher and consultant, 1979—, research coordinator, 1991—. Member of North-South Roundtable, 1978—, Commonwealth Team on Rehabilitation of Uganda, 1979, and United Nations Committee for Development Planning, 1984-85, 1987-90; Food Policy Research Institute, member of board of trustees, 1988—, chair, 1990—; researcher, adviser, and consultant on economic and development issues for various international organizations.

MEMBER: Royal Society of Canada (fellow), Canadian Association of African Studies (president, 1969-71).

AWARDS, HONORS: Gold medal, University of Toronto, 1958; Woodrow Wilson fellowships, 1958-59 and 1959-60; Ford Foundation fellowship, 1960-61; John Simon Guggenheim Memorial fellowship, 1971-72; research grants, Canada Council, 1971-72 and 1974-76; honorary doctor of laws, Dalhousie University, 1988.

WRITINGS:

Peasant Agriculture, Government, and Economic Growth in Nigeria, Irwin, 1966.

(Editor) *Agricultural Planning in East Africa,* East Africa Publishing House, 1968.

International Trade and Economic Development, Penguin Books, 1972.

(Editor) *A World Divided: The Less Developed Countries in the International Economy,* Cambridge University Press, 1976.

International Economic Disorder: Essays in North-South Relations, Macmillan, 1980.

Intra-firm Trade and the Developing Countries, St. Martin's, 1981.

(Editor) *For Good or Evil: Economic Theory and North-South Negotiations,* University of Toronto, 1982.

(Editor) *The IMF and Africa,* International Monetary Fund, 1986.

(Editor) *The Other Side of International Development Policy: Non-Aid Economic Relations with Developing Countries in Canada, Denmark, the Netherlands, Norway and Sweden,* University of Toronto Press, 1990.

The New Global Economy and the Developing Countries: Essays in International Economics and Development, Edward Elgar, 1990.

(Editor) *Trade Policy, Industrialization and Development: New Perspectives,* Clarendon Press, 1992.

Contributor to numerous books, including *Policy Alternatives for a New International Economic Order: An Economic Analysis,* edited by William R. Cline, Praeger, 1979; *Multinationals beyond the Market: Intra-firm Trade and the Control of Transfer Pricing,* edited by Robin Murray, Harvester Press, 1981; *Canada and the Multilateral Trading System,* edited by John Whalley, University of Toronto Press, 1985; *The International Monetary System and Its Reform, Part II,* edited by Sidney Dell, North-Holland, 1987; *Handbook of Development Economics,* Volume II, edited by H. B. Chenery and T. N. Srinivasan, Elsevier Science, 1989. Contributor of articles and reviews to journals, including *World Development, Canadian Journal of Development Studies, African Development, American Economic Review, World Politics, International Organization, Journal of Development Economics, Economic Journal, Canadian Journal of Economics, East African Economic Review,* and *Canadian Journal of African Studies.* Member of journal editorial boards, including *World Development,* 1973—, *Journal of Development Economics,*

1976-90, *International Organization,* 1979-85, *Eastern Africa Economic Review,* 1985—, *Journal of Economics and International Relations,* 1986—, and *Tanzania Journal of Economics,* 1987—.

Some of Helleiner's books have been translated into Spanish and Japanese.

WORK IN PROGRESS: Editing *Trade Policy and Industrialisation in Turbulent Times,* completion expected in 1993; articles on economics, trade, and development.

*   *   *

HELLYER, A(rthur) G(eorge) L(ee)   1902-1993
(Arthur Hellyer)

OBITUARY NOTICE—See index for *CA* sketch: Born December 16, 1902, in Bristol, England; died January 28, 1993, in Sussex, England. Gardener, editor, and writer. As the author of nearly thirty books on gardening, Hellyer is regarded as one of the foremost authorities in the field of horticulture. Afflicted with a respiratory problem as a student at London's Dulwich College, Hellyer took the advice of colleagues and left school for a job on a tomato farm. After spending nearly a dozen years in various occupations in the nursery industry, Hellyer became an assistant editor of *Commercial Horticulture* in 1929. He later held editing positions at both *Amateur Gardening* and *Gardening Illustrated.* In addition to writing such works as *The Amateur Gardener* and *Climbing and Wall Plants,* Hellyer revised *Sander's Encyclopaedia of Gardening,* originally released in 1895. He also penned gardening titles under the name Arthur Hellyer, including *Bulbs Indoors* and *Gardens of Genius.* His awards and honors include the Victoria Medal of Honour from the Royal Horticultural Society and appointment, as a fellow, to the Linnean Society.

OBITUARIES AND OTHER SOURCES:

BOOKS

Who's Who, 145th edition, St. Martin's, 1993, p. 857.

PERIODICALS

Times (London), February 1, 1993, p. 17.

*   *   *

HELLYER, Arthur
See HELLYER, A(rthur) G(eorge) L(ee)

HELMINSKI, Camille Adams   1951-

PERSONAL: Born October 16, 1951, in Jacksonville, FL; daughter of Lee (an artist) and Mildred (Stockton) Adams; married Edmund Kabir Helminski (a publisher), October 19, 1974; children: Matthew, Shams, Cara. *Education:* Received B.A. from Smith College.

ADDRESSES: Home—RFD 4, Box 600, Putney, VT 05346. *Office*—Threshold Books, 139 Main St., Brattleboro, VT 05301.

CAREER: Threshold Books, Brattleboro, VT, codirector, 1981—. The Threshold Society, codirector, 1985—; ALIF International, vice president, 1992—.

MEMBER: National Association for Female Executives, National Organization for Women, Wilderness Society, Audubon Society, Amnesty International.

WRITINGS:

(Translator with Edmund Kabir Helminski) Maulana Jalal al-Din Rumi, *Rumi—Daylight: A Daybook of Spiritual Guidance,* Threshold Books, 1990.
(Translator with Helminski and Ibrahim Al-Shihabi) As'ad Ali, *Happiness without Death: Desert Hymns,* Threshold Books, 1991.
(Translator with Refik Algan) Ahmet Hilmi, *Awakened Dream: Raji's Journeys with the Mirror Dede,* Threshold Books, 1993.

WORK IN PROGRESS: Songs of Gabriel's Wing: Reflections and Prayers; writings of women in Sufism, past and present.

*   *   *

HELYAR, John   1951-

PERSONAL: Born in 1951; son of Richard and Margaret Helyar; married Betsy Morris (a reporter). *Education:* Attended Boston University.

ADDRESSES: c/o HarperCollins, 10 East Fifty-third St., Seventh Floor—Author Mail, New York, NY 10022.

CAREER: Journalist and author. Worked for various newspapers, including the *Fitchburg-Lemonister Sentinel and Enterprise,* and worked for the States News Service; *Wall Street Journal,* worked in the paper's Philadelphia and Chicago bureaus before becoming deputy bureau chief of Atlanta bureau, c. 1980-89; *Southpoint* (magazine), senior editor of business section, beginning in 1989.

AWARDS, HONORS: Gerald Loeb Award in Distinguished Business and Financial Journalism for deadline writing, with Bryan Burrough, 1989, for series of articles on the leveraged buy-out of RJR Nabisco Inc.

WRITINGS:

(With Bryan Burrough) *Barbarians at the Gate: The Fall of RJR Nabisco,* Harper, 1990.

Also author of *Baseball Business,* McKay.

ADAPTATIONS: Barbarians at the Gate was adapted as a television film starring James Garner, HBO, 1993.

SIDELIGHTS: When John Helyar of the *Wall Street Journal* teamed with colleague Bryan Burrough to tell the story of the leveraged buy-out of RJR Nabisco, Inc. that occurred in 1988, they created a series of articles in the *Journal* that garnered them the prestigious Gerald Loeb Award. Even though Helyar left the *Wall Street Journal* in 1989 to become senior editor of *Southpoint* magazine's business section, he and Burrough decided to explore the story in even greater detail in their 1990 book, *Barbarians at the Gate: The Fall of RJR Nabisco.* The volume became a huge success, attaining the top spot on the *New York Times* best-seller list for nonfiction. Critics acclaimed the work as well; several echoed the sentiments of Judith H. Dobrzynski, who proclaimed it a "masterful account" in *Business Week.*

In *Barbarians at the Gate,* Helyar and Burrough explain that the leveraged buy-out of RJR Nabisco began in the mind of the company's own president, F. Ross Johnson, who secretly sought to purchase the company's stock at inflated prices. He thought he and his allies within the company would become extremely wealthy because of the deal. But when Johnson's negotiations with Henry Kravis of Kohlberg Kravis Roberts & Company—an expert in leveraged buy-outs—broke down, Kravis decided to enter the competition to buy RJR Nabisco himself. The bidding became more fierce, other potential purchasers entered the fray, Johnson eventually dropped out, and Kravis finally acquired the company. Acknowledging the journalists' methodical presentation of the story, a reviewer for the *Economist* observed that Helyar and Burrough "have done a solid job of American reportage" reconstructing all the various moves and countermoves. "They tell a good story without getting bogged down in analysis. They have also managed to interview nearly all the big players, often extensively." Scot J. Paltrow in the *Los Angeles Times Book Review* further noted that the authors' "writing is unflawed," and Patricia O'Toole in the *New York Times Book Review* asserted that *Barbarians at the Gate* has "all the suspense of a first-rate thriller."

BIOGRAPHICAL/CRITICAL SOURCES:

BOOKS

Bestsellers 90, Issue 3, Gale, 1990, pp. 7-9.

PERIODICALS

Business Week, January 29, 1990, p. 16.
Economist, January 20, 1990.
Los Angeles Times Book Review, January 28, 1990, pp. 1, 13.
New York Times Book Review, January 21, 1990, p. 7.
Times Literary Supplement, August 10, 1990, p. 846.
Washington Post Book World, January 14, 1990.*

* * *

HENDERSON, William Darryl 1938-

PERSONAL: Born August 26, 1938, in Trail, British Columbia, Canada; son of William Roland (a teacher) and Flora McDonald (a teacher and psychologist; maiden name, McCallum) Henderson; married first wife, Marilyn, 1964 (divorced, 1982); married Mary Ann Gutman (a librarian), December 5, 1985; children: Darryl Gregory, Timothy Michael. *Education:* Attended University of Vienna, 1959-60; Stanford University, B.A., 1961; University of Pittsburgh, Ph.D., 1971; graduated (with honors) from U.S. Army Command and General Staff College, 1974; graduated from National War College, 1983. *Politics:* Independent.

ADDRESSES: Home—19880 Lark Way, Saratoga, CA 95070.

CAREER: U.S. Army, career officer, serving in Korea and Vietnam as infantry commander, 1961-88, retiring as colonel. U.S. Military Academy, assistant professor, 1970-74; other military assignments include deputy commander of Joint Security Area for Panmunjom, Korea, staff assistant in Office of the Deputy Secretary of Defense, executive assistant to the assistant secretary of defense legislative affairs, senior adviser to a major Army Reserve command, senior arms control planner on International Military Staff, Headquarters, North Atlantic Treaty Organization (NATO), and commander of U.S. Army Research Institute for the Behavioral and Social Sciences. Appointed member of President's Commission on the Assignment of Women in the Armed Forces; consultant to Canadian Department of Justice and Canadian Defense Department.

AWARDS, HONORS: Purple Heart, Legion of Merit, Bronze Star, Combat Infantryman's Badge, Meritorious Service Medal with two oak leaf clusters, Air Medal, Joint Service Commendation Medal with oak leaf cluster, and Army Commendation Medal with oak leaf cluster.

WRITINGS:

(Associate editor) *Handbook of World Conflicts,* University of Pittsburgh Press, 1970.

Why the Viet Cong Fought: A Study of Motivation and Control in a Modern Army in Combat, Greenwood Press, 1979.
Cohesion: The Human Element in Combat, National Defense University Press, 1985.
The Hollow Army: How the U.S. Army Is Oversold and Undermanned, Greenwood Press, 1990.

Contributor to books, including *The Study of Leadership,* U.S. Military Academy Press, 1974; and *The Political Education of Soldiers,* edited by Morris Janowitz, Sage Publications, 1983. Contributor to periodicals.

WORK IN PROGRESS: A political novel about a future coup in the United States; research on women in the military.

* * *

HENLE, Fritz 1909-1993

OBITUARY NOTICE—See index for *CA* sketch: Born June 9, 1909, in Dortmund, Germany; immigrated to the United States, 1936, naturalized citizen, 1942; died of a heart attack, January 31, 1993, in San Juan, Puerto Rico. Photographer and writer. After studying photography in Munich, Henle traveled to the United States, where he earned a reputation for his black-and-white representations. His work appeared in such magazines as *Life, Harper's Bazaar,* and *Mademoiselle.* His first book of travel photography, a work that focused on Japan, was published in 1937. In 1948, he moved to St. Croix in the U.S. Virgin Islands and worked on numerous other travel books on locales including China, Mexico, Hawaii, and the Caribbean. Henle also wrote instruction books on his craft, including *Fritz Henle's Guide to Rollei Photography.*

OBITUARIES AND OTHER SOURCES:

BOOKS

Who's Who in American Art 1991-1992, 19th edition, Bowker, 1990, p. 490.

PERIODICALS

Chicago Tribune, February 7, 1993.
New York Times, February 5, 1993, p. A18.

* * *

HERDING, Klaus 1939-

PERSONAL: Born December 27, 1939, in Munich, Germany; son of Otto Herding (a professor); married Helga Reichardt, 1980; children: Maruta. *Education:* Attended University of Tubingen, 1960-61, University of Munich,

1962-64, University of Lille, 1963, and University of Aix-en-Provence, 1965; University of Munster, Ph.D., 1968; University of Hamburg, "Habilitation" degree, 1977.

ADDRESSES: Home—Hamburg, Germany. *Agent*—Kunstgeschichtliches Institut, Hausener Weg 120, D-6000 Frankfurt 90, Germany.

CAREER: National Gallery, Berlin, Germany, assistant to the director, 1968-70; Technische and Free University of Berlin, Berlin, assistant professor of art history, 1971-74; University of Hamburg, Hamburg, Germany, professor of art history, 1975-92, head of faculty of cultural sciences, 1987-88; University of Frankfurt, Frankfurt, Germany, professor of art history, 1993—. Guest professor at University of Bordeaux, 1977-78, University of Marburg, 1980, University of Zurich, 1981, and Graduate School and University Center of the City University of New York, 1985; L'Ecole des Hautes Etudes, Paris, director of studies and guest professor, 1988-90; scholar at the Getty Center, 1992-93. Elected member of the Hamburg Council for Preserving Monuments, 1976-82.

WRITINGS:

Pierre Puget: Das bildnerische Werk, Mann, 1970.

Propylaen Kunstgeschichte (title means "The History of Art"), Jahrhundert, 1970.

(With H. E. Mittig) *Kunst und Alltag im NS-System* (title means "Art and Everyday Life during the National Socialist Era"), Anabas, 1975.

Egalitaet und Autoritaet in Courbets Ladschaftsmalerei (title means "Courbet's Landscape Painting"), Stadel-Jahrbuch, 1975.

(Coeditor with Werner Hofmann) *Courbet und Deutschland* (title means "Courbet and Germany"), Du Mont, 1978.

(Editor) *Realismus als Widerspruch* (title means "Contradictions in Realism"), Suhrkamp, 1978, reprinted 1984.

(With Gunter Otto) *Karikaturen: Nervoese Auffangsorgane des inneren und aeusseren Lebens* (title means "Caricatures"), Anabas, 1980.

Malerei und Theorie (title means "Painting and Theory"), Staedtische Galerie im Staedelschen Kunstinstitut, 1980.

(Coeditor) *Das Courbet-Colloquium im Staedel* (title means "The Courbet Symposium"), [Frankfurt], 1980.

(Coeditor) *Courbet, Gustave, 1819-1877: Les Voyages Secrets de Monsieur Courbet* (title means "The Secret Travels of Gustave Courbet"), Staatliche Kunsthalle Baden-Baden, 1984.

(Editor, translator, and author of introduction) *Proudhon's Art Theory,* [Berlin], 1988.

La Revolution Francaise et l'Europe (title means "Europe and the French Revolution"), [Paris], 1989.

(With Rolf Reichardt) *Die Bildpublizistik der Franzoesischen Revolution* (title means "Broadsheets and Graphics of the French Revolution"), Suhrkamp, 1989.

Im Zeichen der Aufklarung (title means "Under the Sign of Enlightenment"), Fischer Taschenbuch, 1989.

Courbet: To Venture Independence, Yale University Press, 1991.

Also author of *Picasso, Les Demoiselles d'Avignon,* 1992. Contributor to periodicals, including the *Art Bulletin, Burlington Magazine, la Gazette des Beaux-Arts,* and *Pantheon.* Wrote screenplays on French realist painter Gustave Courbet and Belgian surrealist painter Rene Magritte. Coeditor of series, *Kunstwissenschaftliche Forschungen des Ulmer Vereins,* 1970-82, and editor of series *Kunststueck,* 1984-92. Member of consultative committees of *Pantheon, Kritische Berichte, Art History,* and the series *Memoires.*

*　　　*　　　*

HERMAN, Bernard L. 1951-

PERSONAL: Born in 1951.

ADDRESSES: Office—Department of History, University of Delaware, Newark, DE 19716.

CAREER: Worked as professor of history at University of Delaware, Newark; writer.

WRITINGS:

Architectural and Rural Life in Delaware, 1700-1900, University of Tennessee Press, 1987.

(With Svend E. Holsoe) *A Land and Life Remembered: Americo-Liberian Folk Architecture,* afterword by Rodger P. Kingston, photographs by Max Belcher, University of Georgia Press, 1988.

The Stolen House: Material Culture, History, and Metaphor in the Early Republic, University Press of Virginia, 1992.

SIDELIGHTS: Bernard L. Herman is a historian specializing in American architectural developments. Among his work is *The Stolen House: Material Culture, History, and Metaphor in the Early Republic,* which Noel Perrin described in the *New York Times Book Review* as "a curious and mostly quite interesting book." Perrin contended that Herman's purpose with *The Stolen House* "is to pin down the meanings that objects like houses and trees had for people 200 years ago," and he observed that Herman "is especially interested in the ways those meanings varied by social class." According to Perrin, the readers who are tolerant of Herman's "academic" theorizing in *The Stolen House* "will be richly rewarded."

BIOGRAPHICAL/CRITICAL SOURCES:

PERIODICALS

New York Times Book Review, July 12, 1992, p. 11.*

* * *

HERSEY, John (Richard) 1914-1993

OBITUARY NOTICE—See index for *CA* sketch: Born June 17, 1914, in Tientsin, China; died March 23, 1993, in Key West, FL. Educator, journalist, novelist, and author. Hersey began his writing career as a journalist, first as an editor at *Time* magazine, then as a foreign correspondent during World War II. He came to teaching in 1971, spending 18 years as a professor of writing at Yale University and the Massachusetts Institute of Technology. Hersey wrote numerous books and novels, winning a Pulitzer Prize in 1945 for *A Bell for Adano,* a book which recounts the effect of an American military presence in World War II Italy. Although also a novelist, Hersey was most admired for his nonfiction work, particularly his coverage of the atomic bombing of Hiroshima, Japan, in the book *Hiroshima* and, in *The Algiers Motel Incident,* events stemming from the race riots in Detroit. Hersey was best known for his examinations of World War II events, however. As author James Michener stated in the *Detroit Free Press,* "John Hersey's writing about the moral problems in World War II was of the highest quality. . . . Those of us who participated in that war at any level recognize the gravity of what he was attempting." Among Hersey's other successful publications are *Men on Bataan, Blues, Life Sketches,* and *Antonietta.*

OBITUARIES AND OTHER SOURCES:

BOOKS

Who's Who, 145th edition, St. Martin's, 1993.

PERIODICALS

Detroit Free Press, March 25, 1993, p. 6B.

* * *

HEYMAN, Josiah McC(onnell) 1958-

PERSONAL: Born September 23, 1958, in Oklahoma City, OK; son of Louis (a geologist) and Sarah (a biochemist; maiden name, McConnell) Heyman; married Merlyn Deluca (a homemaker), April 12, 1985; children: Robert Louis. *Education:* Johns Hopkins University, B.A., 1980; City University of New York, Ph.D., 1988. *Politics:* Democrat.

ADDRESSES: Home—401 2nd St., Houghton, MI 49931. *Office*—Department of Social Sciences, Michigan Technological University, Houghton, MI 49931.

CAREER: Michigan Technological University, Houghton, assistant professor of anthropology, 1989—.

MEMBER: Latin American Studies Association, American Anthropological Association.

WRITINGS:

Life and Labor on the Border, University of Arizona Press, 1991.

WORK IN PROGRESS: Research on the U.S. Immigration and Naturalization Service at the Mexico-U.S. border.

SIDELIGHTS: Josiah McC. Heyman told *CA:* "I lived in Agua Prieta, Sonora, Mexico, for nearly two years, 1984 to 1986. There I played baseball, went to baptismal parties, visited houses during days and evenings, attended political rallies, drove back and forth across the international border, and carried out in-depth life histories with nearly one-hundred persons that were from twenty to eighty years old. Subsequently, I have returned to the U.S. side of the border for a period of six months, where I interviewed over one-hundred persons who work for the U.S. Immigration and Naturalization Service.

"I am fascinated, first of all, by people; I enjoy nothing more than talking to them, no matter who they are or what they are doing. I am furthermore concerned with understanding the institutional arrangements within which these people live their lives—their work, their nationality, their neighborhood—, which set these personally fascinating individuals against each other in sometimes disturbing manners."

* * *

HIBBERT, Eleanor Alice Burford 1906-1993
(Eleanor Burford; pseudonyms: Philippa Carr, Elbur Ford, Victoria Holt, Kathleen Kellow, Jean Plaidy, Ellalice Tate)

OBITUARY NOTICE—See index for *CA* sketch: Born in 1906, in Kennington, London, England; died January 18, 1993, on a cruise ship in the Mediterranean. Author. In addition to writing historical, Gothic, and romantic novels, Hibbert was perhaps best known by her pseudonyms Jean Plaidy, Victoria Holt, and Philippa Carr. A prolific author, she produced more than 150 books during her lifetime. Hibbert began her literary career writing short stories and was eventually encouraged to create romance novels by her agent. Writing as Jean Plaidy, she published her first novel, *Beyond the Blue Mountains* in 1947. Under this name, she recreated English history and royalty in over ninety novels, such as *Murder Most Royal, Queen in Waiting,* and *Victoria Victorious.* As Victoria Holt, Hibbert wrote Gothic novels with more adventurous heroines, beginning in 1960 with *Mistress of Mellyn* and including the posthumously published *The Black Opal.* Family sagas, historical backgrounds, and extraordinary romance were the domain of Hibbert's pseudonym Philippa Carr, featuring such novels as *The Miracle at St. Bruno's* and *The Adulteress.* Hibbert also published children's books, including *The Young Elizabeth* and *Meg Roper: Daughter of Sir Thomas More,* both under the pseudonym Jean Plaidy.

OBITUARIES AND OTHER SOURCES:

BOOKS

The Writers Directory: 1992-1994, St. James Press, 1992.

PERIODICALS

Chicago Tribune, January 24, 1993, sec. 2, p. 7.
Los Angeles Times, January 22, 1993, p. A22.
Times (London), January 21, 1993, p. 19.
Washington Post, January 21, 1993, p. B7.

*   *   *

HIBBING, John R.   1953-

PERSONAL: Born December 31, 1953; married; children: three. *Education:* Dana College, B.S., 1976; University of Iowa, M.A., 1978, Ph.D., 1980.

ADDRESSES: Office—Department of Political Science, University of Nebraska—Lincoln, Lincoln, NE 68588-0328.

CAREER: Oakland University, Rochester, MI, visiting instructor in political science, 1980-81; University of Nebraska—Lincoln, assistant professor, 1981-85, associate professor, 1985-90, professor of political science, 1990—, chair of department, 1991—. University of Essex, fellow in science and government, 1984-85; Institute of Regional Studies in Budapest, Hungary, visiting professor, 1990.

MEMBER: International Political Science Association (member of executive council, 1991-94), Midwest Political Science Association (member of executive council, 1987-90).

AWARDS, HONORS: Grants from National Science Foundation, 1980, 1987-88, and 1992-93; fellow in England, North Atlantic Treaty Organization, 1984-85; grants from Dirksen Congressional Center, 1986 and 1988; CQ Press Award, 1987.

WRITINGS:

(Editor with John G. Peters) *The Changing World of the U.S. Senate,* University of California Institute of Governmental Studies, 1990.
Congressional Careers: Contours of Life in the U.S. House of Representatives, University of North Carolina Press, 1991.

Work represented in anthologies, including *Elected Politicians and Their Careers,* edited by Shirley Williams and Edward Lascher, Harvard University Press, 1991; *Modern Parliaments,* edited by Gary W. Copeland, University of Oklahoma Press, 1991; and *Human Rights in Eastern and Central Europe,* edited by David P. Forsythe, 1992. Contributor of articles to political science journals. *Legislative Studies Quarterly,* member of editorial board, 1984-86 and 1990-92, coeditor, 1992-94; *American Politics Quarterly,* associate editor, 1987-90, coeditor, 1991-92; also member of editorial board for *American Political Science Review,* 1985-89, and *American Journal of Political Science,* 1991-93.

WORK IN PROGRESS: Congressional Elections, with John R. Alford; *Disconnecting the Electoral Connection,* with Rebekah Herrick and Michael K. Moore; *The Decline in Trust of a Crumbling Regime: Hungary, 1985-1990* and *Elite Circulation in a Peaceful Revolution: Hungary, 1990,* both with Ivan Volgyes; *The History of Congressional Careers;* and *Public Perceptions of the U.S. Congress,* with Elizabeth Theiss-Morse.

*   *   *

HIGHTOWER, Lynn S.

PERSONAL: Born in Chattanooga, TN. *Education:* Received B.A. from University of Kentucky. *Avocational interests:* Canoeing, riding horses, eating M&Ms.

ADDRESSES: Home—Lexington, KY. *Agent*—Matthew Bialer, William Morris Agency, 1350 Ave. of the Americas, New York, NY 10019.

CAREER: Full-time fiction writer.

MEMBER: Horror Writers of America, Mystery Writers of America, Science Fiction Writers of America, Sisters in Crime.

WRITINGS:

Alien Blues (part of "David Silver" series), Ace Books, 1991.
Satan's Lambs, Walker & Co., 1992.
Alien Eyes (part of "David Silver" series), Ace Books, 1993.

Short stories represented in several anthologies, including *Women of Darkness II,* Tor Books, 1990; *Final Shadows,* Doubleday, 1991.

WORK IN PROGRESS: Working on more "David Silver" books; also writing a mystery novel.

SIDELIGHTS: Lynn S. Hightower told *CA:* "I like to combine genres—take what I like out of every genre and put it all in one story. As you can see, I take the kitchen-sink approach to writing. A lot of my work includes dead bodies, aliens, and dark and stormy nights—though *Satan's Lambs* is strictly a mystery. I tried to slip a ghost into the story, but my editor wisely called the plot police." Hightower also said that she shares her office with two cats and an iguana named Earl.

*   *   *

HILL, Walter 1942-

PERSONAL: Born January 10, 1942, in Long Beach, CA. *Education:* Attended the University of Americas, Mexico City, 1959-60; Michigan State University, B.A., 1962, M.A., 1963.

ADDRESSES: Agent—Jeff Berg, International Creative Management, 8899 Beverly Blvd., Los Angeles, CA 90048.

CAREER: Filmmaker and screenwriter. Director of motion pictures, including *The Long Riders,* 1980; *Brewster's Millions,* 1985; *Crossroads,* 1986; *Extreme Prejudice,* 1987; *Johnny Handsome,* 1989; and *Another Forty-eight Hours,* 1990. Producer of motion pictures, including *Alien,* 1979; *Aliens,* 1986; *Blue City,* 1986; and *Alien III,* 1992. Coexecutive producer and director for television series *Tales from the Crypt,* Home Box Office, 1989.

WRITINGS:

SCREENPLAYS

Hickey and Boggs, United Artists, 1972.
The Getaway (adapted from the novel by Jim Thompson), National General, 1972.
The Thief Who Came to Dinner, Warner Brothers, 1973.
The Mackintosh Man, Warner Brothers, 1973.
(With Tracy Keenan Wynn and Lorenzo Semple) *The Drowning Pool* (adapted from the novel by Ross Macdonald), Warner Brothers, 1975.
(With Bruce Henstell and Bryan Gindorff; and director) *Hard Times,* Columbia, 1975.
(And director) *The Driver,* Twentieth Century-Fox, 1978.
(With David Shaber; and director) *The Warriors* (adapted from the novel by Sol Yurick), Paramount, 1979.
(With Michael Kane and David Giler; and director) *Southern Comfort,* Twentieth Century-Fox, 1981.

(With Larry Gross, Roger Spottiswoode, and Steven E. De Souza; and director) *Forty-eight Hours,* Paramount, 1982.
(With Gross; and director) *Streets of Fire,* Universal, 1984.
(With Lukas Heller) *Blue City,* Paramount, 1986.
(With Harry Kleiner and Troy Kennedy Martin; and director and producer) *Red Heat,* TriStar, 1988.
(With David Giler and Larry Ferguson) *Alien III* (based on a story by Vincent Ward), Twentieth Century-Fox, 1992.

Also writer of episodes for television series *Tales from the Crypt,* Home Box Office, 1989.

SIDELIGHTS: Walter Hill is a filmmaker whose stylish action films are often distinguished by a sharp juxtaposition of humor and violence. He began his career as a screenwriter in 1965, and also supported himself by working as a production assistant and assistant director. In the latter capacity Hill worked on the romantic thriller *The Thomas Crown Affair* in 1968, and the next year he assumed similar duties on Woody Allen's comedy *Take the Money and Run.* After completing these projects, Hill concentrated on screenwriting, and in 1972 two of his scripts were produced, *Hickey and Boggs,* a grim thriller, and *The Getaway,* a violent action film directed by genre master Sam Peckinpah. The next year saw production of Hill's *The Thief Who Came to Dinner,* a crime comedy about a computer whiz who becomes a high-society jewel thief, and *The Mackintosh Man,* a gloomy spy drama directed by John Huston. Hill also cowrote the screenplay for 1975's *The Drowning Pool,* which featured Paul Newman as a resourceful private detective.

In 1975 Hill made his debut as writer-director with *Hard Times,* a grim drama about a boxer and a con artist who team up during the Depression. His next effort, *The Driver,* featured Ryan O'Neal as a famed getaway driver who attempts to elude a determined police detective. Vincent Canby, reviewing *The Driver* in the *New York Times,* was critical of the cliched portrayals in the film, terming the movie "singularly unexciting and uninvolving."

Hill followed *The Driver* with *The Warriors,* a violent chase film set in the street-gang milieu of New York City. The story follows a hapless band of street toughs, the Warriors, who are wrongly accused of murdering an ambitious gang leader. Trapped in unfamiliar surroundings and hunted by a host of rival gangs, the Warriors must battle their way through various enemy territories to reach the safety of their home turf. The trek provides for an exhausting night of mayhem and chase which concludes in a showdown with those who actually committed the initial murder.

Critical response to *The Warriors* was mixed, with many initial reviews objecting to the considerable violence in the film. This response seemed prophetic when riots broke out at several theaters showing the movie. Three people were killed in the sporadic violence, and authorities discussed banning the film in several locations. After this uproar had subsided, critics took a more careful look at *The Warriors.* *Saturday Review* contributor Robert F. Moss continued to decry the film's violence. "Bashing someone's head in," the critic wrote, "is almost equivalent to a casual work-out at the gym." *Film Quarterly* reviewer Terrence Rafferty, on the other hand, called it Hill's "most optimistic film," emphasizing the strong bonds that exist between members of the Warriors. "They're racially mixed, they don't have a uniform, they're not one of the large, powerful gangs," Rafferty noted. "What binds them is their friendship, their loyalty to each other." Regardless of the critical debate, a sizeable audience was drawn to *The Warriors,* and it became a cult favorite in the years following its release.

In 1980 Hill directed *The Long Riders,* a film about the notorious James-Younger gang of the late 1800's. In a unique move, Hill cast real-life siblings to portray the brothers in the gang, including James and Stacy Keach as Frank and Jesse James, David, Keith, and Robert Carradine as the Younger brothers, and Randy and Dennis Quaid as Ed and Clell Miller. The film was well received by a number of critics, and it won Hill comparisons to many acclaimed directors, including everyone from John Ford to Sam Peckinpah to Howard Hawks to Raoul Walsh. *Time*'s Richard Schickel affirmed that "Hill is very much in the American grain, the inheritor of the Ford-Hawks-Walsh tradition of artful, understated action film making." *New York*'s David Denby, while expressing some reservations about *The Long Riders,* nonetheless described portions of the movie as "rapturously beautiful," and proclaimed it "the best-directed American movie of the year."

Hill's next film, *Southern Comfort,* concerns a National Guard unit that is attacked by Cajuns while conducting military exercises in the Louisiana bayou. Like much of Hill's canon, the film—which he also cowrote—is an examination of desperate men in a violent situation. *Chicago Tribune* reviewer Gene Siskel described *Southern Comfort* as being "about nothing less than when its OK to kill another human being." The critic found this dark justification of violence to be "absolutely riveting," and called *Southern Comfort* "the best Hill film of all."

Forty-eight Hours, Hill's 1982 comedy-action film, is probably his most popular work. Here a gruff white police officer allies himself with a wise-cracking black convict to apprehend a gun-wielding psychopath, the convict's former partner in crime. Much of the film is based on a series of chases and searches through San Francisco, with the unlikely heroes exchanging insults and, eventually, blows. One of the film's most popular scenes occurs when the

convict, played by comedian Eddie Murphy, pretends to be a police officer, gleefully insulting the bigoted patrons of a country-western bar. This episode, declared Janet Maslin in her *New York Times* appraisal, is "destined to become a classic." The critic also praised the film's memorable characters and pronounced the movie "highly entertaining." Pauline Kael, writing in *New Yorker,* expressed some dissatisfaction with *Forty-eight Hours,* but also found the film to be "excitingly paced; it hooks you at the start and never lets up." The movie's public appeal became clear when it ranked as one of the most commercially successful productions of the year.

Hill remained active in the action genre with *Streets of Fire,* his 1984 film in which a female rock singer is abducted in mid-performance by a band of gruesome bikers. The singer's ex-boyfriend, a glowering soldier of fortune, then takes action, tracking down the kidnappers. Critical reaction to the film was uneven, with many finding the story overbearing and excessively violent. Hill next completed *Brewster's Millions,* in which a minor-league baseball player (played by popular comic actor Richard Pryor) stands to inherit $300 million if he can first spend $30 million within thirty days. This film, which Hill directed from a script by Herschel Weingrod and Timothy Harris, was generally dismissed by critics. Sheila Benson, for instance, wrote in the *Los Angeles Times* that "the fun wears off fast and a faint distaste takes over as millions spill away into nothing."

In 1986 Hill directed *Crossroads,* a film about a young white guitarist obsessed with the blues. He is particularly fascinated by the legend of blues great Robert Johnson, who is said to have sold his soul to the devil to gain his prodigious musical talents. The young man seeks out an aging contemporary of Johnson's and, with the old man in tow, returns to the crossroads where Johnson made his fated deal. The film concludes with the young guitarist and the old man confronting the devil in a musical showdown. *Crossroads* did average business but fared poorly with critics. Paul Attanasio, writing in the *Washington Post,* found the film "drab and predictable" and wondered if "Hill has become a stranger to his own sensibility."

The director returned to action films in 1987 with *Extreme Prejudice,* the story of old friends who meet again on the dusty Texas-Mexico border. In the course of the film one of the men, an incorruptible Texas Ranger, must confront his friend who has become a drug dealer. Their bond is soon undone, and the two men confront each other in a violent showdown.

Hill's next film, *Red Heat,* was another action film, this one focusing on the unlikely union of a humorless Moscow police officer and his cynical, wisecracking Chicago counterpart. These lawmen have teamed to apprehend a Soviet drug dealer who has escaped from his country and fled to Chicago. Like *Forty-eight Hours, Red Heat* is a chase film in which seemingly incompatible partners establish a strong bond while tracking a deadly foe. *Los Angeles Times* reviewer Michael Wilmington termed the film "a really bizarre variation on the urban crime melodrama." Though he considered the film "above average," for this genre, Wilmington found that *Red Heat* "doesn't have the human levels and depth" of some of Hill's previous films. Vincent Canby, in his *New York Times* review, gave the movie a mixed review. "*Red Heat,*" Canby wrote, "is a topically entertaining variation on the sort of action-adventure nonsense that plays best on television."

In 1989 Hill completed directorial duties on *Johnny Handsome,* a film which centers on a convict whose face has been disfigured since birth. Early in the film Johnny is betrayed by his partners in crime and sent to prison. There a prison doctor theorizes that Johnny's horrible disfiguration led to his life of crime. If this deformity is corrected, the doctor believes, Johnny can return to society and forsake crime. After the operation, Johnny gains his release and tries to live an honest life. When he falls in with his former criminal colleagues, however, he attempts to exact revenge for their earlier betrayal.

Hill followed *Johnny Handsome* by directing *Another Forty-eight Hours,* a sequel to his greatest commercial success. Here the heroes of the earlier film reunite and embark on another chase interspersed with humor and violence. *Another Forty-eight Hours* failed to receive the critical acclaim of its predecessor, but its public appeal remained intact. The sequel equalled the commercial success of the original *Forty-eight Hours* in the United States, and surpassed it in foreign markets. The warm overseas reception to *Another Forty-eight Hours* illustrated the popularity Hill's films have often achieved outside the United States.

Critics have frequently commented on the strict moral code that exists in Hill's film universe. His characters may exhibit weakness or vice, but there are clear lines as to whether the role is antagonist or protagonist. Despite strong definitions of right and wrong, Hill does not analyze or attempt to justify his characters' thoughts and actions. As he stated in a *Film Comment* interview, "The screen character with his suitcase packed with psychoanalytic motivation bores me." As a result, Hill tends to explain his own protagonists in simple terms. "In my films," he continued, "when somebody puts a gun in your face, character is how many times you blink." *Film Comment* writer Mike Greco made a more careful assessment of the figures in Hill's films, describing them as "characters who are clearly responsible for their actions." The critic also noted that Hill's audience is "manipulated to understand that success and failure, good fortune and calamity are, in

large measure, functions of character." While Hill paints stark cause and effect scenarios in his films, he sees them as more entertaining than realistic. "Movies have their own strange world," Hill stated in *Film Comment,* "and they are very logical within that world. The world we create in movies has more to do with your dream life than it does with the everyday world we live in."

BIOGRAPHICAL/CRITICAL SOURCES:

BOOKS

Dictionary of Literary Biography, Volume 44: *American Screenwriters, Second Series,* Gale, 1986.

PERIODICALS

Chicago Tribune, October 16, 1981; June 4, 1984; June 17, 1988.
Esquire, November, 1981, pp. 116-22.
Film Comment, May-June, 1980, pp. 13-19; March-April, 1983, pp. 9-18.
Film Quarterly, fall, 1982, pp. 20-27.
Los Angeles Times, May 22, 1985; May 2, 1986; June 17, 1988.
Newsweek, July 4, 1988, p. 58.
New York, May 26, 1980, pp. 68-69; June 10, 1985, p. 78; May 11, 1987, pp. 70-74; June 25, 1990, p. 64.
New Yorker, May 26, 1980, pp. 68-69; January 10, 1983, pp. 86-90; April 21, 1986, pp. 100-04; October 16, 1989, p. 110.
New York Times, July 28, 1978; December 8, 1982; June 1, 1984; May 2, 1986; June 17, 1988.
People, June 1, 1984, p. 12; June 10, 1985, p. 12; May 11, 1987, p. 10; October 16, 1989.
Rolling Stone, April 5, 1979, pp. 40-41.
Saturday Review, October, 1980, pp. 14-18.
Sight and Sound, summer, 1982, pp. 194-98.
Time, June 16, 1980, p. 51; December 20, 1982, p. 82; June 25, 1990, p. 77.
Washington Post, March 24, 1986; May 5, 1986; June 17, 1988.

—*Sketch by Les Stone*

*   *   *

HINES, Jeanne 1922-
(Rosamond Royal, Valerie Sherwood)

PERSONAL: Born July 29, 1922, in Moorefield, West Virginia; daughter of Llewellyn and Bess (Heiskell) Brown; married Edward Thomas Hines, October 14, 1943. *Education:* Graduated from Southern Virginia College for Women; attended National Art School. *Politics:* Republican. *Religion:* Protestant. *Avocational interests:*

History, travel, archaeology, geology, astronomy, interesting houses, cats.

ADDRESSES: Home—Ormond Beach, FL. *Office*—c/o Severn House Publishers, Inc., 475 Fifth Ave., New York, NY 10017.

CAREER: Writer. Taught at National Art Academy in Washington, DC; worked as magazine illustrator for ten years; worked as free-lance commercial artist; reporter for the Judge Advocate General of the Air Force and for the Pentagon for six years; conference reporter for several national organizations and societies; reporter of White House conferences.

MEMBER: Daughters of the American Revolution, Daughters of the American Colonists, American Association for the Advancement of Science, National Trust for Historic Preservation.

AWARDS, HONORS: Navy Commendation for Meritorious Civilian Service during World War II; Romantic Times Lifetime Achievement Award, 1987-88; commendation from Harvard University for Conference on the Olmec at Dumbarton Oaks.

WRITINGS:

The Slashed Portrait, Dell, 1973.
Tidehawks, Popular Library, 1974.
Talons of the Hawk, Dell, 1975.
Brides of Terror, Popular Library, 1976.
Scarecrow House, Popular Library, 1976.
The Keys to Queenscourt, Popular Library, 1976.
The Legend of Witchwynd, Popular Library, 1976.
The Third Wife, Popular Library, 1977.

Author of short stories, some of which have been included in textbooks and anthologies. Columnist for periodicals, including the *Washington Star-News* and the *Georgetowner.*

UNDER PSEUDONYM VALERIE SHERWOOD

This Loving Torment, Warner Books, 1977.
These Golden Pleasures, Warner Books, 1977.
This Towering Passion, Warner Books, 1978.
Her Shining Splendor, Warner Books, 1980.
Bold Breathless Love, Warner Books, 1981.
Rash Reckless Love, Warner Books, 1981.
Wild Willful Love, Warner Books, 1982.
Rich Radiant Love, Warner Books, 1983.
Lovely Lying Lips, Warner Books, 1983.
Born to Love, Warner Books, 1984.
Lovesong, Pocket Books, 1985.
Windsong, Pocket Books, 1986.
Nightsong, Pocket Books, 1986.
To Love a Rogue, New American Library, 1987.
Lisbon, New American Library, 1988.

UNDER PSEUDONYM ROSAMOND ROYAL

Rapture, Popular Library, 1979.

WORK IN PROGRESS: "A big historical novel."

SIDELIGHTS: Jeanne Hines, better known to historical romance readers by her pseudonym Valerie Sherwood, has won an audience with tales of adventure and passion. Often set during the seventeenth century, her long novels portray beautiful and courageous heroines who find and lose love with a variety of roguish men, many of them buccaneers. Eschewing rape and graphic violence, Hines has sold more than one million copies of many of her historicals. Under her own name she has also written romantic mystery novels.

Hines told *CA:* "In the course of a long lifetime, I have lived out the dreams of most of my friends: I have traveled, met the great and the near-great, enjoyed the V.I.P. table at top-level conferences, seen my short stories published internationally and published in textbooks and anthologies. I have seen my mystery novels critically acclaimed and my historical novels enthusiastically received by the public. I have enjoyed being a critic (reviewing spy novels in Washington, D.C., was perhaps the most fun), but I felt I must read every word of every book I reviewed. And since they arrived on my desk in enormous boxes, I knew I would eventually go blind under the strain so I gave it up.

"I feel I must have been born under a lucky star, for I was endowed with wonderful parents who were an endless inspiration to me. My interest in history comes naturally, for I was born in a beautiful valley lying between the Alleghenies and the Blue Ridge, bisected by the south branch of the Potomac that flows down to Washington, D.C., a river lined by lovely colonial homes, most of them built by my ancestors (my ancestors owned Fairfax Grant land surveyed by George Washington). I grew up on tales of the Civil War, in which my grandfather, a dashing Confederate Major, reluctantly surrendered his sword at Appomattox and came back to the Valley to marry a doctor's daughter (a celebrated beauty) and ride with his bride to Texas.

"I come from a romantic background. My parents' long love affair was the very stuff of novels—they were married half a lifetime. And I too was lucky in love. I met a man who had been everywhere and done everything, lived a dozen lifetimes in one even before he met me, and we fell in love at first sight. This year we will celebrate our golden wedding anniversary—fifty years in which we have traveled extensively, been in numerous businesses, and enjoyed our many hobbies, such as prospecting for gold, searching for fossils, prowling through digs and archaeological sites across Mexico, having heated discussions of scientific theories in astronomy and geology, and visiting historic places. Genealogy was one of our passionate interests, and even there we were lucky. Through diligent research and endless field trips we managed to trace every single family line for both of us back before the American Revolution. My first ancestor to arrive in North America was Secretary to the Virginia Colony in 1622, and my husband had an ancestor, 'Lad Kirby,' who came over on the *Mayflower* intending to join his relatives already in Virginia.

"Writing has been good to me too. I'm doing work I love, my books have sold millions of copies (I have a dozen *New York Times* bestsellers back-to-back), my fans write me wonderful letters, and the critics have been kind to me. Here are two gems I will share with you: *Publishers Weekly* declared my novel *Rapture* 'a true romantic's wildest dream' and the *New York Times,* in reviewing a novel I had dedicated to my wonderful cat Fuzzy, said unequivocally, 'Fuzzy would be pleased.' I cherish both comments because I believe they're undoubtedly true!"

BIOGRAPHICAL/CRITICAL SOURCES:

BOOKS

Twentieth-Century Romance and Historical Writers, 2nd edition, St. James Press, 1990, pp. 593-94.

*   *   *

HOBSON, J(ohn) Allan 1933-

PERSONAL: Born June 3, 1933, in Hartford, CT; son of John Robert (a patent attorney) and Anne Barnard (Cotter) Hobson; married Joan Merle Harlowe (a museum administrator), June 23, 1956; children: Ian Bruce Harlowe, Christopher Roger Williams, Julia Anne Laird. *Education:* Wesleyan University, A.B. (with honors and distinction), 1955; Harvard University, M.D., 1959.

ADDRESSES: Office—Harvard Medical School, 74 Fenwood Rd., Boston, MA 02115.

CAREER: Certification as diplomate by American Board of Psychiatry and Neurology, 1968; physician licensed in Massachusetts. Bellevue Hospital, New York City, intern in medicine, 1959-60; Massachusetts Mental Health Center, Boston, resident in psychiatry, 1960-61 and 1964-66, senior psychiatrist, 1965-67, director of laboratory of neurophysiology, 1967, principal psychiatrist, 1967—, director of group psychotherapy training program, 1972-80; National Institute of Mental Health, Bethesda, MD, clinical associate, 1961-63; Harvard Medical School, Boston, research associate in physiology department, 1964-67, instructor in psychiatry, 1966-67, associate in psychiatry, 1967-69, assistant professor, 1969-74, associate professor,

1974, professor of psychiatry, 1978—, professor of psychiatry (neuroscience), 1983—, director of behavioral science teaching program, 1980-86; Brown University, Providence, RI, lecturer in psychiatry, 1972-74.

University of Lyon, special fellow of the National Institute of Mental Health, 1963-64; University of Bordeaux, visiting scientist and lecturer, 1973; University of Edinburgh, Sandoz lecturer, 1975; Italian National Health Research Institute, lecturer, 1978; Istituto di Psicologia, Universita degli Studi, Rome, visiting professor, 1983; Rockefeller Foundation scholar in residence, Bellagio Conference and Study Center, 1987; MacArthur Foundation, health programs consultant, 1989-91, member of Mind-Body Interaction Network, 1992—; University of Messina, visiting professor, 1992—. Consultant to Massachusetts Rehabilitation Commission, Peter Bent Brigham Hospital, Beth Israel Hospital, and Brigham and Women's Hospital.

MEMBER: National Institute of Mental Health (member of scientific advisory board, 1981-84), American Association for Advancement of Science, Society for Neuroscience, Sleep Research Society, Association for the Psychophysiological Study of Sleep, U.S. Public Health Service (lieutenant), Sigma Xi.

AWARDS, HONORS: Benjamin Rush Gold Medal for best scientific exhibit, American Psychiatric Association, 1978; Von Humboldt Award, Federal Republic of Germany, 1990; grants from the National Institute of Mental Health and the MacArthur Foundation.

WRITINGS:

(With Robert W. McCarley) *Neuronal Activity in Sleep: An Annotated Bibliography,* UCLA Brain Information Service, 1971, 2nd edition, 1977.
(Editor with Mary A. Brazier) *The Reticular Formation Revisited,* Raven Press, 1979.
(Selector and author of introduction) *States of Brain and Mind and Abnormal States of Brain and Mind,* Birkhauser Boston, c. 1988.
The Dreaming Brain, Basic Books, 1988.
Sleep, Scientific American Library, 1989.
Sleep and Dreams, Carolina Biological Supply, 1992.

Contributor to books, and to *Encyclopedia Britannica;* contributor of articles on the physiology of sleep and dreaming to professional journals. *Sleep Reviews,* contributing editor, 1970-72, associate editor, 1972-73, editor-in-chief, 1973-74, and book review editor, 1975-76. Member of editorial board for *Journal of Cellular and Molecular Neurobiology,* 1980-86, *Archives Italiennes de Biologie,* 1983—, and *Encyclopedia of Neuroscience,* 1985—. Section editor for *Neuroreport,* 1990—.

Hobson's works have been translated into German, Dutch, French, Italian, and Japanese.

WORK IN PROGRESS: A book that attempts to construct and explain a general theory of conscious states, publication expected by Little, Brown in 1994; research on the biological basis of dreaming.

SIDELIGHTS: A professor of psychiatry at Harvard Medical School who has devoted his research and writings to the study of sleep and dreams, J. Allan Hobson earned international attention with his 1988 book, *The Dreaming Brain,* which *American Scientist* contributor John Antrobus hailed as "unquestionably the finest book ever written on the neuropsychology of dreaming sleep." Critics praised Hobson for presenting his fresh and insightful theory in a work accessible to a general audience. In *The Dreaming Brain,* Hobson argues that dreams are physiologically based and that the best approach to analyzing and understanding them is to study the neural mechanisms related to the dreaming process. Yet, the author also acknowledges and appreciates the tantalizing, esoteric quality of dreams. In *The Dreaming Brain,* he writes, "In our dreams, we all become writers, painters and film makers, combining extraordinary sets of characters, actions, and locations into strangely coherent experiences." Drawing on years of clinical research, Hobson challenges long-accepted theories of dreams in his book. *Science* contributor Robert J. Moore remarked that the author's "thesis, simply stated, is that dreams are what they seem to be, fragments of mental activity that occur during sleep."

In *The Dreaming Brain,* Hobson "gives a masterful tour of the history of dream research," according to Lee Dembart in the *Los Angeles Times.* Hobson notes that during the nineteenth and twentieth centuries, two separate approaches, neurological and psychological, were used to explain dreaming. Austrian psychoanalyst Sigmund Freud, in his 1900 work *The Interpretation of Dreams,* originated the psychoanalytical theory of dreams by categorizing them as the disguised expressions of the unconscious, thus necessitating interpretation. Hobson, however, does not believe in the need for interpretation; for him dreams are transparent. Whereas Freud attributed the sometimes bizarre nature of dreams to the attempts of the ego to disguise or censor unconscious thoughts, Hobson theorizes that such strange content is the result of the brain trying to make sense of random stimuli it receives. Hobson further maintains that advances in the knowledge of brain structure and biochemistry invalidate portions of Freud's theory. And, the author believes that dreaming is inherently healthy, rather than neurotic as Freud suggested.

In *The Dreaming Brain,* Hobson points out that the average person devotes fifty thousand hours to dreaming in a lifetime; most of these dreams, however, are forgotten. The author has recorded his own dreams in a journal for decades and offers excerpts of his entries throughout the book. *London Review of Books* contributor Jeffrey Saver remarked that this is "unique to the field of dream studies: the subjective dream report." Hobson also includes some descriptions of the more than two hundred dreams that were chronicled by a Washington, D.C., scientist in 1939. In addition, Hobson has helped supervise laboratory experiments in which subjects are awakened to describe their dreams.

Hobson uses his painstaking research—as well as previous studies that have related dreams to increased neural activity—to support the "activation-synthesis" theory of dreaming that he and fellow Harvard Medical School staffer Robert W. McCarley introduced in 1977. This model attempts to show how dreams result from states and processes within the brain. The author maintains that dreams begin when a particular group of nerve cells in the brain stem is activated. Hobson claims in *The Dreaming Brain* that the brain, "inexorably bent upon the quest for meaning," takes the signals it receives and tries to make logical associations. It is this aspect of dreaming—how signals are arranged to form a storyline—that Hobson believes reveals the dreamer's "drives, fears and associations."

Though the Hobson-McCarley theory of dream activity leaves some questions unanswered—whether, for instance, dreams can ever be reliably interpreted as symbolic or metaphorical messages—it is widely accepted for the explanations it does present. Saver pointed out that "the purpose of dreaming may so far have eluded scientific investigation, but Hobson, in the theory outlined in *The Dreaming Brain,* has provided a fully satisfactory initial model of the mechanism for the generation of the dream state." The reviewer further remarked that "Hobson has helped loosen the Freudian shackles which have hitherto hobbled mind-brain theorists," and added, "he has created an exemplary model for a unified theory of all human mental activity." Though Gina Kolata complained in the *New York Times Book Review* of Hobson's "overly technical and clumsy style," *Los Angeles Times* contributor Dembart commended the author for his "elegant style both in thought and expression." Dembart concluded that *The Dreaming Brain* "presents a coherent, experimental, non-Freudian theory of dreaming that is full of evidence, argument and passion."

Hobson is also the author of *Sleep,* which is a detailed treatment of various aspects of sleep, including sleep's neurological, evolutionary, behavioral, and psychological features. In addition, the book covers dreaming, disordered sleep, and the functions of sleep. Aimed at the general reader, *Sleep* is an "attractive book" that is "sumptuously illustrated," according to Jacob Empson in the *Times Higher Education Supplement.* Wallace B. Pickworth noted in *Science Books and Films* that the work "will interest both the lay reader and the scientist," and that it is "highly recommended to those interested in a general overview of current topics in sleep and dream research."

BIOGRAPHICAL/CRITICAL SOURCES:

BOOKS

Hobson, J. Allan, *The Dreaming Brain,* Basic Books, 1988.

PERIODICALS

American Scientist, May-June, 1989, p. 294.
London Review of Books, August 4, 1988, pp. 11-12.
Los Angeles Times, April 22, 1988.
Newsweek, August 14, 1989, pp. 41-44.
New York Review of Books, June 15, 1989, pp. 28-32.
New York Times Book Review, March 27, 1988, p. 36.
Science, May 20, 1988, pp. 1078-79.
Science Books and Films, January/February, 1990, p. 128.
Times Higher Education Supplement, October 27, 1989.

*   *   *

HODGKIN, Alan (Lloyd)   1914-

PERSONAL: Born February 5, 1914, in Banbury, England; son of George Hodgkin (a bank secretary) and Mary (Wilson) Smith; married Marni Rous (in publishing), March 31, 1944; children: Sarah Hayes, Deborah, Jonathan, Rachel. *Education:* Attended Trinity College, Cambridge.

CAREER: Trinity College, Cambridge, England, fellow, 1936—, master, 1978-84; Cambridge University, Cambridge, began as instructor, became professor of physiology, 1938-81; University of Leicester, Leicester, England, chancellor, 1971-84. *Military service:* Royal Air Force, 1939-45; worked on concept and design of airborne radar.

MEMBER: Physiological Society, Royal Society (president, 1970-75).

AWARDS, HONORS: Nobel Prize for Physiology or Medicine (with Sir John Carew Eccles and Andrew F. Huxley), Noble Foundation, 1963, for studies of the ionic mechanisms in the nerve cell membrane; Copley Medal, Royal Society, 1965; Helmerich Prize, 1988.

WRITINGS:

Conduction of Nervous Impulse, Liverpool University Press, 1964.
Biographical Memoir of Lord Adrian, Royal Society, 1976.
(With others) *Pursuit of Nature,* Cambridge University Press, 1976.
Chance and Design: Reminiscences of Science in Peace and War, Cambridge University Press, 1992.

Also author of *Starting Again,* an autobiography. Contributor to periodicals, including *Journal of Physiology.*

*   *   *

HOLT, Victoria
See HIBBERT, Eleanor Alice Burford

*   *   *

HORNE, Gerald   1949-

PERSONAL: Born January 3, 1949, in St. Louis, MO; son of Jerry (a truck driver) and Flora (a maid) Horne. *Education:* Princeton University, B.A., 1970; University of California, Berkeley, J.D., 1973; Columbia University, Ph.D., 1982. *Politics:* Peace and Freedom Party.

ADDRESSES: Home—972 West Campus Point Ln., Goleta, CA 93117. *Office*—c/o Black Studies, University of California, Santa Barbara, Santa Barbara, CA 93106.

CAREER: Writer, lawyer, journalist. Former executive director of National Conference of Black Lawyers; conducted human rights investigations in West Bank/Gaza and Philippines. Chair of Peace and Freedom Party.

WRITINGS:

Black and Red: W. E. B. Du Bois and the Afro-American Response to the Cold War, 1944-1963, State University of New York Press, 1985.
Communist Front? The Civil Rights Congress, 1946-1956, Fairleigh Dickinson University Press, 1988.
Studies in Black: Progressive Views and Reviews of the African American Experience, Kendall/Hunt, 1992.
Reversing Discrimination: The Case for Affirmative Action, International Publishers, 1992.

Also contributor to *Thinking and Rethinking U.S. History,* Council on Interracial Books for Children, 1988.

*   *   *

HORTON, Myles   1905-1990

PERSONAL: Born July 5, 1905, in Savannah, TN; died of a brain tumor, January 19, 1990, in New Market, TN; married Zilphia Johnson (deceased); married Aimee Isgrig (divorced); children: Thorsten, Charis. *Education:* Attended Cumberland Presbyterian College and Union Theological Seminary.

CAREER: Educator and writer. Highlander Folk School, Monteagle, TN (later the Highlander Research and Education Center in New Market, TN), founder and head, beginning in 1932.

AWARDS, HONORS: Received Rothko Chapel Award for Commitment to Truth and Freedom, 1986; Robert F. Kennedy Book Award, 1991, for *The Long Haul.*

WRITINGS:

(With Frank Adams) *Unearthing Seeds of Fire: The Idea of Highlander,* J. F. Blair, 1975.
(With Paulo Freire) *We Make the Road by Walking: Conversations on Education and Social Change,* edited by Brenda Bell, John Gaventa, and John Peters, Temple University Press, 1990.
(With Judith Kohl and Herbert Kohl) *The Long Haul: An Autobiography,* Doubleday, 1990.

SIDELIGHTS: Myles Horton founded the controversial Highlander Folk School in 1932 in Monteagle, Tennessee. It was a school intended to educate the working class; in the words of Alfonse A. Narvaez in the *New York Times,* Horton "taught thousands of blacks and whites to challenge entrenched social, economic and political strictures of a segregated society." Over the years as head of Highlander, Horton worked with labor unions and civil rights organizations to promote socialist goals, but he was always independent in his beliefs and frequently differed from the doctrine of official left-wing groups. On the occasion of Highlander's fortieth anniversary, Horton said, as quoted by Narvaez: "We believe that education leads to action. . . . If you advocate just one action, you're an organizer. We teach leadership here. Then people go out and do what they want." Horton expounded his educational theories in two books that he co-authored—*Unearthing Seeds of Fire: The Idea of Highlander* and *We Make the Road by Walking: Conversations on Education and Social Change.* Before his death in 1990 he completed work on his autobiography, *The Long Haul.*

Horton was born July 5, 1905, in Savannah, Tennessee. His family was very religious, and he entered Cumberland Presbyterian College when he was a young man. From there he went to Union Theological Seminary in New York City, where he was introduced to the ideas of Christian socialism and Marxism. Horton returned to Tennessee determined to put some of those theories to use, and with fellow southerners such as Don West, James A. Dombrowski, and John Thompson, he founded the Highlander Folk School.

Throughout his years at Highlander, Horton had to deal with a large amount of controversy. During the 1950s, he was accused of being a Communist. Highlander was one of the few schools at that time in the South to have blacks and whites integrated in classes, and many area residents objected to this then-progressive practice. As a result, the school was firebombed and was eventually seized by the Tennessee state government on trumped-up charges of selling alcohol. Undaunted, Horton moved Highlander to a new location—eventually the school became the Highlander Research and Education Center in New Market, Tennessee.

Horton described these experiences and more in the autobiography he penned with the help of Judith and Herbert Kohl, *The Long Haul.* Reviewing the work in the *Washington Post,* Martin Bauml Duberman lamented the fact that it contained "neither the details of governance, financing, housing and diet, nor any accounting of the interpersonal tensions that come from close-quarter living—and how those tensions were resolved" at the school. Yet he praised the sections "about the residential workshops for grass-roots leaders which were at the core of Highlander's learning process," and concluded that "what *The Long Haul* does give us is enough piecemeal information about Myles Horton's public actions and philosophy to underscore our view of him as a deeply honest, brave man with an unwavering commitment to the oppressed."

BIOGRAPHICAL/CRITICAL SOURCES:

BOOKS

Horton, Myles, Judith Kohl, and Herbert Kohl, *The Long Haul: An Autobiography,* Doubleday, 1990.

PERIODICALS

Nation, February 19, 1990, p. 224; November 12, 1990, pp. 566-570.
New York Times, January 20, 1990.
New York Times Book Review, May 20, 1990.
Washington Post, April 8, 1990, p. 9.*

*   *   *

HORWITZ, Tony   1958-

PERSONAL: Born June 9, 1958, in Washington, DC; married Geraldine Brooks (a reporter), December, 1984. *Education:* Attended Brown University and Columbia University Graduate School of Journalism.

ADDRESSES: Office—Wall Street Journal, 200 Liberty St., New York, NY 10281.

CAREER: News-Sentinel, Fort Wayne, IN, reporter, 1983-84; *Wall Street Journal,* New York City, reporter, 1989—; writer. United Woodcutters Association, labor organizer, 1982-83; *Sydney Morning Herald,* reporter, 1985-87.

AWARDS, HONORS: Hal Boyle Award, with Geraldine Brooks, for best daily newspaper or wire service reporting from abroad, Overseas Press Club, 1990, for coverage of Persian Gulf crisis.

WRITINGS:

One for the Road: Hitchhiking through the Australian Outback, Vintage Books, 1987.

Baghdad without a Map, and Other Misadventures in Arabia, Dutton, 1991, revised edition with new epilogue, Plume, 1991.

Contributor to periodicals, including *Harper's, Playboy,* and *Washington Monthly.*

SIDELIGHTS: Tony Horwitz is a *Wall Street Journal* reporter who has won acclaim for both his newspaper work and his books on foreign lands. In his first volume, *One for the Road: Hitchhiking through the Australian Outback,* Horwitz recounts his arduous and often humorous experiences traveling across Australia's hot, barren desert region in 1986. Horwitz relates that pubs, and their refreshing beer, provided him with valuable sustenance throughout his trek. Beer is the national drink in Australia's Northern Territory, and references to the beverage frequently crop up. The distance between two points, for instance, might be referred to as a "six-pack" (one beer for every eight minutes of travel time) or it might cost "a carton" to have one's car tail pipe fixed. *One for the Road,* according to a *Publishers Weekly* reviewer, "is as much a chronicle of the pubs along the way as of the scenery." The critic went on to praise the book, commending Horwitz's "wry style and . . . eye for absurdity."

Horwitz is also author of *Baghdad without a Map, and Other Misadventures in Arabia,* an account of his travels through more than a dozen Middle Eastern countries, including Egypt, Yemen, Lebanon, and Libya, during the late 1980s. In this book Horwitz relates amusing and sometimes unnerving experiences, including a harrowing boat ride across the heavily mined Strait of Hormuz and a show featuring incompetent belly dancers. In one instance, Horwitz was present at a rally in Teheran, Iran, where men were marching and shouting "death to America." The author eventually found a demonstrator who spoke English; the man told Horwitz that "it has always been my dream" to go to Disneyland and "take my children on the tea-cup ride." After expressing his sentiments about the famous American theme park, the demonstrator returned to his anti-American chant.

From his various experiences Horwitz created "a very funny and frequently insightful look at the world's most combustible region," wrote Barry Gewen in the *New York Times Book Review.* John Haman, in his review for the *Washington Post Book World,* observed that "Horwitz's inclination is for comedy, but dark realities keep breaking in." Another reviewer, *Time*'s R. Z. Sheppard, described

Horwitz as "observant and witty," and Dick Roraback, in his *Los Angeles Times Book Review* assessment, declared that Horwitz's *Baghdad without a Map* constitutes some "tentative, bewildered but often good-natured steps toward exploring the character of America's new adversaries—and allies—among the Arab legion."

BIOGRAPHICAL/CRITICAL SOURCES:

PERIODICALS

Library Journal, August, 1988, p. 158.
Los Angeles Times Book Review, January 12, 1991, p. 9.
New York Times Book Review, February 17, 1991, p. 6.
Publishers Weekly, April 29, 1988, p. 69.
Time, February 25, 1991, pp. 73-74.
Washington Post Book World, March 3, 1991, pp. 4-5.

*   *   *

HOURANI, A. H.
See HOURANI, Albert (Habib)

*   *   *

HOURANI, Albert (Habib)   1916(?)-1993
(A. H. Hourani)

PERSONAL: Born c. 1916 in Manchester, England; died January 17, 1993, in Oxford, England. *Education:* Attended Oxford University.

CAREER: Taught at the American University of Beirut, Lebanon; worked at the Royal Institute of International Affairs, beginning in 1939; Oxford University, Oxford, England, lecturer in modern Middle East history, 1958-80, director of Middle East Center, beginning in 1958; writer. Visiting professor at Harvard University, University of Chicago, and other universities in Europe and the Arab world.

WRITINGS:

(As A. H. Hourani) *Syria and Lebanon,* [Lebanon], 1946.
(As A. H. Hourani) *Minorities in the Arab World,* 1947, reprinted, AMS Press, 1982.
Arabic Thought in the Liberal Age, 1798-1939, Cambridge University Press, 1962.
(Editor with S. M. Stern) *The Islamic City,* University of Pennsylvania Press, 1970.
Islamic Philosophy and the Classical Tradition: Essays Presented by His Friends and Pupils to Richard Walzer on His Seventieth Birthday, University of South Carolina Press, 1972.
Europe and the Middle East, University of California Press, 1980.
A History of the Arab Peoples, Belknap Press, 1991.

Islam in European Thought, Cambridge University Press, 1991.

Advisory editor for *The Cambridge Encyclopedia of the Middle East and North Africa,* Cambridge University Press, 1988.

SIDELIGHTS: A prominent Middle East scholar, Albert Hourani established himself as an incisive observer and analyst of Arabic and Islamic peoples and places. He published his first book, *Syria and Lebanon,* in 1946 and followed with *Minorities in the Arab World* and *Arabic Thought in the Liberal Age, 1789-1939.* Writing in the *Los Angeles Times Book Review,* Edward W. Said described Hourani's early works as "classics, mined by both scholars and general readers for their scope and their fastidiously refined attention to the fabric of Arab life."

In 1970 Hourani collaborated with S. M. Stern in editing *The Islamic City,* which is comprised of essays originally presented in 1965 at a conference at Cambridge University. The papers included in the book address various aspects of Islamic cities, including the developmental and the cultural. A *Times Literary Supplement* reviewer deemed *The Islamic City* "an essential contribution to Islamic studies" and added that the volume "will be welcomed by anyone interested in the subject."

Hourani is probably best known to the general public for his 1991 book *A History of the Arab Peoples,* which became a best-seller after the Persian Gulf War, a conflict prompted by Iraq's invasion of Kuwait. In the book, Said noted in the *Los Angeles Times Book Review,* "the whole story of the Arab people is laid out before us." The reviewer observed that "Hourani's is a worldly and, for the most part, a secular history," and he contended that the book constitutes "a genuinely readable, genuinely responsive history of the Arabs as . . . many of them would want to be known to non-Arabs." Another enthusiast, L. Carl Brown, wrote in the *New York Times Book Review* that *A History of the Arab Peoples* "is a splendid achievement that can be read with profit by rank beginners and jaded specialists." Brown called Hourani "one of the most distinguished scholars of the Arab world and the Middle East" and added that the history volume is "written with grace and wisdom." Similarly, Thomas W. Lippman reported in the *Washington Post Book World* that "Hourani is able to explain, concisely, matters of surpassing difficulty," and Robert Irwin, in his review for the *Times Literary Supplement,* acknowledged that Hourani "delivers a grand story in a deceptively quiet and gentle tone." Irwin noted that *A History of the Arab Peoples* is not an "events-based narrative" or an "operatic history," but rather "a vision of the great journey of the Arab peoples . . . through history."

Hourani is also author of *Islam in European Thought,* which "offers the reader troubled meditations on the ori-

gins and development of Islamic studies in Europe from the Middle Ages onwards," related a *Times Literary Supplement* reviewer. Malise Ruthven, reviewing *Islam in European Thought* in *New Statesman and Society,* noted that at the time Hourani was "our greatest living historian of the Middle East" and added that he had "an understanding of both western and Arab-Muslim intellectual traditions unmatched in his generation."

BIOGRAPHICAL/CRITICAL SOURCES:

PERIODICALS

Economist, May 23, 1981, p. 101; March 2, 1991, p. 83.
Globe and Mail (Toronto), April 6, 1991, p. C8.
International Journal of Middle East Studies, November, 1984, pp. 553-63.
Los Angeles Times Book Review, February 17, 1991, pp. 1, 8.
New Statesman and Society, February 22, 1991; April 26, 1991, pp. 29-30.
New York Review of Books, September 26, 1991.
New York Times Book Review, March 31, 1991, p. 3.
Times Literary Supplement, September 11, 1970, p. 1003; September 19, 1980, p. 1042; February 22, 1991, p. 5; July 15, 1991, p. 25.
Washington Post Book World, March 31, 1991.

OBITUARIES:

PERIODICALS

Los Angeles Times, January 23, 1993, p. A22.*

* * *

HOUSEWRIGHT, Wiley L.   1913-

PERSONAL: Born October 17, 1913, in Wylie, TX; son of Jick (in business) and Lillie D. (a homemaker; maiden name, Townsend) Housewright; married Lucilla Gumm (a homemaker). *Education:* University of North Texas, B.S., 1934; Columbia University, M.A., 1938; New York University, Ed.D., 1942. *Politics:* Democrat. *Religion:* Protestant. *Avocational interests:* Travel, swimming.

ADDRESSES: Home—515 S. Ride Rd., Tallahassee, FL 32303. *Office*—School of Music, Florida State University, Tallahassee, FL 32306.

CAREER: New York University, New York City, lecturer, 1942; University of Texas, Austin, assistant professor of music, 1946-47; Florida State University, Tallahassee, 1947-79, began as professor of music, became dean; summer session professor at Indiana University, 1955, and University of Michigan, 1960; writer. Consultant to Educational Testing Bureau and international music festivals; Ford Foundation, member of the advisory board on humanities and the arts; U.S. Department of State, member of the academic advisory panel. *Military service:* U.S. Army, 1943-46, served in Medical Administrative Corps; first lieutenant; received Distinguished Service Medal.

MEMBER: Music Educators National Conference (president, 1968-70), American Musicological Society, Music Library Association, Florida Economics Club.

WRITINGS:

(Editor with Carl Ernst and Rose Marie Grentzer) *Birchard Music Series,* Summy-Birchard, 1961.
A History of Music and Dance in Florida, 1565-1865, University of Alabama Press, 1991.

Contributor to *Libraries, History, Diplomacy, and the Performing Arts,* edited by Israel Katz, Pendragon Press (Pendragon, NY), 1991. Author of numerous monographs and articles.

WORK IN PROGRESS: An anthology tentatively titled *Music of Early Florida.*

*　　*　　*

HOY, Claire　1940-

PERSONAL: Born July 21, 1940, in Brockville, Ontario, Canada; son of David and Jenny (Richmire) Hoy; married Beverly Sykes, June 1, 1963 (died June 2, 1976); married Lydia Huber (a writer), May 15, 1982; children: (first marriage) Paul, Kathy; (second marriage) Zachary, Clayton, Scarlet. *Education:* Ryerson Polytechnic Institute, B.A., 1964. *Religion:* Presbyterian.

ADDRESSES: Home—23 Clarendon Ave., Ottawa, Ontario, Canada K1Y 0P3. *Office*—Parliamentary Press Gallery, R. 350 North Centre Block, Parliament Hill, Ottawa, Ontario, Canada K1A 0A6.

CAREER: Toronto Telegram, Toronto, political columnist, 1966-70; *Toronto Star,* Toronto, political columnist, 1970-74; *Toronto Sun,* Toronto, political columnist and bureau chief, 1975-87; Global Television Network, Toronto, Canada, political columnist, 1980; *Southern News,* free-lance columnist, 1988—. Frequent panelist and commentator on Canadian television and radio; lecturer.

WRITINGS:

Bill Davis: A Biography, Methuen, 1985.
Friends in High Places: Politics and Patronage in the Mulroney Government, Key Porter Books, 1987.
Margin of Error: Pollsters and the Manipulation of Canadian Politics, Key Porter Books, 1989.
(With Victor Ostrovsky) *By Way of Deception: The Making and Unmaking of a Mossad Officer,* St. Martin's,

1990, published in Canada as *By Way of Deception: A Devastating Insider's Portrait of the Mossad,* Stoddart Publishing, 1990.
Clyde Wells: A Political Biography, Stoddart Publishing, 1992.

SIDELIGHTS: Claire Hoy is a well-known political commentator and author of several related books, including *Bill Davis,* a biography of the former Ontario premier. His second book, *Friends in High Places: Politics and Patronage in the Mulroney Government,* a biography of Canadian Prime Minister Brian Mulroney, details what Hoy perceives as the mistakes Mulroney made in his first years in office. "On turning the last page of this book," wrote Peter Desbarats in the *Globe and Mail,* "there's a feeling that 357 pages were hardly enough to contain all the follies and stupidities and misdeeds crammed within." *Quill and Quire* contributor Paul Park commented, "In the kennel of Canadian journalism, Claire Hoy is a pit-bull terrier." The extensive attacks on the Mulroney government throughout the book delayed its publication until legal issues could be cleared up. The resulting text is less inflammatory than the original, but Desbarats still admitted that *Friends in High Places* "will ensure that Claire Hoy has almost no friends in high places, and that probably suits him just fine."

Writing of his book *Margin of Error: Pollsters and the Manipulation of Canadian Politics,* Hoy told *CA* that the 1988 Canadian election was "perhaps the most bitter and certainly the most overpolled election in Canadian history." During the election, Canadians were barraged with polls, twenty-six at the national level and more than two hundred at local levels. Hoy examines the effects that polls can have on public opinion, and also scrutinizes the link between the media and polls as newspapers obtain stock in polling companies and as journalists incorrectly report poll results. Bodine Williams, writing in the *Globe and Mail,* summarized *Margin of Error* as "a call for ethics in the gathering and reporting of public opinion" and called it "a useful book, especially for political science students and campaign junkies." "Polls," wrote I. M. Owen in *Books in Canada,* "are well worth following with interest. But don't look at another until you've read this book."

Hoy told *CA:* "I am a well-known, right-of-centre, acerbic columnist and commentator on Canadian political affairs. My 1987 book *Friends in High Places,* a controversial look at Prime Minister Brian Mulroney's difficult first two years in office, was the top-selling Canadian hardcover book that year.

"My background flows from a conservative upbringing in the small border town of Prescott, Ontario, across the St. Lawrence River from Ogdensburg (where I became an incurable New York Yankees fan). I come from solid United

Empire Loyalist stock, Presbyterian, and hence view big government, and for that matter big unions and big business, with suspicion.

"I write frequently on the moral issues, e.g. abortion, and am constantly offended by dishonesty and deceit, vigorously attacking it on a regular basis. My reputation is one of a rough, unforgiving journalist who does not shy away from publishing personal information about politicians, however embarrassing it might be. This has not made me universally popular with either politicians or other journalists—it being almost unCanadian, of course, to hold strong views and express them—but since I would never have a politician in my house, the fact that my writing upsets them is of no concern, particularly since throughout my career my style has attracted consistently large reading and listening audiences."

Hoy is also the author, with Victor Ostrovsky, of *By Way of Deception: The Making and Unmaking of a Mossad Officer.* Please refer to Ostrovsky's sketch in this volume for additional sidelights.

BIOGRAPHICAL/CRITICAL SOURCES:

PERIODICALS

Books in Canada, January, 1988, pp. 29-30; January, 1990, pp. 40-41.
Globe and Mail (Toronto), April 27, 1985; November 14, 1987; December 2, 1989, p. C8.
Maclean's, December 4, 1989.
Quill and Quire, July, 1987; November, 1987.

*   *   *

HOY, Nina
See ROTH, Arthur J(oseph)

*   *   *

HUNTER, Matthew
See STONE, Rodney

*   *   *

HUXLEY, Anthony J(ulian) 1920-1992

OBITUARY NOTICE—See index for *CA* sketch: Born December 2, 1920, in Oxford England; died December 26, 1992, in London, England. Horticulturalist, botanist, and writer. The son of noted biologist Sir Julian Huxley and the nephew of prolific author Aldous Huxley, Anthony Huxley became well known in his own right as a significant contributor of published work on horticulture and botany. Although exposed to the natural world through his father, who was at one time secretary of the London Zoo, Anthony Huxley chose to study English literature at Trinity College of Cambridge. After conducting research in the Royal Air Force, Huxley worked for the British Overseas Airways Corporation. In 1949 he began an association with the periodical *Amateur Gardening,* which lasted more than twenty years. In 1971 he retired from his position as editor of the magazine and turned to writing full time. An avid traveler, Huxley occasionally used his experiences in such places as the Mediterranean to inform his work. The numerous books that he wrote and edited focus on a wide variety of plants—both those raised domestically and those suited to a natural habitat. For his contributions to the field, he received both the Veitch Memorial Medal and the Victoria Medal of Honour from the Royal Horticultural Society.

OBITUARIES AND OTHER SOURCES:

BOOKS

The Writers Directory: 1992-1994, St. James Press, 1991, p. 492.

PERIODICALS

Times (London), December 31, 1992, p. 19.

*   *   *

HYDE-PRICE, Adrian 1957-

PERSONAL: Born December 29, 1957, in Plymouth, Devon, England; son of Geoffrey (a naval officer) and Betty (a nurse and health visitor; maiden name, Westmoreland) Hyde-Price. *Education:* University of Wales, University College of Wales, Aberystwyth, B.S.C.; University of Kent at Canterbury, Ph.D.

ADDRESSES: Home—Southampton, England. *Office*—Department of Politics, University of Southampton, Southampton SO9 5NH, England.

CAREER: University of Southampton, Southampton, England, lecturer in politics; writer.

WRITINGS:

European Security beyond the Cold War, Sage Publications, 1991.
The New International Politics of East Central Europe, Manchester University Press, in press.

WORK IN PROGRESS: Research on security in Eastern Europe and the former Soviet Union; research on war, politics, and society.

I-J

IDOL, John L(ane), Jr. 1932-

PERSONAL: Born October 28, 1932, in Deep Gap, NC; son of John Lane (a carpenter) and Annie (a homemaker and salesperson; maiden name, Watson) Idol; married Marjorie South (a secretary), November 24, 1955. *Education:* Appalachian State Teachers College (now State University), B.S. (magna cum laude), 1958; University of Arkansas, M.A., 1961, Ph.D., 1965. *Politics:* Democrat. *Religion:* Unitarian-Universalist. *Avocational interests:* Birdwatching, book collecting, gardening, photography, family history.

ADDRESSES: Home—P.O. Box 1138, Clemson, SC 29633. *Office*—Department of English, 607 Strode Tower, Clemson University, Clemson, SC 29634-1503.

CAREER: English teacher, 1958; Clemson University, Clemson, SC, English teacher, 1964—. Clemson Area Arts Council, president of Friends of the Clemson Community Library; Accommodations Tax Advisory Committee, chair; member of Foothills Chorale; member of Anderson Area Lupus Subchapter. *Military service:* U.S. Air Force, electronics technician, 1951-55; became airman first class.

MEMBER: Modern Language Association of America, Nathaniel Hawthorne Society (president, 1984-86), Thomas Wolfe Society (president, 1981-83), American Name Society, Melville Society, American Association of University Professors, Society for the Study of Southern Literature (vice president, 1993-95), Mark Twain Circle, Southeastern Conference on Linguistics, Southeastern Renaissance Conference, South Atlantic Modern Language Association, Southeastern Name Society (president, 1988-91), Philological Association of the Carolinas (president, 1984), Phi Beta Kappa (president of Piedmont Area association, 1981-83, 1989-91), Phi Kappa Phi, Omicron Delta Kappa, Sigma Tau Delta.

AWARDS, HONORS: Zelda Gitlin Literary Award; Citation of Merit, Thomas Wolfe Society; Distinguished Service Award, Nathaniel Hawthorne Society; Award of Merit, South Carolina chapter of American Association of University Professors; Honored Teacher Award, Philological Association of the Carolinas.

WRITINGS:

(Editor with Sterling Eisiminger) *Why Can't They Write? A Symposium on the State of Written Communication,* University Press of America, 1979.

(Editor) Thomas Wolfe, *K-19: Salvaged Pieces,* Thomas Wolfe Society, 1983.

(Editor with Louis D. Rubin, Jr.) Thomas Wolfe, *Mannerhouse,* Louisiana State University Press, 1985.

(Editor) Thomas Wolfe, *The Hound of Darkness,* Thomas Wolfe Society, 1986.

A Thomas Wolfe Companion, Greenwood Press, 1987.

(With Rita K. Gollin and Sterling Eisiminger) *Prophetic Pictures: Nathaniel Hawthorne's Knowledge and Uses of the Visual Arts,* Greenwood Press, 1991.

(Editor with Melinda M. Ponder and others) *Women's Effect on Hawthorne and Hawthorne's Effect on Women,* University of Massachusetts Press, 1993.

Contributor of poems to magazines and newspapers, including *Thomas Wolfe Review, Journal of Rheumatology, Pembroke,* and *Ruminator.* Past editor, *Nathaniel Hawthorne Review.*

WORK IN PROGRESS: Nathaniel Hawthorne: Contemporary Reviews, with Buford Jones, for Cambridge University Press; editing Thomas Wolfe's *The Party at Jack's,* with Suzanne Stutman, University of North Carolina Press; original poems for a cycle of beast fables.

SIDELIGHTS: John L. Idol, Jr., told *CA:* "During my senior year in high school, my older brother, who was taking a college course in the American novel, brought home a thick novel and said, 'Here, John, is something you'll really enjoy. It's about a mountain family from North Carolina.' He'd already introduced me to F. Scott Fitzgerald, Ernest Hemingway, and William Faulkner, and would later share John Steinbeck and Erskine Caldwell with me. It was Thomas Wolfe who spoke most directly to me, however. I didn't hear everything Wolfe had to say, obviously, since I stuck with my plan to study electrical engineering.

"About the same time I started reading Wolfe, I came upon the poetry of William Butler Yeats and began scribbling imitative lines. Wolfe and Yeats and other writers gave me much companionship during a four-year hitch in the U.S. Air Force. When I entered college, it was not to engineering, but to English that I turned.

"One of my professors, David Reid Hodgin, had been a student at the University of North Carolina when Wolfe was there. Hodgin refired my interest in Wolfe and the American novel. My studies in American novels continued under Blair Rouse, an expert on Ellen Glasgow, at the University of Arkansas. There, I also met David B. Kesterson, who later would become a cofounder of the Nathaniel Hawthorne Society. Our work under Professor Rouse led us to full devotion to the American novel.

"Thirty years of scholarly and editorial work have not left much room for poetry, though I have continued to write it, and to teach a course in seventeenth-century British verse at Clemson University. Poetry will be the chief passion of my retirement. I'll write more of it, read a hell of a lot more than I'll write, and turn critic and scholar only when I find something truly worth saying. I have too many trees on my conscience as it is. Planting a good many trees and coaxing out a few poems should be work enough for retirement. But, of course, I won't leave well enough alone."

*   *   *

INGLIS, Brian (St. John) 1916-1993

OBITUARY NOTICE—See index for *CA* sketch: Born July 31, 1916, in Dublin, Ireland; died February 11, 1993. Television commentator, editor, and writer. Inglis studied at Oxford and served as a flyer in the Coastal Command during World War II before becoming affiliated with the *Irish Times.* After earning a Ph.D., Inglis wrote for the *Daily Sketch* then became an assistant editor for the London *Spectator.* In 1959, he became editor of the paper and held the position for three years. A successful sideline career as a regular on the television program *What the Papers Say* afforded him the financial stability to give up his

editor post in 1962 so that he could devote more time to his writing. He later became a commentator on *All Our Yesterdays,* another television show. Much of Inglis's early writing focuses on Irish topics, and his controversial biography of Roger Casement, a British native who played an important role in rebellions in Ireland, earned him reproach from some people because in it Inglis made allegations that Casement was a homosexual. Inglis's later work, which includes *The Diseases of Civilisation, The Power of Dreams,* and *Trance: A Natural History of Altered States of Mind,* shows his interests in both medicine and the paranormal. Inglis's autobiography, *Downstart,* was published in 1990.

OBITUARIES AND OTHER SOURCES:

BOOKS

The Writers Directory: 1992-1994, St. James Press, 1991, p. 497.

PERIODICALS

Times (London), February 13, 1993, p. 17.

*   *   *

ISLAS, Arturo 1938-1991

OBITUARY NOTICE—See index for *CA* sketch: Born May 24, 1938, in El Paso, TX; died of AIDS, February 15, 1991. Educator and writer. As an American of Mexican descent, Islas fought for the recognition of Chicano literature throughout his life. A scholarship student, Islas graduated from Stanford University and later became a member of Phi Beta Kappa. Between 1960 and 1963, he fulfilled the requirements for a doctorate degree, but did not write a dissertation. He later worked in a hospital and at an adult school in San Francisco, California, where he taught classes in speech and literature. In 1971—after completing his doctorate—he became an assistant professor at his alma mater and was granted a full professorship of American and Chicano literatures in 1986. During his career at Stanford, he was a notable presence at conferences that promoted the literature of women and minority groups. In 1976, he completed a work which he called "Dia de los Muertos/Day of the Dead." The novel, which focuses on a Mexican family living on the border of their home country and the United States, was eventually published in 1984 as *The Rain God.* Islas received the Southwest Book Award for fiction for a revised version of the novel in 1986. He featured the same characters in a second novel, *Migrant Souls,* released in 1990.

OBITUARIES AND OTHER SOURCES:

BOOKS

Dictionary of Literary Biography, Volume 122: *Chicano Writers, Second Series,* Gale, 1992, pp. 146-54.
Who's Who among Hispanic Americans, 1991-92, 1st edition, Gale, 1991, p. 198.

*   *   *

JACKSON, Marian J. A.
  See ROGERS, Marian H.

*   *   *

JAMES, David N. 1952-

PERSONAL: Born June 17, 1952, in Iowa City, IA; son of Harold E. James (co-owner of family pharmacy) and Evelyn F. James (co-owner of family pharmacy); married Jeanne Thomson (an attorney), August 18, 1979. *Education:* Carleton College, B.A., 1975; Vanderbilt University, M.A., 1979, Ph.D., 1981.

ADDRESSES: Office—Department of Philosophy, Old Dominion University, Norfolk, VA 23529-0083.

CAREER: State University of New York at Stony Brook, teacher of philosophy, 1981-82; Longwood College, Farmville, VA, assistant professor of philosophy, 1982-87; Old Dominion University, Norfolk, VA, assistant professor of philosophy, 1987-93, associate professor of philosophy, 1993—. Eastern Virginia Medical School, member of institutional review board, 1992-95; Lake Taylor Hospital, member of ethics advisory board, 1992-95.

MEMBER: Virginia Philosophical Association (president, 1990-91).

AWARDS, HONORS: Griffith Award, 1984, for a paper on neo-Aristotelian virtue ethics.

WRITINGS:

(Editor with Judith Andre) *Rethinking College Athletics,* Temple University Press, 1991.

Contributor to philosophy journals.

WORK IN PROGRESS: A Study of Kant's "Doctrine of Virtue."

*   *   *

JAMES, Frederick
  See MARTIN, William

JANEWAY, Eliot   1913-1993

OBITUARY NOTICE—See index for *CA* sketch: Born January 1, 1913, in New York, NY; died February 8, 1993, in New York, NY. Economist and writer. After graduating from Cornell University, Janeway spent the early years of the Great Depression studying at the London School of Economics. Early in his career, he contributed a series of columns to *Nation* magazine which forecasted the inventory recession of the late 1930s. On the basis of his early work, Janeway was hired by Henry R. Luce, the publisher of such periodicals as *Time* and *Fortune.* Between 1944 and 1948, Janeway's articles appeared in these national publications on a regular basis. In addition to contributing to various periodicals, he also traveled the lecture circuit and appeared on numerous television shows. He was dubbed "Calamity Janeway" for his regularly bleak forecasts of activity on the American stock market. During the late 1950s, he served as an informal adviser and fund raiser for Senator Lyndon B. Johnson. Janeway broke his association with the politician when Johnson, who had become president by that time, increased support for the Vietnam War in the mid-1960s without what Janeway felt was a solid method to raise money for the war effort. Throughout his career, Janeway remained convinced that political actions have a great effect on the economy, and in such books as *The Economics of Crisis: War Politics and the Dollar* and 1989's *Economics of Chaos: On Revitalizing the American Economy* he made various recommendations to individuals and institutions in the nation's capital.

OBITUARIES AND OTHER SOURCES:

BOOKS

The Writers Directory: 1992-1994, St. James Press, 1991.

PERIODICALS

Chicago Tribune, February 9, 1993, section 1, p. 11.
Los Angeles Times, February 10, 1993, p. A26.
New York Times, February 9, 1993, p. B7.
Times (London), February 13, 1993, p. 17.
Washington Post, February 10, 1993, p. D5.

*   *   *

JANSEN, Sharon L.   1951-

PERSONAL: Born July 9, 1951; daughter of Edgar R. and Helen Jean (Arenz) Jansen; married Stephen S. Jaech (divorced, 1989); children: Kristian Jansen Jansen. *Education:* California Lutheran College, B.A. (summa cum laude), 1972; University of Washington, Seattle, M.A., 1973, Ph.D. (with honors), 1980.

ADDRESSES: Home—706 Fifth St., Steilacoom, WA 98388. *Office*—Department of English, Pacific Lutheran University, Tacoma, WA 98447.

CAREER: Fort Steilacoom Community College, Tacoma, WA, part-time instructor in English, 1975-79; Pacific Lutheran University, Tacoma, assistant professor, 1980-86, associate professor of English, 1986—.

AWARDS, HONORS: Grants from National Endowment for the Humanities, 1985, and Evangelical Lutheran Church in America, 1988-89, 1991-92.

WRITINGS:

Political Protest and Prophecy under Henry VIII, Boydell & Brewer, 1991.
(With Kathleen Jordan) *The Welles Anthology (Ms. Rawlinson C.813): A Critical Edition,* Medieval and Renaissance Texts and Studies, 1991.

Work represented in anthologies, including *King Arthur through the Ages,* edited by Valerie M. Lagorio and Mildred Leake Day, (New York), 1990; and *Medieval England: An Encyclopedia,* edited by Paul E. Szarmach, Garland Publishing, 1993. Contributor of more than a dozen articles and reviews to periodicals, including *Frontiers: A Journal of Women Studies, English Literary Renaissance, Sixteenth Century Journal, Rhetoric Review, Shakespeare Quarterly,* and *Anglo-Welsh Review.*

*   *   *

JOENSSON, Reidar   1944-

PERSONAL: Born June 14, 1944, in Malmoe, Sweden; son of Yngve and Wega Joensson; married Donna Matson (a writer); children: Jesper, Janna, Aiden. *Religion:* None.

ADDRESSES: Home—3854 Clayton Ave., Los Angeles, CA 90027. *Agent*—(books) Rosalie Siegel, 111 Murphy Dr., Pennington, NJ 08534; (screenplays) Nancy Nigrosh, c/o The Gersh Agency, 232 North Canon Dr., Beverly Hills, CA 90210.

CAREER: Writer. Director for stage, radio, and television works, including presentations of his own *Kvinnoburen, Soendag . . . fruktansvaerda soendag, Arvet,* and *Jungfruresan.* Former instructor in dramaturgy at Institute for the Dramatic Arts; has held numerous advisory and administrative positions in the field of the arts; founder of several alternative theater groups. *Military service:* Served for fourteen months in the Navy.

MEMBER: Academy of Motion Picture Arts and Sciences, Writers Guild of America, Writers Guild of Sweden.

AWARDS, HONORS: Numerous writing awards, including an annual lifetime grant from Writer's Fund; *Mitt liv som hund* received both a Golden Globe, for best foreign-language film, and an Academy Award nomination, for best screenplay based on material from another medium.

WRITINGS:

Levande livet! (title means "Real Life!"), Norstedt (Stockholm), 1976.
(With Hakan Bostrom) *Fem pjaser for amatorteaterbruk,* Forfattarforl (Stockholm), 1977.
Hemmahamn och Sjofolk, PAN/Norstedt, 1977.
(With Ove Wall) *Emilia Emilia! En pjas,* Forfattarforl, 1978.
(With others) *Kvinnliga brottstycken: texter fran skrivarverkstaden pa Hinseberg,* Forfattarforl, 1980.
Mitt liv som hund (novel), [Sweden], 1983, translation by Eivor Martinus published as *My Life as a Dog,* Farrar, Straus, 1990.
(With Lasse Hallstroem, Pelle Berglund, and Brasse Braennstrocm) *Mitt liv som hund* (screenplay based on his novel; also known as *My Life as a Dog*), Svensk Filmindustri, 1987, translated by Kersti French and published as a book, Faber & Faber.
En hund begraven (novel; title means "Burial of a Dog"), translation by Marianne Ruuth published as *My Father, His Son,* Arcade, 1991.

Also author of the fictional works *Endast for vita* (title means "For Whites Only"), 1969; *En vaeldig borg* (title means "A Mighty Fortress"), 1970; *En borgares doed* (title means "Death of a Bourgeois"), 1971; and *Hemmahamn* (title means "Home Port"), 1973. Author of the stage plays *Vaelkommen hem!* (title means "Welcome Home!"), 1971; *Liten Karin* (title means "Little Karin"), 1973; *Upptaeckarna* (title means "The Discoverers"), 1973; *Sjoefolk* (title means "People at Sea"), 1974; *Familjen Larsson* (title means "The Larsson Family"), 1974; and *Kvinnoburen* (title means "Women in a Cage"), 1980. Author of the television plays *Sektionen* (title means "The Section"), 1976; *Resenaererna* (title means "The Travelers"), 1976; *Till Alfhild* (title means "For Alfhild"), 1979; *Soendag. . . fruktansvaerda soendag* (title means "Miserable Sundays"), 1980; and *Arvet* (title means "The Inheritance"), 1980. Author of the radio play *Den 24 december* (title means "The 24th of December"), 1974. Author of the film *Jungfruresan* (title means "Maiden Voyage"), 1988; and the poetry collection *Svenska bilder* (title means "Swedish Pictures"), 1976. Author of *Roester from ett varv* (title means "Voices from a Shipyard"), 1978, and *Kvinnliga brottstycken* (title means "Words of Women in Prison"), 1980.

Mitt liv som hund has been published in numerous languages, including French, German, and Japanese.

WORK IN PROGRESS: With wife, Donna Matson, *The Hunt,* a screenplay, for Imagine Entertainment.

SIDELIGHTS: After releasing several works in Sweden, Reidar Joensson received international acclaim for his 1983 novel *Mitt liv som hund,* which was adapted for film in 1987 and published as *My Life as a Dog* in 1990. The novel focuses on Ingemar Johansson, a thirteen-year-old boy who is struggling to come to terms with the impending loss of his mother to tuberculosis. Since his mother must occasionally spend time in a sanatorium and his father works outside of the country, Ingemar and his siblings are regularly placed in the care of relatives. In addition to being separated from his parents, the boy also loses contact with the family dog, Sickan, who—Ingemar believes—is being kept in a kennel. The boy receives little information about his mother and his dog and occasionally makes connections between Sickan's situation and the plight of Laika, a Russian dog who starved aboard a Soviet spacecraft in 1958.

Joensson provides his protagonist with an active mind. In one scene, Ingemar pretends that he marries his imaginary friend, Little Frog, and establishes a family life in the district of Happy Hills. At a local junkyard, the boy hunts for treasure that will gain him respect in the eyes of his mother. Ingemar envisions newspaper headlines that read "Young Hero Sends His Sick Mother to Exclusive Resort in Switzerland." Commenting on the energy that Joensson lends to *My Life as a Dog,* Kathryn Morton of *Washington Post Book World* praised the work for its "vigorous inventiveness."

After his mother's death, Ingemar begins to exhibit canine behavior, growling occasionally, guarding the family's empty house, and biting people. "It felt good to be a dog," Joensson writes, "but a bit insecure perhaps. My body was completely relaxed, but at the same time ready to attack at a moment's notice." Later in the novel, Ingemar's brother finds out about the fate of the family dog. Sickan was not sent to a kennel as the children had been told; he was killed. The lie helps Ingemar to understand that, in addition to having false impressions about the fate of his dog, he has harbored misperceptions about his mother. He dismisses earlier thoughts of her as a model of perfection and realizes that he and his siblings, the dog, and his mother's relationship with her husband may have all been encumbrances to her. Michael J. Rosen of the *New York Times Book Review,* while expressing some reservations about the translation of the original text, remarked that *My Life as a Dog* "plucks as intensely as an abandoned puppy at our human heartstrings."

Joensson worked with three other writers on a screenplay adaptation of his novel. The movie garnered critical acclaim from several reviewers who acknowledged it as one of the best foreign films ever released in the United States. When the novel *My Life as a Dog* was published in English translation in 1990—a few years after the release of the foreign film—several reviewers noted differences between the works. Whereas the original text is presented through the eyes of Ingemar, the movie only occasionally employs a first-person narrator. Additionally, the chapters of the book alternate between the years 1957 and 1958, while the film follows a stricter chronology. Despite these differences, reviewers did not think that the changes detracted substantially from the quality of either story. Rather, each work was valued for its own merits. Morton of the *Washington Post Book World* remarked, "Those familiar with the simplified, gentle movie will be surprised by the book's wider scope—and by the many haunting scenes and outrageous events that never made it onto the screen." Still, the novel lacked, in Morton's opinion, "a glowing remembered scene from which the lonely boy can take comfort knowing he was his mother's delight", which is supplied by the film.

Joensson followed *My Life as a Dog* with a sequel, *My Father, His Son,* in which Ingemar, now thirty years old, is involved in a difficult marriage and separates from his wife in order to gain a clearer understanding of who he is. Throughout the story, the main character recounts various adventures which occurred in his past while he was traveling aboard a steam tramper and searching for his father in exotic locales. Their eventual reunion on the coast of Africa turns out to be a disappointment, with Ingemar unsuccessfully trying to tap into his father's true emotions. Nicholas A. Basbanes called *My Father, His Son* "cleverly textured"; and a writer for the *Los Angeles Times Book Review* acknowledged that "what seems to be a rollicking, picaresque novel, comic and gruesome by turns, is actually a sophisticated meditation on how child victims slip seamlessly into being adult victimizers."

BIOGRAPHICAL/CRITICAL SOURCES:

BOOKS

Joensson, Reidar, *My Life as a Dog,* translated by Eivor Martinus, Farrar, Straus, 1990.

PERIODICALS

Los Angeles Times Book Review, November 10, 1991, p. 6.
New Republic, May 25, 1987.
New York Times Book Review, July 8, 1990, p. 8; December 8, 1991, p. 24.
Times Literary Supplement, October 13, 1989, p. 1132.
Washington Post Book World, June 24, 1990.

—Sketch by Mark F. Mikula

JOHNSON, Greg 1953-

PERSONAL: Born July 13, 1953, in San Francisco, CA; son of Raymond F. (co-owner of a construction company) and Jo Ann (co-owner of a construction company; maiden name, Untersee) Johnson. *Education:* Southern Methodist University, B.A., 1973, M.A., 1975; Emory University, Ph.D., 1980. *Politics:* Liberal Democrat.

ADDRESSES: Home—1607 Defoors Walk, Atlanta, GA 30318. *Office*—Kennesaw State College, English Department, P.O. Box 444, Marietta, GA 30061. *Agent*—Diane Cleaver, Sanford J. Greenburger Associates, 55 Fifth Ave., 15th Floor, New York, NY 10003.

CAREER: Kennesaw State College, Marietta, GA, associate professor of English, 1989—; writer. Has also taught at Emory University and the University of Mississippi.

MEMBER: PEN, National Book Critics Circle.

AWARDS, HONORS: O. Henry Award for short fiction, 1986; Greg Johnson was named Georgia Author of the Year for his work on *Distant Friends,* 1991; National Endowment for the Humanities summer stipend, 1993.

WRITINGS:

Emily Dickinson: Perception and the Poet's Quest (criticism), University of Alabama Press, 1985.
Understanding Joyce Carol Oates (criticism), University of South Carolina Press, 1987.
Distant Friends (stories), Ontario Review Press, 1990.
A Friendly Deceit (stories), Johns Hopkins University Press, 1992.
Pagan Babies (novel), Dutton, 1993.
Aid and Comfort (poems), University Press of Florida, 1993.
Joyce Carol Oates: A Study of the Short Fiction, Twayne/Macmillan, in press.

Contributor of reviews to periodicals, including the *Georgia Review* and *New York Times Book Review.*

WORK IN PROGRESS: A novel, *Night Journey,* completion expected in 1994; an authorized biography, *Joyce Carol Oates: A Life in Writing,* for Dutton, completion expected in 1995.

SIDELIGHTS: Fiction writer Greg Johnson garnered critical acclaim with his story collections, *Distant Friends* and *A Friendly Deceit,* and with his 1993 novel, *Pagan Babies.* "My work deals with the complexities of human relationships; very little is autobiographical, as I enjoy exploring the consciousness of fictional characters seemingly antithetical to myself," Johnson told *CA.* "In my two collections, the stories are equally divided between male and female protagonists and focus on people of all ages and backgrounds." Reviewers praised the author for cre-

ating stories that handle subjects such as unhappy relationships, childhood cruelty, and suicide without melodrama. In a *Washington Post Book World* assessment of *Distant Friends,* Dennis Drabelle dubbed the collection "a polished first book," and noted that Johnson "writes precisely and dramatically, with an ear cocked for the momentum that can build up within the borders of a single sentence." *New York Times Book Review* contributor Carol Verderese remarked on the book's "elegiac tone" and noted that the stories "have a breathtaking cumulative power." Reviewing *A Friendly Deceit,* Pinckney Benedict wrote in Chicago *Tribune Books* that Johnson "proves his mettle as a writer" with his second collection. The best stories in the book, according to *New York Times Book Review* contributor Elizabeth Ferber, are the ones in which "Johnson offers keen observations on contemporary life."

Johnson's novel, *Pagan Babies,* "deals with a man and a woman growing up Catholic in America and explores in detail their close but often turbulent relationship over three decades," the author told *CA.* As the novel progresses, Janice and Clifford's friendship weathers their sexual encounters, Janice's miscarriage and abortions, Clifford's discovery that he's gay, and their attraction to the same man. According to Carolyn See in the *Los Angeles Times, Pagan Babies* is "an honest look at several varieties of hell, from the third grade to grim gay bars, but it's suffused with a wistful hope of Heaven." Bernard Welt wrote in *Washington Post Book World* that *Pagan Babies* is "a first novel that manages to combine deeply serious intent with compulsive readability," and that the book "has all the traditional virtues of well-crafted fiction." Welt particularly praised how Johnson "neatly . . . manages the trick of alternating between two nimbly differentiated points of view." Though *Southern Voice* contributor Nicola Griffith found Johnson's use of alternating viewpoints and hindsight "a short story teller's technique," the critic noted that midway through the novel "Johnson's technique starts to make sense. . . . What started as a jerky, not very sympathetic portrait of a gay man and a straight woman who seem to have nothing in common, becomes a powerful and compassionate examination of the way people need each other."

Johnson commented to *CA* about *Pagan Babies:* "Although I went to a Catholic school like Janice and Clifford, the novel is not really autobiographical: they lead much more dramatic, and often traumatic, lives than I do. I intended for their experience as rebellious outsiders to reflect much of the turmoil in American culture generally during the 1960s, 1970s, and 1980s." After Johnson finished the novel, "I thought about Janice and Clifford . . . and thought that I had split myself apart," he told Rebecca Ranson in the *Southern Voice.* "Each of them has characteristics that I have. I'm not like either, not as extreme. . . . I live a pretty quiet writer's life. . . . Growing up Catholic was first-hand experience. Growing up gay I knew." Another autobiographical aspect of *Pagan Babies* is the death of Clifford's friend after the friend contracts AIDS (acquired immunodeficiency syndrome). A friend of Johnson's died of AIDS in 1982; the author wrote several poems about this friend and his poetry collection, *Aid and Comfort,* is primarily concerned with the disease. Johnson told Ranson that AIDS has become "more and more a dramatic, pressing subject, more important to write about."

About his work in general, Johnson observed to *CA* that "reviewers tend to feel that my fiction is 'grim' or 'dark,' and I suppose I do explore the more turbulent dimensions of family life, love relationships, and psychological experience generally. Yet personally I'm very optimistic and actively engaged in my work; I can't imagine doing anything else."

BIOGRAPHICAL/CRITICAL SOURCES:

PERIODICALS

Los Angeles Times, February 8, 1993.
New York Times Book Review, December 9, 1990, p. 24; August 9, 1992, p. 21.
Southern Voice, February 11, 1993.
Tribune Books (Chicago), July 5, 1992, pp. 1, 10.
Washington Post Book World, January 6, 1991, p. 9; March 21, 1993.

* * *

JOHNSON, Richard
See RICHARDSON, John

* * *

JONAS, Hans 1903-1993

OBITUARY NOTICE—See index for *CA* sketch: Born May 10, 1903, in Moenchengladbach, Germany; immigrated to Canada, then to the United States, 1955, naturalized citizen, 1960; died February 5, 1993, in New Rochelle, NY. Educator, philosopher, and writer. In 1933, Jonas, a member of the Jewish faith, left Nazi Germany and taught in Jerusalem. He joined the British Army and served in World War II, then returned to Jerusalem, where he entered the ranks of the Israeli military. He later traveled to North America and eventually settled in the United States, where he joined the staff of Manhattan's New School for Social Research in the mid-1950s and became chair of the philosophy department. During his

long-time association with the institution, Jonas became Alvin Johnson Professor of Philosophy, a position which he held for ten years. Jonas gained national attention in 1964 when he chastised his former mentor in Germany—the well-known philosopher Martin Heidegger—for supporting the cause of the Nazis. Jonas's philosophical works, which include *The Phenomenon of Life* and *Philosophical Essays: From Ancient Creed to Technological Man,* cover such wide-ranging topics as the value of religion and the necessity of ethics in the field of medicine.

OBITUARIES AND OTHER SOURCES:

PERIODICALS

Chicago Tribune, February 7, 1993.
New York Times, February 6, 1993, p. 9.
Times (London), February 11, 1993, p. 19.

* * *

JONES, John (Henry) 1942-

PERSONAL: Born April 29, 1942, in Lingfield, Surrey, England; son of Albert Reginald (a gardener) and Ivy Olive (a homemaker) Jones; married Patricia Beryl Hebdon (a play-group supervisor), 1966; children: Nicholas, Peter, Jeremy. *Education:* Balliol College, Oxford, B.A., 1965, M.A., D.Phil., 1967. *Politics:* "Vacillatory." *Religion:* Church of England.

ADDRESSES: Office—Balliol College, Oxford University, Oxford OX1 3BJ, England.

CAREER: Oxford University, Oxford, England, junior research fellow in biological sciences at Balliol College, 1966-68, official fellow and tutor in organic chemistry, 1968—, university lecturer in organic chemistry, 1970—, dean of Balliol College, 1972—, archivist of Balliol College, 1981—. Kerth Rae Trust, member, 1980—; Balliol College Boat Club Fund, trustee, 1971—.

MEMBER: European Peptide Society, Royal Society of Chemistry (fellow), Royal Historical Society (fellow).

WRITINGS:

Balliol College: A History, 1263-1939, Oxford University Press, 1988.
The Chemical Synthesis of Peptides, Oxford University Press, 1990.
Amino Acids and Peptide Synthesis, Oxford University Press, 1992.
The Records of Balliol College, Oxford, Chadwyck-Healey, 1992.

Contributor of about a hundred articles to scientific periodicals and twenty articles to history journals. Editor, *Eu-*

ropean Peptide Society Newsletter, 1990—, and *Specialist Periodical Reports on Amino Acids and Peptides.*

* * *

JONES, Merry Bloch 1948-

PERSONAL: Born September 29, 1948, in Chicago, IL; daughter of Herman S. (a research chemist) and E. Judith (a homemaker and teacher; maiden name, Kahn) Bloch; married Dobroslav M. Valik (a dentist), June 16, 1973 (divorced, September, 1978); married Robert Llewellyn Jones (a lawyer), July 26, 1987; children: (second marriage) Baille Ariel Esther, Neely Meredith Samantha, a stepson, and a stepdaughter. *Education:* Cornell University, B.A. (with honors), 1970; University of Pennsylvania, M.A., 1972.

ADDRESSES: Home—1619 Winston Rd., Gladwyne, PA 19035. *Agent*—Connie Clausen, Connie Clausen Associates, 250 East 87th St., New York, NY 10128.

CAREER: Writer, 1989—. Video producer, scriptwriter, and consultant, 1975—; operator of a video production company, 1980-89. Worked as producer and director for WKBS-TV; staff communication consultant for Sun Co.; instructor at Temple University; assistant producer for WCAU-TV and KYW-TV; seminar leader; guest on television and radio talk shows.

MEMBER: Authors Guild, Philadelphia Writers Organization.

AWARDS, HONORS: Video awards from Society for Technical Communication and International Association of Business Communicators.

WRITINGS:

(With Jo Ann Schiller) *Stepmothers: Keeping It Together with Your Husband and His Kids,* Birch Lane Press, 1992.
Birthmothers, Chicago Review Press, 1993.

Contributor to magazines and newspapers, including *American Woman, Woman's Own,* and *Philadelphia.*

WORK IN PROGRESS: Research on "unplanned" female roles, including that of mother-in-law; research on "how we deal with the unexpected in roles and relationships."

SIDELIGHTS: Merry Bloch Jones told *CA:* "I began *Stepmothers* because I was frustrated by my own experience as a stepmother. I felt isolated, guilty, and powerless. Through research I learned I wasn't alone. I teamed up with another stepmom, and we wrote about the collective experiences of a number of similarly stymied women.

"The process of writing *Stepmothers* made me realize how many of us are dealing with roles and relationships for which we are not prepared. *Birthmothers* explores what happens to women after they have relinquished babies for adoption. It examines the effects of surrender and identifies patterns that will help birthmothers, their families, adoptees, and adoptive parents prepare for and/or cope with the scars of relinquishment.

"Although I've always written, my writing was focused on client needs from 1972 until 1989, when my second child was born. Since then I've been working at home, concentrating on issues and topics that seem true to me. I plan to continue writing, concentrating on the quiet struggles of 'regular people.' "

* * *

JONSSON, Reidar
See JOENSSON, Reidar

* * *

JORDAN, Robert
See RIGNEY, James Oliver, Jr.

* * *

JORDEN, William John 1923-

PERSONAL: Born May 3, 1923, in Bridger, MT; son of Hugh G. (a contractor) and Jane Ann (Temple) Jorden; married Eleanor Harz, 1944 (divorced); married V. Mildred Xiarhos, 1972; children: (first marriage) William Temple, Eleanor Harz, Marion Telva. *Education:* Yale University, B.A. (with honors), 1947; Columbia University, M.S., 1948. *Avocational interests:* Cabinet making, golf, travel, reading.

ADDRESSES: Home—5934 Frazier Lane, McLean, VA 22102.

CAREER: Vineyard Gazette, Edgartown, MA, reporter, 1947; New York *Herald Tribune,* New York City, member of news staff, 1948; Associated Press, foreign correspondent in the Far East, 1948-52; *New York Times,* foreign correspondent in Japan and Korea, 1952-55, Moscow bureau chief, 1956-58, diplomatic correspondent in Washington, DC, 1958-61; U.S. Department of State, Washington, DC, member of Policy Planning Council, 1961-62, special assistant to under secretary of state, 1962-65, deputy assistant secretary of state for public affairs, 1965-66, member and spokesperson of U.S. delegation to the Vietnam Peace Talks in Paris, France, 1968-69, U.S. Ambassador to Panama, 1974-78; U.S. National Security Council, Washington, DC, member of senior staff, 1966-68 and 1972-74; assistant to President Lyndon B. Johnson, 1969-72; Lyndon B. Johnson Library, Austin, TX, scholar in residence, 1978-80; writer. *Military service:* U.S. Army, 1943-45.

MEMBER: Academy of Political Science, Council on Foreign Relations, Foreign Correspondents of Japan (president, 1952-53), Authors Guild, Washington Golf and Country Club, Yale Club of Washington.

AWARDS, HONORS: Pulitzer traveling fellow, 1948-49; Council on Foreign Relations fellow, 1955-56; cowinner of Pulitzer Prize for overseas reporting, 1958; Grand Cross, Order of Vasco Nunez de Balboa (Republic of Panama), 1978; Distinguished Honor Award, U.S. Department of State, 1978.

WRITINGS:

(With Hugh Borton and others) *Japan between East and West,* Harper, 1957.
Panama Odyssey, University of Texas Press, 1984.

WORK IN PROGRESS: Working on a novel, completion expected in 1994.

SIDELIGHTS: Panama Odyssey presents William John Jorden's account of the negotiations that resulted in the Panama Canal treaties of 1978. The accord granted the Republic of Panama greater sovereignty over the canal and ended seventy-three years of United States control over the strategic waterway. A veteran diplomat who served under presidents John F. Kennedy, Lyndon Johnson, Richard Nixon, Gerald Ford, and Jimmy Carter, Jorden was exposed to the long-running negotiations over the canal early in the process. He eventually became the U.S. Ambassador to Panama in the years leading up to the treaties' ratification, where he played an integral role in the successful completion of the pact. *Panama Odyssey* details his insights and first-hand experience in the negotiation process, resulting in a book that *Washington Post Book World* critic William V. Shannon championed as "the definitive account of the subject."

In addition to chronicling the treaty negotiations, *Panama Odyssey* explores the historical legacy of the canal. The isthmus of Panama was originally a part of Colombia, and when U.S. officials requested a grant of land to build the canal in 1903, the Columbian government refused. Residents of Panama who favored the canal soon led an uprising against Columbia, and with the help of an American warship, they won their independence. A treaty was quickly signed between the United States and the newly established Republic of Panama, and the U.S. was given control of the canal zone. Because of this maneuvering on the part of the United States, the canal was viewed by many Latin Americans as a product of U.S. imperialism. In 1964 rioting broke out in Panama in protest of the American control of the waterway, and officials in Washington became concerned about the security of the Panama holdings. Negotiations on a new set of canal treaties soon began under the direction of President Johnson, but as Jorden explains, the process was a long one.

The bargaining between the two countries took fourteen years to complete, with the new treaties being pursued by four successive U.S. presidents. Many people in the United States were opposed to foreign control of the canal because of the strategic importance of the waterway. Supporters of the new treaties countered that continued U.S. control of the canal would create unrest in the region. The final Senate vote on the treaties was a close one, and passage was won only with intensive lobbying by supporters, including Jorden himself. The issue was also of vital importance to the Panamanian negotiators, and the author's account includes their thoughts and recollections of the diplomatic process.

Several critics found that *Panama Odyssey* provided a very thorough treatment of the subject. "Jorden's study of the new canal treaties is massive," wrote *Los Angeles Times Book Review* critic Frank del Olmo, ". . . .and authoritative. We are unlikely to have a more definitive account of the diplomacy that went into those treaties." Reviewers were divided, however, on how much information was too much. "While his book will be invaluable for students of diplomacy and Latin American affairs," del Olmo continued, "it is far too detailed and narrowly focused for the general reader." Bernard Gwertzman, writing in the *New York Times,* noted that "Jorden could probably have used a good editor to cut away excess anecdote and detail," but the commentator upheld the book's importance. "For aficionados of diplomatic reporting," Gwertzman wrote, "this is the 'sleeper' book of the year, which gives the reader one of the rare opportunities to be invited into a crucial set of negotiations." Shannon, in *Washington Post Book World,* was also enthusiastic about Jorden's chronicle, pointing out that "the book flows in a smoothly readable, well-organized and always clear manner." The critic also found that Jorden's account offers a clear and persuasive opinion about the treaties. "Anyone who still doubts that [President Carter's] canal treaties were in this country's best interest need only join Jorden in his *Panama Odyssey.* His gusto and his overwhelming mastery of his subject are irresistible."

BIOGRAPHICAL/CRITICAL SOURCES:

PERIODICALS

Los Angeles Times Book Review, June 24, 1984, p. 7.
New York Times, July 28, 1984.

New York Times Book Review, July 29, 1984, p. 26.
Washington Post Book World, June 24, 1984, p. 1.

*　　*　　*

JOSEPH, Helen (Beatrice May)   1905-1992

OBITUARY NOTICE—See index for *CA* sketch: Born April 8, 1905, in Midhurst, Sussex, England; immigrated to South Africa, 1946; died of complications from a stroke, December 25, 1992 (one source says December 24), in Johannesburg, South Africa. Educator, social worker, activist, and writer. After graduating with honors from the University of London in 1927 and teaching in India for three years, Joseph moved to South Africa, where she later became a social worker in Johannesburg and Cape Town. She helped found the Congress of Democrats, the white wing of the African National Congress, and in the mid-1950s, fought for an end to racial discrimination in South Africa by supporting the Congress's Freedom Charter. She later marched in Pretoria to challenge the adopted policy that required blacks to carry passes in some of the city's governmentally controlled buildings, and was arrested for treason. For more than three decades she was beleaguered by the South African government for continually and vehemently protesting apartheid, the governmentally sanctioned policy that promotes discrimination against blacks by the white minority. Between 1957 and 1990, the government restricted her behavior by placing her under house arrest, and at various times she was only allowed her one visitor at a time. In 1963, *If This Be Treason,* an account of her successful legal battle against the South African government, was published. Joseph also wrote about her fight against apartheid in *Tomorrow's Sun* and *Side by Side.*

OBITUARIES AND OTHER SOURCES:

PERIODICALS

Chicago Tribune, December 26, 1992.
Los Angeles Times, December 26, 1992, p. A38.
New York Times, December 26, 1992, p. 10.
Washington Post, December 26, 1992, p. B4.

*　　*　　*

JOYCE, Christopher   1950-

PERSONAL: Born February 24, 1950, in Chicago, IL; son of Richard Bruce (a foreign service officer) and Dorothy (Prock) Joyce; married December 8, 1991; wife's name, Melissa; children: Natasha Dorothy. *Education:* George Washington University, B.A., 1972. *Politics:* "Mercurial." *Avocational interests:* Sailing, camping, fishing.

ADDRESSES: Agent—Kristine Dahl, International Creative Management, 40 West 57th St., New York, NY 10010.

CAREER: Capitol Publications, Washington, DC, reporter and editor, 1974-77; McGraw-Hill Publications, Washington, DC, reporter and editor, 1977-81; *New Scientist* magazine, Washington, DC, U.S. editor, 1981-91; National Public Radio, Washington, DC, part-time editor, 1992—.

MEMBER: National Association of Science Writers.

WRITINGS:

(With Eric Stover) *Witnesses from the Grave: The Stories Bones Tell,* Little, Brown, 1991.

Also contributor of an essay to *Mysteries of Life and the Universe: New Essays from America's Finest Writers on Science,* edited by William H. Shore, Harcourt, 1992. Contributor of articles to periodicals.

WORK IN PROGRESS: A book titled *Through the Green Fuse: The Search for New Medicines from the Rain Forests.*

SIDELIGHTS: In their book *Witnesses from the Grave: The Stories Bones Tell,* authors Christopher Joyce and Eric Stover explore the world of forensic anthropology—the study of human bones for police investigation. The primary focus of their book is the dramatic, if grisly, career of forensic anthropologist Clyde Collins Snow, whose success in identifying victims has made him a leader in the field. Snow started in the field at an early age by following his physician father to crime scenes and morgues. As an adult he worked for the Federal Aviation Administration (FAA) as a plane crash investigator, determining the cause of death of victims and identifying bodies. Although Snow eventually left the FAA, he continues conducting investigations on a free-lance basis.

In *Witnesses from the Grave,* Joyce and Stover "skillfully outline how one measures bones to reveal the time, place, and manner of a person's death as well as the physical features that person possessed in life," wrote *New York Times Book Review* critic Malcolm W. Browne. The authors also chronicle many of the cases that Snow and his colleagues investigated, including the identification of the remains of German concentration camp doctor Josef Mengele, the victims of Chicago mass murderer John Wayne Gacy, the 273 fatalities of a 1979 plane crash at Chicago's O'Hare Airport, and a woman murdered by her husband, a Chicago butcher, who attempted to dispose of her body in a sausage grinder. The book's most gruesome and telling story, according to critics, however, is the authors' account of the forensic work Snow carried out in Argentina, where ten thousand men, women, and children were killed and buried in mass graves during the military junta rule from 1976 to 1983. Joyce and Stover evoke the scene Snow encountered: "Scores of skeletons . . . lay in small mesas carved out of the ground. In some places, bones were jumbled together in heaps like a game of pickup sticks . . . Many of the skulls showed single gunshot wounds to the head." Using the unearthed bones as evidence, Snow assisted authorities in placing some of the men responsible for the massacre behind bars. The role of anthropology in this police work received considerable attention. Dental x-rays, once perceived as a nearly infallible means of identification, have fallen under criticism due to a discovery of some dentists who falsify records for tax purposes, leaving skeletons and skulls the more precise choice in investigations. "Bones make good witnesses," Snow comments in the book, "Although they speak softly, they never lie and they never forget."

Joyce told *CA:* "I like to write about unconventional scientists in the pursuit of unusual knowledge in hard-to-reach places. Science is no more complex than simply exploring the universe with an open mind, just as writers of fiction do, and there's no reason science can't read like fiction. That is how I try to write it."

BIOGRAPHICAL/CRITICAL SOURCES:

BOOKS

Joyce, Christopher, and Eric Stover, *Witnesses from the Grave: The Stories Bones Tell,* Little, Brown, 1991.

PERIODICALS

Chicago Tribune, January 30, 1991, section 2, p. 13.
New York Times Book Review, January 20, 1991, p. 11.
Washington Post Book World, January 13, 1991, p. 7.

JUDIS, John B. 1941-

PERSONAL: Born September 25, 1941, in Chicago, IL; son of Hilliard (in sales) and Ruth (a fashion designer; maiden name, Gisnet) Judis; married Susan Pearson (a dentist), October 24, 1977; children: Hilary, Eleanor. *Education:* University of California, Berkeley, B.A., 1963, M.A., 1965. *Religion:* Jewish.

ADDRESSES: Home and office—11201 Valley View Ave., Kensington, MD 20895. *Agent*—Kathy P. Robbins, Robbins Office, Inc., 2 Dag Hammarskjold Plaza, 866 Second Ave., 12th Floor, New York, NY 10017.

CAREER: Writer.

WRITINGS:

William F. Buckley, Jr.: Patron Saint of the Conservatives, Simon & Schuster, 1988.
Grand Illusion, Farrar, Straus, 1992.

Washington correspondent, *In These Times,* 1976—. Contributing editor, *New Republic,* 1982—.

WORK IN PROGRESS: Twilight of the Idols: The Rise and Decline of the American Political Establishment, completion expected in 1996.

BIOGRAPHICAL/CRITICAL SOURCES:

PERIODICALS

New York Times Book Review, May 15, 1988, p. 12.
Washington Post Book World, May 1, 1988, p. 1.

K

KADOHATA, Cynthia 1956(?)-

PERSONAL: Born c. 1956 in Chicago, IL. *Education:* Attended Los Angeles City College; received degree from University of Southern California; attended graduate programs at the University of Pittsburgh and Columbia University.

ADDRESSES: Agent—Andrew Wylie, Wylie, Aitken & Stone, Inc., 250 West 57th St., Suite 2106, New York, NY 10107.

CAREER: Writer. Worked variously as a department store clerk and waitress.

AWARDS, HONORS: Whiting Writer's Award from the Mrs. Giles Whiting Foundation; a grant from the National Endowment for the Arts.

WRITINGS:

The Floating World, Viking, 1989.
In the Heart of the Valley of Love, Viking, 1992.

WORK IN PROGRESS: A novel concerning the friendship of two women.

SIDELIGHTS: Cynthia Kadohata's background and experience are mirrored in her novels about young Asian American women coming of age. Kadohata grew up in a family that moved often—to Illinois, Michigan, Georgia, Arkansas, and California. These experiences of travelling from town to town and state to state are a basic element of her first novel, *The Floating World.* In her second novel, *In the Heart of the Valley of Love,* she uses other autobiographical material. In a *Publishers Weekly* interview with Lisa See, Kadohata related that she has always had "paranoid dreams" about the future and writing the science fiction novel *In the Heart of the Valley of Love* "may have purged my fears." One episode in this book is based on a serious accident Kadohata experienced; a car jumped a curb and hit her, mangling her right arm. The author told See that writing about the incident was a way of dealing with it: "I thought this was a way for me to come out of the closet, in a sense. I have friends who have never seen my arm." Kadohata added that because she uses her own experiences in her writing, the distinction between reality and fiction is sometimes confusing. She pointed out that "sometimes I can't remember if something has happened to me or to my character. My memories become their memories, and their memories become mine."

Kadohata's 1989 novel, *The Floating World,* is told through the voice of twelve-year-old Olivia. The story depicts the journey of a Japanese American family searching for economic and emotional security in post-World War II America. Kadohata uses Olivia's character to portray the family dynamics and interactions that occur as they travel, eat, and even sleep in the same room together. In a passage that reveals the significance of the book's title, Olivia explains this itinerant life: "We were travelling then in what she [Obasan, Olivia's grandmother] called *ukiyo,* the floating world. The floating world was the gas station attendants, restaurants, and jobs we depended on, the motel towns floating in the middle of fields and mountains. In old Japan, *ukiyo* meant the districts full of brothels, tea houses and public baths, but it also referred to change and the pleasures and loneliness change brings. For a long time, I never exactly thought of us as part of any of that, though. *We* were stable, travelling through an unstable world while my father looked for jobs."

In addition to the physical journey, Kadohata illustrates Olivia's internal journey in *The Floating World.* Due to the close quarters of her family's living arrangements, Olivia is exposed to adult issues at an early age. She witnesses the tension that exists between her parents, their quiet arguments, and even their love making. In addition, she is constantly subjected to her eccentric grandmother's frequently abusive behavior. Finally the family finds a stable home in Arkansas where Olivia matures from young teen to young adult. It is during this time that she learns to understand the ways of her parents and grandmother and to develop her own values. *Los Angeles Times Book Review* contributor Grace Edwards-Yearwood commended this portrayal, pointing out that "Kadohata writes compellingly of Olivia's coming of age, her determination to grow beyond her parents' dreams."

The Floating World was met with favorable reviews. Diana O'Hehir in the *New York Times Book Review* claimed that Kadohata's "aim and the book's seem to be one: to present the world affectionately and without embroidery. To notice what's there. To see it as clearly as you can." Caroline Ong, a *Times Literary Supplement* contributor, defined the narrative of *The Floating World* as "haunting because of its very simplicity and starkness, its sketchy descriptions fleshing out raw emotions and painful truths." Susanna Moore, writing in the *Washington Post Book World,* judged that *The Floating World* would be a better book if it had been written in the style of a memoir. But, she conceded that "Kadohata has written a book that is a child's view of the floating world, a view that is perceptive, unsentimental and intelligent." *New York Times* critic Michiko Kakutani praised Kadohata's ability to handle painful moments with humor and sensitivity. The reviewer concluded these "moments not only help to capture the emotional reality of these people's lives in a delicate net of images and words, but they also attest to Ms. Kadohata's authority as a writer. *The Floating World* marks the debut of a luminous new voice in fiction."

Kadohata's second book, 1992's *In the Heart of the Valley of Love,* is a futuristic novel concerning survival and quality of life in Los Angeles in the year 2052. In this world Kadohata pits the haves and have-nots against one another. Both are gun-toting communities without morals, law, or order. Amidst this chaos, the main character, a nineteen-year-old orphan of Asian and African descent named Francie, relates her story of endurance. Some critics were less impressed with *In the Heart of the Valley of Love* than with *The Floating World.* Barbara Quick in the *New York Times Book Review* maintained that the book lacks conviction and imagination, and the main character, with only a few alterations, is the same as Kadohata's main character in her first novel. In a similar vein, Michiko Kakutani argued that "unfortunately, Ms. Kadohata's vision of the future is not sufficiently original or compelling. . . . *Heart of the Valley* is an uncomfortable hybrid: a pallid piece of futuristic writing, and an unconvincing tale of coming of age." The reviewer noted, however, that "the writing in this volume is lucid and finely honed, often lyrical and occasionally magical." Other reviewers were thoroughly impressed by Kadohata's work.

Los Angeles Times Book Review contributor Susan Heeger lauded Kadohata as "masterful in her evocation of physical, spiritual and cultural displacement. . . . The message of this marvelous though often painful book is that our capacity to feel deep emotion—our own and others'—just might bind us together, and save us from ourselves."

Some critics have hailed Kadohata as a new voice for Japanese Americans. Writing in the *Globe and Mail,* Rui Umezawa praised her work: "This is perhaps the greatest joy in reading works of writers from this newly formed tradition. The reader gets a view of another culture from both the inside and the outside. Concepts previously thought foreign suddenly become accessible—at times even moving—making a mockery of pessimistic academics who declare that true understanding of another culture is an impossible dream." In the interview with See, Kadohata summarized her thoughts about the significance of being an Asian American writer: "For the first time in my life, I saw that there could be expectations of me not only as a writer but as an Asian American writer. On the one hand, I felt like, 'Leave me alone.' On the other hand, I thought, 'This is a way I can assert my Asianness.' I wrote the book, and I'm Asian, and I'm the only person who could have written it."

BIOGRAPHICAL/CRITICAL SOURCES:

BOOKS

Kadohata, Cynthia, *The Floating World,* Viking, 1989.

PERIODICALS

Globe and Mail (Toronto), August 5, 1989.
Los Angeles Times Book Review, July 16, 1989, p. 12; August 23, 1992, pp. 1, 8.
New York Times, June 30, 1989, p. C27; July 28, 1992, p. C15.
New York Times Book Review, July 23, 1989, p. 16; August 30, 1992, p. 14.
Publishers Weekly, August 3, 1992, pp. 48-49.
Times Literary Supplement, December 29, 1989, p. 1447.
Washington Post Book World, June 25, 1989, pp. 5, 7; August 16, 1992, p. 5.*

—*Sketch by Pamela S. Dear*

*   *   *

KALENIK, Sandra   1945-1993

OBITUARY NOTICE—See index for *CA* sketch: Born October 6, 1945, in Fairfield, CT; died of cancer, February 22, 1993, in Arlington, VA. Educator, bank executive, businessperson, and writer. Kalenik led a varied career that began in the late 1960s, following her graduation from Ohio State University. She worked as a copywriter for such organizations as the Adams Group, then turned to free-lance writing in 1972. Seven years later she founded and managed the Laughing Stock, a comedy club in the nation's capital. She later taught English and technical writing at the University of the District of Columbia and held several positions with public relations and advertising firms. During the mid- to late 1980s, she served as senior vice president for Washington Federal Savings Bank. In addition to contributing to numerous periodicals, Kalenik wrote plays such as *Life in a Mayonnaise Jar* and *On Behalf of the Laugh,* and, with Jay S. Bernstein, the book *How to Get a Divorce.*

OBITUARIES AND OTHER SOURCES:

BOOKS

Who's Who of American Women, 16th edition, Marquis, 1988, p. 418.

PERIODICALS

Washington Post, February 26, 1993, p. D4.

*   *   *

KALMAN, Laura 1955-

PERSONAL: Born in 1955.

ADDRESSES: Office—Department of History, University of California at Santa Barbara, Santa Barbara, CA 93106.

CAREER: Lawyer, educator, and writer. University of California, Santa Barbara, professor of history.

WRITINGS:

Legal Realism at Yale, 1927-1960, University of North Carolina Press, 1986.
Abe Fortas (biography), Yale University Press, 1990.

SIDELIGHTS: Historian Laura Kalman is best known as the author of *Abe Fortas,* a biography of the influential lawyer who became a member of the U.S. Supreme Court during the administration of President Lyndon Johnson. In this biography Kalman recounts how Fortas proved himself a formidable force while a law student at Yale, where he particularly impressed professor William O. Douglas. During the presidency of Franklin Roosevelt, Douglas helped shape New Deal strategies for recovering from the Great Depression. Fortas accompanied Douglas to Washington, D.C., and eventually established a law firm there. As an attorney, Fortas proved skillful in guiding businesses through post-New Deal regulations. In the ensuing years, Fortas maintained a position of relative power in the capital, becoming a confidant of President Johnson in the 1960s. Despite Fortas's considerable influ-

ence, Kalman notes that, as a Jew, he also remained somewhat of an outsider.

Fortas's career peaked when Johnson named him to the Supreme Court. He joined former mentor Douglas on the court and served under Chief Justice Earl Warren beginning in 1965. After assuming his duties as a justice, Fortas maintained ties with his former partners and continued to advise President Johnson, thus committing what many considered to be breaches of judicial ethics. Fortas was undone when he was nominated as chief justice, whereupon Senate hearings exposed his questionable dealings with Johnson and others. He resigned from the court in 1969 after allegations of financial impropriety.

Reviewers generally found *Abe Fortas* to be a noteworthy biography. *New York Times Book Review* contributor Steven V. Roberts deemed *Abe Fortas* "a good book," and Frank Mankiewicz, writing in *Los Angeles Times Book Review,* pronounced it "well-researched and insightful." Eugene Hickok commented in *Insight* that with *Abe Fortas* Kalman "provides a worthwhile glimpse" into Washington's close-knit system of lobbyists and lawyers. And E. Barrett Prettyman, Jr., wrote in *Washington Post Book World* that Kalman "seems to have diligently plowed every field in an effort to capture the essence of this variegated man."

BIOGRAPHICAL/CRITICAL SOURCES:

PERIODICALS

American Historical Review, October, 1987, pp. 1050-51; February, 1992, p. 315.
Insight, December 10, 1990, p. 63.
Los Angeles Times Book Review, November 18, 1990, p. 7.
New Republic, January 28, 1991.
New York Times Book Review, November 11, 1990, p. 19; November 3, 1991, p. 15.
Washington Post Book World, October 21, 1990, p. 6.*

*   *   *

KANE, Leslie 1945-

PERSONAL: Born March 12, 1945; daughter of Philip Rubin (a pharmacist) and Mini Beyer (a homemaker); married Stuart Kane (a company vice-president), December 14, 1969; children: Pamela, David. *Education:* Brooklyn College of the City University of New York, B.A. (cum laude), 1966; Fairleigh Dickinson University, M.A. (summa cum laude), 1975; New York University, Ph.D. (with distinction), 1979.

ADDRESSES: Home—Newton Centre, MA. *Office*—Department of English, Massachusetts State College at Westfield, Westfield, MA 01086.

CAREER: Massachusetts State College at Westfield, assistant professor, 1979-84, associate professor, 1985-89, professor of English, 1989—. Massachusetts Institute of Technology, adjunct professor, 1983; Babson College, visiting lecturer, 1985-86.

AWARDS, HONORS: Grants for research at University of Reading, 1988, 1990.

WRITINGS:

The Language of Silence: On the Unspoken and the Unspeakable in Modern Drama, Fairleigh Dickinson University Press, 1984.
(Editor and contributor) David Mamet: A Casebook, Garland Publishing, 1992.
(Editor) Isaac Horovitz: Critical Approaches, Greenwood Press, 1993.

Work represented in anthologies, including Feminist Focus: The New Women Playwrights, edited by Enoch Brater, Oxford University Press, 1989; Public Issues, Private Tensions: Contemporary American Dramatists, edited by Matthew Roudane, AMS Press, 1992; and Marsha Norman: A Casebook, in press. Contributor of articles and reviews to scholarly journals.

WORK IN PROGRESS: Weasels and Wisemen: Jewish Identity in Harold Pinter and David Mamet.

SIDELIGHTS: Leslie Kane told CA: "Throughout my career in academe, I have maintained a scholarly interest in the work of Anton Chekhov, Samuel Beckett, and Harold Pinter, expanding my focus to include the work of contemporary American playwrights such as Marsha Norman, Lanford Wilson, David Mamet, and Israel Horovitz, all of whom owe much to European influence. Critical essays in scholarly journals, collected editions, and my book The Language of Silence reflect my continuing examination of linguistic structure and self-sustaining fictions. Increasingly I have developed an interest in Jewish subtext and Holocaust studies, and my current research reflects my obsession with the topic.

"Typically I juggle numerous projects simultaneously. Hopefully, my insight that seemingly endless speech is weighted with ethnic, moral, and personal baggage empowers me to write articulately about playwrights whose social consciousness raises our own."

* * *

KANIN, Michael 1910-1993

OBITUARY NOTICE—See index for CA sketch: Born February 1, 1910, in Rochester, NY; died of congestive heart failure, March 12, 1993, in Los Angeles, CA. Artist, entertainer, producer, playwright and screenwriter. Kanin was perhaps best known as the coauthor, with Ring Lardner, Jr., of the 1942 Academy Award-winning screenplay Woman of the Year, which introduced audiences to the highly successful screen team of Katharine Hepburn and Spencer Tracy. A scenic artist, musician, and entertainer during the thirties, Kanin eventually sustained an eye injury that turned his focus to writing. He wrote numerous screenplays, many with his wife Fay Mitchell, including Sunday Punch, Rhapsody starring Elizabeth Taylor, and Cabbages and Kings. Kanin was the author of other screenplays, including Panama Lady, The Outrage, and, with Ben Starr, How to Commit Marriage. He also produced and directed movies and plays, such as A Double Life for Universal in 1947 and the play Goodbye, My Fancy. Rashomon and the musical The Gay Life are counted among Kanin and Mitchell's Broadway productions. Kanin was also the founder of the Michael Kanin Original Playwrighting Awards for the American College Theater Festival and a charter member of the Writers Guild of America West.

OBITUARIES AND OTHER SOURCES:

BOOKS

Who's Who in Entertainment, Marquis, 1992.

PERIODICALS

Chicago Tribune, March 16, 1993, section 1, p. 10.
Los Angeles Times, March 15, 1993, p. A20.
New York Times, March 16, 1993, p. B6.

* * *

KAURISMAKI, Aki 1957-

PERSONAL: Born in 1957.

CAREER: Screenwriter, director, and producer of motion pictures. Affiliated with Villealfa Film Productions, Helsinki, Finland; has also worked variously as a film critic, actor, and assistant director. Codirector of films with brother Mika Kaurismaki, including Saimaa Gesture, 1981. Director of music videos, including Rocky VI, Thru' the Wire, and L.A. Woman, all 1986.

AWARDS, HONORS: Jussi awards (Finland) for best first film and best script and diplomas from FILMEX, Nordische Filmtage, and the Karlovy Vary International Film Festival, all 1983, for Crime and Punishment; special award from the Hong Kong International Film Festival, 1984, for Calamari Union; Jussi Award for best Finnish film, 1986, for Shadows in Paradise.

WRITINGS:

SCREENPLAYS

(With brother, Mika Kaurismaki) *Arvottomat* (also known as *The Worthless*), Villealfa, 1982.

(With Pauli Pentti; and director) *Rikos ja rangaistus* (adapted from the novel *Crime and Punishment* by Fyodor Dostoyevsky), Villealfa, 1983, released in the U.S. as *Crime and Punishment.*

(With Mika Kaurismaki) *Klaani—Tarina sammokoitten suvusta* (also known as *The Clan: Tale of the Frogs*), Villealfa, 1984.

(And director) *Calamari Union*, Villealfa, 1984.

(And director) *Varjoja Paratiisissa*, Villealfa, 1986, released in the U.S. as *Shadows in Paradise.*

(And director) *Hamlet liikemaailmassa*, Villealfa, 1987, released in the U.S. as *Hamlet Goes Business.*

(And director) *Ariel*, Villealfa, 1988.

(And director) *Leningrad Cowboys Go America*, Orion, 1990.

(And director) *I Hired a Contract Killer*, Villealfa/ Swedish Film Institute, 1990.

(And director) *Tulitikkutehtaan tyutto*, Villealfa/Swedish Film Institute, 1990, released in the U.S. as *The Match Factory Girl*, Kino International, 1992.

(And director) *La Vie de boheme* (also known as *Bohemian Life;* adapted from a novel by Henri Murger), Christa Saredi Films, 1992.

Also writer and director of short films, including *The Liar, Jackpot Two,* and *Those Were the Days.*

SIDELIGHTS: Aki Kaurismaki is one of Finland's most prominent filmmakers, and he is generally ranked among the cinema's most accomplished—and prolific—artists to have appeared since the early 1980s. Kaurismaki's films have been compared to those of French directors Jean-Luc Godard (*Breathless*) and Robert Bresson (*Mouchette*) and American independent filmmaker Jim Jarmusch (*Mystery Train*). Kaurismaki, however, is hardly a household name among the mainstream film-going audience; much of his work has yet to be distributed in the United States. His style, often described as sparse and ironic, relies substantially on deadpan humor, and his subject matter frequently involves the plight of the working class. Many critics commend Kaurismaki for bucking conventional cinematic logic and avoiding the tried-and-true practices of commercial filmmaking. Caryn James described Kaurismaki in the *New York Times* as the "bad boy of Finnish cinema," adding that he is "an original and commanding talent."

Kaurismaki first combined his talents as a director and writer to create the 1983 feature *Crime and Punishment,* an adaptation of Fyodor Dostoyevsky's classic novel about a student who commits murder and then finds him-

self hunted by an ingenious police inspector. Kaurismaki changed several key elements of Dostoyevsky's story while maintaining the novel's spirit. In the film the protagonist, renamed Rahikainen from the book's Raskolnikov, murders not a greedy old woman but an influential businessman who killed Rahikainen's fiance in a hit-and-run accident but was acquitted. A cat-and-mouse game is played out as the police gather evidence against the tormented antihero. Kaurismaki set his version of *Crime and Punishment* in contemporary Helsinki, Finland, and directed his film in a manner described by critics as reminiscent of minimalist master Bresson, who has also gone to Dostoyevsky for film subjects. The film is seen as somewhat less humorous than the director's ensuing works, as it is more concerned with psychological drama than with the sardonic social commentary that his later films evidence. *New York Times* writer James, contrasting *Crime and Punishment* with subsequent works by Kaurismaki, found it relatively "classical in its spareness and its serious tone."

In the same *New York Times* piece, James described *Calamari Union*, Kaurismaki's next work, as "gleefully absurdist." In this film, a band of seventeen hooligans, all of whom bear the name Frank, aspire to gangsterdom in the mythic Hollywood tradition. The narrative follows the Franks (as their gang is known) in their attempt to get across town to a hip night-spot. Kaurismaki presents the film as a study of character and environment rather than a simple linear story. Among the quirky band is a Frank who is preoccupied with quoting actor Robert De Niro's lines from director Martin Scorsese's intense, violent drama *Taxi Driver.* James summarized the film as a "chaotic mix of [Scorsese's film] *Mean Streets* and the Marx Brothers." The critic added that "Mr. Kaurismaki takes over the American gangster film and flavors it with his improbable humor."

Kaurismaki followed *Calamari Union* with *Shadows in Paradise,* the first installment of a trilogy of films chronicling Finnish working-class life. Here a garbage truck driver, Nikander, romances a woman employed as a supermarket cashier. Their modest courtship, carried out amid markets, bingo parlors, and spare apartments, is a low-key, stop-and-go venture, with the cashier reluctant to commit to a relationship. But after she is unfairly dismissed from her job, the woman steals the store's cash box and returns to her suitor. Together, they run away.

For his next film, *Hamlet Goes Business,* completed in 1987, Kaurismaki attempted a more experimental venture. This sardonic film transposes William Shakespeare's classic play *Hamlet* from long-ago Denmark to contemporary Finland, where parasitic bourgeoisie vie for personal and professional authority. Maintaining the basic structure of Shakespeare's story, Kaurismaki replaces Shakespearean language with the kind of colloquial dialogue often found on daytime soap operas. The movie is also shot through with Kaurismaki's trademark stoic humor. The odd combination of often broad comedy with Shakespeare's classic tale led *Interview* critic Luc Sante to describe the film's overall result as "The Three Stooges . . . directed by Ingmar Bergman." Sante credited *Hamlet Goes Business* with exhibiting "exquisite poker-faced japery." Although it is among Kaurismaki's lesser-known productions, *Hamlet Goes Business* is considered by some critics to be a unique and provocative achievement.

Kaurismaki's next film, *Ariel,* is one of his most widely known and is the second part of the trilogy begun with *Shadows in Paradise.* In its depiction of life among the working class it recalls the earlier film, but it features decidedly more violent action. The film's hero is a miner, Taisto, who finds himself unemployed when the mine he works in closes. He is given a car by a fellow miner, who commits suicide moments afterward. After hearing his coworker shoot himself in a diner's bathroom, Taisto placidly gets up, leaves the diner, and departs for Helsinki. During his journey Taisto is mugged and robbed. Upon reaching Helsinki, he meets and becomes romantically involved with a meter maid, but a chance encounter with one of his earlier assailants results in his own imprisonment. Undaunted, the meter maid vows to remain with him. Taisto, with his cellmate, eventually breaks out of prison, but the fugitives soon find themselves up against other treacherous foes. During an altercation, Taisto's cellmate is murdered. That death is immediately avenged, whereupon the hero reunites with his lover and her child, and in one of the film's few uplifting moments, they escape the country.

Like much of his previous work, Kaurismaki's *Ariel* serves less as a narrative than an examination of the common worker. With the film, which Kaurismaki completed in 1988, he gained his first substantial success in the United States. Vincent Canby, in his *New York Times* appraisal, hailed the film as "unusually original." *New Yorker* contributor Terrence Rafferty deemed *Ariel* an "antic, briskly dreamlike road movie." Reviewer Stanley Kauffmann wrote in *New Republic* that *Ariel* is "detached, precise, mocking" and a "seemingly impassive story with a kind of dread absurdist humor." Stuart Klawans stated in his *Nation* review that "*Ariel* is an original, and so is its director."

Leningrad Cowboys Go America was released in the United States soon after the success of *Ariel.* Like the earlier *Calamari Station, Leningrad Cowboys Go America* involves a band of unusual men bound together by a common interest. The Leningrad Cowboys are a collection of hapless pop musicians—each sporting identically distorted Elvis-like hairstyles—advised by a Helsinki impre-

sario to seek their fortunes in the United States. Once stateside, they meet with a New York promoter, who tells them about the big plans he has for their American debut, including a massive concert at Madison Square Garden. After taking one listen to the band's music, however, he immediately books them for a wedding in Mexico. The musicians set off on a trek that takes them to various American locales where their own peculiarities are inevitably matched by the characters they encounter. As they tour, the Leningrad Cowboys manage to adapt their polka-from-hell style to one that resembles American popular music. The change in genre gives the musicians some hope of gaining a measure of success. *New York Times* critic Vincent Canby wrote that *Leningrad Cowboys Go America* "isn't much more than a shaggy-dog story," but he added that "the singular voice of the man who made it remains strong and clear."

In 1990 Kaurismaki wrote and directed *I Hired a Contract Killer,* an English-language comedy in which a clerk loses his job, becomes despondent, and decides to end his life. In this attempt, as with most of his undertakings, the clerk fails miserably. He finds his solution by contracting a hit man to put him out of his misery. After engaging the contract killer, however, the hapless protagonist falls in love and decides he wants to live. This, of course, is not easily done, and he eventually finds himself desperately dodging his murderous tracker. Canby, in his *New York Times* review, noted the film's "playful suspense plot" and its "striking" cinematography of "rich deep colors [that] suggest the artifice of the suspense genre."

Among Kaurismaki's other films of the 1990s is *The Match Factory Girl,* the third and concluding piece of the trilogy including *Shadows in Paradise* and *Ariel.* The heroine of this film is a teenager, Iris, living with her oblivious parents and working in a grossly exploitive system. Iris's job is a bland monotonous exercise of affixing labels to boxes of matches, and her home life is equally full of grayness and drudgery. Her only escape is to go dancing, an event that usually finds her sitting alone with no dancing partner. Only when Iris takes part of her meager paycheck and buys a cheap red dress does she attract a suitor. A one-night fling results in pregnancy, but the man will have nothing further to do with her. The man's rejection of Iris spurs a rebellion in her that results in revenge and escape.

Expanding on his observational and deadpan style, Kaurismaki relates *The Match Factory Girl* with a minimum of dialogue. Light and music cues take the place of verbal communication, portraying Iris's bleak existence in stark visual scenes. Despite the heavy emotional pall that hangs over the film, critics have pointed out Kaurismaki's sly and darkly-shaded humor. They were also quick to note that this humor may not be perceived by all who view the film. "Only those who are responsive to Kaurismaki's astringent style . . . will believe that this is a comedy," reported Kauffmann in the *New Republic.* J. Hoberman affirmed in the *Village Voice* that *The Match Factory Girl* is Kaurismaki's "bleakest" comedy, a film "rationalizing human misery, as it hums with relentless logic." Hoberman concluded that "*The Match Factory Girl* refuses to declare itself either Euro art film or American-style B-movie—it's a triumphant, near-perfect synthesis of both."

Aside from producing scripts for his own projects as director, Kaurismaki has written screenplays with his brother, Mika Kaurismaki, who is also a noted filmmaker. Critics have noted that the siblings constitute virtually the entire Finnish film industry. Notable among their collaborations are *The Worthless,* in which a hapless dishwasher falls in with a female fugitive, and *The Clan: Tales of the Frogs,* wherein a robust family resorts to crime in the Finnish countryside.

Kaurismaki has been praised by critics and viewers of his films as a master of dark and deadpan comedy. His films find characters existing in some of the most morally and socially bankrupt environs; and yet, perhaps because they have lived with it all their lives, these individuals are not crushed by their misfortunes. James described the filmmaker in the *New York Times* as a model for his own cinematic characters: "a droll personality stingy with words yet offering vast irony through his impassive presence." The sheer bluntness with which Kaurismaki presents stoic characters amidst catastrophic personal tragedy and hardship has led many critics to label him the leader of a new school of European cinema. His use of minimal camera movement and quick elliptical jumps is often described as a mixture of the techniques innovated by the French New Wave directors Godard and Bresson and the camp excess of American B-movies. Most critics acknowledge, however, that these derivations are merely the basic ingredients of a film style that takes the best of past filmmaking and forges a new and bracing style. In the *New York Times,* James described Kaurismaki as "more than a prolific upstart or a local curiosity; he is an original and commanding talent among international film makers." Writing in *New Republic,* Kauffmann said of Kaurismaki, "Of prodigal, high-handed talent he has no lack." And Vincent Canby, in a *New York Times* article, declared that "Mr. Kaurismaki could well turn out to be the seminal European film maker of the 1990s."

BIOGRAPHICAL/CRITICAL SOURCES:

PERIODICALS

Chicago Tribune, July 7, 1991.
Christian Science Monitor, November 6, 1990, p. 13.
Interview. April, 1989, p. 114.
Los Angeles Times, February 22, 1989.

Nation, August 13, 1990, p. 179; December 10, 1990, p. 744.
New Republic, August 20, 1990, pp. 24-25; November 12, 1990, pp. 26-27.
New Yorker, August 27, 1990, pp. 91-92.
New York Times, September 24, 1989, p. 71; August 10, 1990, p. C10; August 23, 1990, p. C15; October 3, 1990, p. C13; November 2, 1990, p. C25; October 10, 1992.
Village Voice, November 10, 1992, p. 59.
Washington Post, September 21, 1990, p. B4.*

—*Sketch by Les Stone*

*   *   *

KEIL, Charles 1939-

PERSONAL: Born August 12, 1939, in Norwalk, CT; son of Carl and Marcia (Rudd) Keil; married Angeliki Vellou (a writer); children: Aphrodite, Carl. *Education:* Yale University, B.A., 1961; University of Chicago, M.A., 1964, Ph.D., 1979. *Politics:* "Green." *Religion:* "12/8 Path."

ADDRESSES: Home—81 Crescent Ave., Buffalo, NY 14214. *Office*—Department of American Studies, State University of New York at Buffalo, Buffalo, NY 14260.

CAREER: State University of New York at Buffalo, assistant professor, 1970-71, associate professor, 1971-83, professor of American studies, 1983—, instructor in Upward Bound Program, 1968, Henry Adams fellow, 1968-70; director of graduate studies, 1970-77 and 1979-82, acting chair of American studies department, 1978-79 and 1992, director of undergraduate studies, 1986-89. Central Community School, cofounder, 1970; Trent University, visiting lecturer, 1982 and 1983; WBFO, cohost of "The Beautiful River: A Green Variety Hour," 1989-91; member of board of directors and president of Musicians United for Superior Education, Inc., 1990—; consultant to public schools in several states; lecturer. Member of various musical groups including Outer Circle Orchestra, 1970-89; Azucar, 1988-89; Biocentrics, 1990—; and 12/8 Path Marching Band, 1991—. Organizer for New American Movement, 1974-83, Buffalo Greens, 1985—, and Parkside Greens, 1989—.

MEMBER: United University Professionals, Society for Ethnomusicology, Polish Community Center, American Committee to Keep Biafra Alive (president, Buffalo chapter, 1968-70).

AWARDS, HONORS: Woodrow Wilson fellow, University of Chicago, 1961-62; Ford Foundation fellow in African studies, Indiana University, 1962-63; National Institute of Mental Health fellow, University of Chicago,

1963-64; Roy D. Albert Prize for best master's thesis, University of Chicago, 1963-64; research fellow, Foreign Area Fellowship Program, 1965-67; Rockefeller Foundation research grant, 1975; John Simon Guggenheim fellow, 1979-80; Chicago Folklore Prize cowinner, 1980, for *Tiv Song*; senior fellow, University College Curriculum Committee, 1986-89.

WRITINGS:

Urban Blues, University of Chicago Press, 1966, revised edition, 1992.

Tiv Song, University of Chicago Press, 1979.

(With wife, Angeliki Keil, and Richard Blau) *Polka Happiness,* Temple University Press, 1992.

(Editor with Sue Crafts and Dan Cavicchi) *My Music,* Wesleyan University Press, 1993.

(With Steve Feld) *Music Grooves,* University of Chicago Press, in press.

(With A. Keil and R. Blau) *Polka Perspectives,* University Chicago Press, in press.

Contributor to books, including *Folk Music and Modern Sound,* edited by William Ferris and Mary Hart, University of Mississippi Press, 1982; *The Social Science Encyclopedia,* edited by Adam and Jessica Cooper, Routledge and Kegan Paul, 1985; and *Popular Culture in America,* edited by Paul Buhle, University of Minnesota Press, 1987. Contributor of articles and poetry to periodicals, including *Cultural Anthropology, New York Folklore, Ethnomusicology, Journal of Ethnic Studies, Africa Today, Journal of Aesthetics and Art Criticism, Prodigal, New York Times Magazine, Pure Light, Social Anarchism,* and *Trumpeter.* Member of editorial board for *Dialectical Anthropology,* 1983—, and *Works and Days,* 1984—; editor of *Echology,* 1986-91, and *Museletter,* 1990—; editorial assistant for *Buffalo Reevaluation Counseling Newsletter,* 1987-88.

Urban Blues has also been translated into Japanese.

WORK IN PROGRESS: Sociomusicology: A Participatory Approach, a collection of articles in Greek translation, for Apopira Publications; *The Instruments,* with A. Keil; *The Jazz Rhythm Section;* "Gypsy Fullstop," an epic poem; and an article updating "participatory discrepancy" theory and research.

SIDELIGHTS: Charles Keil told *CA:* "I usually write from a sense of moral indignation, to correct a big injustice, to be sure that people who have been ignored or slighted are at least partially heard from and partially understood. After listening hard to John Coltrane, Malcolm X, and thousands of other strong and distinctive voices from Afro-America in the early 1960s, I was outraged that most white people were still thinking about black people as cultureless, carbon copies of white people and made in America: hence, my first book, *Urban Blues.* Similar moti-

vations kept me and my collaborators plugging away at Polish-American polka studies for the better part of two decades: no books on the subject existed, awareness of ethnic working class cultures being simply non-existent for most people. Singing the unsung—sums up a lot of my writing.

"I am very proud of the fact that since *Urban Blues* (an M.A. thesis) and *Tiv Song* (a Ph.D.thesis), all 'my' books have been collaborative efforts: *Polka Happiness* with Angie Keil and Dick Blau, *Polka Perspectives* with Angie Keil and Dick Blau, *Music Grooves* with Steve Feld, *My Music* with Sue Crafts, Dan Cavicchi and many graduate and undergraduate students, and *The Instruments* with Angie Keil. It takes longer to work closely with others, but the results are richer, the loss of one's individual voice an utterly false fear. Currently I am most interested in helping more children to become musical."

*   *   *

KELLOW, Kathleen
   See HIBBERT, Eleanor Alice Burford

*   *   *

KELLY-BENJAMIN, Kathleen

PERSONAL: Education: St. John's University, Jamaica, NY, B.A., 1973; C. W. Post College, Long Island University, M.A., 1977; Graduate Center of the City University of New York, Ph.D., 1989.

ADDRESSES: Home—1006 Wabash Rd., Palm Bay, FL 32909. *Office*—Department of Science Education, Florida Institute of Technology, 150 West University Blvd., Melbourne, FL 32901.

CAREER: High school mathematics teacher in New York at schools in Hicksville, College Point, and New York City, 1973-79; Higher Achievement Program, New York City, program director and mathematics teacher, 1979-81; Kelly Gabler Test Preparation, New York City, director and mathematics teacher, 1982-85; Hunter College of the City University of New York, New York City, adjunct lecturer in education, 1986-89; Jersey City State College, Jersey City, NJ, assistant professor of education, 1989-90; Florida Institute of Technology, Melbourne, assistant professor of mathematics education, 1990—. Borough of Manhattan Community College, adjunct lecturer, 1985-87; Brevard Community College, guest lecturer, 1991. Center for Advanced Study in Education, research assistant, 1986-87; BellSouth Educational Technology Research Center, project director, 1990—; Center for Excellence in Mathematics, Science, Computers, and Technology, member of board of directors, 1990-92; Brevard Women's Center, guest lecturer, 1991, coordinator of lecture series, 1992; workshop leader; consultant to Integrated Software. City of New York, member of Chancellor's Advisory Committee on Improving Opportunities for Minorities and Women in Science and Mathematics, 1987; Center for Women Policy Studies, member of Educational Equity Policy Studies Program Roundtable, 1988; Mathematical Sciences Education Board, member of National Summit on Mathematics Assessment, 1991.

MEMBER: American Educational Research Association, American Psychological Association, National Council of Teachers of Mathematics, Florida Association of Mathematics Supervisors, Florida Educational Research Association, Florida Council of Teachers of Mathematics.

WRITINGS:

A Young Woman's Guide to Better SAT Scores: Fighting the Gender Gap, Bantam, 1990.

Contributor to books, including *Advances in Program Evaluation,* Volume I: *Effects of Changes in Assessment Policy,* edited by R. L. Stake, 1991.

*   *   *

KEMENY, John G(eorge)   1926-1992

OBITUARY NOTICE—See index for *CA* sketch: Born May 31, 1926, in Budapest, Hungary; immigrated to the United States, 1940, naturalized citizen, 1945; died of a heart attack, December 26, 1992, in Lebanon, NH. Mathematician, educator, and writer. Kemeny helped developed the BASIC (Beginner's All-Purpose Symbolic Instruction Code) language for computers, which afforded students a quicker understanding of electronic programming and created a foundation for the sophisticated programming that was to come. A research assistant to prolific scientist Albert Einstein, Kemeny completed an accelerated course of study when he earned a mathematics doctorate from Princeton University at the age of twenty-three. Four years later, he was granted a full professorship at Dartmouth College and quickly ascended to the chair of the mathematics department. In 1970, he was appointed the president of the institution and served in that role for more than a decade, guiding Dartmouth through important changes. Under his leadership, the institution began accepting female students in 1972, adopted a trimester school schedule, and increased a push for minority enrollment. In 1979, under the administration of President Jimmy Carter, Kemeny served as chair of a commission assigned to investigate the Three Mile Island power plant accident. Kemeny authored or coauthored numer-

ous books on mathematics and computing, including *Introduction to Finite Mathematics, Man and the Computer: A New Symbiosis, Computing for a Course in Finite Mathematics,* and *Structured BASIC Programming.*

OBITUARIES AND OTHER SOURCES:

BOOKS

The Writers Directory: 1992-1994, St. James Press, 1991, p. 534.

PERIODICALS

Los Angeles Times, December 28, 1992, p. A22.
New York Times, December 27, 1992, p. L40.
Washington Post, December 28, 1992, p. B6.

*   *   *

KENNEDY, Caroline (Bouvier)   1957-

PERSONAL: Born in 1957; daughter of John Fitzgerald Kennedy (former President of the United States) and Jacqueline Kennedy Onassis (an editor; maiden name, Bouvier); married Edwin Arthur Schlossberg (a museum exhibit designer), July 19, 1986; children: Rose, Tatiana, Jack. *Education:* Radcliffe College, B.A., 1980; Columbia University Law School, J.D., 1988. *Religion:* Catholic.

CAREER: Lawyer and writer. Metropolitan Museum of Art, New York City, researcher and associate film producer, 1980-85; John Fitzgerald Kennedy Library, Boston, MA, member of board of trustees, 1983.

WRITINGS:

(With Ellen Alderman) *In Our Defense: The Bill of Rights in Action,* Morrow, 1991.

Contributor to periodicals, including *Newsweek* and *Redbook.*

SIDELIGHTS: Caroline Kennedy and Ellen Alderman's 1991 book *In Our Defense: The Bill of Rights in Action,* which became a national best-seller, examines the first ten amendments to the U.S. Constitution on their two-hundredth birthday. The idea for the book developed when the two lawyers, who were then classmates at Columbia University Law School, read a poll that found more than half of the Americans questioned were unable to identify the Bill of Rights. *In Our Defense,* written as a response to this statistic, highlights recent cases that illustrate how each amendment is interpreted in the courtroom and how far each extends. Critics have compared the chapters in the book to short stories that evoke the often odd experiences of the individuals involved in the cases. Reviewers have also praised the manner in which the book emphasizes the humanity of these people, rather than reducing them to the faceless status often reserved for litigants.

One of the most frequently cited examples is the case of Jacqueline Bouknight, a Baltimore woman who, when suspected of abusing her son and ordered to bring him to court, refused to do so because she felt the order violated her Fifth Amendment right against self-incrimination. Withholding the details of her son's whereabouts even after the court ruled that its request was constitutional, Bouknight was jailed on contempt of court charges while her son remained missing. Her argument questions the law's effectiveness with respect to child abuse cases and is an example of how Kennedy and Alderman stress the Bill of Rights's influence on everyday American life.

Kennedy told Carol Clurman in *USA Weekend* that she and Alderman "want people to realize that the Bill of Rights is not just a dusty document, but really has a human face." *Chicago Tribune* contributor Stephanie B. Goldberg wrote: "In the end, one can simplify the law and one can glamorize it with sexy cases, but at its heart is a process of rigorous analysis. Because Alderman and Kennedy are good lawyers, that is what *In Our Defense* does best."

BIOGRAPHICAL/CRITICAL SOURCES:

PERIODICALS

Chicago Tribune, February 26, 1991, section 2, p. 3.
Detroit Free Press, February 10, 1991.
McCall's, September, 1987, pp. 15, 19-20; November, 1991, pp. 126, 188-190.
New York Times, February 8, 1991, p. B16.
People, August 4, 1986, p. 30.
USA Weekend, February 1, 1991, pp. 4-5.

*　　*　　*

KENNEDY, Liv 1934-

PERSONAL: Born April 20, 1934, in Port Neville, British Columbia, Canada; daughter of Ingebrigt and Ferdinanda (Mathiesen) Hansen; married Edward J. Suttle, 1952 (marriage ended, 1963); married Charles F. Kennedy, 1964 (marriage ended, 1978); married Hugh C. McIntyre (a writer), May 22, 1987; children: (first marriage) Curtis A. *Education:* Attended Falkener Smith's Academy of Art, Vancouver, British Columbia, 1951-52, University of British Columbia, Langara College, and Simon Fraser University. *Religion:* Christian.

ADDRESSES: Home and office—Box 14, 3600 Outrigger Rd., Nanoose Bay, British Columbia, Canada V0R 2R0; and P.O. Box 91405, West Vancouver, British Columbia, Canada V7V 3P1.

CAREER: Dalcraft Ltd., commercial artist, 1950-55; Grouse Mountain Resorts Ltd., ski instructor, 1955-63; free-lance writer and photographer, 1968—. Strasser Travel, professional tour escort and travel consultant, 1973—; Jib Set Sailing School, sailing instructor, 1974-78; Maritime Museum of Vancouver, coordinator of the annual series "Offshore Cruising Adventures," 1976—; Canadian Broadcasting Corp., yachting correspondent and broadcaster for *Good Morning Radio,* 1977—. Malaspina College, photojournalism teacher, 1992.

MEMBER: Periodical Writers Association of Canada, Blue Water Cruising Association (founding member), Fairwinds Golf and Country Club (charter member), Schooner Cove Yacht Club, Sons of Norway (Solstrand Lodge).

AWARDS, HONORS: First Prize, People and Places Contest, *Lens and Shutter,* 1978; grant from Canada Council.

WRITINGS:

(Coauthor) *Vancouver Once upon a Time,* privately printed, 1974.
Coastal Villages, Harbour Publishing, 1991.

Author of "Offshore People," a regular column in *Pacific Yachting* and, later, *Boat World,* 1971—. Contributor of articles and photographs to magazines in the United States and Canada, including *Sea, Sailing Canada, Weekend, Yachting USA, Photo Life,* and *Motor Boat and Sailing.*

SIDELIGHTS: Liv Kennedy told *CA:* "I have spent as much of my life on the water as on the land. I was born aboard the Coast Mission ship *Columbia* and grew up in the logging camps and fishing villages of the British Columbia coast. My parents came from the Lofoten Island area of northern Norway. They were among the early settlers to pioneer the coast of British Columbia.

"I have traveled extensively by small boat over the oceans of the world, including a four-year circumnavigation of the world between 1965 and 1969, with Charles Kennedy and my son Curtis, aboard the thirty-seven-foot cutter *Kelea.* We were the first Canadian family to make such a voyage. During those years under sail, I helped supplement the family income by writing articles about the adventures of cruising around the world in a small boat.

"Since returning to British Columbia, I have written about other people who make ocean voyages aboard small boats. Besides yachting, I take a special interest in the coastal history. I have cruised the coast of British Columbia for many years, taking photographs and researching its early history.

"I began keeping a diary as a child, while I was living on our family homestead on northern Quadra Island. At the age of eleven, I submitted my first news item to the *Westcoast Fisherman*. It was printed on the front page, along with the picture I had taken with my first camera, a baby Brownie. My main interest, however, was our domestic animals: the cow, horses, goats, pet pig, chickens, ducks, and geese. They received a daily entry in the diary, as did the wild animals and birds of the forest that surrounded our homestead. As many children are, I was vividly concerned about the mistreatment of some of these species: killing chickens and pigs in order to eat, hunting down cougars with dogs just to kill them, and slaughtering horses when they were no longer fit for work.

"My husband and I are now vegetarians. This came about while we were having a coffee in an outdoor cafe in a village on the Adriatic coast of what is now Croatia. Unknown to us, there was an abattoir nearby. To our dismay, a poor, little pig ran among the tables of the cafe, screaming until his pursuers eventually pinned him to the ground. My mission on earth is to help people understand the animals that share this earth with us."

BIOGRAPHICAL/CRITICAL SOURCES:

PERIODICALS

Globe and Mail (Toronto), February 1, 1992, p. A12.

*   *   *

KENNEDY, Nigel (Paul) 1956-

PERSONAL: Born December 28, 1956, in Brighton, England; son of John (a cellist) and Scylla (a piano teacher; maiden name, Stoner) Kennedy. *Education:* Attended Yehudi Menuhin School, beginning in 1964, and Juilliard School of Performing Arts, beginning c. 1972. *Avocational interests:* Golf, football, cricket.

ADDRESSES: Home—Malvern Hills, England. *Agent*—John Stanley Media Management, 28 Nottingham Pl., London W1M 3FD, England.

CAREER: Violinist. Kennedy's classical recordings, all released by Angel/EMI, include Sir Edward William Elgar's *Violin Concerto in B Minor, Op. 61*, 1984; Bela Bartok's *Sonata for Solo Violin* and Duke Ellington's *Mainly Black*, 1986; Felix Mendelssohn's *Violin Concerto in E Minor, Op. 64* and Max Bruch's *Violin Concerto in G Minor, Op. 26*, 1986; Jean Sibelius's *Violin Concerto* and *Symphony No. 5*, 1986; Sir William Turner Walton's *Violin Concerto* and *Viola Concerto*, 1987; and Antonio Vivaldi's *The Four Seasons*, 1989. He has also performed on the albums *Nigel Kennedy: Let Loose*, released by EMI; *Nigel Kennedy Plays Jazz*, released by Chandos; *Once Upon a Long Ago*, released by EMI; *Strad Jazz*, released by Chandos; and *Just Listen*, EMI, 1992. Has appeared with numerous symphony orchestras and has conducted the St. Paul Chamber Orchestra.

AWARDS, HONORS: Best Classical Record, British Record Industry Awards, and Record of the Year nomination, *Gramophone,* both 1985, both for recording of Sir Edward William Elgar's *Violin Concerto in B Minor, Op. 61;* Guinness Book of Records, 1990, for sustaining the recording of Antonio Vivaldi's *The Four Seasons* at No. 1 on the United Kingdom Classical Chart for over one year; Golden Rose of Montreaux, 1990; Variety Club Showbusiness Personality of the Year, 1991; honorary D.Litt., University of Bath, 1991.

WRITINGS:

Always Playing (autobiography), St. Martin's, 1992.

BIOGRAPHICAL/CRITICAL SOURCES:

BOOKS

Contemporary Musicians, Volume 8, Gale, 1993, pp. 146-148.

PERIODICALS

Chicago Tribune, January 16, 1989, section 5, p. 3; January 18, 1989, section 1, p. 18; August 21, 1989, section 1, p. 16; October 23, 1989, section 1, p. 14; April 24, 1991, section 1, p. 22.
Los Angeles Times, November 20, 1988, section C, p. 78; May 12, 1991, section CAL, p. 4; May 12, 1991, section CAL, p. 70; January 24, 1992, section F, p. 8.
Maclean's, May 26, 1986, p. 54; May 18, 1992, p. 55.
New Statesman, December 18, 1987, p. 37.
New York Times, May 29, 1988, section 2, p. 23; April 21, 1989, section C, p. 19; April 21, 1991, section 2, p. 27; April 12, 1992, section 2, p. 23; April 18, 1992, section A, p. 11.
Washington Post, March 2, 1988; May 10, 1991, section C, p. 2; May 13, 1991, section B, p. 1; July 26, 1992, section G, p. 4.*

*   *   *

KILPATRICK, Andrew 1943-

PERSONAL: Born April 17, 1943, in Washington, DC; son of Carroll (a newspaper correspondent) and Frances (a schoolteacher; maiden name, Williams) Kilpatrick; married Kay Gauntt, June 4, 1974 (divorced September 1, 1987); married Pat Terrell (a director of marketing), March 1, 1992; children: Jack, Anna. *Education:* Washington and Lee University, B.A., 1965; University of Vermont, M.A., 1968. *Politics:* "Middle of the road." *Religion:* Episcopalian. *Avocational interests:* Walking, reading. "I am an old, retired Boston Marathon runner, with emphasis on old and retired."

ADDRESSES: *Home*—20 Montcrest Dr., Birmingham, AL 35213. *Office*—Prudential Securities, Inc., Financial Center, 505 20th St. N., Suite 1000, Birmingham, AL 35203. *Agent*—Robin Straus, Robin Straus Agency, 229 East 79th St., New York, NY 10021.

CAREER: U.S. Peace Corps, Washington, DC, volunteer in India, 1965-67; *Raleigh News and Observer*, Raleigh, NC, copy editor, 1971-72; *Birmingham News*, Birmingham, AL, reporter, 1972-84; *Birmingham Post-Herald*, Birmingham, business reporter, 1984-92; Prudential Securities, Inc., Birmingham, stockbroker, 1992—. *Military service:* U.S. Navy, 1968-71; became lieutenant junior grade.

WRITINGS:

Warren Buffett: The Good Guy of Wall Street, Donald I. Fine, 1992.

WORK IN PROGRESS: A more definitive work on Warren Buffett.

SIDELIGHTS: Andrew Kilpatrick told *CA:* "I wrote my book about investor Warren Buffett because I was absolutely taken with Mr. Buffett's impeccable ethics and his extraordinary sense of humor, in addition to his fabled investing success. Quite frankly, I think he's the most interesting person in the country."

*   *   *

KING, Laurie R. 1952-

PERSONAL: Born September 19, 1952, in Oakland, CA; married Noel Q. King (a professor emeritus), 1977; children: Nathanael, Zoe. *Education:* University of California, Santa Cruz, B.A., 1977; Graduate Theological Union, Berkeley, CA, M.A., 1984.

ADDRESSES: *Agent*—Linda Allen, 1949 Green St. No. 5, San Francisco, CA 94123.

CAREER: Writer.

WRITINGS:

A Grave Talent (mystery novel), St. Martin's, 1993.

WORK IN PROGRESS: Mystery novels *With Child* and another, tentatively titled *The Beekeeper's Apprentice*, publication of both expected by 1994.

KINGSLEY, April 1941-

PERSONAL: Born February 16, 1941, in New York, NY; daughter of Kingdon Edward and Grace (Haddock) Kingsley; married Budd Hopkins, 1973; children: Grace. *Education:* Queens College of the City University of New York, A.A.S., 1960; New York University, B.A., 1966, M.A., 1968; Graduate School and University Center of the City University of New York, A.B.D. and M.Phil., 1986. *Avocational interests:* Fishing.

ADDRESSES: *Home and office*—246 West 16th St., New York, NY 10011; (summer) RR 1 Trotting Pk., Wellfleet, MA 02667.

CAREER: Park Place Gallery, assistant director, 1965-66; Museum of Modern Art, New York City, curatorial assistant, 1969-71; Pasadena Art Museum, NY, associate curator, 1971-72; School of Visual Arts, NY, instructor, 1973-91; Sculpture Center, NY, curator, 1980-89; Franz Kline Catalogue Raisonnee, project director, 1986—. Visiting lecturer at Pratt Institute, spring, 1979; adjunct faculty member at Rhode Island School of Design, 1982; City University of New York, adjunct professor, 1985-87, adjunct professor at Queens College, 1985.

MEMBER: International Association of Art Critics, College Art Association.

AWARDS, HONORS: Institute of Fine Arts fellowship, 1966; Ford Foundation fellowship, 1967.

WRITINGS:

(Editor) *Adolf Gottlieb: Works on Paper*, American Federation of Arts, 1985.
The Turning Point: The Abstract Expressionists and the Transformation of American Art, Simon & Schuster, 1992.

Works represented in catalogues, including *The Interior Self: Three Generations of Expressionists View the Human Image*, Montclair Art Museum, 1987; *Hundred Years of American Paintings: The Montclair Art Museum Collection*, Hudson Hills, 1989; *Michael Loew*, Landau Fine Arts, 1990; *Michael Rubin*, Philip Samuels Fine Art, 1990; and *Julius Tobias*, State University of New York at Stonybrook, 1992. Contributor to periodicals, including *Art Gallery, Art News, Artforum, Art International*, and *Newsweek*. Coeditor of *Art Express* (magazine), 1981-82.

*   *   *

KINNEY, Francis S(herwood) 1915-1993

OBITUARY NOTICE—See index for *CA* sketch: Born November 2, 1915, in New York, NY; died of complications from Alzheimer's disease, January 4, 1993, in Nesconset, NY. Naval architect and writer. After graduating from Princeton University in 1938, Kinney began a lengthy career in naval architecture. For more than thirty years he held the position of senior designer at Sparkman and Stephens, and in the late 1970s penned *You Are First: The Story of Olin and Rod Stephens of Sparkman & Stephens*. The work details the history of the naval architectural firm, which crafted many of the 12-Meter yachts used in the America's Cup race. Kinney also wrote the seventh and eighth editions of *Skene's Elements of Yacht Design*.

OBITUARIES AND OTHER SOURCES:

PERIODICALS

New York Times, January 6, 1993, p. B6.

*   *   *

KITCH, Sally L. 1946-

PERSONAL: Born May 16, 1946, in Baltimore, MD; daughter of George J. (an attorney) and Mabel (a government worker; maiden name, Shelby) Leibowitz; married Thomas D. Kitch; children: Aaron Wells and Justin Shelby (twins). *Education:* Cornell University, A.B. (with honors), 1967; University of Chicago, M.A., 1968; Emory University, Ph.D., 1984.

ADDRESSES: Home—Columbus, OH. *Office*—Center for Women's Studies, 186 University Hall, 230 North Oval Mall, Ohio State University, Columbus, OH 43210-1311.

CAREER: Wichita State University, Wichita, KS, instructor, 1969-78, assistant professor, 1978-87, associate professor of women's studies, 1987-92, director of Center for Women's Studies, 1988-92; Ohio State University, Columbus, professor of women's and comparative studies and director of Center for Women's Studies, 1992—. Kansas Committee for the Humanities, field humanist, 1975-79. University Press of Kansas, member of editorial board, 1990-92.

MEMBER: National Women's Studies Association (Midwest regional coordinator, 1977-79), Phi Beta Kappa.

AWARDS, HONORS: Grants from National Endowment for the Humanities, 1987 and 1988; Book Award from National Women's Studies Association and University of Illinois Press, 1987, for *Chaste Liberation: Celibacy and Female Cultural Status;* Helen Hooven Santmyer Prize in Women's Studies, Ohio State University Press, 1990, for *This Strange Society of Women: Reading the Letters and Lives of the Woman's Commonwealth.*

WRITINGS:

(Co-editor and contributor) *Design for Equity: Women and Leadership in Higher Education,* Education Development Center, U.S. Department of Education, 1980.
(Co-author) *The Source Book: An Inductive Approach to Composition,* Longman, 1981.
Chaste Liberation: Celibacy and Female Cultural Status, University of Illinois Press, 1987.
This Strange Society of Women: Reading the Letters and Lives of the Woman's Commonwealth, Ohio State University Press, 1993.

Work represented in books, including *Intrigue in the Garden: Essays on the History of Exegesis of Genesis 1-3,* edited by Gregory A. Robbins, Edwin Mellen, 1988; *On Peace, War, and Gender: A Challenge to Genetic Explanations,* edited by Anne Hunter, Feminist Press, 1991; and *Continental, Latin American, and Francophone Women Writers, 1988-1989,* Volume III, University Press of America, 1993. Contributor of articles and reviews to professional periodicals.

WORK IN PROGRESS: Co-editor of *We're All in This Alone: Career Women's Challenges and Constraints,* and author of the contribution "The Feminist Factor," for Sage Publications; "Of Roots and Motherlands," a chapter to be included in a book on psychological theory and women's literature.

*   *   *

KLECK, Gary 1951-

PERSONAL: Born March 2, 1951, in Lombard, IL; son of William Gordon (a manager) and Muriel Joyce (a homemaker; maiden name, Edwards) Kleck; married Diane Gomez (a supervisor), June 20, 1981; children: Matthew Gomez, Tessa Gomez. *Education:* University of Illinois at Urbana-Champaign, A.B., 1973, A.M., 1975, Ph.D., 1979. *Politics:* Liberal Democrat.

ADDRESSES: Home—1003 Piedmont Dr., Tallahassee, FL 32312. *Office*—School of Criminology and Criminal Justice, Florida State University, Tallahassee, FL 32306.

CAREER: Florida State University, Tallahassee, instructor, 1978-79, assistant professor, 1979-84, associate professor, 1984-91, professor of criminology and criminal justice, 1991—.

MEMBER: American Society of Criminology, American Sociological Association, American Civil Liberties Union, Common Cause, Natural Resources Defense Council.

WRITINGS:

Point Blank: Guns and Violence in America, Aldine de Gruyter, 1991.

Contributor to periodicals, including *American Sociological Review* and *American Journal of Sociology.*

WORK IN PROGRESS: Research on the dynamics of violent interactions.

* * *

KLEIN, George 1925-

PERSONAL: Born July 28, 1925, in Budapest, Hungary. *Education:* Karolinska Institute, M.D., 1951; University of Chicago, D.Sc. (with honors), 1966; University of Debrecen, M.D. (with honors), 1988; Hebrew University, Ph.D., 1989.

ADDRESSES: Office—Department of Tumor Biology, Karolinska Institute, Box 60400, S-104 01 Stockholm, Sweden.

CAREER: Budapest University, Budapest, Hungary, instructor in histology, 1945, instructor in pathology, 1946; Karolinska Institute, Stockholm, Sweden, research fellow, 1947-49, assistant professor of cell research, 1951-57, professor of tumor biology and department head, 1957—. Institute for Cancer Research, guest investigator, 1950; Stanford University, visiting professor, 1961; Harvard University, Dunham Lecturer, 1966; American Association of Cancer Research, Clowes Memorial Lecturer, 1967; Swedish Medical Association, Lennander Lecturer, 1967; Hebrew University, visiting professor, 1973—; University of Arizona, Donald Wae Waddel Lecturer, 1991.

MEMBER: Royal Swedish Academy of Sciences, Nobel Assembly of Karolinska Institute, Scientific Advisory Council of the Swedish Medical Board, National Academy of Sciences of the United States, American Philosophical Society, Hungarian Academy of Sciences, American Association of Immunologists, French Society of Immunology, American Association for Cancer Research, American Academy of Arts and Sciences.

AWARDS, HONORS: Bertha Goldblatt Teplitz Award (with Eva Klein), 1960; Danish Pathological Society Prize, 1967; Fogarty Scholar, National Institute of the Humanities, 1972; Rabbi Shai Shacknai Prize in Tumor Immunology, 1972; Bertner Award, 1973; Annual Award, American Cancer Society, 1973; Harvey Lecturer, 1973; Prix Griffuel, 1974; Harvey Prize, 1975; Gardner Award, 1976; Behring Prize, 1977; Bjoerken Prize, 1978; Sloan Prize, General Motors Cancer Research Foundation, 1979; Santa Chiara Academy Award, 1979; Erik

Fernstroem Prize (with Klein), 1983; Anniversary Prize, Swedish Medical Association, 1983; Letterstedt Prize, Royal Swedish Academy of Sciences, 1989; Dobloug Prize, Swedish Academy of Literature, 1990; Lisl and Leo Eitinger Prize, Oslo University, 1990.

WRITINGS:

(Editor) *Viral Oncology,* Raven Press, 1980.

(Editor) *Oncogene Studies,* Raven Press, 1982.

(Editor) *The Transformation-Associated Cellular p53 Protein,* Raven Press, 1982.

DNA-Virus Oncogenes and Their Action, Raven Press, 1983.

Istaellet foer Hemland, Bonniers (Stockholm), 1984.

Mechanisms of Neoplastic Transformation at the Cellular Level: Advances in Viral Oncology, Raven Press, 1984.

(Editor) *Viruses as the Causative Agents of Naturally Occurring Tumors,* Raven Press, 1985.

Ateisten och den Heliga Staden, Bonniers, 1987.

(Editor) *Analysis of Multistep Scenarios in the Natural History of Human or Animal Cancer,* Raven Press, 1987.

(Editor) *Experimental Approaches to Multifactorial Interactions in Tumor Development,* Raven Press, 1987.

Pieta, Bonniers, 1989, MIT Press, 1992.

Tumorigenic DNA Viruses, Raven Press, 1989.

The Atheist and the Holy City: Encounters and Reflections, MIT Press, 1990.

(With Per Ahlmark) *Motstaandet,* Bonniers, 1991.

Editor of *Advances in Cancer Research* series, Academic Press. Contributor to periodicals.

* * *

KLEIN, Philip Shriver 1909-1993

OBITUARY NOTICE—See index for *CA* sketch: Born June 10, 1909, in Allentown, PA; died of heart failure, February 15, 1993, in State College, PA. Educator, historian, and author. Klein, a historian known for his expertise on President James Buchanan, began his lengthy teaching career in the late 1930s. After earning his doctorate in history from the University of Pennsylvania, Klein taught at Franklin and Marshall College for several years. In 1941 he became an assistant professor at Pennsylvania State University. After a stint with the military during World War II, Klein returned to Pennsylvania State University. He chaired the history department from 1953 to 1956 and was named professor emeritus in 1972. Klein served at various times as president of the Historical Foundation of Pennsylvania and the Pennsylvania Historical Association. He is credited with writing what many consider to be the most authoritative biography on President James Buchanan. In the book, Klein argues that—contrary to what many historians believe—Buchanan was a very effective president, due in part to his attempts to prevent the U.S. Civil War. In addition to *President James Buchanan,* Klein wrote such titles as *A History of Pennsylvania* with Ari Hoogenboom, and *History of the United States,* with A. C. Bining.

OBITUARIES AND OTHER SOURCES:

BOOKS

International Authors and Writers Who's Who, 9th edition, [and] *International Who's Who in Poetry,* 6th edition, Melrose, 1982, p. 350.

PERIODICALS

New York Times, March 3, 1993, p. B12.

*   *   *

KLIEMAN, Charles   1940-

PERSONAL: Born November 5, 1940, in Philadelphia, PA; son of Paul and Harriet (Lean) Klieman; children: Michael, Valerie. *Education:* Ursinus College, B.S., 1962; Jefferson Medical College, M.D., 1967.

ADDRESSES: Home—79 Cypress Way, Rolling Hills Estates, CA 90274. *Office*—12291 East Washington Blvd., Whittier, CA 90606.

CAREER: Cardiovascular surgeon, Los Angeles, CA, 1974—. Director, owner, and president of various companies; inventor.

MEMBER: "Most medical societies of my profession."

WRITINGS:

Save Your Arteries, Save Your Life, Warner, 1987.
If It Runs in Your Family: Heart Disease, Bantam, 1991.

WORK IN PROGRESS: Two novels; *Metaphysics and Medicine.*

*   *   *

KLINGENSTEIN, Susanne (Schloetelburg)   1959-

PERSONAL: Born April 17, 1959, in Baden-Baden, Germany; daughter of Horst (a writer) and Margaretha (an executive; maiden name, Gruninger; present surname, Huettemann) Schloetelburg. *Education:* Attended University of Stirling, 1979-80; University of Mannheim, B.A., 1980; Brandeis University, M.A. (English), 1983; University of Heidelberg, M.A. (English), 1984, M.A.

(German), 1985, Ph.D. (summa cum laude), 1990. *Religion:* Jewish.

ADDRESSES: Home—59 Joy St., Boston, MA 02114. *Office*—Department of Writing and Humanistic Studies, E14-333, Massachusetts Institute of Technology, Cambridge, MA 02139.

CAREER: Bibliographisches Institut, Mannheim, Germany, editorial assistant and proofreader, summers, 1980-83; Astronomisches Rechen-Institut, Heidelberg, Germany, proofreader, 1983-85; University of Mannheim, Mannheim, Germany, temporary assistant professor of English, 1986-87; Harvard University, Cambridge, MA, instructor, 1989-90, lecturer in English and American literature, 1990-92; Massachusetts Institute of Technology, Cambridge, assistant professor of writing and humanistic studies, 1993—. Consultant to H. Aschebourg and Co.

MEMBER: Modern Language Association of America, Association for Jewish Studies, American Studies Association, English Institute, Deutsche Gesellschaft fuer Amerikastudien, Northeast Modern Language Association.

AWARDS, HONORS: German state scholar in Scotland, 1979-80; fellow of German Academic Exchange Service, 1982-83 and 1987-88, German Marshall Fund, 1988, and Memorial Foundation for Jewish Culture, 1991-92; grant from Deutsche Forschungsmeinschaft, 1993-94.

WRITINGS:

Jews in the American Academy, 1900-1940: The Dynamics of Intellectual Assimilation, Yale University Press, 1991.

Work represented in anthologies, including *The Other New York Jewish Intellectuals,* edited by Carole Kessner, New York University Press; *Reconfiguring Jewish American Identity: Literary and Cultural Essays in Autobiographical Mode,* edited by Shelley Fisher-Fishkin and Jeffrey Rubin-Dorsky, University of Wisconsin Press; and *Reference Guide to Short Fiction,* edited by Noelle Watson, Gale. Contributor of articles and reviews to periodicals, including *Die Zeit* and *The New Leader.*

WORK IN PROGRESS: Rethinking Home: The Cultural Work of Jewish Critics in the Literary Academy; research on American academic history and American Jewish literature.

*   *   *

KNAPP, J(ohn) Merrill   1914-1993

OBITUARY NOTICE—See index for *CA* sketch: Born May 9, 1914, in New York, NY; died of prostate cancer,

March 7, 1993, in Princeton, NJ. Educator, editor, and writer. Remembered as an authority on composer George Frederick Handel, Knapp served as an instructor in the music department of Princeton University for more than four decades. He received his undergraduate degree from Yale University in the mid-1930s, traveled to California, then returned to his alma mater to serve as assistant director of the glee club. Later, he earned his master's degree from Columbia University. He served in the U.S. Navy during World War II and, upon completion of his tour of duty, began his lengthy affiliation with Princeton University. In 1961, he was appointed full professor. During his association with the university, he led the glee club, chaired the music department, and, during the 1960s, acted as dean of the college. Knapp's literary work includes 1987's *Handel's Operas 1704-1726,* coauthored with Winton Dean, the editing of two volumes of the complete works of Handel, and books on opera and vocal work.

OBITUARIES AND OTHER SOURCES:

BOOKS

Who's Who in Entertainment, Second Edition, Marquis, 1992, p. 354.

PERIODICALS

New York Times, March 10, 1993, p. B7.

* * *

KNEBEL, Fletcher 1911-1993

OBITUARY NOTICE—See index for *CA* sketch: Born October 1, 1911, in Dayton, OH; committed suicide February 26, 1993, in Honolulu, HI. Journalist and author. Knebel was perhaps best known for his Cold War thriller, *Seven Days in May,* written with Charles W. Bailey, and for his satiric syndicated daily column, "Potomac Fever," which he wrote for thirteen years beginning in 1951. He began his writing career as a reporter for local newspapers, including the *Coatesville Record* in Coatesville, PA. In 1936, he joined the *Cleveland Plain Dealer,* becoming the Washington correspondent a year later. Knebel's books, mostly novels, include *Night of Camp David* for which he won an Ohioana Book Award in 1966, *Trespass, Dark Horse, Crossing in Berlin,* and *Before You Sue,* a work of nonfiction.

OBITUARIES AND OTHER SOURCES:

BOOKS

Contemporary Novelists, 5th edition, St. Martin's, 1991.

PERIODICALS

New York Times, February 28, 1993, p. 44.

Washington Post, February 28, 1993, p. B7.

* * *

KOFORD, Kenneth J. 1948-

PERSONAL: Born December 30, 1948, in Hollywood, CA; son of Kenneth Harold (a geologist) and Theresa Amelia (Sutton) Koford. *Education:* Yale University, B.A., 1970; University of California, Los Angeles, Ph.D., 1977.

ADDRESSES: Home—281 Beverly Rd., Newark, DE 19711. *Office*—Department of Economics, University of Delaware, Newark, DE 19716.

CAREER: University of Delaware, Newark, began as assistant professor, became associate professor of economics and political science.

WRITINGS:

(Editor with James Butkiewicz and Jeffrey B. Miller) *Keynes' Economic Legacy: Contemporary Macro-Economic Theories,* Praeger, 1988.
(Editor with Jeffrey B. Miller) *Social Norms and Economic Institutions,* University of Michigan Press, 1991.

WORK IN PROGRESS: Research on macro-economic policy and on reform in Eastern Europe.

* * *

KOWALEWSKI, Michael (John) 1956-

PERSONAL: Surname is pronounced "*ko*-wa-les-ki"; born November 2, 1956, in San Francisco, CA; son of Edward John (a laboratory technician) and Suzanne (a teacher's aide; maiden name, Thome) Kowalewski; married Catherine Anne Oates, June 25, 1983; children: Nicholas Edward, Sarah Marie. *Education:* Amherst College, B.A., 1978; Rutgers University, M.A., 1982, Ph.D., 1986. *Politics:* Democrat. *Religion:* Roman Catholic. *Avocational interests:* Running, photography, travel, brewing beer.

ADDRESSES: Home—Northfield, MN. *Office*—Department of English, Carleton College, Northfield, MN 55057.

CAREER: High school English teacher in Duluth, MN, 1978-79; Princeton University, Princeton, NJ, assistant professor of English, 1986-91; Carleton College, Northfield, MN, assistant professor of English, 1991—.

MEMBER: Modern Language Association of America, American Literature Association, Western Literature Association, California Studies Association.

AWARDS, HONORS: Fellow of American Council of Learned Societies, 1988-89.

WRITINGS:

(Editor) *Temperamental Journeys: Essays on the Modern Literature of Travel,* University of Georgia Press, 1992.
Deadly Musings: Violence and Verbal Form in American Fiction, Princeton University Press, 1993.

Contributor to *American Literary History.*

WORK IN PROGRESS: Editing *Reading the West: New Essays on the Literature of the American West,* for Cambridge University Press; a book-length study of California writers, painters, photographers, and filmmakers.

SIDELIGHTS: Michael Kowalewski told *CA:* "I have organized reading marathons for a number of years, at both Carleton and Princeton. These are all-day and all-night readings of unwieldy works that aren't often taught in classes. Designed to help recover the lost art of reading aloud, past marathons have used Thomas Pynchon's *Gravity's Rainbow,* Henry Fielding's *Tom Jones,* and John Barth's *Giles Goat Boy.*"

*   *   *

KRINGLE, Karen   1947-

PERSONAL: Born February 15, 1947, in Rice Lake, WI; daughter of Leonard G. (a farmer and politician) and Gladys A. (a teacher; maiden name, Ludwig-Larsen) Kringle; partner of Grace A. Wood (a dairy farmer). *Education:* Attended Stout State University (now University of Wisconsin—Stout), 1966-68, and University of Wisconsin—Madison, 1967-69. *Politics:* Independent. *Religion:* "Non-traditional."

ADDRESSES: Home—Rice Lake, WI. *Office*—c/o Kelly Kager, P.O. Box 300170, Minneapolis, MN 55403.

CAREER: Rice Lake Public Library, Rice Lake, WI, staff member, 1965-70; dairy farm worker near Rice Lake, 1972-80, farm owner, 1980—. Charlton Publications, crossword puzzle constructor, 1972-84. Rice Lake Farmers Union Cooperative, member of board of directors, 1980-86; member of Barron County Farm Bureau, Barron Electric Cooperative, and Barron-Washburn Dairy Herd Improvement Council. Has also worked variously as a drugstore clerk, chauffeur, chambermaid, and waitress.

WRITINGS:

Vital Ties, Spinsters, Ink, 1992.

WORK IN PROGRESS: Neighbors and Friends, a novel set in rural Wisconsin, completion expected in 1994; ongoing research on regional history, with emphasis on a nineteenth-century lumbering company and its impact on the regional economy and environment.

SIDELIGHTS: Karen Kringle told *CA:* "As a life-long rural resident of Wisconsin, my aim in writing is to provide some 'insider' information to urban readers about what it's like to live and work with the soil and with animals. This work is very trying (a seven-day-a-week affair) and, while I try to write on a regular basis, it is difficult to find the time, especially uninterrupted time. Because of this, I schedule my writing very early in the morning, often as early as 3:30 a.m. It is a quiet time, with no one else awake, and I've come to treasure it."

*   *   *

KRONEN, Steve   1953-

PERSONAL: Born September 2, 1953, in Cleveland, OH; son of Phil (in sales) and Janet (in sales; maiden name, Bernstein; present surname, Eisenberg) Kronen; married Ivonne Lamazares (an associate professor), October 19, 1991. *Education:* Warren Wilson College, M.F.A., 1988. *Politics:* "Fairly far to the left." *Religion:* "Omni (or perhaps none—I'm not sure—or Jewish, I guess.)"

ADDRESSES: Home and office—5838 Southwest 74th Tr., No. 104, South Miami, FL 33143.

CAREER: Licensed massage therapist in Miami, FL, 1982—. Miami Dade Community College, part-time composition teacher. Recording for the Blind, reader, 1988—.

MEMBER: Florida State Massage Therapy Association, Amnesty International.

AWARDS, HONORS: Grand prize, Academy of American Poets College Competition, 1982; artists fellow, Florida Arts Council, 1989.

WRITINGS:

Empirical Evidence, University of Georgia Press, 1992.

WORK IN PROGRESS: A book of new poems, tentatively titled *The Wide World.*

SIDELIGHTS: Steve Kronen told *CA:* "I cannot differentiate those events in my life that make me a writer from those that don't; they all contribute to who I am and, therefore, to what I write. I suspect I write because I can. Had I been able to take apart car engines and put them back together, I may very well have been a car mechanic, or perhaps a writing car mechanic.

"I grew up in a reformed Jewish household, my parents separating when I was seventeen (and eventually divorcing). I left home in 1973 at nineteen, lived in Gainesville,

Florida, for three years, and at Kripalu Yoga Ashram in Sumneytown, Pennsylvania, for three years, studied calligraphy in New York City for two years, and spent six months in San Francisco, California. Back in Miami in 1981, I decided I would concentrate on writing poetry. That is what I always wanted to do and had, indeed, done off and on through the years, reading the masters and teaching myself to write sonnets as a teenager and young man. The primary influences on my poetry have been John Keats, T. S. Eliot, Wilfred Owen, John Donne, Matthew Arnold (especially 'Dover Beach'), Robert Frost, Don Justice, and Richard Wilbur.

"I've been a licensed massage therapist since 1982, which is how I make my living, and which affords me a flexible enough schedule to write. I teach composition part-time at Miami Dade Community College. I've been a tax resister for the last eight years (which is how long I've made enough money actually to pay taxes) in protest against our government's military and economic policies. It seems more materially and morally practical to refuse to give them the money in the first place than to give it to them and then protest about how they spend it. Likewise, during the Vietnam War I refused to register for the draft. Again, it seemed best not to get involved with nincompoops in the first place—and such dangerous nincompoops. Although my politics are fairly far to the left, I've little sympathy with those on the left who defend Cuba's Fidel Castro or other despots who claim to be for the people. I think it behooves us as human beings to support justice, food in the belly, roof over the head, human rights, and democracy. It's my fervent hope that Republican former presidents George Bush and Ronald Reagan end up making license plates as they deserve.

"All of my activities inform my poetry somehow. I think all good poetry tries ultimately to explain just how our human hearts have come to such a pass, and how we learn compassion thereby. That is what I try to do with my poetry, hopefully with enough technical expertise that any given poem stands up as a good piece of writing."

*   *   *

KUTNER, Luis   1908-1993

OBITUARY NOTICE—See index for *CA* sketch: Born June 9, 1908, in Chicago, IL; died of heart failure, March 1, 1993, in Chicago. During a career that spanned more than sixty years, Kutner became one of the most notable human rights lawyers of the twentieth century. As cofounder of Amnesty International and the founder of World Habeas Corpus, Kutner fought for international policies which would protect individuals against dubious imprisonment. His clients included poet Ezra Pound, who

was kept in a mental hospital after he was judged to be mentally incompetent to defend himself against allegations that he consorted with the Fascist Italian government. At the request of author Ernest Hemingway, Kutner argued Pound's case and obtained his release. He was also instrumental in defending such notable figures as Hungarian Cardinal Josef Mindszenty and past Congo President Moise Tshombe against grave charges. In the late 1920s he developed the first living will in response to the victim of a crime who died a painful death from gangrene. Under the conditions of a living will, prospective patients deny their caretakers the right to continue life-support systems beyond a certain time limit. In addition to his writings on the legal system, Kutner penned works of fiction, plays, and such volumes of poetry as *Moon Splashed* and *Red Wine and Shadows*.

OBITUARIES AND OTHER SOURCES:

BOOKS

Who's Who in American Law, 4th edition, Marquis, 1985, p. 313.

PERIODICALS

Chicago Tribune, March 3, 1993.
Los Angeles Times, March 6, 1993, p. A25.
New York Times, March 4, 1993, p. B9.
Times (London), March 5, 1993, p. 19.

*   *   *

KYNDRUP, Morten   1952-

PERSONAL: Born November 7, 1952, in Copenhagen, Denmark; son of Niels (a college principal) and Bitten (a social worker) Kyndrup; married Dorthe Iversen (a counselor and advisory officer); children: Lea; stepchildren: Jonas Iversen. *Education:* Aarhus University, mag.art., 1978, D.Phil., 1992.

ADDRESSES: Home—Sjaellandsgade 67, DK-8000 Arhus C, Denmark. *Office*—Aarhus Universitet, DK-8000 Arhus C, Denmark.

CAREER: Aarhus University, Aarhus, Denmark, associate professor of literature, 1982-88, docent, 1988—. Cofounder of Center for Interdisciplinary Aesthetic Studies; committee member of Aarhus Kunstmuseum and Aarhus Universitetsforlag (Aarhus University Press).

AWARDS, HONORS: Post-graduate scholarship, Aarhus University, 1978-82.

WRITINGS:

Dansk Socialistisk litteratur i 70erne, Akademisk Forlag, 1980.
Aestetik og Litteratur, Arkona, 1982.

Tid til: 12 historier fra mandens verden (short stories), Arkona, 1982.

(With Claus P. Staehr) *Realismebegrebet i den moderne litteraturteoretiske debat,* three volumes, Akademisk Forlag, 1982.

(Editor with Anders Troelsen) *Kulturarbejde og tvaera-estetik,* Aarhus Universitet, 1984.

Det Postmoderne, Gyldendal, 1986.

(Editor with Andersen and others) *Fortaelling og erfaring,* Aarhus University Press, 1988.

Framing and Fiction: Studies in the Rhetoric of Novel, History, and Interpretation, Aarhus University Press, 1992.

SIDELIGHTS: Morten Kyndrup told *CA:* "I am involved both in art and art sciences. I have worked as a musician, published poetry and short stories, and during my late years I have written the lyrics of several major musical works. On the basis of my education in comparative literature, I have had an extensive academic career. I am a co-founder of the Center for Interdisciplinary Aesthetic Studies, a special line of studies at Aarhus University, which makes it formally possible to combine elements from comparative literature, dramaturgy, musical science, and art history.

"*Framing Fiction: Studies in the Rhetoric of Novel, History, and Interpretation,* my first book in English, also combines a number of these interests. It mounts a number of analyses of European and American novels from Denis Diderot to Paul Auster into a musical form, which thereby also illustrates the basic problems of the writing of art history and the basic questions of interpretation."

L

LACK, Paul D. 1944-

PERSONAL: Born September 7, 1944, in St. Louis, MO; son of Paul E. (a teamster) and Catherine M. (a cafeteria worker) Lack; married Katha Lynn Walker, June 3, 1967 (divorced August 4, 1992); children: J. Spence, K. Brooke. *Education:* McMurry College, B.A., 1966; Texas Tech University, M.A., 1969, Ph.D., 1973. *Politics:* Democrat. *Religion:* United Methodist. *Avocational interests:* Sports.

ADDRESSES: Home—2715 Southwest Dr., No. 109, Abilene, TX 79605. *Office*—Institute of Research, Box 638, McMurry University, Abilene, TX 79697.

CAREER: McMurry University, Abilene, TX, professor of history, 1971—, vice president for institutional research and planning, 1989—. Museums of Abilene, president-elect, 1992.

MEMBER: Southern Historical Association, Texas State Historical Association.

AWARDS, HONORS: H. Bailey Carroll Award, Texas State Historical Association, 1966.

WRITINGS:

(Coauthor) *Black Leaders in Texas,* Texas State Historical Association, 1982.
(Coauthor) *Texas through Time,* Texas A & M University Press, 1990.
The Texas Revolutionary Experience, Texas A & M University Press, 1992.

WORK IN PROGRESS: Editing *From Virginia to Texas: The Diary of William F. Gray;* coauthor of *Tejanos in Rebellion;* researching the rebellion of Vicente Cordoba, 1838-39.

LAMB, Christina 1965-

PERSONAL: Born May 15, 1965, in London, England; daughter of Kenneth Ernest Edward (an accountant) and Anne (an information technology trainer; maiden name, Wilson) Lamb. *Education:* Oxford University, B.A., 1987. *Politics:* "Left of center." *Religion:* "Still waiting to see the light."

ADDRESSES: Home—Rio de Janeiro, Brazil. *Office*—Foreign Desk, *Financial Times,* 1 Southwark Bridge, London SE1 9HL, England. *Agent*—Gill Coleridge, 20 Powis Mews, London W11, England.

CAREER: Central Television, Birmingham, England, trainee reporter, 1987-88; *Financial Times,* London, England, correspondent from Pakistan and Afghanistan, 1988-90, and Brazil, 1990—.

AWARDS, HONORS: Named Young Journalist of the Year, British Press Awards, 1989; shared Reporter of the Year Award, 1991; award for periodical writing, Amnesty International, 1992.

WRITINGS:

Waiting for Allah, Hamish Hamilton, 1991.

WORK IN PROGRESS: The Last Happy Nation, a book about Brazil.

* * *

LAMB, Wally 1950-
(Walter Lamb)

PERSONAL: Born October 17, 1950, in Norwich, CT; son of Walter A. (a utility superintendent) and Anna (a homemaker; maiden name, Pedace) Lamb; married Christine Grabarek (an elementary school teacher), July 1, 1978;

children: Jared, Justin. *Education:* University of Connecticut, B.A., 1972, M.A., 1977; Vermont College, M.F.A., 1984. *Politics:* "Left of center." *Religion:* "Questioning Catholic." *Avocational interests:* Racquetball, running, rock and roll.

ADDRESSES: Home—63 Lewiston Ave., Willimantic, CT 06226. *Agent*—Linda Chester, Linda Chester Literary Agency, 1035 Fifth Ave, New York, NY 10028.

CAREER: Norwich Free Academy, Norwich, CT, English teacher, 1972-88, writing center director, 1988—; writer. Fresh Air Fund, host parent, 1982—; member of the board of directors of the public library in Willimantic, CT, 1988—.

MEMBER: Poets & Writers, National Education Association, Literary Network, Connecticut Voices, Connecticut Council of Teachers of English, Phi Beta Kappa.

AWARDS, HONORS: Literature grant, Connecticut Commission on the Arts, 1988; Teacher of the Year, Norwich Free Academy, 1989; William Peden Prize in fiction, University of Missouri, and Pushcart Prize, both 1990, both for short story "Astronauts"; national winner, Thanks to Teachers Excellence Award, 1990; Connecticut Commission on the Arts, visiting artist, 1987—; fellowship from National Endowment for the Arts, 1993.

WRITINGS:

(Editor under name Walter Lamb) *Always Begin Where You Are* (poetry textbook), McGraw, 1979.
She's Come Undone (novel), Pocket Books, 1992.

Work represented in several anthologies, including *Streetsongs: New Voices in Fiction*, Longstreet Press, 1990; *Pushcart Prize XV: Best of the Small Presses, 1990-91*, edited by Bill Henderson, Pushcart Press, 1990; and *Best of the Missouri Review, 1978-1990*, University of Missouri Press, 1991.

WORK IN PROGRESS: A novel, with completion expected in 1994.

SIDELIGHTS: Wally Lamb's debut novel, *She's Come Undone,* has been praised by reviewers as a humorous and poignant account of a woman's struggle to overcome a lifetime of unfortunate circumstances. "This is a tragicomic tale of a quirky, loveable, smart-mouthed survivor," wrote Susan Larson in the New Orleans *Times-Picayune,* adding that "this big, warm, embracing book is filled with a generous love and understanding of women." The book is narrated by Dolores Price, who reflects on the important events in her life. As Lamb explained it to *CA,* the use of a female narrator was not a conscious choice on his part. "The focal character of my novel . . . came to me initially as a voice inside my head," the author said, "an unnamed, self-deprecating woman joking about her recently failed marriage. As I began to invent a life around the voice, I had no idea that I was starting a novel or that the story would take me eight-and-a-half years to complete."

Dolores's story begins when she is a child. She endures her parents' failing marriage for several unhappy years before a divorce lands her mother in a state mental hospital and sends Dolores to live with a grandmother. The child's time there is also far from happy; she receives little comfort from her distant grandmother and is later raped by a neighbor. By the time she leaves for college, Dolores has become obese and withdrawn. Her fixation on her roommate's boyfriend, Dante Davis, offers little hope of satisfaction, and she eventually attempts to take her own life. Dolores, following in her mother's footsteps, winds up in a mental hospital. But unlike her mother, Dolores uses the experience as a means of reinventing herself. She loses weight, hatches a plan to win Dante's heart, and upon her release, she makes this dream a reality. Further misfortune awaits her after she is married, but Dolores proves herself a durable survivor who is able to carry on.

Though *She's Come Undone* is loaded with potentially grim material, critics have praised Lamb's use of comedy to lighten the story. Hilma Wolitzer, reviewing the novel in the *New York Times Book Review,* found that "its pleasures lie primarily in its lively narrative and biting humor," and the critic also characterized *She's Come Undone* as "an ambitious, often stirring and hilarious book." While Wolitzer did note several "excesses" regarding the inclusion of "topical plot turns" such as AIDS, abortion, and infertility, she found Dolores an engaging character who holds the reader's attention. "Excess is tolerable," Wolitzer wrote, when "characters are . . . endearing to the reader, as Dolores Price is, even in her most self-deprecatory moments."

The publication of *She's Come Undone* came eleven years after Lamb's literary career got off to a memorable start. "I began writing fiction on Memorial Day, 1981," Lamb told *CA,* "the morning our first child was born. After an 'all-nighter' in the delivery room, my wife and baby son were sleeping, and I ran home to grab a quick shower. I don't pretend to understand the chemical or psychological mix of adrenalin, exhaustion, and shower water which produced for me that morning the first fictional voice I ever heard: that of a wiseguy teenager complaining about his summer job as an ice cream vendor. By instinct, I jumped out of the shower, ran naked down the hallway, and scrawled on a piece of paper what the voice had said. About a month later—after I'd become proficient with diaper pins and carseat buckles—the jotted note resurfaced and I began what became my first story, 'Mister Softee,' which was published in *Northeast* magazine three years later."

Though the publication of *She's Come Undone* has established Lamb as a professional writer, he continues to teach high school in Connecticut. He has found that the two pursuits often complement one another. "My work as a writer has altered the way I teach," he explained to *CA.* "During my first years in the classroom, I taught writing by assigning topics and due dates and then evaluating my students' efforts, penning copious marginal comments about what each writer *might* have done to make the work more effective. My students, who rightfully assumed that their papers were, at that point, *faits accompli,* usually skipped the comments and flipped immediately to the grade. As I committed myself increasingly to fiction writing, I began to see that the most meaningful assignments come from the writer herself or himself and that feedback is helpful when the writing is ongoing, not after it's finished. With that in mind—and with the endorsement of the school administration—I designed and implemented the Academy's writing center. At the center, students are empowered by their own creative instincts and function both as creators and critics of writing—their own and others'. Teachers are trained to facilitate rather than dictate and are encouraged to write alongside their students and to submit their work to the critical process."

Lamb's interest in the work of other contemporary artists has helped him better understand the themes in his own writing. "Writers whose work I reread and study include Anne Tyler, Andre Dubus, Margaret Atwood, John Updike, Toni Morrison, Harper Lee, Alice Walker, Gabriel Garcia Marquez, Flannery O'Connor, and Joseph Campbell," Lamb explained. "These writers shake me up—disturb me in honest ways that allow me to hold onto hope. My fiction is equally informed by other media: the unpredictable lyrics of Laurie Anderson and John Prine; the unexpected juxtaposition of artists Pablo Picasso and Rene-Francois-Ghislain Magritte; the edgy comedy of collaborators Lily Tomlin and Jane Wagner. For better or worse, television also fuels my work. I watch TV with a wary eye, acknowledging its influence without ever trusting it. I'm most responsive to artists who juggle three balls in the air: hope, pain, and humor. I aim for just such a juggling act in my own fiction."

The presence of conflicting emotions runs through many facets of Lamb's life, and it has proved a driving force in his writing. "As a father and teacher, I'm both hopeful and afraid," he told *CA,* "and I think my stories reflect this. My three callings—fathering, teaching and fiction writing—are Siamese triplets joined at the head and heart, impossible to separate. I write because complacency disturbs me in the face of the world's pain and because sometimes voices other than my own talk inside my head. I recognize these as gifts and follow."

BIOGRAPHICAL/CRITICAL SOURCES:

PERIODICALS

Times-Picayune (New Orleans), July 28, 1992.
New York Times Book Review, August 23, 1992.

*　　*　　*

LAMB, Walter
See LAMB, Wally

*　　*　　*

LAMBDIN, Dewey (W.)　1945-

PERSONAL: Born January 21, 1945, in San Diego, CA; son of Dewey W. (a U.S. Navy lieutenant commander) and Edda A. (a schoolteacher; maiden name, Ellison) Lambdin; married Melinda Phillips, July 1971 (divorced October, 1974); married Julie Dawn Pascoe, October, 1984 (divorced November, 1986). *Education:* Attended University of Tennessee at Knoxville, 1963, and Cumberland College, 1964-65; Montana State University, B.S., 1969. *Politics:* Democrat. *Religion:* Episcopalian. *Avocational interests:* Sailboats, photography, military history, banjo.

ADDRESSES: Home and office—141 Neese Dr., Apt. G-20, Nashville, TN 37211. *Agent*—Wieser & Wieser, 118 East Twenty-fifth St., New York, NY 10010.

CAREER: WMC-TV 5, Memphis, TN, assistant director, 1969-72, producer and director, 1972-81; WPTY-TV 24, Memphis, production manager, 1981-84; free-lance camera and light technician and director, Nashville, TN, 1984-87; Admark Advertising, Nashville, writer and producer, 1987; writer.

MEMBER: American Film Institute, National Academy of Television Arts and Sciences, U.S. Naval Institute, U.S. Navy Memorial Foundation, Cousteau Society, National Maritime Museum (Greenwich, England).

WRITINGS:

HISTORICAL NOVELS

The King's Coat, Donald I. Fine, 1989.
The French Admiral, Donald I. Fine, 1990.
The King's Commission, Donald I. Fine, 1991.
The King's Privateer, Donald I. Fine, 1992.
The Gun Ketch, Donald I. Fine, 1993.

OTHER

Contributor of book reviews to the Nashville *Banner.*

WORK IN PROGRESS: Empires, a novel set in the Caribbean, circa 1492; research on the effects of ocean pollution on marine mammals for a novel, *The Selkie.*

SIDELIGHTS: The military and amorous adventures of Alan Lewrie, a fictional member of the British Royal Navy during the 1700s, have gained novelist Dewey Lambdin enthusiastic reviews. His books focusing on Lewrie have been praised by critics for their historical accuracy, exciting sea battles, and likable hero. Lambdin's first novel, *The King's Coat,* published in 1989, narrates Lewrie's inauspicious beginnings; illegitimate son of an English lord, the seventeen-year-old boy is forced into naval service as part of a plot by his father to disinherit him. The hardships of life at sea during wartime eventually turn Lewrie into an able seaman, but he also finds time to exercise his innate talent for womanizing. A *Kirkus Reviews* contributor found Lambdin's tale to contain all the necessary ingredients of a successful sea adventure, calling the book "wonderful stuff." Reviewer C. Robert Nixon maintained in *Library Journal* that the author "demonstrates a good enough grasp of sailing and 18th-century sea warfare to satisfy readers of this genre."

The further exploits of Lewrie are recorded in Lambdin's 1990 *The French Admiral,* in which the midshipman becomes involved with the siege of Yorktown during the American Revolution. A *Publishers Weekly* reviewer noted the novel's "colorful characters, . . . gripping plot and firm historical background." In *The King's Commission,* published in 1991, Lewrie rises to the rank of lieutenant, sails the Caribbean, engages in a few romantic affairs, and eventually earns command of his own ship. C. Robert Nixon, in a review of *The King's Commission* in *Library Journal,* commended Lambdin's "combination of technical and historical accuracy." Lewrie journeys to India and China in Lambdin's fourth novel, *The King's Privateer.* During the course of the work, the hero chases pirates and encounters his former nemesis—his father, Sir Hugo Willoughby. A fifth novel entitled *The Gun Ketch* was published by Lambdin in 1993. Many reviewers of Lambdin's work have compared the Lewrie books to the classic sea stories of C. S. Forester, which featured the character of Horatio Hornblower. Newgate Callendar declared in his *New York Times Book Review* assessment of *The King's Privateer* that Lambdin "has started a series that can stand up very well against the stories of the master."

Lambdin told *CA:* "I started writing as play one rainy day when I was ten; I then was forced to write extensively at military school and in college and found that it was still 'fun.' My freshman final English essay, 'Preparedness Prevents War?,' was published in the University of Tennessee's *Theme Vault* in 1963 and in *Themes for Study* at Ithaca College in 1964, which whetted my appetite for writing and boosted my ego.

"I was influenced early in my life by the writing of Ernest Hemingway and later by authors such as George McDonald Fraser (author of the 'Flashman' series), C. S. Forester, Tobias Smollett, Henry Fielding, and Robert Glass Cleland. I've always preferred to keep a tongue-in-cheek mix in my adventures, to avoid unrelieved, stark, square-jawed drama. I like heroes with feet of clay and sins and 'warts'—people whose personal lives have nothing to do with their public image and who conquer adversity in spite of all. Military school, college dorms, and the fraternity of Kappa Sigma introduced me to many grand people who weren't true images of heroes—just normal ne'er-do-wells, like Rudyard Kipling's 'gentlemen rankers.' And I've found that some of the greatest atrocities were committed by decent people for the best reasons, while some of the most heroic deeds were accomplished by the worst people for the worst reasons! I like to keep that paradox alive.

"The Alan Lewrie series of naval adventures began in 1981 when, after bingeing on *all* of C. S. Forester and Alexander Kent's 'Bolitho' series, I uttered those infamous words: 'I bet I could do just as well!' I decided to create a hero who was an eighteenth-century character, not a twentieth-century transplant such as Hornblower or Bolitho, with their Victorian and public school outlooks. Gary Jennings was an influence as well. The research is half the fun of getting there, since I dread letters or phone calls from anyone who wants to ream me for making a historical error; I enjoy reading and learning anyway.

"While I live in the South (most of my relatives were farmers, railroad men, or coal-miners) and would never even consider living anywhere else (except closer to the ocean), I don't consider myself a southern writer. I love ships and the sea, courtesy of the U.S. Navy and my dad; Celtic music, thanks to being Welsh-Scots-English-Irish; sailing, thanks to Derek Rooke of Memphis; cats, thanks to Babcock, my first Siamese; books, reading, and history, thanks to my mom and dad."

BIOGRAPHICAL/CRITICAL SOURCES:

PERIODICALS

Kirkus Reviews, May 1, 1989, p. 651.

Library Journal, May 1, 1989, p. 99; March 15, 1990, p. 113; March 1, 1991, p. 117; May 1, 1992, p. 118.

New York Times Book Review, April 26, 1992, p. 21.

Publishers Weekly, April 28, 1989, p. 61; March 9, 1990, p. 53; February 1, 1991, p. 67; February 24, 1992, p. 44.

LAMMERS, Wayne P. 1951-

PERSONAL: Born December 5, 1951, in Lodi, OH; son of Richard L. (a missionary) and Martha (a missionary; maiden name, Lewis) Lammers; married January 16, 1975; wife's name, Cheryl (a social worker); children: Michael Jonathan. *Education:* Sophia University (Tokyo), B.A., 1976; University of Michigan, M.A., 1980, Ph.D., 1987. *Politics:* "Progressive and green." *Religion:* "None."

ADDRESSES: Home and office—14960 Southwest Ninety-second Ave., Tigard, OR 97224.

CAREER: University of Wisconsin, Madison, assistant professor of Japanese, 1984-90; self-employed translator and consultant, 1989—; Lewis and Clark College, Portland, OR, assistant professor of Japanese, 1990-92; Mangajin Inc., Atlanta, GA, translations editor, 1991—.

MEMBER: Association for Asian Studies, Association of Teachers of Japanese (secretary, 1984-90).

AWARDS, HONORS: PEN Center USA West Literary Award for translation, 1993, for *Still Life and Other Stories.*

WRITINGS:

The Tale of Matsura: Fujiwara Teika's Experiment in Fiction, University of Michigan Center for Japanese Studies, 1992.
(Translator) Junzo Shono, *Still Life and Other Stories,* Stone Bridge Press, 1992.
(Translator) Ooka Shohei, *Furyoki* (novel; title means "POW Journal,") Pacific Basin Institute, Library of Japan, in press.

SIDELIGHTS: Wayne P. Lammers told *CA:* "As a literary translator in an era when contacts between different cultures are increasing exponentially, I like to remind people that reading translated literature from other countries is one of the least taxing ways to learn about other cultures."

*   *   *

LANDRETH, Marsha Ann 1947-

PERSONAL: Born December 16, 1947, in Denver, CO; daughter of A. Neil Ross (a journalist) and Pauline Bircher Burns; married Knute Landreth (a doctor), March 21, 1969 (divorced, April, 1991); children: Brant Thomas, Ross Stuart. *Education:* University of Northern Colorado, B.A., 1969.

ADDRESSES: Agent—The Kopaloff Company, Inc., 1930 Century Park West, Suite 403, Los Angeles, CA 90067.

CAREER: Teacher, 1969-81; writer, 1987—.

MEMBER: International Association of Crime Writers, Western Writers of America, Mystery Writers of America, Sisters in Crime.

WRITINGS:

William T. Sherman (biography), W. H. Smith, 1990.
Holiday Murders (mystery), Walker & Co., 1992.
French Creek (western), M. Evans, 1993.
A Clinic for Murder (mystery), Walker & Co., 1993.
The Healers (first book in a series), New American Library, 1993.

WORK IN PROGRESS: Mackenzie York, Esq.; an original screenplay.

*   *   *

LANE, Abbe 1935-

PERSONAL: Born December 14, 1935, in Brooklyn, NY; daughter of Abby (in the clothing business) and Grace (a homemaker) Lane; married Xavier Cugat (a bandleader), c. 1952 (divorced, 1964); married Perry Leff (an investor), December 16, 1964; children: (second marriage) Andrew, Steven.

ADDRESSES: Home—Holmby Hills, CA; Maui, HI; Malibu, CA; and Aspen, CO. *Office*—444 N. Faring Rd., Los Angeles, CA 90077. *Agent*—Ed Victor, 162 Wardour St., London W1V 3AT, England.

CAREER: Entertainer and writer. Professional singer, dancer, and recording artist appearing and recording with the Xavier Cugat orchestra and as a solo performer; actress appearing in plays, including *Bonanza Bound* and *Oh, Captain;* actress on television shows in England, including *The Abbe Lane Special,* and on programs throughout Europe and Latin America; actress in films, including numerous Italian motion pictures.

AWARDS, HONORS: Antoinette Perry Award nomination, for *Oh, Captain.*

WRITINGS:

But Where is Love?, Warner Books, 1993.

WORK IN PROGRESS: A second novel.

*   *   *

LARDY, Nicholas R. 1946-

PERSONAL: Born April 8, 1946; son of Henry (a professor) and Annrita (a homemaker; maiden name, Dresselhuys) Lardy; married Barbara Dawe, 1970; children: Elizabeth, Lillian. *Education:* University of Wisconsin, B.A., 1968; University of Michigan, Ph.D., 1975.

ADDRESSES: Home—3802 110th Pl. N.E., Bellevue, WA 98004. *Office*—Henry M. Jackson School of International Studies, University of Washington, DR-05, Seattle, WA 98195.

CAREER: University of Michigan Center for Chinese Studies, Ann Arbor, MI, postdoctoral scholar, 1975; Yale University, New Haven, CT, 1975-83, began as assistant professor, became associate professor of economics, assistant director of Economic Growth Center, 1979-82; University of Washington, Seattle, associate professor, 1983-85, professor of international studies, 1985—, chair of China program, Jackson School of International Studies, 1984-89, director of Jackson School of International Studies, 1991—. National Committee on United States-China Relations, member of board of directors; Committee on Scholarly Communication with the People's Republic of China, vice-chair; Committee on International Relations Studies with the People's Republic of China, member.

MEMBER: American Economic Association, Association for Comparative Economic Studies, Association for Asian Studies.

AWARDS, HONORS: Grants from Yale University Concilium on International and Area Studies, 1976 and 1978, Social Science Research Council and American Council of Learned Societies Joint Committee on Contemporary China, Subcommittee on Research on the Chinese Economy, 1976 and 1978-79, Luce Fund for Asian Studies, Henry R. Luce Foundation, 1980-82, and International Economics Division, U.S. Department of Agriculture, 1984-86; research fellowship, American Council of Learned Studies and the Social Science Research Council, 1989-90.

WRITINGS:

(Editor) *Chinese Economic Planning: Translations from Ching-Chi Yen-Chiu,* M. E. Sharpe, 1978.
Economic Growth and Distribution in China, Cambridge University Press, 1978.
Agriculture in China's Modern Economic Development, Cambridge University Press, 1983.
Agricultural Prices in China, World Bank, 1983.
(Editor with Kenneth R. Lieberthal) *Chen Yun's Strategy for China's Development: A Non-Maoist Alternative,* M. E. Sharpe, 1983.
Foreign Trade and Economic Reform in China, 1978-1990, Cambridge University Press, 1992.

Works represented in anthologies, including *China's Development Experience in Comparative Perspective,* edited by Robert F. Dernberger, Harvard University Press, 1980;

Agriculture in Third World Development, edited by Carl Eicher and John Staatz, Johns Hopkins University Press, 1984; *The Cambridge History of China,* edited by John King Fairbank and Roderick MacFarquhar, Cambridge University Press, 1987; and *Economic Cooperation in the Asia-Pacific Region,* edited by John P. Hardt and Young C. Kim, Westview Press, 1990. Contributor of articles and reviews to periodicals, including *American Journal of Agricultural Economics, Journal of Economic History,* and *Science.* Member of editorial boards of *China Economic Review, China Quarterly,* and *Journal of Comparative Economics.*

WORK IN PROGRESS: Research on foreign trade and economic reform in China.

*   *   *

LARGE, David C.
    See LARGE, David Clay

*   *   *

LARGE, David Clay   1945-
    (David C. Large)

PERSONAL: Born August 13, 1945, in Scottfield, IL; son of Henry Ranney (a physician) and Lois (Altman) Large; married Jacque Lysons, October 10, 1966 (divorced, 1977); married Margaret Wheeler (a teacher), May 24, 1980; children: Joshua. *Education:* University of Washington, Seattle, B.A., 1967; University of California, Berkeley, M.A., 1969, Ph.D., 1974. *Avocational interests:* Long distance running, racquetball, backpacking, skiing, fly fishing, wine tasting and collecting, reading contemporary fiction.

ADDRESSES: Home—721 West Koch, Bozeman, MT 59715. *Office*—Department of History, Montana State University, Bozeman, MT 59717.

CAREER: Smith College, Northhampton, MA, assistant professor of history, 1973-78; Yale University, New Haven, CT, assistant professor of history, 1978-83; Montana State University, Bozeman, assistant professor of history, 1983-88, professor of history, 1988—; writer.

MEMBER: American History Association, Conference Group of Central European Historians, Phi Beta Kappa.

AWARDS, HONORS: Woodrow Wilson fellowship, 1967; Ford Foundation fellowship, 1968-71; Fulbright fellowship, 1972; Morse fellowship from Yale University, 1982; National Endowment for the Humanities fellowship, 1986; German Marshall Fund fellowship, 1990.

WRITINGS:

The Politics of Law and Order: A History of the Bavarian Einwohnerwehr, American Philosophical Society, 1980.

(As David C. Large; editor with William Weber) *Wagnerism in European Culture and Politics,* Cornell University Press, 1984.

Between Two Fires: Europe's Path in the 1930s, Norton, 1990.

(With Felix Gilbert) *History of Modern Europe Series, Volume 6: The End of the European Era, 1890 to the Present,* 4th edition, 1991.

(Editor) *Contending with Hitler: Varieties of German Resistance in the Third Reich,* Cambridge University Press, 1992.

Contributor to periodicals, including *Journal of the History of Ideas.*

WORK IN PROGRESS: Germans to the Front: West German Rearmament in the Adenauer Era, Birthplace of Nazism: Munich from Ludwig I to Hitler, and *Germany's Metropolis: A History of Modern Berlin.*

SIDELIGHTS: David Clay Large is a historian specializing in the nineteenth and twentieth centuries. He is perhaps best known as editor, with William Weber, of *Wagnerism in European Culture and Politics,* a collection of essays examining the significance of opera composer Richard Wagner's music and thought in the development of Europe. D. J. R. Bruckner, writing in the *New York Times,* affirmed that "this exploratory examination of the extraordinary wave of Wagnerism that washed over Europe for generations is a salutary undertaking," and he added that the volume "is rich in suggestions and insights and, while the essays are a bit uneven, most are very good reading." Another critic, James Joll, wrote in the *New York Review of Books* that *Wagnerism in European Culture and Politics* "provides a valuable introduction to an important . . . aspect of European cultural history during the last quarter of the nineteenth century." And *Times Literary Supplement* reviewer Peter Heyworth noted that the collection compiled by Large and Weber "contains much fascinating information not readily available elsewhere."

Among Large's other works is *Between Two Fires: Europe's Path in the 1930s,* an analysis of lesser-known events that exerted substantial effect on European culture and politics. Among Large's subjects in this work are the Stavisky scandal, in which the French government was implicated in the deeds of a swindler; the Austrian civil war of 1934, in which right- and left-wing extremists clashed; and a protest march conducted by unemployed shipyard workers in England in 1936. "To the amateur historian," observed Frank J. Prial in the *New York Times*

Book Review, "much of the value of Mr. Large's book is his recounting of events that everyone has heard of but knows little about." Prial, in acknowledging Large's "sense of drama," concluded that the historian "knows how to write: he recognizes a good quotation or anecdote."

BIOGRAPHICAL/CRITICAL SOURCES:

PERIODICALS

New York Review of Books, January 31, 1985, pp. 9-10.
New York Times, January 5, 1985.
New York Times Book Review, February 25, 1990, p. 30.
Times Literary Supplement, May 17, 1985, p. 538; October 12, 1990, p. 1095.
Washington Post Book World, April 8, 1990, p. 10.

*   *   *

LAROQUE, Francois G. 1948-

PERSONAL: Born April 26, 1948, in Paris, France; son of Jean (a judge) and Jacqueline (a radiologist; maiden name, Renault); married Yolande Duech (a dentist), April 28, 1972; children: Stephanie, Charlotte. *Education:* Attended the Sorbonne, 1968-72; attended St. John's College, Oxford, 1969-70. *Religion:* Catholic.

ADDRESSES: Home—18 rue du Tartelet, Boullay-les-Troux 91470, France. *Office*—Institut du Monde Anglophone, Universite de Paris III, Sorbonne Nouvelle, 5 rue de l'Ecole-de-Medecine, 75006 Paris, France.

CAREER: Universite Paul Valery, Montpellier, France, assistant professor, 1973-80, associate professor, 1980-88, professor of English, 1988-90; Universite de Paris III (Sorbonne Nouvelle), Paris, France, professor of English, 1991—. *Military service:* Served in French Army, 1971-72.

MEMBER: International Shakespeare Association, International Association of University Professors of English, Shakespeare Conference.

WRITINGS:

Shakespeare et la fete, Presses Universitaires de France, 1988, translated by Janet Lloyd as *Shakespeare's Festive World: Elizabethan Seasonal Entertainment and the Professional Stage,* Cambridge University Press, 1991.

(With Alain Morvan and Andre Topia) *Anthropologie de la litterature anglaise,* Presses Universitaires de France, 1991.

Shakespeare comme il vous plaira, Gallimard, 1991.

Histoire de la litterature anglaise, Presses Universitaires de France, 1993.

Les comedies de Shakespeare, Presses Universitaires de France, in press.

WORK IN PROGRESS: *Theatre elisabethain,* for Gallimard, completion expected 1997; *Shakespeare: Oeuvres completes,* for Livre de Poche, completion expected 2004.

SIDELIGHTS: Francois G. Laroque told *CA:* "*Shakespeare's Festive World,* first published in French under the title *Shakespeare et la fete,* was a rewritten version of my 1985 doctoral dissertation. Particularly helpful for this work were the Centre d'Etudes et de Recherches Elisabethaines in Montpellier, France; the Shakespeare Institute and the Shakespeare Centre in Stratford-upon-Avon, England; the Folger Library in Washington, D.C.; as well as various other institutions.

"The general motivation for this book was that C. L. Barber's famous monograph, *Shakespeare's Festive Comedy,* needed updating and that the pioneering work of several 'new' historians could be used to shed light on some aspects of literature. The notion of an archaeology of drama was also inspired by N. Foucault's *Les mots et les choses* and *Une archeologie du savoir.*

"Personal circumstances for being involved in this type of research are certainly related to my long-standing interest in Catholic rituals and folklore. I discovered Midsummer bonfires, Morris dancing, and Guy Fawkes' Day while I was studying in Oxford and discovering Shakespeare's plays in London and Stratford. My involvement in the festive student demonstrations in May of 1968 in Paris may also have something to do with all this."

*   *   *

LAURENCE, Janet 1937-

PERSONAL: Born December 3, 1937; daughter of Roy John (a timber merchant and radio producer) and Ruth Doris (a homemaker; maiden name, Gustafsson) Duffell; married Keith Ronald Laurence (a financial advisor), October 15, 1969; stepchildren: Justin Noel, Timothy John. *Education:* Open University, B.A., 1979. *Politics:* Conservative. *Religion:* Lutheran. *Avocational interests:* History of cooking, theatre, history, gardening, interior decoration.

ADDRESSES: *Home and office*—The Grooms, East Lydford, Somerton, Somerset TA11 7HD, England. *Agent*—Michael Thomas, A. M. Heath & Co. Ltd., 79 St. Martin's Lane, London WC2N 4AA, England.

CAREER: J. Walter Thompson (advertising agency), London, England, secretary, 1956-59; secretary in New York City and San Francisco, CA, 1959-60; Max Wilson (travel entrepreneur), personal assistant, 1960-65; Nielson, McCarthy (public relations firm), executive, 1965-70; free-lance public relations consultant; writer. Cooking in-

structor in own home, 1980-83. Chair of Consumers' Committees for England, Wales, and Great Britain.

MEMBER: Guild of Food Writers, Crime Writers' Association, Mystery Writers of America.

WRITINGS:

"DARINA LISLE" CRIME NOVELS

A Deepe Coffyn, Macmillan, 1989, Doubleday, 1990.
A Tasty Way to Die, Macmillan, 1990, Doubleday, 1991.
Hotel Morgue, Macmillan, 1991, Doubleday, 1992.
Recipe for Death, Macmillan, 1992, Doubleday, 1993.
Death and the Epicure, Macmillan, 1993.

COOKBOOKS

A Little French Cookbook, Appletree Press, 1989.
A Little Scandinavian Cookbook, Appletree Press, 1990.
A Little Coffee Cookbook, Appletree Press, 1992.
Just for Two, Hodder & Stoughton, 1992.

OTHER

A Taste of Somerset Guide to Good Food and Drink, Good Books, 1989.

Author of weekly cookery column for the *Daily Telegraph,* 1983-86.

WORK IN PROGRESS: An untitled novel, to be published under a pseudonym by Headline in 1993; a general crime novel and a sequel to the novel to be published by Headline in 1993; *Appetite for Death,* the sixth Darina Lisle crime novel, publication expected spring, 1994; a general cookery book with a leading British chef.

SIDELIGHTS: Janet Laurence told *CA:* "Writing and food have dominated my life, but it took many years for either to provide me with a profession. I worked as a secretary for a number of years, graduating into a position as personal assistant for a travel tycoon before joining a public relations company as an executive. Both careers gave valuable and enjoyable opportunities for travel and eating in first-class restaurants.

"Marriage gave the chance for learning more about food and cooking as we entertained frequently and I found my interest was not always matched by my technical skill. My Swedish mother's marvelous cooking influenced each of her four children. We all love food, and my brother Michael became a top hotel manger, spending two years in the kitchens of London's Savoy Hotel in the process. I enjoyed attending courses and teaching myself to cook. When my husband and I bought a large house in the West Country in 1978, it had to earn its living in some way, and I decided to run four-day residential cookery courses for teenagers. Their popularity led to other courses and a new career.

"Ever since I can remember I have scribbled stories and books, mostly unsuccessfully, and it was my interest in writing that had led to finding a job in public relations. I turned to writing on cookery and for several years produced a weekly cookery column for the *Daily Telegraph,* a national newspaper in the United Kingdom. Then I attended a creative writing course that produced the first page of my first detective novel, *A Deepe Coffyn,* which combined my love of food with my interest in crime fiction. Cordon bleu cook Darina Lisle was born and has so far appeared in five novels, each set in a different area of the food world, and the sixth is being written at present.

"Alongside the crime novels I have also written cookery books, including *Just for Two,* which contains recipes and advice for meals *a deux.* I have just finished my first general novel, as yet untitled, which will appear under a pseudonym. Books seem to be queuing up to get written; I no sooner finish one than I am on to the next. I started late and have a lot of catching up to do. A long-cherished ambition is to write a history of cooking, but time for research at the moment is limited.

"As a novelist, my aim is to entertain with believable stories rooted in character. As a cookery writer, I want to introduce readers to enjoyable eating and better cooking, with lots of tips on technique. I am pretty disciplined once I start a book, with set daily targets that I hope to exceed. I start in the early morning and continue as long as I can, working straight onto a word processor. We have a house in France that is wonderful for writing; it's so quiet with none of the interruptions that interfere with my day's output in England. These interruptions can involve family and friends, but also the government food committee I chair, the cookery demonstrations I occasionally agree to, political campaigning for elections, food for charity events, and sundry other activities.

"My family consists of my husband, retired now from his financial consultancy, and two stepsons, both now grown up and one living and working in the United States. My husband and I love traveling, seeing friends, spending time in France, gardening there and in England, visiting the theatre and art galleries, and reading. Our Somerset life often provides background material for my books."

BIOGRAPHICAL/CRITICAL SOURCES:

PERIODICALS

Kirkus Reviews, November 15, 1989, p. 1636; December 15, 1990, p. 1712.
Library Journal, January, 1991, p. 159.
New York Times Book Review, February 18, 1990, p. 23.
Publisher's Weekly, November 24, 1989, p. 60.
Times (London), May 3, 1990.
Times Literary Supplement, July 21, 1989, p. 810.

LAYMAN, Carol Spurlock 1937-

PERSONAL: Born January 27, 1937, in Vernon, IN; daughter of Richard T. (a factory laborer) and Virginia (a homemaker; maiden name, Cadby) Spurlock; married Donald G. Layman (in quality control), May 27, 1956; children: Shelley Layman Green, Doug. *Politics:* Independent. *Religion:* Protestant. *Avocational interests:* Nature.

ADDRESSES: Home—Rt. 4, Box 67, North Vernon, IN 47265. *Office*—Still Waters Press, P.O. Box 47, North Vernon, IN 47265-0047.

CAREER: Writer. Conducts wildlife lessons and boat rides for school children.

MEMBER: Publishers Marketing Association, Mid-American Publishers Association.

WRITINGS:

Growing Up Rich in Vernon, Indiana, Still Waters Press, 1992.

WORK IN PROGRESS: The Copper Kettle: Isaac McCoy's Life and Times, a fictionalized biography of Isaac McCoy (1784-1846), missionary to the Indians, publication expected in 1994.

SIDELIGHTS: Carol Spurlock Layman told *CA:* "Firmly believing that a woman can have it all, as long as she doesn't try to have it all at once, I delayed my second career (writing) until I had finished my first career, which was rearing two children. Then, having barely begun, I put writing aside for five more years to help my husband create a forty-five-acre wildlife habitat and build our home, with our own hands, in the middle of it. I have yet to regret these decisions.

"Having entered the writing landscape too late to participate in the rebellions of the 1970s, I shall have to rebel against the 1990s by writing life-affirming books. This is my pledge: I shall not add one additional ounce of sleaze to the environment. I feel controversial already.

"More seriously, my books will be American history, but they will be written in such a style that even those who don't like to read history will find them suitable. It is happening already with *Growing Up Rich in Vernon, Indiana,* a humorous slice of American small-town life from the 1940s and 1950s. I call this genre sugar-coated history.

"I interrupted page 812 of my 'big' book to write the Vernon book. Promoting the big book, *The Copper Kettle: Isaac McCoy's Life and Times,* will be a challenge, but I love a challenge. I must persuade the reader to open his or her mind, if this is necessary for the reader to get past the fact that the protagonist is a nineteenth-century Baptist missionary to the American Indians. Every reader whose mind is open will behold a fascinating and undiscovered vein of American history."

*   *   *

LEE, Gentry 1942-

PERSONAL: Born March 29, 1942, in New York, NY; son of Harrell Estes (a journalist) and Peggy (Harding) Lee; married Stacey Kiddoo (a homemaker), July 13, 1985; children: Robert, Patrick, Michael, Travis. *Education:* Attended the University of Texas at Austin, Massachusetts Institute of Technology, and the University of Glasgow.

ADDRESSES: Agent—Russ Galen, Scott Meredith Literary Agency, 845 Third Ave., New York, NY 10022.

CAREER: Writer and aerospace engineer.

WRITINGS:

WITH ARTHUR C. CLARKE; SCIENCE FICTION

Cradle, Warner Books, 1989.
Rama II, Bantam, 1989.
The Garden of Rama, Bantam, 1991.

WORK IN PROGRESS: Rama Revealed with Arthur C. Clarke; three science fiction novels.

SIDELIGHTS: Gentry Lee is best known for his collaborations with noted science fiction writer Arthur C. Clarke, whose novel *2001: A Space Odyssey* was adapted for film by director Stanley Kubrick. Lee first collaborated with Clarke on *Cradle,* in which an intrepid reporter, Carol Dawson, investigates a military project and uncovers evidence of an extraterrestrial spacecraft. The aliens, Dawson eventually learns, are interplanetary environmentalists who have arrived on earth to save various endangered species. Before the aliens can successfully complete their mission, though, they must first restore their damaged craft. Meanwhile, military officials and a band of loathsome opportunists all try to capture the benevolent space travelers.

In 1989 Lee again teamed with Clarke for *Rama II,* a sequel to Clarke's *Rendezvous with Rama,* for which he had received the prestigious Nebula and Hugo awards. Rama itself is a mysterious cylindrical spacecraft that roams the universe. In *Rama II* a team of scientists is assembled to explore Rama as it nears Earth. The various team members soon become embroiled in a range of personal intrigues, and in their professional capacities they fail to identify the actual Ramans. Officials on Earth, however, have concluded that the roaming spaceship constitutes a threat, and they attempt to destroy it.

Lee and Clarke followed *Rama II* with *The Garden of Rama,* in which the ship once again approaches Earth,

this time with intentions of obtaining a greater sampling of humanity. Deceitful world leaders respond to Rama by surrendering a sizeable group—more than two thousand citizens—whose members soon enough reveal humanity's apparently unending social ills, including crime, bigotry, and alienation. Meanwhile, Earthlings previously aboard Rama uncover the ship's purpose as a station designed to catalog various life forms in a specific region of the galaxy. Gerald Jonas, in his appraisal for the *New York Times Book Review,* noted that reading *The Garden of Rama* brought him a "little shiver of delight."

BIOGRAPHICAL/CRITICAL SOURCES:

PERIODICALS

Analog Science Fiction—Science Fact, December 15, 1988, pp. 184-85.
New York Times Book Review, December 31, 1989, p. 4; September 1, 1991, p. 13.

*   *   *

LEFCOURT, Peter 1941-

PERSONAL: Born December 19, 1941, in New York. *Education:* Union College, B.A., 1962.

ADDRESSES: Office—999 North Doheny Dr., Suite 906, Los Angeles, CA 90069. *Agent*—(Film and television) Ken Gross, Paradigm, 10100 Santa Monica Blvd., Los Angeles, CA 90067; (books) Esther Newberg, International Creative Management, 40 West Fifty-Seventh St., New York, NY 10019.

CAREER: Producer and writer. Producer of television series *Cagney and Lacey,* 1983-84.

MEMBER: Academy of Television Arts and Sciences, Authors Guild, Dramatists Guild, Writers Guild of America, West.

AWARDS, HONORS: Cagney and Lacey received an Emmy Award nomination for best drama series, Academy of Television Arts and Sciences, 1984, and an Emmy Award for best drama series, 1985; Ohio State Broadcasting Award, 1987, for *Cracked Up;* Dramalogue Award for Playwriting, 1990, for *Only the Dead Know Burbank.*

WRITINGS:

NOVELS

The Deal, Random House, 1991.
The Dreyfus Affair, Random House, 1992.

STAGE PLAYS

Only the Dead Know Burbank, produced in Los Angeles at Actors' Alley Repertory Theatre, 1990.

Sweet Talk, produced in Los Angeles at Actors' Alley Repertory Theatre, 1991.

La Ronde de Lunch, produced in Los Angeles at Actors' Alley Repertory Theatre, 1992.

OTHER

Has also written scripts for film and television, including *Inherit the Mob; American Dream; Rivkin: Bounty Hunter; Bulba; The Devlin Connection; Remington Steele; Scarecrow and Mrs. King; Two Marriages; Cagney and Lacey; I Had Three Wives; Monte Carlo, Parts I and II; Cracked Up; Fine Things; The Women of Windsor; Psych Ward;* and *Studio 5 B.* Contributor of poetry to periodicals, including *Exquisite Corpse, Galley Sail Review, Hawaii Review, California State Poetry Quarterly,* and *Lactuca.* Contributor of fiction to periodicals, including *Redbook* and *Mind Scapes.*

WORK IN PROGRESS: A novel.

SIDELIGHTS: Peter Lefcourt began rising to prominence as a television writer and producer during the 1980s. He produced *Cagney and Lacey,* the Emmy-winning drama series about the plight of two female police detectives, and he also wrote scripts for that show, in addition to penning episodes for other series, including *Remington Steele* and *Scarecrow and Mrs. King.* As the 1990s began, Lefcourt branched out into other genres, writing a play, *Only the Dead Know Burbank,* that met with critical acclaim when it was staged in Los Angeles, California. His first novel, *The Deal,* was published in 1991 and was hailed by reviewers for its humorous, irreverent look at the world of Hollywood filmmaking. Lefcourt's second novel, *The Dreyfus Affair,* was also well received.

The Deal concerns a failing film producer, Charlie Berns, who is about to commit suicide by asphyxiating himself with fumes from his Mercedes when his nephew shows up with a film script for him to produce. The script is about English politics under Queen Victoria, and features as its unlikely hero Victoria's Prime Minister Benjamin Disraeli. Charlie manages to get the film into production, but the project undergoes many changes until it becomes an action-adventure film featuring a famous African American martial arts star. Judith Rascoe in the *New York Times Book Review* called the novel "a good-natured romp through the dream factory" and further noted that *The Deal* "is full of affable inside jokes that aren't so deep inside that a regular viewer of *Entertainment Tonight* can't enjoy them." In a similar vein, a critic for *Publishers Weekly* asserted that "Lefcourt's first novel is a hilariously entertaining insider's look at the business of making movies."

Lefcourt sets his 1992 novel *The Dreyfus Affair* in the world of professional baseball. The book's protagonist,

Randy Dreyfus, is a major-league shortstop who is disturbed by the fact that he is falling in love with his second baseman. Dreyfus eventually gives into his feelings, which are reciprocated. All goes well until the two are recorded sharing a kiss by a hidden security camera. The lovers are banned from baseball for life, just as their team is about to enter the World Series. "But, as all true fans know, the game's not over till it's over," concluded Katrine Ames, reviewing the novel in *Newsweek.* Ames also praised the book as "exceptionally funny." Despite the slightly controversial subject matter of *The Dreyfus Affair,* many critics echoed the sentiments of *Library Journal*'s Marylaine Block, who called the work "thoroughly likeable."

Lefcourt told *CA:* "Writing is like going to the dentist—it feels good when you're finished."

BIOGRAPHICAL/CRITICAL SOURCES:

PERIODICALS

Library Journal, April 1, 1992, pp. 146, 148.
Newsweek, June 22, 1992, p. 54.
New York Times Book Review, June 2, 1991, p. 12.
Publishers Weekly, February 22, 1991, p. 211.
Times (London), February 29, 1992, p. 34.

*   *   *

LEIBOVITZ, Annie 1949-

PERSONAL: Full name, Anna-Lou Leibovitz; born October 2, 1949, in Westbury, CT; daughter of Sam (a U.S. Air Force colonel) and Marilyn (a modern-dance instructor) Leibovitz. *Education:* San Francisco Art Institute, B.F.A., 1971; studied photography with Ralph Gibson. *Avocational interests:* Bicycling, hiking.

ADDRESSES: Home—New York, NY. *Office*—Annie Leibovitz Studio, 55 Vandam St., New York, NY 10013. *Agent*—Jim Moffat, Art & Commerce, 108 West 18th St., New York, NY 10011.

CAREER: Kibbutz Amir, Israel, member of archaeological team excavating King Solomon's temple, 1969; *Rolling Stone* (magazine), San Francisco, CA, and New York City, photographer, 1970-73, chief photographer, 1973-83; *Vanity Fair* (magazine), New York City, contributing photographer, 1983—; Annie Leibovitz Studio, New York City, owner. Tour photographer for rock band the Rolling Stones, 1975; World Cup Games, Mexico, poster photographer, 1986; American Ballet Theater, portrait photographer for fiftieth anniversary tour book, 1989; White Oak Dance Project, documentary photographer, 1990; Mary Boone Gallery, portrait photographer, 1990; advertising photographer for American Express, Arrow, Beef Industry Council, Christian Brothers, the Gap,

Honda, Rose's Lime Juice, and *U.S. News and World Report;* photographer for movie posters, record album covers, and book covers. Exhibitions include Sidney Janis Gallery, New York City, 1983, and tour of U.S. and European cities, 1983-85; Sidney Janis Gallery, 1986, and tour, 1986-89; Arles Festival, France, 1986; James Danziger Gallery, New York City, 1991; National Portrait Gallery, Washington, DC, 1991, then International Center of Photography, New York City, 1991, and tour of U.S., European, and Far East cities, 1991-93.

AWARDS, HONORS: Photographer of the Year, American Society of Magazine Photographers, 1984; Innovation in Photography Award, American Society of Magazine Photographers, 1987; Clio Award, Clio Enterprises, and Campaign of the Decade, *Advertising Age,* both 1987, and Infinity Award for applied photography, International Center of Photography, 1990, all for photography for American Express "Portraits" advertising campaign.

WRITINGS:

(Editor) *Shooting Stars,* Straight Arrow Books, 1973.
Photographs, Pantheon, 1983.
(With others) *Visual Aid,* edited by James Danziger, foreword by Cornell Capa, Pantheon, 1986.
(Photographer) Alan Olshan, editor, *American Ballet Theatre: The First Fifty Years,* Dewynters PLC, 1989.
(Photographer) Jim Henke, *Human Rights Now!,* Amnesty International, 1989.
Photographs—Annie Leibovitz, 1970-1990, HarperCollins, 1991.
Misha and Others: Photographs, Smithsonian Institution Press, 1992.

Contributor of photographs to periodicals, including *Bunte, Cambio 16, El Europeo, Elle, Epocha, Esquire, Interview, Le Nouvel Observateur, Life, Ms., Newsweek, New York Times Magazine,* London *Observer, Paris Match, Stern,* London *Sunday Times, Switch, Time, Vogue,* and *Zeit.*

SIDELIGHTS: Best known for her bold, colorful photographs for the cover of *Rolling Stone* magazine, Annie Leibovitz is "the portraitist of the rock generation," wrote Mary Ann Tighe in the *Washington Post Book World.* Her famous subjects have ranged from rock legend Chuck Berry to former U.S. President Richard Nixon. Often her portraits capture the essence of her subjects' images or dig beneath the veneer of fame to reveal unexpected vulnerability. Some pictures, notably nudes such as her 1991 *Vanity Fair* cover shot of pregnant actress Demi Moore, have sparked controversy. Leibovitz's subjects have appeared smeared with mud or covered with roses, naked or swathed in yards of cloth, impeccably made-up or wildly disheveled. Through hundreds of attention-getting im-

ages, Leibovitz "has helped define the nature of stardom in a star-struck age," asserted Charles Hagen in *ARTnews.*

Reviewers expressed various opinions on what made Leibovitz's photographs stand out. In Hagen's *ARTnews* article, critic Andy Grundberg asserted that Leibovitz "exaggerates the distinctive characteristics of [her subjects'] public images in a way that's funny and deflating." Hagen was impressed by how "physical" her portraits are: "Leibovitz gets her sitters to use their whole bodies." In a similar vein, several writers traced Leibovitz's success to her skill at getting her subjects actively involved in their photo sessions. As Laurence Shames put it in *American Photographer,* "What sets Leibovitz apart . . . has almost nothing to do with her handling of the camera, and almost everything to do with her handling of the subject."

By 1991 Leibovitz had attained such stature that the International Center for Photography and the National Portrait Gallery in Washington, D.C., mounted a retrospective of her twenty-year career—only the second time such an exhibition was held for a living photographer. Record crowds turned out for the show. The total attendance for its five-week run at the Portrait Gallery equaled a year's normal attendance at the gallery, or around three hundred thousand. Leibovitz's career was also celebrated in an accompanying book of more than two hundred pages titled *Photographs—Annie Leibovitz, 1970-1990.* Reviewing the book for the *New York Times Book Review,* Christine Schwartz dubbed the photographer "the modern equivalent of a court painter." Echoing Tighe's opinion that the significance of Leibovitz's work hinges on the public's love of celebrities, she nevertheless commended Leibovitz's ability to "achieve the combination of glamour, intimacy and wit we demand of celebrity pictures." To Schwartz, the collection confirms Leibovitz as "our day's most gifted photographer of the stars." Richard Lacayo, writing in *Time,* assessed her portraits with reservations, finding them somewhat paradoxical. Asserted Lacayo, "Leibovitz's best-known work . . . tries to twit propriety in the slickest possible style." In a more favorable appraisal, Maddy Miller of *People,* noting that Leibovitz is "still making waves," suggested that "this extraordinary 20-year retrospective may quickly be eclipsed by the photographer's continuing triumphs."

BIOGRAPHICAL/CRITICAL SOURCES:

BOOKS

Leibovitz, Annie, *Photographs,* Pantheon, 1983.
Leibovitz, Annie, *Photographs—Annie Leibovitz, 1970-1990,* HarperCollins, 1991.
Marcus, Adrianne, *The Photojournalist, Mary Ellen Mark and Annie Leibovitz,* Crowell, 1974.
Newsmakers 88, Cumulation, Gale, 1988, pp. 248-49.

PERIODICALS

Adweek, February 1, 1988.
American Photographer, January, 1984, pp. 38-39, 44-59; February, 1988.
Art in America, April, 1984.
ARTnews, March, 1992, pp. 90-95.
Arts, February, 1984.
Chicago Tribune, December 23, 1983; May 5, 1991, p. 1.
Christian Science Monitor, November 17, 1983.
Esquire, December, 1991, pp. 124-33.
Harper's Bazaar, June, 1984, pp. 146-47, 180.
Los Angeles Times, November 9, 1983.
Newsday, December 4, 1983.
New York, September 19, 1983, pp. 88-89; March 14, 1988, pp. 24, 26, 28.
New York Daily News, November 30, 1986, p. 3.
New York Times, October 9, 1983.
New York Times Book Review, October 23, 1983, p. 31; January 26, 1992, p. 20.
New York Woman, September, 1988, p. 100.
People, November 18, 1991, p. 31.
Publishers Weekly, November 16, 1990, pp. 34-35.
Rolling Stone, January 22, 1981, p. 5.
Time, September 30, 1991, pp. 72-74.
Vanity Fair, September, 1991.
Wall Street Journal, September 10, 1987.
Washington Post, December 4, 1984, p. 1; April 19, 1991, p. 1.
Washington Post Book World, November 27, 1983, pp. 5, 9, 11.

* * *

LEIGH, Richard (Harris) 1943-

PERSONAL: Born August 16, 1943, in New Jersey. *Education:* Tufts University, B.A., 1965; University of Chicago, M.A., 1967; State University of New York at Stony Brook, Ph.D., 1970.

ADDRESSES: Agent—Barbara Levy, 21 Kelly St., London NW1 8PG, England.

CAREER: Simon Fraser University, Vancouver, British Columbia, special collections librarian, 1970-72; writer.

MEMBER: Pushkin Prize Programme in Ireland (co-founder).

AWARDS, HONORS: "Madonna" was chosen as one of the best short stories of 1982 by *Random Review.*

WRITINGS:

WITH MICHAEL BAIGENT

(And with Henry Lincoln) *The Holy Blood and the Holy Grail,* Delacorte, 1982.

(And with Lincoln) *The Messianic Legacy,* Holt, 1986.
The Temple and the Lodge, J. Cape, 1989.
The Dead Sea Scrolls Deception, Summit Books, 1991.

OTHER

Contributor of introductions to books, including *Song of a Man Who Came Through,* by Douglas Lockhart, 1978. Contributor of short stories, including "Madonna," to anthologies and journals.

SIDELIGHTS: Richard Leigh's collaborative studies have put forth several controversial theories regarding Western religion and history. His books—written with Michael Baigent and Henry Lincoln—often focus on the origins of Christianity, offering reinterpretations of religious history and sometimes alleging conspiracies on the part of church leaders. Leigh and his coauthors have drawn fire for their assertions, being scorned by both religious authorities and many book reviewers. They have also attracted a large number of readers who are interested in their dramatic investigations of the past.

The Holy Blood and the Holy Grail and its sequel, *The Messianic Legacy,* contend that Jesus Christ, rather than being the crucified and resurrected son of God, was instead a worldly leader of the Nazarene Party, a group opposed to Roman rule. Jesus, the authors maintain, married Mary Magdalene and had several children. His descendants eventually resettled in France, established a principality, and centuries later formed the Order of Sion, a secret society that still exists. During the First Crusade, members of this society occupied Jerusalem and obtained the holy grail, an artifact which proves Jesus's true identity. The grail was later returned to France, where it was kept by the Order of Sion and by their successors, the Knights Templar. Over the centuries the Roman Catholic church has attempted to cover up the truth about Jesus's descendants, the authors allege, because their existence refutes church doctrine regarding Jesus's life and works. Despite this opposition, the Order of Sion continues to guard the grail, waiting for their opportunity to establish Jesus's heir as the monarch of a united Europe.

In *The Temple and the Lodge,* Leigh and Baigent take up the story of the Knights Templar, who had played a role in their earlier analysis of the holy grail. It is generally believed that the Templars were first established in 1120 to guard Christian pilgrims traveling to the Middle East. By the 1300s they had become a powerful army with land holdings in Europe and the Middle East, but when they were banned by Pope Clement V in 1308, the order was thought to have come to an end. *The Temple and the Lodge,* on the other hand, claims that the Knights Templar relocated to Scotland after being suppressed by the pope and that they played a vital role in subsequent events, including military struggles for control of Great Britain.

The book also contends that the Templars are connected to the Freemasons—a secretive organization that began in England in the 1600s and continues to the present. Freemasonry eventually spread throughout Europe and America, boasting such well-known members as George Washington and Benjamin Franklin. The Freemasons' large and powerful membership, the authors maintain, had a profound impact on historical events after 1700, thereby perpetuating the influence of the Templars.

In *The Dead Sea Scrolls Deception,* Leigh and Baigent returned to the subject of early Christianity. The book concerns the ancient scrolls that were found in caves near the Dead Sea in 1947. Since their discovery, the scrolls have been studied by a select group of researchers at the Ecole Biblique in Jerusalem whose findings have yet to be published. The scrolls are thought to be the work of the Qumran community, dating either to the period before Christ is believed to have lived, or else to the years shortly after his death. Leigh and Baigent subscribe to the latter view, upholding the theories of Robert Eisenman, a professor at California State University, Long Beach. Eisenman believes that the scrolls were written by one of the first Christian organizations, the Zealots, a group led by Jesus's brother James. Proclaiming the documents an authentic chronicle of the early church, *The Dead Sea Scrolls Deception* suggests that the scrolls contain information about Jesus and the early Christians that contradicts later Christian doctrine. Unwilling to let this damaging information become public, the Catholic church and others have been involved in a conspiracy to prevent the scrolls from being published.

Many critics have been skeptical about the claims that Leigh and his collaborators have made in their books. Michele Roberts's review in *New Statesman and Society* concluded that "it's easy to dismiss the central thesis of *The Messianic Legacy,*" while the *Washington Post*'s Martin E. Marty sounded a similar note regarding *The Holy Blood and the Holy Grail,* terming it a "sensational and sensationally misguiding book." The primary complaint these critics make is that the books lack legitimate proof of the authors' theories. "Their technique is shameful," wrote Marty in assessing *The Temple and the Lodge.* "It belongs to the plant-a-suggestion-in-the-readers'-minds-and-then-pretend-you've-proven-something schools. They ask us to imagine and entertain various possibilities, and then act as if these possibilities have thus been established." Peter Jones, reviewing *The Dead Sea Scrolls Deception* in the London *Times,* was equally harsh, declaring that "this theory is simply paranoid, and the two chapters of 'research' produce not one jot of evidence."

Despite these criticisms, several reviewers have indicated that Leigh and his coauthors produce very entertaining works. "The inquiry presented here is an interesting me-

lange of the factual and the imagined," wrote Genevieve Stuttaford in her *Publishers Weekly* review of *The Messianic Legacy; Newsweek*'s Sharon Begley found that *The Dead Sea Scrolls Deception* "spins a lively tale of one controversial interpretation of the scrolls." John Ray's review of *The Dead Sea Scrolls Deception* in the *Times Literary Supplement* also suggests that a positive development may result from the popular interest in the book. "If it succeeds in advancing the publication of the material from Qumran," Ray wrote, "it will have achieved genuine good." In 1991 the Huntington Library in California announced that it would release microfilm copies of the scrolls. While this action cannot be directly attributed to the appearance of *The Dead Sea Scrolls Deception,* the release of the scrolls should provide a new perspective on Leigh and Baigent's controversial religious theories.

BIOGRAPHICAL/CRITICAL SOURCES:

PERIODICALS

Globe and Mail (Toronto), July 15, 1989.
New Statesman and Society, December 19, 1986, p. 66.
Newsweek, March 2, 1992, p. 67.
New York Times, February 12, 1992.
Publishers Weekly, September 25, 1987, p. 90.
Times (London), April 6, 1989; May 18, 1991, p. 22.
Times Literary Supplement, January 22, 1982, p. 69; May 24, 1991.
Washington Post, January 19, 1990.*

—*Sketch by Jeff Hill*

*   *   *

LESSER, Wendy 1952-

PERSONAL: Born March 20, 1952, in Santa Monica, CA; daughter of Murray (an engineer and writer) Lesser and Millicent (a writer; maiden name, Gerson) Dillon; married Richard Rizzo (a professor and writer), January 18, 1985; children: Nicholas Rizzo. *Education:* Harvard University, B.A., 1973; King's College, Cambridge, M.A., 1975; University of California, Berkeley, Ph.D., 1982. *Politics:* "Left-leaning Democrat." *Religion:* "Secular Jew."

ADDRESSES: Office—*Threepenny Review,* P.O. Box 9131, Berkeley, CA 94709. *Agent*—Gloria Loomis, Watkins Loomis Agency, Inc., 133 East Thirty-fifth St., Suite 1, New York, NY 10016.

CAREER: Lesser & Ogden Associates (a public policy consulting firm), Berkeley, CA, partner, 1977-81; *Threepenny Review,* Berkeley, founding editor, 1980—; writer. Consultant to nonprofit organizations, including the National Endowment for the Arts and San Francisco Foundation.

AWARDS, HONORS: Fellowships from the National Endowment for the Humanities, 1983, 1991, and the John Simon Guggenheim Memorial Foundation, 1988; Rockefeller Foundation Bellagio Residency, 1984.

WRITINGS:

The Life below the Ground: A Study of the Subterranean in Literature and History, Faber & Faber, 1987.

His Other Half: Men Looking at Women through Art, Harvard University Press, 1991.

(Editor) *Hiding in Plain Sight: Essays in Criticism and Autobiography,* Mercury House, 1993.

Pictures at an Execution, Harvard University Press, in press.

Contributor of book reviews to periodicals.

SIDELIGHTS: Founding editor of the literary quarterly *Threepenny Review,* Wendy Lesser is the author of *The Life below the Ground: A Study of the Subterranean in Literature and History* and *His Other Half: Men Looking at Women through Art.* In *The Life below the Ground,* Lesser writes that she intends her book to be "an idiosyncratic meditation on the idea of the underground." She explores the use of the subterranean as a setting and metaphor in various works of the past 200 years, including such disparate ones as Lewis Carroll's *Alice's Adventures in Wonderland,* Steven Spielberg's film *Indiana Jones and the Temple of Doom,* Dante's *Inferno,* the writings of Franz Kafka and Graham Greene, and the movies of Alfred Hitchcock. Though some critics judged that Lesser sometimes strains to create parallels between widely different works, others praised the author's subject choice. *Los Angeles Times Book Review* contributor Brian Stonehill commented that Lesser "practices intelligent and informed *cultural* criticism. . . . [She] digs for meaning; she mines remarkable merit; and shows us, once again, the earth-shaking power of ideas."

In her 1991 collection, *His Other Half,* Lesser "bases her group of essays on the idea that certain male artists are in search of their own lost or hidden female selves, and that the success of their search can be measured by the way such rescued selves are freed by the artist and given independent life in his works of art," according to *New York Times Book Review* contributor Anne Hollander. As in *The Life below the Ground,* Lesser communicates her theme by discussing a wide variety of art, including the paintings of Edgar Degas, the photographs of Cecil Beaton, the films of Alfred Hitchcock, the novels of Henry James and D. H. Lawrence, and the poetry of Randall Jarrell. In her examination of male artists' portrayal of women, Lesser takes what some reviewers regard as an unorthodox feminist approach. "In defiance of feminists and women's studies, [Lesser] chooses to examine the feminine bent through the prism of male consciousness, so that even

when the woman in question is actual, like [actress] Marilyn Monroe, she discusses her only as an artefact, through her 'creators,' " noted Marina Warner in the *Times Literary Supplement.*

Critics responded enthusiastically to *His Other Half,* often citing Lesser's originality, insight, and engaging style. *Chicago Tribune* reviewer Joseph Coates, for instance, commented that "it isn't often that a critic can recommend a work of criticism as entertainment, but Wendy Lesser's refreshingly personal approach saves her from any kind of specialized deadness." Warner judged *His Other Half* to be "an arresting work of criticism," adding that "Lesser writes with volatile wit, an eager, almost breezy confidence and a palpable pleasure in reading and looking and analysing—and in the suppleness of her own cleverness."

Lesser told *CA:* "When I look for my books on the shelves of bookstores, I often find them in a category called 'Cultural Criticism,' and some people therefore refer to me as a culture critic (whatever that is). But I prefer to think of myself as a writer who began as a literary critic and expanded outward to include other subjects as well. For me, this signifies a respect for specificity over vague 'cultural' pronouncements and an acknowledgement that literature, as T. S. Eliot said, is related 'not to "life," as something contrasted to literature, but to all the other activities, which, together with literature, are the components of life.' "

BIOGRAPHICAL/CRITICAL SOURCES:

BOOKS

Lesser, Wendy, *The Life below the Ground: A Study of the Subterranean in Literature and History,* Faber & Faber, 1987.

PERIODICALS

Chicago Tribune, March 21, 1991, section 2, p. 3.
Los Angeles Times Book Review, February 14, 1988, p. 11.
New York Times Book Review, November 22, 1987, p. 26; April 7, 1991, p. 15.
Times Literary Supplement, June 7, 1991, pp. 9-10.
Washington Post Book World, March 10, 1991, p. 5.

*　　*　　*

LETNANOVA, Elena 1942-

PERSONAL: Born October 23, 1942, in Pressburg (now Bratislava), Czechoslovakia; daughter of Julius Letnan (a music composer) and Elena (Ivaskova) Letnanova (a teacher); married Andrej Mraz (a mathematician, philosopher, and writer), 1966, (divorced, 1980); children: Juliana Mrazova. *Education:* Studied architecture at Supreme

School of Technique, 1960-62; College of Musical Arts, Bratislava, master's degree, 1966; Frederic Chopin Academy of Music in Warsaw, postgraduate studies, 1966-68; attended Hochschule fuer Musik, Munich, 1970-71; University of Jan Amos Komensky, Ph.D., 1979. *Politics:* "Anticommunist." *Religion:* "Baptized as Augsburg-Lutheran." *Avocational interests:* Fine arts, philosophy, judo, chess, theater, poetry, mountain hiking, politics, and gliding.

ADDRESSES: Home—Mozartova II, 81104 Bratislava, Czechoslovakia. *Office*—University of Jan Amos Komensky, Lekarska Fakulta, Katedra Jazvkov, Sasinkova 4/a, 81108 Bratislava, Czechoslovakia. *Agent*—Slovak Literary Agency, Partizanska 21, 81530 Bratislava, Czechoslovakia.

CAREER: Piano soloist and accompanist, 1966-74 and 1985—; University of Jan Amos Komensky, Nitra, Czechoslovakia, 1968-70, began as lecturer, became assistant professor; Slovconcert Agency, Bratislava, Czechoslovakia, concert pianist, 1970-74; State Conservatory of Music, Bratislava, professor of music, 1974-75; University of Jan Amos Komensky, Bratislava, 1974-84, began as assistant professor, became associate professor in department of musicology; piano teacher in Rome, Italy, 1984-85; Barnes Constructural Engineers, Arlington, TX, draftsperson, 1985; teacher and concert performer in Texas and Colorado, 1985-87; University of Dayton, Dayton, OH, associate professor of piano and head of piano area, 1987-92; University of Jan Amos Komensky, assistant professor, 1992—. Performed in Czechoslovakian films *Outstanding Women Artists* and *Jan Zelibsky,* 1973.

MEMBER: Slovak Union of Composers and Performers, Music Teachers National Association, and European Piano Teachers Association (London), among others.

AWARDS, HONORS: Special prize, State Chopin Competition at Marianske Lazne, 1965; Deutcher Akademischer Austauschdienst Grant, 1970-71; grant from Slovak National Music Fund, 1972, for premiere of Juraj Hatrik's piano concerto; Medal of Slava Vorlova, National Festival of Music in Nachod, 1974, for outstanding performances; grant from Marguerite Wilbur Foundation, 1987-88; grants from Artsdayton, 1987 and 1989, for production of "Kandinsky-Mussorgsky: Pictures at an Exhibition," a multimedia event at Boll Theater, University of Dayton, and research on nineteenth-century performance treatises and aesthetics.

WRITINGS:

(Translator) Aleksandr I. Solzhenitsyn, *Message from Exile,* [Bratislava], 1979.

Piano Interpretation in the Seventeenth, Eighteenth, and Nineteenth Centuries: A Study of Theory and Practice Using Original Documents, McFarland, 1991.

Also author of short stories, including "Richter," "Escape," and "One Day of E. L." Contributor to periodicals, including *Pravda, Musical Horizons, Musical Life, Praca, Piano Quarterly, Royal Music Journal,* and *Kulturny Zivot.*

WORK IN PROGRESS: Homo Ludens, origin of the play viewed through physiological, sociological, historical, and aesthetical theories of Huisinga, Plechanov, and others.

SIDELIGHTS: Elena Letnanova is an acclaimed pianist, writer, and teacher of music. She has performed at numerous places worldwide, including Carnegie Hall's Weill Recital Hall, in a career that spans more than twenty years. Letnanova was an active anticommunist, and as a result of her opposition to the Russian invasion of Czechoslovakia she was not allowed to perform for a decade by the Czech government. Letnanova fled to Italy in 1984, where she lived in a refugee camp with her daughter while waiting for sponsorship into the United States. She later returned to Czechoslovakia, where she accepted a teaching position at the University of Jan Amos Komensky.

Letnanova told *CA:* "I began to write for myself as a corollary to my painting and professional musicianship as a student. I started to write because I felt a strong need to express my critical views of Czechoslovakian society in the late 1960s. I started with short stories that I kept in my drawer, and at the same time I was editing the short stories of my ex-husband. I feverishly chronicled events, sometimes in random snatches. Mainly I was a mood painter and monologist in stories. When I was teaching at university I found there a fertile ground for observing the treasons and masques of the characters that would populate my writings. I found striking resonance in the works of George Orwell, Franz Kafka, and Saul Bellow. I have been fascinated, negatively, by the quick adaptability of weak people inside and outside of the communistic party under and before the regime of Vaclav Havel. The abandoning of man's identity and the general apathy of my society became the *spiritus movens* of my writings.

"My work was also influenced by my nearest friends and by writers: Dominik Tatarka, Milan Simecka, Vaclav Havel, and Karol Capek. The musicological works were derived from practical needs and improper renditions of Renaissance and baroque music."

LEWIS, Michael 1960-

PERSONAL: Born October 15, 1960, in New Orleans, LA; son of J. Thomas (a corporate lawyer) and Diana (a community activist; maiden name, Monroe) Lewis. *Education:* Princeton University, B.A., 1982; London School of Economics and Political Science, M.A., 1985.

ADDRESSES: Home—London, England. *Agent*—Albert Zuckerman, Writers House, 21 West Twenty-sixth St., New York, NY 10010.

CAREER: Salomon Brothers, New York City, bond salesman, 1984-88; writer.

WRITINGS:

Liar's Poker: Rising through the Wreckage on Wall Street, Norton, 1989.
Pacific Rift: Adventures in the Fault Zone between the U.S. and Japan, Whittle Communications, 1991.
The Money Culture (articles and essays), Norton, 1991.

Contributor to periodicals, including *New Republic, New York Times, Spectator,* and *Washington Post.*

WORK IN PROGRESS: A novel.

SIDELIGHTS: Michael Lewis became a top bond salesman for Wall Street's Salomon Brothers firm before resigning in 1988 to become a writer. In 1989 Lewis published his first book, *Liar's Poker: Rising through the Wreckage on Wall Street,* in which he recounts his own experiences in the stocks-and-bonds field. A successful bond trader, Lewis contends, is one who is shrewd and willing to risk substantial funds in order to realize ever-greater profits. Lewis also observes, however, that a successful company cannot practice similarly cavalier management, and in *Liar's Poker* he charts the demise of Salomon Brothers as a key firm in bond trading. According to Lewis, internal competition, greed, and a lack of long-range planning all served to undo Salomon Brothers, which suffered major losses in October, 1987, when the value of stocks unexpectedly plummeted.

Liar's Poker generally won acclaim as an incisive, often funny insider's perspective on Wall Street practices. Chicago *Tribune Books* reviewer William Brashler, for instance, described Lewis's book as "sort of a financial locker room yarn," and *Los Angeles Times Book Review* critic Scot J. Paltrow deemed it "an insightful and extremely readable sort of non-fiction satire." Another critic, Richard L. Stern, noted in the *New York Times Book Review* that Lewis is "obviously as good a writer as he was a bond salesman."

Lewis followed *Liar's Poker* with *Pacific Rift: Adventures in the Fault Zone between the U.S. and Japan,* in which he compares and contrasts the business practices of two men: a Japanese real-estate representative in New York City and an American insurance seller. In *Pacific Rift,* as Frank Gibney reported in the *New York Times Book Review,* Lewis substantiates "the obvious fact that Japanese and American ways of doing business are often very different." America, he asserts, has developed a deviant capitalism, one dependent on federal regulation that is, in turn, alarmingly negative in its effects. But Japan, Lewis contends, has practiced a more traditional capitalism, which depends largely on private businesses. In addition, according to Lewis, Japanese culture has maintained its emphasis on conservative values. "In other words," as George Gilder noted in the *Washington Post Book World,* "Japan wins through low taxes, firm families, rigorous schools and hard work." Gilder found *Pacific Rift* a sobering analysis.

Lewis is also author of *The Money Culture,* a collection of articles and essays. In these pieces Lewis, according to a *Washington Post Book World* reviewer, "finds a common thread: not merely of acquisitiveness but of 'an entire culture based on entitlement,' from the greedy 25-year-olds of Wall Street . . . to the relatively impecunious ordinary Americans lining up for financial get-rich-quick schemes." Gary Weiss, in his *Business Week* review of *The Money Culture,* described Lewis as "entertaining" and added that "the durability of Lewis's prose is impressive."

BIOGRAPHICAL/CRITICAL SOURCES:

PERIODICALS

Bestsellers 90, Volume 2, Gale, 1990, pp. 50-51.
Business Week, October 6, 1991, p. 3.
Economist, November 18, 1989, p. 107.
London Review of Books, December 21, 1989, p. 16.
Harvard Business Review, January, 1992, p. 32.
Los Angeles Times Book Review, November 5, 1989, p. 19; October 7, 1990, p. 14.
Nation, December 24, 1990, p. 817.
New York Times Book Review, October 29, 1989; September 30, 1990, p. 46; May 24, 1992, pp. 10-12.
Time, November 6, 1989, p. 103; February 19, 1990, p. 71.
Times Literary Supplement, February 9, 1990, p. 140; February 28, 1992, pp. 5-6.
Tribune Books (Chicago), November 26, 1989; October 14, 1990, p. 8.
Washington Post Book World, March 3, 1991, pp. 11-12.

*   *   *

LIM, Shirley Geok-lin 1944-

PERSONAL: Born December 27, 1944, in Malacca, Malaysia; immigrated to the United States, 1969; daughter of Chin Som (a petition writer) and Chye Neo (a homemaker; maiden name, Ang) Lim; married Charles Bazerman (a professor), November, 1972; children: Gershom Kean. *Education:* University of Malaya, B.A. (with first class honors), 1967, graduate study, 1967-69; Brandeis University, M.A., 1971, Ph.D., 1973.

ADDRESSES: Home—574 Calle Anzuelo, Santa Barbara, CA 93111. *Office*—Department of English, University of California, Santa Barbara, CA 93106.

CAREER: University of Malaya, Kuala Lumpur, part-time lecturer, 1967-69; Queens College of the City University of New York, Flushing, NY, teaching fellow, 1972-73; Hostos Community College of the City University of New York, Bronx, NY, assistant professor, 1973-76; Westchester Community College of the State University of New York, Valhalla, associate professor, 1976-90; University of California, Santa Barbara, professor of Asian American studies and English, 1990—. Universiti Sains, part-time lecturer, 1974; National University of Singapore, visiting fellow, 1982, writer in residence, 1985, Asia Foundation fellow at Centre for Advanced Studies, 1989; Graduate Center of the City University of New York, Mellon fellow, 1983, 1987; University of California, Irvine, minority discourses fellow at Interdisciplinary Research Center, 1993. East-West Center (Honolulu, HI), writer in residence, 1988; gives poetry readings and workshops. Member of New York Governor's Commission on Libraries, 1990—.

MEMBER: International P.E.N., Modern Language Association of America (member of executive committee, Division on Literature in English Other Than British and American, 1986-90; founder of Discussion Group on Asian American Literature, 1985, and chair of its executive committee, 1989; member of executive committee, Division on Ethnic Literature, 1993-97), American Studies Association, Association for Asian American Studies, National Women's Studies Association, Multi-Ethnic Literatures of the United States (MELUS), National Association for Ethnic Studies, American Association of Australian Literary Studies, Coordinating Council of Literary Magazines (member of board of directors, 1983-88; chair, 1986-87; member of executive council, 1987-88), Association for Commonwealth Languages and Literatures, Asian American Faculty and Staff Association of the University of California, Santa Barbara (chair, 1992).

AWARDS, HONORS: Vienna international fellow, 1969-72; Fulbright scholar, 1969-72; grants from National Endowment for the Humanities, 1978, 1987; Commonwealth Poetry Prize, 1980, for *Crossing the Peninsula;* fellow of Institute of Southeast-Asian Studies, 1985-86; *Asia Week* short story prize, 1986; grant from Westchester Foundation, 1987; American Book Award, 1989, for *The Forbidden Stitch.*

WRITINGS:

Crossing the Peninsula and Other Poems, Heinemann (Kuala Lumpur, Malaya), 1980.

Another Country and Other Stories, Times Books International (Singapore), 1982.

No Man's Grove and Other Poems, National University of Singapore, 1985.

Modern Secrets: New and Selected Poems, Dangaroo Press (Aarhus, Denmark), 1989.

(Coeditor and author of introduction) *The Forbidden Stitch: An Asian American Women's Anthology,* Calyx Books, 1989.

(Editor) *Approaches to Teaching Kingston's "The Woman Warrior",* Modern Language Association Press, 1991.

(Coeditor) *Reading Asian American Literatures,* Temple University Press, 1992.

(Co-editor) *One World of Literature: An Anthology of Contemporary Global Literature,* Houghton, 1992.

Nationalism and Literature: English-Language Writers from the Philippines and Singapore, New Day Publishers (Quezon City, Philippines), 1993.

Work represented in dozens of anthologies, including *Rim of Fire: Short Stories from the Pacific Rim,* edited by Calderon, Random House, 1992; *Birth and the Literary Imagination: A Cross-Cultural Anthology,* edited by Alice Deakins, Feminist Press, 1993; and *Unbecoming Daughters of the Empire,* edited by Anna Rutherford and Shirley Chew, Dangaroo Press, 1993. Contributor of more than a hundred articles, stories, poems, and reviews to periodicals in the United States and abroad, including *New Literary History, Journal of Commonwealth Literature, Commentary,* and *Insight. Feminist Studies,* coeditor, 1993, and member of editorial board; founder and editor of *Asian America: Journal of Culture and the Arts,* 1992—; member of editorial board, *MELUS,* 1993; advisory editor of *Reconstructing American Literature* and *Composition Review.*

WORK IN PROGRESS: That Farther Country: A Novel in Three Movements—Circling, Crossing, Landing, completion expected in 1994; *Broken English,* poems, 1994; *Postcolonial Asian/American,* collected essays; research on Asian American gender issues and representations, migrant and diaspora literatures, subaltern cultural studies, Southeast Asian literatures, postcolonial and women's autobiographies, and minorities and the visual arts.

SIDELIGHTS: Shirley Geok-lin Lim told *CA:* "I was born in a tropical colony of the British Empire. The English language was only one of three (Malay and Hokkien being the other two) languages that surrounded me but it is my language of choice. As a Chinese/Malaysian/American, the only constant in my life has been my relationship with this 'imperial' language, a language which originated in the soil of Anglo-Saxon speech and flourished on the Shakespearean stage but which, to my mind, now plainly belongs to the entire human species, like rice, cotton, or paper.

"Much of my writing life is composed of negotiating multiple identities, multiple societies, multiple desires, and multiple genres. I have published poetry, short fiction, criticism, and autobiographical essays, and I have been working on a novel for a long time. I am an Asian, a Westerner, and a woman, and I have known desperate hunger, in the presence of which one must be committed to speak. Singleness of self, the ideal of the autonomous individual, or the pure racialized community, is an impossible project for a multiple immigrant like me. I am currently writing a book of memoirs on the post-colonial geographies of Malaysia."

*   *   *

LIPTON, Eunice

PERSONAL: Born in New York City; daughter of Louis (a salesperson and entrepreneur) and Trudy (a bookkeeper; maiden name, Kirschenbaum) Lipton; married Ken Aptekar (a painter), May 31, 1984. *Education:* City College of the City University of New York, B.A., 1962; New York University, M.A., 1965, Ph.D., 1975. *Politics:* "Leftist." *Religion:* Jewish.

ADDRESSES: Home—201 West 85th St., No. 7E, New York, NY 10024. *Agent*—Gloria Loomis.

CAREER: University of Rhode Island, Kingston, instructor in art history, 1965-67; Bard College, Annandale-on-Hudson, NY, instructor in art history, 1970-72; Hunter College of the City University of New York, New York City, began as lecturer, became assistant professor of art history, 1973-78; Parsons School of Design, New York City, lecturer in art history, 1978-80; State University of New York at Binghamton, associate professor of art history, 1980-88. Williams College and Clark Art Institute, Robert Sterling Clark Visiting Professor, 1986; School of the Art Institute of Chicago, visiting artist, 1988. Fantastic Coalition of Women in the Arts, organizing member, 1989—; New York University, member of Institute for the Humanities seminar on sexuality, gender, and consumer culture, 1987—; Artists Meeting for Cultural Change, member, 1974-77.

MEMBER: College Art Association (organizing member of Caucus for Marxism and Art, 1976-80).

AWARDS, HONORS: Schuster Award from Hunter College of the City University of New York, 1976, for Degas/laundress project; grants from American Council of

Learned Societies, 1978, 1987; award for nonfiction literature, New York Foundation for the Arts, 1990, for a memoir of Victorine Meurent; resident of Dejerassi Foundation, 1991; award for nonfiction literature, Ludwig Vogelstein Foundation, 1991, for *Alias Olympia;* resident of Ucross Foundation and Rockefeller Foundation Study and Conference Center, Bellagio, Italy, 1992.

WRITINGS:

Picasso Criticism, 1901-1939: The Making of an Artist-Hero, Garland Publishing, 1976.
Looking into Degas: Uneasy Images of Women and Modern Life, University of California Press, 1986.
Alias Olympia: A Woman's Search for Manet's Notorious Model and Her Own Desire, Macmillan, 1993.

Work represented in anthologies, including *The Decade Show: Frameworks of Identity in the 1980s,* New Museum (New York City), 1990. Contributor of more than twenty articles and reviews to art journals and other periodicals. Member of editorial board, *Genders,* 1987—.

WORK IN PROGRESS: A book about Jewish identity, focusing on four French Jewish artists before, during, and after the Dreyfus Affair.

BIOGRAPHICAL/CRITICAL SOURCES:

PERIODICALS

Times Literary Supplement, August 28, 1987, p. 923.

*   *   *

LLEWELLYN, Sam 1948-

PERSONAL: Born August 2, 1948, in the Isles of Scilly; son of William Somers (an Anglican bishop) and Innis Dorrien Smith Llewellyn; married Karen Margaret Wallace (a writer), 1975; children: William, Martin. *Education:* St. Catherine's College, Oxford, B.A., 1970, M.A., 1973. *Politics:* "Tory anarchist." *Avocational interests:* Wine, sailing.

ADDRESSES: Agent—Jon Johnson, Clerkenwell House, 45-47 Clerkenwell Green, London EC1R 0HT, England.

CAREER: Musician and writer. Director of Arch Books.

MEMBER: League of Nightrunners, Baverstock Orpheans.

WRITINGS:

THRILLERS

Dead Reckoning, Michael Joseph, 1987, Summit Books, 1988.
Blood Orange, Summit Books, 1989.
Death Roll, Michael Joseph, 1989, Summit Books, 1990.

Dead Eye, Michael Joseph, 1990, Summit Books, 1991.
Blood Knot, Michael Joseph, 1991, Pocket Books, 1992.
Riptide, Michael Joseph, 1992.
Clawhammer, Michael Joseph, 1993.

CHILDREN'S BOOKS

Pegleg, illustrations by Robert Bartelt, Dent, 1989.
Pig in the Middle, illustrations by Michael Trevithick, Walker, 1989.
The Rope School, Walker, in press.

OTHER

Gurney's Revenge, Arlington Books, 1977.
Gurney's Reward, Corgi Books, 1979.
Gurney's Release, Arlington Books, 1979.
Hell Bay (novel), Ballantine, 1980.
The Last Will and Testament of Robert Louis Stevenson, Arlington, 1981.
Yacky dar Moy Bewty!: A Phrasebook for the Regions of Britain (with Irish Supplement), illustrations by Nigel Paige, Elm Tree, 1985.
Small Parts in History (nonfiction), Sidgwick & Jackson, 1985.
The Worst Journey in the Midlands (nonfiction), illustrations by Chris Aggs, Heinemann, 1985.
Sea Story (novel), St. Martin's, 1987.

Contributor to periodicals.

WORK IN PROGRESS: A thriller set in the high latitudes of the northern hemisphere, completion expected 1994.

SIDELIGHTS: Sam Llewellyn is an avid sailor who has won recognition with his various writings, notably thrillers, set at sea. Among his earliest entries in the genre is *Dead Reckoning,* in which a yacht designer discovers that his racing craft are being sabotaged. Determined to prove the actual safety of his designs, the hero willingly risks his life by entering a key competition. Newgate Callendar, in his regular *New York Times Book Review* appraisal of crime fiction, noted that in *Dead Reckoning* "the writing is clear and the mystery carefully plotted."

In another thriller, *Blood Orange,* Llewellyn writes about a racing trio undone when their yacht founders, and one of the crew, Alan, is believed drowned. The two surviving sailors, James and Ed, continue with their lives, though Ed himself is suspected of playing a part in Alan's drowning. James, however, suddenly discovers the missing Alan aboard another yacht. But before James can address him Alan vanishes. Soon afterward Alan is truly found dead. When another of James's acquaintances suffers a boating mishap, he begins to suspect a conspiracy of foul play.

Llewellyn's other thrillers include *Death Roll,* another tale of seaside sabotage, and *Blood Knot,* in which a former journalist is framed with the drowning of a Soviet sailor.

In the course of the latter story the hero discovers a considerable plot in Estonia, and in unraveling events he finds himself uncovering the circumstances of his own father's mysterious demise.

Aside from thrillers, Llewellyn's writings include children's tales and books of humor. His juvenile volume *Pig in the Middle,* for instance, concerns a seal pup stranded in a lagoon. While a prosperous fisherman contends that his livelihood is threatened by the seal's presence, a young boy, plagued with a constantly inebriated father and a mean-spirited mother, finds that his own troubled life is somehow enriched by the same creature. Brian Alderson, writing in the London *Times,* proclaimed that *Pig in the Middle* "reads like an old-time yarn."

Among Llewellyn's earliest volumes is *Yacky Dar Moy Bewty!: A Phrasebook for the Regions of Britain (with Irish Supplement),* in which he proposes that Britain be divided by dialect into nine specific regions. Basil Boothroyd, in his review for the London *Times,* affirmed that Llewellyn "has a good and funny idea," and he added that the author "pursues it with industry and a keen feeling for the absurd."

In addition, Llewellyn has produced *The Worst Journey in the Midlands,* an account of his arduous, three-hundred mile rowboat voyage from Wales to Westminster on the Severn River. Though Llewellyn sometimes found himself in dangerous circumstances—at one point he suffered a head injury when he was pitched from his vessel—he nonetheless shows considerable humor in the retelling.

Another of Llewellyn's nonfiction volumes is *Small Parts in History,* in which, as Boothroyd reported in the London *Times,* the author "has . . . hit on the witty idea of digging up nonentities who have played small parts in high matters." Among the seventy-seven subjects in this book are Alexander Selkirk, the shipwrecked sailor who served as the inspiration for Daniel Defoe's classic character Robinson Crusoe. Llewellyn reports that after being rescued, Selkirk commenced a life of philandering and rowdiness. Boothroyd appraised the contents of *Small Parts in History* as "appetizing bedside snacks."

Llewellyn told *CA:* "I have always lived on, by, in, or under the sea, and I have taken great pleasure in telling stories about it. It is always good to have an excuse to spend a lot of the year on a boat."

BIOGRAPHICAL/CRITICAL SOURCES:

PERIODICALS

Armchair Detective, fall, 1989, p. 371.
Los Angeles Times Book Review, February 24, 1985.

New York Times Book Review, May 22, 1988, p. 28; April 9, 1989, p. 42; May 27, 1990, p. 27; April 28, 1991, p. 24; October 11, 1992, p. 27.

Times (London), November 14, 1985; June 4, 1987.

Times Educational Supplement, January 6, 1989, p. 26; July 14, 1989, p. 26.

Times Literary Supplement, July 21, 1989, p. 810.

Tribune Books (Chicago), April 24, 1988, p. 7; April 9, 1989, p. 4.

* * *

LLOYD, (Mary) Norris   1908-1993

OBITUARY NOTICE—See index for *CA* sketch: Born September 1, 1908, in Greenwood, SC; died February 10, 1993, in Winnetka, IL. Author and social activist. Lloyd was a participant in protests during the 1960s and 1970s, fighting for racial equality in the Civil Rights Movement and against the Vietnam War. She also wrote several works that were either written for or about children, including *Desperate Dragons, Billy Hunts the Unicorn, Katie and the Catastrophe, The Village That Allah Forgot,* and *A Dream of Mansions.*

OBITUARIES AND OTHER SOURCES:

PERIODICALS

Chicago Tribune, February 15, 1993, sec. 1, p. 11.

* * *

LOEWALD, Hans W.   1906-1993

OBITUARY NOTICE—See index for *CA* sketch: Born January 19, 1906, in Colmar, France; immigrated to the United States, 1939; died January 9, 1993, in Hamden, CT. Psychoanalyst, educator, and writer. After receiving an education in Europe—culminating in the receipt of his M.D. from the University of Rome in the mid-1930s—Loewald moved to the United States, where he trained further at Rhode Island State Hospital and the University of Maryland Hospital. His subsequent career spanned more than forty years and included teaching posts in psychiatry at University of Maryland's Medical School, as well as at Yale Medical School and the Yale Child Study Center. For part of the time that he was teaching, he also practiced psychotherapy in New Haven, Connecticut. For his contributions to the field of psychoanalysis, Loewald received the Laughlin Award, bestowed by the American College of Psychoanalysis, and in 1991 the Mary S. Sigourney Fund Award. Loewald's published works include *Psychoanalysis and the History of the Individual, Papers on Psychoanalysis,* and *Sublimation: Inquiries into Theoretical Psychoanalysis.*

OBITUARIES AND OTHER SOURCES:

PERIODICALS

New York Times, January 13, 1993, p. A19.

* * *

LOOMIS, Susan Herrmann   1955-

PERSONAL: Born August 27, 1955, in Orlando, FL; married Michael Loomis, 1983; children: Joseph. *Education:* University of Washington, Seattle, B.A., 1977; Ecole de Cuisine La Varenne, grand diplome, 1981.

ADDRESSES: Agent—Susan Lescher, Lescher & Lescher Ltd., 67 Irving Pl., New York, NY 10003.

CAREER: Wenatchee World, Wenatchee, WA, reporter, 1977; North Central Washington Museum, Wenatchee, director of public relations, 1978; Cabrini Hospital, Seattle, WA, assistant director of public relations, 1979-80; Ecole de Cuisine La Varenne, Paris, France, member of editorial staff, 1981-82; Village Voice Cafe-Librairie, Paris, chef and manager, 1982-83; free-lance writer, 1983-84; International Association of Cooking Professionals, editor, 1985-86; free-lance writer, 1986—.

WRITINGS:

(With Patricia Wells) *The Food Lover's Guide to Paris,* Workman Publishing, 1984.

Paris in Your Pocket, Barron's, 1985.

The Great American Seafood Cookbook, Workman Publishing, 1988.

Farmhouse Cookbook, Workman Publishing, 1991.

Seafood Celebrations, Workman Publishing, 1993.

Contributor of articles and reviews to magazines and newspapers, including *Bon Appetit, Food and Wine, Ladies' Home Journal, Gourmet, New York Times,* and *Travel Holiday.* Editor, *Commentary,* 1985-86; contributing editor, *Seafood Business,* 1987—.

WORK IN PROGRESS: French Country Food.

* * *

LOVELL, Mary S(ybilla)   1941-

PERSONAL: Born October 23, 1941, in Prestatyn, Wales; daughter of William G. and Mary Catherine (Wooley) Shelton; married Clifford C. Lovell, October 22, 1960 (divorced, 1974); married Geoffrey A. H. Watts, July 11, 1992; children: Graeme, Robert. *Politics:* Conservative. *Religion:* Church of England. *Avocational interests:* Flying, sailing, foxhunting, history.

ADDRESSES: Home and office—Stroat House, Stroat, Gloucestershire NP6 7LR, England. *Agent*—Robert Ducas, 350 Hudson St., New York, NY 10010.

CAREER: Worked as an accountant and business director, 1963-83, and as a technical writer and documentation manager, 1983-86; writer, 1986—.

MEMBER: Society of Authors, Royal Overseas League, New Forest Hunt Club, R. S. Surtees Society, Master of Foxhounds Association.

WRITINGS:

A Hunting Pageant, Saiga, 1981.
Cats as Pets, Saiga, 1982.
Straight on Till Morning: The Biography of Beryl Markham, St. Martin's, 1987.
(Editor) Beryl Markham, *The Splendid Outcast* (stories), North Point, 1987.
The Sound of Wings: The Life of Amelia Earhart, St. Martin's, 1989.
Cast No Shadow: The Life of the American Spy Who Changed the Course of World War II, Pantheon, 1992.

Contributor to periodicals, including *Cosmopolitan* and *Marie Claire.*

Some of Lovell's works have been translated into French, German, and Danish.

WORK IN PROGRESS: A biography of "Jane Digby, a Victorian adventuress."

SIDELIGHTS: British writer Mary S. Lovell has received acclaim for her biographical portraits of female adventurers. The first of these books, *Straight on Till Morning: The Biography of Beryl Markham,* documents the life of the colorful, tempestuous pilot who in 1936 became the first person to fly solo from England to North America. Markham grew up in Africa, was married three times, knew how to repair an airplane engine, and had trained several successful racehorses. She was, according to Lovell, a beautiful, strong, eccentric woman with a magnetic personality. Jonathan Yardley wrote in the *Washington Post Book World* that Markham "seems, in fact, to have been a character rarely encountered in life or in art: the female equivalent of a rogue."

Lovell penned the biography after meeting Markham in 1986 and caring for the aging woman during the final months of her life. The author described Markham as "highly intelligent and totally single-minded" in an interview with London *Times* reviewer Sally Brompton, and added that Markham was "the most important person I've ever met in my life." *New York Times Book Review* contributor Diane Ackerman observed that *Straight on Till Morning* "is the story of a phenomenal life told convinc-

ingly by someone fascinated by her subject. . . . every page is filled with revelations, gossip and fascinating details about Markham and the people she knew." Ackerman further commented that "Lovell's superbly researched biography is likely to be definitive."

Lovell followed *Straight on Till Morning* with *The Sound of Wings: The Life of Amelia Earhart.* The biography recounts the exploits of Earhart, the aviator who gained fame by becoming the first woman to complete a solo flight across the Atlantic Ocean in 1932. Earhart's unexplained disappearance while flying over the Pacific in 1937 has long been a source of mystery, but as Lovell told *CA,* *The Sound of Wings* is "*not* a theory on her disappearance." The book is, instead, a biography that follows Earhart from her quiet childhood to her years of celebrity in the 1930s. Rhoda Koenig described the story of Earhart's life as "extraordinary," in her *New York* review, and she declared that Lovell writes about Earhart with "expertise and understanding." Similarly, *New York Times Book Review* contributor David M. Kennedy noted that Earhart's "life and death were the stuff of tragedy" and reported that Lovell manages to "vividly evoke that tragic aspect." *The Sound of Wings,* the critic added, provides "fascinating detail both on Earhart's relationship with her husband . . . and on technical aspects of her final flight."

Lovell is also the author of *Cast No Shadow: The Life of the American Spy Who Changed the Course of World War II,* which was published in 1992. *Cast No Shadow* chronicles the life of Amy Elizabeth Thorpe Pack, who spied for the Allies during World War II, often getting privileged information by seducing enemy officers. The American wife of a British diplomat, Pack was able to produce Italian and French Vichy code books for the Allies. Brooke Kroeger, reviewing *Cast No Shadow* in the *New York Times Book Review,* commended Lovell's "fast-paced narrative" and vivid descriptions.

Lovell told *CA:* "Writing a biography is writing history. One is therefore obliged to stick ruthlessly to the facts, so it is not surprising that two-thirds of my work on any book consists of research. If I find a piece of information that I cannot substantiate elsewhere—hearsay, for example—I will only use it if it seems absolutely vital to the story and in those cases I quote that source and stress that I have been unable to substantiate it. My books contain thousands of facts relating to my subjects and the times in which they lived, and I receive hundreds of letters from readers, but I get very few letters suggesting corrections, though I do get offered additional information for which I am always grateful. I enjoy writing about adventurous women, especially those who managed to break out of the conventional mold allotted to them, before women enjoyed today's freedoms."

BIOGRAPHICAL/CRITICAL SOURCES:

PERIODICALS

Los Angeles Times Book Review, October 4, 1987, pp. 3, 12.

New York, December 4, 1989.

New York Times, August 15, 1987.

New York Times Book Review, August 23, 1987, p. 1; November 26, 1989, pp. 1, 28-29; June 21, 1992, p. 16.

Time, October 5, 1987.

Times (London), July 15, 1987.

Tribune Books (Chicago), September 27, 1987, p. 6; December 10, 1989, p. 1.

Washington Post Book World, August 30, 1987, p. 3; June 26, 1988, p. 12.

* * *

LOWENTHAL, Leo   1900-1993

OBITUARY NOTICE—See index for *CA* sketch: Born November 3, 1900, in Frankfurt, Germany; died of pneumonia, January 21, 1993, in Berkeley, CA. Sociologist, literary theorist, educator, and author. Lowenthal worked as a researcher at the Institute of Social Research and as director of research for Voice of America, a project of the U.S. Department of State and the U.S. Information Agency, before accepting a faculty position in the sociology department at the University of California at Berkeley in 1956. During his twelve-year tenure at the university, Lowenthal focused on the role of literature in society, and he continued to lead graduate discussions on literature after his retirement in 1968. He published a number of works in his area of specialty, including *Literature and the Image of Man: Sociological Studies of the European Drama and Novel, 1600-1900, Literature, Popular Culture, and Society,* and the four-volume *Communication in Society.* In 1987 he produced a book of memoirs entitled *An Unmastered Past: Autobiographical Reflections.*

OBITUARIES AND OTHER SOURCES:

BOOKS

The Writers Directory: 1992-1994, St. James Press, 1992.

PERIODICALS

New York Times, January 25, 1993, p. B9.

* * *

LUBOW, Arthur   1952-

PERSONAL: Born September 18, 1952, in New York, NY; son of Harold (an accountant) and Yetta (a schoolteacher; maiden name, Gottlieb) Lubow. *Education:* Harvard University, A.B., 1974; attended Cambridge University, 1974-75.

ADDRESSES: Home—New York, NY. *Office—New Yorker,* 20 West Forty-third St., New York, NY 10036. *Agent*—Peter Matson, Sterling Lord Literistic, Inc., One Madison Ave., New York, NY 10010.

CAREER: People, New York City, writer, 1979-84; *Vanity Fair,* New York City, writer, 1987-88, contributing editor, 1991-92; *New Yorker,* New York City, writer, 1992—.

WRITINGS:

The Reporter Who Would Be King, Scribner, 1992.

* * *

LUNG, Chang
See RIGNEY, James Oliver, Jr.

* * *

LYFORD, Joseph Philip   1918-1992

OBITUARY NOTICE—See index for *CA* sketch: Born August 4, 1918, in Chicago, IL; died December 2, 1992, in Orinda, CA (one source says Rheem, CA). Educator, journalist, and author. Considered a pioneer in the application of sociological theories to the reporting of urban affairs, Lyford worked as a journalist for several organizations from the late 1930s to the early 1950s, including the *Boston Post* and the International News Service. He also worked as press secretary to Connecticut governor Chester Bowles and served as executive secretary to U.S. Senator William Benton; aspiring to political office himself, Lyford made unsuccessful bids for a U.S. House of Representatives seat in 1952 and 1954. He received national acclaim in the 1960s for his journalistic portraits of small town and urban life in the books *The Talk in Vandalia* and *The Airtight Cage.* Lyford was awarded a Sidney Hillman Foundation Award for *The Airtight Cage* in 1967. He continued his interest in urban affairs as a professor of journalism at the University of California from 1966 to 1983. Lyford was also the author of 1981's *The Berkeley Archipelago.*

OBITUARIES AND OTHER SOURCES:

BOOKS

Lyford, Joseph Philip, *The Airtight Cage,* Harper, 1966.

Who's Who in Writers, Editors, and Poets, 1989-1990, December Press, 1989, p. 323.

PERIODICALS

Chicago Tribune, December 5, 1992, section 2, p. 19; December 6, 1992, section 2, p. 8.
Los Angeles Times, December 5, 1992, p. A26.
New York Times, December 4, 1992, p. D19.

*　　*　　*

LYON, Bentley   1929-

PERSONAL: Born September 28, 1929, in Dayton, OH; son of Charles B. and Elizabeth (a teacher and Navy payroll clerk; maiden name, Savage) Lyon; married Mary Ann Hayes, 1956 (died February 20, 1970); married Elizabeth J. (a sculptor), August 23, 1971; stepchildren: three. *Education:* University of California, Berkeley, B.S., 1952. *Politics:* "Registered Democrat since 1951; vote according to candidates and stands on issues." *Religion:* None. *Avocational interests:* Dixieland jazz, race-walking.

ADDRESSES: Home—3416 El Toboso Dr. N.W., Albuquerque, NM 87104. *Agent*—Jack N. Albert, New York, NY; Destiny Marquez, California.

CAREER: U.S. Forest Service, worked in prevention and control of forest fires, seasonally, 1947-52, full time, 1952-85; writer. Involved in neighborhood watch program, 1986—. *Military service:* U.S. Marine Corps, 1952-54, served in Korea; became first lieutenant.

MEMBER: Rio Grande Jazz Society, New Mexico Racewalkers.

AWARDS, HONORS: Citation for Outstanding Service in Fire Management, U.S. Forest Service and National Association of State Foresters, 1984.

WRITINGS:

(Editor, compiler) *Wildland Fire Management Terminology,* FAO Rome, 1985.

White Crow, St. Martin's, 1989.
Summer Stalk, St. Martin's, 1992.

Wildland Fire Management Terminology has also been published in four other languages.

WORK IN PROGRESS: A book tentatively titled, *Murder at the Jazz Band Ball,* completion expected in 1994.

SIDELIGHTS: Bentley Lyon told *CA:* "I consider myself first a forester (by education and vocation), then a musician (by the need for that style of self-expression), then an aging athlete. I was the first wrestler from a school west of the Rockies to win an individual National Collegiate Athletic Association championship. I later became a runner and, finally, a race-walker. Novels came along after these things, perhaps as a latent objection to having to write reports and letters according to the Government Style Manual.

"The taxpayers send me money every month, so I don't have to write to eat. But I do owe my readers the truth as I see it, if only through fiction. My first two novels make use of my professional background: 'forestry thrillers,' I tell my friends jokingly, the term being an apparent oxymoron. My fourth book, tentatively titled *Murder at the Jazz Band Ball,* does the same vis-a-vis my interest in music. In each case it's a chance to take readers backstage for a journey they probably missed during their own lives.

"Aside from making money and becoming famous by writing, I suppose most fiction writers are motivated by the desire to entertain, educate, and perhaps influence their readers. But I'm certain I'm not the first writer to discover that the art has its greatest impact on the writer himself. A writer soon finds himself seeing, smelling, hearing, thinking more acutely, and more carefully weighing human motivation. Full perception and comprehension of reality, of course, can never be attained. That is why the perfect novel can never be written."

M

MacARTHUR, John R. 1956-

PERSONAL: Born June 4, 1956, in New York, NY; son of John Roderick MacArthur and Christiane Jacqueline (L'Etandart) MacArthur; married Renee Khatami; children: Sophie. *Education:* Columbia University, B.A., 1978.

ADDRESSES: Home—151 Central Park West, New York, NY 10023. *Office*—666 Broadway, New York, NY 10012. *Agent*—Denise Shannon, Georges Borchardt, Inc., 136 E. 57th St., New York, NY 10022.

CAREER: Wall Street Journal, New York City, reporter, 1977; *Washington Star,* Washington, DC, reporter, 1978; *Bergen Record,* reporter, 1978-79; *Chicago Sun-Times,* Chicago, IL, reporter, 1979-82; United Press International, assistant foreign editor, 1982; Harper's Magazine Foundation, New York City, president and publisher of *Harper's,* 1983—. Cofounder of the Article 19 International Centre on Censorship, London, 1986; director of the Committee to Protect Journalists, the J. Roderick MacArthur Foundation, and the Death Penalty Information Center; fellow at the New York Institute for the Humanities.

WRITINGS:

Second Front: Censorship and Propaganda in the Gulf War, Hill & Wang, 1992.

Contributor of articles to several newspapers and magazines, including *New York Times, Wall Street Journal,* Toronto *Globe and Mail, Los Angeles Times, Progressive,* and *Washington Journalism Review.*

SIDELIGHTS: Since becoming publisher of *Harper's* in 1983, John R. MacArthur has been active in the fight against censorship in the United States and around the world. He initiated and helped organize the PEN/Article 19/Authors Guild reading and rally for Salman Rushdie (author of the controversial book *The Satanic Verses*) in New York in February 1989.

*   *   *

MACHOR, James L(awrence) 1950-

PERSONAL: Born October 13, 1950, in Cleveland, OH; son of Lawrence Joseph (a carton-die maker) and Helen (a homemaker; maiden name, Soltis) Machor; married, wife's name Nancy Ann (a teacher), May 13, 1972; children: Travis James. *Education:* Ohio University, B.A., 1972; University of Idaho, M.A., 1974; University of Illinois, Ph.D., 1980. *Politics:* Independent. *Religion:* Agnostic.

ADDRESSES: Home—1507 Leavenworth St., Manhattan, KS 66502. *Office*—Department of English, Denison Hall, Kansas State University, Manhattan, KS 66506.

CAREER: Ohio State University at Lima, assistant professor, 1980-86, associate professor of English, 1986-90; Kansas State University, Manhattan, associate professor of English, 1990—.

MEMBER: Modern Language Association of America, American Studies Association, American Literature Association, Western Literature Association.

AWARDS, HONORS: Fellow of National Endowment for the Humanities, 1986; Fulbright fellow at University of Brussels, 1991.

WRITINGS:

Pastoral Cities: Urban Ideals and the Symbolic Landscape of America, University of Wisconsin Press, 1987.

(Editor and contributor) *Readers in History: Nineteenth-Century American Literature and the Contexts of Response*, Johns Hopkins University Press, 1993.

Contributor of articles and reviews to periodicals. Associate editor, *Studies in the Novel*, 1992-93.

WORK IN PROGRESS: Informed Reading and the Interpretive Contexts of American Fiction (tentative title).

SIDELIGHTS: James L. Machor told *CA:* "As is the case for many authors, my interest in writing has developed from my experiences. *Pastoral Cities* resulted from my having grown up in a large city and from my continued fascination with urban life, with its meaning and with the problems it presents in defining who we are, both individually and collectively. I've often been uneasy with 'definitive' interpretations, with the authority of official responses—thus, my current work in the relation between interpretive practices and American fiction, particularly in the nineteenth century when ways of reading were in place that are quite 'foreign' to us today. One could say, in fact, that forms of interpretation, whether of texts or of places, have always been at the center of my interests."

*   *   *

MACOUREK, Milos 1926-

PERSONAL: Born December 2, 1926, in Kromeriz, Czechoslovakia; son of Judr Alois Macourek (a notary) and Frantiska Macourkova; married Jirina Ruzickova (a music professor), September, 1947; children: Martin, Marek. *Politics:* "Without." *Religion:* "Without." *Avocational interests:* Music, the art of painting.

ADDRESSES: Home—14700 Prague 4, Podolska 1490, Czechoslovakia. *Agent*—Divadelni A Literarni Agentura (DILIA), 120 00 Prague 2, Polska 1, Czechoslovakia.

CAREER: Film Studio Barrandov, Prague, Czechoslovakia, dramaturgist and scenarist, 1960; full-time writer, 1980—. Worked variously as a subsidiary worker, 1946, an editor at a publishing company, 1947, a secretary for a trade union headquarters, 1950, and a lecturer in a trade union school, 1953. Director, with Adolf Born and Jaroslav Doubrava, of *Imago*, 1985, *Mindrak,* and others. *Military service:* Served in Czechoslovakia, 1948-50; administration.

MEMBER: Czechoslovak Writers Federation, Czechoslovak Dramatic Artist Federation.

AWARDS, HONORS: Mack Senett Prize (Switzerland), and Gold Star award (Terst), both 1966, for *Kdo chce zabit Jesii?;* Grand Prix (France), and Main Prize (Germany), both 1966, for *Jak si opatrit hodne dite;* Best Book Loisirs

Jeunes diploma, French Minister for the Youth, Sport, and Free Time Employment, 1980, for *Le telephone enchante,* a French translation of *Mach a Sebestova;* Grand Prix (Spain), Critics' Prize (Brazil), and prize from Terst, all 1981, for *Monstrum z galaxie Arcana;* Main Prize (Canada), 1982, Grand Prix (Spain), 1982, and Grand Prix (Finland), 1983, all for *Mindrak;* recipient of other awards.

WRITINGS:

SCREENPLAYS

(And director with Stanislav Latal) *Jak si opatrit hodne dite* (animated cartoon; title means "How to Provide Oneself with a Good Child"), Studio Jiriho Trnky (Prague), 1966.

Kdo chce zabit Jesii? (comedy; title means "Who Wants to Kill Jessie?"), directed by Vaclav Vorlicek, Film Studio Barrandov (Prague), 1966.

(With Oldrich Lipsky) *Stastny konec* (comedy/drama; based on a story by Macourek; title means "Happy End"), directed by Lipsky, Film Studio Barrandov/ Continental Distributing, 1968.

Pane, vy jste vdova (comedy; title means "Sir, You Are a Widow"), directed by Vaclav Vorlicek, Film Studio Barrandov, 1971.

Bourlive vino (comedy; title means "Wild Wine"), directed by Vaclav Vorlicek, Film Studio Barrandov, 1975, published in Russian as *Burljasce vino,* Iskustvo (Moscow), 1982.

(And director with Adolf Born and Jaroslav Doubrava) *Mindrak* (animated cartoon; title means "A Complex of Inferiority"), Bratri v triku (Prague), 1981.

Monstrum z galaxie Arcana (comedy; title means "A Monster from the Galaxy of Arcana"), directed by Dusan Vukotic, Film Studio Barrandov/Zagreb (Yugoslavia), 1981.

Also author of other screenplays.

SCREENPLAYS; FOR CHILDREN

Arabela (thirteen-part television serial), directed by Vaclav Vorlicek, Czechoslovak Television (Prague) and Westdeutscher Rundfunk (Cologne), 1981.

(Written and directed with Adolf Born and Jaroslav Doubrava) *Mach a Sebestova* (thirteen-part animated serial; title means "Mach and Sebestova"), Bratri v triku, 1983.

Letajici Ferdinand (six-part television serial; title means "The Flying Ferdinand"), directed by Vaclav Vorlicek, Czechoslovak Television (Prague) and Westdeutscher Rundfunk (Cologne), 1984.

(Written and directed with Adolf Born and Jaroslav Doubrava) *Mach a Sebestova, K Tabuli!* (collection of seven *Mach a Sebestova* shorts and a new episode; title means "Mach and Sebestova, Come to the Blackboard Please!"), Kratky Film/Bratri v triku, 1985.

Bambinot (six-part television serial), directed by Jaroslav Dudek, Czechoslovak Television (Prague) and Westdeutscher Rundfunk (Cologne), 1984.

Krecek v nocni kosili (six-part television serial; title means "Hamster in a Nightgown"), directed by Vaclav Vorlicek, Czechoslovak Television (Prague) and Westdeutscher Rundfunk (Cologne), 1987.

(Written and directed with Adolf Born and Jaroslav Doubrava) *Zofka* (thirteen-part animated television serial; title means "Sophia"), Bratri v triku, 1987.

OTHER; FOR CHILDREN

Jednicky ma papousek (play; title means "The Parrot Has Got the Best Marks"), produced at Na Zabradli, Prague, 1959.

Jakub a dve ste dedecku (fairy tale; title means "Jacob and Two Hundred Grandfathers"), illustrated by Bohumil Habart, Statni nakl. detske knihy (Prague), 1963.

Mravenecnik v pocetnici (fairy tale; title means "An Anteater in an Arithmetic Book"), illustrated by Miroslav Stepanek, Statni nakl. detske knihy, 1966.

Pohadky (consists of *Jakub a dve ste dedecku* and *Mravenecnik v pocetnici;* title means "Fairy Tales"), illustrated by Vaclav Sivko, Mlada fronta, 1971, revised edition, illustrated by Adolf Born, Albatros (Prague), 1984, translation by Marie Burg published as *Curious Tales,* Oxford University Press, 1980.

Svete, div se! (poetry; title means "Hear, Oh Hear!"), illustrated by Adolf Born, Albatros, 1974.

Mach a Sebestova (fairy tale; title means "Mach and Sebestova"), illustrated by Adolph Born, Albatros, 1982, translation by Dagmas Herrmann published as *Max and Sally and the Phenomenal Phone,* Wellington Publishing, 1989.

Maerchenbraut (novel; based on a television serial; title means "Fairy Tale Bride"), Verlagsgesellschaft Schulfernsehen (Cologne), 1984.

Der fliegende Ferdinand (novel; based on a television serial; title means "The Flying Ferdinand"), Verlagsgesellschaft Schulfernsehen, 1984.

Mach a Sebestova has been translated into French, German, Japanese, and Dutch.

OTHER

Clovek by neveril svym ocim (poetry; title means "One Would Not Believe One's Eyes"), Ceskoslovensky spisovatel (Prague), 1958.

Zivocichopis (fable; title means "Zoology"), Ceskoslovensky spisovatel, 1962.

Zirafa nebo tulipan? (title means "A Giraffe or a Tulip?"), illustrated by Adolf Hoffmeister, Mlada fronta (Prague), 1964.

Hra na Zuzanku (play; title means "Let Us Play a Little Susan"), produced at Na Zabradli, Prague, 1967.

Do rise Inku (travel guide; title means "To the Realm of Incas"), photographs by Jiri Havel, Pressfoto (Prague), 1976.

Slovnik ceskych spisovatelu (title means "Encyclopedia of Czech Writers"), Ceskoslovensky spisovatel, 1986.

Filmove profily (title means "Film Profiles"), CS Filmovy ustav (Prague), 1986.

Laska a delove koule (story and fable; title means "Love and the Cannonballs"), Ceskoslovensky spisovatel, 1989.

Also author of other feature films, animated films, and television serials. *Hra na Zuzanku* has been translated into German and Spanish. Macourek's other works have been translated into French, German, Hungarian, Polish, Serbo-Croatian, Slovak, English, Russian, Japanese, Dutch, Spanish, Lithuanian, and Estonian.

WORK IN PROGRESS: Arabela se vraci (twenty-six part television serial; title means "Arabella Is Coming Back"), directed by Vaclav Vorlicek, Czechoslovak Television (Prague), and Westdeutscher Rundfunk (Cologne); *Mach a Sebestova na prazdninach* (fairy tale; title means "Mach and Sebestova on Holidays"), illustrated by Adolf Born.

SIDELIGHTS: Milos Macourek told *CA:* "Even when I am writing mostly for adults, I feel like a storyteller. The first step in my productions is fantasy and humor—sometimes very black. I like films in high spirits, animated, especially in which my fantasy has the highest upsurge and with the help of picture, movement, and music to amplify its effect."

BIOGRAPHICAL/CRITICAL SOURCES:

PERIODICALS

Times Educational Supplement, October 3, 1980, p. 25.

*　　　*　　　*

MAHER, Mary 1940-

PERSONAL: Born November 9, 1940, in Chicago, IL; daughter of James (an attorney) and Bonnie (a homemaker; maiden name, Burns) Maher; married Des Geraghty, January, 1969 (separated, 1979); children: Maeve, Nora. *Education:* Attended Convent of the Sacred Heart, 1954-58; attended Barat College, 1958-62. *Politics:* "A socialist and feminist."

ADDRESSES: Home—28 Annavilla, Dublin 6, Ireland. *Office*—Irish Times Ltd., Dublin 2, Ireland. *Agent*—

Christine Green, 2 Barbon Close, Great Ormond St., London WC1, England.

CAREER: Chicago Tribune, Chicago, IL, feature writer, 1962-65; *Irish Times,* Dublin, Ireland, worked variously as feature writer, reporter, assistant news editor, women's editor, and assistant chief sub-editor, 1965—; homemaker.

WRITINGS:

The Devil's Card, St. Martin's, 1992.

WORK IN PROGRESS: Working on a novel on the women's movement.

SIDELIGHTS: Mary Maher told *CA:* "I grew up in the very secure world of Irish Chicago and was a product of Catholic schools and green dye in the river every March 17. It is not a legacy everyone escapes from lightly, although not everyone feels a strong need to return to the source of all identity for further inspection. I did feel that need. But even more urgently, I felt the need to get something unusual in the way of journalistic experience that might release me from the genteel ghetto of the women's pages, which is where reporters of the wrong sex were consigned in the 1960s. I left the *Chicago Tribune* in November 1965 for Ireland and a three-month probationary position on the *Irish Times* in Dublin.

"I never went back, and I am still with the *Irish Times.* Over the intervening years, as this small, eccentric newspaper and country have gone through immense social change, I settled down, had children, and served my time as a reporter, feature writer, columnist, assistant news editor, and copy editor.

"I have written a great deal, in magazine features and in short stories, on the areas I have been most closely involved in—civil rights, trade unions, the women's liberation movement, and the links between Ireland and America. My first novel, *The Devil's Card,* is very much in the last category and is based on a true story of nineteenth-century Chicago that remains a tragic mystery."

*　　*　　*

MAL
See HANCOCK, Malcolm

*　　*　　*

MALANOWSKI, Jamie 1953-

PERSONAL: Born June 15, 1953, in Baltimore, MD; son of Clemens S. (a machinist) and Irene Helen (a homemaker; maiden name, Glodek) Malanowski; married Vir-

ginia M. Jackson (a midwife), May 24, 1975; children: Molly, Cara. *Education:* La Salle College, B.A., 1975; University of Pennsylvania, M.A., 1977.

ADDRESSES: Home—889 Pleasantville Rd., Briarcliff, NY 10510. *Office*—*Spy,* 5 Union Sq. W., New York, NY 10003.

CAREER: Spy, New York City, national editor, 1986—.

WRITINGS:

(With Susan Morrison) *Spy High,* Doubleday, 1991. *Mr. Stupid Goes to Washington,* Birch Lane Press, 1992.

Author of the play *This Happy, Happy Land,* 1993.

*　　*　　*

MANAKA, Matsemela 1956-

PERSONAL: Born, June 20, 1956, in Alexandra Township, South Africa; son of Gilbert and Nelly Manaka; married in 1984; wife's name, Nomsa; children: Maakomela, Mthutezeli.

ADDRESSES: Home—Soweto, South Africa. *Office*—Ekhaya Soweto Museum, 973 Phase 3, Diepkloof 1864, Soweto, South Africa. *Agent*—c/o PEN, 568 Broadway, 4th floor, New York, NY 10012.

CAREER: Writer, artist, director, producer, and performer. Worked as a teacher at Madibane High School, Ithuteng Commercial College, Madibane Adult Education, Masisizane Community College for Secretarial Practice; Soyikwa Institute of African Theatre, Soweto, South Africa, founder and teacher; Funda Arts Centre, Soweto, acting and directing teacher. Director of stage productions, including *Shaka: An Excerpt from Ogun Abibman,* written by Wole Soyinka, 1980, *Dark Voices,* written by Zakes Mda, 1984, *Buwa,* written by Caiphus Semenya, 1986-88, and *Nkosi: The Healing Song,* written by Mothobi Mutloatse, 1992; producer of stage productions, including *eGoli* and *Blues Afrika Cafe.* Artwork presented in numerous exhibitions in South Africa and Europe, 1978-1992, including shows at Commonwealth Institute, London, England, 1981, Alliance Francaise, Cape Town, South Africa, 1984, and Berman Gallery, Johannesburg, South Africa, 1992. Ekhaya Soweto Neighborhood Museum, Soweto, founder and curator. Affiliated with Raven Press.

AWARDS, HONORS: Freedom-to-Write Award, PEN, 1987; Edinburgh Fringe First Award for productions of *Pula* and *Imbumba.*

WRITINGS:

PLAYS

(Coauthor with members of Creative Youth Association) *The Horn,* produced in South Africa, 1977.

eGoli (title means "City of Gold"), produced in South Africa, 1978.

Blues Afrika, produced in West Germany, 1980.

Pula (title means "Rain"), produced in South Africa, 1982, produced in London, 1984.

Imbumba, produced in London, 1984.

Children of Asazi (one-act), produced Off-Broadway, 1986.

(And director) *Domba, the Last Dance,* produced in South Africa, 1986.

(With Motsumi Makhene and Peter Boroko) *Goree* (musical; book by Manaka; music by Manaka, Makhene, and Boroko), produced in New York City, 1989.

Also author and director of *Vuka,* 1981, *Toro the African Dream,* 1987, *Blues Afrika Cafe,* 1990, *Ekhaya Museum of Soweto,* 1991, and *Yamina,* 1993.

OTHER

Coauthor, with Ratshaka Ratshitanga, Mark Newman, and Eddie Wes, of the film screenplay *Two Rivers;* author of the screenplay *Kiba: The Beat Between.* Editor of *Staffrider,* 1979-82.

SIDELIGHTS: Matsemela Manaka is a leading black playwright in South Africa. Long associated with the Soyikwa Institute of African Theatre in Soweto, Manaka is known for his Afrocentric—and sometimes controversial—works, which he has successfully presented at home despite South Africa's racist apartheid policy. Manaka began as a playwright in the late 1970s with such productions as *The Horn, Imbumba,* and *eGoli* (which means "City of Gold," a reference to Johannesburg). He discussed his creative philosophy in an interview with T. Philemon Wakashe in *Drama Review:* "Serious theatre in South Africa has to have an effect on black people. It has to stop simply describing. People say I'm changing, that my plays are no longer as radical as before. No, I say, my plays are now focusing on human experience. . . . I am examining the conflict of the South African experience, a human experience that is not limited to me as a black South African."

In 1984 the Soyikwa company presented *Imbumba* with another Manaka play, *Pula* (the title means "Rain"), as a double bill in London. *Imbumba* concerns life on a prison farm. *Pula* uses song, dance, and mime to tell the story of a young black and his experiences in Johannesburg. Anthony Masters, writing in the London *Times,* found himself in "awe at the pain and anger" expressed by the performers in the production.

Manaka's *Children of Asazi* was presented in New York City in 1986 as part of a festival called "Woza Africa!" (which means "Arise Africa!"). Like many of Manaka's plays, *Children of Asazi* incorporates chanting and other ethnic devices. This play, a love story set against the South African government's destruction of a black community, is written, according to the *New York Times*'s Mel Gussow, "with a kind of homely poetry." Gussow found the festival production was "performed with a forthright sincerity."

Among Manaka's other plays produced in the United States is *Goree,* which was presented in New York City in 1989. This work, a musical, concerns a girl who embarks to find a women renowned as Africa's finest singer and dancer. When the girl becomes stranded on Goree, an island, she befriends a woman who, in turn, teaches her to sing and dance. *New York Times* reviewer Wilborn Hampton found the work juvenile but "entertaining."

Manaka told *CA:* "For me, theatre as a totality of the arts has become a way of life. It is a ritual without which my life would be empty. It is a ritual from which we derive the comfort and hope that one day the wounds of our people will be healed. As a writer, I see myself as a custodian of the past for the future. We are historians, educators, and liberators. As the saying goes—'a book is a universe.' We are engaged in the universal dialogue to bring an end to human suffering and let peace prevail."

BIOGRAPHICAL/CRITICAL SOURCES:

PERIODICALS

Drama Review, winter, 1986, pp. 48-50.
New York Times, August 31, 1986; September 26, 1986; October 5, 1986.
Times (London), March 15, 1984; September 24, 1989.

*   *   *

MANDEL, Charlotte 1925-

PERSONAL: Born April 1, 1925, in New York, NY; daughter of Louis (a postal worker) and Rose (a homemaker; maiden name, Steckel) Lifschutz; married Irwin D. Mandel (a dental researcher and professor), April 1, 1944; children: Carol, Nora, Richard. *Education:* Brooklyn College (now of the City University of New York), B.A., 1944; Montclair State College, M.A., 1977.

ADDRESSES: Home—Cedar Grove, NJ. *Office*—c/o Saturday Press, Inc., P.O. Box 884, Upper Montclair, NJ 07043.

CAREER: Saturday Press, Inc., Upper Montclair, NJ, editor, 1981—. Adult School of Montclair, teacher of poetry courses and workshops; gives public readings.

MEMBER: International League for Peace and Freedom (president of Essex County branch, 1964-66), International PEN, National Book Critics Circle, Poetry Society of America, Modern Language Association of America, Associated Writing Programs.

AWARDS, HONORS: Bernice Kavinoky Isaacson Poetry Award, New School for Social Research, 1972; winner of five competitions, William Carlos Williams Poetry Center, 1972-76; fellowships from Millay Colony, 1978, New Jersey State Council on the Arts, 1980 and 1983, and Virginia Center for the Creative Arts, 1980 and 1983; Yaddo fellow, 1985, 1986, 1989, 1990, and 1992; winner of Open Voices Competition, Writer's Voice, 1986; fellow at Villa Montalvo Center for the Arts, 1988; Women of Achievement Award, New Jersey Business and Professional Women, 1988; fellow of Geraldine R. Dodge Foundation at Yaddo, 1989.

WRITINGS:

(Editor) David de Leeuw, *I Could See the Rainbow on My Pillow: Poems in Conversation,* Lawton Press, 1980.
A Disc of Clear Water (poems), Saturday Press, 1981.
(Editor with Maxine Silverman) *Saturday's Women: The Eileen W. Barnes Award Anthology,* Saturday Press, 1982.
Doll (poem), Salt-Works Press, 1986.
The Life of Mary (poem-novella; performed in a staged reading in New York City, at Bill Bace Gallery, 1990), foreword by Sandra M. Gilbert, Saturday Press, 1988.
Keeping Him Alive (poems), Silver Apples Press, 1990.
The Marriages of Jacob (poem-novella), Micah, 1991.

Work represented in anthologies; contributor of articles, poems, stories, and reviews to periodicals, including *Iowa Review, Greenfield Review, Short Fiction by Women, Women's Studies, Prairie Schooner,* and *Stone Country.* Mandel has recorded the audio tape *The Life of Mary,* with music by David Hauer, Saturday Press, 1993.

WORK IN PROGRESS: A novella set in Brooklyn during World War II; a long, autobiographical poem "using cinematic time shifts"; research on newspapers and photography of the 1930s and 1940s.

SIDELIGHTS: Charlotte Mandel told *CA:* "Each new poem on the page astonishes me as a voice to which I must listen. A story or essay will live apart, independent of my nurture. For me, the challenge then begins afresh—to articulate the experience of muteness. Until midlife, my working identity was entirely that of wife-mother-daughter: a role attached to the needs of others. I still value those parts of my identity, but I incorporate them into my work as poet, writer, editor, and independent scholar. I am the founding editor of the Eileen W. Barnes Award, sponsored by Saturday Press to publish first books by women poets over forty."

Mandel continued: "Metaphor can be a magical key to discovery and communication, or a word game of hide and seek. A poem must be uncompromisingly honest, or else it simply will not work." In a review of Mandel's first collection, *A Disc of Clear Water, New Directions for Women* contributor Anne Blackford wrote that Mandel's poems "demand energy from the reader, the unwinding of bandages or shrouds . . . from our eyes. We begin to see and hear language that is pared down and not easy, but always alive."

"In two poem-novellas, *The Life of Mary* and *The Marriages of Jacob,* I wanted to give voice to biblical women sealed into attitudes projected upon them; their stories control present-day lives," Mandel told *CA.* In the foreword to *The Life of Mary,* Sandra M. Gilbert stated that the book "juxtaposes the story of the conception, pregnancy, and maternity that change the life of a contemporary Mary with a set of reflections on the motherhood of the biblical Mary. . . . Mandel's long poem also mediates beautifully between . . . the 'great time' in which divine, mythic events occur . . . and the ongoing historical time in which we all live."

BIOGRAPHICAL/CRITICAL SOURCES:

BOOKS

Mandel, Charlotte, *The Life of Mary,* foreword by Sandra M. Gilbert, Saturday Press, 1988.

PERIODICALS

Choice, June, 1992.
New Directions for Women, January/February, 1982.

*   *   *

MANKIEWICZ, Joseph L(eo) 1909-1993

OBITUARY NOTICE—See index for *CA* sketch: Born February 11, 1909, in Wilkes-Barre, PA; died of heart failure, February 5, 1993, in Mount Kisco, NY. Producer, director, and screenwriter. Academy Award-winner Mankiewicz was well-known for his writing and directing talents in films such as *The Keys of the Kingdom Cleopatra,* and *The Barefoot Contessa.* He began his career in the film industry writing subtitles for silent foreign films. Hired by the Paramount studio in 1929, he gradually moved from writing subtitles to dialogue to crafting entire screenplays, including, with others, *Skippy* and *This Reckless Age.* Mankiewicz's producing debut came in 1936 with *Fury* and was followed by *The Philadelphia Story* and *Woman of the Year.* Eventually, Mankiewicz began directing, and such films as *Dragonwyck* and *The Ghost and Mrs. Muir* received his touch. In the ensuing years, Mankiewicz was involved with other successful films, writing and directing 1949's *A Letter to Three Wives* and *All about Eve* in 1950; he received the Academy Awards for best direction and best screenplay for both films. His last film was *Sleuth* in 1972. Quoted in the *New York Times*, Mankiewicz summarized his career, stating, "I've lived without caring what anybody thought of me. I followed very few of the rules. I think I've written some good screenplays, gotten some good performances and made some good movies."

OBITUARIES AND OTHER SOURCES:

BOOKS

Dictionary of Literary Biography, Volume 44: *American Screenwriters, Second Series*, Gale, 1986.
Who's Who, 144th edition, St. Martin's, 1992.

PERIODICALS

Chicago Tribune, February 7, 1993, sec. 2, p. 6.
Los Angeles Times, February 6, 1993, p. A24.
New York Times, February 6, 1993, p. P10.
Times (London), February 8, 1993, p. 17.
Washington Post, February 6, 1993, p. B4.

*   *   *

MANN, Arthur   1922-1993

OBITUARY NOTICE—See index for *CA* sketch: Born January 3, 1922, in Brooklyn, NY; died February 7, 1993, in Chicago, IL. Historian, educator, and author. A noted historian, Mann was the author of a number of books on American politics, including his highly praised volumes on New York mayor Fiorello La Guardia. Mann's *La Guardia: A Fighter against His Times, 1882-1933* and *La Guardia Comes to Power: 1933* were applauded by reviewers for their thorough scholarship and straightforward prose. The author's academic career spanned more than forty years and included positions at the Massachusetts Institute of Technology, Smith College, and the University of Chicago, where he became Preston and Sterling Morton Professor of History in 1971. Other books by Mann include *Yankee Reformers in the Urban Age, History and the Role of the City in American Life,* and *The One and the Many: Reflections on the American Identity.*

OBITUARIES AND OTHER SOURCES:

BOOKS

Who's Who in the World, 11th edition, Marquis, 1991, p. 681.

PERIODICALS

New York Times, February 9, 1993, p. B6.

MANN, Robert   1958-

PERSONAL: Born September 2, 1958, in Beaumont, TX; son of Robert T. (a minister) and Charlene Wellhausen Mann; married Cynthia Horaist (a small-business owner), December 18, 1992. *Education:* Northeast Louisiana University, B.A., 1981. *Politics:* Democrat. *Religion:* Disciples of Christ.

ADDRESSES: Home—4336 Fleet Dr., Baton Rouge, LA 70809. *Agent*—Clyde Taylor, Curtis Brown Ltd., 10 Astor Place, New York, NY 10003.

CAREER: Monroe News-Star, Monroe, LA, reporter, 1981-83; *Shreveport Journal*, Shreveport, LA, political writer, 1983-85; U.S. Senator Russell Long, Washington, DC, press secretary, 1985-87; U.S. Senator John Breaux, Washington, DC, press secretary, 1987—. Press secretary for U.S. Senator J. Bennett Johnston's 1990 reelection campaign.

MEMBER: U.S. Senate Press Secretaries Association (president, 1991-92).

AWARDS, HONORS: Louisiana-Mississippi Associated Press Award, best general feature, c. 1983.

WRITINGS:

Legacy to Power: Senator Russell Long of Louisiana, Paragon House, 1992.

SIDELIGHTS: A press secretary for U.S. Senator Russell Long from 1985 to 1987, Robert Mann combined his political and personal interests to write 1992's *Legacy to Power: Senator Russell Long of Louisiana.* An authorized biography, the book contains research into the highlights, as well as the darker areas, of the life and career of Long, the son of powerful Louisiana governor Huey Long. Unlike his father, who was known for his ruthless political tactics, Russell Long achieved success during his nearly forty-year tenure on Capitol Hill with his ability to build friendly alliances and with his plain-speaking manner. He eventually became the most powerful member of the Senate, serving as chair of the Finance Committee and defending such causes as Social Security and Medicaid. Reviewers noted that although Mann's work was subject to the approval of Long, the volume does include some discussion of the senator's more unappealing characteristics. While considered a moderate overall, Long opposed several issues which threatened the status quo, including civil rights and energy and tax reform. *Legacy to Power* also addresses Long's struggle with alcoholism, although Mann acknowledged in his book that several passages dealing with this subject were deleted due to Long's disapproval.

Reviewers were generally pleased with Mann's depiction of Long. *Monroe News-Star* writer Bodie McCrory stated that several prominent political figures had praised the work; he quoted former president Richard Nixon's description of *Legacy to Power* as "a fascinating portrayal of a remarkable political life." Although a *Publishers Weekly* critic complained of a lack of "meaningful analysis" in the book, a *Kirkus Reviews* contributor considered *Legacy to Power* to be "adroitly told" and "an absorbing account of one of America's great *eminences grises*." Jack Wardlaw, writing in the *New Orleans Times-Picayune,* declared that Mann's book "is a remarkably candid one, not shrinking from discussion of some of the more controversial aspects of Long's career." Acknowledging the limits imposed on Mann by his chosen genre, Wiley W. Hilburn, Jr., in the *Shreveport Times* surmised, "though this is an authorized biography, the author has produced an evenhanded, clear-eyed, often eloquent portrait of the complex Russell."

Mann told *CA:* "My professional career has always been a mixture of politics and journalism. As a reporter for two newspapers in Louisiana, I developed a keen interest in government and politics. As political writer for the *Shreveport Journal* in 1983, I traveled extensively with the two major candidates (Democrat Edwin Edwards and incumbent Republican Dave Treen) and won the Louisiana-Mississippi Associated Press Award for best general feature for my profile of Edwards. My campaign reporting attracted the attention of Senator Russell Long of Louisiana, who asked me to join his staff as press secretary in 1985. When Long retired two years later, his successor, John Breaux, appointed me press secretary, a position I still hold.

"Even though I had left journalism for politics, I never lost my appetite for writing. But the kind of writing demanded in my Senate job was never particularly challenging. It was for that reason I began to consider writing a biography—my favorite genre—about a political figure. Because no one had yet tackled Russell Long, I approached him with the idea of his cooperation on an authorized biography.

"I understood that writing an authorized biography was not the best way to debut on the literary scene, but I knew that a well-written book could help me establish the credentials to write again. My goal was to publish an authorized account of Long's life, while maintaining my objectivity as best I could. With minor exceptions, I believe I accomplished this goal, evidenced by reviews which have noted the difficult issues—Long's civil rights record and his drinking problem—discussed in the book.

"I hope to soon begin another book project, this time on the topic of the U.S. Senate during the 1950s and 1960s. With Senator Breaux's cooperation (I now hold a part-time position), I will be able to devote more of my energies to writing. For my first book, I was forced to write and conduct research at night and on weekends, a routine not conducive to a normal lifestyle. I now hope that my new routine will give me more time to write and research in a more reasonable atmosphere."

BIOGRAPHICAL/CRITICAL SOURCES:

BOOKS

Mann, Robert, *Legacy to Power: Senator Russell Long of Louisiana,* Paragon House, 1992.

PERIODICALS

Kirkus Reviews, August 15, 1992, p. 1042.
Monroe News-Star (Louisiana), December 6, 1992.
New Orleans Times-Picayune, January 6, 1993.
Publishers Weekly, August 3, 1992, p. 53.
Shreveport Times, November 8, 1992.

*   *   *

MANNING, Martin
    See SMITH, R(eginald) D(onald)

*   *   *

MARA, Barney
    See ROTH, Arthur J(oseph)

*   *   *

MARCHAM, Frederick George   1898-1992

OBITUARY NOTICE—See index for *CA* sketch: Born November 20, 1898, in Reading, England; died December 16, 1992, in Ithaca, NY. Educator, sports administrator, politician, author. Marcham, a specialist in the British Constitution, began teaching in the history department at Cornell University in 1924; during his sixty-eight year tenure there he became a full professor, served as Goldwin Smith Professor of English History, and acted as chair of the department for two terms. In addition, he was active in sports-related activities, both as a boxing coach and as the first chair of the Ivy League athletic eligibility committee. He served as mayor of Cayuga Heights, NY, from 1957 to 1988. Marcham's writings include *History of England, A Constitutional History of Modern England,* and, with Carl Stephenson, *Sources of English Constitutional History.* He was also the editor of *Louis Agassiz Fuertes and the Singular Beauty of Birds.*

OBITUARIES AND OTHER SOURCES:

BOOKS

Who's Who in America, 40th edition, Marquis, 1978.

PERIODICALS

New York Times, December 19, 1992, p. 12.

* * *

MARGOLIS, Nadia 1949-

PERSONAL: Born April 27, 1949, in Neuilly-sur-Seine, France; daughter of Morton Margolis (a college professor and artist) and Diane Seyfort-Ruegg Kensler (a homemaker); married Peter K. Marshall (a college professor), May 23, 1984. *Education:* University of New Hampshire, B.A., 1971; Stanford University, Ph.D., 1977. *Politics:* Democrat. *Religion:* Jewish. *Avocational interests:* Cycling, squash, hiking, drawing, and painting.

ADDRESSES: Home—75 Amherst Rd., Leverett, MA 01054. *Office*—Department of French and Italian, Herter Hall, University of Massachusetts, Amherst, MA 01003.

CAREER: Stanford University, Stanford, CA, lecturer, 1976-77; Wheel Power, Exeter, NH, bicycle mechanic, 1977; *Speculum,* Cambridge, MA, editorial assistant, 1977-78; Amherst College, Amherst, MA, assistant professor, 1978-85; University of Utah, Salt Lake City, UT, associate professor of French, 1985-89; writer. Illustrator and artist for textbooks and posters, 1976—; U.S. Cycling Federation, official and administrative assistant for Junior World Championships, 1978; *Christine de Pizan's Society Newsletter,* editor, 1991—; member of Bicycle Safety Committee in Amherst, MA.

MEMBER: International Courtly Literature Society, Modern Language Association, Medieval Academy of America, Societe Rencesvals.

AWARDS, HONORS: Independent scholar, National Endowment for the Humanities, 1981-82; faculty research grant, University of Utah, 1988.

WRITINGS:

(Contributor and translator) Elizabeth Petroff, editor, *Medieval Women's Visionary Literature,* Oxford University Press, 1986.
Joan of Arc in History, Literature and Film, Garland, 1990.
(Translator with Thelma Fenster) Christine de Pizan, *Book of the Duke of True Lovers,* Persea, 1991.
(Editor with E. J. Richards, and others) *Reinterpreting Christine de Pizan,* University of Georgia, 1992.

Also wrote and illustrated a bike safety manual for the Bicycle Safety Committee in Amherst.

WORK IN PROGRESS: A translation of Flora Tristan's *Mephis,* 1995. "A novel on Russian Jewish immigrant artists, several generations, struggling to make it without selling out (in various senses of the term), set in Boston (1895-1990)." Researching various topics in later medieval French and Italian literature.

* * *

MARKS, Richard Lee 1923(?)-

PERSONAL: Born c. 1923.

ADDRESSES: Agent—c/o Watkins Loomis Agency, 150 East 35th St., Suite 530, New York, NY 10016.

CAREER: Writer. Worked in petroleum fields.

WRITINGS:

Three Men of the Beagle (nonfiction), Knopf, 1991.

SIDELIGHTS: Richard Lee Marks's *Three Men of the Beagle* is a somewhat speculative account of naturalist Charles Darwin's naval voyage to South America, where he made some of the discoveries that led him to write *The Origin of the Species.* Darwin's epochal work included his theory of evolution and a discussion of natural selection—the process by which organisms best suited to their environment survive to pass on their traits to successive generations. Accompanying Darwin on his voyage was Robert Fitzroy, who captained the vessel. Fitzroy later became a seminal meteorologist and served as governor of New Zealand before killing himself at age fifty-nine. The third man referred to in the book's title is Jemmy Button, a Tierra del Fuego Indian who was brought by Darwin and Fitzroy back to England. Robert Kanigel, writing in the *Los Angeles Times Book Review,* reported that the three men's "tangled relationship . . . is the basis for this rich story, filled with blood, violence, starvation, shipwrecks, and all the other wonderful stuff of a great adventure yarn." *Washington Post Book World* reviewer Matt Schudel reported that *Three Men of the Beagle* is "intriguing" and constitutes "a provocative study."

BIOGRAPHICAL/CRITICAL SOURCES:

PERIODICALS

Booklist, April 15, 1991.
Library Journal, April 1, 1991, p. 136.
Los Angeles Times Book Review, June 9, 1991, p. 12.
Publishers Weekly, February 15, 1991, p. 82.
Washington Post Book World, April 14, 1991, p. 8.*

* * *

MARSHAK, Robert Eugene 1916-1992

OBITUARY NOTICE—See index for *CA* sketch: Born October 11, 1916, in New York, NY; drowned, December

23, 1992, in Cancun, Mexico. Physicist, educator, administrator, and author. Marshak made several important contributions to the field of physics and was a member of the team that created the first atomic bomb. As a graduate student with Professor Hans Bethe of Cornell University, he received attention for making advances in the understanding of how stars generate heat. After finishing his doctorate, Marshak began teaching at the University of Rochester, taking a leave of absence in the 1940s to work on the U.S. government's atomic bomb project led by J. Robert Oppenheimer at Los Alamos, New Mexico. During this time he served as chief deputy in theoretical physics for the project and developed a theory of shock waves that became known as the "Marshak wave." Marshak returned to the University of Rochester after World War II and led efforts for scientific cooperation with scientists in Soviet-bloc countries. In 1970 he accepted a position as president of the City University of New York. The school experienced racial and economic turmoil during Marshak's stay, but he attempted to preserve the institution's original mission of providing education to the socially disadvantaged by opening admissions to all high-school graduates. The program was later abandoned, and in 1979 he resigned his post and accepted a position as university distinguished professor of physics at Virginia Polytechnic Institute and State University. He was the recipient of many awards, including three Guggenheim fellowships and the first award for international scientific cooperation given by the American Association for the Advancement of Science. He wrote, cowrote, and edited several scientific texts, including *Our Atomic World, Introduction to Elementary Particle Physics, Perspectives in Modern Physics, Theory of West Interactions in Particle Physics,* and *Conceptual Foundation of Modern Particle Physics,* which was in press at the time of his death. Marshak also penned a book about his years at the City College of New York entitled *Academic Renewal in the 1970s: Memoirs of a City College President.*

OBITUARIES AND OTHER SOURCES:

BOOKS

Who's Who in America, 46th edition, Marquis, 1990.

PERIODICALS

Chicago Tribune, December 25, 1992, section 2, p. 10.
Los Angeles Times, December 25, 1992, p. A30.
New York Times, December 25, 1992, p. A29.
Washington Post, December 25, 1992, p. D6.

MARSHALL, George N(ichols) 1920-1993

OBITUARY NOTICE—See index for *CA* sketch: Born July 4, 1920, in Bozeman, MT; died of heart failure, February 15, 1993, in Chapel Hill, NC. Minister and author. Ordained a Unitarian-Universalist minister in 1943, Marshall eventually became the head of the Church of the Larger Fellowship, an unconventional sect in which members are joined by mail, phone, computer, video, publications, or other media rather than a central place of worship. He wrote a number of religious works, including *Church of the Pilgrim Fathers, Buddha: His Quest for Serenity,* and *Facing Death and Grief.* A founding member of the American Friends of Albert Schweitzer, Marshall published two books about the humanitarian: *On an Understanding of Albert Schweitzer* and, with David Poling, *Schweitzer, A Biography.*

OBITUARIES AND OTHER SOURCES:

BOOKS

Who's Who in Religion, 4th edition, Marquis, 1992.

PERIODICALS

New York Times, February 27, 1993, p. 27.

*   *   *

MARSHALL, Peter (H.) 1946-

PERSONAL: Born August 23, 1946, in Bognor Regis, England; son of William Cyril (a horse trainer) and Vera Ida (Payne) Marshall; married Jenny Therese Zobel (a radio broadcaster); children: Emily, Dylan. *Education:* University of London, England, B.A., 1970; University of Sussex, M.A., 1971, Ph.D., 1977.

ADDRESSES: Agent—Zena Publications, Garth-Y-Foel, Croesor, Penrhyndeudraeth, Gwynedd, Wales, UK.

CAREER: College St. Michel, Dakar, Senegal, West Africa, English teacher, 1966-67; Extramural Department, University of London, England, tutor in philosophy and literature, 1974-80; Extramural Department, University College of North Wales, tutor in philosophy, 1981—. Served as a cadet-purser on the P & O/Orient Line, British Merchant Navy, 1964-66.

WRITINGS:

William Godwin, Yale University Press, 1984.
Journey through Tanzania, photographs by Mohamed Amin and Duncan Willetts, Bodley Head, 1984.
Into Cuba, photographs by Barry Lewis, Alfred Van der Marck Editions, 1985.
Cuba Libre, Gollancz, 1987.
(Editor and author of introduction) William Godwin, *Damon and Delia,* Zena, 1988.

(Editor and author of introduction) *The Anarchist Writings of William Blake,* Freedom Press, 1988.

Demanding the Impossible: A History of Anarchism, HarperCollins, 1991.

Nature-Wise: An Exploration of Ecological Thinking, Simon & Schuster, 1992.

Contributor of articles and book reviews to periodicals, including *Africa Guide, Asia and Pacific Yearbook, Latin America and Caribbean Yearbook, New Internationalist,* and *The Traveller.*

WORK IN PROGRESS: A Voyage around Africa; a book to be published by Simon & Schuster and a related television series to be broadcast on British television.

SIDELIGHTS: British educator Peter Marshall is noted for his biography of the radical eighteenth-century British philosopher William Godwin. Marshall's strong desire to keep the ideas of England's more famous political theorists accessible to the public has also prompted him to edit several works, including Godwin's *Damon and Delia* and *The Anarchist Writings of William Blake,* for the modern reader.

Marshall's biographical portrait of Godwin recounts events in the philosopher's life and provides a detailed summary of all work published by Godwin over the course of his political career. *William Godwin* includes detailed explications of Godwin's more notable novels and of Godwin's biography of British poet and author Geoffrey Chaucer. In addition Marshall provides his readers with an examination of Godwin's most significant philosophical work, *An Enquiry Concerning Political Justice.* Although finding Marshall's biography somewhat excessive in its thoroughness, *New York Times Book Review* contributor David Bromwich maintained that *William Godwin* "is interesting. It brings back a thinker who was at once visionary and confident, and who had the good fortune to write when utopian ideas did not seem utopian." Biographer Don Locke commented in the *Times Literary Supplement,* "Marshall's *William Godwin* is a comprehensive and scholarly, if somewhat pedestrian, account of the man, his writings, and his doings, fully informed by recent research and with a clear sense of the personal origins of Godwin's thought."

More recently, Marshall has broadened his study to include not only Godwin but other radical political theorists. *Demanding the Impossible: A History of Anarchy,* published in 1991, includes Godwin's vision of an anarchist society as one of many political theories by such members of the anarchist school as Mikhail Bakunin, Gabriel de Foigny, Wilhelm von Humboldt, and Ayn Rand. The volume was praised by reviewers for the breadth of its study and Marshall's scholarly approach. *Observer* reviewer David Widgery described *Demanding the Impossi-*

ble as a "scrupulous and comprehensive elucidation of anarchist ideas from sixth-century-B.C. Taoism through to Chomsky, Bookchin, the eco-anarchists and the anarcha-feminists." And James Joll, writing in the *Times Literary Supplement,* noted that "Peter Marshall's wide survey comes at the right moment when so many other ideologies have collapsed, and his concluding discussion of anarchism in relation to world ecological problems . . . suggests that, for all its past failures, anarchism in some form or another still provides suggestions as to how a different and better society might be organized."

BIOGRAPHICAL/CRITICAL SOURCES:

PERIODICALS

New York Times Book Review, October 21, 1984, pp. 24-25.

Observer, January 26, 1992, p. 54.

Times Literary Supplement, September 21, 1984, p. 1061; January 10, 1992, pp. 3-4.*

*   *   *

MARTIN, Oliver
See SMITH, R(eginald) D(onald)

*   *   *

MARTIN, William   1950-
(Frederick James)

PERSONAL: Born May 13, 1950, in Cambridge, MA; son of William E. (a communications manager) and Charlotte L. (a homemaker) Martin; married Christine Kunz (a chemist), August 4, 1973; children: three. *Education:* Harvard University, B.A., 1972; University of Southern California, M.F.A., 1976.

ADDRESSES: Agent—Robert Gottlieb, William Morris Agency, 1350 Avenue of the Americas, New York, NY 10019.

CAREER: Writer.

MEMBER: Writers Guild, Authors Guild, Mystery Writers of America, Massachusetts Historical Society.

AWARDS, HONORS: David McCord Prize, Harvard College, 1972; CBS fellow, University of Southern California, 1975; Hal Wallis screenwriting fellow, University of Southern California, 1976.

WRITINGS:

NOVELS

Back Bay, Crown, 1980.
Nerve Endings, Crown, 1984.

The Rising of the Moon, Crown, 1987.
Cape Cod, Warner Books, 1991.

OTHER

(Under pseudonym Frederick James) *Humanoids from the Deep* (screenplay), New World Pictures, 1980.
George Washington: The Man Who Wouldn't Be King (television play; part of series, *The American Experience*), PBS, 1992.

WORK IN PROGRESS: Annapolis, a novel about an American naval family and America's military history.

SIDELIGHTS: William Martin is a writer who has won acclaim with his novels set in New England. He began his literary career in 1980 with *Back Bay,* the multigenerational tale of a Boston family and a missing tea set. The family is the Pratts, whose mercantile ancestor once sought to purchase a silver tea set created by Paul Revere for President George Washington. When the White House burned during the War of 1812, the tea set was stolen. The thieves embarked for Boston, where wealthy Horace Taylor Pratt had arranged to purchase the stolen property. But the thieves, while approaching Boston by ship, fought and killed each other. During the fight, the tea set fell into the harbor. Several generations later, history student Peter Fallon, a descendent of Horace Taylor Pratt, determines to recover the tea set from the harbor bottom. William J. Leonard, in his review of the novel for *America,* described Martin's debut novel as "a grand story . . . packed with action," and he added that it is "an impressive achievement." And Kathy Taflinger in the *Cincinnati Enquirer* remarked that "reading *Back Bay* is almost like watching an artist paint a picture—the longer you watch, the clearer the image. The more you read of this 437-page novel, the more interesting it gets."

Martin followed *Back Bay* with *Nerve Endings,* in which kidney recipient Jim Whiting, an advertising copywriter, becomes obsessed with the dead donor, who died in a boating explosion. Whiting soon discovers that the donor, film producer Roger Darrow, had planned to expose considerable corruption that he had recently uncovered in the cable television business. With Darrow's widow, Whiting embarks on a cross-country adventure to undo Darrow's murderous foes. *Detroit Free Press* reviewer Ellen Creager proclaimed *Nerve Endings* "a good tale for a dreary afternoon."

In his next novel, *The Rising of the Moon,* Martin writes about events immediately preceding the Easter Rising that resulted in the separation of Northern Ireland from Ireland in 1916. The novel's hero is Padraic Starr, an Irish rebel who has arrived in Boston to procure arms and volunteers for the impending rebellion back home against the British. He soon joins forces with his cousin, Tom Tracy;

the cousin's Zionist lover, Rachel; and a sympathetic priest. After various adventures, including a train robbery, the heroes begin their harrowing journey through storm-tossed seas and past prowling German submarines. Joanne Omang reported in the *Washington Post* that the novel provides readers with "a few hours of fast-paced entertainment." And Charles J. Cannon in the *Seattle Post-Intelligencer* noted that *The Rising of the Moon* "is a gem of a read, a marvelous adventure not to be missed."

Martin's *Cape Cod,* which appeared in 1991, is an epic novel of Cape Cod and its inhabitants from the Mayflower landing to present times. The novel is structured by a long-lived rivalry between the Bigelows and the Hilyards, two families whose members begin quarreling before they plan to go to America. The clash, centered largely on disputed ownership of Jack's Island, continues throughout the ensuing decades, and it culminates with the Bigelow family's efforts to construct housing on the contested property while the Hilyards hope to keep the island natural and undeveloped. "Engrossing and entertaining," according to Charla Gabert in the *Boston Sunday Herald, Cape Cod* "is packed with history, action, adventure, romance, sex and intrigue—something for everyone." Gabert also commended Martin for his ability to combine the historical and fictional elements in the text, remarking, "The result is a rich and satisfying concoction that, like the best of historical fiction, delights as it educates." The book was also praised by David Forsmark of the *Flint Sunday Journal,* who ranked Martin's historical fiction with that of such notables in the genre as James Michener and Kenneth Roberts.

In addition to writing novels, Martin penned the screenplay *Humanoids from the Deep* under the pseudonym Frederick James. Of his experience in trying to enter the film industry, Martin told *CA:* "Like most everyone who has sought to break into Hollywood during the last three decades, I spent time in producer Roger Corman's postgraduate, guild-minimum school for low budget filmmaking. I did not, however follow in the footsteps of Francis Coppola or Jack Nicholson or many of the other Corman novices, because, in the same season that the film was released, my first novel was published and I was set free."

In 1992, the television program *American Experience* broadcast *George Washington: The Man Who Wouldn't Be King,* another work by Martin. "In this film, I did not have the luxury of a fictional character through whom I could see history," the author told *CA.* "Instead I appeared as the historical novelist and narrator searching for the man behind the myth." *George Washington* received acclaim from critics, including Jeff Silverman of *Variety,* who called the piece "a fascinating and fluid portrait of a complicated man." And Geoffrey C. Ward in *American Heritage* praised the writing, remarking that "Martin prove[s] an amiable guide" to the places and events in the life of the former president.

Martin told *CA:* "The simple truth I learned at the start of my career and have never forgotten is this: people like stories. Readers (and viewers) like to be taken on a journey to a place they have never been, where the foreign seems familiar and the familiar seems unique.

"I like to take them into the past because it's a good place to study human nature, which always seems familiar no matter how unique the time or place may be. Moreover, most historical events can be examined as though they were stories. There are inciting incidents, rising and falling actions, crises, resolutions, denouements. So I can never complain about writer's block, because I always have a structure. And finally, I am fascinated by our own relationship to history, to the most world-shaking of events and the most private decisions of our own ancestors. History reaches for both of these poles, but often, it is the historical novelist who is able to grasp them both at the same time.

"So I tell stories. In the process, I take people through time, across space, and—if I'm doing my job well—toward a deeper understanding of the things that make us all human."

BIOGRAPHICAL/CRITICAL SOURCES:

PERIODICALS

America, May 24, 1980, pp. 447-48.
American Heritage, February/March, 1983, p. 16.
Boston Sunday Herald, March 31, 1991.
Christian Science Monitor, May 6, 1991.
Cincinnati Enquirer, February 24, 1980.
Detroit Free Press, March 4, 1984.
Detroit News, February 9, 1980.
Flint Sunday Journal, July 7, 1991.
Los Angeles Times, March 11, 1991, p. E6.
New York Times Book Review, February 19, 1984, p. 22; July 12, 1987, p. 20.
Seattle Post-Intelligencer, April 23, 1987.
Variety, November 18, 1992.
Washington Post, March 17, 1987.
Washington Post Book World, February 5, 1984, p. 13.

* * *

MARTINI, Steve(n Paul) 1946-

PERSONAL: Born February 28, 1946, in San Francisco, CA; son of Ernest R. and Rita M. Martini; married April 3, 1976; wife's name, Leah; children: one. *Education:* University of California, Santa Cruz, B.A., 1968; University of the Pacific, McGeorge School of Law, J.D., 1974.

ADDRESSES: Agent—John Hawkins & Associates, 71 West Twenty-third St., Suite 1600, New York, NY 10010.

CAREER: Los Angeles Daily Journal, journalist and State House correspondent in Sacramento, CA, 1970-75; lawyer in private practice, Sacramento, 1975-80; state attorney for various agencies, including State Department of Consumer Affairs, also served as deputy director of the State Office of Administrative Hearings and as special counsel for California Victims of Violent Crimes Program, all 1980-91; full-time writer, 1991—.

WRITINGS:

MYSTERIES

The Simeon Chamber, Donald I. Fine, 1988.
Compelling Evidence (Book-of-the-Month Club selection), Putnam, 1992.
Prime Witness, Putnam, 1993.

SIDELIGHTS: Former journalist and attorney Steve Martini is a writer of suspense fiction that is influenced by his professional experience. His first novel, *The Simeon Chamber,* concerns a San Francisco, California, lawyer, Sam Bogardus, who discovers that one of his clients, Jennifer Davies, possesses pages that may be from the long lost diaries of sixteenth-century explorer Sir Francis Drake. Not long after this discovery, Bogardus and Davies find themselves in considerable danger. Pursued by unsavory characters eager to gain possession of the documents, the attorney and his client embark on a wild chase that takes them throughout the San Francisco Bay Area. Their trail eventually leads to the San Simeon castle built by publishing magnate William Randolph Hearst. At San Simeon, Bogardus uncovers a secret black market agenda from World War II and its relationship to Jennifer's documents. A contributor for *Kirkus Reviews* called the novel "generally rousing," and a *Publishers Weekly* reviewer described *The Simeon Chamber* as a "fast read" that features a "stunning finale."

Martini is also author of *Compelling Evidence,* a novel about love and murder among law professionals. The novel's hero and narrator is Paul Madriana, an attorney who lost his position with a major firm after it was discovered that he was having an affair with the wife of Ben Potter, his boss and mentor. When Potter is found dead on the eve of his appointment to the U.S. Supreme Court, the police suspect murder. Potter's wife—and Madriana's former lover—is arrested and charged with her husband's death. The plot thickens when Madriana is recruited as a member of the woman's defense team. When the chief defense counsel fumbles the inquest and subsequently bails out of the case, Madriana is left as the woman's sole lawyer. Matters become worse for the attorney as he realizes he has become a pawn in a much larger game, with stakes that are higher than a prison term. While a *Publishers Weekly* reviewer found the author's technical language stifling at times, Martini was applauded for writing a "refreshingly candid legal procedural." *Los Angeles Times* reviewer Charles Champlin praised *Compelling Evidence* for its "sheer storytelling professionalism." Commending the author's skill in evoking courtroom drama, *New York Times Book Review* contributor Marilyn Stasio opined that "on his feet and in front of a jury, Mr. Martini speaks in a commanding voice."

Martini told *CA:* "Full-time fiction writing had been my dream for many years, since college and particularly since my days as a journalist twenty years ago. For those who wish to make such a career for themselves there is only one known formula: consistent and diligent effort over an extended period of time. For me the mix of law and fiction was natural as I had been writing in the field during my career as a journalist, covering the courts, the legislature, and various other governmental agencies. Later, having engaged in the practice of law, I was able to bring to bear that experience in order to craft credible trial and courtroom fiction. For me, a good courtroom story must cut very close to the bone of reality to have true value."

BIOGRAPHICAL/CRITICAL SOURCES:

PERIODICALS

Kirkus Reviews, August 1, 1988, p. 1089.
Los Angeles Times Book Review, March 8, 1992, p. 8.
New York Times Book Review, March 22, 1992, p. 22.
Publishers Weekly, September 2, 1988, p. 90; November 29, 1991, p. 43.

*   *   *

MARTON, Kati (Ilona) 1949-

PERSONAL: Born April 3, 1949, in Budapest, Hungary; daughter of Endre (a journalist and professor) and Ilona (a journalist) Marton; married Peter Jennings (a journalist), September, 1979; children: Elizabeth, Christopher. *Education:* Attended Wells College, 1965-67, and the Sorbonne and the Institut des Etudes de Sciences Politiques, Paris, 1967-68; George Washington University, B.A., 1969, M.A., 1971.

ADDRESSES: Home—New York, NY. *Agent*—Amanda Urban, International Creative Management, 40 West Fifty-seventh St., New York, NY 10019.

CAREER: National Public Radio, Washington, DC, reporter, 1971-72; WCAU-TV, Philadelphia, PA, news writer and reporter, 1973-77; ABC News, foreign correspondent and bureau chief based in Bonn, West Germany (now Germany), 1977-79; *Sunday Times,* London, En-

gland, columnist, 1983-85; writer. Also reporter for Public Broadcasting Service (PBS-TV), *Atlantic Monthly, London Times,* and *New Republic;* visiting scholar at the Freedom Forum Media Studies Center, Columbia University, 1991-92.

AWARDS, HONORS: Channel 10 Award for reporting, 1973; George Foster Peabody Award, 1973, for a documentary on China; Philadelphia Press Association Award for best television feature story, 1974; Gannett fellow, 1988.

WRITINGS:

Wallenberg (biography), Random House, 1982.
An American Woman (novel), Norton, 1987.
The Polk Conspiracy: Murder and Cover-up in the Case of CBS News (nonfiction), Farrar, Strauss, 1990.

Contributor of articles to periodicals, including *Vanity Fair, Wall Street Journal,* and *Newsweek.*

WORK IN PROGRESS: A book about the life and assassination of Count Folke Bernadotte, the first United Nations mediator to the Arab and Jewish communities in the Middle East.

SIDELIGHTS: Ranging from biography to fiction, Kati Marton's writings often draw on politics, history, and her experience as a journalist. The Hungarian-born author's first book, *Wallenberg,* is a biography of Raoul Wallenberg, a Swedish diplomat who single-handedly saved thousands of Hungarian Jews from death at the hands of German Nazis during World War II. Without legal authority or ulterior motive, Wallenberg secured the release of Jews en route to death camps by claiming that they were Swedes under the protection of the Swedish government. Wallenberg disappeared when the Soviet Army invaded Budapest near the end of the war, and he reportedly died in a Soviet prison in 1947. But his biographers, including Marton, have not ruled out the possibility that the Swede is still alive. Marton's *Wallenberg* garnered a favorable reaction from critics. In a review of several Wallenberg biographies, *Washington Post Book World* contributor Charles Fenyvesi judged that Marton "excels in descriptions of her native Hungary and the Soviet gulag; her book has the most sensitive treatment of the personalities involved. It is the best written of the four and may well become the standard Wallenberg biography."

Marton's Hungarian heritage provided the basis for her next work, the 1987 novel *An American Woman.* Like the author, the book's central character, Anna Bator, is a Hungarian-born American journalist who works as a correspondent in Eastern Europe. Anna's parents, like Marton's parents, are both journalists who were imprisoned in Communist Hungary in the 1950s after they were accused of being in league with the U.S. Central Intelligence

Agency. Freed during the Hungarian Revolution of 1956, Marton's parents emigrated with their daughters to Chevy Chase, Maryland, in 1959. Marton returned to her native country in the 1970s to do a series for ABC News, and told *Washington Post* writer Stephanie Mansfield that "it was a very emotionally wrenching experience. It really felt as though I had never left. I had changed but nothing there had changed."

Anna comes to a similar realization in *An American Woman,* and she uses her time in Hungary to unearth the past that her father, Alex, refuses to discuss. In doing so, the heroine becomes involved in romance and political intrigue, discovers that her father was Jewish, and, after breaking a story about a planned invasion of Poland by Soviet-backed forces, eventually lands in prison. Interspersed with Anna's story are flashbacks of her family's life in the 1950s. "Anna's account of her parents' arrest by the Hungarian secret police, their search of the family's apartment and her father's letters from prison make for compelling reading," noted Helen Epstein in the *Washington Post.* "The themes of reclamation and repetition—the child repeating the life events of the parents—are fascinating, and the novel moves quickly to a surprising close."

Though other critics found *An American Woman* to be lacking in character development and focus, several reviewers commented on the authenticity of the novel. Toronto *Globe and Mail* contributor Judy Stoffman, for instance, assessed that "the details of a reporter's working life in an Eastern bloc country ring true, as does Marton's description of the discomfort of the accent-free immigrant, the person who passes for native-born but knows herself to be different." Writing in the *New York Times Book Review,* Nina Darnton called *An American Woman* "a lively cold war story, told with sensitivity and intelligence." Marton commented on the personal nature of her novel to Mansfield, declaring that "nobody else could have written this book." The author explained that she transformed her experience into a novel rather than an autobiography because "it seems to me that writing a novel, one can be far more truthful."

A search for the truth also propels Marton's third book, *The Polk Conspiracy: Murder and Cover-up in the Case of CBS News,* which is a nonfiction account of the events surrounding the demise of respected American correspondent George Polk in Greece in 1948. According to official reports, Polk was killed by Greek Communists while covering the civil war between Communist insurgents and the American-backed right-wing Greek government. A journalist with reported Communist sympathies confessed to being a conspirator in the murder—after being tortured by the Greek police—but later recanted. Using previously classified information from the U.S. Federal Bureau of Investigation, Central Intelligence Agency, and State De-

partment, Marton argues that it was actually the Greek government who had Polk killed, and that the U.S. participated in a cover-up so as to maintain a friendly relationship with its anti-Communist ally.

The Communists, Marton maintains, had no motive to kill Polk, who was critical of the Greek government and who had planned to interview the guerrillas in northern Greece around the time he was murdered. According to Marton, however, the Greek government did have a motive: a few days before his death, Polk accused Greek foreign minister Constantine Tsaldaris of illegally transferring twenty-five thousand dollars into a New York bank account and threatened to break the story, which would be an embarrassment to the Greek government and which could damage U.S.-Greek relations. Polk never did report on the scandal, though, because shortly after his confrontation with Tsaldaris his body washed ashore at Salonika Bay. The U.S. launched an investigation, but members of the probe ensured that the outcome aligned with America's political interests rather than the truth, Marton asserts in *The Polk Conspiracy.* "Mr. Polk's Government and his colleagues sacrificed him for political expediency," Marton told Roger Cohen in the *New York Times.* "I think America betrayed one of its most gifted correspondents."

Though *Washington Post Book World* contributor Joseph E. Persico commented that "Marton's circumstantial case is . . . stronger than her factual case," several critics found the author's evidence compelling and praised *The Polk Conspiracy.* In the *Los Angeles Times Book Review,* Murray Fromson called Marton's book "an impressive work of investigative reporting" and an "engrossing expose." Persico declared that "the Polk case is more than a tale of covered-up murder. In Kati Marton's skilled hands it becomes a parable of the endless struggle between the truth and political expedience." *The Polk Conspiracy* is "a true life-and-death account that reads like a thriller," according to *New York Times* reviewer Herbert Mitgang. And, writing in the *New York Times Book Review,* Michael Janeway judged that "Marton tells the story of George Polk's life skillfully, reminding us how lonely, perilous and heroic a reporter's lot can be."

BIOGRAPHICAL/CRITICAL SOURCES:

PERIODICALS

Globe and Mail (Toronto), August 15, 1987.
Los Angeles Times Book Review, September 30, 1990, p. 1.
New York Times, October 13, 1990; October 17, 1990.
New York Times Book Review, May 24, 1987, p. 12; October 28, 1990, p. 3.
Tribune Books (Chicago), March 29, 1987, p. 6.
Washington Post, April 25, 1987; April 28, 1987.

Washington Post Book World, June 20, 1982, p. 8; September 30, 1990, p. 4.

—*Sketch by Michelle M. Motowski*

*   *   *

MASTERSON, Daniel M.   1945-

PERSONAL: Born January 26, 1945; son of Laurence P. and Josephine Masterson; married in 1972; children: three. *Education:* University of Illinois at Urbana-Champaign, B.A., 1967; Michigan State University, M.A., 1968, Ph.D., 1976; also attended University of Barcelona, 1971.

ADDRESSES: Home—11 King Court, Annapolis, MD 21401. *Office*—Department of History, 356 Sampson Hall, United States Naval Academy, Annapolis, MD 21402-5044.

CAREER: High school social studies teacher in Dolton, IL, 1968-71; Michigan State University, East Lansing, instructor in history, 1970-75; U.S. Naval Academy, Annapolis, MD, assistant professor, 1979-83, associate professor of history, 1983—. Visiting assistant professor of history, North Carolina State University, 1975, Marietta College, 1976-77, and State University of New York College at Oswego, 1977-78; Ohio Commission on Allied Health Education, program coordinator, 1979.

MEMBER: Conference on Latin American History, Association of Third World Studies, Mid-Atlantic Council on Latin American Studies (member of executive council, 1991), Washington Area Modern Latin American Historians Association, U.S. Commission on Military History, Phi Alpha Theta.

AWARDS, HONORS: Fellow of the National Endowment for the Humanities at Stanford University, 1978, and Cornell University, 1990; grant from Franklin and Eleanor Roosevelt Institute, 1991.

WRITINGS:

(Editor with John F. Bratzel, and contributor) *The Underside of Latin American History* (monograph), Latin American Studies Center, Michigan State University, 1977.
(General editor) *Naval History: The Sixth Symposium of the United States Naval Academy,* Scholarly Resources, 1987.
Militarism and Politics in Latin America: Peru from Sanchez Cerro to Sendero Luminoso, Greenwood Press, 1991.

Work represented in anthologies, including *Encyclopedia of Latin American History.* Contributor of articles and reviews to periodicals, including *Christian Century.* Associate editor, *Journal of Third World Studies.*

Militarism and Politics in Latin America: Peru from Sanchez Cerro to Sendero Luminoso has been translated into Spanish.

WORK IN PROGRESS: Unwanted Immigrants: The Japanese in Latin America, 1880-1950, with Sayaka Funada and John F. Bratzel, publication by Paragon House expected in 1995; research on Peru's "Shining Path" and state policy.

*   *   *

MATSUDA, Mari J.

PERSONAL: Education: Arizona State University, B.A., 1975; University of Hawaii, J.D., 1980; Harvard University, LL.M., 1983.

ADDRESSES: Office—Law Center, Georgetown University, 600 New Jersey Ave. NE, Washington, DC 20001.

CAREER: University of California, Los Angeles, professor of law; affiliated with Georgetown University, Washington, DC.

WRITINGS:

(Editor) *Called from Within: Early Women Lawyers of Hawaii,* University of Hawaii Press, 1992.
(With Crenshaw, Delgado, and Lawrence) *Words That Wound,* Westview, 1992.

WORK IN PROGRESS: Research on legal history, women's studies, and Asian Americans.

*   *   *

MATSUURA, Kumiko   1955-

PERSONAL: Born January 15, 1955, in Tokushima, Japan; daughter of Yoshio (in business) and Sakae (a homemaker) Matsuura; married Joachim Wilhelm Mueller (a member of the United Nations staff), March 14, 1991. *Education:* Pontificia Universidade Catolica, Rio de Janeiro, B.B.A., 1978, postgraduate certificate in systems analysis, 1985, postgraduate certificate in finance, 1986; attended Instituto Maua de Tecnologia, Sao Paulo, 1981; Fordham University, M.B.A., 1989.

ADDRESSES: Home—Rudolfsplatz 2/29, 1010 Vienna, Austria. *Office*—Strategy, Policy, and Planning Office, United Nations Industrial Development Organization, P.O. Box 400, Room D-2213, A-1400 Vienna, Austria.

CAREER: Villares Industrias de Base, Sao Paulo, Brazil, chief of Production Planning Section, 1976-80; Sebep

(Montreal Engenharia and Baker/Hughes) Oil Service Co., Rio de Janeiro, Brazil, technical planning officer, chief planner, coordinator of system development, and manager of Corporate Financial Planning and Control Division, 1981-87; United Nations, New York City, program budget officer and systems analyst in Budget Division, 1987-90; United Nations Industrial Development Organization, Vienna, Austria, program planning officer in Strategy, Policy, and Planning Office, 1990—. Mackenzie University (Sao Paulo), assistant professor, 1985-86; consultant to Coopers & Lybrand.

MEMBER: Beta Gamma Sigma.

WRITINGS:

Japanese Direct Investment in the U.S.A.: The Case of the Banking/Financial Industry, Pan-Pacific Management Association, 1990.

Coeditor, *Annual Review of United Nations Affairs,* Oceana, 1988—.

* * *

MAYER, Jean 1920-1993

OBITUARY NOTICE—See index for *CA* sketch: Born February 19, 1920, in Paris, France; died of a heart attack, January 1, 1993, in Sarasota, FL. Nutritionist, educator, administrator, adviser, and author. Mayer, a prominent researcher and activist for improved nutritional standards in the United States and in Third World countries, was instrumental in expanding food stamp and school lunch programs in the United States. His leadership as president and chancellor of Tufts University transformed the liberal arts school into an internationally recognized institution of research on nutritional and environmental issues. Born in France, Mayer emigrated to the United States after heroic service with the Free French, French Resistance, and British intelligence forces during World War II. He received several military decorations for his wartime actions, including the Croix de Guerre. After earning a Ph.D. from Yale University in the late 1940s, Mayer began a twenty-five year career at Harvard University. His pioneering research on obesity and hunger resulted in several important finds, including his discovery of the relationship between hunger and glucose levels in the blood. He served as an adviser on nutritional issues to presidents Richard M. Nixon, Gerald R. Ford, and Jimmy Carter; lead relief missions to Africa, India, Ghana, and other countries; and acted as adviser to many organizations, including the United Nations. In 1976 he became president of Tufts University, establishing the nation's first graduate school of nutrition and expanding other graduate and undergraduate programs there. He received presidential

awards from President George Bush in 1989 and 1992 for his work on hunger, environmental, and conservation issues. Mayer was a prolific writer who wrote a syndicated nutrition column for several years in addition to producing hundreds of scientific papers and several books. His works include *Appetites and the Many Obesities, Overweight: Causes, Cost, Control, Human Nutrition: Its Physiological, Medical, and Social Aspects,* and *A Diet for Living.* He was also editor and coeditor of a number of books, including *Health and the Patterns of Life, Food and Nutrition in Health and Disease,* and *Food and Nutrition in a Changing World.*

OBITUARIES AND OTHER SOURCES:

BOOKS

Who's Who in the World, 11th edition, Marquis, 1991.

PERIODICALS

Los Angeles Times, January 3, 1993, p. A22.
New York Times, January 2, 1993, p. 9.
Times (London), January 4, 1993, p. 17.

* * *

McCABE, Peter 1945-

PERSONAL: Born November 7, 1945, in England. *Education:* Cambridge University, B.A., 1967.

ADDRESSES: Agent—Loretta Barrett, Barrett Books, 101 Fifth Ave., New York, NY 10003.

CAREER: Writer.

WRITINGS:

Apple to the Core, Pocket Books, 1972.
Bad News at Black Rock: The Sell-Out of CBS News, Arbor House, 1987.
City of Lies, Morrow, 1993.

* * *

McCAULEY, Sue 1941-

PERSONAL: Born December 1, 1941, in Dannevirke, New Zealand; daughter of James McDougal (a farmer) and Violet (a teacher; maiden name, Montgomery) McGibbon; married Denis McCauley, 1962 (divorced, 1974); married Pat Hammond (in forestry), October 26, 1979; children: (first marriage) Nathan, Keely. *Politics:* "Left." *Religion:* Agnostic.

ADDRESSES: Home—P.O. Box 18, Okaihau, Northland, New Zealand. *Agent*—Ray Richards, P.O. Box 31, 240 Milford, Auckland, New Zealand.

CAREER: Dannevirke Public Hospital, New Zealand, nurse's aide, 1958-59; New Zealand Broadcasting Service, Napier, copywriter, 1959-60; *Listener,* Wellington, New Zealand, journalist, 1960-62; worked as a waitress in Melbourne, Australia, 1962-63; Taranaki *Herald,* New Plymouth, New Zealand, reporter, 1963-64; *Christchurch Press,* Christchurch, New Zealand, reporter, 1964-65; free-lance writer. University of Auckland, writer in residence, 1986.

MEMBER: PEN, New Zealand Writers' Guild.

AWARDS, HONORS: Wattie Book of the Year Award, Book Publishers Association of New Zealand, 1982, and New Zealand Book Award for Fiction, 1983, both for *Other Halves;* Mobil Radio Award for Drama, 1982, for "The Ezra File"; "The Ordinary Girl" was a runner-up in the Year of the Child competition.

WRITINGS:

NOVELS

Other Halves, Hodder & Stoughton, 1982, Penguin, 1985.
Then Again, Hodder & Stoughton, 1988.
Bad Music, Hodder & Stoughton, c. 1990.

TELEVISION PLAYS

"As Old as the World," Television New Zealand (TVNZ), 1968.
"Friends and Neighbours," TVNZ, 1973.
"The Shadow Trader" (series), TVNZ, 1989.
"Shark in the Park" (episodic), TVNZ, 1991.
"Married," TVNZ, 1993.
"Matrons of Honour," TVNZ, 1993.
(With Greg McGee) "Marlin Bay" (episodic), TVNZ, 1993.

RADIO PLAYS

"The Obituary," Radio New Zealand (RNZ), 1967.
"The Evening Out," RNZ, 1968, American Broadcasting Corporation (ABC), 1970.
"Robbie," RNZ, 1972.
"Crutch," RNZ, 1975, British Broadcasting Corporation (BBC), 1980.
"Minor Adjustment," RNZ, 1975.
"Some without a Sigh," RNZ, 1975.
"Letters to May," RNZ, 1977.
"The Ordinary Girl," RNZ, 1978.
"When Did He Last Buy You Flowers?," RNZ, 1980, BBC, 1984.
"The Voice Despised," RNZ, 1980.
"The Missionaries," RNZ, 1981.
"Isobel, God, and the Cowboy," RNZ, 1981.
"The Ezra File," RNZ, 1982.
"Thank You Buzz Aldrin," RNZ, 1982.
"The Man Who Sleeps with My Mother," RNZ, 1983.
"Family Ties," RNZ, 1986.

"Waiting for Heathcliff " (adaptation of McCauley's stage play of the same title), RNZ, 1992.

OTHER

Other Halves (screenplay; adapted from McCauley's novel of the same title), Findlayson-Hill Production, 1984.
Waiting for Heathcliff (play), produced in Christchurch, New Zealand, 1988.
(Editor) *Erotic Writing,* Penguin, 1992.

Contributor of articles, stories, and television, radio, and book reviews to periodicals. Columnist for *Thursday* magazine.

WORK IN PROGRESS: A screenplay; a novel.

SIDELIGHTS: New Zealander Sue McCauley, whose fiction includes radio and television plays, is best known in the United States for her novels *Other Halves, Then Again,* and *Bad Music. Other Halves* concerns Liz, a white, middle-class suburban homemaker, and Tug, a black aborigine teenager who calls the inner-city streets of Auckland, New Zealand home. The two meet at a mental institution, where Liz is admitted after faking a suicide attempt and where Tug goes to avoid being charged with a burglary. As the story progresses, Liz and Tug leave the mental institution and become lovers, meanwhile contending with their racial, age, and class differences.

Praised as a romantic novel with well-drawn characters, *Other Halves* won New Zealand's Wattie Book of the Year Award in 1982. Though some critics commended McCauley's understanding of the social issues her book addresses, *Washington Post* contributor Susanna Nicholson opined that the author "whitewashes [her story] with sermons on 'how the other half lives.' " Nicholson did acknowledge, however, that "Tug is a wonderful character, protean, exuberant and foulmouthed." The relationship between Tug and Liz "is presented movingly and divertingly," according to *Times Literary Supplement* contributor Robert Brian. *Other Halves,* Brian continued, "is not only a good love story but also good ethnography. More convincingly than any urban anthropologist McCauley lets us into the squalid nooks and crannies" of Auckland. The reviewer concluded that *Other Halves* is a "fine novel."

McCauley followed *Other Halves* with *Then Again,* which was published in 1988. The book concerns a motley group of characters who retreat to an island off the coast of New Zealand to escape the stressful effects of materialistic, corrupt, industrialized society. Among the island's inhabitants is Maureen, a single mother on welfare; Keith, a former journalist who drinks too much; and Josie, a beautiful, overweight woman whose several bad marriages have made her wary of marrying Geoff, her lover of seven years. McCauley's characters, according to reviewers, are credible and well-rounded. And though the author's "preaching" sometimes "clouds the story," according to Andrea Stevens in the *New York Times Book Review,* "her portraits, especially of the women, stand out above the fog." A *Publishers Weekly* critic declared that "by no means a polemic, [*Then Again*] is alternately tragic and uproariously funny, and always engrossing."

McCauley told *CA:* "After nearly twenty years of earning a semblance of a living as a free-lance writer, the local success of my first novel has suddenly made me 'established' and apparently of interest! I still regard myself as a 'commercial' writer—I'm obliged to earn a living from my work, having no other marketable skills or talents.

"I read that I write social realism and concentrate on the underdog—but in fact I have simply always written (journalism apart) about the people and environments I know best. I almost always write with a bright hope but no real expectation that I may put a small dent in the prevailing social order."

BIOGRAPHICAL/CRITICAL SOURCES:

PERIODICALS

New York Times Book Review, September 18, 1988, p. 32.
Publishers Weekly, March 4, 1988, p. 100.
Times Literary Supplement, April 8, 1983, p. 360.
Washington Post, August 13, 1985.

*   *   *

McCLINTON, Katharine Morrison   1899-1993

OBITUARY NOTICE—See index for *CA* sketch: Born January 23, 1899, in San Francisco, CA; died of heart failure, January 27, 1993, in Manhattan, NY. Art critic, lecturer, and author. An expert on collecting art and antiques, McClinton worked as a lecturer at the University of California and at the Fine Arts Gallery in San Francisco in the 1920s and 1930s. She also served in the 1930s as art critic for the *San Diego Sun* and as a member of the editorial staff of *McCall's* magazine. Author of more than thirty books, her most popular works were those on the Art Deco movement, particularly *Art Deco for Collectors* and *Lalique for Collectors.* Other books published by McClinton include *Antique Collecting, The Changing Church: Its Architecture, Art, and Decoration,* and *Collecting American Victorian Antiques.*

OBITUARIES AND OTHER SOURCES:

PERIODICALS

New York Times, January 31, 1993, p. 44.

McCORMACK, Arthur Gerard   1911-1992

OBITUARY NOTICE—See index for *CA* sketch: Born August 16, 1911, in Liverpool, England; died December 11, 1992. Priest, population expert, and author. McCormack, a Roman Catholic priest whose views on population control conflicted with Catholic doctrine, earned international respect for his work to address the problem of world poverty. An adviser on population and developing countries to the Second Vatican Council in the 1960s, McCormack was instrumental in drafting the Church's plan to encourage progress and social justice throughout the world. He remained in Rome to work for the Pontifical Commission for Justice and Peace, but his support of artificial birth control as a means of curbing poverty in Third World countries caused him to lose favor with some Church officials, and he resigned his post in the 1970s. McCormack continued to focus on population issues, serving as a consultant to the World Population Congress in Bucharest from 1971 to 1975 and as a delegate to the 1984 non-governmental population conference in Mexico City, where he gave the concluding address. He published several books in his field of interest, including *People, Space, Food, World Poverty and the Christian, The Population Problem, The Population Explosion and Christian Concern,* and *Multinational Investment: Boon or Burden for the Developing Countries.*

OBITUARIES AND OTHER SOURCES:

BOOKS

Who's Who, 144th edition, St. Martin's, 1992, p. 1169.

PERIODICALS

Times (London), January 2, 1993, p. 15.

*   *   *

McCOWN, Edna   1947-

PERSONAL: Born August 27, 1947, in Florence, SC; daughter of William Robert (in sales) and Ernestine (a homemaker; maiden name, Allen) McCown. *Education:* Duquesne University, M.A., 1974; State University of New York at Stony Brook, Ph.D., 1982. *Politics:* Democrat.

ADDRESSES: Home—19 West 70th St., No. 4R, New York, NY 10023.

CAREER: Goethe House, New York City, worked in language department, 1982-86; translator.

MEMBER: International P.E.N.

WRITINGS:

TRANSLATOR

Erich Hackl, *Aurora's Motive* (novel), Knopf, 1988.

Hackl, *Farewell, Sidonia* (novel), Fromm International, 1991.

Gert Hofmann, *Before the Rainy Season* (novel), Grove, 1991.

Felix Mettler, *The Wild Boar* (novel), Fromm International, 1992.

Alfred Doeblin, *Destiny's Journey* (memoir), Paragon House, 1992.

Thomas Huerlimann, *The Couple* (novella), Fromm International, 1992.

Other translations include the novel *Die Wachsfluegelfrau,* by Eveline Hasler, 1993.

*   *   *

McCUNE, Shannon   1913-1993

OBITUARY NOTICE—See index for *CA* sketch: Born April 6, 1913, in Sonch'on, Korea; died of congestive heart failure, January 4, 1993, in Gainesville, FL. Geographer, educator, administrator, and author. An expert on Asian geography, McCune held several governmental and academic positions in his area of specialty. A professor of geography at Ohio State University and Colgate University in the 1940s and 1950s, McCune also served during this time in India and China with the Foreign Economic Administration, earning a Presidential Medal of Freedom in 1946. McCune was named provost of the University of Massachusetts in 1955, leaving that post to serve as the first civil administrator of Japan's Ryukyo Islands from 1962 to 1964. Upon returning to the United States, he was named president of the University of Vermont. McCune also acted as an educational consultant for the United Nations mission in West Irian, directed the American Geographical Society for two years, and was director of the education department of the United Nations Educational, Scientific, and Cultural Organization (UNESCO). McCune returned to teaching at the University of Florida in Gainesville in 1969 and was named professor emeritus in 1979. His published works include *Korea's Heritage: A Regional and Social Geography, Views of the Geography of Korea, 1935-1960, Islands in Conflict in East Asian Waters,* and *Intelligence on the Economic Collapse of Japan in 1945.*

OBITUARIES AND OTHER SOURCES:

BOOKS

Who's Who in America, 46th edition, Marquis, 1990.

PERIODICALS

New York Times, January 8, 1993, p. A16.
Washington Post, January 9, 1993, p. B7.

*   *   *

McEVILLEY, Thomas   1939-

PERSONAL: Born July 13, 1939; son of Thomas McEvilley (an artist; in business) and Katherine (a social worker; maiden name, Bartlett) Friede; married Marion McMillen, 1961 (divorced, 1986); married Maura Sheehan (an artist), September, 26, 1992; children: Thomas, Alexander (deceased), Monte. *Education:* University of Cincinnati, B.A. (magna cum laude), 1963; University of Washington, M.A., 1965; University of Cincinnati, Ph.D. (with high honors), 1968. *Politics:* Democrat. *Religion:* Atheist.

ADDRESSES: Home—Box 20752, Tompkins Square Station, New York, NY 10009.

CAREER: Rice University, Houston, TX, associate professor, 1970—. Visiting professor at School of the Art Institute of Chicago, 1985-86, and Yale University, School of Art, 1991-92. Public speaker, visiting critic, and moderator and panel member on art issues. Art exhibitions include *The 84 Seasons* at Oil and Steel Gallery, New York, 1984, and the sound installations *Burn* and *The Black Box* at Middleberg, Holland, October, 1984. Has given poetry readings in Ohio, Ireland, and New York. Television appearances include several British Broadcasting Corporation programs on art.

MEMBER: Phi Beta Kappa.

AWARDS, HONORS: Critics grant, National Endowments for the Arts, 1984-85; Frank Jewett Mather Award, distinguished critic of the year, College Art Association, 1993.

WRITINGS:

Partygoing (novel), Award Books, 1964.

Wakerobin (novel), Award Books, 1965.

The Impregnation of the Guggenheim Museum, Solomon R. Guggenheim Foundation (New York), 1982.

44 Four-Line Poems, Full Court Press, 1982.

Pat Steir: The Breughel Series, A Vanitas of Style, Minneapolis College of Art and Design, 1985.

Ulay and Marina Abramovic: Modus Vivendi, Stedelijk Museum (Eindhoven, Holland), 1985.

Les Levine: Billboard Projects: BLAME GOD, Institute of Contemporary Arts (London), 1985.

Focus on the Image: Selections from the Rivendell Collection, Art Museum Association of America (New York), 1986.

Janis Kounellis, Museum of Contemporary Art (Chicago), 1986.

Julian Schnabel, The Whitechapel Gallery (London), 1986, revised edition, Whitney Museum (New York), 1987.

North of Yesterday (novel), McPherson, 1987.

Lucas Samaras: Objects and Subjects 1969-1986, Abbeville Press, 1988.

(With Ulay and Marina Abramovic) *The Lovers,* Stedelijk Museum, 1989.

(With Eric Orr and James Lee Byars) *Zero Mass,* Kaleidoscope Press, 1989.

William Anastasi, Scott Hanson Gallery (New York), 1989.

Georg Baselitz: Sculpture "Forty-Five," Pace Gallery, 1990.

Art and Discontent: Theory at the Millennium, Documentext, 1991.

Dennis Oppenheim: And the Mind Grew Fingers, Abrams, 1991.

Art and Otherness: Crisis of Cultural Identity, McPherson, 1992.

The Exile's Return: Redefining Painting for the Post-Modern Age, Cambridge University Press, 1993.

Yves Klein: Conquistador of the Void, Schirmer-Mosel Verlag (Berlin), 1993.

(With Amiri Baraka) *Thornton Dial: The Tiger Paintings,* Abrams, 1993.

The Arimaspea (novel), McPherson, 1993.

Pat Steir: The Water Paintings, Abrams, in press.

Contributor to books, including *Theories of Contemporary Art,* edited by Richard Hertz, Prentice Hall, 1984; *Africa Explores: Twentieth Century African Art,* edited by Susan Vogel, TeNeues Publishing Co., 1991; *Allocations: Art for a Natural and Artificial Environment,* Distributed Art Publishers, 1992; and *Tantra and Culture,* Mellen Press, 1993. Contributor of articles, poetry, short stories, and translations to periodicals, including *Artforum, Contemporanea, American Journal of Philology, Phoenix, Philosophy East and West, Hermes, Krisis,* and *Midwest.* Contributing editor to *Artforum,* 1982—, and editor in chief of *Contemporanea,* 1990. Author of essays for exhibition catalogues and audiocassette tapes for exhibitions.

McEvilley's works have been translated into French, German, Italian, Spanish, Greek, Turkish, Chinese, and Japanese.

WORK IN PROGRESS: The Garden of the Graces: Sapphic Imagery and the Bronze Age; The Shape of Ancient Thought: A Comparative Study of Greek and Indian Philosophies and Their Roots in the Bronze Age.

SIDELIGHTS: Thomas McEvilley told *CA:* "As a Classicist, I have a great love for the roots of Western civilization; at the same time, as an Orientalist I appreciate the selfhood of the so-called Other. This fusion informs all my work—creative writing, art criticism, and scholarship.

"Writing novels out of a deep respect for the seriousness of the novel in the Western tradition, I still have felt it important to open the novel up to multicultural modes of expression. My novel, *The Arimaspeia,* acts out this compulsion.

"As a critic, my deep love for the Western forms of visual expression collides with my sense of the damage that Western self-absorbedness has wrought upon the world. I advocate in many writings (such as *Art and Otherness*) an attempt on the part of white Westerners to deliberately open themselves to the visual selfhoods of other cultures—not to abandon one's own culture, but to relativize it.

"As a scholar I have been keenly aware of the repressed record of cross-cultural influences. My principal work—*The Shape of Ancient Thought: A Comparative Study of Greek and Indian Philosophies*—goes against the grain of parochial exclusionism so long practiced by Western specialized scholars. Its ultimate aim is to revive the nineteenth-century practice of studying Greek, Latin, and Sanskrit in the same curricula.

"Much of my recent work in these (and other) fields has dwelt upon the precise awareness both of cultural stereotypes and of a path of thought and feeling that may go beyond them."

*   *   *

McGRATH, Earl James 1902-1993

OBITUARY NOTICE—See index for *CA* sketch: Born November 16, 1902, in Buffalo, NY; died January 14, 1993, in Tucson, AZ. Educator, administrator, and author. McGrath's long career in the field of education included his role as the Commissioner of Education under presidents Harry S. Truman and Dwight D. Eisenhower. A professor at the State University of New York at Buffalo and other schools, McGrath also served as the head of such academic institutions as the State University of Iowa, the University of Kansas City, the Institute of Higher Education at Columbia Teachers College, Eisenhower College, and the Higher Education Center at Temple University. McGrath wrote several books on the subject of education, including *Education, the Wellspring of Democracy, Liberal Education in the Professions,* and *The Graduate School and the Decline of Liberal Education.*

OBITUARIES AND OTHER SOURCES:

BOOKS

Who's Who in the World, 11th edition, Marquis, 1991, p. 709.

PERIODICALS

Chicago Tribune, February 7, 1993, section 2, p. 6.
New York Times, February 5, 1993, p. A18.

*   *   *

McGURK, Slater
See ROTH, Arthur J(oseph)

*   *   *

McHENRY, Leemon B.   1956-

PERSONAL: Born September 1, 1956, in Camp Lejeune, NC. *Education:* University of Southern Mississippi, B.A., 1978, M.A., 1981; attended Louisiana State University, 1978, and London School of Economics and Political Science, London, 1979; University of Edinburgh, Ph.D., 1984. *Avocational interests:* Fencing, surfing, flying.

ADDRESSES: Home—831 1/2 Woodlawn Ave., Springfield, OH 45504. *Office*—Department of Philosophy, Wittenberg University, P.O. Box 720, Springfield, OH 45501.

CAREER: Old Dominion University, Norfolk, VA, adjunct assistant professor, 1985-86; St. Leo College, St. Leo, FL, adjunct assistant professor, 1985-86; Davidson College, Davidson, NC, visiting assistant professor, 1986-88, member of pre-medical review committee, 1987-88, adviser for students' philosophy society; Central Michigan University, Mt. Pleasant, MI, visiting assistant professor, founder of and adviser for fencing club, 1988-90, member of visiting speaker committee, 1989-90, adviser for students' philosophy society; Wittenberg University, Springfield, OH, assistant professor, founder of and adviser for fencing club, 1990—, member of Quine Conference committee, 1991-92, visiting speaker committee, 1991—, and international education committee, 1992—, faculty adviser for Phi Sigma Tau Honor Society in Philosophy. Affiliated with National Endowment for the Humanities Summer Institute on Nagarjuna and Buddhist Thought, University of Hawaii, 1989. Manuscript consultant for *Choice,* State University of New York Press, and Macmillan Publishing Company.

MEMBER: American Philosophical Association, Mind Association, Society for the Advancement of American Philosophy, Society for the Study of Process Philosophies, Phi Kappa Phi.

AWARDS, HONORS: Outstanding Graduate Student in Philosophy, University of Southern Mississippi, 1980; Overseas Research Students Award, Committee of Vice-Chancellors and Principals of the Universities of the United Kingdom, 1982-84; Annual Essay Prize, North Carolina Philosophical Society, 1987; research grants from Davidson College, 1987, Central Michigan University, 1989, Matchette Foundation, 1991, and Wittenberg University, 1993.

WRITINGS:

Whitehead and Bradley: A Comparative Analysis, edited by Robert Cummings Neville, State University of New York Press, 1991.
(Editor with Frederick Adams, and contributor) *Reflections on Philosophy: Introductory Essays,* St. Martin's, 1993.

Contributor to Victor Lowe's *Alfred North Whitehead: The Man and His Work, Volume II: 1910-1947,* edited by J. B. Schneewind, Johns Hopkins University Press, 1990. Contributor of articles and reviews to professional journals, including *Choice, Journal of Speculative Philosophy, Southern Journal of Philosophy, Review of Metaphysics,* and *Philosophical Books.*

WORK IN PROGRESS: Editing *Philosophy: Classic and Contemporary Readings,* with Frederick Adams, for St. Martin's; *The Event Universe: Revisionary Metaphysics Reconsidered,* a monograph; several scholarly articles; research on the philosophy of physics, theories of time, and cosmology.

*   *   *

McKERNAN, Victoria   1957-

PERSONAL: Born November 19, 1957, in Washington, DC; daughter of John V. (an army security agent) and Helen (Krzykowski) McKernan. *Education:* George Washington University, B.A., 1982.

ADDRESSES: Home and office—1421 Columbia Rd. N.W., No. 404, Washington, DC 20009. *Agent*—Matt Bialer, William Morris Agency, 1350 Avenue of the Americas, New York, NY 10019.

CAREER: Writer. Has held more than fifty occupations. Certified scuba diving instructor.

WRITINGS:

Osprey Reef (mystery), Carroll & Graf, 1990.
Point Deception (mystery), Carroll & Graf, 1992.

Contributor to periodicals, including *Newsweek* and *Washington Post.*

WORK IN PROGRESS: Crooked Island, another mystery; *Gideon,* a novel "about a bilingual, ambidextrous hermaphrodite"; children's books.

SIDELIGHTS: Victoria McKernan is a mystery writer who made her literary debut in 1990 with *Osprey Reef.* The novel introduces crime-solving heroine Chicago Nordejoong, whom Candy Sagon described in the *Washington Post* as "a sharp-tongued, scuba-diving young woman with a pet boa who eats lima bean sandwiches and cream of mushroom soup out of a can." Nordejoong is a notoriously poor cook: In *Point Deception,* McKernan's second mystery, Nordejoong is described by her lover as a culinary incompetent who would fail to prepare toast properly even if instructions were printed on the bread slices. Nordejoong is also the heroine of McKernan's forthcoming *Crooked Island,* in which Florida is threatened by both a hurricane and a malaria epidemic.

When asked what inspired her to write mysteries, McKernan told Sagon that she was once desperate for reading material while on a yacht. "I had run out of books and I was looking around the boat for something else to read when I found a mystery," she related. "I read it and thought, 'I could do this.'"

McKernan told *CA:* "After many years of vagabond bliss and at least fifty different jobs, from manual labor to dancing in an opera, I am currently *almost* making enough from various writings to live on. I wrote my first mystery as something of an exercise and a way to get my foot in the publishing door, but soon discovered I really liked the genre and was good at it. After many years of working on my 'real literature' I was always coming up against the same criticism: exciting stuff, but too 'all over the place.' Then one summer while crewing on a yacht and desperate for reading material, I picked up my first mystery and realized here was a genre that demanded good narrative structure, plot development, and prosaic restraint. Of course, I also had a good idea for a protagonist and story, based on my scuba-diving adventures.

"Chicago Nordejoong, heroine of *Osprey Reef* and *Point Deception,* is a sharp-tongued, independent young woman who grew up on merchant ships, now lives on her sailboat with her pet boa constrictor, and teaches scuba diving. A bit of a social misfit, Nordejoong stumbles into a tempestuous partnership with Alex Sanders, an ex-government agent.

"I base my books around scuba diving because the underwater world is a place I love and know well, and it is a place unknown and intriguing to most people. I also wanted to write a really good underwater fight scene,

shark attack, escape from a sunken cave, and daring nighttime rescue, all of which wound up in the first two books.

"The adventure and suspense are important elements of my books, but I still believe characters are paramount. What you have essentially, in a mystery or any other novel, is a story about people dealing with, and resolving, a certain conflict. As a reader, I will follow an interesting character anywhere and abandon the most artful plot if the character is one-dimensional or cliched.

"Nordejoong and Sanders are also the protagonists of the forthcoming *Crooked Island,* which revolves around maritime pharmacology, a hurricane, and a malaria epidemic in Florida."

BIOGRAPHICAL/CRITICAL SOURCES:

PERIODICALS

Mystery Scene, September/October, 1992.
Washington Post, December 20, 1990, p. E1; September 30, 1992.

*   *   *

McLOUGHLIN, William G.   1922-1993

OBITUARY NOTICE—See index for *CA* sketch: Born June 11, 1922, in Maplewood, NJ; died of liver cancer, January 4, 1993, in Providence, RI. Historian, educator, and author. A professor of history and religion at Brown University for almost forty years, McLoughlin researched and wrote about topics such as religion in early and modern America, the history of Rhode Island, and the Cherokee nation. He earned a Fulbright scholarship, a Guggenheim fellowship, and a National Endowment for the Humanities fellowship during his career. McLoughlin's published works include *New England Dissent, 1630-1833: The Baptists and the Separation of Church and State, Revivals, Awakenings, and Reform,* and *After the Trail of Tears: The Cherokees, 1839-1880,* which was in press at the time of his death.

OBITUARIES AND OTHER SOURCES:

BOOKS

Who's Who in America, 43rd edition, Marquis, 1984.

PERIODICALS

New York Times, January 6, 1993, p. B6.

*   *   *

McMILLAN, Terry (L.)   1951-

PERSONAL: Born October 18, 1951, in Port Huron, MI; daughter of Edward McMillan and Madeline Washington

Tillman; children: Solomon Welch. *Education:* University of California, Berkeley, B.S., 1979; Columbia University, M.F.A., 1979.

ADDRESSES: Home—Free at Last, P.O. Box 2408, Danville, CA 94526. *Agent*—Molly Friedrich, Aaron Priest Literary Agency, 122 East Forty-second St., Suite 3902, New York, NY 10168.

CAREER: University of Wyoming, Laramie, instructor, 1987-90; University of Arizona, Tucson, professor, 1990-92; writer.

MEMBER: PEN, Author's League.

AWARDS, HONORS: National Endowment for the Arts fellowship, 1988.

WRITINGS:

Mama (novel), Houghton, 1987.
Disappearing Acts (novel), Viking, 1989.
(Editor) *Breaking Ice: An Anthology of Contemporary African-American Fiction,* Viking, 1990.
Waiting to Exhale (novel), Viking, 1992.

Contributor to *Five for Five: The Films of Spike Lee,* Stewart, Tabori, 1991.

SIDELIGHTS: "Terry McMillan has the power to be an important contemporary novelist," stated Valerie Sayers reviewing *Disappearing Acts* in the *New York Times Book Review* back in 1989. "Watch Terry McMillan. She's going to be a major writer," predicted a short but positive review of the same novel in *Cosmopolitan.* McMillan had already garnered attention and critical praise for her first novel, *Mama,* which was published in 1987. Over the next five years, these predictions began to come true. In 1992 McMillan saw the publication of *Waiting to Exhale,* her third novel. Her publisher sent her on a twenty-city, six-week tour, and McMillan appeared on several popular television programs including the *Oprah Winfrey Show,* the *Arsenio Hall Show,* and *Today.*

"Seriously, I just don't get it; I really don't," the author mused during an interview with Audrey Edwards for *Essence.* But McMillan's honest, unaffected writings have clearly struck a chord with the book-buying public. Paperback rights for *Waiting to Exhale* fetched a hefty $2.64 million, making the deal with Pocket Books the second largest of its kind in publishing history. And in September of 1992, Twentieth Century-Fox optioned the book for film.

McMillan grew up in Port Huron, Michigan, a city approximately sixty miles northeast of Detroit. Her working-class parents did not make a point of reading to their five children, but McMillan discovered the pleasure of reading as a teenager shelving books in a local library.

Prior to working in the library, she had no exposure to books by black writers. McMillan recalled feeling embarrassed when she saw a book by James Baldwin with his picture on the cover. In a *Washington Post* article, she was quoted as saying, "I . . . did not read his book because I was too afraid. I couldn't imagine that he'd have anything better or different to say than [German essayist and novelist] Thomas Mann, [American writer] Henry Thoreau, [American essayist and poet] Ralph Waldo Emerson. . . . Needless to say, I was not just naive, but had not yet acquired an ounce of black pride."

Later, as a student at a community college in Los Angeles, McMillan immersed herself in most of the classics of African-American literature. After reading Alex Haley's *Autobiography of Malcolm X,* McMillan realized that she had no reason to be ashamed of a people who had such a proud history. At age twenty-five, she published her first short story. Eleven years after that, her first novel, *Mama,* was released by Houghton Mifflin.

McMillan was determined not to let her debut novel go unnoticed. Typically, first novels receive little publicity other than the press releases and galleys sent out by the publisher. When McMillan's publisher told her that they could not do more for her, McMillan decided to promote the book on her own. She wrote over three thousand letters to chain bookstores, independent booksellers, universities, and colleges. Although what she was doing seemed logical in her own mind, the recipients of her letters were not used to such efforts by an author. They found her approach hard to resist, so by the end of the summer of 1987 she had several offers for readings. McMillan then scheduled her own book publicity tour and let her publicist know where she was going instead of it being the other way around.

By the time *Waiting to Exhale* was published, it was the other way around. The scene at a reading from the novel was described in the *Los Angeles Times* this way: "Several hundred fans, mostly black and female, are shoehorned into Marcus Bookstore on a recent Saturday night. Several hundred more form a line down the block and around the corner. The reading . . . hasn't begun because McMillan is greeting those who couldn't squeeze inside. . . . Finally, the writer . . . steps through the throng."

McMillan had come a long way since the publication of her first novel, which started out as a short story. "I really love the short story as a form," stated McMillan in an interview with *Writer's Digest.* "Mama" was just one of several short stories that McMillan had tried with limited success to get into print. Then the Harlem Writer's Guild accepted her into their group and told her that "Mama" really should be a novel and not a short story. After four weeks at the MacDowell artists colony and two weeks at the Yaddo colony, McMillan had expanded her short story into over four hundred pages. When her agent suggested certain revisions to the book, McMillan questioned whether the woman truly understood what the book was about.

Frustrated by this and by certain events taking place in her personal life, McMillan took things into her own hands and sent her collection of short stories to Houghton Mifflin. Hoping that she would at least get some free editorial advice, McMillan was surprised when the publisher contacted her about the novel she had mentioned briefly in her letter to them. She sent them pages from *Mama* and approximately four days later got word from the Houghton Mifflin that they loved it.

Mama tells the story of the struggle Mildred Peacock has raising her five children after she throws her drunkard husband out of the house. The novel begins: "Mildred hid the ax beneath the mattress of the cot in the dining room." With those words, McMillan's novel becomes "a runaway narrative pulling a crowded cast of funny, earthy characters," stated Sayers in the *New York Times Book Review*. Because of McMillan's promotional efforts, the novel received numerous reviews—the overwhelming majority of which were positive—and McMillan gave thirty-nine readings. Six weeks after *Mama* was published, it went into its third printing.

Disappearing Acts, her second novel, proved to be quite different from *Mama*. For *Disappearing Acts,* McMillan chose to tell the story of star-crossed lovers by alternating the narrative between the main characters. Zora Banks and Franklin Swift fall in love "at first sight" when they meet at Zora's new apartment, where Franklin works as part of the renovating crew. Zora is an educated black woman working as a junior high school music teacher; Franklin is a high-school dropout working in construction. In spite of the differences in their backgrounds, the two become involved, move in together, and try to overcome the fear they both feel because of past failures in love.

Writing in the *Washington Post Book World,* David Nicholson pointed out that although this difference in backgrounds is an old literary device, it is one that is particularly relevant to black Americans: "Professional black women complain of an ever-shrinking pool of eligible men, citing statistics that show the number of black men in prison is increasing, while the number of black men in college is decreasing. Articles on alternatives for women, from celibacy to 'man-sharing' to relationships with blue-collar workers like Franklin have long been a staple of black general interest and women's magazines."

McMillan expressed her thoughts on this issue in an article she wrote entitled "Looking for Mr. Right" for the February, 1990, issue of *Essence*. "Maybe it's just me, but I'm finding it harder and harder to meet men. . . . I grew up and became what my mama prayed out loud I'd become: educated, strong, smart, independent and reliable. . . . Now it seems as if carving a place for myself in the world is backfiring. Never in a million years would I have dreamed that I'd be 38 years old and still single."

Throughout the rest of the article, McMillan discusses how she had planned to be married by age twenty-four but found herself attending graduate school instead. She ended up loving and living with men who did not, as she puts it, "take life as seriously as I did." When she was thirty-two years old, she gave birth to her son, Solomon. Shortly after that she ended a three-year relationship with her son's father. Since then McMillan had been involved in what she called "two powerful but short-lived relationships," both of which ended when, without any explanation, the man stopped calling.

McMillan believes that "even though a lot of 'professional' men claim to want a smart, independent woman, they're kidding themselves." She thinks that these men do not feel secure unless they are with passive women or with women who will "back down, back off or just acquiesce" until they appear to be tamed. "I'm not tamable," declared McMillan in *Essence*. In response to a former boyfriend who told her that it is lonely at the top, McMillan replied, "It is lonely 'out here.' But I wouldn't for a minute give up all that I've earned just to have a man. I just wish it were easier to meet men and get to know them."

Reviewers commended McMillan on her ability to give such a true voice to the character of Franklin in *Disappearing Acts*. One reviewer for the *Washington Post Book World* called the novel "one of the few . . . to contain rounded, sympathetic portraits of black men and to depict relationships between black men and black women as something more than the relationship between victimizer and victim, oppressor and oppressed." In the *New York Times Book Review,* another reviewer stated: "The miracle is that Ms. McMillan takes the reader so deep into this man's head—and makes what goes on there so complicated—that [the] story becomes not only comprehensible but affecting." Not only did McMillan's second novel win critical acclaim, it also was optioned for a film; McMillan eventually wrote the screenplay for Metro-Goldwyn-Mayer.

Leonard Welch, McMillan's former lover and the father of their son, also found that portions of *Disappearing Acts* rung true—so true, in fact, that in August of 1990 he filed a $4.75 million defamation suit against McMillan. Welch claimed that McMillan used him as the model for the novel's main male character, and therefore the book defamed him. The suit also named Penguin USA (parent company of Viking, the publisher of the book) and Simon & Schuster (publisher of the book in paperback) as defendants.

The suit alleged that McMillan had acted maliciously in writing the novel and that she had written it mainly out of vindictiveness and a sense of revenge toward Welch. In addition to believing that the novel realistically portrayed his three-year relationship with McMillan, Welch claimed that he suffered emotional stress. McMillan had dedicated the book to their son, and Welch feared that Solomon would believe the defamatory parts of the novel when he was old enough to read it.

Martin Garbus, the lawyer for Penguin USA, maintained that if McMillan had been an obscure writer who wrote an obscure book, then there would not have been a lawsuit at all. One of McMillan's writing peers was quoted in the *Los Angeles Times* as saying, "I think it's just part of the general nastiness of the time, that people see someone doing well and they want part of it."

The suit raised the issue of the delicate balance fiction writers must maintain. Many novelists draw on their experiences when writing, and most feel that they have an obligation to protect the privacy of an individual. In the *Los Angeles Times,* Garbus explained: "What Terry McMillan has done is no different than what other writers have done. It has to be permissible to draw on your real-life experiences. Otherwise, you can't write fiction." Most people involved in the suit, including Welch's lawyer, agreed that a victory for Welch could set an unfortunate precedent that would inhibit the creativity of fiction writers.

In April of 1991, the New York Supreme Court ruled in McMillan's favor. As reported in the *Wall Street Journal,* the judge in the case wrote that although "the fictional character and the real man share the same occupation and educational background and even like the same breakfast cereal . . . the man in the novel is a lazy, emotionally disturbed alcoholic who uses drugs and sometimes beats his girlfriend." The judge declared that "Leonard Welch is none of these things."

In 1990 Viking published *Breaking Ice: An Anthology of Contemporary African-American Fiction.* Edited by Mc-Millan, the anthology came into being as a result of the anger she experienced after reading a collection of short stories that did not include any black or Third World writers. Her research and book proposal were the first steps in correcting what McMillan felt was the publishing industry's neglect of black writers. She received almost three hundred submissions for the anthology and chose fifty-seven seasoned, emerging, and unpublished writers.

In reviewing *Breaking Ice* for the *Washington Post Book World,* author Joyce Carol Oates characterized the book

as "a wonderfully generous and diverse collection of prose fiction by our most gifted African-American writers." Oates credited McMillan's judgment for selecting such "high quality of writing . . . that one could hardly distinguish between the categories [of writers] in terms of originality, depth of vision and command of the language."

McMillan's third novel, *Waiting to Exhale,* tells the stories of four professional black women who have everything except for the love of a good man. The overall theme of the book is men's fear of commitment; a subtheme is the fear of growing old alone. The novel has hit a nerve with its readers—both male and female. Many women seem to identify with McMillan's characters; so do some men. According to the *Los Angeles Times,* one black male from an audience of over two thousand proclaimed: "I think I speak for a lot of brothers. I know I'm all over the book. . . . All I can say is, I'm willing to learn. Being defensive is not the answer." This is precisely the response to the book that McMillan was hoping to get. She wants people to understand that she is not trying to offend or insult black males. She just wants men to be aware of the things they do that make it difficult for women to love them.

One issue that emerged from many reviews of McMillan's earlier books is the amount of profanity she uses. *Waiting to Exhale* met with the same criticism. One critic called her characters male-bashing stand-up comedians who use foul language. For McMillan, reproducing her characters' profane language is her way of staying close to them. She believes that basically the language she uses is accurate. She told *Publishers Weekly:* "That's the way we talk. And I want to know why I've never read a review where they complain about the language that male writers use!"

For her portrayal of feisty, tough, black heroines, McMillan has been compared to acclaimed black women writers Alice Walker, Gloria Naylor, and Zora Neale Hurston. McMillan acknowledges the compliment but asserts in the introduction to *Breaking Ice* that her generation of black writers is "a new breed, free to write as we please . . . because of the way life has changed." Life has changed for her generation but it has also stayed the same for many women in one fundamental way: the search for happiness and fulfillment continues. In an article in the *Los Angeles Times,* McMillan maintained: "A house and a car and all the money in the bank won't make you happy. People need people. People crave intimacy."

Ever mindful of the fleeting nature of fame, McMillan views her celebrity status with a clear eye and remains focused on her mission as a writer. "This won't last," she stated in *Essence.* "Today it's me. Tomorrow it will be somebody else. I always remember that."

BIOGRAPHICAL/CRITICAL SOURCES:

BOOKS

Contemporary Literary Criticism, Gale, Volume 50, 1988, Volume 61, 1991.

McMillan, Terry, *Mama,* Houghton, 1987.

McMillan, editor, *Breaking Ice: An Anthology of Contemporary African-American Fiction,* Viking, 1990.

PERIODICALS

Callaloo, summer, 1988, pp. 649-50.

Cosmopolitan, August, 1989.

Detroit News, September 7, 1992.

Emerge, September, 1992.

Essence, February, 1990; October, 1992.

Esquire, July, 1988, pp. 100, 102, 104.

Los Angeles Times, February 23, 1987; October 29, 1990, section E, p. 1; June 19, 1992.

New York Times Book Review, February 22, 1987, p. 11; August 6, 1989, p. 8; May 31, 1992, p. 12.

New York Times Magazine, August 9, 1992, p. 20.

People, July 20, 1992.

Publishers Weekly, May 11, 1992; July 13, 1992; September 21, 1992.

Tribune Books (Chicago), September 23, 1990, p. 1; May 31, 1992, p. 6.

Village Voice, March 24, 1987, p. 46.

Wall Street Journal, April 11, 1991.

Washington Post, November 17, 1990, section D, p. 1.

Washington Post Book World, August 27, 1989, p. 6; September 16, 1990, p. 1; May 24, 1992, p. 11.

Writer's Digest, October, 1987.

—*Sketch by Debra G. Darnell*

*　　*　　*

MEAD, Christopher Curtis 1953-

PERSONAL: Born April 30, 1953, in New Haven, CT; son of William Curtis (a professor) and Katherine (a museum director; maiden name, Harper) Mead; married Michele Penhall (a writer), October 20, 1990. *Education:* University of California, Riverside, B.A. (summa cum laude), 1975; University of Pennsylvania, M.A., 1978, Ph.D., 1986.

ADDRESSES: Home—4504 Sunningdale Ave. N.E., Albuquerque, NM 87110. *Office*—Department of Art and Art History, University of New Mexico, Albuquerque, NM 98131.

CAREER: University of New Mexico, Albuquerque, lecturer, 1980-86, assistant professor, 1986-89, associate professor of art and art history, 1989—, head of department, 1992—. Rice University, guest curator, 1993.

MEMBER: Society of Architectural Historians, College Art Association, Phi Beta Kappa.

AWARDS, HONORS: Samuel H. Kress fellow, 1988; Faculty Achievement Award, Burlington Resources Foundation, 1992.

WRITINGS:

Space for the Continuous Present in the Residential Architecture of Bart Prince, University of New Mexico Art Museum, 1989.

(Editor and author of introduction) *The Architecture of Robert Venturi,* University of New Mexico Press, 1989.

Houses by Bart Prince: An American Architecture for the Continuous Present, University of New Mexico Press, 1991.

Charles Garnier's Paris Opera: Architectural Empathy and the Renaissance of French Classicism, MIT Press, 1991.

Contributor to books, including *Gallery Works: Bart Prince,* Farish Gallery, Rice University, 1993. Contributor of articles and reviews to periodicals, including *New Mexico Architecture, New Mexico Historical Review, Art Bulletin,* and *Art Space.* Co-editor, *New Mexico Studies in the Fine Arts,* 1982.

WORK IN PROGRESS: Bart Prince: The American Practice of Organic Architecture; Victor Baltard: City Architect of Nineteenth-Century Paris, a monograph.

*　　*　　*

MEDICINE-EAGLE, Brooke 1943-

PERSONAL: Born April 24, 1943, in Thermopolis, WY. *Education:* University of Denver, B.A., 1965; Mankato State University, M.A.; doctoral study at Humanistic Psychology Institute. *Politics:* Liberal. *Religion:* "Native American spirituality." *Avocational interests:* Wilderness backpacking, horseback riding, beading and traditional arts.

ADDRESSES: Office—Sky Lodge, P.O. Box 121, Ovando, MT 59854. *Agent*—Wabun Wind, P.O. Box 199, Devon, PA 19333.

CAREER: Elementary and high school teacher, 1965-68; San Francisco State University, San Francisco, CA, professor of Native American studies, 1975-76; self-employed teacher and consultant in the United States and abroad, 1978—. Singer and songwriter for Harmony Network; consultant in sacred ecology and sustainable design.

MEMBER: Phi Beta Kappa.

AWARDS, HONORS: Ford Foundation fellow.

WRITINGS:

Buffalo Woman Comes Singing, Ballantine, 1991.

Work represented in anthologies, including *The Woman-spirit Sourcebook,* edited by Patrice Wynne, Harper, 1988; *Healers on Healing,* edited by Richard Carlson and Benjamin Shield, J. P. Tarcher, 1989; and *Childlessness Transformed: Stories of Alternative Parenting,* edited by Jane English, Earth Heart, 1989. Contributor to periodicals, including *Wildfire, Woman of Power, Self Discovery: Arizona Magazine for Mind, Body, and Spirit, Shaman's Drum, American Theosophist,* and *White Clouds Poetry Revue.*

AUDIO TAPES

Tape cassettes for New Dimensions Radio include *The Indian Medicine Way, Earth Is Our Mother, The Rainbow Warrior, Spirit Dance, Native Visions: Healing the Heart,* and *Tales of White Buffalo Woman.*

WORK IN PROGRESS: Song of the Seven Shields, a teaching story of American native ways.

SIDELIGHTS: Brooke Medicine-Eagle told *CA:* "Two days after my birth in the hot springs town of Thermopolis, Wyoming, near where my mother had been raised, I was brought home to our self-sufficient ranch on my home reservation, the Crow Reservation in southeastern Montana. There my parents, my brother, and I lived in relative isolation, our days filled with the tasks of making a life raising cattle and horses and the crops that fed them and us. Much of my basic sacred ecological framework developed in those years in the beauty of the wilderness, where I did every possible kind of work, from building barns to basic veterinary work, from carrying water from our spring to keeping house in our old log home— and making do with what we had. We had no electricity or running water for most of the years of my childhood, so my early experience was very much like what many people lived in the late 1800s.

"That background, and my experience of being in San Francisco in the fading days of the hippie era, when a whole new consciousness was being born, have given me a broader base of understanding than that spanned by most of my contemporaries. This foundation was enhanced by my native background, though I was raised in a white world; by the relative poverty of my childhood, though I received a scholarship to an elite school for college; by being taught at home for the first years of my schooling and then becoming a teacher myself; and by spending time with wise teachers from many places around the world. All this has given me a varied and enriching experience, and it helped form my identification as a 'rainbow' teacher: a person who is global in feeling and devotion, whose love is for Mother Earth and *all* her children, whose connections are among and between many groups and ways, rather than within one specific way.

"I began writing as a way to share with more and more interested people the understandings from my experience, especially those things with native influence. I believe that the understanding of how to live in harmony with all things in the circle of life is vital information for all people in this time of ecological and social crisis; and if my words can be helpful, I am glad to share them. I want my writings to stimulate my readers to action in service of their own wholeness and that of the entire circle of life, rather than simply to entertain them.

"My work in progress is a fiction work, in which ways of Earth peoples are shared through the eyes of a young girl learning her tribe's spiritual ways. Writing is a real joy for me; I seem to have a 'channel' in my brain that can be turned on at will, to pour forth the story. I am as interested in reading what comes out on the page as are most of my readers!"

BIOGRAPHICAL/CRITICAL SOURCES:

PERIODICALS

East West Journal, January, 1979, p. 42; November, 1981, p. 31; January, 1982, p. 24.
New Age Journal, May, 1983.
Whole Life Times, September, 1982.
Wildfire, Volume IV, number 1, 1988, p. 32.

*   *   *

MEHAFFEY, Karen Rae   1959-

PERSONAL: Born March 16, 1959, in Ann Arbor, MI; daughter of Donald R. (a marketing executive) and Betty Jane (a secretary and homemaker) Forsyth; married Colin H. Mehaffey (a processing engineer), October 21, 1989. *Education:* University of Michigan—Dearborn, A.B. (with honors), 1981; University of Michigan, A.M.L.S., 1982.

ADDRESSES: Home—14500 Prospect, Apt. 210, Dearborn, MI 48126. *Office*—Cardinal Szoka Theological Library, Sacred Heart Major Seminary, 2701 West Chicago Blvd., Detroit, MI 48206.

CAREER: Gale Research Co., Detroit, MI, research assistant for *Literary Criticism,* 1982-83, research coordinator, 1983-84; University of Michigan—Dearborn, library assistant in archives, 1985; high school music teacher and head librarian in Detroit, 1986-88; Sacred Heart Major Seminary, Detroit, assistant librarian in cataloging and technical services, Cardinal Szoka Theological Library, 1988—, acting head librarian, 1992—. Professional vocalist (mezzo soprano), 1980—. National Women's History Network, member of speaker's bureau; Historic Fort Wayne, member of Detroit volunteer program, 1987—; Greenmead Historic Village, volunteer worker, 1987—; member of Seventeenth Michigan Volunteer Infantry, 1987—, and Ladies Soldiers Friend Society, 1992—.

MEMBER: American Library Association (and its Technical Services Roundtable), Catholic Library Association, History Education Association, American Friends of the Vatican Library, Michigan Library Association.

WRITINGS:

Victorian American Women, 1840-1880: An Annotated Bibliography, Garland Publishing, 1992.

Contributor of articles and reviews to journals, including *Victorian Revue* and *Michigan Historical Review.* Contributing editor, *Camp Chase Gazette,* 1988—, and *Civil War Lady,* 1992—.

WORK IN PROGRESS: Womanhood in Victorian America, 1840-1880, for Garland Publishing, completion expected in 1994; *Women in the American Civil War, 1861-1865: A Select, Annotated Bibliography,* Greenwood Press, 1995; research on the genre of consolation literature written for women in the United States from 1800 to 1880, and on mourning traditions and fashions; research on etiquette, social activities, and the domesticity of the middle-class woman in America, 1840-1880, with an emphasis on the Civil War era.

SIDELIGHTS: Karen Rae Mehaffey told *CA:* "My interest in Victorian American women's studies comes from a life-long love for cultural history. Raised in the Detroit area, I come from a family of teachers, loggers, and automotive industry employees, and this eclectic background made me develop a love of all things American. While other children spent summer vacations visiting amusement parks, my parents took me to Williamsburg, Sturbridge Village, and national battlefields. I worked at Greenfield Village, the open-air museum in Dearborn, Michigan, during high school and college, and developed an ability to interpret history to the public. This deepened my respect for the women of our collective American past, and how hard they worked to create a home and raise a family.

"After completing my education, I developed an interest in Civil War living history, a hobby pursued by thousands of people across the United States. After joining a local organization, I found it would be necessary to research and document almost everything about Victorian women's lives, in order to create the appropriate clothing and persona for a re-enactment of this historical period for the public. In doing so, I also found that much of the information I sought on women had not been documented by twentieth-century historians and writers, and much of what is available is inaccurate or poorly written. This set me on a course to pursue Victorian women's studies.

"My hobby has now grown into a second profession, and has influenced me to write for a variety of small press specialty journals and academic journals, and to write books. I also lecture on my research, but tend to make presentations in period garb, in order to increase the audience's understanding of the Victorian lady of the mid-century.

"In my writing, I hope to help people access, understand, and appreciate the American woman of the nineteenth century, and to increase awareness of the growing field of women's studies."

*   *   *

MELMAN, Yossi (Bili) 1950-

PERSONAL: Born December 27, 1950, in Zabrze, Poland; immigrated to Israel; son of Yitzhak (an industrialist) and Anna (a homemaker; maiden name, Horwitz) Melman; married Billie Rosenzweig (a historian), July 6, 1976; children: Yotam-Dov, Daria. *Education:* Hebrew University of Jerusalem, B.A., 1976; attended Harvard University, 1989-90. *Religion:* Jewish.

ADDRESSES: Home—13 Karni St., Ramat-Ativ, 69025 Tel Aviv, Israel. *Office*—*Ha'aretz,* 21 Schocken St., 61001 Tel Aviv, Israel. *Agent*—Scott Meredith Literary Agency, 845 Third Ave., New York, NY 10022.

CAREER: Kol Israel (radio), Jerusalem, Israel, economic correspondent, 1975-80; *Ha'aretz* (daily newspaper), Tel Aviv, Israel, European correspondent in London, 1980-84, special correspondent, 1989—; *Davar* (daily newspaper), Tel Aviv, chief diplomatic correspondent, 1984-89. *Jane's Defence Weekly,* Israeli correspondent, 1984-87; *Glasgow Herald,* Israeli correspondent, 1984-89. Lecturer on Israel and other subjects. *Military service:* Israeli Defence Forces, 1969-72.

MEMBER: National Federation of Israeli Journalists.

AWARDS, HONORS: The Master Terrorist: The True Story of Abu Nidal was selected by the *New York Times* as a notable paperback of 1987; Overseas Press Club of America award, 1987; Nieman fellow in journalism, Harvard University, 1989-90; *Every Spy a Prince: The Complete History of Israel's Intelligence Community* received an award from the *New York Times* in 1990.

WRITINGS:

The CIA Report on Israel's Intelligence Community (in Hebrew), Zabam, 1982.
The Master Terrorist: The True Story of Abu Nidal, Adama, 1986.

(With Dan Raviv) *Behind the Uprising: Israelis, Jordanians, and Palestinians,* Greenwood Press, 1989.

(With Raviv) *The Imperfect Spies,* Sidgwick & Jackson, 1989, published in the United States as *Every Spy a Prince: The Complete History of Israel's Intelligence Community,* Houghton, 1990.

The New Israelis: An Intimate View of a Changing People, Birch Lane Press, 1992.

(With Raviv) *Friends in Deed: Inside the U.S.-Israel Alliance,* Hyperion, in press.

Also author of *A Profile of a Terrorist Organization,* in Hebrew. Contributor of articles and editorials to the *Washington Post, New York Times, Los Angeles Times, Boston Globe, Newsweek,* and *International Herald Tribune.*

SIDELIGHTS: As a correspondent for the Israeli state radio service, major newspapers in Tel Aviv, and periodicals in Great Britain and the United States, Yossi Melman has developed a reputation as one of Israel's leading journalists. He has written and lectured on Israel and its society, Arab-Israeli conflicts, the Palestinian uprising, defense concerns, the Israeli intelligence community, Israeli-American relations, Europe, and other issues. Melman's first book published in English explores an issue that plagues the Middle East: terrorism.

In *The Master Terrorist: The True Story of Abu Nidal,* Melman profiles the elusive Palestinian responsible for numerous terrorist attacks against Arab moderates and Westerners. Abu Nidal, whose name means "father of the struggle," was born Sabri al-Banna in 1937 into a family of wealthy landholders in Palestine. However, his family lost everything when Israel was born in 1948 and the new nation seized much Palestinian land, including the family's property. Young Sabri spent several years in a refugee camp in the Gaza Strip. "Melman writes that terrorists are not born but made in places like the Palestinian refugee camps in Lebanon," noted John Kifner in the *New York Times Book Review.*

Such was the case for Sabri al-Banna. In *The Master Terrorist,* Melman explains how Sabri emerged from the camp to study in Jerusalem and Cairo, Egypt. The Palestinian then moved to Saudi Arabia to work, but soon turned to political agitation. He was deported from Saudi Arabia and Sudan for his activities. He eventually joined the Palestine Liberation Organization (PLO) and served for a period as chief of its office in Iraq. Dissatisfied with the PLO's trend toward moderation, he left in the early 1970s to found the more militant Abu Nidal Group.

Melman further shows that over the next twelve years, Abu Nidal and his organization carried out more than eighty attacks in Europe and the Middle East. Behind a veil of secrecy and front organizations such as Black September, Black June, and the Revolutionary Command, the terrorist masterminded the 1973 assassinations of the U.S. Ambassador to Sudan and a European diplomat, the 1982 assassination of the Israeli Ambassador to Great Britain, the 1985 murder of sixty passengers on board an Egyptian airliner, and the shootings at the El Al (Israeli airline) counters in Rome, Italy, and Vienna, Austria, that left nineteen people dead. In his book, Melman "provides a powerful portrait of a violent mind and of one of the world's most dangerous individuals," commented Herbert Mitgang in the *New York Times.*

Since breaking with the PLO, Abu Nidal has established ties with Syria, Iraq, Lebanon, Libya, and other Middle Eastern nations. And, as Mitgang noted, Melman's book offers "an inside view of the workings of the Palestine Liberation Organization and other terrorist groups, complete with infrastructure, names and places." The difficulty that Melman faces in his profile is the same difficulty faced by counter-terrorist organizations. As Kifner pointed out, "because of the secrecy with which Abu Nidal guards his structure of small, isolated cells, we get little more than a glimpse of his organization's training, recruitment of students and discipline, or of the hard nature of the man himself." *Maclean's* contributor Michael Posner commented that the book "raises as many questions as it answers." Still, he concluded, "Melman's interim report on one of the world's leading exponents of terrorism offers an excellent introduction."

Melman has collaborated with Columbia Broadcasting System (CBS) News correspondent Dan Raviv on two other books about Israel and the Middle East. For more information about *Behind the Uprising: Israelis, Jordanians, and Palestinians* and *Every Spy a Prince: The Complete History of Israel's Intelligence Community,* see Dan Raviv's entry in this volume.

BIOGRAPHICAL/CRITICAL SOURCES:

PERIODICALS

Los Angeles Times Book Review, April 29, 1990; July 29, 1990.
Maclean's, January 19, 1987.
New Statesman, August 30, 1991.
New York Times, August 8, 1986; July 14, 1990.
New York Times Book Review, September 14, 1986; July 8, 1990.
Times Literary Supplement, January 26, 1990.
Washington Post Book World, August 12, 1990.

*   *   *

MEREDITH, Scott   1923-1993

OBITUARY NOTICE—See index for *CA* sketch: Born November 24, 1923, in New York, NY; died of cancer,

February 11, 1993, in Manhasset, NY. Literary agent, editor, and writer. Cofounder of the Scott Meredith Literary Agency, Meredith was known for introducing the concept of auctioning manuscripts to publishers in the 1950s. During his career, the agent had such notable clients as Norman Mailer, P. G. Wodehouse, Arthur C. Clarke, Margaret Truman, Carl Sagan, Spiro T. Agnew, and Judith Campbell Exner. Meredith also edited a number of anthologies and wrote several books, including *Writing to Sell, George S. Kaufman and His Friends,* and *Louis B. Mayer and His Enemies.*

OBITUARIES AND OTHER SOURCES:

BOOKS

The Writers Directory: 1992-1994, St. James Press, 1992, p. 671.

PERIODICALS

Los Angeles Times, February 15, 1993, p. A26.
New York Times, February 13, 1993, p. 10.
Times (London), February 17, 1993, p. 17.

* * *

MERRIMAN, Catherine 1949-

PERSONAL: Born April 28, 1949, in London, England; daughter of Charles Roycroft (a psychoanalyst) and Chloe Aldridge (a psychiatrist; maiden name, Majolier); married Christopher Merriman (a housing officer), September 12, 1970; children: Roger, Chloe. *Education:* University of Kent at Canterbury, B.A. (with honors), 1970. *Politics:* "Greenish Labour." *Religion:* None.

ADDRESSES: Home—Tankers Row, Railwayside, South Clydach, Abergavenny, Gwent NP7 0RD, Wales.

CAREER: Senior assistant statistician for civil service offices in London, England, and Gwent, Wales, 1970-75; Ecoropa (environmental organization), Crickhowell, Powys, Wales, part-time administrative worker, 1987—. Abergavenny Women's Aid, volunteer worker, 1980-91.

MEMBER: Society of Authors, Welsh Academy (associate member).

AWARDS, HONORS: Runner-up for Welsh Book of the Year Award, 1992, for *Silly Mothers;* Ruth Hadden Memorial Award, 1992, for *Leaving the Light On.*

WRITINGS:

Silly Mothers (stories), Hound, 1991.
Leaving the Light On (novel), Gollancz, 1992.

Work represented in anthologies, including *Iron Women,* 1991; and *The New Penguin Book of Welsh Short Stories,* Penguin, 1993. Contributor of stories and poems to periodicals, including *New Welsh Review, New England Review,* and *Everywoman.* Stories have been broadcast by BBC-Radio.

WORK IN PROGRESS: A contemporary novel about male competition and violence.

SIDELIGHTS: Catherine Merriman told *CA:* "Although I am English, I moved in my early twenties to South Wales, where my husband and I live in a stone cottage on a disused railway line halfway up a small mountain. We share the property with our two children, our two dogs, and assorted motor bikes.

"I had no thought of being a writer until I was thirty-five. In my twenties I was a government statistician, but gave it up for a succession of temporary part-time jobs when my children were born. With hindsight, I feel that, up to the age of thirty-five, I was absorbing input—from books, film, radio, people, and life experiences—and that I simply reached a point when I became 'full' and urgently needed to produce output. The pressure to write came suddenly and, at first, was very intense. Both my novels owe much to the eleven years I spent as a volunteer worker for a women's aid group, though neither draws explicitly on my experiences.

"*Leaving the Light On* is a novel of power relationships and the different ways we care for or about other people, and my second novel is primarily concerned with male-to-male competition and aggression. I do not, however, in either my novels or short stories, set out with the intention of making political or sociological points. The stories come first, and what I am trying to say becomes apparent to me as I mold the narrative. I write for myself, and when I read fiction, I want to be engaged by characters and gripped by story lines, so that is how I try to write.

"My short stories are carefully crafted, with nearly always a beginning, middle, and end, because that's the sort of tidy-minded, eye-on-the-ball person I am, but they are not always naturalistic, and can be about anything. I'm as happy writing about a woman who can fly, or who is invisible to herself in mirrors, as I am writing about a child's lust for danger, or bikers out dead-sheep-stealing on the Welsh hills for an evening barbecue."

* * *

MICOU, Paul 1959-

PERSONAL: Surname pronounced "mee-*koo*"; born April 22, 1959, in San Francisco, CA; son of Paul (an attorney) and Ann (an editor; maiden name, McKiastry) Micou; married Anna Ulrika Nilsson (a management consultant), October 6, 1990. *Education:* Harvard University, B.A., 1981.

Addresses: Office—Transworld Publishers, 61-63 Uxbridge Rd., Ealing, London W5 55A, England. *Agent*—Arthur Goodhart, 3 Vicarage Gate, London W8 4HH, England.

CAREER: Writer.

WRITINGS:

The Music Programme (novel), Bantam, 1989.
The Cover Artist (novel), Bantam, 1990.
The Death of David Debrizzi (novel), Bantam, 1991.
Rotten Times, Bantam, 1992.

SIDELIGHTS: Paul Micou's first book, *The Music Programme,* is a comic novel set in Africa. The plot concerns a cultural aid program funded by the United States which is being exploited by a number of bureaucrats, musicians, and other residents of an African country. A congressional envoy, Charles "Crack" McCray, is sent to investigate the situation and soon encounters a series of humorous entanglements. John Nicholson, reviewing *The Music Programme* in the London *Times,* noted the "confidence" of Micou's writing and compared the author to acclaimed humorous fiction writer William Boyd. "*The Music Programme,*" Nicholson wrote, "is, without doubt, the funniest first novel to come my way since William Boyd's *A Good Man in Africa.*"

The Cover Artist, Micou's next novel, follows magazine illustrator Oscar Lemoine as he circulates among the elite of European high society. While Lemoine receives attention for his caricatures of nudes, his dog, Elizabeth, is also an artist, creating expressionist paintings with a canine touch. In his 1991 novel, *The Death of David Debrizzi,* Micou returns to the music world, recounting the story of the title character, a promising pianist whose rise to prominence creates a rift between his two music teachers.

BIOGRAPHICAL/CRITICAL SOURCES:

PERIODICALS

Times (London), March 16, 1989; March 8, 1990.
Times Literary Supplement, June 28, 1991, p. 19.

*   *   *

MIKALSON, Jon D.   1943-

PERSONAL: Born August 1, 1943, in Milwaukee, WI; son of John M. and Evelyn K. Mikalson; married Mary Villemonte, August 28, 1966; children: Melissa, Jacquelyn. *Education:* University of Wisconsin—Madison, B.A.,

1965; attended American School of Classical Studies, Athens, 1968-69; Harvard University, Ph.D., 1970.

ADDRESSES: Home—Route 3, Box 430, Crozet, VA 22932. *Office*—Department of Classics, 146 New Cabell Hall, University of Virginia, Charlottesville, VA 22903.

CAREER: University of Virginia, Charlottesville, assistant professor, 1970-77, associate professor, 1977-84, professor of classics, 1984—.

MEMBER: American Philological Association, Classical Association of the Middle West and South, Classical Association of Virginia (past president).

WRITINGS:

The Sacred and Civil Calendar of the Athenian Year, Princeton University Press, 1975.
Athenian Popular Religion, University of North Carolina Press, 1985.
Honor Thy Gods, University of North Carolina Press, 1991.

WORK IN PROGRESS: For Health and Safety: Religion in Hellenistic Athens.

*   *   *

MILLER, Judith   1948-

PERSONAL: Born in 1948, in New York, NY. *Education:* Attended Ohio State University and Barnard College; received M.A. from Princeton University.

ADDRESSES: Office—New York Times, 229 West 43rd St., New York, NY 10036.

CAREER: New York Times, New York City, reporter, editor, and correspondent, 1977—, began as reporter on the Securities and Exchange Commission, became Cairo, Egypt, bureau chief in 1983, became correspondent in Paris, France, in 1986, currently senior writer in New York. Free-lance journalist, 1976.

WRITINGS:

One, by One, by One: Facing the Holocaust, Simon & Schuster, 1990.
(With Laurie Mylroie) *Saddam Hussein and the Crisis in the Gulf,* Random House, 1990.

Contributor to the *Progressive, New Republic, Foreign Affairs,* and many Middle Eastern journals. Also contributor to National Public Radio.

SIDELIGHTS: Since she joined the *New York Times* in 1977, Judith Miller has been a consistent contributor of reports and features on European and domestic politics and media. But she is best known for her work as a bureau chief in Cairo, Egypt, and as a special correspondent in the Middle East during the 1980s. She covered events such as the suicide attack on the Marine Corps barracks in Beirut, Lebanon, the hijacking of the cruise ship *Achille Lauro* and subsequent murder of Jewish passengers, the bombing of the U.S. embassy in Kuwait, and the Arab-Israeli peace process.

Miller's interview credits include most of the major players in Middle Eastern politics. She has provided *Times* readers with interviews of Jordan's King Hussein, former Israeli Prime Minister Shimon Peres, Egyptian President Hosni Mubarak, and Yasir Arafat of the Palestine Liberation Organization. Perhaps her biggest scoop came with the private interview that she secured with Libyan leader Muammar Qaddafi and her series of articles on the man and his country. "He has his own kind of bizarre ideology, a vision of an Islamic Utopia that he's creating in Libya. He's sincere about that," Miller told Joan Juliet Buck in a *Vogue* profile. Added Miller, "Qaddafi comes across in many ways as uneducated and so incredibly naive that it's hard to believe this guy is a killer, which he is."

Miller's experience in the Middle East has not only given her insights into the politics and personalities of that region, but also into the dilemma so closely associated with the Middle East in the minds of Westerners: terrorism. "I think . . . that part of the reason I feel so strongly about terrorism is that I've now covered enough of it to last me a lifetime," she explained in *Vogue*. "Terrorists are not all that clever. Some are well-organized, but I think that in lots of instances they've been as effective as they have because governments have acted stupidly." Miller offered the following advice: "The civilized world simply has to draw the line and say it's not true that one man's terrorist is another man's freedom fighter, because terrorism has a distinct and a specific meaning, and it is the wanton killing and deliberate murders of noncombatants, civilians, innocent people not involved in your conflict to inspire fear for political goals."

Miller has used her newspaper writing as a springboard for two books. Her first book grew out of a feature on the Holocaust—the slaughter of Jews by the Nazis during World War II—that she wrote while a correspondent in Paris in the mid-1980s. The resulting book, *One, by One, by One: Facing the Holocaust,* is, according to *New York Times Book Review* contributor Eli N. Evans, "a timely, provocative and in many respects deeply disturbing book about the ways in which five European countries and the United States are forgetting, distorting and politically manipulating the memory of the Holocaust." "She has discovered, to her dismay," wrote Eward Norden in *Commentary,* "that in Germany, Austria, Holland, France, and the USSR, the facts of the Holocaust are being cooked, that history is being mythologized for local consumption and political purposes."

Miller scrutinizes efforts in Germany at historical revisionism, especially in the wake of German reunification. She throws a spotlight on the election of former Nazi Kurt Waldheim as president of Austria to show that country's inability to come to terms with its collaboration. She contrasts the public celebration of the Dutch resistance and Holocaust victim and diarist Anne Frank with the disturbing fact that only twenty-five percent of Dutch Jews survived World War II. She finds France's uneasy memory of its role in Jewish deportations revived by the trial of Nazi war criminal Klaus Barbie. She discovers that the tragedy suffered by Russian Jews was overshadowed by the deaths of twenty million Russians. Finally, Miller looks at American remembrances of the Holocaust in events such as President Ronald Reagan's visit to the Bitburg Cemetery (where Nazis had been buried) and in the heated debate surrounding the U.S. Holocaust Memorial Museum in Washington, D.C.

"Judith Miller has had access that few freelance writers could equal," commented Evans. "She has taken her mission seriously and has written a troubling and thought-provoking exploration into a dark world of memory and redemption." Her mission, as Norden put it, is to call on all of these countries and others "to tell themselves and their children the whole truth, and to do this before the last collaborators with the Nazis and the last Jewish survivors are gone." "Unless we can keep it in mind that the Holocaust was comprised of the suffering of individuals, each with a face and name," added Norden, "ignorance and forgetfulness will prevail, depriving Jews and Gentiles of their 'surest defense' against the repetition of 'such gigantic cruelty.' "

Miller's second book, *Saddam Hussein and the Crisis in the Gulf,* was coauthored with Harvard scholar Laurie Mylroie as a quick response to the 1990 Iraqi invasion of Kuwait. "Written in three weeks and published in a fourth," wrote Stephen R. Shalom in the *Nation*, "[it] appeared a few months before the U.S. attack on Iraq." "While largely a synthesis of others' work, their book puts much essential background material on Iraq into one volume," commented Stanley Reed in *Business Week*. Miller and Mylroie profile the man that they call the Iraqi "Godfather," a man born into poverty in 1937 in a small village one hundred miles north of Baghdad. They outline his youth and then his emergence into the national scene in Iraq as a hit man for the Baath Party, which was struggling to control the country after the fall of King Faisal II in 1958.

When the Baathists finally seized power in 1963, Hussein took a position as interrogator and torturer. After a fall from grace and two years in prison, he reemerged to found a Baathist security force. On the inside with his own power base, Hussein continued his ruthless rise to the top. In 1979 he became president of Iraq and leader of the Baath Party and proceeded to execute hundreds of his opponents in the party. "The mechanics of Mr. Hussein's rise and his maintenance of power are skillfully described in *Saddam Hussein and the Crisis in the Gulf,* as is the history of Iraq's acquisition of weapons of mass destruction," wrote Marvin Zonis in the *New York Times Book Review.*

The book also covers the U.S. policy toward Iraq during Hussein's reign. It is this aspect of the book with which Shalom found fault. He especially found Mylroie's criticism of the United States for its pro-Baghdad stance prior to the invasion inconsistent. In her previous writings, noted Shalom, "Mylroie didn't just misjudge Iraq. She served as an apologist for and supporter of Saddam Hussein, a man whom after the invasion of Kuwait she presented as eternally evil. This transformation precisely parallels the official policy of the U.S. government." Zonis conceded that the authors miss some opportunities with this book, but in his assessment, "What they do deliver, however, is a frequently riveting account of how Saddam Hussein, ruthless visionary that he is, has driven his country and manipulated much of the world to satisfy his grandiose ambitions."

BIOGRAPHICAL/CRITICAL SOURCES:

BOOKS

Miller, Judith, and Laurie Mylroie, *Saddam Hussein and the Crisis in the Gulf,* Random House, 1990.

PERIODICALS

Business Week, November 26, 1990, pp. 12, 14.
Commentary, August, 1990, pp. 62-64.
Current History, January, 1991.
Nation, February 25, 1991, pp. 241-43.
New York Review of Books, December 20, 1990.
New York Times Book Review, April 29, 1990; November 11, 1990, p. 7.
Publishers Weekly, March 16, 1990, p. 57.
Time, May 14, 1990, p. 89.
Vogue, August, 1986, pp. 323, 377-79.*

—*Sketch by Bryan Ryan*

* * *

MISH, Charles C(arroll) 1913-1992

OBITUARY NOTICE—See index for *CA* sketch: Born June 27, 1913, in Williamsport, PA; died of a heart attack, December 30, 1992, in Washington, DC. Educator and editor. Mish, a specialist in seventeenth-century literature,

served as professor of English at the University of Maryland from 1946 to 1984. In 1963 he edited *Short Fiction of the Seventeenth Century,* which was also published as *Anchor Anthology of Short Fiction of the Seventeenth Century.* In addition, Mish was the editor of *English Prose Fiction, 1600-1700: A Chronological Checklist* and *Restoration Prose Fiction, 1666-1700: An Anthology of Representative Pieces.*

OBITUARIES AND OTHER SOURCES:

PERIODICALS

Washington Post, January 7, 1993, p. B6.

* * *

MITCHELL, Joseph B(rady) 1915-1993

OBITUARY NOTICE—See index for *CA* sketch: Born September 25, 1915, in Fort Leavenworth, KS; died of congestive heart failure, February 17, 1993, in Washington, DC. Military officer, historian, and author. After serving in the U.S. Army for eighteen years, Mitchell became a historian with the American Battle Monuments Commission, later accepting a position as curator of the Fort Ward Museum in Alexandria, Virginia. He was an officer in several historical organizations, including the Civil War Round Table of Alexandria, the Alexandria Historical Society, the Civil War Round Table, the American Revolution Round Table, Sons of Confederate Veterans, and the Military Order of Stars and Bars. Mitchell contributed to numerous periodicals and encyclopedias and penned books on military topics. In 1962 he was presented with a best book award from the American Revolution Round Table of New York for his *Decisive Battles of the American Revolution.* He also wrote *Decisive Battles of the Civil War, Twenty Decisive Battles of the World,* and *The Badge of Gallantry: Recollections of Civil War Congressional Medal of Honor Winners.*

OBITUARIES AND OTHER SOURCES:

BOOKS

Who's Who in the South and Southwest, 23rd edition, Marquis, 1991.

PERIODICALS

Washington Post, February 24, 1993, p. C7.

* * *

MITCHELL, Reid 1955-

PERSONAL: Born April 16, 1955, in Georgia; son of E. T. and Virginia (Adams) Mitchell; married Liza Buurma (a playwright), 1989. *Education:* Attended University of New Orleans, College of William and Mary, and University of California, Berkeley. *Avocational interests:* Rhythm and blues guitar.

ADDRESSES: Office—Department of History, University of Maryland, Baltimore County, 5401 Wilkens Ave., Catonsville, MD 21228.

CAREER: Princeton University, Princeton, NJ, assistant professor of history, 1986-93; University of Maryland, Baltimore County, Catonsville, assistant professor of history, 1993—.

WRITINGS:

Civil War Soldiers, Viking, 1988.
Vacant Chair, Oxford University Press, 1993.

WORK IN PROGRESS: A one-volume history of the Confederacy; a novel set during the Civil War.

BIOGRAPHICAL/CRITICAL SOURCES:

PERIODICALS

Tribune Books (Chicago), October 9, 1988, p. 3.

* * *

MNOOKIN, Robert H(arris)   1942-

PERSONAL: Born February 4, 1942; married Dale Seigel; children: Jennifer Leigh, Allison Heather. *Education:* Harvard University, A.B. (magna cum laude), 1964, LL.B. (magna cum laude), 1968.

ADDRESSES: Home—430 El Escarpado, Stanford, CA 94305. *Office*—Stanford Center on Conflict and Negotiation, Stanford Law School, Stanford, CA 94305.

CAREER: Admitted to the California Bar and District of Columbia Bar. U.S. Court of Appeals, District of Columbia Circuit, law clerk to Judge Carl McGowan, 1968-69; Supreme Court of the United States, law clerk to Justice John M. Harlan, 1969-70; Howard, Rice, Nemerovski, Canady, Robertson & Falk, San Francisco, CA, associate attorney, 1970-72, associate attorney of counsel, 1972—; University of California, Berkeley, acting professor and director of childhood and government project at Earl Warren Legal Institute, 1972-74, professor of law, 1975-81; Stanford University, Stanford, CA, visiting professor, 1980-81, professor, 1981-87, Adelbert H. Sweet Professor of Law, 1987—, director of Center on Conflict and Negotiation, 1988—, fellow of Center for Advanced Study in the Behavioral Sciences, 1981-82, chair of Jewish Community Federation, 1984-86; Harvard University, Cambridge, MA, visiting professor of law, 1990-91. Harvard Overseer's Committee to Visit the Law School, mem-

ber, 1972-78; Berkeley Public Library, member of board of trustees, 1972-80, chairman, 1974-76, vice-chairman, 1976-78; Oxford University, Wolfson College, visiting fellow in Centre for Socio-Legal Studies, 1978; Head-Royce School, member of board of trustees, 1979-80; National Academy of Sciences, member of committee on Child Development Research and Public Policy, 1979-84, member of panel on adolescent pregnancy and childbearing, 1984-89; Stanford Hillel Foundation, member of executive board, 1986, president, 1989; member of American Law Institute, Asia/Pacific Center for Resolution of International Business Disputes, and Center for Public Resources.

MEMBER: American Bar Association, International Society on Family Law (member of executive council, 1981-85), California Bar Association, San Francisco Bar Association.

AWARDS, HONORS: Fulbright scholar, 1964-65; award for distinguished contributions to child advocacy, American Psychological Association, 1983; award for outstanding leadership in the protection of children's rights, National Center for Youth Law and Youth Law Center, 1986.

WRITINGS:

Child, Family, and State: Problems and Materials on Children and the Law, Little, Brown, 1978, 2nd edition (with K. Weisberg), 1989.
In the Interests of Children: Advocacy, Law Reform and Public Policy, W. H. Freeman, 1985.
(With Eleanor E. Maccoby) *Dividing the Child: Social and Legal Dilemmas of Custody,* Harvard University Press, 1992.

Contributor to books, including *Providing Civil Justice for the Child,* edited by H. Geech and E. Szwed, Edward Arnold, 1984; *In the Interests of Children: Advocacy, Law Reform and Public Policy,* W. H. Freeman, 1985; *Impact of Divorce, Single Parenting, and Stepparenting on Children,* edited by M. Hetherington and J. Arasten, Lawrence Erlbaum, 1988; *Divorce Reform at the Crossroads,* edited by S. Sugarman and H. Kay, Yale University Press, 1990. Contributor to numerous journals, including *Harvard Educational Review, Journal of the American Academy of Child Psychiatry, Harvard Law School Bulletin, Yale Law Journal, Stanford Lawyer, Journal of Political Economy, Wall Street Journal, Stanford Law Review,* and *Negotiation Journal.*

MOHR, Richard D(rake) 1950-

PERSONAL: Born October 24, 1950, in Portland, OR; son of Theodore Owen (in sales) and Elaine (a schoolteacher) Mohr; partner of Robert W. Switzer (a clerk), since May 20, 1978. *Education:* University of Chicago, B.A., 1972; University of Toronto, M.A., 1973, Ph.D., 1977.

ADDRESSES: Office—105 Gregory Hall, University of Illinois at Urbana/Champaign, 810 South Wright St., Urbana, IL 60801.

CAREER: University of Illinois at Urbana/Champaign, professor of philosophy.

WRITINGS:

The Platonic Cosmology, E. J. Brill, 1985.
Gays/Justice: A Study of Ethics, Society, and Law, Columbia University Press, 1988.
Gay Ideas: Outing and Other Controversies, Beacon Press, 1992.

Between Men—Between Women: Lesbian and Gay Studies from Columbia University Press, founding editor, general editor, 1989-91.

WORK IN PROGRESS: The Little Book of Gay Rights; Plato's Republic—and Ours; research on First Amendment issues and on the "cultural wars."

SIDELIGHTS: Richard D. Mohr told *CA:* "I have a secret life as a classicist. In 1985 I wrote a very obscure book on very obscure matters in Plato's cosmology. Then I started writing on gay moral and political issues. My 1988 book, *Gays/Justice,* defends a liberal understanding of the relationship between citizen and government. It addresses constitutional rights, civil rights, the crisis of acquired immune deficiency syndrome, and political strategy. In light of the book's success, I became the founding editor of the journal *Between Men—Between Women,* the first institutionalized form of gay studies in America.

"Then I started writing on current controversies within the gay community. This project became my 1992 book, *Gay Ideas,* one chapter of which, in a general rumination about masculinity, discusses images by the gay eroticists Robert Mapplethorpe, Rex, and Tom of Finland. The illustrations in this chapter caused the manuscript to crash and burn through the university presses. Their behavior was shameful. Beacon Press heroically came to the book's rescue. It turns out that on free speech issues, religion and free enterprise did better than the so-called marketplace of ideas—the universities. Beacon, in turn, had difficulty finding a printer for the book. Twenty-three printers, including all of their usual ones and even the printer of Madonna's *Sex,* refused to touch the book.

"I have a number of book projects in mind. One is a little book on gay rights, pitched at a general audience. One is a book on Plato's *Republic,* a project that would try to redo for the millennium Karl Popper's *Open Society and Its Enemies.* Finally, I want to write, from a liberal perspective, a book on the cultural wars."

*   *   *

MORGAN, Edward P(addock) 1910-1993

OBITUARY NOTICE—See index for *CA* sketch: Born June 23, 1910, in Walla Walla, WA; died of complications of lung cancer, January 27, 1993, in McLean, VA. Journalist and author. Morgan received a George Foster Peabody Award in 1956 for his American Broadcasting Corporation (ABC) radio program, *Edward P. Morgan and the News.* He began his career as a newspaper correspondent and associate editor for papers including the *Chicago Daily News* during the 1930s and 1940s. Morgan later worked as a correspondent for Columbia Broadcasting System (CBS), becoming director of radio and television news before moving to American Broadcasting System (ABC) as television news anchor. In this capacity Morgan covered the assassination of U.S. President John F. Kennedy and maintained his composure while reporting on the disastrous collision of two luxury liners although he was aware that his fourteen-year-old daughter was on board one of them. A critic of commercial news even as he participated in it, Morgan later joined public television in its experimental stages, delivering a ground-breaking feature on racial relations in the United States. His news broadcasting honors include the Alfred I. DuPont and George Polk Awards. Morgan was the editor of *This I Believe* and the author of *Clearing the Air.*

OBITUARIES AND OTHER SOURCES:

BOOKS

Biographical Dictionary of American Journalism, Greenwood, 1989.
Encyclopedia of Twentieth-Century Journalists, Garland Publishing, 1986.
Who's Who in the South and Southwest, Marquis, 1976.

PERIODICALS

Chicago Tribune, January 30, 1993, section 2, p. 19.
Los Angeles Times, January 30, 1993, p. A24.
New York Times, January 29, 1993, p. A18.
Washington Post, January 29, 1993, p. B5.

MORLEY, Margaret 1941-

PERSONAL: Born September 23, 1941, in Boston, MA; daughter of Felix J. (an electrical engineer) and Margaret (a bookkeeper; maiden name, Conley) Gudejko; married Sheridan Morley, 1965 (divorced, 1991); children: Hugo, Alexis, Juliet. *Education:* Emmanuel College, B.A., 1963; University of Hawaii at Manoa, M.F.A., 1964. *Avocational interests:* Golf.

ADDRESSES: Home—Bracknell, Berkshire, England. *Agent*—Michael Shaw, Curtis Brown, 162-168 Regent St., London W1R 5TB, England.

CAREER: Writer.

WRITINGS:

A Friend in Need, Robson Books, 1976.
The Films and Faces of Laurence Olivier, Citadel, 1978.
Larger Than Life (biography of Robert Morley), Robson Books, 1979.
Ten Days in China, Aiden Ellis, 1986.
Celia Eden, Aiden Ellis, 1987.
The Summer Woods, Hodder & Stoughton, 1990.
Wild Spirit: The Story of Percy Bysshe Shelley, Hodder & Stoughton, 1992.

Contributor to periodicals. Film critic, *Woman's Journal.*

SIDELIGHTS: Margaret Morley told *CA:* "I suppose I have spent my career working through the recognized genres. In the seventies I concentrated on journalism (interviews for magazines with actors such as Sean Connery and writers like Daphne DuMaurier). I was also a film critic and a general arts reporter, and I published short stories.

"Since then I have published books which include biography, travel, family saga, novella, and historical nonfiction. I have also worked on humor, collaborating with my late father-in-law, Robert Morley, and done some work ghosting for actors. At the moment, I am working on a contemporary novel, the heroine of which is an everyday psychopath, and I am researching further into the eighteenth century."

*   *   *

MORRIS, Roger 1938-
(Suetonius)

PERSONAL: Born January 15, 1938, in Kansas City, MO; son of Paul M. (a broker) and Cathrine (in business; maiden name, Transue) Morris; married Karin Hedlund, November 21, 1959 (divorced November 7, 1977); married Kathrin Erickson, February 10, 1978; children: Peter Hedlund, Zoe Kristine, Ethan Taylor, David Giles, Dylan

Cardinal. *Education:* University of Missouri—Kansas City, A.B. (summa cum laude), 1960; attended Moscow State University, 1963-64; Harvard University, Ph.D., 1973. *Politics:* Independent. *Religion:* Christian Science.

ADDRESSES: Home and office—1225 Seville Rd., Santa Fe, NM 87501. *Agent*—Sobel Weber Associates, Ltd., 146 East 19th St., New York, NY 10003.

CAREER: Harvard University, Cambridge, MA, teaching fellow in government, 1965-66; U.S. Department of State, Washington, DC, U.S. Foreign Service Officer and executive secretariat of secretary of state, 1966-67; White House, Washington, DC, staff member, 1967; National Security Council, Washington, DC, staff member, 1968, senior staff member, 1968-70; legislative assistant for U.S. Senator Walter Mondale, 1970-72; Carnegie Endowment for International Peace, Washington, DC, director of policy studies, 1972-74; writer. Oxfam America, member of board of directors, 1975-78; U.S. Agency for International Development, consultant, 1978-79; New Mexico Project for Investigative Reporting, director, beginning in 1982; KNME-TV, coproducer and host of *At Week's End,* a public affairs program, 1989—; University of New Mexico, adjunct professor of political science and general honors, 1990—; Sunmount Syndicate, co-owner, editor, and columnist, 1990—; member of board, National Council of International Visitors; member of board, Western Issues, Inc.; frequent speaker before civic organizations and university audiences.

AWARDS, HONORS: Woodrow Wilson National Fellow, Harvard University, 1960-61; Ford Foundation Research Fellow, British Museum, University of London, 1964-65; prizes for investigative journalism, public service, and newswriting, New Mexico Press Association, 1980 and 1981; first prize, investigative reporting, National Newspaper Association, 1982; National Awards for Distinguished Investigative Journalism *Pro Bono Publico,* Investigative Reporters and Editors, 1982 and 1985; Guy Rader Award for Medical Reporting, 1984; Bronze Medal, "Finest Reporting All Media Nationwide," Investigative Reporters and Editors, 1985; National Book Award Silver Medal, nonfiction, and National Critics Circle finalist, biography, both 1990, for *Richard Milhous Nixon: The Rise of an American Politician; Richard Milhous Nixon: The Rise of an American Politician* was named a *New York Times* Notable Book of the Year, 1990; Pulitzer Prize nominee, commentary and interpretative journalism, 1991; Society of American Historians fellow, 1992; National Endowment for the Humanities fellow, 1993; Guggenheim Fellow, 1993-94.

WRITINGS:

(With Kay Miller and others) *Passing By: The U.S. and Genocide in Burundi,* Carnegie Endowment, 1973.

(With Hal Sheets) *Disaster in the Desert: Humanitarian Relief in the African Drought,* Carnegie Endowment, 1974.

Uncertain Greatness: Henry Kissinger and American Foreign Policy, Harper, 1977.

Haig: The General's Progress, G. P. Putnam's, 1982.

The Devil's Butcher Shop: The New Mexico Prison Uprising, F. Watts, 1983.

Richard Milhous Nixon: The Rise of an American Politician (volume one of an intended three-part series), Holt, 1990.

Promises of Change: Image and Reality in the Clinton Presidency, Holt, 1993.

Author of a series of articles, under the pseudonym Suetonius, for *New Republic,* 1976-77; contributor of more than three hundred articles to periodicals, including *Columbia Journalism Review, Nation, Newsday,* and Santa Fe *Reporter;* regular op-ed contributor to *Los Angeles Times* and *Arizona Republic; New Republic,* contributing editor, beginning in 1981; Santa Fe *Reporter,* contributing editor, beginning in 1982; syndicated columnist for twelve New Mexico newspapers.

WORK IN PROGRESS: Richard Milhous Nixon: Crucible of Power, 1953-1960.

SIDELIGHTS: While serving on the U.S. National Security Council in the late 1960s, Roger Morris worked with several political figures who were part of the administrations of presidents Richard M. Nixon and Lyndon B. Johnson. Morris resigned from his National Security Council position in 1970, after disagreeing with a decision to send U.S. troops into Cambodia during the Vietnam War. He draws on his experiences in the White House in writing biographies about Henry Kissinger, assistant for national security for President Nixon and later secretary of state; Alexander Haig, who served as White House chief of staff in the early 1970s; and President Nixon.

In *Uncertain Greatness* Morris discusses the White House career of Henry Kissinger, focusing on the foreign policies Kissinger helped shape while serving as security adviser to President Nixon. According to Don Oberdorfer of the *Washington Post Book World,* "Kissinger is depicted as egotistical, cynical, tyrannical, callous—and brilliant" in the biography. Throughout the book Morris suggests that various weaknesses in the president's character—including a drinking habit—contributed to the advancement of Kissinger's political career and to the impression that he was at times the "de facto president." In 1973, Kissinger was appointed secretary of state and held the position through the end of Nixon's tenure and into the years of Gerald Ford's presidency.

Reviewers noted that observations presented in *Uncertain Greatness* on both politics in Africa and the conflict in

Vietnam are especially revealing. In the late 1960s, when the West African province of Biafra tried to break from its ruling country, Nigeria, many of the secessionists were starved to death. Morris shows how such atrocity was ignored or dismissed by many in the U.S. State Department, which sided with the Nigerian forces during the civil war. Kissinger, speaking on behalf of the president, related Nixon's desire to help the citizens of Biafra, but little was done to alleviate their suffering. Morris also contends that as assistant to President Nixon, Kissinger helped perpetuate the Vietnam War through the late 1960s and early 1970s. While some reviewers faulted Morris for not providing adequate documentation for his allegations in *Uncertain Greatness, Nation* contributor Alex Beam deemed the book "an engrossing upstairs-downstairs account of the Kissinger era." And Oberdorfer of *Washington Post Book World* lauded its "flashes of brilliance and much uninhibited 'truth telling.' "

Morris's *Haig: The General's Progress* details the life of Alexander Haig, who served as White House chief of staff under President Nixon. Nicholas Lemann in the *New York Times Book Review* complimented Morris for the biography, noting that he possesses "a vivid writing style and an admirable familiarity with the public record." The author tells of how Haig was raised in an affluent suburb of Philadelphia, Pennsylvania, the son of an aspiring lawyer who passed away before Haig became a teenager. After attending the University of Notre Dame for a short time, he transferred to West Point, where he trained for a military career. Haig graduated with a mediocre class rank, served in both the Korean and Vietnam wars, and, during peacetime, worked a number of jobs which resulted in his eventual position as White House chief of staff. "Morris's view of Mr. Haig is entirely unflattering, while very much giving the general his due as a skillful climber," noted Lemann.

Throughout *Haig: The General's Progress* Morris offers insight into various suspicious events that occurred during the Nixon presidency in which Haig might have played a part. He attempts to explain Haig's possible involvement in the "red alert" of October 24, 1973, when American troops in several countries were ordered to prepare for potential war with the Soviet Union. He also questions Haig's behavior after the president was forced to resign in the wake of the Watergate scandal, during which agents connected with the Committee to Re-elect the President were discovered breaking into Democratic National Headquarters. Morris argues that Haig might have been involved with a plan to seize control of political power in the waning days of the Nixon presidency. The author also explains that after Watergate both Haig and Henry Kissinger made ardent efforts to keep their personal files from being reviewed by members of the new administration headed by President Ford. "To read Morris' work is to be plunged back almost immediately into the poisonous intrigues of the Nixon White House and to be confronted once again with mysterious, evil and still-unexplained questions," remarked Harrison E. Salisbury in *Chicago Tribune Book World.*

Morris's 1990 publication, *Richard Milhous Nixon: The Rise of an American Politician,* documents the early personal life and political career of the former president. Instead of centering on Nixon's tenure as the nation's leader, Morris focuses on his subject's ascendancy to the U.S. vice presidency, charting his childhood, his educational background, and his early involvement in lesser-known political campaigns. Morris describes various events that contributed to the formation of Nixon's character, showing how he handled the deaths of two of his brothers due to illness, how as an adolescent he woke up at four in the morning to purchase produce at the farmers' market for his father's store, and how he broke into a dean's office with fellow law students at Duke University in order to sneak an early glimpse at his grades. Morris also provides insight into Nixon's relationship with Thelma Patricia Ryan, who, although not initially attracted to him, ultimately married him after he ardently pursued a relationship with her.

In regard to politics, Morris recounts the California congressional election of 1946, in which Nixon defeated Jerry Voorhis, an incumbent candidate who was widely respected. According to Alan Brinkley of *New Republic,* Morris's depiction of the race "is a masterpiece of reconstruction—particularly in its portrait of the political climate of Southern California of the late 1940s." The biographer writes of the vast amounts of money that were contributed to the campaign from disparate and sometimes untraceable sources and of Nixon's own active participation in the orchestration of the campaign. Morris notes that "so complete was his [Nixon's] attention to detail, so insistent the control that the candidate himself even decided the precise telephone poles and other locations" to post publicity flyers. During debates between the two candidates, Nixon made certain that he had vociferous supporters in the crowd who denounced his opponent. According to the author, Nixon took his campaign manager's advice and suggested that Voorhis was a Communist at a time when Americans were highly suspicious of anti-American sympathies. Morris also covers Nixon's bid for election to the Senate in 1950 against Helen Gahagan Douglas in a campaign that made use of many of the same strategies that helped Nixon in his congressional victory.

Morris reveals that as a senator, Nixon appeased various factions of the Republican party in order to gain support as a possible running mate for presidential candidate Dwight D. Eisenhower. During his tenure as senator,

Nixon also made use of a fund established to cover his political expenses. Morris investigates the controversy surrounding these contributions, which arose when journalists, who found out about the money pool in 1952, wondered why Nixon had been keeping it a secret. While Morris acknowledges that it was normal and legal practice to maintain such a fund, he regards its existence as further evidence of the questionable methods used by Nixon to finance his political career.

For his biography of the former president, Morris received National Book Award Silver Medal in nonfiction and received praise from several reviewers. Kevin Starr of the *New York Times Book Review* commended Morris, acknowledging that "*Richard Milhous Nixon* is a massive, powerful biography, absorbing in its research and in its skillful use of anecdote and illustrative detail." And Brinkley of *New Republic* regarded Morris's book on the former president as "the most thorough and sensitive account of Nixon's youth and early career, and the most revealing portrait of the man, anyone has yet written."

In addition to his political biographies, Morris has written other nonfiction works, including *The Devil's Butcher Shop.* The title refers to the New Mexico State Penitentiary in Santa Fe, where a riot occurred on February 2, 1980. Published in 1983, the book chronicles the uprising in which at least thirty-three men were murdered and numerous others were tortured physically and mentally. Morris provides background information on the prison, discussing several factors that contributed to the eventual calamity. He describes how inmates were abused—from physical tortures and medical mistreatment to more subtle emotional and mental torment. The author also notes how the penitentiary itself was poorly designed and overcrowded, and how prison officials often committed criminal acts of their own, including theft and fraud. Praising Morris for providing coverage of the event that newspapers were not willing to offer, David C. Anderson of the *New York Times Book Review* called *The Devil's Butcher Shop* "a riveting, upsetting and ultimately enraging investigation."

Roger Morris told *CA:* "As a boy growing up in the Middle West, my abiding ambition was to be a diplomat, though my education and experience nurtured an equal love (and perhaps greater respect, even then) for writing and writers. An extraordinarily fortunate and revealing experience at the upper levels of foreign policy and politics in Washington, D.C., impressed upon me the importance of portraying that world with independence and honesty—and led naturally to my writing. My books on national and international issues are informed, in part, by my personal experience and by commitment to uncompromising scholarship. The book about the Santa Fe prison riot grew out of my almost accidental local reporting on the subject and a genuine fascination and love for New Mexico. All my work is inspired, I suppose, by an enduring faith, despite so much evidence to the contrary, in the ultimate responsiveness and goodness of American democracy. My writing owes so many debts—to teachers and colleagues, to my agent and editors, to other writers as models and masters, of course to my family, and most of all to my collaborator, sensibility and conscience, my wife Kathy."

BIOGRAPHICAL/CRITICAL SOURCES:

BOOKS

Morris, Roger, *Richard Milhous Nixon: The Rise of an American Politician,* Holt, 1990.

PERIODICALS

Atlantic Monthly, February, 1978, p. 92.
Chicago Tribune Book World, July 18, 1982, p. 1.
Economist, December 9, 1989, pp. 95-96.
Nation, October 15, 1977, pp. 376-77
New York Times, November 11, 1989.
New York Times Book Review, August 15, 1982, p. 9; February 26, 1984; November 12, 1989, p. 1.
New Republic, October 1, 1990, pp. 28-35.
Spectator, February 25, 1978, pp. 21-22
Time, November 6, 1989, pp. 100-02.
Washington Post Book World, August 28, 1977, p. 1; July 18, 1982, p. 1.

—*Sketch by Mark F. Mikula*

*   *   *

MOSS, Jeff(rey)

PERSONAL: Born in New York, NY; son of an actor and a writer; married; children: one son. *Education:* Received degree from Princeton University. *Avocational interests:* Theatre.

ADDRESSES: Home—New York, NY.

CAREER: Columbia Broadcasting System (CBS-TV), New York City, began as production assistant for television program *Captain Kangaroo,* became writer for *Captain Kangaroo;* Children's Television Workshop, New York City, head writer and composer/lyricist for *Sesame Street,* beginning in 1969, currently staff writer for *Sesame Street;* children's book author in New York City, c. 1989—. Composer and lyricist for film *The Muppets Take Manhattan,* Tri-Star, 1984; contributor of music and lyrics to numerous *Sesame Street* song albums. *Military service:* U.S. Army.

AWARDS, HONORS: Emmy Awards—outstanding achievement in a children's program, both 1969, for music

and lyrics for *Sesame Street* episode "This Way to Sesame Street" and writing for episode "Sally Sees Sesame Street"; Emmy Award—individual achievement in a children's program, 1973, for *Sesame Street;* Emmy Awards—writing in a children's series, 1982, 1983, 1984, 1985, 1986, 1987, 1988, 1989, and 1990, all for *Sesame Street;* Emmy Awards—music composition in a children's program, 1982 and 1989, both for *Sesame Street.*

Grammy Awards—recording for children, 1972, for *Sesame Street II,* 1980, for *The People in Your Neighborhood,* and 1984, for *The Muppets Take Manhattan—the Original Soundtrack;* Academy Award nomination—original song score, 1984, for *The Muppets Take Manhattan.*

WRITINGS:

The Butterfly Jar: Poems, illustrated by Chris Demarest, Bantam, 1989.
The Other Side of the Door: Poems, illustrated by Demarest, Bantam, 1991.
The Sesame Street Book of Poetry, illustrated by Bruce McNally, Random House/Children's Television Workshop, 1991.
Bob and Jack: A Boy and His Yak (picture book), illustrated by Demarest, Bantam, 1992.
The Sesame Street Songbook, Macmillan, 1992.

UNDER NAME JEFFREY MOSS

(With others) *The Sesame Street Treasury: Featuring Jim Henson's Sesame Street Muppets,* illustrated by Tom Cooke and others, Random House/Children's Television Workshop, 1973.
(With Norman Stiles and Daniel Wilcox) *The Sesame Street ABC Storybook: Featuring Jim Henson's Muppets,* illustrated by Peter Cross and others, Random House, 1974.
(With Emily Perl Kingsley and David Korr) *The Sesame Street Book of Fairy Tales: Featuring Jim Henson's Muppets,* illustrated by Joe Mathieu, Random House, 1975.
Oscar's Book, illustrated by Michael Gross, Western Publishing, 1976.
People in Your Neighborhood, illustrated by Richard Brown, Western Publishing/Children's Television Workshop, 1983.
People in My Family, illustrated by Carol Nicklaus, Western Publishing/Children's Television Workshop, 1983.
(With others) *The Songs of Sesame Street in Poems and Pictures: Featuring Jim Henson's Sesame Street Muppets,* illustrated by Normand Chartier, Random House/Children's Television Workshop, 1983.

Author of book, music, and lyrics for two musical plays, both produced by the Princeton Triangle Club; contributor of poems to anthologies, including *Free to Be . . . a Family,* by Marlo Thomas et al., Bantam, 1990.

WORK IN PROGRESS: Zoo Fantasy, a screenplay for Francis Ford Coppola.

SIDELIGHTS: "I think my main goals in whatever I do are to entertain the audience, and to teach them a little bit, leave them a tiny bit better off than when I found them," Jeff Moss said in an interview with *Something about the Author (SATA).* Moss—the original head writer and composer/lyricist for the groundbreaking children's television series *Sesame Street*—has penned many of the program's best known songs, including "Rubber Duckie" and "The People in Your Neighborhood." More recently, he has published two volumes of poetry for young people, *The Butterfly Jar* and *The Other Side of the Door,* and a story in verse, *Bob and Jack: A Boy and His Yak.* In both his television work and his books, the award-winning writer has succeeded in making children and their parents laugh while they gain some new insight into themselves and the world around them.

Although he only recently became a parent, Moss believes that his childlike perspective arises from observing children, as well as from his strong memories of his own childhood. But more importantly, he commented, "I don't look at writing for children as that different than writing for anybody else. The emotions that you write about are for the most part the same as you would write about for anybody. You just do it with a vocabulary of experience that children will understand." Moss also derives inspiration from watching adults, for, as he explained, "All of us have a great deal of the child left in us, and some of us show it more than others."

Moss began writing poetry and music at an early age. His father, an actor, and his mother, who had been a writer for a time, filled their home with recordings of classical music and Broadway show tunes. The young Moss studied piano and read a great deal. During a road trip with his father at the age of eight or nine, he discovered crossword puzzles for the first time and felt as though they had been created for him. On the subject of words, Moss told *SATA,* "I have always loved them and I still love them. When I'm sitting around, I play with them in my head, the way other people think about—I don't know—cars. I think a certain amount of that is just born into you. I think I would love words no matter what I did for a living—if I were a factory worker, or a doctor, or whatever."

Remembering a party he held for the publication of his first collection of poetry, *The Butterfly Jar,* in 1989, Moss recalled, "My stepson, who was then ten or eleven, somehow had found this old box of stuff from when I was six years old, and found, in fact, a little poem I had written, along with a drawing that I had done to go with it. And

he said that he could see very clearly, even when I was six, why I had become a writer—and also why I had not become an illustrator."

As a teenager, Moss realized that his peers were not interested in the kinds of music he had studied. He continued composing, but added rock 'n' roll songs to his repertoire. In college, he became involved with the Princeton Triangle Club, a student-run musical comedy group which toured major theatres throughout the country. Moss wrote the book, music, and lyrics for two Princeton Triangle revues, and also appeared in them.

After graduating from Princeton, Moss was offered two positions with Columbia Broadcasting System (CBS) television. One was in the news department, and the other was for the children's program *Captain Kangaroo.* He told *SATA,* "I hadn't seen *Captain Kangaroo,* and I had seen the news, so I said, 'let me try *Captain Kangaroo.'* " This show, which appeared from 1955 to 1984, was the longest-running children's series in television history. Moss worked as a production assistant for less than a year before leaving to serve in the army. Six months later, he returned to the show as a writer, and stayed on for two years. He decided at that point to leave television and do some "serious" writing.

Some of Moss's colleagues at *Captain Kangaroo* were also leaving CBS, hoping to start a new children's series on public television. The idea that would become *Sesame Street* had begun to take shape in the minds of a number of artists and educators in the mid-1960s. Included in the group were Joan Ganz Cooney, who served as the executive director of the Children's Television Workshop, Gerald S. Lesser, who chaired the board of advisors, Joe Raposo, who became the musical director, famed puppeteer Jim Henson, and many others. They all shared the belief that television could be a positive influence in the lives of preschoolers. Their goal—which had never been successfully accomplished—was to create a television program which would be entertaining to young children, and which would also introduce some basic educational concepts.

Moss was invited to join the effort as head writer and composer/lyricist. Although he initially refused the offer, the others continued to pester him. Finally, Moss agreed to come to the studio to see for himself what they were trying to do, "and I saw two things. What they were trying to do was wonderful. But it was a strangely financed thing. Because it was public money, they paid very, very low salaries to everybody, but there was a lot of money available, so that whatever you wrote could get produced tremendously well. Plus, half the cast was black. This was in 1969, and it meant a lot to me back then. And it was only going to be for six months, and I said, 'well, let me see.' "

Moss has since spent more than two decades as a writer and composer for the series, producing *Sesame Street* books and records as well as creating some of the show's most memorable characters and songs. In *Children and Television: Lessons from Sesame Street,* Gerald S. Lesser refers to the original *Sesame Street* artists' contributions as "different forms of creative genius." The show's educational focus has evolved a great deal over the years; while the earlier episodes stress reading and math skills, the later ones deal more with emotional and social issues. The program's content—based on the findings of an ongoing research team which observes preschoolers watching television—includes a variety of different kinds of segments. Brief animated sketches are linked with neighborhood scenes by a connection with certain letters and numbers, or by a visual or conceptual theme. The street itself appears several times throughout each episode, and its residents—who come from diverse racial and ethnic backgrounds—invite viewers to become a part of their safe, accepting world. In addition, there are segments which introduce the viewer to environments which he or she may not have the opportunity to visit.

Among *Sesame Street*'s strongest attractions for both young children and adults are the "Muppets," which were created when Jim Henson and his associates combined aspects of marionettes and puppets. Through a collaborative effort between writers, composers, and puppeteers, the Muppets are transformed from lifeless objects into highly realistic characters, many of whom express a full range of human emotions. The brightly-colored animals and monsters—who talk and sing like people—have the dual ability to charm children with their cute, fuzzy quality and captivate adults with their irreverent yet innocent humor.

The Muppets have played a major role in Moss's experience as a *Sesame Street* writer. He considers them to be "a lot more real than the great majority of characters on television. A lot of them have a little more depth and interest to them than, say, a lot of the sitcoms." Moss explained that even if the puppeteer is in plain sight, the Muppet seems so real that the viewer will often forget that the person is there. When children visit the studio, they often talk only to the Muppet. "And the kid will send back the message the next day: 'say hi to the Count for me—and the Count's friend,' and that will be the puppeteer." Moss once asked Frank Oz, the master puppeteer who plays Miss Piggy, " 'how did you get her to do that expression without moving or changing the eyes?' The answer is if you slow down the film and look at it, she really isn't changing her expression, you just believe that she is because they are all so wonderful at what they do."

By coming up with ideas for characters, just as a fiction writer would do, Moss contributed to the development of two important Muppets—Cookie Monster and Oscar the Grouch—and paved the way for countless others. In the early days of the program, according to Moss, all the monster Muppets were scary, and none of them talked. One day, Moss picked up the monster Muppet which he called "Boggle Eyes," and wondered what it would be like as a humorous character—perhaps with a childlike obsession. When the writer shared his idea, he was told to try it out, but not to give the creature too much to say. At Cookie Monster's debut rehearsal, the Muppet said just two words: "milk" and "COOOOOOOOOKKKKK-KIEEEEEEEEE." The reaction was extremely favorable; as Moss told *SATA,* "Everybody fell off their chairs, and I went back and wrote some more. Obsessive characters are always interesting."

Moss is perhaps best known for the many songs he composed for the *Sesame Street* Muppets. His most famous song, written for the Ernie character, is a tribute to bath toys and special friends: "Rubber Duckie, you're the one/ you make bath time lots of fun/ Rubber Duckie, I'm awfully fond of you." Another favorite, "I Love Trash," was inspired by the lovable green master of gripes, Oscar the Grouch, who lives in a garbage can and detests sunshine, pleasantness, and people. From the beginning, Moss was infinitely pleased with the way in which his musical scores were translated into Muppet performances. "The first song I wrote—which was very early on, of course, the second week I came to work—was called 'Five People in My Family.' I remember going there and watching it taped. I think if a writer sees something that he does performed, and it's eighty percent of what he wants it to be, you're just very, very happy. That was the first song I'd written, and Joe [Raposo] arranged it, and I went and saw it done, and said, 'gee, that's about 103 percent.' A total pleasure."

By the mid-1970s, *Sesame Street* had gained worldwide popularity. While still remaining faithful to their beginnings, the Muppets began moonlighting as stars of their own syndicated prime-time variety series, *The Muppet Show.* The program was extremely popular, eventually reaching viewers in more than one hundred countries, and its success led to several major motion pictures, including *The Muppet Movie, The Great Muppet Caper,* and *The Muppets Take Manhattan.* Moss would receive both an Academy Award nomination and a Grammy Award for the soundtrack to *The Muppets Take Manhattan.* Also in the mid-1970s, Moss stopped writing for television in order to concentrate on composing songs for *Sesame Street* record albums. He later returned to the program as a staff writer, and is now contributing about three months out of every year to the series. "They're nice enough to let me do pretty much what I want, whenever I want," he said of the current *Sesame Street* staff, "and it's still a lot of fun. It's a wonderful home base—it's like a family."

Moss's main activity now is writing books of humorous rhymed verse. The author stresses that his poems—like his work for *Sesame Street*—are intended not simply for children, but for families. It is important to him that his work be enjoyable to all ages, "with the family as the target and the children the bull's-eye." Moss explained this with a comparison to his work for *Sesame Street*: "If the subject's about the letter *D*, you're not going to have a thirty year old say, 'Oh, thank God this show about the letter *D* is on,' but you will have the thirty year old be able to watch the television set and say, 'hey, that's a real entertaining bit about the letter *D*,' and the poems are more like that."

When Moss began writing poetry on his own, he was not intending to publish a collection. Though he had been writing for children's television for many years, he had no children of his own at the time, and was unacquainted with contemporary literature for young people. But he was asked to write a few poems for an anthology, "and I really enjoyed it. And the next time I had a free period in my schedule, I said, 'well, let's see if I can do a few more.' I didn't know where it would lead, and then I had a half a dozen. I said, 'well, let's keep going,' and then I was about a third of the way through and I said, 'well, I think I'll just keep going until I have a book.'"

In terms of a unifying concept for the work, Moss told *SATA*, "I think I had an idea for 'The Butterfly Jar,' which was just one of the poems, and then when I had written that, it seemed like that was what the book was about, as much as anything else." The title poem portrays the world of the imagination in a very poignant way: "And there are things inside my head / Waiting to be thought or said / Dreams and jokes and wonderings are / Locked inside, like a butterfly jar." The poem sets the stage for other cleverly rhymed, energetic pieces—ranging in tone from the very silly to the very serious—which look at commonplace, universal situations from a young person's perspective.

In *The Butterfly Jar*, Moss continues to communicate the values he supported as a *Sesame Street* writer. His funny themes and wordplay work together with Chris Demarest's whimsical illustrations to illuminate a range of feelings with which most people can identify. "Meeting Strangers" is narrated by a shy monster character who epitomizes the fear of not being liked or accepted by others. "They act like I'm a monster / When I'm the one who's new. / They never smile at me and say, / Why, hi there, how are you?" In "This and That," Moss picks up on the visual format *Sesame Street* uses to illustrate simple concepts. The poem demonstrates the notion of relative size by contrasting large, bold type with smaller, lighter type. Comprised of short, repeated sounds, the poem is both fun to look at and fun to read aloud. The poem, "I Don't Want to Live on the Moon," which was recorded

as a song by the renowned Muppet Kermit the Frog on a *Sesame Street* album, celebrates the joy of visiting new places, as well as the comfort of returning home. "Though I'd like to look down at the earth from above, / I would miss all the places and people I love. / So although I might like it for one afternoon / I don't want to live on the moon."

Moss told *SATA* of his experience with the poem "Grandma's Kisses": "When I wrote it, I thought, 'This is very personal—the way my grandma used to try to kiss me when I was a kid.' Well, it turns out that every child in the world has somebody who wants to kiss them in a very wet, juicy way, whom they don't want to be kissed by." The author added, "You don't really realize you're speaking to as many people as you are, and that's always fun—to be surprised. I go to a school or a convention or wherever and I say, 'Is there anybody here who has somebody who really loves to kiss them but they're not really crazy about being kissed by?' And they start squealing and eight hundred hands go up, so you've really touched a nerve."

Reviewers found *The Butterfly Jar* interesting and enjoyable, although one felt that some of the pieces might be more successful in performance than in print. In her review for *School Library Journal*, Barbara S. McGinn called the poems "slightly wacky" and "fun-to-read." A *New York Times Book Review* contributor termed the book "an appealing collection." Several critics compared *The Butterfly Jar* to Shel Silverstein's book *Where the Sidewalk Ends*, on account of its design, which leaves a lot of white space on each page. However, Kathryn LaBarbera, writing in *Booklist*, found Moss's work "more optimistic and less irreverent" than that of Silverstein. Moss told *SATA*, "I'm pleased that they put me in the league with somebody who is as much an institution as [Silverstein] is. I think my poems have a little bit more to do with day-to-day real living than his."

Moss's 1991 book, *The Other Side of the Door*, which is illustrated by Demarest and similar in format to *The Butterfly Jar*, may be viewed as a more adventurous collection. Whereas the cover of *The Butterfly Jar* presents a light, carefree scene, *The Other Side of the Door* has a more daring, mysterious look. The title piece promises that "I can be a different me," and "there's no place I can't explore," for "everything can happen, / on the other side of the door." In the poem "Pictures of Grampa," a child describes the death of a grandfather, and the grandmother's subsequent journey from grief to recovery. The poem "Babies" promotes acceptance of new siblings by offering a different way of looking at things: "Even your teacher who's so smart at school / Would lie in her playpen and gurgle and drool. / So love your new sister and please don't forget / Even *you* were once tiny and noisy and wet." And "Bad Mood" portrays an experience everyone has had: "Please don't write, please don't phone, / Please just leave me alone / In this big deep dark hole that I've dug." Toward the end of *The Other Side of the Door,* Moss begins to experiment with form. His poems imitate other types of short texts with which children are familiar, such as a multiple choice question and a letter. There is also a word game in which the reader completes the poem by choosing words to fill in the blanks.

Bob and Jack: A Boy and His Yak, Moss's 1992 publication, is a story written in verse that spans an entire life cycle in its celebration of friendship. As a child, Jack shares many adventures with Bob, his pet yak. But when it comes time for Jack to leave for college, the two begin a separation process that is completed when Bob dies. Jack goes on to marry and start a family, and eventually gives his daughter a pet yak of her own. A *Publishers Weekly* reviewer appreciated the book's "eminent readability and sweet message."

Moss's recent projects provide certain pleasures that were lacking in his work for television, he told *SATA.* With book writing, "you know you're going directly to your audience. There is nothing in between, so you don't have to take into consideration a performer," Moss explained. In addition, there's "a different kind of excitement to hear somebody read your stuff out loud. I've been in a house where the kid didn't know that I wrote the book, and will say to his mother, 'Read me to sleep with *The Butterfly Jar,*' which is the absolute pleasure. It's not the same as television, because with television, you're not in the room, for the most part, when anybody's watching. Even though a couple million people may be watching, you're not with them. The books are so personal, so one-on-one—I mean I can read to a kid or go out to sign books or whatever, and you're coming into direct contact with somebody, you've spoken to them. It's a true pleasure.

"Where I've been luckiest is—it happened twice—to be in a bookstore where somebody is buying your book, or to hear somebody singing your song. To know people are getting a kick out of what you've done; they don't know who you are, but they know that you've done it—and it's very rewarding. I think kids are the one audience that's straightforward and honest in their reaction to everything. So you know that if you're doing well with them, they're not just saying it to be nice."

BIOGRAPHICAL/CRITICAL SOURCES:

BOOKS

Lesser, Gerald S., *Children and Television: Lessons from Sesame Street,* Vintage Books, 1974, p. 240.

PERIODICALS

Booklist, February 1, 1990, p. 1093.
Detroit Free Press, November 18, 1992.
Kirkus Reviews, November 15, 1989, p. 1674.
New York Times Book Review, March 4, 1990, p. 33.
Publishers Weekly, October 19, 1992, p. 75.
School Library Journal, March, 1984, p. 148; July, 1990, p. 86.

OTHER

Moss, Jeff, telephone interview with Joanna Brod for *Something about the Author,* conducted August 27, 1992.

—*Sketch by Joanna Brod*

*   *   *

MOULIN, Annie 1946-
(Marie-Annie Moulin)

PERSONAL: Born April 26, 1946, in Le Breuil-sur-Cooze, France; daughter of Denis and Therese (Fournier) Moulin; married Max Bourret (a teacher), 1989. *Education:* University of Clermont-Ferrand, Licence d'Histoire, 1966, Agregation d'Histoire, 1968, Docteur en Histoire, 1985.

ADDRESSES: Office—U.F.R. Lettres, Universite de Clermont II, 29 Blvd. Gergovia, 63037 Clermont-Ferrand, France.

CAREER: University of Clermont II, Clermont-Ferrand, France, *maitre de conference d'histoire contemporaine,* 1989—.

WRITINGS:

(Under name Marie-Annie Moulin) *Les macons de la haute-marche au XVIIIe siecle,* Institut d'Etudes du Massif Central, 1986.
Les paysans dans la societe francaise, Le Seuil, 1988, translation by M. C. Cleary and M. F. Cleary published as *Peasantry and Society in France since 1789,* Cambridge University Press, 1991.

WORK IN PROGRESS: A book about industrial development during World War I.

*   *   *

MOULIN, Marie-Annie
See MOULIN, Annie

MOWITT, John 1952-

PERSONAL: Born August 17, 1952, in Lakewood, OH; son of John William (in business) and Arlene Vesta (Lange) Mowitt; married Winifred Woodhull, 1984 (marriage ended, July 19, 1989); married Jeanine Carol Ferguson (a student), August 28, 1989; children: (first marriage) Rachel Woodhull, Rosalind Frances Mowitt. *Education:* Miami-Dade Community College, A.A., 1972; Florida International University, B.A., 1974; University of Wisconsin—Madison, Ph.D., 1982. *Politics:* "Socialist-Feminist." *Religion:* "None."

ADDRESSES: Office—Ford Hall, University of Minnesota—Twin Cities, Minneapolis, MN 55455.

CAREER: University of Minnesota—Twin Cities, Minneapolis, associate professor, 1990—; writer.

MEMBER: Modern Language Association.

WRITINGS:

Text: The Genealogy of an Antidisciplinary Object, Duke University Press, 1992.

WORK IN PROGRESS: Percussion: Drumming, Beating, Striking.

* * *

MUGNY, Gabriel 1949-

PERSONAL: Born August 16, 1949, in Fribourg, Switzerland; son of Arthur and Marthe Mugny; married Carmen Roca (a musician); children: Fanny, Esther, Fiona. *Education:* Received Ph.D. from University of Geneva.

ADDRESSES: Home—9 route de Drize, CH-1227 Carouge, Geneva, Switzerland.

CAREER: University of Geneva, Geneva, Switzerland, professor of social psychology.

WRITINGS:

The Power of Minorities, Academic Press, 1982.
(With W. Doise) *The Social Development of the Intellect,* Pergamon, 1984.
(Editor with S. Mosconcis and E. Van Avermaet) *Perspectives on Minority Influence,* Cambridge University Press, 1985.
(With E. Carugati) *Social Representations of Intelligence,* Cambridge University Press, 1989.
(With G. A. Perez) *The Social Psychology of Minority Influence,* Cambridge University Press, 1991.
(Editor with M. von Cranach and W. Doise) *Social Representations and the Social Bases of Knowledge,* Hans Huber (Bern, Switzerland), 1992.

WORK IN PROGRESS: Social Influence: The Conflict Elaboration Theory, with G. A. Perez and others.

SIDELIGHTS: Gabriel Mugny told *CA:* "I have developed a socio-constructivist approach to cognitive development, social influence processes, and persuasion. In a 'European style,' I approach social psychological phenomena linked to intellective tasks (in children and adults) and perceptual and opinion tasks (racism, xenophobia, tobacco consumption, pollution, abortion, et cetera) in terms of the constructive effects of sociocognitive conflicts."

* * *

MURRAY, Gale Barbara 1945-

PERSONAL: Born in 1945. *Education:* Barnard College, B.A. (cum laude), 1966; Columbia University, M.A., 1970, M.Phil., 1977, Ph.D. (with distinction), 1978.

ADDRESSES: Home—1202 North Institute, Colorado Springs, CO 80903.

CAREER: Brooklyn College of the City University of New York, Brooklyn, NY, adjunct instructor, 1972-73, adjunct assistant professor of art history, 1973-74 and 1975; Oberlin College, Oberlin, OH, visiting instructor in art, spring, 1976; Colorado College, Colorado Springs, instructor, 1976-78, assistant professor, 1978-84, associate professor, 1985-90, professor of art, 1991—, department head, 1992—.

AWARDS, HONORS: Fulbright fellow in France, 1971-72; grants from French Government, 1975, American Council of Learned Societies, 1983, and American Philosophical Society, 1989-90.

WRITINGS:

Toulouse-Lautrec: The Formative Years, 1878-1891, Oxford University Press, 1991.
(Editor) *Toulouse-Lautrec: A Retrospective,* Macmillan, 1992.

Work represented in anthologies, including *The Letters of Henri de Toulouse-Lautrec,* edited by Herbert Schimmel, Oxford University Press, 1991. Contributor of articles and reviews to arts journals.

* * *

MYERS, Bernard S(amuel) 1908-1993

OBITUARY NOTICE—See index for *CA* sketch: Born May 4, 1908, in New York, NY; died of pneumonia, February 28, 1993, in Brooklyn, NY. Art historian, educator, editor, and author. Myers was a lecturer in architecture, education, and fine arts at colleges including New York University and City College of New York from 1930 to 1958. He later spent seventeen years as editor-in-chief of art books at McGraw-Hill Book Co., serving as consulting editor for their sixteen-volume *Encyclopedia of World Art.* Myers also acted as senior consulting editor for the *Random House Companion to Painting and Sculpture* and was the author of *Problems of the Younger Artist.*

OBITUARIES AND OTHER SOURCES:

BOOKS

Author's and Writer's Who's Who, sixth edition, Hafner Publishing, 1971.
International Authors and Writers Who's Who, seventh edition, Melrose, 1976.
Who's Who in America, Marquis, 1984.

PERIODICALS

New York Times, March 3, 1993, p. B12.

N-O

NAGEM, Monique F. 1941-

PERSONAL: Born May 24, 1941, in Paris, France. *Education:* McNeese State University, B.A., 1962, M.A., 1973; University of Texas at Austin, Ph.D., 1986.

ADDRESSES: Home—1115 Ryan St., Lake Charles, LA 70601-5352. *Office*—Department of Languages, McNeese State University, Lake Charles, LA 70609-2655.

CAREER: McNeese State University, Lake Charles, LA, associate professor of languages, 1981—.

MEMBER: American Translators Association, American Literary Translators Association, American Association of Teachers of French, Beckette Society.

WRITINGS:

(Translator) Chantal Chawaf, *Redemption,* Dalkey Archive Press, 1992.
(Translator) Chantal Chawaf, *Mother Love, Mother Earth,* Garland Publishing, 1992.

WORK IN PROGRESS: Translating *Copies Conformes* by Monique LaRue and *Le Vieux de la Montagne* by Habib Tengour.

*   *   *

NAJ, Amal K. 1951-

PERSONAL: Born June 17, 1951, in India; son of Anil Kumar and Biva (Rani) Nag. *Education:* Queen's University of Belfast, B.Sc. (with honors), 1975.

ADDRESSES: Home—196 East 75th St., Apt. 7D, New York, NY 10021. *Agent*—Richard S. Pine, Arthur Pine Associates, Inc., 250 West 57th St., New York, NY 10019.

CAREER: Wall Street Journal, New York City, staff reporter, 1978—.

WRITINGS:

Peppers: A Story of Hot Pursuits, Knopf, 1992.

WORK IN PROGRESS: A work of fiction.

*   *   *

NATHANSON, Paul 1947-

PERSONAL: Born June 20, 1947, in New York, NY; son of Solomon (an engineer and real estate appraiser) and Roslyn Helen (a dietician and braille transcriber; maiden name, Singer) Nathanson. *Education:* McGill University, B.A., 1968, M.L.S., 1971, B.Th., 1978, Ph.D., 1989; Concordia University, M.A., 1979. *Religion:* Judaism. *Avocational interests:* History, India, Russia, art, and opera.

ADDRESSES: Home—4854 Cote Des Neiges, Apt. 605, Montreal, Quebec, Canada H3V 1G7. *Office*—McGill Centre for Medicine, Ethics, and Law, 3690 Peel St., Montreal, Quebec, Canada H3A 1W9.

CAREER: Jewish Public Library, Montreal, Quebec, Canada, cataloguer, 1972-73 and 1974-76; National Gallery of Canada, Ottawa, Ontario, cataloguer, 1973-74; Vancouver School of Theology, Vancouver, British Columbia, Canada, librarian and instructor, 1979-82; Bishop's University, Lennoxville, Quebec, instructor, 1984; McGill University, Montreal, instructor, 1988, Centre for Medicine, Ethics, and Law, coinvestigator, 1988-90, Faculty of Religious Studies and Centre for Medicine, Ethics, and Law, senior research associate, 1990—. Lecturer, speaker, and writer.

MEMBER: American Academy of Religion, Popular Culture Association.

AWARDS, HONORS: University scholarship, 1968, 1977, and 1978, Sir William MacDonald scholarship, 1968, H.

W. Wilson scholarship, 1970, Birks award (for highest standing), 1978, and McConnell fellowship, 1983-86, all from McGill University; Ellegood Jubilee scholarship, 1977, and Lobley prize, 1978, both from Montreal Diocesan Theological College; grants from McGill Centre for Medicine, Ethics, and Law, 1988-90, 1989, 1990-93, 1991, and 1992, and from Ministere de l'enseignement superieur et de la science, 1984-86.

WRITINGS:

Over the Rainbow: The Wizard of Oz as a Secular Myth of America, State University of New York Press, 1991.

Coauthor, with Katherine Young and Margaret Somerville, of *The Future of Nature: New Reproductive Technologies and the Symbolic Frontier,* 1993; and with Young, of *Beyond the Fall of Man: From Ideology to Dialogue in the Conflict over Masculine Identity,* 1993. Contributor to periodicals, including *Journal of Popular Culture, Hikmat, Ecumenist, Viewpoints,* and *Arc.*

WORK IN PROGRESS: Researching religion and art, men's studies, and gender and ethics.

SIDELIGHTS: Paul Nathanson told *CA:* "My motivation for writing a book about *The Wizard of Oz* has two sources. In the first place, I have always been fascinated by movies. But my work has not been focused on art films, characterized by innovative techniques, idiosyncratic forms, and hostility toward cultural norms. I am more interested in popular movies, those that are massively and enduringly popular. Because movies of this kind do not fit prevalent definitions of art, they are usually dismissed in one way or another as bad art. That is, they are trivialized as entertaining diversions for the masses, challenged as banal commercial exploitation, or attacked as sinister ideological propaganda. My own experience suggests to me that these approaches are inadequate. They either ignore the importance of fantasy or reduce people to passive victims of conspiracies. I am not a mindless zombie, a passive consumer, or a helpless victim when I go to the movies. So what really happens in darkened theaters when popular movies are shown? The phenomenon has been likened to dreaming: popular movies are 'collective daydreams' in which our deepest hopes and darkest fears, those pertaining to both ourselves and our communities, are explored and experienced symbolically. It seems to me, though, that movies are not only like daydreams but also like myths: traditional stories about origin, destiny, and identity that are told by communities.

"That brings me to the other source of my interest in *The Wizard of Oz:* my work in the field of religious studies. Myth, after all, is a characteristic expression of religion. But no one goes to the movies with this in mind. What, then, is the relation between popular movies and myths?

I suggest that popular movies come to function in a modern and ostensibly secular society very much the way myths do in traditional and religious societies. They have become the cultural property of nearly everyone primarily because of the evocative power of their underlying themes. This is nothing new. At all times and in all places, people have told stories—myths—to explore the fundamental paradoxes of everyday life. These myths are generated by the universal need to create meaning and order in a world that includes both good and evil, birth and death, nature and culture, male and female, familiar and alien, us and them. What is new in our culturally fragmented society, however, is the desirability of trying to do this *outside* the context of any one traditional religion. The movies that I find most interesting are those that recapitulate in secular terms, and usually by default rather than by design, myths that have played a profound role over the centuries in shaping the way we think about ourselves, our place in society, and our place in the cosmos.

"One of the most significant motifs in these movies, including *The Wizard of Oz,* is home—especially returning home. Even in the West, history has been understood as a process of returning home to a paradise beyond history. My interest in this is probably due to the fact that I am Jewish. Returning home is a central theme not only in the biblical texts (return from historical exile to the promised land; return from trans-historical exile to the eschatological holy land of messianic times) but also the rabbinic tradition that emerged from it (return of the soul to God through repentance; return to the primary events in sacred history on the sabbath and festivals; return of the soul to Eden after death).

"My interest in the theme of returning home is also due to my interest in America. Although I was born in New York, my parents are Canadian. We returned to Canada when I was an infant. During the Vietnam War, however, I spent a year in New York, taking the precaution of renouncing my American citizenship before going. Years later, amnesties were offered to deserters, but not to people like me. My imagination continues to be haunted by the United States. I consider myself a kind of 'exile.' This stimulates my interest in the whole notion of exile, and particularly in another group of people who, for very different reasons, considered themselves exiles: the Europeans who set off three hundred years ago for the New World as members of a New Israel returning to a New Promised Land in what they believed was a New Eden. Once there, especially after the Civil War, these people began to realize that they had been expelled once again from paradise into a world of conflict and confusion. But the hope of return remained firm in terms both religious (the future America as a millenarian version of the primeval garden) and secular (the future America as a technological and utopian version of the heavenly city). This profound desire to wipe the slate clean and start over again lies at the heart not only of American civilization but of western civilization since biblical times.

"I am also interested in secular myths about coming of age. This is the explicit theme of *The Wizard of Oz.* In a current project, I have found that it is an implicit theme of another classic movie, *Rebel without a Cause.* My interest now, though, is focused more specifically on the problems presented by coming of age for *men:* the formation of masculine identity and the presentation of manhood in both popular and elite (academic) culture. This is the subject of a book that I am writing with my colleague, Katherine Young. Moreover, my scope of inquiry now includes television shows, comic strips, romance novels, and popular magazines, as well as movies."

*   *   *

NEHRING, James 1958-

PERSONAL: Born October 29, 1958, in New York, NY; son of Robert E. (in insurance and real estate management) and Mary (a homemaker; maiden name, Stafford) Nehring; married Laurie A. Sutherland (an information specialist), August 25, 1984; children: Rebecca, Abigail. *Education:* University of Virginia, B.A. (with high distinction), 1980; Brown University, M.A.T., 1982.

ADDRESSES: Home—25 Oakwood Place, Delmar, NY 12054. *Agent*—Susan Romer, Don Congdon Associates, 156 Fifth Ave., Suite 625, New York, NY 10010.

CAREER: Pine Bush Central Schools, Pine Bush, NY, teacher, 1982-85; Voorheesville Schools, Voorheesville, NY, teacher, 1985-86; Bethlehem Central Schools, Delmar, NY, teacher, 1986-92.

MEMBER: National Council of the Social Studies.

WRITINGS:

Why Do We Gotta Do This Stuff, Mr. Nehring?, M. Evans, 1989.
The Schools We Have, the Schools We Want, Jossey-Bass, 1992.

Book review editor, *Social Science Record.*

WORK IN PROGRESS: A novel about best friends.

*   *   *

NELSON, Peter N. 1953-

PERSONAL: Born February 8, 1953, in Minneapolis, MN; son of Newell N. (an economist) and Lois (a homemaker and secretary; maiden name, Jacobson) Nelson; married Diane Porcella, July 8, 1989. *Education:* St. Olaf College, B.A. in English and B.A. in art (cum laude), 1975; University of Iowa, M.F.A., 1979. *Politics:* Independent. *Avocational interests:* "In my spare time I play with my dog, work in the garden, paint or draw, and I sometimes play piano in a country-western dance band."

ADDRESSES: Agent—Alice Martell, 555 Fifth Ave., New York, NY 10017.

CAREER: Free-lance journalist, 1981—. Teacher of creative writing at Rhode Island School of Design and St. Lawrence University.

AWARDS, HONORS: James Michener Fellowship, 1981; Rhode Island State Arts Council grant for fiction, 1985; Massachusetts Artists Foundation Fellowship in playwriting, for *Crazytime;* Edgar Award nomination, Mystery Writers of America, 1992, for *Scarface.*

WRITINGS:

YOUNG ADULT NOVELS

Sylvia Smith-Smith, Crosswinds, 1987.
Fast Lane West, Simon & Schuster, 1991.
Night of Fire, Simon & Schuster, 1991.
Scarface, Simon & Schuster, 1991.
Deadly Lessons, Simon & Schuster, 1992.
Dangerous Waters, Simon & Schuster, 1992.
Double Dose, HarperCollins, 1992.
First to Die, HarperCollins, 1992.

OTHER

Real Man Tells All (collected columns), Viking, 1987.
Marry Like a Man, New American Library, 1992.

Also author of the screenplay *Crazytime.* Contributor of the "His" column to *Mademoiselle.* Contributor to periodicals, including *Esquire, Harpers, New England Monthly, Redbook,* and *Special Report.*

SIDELIGHTS: Peter N. Nelson commented: "I was born on the eighth of February, 1953, in Minneapolis, Minnesota, the second of four children. My father, Newell N. Nelson, worked as an economist for General Mills until retiring in 1987. My mother, Lois, was a mother and later a secretary until she retired in 1989. I attended Washburn High School, in Minneapolis, and later St. Olaf College, in Northfield, Minnesota, majoring in art and English, bachelor degrees cum laude, 1975, my studies including a year at St. Peter's College in Oxford, England. I taught English and studied poetry at the University of Arizona, in Tucson, from 1976 to 1977, but transferred to the University of Iowa Writers' Workshop, in Iowa City, where I finished an M.F.A. in poetry in 1979. By the time I finished my degree, I was writing only fiction. In 1981, I received a James Michener Fellowship, an award given to promising first novelists, and moved to Portland, Oregon.

"The grant, which lasted a year and a half, bought me the time to establish myself as a free-lance writer. My very first publication appeared in *Esquire* in 1982, after which I moved to Providence, Rhode Island, where I taught creative writing at the Rhode Island School of Design (briefly), while making frequent trips to New York City to find magazine work. I continued to write both fiction and nonfiction throughout the 1980s. In 1992, I taught creative writing at St. Lawrence University in Canton, New York.

"My nonfiction has appeared in the Chicago *Tribune, Elle, Esquire, Glamour, Mademoiselle, Men's Life, Mother Jones, New England Monthly, Northwest Orient, Outside, Rolling Stone,* and other magazines, and for two years I wrote the 'His' column for *Mademoiselle,* those columns collected in a volume called *Real Man Tells All.*

"My short stories appearing in *Seventeen* were collected in a volume named after the title character, Sylvia Smith-Smith, a girl whose mother had the same last name as her father but refused to take it when they married. Simon & Schuster has published the next five books of the series as well as a reprint of the original volume. Sylvia Smith-Smith was based on a real girl I knew named Marah who hated anchovies. One night at dinner, when Marah was perhaps twelve years old, her stepfather and I tried to get her to eat a single anchovy. We each took a ten dollar bill from our wallets and laid the money on the table before her—hers for the consumption of a mere hairy fish. She refused, though twenty dollars is a lot of money for a twelve year old, even today. I admired her gumption so much that I wanted to put it into a story, and so Sylvia was born.

"How the career writing Sylvia Smith-Smith stories and books (as well as other young adult material) came about is equally accidental. I sold the first Sylvia story to *Seventeen* magazine. After it was published, my agent called to say *Seventeen* really liked it and wondered if I had any more Sylvia stories. I said I did not. My agent, sounding puzzled, thought I did and advised me that, if I did, I should send them to *Seventeen.* I thought, well, 'duh' . . . and said I would. If I were to write another. I had no plans to do so. Several months later the fiction editor from *Seventeen* called and said, 'I don't want to pressure you, but the story is scheduled for March, and we need to know what it's about so we can get the art department started.' 'What *what's* about?' I asked. They had thought they'd assigned another Sylvia story, commissioned one, I should say, but my agent (my first one—I've since gotten another, for obvious reasons) had failed to accurately convey the message. 'Give me a week,' I told the fiction editor. I

wrote one story, wasn't thrilled with it, wrote a second which I liked better, all in a week, mailed them both, and *Seventeen* bought them both. Three stories became a series, which became a book, which became a series of books.

"HarperCollins has published a second series of young adult novels. *First to Die, Double Dose,* and *Third Degree* are the titles of the first three books. Three more are scheduled for 1993, and the series has been optioned by Viacom Productions as a possible television series."

*   *   *

NEWHALL, Beaumont   1908-1993

OBITUARY NOTICE—See index for *CA* sketch: Born June 23, 1908, in Lynn, MA; died of complications from a stroke, February 26, 1993, in Santa Fe, NM. Historian, curator, educator, and author. Newhall's *The History of Photography, 1839 to the Present,* which grew out of his 1937 exhibition and was revised throughout his life, is a celebrated work in the field of photography history. Hired as a librarian at the Museum of Modern Art in 1935, Newhall was appointed the first curator of its newly created photography department in 1940. Eight years later Newhall left the museum to become a curator at the George Eastman House, now known as the International Museum of Photography, where he served as director for thirteen years. He was a professor of art at the University of New Mexico in Albuquerque from 1971 until 1984, when he was named professor emeritus. A prolific author, Newhall wrote *In Plain Sight* and *Supreme Instants: The Photography of Edward Weston,* and was the editor of *Photography: Essays and Images.*

OBITUARIES AND OTHER SOURCES:

BOOKS

Contemporary Photographers, second edition, St. James Press, 1988.
International Authors and Writers Who's Who, eleventh edition, International Biographical Centre, 1989.
Who's Who in America, Marquis, 1992.
The Writers Directory: 1990-1992, St. James Press, 1990.

PERIODICALS

Chicago Tribune, February 28, 1993, section 2, p. 6.
Los Angeles Times, February 27, 1993, p. A24.
New York Times, February 27, 1993, p. 27.

NEWHALL, David S(owle) 1929-

PERSONAL: Born July 26, 1929, in Burlington, VT; son of Chester A. (a physician and professor of anatomy) and Nella Perry (a homemaker; maiden name, Tillotson) Newhall; married Edna Newton (a homemaker), 1952; children: Rebecca Newhall Falby, John, Jesslyn, Melissa Yu, David Chester. *Education:* University of Vermont, B.A., 1951; Harvard University, A.M., 1956, Ph.D., 1963. *Religion:* Presbyterian. *Avocational interests:* Railroads, the church choir, classical music, college athletics.

ADDRESSES: Home—634 North Third St., Danville, KY 40422. *Office*—Department of History, Centre College, Danville, KY 40422.

CAREER: University of Vermont, Burlington, instructor, 1959-63, assistant professor of history, 1963-66; Centre College, Danville, KY, assistant professor, 1966-67, associate professor, 1967-70, professor of history, 1970—, National Endowment for the Humanities Distinguished Professor, 1987-91. *Military service:* U.S. Army, 1951-53; served in Korea; received Combat Medical Badge.

MEMBER: World History Association, Society for French Historical Studies, Southern Historical Association, Ohio Valley World History Association, Phi Beta Kappa, Phi Alpha Theta, Omicron Delta Kappa.

WRITINGS:

Clemenceau: A Life at War, Edwin Mellen, 1991.

Work represented in books, including *Historical Dictionary of the Third French Republic,* edited by Patrick Hutton, Greenwood Press, 1986; *The Kentucky Encyclopedia,* University Press of Kentucky, 1992; and *Leaders of the World,* Gale, 1993.

WORK IN PROGRESS: Research on Vermont in the Civil War.

*   *   *

NINGKUN, Wu 1921-

PERSONAL: Born September 14, 1921, in Yangzhou, China; married Yikai Li (a college instructor), July 8, 1954; children: Yiding, Yimao Norman, Yicun. *Education:* Attended Southwestern University, 1939-41; Manchester College, B.A., 1948; University of Chicago, M.A., 1949, Ph.D., 1951.

ADDRESSES: Home—3341 Buchanan St. No. 301, Mt. Ranier, MD 20712.

CAREER: Institute of International Relations, Beijing, China, professor of English, 1956-92; writer.

WRITINGS:

A Single Tear, Atlantic Monthly Press, 1992.

Translator of works into Chinese, including *The Great Gatsby,* by F. Scott Fitzgerald, 1980, and *Short Stories of Henry James,* by Henry James, 1983. Contributor of "From Half-Step Bridge to Cambridge" to *Cambridge Review,* 1986.

*   *   *

NITZE, Paul H(enry) 1907-

PERSONAL: Born January 16, 1907, in Amherst, MA; son of William A. (an educator) and Anina Hilken Nitze; married Phyllis Pratt, December 2, 1932 (deceased); married Elisabeth Scott Porter, January 23, 1993; children: (first marriage) Heidi, Peter, William, Phyllis Anina Nitze Thompson. *Education:* Harvard University, B.A. (cum laude), 1928, graduate study, 1937-38. *Religion:* Episcopalian.

ADDRESSES: Home—3120 Woodley Rd. N.W., Washington, DC 20008. *Office*—Paul H. Nitze School of Advanced International Studies, Johns Hopkins University, 1619 Massachusetts Ave., Suite 811, Washington, DC 20036. *Agent*—Sterling Lord Literistic Inc., One Madison Ave., New York, NY 10010.

CAREER: Affiliated with Dillon, Read & Co. (an investment banking firm), New York City, 1929-38, vice-president, 1939-41; U.S. Department of State, Washington, DC, deputy director of Office of International Trade Policy, 1946-48, deputy assistant secretary of state for economic affairs, 1948-49, deputy director of policy planning staff, 1949, director of policy planning staff, 1950-53, head of U.S. delegation to intermediate-range nuclear forces negotiations with the Soviet Union, 1981-84, special adviser on arms control to president and secretary of state, 1985-89, ambassador at large, 1986-89; Foreign Service Education Foundation, Washington, DC, president, 1953-61; U.S. Department of Defense, Washington, DC, assistant secretary for international security affairs, 1961-63, secretary of the Navy, 1963-67, deputy secretary of defense, 1967-69, representative of secretary of defense on U.S. delegation to Strategic Arms Limitation Talks (SALT) with the Soviet Union, 1969-74; Johns Hopkins University, Paul H. Nitze School of Advanced International Studies, Washington, DC, diplomat-in-residence, 1989—. P. H. Nitze & Co., Inc., president, 1938-39; Office of Coordinator of Inter-American Affairs, financial director, 1941-42; Board of Economic Warfare, chief of metals and minerals branch, 1942-43; Foreign Economic Administration, director of foreign procurement and development branch, 1943-44; U.S. Strategic Bombing Survey, director, 1944-45, vice chairman, 1945-46; consultant on defense policy and U.S./Soviet strategic relationship for various government departments and private firms, 1975-81; Committee on the Present Danger, chairman of policy studies, 1978-81.

Johns Hopkins University, chairman of advisory council of School of Advanced International Studies (now Paul H. Nitze School of Advanced International Studies), 1954-81, member of advisory council, 1981—, trustee, 1969-81, trustee emeritus, 1981—; trustee of Aspen Institute for Humanistic Studies, 1954—, and George C. Marshall Research Foundation, 1954—; Harvard University, member of board of overseers, 1967-72. Member of boards of directors of Aspen Skiing Corporation, 1946-81, Schroder's Inc., 1969-81, American Security & Trust Company, 1970-81, Ethics and Public Policy Center, 1970-81, Atlantic Council of the United States, 1970—, and Twentieth Century-Fox Film Corporation, 1978-81. Director of Washington Opera, Desert Music Festival, Bethlehem Bach Festival, and the Aspen Institute.

AWARDS, HONORS: Medal of Merit from President Harry Truman, 1945; U.S. Department of Defense, Medal for Distinguished Public Service, 1973, and Bronze Palm, 1977; George C. Marshall Medal, Association of the U.S. Army, 1985; Presidential Medal of Freedom, U.S. Executive Office of the President, 1985; Knight Commander's Cross (Badge and Star) of Order of Merit, Federal Republic of Germany, 1985; Order of Merit, Italy, 1988; Secretary General's Atlantic Award (Man of the Year), North Atlantic Treaty Organization, 1988; Royal Belgium Order of the Crown, 1989; Jefferson Award for public service by an elected or appointed official, American Institute for Public Service, 1989; Burkett Miller Award, University of Virginia, 1989; Gold Medal Award, National Institute of Social Sciences, 1989; Eric M. Warburg Award, Atlantik-Bruecke, 1990; Edward Weintal Prize for Diplomatic Reporting, Special Citation, Georgetown University Institute for the Study of Diplomacy, 1990, and Adolphe Bentinck Prize, 1991, both for *From Hiroshima to Glasnost: At the Center of Decision—A Memoir;* Theodore Roosevelt Distinguished Service Medal, Theodore Roosevelt Association, 1990; Sylvanus Thayer Award, U.S. Military Academy, 1991; inducted into Aspen Hall of Fame, 1991; Distinguished Alumnus Award, The U-High Laboratory School, University of Chicago, 1991; Grosse Goldene Ehrenzeichen des Landes Steiermark mit dem Stern, 1991; honorary degrees from Johns Hopkins University, 1986, Harvard University, 1986, Amherst College, 1989, Williams College, 1989, Pratt Institute, and New School for Social Research.

WRITINGS:

U.S. Foreign Policy, 1945-1955, Foreign Policy Association, 1956.

Political Aspects of a National Strategy, Washington Center of Foreign Policy Research, 1960.

The Recovery of Ethics, Church Peace Union, 1960.

(With John F. Lehman and Seymour Weiss) *The Carter Proposals: Some Basic Questions and Cautions,* Center for Advanced International Studies, University of Miami, 1977.

(With Leonard Sullivan, Jr., and Atlantic Council's Working Group on Securing the Seas) *Securing the Seas: The Soviet Naval Challenge and Western Alliance Options,* Atlantic Council of the United States, 1978.

Paul H. Nitze on Foreign Policy (speeches, lectures, and articles), edited by Kenneth W. Thompson and Steven L. Rearden, Miller Center, University of Virginia/ University Press of America, 1989.

(With Ann M. Smith and Steven L. Rearden) *From Hiroshima to Glasnost: At the Center of Decision—A Memoir,* Grove Weidenfeld, 1989.

Tension between Opposites: The Theory and Practice of Politics, Scribner, 1993.

Contributor to books, including *Theoretical Aspects of International Relations,* edited by William T. R. Fox, University of Notre Dame Press, 1959; *Defending America,* Basic Books, 1977; and *American Defense Annual, 1986-1987,* edited by Joseph Kruzel, Heath, 1986. Contributor to numerous periodicals, including *American Legion, Atlantic Community Quarterly, Comparative Strategy, Fletcher Forum, Foreign Affairs, Foreign Policy, International Security, Journal of International Relations, New York Times, New York Times Magazine, Review of Politics, Washington Post,* and *Worldview.*

WORK IN PROGRESS: Research on events in the North Atlantic Treaty Organization, the U.S.S.R., and Eastern Europe.

SIDELIGHTS: During a political career stretching through five decades, Paul H. Nitze became known for his powerful influence on American defense policies. As Robert L. Beisner noted in a *Washington Post Book World* article, "Nitze's handprints are all over American national security policies since 1945." He first became involved in military matters in the 1940s, during World War II; with the Strategic Bombing Survey Nitze helped analyze the effectiveness of bombing raids in Europe and determine what kinds of attack would most hinder the Japanese. According to Stanley Hoffmann, writing in the *New York Review of Books,* Nitze's report suggested that the use of atomic bombs in Hiroshima and Nagasaki might have been unnecessary. In 1950 he set a lasting course for

American-Soviet relations during the long conflict known as the cold war, stating in a National Security Council report that the United States needed to counter Soviet expansionism by increasing its own military might. Such promotion of the military, however, found its balance in Nitze's repeated efforts under President Ronald Reagan to make a nuclear arms reduction treaty with the U.S.S.R. His famed behind-the-scenes "walk in the woods" with a Soviet negotiator in 1982 almost resulted in a compromise, but the countries' leaders rejected the proposed agreement. Later, when Reagan and Soviet leader Mikhail Gorbachev discussed arms control in Reykjavik, Iceland, Nitze received some of the credit for the two countries' first faltering steps toward a pact. Altogether, Nitze's was "a long, admirable life in public service," in the opinion of *Los Angeles Times Book Review* contributor Gregory F. Treverton.

In 1989 Nitze published a memoir of his career, *From Hiroshima to Glasnost: At the Center of Decision.* Written with Ann M. Smith and Steven L. Rearden, the book touches on the wide-ranging experiences of "the consummate cold warrior," as Walter Isaacson dubbed Nitze in the *New York Times Book Review.* Critics welcomed the author's occasional revelations about his life, but several regretted what they judged the memoir's overall impersonality and reticence. Observed Hoffmann, "One suspects that he knows a great deal about the sociology and psychology of the establishment," for example, "but that this is the last subject he wants to discuss with outsiders." Still, the critic asserted, *From Hiroshima to Glasnost* is valuable because it "describes Nitze's positions" and "raises issues that remain important." Hailing Nitze's uncommon personal integrity and boldness, James O. Goldsborough mused in Chicago *Tribune Books* that the book suffered somewhat from having been transcribed from oral accounts. "I can't help but think what this memoir might have been had Nitze, a cultivated man, written it himself, striving for the right words to recapture the adventure that has been his life." Despite reservations, Isaacson summarized Nitze's autobiography as "a solid and respectable diplomatic tome, one that adds a bit of wisdom and insight . . . to the history of the cold war that he helped wage."

Nitze told *CA:* "In early September 1945 I arrived in Japan with the United States Strategic Bombing Survey to study the effects of the two atomic bombs exploded over the cities of Hiroshima and Nagasaki. The sky was a delicate pale blue as we flew in over Tokyo Bay, with Fujiyama on the left and directly ahead a small island rising out of the mist. From the air, Japan was an exquisite jewel in the setting sun. On the ground, the devastation was readily apparent; whole cities had been burned to the ground, and the people, far from being the enemy we had

fought so long and hard, appeared graceful and hardworking, but they were confused and totally demoralized. My own confusion rose to confound me; like most Americans during World War II, I hated the Japanese for their sneak attack on Pearl Harbor. The Japanese, on the other hand, seemed to bear no malice to the members of the American occupation forces despite the devastation of their cities.

"There is no question that the destruction in Hiroshima and Nagasaki was severe, with over one hundred thousand people killed in the two cities. On the other hand, over eighty thousand were killed and nearly sixteen square miles destroyed in Tokyo alone in one firebomb raid earlier that year. The significance of the atomic bomb was that it compressed the power of many conventional bombs into one bomb, thereby increasing enormously the effectiveness of a single B-29 bomber. It would have taken 210 bombers, each carrying ten tons of high explosives and incendiaries, to equal the effects of the single atomic bomb at Hiroshima, and 120 bombers at Nagasaki.

"Thus began my dedication to national security matters and strategic nuclear policy in particular. My memoir was written forty-five years later with the hope that I had something to say, either by example or from the mistakes that were made, to the new generation coming into positions of influence. Overall, I would say that my generation can take a certain pride in our accomplishments: a war was won; Europe and the Far East, shattered by that war, were largely restored; the spread of totalitarianism was checked; and a third world war has been avoided. The containment policy, formed and implemented after World War II, can be declared a success now that the Communist party in the Soviet Union has turned its eye inward and decided it didn't like what it saw. Uncertainties remain, however, and it is important that a new generation of policymakers continues to act with wisdom and determination. I hope that some of our experiences may provide useful insights to them. At any rate, I am grateful for the opportunity I had to participate in the history of a fateful era."

BIOGRAPHICAL/CRITICAL SOURCES:

BOOKS

Callahan, David, *Dangerous Capabilities: Paul Nitze and the Cold War,* HarperCollins, 1990.

Nitze, Paul H., Ann M. Smith, and Steven L. Rearden, *From Hiroshima to Glasnost: At the Center of Decision—A Memoir,* Grove-Weidenfeld, 1989.

Talbott, Strobe, *The Master of the Game: Paul Nitze and the Nuclear Peace,* Knopf, 1988.

PERIODICALS

Los Angeles Times Book Review, January 7, 1990, p. 11.

New York Review of Books, November 23, 1989, pp. 13-17.
New York Times Book Review, October 15, 1989, p. 15.
Tribune Books (Chicago), November 12, 1989, p. 5.
Washington Post Book World, October 22, 1989, p. 11.

*   *   *

NOLAN, Janne E.

PERSONAL: Born in Paris, France; U.S. citizen; married Barry Blechman (a defense analyst); children: Emilie; stepchildren: Jennifer, Allison. *Education:* Antioch College, B.A., 1975; Fletcher School of Law and Diplomacy, M.A., 1977, Ph.D., 1982.

ADDRESSES: Home—1742 Swann St. N.W., Washington, DC, 20009. *Office*—Brookings Institution, 1775 Massachusetts Ave. N.W., Washington, DC 20036.

CAREER: U.S. Arms Control and Disarmament Agency, Washington, DC, specialist in technology transfer policy and delegate to U.S.-Soviet negotiations on arms transfer limitations, 1977-80; Science Applications International Corp., McLean, VA, senior consultant, 1982-83; Brookings Institution, Washington, DC, senior fellow, 1987—; Georgetown University, Washington, DC, adjunct professor, 1989—; also affiliated with Georgetown Center for Strategic and International Studies, Stanford University Center on International Security and Arms Control, and Harvard University Center for Science and International Affairs. U.S. Senate Armed Services Committee, senior designee, 1983-86. Advisor to congressional and presidential election campaigns, 1982-92; testified before U.S. Senate and House of Representatives; consultant to U.S. Department of State, U.S. Department of Defense, Kettering Foundation, U.S. Office of Technology Assessment, and Institute for Defense Analysis.

MEMBER: International Institute for Strategic Studies, Council on Foreign Relations, American Academy of Arts and Sciences (member of board of directors), American Association for the Advancement of Science (member of board of directors, Committee on International Security and Arms Control), Institute for Foreign Policy Analysis.

WRITINGS:

Military Industry in Taiwan and South Korea, Macmillan, 1986.
Guardians of the Arsenal: The Politics of Nuclear Strategy, Basic Books, 1989.
Trappings of Power: Ballistic Missiles in the Third World, Brookings Institution, 1991.

Contributor to periodicals, including *Foreign Affairs, Foreign Policy, New Republic,* and *Scientific American.* Member of editorial board, *Bulletin of Atomic Scientists.*

WORK IN PROGRESS: Editing a book about the future of the international security regime; research for a book about the future of American nuclear forces, for Brookings Institution.

BIOGRAPHICAL/CRITICAL SOURCES:

PERIODICALS

New York Times Book Review, December 24, 1989, p. 11.

*   *   *

NORDHAUG, Odd   1953-

PERSONAL: Born February 9, 1953, in Oslo, Norway; son of Alf and Ragnhild Nordhaug; married Turid Wallestad (a high school teacher), November 17, 1978; children: Ingerid W., Fishild W. *Education:* Norwegian School of Economics, M.Sc., 1976; University of Bergen, B.A., 1977, M.A., 1980; University of Oslo, D.Phil., 1989.

ADDRESSES: Home—Amundsleitet 75, Bergen-Ulset 5095, Norway. *Office*—Norwegian School of Economics, Breiviken 2, Bergen 5035, Norway.

CAREER: University of Bergen, Bergen, Norway, research assistant, 1977-79, assistant professor, 1981-83; Norwegian School of Economics, Bergen, began as associate professor, became professor, 1984—, program director, 1985-91. *Bergensavisen* (daily newspaper), chair of board. *Military service:* Royal Norwegian Navy, 1980-81; became quartermaster.

MEMBER: Academy of Management, Strategic Management Society.

WRITINGS:

(Editor) *Makt i Norge,* (title means "Power in Norway"), Fagbokforlaget, 1983.
Effekter av personalopplaering: Individ og organisasjon (title means "Training: Individual and Organization"), NVI/Tapir, 1985.
(With P. Langseth and H. Werring) *Personaladministrasjon* (title means "Personnel Administration"), TANO, 1988.
Kompetansestyring (title means "Competence Governance"), TANO, 1990.
The Shadow Educational System: Adult Resource Development, Oxford University Press/Norwegian University Press, 1991.
Ledelse av menneskelige ressurser (title means "Human Resource Management"), TANO, 1993.
Human Resources in Organizations, Norwegian University Press/Oxford University Press, 1993.

Also author, with T. Colbjornsen and O. Korsnes, of *Fagbevegelsen: Interesseorganisasjon og administrator* (title means "Trade Unions: Interest Organizations and Regulators"), Norwegian University Press. Work represented in several anthologies, including *Kompetanse, organisasjon og ledelse* (title means "Competence, Organization, and Management"), TANO, 1987; *Strategisk personalledelse* (title means "Strategic Human Resource Management"), TANO, 1990; and *Laering i organisasjoner* (title means "Learning in Organizations"), TANO, 1990. Contributor to books, including *Rekindling Commitment in Adult Education,* edited by R. Hoghielm, Stockholm Institute of Education, 1984; *Perspectives on Continuing Education in Europe,* edited by P. Jarvis, NIEA, 1992; and *Livslang laering* (title means "Lifelong Learning"), edited by J. Kvam, Tapir, 1992. Contributor of articles to periodicals, including *Journal of General Management, International Journal of Human Resource Management, Adult Education Quarterly, International Journal of Lifelong Education,* and *Human Resource Management Journal.*

*   *   *

O'CONNOR, Robert 1959-

PERSONAL: Born October 25, 1959, in New York, NY; son of Thomas Francis (a physician) and Mary Theresa (a registered nurse; maiden name, Harnett) O'Connor; married Donna Marsh (a writer and teacher), August 18, 1984; children: Vanessa Lang, James. *Education:* State University of New York College at Oswego, B.A., 1982; Syracuse University, M.A., 1985. *Religion:* Roman Catholic.

ADDRESSES: Home—Liverpool, NY. *Office*—Department of English, 38 Swetman Hall, State University of New York College at Oswego, Oswego, NY 13126. *Agent*—Amanda Urban, International Creative Management, 40 West 57th St., New York, NY 10019.

CAREER: State University of New York College at Oswego, lecturer in fiction, drama, and literature, 1985—. Syracuse University, university fellow, 1982-84, instructor, 1985-91; Auburn Correctional Facility, instructor, 1990-92.

WRITINGS:

Buffalo Soldiers (novel), Knopf, 1993.

Also author, with Leigh Allison Wilson, of the screenplay *Wind,* based on Wilson's novella, for John Bloomgarten Productions.

SIDELIGHTS: Robert O'Connor told *CA:* "My parents lived in Eastchester, New York, a suburb of New York City, and I went to Immaculate Conception grammar school, where my father had gone when he was a boy. I think going to a Catholic grammar school, with its cons-

tant emphasis on moral examination and the possible treachery on the surface of things, is something that influences one's writing in the deepest way. I remember at one point considering the priesthood, but deciding that the Christian religion could not be that hard up.

"I attended Eastchester High School, and worked part-time in a karate school, receiving a black belt and teaching self-defense to adults. Part of my understanding that the world can be constructed in stories came from listening to my students, who were older than I, talk about having been to war, having been in love, and the various paths and adventures their lives had taken. It was like taking a graduate course in life while I was still trying to grasp the basics. One of my students, whose story was eventually recorded in *Buffalo Soldiers,* told me about having been to Vietnam twice. 'They made you go twice?' I asked, incredulous. 'I volunteered,' he said. 'I enjoyed it.' In all other respects, he was a very normal individual, not even a particularly good fighter, nothing at all like the cliched image of the dramatically disturbed Vietnam veteran, although some of them attended the karate school, too. It was then I realized that many stories were not being told, and I resolved to tell them.

"*Buffalo Soldiers* is a book about Specialist Ray Elwood, a clerk in the U.S. Army station in Germany, who has lost his moral base and is in search of redemption. I think that the feeling we are in a fallen world, and that one must fight to regain one's moral balance, is a theme that strikes a resonant chord in me, as well as in other writers that I admire, notably Flannery O'Connor, John Cheever, Anton Chekhov, Fyodor Dostoevsky, and Graham Greene.

"When I began teaching in Oswego, I saw a lot of students who had missed Vietnam, but had joined the Army. They had served in Germany and told stories of a war going on within the Army, a secret war that involved race and drugs and power, and that nobody else was writing about. These stories had clear allegorical implications about what was going on here in the streets of this country. I think one of the things that people try to do as writers is tell the secrets. In doing that, the writer can show the unshowable, speak the unspeakable, no matter how unpleasant that can be. This accounts for much of the rawness, as well as the humor, in my book. The analogy I use is that fiction tries to hold up a mirror to society. If one doesn't like the image, one shouldn't try to change the mirror, but rather change what is causing the reflection.

"Toward the end of writing *Buffalo Soldiers* (which took four years), I began teaching at a maximum security prison in upstate New York. There, I was able to confirm some of my suspicions about the present-tense nature of crime, the essential visceral excitement of it, and that the use of second-person narrative in my book was thematically as well as technically justified. Many times interviewers have asked how I found out or knew about a particular bit of information, with the implication that a person must have experienced something personally in order to write about it. This is a journalistic conception of literature; it ignores the deeper wellsprings from which the fiction draws. In truth, the easiest things to gather are the facts; what is difficult is to know what is in someone's heart. This curiosity to know is part of the advice I give younger writers: Don't write what you know, (this is the worst and most reductive advice one can give beginning writers) but rather write what you don't know about what you know. This implies the mystery that lies at the heart of fiction, and was among the best and most inspirational advice I had been given and try to pass on now."

BIOGRAPHICAL/CRITICAL SOURCES:

PERIODICALS

Los Angeles Times, February 22, 1993.
New York Times, January 21, 1993.
Observer, February 21, 1993.

*   *   *

OLMERT, Michael 1940-

PERSONAL: Born March 8, 1940, in Washington, DC; son of Kenneth R. (a management analyst) and Mercedes (Drain) Olmert; married Meg Daley (a television producer), September 1, 1988; children: Michael, Anthony B., Patrick. *Education:* University of Maryland at College Park, B.A., 1962, Ph.D., 1980; Georgetown University, M.A., 1965; attended Christ Church, Oxford, 1983, 1987, 1988, and 1990. *Politics:* Democrat. *Religion:* Roman Catholic.

ADDRESSES: Home and office—1841 Columbia Rd. S.W., Apt. 603, Washington, DC 20009. *Agent*—Leona Schecter, 3748 Huntington St., Washington, DC 20015.

CAREER: Institute for Defense Analyses, Arlington, VA, editor, 1964-66; Arinc Research, Annapolis, MD, editor, 1966-68; Resource Management Corp., Bethesda, MD, director of publications, 1968-72; free-lance writer, 1972—. Catholic University, lecturer, 1981; University of Maryland at College Park, instructor in English, 1986—.

WRITINGS:

The Tradition of Sport in Medieval Literature, University of Maryland Press, 1980.
The Official Guidebook to Williamsburg, Colonial Williamsburg Foundation, 1985.
The Smithsonian Book of Books, Smithsonian Institution Press, 1992.

Author of educational film scripts, including *Aidan and Otto,* National Geographic Educational Films, 1990; *American Immigration,* National Geographic Educational Films, 1991; *Colonial Multiculturalism,* National Geographic Interactive Media, 1992; and *Eastern European Business,* U.S. Information Agency, 1993. Columnist for *Smithsonian,* 1981-88. Contributor of articles and reviews to magazines and newspapers, including *Chaucer Review, American Transcendental Quarterly, Archaeology, Science, Horticulture,* and *Sports Illustrated.*

FOR TELEVISION

Wildebeest Migration, The Discovery Channel, 1990.
Amazing Games, ESPN, 1991.
Science Bowl 1992, PBS, 1992.
For the Living: The Opening of the Holocaust Museum, WETA-TV, 1993.

Writer of episodes for the series *Smithsonian World,* broadcast by PBS, including "Islam," 1987, "Elephant on the Hill: Art vs. Technology," 1987, "Latin American Voices," 1987, and "Nigerian Art," 1990; also author of episodes for the series National Geographic *Explorer,* including "Falcon and Falconer," 1985, "Brazil Naturalists," 1986, "Killer Bees," 1986, "Dolphin Talk," 1986, "Hog Island Cattle Roundup," 1986, "Herculaneum," 1986, "Monhegan Lobstermen," 1986, "Tabasco," 1986, "Caesarea Archaeology," 1987, "Opal Mines of Australia," 1988, "Kronan: Swedish Underwater Archaeology," 1988, "Nineteenth-Century Time Capsule," 1989, "Winter in Yellowstone," 1989, "Mardy Murie: Historic Environmentalist," 1989, "Shark Trackers," 1989, and "Gauchos," 1991. Author of twelve dramatic monologues for *D.C. History Moments,* WETA-TV, 1991.

WORK IN PROGRESS: Baseline Jumper, a novel; *Points of Origin,* essays on historicism; *Greek Mythology,* a film script; *Aphrodite,* a film script.

SIDELIGHTS: Michael Olmert told *CA:* "The single most important rule in writing is 'Don't bore yourself!'—a line I learned from John Mortimer. It also helps to feel, every time you sit down to write, that you're doing something brand new, something that's never been done before in just this way. Writing for television documentaries is perfect training for improving the pace of writing for print. The best training of all, however, is reading good stuff."

*   *   *

O'NEAL, Reagan
See RIGNEY, James Oliver, Jr.

O'REILLY, Jackson
See RIGNEY, James Oliver, Jr.

*   *   *

OSTROVSKY, Victor 1949-

PERSONAL: Born November 28, 1949, in Edmonton, Alberta, Canada; married; wife's name, Bella; children: Sharon, Leeorah.

ADDRESSES: Home—Ottawa, Canada.

CAREER: The Institute for Intelligence and Special Operations (Mossad), Israel, case officer, 1984-86. Worked variously as a painter, graphic designer, stained-glass window maker, and carpet salesperson. *Military service:* Served in Israeli Army, until 1971, and Israeli Navy, 1977-81; became second lieutenant.

WRITINGS:

(With Claire Hoy) *By Way of Deception: The Making and Unmaking of a Mossad Officer,* St. Martin's, 1990, published in Canada as *By Way of Deception: A Devastating Insider's Portrait of the Mossad,* Stoddart Publishing, 1990.
Lion of Judah (novel), St. Martin's, 1993.

By Way of Deception has been translated into numerous languages, including Arabic, Danish, Dutch, French, German, Greek, Italian, Norwegian, Spanish, and Turkish.

SIDELIGHTS: By Way of Deception: The Making and Unmaking of a Mossad Officer, by Victor Ostrovsky and Claire Hoy, made headlines in September, 1990, when it was temporarily banned from bookshelves in both the United States and Canada. The U.S. decision to repress the book at Israel's request was the first time any book had been suppressed by a foreign power before being released. However, the ban, enforced by the New York State Supreme Court on September 12 at 1 o'clock a.m., contradicted the U.S. Constitution's First Amendment guarantee of free speech and press, and the court lifted the restriction approximately forty hours after it was ordered (the Canadian ban was lifted five days later). Israel had argued that, if the book were released, lives would be endangered. The source of this fear was the subject matter of the book: the Mossad (officially called *Ha Mossad, le Modiyn ve le Tafkidim Mayuhadim,* which means "The Institute for Intelligence and Special Operations") is Israel's special intelligence agency, and Ostrovsky and Hoy's book was perceived to threaten the security of Mossad agents around the world. Ostrovsky was in Mossad employ from December, 1984, to March, 1986, and the release of the book clearly violated a contract that Ostrovsky had signed with the Mossad forbidding him to publish inside information, a crime punishable by imprisonment in Israel. But because Ostrovsky felt that the Mossad was working against the good of Israel, he took his story to prominent Canadian journalist Claire Hoy, and the result of their collaboration is *By Way of Deception,* a phrase that comes from the Mossad motto, "By way of deception, thou shalt do war." In the forward of the book, Ostrovsky writes, "The twisted ideals and self-centered pragmatism that I encountered inside the Mossad, coupled with this so-called team's greed, lust, and total lack of respect for human life, . . . motivated me to tell this story."

Ostrovsky, who holds dual Canadian and Israeli citizenship, was born in Canada but moved with his mother to Israel when he was six. After shuttling between Israel and Canada as a youth, Ostrovsky finally settled in Holon, near Tel Aviv, with his maternal grandparents when his mother returned to Canada. At age seventeen, Ostrovsky entered the army for his compulsory term and left as the youngest officer in the Israeli military. In 1971, after his service, he returned to Canada and worked variously in advertising and carpet sales. But he once again returned to Israel in 1977 and joined the navy.

Ostrovsky was contacted by military officials while serving in the navy and given a series of tests, both psychological and physical, for reasons kept secret from him. The secrecy signalled to him that the Mossad was involved. When Ostrovsky finally learned that training for the position would require that he be away from his family except for a visit every two or three weeks, he told his interviewer that he was no longer interested. He and his wife, Bella, were harassed over the phone for the next eight months, but Ostrovsky wrote in the book that "since I was already serving in the military, I didn't feel as if I was neglecting my country."

In 1981, Ostrovsky left the navy and set up a business selling stained glass windows. But in October, 1982, he was contacted by the military again. This time, after an extensive and time-consuming series of tests that included a six-hour scrutiny of his wife, Ostrovsky was hired for what did turn out to be the Mossad. As an employee, he learned that the first series of tests he had undergone was for a position in the *kidon,* an assassination unit. Other information he gathered while an officer in the Mossad prompted him to write *By Way of Deception.* As Hoy wrote in the forward, "One of the main themes of this book is Victor's belief that the Mossad is out of control, that even the prime minister, although ostensibly in charge, has no real authority over its actions and is often manipulated by it into approving or taking actions that may be in the best interest of those running the Mossad, but not necessarily in the best interests of Israel."

Ostrovsky's claims in the book are serious and far-reaching. He states that the Mossad has a spying operation, called Al, stationed in the United States, and argues that Al was responsible for the resignation of United Nations Ambassador Andrew Young in 1979 because he was empathetic to the Palestine Liberation Organization (PLO), a long-standing enemy of Israel. But the most sensational and widely discussed claim is that, in 1983, the Mossad knew that Shiite Muslims had hidden an atypically large load of explosives in a Mercedes truck but failed to pass on a detailed warning of an imminent attack to the U.S. and other countries. Because of the unusual destructive potential, Ostrovsky says that the Mossad knew that the target could only have been one of several locations, including a U.S. compound in Lebanon. The suicide mission claimed the lives of 241 U.S. Marines and 58 French paratroopers. *Washington Post* writers Howard Kurtz and William Claiborne reported that, according to Ostrovsky, the head of the Mossad said, "We're not there to protect Americans. They're a big country." *Los Angeles Time Book Review* contributor James Bamford quoted Ostrovsky as writing, "The general attitude about Americans was: 'Hey, they want to stick their nose into this Lebanon thing, let them pay the price.' "

Ostrovsky was released from the Mossad in 1986 after he helped force down a plane supposedly full of PLO officials who turned out not to be on board. The Israeli government, embarrassed by the incident, has attacked Ostrovsky on this issue, claiming that *By Way of Deception* was written to revenge his dismissal. The book was called "an amalgam of lies and inventions based on very few facts," by Avi Pazner, then-Prime Minister Yitzhak Shamir's spokesman, as David Todd quoted in *Maclean's.* Israel has also allegedly attempted to malign Ostrovsky's character.

Ostrovsky went into hiding after being threatened by men he claims were Mossad agents. He feared the same fate as Mordechai Vanunu, an Israeli nuclear technician who sold information on a nuclear weapons installation to a London newspaper. Mossad agents apparently kidnapped Vanunu in Rome and took him back to Israel, where he was sentenced to eighteen years in prison. Ostrovsky's fear was echoed by officials at Stoddart Publishing and coauthor Hoy. But after about nine days of hiding, Ostrovsky returned to his home in Ottawa. Kurtz and Claiborne reported that Ostrovsky said: "Enough is enough. I'm not going to hide under a rock any more. If they [the Mossad] grab me, it's up to the Canadian government and Israel whether or not I'm forced to go back."

Though the book's credibility is supported by the extensive and immediate measures the Israeli government took to suppress it, many of Ostrovsky's claims have drawn criticisms from reviewers. Often cited is Ostrovsky's ex-planation of his release. He writes that he fulfilled his obligations in forcing down the PLO plane and is merely a scapegoat, but *New York Times Book Review* contributor David Wise wrote that "it is not entirely clear why he would have been blamed." James Littleton, writing in the Toronto *Globe and Mail,* commented that the book "leaves a disturbing sense of doubt. . . . The mental alarm bells ring louder at the sight of the extensive use of quoted dialogue purportedly occurring in scenes in which Ostrovsky could not have been present." These scenes fill the second half of the book, incidents which Ostrovsky affirms he learned of because he had free access to the Mossad's computers and because the training that he underwent often used real-life descriptions of previous Mossad operations. The first half of *By Way of Deception* is an account of the Ostrovsky's training, "serving as a veritable manual of Mossad craft," Bamford wrote, describing "how to establish a cover, evade surveillance, plant a bug and all the other tricks of the trade." "The book is strongest in its grunt's-eye view of the Mossad," *Newsweek* contributor Tom Masland appraised. "Ostrovsky's firsthand account of a three-year apprenticeship in the art of spying has the immediacy of a novel."

BIOGRAPHICAL/CRITICAL SOURCES:

BOOKS

Ostrovsky, Victor, and Claire Hoy, *By Way of Deception: The Making and Unmaking of a Mossad Officer,* St. Martin's, 1990.

PERIODICALS

Detroit Free Press, November 11, 1990.
Detroit News, November 7, 1990.
Globe and Mail (Toronto), September 15, 1990; September 29, 1990.
Los Angeles Times Book Review, October 14, 1990, p. 13.
Maclean's, September 24, 1990, p. 60.
Nation, October 22, 1990, pp. 458-460.
Newsweek, September 24, 1990, pp. 33-34.
New York Times, September 24, 1990.
New York Times Book Review, October 7, 1990, pp. 12-13.
Washington Post, September 14, 1990; September 15, 1990.*

—*Sketch by Roger M. Valade III*

*   *   *

OTTO, Whitney 1955-

PERSONAL: Born March 5, 1955, in Burbank, CA; daughter of William B. Otto, Sr. (an electrical engineer) and Constance D. Vambert (a professional public speaker; maiden name, di Silvestro); married John A. Riley, December 8, 1991; children: Samuel Morganfield Riley. *Education:* Attended Raymond College, University of the Pacific, 1973-74, and San Diego State University, 1974-75; University of California, Irvine, B.A., 1987, M.F.A., 1990. *Politics:* "Yes. Predictably liberal." *Avocational interests:* Making boxes and screens.

ADDRESSES: Agent—Joy Harris, Robert Lantz-Joy Harris Literary Agency, 156 Fifth Ave., New York, NY 10010.

CAREER: Affiliated with the University of California, Irvine, 1975-78; bookkeeper in San Francisco, CA, 1980-86; University of California, Irvine, instructor in creative writing and composition, 1987-89; Irvine Valley College, instructor in composition, 1990.

MEMBER: PEN.

AWARDS, HONORS: Art Siedenbaum Award nomination for first novel, *Los Angeles Times,* 1990.

WRITINGS:

How to Make an American Quilt, Villard Books, 1991.

ADAPTATIONS: How to Make an American Quilt has been adapted into two audiocassettes, read by Judith Ivey, Random Audio, 1992.

WORK IN PROGRESS: A novel, publication expected in 1994; *The Quilt Book.*

SIDELIGHTS: While working toward her Master's of Fine Arts degree at the University of California at Irvine, Whitney Otto wrote a short story that used the practice of quilting as a metaphor for events in the lives of its characters. On the advice of Donald Heiney, a university faculty member and writer, she eventually expanded the work into a novel, *How to Make an American Quilt.* The narrative relates the stories of a group of women that regularly meets in the small California town of Grasse—just outside Bakersfield—to sew. Their current project involves making a quilt that they intend to give as a wedding present to Finn Bennett-Dodd, the twenty-six-year-old woman who narrates the story. Finn's grandmother, Hy Dodd, and great aunt, Glady Joe Cleary, are among members of the quilting circle who tell about their marriages, their relationships with family and friends, and their connections to one another in separate chapters of the novel. Interspersed between each story are bits of information about the history of quilting and sets of sewing instructions.

David McLellan, in an article printed in the *Los Angeles Times,* referred to an interview in which Otto spoke about the use of the quilt in her novel: "It fascinated me—the idea that each patch, for example, has its own life or wholeness to it and when you join them together you get another sense of wholeness. Quilting also interested me as an urge, or impulse; people have to be joined in marriage, or friendship, or love, or to join clubs. . . . When I wrote the short story, I just sort of wrote it and didn't think about all these things. When I finished it, I thought it's like this metaphor of coming together and looking at each woman and talking about friendship, marriage, children, and lives that pull apart." Otto told *CA* that "the impulse to join is countered by the equally strong impulse to be singular or solitary. And I feel that the lives of my characters are driven by these contradictory desires. A quilt, metaphorically, can be an illustration of fusion and separation." Barbara Fisher in the *Washington Post* praised the author for her use of the practice of quilting in her novel, stating that "Otto has made this metaphor personal and vivid. The quilting analogy seems so right, one wonders why it has never been made before."

Upon its release, *How to Make an American Quilt* elicited praise from several reviewers. Judith Freeman in the *Los Angeles Times Book Review* commended Otto for the economy and efficiency used in depicting the characters, noting that "one of the truly remarkable things about this novel is how powerfully, and succinctly, an entire life can be portrayed in just a few pages." A reviewer for *Publishers Weekly* also lauded Otto, acknowledging that *How to Make an American Quilt* is a "remarkable first novel" that is "imaginative in concept and execution." In the *Los Angeles Times Book Review,* Freeman also complimented Otto on her literary debut, pointing out that the novel includes "beautiful individual stories, stitched into a profoundly moving whole. There is a sense of history here, a feeling for quilting that elevates this somewhat arcane, feminine activity to a level of Zen-like wonder."

Otto told *CA:* "In terms of my writing style, I think I am a maker of collages, in a way. I tend to fashion things by juxtaposition, overlapping, working through the larger structure piece by piece. I love being a writer and agree with James Baldwin, who said, 'I consider that I have many responsibilities, but none greater than this: to last, as Hemingway says, and get my work done. I want to be an honest man and a good writer.' "

BIOGRAPHICAL/CRITICAL SOURCES:

PERIODICALS

Detroit Free Press, March 17, 1991.
Globe and Mail (Toronto), April 6, 1991, p. C7.
Los Angeles Times, March 28, 1991, p. E7.
Los Angeles Times Book Review, March 24, 1991, p. 3.
New York Times Book Review, March 24, 1991, p. 10.
Publishers Weekly, February 8, 1991, p. 46.
Times (London), July 18, 1991, p. 14.
Times Literary Supplement, July 26, 1991, p. 19.
Tribune Books (Chicago), April 28, 1991, pp. 6-7.

Washington Post, May 27, 1991, p. C3.

P-Q

PACK, Spencer J. 1953-

PERSONAL: Born September 4, 1953; married Susan Solomon. *Education:* Franconia College, B.A., 1975; University of Toronto, M.A., 1978; University of New Hampshire, Ph.D., 1983.

ADDRESSES: Home—27 Little Bay Ln., Branford, CT 06405. *Office*—Department of Economics, #5554, Connecticut College, New London, CT 06320.

CAREER: Connecticut College, New London, instructor, 1981-83, assistant professor, 1983-88, associate professor of economics, 1988—, chair of department, 1988-91. Yale University, visiting associate professor, 1990-91.

AWARDS, HONORS: Dana Fellow Grant, Yale University, 1990.

WRITINGS:

Reconstructing Marxian Economics: Marx Based upon a Sraffian Commodity Theory of Value, Praeger, 1985.
Capitalism as a Moral System: Adam Smith's Critique of the Free Market Economy, Edward Elgar, 1991.

Work represented in anthologies, including *Aristotle (384-322 BC): Pioneers in Economics,* edited by Mark Blaug, Edward Elgar, 1991. Contributor of articles and reviews to periodicals, including *History of Political Economy.*

*   *   *

PAGE, Louise 1955-

PERSONAL: Born in 1955, in London, England. *Education:* Attended Birmingham University and Cardiff University.

ADDRESSES: Agent—Phil Kelvin, Goodwin Associates, 12 Rabbit Row, London W8 4DX, England.

CAREER: Playwright. Writer in residence at Royal Court Theatre, London, England, 1982-83.

AWARDS, HONORS: Received George Devine Award for *Salonika;* named a promising playwright by *Plays and Players,* 1985.

WRITINGS:

PLAYS

Salonika (produced in London, 1982), Methuen, 1983.
Real Estate (produced in 1984), Methuen, 1985.
Golden Girls (produced in 1984), Methuen, 1985.
Beauty and the Beast (produced at Women's Playhouse Trust, 1985), Methuen, 1986.
Diplomatic Wives, Methuen, 1989.
Plays One (contains *Tissue, Salonika, Real Estate,* and *Golden Girls*), Methuen, 1990.

Also author of the plays *Want Ad,* 1977, *Tissue,* 1978, *Hearing,* 1979, *Housewives,* 1981, *Falkland sound/Voces de Malvinas,* 1983, and *Goat,* 1986. Works represented in anthologies, including *Plays by Women.*

OTHER

Also author of works for radio and television.

SIDELIGHTS: Louise Page is a celebrated playwright whose works concern social issues, often those specific to women. She began her career in 1978 with *Tissue,* a drama about a woman stricken with breast cancer. The next year Page presented *Hearing,* in which a deaf woman shares an evening of drinking and dancing with an increasingly hard-of-hearing mechanic, then returns with him to a factory and destroys the machinery responsible for his hearing loss. Sally Aire, writing in *Plays and Players,* affirmed that *Hearing* provides "a valuable contribution to our awareness of the kind of social problem which we are often only too happy to be able to ignore." And in her 1981 production *Housewives,* Page relates the particular difficulties encountered by a woman seeking election to Britain's Parliament. She loses the contest to another woman who is more physically appealing.

Page's 1983 play *Salonika* is among her best known. In this dreamlike work, an aging woman travels to Greece with her mother to find the grave of her father, a soldier who died there during World War I. But they find the man himself, ghost-like, still young and in uniform. His memories, however, are of his own death. In addition, he is distraught by the presence of his widow's other traveling companion, her septuagenarian suitor. Robert Cushman, in his review for the *Observer,* described *Salonika* as "a dark but thoroughly undepressing piece" and he proclaimed it "the best to arrive in London in months." Edith Oliver wrote in the *New Yorker* that the play's mood "is maintained throughout, and its spell holds long after the play is over."

Page followed *Salonika* with the dramatic *Falkland sound/Voces de Malvinas,* which she developed from actual letters and interviews relating to the Falkland Islands conflict between England and Argentina in the early 1980s. In the play, Page again conveys her concerns for the devastating effects—on both individuals and society at large—of warfare and its aftermath.

In *Real Estate,* a drama centering on complex family relationships, Page writes of a mother and daughter, Gwen and Jenny, who meet after a twenty-year separation. Gwen blames her own miscarriage on her daughter, who had abruptly left home, believing that Jenny's leaving caused it. When mother and daughter meet again, it is the daughter who is pregnant, a situation which inspires a different set of expectations, particularly from Gwen's husband (even though he is not Jenny's father). *Spectator* reviewer Giles Gorden noted that the characters in *Real Estate* are ordinary people who "become special, extraordinary, because of the dignity [Page] endows them with." And Mel Gussow, in his *New York Times* assessment, declared that *Real Estate* "is buttressed by its humanity."

Golden Girls, Page's next play, is set in the world of athletics. Its principals are four women who aspire to run together as a relay team in the Olympic Games. In this work Page addresses a wide range of sports-related topics, including drug use, training methods, and sponsorship. Naseem Khan noted in *New Statesman* that in *Golden Girls* Page "deftly weaves together a great deal of material," much of which, Khan declared, "is personal, human, funny." And the characters, Khan added, are "vivid and credible." London *Times* critic Irving Wardle affirmed that the play succeeds in depicting "a group of women

passionately involved in an activity that drives out conventionally assumed female preoccupations."

Beauty and the Beast, which appeared on the British stage in 1986, is Page's relatively straightforward recounting of the French fairy tale in which a beautiful young woman, held captive by a cruel—but actually pitiful—beast, eventually falls in love with him, thereby relieving him of a curse that suppressed his true, handsome features. "The story of *Beauty and the Beast* is a simple one," observed Jeanette Winterson in the *Times Literary Supplement,* "and Louise Page leaves it uncluttered."

Among Page's subsequent plays is *Goat,* a 1986 work about nuclear war, and *Diplomatic Wives,* a 1989 production. In addition, she has written works for both radio and television.

BIOGRAPHICAL/CRITICAL SOURCES:

BOOKS

Betsko, Kathleen, and Rachel Koenig, *Interviews with Contemporary Women Playwrights,* Beech Tree, 1987, pp. 353-64.
Contemporary Literary Criticism, Volume 40, Gale, 1986, pp. 350-56.

PERIODICALS

Drama, summer, 1979, p. 66.
New Statesman, May 18, 1984, p. 30; June 29, 1984, p. 29; April 15, 1985, p. 95; January 10, 1986, pp. 31-32.
New York, April 15, 1985, p. 95; January 11, 1988, p. 58.
New Yorker, April 15, 1985, p. 96; December 14, 1987, p. 119.
New York Times, March 6, 1985, p. C20.
Observer, August 8, 1982, p. 27.
Plays and Players, July, 1979, pp. 32-33; February 18, 1983, pp. 16-18.
Spectator, May 19, 1984, p. 348.
Times (London), August 3, 1982, p. 7; April 30, 1985, p. 10; January 10, 1986, p. 39.
Times Literary Supplement, January 10, 1986, p. 39.*

*   *   *

PAGE, Penny B(ooth)   1949-

PERSONAL: Born March 1, 1949, in Atlanta, GA; daughter of Howard Douglas Booth (an electrical engineer) and Edith Ann Pennington; married Danny Floyd Page, December 27, 1966 (divorced March 21, 1978); married Mark Edward Lender (a historian), July 30, 1983; children: (first marriage) Scott Matthew. *Education:* Livingston College, B.A., 1977; Rutgers University, M.L.S., 1978.

ADDRESSES: Home—91 Upland Ave., Metuchen, NJ 08840. *Office*—Rutgers Center of Alcohol Studies, Smithers Hall, Busch Campus, Piscataway, NJ 08855-0969.

CAREER: Rutgers Center of Alcohol Studies, New Brunswick, NJ, bibliographic assistant, 1977-78, research assistant, 1978-81, librarian, 1981—. Rutgers Center of Alcohol Studies, member of executive committee, 1979-81, member of library planning committee, 1983-84, chair of search committee for alcohol studies bibliographer, 1986, member of operations committee, 1987—, member of search committee for director of prevention, 1990-91; Rutgers University Libraries, member of emergency planning committee, 1983-84, member of technical services special interest group, 1983-85, member of personnel policy and affirmative action committee, 1987-88. Librarians and Information Specialists in Addictions, member, 1980-81; Substance Abuse Librarians and Information Specialists, chair, 1984-85, vice chair, 1985-87, archivist, 1987—, member of steering committee, 1989—; New Jersey Library Association, member of committee on institutes, 1984-87, member of committee on scholarship, 1985—, member of committee on honors and awards, 1985—, member of committee on research methods, 1987—, member of history and bibliography section, 1990—. Health and Psychosocial Instruments File (online database), member of advisory board, 1987—; National Council on Alcoholism, member of publications advisory task force, 1988-89; Highland Park Public Library, member of board of trustees, 1989-90; National Institute on Alcohol Use and Alcoholism, member of thesaurus advisory committee, 1989—. Speaker at conferences and workshops.

MEMBER: American Library Association, Alcohol and Temperance History Group, Alcohol and Drug Study Group.

AWARDS, HONORS: Grant from New Jersey Department of Higher Education, 1988; research award from New Jersey Library Association, 1989.

WRITINGS:

Alcohol Use and Alcoholism: A Guide to the Literature, Garland Publishing, 1986.
Children of Alcoholics: A Sourcebook, Garland Publishing, 1991.

Contributor to books, including *Past and Present: Lives of New Jersey Women,* Scarecrow, 1990; contributor of articles and book reviews to periodicals, including *Alcohol Health and Research World, Reference Services Review, British Journal of Addiction,* and *Journal of Alcohol and Drug Education. Substance Abuse Index and Abstracts,* member of editorial board, 1987-89; *New Jersey Libraries,*

member of editorial committee, 1989—, editor of research column, 1991—.

*　　*　　*

PAGLIA, Camille (Anna) 1947-

PERSONAL: Born April 2, 1947, in Endicott, NY; daughter of Pasquale (a professor of Romance languages) and Lydia Paglia. *Education:* State University of New York, Binghamton, B.A., 1968; Yale University, M.Phil., 1971, Ph.D., 1974.

ADDRESSES: Home—Swarthmore, PA. *Office*—Department of Humanities, University of the Arts, 320 South Broad St., Philadelphia, PA 19102. *Agent*—Lynn Nesbit, Janklow and Nesbit, 598 Madison Ave., New York, NY 10022.

CAREER: Bennington College, Bennington, VT, faculty member in Literature and Languages Division, 1972-80; Wesleyan University, Middletown, CT, visiting lecturer in English, 1980; Yale University, New Haven, CT, fellow of Ezra Stiles College, 1981, visiting lecturer in comparative literature, 1981 and 1984, visiting lecturer in English, 1981-83, fellow of Silliman College, 1984; Philadelphia College of Performing Arts (became University of the Arts), Philadelphia, PA, assistant professor, 1984-86, associate professor, 1987-91; professor of humanities, 1991—.

AWARDS, HONORS: National Book Critics Circle Award nomination for criticism, 1991, for *Sexual Personae: Art and Decadence from Nefertiti to Emily Dickinson.*

WRITINGS:

Sexual Personae: Art and Decadence from Nefertiti to Emily Dickinson, Yale University Press, 1990.
Sex, Art, and American Culture: Essays, Vintage Books, 1992.

WORK IN PROGRESS: A second collection of essays and a second volume of *Sexual Personae.*

SIDELIGHTS: Camille Paglia's unorthodox feminist views on the role of sexuality in the development of art and culture in Western civilization became the subject of heated debate with the publication of her first book, *Sexual Personae: Art and Decadence from Nefertiti to Emily Dickinson,* in 1990. In the book, and in her subsequent media statements and campus appearances across the country, Paglia has aroused controversy by accusing the contemporary feminist establishment of suppressing the aesthetics of art and beauty and the dangers of sexuality; she warns that historical reality is being ignored in the push for change. Paglia has in turn been criticized by some for her statements on issues such as date rape, pornography, and educational reform. A selection of her many articles, interviews, and lectures appears in the 1992 publication, *Sex, Art, and American Culture.*

Paglia posits in *Sexual Personae* that "the amorality, aggression, sadism, voyeurism, and pornography in great art have been ignored or glossed over by most academic critics." She highlights the appearances of such themes in order "to demonstrate the unity and continuity of Western culture" and disprove the modernist idea that culture is fragmented and meaningless. Terry Teachout in the *New York Times Book Review* stated that "to this end, *Sexual Personae* serves as an illustrated catalogue of the pagan sexual symbolism that Ms. Paglia believes to be omnipresent in Western art." Paglia outlines a number of sexually-charged figures which she calls "sexual personae," a term that *Nation* contributor Mark Edmundson defined as "erotic archetypes, figures that compel sexual fascination from all perceivers, whatever their professed erotic preferences." These archetypes include the femme fatale, the Great Mother, the vampire, and the hermaphrodite.

Paglia's application of her theory to authors such as the Marquis de Sade, Samuel Taylor Coleridge, and Emily Dickinson proved interesting to many reviewers. "Her fascination with 'perversity' in literature brings her to some startling interpretations," acknowledged Lillian Faderman in the *Washington Post Book World.* The reviewer also observed that Paglia's "discussion of the sexual ambiguities and obsessions that critics have ignored or minimized in major American writers is especially compelling." Walter Kendrick, in his *Voice Literary Supplement* assessment, applauded Paglia's "detailed, subtle readings of [Oscar Wilde's] *The Picture of Dorian Gray* and *The Importance of Being Earnest* and a delicious hatchet job on Emily Dickinson, whom Paglia reads as 'that autoerotic sadist,' 'Amherst's Madame de Sade.' "

The author's interest in the sexual element throughout Western history is based on the basic duality or struggle she sees underlying this culture. Using a comparison based on Greek mythology, Paglia comments that the rational, Apollonian force of humanity that creates the order of society is constantly striving to protect itself from the Dionysian, or dark, chaotic forces of nature. She describes the Dionysian element as "the chthonian [earth-bound] realities which Apollo evades, the blind grinding of subterranean force, the long slow suck, the murk and ooze." And despite all the grand scientific and philosophical achievements of Western logic, this irrational pagan force of nature continually wells up, revealing itself in sex, art, and other aspects of popular culture, theorizes Paglia. Sex, especially, reveals these tensions: "Sex is the point of contact between man and nature, where morality and good intentions fall to primitive urges."

This unwieldy instinct unleashes the darker forces that Paglia claims are ignored by mainstream feminists and others who idealize sex as inherently pure, positive, and safe. The perversities that occur in sexual behavior are not caused by social injustice, maintains Paglia, but by natural forces that have not been properly contained by society's defenses. The artifice of society, which is exemplified in the classic works of art, literature, and philosophy of Western culture, is given the highest status by Paglia for this role of protecting and advancing humanity. "Much of western culture is a distortion of reality," she says in *Sexual Personae.* "But reality *should* be distorted; that is, imaginatively amended." Mark Edmundson summarized Paglia's idea that "the glory of art lies in its power to extemporize fictive identities—the personae—that swerve away from biology's literal insistence on what we are. . . . Decadence ritualizes, and thus subdues, erotic violence."

This favorable view of decadence and pornography has set Paglia in direct opposition to the opinions of many in academic and feminist circles. Feminist thought that condemns pornography as the imposition of social prejudice on the inherent goodness of sexuality is decried by Paglia as naive. She accuses feminists with these beliefs of uncritically accepting the ideals of eighteenth-century French philosopher Jean-Jacques Rousseau, who paired nature with freedom and nobility and considered the structures of society oppressive. Paglia's view is that "feminism has exceeded its proper mission of seeking political equality for women and has ended by rejecting contingency, that is, human limitation by nature or fate." Paglia's own brand of feminism, which she outlined in a lecture given at the Massachusetts Institute of Technology, as published in *Sex, Art, and American Culture,* is not based on the Rousseauian idealism which she says was revived in the 1960s, but on the practical realities of sex and culture. She cites as her formative feminist heroes pilot Amelia Earhart, actress Katharine Hepburn, and French theorist Simone de Beauvoir.

Paglia also asserts that "nature's burden falls more heavily on one [the female] sex," that women's natural identity does not create the same type of tension that is found in men. Overwhelmed by the powerful psychological domination of the mother and her relationship with the life and death forces of the earth, men turn to cerebral achievement in an attempt to establish a separate identity from the female and protect themselves from the primal elements, posits Paglia. Statements such as Paglia's widely quoted line, "If civilization had been left in female hands, we would still be living in grass huts," were interpreted by some reviewers to be a rationalization for limiting women's role in society to that of a passive object. Lillian Faderman, in her review of *Sexual Personae* suggested,

"Paglia believes that there is indeed a basis for sexual stereotypes that is biological and firmly rooted in the unconscious." Helen Vendler was also concerned that Paglia's theory does not allow for women to participate in cultural achievement equally with men: "To Paglia, women writers remain 'chthonic,' earthbound, and swamp-like, unable to rise to such inventive Apollonian designs," she declared in *New York Review of Books.*

Anticipating such reactions in her introduction to *Sexual Personae,* Paglia asserts that women actually hold a privileged status of power in relation to men: "I reaffirm and celebrate woman's ancient mystery and glamour. I see the mother as an overwhelming force who condemns men to lifelong sexual anxiety, from which they escape through rationalism and physical achievement." In addition, she argues that the power of Apollonian society is, or should be, just as accessible to women as to men. Responding to Vendler in the *New York Review of Books,* Paglia claimed that *Sexual Personae* had been misread and misunderstood by Vendler and others. "From first chapter to last, my thesis is that all writing, all art is Apollonian. Every woman who takes pen or brush in hand is making an Apollonian swerve away from nature, even when nature is her subject."

The untraditional subject and style of the *Sexual Personae,* despite the reservations of some critics, was widely praised. Faderman called *Sexual Personae* "a remarkable book, at once outrageous and compelling, fanatical and brilliant. As infuriating as Paglia often is, one must be awed by her vast energy, erudition and wit." Teachout commented that Paglia "is an exciting (if purple) stylist and an admirably close reader with a hard core of common sense. For all its flaws, her first book is every bit as intellectually stimulating as it is exasperating." Edmundson concluded that in exploring the issue of sexuality and sexual personae in culture Paglia "has found a part of the story that no one is telling. It's a splendid and exhilarating find, and makes for a brilliant book." In *Sexual Personae,* Paglia promised a second volume that will focus on similar themes in popular culture since the turn of the century, particularly Hollywood films and rock music.

In addition to pursuing this work, in 1992 Paglia published *Sex, Art, and American Culture,* a collection of her articles, interviews, and lectures. Included are commentaries on pop-star Madonna, whom Paglia considers "the true feminist" for the street-smart brand of sexuality that fills her rock songs and music videos. "Madonna has taught young women to be fully female and sexual while still exercising control over their lives," Paglia asserts in "Madonna I: Animality and Artifice." In other essays she discusses actress Elizabeth Taylor, artist Robert Mapplethorpe, professor Milton Kessler, and others in the public eye. Also included are Paglia's further indictments of cer-

tain academic trends, particularly women's studies and French deconstructionist theory, as found in the essays "Junk Bonds and Corporate Raiders" and "The M.I.T. Lecture."

Two chapters of *Sex, Art, and Modern Culture* are devoted to date rape, which Paglia contends is an ethical violation that contemporary feminists do little to prevent. "Rape is an outrage that cannot be tolerated in civilized society," she posits in "Rape and Modern Sex War." "Yet feminism, which has waged a crusade for rape to be taken more seriously, has put young women in danger by hiding the truth about sex from them." Rather than relying on grievance committees to solve the problem of rape on campuses and elsewhere, Paglia feels the solution lies in informing women about the "what is for men the eroticism or fun element in rape" so that by understanding rape, women can learn to protect themselves from it by using "common sense." In other essays, Paglia, a libertarian, outlines her beliefs that the state should not intrude into the private realm; she is pro-choice and supports decriminalization of prostitution and legalization of drugs. Arguing that Paglia's is an unconventional but important voice, a *Publishers Weekly* reviewer concluded that in *Sex, Art, and Culture* the author presents "an ambitious range of art and ideas, her invocation of primal sexuality adding a missing element to critical debates."

BIOGRAPHICAL/CRITICAL SOURCES:

BOOKS

Contemporary Literary Criticism, Volume 68, Gale, 1991, pp. 303-20.
Paglia, Camille, *Sex, Art, and American Culture: Essays,* Vintage Books, 1992.
Paglia, *Sexual Personae: Art and Decadence from Nefertiti to Emily Dickinson,* Yale University Press, 1990.

PERIODICALS

Nation, June 25, 1990, pp. 897-99.
Newsweek, September 21, 1992, p. 82.
New York, March 4, 1991, pp. 22-30.
New York Review of Books, May 31, 1990, pp. 19-25; August 16, 1990, p. 59.
New York Times Book Review, July 22, 1990, p. 7.
Publishers Weekly, August 17, 1992.
Time, January 13, 1992, pp. 62-63.
Times (London), April 13, 1991, pp. 10-11.
Times Literary Supplement, April 20, 1990, p. 414.
Village Voice, September 29, 1992, pp. 92-94.
Voice Literary Supplement, March, 1990, p. 7.
Washington Post Book World, February 18, 1990, p. 5.

—*Sketch by Marie Ellavich*

PALLONE, Dave 1951-

PERSONAL: Born October 5, 1951, in Waltham, MA; son of Carmine and Michelina (Gallo) Pallone. *Education:* Attended Umpire Development Program (St. Petersburg, FL), 1971.

ADDRESSES: Home—Washington, DC. *Office*—c/o Acton and Dystel, 928 Broadway, New York, NY 10010.

CAREER: National League baseball umpire, 1979-88; writer.

WRITINGS:

(With Alan Steinberg) *Behind the Mask: My Double Life in Baseball* (memoir), Viking, 1990.

SIDELIGHTS: Dave Pallone is known for the controversies surrounding his ten-year stint as a major-league baseball umpire. He worked for several years in various minor leagues and entered the majors in 1979, only after its unionized umpires engaged in a strike for better wages. Once hired into the National League, Pallone readily found himself the subject of abuse and disdain. Players, for instance, were quick to question his qualifications. "They were trying to show that I didn't deserve to be there," Pallone recalled to *Los Angeles Times*'s David Colker in 1990. When the strike ended, Pallone was retained by the league. This action drew the ire of unionized umpires, many of whom would pointedly ignore and avoid him.

In the major leagues Pallone developed a reputation as a volatile, no-nonsense umpire. For example, in St. Louis he responded to calls from the Cardinal dugout by banishing all of the team's non-starting players to the locker room. However, his most notorious encounter came in 1988 against Pete Rose, the legendary player who was managing the Cincinnati Reds. Amid a heated exchange, Pallone banished Rose from the field. Pallone then turned away from Rose, who in response shoved him. This act prompted the personal intercession of baseball commissioner Bart Giamatti, who found Rose guilty of gross misconduct and both suspended him for thirty days and fined him ten thousand dollars. In addition Giamatti charged Pallone one hundred dollars for losing self-control. Agreeing that he was partly culpable, Pallone demanded a higher penalty, whereupon he was assessed for an additional nine hundred dollars.

While meeting with Giamatti, Pallone acknowledged his volatile temperament. He attributed it partly to his anxiety over keeping his homosexuality a secret. According to Pallone, Giamatti expressed no concern as long as Pallone maintained his credibility on the baseball field. But only a few months after meeting with the commissioner, Pallone was summoned again. At this second meeting, Giamatti disclosed that Pallone had been linked to a gay sex ring involving teenagers in New York State. The commissioner requested that Pallone commence voluntary leave. He yielded to the request, and his contract was never renewed.

In 1990 Pallone, whom Colker described in the *Los Angeles Times* as "one of the most hated umpires in the history of major league baseball," published a memoir *Behind the Mask: My Double Life in Baseball*. In his novel, he discusses the many controversies surrounding his career. "My book," he told Colker, "is about a little boy who dreamed of being in baseball, got his dream, and then had it taken away from him." *Sports Illustrated* reviewer Steve Rushin found the book self-serving and declared that it had been produced "for the fulfillment of the author, not the reader." But Pallone himself emphasizes that *Behind the Mask* hardly signifies an end in itself. "My goal," he told Colker, "is to become a good spokesperson for the gay community."

BIOGRAPHICAL/CRITICAL SOURCES:

BOOKS

Pallone, Dave, and Alan Steinberg, *Behind the Mask: My Double Life in Baseball,* Viking, 1990.

PERIODICALS

Los Angeles Times, June 22, 1990.
New York Times Book Review, July 22, 1990, p. 21.
Sporting News, July 23, 1990, p. 6.
Sports Illustrated, July 23, 1990, p. 13.

*   *   *

PALUDI, Michele A. 1954-

PERSONAL: Born June 13, 1954, in Schenectady, NY; daughter of Michael and Antoinette Paludi. *Education:* Union College, Schenectady, NY, B.S., 1976; University of Cincinnati, M.A., 1978, Ph.D., 1980. *Religion:* Roman Catholic.

ADDRESSES: Office—Michele Paludi and Associates, 1606 Lenox Rd., Schenectady, NY 12308.

CAREER: Michele Paludi and Associates (consultants in sexual harassment), Schenectady, NY, principal. Kent State University, Kent, OH, visiting assistant professor, 1981-82, assistant professor, 1982-85, associate professor of psychology, 1985-88; Hunter College of the City University of New York, New York City, visiting associate professor, 1986-92, professor of psychology, 1992—, director of Women's Studies Program, 1991-92; Union College, Schenectady, visiting professor of psychology, 1992—. Host and producer of the show *Gender Matters;*

guest on programs such as *Sonya Friedman Live* and *Talk Live.*

AWARDS, HONORS: Emerging Leader Award, American Psychological Association's Committee on Women, 1988; Progress in Equity Award, American Association of University Women, 1992; Woman of Vision Award for Advocacy, Young Women's Christian Association, 1992; Gustavus Myers Award, outstanding book on human rights, 1992, for *Ivory Power.*

WRITINGS:

(Editor) *Ivory Power: Sexual Harassment on Campus,* State University of New York Press, 1990.
(Editor with G. A. Steuernagel) *Foundations for a Feminist Restructuring of the Academic Disciplines,* Haworth, 1990.
Exploring/Teaching the Psychology of Women: A Manual of Resources, State University of New York Press, 1990.
(With R. B. Barickman) *Academic and Workplace Sexual Harassment: A Resource Manual,* State University of New York Press, 1991.
(With J. A. Doyle) *Sex and Gender: The Human Experience,* W. C. Brown, 1991.
The Psychology of Women, W. C. Brown, 1992.
(Editor with F. L. Denmark) *Handbook on the Psychology of Women,* Greenwood Press, 1993.

Work represented in books, including *Victimization: An International Perspective,* edited by E. Viano, Springer Publishing, 1992. Contributor to *Journal of the National Association of Women Deans, Counselors, and Administrators.*

WORK IN PROGRESS: Editing *Working Nine to Five: Women, Men, Sex, and Power,* for State University of New York Press.

*   *   *

PARKER, Leslie
See THIRKELL, Angela (Margaret)

*   *   *

PARKER, Michael 1959-

PERSONAL: Born February 6, 1959, in Silver City, NC; son of James H. (a newspaper editor) and Hallie (a teacher and counselor; maiden name, McLean) Parker; married; wife's name, Catharine; children: Emma. *Education:* University of North Carolina at Chapel Hill, B.A., 1984; University of Virginia, M.F.A., 1988.

ADDRESSES: Office—c/o Publicity Director, Macmillan Publishing Co., 866 Third Ave., New York, NY 10022.

CAREER: University of North Carolina at Greensboro, assistant professor, 1992-93.

WRITINGS:

Hello Down There, Macmillan, 1993.
Golden Hour (novella and stories), Scribner, in press.

WORK IN PROGRESS: The Geographical Cure, a novel.

SIDELIGHTS: Michael Parker's first novel, *Hello Down There,* centers on Edward Keane, a morphine addict who lives alone outside a North Carolina town in the 1950s. Keane, the son of influential parents, fell into this state of disrepute after being involved in a car accident that killed his wealthy fiancee. He is lured out of his isolation and addiction by seventeen-year-old Eureka Speight, whose desire to hear tales of imagination is matched by Keane's desire to tell them. Keane claims, in fact, that his true addiction is to metaphors. Frederick Busch described *Hello Down There* in his *New York Times Book Review* assessment as "a serious, memorable novel," particularly noting Parker's "love of clear, crisp, pungent language." Many reviewers also commented on the similarities between Parker's prose and the writing of other Southern authors such as Cormac McCarthy and William Faulkner. A *Kirkus Reviews* contributor observed that *Hello Down There* contained "the same bitter humor and nihilistic denouement" as Faulkner's novel *Sanctuary,* and a *Publishers Weekly* reviewer stated that the novel "is Southern gothic intrigue and eccentricity at its best."

BIOGRAPHICAL/CRITICAL SOURCES:

PERIODICALS

Booklist, February 5, 1993.
Boston Globe, February 14, 1993.
Kirkus Reviews, December 1, 1992, p. 1452.
Library Journal, December, 1992.
New York Times Book Review, February 21, 1993, p. 10.
Publishers Weekly, November 23, 1992, p. 52.

*   *   *

PARKER, Una-Mary 1930-

PERSONAL: Born March 30, 1930, in London, England; daughter of Hugh Power (in business) and Laura (Walker-Harrdwer) Nepean Gubbins; married Archie Parker (a photographer), October 6, 1951 (deceased); children: Diana Parker Hobart, Philip. *Education:* Educated privately. *Politics:* Conservative. *Religion:* Church of England.

ADDRESSES: Home—42 Trevor Sq., London SW7 1EW, England. *Office*—9 Cheval Place, London SW7 1DY, England. *Agent*—Susan Zeckendorf, 171 West 57th St., New

York, NY 10019; and Abner Stein, 10 Roland Gardens, London SW7 3PH, England.

CAREER: Novelist. Worked as a journalist.

WRITINGS:

Riches, New American Library, 1987.
Scandals, New American Library, 1988.
Temptations, New American Library, 1989.
Enticements, New American Library, 1991.
The Palace Affair, Signet Books, 1992.
Forbidden Feelings, Headline, 1993.
Only the Best, Headline, in press.

Former social editor, *Tatler.*

WORK IN PROGRESS: A Guilty Pleasure, for Headline, publication expected in 1995; *Objects of Desire,* a saga, for Headline, publication expected in 1996.

SIDELIGHTS: Una-Mary Parker told *CA:* "Ever since I can remember, I wanted to be a writer. At the age of ten I had a children's story published in the *Weekly Scotsman,* and that was it! Although I pursued a career as a journalist, while bringing up my son and daughter, it was at the back of my mind all the time that, one day, I would become a novelist. Now I consider myself to be supremely lucky to be earning a living by doing what I really want to do.

"I keep normal office hours, working in the public relations offices of my daughter, as I like the buzz of other people working around me, and I type my books directly on an electric typewriter. So far, my books have gone into nine languages, and four have been sold to an audio books company. There is talk at present that one will be made into a television mini-series.

"I read everything I can lay my hands on, from Emile Zola to Jackie Collins, Charlotte Bronte, and Ruth Rendell. I advise anyone wanting to be a writer to read as much as possible. This is the best way to learn, apart from constant practice."

*   *   *

PARKINSON, C(yril) Northcote   1909-1993

OBITUARY NOTICE—See index for *CA* sketch: Born July 30, 1909, at Barnard Castle, County Durham, England; died March 9 (one source says March 10), 1993, in Canterbury, England. Historian, educator, and author. Parkinson coined the phrase, "Work expands so as to fill the time available for its completion," which he originally publicized in a 1955 article in the *Economist.* The article attracted a great deal of attention and Parkinson's best-selling 1958 work *Parkinson's Law,* a blend of economics

and satire that further examines the subject, was adapted as a musical by the British Broadcasting Corporation (BBC). Parkinson began his career as a teacher at Cambridge University in the 1930s. It was during his military service in World War II that he first made the observation concerning work and time that brought him fame. After the war he taught naval history at the University of Liverpool and was the Raffles Professor of History at the University of Malaya. Parkinson published more than sixty books, including *Mrs. Parkinson's Law* and *The Law of Longer Life,* and scholarly works such as *Britain in the Far East: The Singapore Naval Base* and *War in the Eastern Seas, 1793-1815.*

OBITUARIES AND OTHER SOURCES:

BOOKS

Current Biography, H. W. Wilson, 1960.
International Who's Who, fifty-third edition, Europa, 1989.
Who's Who, 145th edition, St. Martin's Press, 1993.
Writers Directory: 1990-1992, St. James Press, 1990.

PERIODICALS

New York Times, March 12, 1993, p. A19.
Times (London), March 11, 1993, p. 23.
Washington Post, March 12, 1993, p. B7.

*   *   *

PARNELL, Mary Davies   1936-

PERSONAL: Born September 6, 1936, in Trehafod, Wales; daughter of John (a carpenter and shopkeeper) and Sarah (a homemaker and shopkeeper; maiden name, Richards) Davies; married Michael Parnell (a biographer), October 16, 1961 (died September 17, 1991); children: Richard Aaron, Sarah Kathryn. *Education:* University College of Wales, B.A., 1959; University of Wales College of Cardiff, Diploma in Education, 1960. *Politics:* "Center-right." *Religion:* Protestant. *Avocational interests:* Racket sports, watching rugby football, cycling.

ADDRESSES: Home—9 Radyr Court Rise, Llandaff, Cardiff, South Glamorgan CFS 2QH, Wales. *Office*—*New Welsh Review,* 49 Park Place, Cardiff, South Glamorgan CF1 3AT, Wales.

CAREER: Worked as a French teacher; *New Welsh Review,* Cardiff, South Glamorgan, Wales, editorial assistant.

WRITINGS:

Block Salt and Candles: A Rhondda Childhood, Dufour, 1992.

WORK IN PROGRESS: A semi-autobiographical book about her grammar-school days.

SIDELIGHTS: Mary Davies Parnell told *CA:* "I taught French for too long and finally decided to rejoin the world of human beings. I started writing when, after a power cut, I began reminiscing about the days before electric light. I was later persuaded to write down my memories. My most productive writing time and place is in bed between six-thirty and seven-thirty in the morning."

* * *

PAUL, Celeste 1952-

PERSONAL: Born June 4, 1952, in Bethlehem, PA; daughter of Roy A. and Eleanor F. (Kauffman) Paul; married Charles A. Sefranek (an electrical engineer); children: Louis, James, Jeffrey, Allen. *Education:* Received R.N. from Allentown Hospital School of Nursing. *Religion:* Roman Catholic.

ADDRESSES: Home—Portsmouth, RI 02871. *Agent*—Donald Maass, 304 West 92nd St., No. 8P, New York, NY 10025.

CAREER: Free-lance writer. Worked as registered nurse, tour guide, weaver and spinner, writer of greeting cards, classified advertisement taker for a newspaper, and as vine pruner and harvester for a local vineyard.

MEMBER: Horror Writers of America, Newport Writers Forum.

WRITINGS:

The Berlin Covenant, Penguin, 1992.

SIDELIGHTS: Celeste Paul told *CA:* "I began writing during a difficult period in my life. The writing became a tension reliever and helped me to hang on to my sanity until times got better.

"Because I am a devoted fan of Stephen King and Dean Koontz, it was only natural for me to write in the fields of horror and suspense. I would like to say I was an instant success, but alas, that was not so. It took seven years and three failed novels before I sold my first book, then another two years before I saw the book in print.

"My advice for aspiring writers is: write every day. Set a goal for the day, either a number of words or a number of pages, and stick to it. If you write just one page a day, by the end of the year, you will have a book! Unless you are independently wealthy, find a job that will support you; success may take years. Be patient, and don't give up. Join a writers' group in your area that will help you meet others who are going through the same struggles that you are. Good luck!"

PENCAVEL, John (H.) 1943-

PERSONAL: Born November 12, 1943, in London, England; immigrated to United States, 1966; son of Harold and Norma (Abate) Pencavel; married Louise Smith, August, 1978; children: Christopher, Alice, Matthew. *Education:* University College, London, B.S. (with first class honors), 1965, M.S. (with distinction), 1966; Princeton University, Ph.D., 1969.

ADDRESSES: Home—20 Sneckner Ct., Menlo Park, CA 94025. *Office*—Department of Economics, Stanford University, Stanford, CA 94305-6072.

CAREER: Princeton University, Princeton, NJ, affiliated with Industrial Relations Section, 1968-69; Stanford University, Stanford, CA, professor of economics, 1969—.

AWARDS, HONORS: Jane Eliza Proctor Visiting Fellow, Princeton University, 1966-67; National fellow, Hoover Institution on War, Revolution, and Peace, 1972-73; Guggenheim fellow, 1987-88.

WRITINGS:

An Analysis of the Quit Rate in American Manufacturing Industry, Princeton University Press, 1970.
Labor Markets under Trade Unionism: Employment, Wages, and Hours, Basil Blackwell, 1991.

Work represented in anthologies, including *Advances in the Theory and Measurement of Unemployment,* edited by Yoram Weiss and Gideon Fishelson, Macmillan, 1990; *Productivity and Higher Education,* edited by Richard Anderson and Joel Myerson, Peterson's Guides, 1992; and *American Higher Education and National Growth,* edited by William E. Becker and Darrell Lewis, Kluwer, 1992. Contributor of articles and reviews to periodicals, including *American Economic Review* and *Journal of Economic Education. Journal of Economic Literature,* associate editor, 1982-85, editor, 1986—.

WORK IN PROGRESS: Papers on worker cooperatives and hours of work for publication in academic journals.

* * *

PERCY, John R(ees) 1941-

PERSONAL: Born July 10, 1941, in Windsor, England; son of George Francis and Christine (Holland) Percy; married Maire Ede Robertson (a scientist), June 16, 1962; children: Carol Elaine. *Education:* University of Toronto, B.Sc., 1962, M.A., 1963, Ph.D., 1968. *Politics:* "Variable." *Religion:* None. *Avocational interests:* Travel, music.

ADDRESSES: Home—381 Prince Edward Dr., Toronto, Ontario, Canada M8X 2L6. *Office*—Erindale College,

University of Toronto in Mississauga, 3359 Mississauga Rd. N., Mississauga, Ontario, Canada L5L 1C6.

CAREER: University of Toronto in Mississauga, Erindale College, Mississauga, Ontario, Canada, assistant professor, 1968-73, associate professor, 1973-78, professor of astronomy, 1978—, associate dean for sciences and vice principal for research and graduate studies, 1989—. Ontario Science Centre, vice chair of board of trustees; Commission on the Teaching of Astronomy, vice president, 1991-94.

MEMBER: International Astronomical Union (president of Commission on Variable Stars, 1991-94), Royal Canadian Institute (president, 1985-86), Royal Astronomical Society of Canada (president, 1978-80), American Association of Variable Star Observers (president, 1989-91), Science Teachers Association of Ontario (honorary president, 1988-91).

AWARDS, HONORS: Royal Jubilee Medal, 1977.

WRITINGS:

(Editor) *The Study of Variable Stars Using Small Telescopes,* Cambridge University Press, 1986.

(With W. A. Andrews, Elgin Wolfe, and others) *Science 10: An Introductory Study,* Prentice-Hall Canada, 1988.

(Editor with Jay Pasachoff) *The Teaching of Astronomy,* Cambridge University Press, 1990.

(Editor with Janet Mattei and Christiaan Sterken) *Variable Star Research: An International Perspective,* Cambridge University Press, 1991.

WORK IN PROGRESS: A book on variable stars, for Cambridge University Press; research on variable stars, stellar evolution, and science education.

SIDELIGHTS: John R. Percy told *CA:* "Astronomy has a special appeal to people young and old; as the mathematician Poincare said, 'it shows how small our body, how large our mind.' Unfortunately, astronomy plays only a minor role in our education system; my successful effort to add more astronomy to my provincial science curriculum led to the book *Science 10.*

"The opportunity to meet and work with kindred spirits from all over the world is one of the most satisfying aspects of my career as an astronomy professor. *The Teaching of Astronomy* was the proceedings of an international conference which I organized in 1988 under the auspices of the International Astronomical Union. It brought together a hundred-sixty astronomy educators from thirty countries, in one of the most enjoyable weeks of my professional life.

"Astronomy is unique in the extent to which skilled amateurs can contribute to it. For instance, amateurs make

systematic measurements of the changing brightness of thousands of variable stars—my main research interest. Their measurements provide an important, lasting record of the behavior of these often unpredictable stars. Both *The Study of Variable Stars Using Small Telescopes* and *Variable Star Research* are based on conferences which I organized to instruct and inspire these amateur researchers, and to provide them with feedback on how their measurements contribute to our understanding of the stars."

*   *   *

PERRY, Paul 1950-

PERSONAL: Born July 8, 1950, in Phoenix, AZ; son of Jewel F. (an insurance agent) and Esther Ida (a homemaker; maiden name, Stanwick) Perry; married Sandy Phipps, 1969 (divorced, 1974); married Darlene Joy Bennett (a homemaker), September 30, 1979; children: (first marriage) Paul; (second marriage) Paige-Marie, Reed. *Education:* Arizona State University, B.A., 1972. *Politics:* "Democrat bordering on Libertarian." *Religion:* Protestant.

ADDRESSES: Home and office—8215 East Gary Rd., Scottsdale, AZ 85260. *Agent*—Nat Sobel, Sobel Weber Associates, Inc., 146 East Nineteenth St., New York, NY 10003.

CAREER: Runner's World, Mountain View, CA, managing editor, 1978-80; *Running,* Eugene, OR, editor-in-chief, 1980-83; *American Health,* New York City, executive editor, 1984-88; writer.

AWARDS, HONORS: Gannett Foundation Media Center Scholar.

WRITINGS:

(With Raymond Moody) *The Light Beyond,* Bantam, 1988.

(With Melvin Morse) *Close to the Light,* Villard, 1990.

(With Herman Hellerstein) *Healing Your Heart,* Simon & Schuster, 1990.

(With Ken Babbs) *On the Bus,* Thunder's Mouth Press, 1990.

(With Moody) *Coming Back,* Bantam, 1991.

(With Morse) *Transformed by the Light,* Villard, 1992.

Fear and Loathing: The Strange and Terrible Saga of Hunter S. Thompson, Thunder's Mouth Press, 1992.

Contributor to periodicals, including *American Health, Reader's Digest,* and *USA Weekend.* Consulting editor to periodicals, including *Outside, Men's Journal,* and *Runner.*

SIDELIGHTS: "I write on a wide variety of topics," Paul Perry told *CA,* and a sampling of the author's works proves his point. Frequently collaborating with experts in various fields, Perry has published books that range from preventative medicine (*Healing Your Heart*) to accounts of counterculture heroes such as Ken Kesey and Hunter S. Thompson. A recurring interest for Perry is the topic of temporary death, and he has devoted several books to the subject. *Closer to the Light,* which placed on the *New York Times* best-seller list for several weeks in late 1990, recounts the tales of various children who came close to dying, then survived to tell of their unusual experiences. A companion book, *Transformed by the Light,* followed in 1992, examining the long-term effects of such experiences.

On the Bus, which Perry cowrote with Ken Babbs, focuses on the influential bus trip made by novelist Ken Kesey and the Merry Pranksters in the summer of 1964. Using the royalties from his first two novels, *One Flew over the Cuckoo's Nest* and *Sometimes a Great Notion,* Kesey financed a trip from California to New York aboard a bright, multicolored bus. Accompanying Kesey were the Merry Pranksters, a band of like-minded individuals culled from graduate writing classes that the author taught. The Prankster's purpose was, ostensibly, to travel America's highways, shoot vast quantities of film, take mind-altering drugs such as LSD, and distill a new medium of literary and artistic expression. The Prankster's high jinks on the road included dropping acid in the desert, visiting fellow LSD guru Timothy Leary, and meeting up with a Hell's Angels biker gang for a dangerous night of partying. Perry and Babbs, who was a member of the Pranksters, use the recollections of the participants, detailed photographs, and news clippings from the times to document Kesey's trek.

The journey of Kesey and the Merry Pranksters, which was hailed by many as the launch of the hippie era, has already been the subject of various literary works, including Tom Wolfe's popular *Electric Kool-Aid Acid Test* and Kesey's own *Further Inquiry.* "Kesey's book documents those days," noted *New Time*'s Dave Walker, comparing Perry's account with Kesey's. "Paul Perry tries to explain their continuing attraction." Walker added that "Perry tries for the wide angle in [*On the Bus*], and succeeds for all who were merely fellow-travelers 'on the bus' or who first got turned on to the new transportation possibilities revealed in Tom Wolfe's 'electric' book." Charles Bowden, writing in the *Los Angeles Times Book Review,* reported that *On the Bus* provides "a handy history of LSD, and a chronicle of Kesey and the Pranksters after the bus ride—the acid tests, the busts, and the eventual descent of the band into relatively ordinary lives."

Perry investigated another counterculture icon in his 1992 biography *Fear and Loathing: The Strange and Terrible Saga of Hunter S. Thompson.* Thompson gained notoriety in the 1960s as the foremost practitioner of "gonzo jour-

nalism." The author's unconventional books and feature articles were highlighted by quirky observations and often focused on his own misadventures while covering the stories. Thompson's writing also dealt with his legendary status as a consumer of drugs and alcohol, with *Fear and Loathing in Las Vegas*—an account of the author's drugged visit to the Nevada gambling mecca—becoming a cult favorite. While Perry's biography further documents Thompson's overindulgence in controlled substances, the book also probes other aspects of his life, including the physical abuse of his wife and his proclivity for threatening people with handguns.

Tom Graves, writing in *New York Times Book Review,* gave the biography a mixed review. While noting that Perry "comes up woefully short" in documenting Thompson's later career, the critic found that Perry "convincingly recounts Mr. Thompson's troubled youth and his struggles as a journeyman writer." Perry's chronicle of Thompson's life has several competitors; two other biographies, *Hunter: The Strange and Savage Life of Hunter S. Thompson* by E. Jean Carroll and *When the Going Gets Weird: The Twisted Life and Times of Hunter S. Thompson* by Peter O. Whitmer, both appeared in 1993. Comparing the three biographies in *Details,* David Streitfeld praised Perry's account, recommending it as "the one to read."

Discussing his biography of Thompson, Perry told *CA:* "This is a traditional biography that traces Hunter's life from childhood. But it is also untraditional in the sense that I write about my own rather bizarre dealings with Hunter. In 1980, as the editor of *Running* magazine, I commissioned Hunter to cover the Honolulu Marathon and spent a considerable amount of time with the self-proclaimed 'doctor of journalism,' pulling the story out of him. Like so many other people who have read the works of Thompson, I thought he over-stated his drug use. But after spending time with him, I realized that he has always understated his amount of pharmaceutical abuse. He calls himself 'the last of the old time drug addicts,' and I can certainly vouch for the fact that he lives up to that reputation.

"Despite the many difficulties in dealing with Hunter, we stayed in touch long after the Honolulu Marathon piece was published in *Running.* In fact, he eventually lengthened the marathon piece and turned it into a book entitled *The Curse of Lono.* We later tried working together again, developing a book idea that would cure Hunter of his addictions to drugs, alcohol, and cigarettes by replacing them with compulsive fitness activities like running and other forms of exercise. The plan was to have him attend the Pritikin Longevity Center and other similar clinics to help him kick his habits. Hunter was fond of the idea, but it was shot down by a publisher at Summit Books who inexplicably felt that involvement in such a healthy endeavor would prove dangerous for Hunter."

BIOGRAPHICAL/CRITICAL SOURCES:

PERIODICALS

Details, February, 1993, p. 87.
Los Angeles Times Book Review, October 21, 1990, pp. 4, 7.
New Times, November 28, 1990, pp. 22, 34-42.
New York Times Book Review, December 9, 1990; January 17, 1993, p. 24.
Washington Post Book World, November 18, 1990, p. 1.

*   *   *

PESSEN, Edward 1920-1992

OBITUARY NOTICE—See index for *CA* sketch: Born December 31, 1920, in Brooklyn, NY; died of a heart attack, December 22, 1992, in Miami, FL. Historian, educator, and author. Pessen received a Pulitzer Prize nomination for *Most Uncommon Jacksonians: The Radical Leaders of the Early Labor Movement* and a National Book Award nomination for *Riches, Class, and Power before the Civil War.* After serving in the United States Army in World War II, Pessen received his doctorate in history from Columbia University. He then spent fourteen years as professor of history and department chair at Staten Island Community College. Pessen joined the faculty of the City University of New York in 1968 and was named distinguished university professor of history in 1972. Specializing in the Jacksonian period and the study of social mobility, Pessen was the author of *The Many-Faceted Jacksonian Era* and *The Log Cabin Myth: The Social Backgrounds of the Presidents.* He also wrote *Losing Our Souls: The American Experience in the Cold War.*

OBITUARIES AND OTHER SOURCES:

BOOKS

International Authors and Writers Who's Who, eleventh edition, International Biographical Centre, 1989.
Who's Who in America, Marquis, 1992.
Who's Who in Writers, Editors, and Poets, 1989-1990, December Press, 1989.
Writers Directory: 1990-1992, St. James Press, 1990.

PERIODICALS

New York Times, December 24, 1992, p. B7.

PETERS, Ralph 1952-

PERSONAL: Born April 19, 1952, in Pottsville, PA; married Marion Ann Martin, 1982. *Education:* Received M.A. from St. Mary's University; attended United States Army Command and General Staff College, U.S. Army Russian Institute, and other military schools and institutions.

ADDRESSES: Agent—Robert Gottlieb, William Morris Agency, 1350 Avenue of the Americas, New York, NY 10019.

CAREER: U.S. Army, 1976—; commissioned, 1980; present rank, major. Writer.

WRITINGS:

NOVELS

Brave Romeo, Richard Marek, 1981.
Red Army, Pocket Books, 1989.
The War in 2020, Pocket Books, 1991.
Flames of Heaven, Pocket Books, 1993.

OTHER

Also author of articles and essays on military subjects.

WORK IN PROGRESS: A novel.

SIDELIGHTS: Ralph Peters is a U.S. Army military intelligence officer who has also achieved success with his political thrillers. His first novel, *Brave Romeo,* concerns Jack Thorne, a poetry-writing guerrilla fighter who becomes an intelligence officer and uncovers evidence of a right-wing conspiracy in Germany. Unable to convince his superiors of the terrorist operation's grave threat to Western security, the hero teams instead with a left-wing student who personally challenges the conspirators after having been accused of masterminding an act of aggression that they conducted. Alan Cheuse, writing in the *New York Times Book Review,* deemed *Brave Romeo* "worth reading."

Peters followed *Brave Romeo* with *Red Army,* a story set during World War III in which Soviet forces in Central Europe overwhelm North Atlantic Treaty Organization (NATO) troops. But unlike similar works in the genre, *Red Army*'s perspective is that of the Soviet fighters: an infantryman, fearing separation from his fellow soldiers, charges into the darkness where the enemy, presumably, awaits; a tank commander, motivated by cowardice, commits a heroic act; and an accomplished general ponders the significance of his Jewish background. *Newsweek* reviewer Harry Anderson hailed *Red Army* as "a very engaging read" and added that "it is hard to imagine a better portrayal of modern war."

The War in 2020, Peters's third novel, was described by Donovan Fitzpatrick in the *New York Times Book Review* as "a terrifying vision of global conflict in the 21st century." In this novel Peters presents a chaotic, high-technology conflict in which Israel is destroyed by nuclear and chemical bombs, American forces are undone in Africa, and Moslems armed with Japanese weapons threaten to overwhelm the Soviet Union, which is already teetering towards civil war. *Washington Post* reviewer David Morrell, while objecting that *The War in 2020* "tends to reinforce national stereotypes," conceded that it serves as "a diverting action novel."

Peters told *CA:* "Those who are unwilling to risk their lives usually don't have lives worth risking."

BIOGRAPHICAL/CRITICAL SOURCES:

PERIODICALS

New Republic, June 23, 1982.
Newsweek, May 22, 1989, pp. 88-89.
New York Times Book Review, March 22, 1981; June 18, 1989, p. 20; May 5, 1991, p. 25.
Washington Post, April 11, 1991, p. D3.

*   *   *

PETERSON, Fred W.   1932-

PERSONAL: Born May 25, 1932, in Chicago, IL; son of Frederick William (a mechanic) and Crystal Mabel (a telephone operator); married Vasilikie Demos (a college professor); children: Kristin, Karl, Caleb. *Education:* St. Olaf College, B.A., 1954; Luther Theological Seminary, B.Th., 1957; University of Minnesota, Ph.D., 1961. *Politics:* Democrat.

ADDRESSES: Home—1007 Idaho Ave., Morris, MN 56267. *Office*—University of Minnesota, Morris, MN 56267.

CAREER: University of Minnesota, Morris, professor of art history, 1961-92; writer.

MEMBER: College Art Association, Society for Architectural History, Vernacular Architecture Forum.

WRITINGS:

Homes in the Heartland, University Press of Kansas, 1992.

WORK IN PROGRESS: Researching the German-American community and origins of balloon frame construction.

PEYO
See CULLIFORD, Pierre

*   *   *

PHELPS, Barry   1941-

PERSONAL: Born January 26, 1941, in Leicester, England; married in 1964; children: Rupert, Cecily. *Education:* Attended City of London College. *Avocational interests:* British political history, bibliography, travel, rugby, jogging, chess.

ADDRESSES: Home—25 Kenway Rd., London SW5 0RP, England. *Office*—Suite 49, New House, 67 Hatton Garden, London EC1N 8JY, England. *Agent*—Anne Dewe, Andrew Mann Ltd., 1 Old Compton St., London W1V 5PH, England.

CAREER: Laing & Cruickshank, London, England, stockbrokers' authorized clerk; Union Acceptances, Johannesburg, South Africa, portfolio manager; Guinness Mahon, London, portfolio manager and investment analyst; M&G Unit Trust Group, investment research manager, 1968-69; Keyser Ullmann, investment manager, 1969-71; *Euromoney,* began as deputy editor, became editor, 1971-73; *Daily Mail,* London, assistant city editor of City Page, 1973-83; Broad Street Associates Ltd., executive director, 1983-86; Abbatt Phelps Tanous Ltd. (financial public relations consultants), founder, 1986, partner, 1986-88; MMI Strategic Communications, executive director, 1988-90; Capital Markets Partners Ltd., director, 1990—. APT Data Services Ltd., chairman, 1985—; Politics International Ltd., director and consultant, 1986-89. Consultant to Ribstone Ltd. Westminster City Council, member of Finance, Town Planning, and Establishment Committees, 1968-71. *Military service:* Territorial Army, 1958-67.

MEMBER: Society of Investment Analysts, Royal Statistical Society (fellow), British Institute of Management.

WRITINGS:

The Inflation Fighter's Handbook, Daily Mail, 1975.
Power and the Party (nonfiction), Macmillan, 1982.
P. G. Wodehouse: Man and Myth, Constable, 1992.

Also author of the privately printed *Wooster of Yaxley and Wodehouse of Kimberley: Parallel Peerages,* 1992.

WORK IN PROGRESS: Posthumous Assassination, a biography of former British prime minister Stanley Baldwin.

PHILLIPS, Julia (Miller) 1944-

PERSONAL: Born April 7, 1944, in New York City; daughter of Adolph (a physicist) and Tanya Miller; married Michael Phillips (a producer; divorced); children: Kate Elizabeth. *Education:* Mt. Holyoke College, B.A., 1965.

ADDRESSES: Office—c/o Writers Guild, 8955 Beverly Blvd., Los Angeles, CA 90048.

CAREER: Film producer and author. Began career at *McCall's* (magazine), New York City, as a production assistant, and Macmillan Publications, New York City, as a copywriter; *Ladies Home Journal,* New York City, editorial assistant, 1965-69, later became associate editor; Paramount Pictures, New York City, East Coast story editor, 1969; affiliated with Mirisch Productions, New York City, 1970; First Artist Productions, New York City, creative executive, 1971; cofounder of Bill/Phillips Productions and Ruthless Productions, Los Angeles, CA, 1971.

Producer of films, sometimes with others, including *Steelyard Blues,* Warner Bros., 1972; *The Sting,* Universal, 1973; *Taxi Driver,* Columbia, 1976; *The Big Bus,* Paramount, 1976; *Close Encounters of the Third Kind,* Columbia, 1977; *The Beat,* Vestron, 1988; and *Don't Tell Mom the Babysitter's Dead,* Warner Bros., 1991.

MEMBER: Academy of Motion Picture Arts and Sciences, Writers Guild.

AWARDS, HONORS: Katherine McFarland Short Story Award, 1963; Short Story Award from Phi Beta Kappa, 1964; Academy Award, Best Picture, 1974, for *The Sting;* Palm d'or (Best Picture Award), Cannes International Film Festival, 1976, for *Taxi Driver.*

WRITINGS:

You'll Never Eat Lunch in This Town Again, Random House, 1990.

Also author of various short stories.

SIDELIGHTS: Julia Phillips became the first woman producer ever to have a film win an Academy Award for best picture in 1974. *The Sting* garnered the honor for her and her coproducers—husband Michael Phillips and partner Tony Bill. After this triumph, she went on to produce two more successful films, *Taxi Driver* and *Close Encounters of the Third Kind* before drug problems and disagreements with Hollywood's powerful people scuttled her career. Phillips tells this story—and reveals a lot of gossip about film industry celebrities—in her 1990 best-seller, *You'll Never Eat Lunch in This Town Again.*

Before becoming involved in the film industry, Phillips worked in publishing in New York City. In various editorial capacities, she was employed by magazines such as *McCall's* and *Ladies Home Journal* and by Macmillan Publications. While still studying for her bachelors' degree at Mt. Holyoke College, Phillips won a few prizes for her short fiction. But during the late 1960s, she started working for film companies in New York, and eventually moved to Los Angeles, California, with her husband Michael and their partner Tony Bill to form their own production company.

The trio's first major effort was the 1972 film *Steelyard Blues,* but the following year they found major critical and popular success with *The Sting,* which was directed by George Roy Hill and stars Paul Newman and Robert Redford. After *The Sting* won the best picture Oscar in 1974, more career opportunities became available to the partnership, but Phillips and her husband parted company with Bill, going on to produce the critically acclaimed film, *Taxi Driver.* Directed by Martin Scorsese and starring Robert DeNiro, *Taxi Driver* garnered the prestigious Palme d'or at the Cannes International Film Festival.

By the time the couple went on to produce director Steven Spielberg's 1977 hit, *Close Encounters of the Third Kind,* their marriage was breaking up. In *You'll Never Eat Lunch in This Town Again,* Phillips admits that her drug problem—she was especially fond of freebasing cocaine—was rather heavy at this time, but she claims she was fired in the late stages of the film's production not because of drugs but "because she demanded a percentage of the movie merchandising rights," according to Joyce Wadler in *People.* After *Close Encounters* and her divorce, Phillips had difficulty finding work; though frank about her cocaine addiction and subsequent recovery in her book, she also blames Hollywood's sexism and hypocrisy for her inaction in the business. *The Beat,* a film released in 1988, was supposed to be Phillips's comeback as a producer, but, as Wadler opined, it was "a flop."

Phillips channeled her anger at her Hollywood cohorts into the writing of *You'll Never Eat Lunch in This Town Again,* because, as Wadler explained, "she desperately need[ed] money." Phillips told Wadler, "I'm just being honest. I didn't write the book to get back in the business. I had to accept the fact that I wasn't in the business before I wrote the book." The resulting volume rushed to the top of the *New York Times's* Best Sellers list, and was labeled "perhaps the most scandalous and vituperative book ever about the movie industry's elite" by Brian D. Johnson in *Maclean's.* Reviewer Nina J. Easton of the *Los Angeles Times* observed that "the index listing under [Phillips's] name probably best sums up" a major portion of *Lunch:* "'Academy Awards of . . . anxiety and nervousness of . . . depressions of . . . dieting of . . . directing of . . . drug bust of . . . drug use of . . . firings of . . . guilt of . . . lateness of . . . loneliness of . . . near-strangulation experiences of . . . pregnancies of . . . rage and anger of

. . . sexual behavior of . . . success of . . . suicidal behavior of . . .' etc. etc." But in addition to an honest discussion of her own life, including the time a drug-dealer boyfriend aimed a semi-automatic rifle at the author and her young daughter, Phillips's book includes gossip about people she has known or worked with, such as Steven Spielberg, Goldie Hawn, Cybill Shepherd, and Warren Beatty.

When *You'll Never Eat Lunch in This Town Again* came out, Phillips was fired from a production job on the film version of novelist Anne Rice's *Interview With the Vampire* by producer David Geffen. She discussed him in an unfavorable light in the book, and he justified dismissing her because of it to Easton: "You think there's a safe space here for creative people to disagree after that? Only a person who wants to get fired would do this." Phillips has found production work in the early 1990s, however—she produced *Don't Tell Mom the Babysitter's Dead*, which was released in 1991.

BIOGRAPHICAL/CRITICAL SOURCES:

BOOKS

Phillips, Julia, *You'll Never Eat Lunch in This Town Again,* Random House, 1990.

PERIODICALS

Interview, February, 1991, p. 32.
Los Angeles Times, March 4, 1991, pp. F1, F12.
Maclean's, April 29, 1991, p. 62.
New York Review of Books, May 16, 1991, pp. 23-26.
New York Times Book Review, March 17, 1991, pp. 3, 17; April 7, 1991, p. 30.
People, March 18, 1991, pp. 103-108.*

—*Sketch by Elizabeth Wenning*

*   *   *

PHILLIPS, Sky 1921-

PERSONAL: Born May 24, 1921, in Washington, DC; daughter of Donald Boyer (a U.S. Army pilot) and Rosamond Holmes (a poet) Phillips; married William Morris Beaven (a U.S. Air Force pilot), June 6, 1942; children: Sky Beaven Katona, Roz Beaven Hickman, Barbara Beaven Rich. *Education:* Attended American University. *Politics:* "Cradle conservative (mellowing)." *Religion:* Episcopalian.

ADDRESSES: Home—6018 Mayfair Ln., Alexandria, VA 22310. *Agent*—Sara Sheppard Landis, 271 Avenue C, New York, NY 10009.

CAREER: Secretary, proofreader, technical editor. President of Air Force Officers' Wives' Club.

MEMBER: Washington Independent Writers, World War II Studies Association.

WRITINGS:

Secret Mission to Melbourne: November 1941, Sunflower University Press, 1992.

WORK IN PROGRESS: "The Luzon Trilogy, which includes a narrative of the 1942 surrender of Americans in the Philippines; prison camps and guerrilla warfare; and eventual victory—employing both actual and fictional characters."

SIDELIGHTS: Sky Phillips told *CA:* "I did not choose my writing path; I was haunted into it. I lived in Manila as a child, where my father was based as an Army pilot prior to World War II, and again in the Philippines during the early 1960s with my husband, an Air Force pilot. Curious about what had happened to my childhood friends and to officers whom I had known and who were captured during the war, I read the war memoirs of Clark Air Base (which is now buried under volcanic ash). I was gripped by the stories of the prisoners of war (POWs), so little known in the United States, and of the Americans who escaped and fought as guerrillas behind the Japanese lines at great cost. I wanted to *read* a *novel* that portrayed this great Greek tragedy truthfully.

"Back in the United States my reading became research. When I interviewed former POWs, they asked me to write their untold story, and I felt that I must try. My goal is to write what Russian author Alexander Isayevich Solzhenitsyn called 'documentary fiction.' That is, to allow the actual historic events to form a framework as accurately as possible, while showing these events through the eyes and sensibility of a fictional participant—thus letting the reader share the emotions behind the dry facts. My first book, *Secret Mission to Melbourne: November 1941,* sets the stage for the Bataan-Corregidor trilogy and introduces my protagonist before war changes his world.

"My working habits are almost monastic; I'm not a prolific writer, so I have given up daytime social life in order to produce. I do walk a morning mile, weather permitting. For influences, the two writers that spring to mind are Joseph Conrad and Rudyard Kipling! As for contemporary writers—I read reviews; but alas, my reading is limited to my field of research. As for advice: don't write unless you must. If you must—do your best and then revise, revise, revise."

*   *   *

PIPER, Jon Kingsbury 1957-

PERSONAL: Born September 6, 1957, in Keene, NH; son of Roy K. (a land surveyor) and Anne (an antiques dealer;

maiden name, Macechok) Piper; married Mary Elizabeth Brown (a homemaker), August 3, 1980; children: Joshua, Emily, Samuel. *Education:* Bates College, B.S., 1979; Washington State University, Ph.D., 1984. *Politics:* Independent. *Religion:* Christian.

ADDRESSES: Home—228 West Falun Rd., Assaria, KS 67416. *Office*—Land Institute, 2440 East Water Well Rd., Salina, KS 67401.

CAREER: Washington State University, Pullman, visiting assistant professor of biology, 1985; Land Institute, Salina, KS, research associate, 1985—, research coordinator, 1989—, member of management team, 1992—. Benedictine College at Marymount, adjunct faculty member, 1989; Kansas State University, adjunct assistant professor; Bethel College (North Newton, KS), member of Sand Prairie Reservation Management Advisory Board, 1988—; Hesston College, member of scientific advisory board for Dyck Arboretum of the Plains, 1992—.

MEMBER: Botanical Society of America, Ecological Society of America, Society for Conservation Biology, Soil Science Society of America, British Ecological Society, Torrey Botanical Club.

AWARDS, HONORS: Grant from Eppley Foundation for Research, 1988.

WRITINGS:

(With J. D. Soule) *Farming in Nature's Image: An Ecological Approach to Agriculture,* Island Press, 1992.

Contributor to scientific journals. Editor, *Land Institute Research Report,* 1986—; member of editorial board, *Journal of Sustainable Agriculture,* 1992—.

WORK IN PROGRESS: Research on the ecology of North American grasslands and forests; the life history, demography, and reproductive strategy of herbaceous perennial plants; the effects of environmental heterogeneity on plant reproductive ecology, interactions between species, and community dynamics; the ecology of agroecosystems and sustainable agriculture.

*   *   *

PLAIDY, Jean
   See HIBBERT, Eleanor Alice Burford

*   *   *

POLLAK, Martha D.   1941-

PERSONAL: Born July 14, 1951, in Sighet, Romania; daughter of Myron (an accountant) and Margaret (an ac-

countant; maiden name, Tessler) Pollak; married Marco Diani (a philosopher), July 27, 1984. *Education:* Cornell University, B.Arch., 1974; Massachusetts Institute of Technology, Ph.D., 1985; also attended Delft University. *Politics:* Democrat. *Religion:* Jewish.

ADDRESSES: Home—2930 North Commonwealth, Chicago, IL 60657. *Office*—310 Henry Hall, University of Illinois at Chicago Circle, Chicago, IL 60680.

CAREER: University of Illinois at Chicago Circle, Chicago, associate professor of the history of architecture, 1983—.

MEMBER: College Art Association, Society of Architectural Historians, Renaissance Society of America.

AWARDS, HONORS: Marraro Prize, American Catholic Historical Association, 1992.

WRITINGS:

Turin, 1564-1680: Urban Design, Military Culture, and the Creation of the Absolutist Capital, University of Chicago Press, 1991.
Military Architecture, Cartography, and the Representation of the Early Modern European City, University of Chicago Press, 1991.

WORK IN PROGRESS: Baroque Cities, completion expected in 1994.

*   *   *

POMEROY, Pete
   See ROTH, Arthur J(oseph)

*   *   *

PONSONBY, Laura   1935-

PERSONAL: Born October 31, 1935; daughter of Matthew and Elizabeth (Bigham) Ponsonby. *Education:* Attended Guildhall School of Music and Drama.

ADDRESSES: Home—17 South End, London W8 6BD, England. *Office*—Royal Botanic Gardens, Kew, Richmond, Surrey TW9 3AB, England.

CAREER: Royal Botanic Gardens, Kew, England, education officer, 1965—. Haslemere Educational Museum, honorary botanist; Grove Park School, governor, 1992—.

MEMBER: National Trust, Haslemere Natural History Society (president, 1983-92), Haslemere Recorded Music Society (vice-president).

WRITINGS:

(With Jane Stubbs) *List of the Flowering Plants and Ferns of Haslemere District* (juvenile), H.M.S.O., 1978.

Marianne North at Kew Gardens, Webb & Bower, 1990.

*   *   *

POWERS, Alan   1955-

PERSONAL: Born February 5, 1955, in London, England; son of Michael (an architect) and Frances (Wilson) Powers; married Susanna Curtis (a proofreader), January 10, 1982; children: Eleanor, William. *Education:* Clare College, Cambridge, B.A., 1977, Ph.D., 1983. *Religion:* Church of England.

ADDRESSES: Home—99 Judd St., London WC1H 9NE, England.

CAREER: Free-lance writer, 1982—. Judd Street Gallery, director, 1985-91; Art Workers Guild, honorary librarian, 1985—; Prince of Wales Institute of Architecture, librarian, 1993—.

MEMBER: Thirties Society (honorary case work officer, 1981-91), Twentieth Century Society, Victorian Society, Georgian Group, Society of Architectural Historians.

WRITINGS:

(With C. Aslet) *The English House,* Viking, 1985.
H. S. Goodhart-Rendel, Architectural Association, 1987.
Oliver Hill, Mouton, 1989.
Shop Fronts, Chatto & Windus, 1989.
Modern Block Printed Textiles, Walker Books, 1992.
In the Line of Development, Heinz Gallery, 1992.

WORK IN PROGRESS: Francis Pollen, Architect; Architecture in Britain, 1890-1940; research on mural painting in Britain since 1900.

SIDELIGHTS: Alan Powers told *CA:* "My academic background is in art history, but I am seldom satisfied for long by sedentary scholarship; hence, my involvement in architectural conservation, printmaking, running my own gallery for five years, and writing. I am looking for synthesis in architecture that lies beyond the stylistic division of modern and traditional."

*   *   *

POWERS, Meredith A(nn)   1949-

PERSONAL: Born February 20, 1949, in Providence, RI; daughter of John M. (a teacher) and Pauline (Kindelan) Powers; married Gerard A. Cyr (an attorney and literary agent), 1977 (marriage ended, 1987); children: Gabriel. *Education:* Albertus Magnus College, B.A., 1971; Rhode Island College, M.A.T., 1975; University of Rhode Island, Ph.D., 1988.

ADDRESSES: Home—47 Blackstone Blvd., Providence, RI 02906. *Agent*—Gerard A. Cyr, Rivkin, Baker & Braverman.

CAREER: Junior high school English teacher, 1972-75; Joseph Case High School, teacher of remedial English, world literature, and a writing workshop, 1975-93. Valley Hospice, member of advisory board, 1991—.

MEMBER: Swansea Educators Association (president, 1992—).

WRITINGS:

The Heroine in Western Literature, McFarland and Co., 1991.

Author of a weekly column in *New Bedford Standard Times,* 1971-72. Contributor to *International Journal of Family Counseling* and *Kliat Audiobook Guide.*

WORK IN PROGRESS: A novel; a study of the effectiveness of using unabridged recorded classics as part of literary instruction at the secondary school level.

SIDELIGHTS: Meredith A. Powers told *CA:* "I spend every day struggling to find time to write. My time is spent teaching but, like a stubborn organism, the will to write asserts itself every day in everything and remains too little satisfied."

*   *   *

PRICE, Adrian Hyde
See HYDE-PRICE, Adrian

*   *   *

PRIEST, Lisa   1964-

PERSONAL: Born January 20, 1964, in Windsor, Ontario, Canada; daughter of Arthur Bernard (a toolmaker) and Barbara (a homemaker) Priest. *Education:* Received B.A. (with honors) from University of Windsor. *Politics:* None. *Religion:* "Anglican (not practicing)."

ADDRESSES: Home—28 West Lynn Ave., Toronto, Ontario, Canada M4C 3V8. *Office*—1 Yonge St., Toronto, Ontario, Canada M5E 2E6.

CAREER: Worked as a reporter for *Windsor Star,* Windsor, Ontario, for two years, and *Winnipeg Free Press,* Winnipeg, Manitoba, Canada, for two and a half years; *Toronto Star,* Toronto, Ontario, medicine and health policy writer.

AWARDS, HONORS: Arthur Ellis Award for best nonfiction, Crime Writers of Canada, 1990.

WRITINGS:

Conspiracy of Silence, McClelland & Stewart, 1989.
Women Who Killed, McClelland & Stewart, 1992.

ADAPTATIONS: Conspiracy of Silence was adapted into a Canadian Broadcasting Corp. (CBC) television miniseries.

SIDELIGHTS: Lisa Priest told *CA:* "My first book, *Conspiracy of Silence,* is about the hushed up murder of a Cree Indian girl in a small northern Manitoba community. White members of the community knew who the killer was, but no one bothered to tell the police. Sixteen years after the 1971 murder, one police officer in Thompson determined to find out the truth. He travelled to the murder site, interviewed people, placed newspaper ads, and used wiretaps until three of the four men involved were arrested. Eventually, two men—charged with murder—went to trial, and only one was convicted. I wrote the book because I was outraged by the injustice of the case, and I wanted people to see that racism exists in this country. I had only three months to write the book, and I scrambled, working sixteen hours a day. I was twenty-four at the time and ambitious to make my mark in life. My second book, *Women Who Killed,* an anthology of eleven women who killed in Canada, was published in May, 1992. My goal is to write books that have social significance and provide insight into the Canadian psyche. Too often, Canadians view themselves as peaceful, tolerant people, but there are cases—like Betty Osborne's—which show that that just isn't the case. I work full time as a newspaper reporter with the *Toronto Star,* where I cover medicine and health policy."

*   *   *

PRIEST, Stephen 1954-

PERSONAL: Born August 22, 1954, in Oxford, England; son of Arthur Priest. *Education:* Cambridge University, B.A. (with honors), 1980, M.A. (with honors), 1984.

ADDRESSES: Office—Department of Philosophy, University of Edinburgh, Edinburgh EH8 9YL, Scotland.

CAREER: Council of Europe, Strasbourg, France, press and information administrator, 1977; University of Edinburgh, Edinburgh, Scotland, lecturer in philosophy, director of studies in philosophy. Oxford University, visiting scholar at Wolfson College.

WRITINGS:

Hegel's Critique of Kant, Oxford University Press, 1987.
The British Empiricists, Penguin, 1990.
Theories of the Mind, Houghton, 1991.

WORK IN PROGRESS: Merleau-Ponty: The Arguments of the Philosophers and *How to Think Logically,* both for Routledge & Kegan Paul; research on philosophical problems.

SIDELIGHTS: Stephen Priest told *CA:* "I am a philosopher who thinks of philosophy as the attempt to solve fundamental problems about the nature of existence. My thinking escapes the current neo-Kantian and anti-metaphysical philosophical orthodoxies, whether they are positivist or phenomenological, 'linguistic,' structuralist, or deconstructive. I maintain that putative anti-metaphysical philosophy itself rests on metaphysical assumptions, and that the orthodox view that there is a distinction between analytical and continental philosophical traditions is exaggerated."

*   *   *

PRINCESS ANNE
See ANNE (Elizabeth Alice Louise Windsor), Princess

*   *   *

PUTNAM, Constance E(lizabeth) 1943-

PERSONAL: Born March 2, 1943, in Hanover, NH; daughter of William Frederick (a physician) and Mildred Margaret (a physician's assistant; maiden name, Best) Putnam; married Hugo Adam Bedau (a college professor), June 16, 1990. *Education:* Reed College, B.A., 1965, M.A.T., 1966; doctoral study at Tufts University, 1991—. *Politics:* Democrat. *Religion:* Protestant.

ADDRESSES: Home and office—111 Hayward Mill Rd., Concord, MA 01742.

CAREER: Schoolteacher in Portland, OR, 1965-70, and Hildeshein, Germany, 1971-73; Houghton Mifflin Co., Boston, MA, consulting editor, 1974-81, executive editor of foreign languages, 1981-83; Northeastern University, Boston, director of graphic arts program, 1983-85; freelance writer, editor, and teacher, 1985—. Concord Family Service, member of board of directors, 1990—; member of West Concord Depot Citizens Advisory Commission, 1988-89, Concord Fair Housing Commission, 1989-90, Concord Housing Authority, 1990-91, and Concord-Carlisle Human Rights Council, 1990-92.

MEMBER: National Writers Union.

AWARDS, HONORS: Danforth Foundation fellowships, 1967 and 1968; Graphic Arts Incentive Award, 1984; best article award, International Technical Communications Conference, 1986.

WRITINGS:

German Today 1 Tests, Houghton, 1982.
German Today 2 Tests, Houghton, 1982.
(Translator) *Criminological Research in the Eighties and Beyond,* Max Planck Institute, 1988.
(With Michael L. Radelet and husband, Hugo Adam Bedau) *In Spite of Innocence: Erroneous Convictions in Capital Cases,* Northeastern University Press, 1992.

Contributor to periodicals.

WORK IN PROGRESS: Biographies of physicians Nathan Smith and the author's father, William F. Putnam.

SIDELIGHTS: Constance E. Putnam told *CA:* "With a background in education, specifically in foreign language pedagogy and the teaching of English both to its native speakers and to those learning it as a foreign language, I have, throughout my adult years, been interested in the communication of ideas through the medium of writing. My years in the education division of Houghton Mifflin Company consolidated my abilities as an editor; since then, I have worked in a variety of settings as a teacher of editing and writing skills. I have also continued to edit a wide range of books and articles for numerous writers. All this has heightened my interest in and sensitivity to language.

"When I was a teenager, a family friend made a profound impression on me by saying that the difference between writers and non-writers is that writers write; it is a platitude, to be sure, but that was what finally pushed me to sit down and, not only begin writing seriously, but to take steps to get my own writing published. With encouragement from the then editor of our local weekly paper, I turned myself into a regular columnist, without any prior experience in journalism. I now have a satisfying number of by-lines to my credit in some two dozen magazines and newspapers.

"At the same time, I continued publishing in professional journals, as I had while I was working in the field of foreign language pedagogy. That, in turn, led me to write book reviews on a wider variety of topics, and to explore more seriously topics in human and civil rights. For the local paper, I have written extensively on issues having to do with tolerance and low-income housing, for instance; as an editor, I have worked for a long time on the articles and books my husband (Hugh Adam Bedau) has written on capital punishment. That led me to join him and Michael L. Radelet as a coauthor of the book *In Spite of Innocence.*

"Meanwhile, an interest in the history of medicine and in doctor-patient relationships, spurred by my having become the de facto family archivist when my father (a doc-

tor) died, was growing. I returned to the academic world in 1991 as a doctoral candidate in Tufts University's interdisciplinary doctorate program, where I am concentrating on those two subjects. Medical education, another area of concern and interest to me, and the delivery of primary health care are, needless to say, hot topics in this country now. I have plenty of writing to do."

*   *   *

QUEENAN, Joe 1950-

PERSONAL: Born November 3, 1950, in Philadelphia, PA; son of Joseph and Agnes (McNulty) Queenan; married Francesca Jane Spinner (a certified public accountant), January 7, 1977; children: Bridget, Gordon. *Education:* St. Joseph's College, B.A., 1972. *Politics:* Democrat. *Religion:* Roman Catholic.

ADDRESSES: Home—Tarrytown, NY. *Agent*—Joe Vallecy, 320 Riverside Dr., New York, NY 10012.

CAREER: Barron's, New York City, writer, 1987-89; *Forbes,* senior editor, 1989-90; free-lance writer, 1990—.

WRITINGS:

Imperial Caddy: The Rise of Dan Quayle in America and the Decline and Fall of Practically Everything Else, Hyperion (New York City), 1992.

Contributor to magazines and newspapers, including *Spy, Gentlemen's Quarterly, Movieline, Chief Executive,* and *Time.*

WORK IN PROGRESS: If You're Talking to Me, Your Career Is in Trouble, movie essays.

SIDELIGHTS: Joe Queenan told *CA:* "I write because it beats working in a factory. That's it."

*   *   *

QUINE, Judith Balaban 1932-

PERSONAL: Born in Chicago, IL, 1932; daughter of Barney (a film executive) and Tillie Balaban; married Jay Kanter (an agent), 1953 (divorced); married Tony Franciosa (an actor; divorced); married Don Quine (a karate promoter).

ADDRESSES: Office—c/o Pocket Books, 1230 Avenue of the Americas, New York, NY 10020.

CAREER: Actress, homemaker, and author. Cofounder (with husband Don Quine) of the Professional Karate Association.

WRITINGS:

The Bridesmaids: Grace Kelly, Princess of Monaco, and Six Intimate Friends (nonfiction), Weidenfeld & Nicolson, 1989, Pocket Books, 1990.

WORK IN PROGRESS: A novel.

SIDELIGHTS: When actress Judith Balaban married agent Jay Kanter in 1953, she met one of her husband's more famous clients, silver screen legend Grace Kelly. Kelly was one of the most popular and sought after actresses of the 1950s, starring in such classic films as *The Country Girl, High Society,* and the Alfred Hitchcock thrillers *Dial M for Murder* and *Rear Window.* By the time Kelly married Prince Rainier of Monaco in 1956, Kelly and Balaban had become such close friends that Balaban served as one of six bridesmaids in what many people felt was "the Ultimate Wedding of All Time," in the words of Stephen Birmingham in *Washington Post Book World.* More than thirty years later, Judith Balaban Quine has penned a book about her experience in the royal wedding, her continued friendship with the late Princess Grace of Monaco, who died in a tragic car accident, and the lives of the other bridesmaids who took part in the royal wedding with her. The result, *The Bridesmaids: Grace Kelly, Princess of Monaco, and Six Intimate Friends,* has been widely and favorably reviewed. In this book, Quine is "less a biographer—or autobiographer—and more a chronicler of an era," lauded Jeannine Stein in the *Los Angeles Times.*

In *The Bridesmaids,* Quine offers a very detailed account of the royal nuptials. "Every bow, every bauble, every floral centerpiece, every table setting and every bridesmaid's shortie white kid glove is lovingly described, along with, naturally, the Wedding Dress," explained Birmingham. "If you are a wedding nut . . . then this is the book for you," he added. But Quine tackles more serious issues in the book as well, including the possibilities for disillusionment in the 1950s woman's dream of marrying the right man and living happily ever after. She reveals that the marriage of one of the bridesmaids, former model Carolyn Scott Reybold, ended in a divorce with a fairly large settlement. Reybold, who suffered emotional trauma after her daughter was killed in a car accident, wound up living in a women's shelter in New York City. And about Princess Grace herself, after approximately twenty years of the marriage that caused her to forsake her acting career, Quine writes in her book: "Her maverick sense of adventure seemed all but suppressed, though we could still hear its wings fluttering against the walls, yearning to escape." But while some critics have expressed a wish for more details about the late princess, many praise Quine's kind portrayal of Kelly and the author's lack of desire to pin some horrible scandal—such as the alcoholism alleged in some other treatments—on Princess Grace. Quine explained this to Stein: "I don't think people are trashy, so I don't like to trash them. I wrote about people I know, which meant I cared for them. I wanted to write about what it meant to be alive then, a woman trying to be a wife, a mother, a worker, a person and that's not a trashy experience. That's called being alive."

BIOGRAPHICAL/CRITICAL SOURCES:

BOOKS

Quine, Judith Balaban, *The Bridesmaids: Grace Kelly, Princess of Monaco, and Six Intimate Friends,* Weidenfeld & Nicolson, 1989.

PERIODICALS

Chicago Tribune, June 15, 1989, pp. 1, 3; June 30, 1989.
Los Angeles Times, June 5, 1989.
New York Times Book Review, June 11, 1989, p. 46.
Times Literary Supplement, September 22, 1989, p. 1040.
Washington Post, August 21, 1989.
Washington Post Book World, July 2, 1989, p. 11.*

R

RADELET, Michael L. 1950-

PERSONAL: Born October 24, 1950, in South Bend, IN; son of Louis A. (a professor) and Elizabeth Grace (a homemaker; maiden name, Delaney) Radelet; married Elizabeth Handlos (a community organizer), June 23, 1990; children: Jacob William. *Education:* Michigan State University, B.A., 1972; Eastern Michigan University, M.A., 1974; Purdue University, Ph.D., 1977; postdoctoral study at University of Wisconsin—Madison, 1977-79, and University of New Hampshire, 1989-90.

ADDRESSES: Home—1019 Northwest 36th Terrace, Gainesville, FL 32605. *Office*—Department of Sociology, University of Florida, Gainesville, FL 32611-2036.

CAREER: University of Florida, Gainesville, assistant professor, 1979-84, associate professor, 1984-93, professor of sociology, 1993—.

MEMBER: American Sociological Association, American Society of Criminology.

WRITINGS:

(With Margaret Vandiver) *Capital Punishment in America: An Annotated Bibliography,* Garland Publishing, 1988.

(Editor) *Facing the Death Penalty: Essays on a Cruel and Unusual Punishment,* Temple University Press, 1989.

(With Hugo Adam Bedau and Constance E. Putnam) *In Spite of Innocence: Erroneous Convictions in Capital Cases,* Northeastern University Press, 1992.

(With Kent S. Miller) *Executing the Mentally Ill: The Criminal Justice System and the Case of Alvin Ford,* Sage Publications, 1993.

BIOGRAPHICAL/CRITICAL SOURCES:

PERIODICALS

Washington Post Book World, September 3, 1989, p. 8.

*   *   *

RAVIV, Dan 1954-

PERSONAL: Born September 27, 1954, in New York, NY; son of Benjamin (an engineer) and Esther (a teacher) Raviv; married Dori Phaff (a television researcher), June, 1982; children: Jonathan, Emma. *Education:* Harvard University, B.A., 1976.

ADDRESSES: Office—CBS News, 4770 Biscayne Blvd., Miami, FL 33137. *Agent*—Russell Galen, Scott Meredith Literary Agency, 845 Third Ave., New York, NY 10022.

CAREER: Columbia Broadcasting System (CBS) Radio, Boston, MA, editor, 1974-76; CBS News, New York City, producer, 1976-78, reporter in Tel Aviv, Israel, 1978-80, correspondent in London, England, 1980-92, correspondent in Miami, FL, 1993—.

AWARDS, HONORS: Overseas Press Club of America award, 1987; *Every Spy a Prince: The Complete History of Israel's Intelligence Community* received an award from the *New York Times* in 1990.

WRITINGS:

(With Yossi Melman) *Behind the Uprising: Israelis, Jordanians, and Palestinians,* Greenwood Press, 1989.

(With Melman) *The Imperfect Spies,* Sidgwick & Jackson, 1989, published in the United States as *Every Spy a Prince: The Complete History of Israel's Intelligence Community,* Houghton, 1990.

(With Melman) *Friends in Deed: Inside the U.S.-Israel Alliance,* Hyperion, in press.

Contributor to the *Washington Post, Miami Herald,* and to other newspapers.

SIDELIGHTS: CBS News correspondent Dan Raviv has collaborated with Israeli journalist Yossi Melman on several reports on Israeli affairs for the *Washington Post,* and the team has published two books together. One product of their collaboration is *Behind the Uprising: Israelis, Jordanians, and Palestinians,* a 1989 work that provides background on the *intifada,* the Palestinian uprising against Israeli military rule in the occupied lands. The volume centers "on the clandestine contacts between Israeli and Jordanian leaders since before the foundation of the state of Israel," wrote Helena Cobban in the *Los Angeles Times Book Review.* "The authors, two hard-burrowing . . . journalists, provide a wealth of detail about these contacts, mainly using leaks from Israeli participants."

Raviv and Melman also collaborated on the best-selling *Every Spy a Prince: The Complete History of Israel's Intelligence Community.* The reputation of the Israeli secret services—the Mossad for foreign operations, Shin Bet for domestic operations, and Aman for military intelligence—has grown since the founding of the modern Jewish state in 1948 to make them legendary in the world of espionage. Raviv and Melman attempt to uncover the truth behind the legend in *Every Spy a Prince.* The early members of these organizations were well-educated and cultured and willing to accept the high standards of patriotism and selflessness demanded of them by officials in Israel and by the leaders of the intelligence community. Even as the services grew into more professional institutions and expanded their information-gathering capacity through computers and other technological tools, they continued to add to their mystique by scoring major successes in field operations. In 1956 the Israelis were the first to secure a copy of Soviet leader Nikita Khrushchev's secret speech to the Communist Party Congress in which he discussed the brutality of the Stalin regime. Israeli agents captured Nazi war criminal Adolf Eichmann in 1960 in Argentina. Then, Israel achieved an overwhelming success in the 1967 Six-Day War, largely because of excellent intelligence. In the 1970s, they performed a successful raid on Entebbe, Uganda, to save hostages. At times such as these, the country's spy organizations seemed invincible.

Raviv and Melman gathered much of the information on these operations from former and active agents and "even though some of the Israeli operatives sound boastful," wrote Herbert Mitgang in the *New York Times,* "the book is not propaganda or disinformation. While it is filled with many examples of how Mossad pulled off major coups, the authors are at pains to point out that the Israelis sometimes goofed." Among their failures was their attempt to frame and discredit the new nationalistic government in Egypt in 1954 by bombing American and British embassy buildings. In addition, they were blamed for poor intelligence in not anticipating the 1973 Yom Kippur War. In the 1980s, the intelligence organizations were scandalized by discoveries that they had killed Palestinians arrested for hijacking a bus, recruited American Jonathan Pollard to spy on Israel's ally, and been deeply involved in the Iran-Contra arms-for-hostages operations. As the 1990s began to take shape, the Israeli intelligence community was under scrutiny for exacerbating the problems of the Palestinian uprising.

Raviv and Melman offer *Every Spy a Prince* as a "complete history of Israel's intelligence community," and therefore, they cover a lot of ground. This characteristic of the volume is the target of some of the criticism aimed at it. "Raviv and Melman seem so preoccupied with packing everything into this [book]," commented Steven Luxenberg in the *Washington Post Book World,* "that any sort of analysis or context gets lost. Their approach is too shallow to be good history and too episodic to be complete." *New York Times Book Review* contributor David Wise conceded that "the book is episodic, often fragmented, stuffed with marginal anecdotes that get in the way of the narrative." However, he added that "Mr. Raviv and Mr. Melman have done a remarkable job of penetrating Israel's secret agencies."

Wise found that the authors "break substantial new ground, providing as clear and comprehensive a look at Israeli intelligence as we are likely to get. They perpetuate the legend even while reducing it to a more realistic size—no mean feat in itself. And they tell some wonderful stories." Walter Laqueur offered a similar assessment in the *Times Literary Supplement.* He stated that the work is "the most detailed and reliable history so far of Israeli intelligence. The book is based not on sensational revelations but on diligent research of Israeli publications." Moreover, as David Langsam pointed out in the *New Statesman, Every Spy a Prince* offers a valuable warning: "Melman and Raviv conclude that, while Israel more than most other countries has a need to protect itself, 'what Israeli citizens should realise is that intelligence is simply an extension of their nation's policies. If the policies are faulty, even the best intelligence in the world cannot repair them.'"

For further information on Yossi Melman, see his entry in this volume.

BIOGRAPHICAL/CRITICAL SOURCES:

PERIODICALS

Los Angeles Times Book Review, April 29, 1990; July 29, 1990.
New Statesman, August 30, 1991.
New York Times, August 8, 1986; July 14, 1990.

New York Times Book Review, July 8, 1990.
Times Literary Supplement, January 26, 1990.
Washington Post Book World, August 12, 1990.

—*Sketch by Bryan Ryan*

* * *

REHNQUIST, William H(ubbs) 1924-

PERSONAL: Born October 1, 1924, in Milwaukee, WI; son of William Benjamin and Margery (Peck) Rehnquist; married Natalie Cornell, August 29, 1953; children: James, Janet, Nancy. *Education:* Attended Kenyon College, 1943; Stanford University, B.A. and M.A., 1948, L.L.B., 1952; Harvard University, M.A., 1949. *Religion:* Lutheran.

ADDRESSES: Office—c/o Supreme Court of the United States, 1 First St. NE, Washington, DC 20543.

CAREER: U.S. Supreme Court, Washington, DC, law clerk for Justice Robert H. Jackson, 1952-53; Evans, Kitchel & Jenckes, Phoenix, AZ, attorney, 1953-55; Ragan & Rehnquist, Phoenix, partner, 1956-57; Cunningham, Carson & Messenger, Phoenix, partner, 1957-60; Powers & Rehnquist, Phoenix, partner, 1960-69; U.S. Department of Justice, Office of Legal Counsel, assistant attorney, 1969-71; U.S. Supreme Court, justice, 1972-86, chief justice, 1986—. Member of the National Conference of Commissioners on Uniform State Laws, 1963-69. *Military service:* U.S. Army Air Corps, 1943-46; became sergeant, served in Weather Service in Africa-Middle East Theater.

MEMBER: Order of the Coif, Phi Beta Kappa, Phi Delta Phi.

WRITINGS:

The Supreme Court: How It Was, How It Is, Morrow, 1987.
Grand Inquests: The Historic Impeachments of Justice Samuel Chase and President Andrew Johnson, Morrow, 1992.

Contributor of articles to law journals.

SIDELIGHTS: The chief justice of the U.S. Supreme Court since 1986, William H. Rehnquist has written two books concerning the American judiciary, *The Supreme Court: How It Was, How It Is* and *Grand Inquests: The Historic Impeachments of Justice Samuel Chase and President Andrew Johnson.* In *The Supreme Court,* Rehnquist offers a history of America's highest court from its beginnings to the mid-twentieth century and also reveals the inner workings of the institution today. Supreme Court justices, for instance, "read newspapers and magazines, we watch news on television, we talk to our friends about current events," Rehnquist writes in *The Supreme Court.* "No judge worthy of his salt would ever cast his vote in a particular case simply because he thought the majority of the public wanted him to vote that way, but that is quite a different thing from saying that no judge is ever influenced by the great tides of public opinion that run in a country such as ours." Additionally, the book includes an account of Rehnquist's own introduction to the Court as a clerk for Justice Robert H. Jackson in the 1950s. *The Supreme Court* was well received by critics, who considered it to be an engaging and readable volume appropriate for the general public.

In his 1992 book, *Grand Inquests,* Rehnquist concentrates on the impeachment trials of Supreme Court Justice Samuel Chase in 1805 and President Andrew Johnson in 1868. Both trials, Rehnquist notes, were motivated by politics rather than serious wrongdoing on the part of Chase or Johnson. The chief justice also points out that the acquittals of Chase and Johnson served to discourage future use of impeachment for political reasons and affirmed the political independence of the Supreme Court and the power of the executive branch. Though other historians have studied both trials, *Washington Post Book World* contributor Edwin M. Yoder commented that Rehnquist "brings fresh information and a fresh angle of vision" to his subject. *Grand Inquests,* according to Yoder, "is also incisive, readable and fair-minded. . . . The merits of this engaging and informative book go well beyond its unusual authorship."

BIOGRAPHICAL/CRITICAL SOURCES:

BOOKS

Rehnquist, William H., *The Supreme Court: How It Was, How It Is,* Morrow, 1987.

PERIODICALS

Los Angeles Times Book Review, August 23, 1987, pp. 1, 13.
New York Times Book Review, June 14, 1992, p. 9.
Washington Post Book World, July 12, 1992, p. 11.

* * *

REID, Christopher (John) 1949-

PERSONAL: Born May 13, 1949, in Hong Kong; son of James Theodore (an oil company employee) and Alice Margaret (Dedear) Reid; married Lucinda Catherine Gane (an actress), July 7, 1979. *Education:* Exeter College, Oxford, B.A., 1971. *Politics:* Socialist.

ADDRESSES: Office—c/o Faber & Faber Ltd., 3 Queen Square, London WC1N 3AU, England.

CAREER: Writer and editor. Worked variously as a librarian, actor, filing clerk, theatrical stage worker, freelance journalist, and as a nanny and tutor. Crafts Council, London, England, editor of "News and Reviews" section of *Crafts* magazine, 1979-81; Faber & Faber Ltd., London, publisher, 1986—, poetry editor, 1991—.

AWARDS, HONORS: Eric Gregory Award, 1978; Prudence Farmer Award for poetry (cowinner with Craig Raine), 1978 and 1980; Somerset Maugham Award and Hawthornden Prize, both 1980, both for *Arcadia.*

WRITINGS:

POETRY

Arcadia, Oxford University Press, 1979.
Pea Soup, Oxford University Press, 1982.
Katerina Brac, Faber & Faber, 1985.
In the Echoey Tunnel, Faber & Faber, 1991.

OTHER

(Editor) *The Poetry Book Society Anthology, 1989-1990,* Hutchinson, 1990.

Contributor to periodicals, including London *Sunday Times, London Review of Books,* and *Listener.*

SIDELIGHTS: Since the beginning of his career, Christopher Reid has been considered a member of the "Martian School" of poetry. This group of English poets are distinguished by the perspective their poems adopt in describing their surroundings. According to *Washington Post Book World* critic David Young, the poets of the Martian School "try to look at the world as though they had just arrived from another planet, seeing it new and making it new by powerful and unusual metaphors." Armed with this vision, Reid has produced several acclaimed volumes of poetry that feature new interpretations of common objects, emphasizing a worldview that critics often characterize as witty and playful.

As reviewers have frequently noted, Reid's work depends on his vivid imagination, his ability to make striking comparisons between objects that seem, on first glance, to be unalike. These imaginative metaphors were first displayed in Reid's debut collection, *Arcadia,* which includes a variety of unusual juxtapositions. Reid compares toenail clippers to a sailing ship, a can-opener to "a twirly dragonfly," and a dining table to a cathedral. In another poem, Reid describes a butcher shop as if it were heaven, finding a vision of angels in slabs of pork and comparing the ribs of butchered hogs to "enormous harps."

Published in 1979, *Arcadia* appeared at roughly the same time as the debut by poet Craig Raine, another member of the Martian School. Taken together, the work of the two poets was considered by critics to be an innovative departure for English poetry. "There can be no doubt of their literary-historical significance," wrote Blake Morrison in *New Statesman and Society.* "Raine and Reid are the first mainstream British poets since 1945 to embark on a programme which makes imagination its priority." The critic also noted that "for them imagination is *play*—the mind enjoying itself on life's surfaces rather than burrowing beneath."

While critics such as Morrison praised this novel approach, others found that Reid's emphasis on the surface of events resulted in disappointingly superficial poetry. *Listener*'s Anne Stevenson voiced this opinion in her review of *Arcadia,* stating that "in the end, most of these poems are simply silly." Other reviewers took a more moderate stance regarding the poet's work, expressing appreciation but wondering how Reid and other Martian poets would develop their writing in future works. Alan Brownjohn's review in *Encounter* approved of the "ironical fancies" of the Martians, but speculated that "this ironical stance can't be kept up indefinitely, . . . Raine and Reid will need to move on from these very entertaining and promising beginnings."

Upon the release of *Pea Soup,* the poet's second collection, critics again speculated about Reid's ability to expand the range of his work, and several complained that he had failed to move on to new poetic territory. "The Reid of *Pea Soup* appears unaware of any need for development," wrote Michael Hulse in *Dictionary of Literary Biography,* noting that the style which had made Reid "so obviously different" upon his debut had become "self-parodying" in *Pea Soup.* Similar disappointment was voiced by reviewers such as Martin Booth in *British Book News,* who complained that "the work is abundantly clever but distinctly artless." Other critics were more approving of the collection, however. John Bayley in *London Review of Books* praised that manner in which Reid avoided "implication and afterthought" in the poems, an approach which enhanced the immediacy of the work. "Again and again," the critic wrote of *Pea Soup,* "poetry and meaning meet the moments of our present time head-on, and the resultant collision is intensely exhilarating for the spectator."

Reid's next collection, *Katerina Brac,* found the poet using a fictional identity to create a new approach to his work. The book masquerades as a translated collection of poems by an imaginary Eastern European writer named Katerina Brac. Elaine Feinstein, writing in the *Times Literary Supplement,* saw this as this an interesting approach, writing that "so elaborate a deceit is certainly intriguing." The critic praised the "immediately pleasurable quality" of selected poems in the collection, while noting that behind the guise of the imaginary female poet was a "delicate, dreamy sensibility which is very much that of Reid himself." Bevis Hillier in *Los Angeles Times Book Review* also found the collection satisfying, declaring that Reid "has what the more portentous free verse poets fatally lack: wit. It shows not only in his frequent jokes, but also in his vivacious phrase-making." Hillier also compared Reid to two acclaimed poets of the twentieth century, proclaiming that he "must be counted among the best writers of free verse since [T. S.] Eliot and [W. H.] Auden."

Throughout his career, Reid has been reluctant to divulge information about himself, and the poet is quoted by Hulse as saying that he is "quite happy to be shrouded in mystery so far as my private life is concerned." Hulse also notes that Reid's early poems showed a similar reluctance to address personal events, leading the critic to claim that Reid's "resistance to the autobiographical is almost a phobia." Reviewers have noted a trend toward autobiography in the poet's later works, however. Poems in *Pea Soup* have addressed Reid's relationship with his wife, leading Hulse to speculate that "a more personal note may be entering his work." Reid's wife and her battle against leukemia were also the subject of a poem in his 1991 collection, *In the Echoey Tunnel*.

Whatever subject he is addressing, Reid's work has been seen as an important contribution to contemporary English poetry. "Reid's chief excellence," wrote Bayley in *London Review of Books*, "which makes him one of the best poets of our time for some things, is for making a basic simplicity of theme work itself out through a highly visual and tactile pattern." And Peter Porter in the *Observer* noted that "both Raine and Reid have done poetry a service by trying to make it as interesting as prose. They are out to entertain, to regain poetry's lost readership. . . . In their hands it startles by comparisons, adopts wilful metaphors, and is unapologetic about being clever."

BIOGRAPHICAL/CRITICAL SOURCES:

BOOKS

Contemporary Literary Criticism, Volume 33, Gale, 1985, pp. 348-51.
Dictionary of Literary Biography, Volume 40: *Poets of Great Britain and Ireland since 1960,* Gale, 1985.
Reid, Christopher, *Arcadia,* Oxford University Press, 1979.

PERIODICALS

British Book News, February, 1983, p. 117.
Encounter, November, 1979, pp. 70-77.
Listener, August 16, 1979, pp. 220-21.
London Review of Books, September 16, 1982, p. 14.
Los Angeles Times Book Review, May 11, 1986, p. 6.
New Statesman and Society, July 13, 1979, p. 64.
Observer, October 3, 1982, p. 32.
Times Literary Supplement, March 21, 1986, p. 308.

Washington Post Book World, September 7, 1980, p. 5.

—*Sketch by Jeff Hill*

*   *   *

REINGOLD, Nathan 1927-

PERSONAL: Born March 23, 1927, in New York, NY; son of Benjamin Reingold (a window cleaner) and Fanny (Rosenfeld) Reingold; married Ida Hornstein (a mathematician), January 1, 1955 (deceased); married Ellen G. Miles (an art historian), November 28, 1992; children: Matthew H., Nicholas F. *Education:* New York University, B.A., 1947, M.A., 1948; University of Pennsylvania, Ph.D., 1951. *Religion:* Jewish.

ADDRESSES: Home—4801 Hampden Ln., Bethesda, MD 20804. *Office*—National Museum of American History, Smithsonian Institution, Washington, DC 20560.

CAREER: National Archives, Washington, DC, staff member, 1951-59; Library of Congress, Washington, DC, specialist in the history of science, 1959-66; Smithsonian Institution, Washington, DC, editor of the Joseph Henry Papers, 1966-85, senior historian at National Museum of American History, 1985-93, historian emeritus, 1993—. Yale University, senior post-doctoral fellow, 1960-61; University of Pennsylvania, instructor, 1966, visiting professor of American civilization, 1969; Rockefeller University, Rockefeller Archive Center, member of governing council, 1973-82, 1984-90, special consultant to governing council, 1983-84; Woodrow Wilson International Center for Scholars, adjunct fellow, 1975; International Union of History and Philosophy of Science, Commission on Documentation, president, 1981-93; Rennselaer Polytechnic Institute, Allen Lecturer in the History of Mathematics, 1981; member of various professional committees and advisory councils on history and philosophy of science; chaired and organized numerous conferences in the U.S., Great Britain, Australia, and Italy.

MEMBER: International Academy of the History of Science (corresponding member), American Antiquarian Society, American Association of the Advancement of Science (fellow), American Historical Association, History of Science Society (council member, 1964-67; Pfizer Award committee chair, 1988), Society for History of Technology (member of advisory council, 1962-65), Association for Documentary Editing (director of publications, 1980-81), Phi Beta Kappa (science book award selection committee member, 1966-69), Cosmos Club.

AWARDS, HONORS: Sesquicentennial Medal, Coast and Geodetic Survey, 1956; research grants from American Philosophical Society, 1962-63, National Science Foundation, 1965-66 and 1967-72, National Endowment for the

Humanities, 1973-78, and Lounsbery Foundation, 1982-83; Centennial Medal, National Academy of Sciences, 1963.

WRITINGS:

(Editor) *Science in Nineteenth-Century America: A Documentary History,* Hill & Wang, 1964.
(Editor) *The Papers of Joseph Henry,* five volumes, Smithsonian Institution Press, 1972-85.
(Editor) *Science in America since 1820,* Science History Publications, 1976.
(Editor) *The Sciences in the American Context: New Perspectives,* Smithsonian Institution Press, 1979.
(Editor with wife, Ida H. Reingold) *Science in America: A Documentary History, 1900-1939,* University of Chicago Press, 1981.
(Editor with Marc Rothenberg, and contributor) *Scientific Colonialism: A Cross-cultural Comparison,* Smithsonian Institution Press, 1986.
Science, American Style, Rutgers University Press, 1991.

Contributor to books, including *Nineteenth-Century American Science: A Reappraisal,* edited by George N. Daniels, Northwestern University Press, 1972; *The Pursuit of Knowledge in the Early American Republic,* edited by A. Oleson and S. Brown, Johns Hopkins University Press, 1976; *Expository Science: Forms and Functions of Popularization,* edited by T. Shinn and R. Whitley, Dordrecht, 1985; *The Michelson Era in American Science,* edited by S. Goldberg and R. Stuewer, 1988. Contributor to periodicals, including *Minerva, British Journal for the History of Science, American Archivist, Reviews in American History, History, Nature,* and *American Quarterly.* Editorial board member of *Historical Studies of the Physical Sciences,* 1968-79, and *New York History,* 1973-77; editorial advisory board member of *Isis,* 1971-75, and *Social Studies of Science,* 1974-80.

WORK IN PROGRESS: Associate editor, *American National Biography.*

SIDELIGHTS: Nathan Reingold told *CA:* "I am an academic but not in academe. I am the first person to have worked in our three great natural cultural institutions: National Archives, Library of Congress, Smithsonian Institution. My principal intellectual interest is to place the sciences within the context of American society."

*   *   *

RENEHAN, Edward J(ohn), Jr. 1956-

PERSONAL: Born August 7, 1956, in New York, NY; son of Edward John (a purchasing agent) and Joan (a homemaker; maiden name, Salvesen) Renehan; married Christa

Bartkovick (a graphic artist), August 24, 1985; children: William James, Katherine Eleanor. *Politics:* "Generally left of center."

ADDRESSES: Home—34 New St., Lynbrook, NY 11563. *Agent*—Julian Bach Literary Agency, 22 East Seventy-first St., New York, NY 10021.

CAREER: Writer.

WRITINGS:

(Editor) John Burroughs, *A River View and Other Hudson Valley Essays,* North River, 1981.
John Burroughs: An American Naturalist (biography), Chelsea Green, 1992.
The Secret Six (nonfiction), Crown, in press.

Contributor to periodicals, including *American Scholar, Conservationist,* and *Hudson Valley Magazine.*

SIDELIGHTS: Edward J. Renehan, Jr. is author of *John Burroughs: An American Naturalist,* a biography of the celebrated conservationist and nature writer of the late nineteenth and early twentieth centuries. Robert McCracken Peck, in his *New York Times Book Review* assessment of *John Burroughs,* described the legendary naturalist as "a champion of hard work and simple country living" and quoted the man who was the most popular nature writer of his time on his philosophy: "Wisdom cannot come by railroad or automobile, or aeroplane, or be hurried up by telegraph or telephone, [but only in] simple things, modest wants, agrarian independence and the value of a kinship to place." Renehan explained his own interest in Burroughs to *CA:* "Who could be more fascinating than a pioneer nineteenth-century naturalist and essayist who, long before the stylish environmentalism of our own day, wrote that cities were the 'devil's laboratory' and that, in order to endure, man had to develop a relationship with nature that did not 'vulgarize it and rob it of its divinity'?" Peck praised Renehan's book: "In *John Burroughs,* Mr. Renehan . . . [reveals] a far more complex and interesting man than other biographers have described."

Renehan told *CA:* "I am fascinated by the process of biography and historical narrative. Throughout my schooling, my two great loves were always the subjects of history and composition. Merging these two things, I find my voice as an author.

"The past—and, of particular importance to me, the American past—is full of wonderful untold stories that lay waiting down at the far ends of neglected corridors of memory, ready to enlighten us on the sources of the political and social milieu of our day.

"Today—amid the multitude of environmental, social, and ethical crises that confront us—we desperately need lore from the past that provides models of forbears who, guided by the light of their own sense of justice and truth, went against long odds to stand up for what they believed. We need to be reminded, for example, of George Luther Stearns, a figure in my forthcoming book *The Secret Six.* Stearns was a wealthy Boston merchant in the 1850s who risked literally everything he had (and also risked the gallows) to aid the abolitionist militiaman John Brown. So long as I can bring such men as John Burroughs and Stearns to life in my pages for the education and enlightenment of contemporaries who want their example, I'll feel that I'm doing good work."

BIOGRAPHICAL/CRITICAL SOURCES:

PERIODICALS

New York Times Book Review, December 13, 1992.

*   *   *

RIAHI-BELKAOUI, Ahmed   1943-
(Ahmed R. Belkaoui)

PERSONAL: Born December 1, 1943, in Zaghouan, Tunisia; naturalized U.S. citizen; married; wife's name, Janice; children: Hedi J. *Education:* Lycee Carnot, B.M.E., 1964; Universite de Tunis, H.E.C., 1967; University of Illinois, M.B.A., 1970; Syracuse University, Ph.D., 1973; Society of Management Accountants of Ontario, C.M.A., 1978. *Politics:* "Liberal and progressive." *Religion:* Muslim.

ADDRESSES: Home—253 East Delaware, No. 3G, Chicago, IL 60611. *Office*—College of Business Administration, University of Illinois at Chicago Circle, M/C 006, P.O. Box 802451, Chicago, IL 60680.

CAREER: University of Ottawa, Ottawa, Ontario, began as assistant professor, became associate professor, 1973-79, member of executive committee, 1976-78, associate professor, 1980-81; University of Illinois at Chicago Circle, Chicago, professor of accounting, 1981—, fellow of Honors College, 1982-84, member of executive committee, Social Science Data Archive, 1983-84, member of faculty research board, *Center for Human Resource Management,* 1992—. University of Chicago, visiting associate professor, 1979-80; lecturer at University of Quebec, Syracuse University, Carleton University, Sherbrooke University, University of Venice, University of Kuwait, and Irbid University; consultant to U.S. Army Corps of Engineers, U.S. Office of Personnel Management, and Institute for International Cooperation; manuscript reviewer for periodicals.

MEMBER: American Accounting Association (chair, Cultural Studies and Accounting Research Committee, 1988-89), Judgment and Decision Making Association,

Society of Management Accountants of Ontario, Beta Gamma Sigma.

AWARDS, HONORS: Grant from the government of Tunisia, 1964-67; scholarship from Agency for International Development, 1968-73; Seagram Business Faculty Award, 1973-74.

WRITINGS:

UNDER NAME AHMED R. BELKAOUI; ALL PUBLISHED BY GREENWOOD PRESS, EXCEPT WHERE INDICATED

The Conceptual Foundations of Management Accounting, Addison-Wesley, 1980.

Cost Accounting: A Multidimensional Emphasis, Dryden, 1983.

Industrial Bond Ratings and the Rating Process, 1983.

Socio-Economic Accounting, 1984.

Theorie Comptable, Presses de l'Universite du Quebec, 2nd edition, 1984.

Public Policy and the Problems and Practices of Accounting, 1985.

International Accounting: Issues and Solutions, 1985.

The Learning Curve: A Management Accounting Tool, 1986.

Handbook of Management Control Systems, 1986.

Quantitative Models in Accounting: A Guide to Practitioners, 1987.

The New Environment in International Accounting: Issues and Practices, 1987.

Inquiry and Accounting: Alternative Methods and Research Perspectives, 1987.

The Coming Crisis in Accounting, 1989.

Behavioral Accounting: The Research and Practical Issues, 1989.

Human Information Processing in Accounting, 1989.

Judgment in International Accounting: A Theory of Cognition, Cultures, Language, and Contracts, 1990.

(With Ellen Pavlik) *Determinants of Executive Compensation: Ownership, Performance, Firm Size, and Corporate Diversification,* 1991.

Multinational Management Accounting, 1991.

Multinational Financial Accounting, 1991.

Handbook of Cost Accounting: Theory and Techniques, 1991.

(With Janice Monti-Belkaoui) *Accounting for Economic Dualism,* 1991.

Accounting Theory, Academic Press, 3rd edition, 1992.

Value Added Reporting: The Lessons for the United States, 1992.

The New Foundations of Management Accounting, 1992.

(With Pavlik) *Accounting for Corporate Reputation,* 1992.

Morality in Accounting, 1992.

Work represented in anthologies, including *Cases, Readings, and Exercise in Canadian Financial Management,* edited by A. Kahl and W. Rentz, Holt, 1984. Contributor of numerous articles to periodicals, including *Managerial Finance* and *Journal of Business Finance and Accounting.* Member of editorial board, *Journal of Business Finance and Accounting,* 1985—, *Accounting, Auditing, and Accountability,* 1987-91, and *Middle-East Business and Economic Review,* 1987—; guest editor, *Managerial Finance,* 1991 and 1992.

WORK IN PROGRESS: Control for Quality and *Accounting for the Developing Countries.*

*   *   *

RICARDO, Jack 1940-

PERSONAL: Born January 27, 1940, in New York, NY; son of John (a television repair technician) and Nellie (a homemaker; maiden name, Swintek) Ricardo; companion of Allan. *Education:* Attended New York University. *Politics:* Democrat. *Religion:* "Former Catholic."

ADDRESSES: Home and office—4417 Southwest Sixty-sixth Terr., Davie, FL 33314. *Agent*—Lyle Steele, 511 East Seventy-third St., New York, NY 10021.

CAREER: Writer; *Michael's Thing,* New York City, film critic, early 1970s.

WRITINGS:

Death with Dignity (a mystery), Banned Books, 1991.
(Editor) *Leathermen Speak Out: An Anthology on Leathersex,* Leyland Publications, 1991.
The Night G. A. A. Died: A Mystery, St. Martin's, 1992.
Leathermen Speak Out II, Leyland Publications, 1993.

WORK IN PROGRESS: Steamed to Death, a mystery, and *Sam's Hill,* an epic western.

SIDELIGHTS: Jack Ricardo told *CA:* "I began writing in the early 1970s, as a film critic for *Michael's Thing,* a New York City gay guide. During the rest of the seventies, I was stoned. In the beginning of the 1980s I moved to Florida, cleared my mind of artificial stimulants, and penned my first mystery novel, *Y Murder* which I couldn't sell. After writing another mystery novel, *Smoked Glass,* which also didn't sell, I hit pay dirt. My third mystery novel, *Death with Dignity,* was picked up for publication by Banned Books. That same year, Leyland Publications also published my nonfiction work, *Leathermen Speak Out.* I then acquired an agent and a contract with St. Martin's Press, who published my first hardback Archie Cain mystery novel, *The Night G. A. A. Died,* which is the kick-off for a series of mysteries set in the gay playgrounds of New York City during the promiscuous 1970s."

RICH, Matty 1971-

PERSONAL: Given name, Matthew Satisfield Richardson; born November 26, 1971, in Brooklyn, NY; son of Beatrice Richardson. *Education:* Attended John Jay College and New York University.

ADDRESSES: Agent—Michael Gruber, William Morris Agency, 1350 Avenue of the Americas, New York, NY 10019; Terrie Williams, 1841 Broadway, Suite 914, New York, NY 10023.

CAREER: Screenwriter, director, and producer of motion pictures.

AWARDS, HONORS: Special jury prize, Sundance Film Festival, 1991, for *Straight out of Brooklyn;* NOVA Award, most promising director, Producer's Guild of America, 1992; Independent Spirit Award, 1992; NAACP's Special Award for Filmmaking.

WRITINGS:

(And director) *Straight out of Brooklyn* (screenplay), 1991.

Also author and director of *Ray Mercer vs. Tommy Morrison Pre-fight Profiles,* for TVKO/Time Warner Sports; author of the nonfiction work *Short-term and Long-term Thinking.*

WORK IN PROGRESS: The Forty Thieves, a screenplay; scripts for *Red Hook,* an hour-long television drama being developed for Fox.

SIDELIGHTS: While still a teenager, Matty Rich served as screenwriter, director, and producer of *Straight out of Brooklyn,* his autobiographical film depicting a young man's desperate attempt to escape his violent, crime-ridden environment. *Detroit News* film critic Susan Stark deemed Rich's coming-of-age story "terrifying and tragic." For Rich, such a description was also appropriate for his life. *Straight out of Brooklyn*'s main character was based on Rich's best friend, Lamont, who died of an untreated kidney problem while in a juvenile home. The filmmaker's aunt and uncle both died on Rich's birthday (she had a heart attack in a hospital, he was robbed and shot at a bus stop on his way to see her), and each of the six friends he had as an adolescent also died. Rage about the senselessness of these happenings served as a motivating factor for his screen venture. Rich explained to Richard Corliss in *Time,* "I wasn't interested in film because I love film or some director. . . . I was angry that everybody around me got destroyed, and I wanted to show that everyday struggle."

Rich began making *Straight out of Brooklyn* when he was seventeen years old and employed ingenious methods to pay for the project. Using his sister and mother's credit cards, he financed a short trailer that was featured on a New York radio station, hoping to solicit investors for the movie. By chance, he also met Jonathan Demme, Academy Award-winning director of 1991's *Silence of the Lambs,* who was impressed with Rich's vision and helped him procure funding from television's Public Broadcasting Service (PBS-TV). Made on a budget of $300,000, *Straight out of Brooklyn* was featured at both the Cannes and Sundance film festivals and met with critical and box-office success.

In *Straight out of Brooklyn,* protagonist Dennis Brown lives in a low-income Brooklyn housing project. His father, a Vietnam veteran, is a gas station attendant who blames his economic position on racism and vents his frustrations by drinking to excess and beating his defeated wife who, in turn, tries to shrug off the bruises. This fighting wears on Dennis; he anticipates his father's frequent rages with dread, but attributes both parents' actions to their seemingly inescapable socioeconomic position. In a desperate attempt to halt the cycle of violence and hopelessness, Dennis masterminds a money-making scheme to leave the projects. Along with his friends Larry—played by Rich—and Kevin, Dennis robs a local drug dealer. With a briefcase of money, he dreams of a new life in a safe environment with his family and girlfriend. Rich, however, shows that the problem of poverty cannot be mended with superficial tactics. *Straight out of Brooklyn* ends with Dennis fearing reprisal from the drug dealer and witnessing a family tragedy.

Reviewers and audiences generally lauded Rich's uncompromising portrait of ghetto life in *Straight out of Brooklyn.* Some deemed the work more powerful because of its unhappy ending. Several critics judged Rich's camera work somewhat unpolished, but felt that the emotion and gritty vision he brought to the screen made up for shortcomings in technique. A *Newsweek* writer asserted, "*Straight out of Brooklyn* is a blunt instrument, but that's one reason it works. . . . The violence feels immediate and random. The wrong people die for the wrong reasons; life goes on unaffected." A *Rolling Stone* contributor noted that Rich "carved an unshakable movie out of his rage."

Rich garnered the immediate attention of movie moguls with his first film venture and he welcomed the acclaim *Straight out of Brooklyn* received. The director explained to *Premiere* contributor David Sternbach, "I worked hard for it, and I deserve the recognition of being an up-and-coming filmmaker. I'm not a boy genius. I'm just a young man who had something to say, who wanted to express it on film." Rich, however, puts the attention in perspective: In *Time* he admitted, "If I hadn't done this movie, I'd be just another black kid on the street with a gold tooth and a funny haircut."

BIOGRAPHICAL/CRITICAL SOURCES:

PERIODICALS

Detroit Free Press, June 23, 1991, pp. 1G, 6G; June 28, 1991, pp. 1D, 3D.
Detroit News, June 20, 1991, pp. 1C, 3-4C; June 28, 1991, pp. 3D, 9D.
Ebony, November, 1991, pp. 156-164.
Elle, June, 1991, pp. 60-61.
Newsweek, May 27, 1991, p. 58.
New York Times Magazine, July 14, 1991, pp. 15-19, 38, 40, 44.
Premiere, July, 1991, pp. 20, 26-27.
Rolling Stone, June 13, 1991, p. 108.
Time, June 17, 1991, pp. 64-68.

*   *   *

RICHARDSON, John   1924-
(Richard Johnson)

PERSONAL: Born in 1924, in London, England; father was a general. *Education:* Attended Slade School of Art, London.

ADDRESSES: Home— New York, NY.

CAREER: Art critic, editor, and biographer. *New Statesman,* London, England, art, ballet, and fiction critic; affiliated with Christie's, New York City; vice president of Knoedler's (an art gallery); managing director of Artemis (a consortium of art dealers); exhibition organizer; art adviser.

AWARDS, HONORS: Received Whitbread Award for *A Life of Picasso: Volume I, 1881-1906.*

WRITINGS:

Manet, Phaidon, 1967, revised edition with notes by Kathleen Adler, Salem House, 1984.
(Editor) *The Collection of Germain Seligman: Paintings, Drawings, and Works of Art,* E. V. Thaw, 1979.
(With the collaboration of Marilyn McCully) *A Life of Picasso: Volume I, 1881-1906,* Random House, 1991.

Contributor to *Late Picasso: Paintings, Sculpture, Drawings, Prints, 1953-1972,* University of Washington Press, 1989; contributor to periodicals, sometimes under the pseudonym Richard Johnson, including *New Statesman, New York Review of Books,* and *House and Garden.*

EXHIBITION CATALOGUES

(Editor with Eric Zafran) *Master Paintings from the Hermitage and the State Russian Museum, Leningrad,* M. Knoedler, 1975.
(Preparer) *Corot and Courbet,* D. Carritt, Ltd., 1979.

Through the Eye of Picasso, 1928-1934: The Dinard Sketchbook and Related Paintings and Sculpture, W. Beadleston, 1985.

Contributor to *Douglas Cooper und die Meister des Kubismus* (title means "Douglas Cooper and the Masters of Cubism"), text and catalogue by Dorothy M. Kosinski, Kunstmuseum Basel, 1987; and *Nicolas de Stael in America,* Phillips Collection, 1990.

WORK IN PROGRESS: The second volume of *A Life of Picasso.*

SIDELIGHTS: John Richardson, an art critic, editor, and biographer, told Grace Glueck of the *New York Times:* "Writing about Picasso is a minefield. . . . With him, you have to leave everything open-ended, leave room for another interpretation. You can't slam the door on anything." The master painter Pablo Picasso allegedly thought of his work as his diary, and, using that belief as a premise, Richardson seeks to link the artist's life with his paintings in *A Life of Picasso: Volume I, 1881-1906,* the first installment of a proposed four-volume biography. "Already," he told the *New York Times Book Review,* "people are starting to fictionalize, historicize, politicize, and psychoanalyze [Picasso's] work, and already they are arriving at absurd conclusions because they're not sufficiently familiar with the facts of the artist's life."

Richardson—who has also written a study on the French painter Edouard Manet and criticism for periodicals—became a friend of Picasso while living in the south of France in the 1950s. Because of his relationship with the artist, who died in 1973, the anticipation preceding the publication of *A Life of Picasso* was some of the most heated in the history of biography; both art historians and the general public were anxious to glimpse the intimate look at the revolutionary painter the book promised. *A Life of Picasso* examines Picasso's first twenty-five years, beginning with his childhood in Spain and following him to his first years in Paris. Sometimes able to reconstruct day by day accounts of Picasso's life with the help of research provided by the art historian Marilyn McCully, Richardson attempts to reconcile the many versions of the painter's youth into one truthful, definitive work.

One of the ways Richardson illuminates truth is by eliminating the myths that surround the artist. Richardson writes that Picasso was not a child prodigy—he is often compared to the composer Wolfgang Amadeus Mozart—but that his skill was a result of hard practice. He also notes that Picasso's father, an unsuccessful painter of pigeons who encouraged his son's artistic interests, did not surrender his brush to his son upon witnessing Picasso's ability but continued to paint for many years. In addition, Richardson evokes the rough, bohemian lifestyle Picasso adopted when he traveled to Paris in 1900, and describes the mistresses and artists with whom Picasso associated at the time, a circle that included the writer Gertrude Stein and fellow painter Henri Matisse. Richardson closes the first volume as Picasso prepares to paint *Les Demoiselles d'Avignon,* the canvas that would revolutionize the world of art by introducing the Cubist movement.

Critics found that *A Life of Picasso* met their expectations. "A remarkable achievement . . .," *New York Times Book Review* contributor John Russell wrote. "Not only Picasso himself, but all those with whom he came into close contact—friends, lovers, colleagues, nonentities and men and women of genius—are brought to rounded life." In *Maclean's,* Pamela Young commented that Richardson's "book is a remarkably evocative study of a formidable artist's emerging greatness." Comparing *A Life of Picasso* to Richard Ellmann's National Book Award-winning biography *James Joyce, Time* reviewer Robert Hughes wrote: "Richardson is a born storyteller, with a vivid sense of detail and character that enables him to deal with the large cast of players entangled in Picasso's early life."

Aside from these appraisals of Richardson's ability to bring Picasso and the people with whom he associated to life, Hilton Kramer, writing in the *Washington Post Book World,* praised the critical aspect of Richardson's work: "His analysis of the paintings of the Blue period and the Rose period—the high points of Picasso's achievement in the years covered by this first volume—is the best I have read anywhere, and so is his account of the way Picasso responded to certain earlier artists . . . in his own early work." In the *Los Angeles Times Book Review,* Peter Schjeldahl wrote, "Richardson's strongest suit is a running analysis of Picasso's stylistic evolution that makes [the painters] El Greco, [Francisco] Goya and [Paul] Gauguin as vividly present in the book as any friend or mistress." Kramer also praised the overall impact of *A Life of Picasso:* "This is a book that shows every sign of changing the course of biographical writing about the major figures of the modern movement. . . . If the sheer brilliance of this first installment can be sustained throughout the remainder of the work, Richardson will have written not only one of the great biographies but a book likely to illuminate a good deal . . . about the life of the spirit in this turbulent century."

BIOGRAPHICAL/CRITICAL SOURCES:

PERIODICALS

Los Angeles Times Book Review, February 24, 1991, pp. 1, 9.
Maclean's, April 22, 1991, p. 65.
New York Times, March 19, 1991, pp. C11, C18.
New York Times Book Review, March 3, 1991, pp. 1, 20-21; December 1, 1991, p. 3.
Time, February 19, 1991, pp. 65-66.

Tribune Books (Chicago), February 24, 1991, p. 5.
Washington Post Book World, February 10, 1991, pp. 1, 8.*

—*Sketch by Roger M. Valade III*

*   *   *

RIDLEY, Philip

ADDRESSES: Office—c/o British Academy of Film and Television Arts, 195 Piccadilly, London W1, England.

CAREER: Writer and film director.

AWARDS, HONORS: Smarties Book Prize, 1991.

WRITINGS:

ADULT FICTION

In the Eyes of My Fury (novel), Penguin, 1989.
Flamingoes in Orbit (stories), Hamish Hamilton, 1990.

YOUNG ADULT NOVELS

Dakota of the White Flats, Knopf, 1991.
Krindlekrax; or, How Rushkin Splinter Battled a Horrible Monster and Saved His Entire Neighborhood, illustrated by Gary Hovland, Knopf, 1991.

SCREENPLAYS

The Krays, Miramax, 1990.
(And director) *The Reflecting Skin,* Miramax, 1991.

OTHER

Also author of the play *The Pitchfork Disney,* produced in 1991.

SIDELIGHTS: Philip Ridley has won acclaim for his unsettling explorations of various aspects of childhood in his stories, novels, and plays for the stage and screen. He began his career in 1989 with *In the Eyes of My Fury,* a novel about a boy who uncovers some disturbing secrets regarding his mother's past. In the process, the youth makes some equally discomforting realizations about the destructiveness of his small community's ostensibly righteous morality. London *Times* reviewer Anne Barnes, while expressing some reservations about the novel, conceded that "it is skillfully done."

Ridley followed his first novel with *Flamingoes in Orbit,* a series of horrific stories that frequently concentrate on childhood. In one tale, two boys covet photographs of war atrocities; in another, youths gleefully prod a dolphin with pitchforks. Elsewhere in the collection, a boy begins to giggle uncontrollably while in a classroom listening to a blind Holocaust survivor. The boy is forced to go to the woman's home to apologize, at which time—to her igno-

rance—he tosses her pregnant cat from the twenty-fourth floor. Roz Kaveney, in her *Times Literary Supplement* appraisal, noted thematic similarities among the thirteen tales comprising *Flamingoes in Orbit,* and she declared that "the power of the book, as a whole, derives from the ways in which . . . different voices blend in a single cry of frustration and regret."

Ridley has also written two novels for young adults. *Dakota of the White Flats,* which was published in 1991, is set in a group of apartment buildings in lower-class London. Among the area residents are Dakota Pink, the adventurous ten-year-old girl whose observations provide the book's narration, and Treacle, her companion. As Meg Wolitzer noted in the *New York Times Book Review:* "Everyone here has a slightly surreal quality." Notably peculiar is Dakota's mother, who has spent the last nine years inside her flat, where she is content to consume dumplings and read romance novels while futilely awaiting her husband's return. Other characters include Medusa, a former actress who strolls the area with a shopping cart lined with cabbage leaves, and Henry Twig, a gruesome fellow with an extraordinary fear of silverfish. Wolitzer proclaimed *Dakota of the White Flats* "first-rate entertainment that manages to be tender as well as truly funny."

In *Krindlekrax,* Ridley's next novel for young adults, a meek youth comes to battle a terrifying creature dwelling beneath a neighborhood street. The hero, Rushkin, manages to overcome his reserved nature and save his family and friends. Like *Dakota of the White Flats, Krindlekrax* features a host of bizarre characters, including a demure mother constantly proffering tea and toast and a destructive bully named Elvis.

Though fiction has been the bulk of Ridley's production, he has also distinguished himself in film. In 1990 he produced the script for director Peter Medak's *The Krays,* a crime drama about the monstrous twins that actually reigned in the London underworld during the 1960s. The sadistic brothers, dominated by their frighteningly doting mother, indulge their violent predilections while terrorizing the London club scene, but their demise is not an enviable one. Hal Hinson, in his *Washington Post* review, described *The Krays* as "an Oedipal gangster film" and contended that the film "is most enticing when the psychological atmosphere is thick with unresolved sexual suggestiveness." And Janet Maslin, in her assessment for the *New York Times,* observed that *The Krays* "eerily intertwines the brothers' criminal exploits with their attitudes about love and family."

Ridley both wrote and directed *The Reflecting Skin,* a 1991 drama set in a bleak community in the American Midwest during the end of World War II. Here, young Seth Dove lives a singularly harrowing childhood. His friend has been abducted and murdered by homosexuals. Seth's father, suspected of playing a part in the boy's disappearance, commits suicide by self-immolation. Seth's life is further disrupted by the arrival of his brother, Cameron, who has returned home after participating in nuclear bomb tests in the South Pacific. Once home, Cameron commences an affair with Blue, a widow whom Seth believes to be a vampire who is associated with his friend's demise. *The Reflecting Skin* has been compared to the unnerving and occasionally violent films of director David Lynch.

Among Ridley's other works is *The Pitchfork Disney*, a play about brother-and-sister twins obsessed with their dead parents. The twins, though fully grown, nonetheless are content to behave as children. Their twisted existence together is disrupted by the arrival of an intrusive teenager who chews on live cockroaches. The youth, it is soon disclosed, has himself suffered a traumatic childhood. London *Times* reviewer Benedict Nightingale, who called *The Pitchfork Disney* a "grotesque comedy," averred that Ridley "appears to think of childhood in the same way a joint of meat might think of the slaughterhouse."

BIOGRAPHICAL/CRITICAL SOURCES:

PERIODICALS

American Film, July, 1991, p. 53.
Chicago Tribune, November 9, 1990.
New Statesman and Society, May 11, 1990, p. 40; November 9, 1990, p. 40.
Newsweek, November 26, 1990, p. 78.
New York Times, November 9, 1990.
New York Times Book Review, September 15, 1991, p. 27.
Times (London), February 11, 1989; May 3, 1990; January 7, 1991, p. 14.
Times Educational Supplement, February 24, 1989, p. B8.
Times Literary Supplement, June 22, 1990, p. 674.
Washington Post, November 9, 1990.*

—*Sketch by Les Stone*

*   *   *

RIGNEY, James Oliver, Jr. 1948-
(Robert Jordan, Chang Lung, Reagan O'Neal, Jackson O'Reilly)

PERSONAL: Born October 17, 1948, in Charleston, SC; son of James Oliver and Eva May (Grooms) Rigney; married Harriet Stoney Popham McDougal, March 28, 1981; children: William Popham McDougal. *Education:* The Citadel, B.S., 1974.

ADDRESSES: Home—129 Tradd St., Charleston, SC 29401.

CAREER: U.S. Civil Service, nuclear engineer, 1974-78; free-lance writer, 1978—.

MEMBER: Science Fiction Writers of America.

WRITINGS:

UNDER PSEUDONYM ROBERT JORDAN; "CONAN" FANTASY SERIES; ALL PUBLISHED BY TOM DOHERTY

Conan the Invincible, 1982.
Conan the Defender, 1982.
Conan the Triumphant, c. 1983.
Conan the Unconquered, c. 1983.
Conan the Destroyer, 1984.
Conan the Magnificent, c. 1984.
Conan the Victorious, 1985.

UNDER PSEUDONYM ROBERT JORDAN; "WHEEL OF TIME" FANTASY SERIES

The Eye of the World, Tom Doherty, 1990.
The Great Hunt, Tom Doherty, 1990.
The Dragon Reborn, Tor Books, 1991.
The Shadow Rising, Tor Books, 1992.

OTHER

Author (under pseudonym Reagan O'Neal) of books in the "Fallon" series, including *The Fallon Blood*, 1980; *The Fallon Pride*, 1981; *The Fallon Legacy*, 1982. Also author (under pseudonym Jackson O'Reilly) of *Cheyenne Raiders* (novel), 1982. Contributor, sometimes under pseudonym Chang Lung, to periodicals, including *Library Journal*.

SIDELIGHTS: James Oliver Rigney, Jr., writing under various pseudonyms, is a prolific author of genre fiction. As Robert Jordan, he has produced several fantasy volumes featuring the heroic Conan, a powerful barbarian who roams a magical land of strange creatures and supernatural villains. Among these works—which are based on a character created in the 1950s by Texan Robert Howard—are *Conan the Invincible, Conan the Unconquered*, and *Conan the Triumphant*. Rigney's other writings under the Jordan pseudonym include the "Wheel of Time" fantasy series about the struggle between good and evil in a long-ago land of brutality and sorcery. Among the works in this series are *The Eye of the World, The Great Hunt*, and *The Dragon Reborn*. Rigney has also produced many other writings, including—as Chang Lung—dance reviews.

BIOGRAPHICAL/CRITICAL SOURCES:

PERIODICALS

Fantasy Review, August, 1984, p. 12; September, 1984, p. 30
Science Fiction Review, February, 1983; p. 31; May, 1983, p. 55.*

RINDERLE, Walter 1940-

PERSONAL: Born August 31, 1940, in Vincennes, IN; son of Joseph (in business) and Mildred Rinderle; married Christin Fischer (a registered nurse), 1974; children: Christina, Christopher. *Education:* Attended St. Meinrad College, 1958-62; received M.A. and S.T.L. from State University of Innsbruck; received M.A. and Ph.D. from University of Notre Dame. *Religion:* Roman Catholic.

ADDRESSES: Home—R.R.6, E-2, Vincennes, IN 47591.

CAREER: Vincennes University, Vincennes, IN, instructor, 1969-71; College of the Holy Cross, Worcester, MA, instructor, 1985-87; St. Mary's College, Notre Dame, IN, instructor, 1974-84; Vincennes University, instructor, 1989—.

WRITINGS:

(With Bernard Norling) *The Nazi Impact on a German Village,* University Press of Kentucky, 1992.
Two Hundred Years of Catholic Education in Knox County, Indiana, 1792-1992, Jostens, 1993.

SIDELIGHTS: Walter Rinderle told *CA:* "My major academic interests are local history (United States and Germany), speech, anthropology, English composition, and economics. These are subjects that I have taught over the years.

"I am concerned with social problems, and have given many years of my life to help low-income families and those who are facing rejection. I believe we need to teach our young people that they should care about others—that by giving of themselves, they will find happiness. I think that values, similar to the ten commandments, are important for any society to survive."

*   *   *

RING, Jennifer 1948-

PERSONAL: Born November 18, 1948, in Los Angeles, CA; daughter of George Joseph (in auto sales) and Frances (a writer and editor; maiden name, Kroll) Ring; married Norman Jacobson (a professor), August 24, 1979; children: Johanna, Lillian. *Education:* Attended University of Edinburgh, 1968-69; University of California, Los Angeles, B.A., 1970; attended London School of Economics and Political Science, London, 1970-71; received M.A. and Ph.D. from University of California, Berkeley.

ADDRESSES: Home—3 Lakecrest Dr., Columbia, SC 29206. *Office*—Department of Government and International Studies, University of South Carolina at Columbia, Columbia, SC 29208.

CAREER: Columbia University, New York City, assistant professor of political science, 1979-80; University of California, Berkeley, lecturer in political science, 1981-85; Stanford University, Stanford, CA, lecturer in political science, 1981-85; University of South Carolina at Columbia, associate professor of government and international studies, 1989—.

WRITINGS:

Modern Political Theory and Contemporary Feminism: A Dialectical Analysis, State University of New York Press, 1991.

Contributor to books, including *Competition: A Feminist Taboo?*

WORK IN PROGRESS: The Political Consequences of Thinking: Hannah Arendt's Search for a Worldly Philosophy.

*   *   *

ROBBINS, Lawrence H. 1938-

PERSONAL: Born November 22, 1938; married Martha Edwards; children: four. *Education:* University of Michigan, A.B. and A.M., both 1961; University of California, Berkeley, Ph.D., 1968.

ADDRESSES: Office—Department of Anthropology, Michigan State University, East Lansing, MI 48824.

CAREER: University of California, Berkeley, lecturer, 1964; University of Utah, Salt Lake City, assistant professor, 1967-68; Michigan State University, East Lansing, assistant professor, 1968 and 1971, associate professor, 1972-1976, professor of anthropology, 1977—, currently chair of department of anthropology, coordinator of Consortium for Archaeological Research Center, and adjunct curator of Michigan State University Museum. University of Maryland at College Park, lecturer, 1965; University of Nairobi, visiting research associate, 1969-70; National Museums of Kenya and British Institute, visiting research associate, 1974-75; University of Botswana, visiting lecturer, 1982-83. Has contributed to museum exhibits and research collections.

MEMBER: Southern African Archaeological Society, Society for Africanist Archaeologists in America, American Anthropological Association (fellow), Botswana Society.

AWARDS, HONORS: Grants from National Science Foundation, 1965-66, 1969-70, 1975-77, 1991-92, and 1992, from Michigan State University, 1979, 1985-86, 1990, and 1991-92, and from *National Geographic,* 1987 and 1989; named Outstanding Teacher, Michigan State University Department of Anthropology, 1979 and 1986; Fulbright fellow, 1982-83.

WRITINGS:

The Lothagam Site (monograph), appendix by Brian M. Fagan, Michigan State University Museum, 1974.

(With J. L. Angel, T. W. Phenice, and B. M. Lynch) *Late Stone Age Fisherman of Lothagam Kenya* (monograph), Michigan State University Museum, 1980.

Lopoy, a Late Stone Age Fishing and Pastoralist Settlement West of Lake Turkana, Kenya (monograph), Michigan State University Museum, 1980.

The Archaeologist's Eye: Great Discoveries, Missing Links, and Ancient Treasures, Hale, 1989, published as *Stones, Bones and Ancient Cities: Great Discoveries in Archaeology and the Search for Human Origins,* St. Martin's, 1990.

Work represented in anthologies, including *Adventures of Anthropology,* edited by W. J. Kennedy, West Publishing, 1977, and *From Hunters to Farmers,* edited by J. D. Clark and S. Brandt, University of California Press, 1984. Contributor of numerous articles to periodicals, including *Science, Current Anthropology,* and *Botswana Notes and Records.* Editor of Michigan State University's African Studies Center Monograph series, 1980-82; member of editorial board of Michigan State University Museum Anthropological Publication Series.

The Archaeologist's Eye: Great Discoveries, Missing Links, and Ancient Treasures was translated into Japanese.

*   *   *

ROCHELLE, Mercedes 1955-

PERSONAL: Born March 5, 1955, in St. Louis, MO; daughter of John T. and Antoinette (Marin) Mulderig. *Education:* University of Missouri—St. Louis, B.A. *Avocational interests:* Medieval history.

ADDRESSES: Home—P.O. Box 70, Lambertville, NJ 08530.

CAREER: Writer.

MEMBER: Society for Creative Anachronism.

WRITINGS:

Historical Art Index, A.D. 400-1650, McFarland and Co., 1989.

Mythological and Classical World Art Index, McFarland and Co., 1991.

Post-Biblical Saints Art Index, McFarland and Co., in press.

Contributor to *Military History.*

SIDELIGHTS: Mercedes Rochelle told *CA:* "I started my career as an indexer of artwork by one of those accidents that took me away from what I considered my real interest: medieval history and historical fiction. While writing an article for *Military History* magazine, I spent more time researching the illustrations than constructing the story. I was amazed that I couldn't find any indexes that arranged art by subject; without knowing the artist's name, a researcher was out of luck. I began my first subject index as an answer to the dilemma at hand: trying to find pictures that illustrated the battle of Flodden Field.

"My art indexes are a continuing project to catalog all the narrative and non-genre paintings I can discover in the Western world—a lifetime's work, I suspect. In the indexes (one book per subject), I have arranged the entries chronologically under alphabetically arranged subject headings, complete with the piece's location and other books where the piece is reproduced.

"Ironically, while attempting to make the researcher's job a little easier, I accidentally taught myself how to appreciate and understand art. By now I've studied thousands of paintings, sculptures, frescoes, manuscript illuminations, drawings, and engravings. Because I must study the piece's content, rather than style, I came to understand medieval history in ways I never would have learned through scholarly books. The artists depicted scenes and legends that are practically lost to the modern world. Events I couldn't find in dictionaries and encyclopedias must have been common knowledge to contemporaries.

"It's even more fascinating to watch how themes developed over the centuries, and how certain eras tended to emphasize subjects that earlier or later generations neglected. For instance, after the sixteenth century, we start seeing allegorical paintings about Hercules (choosing between vice and virtue, or his apotheosis), whereas the earlier pieces put him into a much more aggressive, fighting role. Or, St. Christopher was a great favorite in the fifteenth and sixteenth centuries, whereas I found few references to him in the seventeenth and fewer yet in the eighteenth century. Try finding any saints at all in nineteenth-century art; they are comparatively rare, while mythology continued to find its supporters.

"This line of work is beginning to suggest several different directions I might take, and I anticipate delving deeper into subjects I have come to know almost exclusively through art. With a little luck, I may eventually get back to my historical fiction with a more enlightened vision."

*   *   *

ROCKWELL, Theodore (III) 1922-

PERSONAL: Born June 26, 1922, in Chicago, IL; son of Theodore Griffith (an insurance executive) and Paisley (a homemaker; maiden name, Shane) Rockwell; married Mary Juanita Compton (an artist), January 25, 1947; children: Robert C., W. Teed, Larry E., Juanita. *Education:* Princeton University, B.S., 1943, M.S., 1945; attended Oak Ridge School of Reactor Technology, 1947. *Politics:* Independent. *Religion:* Presbyterian.

ADDRESSES: Home and office—3403 Woolsey Dr., Chevy Chase, MD 20815. *Agent*—Perry Knowlton, Curtis Brown Ltd., 10 Astor Pl., New York, NY 10003.

CAREER: Atomic Bomb Project, Oak Ridge, TN, process improvement engineer, 1944-49; U.S. Atomic Energy Commission, director of Nuclear Technology Divisions for the commission and the U.S. Navy, 1949-54, technical director of Admiral Rickover's Nuclear Power Program, 1954-64; MPR Associates, Inc. (engineering firm), Washington, DC, founder, 1964, principal officer, 1964-87; free-lance writer and engineer in Chevy Chase, MD, 1988—. Johns Hopkins University, research associate at Center for Foreign Policy Research, 1965-68. National Artificial Heart Program, non-medical member of advisory group, 1966; Atomic Industrial Forum, chairperson of Reactor Safety Task Force, 1966-72; awarded several patents; consultant to Joint Congressional Committee on Atomic Energy. Public speaker, including lectures at National War College, Smithsonian Institution, Theosophical Society, and National Spiritual Science Center.

MEMBER: American Nuclear Society, U.S. Naval Institute, Naval Submarine League, Parapsychological Association, Institute of Noetic Sciences, National Press Club, Washington Independent Writers, Writers Center, Cosmos Club.

AWARDS, HONORS: Distinguished Civilian Service Medal from U.S. Navy; Distinguished Service Medal from U.S. Atomic Energy Commission; William A. Jump Award for Exemplary Achievement in Public Administration from U.S. Navy and U.S. Atomic Energy Commission; Lifetime Achievement Award (renamed Rockwell Award) from American Nuclear Society; Sc.D. from Tri-State University, 1960.

WRITINGS:

(Editor) *The Reactor Shielding Design Manual,* McGraw, 1956.
(With members of the Naval Reactors Branch, U.S. Atomic Energy Commission) *The Shippingport Pressurized Water Reactor,* Addison-Wesley, 1958.
(With David W. Wainhouse, Bernhard G. Bechhoefer, Harry D. Hughes, and others) *Arms Control Agreements: Designs for Verification,* Johns Hopkins Press, 1968.
The Rickover Effect: How One Man Made a Difference, Naval Institute Press, 1992.

Author of *Vice Versa,* an unpublished trilogy of one-act plays, 1990. Contributor to scientific journals and other periodicals, including *Saturday Evening Post, True, Journal of Parapsychology, Research in Parapsychology, Zetetic Scholar,* and *New Realities.* Co-founder, *Princeton Engineer,* 1941.

WORK IN PROGRESS: A book "intended to show atomic energy through the lives of people involved with it"; a book on "how social action groups, now at war with each other, might work together."

SIDELIGHTS: Theodore Rockwell told *CA:* "I've done writing as far back as I can remember. At Princeton, I worked on the *Princeton Sunday News,* an 'alternative newspaper,' and the *Sovereign,* a literary magazine edited by fellow student Malcolm Forbes, and I was a co-founder of the *Princeton Engineer* which, in 1991, celebrated its fiftieth anniversary of continuous publication. This experience trained me, not only in writing, but also in the allied skills of editing, design, composition, typography, and the like.

"I tried my hand at playwriting as well, working with the Playwrights Forum in Washington. I wrote a trilogy of one-act plays, very different from one another but with a common thread. It was actually given a staged reading, with professional actors and a director, but I was dissatisfied with the ephemeral nature of theater. Once the sounds of a performance die, the piece is gone. I feel more comfortable with a book, which has some permanence. You can achieve that with film, too, but with films the author has no control over the final product.

"As an engineer, I have always been sensitive to the perception that engineers can't write. I was particularly pleased, then, when Connie Buchanan, the editor of Tom Clancy's eminently readable novel *Hunt for Red October,* agreed to critique the original unedited manuscript for *The Rickover Effect* and wrote that it was 'an excellent manuscript by any standards.'

"I have been fortunate in being in on some very exciting and important projects, and in being there from the beginning. In each case, I was able to put down, in the public record, information that was otherwise unavailable and which I thought people should know. First I wrote about the opening of the atomic age in wartime Oak Ridge, Tennessee, and then about the practical harnessing of a fearsome weapon for peaceful purposes.

"I have also been close to the pioneers of consciousness research: mind/body interactions, psychic phenomena, and experiments in altered states of consciousness. This important work is largely ridiculed by mainstream scientists, and its spiritual implications are shunned by most religious leaders. This has led to my interest in how and why we fear new ideas and what can be done to open up our institutions and combat in-fighting among various apostles of social change. In pursuing this interest, I have talked with swamis, yogis, shamans, and lamas (including the Dalai Lama) and have dabbled with fire-walking, metal-bending, and other mind games."

*   *   *

RODARMOR, William 1942-

PERSONAL: Surname is pronounced *Road*-uh-more; born June 5, 1942, in New York City; son of Charles J. (an investment banker) and Virginia (a contractor; maiden name, Haughwout) Rodarmor; married Thaisa Frank (a writer), May 11, 1980; children: Casey (son). *Education:* Dartmouth College, A.B., 1966; Columbia University, J.D., 1969; University of California, Berkeley, M.J., 1984. *Religion:* Zen Buddhist.

ADDRESSES: Home—Oakland, CA. *Office*—*California Monthly,* Alumni House, Berkeley, CA 94720.

CAREER: Lawyer in San Francisco, CA, 1969-70; freelance writer, 1970-86; *PC World,* San Francisco, associate editor, 1986-89; *California Monthly,* Berkeley, managing editor, 1989—. *East Bay Review,* associate publisher, 1975-78. Translator from French, 1971—. California State Bar, inactive member. *Military service:* U.S. Army, 1961-64.

WRITINGS:

TRANSLATOR

Bernard Moltessier, *The Long Way,* Doubleday, 1972.
Fishes of Polynesia, Hachette, 1973.
The Carnivorous Lamb, David Godine, 1984.
Denis Belloc, *Neons,* David Godine, 1991.
Denis Belloc, *Slow Death in Paris,* David Godine, 1992.

OTHER

(Editor) *People Behind the News,* Media Alliance, 1984.
(Editor) *Twelve Myths About World Hunger,* Grove, 1986.

Contributor of articles and reviews to periodicals, including *California Lawyer, East West Journal, CoEvolution Quarterly, Popular Photography,* and *Berkeley Monthly.*

WORK IN PROGRESS: Translating from the French *Savage Nights,* by Cyril Collard, for Quartet Books, and *Catherine Certitude,* by Modiani, for David Godine.

SIDELIGHTS: William Rodarmor told *CA:* "I'm a journalist partly because journalism is a form of subsidized nosiness. I'm a translator because of the pleasure of making good books available to people who couldn't otherwise read them. My most notable accomplishment was sailing solo from Tahiti to Hawaii in 1971. I celebrated my fiftieth birthday by going bungee-jumping."

*   *   *

RODDICK, Anita (Lucia) 1942-

PERSONAL: Born October 23, 1942, in Littlehampton, West Sussex, England; daughter of Henry Perilli (a cafe co-owner) and Gilda De Vita (a cafe co-owner); married Thomas Gordon Roddick (a poet), 1970; children: Justine, Samantha. *Education:* Graduated from Bath College of Education, 1962. *Politics:* "Active: Amuse, Challenge, Teach, Inspire, Vex, and Energize." *Avocational interests:* Music, theatre, film, the arts, travel, "talking to radical thinkers."

ADDRESSES: Office—The Body Shop International PLC, Watersmead, Littlehampton, West Sussex BN17 6LS, England.

CAREER: Co-owner and manager of restaurant, Littlehampton, West Sussex, England, 1962-76; founder of the Body Shop (skin and hair care company), Brighton, Sussex, England, 1976; group managing director of the Body Shop International PLC, Littlehampton, 1984—. Formerly a teacher; worked at clip desk of *Herald Tribune* (Paris office); studied women's rights in Third World countries for the United Nations Labor Organization.

MEMBER: Amnesty International, Cultural Survival, Social Venture Network, Business for Social Responsibility.

AWARDS, HONORS: Veuve Clicquot Business Woman of the Year, 1985; Cognac Otard Achievement of the Year Award and Burson-Marstellar Business Enterprise Award, Confederacy of British Industry, both 1987; received an Order of the British Empire on the Queen's New Year Honours List, and Women of Achievement Award, *Woman's Own,* both 1988; United Nations "Global 500" Environment Award, 1989; named a Woman Who Has Made a Difference, International Women's Forum, 1990; Analysis Award, *Financial Evening Standard,* 1991; World Vision awards, Centre for World Development Education, 1991 and 1992, both for the Body Shop's "Trade Not Aid" Initiatives. Honorary degrees from University of Sussex, 1988, University of Nottingham, 1990, New England College—Sussex, 1991, London Institute, 1991, and University of Portsmouth, 1992.

The Body Shop received the following awards and honors: Communicator of the Year, British Association of Industrial Editors, 1988; Retailer of the Year, Country Natwest, and Marketing Society Award, both 1989; Queen's Award for Export, 1990; Environment Management Award, United Kingdom Award for Employee Volunteering,

Business in the Community, and Employee Volunteering Award, Per Cent Club, all 1991.

WRITINGS:

Body and Soul: Profits with Principles, the Amazing Success Story of Anita Roddick and the Body Shop (autobiography), Crown, 1991, Ebury Press, 1991.

WORK IN PROGRESS: The Body Shop Book.

SIDELIGHTS: "Our business is about two things: social change and action, and skin care. Social change and action come first," British entrepreneur Anita Roddick related to *Forbes* interviewer Jean Sherman Chatzky in 1992. Roddick, the founder and managing director of the Body Shop International PLC, is the author of *Body and Soul: Profits with Principles, the Amazing Success Story of Anita Roddick and the Body Shop.* The autobiographical work describes the author's natural skin and hair care company in terms of her personal philosophy of business. Roddick opened the original Body Shop as a means of supporting her family and promoting environmental and social responsibility; however, the business has proved to be a tremendous financial success as well. As the managing director concentrates on making the world a healthier, more humane place, her franchise has grown to encompass more than nine hundred stores in forty-two countries, with sales of approximately three hundred million dollars in 1992. As Rosemary Clunie expressed in the London *Times Saturday Review,* "Roddick has dared to replace the golden rule of capitalism, 'maximise profits', with a new business paradigm—'have fun; put love where your labour is, go in the opposite direction to everyone else'—and made it more profitable."

The Body Shop was created in 1976 when Roddick's husband decided he wanted to ride a horse from Buenos Aires, Argentina to New York City. Admiring his adventurous spirit, Roddick agreed to sell their restaurant to finance the excursion. This left her with the task of supporting herself and their two daughters. The child of Italian immigrants who owned and operated a cafe, Roddick had developed a business sense early in life. During her travels for the United Nations Labor Organization, she had observed women in Third World cultures using fruit and vegetable oils to cleanse their skin and hair, and believed that British women might be interested in learning about these practices. Roddick decided to sell natural lotions, soaps, and shampoos in a range of sizes so that customers could try new products in small quantities.

The first Body Shop was a small store located between two funeral parlors in Brighton, England. Roddick painted the interior dark green and, with the help of an herbalist, obtained the ingredients necessary to reproduce fifteen preparations as used by indigenous cultures. She packaged them in simple, unembellished plastic containers with hand-written labels, and kept prices down by eliminating advertising from her budget. When the undertakers next door objected to the name "Body Shop," she notified the press, and the resulting publicity brought in customers almost immediately. Despite the odds of failure in such a competitive industry, the Body Shop grew so popular in its first six months that Roddick was soon ready to open a second store.

The company's product line would eventually consist of roughly four hundred items, including carrot moisture cream, pineapple face wash, cucumber cleansing milk, elderflower under-eye gel, and banana hair conditioner, as well as naturally scented oils, soaps, shower gels, and talcum powder. Roddick has also developed shaving cream, aftershave lotion, and other items geared specifically toward men. While most cosmetics companies emphasize beauty, the Body Shop's products are intended to promote health. As Roddick explained to *Life* magazine's Lisa Distelheim, "We can't take a beauty cream too seriously. We don't use the words 'beauty,' 'nourishing,' 'rejuvenating'—all that. The vocabulary is different." She strongly objects to cosmetics companies that claim their products will improve one's social life, and has never created a concoction "that made your breasts larger, your thighs thinner or took the wrinkles off your face," she told *New York Times Magazine.* "We don't make promises of any kind," Roddick claimed in *Newsweek,* "other than to say that our stuff will clean and protect your hair and skin, amen."

The products themselves are a mark of Roddick's commitment to environmental and social responsibility. She does not use ingredients that have been tested on animals, and has instituted a "Trade Not Aid" program with Third World suppliers, paying the same top prices she pays for ingredients that are supplied locally. The packaging is minimal, and the Body Shop offers a discount for refills or returned containers. In addition, the stores use only recycled paper and do not use endangered tropical hardwood in their displays. But to Roddick, it is not enough that her business does not harm the environment; the company must actively strive to help people, animals, and the natural world. The Body Shop storefronts, in addition to promoting the company's merchandise, publicize various issues with which the Body Shop is concerned, including endangered species, whale slaughtering, the dumping of wastes in the North Sea, the depletion of the ozone layer, human rights, homelessness, and acquired immunodeficiency syndrome (AIDS). Inside, shoppers can obtain leaflets providing further information. Using the stores as magnets to draw supporters, the Body Shop has launched a new activist project each year. In 1991, for example, the company worked to preserve the Amazon rain forest and improve the living conditions of Romanian orphans.

Involvement in social action is a strict requirement for the Body Shop's employees, who are paid to do half a day of community service per month. Roddick considers the people who work for the Body Shop to be unique in that for them, "work is about the search for daily meaning as well as daily bread, for recognition as well as cash, stimulation rather than torpor." Roddick shares profits, educates her staff, and tries to provide a healthy, pleasant working environment. She writes in *Body and Soul,* "In business as in life I need to be entertained, to have a sense of family, to be part of a community, to feel constantly the thrill of the unexpected. I have always wanted the people who work for the Body Shop to share those feelings."

In 1984 Roddick and her husband—who had returned from his trek after a year to help with the company's finances—decided that going public would be the next logical step. From that point on, according to Roddick's autobiography, "the Body Shop ceased to exist as just another trading business. It became a force for social change." The company's international status has allowed the entrepreneur to share her vision on a global scale, and she has said that her social conscience always comes before her obligation to shareholders. However, it was not until 1988 that Roddick felt prepared to bring the Body Shop to the United States, and even then, she did so at a gradual pace, owning the stores herself while she adjusted to "the unions, the regulators, and, especially, the malls." But the New York City shop was an instant success, and in 1990, franchises opened in this country.

As Roddick's enterprise expanded, she was careful to duplicate the flavor of the original Body Shop in each new store. "When we became successful, we didn't change anything," she noted in the *New York Times Magazine.* "That's the smartest thing we ever did." She has continued to enforce the early decisions that were dictated by her ideals and her lack of funds. For example, she has never paid for product advertising, relying on interviews and word of mouth to attract business. In addition, all franchisees and their shop staff are involved in some type of community project, and the franchisees are in touch with one another through newsletters and workshops. Like the original store, the franchises are small and painted green, and the products are still packaged in inexpensive containers. The Body Shop continues to offer discounts for refills or returned containers. Cosmetics industry consultant Allan G. Mottus observed in the *New York Times Magazine* that the unique atmosphere of upbeat music, plants, brightly-colored displays, and products available for testing makes the Body Shop "like the soda shop or the bookstore where people just get together. Department stores

are like mausoleums, they're so serious. [Roddick]'s created a festive place."

While the policies and ambiance of the Body Shop have remained consistent, Roddick continues to discover new products during her frequent travels. She has also expanded the company's visibility through a mail-order catalog decorated with large-font, multicolored quotations and phrases identifying the company's values. In addition to skin and hair care products, the catalog features other imaginative items, such as a canvas tote bag sporting the Body Shop logo, gift baskets that may be individually designed by customers, an "endangered species box" with soaps shaped like five different endangered animals, and a "stress kit" containing massage oil and foot lotion. The company also sells posters dealing with recycling, Amnesty International, and other subjects, and offers videotapes on a rent-to-own basis that provide detailed journeys through the history of the Body Shop, the creation of Body Shop products, and the environment.

Roddick's unique combination of spiritual focus and financial reward have attracted a great deal of attention in the business world. "This woman is really going to leave a mark," Mottus predicted. "She's revolutionizing the business with the products she sells and the way she sells them." In addition to being designated an officer of the British Empire by the Queen of England, Roddick was named Business Woman of the Year in 1985 and received the United Nations "Global 500" Environment Award in 1989. Her approximately three hundred million-dollar share in the firm has made her one of the wealthiest women in Great Britain. When asked to explain her success, Roddick told Distelheim, "One answer is that we have an understanding of women. The cosmetics companies are run by men. This company is run on feminine principles." Among these principles is the notion that "gut feeling, instinct and all that are as important as organization and management." Roddick added, "There's very little difference actually between an entrepreneur and a crazy person. I have the ability to convince people, and they follow."

Body and Soul interweaves Roddick's criticism of the cosmetics industry with a discussion of her own business principles and the ways she has applied them throughout the Body Shop's history. The text is complemented by photographs and large, whimsical graphics. Wilda Williams, writing in *Library Journal,* commented, "Some of [Roddick's] ideas, while well-intended . . . are questionable. Still, her passion and her infectious enthusiasm make her book a cut above the usual gray 'How I Succeeded' tomes." McFadyean called the work an "exercise in solipsism" with the author "showing every inch of the way how much she *cares.*" Having investigated the wages and working conditions of Body Shop franchise employees,

McFadyean challenged Roddick's perception that these workers "dream of noble causes." Clunie, on the other hand, lauded the autobiography as "a manual for the 21st century." She added, "To dreamers and idealists, it offers the possibility of contributing to the welfare of society without sacrificing their souls." The reviewer likened Roddick's book to a Body Shop product: "organic, tantalising and aesthetically pleasing."

Roddick told *CA:* "School teaches us to be anonymous—to go through accepted channels. I've never believed that should be so, and it's worked for me. You educate people—especially young people—by stirring their passions."

BIOGRAPHICAL/CRITICAL SOURCES:

BOOKS

Newsmakers 89, Issue 4, Gale, 1989.
International Who's Who, 55th edition, Europa, 1991.
Roddick, Anita, *Body and Soul: Profits with Principles, the Amazing Success Story of Anita Roddick and the Body Shop,* Crown, 1991.

PERIODICALS

Forbes, March 2, 1992, pp. 83-84.
Library Journal, October 1, 1991, pp. 114, 118.
Life, November, 1988, pp. 21-22, 24.
New Statesman and Society, November 15, 1991, p. 44.
Newsweek, February 12, 1990, pp. 65-66.
New York Times Magazine, February 4, 1990.
Time, April 23, 1990, p. 82.
Times Saturday Review (London), October 5, 1991, p. 48.

—*Sketch by Joanna Brod*

*   *   *

ROGERS, Marian H.   1932-
(Marian J. A. Jackson)

PERSONAL: Born October 20, 1932, in Birmingham, AL; daughter of Frank (a realtor) and Margaret (a homemaker; maiden name, Jackson) Bryson; married Dee Oliver Herrick, May 31, 1952 (marriage ended, 1963); married J. Trumbull Rogers, July 1, 1978 (marriage ended, 1985); children: (first marriage) Christy Herrick-Siatsis, Rebecca. *Education:* Attended New York University. *Politics:* Democrat. *Avocational interests:* Duplicate bridge, travel, reading, classical music, dancing, live theatre.

ADDRESSES: Home—New York, NY. *Agent*—Elizabeth Backman, Box 536, Johnnycake Hollow Rd., Pine Plains, NY 12567.

CAREER: Institute of Electrical and Electronics Engineers, New York City, manager of technical services de-

partment, 1970-78; free-lance writer, 1985—. English in Action, member of board of directors; sergeant in local auxiliary police organization.

MEMBER: Authors Guild, Mystery Writers of America, American Crime Writers League, Sisters in Crime.

WRITINGS:

UNDER PSEUDONYM MARIAN J. A. JACKSON

A Miss Danforth Mystery: The Punjat's Ruby, Pinnacle Books, 1990.
A Miss Danforth Mystery: The Arabian Pearl, Pinnacle Books, 1991.
A Miss Danforth Mystery: The Cat's Eye, Pinnacle Books, 1991.
A Miss Danforth Mystery: Diamond Head, Walker and Co., 1992.
A Miss Danforth Mystery: Sunken Treasure (tentative title), Walker and Co., in press.

WORK IN PROGRESS: Another Miss Danforth mystery, for Walker and Co.; research on yachting in the Caribbean in the year 1900; research on New Orleans in the year 1900.

*   *   *

ROGOW, Roberta   1942-

PERSONAL: Born March 7, 1942; daughter of Stanley (a lawyer and actor) and Shirley (a psychologist; maiden name, Heller) Winston; married Murray Rogow (a press agent and writer), November 3, 1963; children: Miriam Ann, Louise Katherine. *Education:* Queens College of the City University of New York, B.A., 1962; Columbia University, M.L.S., 1971. *Politics:* Democrat. *Religion:* Jewish. *Avocational interests:* Needlework, science fiction costuming, songwriting, singing in choir, science fiction conventions.

ADDRESSES: Home—20-33 Carlton Pl., Fair Lawn, NJ 07410. *Office*—Union Public Library, Friberger Park, Union, NJ 07083.

CAREER: Held various positions at Paterson Free Public Library, Paterson, NJ, 1971-82; Ridgefield Public Library, Ridgefield, NJ, children's librarian, 1982-87; Union Free Public Library, Union, NJ, children's librarian, 1987—. Other Worlds Books, editor, publisher, and owner, 1978—.

MEMBER: New Jersey Library Association, Science Fiction Writers of America.

WRITINGS:

Trexindex: An Index to Star Trek Fanzines, Other World Books, 1976.

FutureSpeak: A Fan's Guide to the Language of Science Fiction, Paragon House, 1991.

Also author of five supplements to *Trexindex,* c. 1976-87. Contributor to story anthologies, including *Merovingen Nights #3: Troubled Waters,* DAW Books, 1988; *Merovingen Nights #4: Smuggler's Gold,* DAW Books, 1988; *Merovingen Nights #5: Divine Right,* DAW Books, 1989; and *Merovingen Nights #6: Flood Tide,* DAW Books, 1990. Contributor of stories to periodicals. Editor of magazines, including *Beyond . . . Science Fiction and Fantasy,* 1987-91, and *GRIP,* 1978—.

WORK IN PROGRESS: A murder mystery set in a parallel universe Manhattan.

SIDELIGHTS: Roberta Rogow told *CA:* "I have two full-time careers. By day I am a municipal librarian in New Jersey, as I have been since 1971. Weekends and vacations are devoted to the subculture of science fiction in all its manifestations. The union of librarianship and science fiction led to the writing of *FutureSpeak: A Fan's Guide to the Language of Science Fiction,* published by Paragon House in 1991. In addition to my two careers, I am also the mother of two daughters and the wife of a very cooperative husband.

"I grew up in an upper-middle class Jewish suburban household; my mother was a psychologist and my father was a corporation lawyer. I went through the New York City school system and graduated from Queens College of the City University of New York with a degree in music and theater in 1962. After a decade of musical and acting studies and 'working in show biz' with a variety of fringe groups, I abandoned the elusive dream of stardom. I married Murray Rogow, a theatrical press agent, and temporarily hung up my costumes to give birth to Miriam in 1964 and Louise in 1968.

"I resumed my studies in 1969 at the Columbia School of Library Science, where I earned my master's degree in 1971. My theatrical and musical talents were utilized at the Paterson Free Public Library, Ridgefield Public Library, and Union Free Public Library, where I held positions in the children's and young adults' departments. I also served on several committees of the New Jersey Library Association.

"My second career in science fiction began when I discovered the early novels of Robert Heinlein and the story collections of C. L. Moore. The lure of faraway worlds and strange people drew me into science fiction in its 'silver age.' However, I remained a 'passifan' who only read the stories—until I discovered the world of *Star Trek.* I got hooked and devoured each weekly episode and rerun. A 'Trekker' had been born. At a library convention I met two fellow Trekkers who were active in the committee

that ran the first *Star Trek* conventions. I attended my first convention in 1973, where I found hundreds of devotees who could spend a whole weekend talking 'Trek.' I also discovered 'fanzines,' those non-commercial publications produced by amateur publishers or on copying machines and sold at conventions. In the fanzines, writers could take the *Star Trek* characters and put them in new situations and universes.

"I had always wanted to share my stories. Now I had an audience. There was little or no money to be made from this, but there was the light at the end of the tunnel—I might someday see my writing in print. Two years later, in 1976, one of my stories was accepted and printed; the second career was begun. I plunged into fandom with both feet. I felt that if I could write for fanzines, I could also edit them. My own fanzine, *GRIP,* was begun in 1978. Between 1978 and 1987, I was involved with two other fanzines. I not only published my own magazines, I sold them at conventions. I extended my efforts to promoting items on consignment from other fanzine publishers all over the country.

"Once, after reading the first part of a two-part story in a fanzine, I was unable to find the second half of the continued story. In trying to solve this problem, the librarian in me took over, and I began compiling and publishing *Trexindex: An Index to Star Trek Magazines.* It was a massive effort in which I indexed, by story and author, over 500 titles from the previous ten years. Five supplements of *Trexindex* followed, the last appearing in 1987, when other demands on my time caused me to turn the project over to Bill Hupe, who has since done two more supplements.

"My songwriting, guitar playing, and folksinging talents also found their way into my science fiction life. I began writing and performing parodies about the Star Trek characters, science fiction books and films, and the 'fannish' life (such parodies are called 'filk' songs, from a misprint on a convention songsheet). I have published nine collections of my 'filk' songs and have recorded and produced six audiocassettes, which are sold at science fiction conventions across the United States.

"My writing found a paying market when C. J. Cherryh accepted my story 'Nessus' Shirt' for the 'Shared Universe' anthology *Merovingen Nights #3: Troubled Waters.* More sales followed. I have had stories in four of the *Merovingen Nights* anthologies.

"In addition to my writing and singing activities, I have participated in many other areas of the science fiction world. I have entered my original needlepoints in science fiction convention art shows. I have participated in masquerades, wearing homemade costumes based on science fiction characters that have earned me a wall full of trophies. I have even served on convention committees, running the dealer's room or assisting backstage at the masquerades. All this experience has been distilled into *FutureSpeak,* which uses a dictionary format to clarify the mysterious subculture of science fiction fandom by explaining the words and phrases of its many worlds. Fannish jargon, writers' terminology, and the scientific background materials that make up the 'science' in science fiction are all part of this 'language.' Both 'fans' and 'mundanes' have found *FutureSpeak* both fascinating and informative."

*   *   *

ROKKAN, Elizabeth 1925-

PERSONAL: Surname is accented on the first syllable; born May 26, 1925, in Lampeter, Wales; daughter of William Henry (a theologian and professor of Celtic studies) and Dorothy (a musician and teacher; maiden name, Clough) Harris; married Stein Rokkan (a professor of comparative politics), October 14, 1950; children: Siriol Rokkan Wilson, Bendik. *Education:* University of Wales, University College of Wales, Aberystwyth, B.A. (with honors), 1945, M.A., 1957; attended University of Oslo, 1953-54, University of Michigan and Harvard University, both 1954-55, Stanford University, 1959-60, and Yale University, 1969-70. *Religion:* "Anglican (Church in Wales)."

ADDRESSES: Home—7 Maynard Court, Fairwater Rd., Llandaff, Cardiff CF5 2LS, Wales.

CAREER: Foreign Office, London, England, press archivist in research department, 1945-46; Royal Institute of International Affairs, London, press archivist, 1946-51; Institute for Social Research, Oslo, Norway, secretarial assistant, 1952-53; secretary to cultural attache at American embassy in Oslo, and to U.S. Educational Foundation in Norway, 1953-54; International Research Associates, Inc., New York City, interviewer, 1954-55; U.S. Educational Foundation in Norway, staff member, 1955-56; British Embassy, Oslo, assistant to press reader, 1957-58; University of Bergen, Bergen, Norway, part-time assistant lecturer, 1958-63, lecturer, 1964-86, senior lecturer in English language and civilization, 1986-90. University of Wales, University College of Wales, Aberystwyth, member of education faculty, 1973; University of Tromsoe, guest lecturer, 1980; University of York, lecturer at Language Centre, 1982; University of Wales, St. David's University College, translator in residence and guest lecturer, 1986; University of Washington, Seattle, visiting professor, 1989.

MEMBER: International Political Science Association, International Federation of University Women (delegate to World Congress, 1989), European Association for American Studies, Society for the Advancement of Scandinavian Study, British Association of Scandinavian Studies, University Women's Club.

WRITINGS:

TRANSLATOR

Cora Sandel, *The Leech,* P. Owen, 1960, Ohio University Press, 1986.
Sandel, *Alberta and Jacob* (also see below), P. Owen, 1962.
Sandel, *Alberta and Freedom* (also see below), P. Owen, 1963.
Sandel, *Alberta Alone,* P. Owen, 1965, Orion Press (includes *Alberta and Jacob* and *Alberta and Freedom*), 1966.
Tarjei Vesaas, *The Ice Palace,* P. Owen, 1966, published as *Palace of Ice,* Morrow, 1968, reprinted as *The Ice Palace,* Sun and Moon, 1991.
Sandel, *Krane's Cafe,* P. Owen, 1968, Ohio University Press, 1985.
Vesaas, *The Great Cycle,* University of Wisconsin Press, 1968.
Vesaas, *The Bridges,* P. Owen, 1969, Morrow, 1970.
Vesaas, *The Boat in the Evening,* P. Owen, 1971, Morrow, 1972.
(And author of foreword) Vesaas, *The House in the Dark,* P. Owen, 1976.
Vesaas, *The Bleaching Yard,* P. Owen, 1981.
Johan Borgen, *The Scapegoat,* Norvik Press, 1993.

Translations represented in anthologies, including *An Everyday Story: Norwegian Women's Fiction,* edited by Katherine Hanson, Seal Press (Seattle, WA), 1984; and *View from the Window: Contemporary Norwegian Short Stories,* Norwegian Universities Press, 1986. Contributor of translations to periodicals, including *Literary Review.*

OTHER

Work represented in anthologies. Contributor of articles and reviews to periodicals, including *Poetry Wales, Scandinavica,* and *American Studies in Scandinavia.*

WORK IN PROGRESS: Research on the migration of women through marriage.

*   *   *

ROPES, Linda Brubaker 1942-

PERSONAL: Born July 13, 1942, in Flagstaff, AZ; daughter of Harvey Karl (a lawyer) and Jessie (a homemaker; maiden name, Lee) Mangum; married Thomas A. Brubaker, August 11, 1962 (marriage ended); Leverett H. Ropes (a graphic artist), March 17, 1990; children: (first marriage) Michael A. *Education:* University of Wyoming, B.A., 1965. *Politics:* Democrat. *Religion:* Unitarian-Universalist.

ADDRESSES: Home and office—500 Creekside Ct., Golden, CO 80403.

CAREER: Creative Ink (writing service), Golden, CO, owner, 1981—.

MEMBER: American Society of Trainers and Developers, Colorado Authors League (member of board of directors, 1989-91).

WRITINGS:

The Health Care Crisis in America: A Reference Handbook, ABC-CLIO, 1991.

*   *   *

ROSENBERG, Nancy Taylor 1946-

PERSONAL: Born July 9, 1946, in Dallas, TX; daughter of William Hoyt (an "oil man") and Ethel LaVerne (a homemaker) Taylor; married Calvin Skyrme (divorced, 1984); married Jerry Rosenberg (an investor); children: (first marriage) Forrest Blake, Chessly Lynn Nesci, Gerald Hoyt; (second marriage) Amy Laura, Nancy Beth. *Education:* Attended Gulf Park College and University of California, Los Angeles. *Politics:* "Non-partisan." *Religion:* Jewish.

ADDRESSES: Home—Niguel, CA. *Agent*—Peter Miller, 220 West Nineteenth St., Suite 220, New York, NY 10011.

CAREER: Dallas Police Department, Dallas, TX, police officer, 1971-75; Ventura Police Department, Ventura, CA, community service officer, 1978-81; Ventura County Probation Department, Ventura, deputy probation officer, 1981-84. Video Movie Wholesalers, vice president and owner. Has also worked as a police officer in New Mexico and Arizona, a criminal investigator, and a model.

WRITINGS:

NOVELS

Mitigating Circumstances, Dutton, 1993.
Interest of Justice, Dutton, 1993.
The Eyewitness, Dutton, in press.

SIDELIGHTS: Nancy Taylor Rosenberg told *CA:* "All my life, I planned to become an author. After studying English in college, however, I found myself in many different careers. I was a model, a police officer, a probation officer, and a criminal investigator. These experiences served me well, as I write thrillers set in the criminal justice system.

I am also the mother of five children. Young people appear many times as characters in my novels.

"At the age of forty-five, I decided to pursue my dream by studying writing at the University of California, Los Angeles. One year later my first novel was purchased during a fierce bidding war for what I considered an enormous sum of money. A few days later, the movie rights were sold to Tri Star Pictures and targeted to be Jonathan Demme's next project. The book was also a main selection of the Literary Guild, and it will be printed in thirteen different countries throughout the world. For a writer, this was a dream come true. For me, it was a miracle. It only got better. Approximately six months later, New American Library/Dutton signed me to a four-book contract.

"Many people ask me how I made it as a novelist in such economically poor times, and how any new writer manages to become published. My belief is that any terrific piece of work will find its way into print, but I also believe that hard work and perseverance are the mainstay of the writer. This is not something you can approach as a hobby. You must be as serious and focused with your writing as you would be if you were a surgeon stitching delicate arteries and nerves. Being able to accept criticism, listen to worthwhile suggestions, and tirelessly rewrite are some of the best attributes. Young or unpublished writers of all ages tend to become seduced by their own writing and stubbornly reject suggestions on how they can improve.

"On the specific side, I packaged myself and my work to be commercially attractive and easily assimilated by agents, the first step toward publishing. I included a chapter-by-chapter outline of my novel, enabling agents to follow the plot line without taking the time to read the entire manuscript, and I enclosed sample chapters, allowing them to review my prose and listen to my voice. In addition, I enclosed a photograph of myself, a biography, and comments other fledgling writers had made about my manuscript.

"If you feel compelled to write, you are probably a writer. This driving need to express yourself and tell stories is the distinctive mark of talent. In today's publishing world, however, if you want to produce more than one publishable work, you must discover a niche. Then, as in any business venture, you must examine the work of others in your selected niche. Listen closely to any and all comments made by rejecting agents or publishers. Even though agents are constantly deluged with unsolicited manuscripts to the point where they sometimes let a talented beginner slip right through their fingers, most of them know their stuff. Do not be discouraged. I was rejected by fifteen literary agents long after my novel had been sold, articles had appeared in numerous trade journals and magazines, and the checks were in the bank. Fasten your seat belts, burn the midnight oil, and listen to your inner voice. Good luck!"

*   *   *

ROSENTHAL, Jack (Morris) 1931-

PERSONAL: Born September 8, 1931, in Manchester, England; son of Samuel (a waterproof garment maker) and Leah (Miller) Rosenthal; married Maureen Lipman (an actress), February 18, 1973; children: Amy, Adam. *Education:* Sheffield University, B.A. (with honors). *Avocational interests:* "Filling in forms for publications such as this."

ADDRESSES: Agent—William Morris Agency, 31 Soho Sq., London WIV 5DG, England (or) 151 El Camino Dr., Beverly Hills, CA 90212.

CAREER: Television, theater, and film writer.

MEMBER: Dramatists' Club, British Academy of Film and Television Arts.

AWARDS, HONORS: Television Critics Best Play Award, 1971, for *Another Sunday and Sweet F.A.;* Writer's Guild Best Comedy Series Award, 1971, for *The Lovers;* American International Emmy Award, 1975, for *The Evacuees;* British Academy of Film and Television Arts Best Play awards, 1975, for *The Evacuees,* 1976, for *Bar Mitzvah Boy,* and 1977, for *Spend, Spend, Spend;* Broadcasting Press Guild Best Play awards, 1975, for *The Evacuees,* and 1976, for *Bar Mitzvah Boy;* British Academy of Film and Television Arts Writer's Award, 1976; Royal Television Society Writer's Award, 1976; award from Cannes Film Festival, c. 1980, for *Lucky Star;* Genie Award—best adapted screenplay, Academy of Canadian Cinema and Television, 1980, for *Lucky Star;* award from Cine del Luca [Monte Carlo], c. 1984, for *The Devil's Lieutenant;* Best Fiction Video Award, Rio de Janeiro Film Festival, c. 1987, for *Ready When You Are, Mr. McGill;* San Francisco Film Festival Special Jury Award, c. 1987, for *Day to Remember;* Best Play Award, Prix Europa, c. 1992, for *Bye, Bye, Baby.*

Writer's Guild Best Play Award nomination, c. 1974, for *There'll Almost Always Be an England;* British Academy of Film and Television Arts Best Play Award nominations, c. 1976, for *Ready When You Are, Mr. McGill,* c. 1979, for *The Knowledge,* c. 1982, for *P'tang, Yang, Kipperbang,* and c. 1987, for *London's Burning;* Prix Italia nominations—television, Radiotelevisione Italiana, c. 1978, for *Spend, Spend, Spend,* and c. 1979, for *The Knowledge.*

WRITINGS:

TELEVISION SERIES

Coronation Street, Granada, 1961-69.
That Was the Week That Was, British Broadcasting Corporation (BBC), 1963.
The Dustbinmen, Granada, 1969.
The Lovers, Granada, c. 1971.
Sadie, It's Cold Outside, Thames, 1975.
Red Letter Day, Granada, 1976.

Also writer for *Bulldog Breed,* Granada. Contributed episodes to *The Odd Man, The Verdict Is Yours, The Villains, Pardon the Expression,* and *The Army Game,* all Granada; *Taxi!, BBC Comedy Playhouse,* and *Duchess of Duke Street,* all BBC; and *Mrs. Thursday,* Associated Television Ltd. (ATV).

OTHER TELEVISION WRITING

Green Rub, Granada, 1963.
Pie in the Sky, Granada, 1963.
The Night before the Morning After, ABC, 1966.
Compensation Alice, ABC, 1967.
There's a Hole in Your Dustbin, Delilah, Granada, 1968.
Your Name's Not God, It's Edgar, Granada, 1969.
Another Sunday and Sweet F.A., Granada, c. 1971.
And for My Next Trick, BBC, 1973.
Hot Fat, BBC, 1974.
Polly Put the Kettle On, London Weekend Television (LWT), 1974.
Mr. Ellis versus the People, Granada, 1974.
There'll Almost Always Be an England, Granada, 1974.
The Evacuees, BBC, 1975.
Big Sid, Granada, 1975.
Bar Mitzvah Boy, BBC, 1976.
Ready When You Are, Mr. McGill, Granada, 1976.
Well, Thank You, Thursday, Granada, 1976.
Spend, Spend, Spend (adapted from the book by Vivian Nicholson), BBC, 1977.
Auntie's Niece, BBC, 1977.
Spaghetti Two-Step, Yorkshire, 1977.
P'tang, Yang, Kipperbang, Channel 4 (United Kingdom), 1982.
Mrs. Capper's Birthday (play adaptation), BBC, 1985.
London's Burning, LWT, 1986.
Fools on the Hill, BBC, 1986.
Day to Remember, Channel 4, 1986.
And a Nightingale Sang (play adaptation), Tyne-Tees, 1989.
Bag Lady, Central TV, 1989.
Sleeping Sickness, Central TV, 1991.
Bye, Bye, Baby, Channel 4, c. 1992.

Also author of *Wide-Eyed and Legless,* BBC; *The Devil's Lieutenant* and *The Chain,* both Channel 4; and *The Knowledge,* 1979.

TELEVISION COMPILATIONS

Three Award-Winning Television Plays (contains *Bar Mitzvah Boy, The Evacuees,* and *Spend, Spend, Spend*), Penguin, 1978.
P'tang, Yang, Kipperbang, and Other TV Plays, edited by Alison Leake, Longman, 1984.
The Chain with The Knowledge and Ready When You Are, Mr. McGill, Faber, 1986.
London's Burning: The Screenplay of the Original Film of London's Burning, Robson Books, 1989.

Contributor to *The Television Dramatist,* Elek, 1973, and *First Love,* Channel Four Books, 1984.

SCREENPLAYS

The Lovers, British Lion, 1973.
The Lucky Star (adaptation of a work by Max Fischer), Pickman Films, 1981, Cineworld, 1984.
(With Barbra Streisand) *Yentl,* Metro-Goldwyn-Mayer (MGM)/United Artists (UA), 1983.
P'tang Yang Kipperbang (also released as *Kipperbang*), MGM/UA, 1984.
The Chain, Rank, 1985.

Also author of unproduced screenplays, *Conventions,* Universal, *The Best* and *Gabriela: Clove and Cinnamon,* both Columbia, and *Family Matters,* Warner Brothers. Contributor (uncredited) to *The Prince of Tides,* Columbia, *Continental Divide,* Universal, and *Everybody's All-American.*

STAGE PLAYS

Bar Mitzvah Boy (musical), produced at Her Majesty's Theatre, London, England, 1978.
Smash!, produced in England, 1981.

Also author of the musical *Dear Anyone,* produced at the Cambridge Theatre in London, and *Our Gracie.*

WORK IN PROGRESS: Gypsy and Me, a film, for Orion; *Moving Story,* a drama series, for Paravision; *Mrs. Sherlock Holmes,* a drama series, for Zenith films; *Tortoise,* a television film, for Theatre of Comedy.

SIDELIGHTS: Jack Rosenthal, one of England's most prolific television and film writers, uses comedy to explore contemporary social issues. Rosenthal penned the entire first run of the British series *That Was the Week That Was,* as well as two hundred episodes of *Coronation Street,* during the 1960s and received British Academy of Film and Television Arts Best Play awards for the teleplays *Spend, Spend, Spend, The Evacuees,* and *Bar Mitzvah Boy.*

These scripts were published together in 1978 as *Three Award-Winning Television Plays.*

Rosenthal's feature films include *Yentl,* a 1983 picture that he cowrote with director Barbra Streisand. Streisand, who also starred in the movie with Mandy Patinkin and Amy Irving, had purchased the film rights to Jewish folk author Isaac Bashevis Singer's tale, "Yentl, the Yeshiva Boy," fourteen years earlier, and the film marked her directorial debut. Though set in an early twentieth-century Polish *shtetl* [Jewish town or village], the film retells Singer's story through a contemporary feminist framework. Streisand and Rosenthal set up a complex love triangle through which they examine sex roles and celebrate new possibilities. Several reviewers noted that Streisand's branching out as a director, and her willingness to masquerade as a male character, reflect the potential for expanded gender definitions that *Yentl* proposes. The songs, written by composer Michel Legrand and lyricists Marilyn and Alan Bergman, are sung only by Yentl, and serve as an ongoing monologue defining her private struggle. At times, the action of the film resumes with the song continuing under the dialogue.

The title character is a girl who has inherited a love of learning from her scholarly father. Although it is forbidden for women to study the holy scriptures, and customary for them to remain illiterate, Yentl's father secretly shares his knowledge with her. After he dies, Yentl disguises herself as a boy and travels to another village. Calling herself Anshel, she enrolls in a *yeshiva* [school for studying sacred Jewish texts], where she meets Avigdor, a handsome rabbinical student who admires Anshel's intellect. The two become study partners and close friends, although Yentl disputes Avigdor's slighting remarks about women.

Avigdor introduces Yentl to his fiance, Hadass, an attractive, feminine woman whose only desire is to please her future husband. Both captivated and terrified by Avigdor, Hadass finds Anshel's gentleness alluring. Yentl is torn between disdain and envy for Hadass's sensual charm, and is attracted to Avigdor. He is in love with Hadass, but feels strangely drawn to his friend Anshel as well. Avigdor and Yentl become frequent guests at Hadass's home, until her parents break off the engagement. The grieving Avigdor then implores his closest friend Anshel to marry Hadass in his place.

Yentl feels utterly confused; but seeing no way out of the situation, she proposes to Hadass, who accepts. After the wedding, Yentl avoids sexual relations with Hadass by telling her that they must wait until they are better acquainted. Yentl does, however, teach Hadass about Jewish law, giving her a sense of pride in herself. Finally, Yentl reveals to Avigdor that she is a woman. He can no longer treat her as an equal, and Yentl feels compelled to move on. Whereas Singer's Yentl travels to another *yeshiva* in a new village, Streisand and Rosenthal's Yentl boards a ship for America, where she hopes to find greater freedom. Reviewers found *Yentl*'s story line sensitively and carefully rendered, and felt the film represented an important development in Streisand's career. "It's rare to see such a labor of love, such emotion in almost every frame of a film," Jack Kroll commented in *Newsweek*. Stanley Kauffmann noted in *New Republic* that although the screenplay "gives grounds to those who want to complain of literary infidelity and historical inaccuracy," *Yentl*'s innovative use of songs constituted a breakthrough in filmmaking. Writing in the *Chicago Tribune*, Gene Siskel called *Yentl* "a warm treat for the holidays."

P'tang Yang Kipperbang, another of Rosenthal's feature films, played in the United States under the title *Kipperbang* in 1984. Reviewing the film in the *New York Times*, Janet Maslin noted, "The best things about 'Kipperbang' . . . are the richly evocative look of the production . . . and the screenplay by Jack Rosenthal, which includes some clever turns of phrase." The story concerns the students and staff of a British school in 1948. Fourteen-year-old Alan "Quack Quack" Duckworth, a daydreamer who translates events in his life into reveries about cricket matches, is in love. He plans for his first kiss to occur "early next week at the latest, weather permitting." When Alan is miraculously given a romantic role in the class play, he has the opportunity to make his fantasy a reality. In the midst of this coming-of-age story, the adults who work at the school are involved in less innocent affairs; an English teacher who had a relationship with the headmaster during the war is now involved with a groundskeeper who fought in it. Maslin commented, "The schoolboy nostalgia of 'Kipperbang' is as decorous as an English garden and as colorful as some of the epithets that are bestowed upon the film's leading character."

BIOGRAPHICAL/CRITICAL SOURCES:

BOOKS

Contemporary Dramatists, 3rd edition, St. Martin's, 1982.
International Authors and Writers Who's Who, 12th edition, International Biographical Centre, 1991.
Who's Who, St. Martin's, 1992.

PERIODICALS

Chicago Tribune, December 9, 1983.
Los Angeles Times, November 18, 1983, pp. 1, 16; August 17, 1984.
Maclean's, November 28, 1983, p. 69.
Ms., February, 1984, p. 32.
New Republic, December 19, 1983, pp. 22-23.
Newsweek, November 28, 1983, pp. 109-110.

New Yorker, November 28, 1983, p. 170.
New York Times, November 18, 1983, p. C10; April 4, 1984; April 20, 1984.
Stage, January 13, 1972.
Stage and Television Today, November 26, 1970.
Time, November 21, 1983, p. 93.
Times (London), May 24, 1985.

—*Sketch by Joanna Brod*

*   *   *

ROSNER, Lisa 1958-

PERSONAL: Born June 18, 1958, in New York, NY; daughter of Henry (a doctor) and Lillian (a homemaker; maiden name, Stern) Rosner; married John Theibault (a professor), June 10, 1990; children: Alice Rebecca. *Education:* Princeton University, A.B., 1979; attended University of Edinburgh, 1979-80; Johns Hopkins University, Ph.D., 1985.

ADDRESSES: Office—Historical Studies Program, Stockton State College, Pomona, NJ 08240.

CAREER: Stockton State College, Pomona, NJ, associate professor of history, 1987—.

MEMBER: American Historical Association, History of Science Society, American Association for the History of Medicine, American Society for Eighteenth-Century Studies, Eighteenth-Century Scottish Studies Society.

WRITINGS:

(Editor with Alice Stroup) *Directory of Women in the History of Science, Technology, and Medicine*, History of Science Society, 1991.
Medical Education in the Age of Improvement: Edinburgh Students and Apprentices, 1720-1826, Edinburgh University Press, 1991.
First Look at Quattro Pro 2.0/3.0, Mitchell-McGraw, 1992.
(With Jim Shuman) *Using Quattro Pro 2.0/3.0*, Mitchell-McGraw, 1992.
First Look at Quattro Pro for Windows, Mitchell-McGraw, 1992.

WORK IN PROGRESS: The Two Lives of Alexander Lesassion, a monograph based on the diaries and novel of an army surgeon during the Napoleonic wars, completion expected in 1995.

*   *   *

ROSS, Lillian Hammer 1925-

PERSONAL: Born July 16, 1925, in Los Angeles, CA; daughter of David (a merchant) and Frieda (Kamornick)

Hammer; married Albert Ellis Ross, August 15, 1948 (died January 7, 1991); children: Stephen Frederick, Susan Ross Peterson, David Paul. *Education:* University of California, Los Angeles, B.A., 1948, English as a Second Language teacher credential, 1974, bilingual Spanish/English teacher credential, 1975.

ADDRESSES: Office—c/o Publicity Director, Jewish Publication Society, 1930 Chestnut St., Philadelphia, PA 19103-4599.

CAREER: Los Angeles Unified School district, kindergarten and primary school teacher, 1948-54 and 1964-80. Writer, 1990—.

MEMBER: Society of Children's Book Writers, PEN, Women's National Book Association, Long Beach Authors' Festival.

WRITINGS:

The Little Old Man and His Dreams, Harper, 1990.
Buba Leah and Her Paper Children, Jewish Publication Society, 1991.

Author of the unpublished works *David and the Four White Chickens, Hannah, Also Known as Sarah,* and *Papa Is Coming Home for Pesach.* Also contributor of "A Tall Tale" to *Highlights* magazine, 1989.

WORK IN PROGRESS: "Tales my father told me; tales my mother told me."

SIDELIGHTS: Lillian Hammer Ross commented: "My daughter and son-in-law had set their wedding date for the first night of Hanukkah. Invitations mailed, my ninety-year-old father was hospitalized with heart failure. My mother sat by her husband's bed and every time he opened his eyes, she whispered, 'David, you must be well for Susan's wedding.' My mother and father walked down the aisle at their granddaughter's wedding and two months later, my father died. These events were the motivation for my writing the picture/storybook *The Little Old Man and His Dreams.*

"One weekend, I attended the conference of 'Writers of the Pacific Rim' where Charlotte Zolotow, Children's Editor for Harper and Row, was the main speaker. At intermission, I approached her and asked why it was I received complimentary letters about my writing, but no acceptance of my manuscripts. 'You just haven't met the right editor,' was her reply. At home, I sent my manuscript, *The Little Old Man and His Dreams,* with a covering letter. 'Remember me? I'm the woman you met at the writers conference last December.' One month later, I received a call from Charlotte Zolotow's office, and the following month a contract was signed.

"I set the scene of *The Little Old Man* in Europe when people rode in wagons pulled by their horses. My writing has taken me to a past time of Europe in the early 1900s. I have connected with my parents' past life and brought it into the present so that their great-grandchildren will better understand their cultural heritage."

*   *   *

ROSSOL, Monona 1936-

PERSONAL: Born January 31, 1936, in Madison, WI; daughter of Ben (a booking agent and entertainer) and Alva (an entertainer; maiden name, Topel) Bergor; married John Otto Holzhueter (a historian), 1962 (divorced, 1981). *Education:* University of Wisconsin—Madison, B.S., 1960, M.S., 1962, M.F.A., 1964.

ADDRESSES: Home and office—Arts, Crafts, and Theater Safety, Inc., 181 Thompson St., No. 23, New York, NY 10012-2586.

CAREER: Bjorksten Research Laboratory, Madison, WI, research chemist, 1959-60; University of Wisconsin—Madison, instructor in integrated liberal studies and ceramics, 1961-62, project assistant in civil engineering, 1964-67; Center for Occupational Hazards (now Center for Safety in the Arts), New York City, cofounder, 1977, director of information, 1977-87, president, 1980-86; Arts, Crafts, and Theatre Safety, Inc., New York City, founder and president, 1987—. Ceramics teacher at schools and universities, 1964-80, including Herbert H. Lehman College of the City University of New York, Henry Street Settlement House, and Greenwich House Pottery; proprietor of a ceramic studio in Mazomanie, WI, 1964-77; free-lance art restoration consultant and restorer, 1975-78. Member of New York Committee for Occupational Safety and Health; consultant to J. Paul Getty Conservation Library, Boston Children's Museum, and Museum of Modern Art.

MEMBER: American Industrial Hygiene Association, American Institute for Conservation, American Society for Testing and Materials, American Welding Society, National Fire Protection Association, Artist Craftsmen of New York (president, 1977-81 and 1992), Wisconsin Designer Craftsmen, Pen and Brush.

AWARDS, HONORS: Twenty-third Ceramic National Purchase Award.

WRITINGS:

Stage Fright: Health and Safety in the Theater, Center for Occupational Hazards, 1986.
The Artist's Complete Health and Safety Guide, Allworth Press, 1990.
Safety Training Manual: Our Right to Know Program, Edge Publishing, 1991.

(With Susan Shaw) *Overexposure: Health Hazards in Photography,* Allworth Press, 1991.

(With Ben Bartlett) *Danger: Artist at Work,* Thorpe Publishing [Australia], 1991.

Keeping Clay Work Safe and Legal, National Council on Education for the Ceramic Arts, 1993.

Work represented in anthologies, including *Health Hazards Manual for Artists,* edited by Michael McCann, Foundation for the Community of Artists (New York City), 1978; *The Business of Art,* edited by Lee Caplin, Prentice-Hall, 1982; and *Safety in Museums and Galleries,* edited by F. M. P. Howie, Butterworth, 1987. Author of the columns "Ceramics and Health," in *Ceramic Scope,* 1980-82, and "Accent on Safety," in *Shuttle Spindle and Dyepot,* 1991-92. Contributor to periodicals, including *Surface Design Journal, Creative Ohio, Leonardo, Puppetry Journal,* and *Art Hazards News.* Editor, *Artist-Craftsmen Newsletter,* 1971-73, and *ACTS Facts,* 1987—; safety editor, *Professional Stained Glass,* 1987—.

SIDELIGHTS: Monona Rossol told *CA:* "I was born into a theatrical family, worked as a professional entertainer from age three to seventeen, and left my family to enroll in the University of Wisconsin. I earned a degree in chemistry and got work as a project assistant and research chemist. The money I earned was used to put myself through graduate school, where I earned an M.S. in ceramics and sculpture and an M.F.A. in ceramics and glassblowing, with a minor in music.

"In school I realized that the same acids, solvents, metals, and other chemicals were being used in both the chemistry and art departments. In the art department, however, there were no eye wash fountains, gloves, fume hoods, or other safety equipment. I began to write papers and give graduate seminars on the hazards of art. Both teachers and students walked out of my seminars, and they wouldn't read my papers; they claimed the information 'interfered with' their creativity.

"Death and disease interfere with creativity, too, so I have persisted. Now there are laws (the Occupational Safety and Health Administration Hazard Communication Standard) which require all employees who use toxic materials to attend formal health and safety training sessions. I specialize in these sessions, and much of what I write can be used as training materials. Some of the same people who walked out of my seminars in the sixties have had to sit through them in the nineties.

"My unusual background in the theater and entertainment industries, as an art and science teacher and as a professional artist and craftsperson, allows me to speak and write with understanding for these groups about the hazards of their work, the precautions they must take, and the governmental regulations with which they must comply."

ROTH, Arthur J(oseph) 1925-1993
(Nina Hoy, Barney Mara, Slater McGurk, Pete Pomeroy)

OBITUARY NOTICE—See index for *CA* sketch: Born August 3, 1925, in the Bronx, New York, NY; died of liver cancer, March 5, 1993, in Amagansett, Long Island, NY. Columnist, novelist, and author. Roth was perhaps best known for his *East Hampton Star* column, "From the Scuttlehole," which he wrote for twenty-seven years beginning in 1966. He held various jobs as a budding author, including bartender, coalminer, logger, college English instructor, and truck driver. His first novel, *A Terrible Beauty,* was based on his personal experience in the Irish Republican Army during the 1940s. Roth's other adult works include *The Shame of Our Wounds* and the nonfiction volume, *Eiger: Wall of Death.* He also wrote mystery novels under the pseudonym Slater McGurk, such as *The Grand Central Murders* and *The Big Dig.* But it is for young adults that Roth wrote the majority of his books, including *Wipeout!, The Iceberg Hermit, Two for Survival, Demolition Man,* and *The Caretaker.*

OBITUARIES AND OTHER SOURCES:

BOOKS

Authors of Books for Young People, 3rd edition, Scarecrow, 1990.

Something about the Author Autobiography Series, Volume 11, Gale, 1991.

PERIODICALS

New York Times, March 22, 1993, p. D8.

* * *

ROYAL, Rosamond
See HINES, Jeanne

* * *

RUBIN, Bruce Joel 1943(?)-

PERSONAL: Born c. 1943; son of James (a contractor) and Sondra Rubin; married Blanche Mallins; children: Joshua, Ari. *Education:* Attended Wayne State University, 1960-62, and New York University Film School.

ADDRESSES: Home—San Fernando Valley, CA. *Agent*—Sanford, Skouras, Gross, & Associates, 1015 Gayley, third floor, Los Angeles, CA 90024.

CAREER: National Broadcasting Company (NBC-TV), New York City, assistant film editor in news department; Whitney Museum, New York City, curator in art-film department; writer of motion pictures, beginning in the 1970s.

MEMBER: Writers Guild of America.

AWARDS, HONORS: Writers Guild of America Award nomination, best original screenplay, and Academy Award, best original screenplay, both 1991, both for *Ghost.*

WRITINGS:

SCREENPLAYS

(With Robert Statzel and Phillip Frank Messina) *Brainstorm,* Metro-Goldwyn-Mayer/United Artists, 1983.
Deadly Friend (based on the novel *Friend* by Diana Henstell), Warner Brothers, 1986.
Ghost, Paramount, 1990.
Jacob's Ladder (TriStar, 1990), foreword by Adrian Lyne, Applause Theatre Book Publishers, 1990.

Also contributed to the screenplays *Sleeping with the Enemy* and *The Mrs.*

WORK IN PROGRESS: Writing and directing the film *My Life,* about an American family.

SIDELIGHTS: Bruce Joel Rubin is best known as the Academy Award-winning screenwriter of *Ghost,* one of the top ten grossing films of all time. In addition, he has written the science fiction thriller *Brainstorm,* the horror film *Deadly Friend,* and the image-laden *Jacob's Ladder.* With a payment of one million dollars for the latter script, Rubin joined an elite class of screenwriters able to command six figure paychecks. Rubin has earned this status by creating films that strike a common chord in moviegoers. Critics and fellow filmmakers alike have commented on this key ingredient to Rubin's success: his ability to relate, and his belief in, a world beyond death. Jerry Zucker, the director of *Ghost,* commented to Kirk Honeycutt in the *Los Angeles Times,* "What I loved about the script [for *Ghost*] . . . was that it was written by someone who really believes in the spiritual world and takes these issues seriously."

Growing up in Detroit, Michigan, Rubin developed an early interest in theatrical creation. He and his siblings constructed a stage in their basement and often improvised their own plays. Alongside this growing involvement with drama, Rubin also became fascinated with the relationship between life and death. He recalled an epiphany he had at age five to the *Detroit Free Press*'s Kathy Huffines: "We stopped at an auto accident where a girl my age had been crushed by a car. . . . From that age, I knew death was a part of life." Reaching adulthood, Rubin attended college and eventually earned a degree from New York University's prestigious film school. While there he was a classmate of the now famous directors Martin Scor-

cese (*Raging Bull, Cape Fear*) and Brian DePalma (*Carrie, The Untouchables*), who directed one of Rubin's early scripts titled *Jennifer.* After graduation Rubin worked for a time as a film editor for the National Broadcasting Corporation's (NBC-TV) news department, but he soon became dissatisfied and sought fulfillment elsewhere. Seeking the meaning of life, he travelled the world, visiting such places as Turkey, Iran, Nepal, and Japan. While in India, Rubin experienced the strength of death in spirituality. He witnessed the scores of people who each year flock to holy spots along the Ganges, a river considered sacred, to willfully die and enter a higher plane. Rubin credits this journey with giving him a clearer perception of human existence and adding a spiritual balance to his life. When he returned to the United States he began to craft screenplays that reflected his belief in life, death, and the world beyond.

Brainstorm, Rubin's first major film, is the story of two scientists and the effect their invention has on life after death. Michael and Lillian are researchers who have invented a machine that can record a person's thoughts and sensorial experiences. When another subject is hooked into the machine and the recording is played back, the second person fully relives the first subject's sensations. As they streamline this creation, Michael and Lillian experiment with the possibilities of their invention. They record rollercoaster rides, skydives, and even sexual intercourse. The corporation that has funded Michael and Lillian's research, however, wants to use the machine for military purposes. Having envisioned her invention as a boon to mankind, Lillian is outraged to learn of the company's plan. Alone in her lab one night, she is overcome with fury. The physical strain triggers her heart condition, and she is beset with a massive coronary attack. She realizes that she is dying and, rather than call for help, attaches herself to the machine and records her death. In the days that follow Michael must contend not only with his partner's demise but with a team of government scientists usurping their project. The discovery of Lillian's death tape spurs a power struggle between Michael and the company. While Michael wants to keep the tape from being exploited—and to play it—the government sees the tape as a possible weapon. With the help of his wife, Karen, Michael manages to steal the tape and experience Lillian's death. Critical reaction to the film was mixed. *Time* reviewer Richard Schickel complained that *Brainstorm* lacked "clear purpose and forceful dramatic structure." The *Motion Picture Guide* (*MPG*) viewed the film more favorably, however, commenting on its numerous special effects and its use of humor "to leaven the gritty moments."

Rubin's next project was a 1986 screenplay for horror director Wes Craven, who had previously found fame with his film *A Nightmare on Elm Street.* Titled *Deadly Friend,* it is the story of a teenager who uses his intellect in robot and computer technology to reanimate his recently brain-dead girlfriend. The procedure works, but the girl exhibits far from normal behavior and goes on a murderous rampage. It is up to the young inventor to stop her before the police reach her. The film received mild attention at the box office and was generally regarded by critics as standard horror fare.

The year 1990 proved to be a breakthrough one for Rubin, as two of his scripts became highly successful movies. The first to succeed was *Ghost,* a story of love and suspense beyond death. Sam and Molly are a young, upwardly mobile couple who have just moved into a new apartment together. Although there is a deep emotional and physical bond between them, Sam is unable to tell Molly that he loves her. While returning from a play one night, they are attacked by a vicious mugger. Sam stands up to the attacker and chases him away, but as he returns to Molly, he finds her weeping over a body on the ground. As he approaches, Sam realizes that the body is his, and that the mugger has shot and killed him. Sam is stunned to discover that he is dead and that he is, in fact, a ghost. Although he can still see her, Molly can neither hear nor see Sam. The only contact that the dead man has is with other ghosts, who offer him little assistance or comfort. It is only when Sam happens upon Oda Mae Brown that his circumstances change. Oda Mae is a palm reader, a medium, and a spiritual minister. She is also a con artist and a complete fake with no paranormal abilities—or so she thought. When Sam enters her place of business, Oda Mae is amazed to find that she can hear Sam. The ghost eventually persuades her to aid him in communicating with Molly. The story becomes more complicated when Sam learns that Molly is in danger and he is the only one—with Oda Mae's help—that can save her. The film climaxes with the lovers sharing a brief reunion that transcends the border of life and death.

Ghost started out as a "sleeper," a film that opens without much fanfare but eventually, through word-of-mouth, becomes very popular. By the time its theatrical release ended, *Ghost* had become the top grossing film of 1990 and one of the biggest money-makers in movie history. Critical reaction to *Ghost* was not as enthusiastic—as is often the case with popular movies—but many critics wrote favorably about the film. Janet Maslin, writing in the *New York Times,* commented that *Ghost* is "eccentric enough to remain interesting even when its ghost story isn't easy to believe." Maslin also credited the film's "appealingly offbeat digressions" with keeping the story fresh. The *Washington Post*'s Desson Howe, while grading the movie as "formula-packed" and calculated, admitted that he found *Ghost* "surprisingly entertaining." Another *Washington Post* reviewer, Rita Kempley, described the film as such:

"An old-fashioned fantasy shot through with sentiment, 'Ghost' moves through genres as readily as a phantom through castle walls." In addition to praising the film's multifaceted appeal, Kempley called *Ghost* "emotionally honest."

The other Rubin project to see production in 1990 was *Jacob's Ladder,* a script that he had actually written ten years before. Due to the complex nature of the story, however, it was deemed by many to be unfilmable. It was not until *Jacob's Ladder* was cited by *American Film* as one of the best unproduced scripts in Hollywood that an impetus to film the story got underway. Dealing with elements of good and evil, life and death, and, as the biblical title implies, an ascension to a heavenly place, the story revolves around a man named Jacob Singer. The film begins by depicting Jacob as a foot soldier in Vietnam. As he is shown enjoying a lull in combat with his unit, an unseen enemy descends and attacks the group in a surrealistically violent scene. Jacob is severely wounded. From Vietnam, the story catapults to New York City where Jacob is working as a U.S. postal employee and living with a fiery Latina coworker named Jezzie (short for Jezebel). While this may seem like the beginning of the narrative thread, it is actually a just strand of a much larger weave. It is eventually revealed that Jacob may have previously been, or still is, a well-to-do professional with a doctorate, a beautiful wife, and three young children. His youngest son may or may not have been killed in a tragic accident and this may or may not have driven the family apart. All of this information is questionable, because no sooner is one Jacob Singer presented than another is suggested. At various points in the film, Jacob may still be dying from a bayonet wound on an operating table in Vietnam, he may indeed be a postal worker, or he may be living a life of quiet domesticity with his wife and children. The viewer is left to discern reality from illusion.

The unifying theme in *Jacob's Ladder* is one of hallucinatory (or real) intrusion and moral struggle. Whichever Jacob is being depicted, there are horrifying images from other lives and other realms intruding. Riding a subway car, Jacob sees the other passengers as demons, indicating that evil forces may be trying to claim him. At one point it is suggested that Jacob is a victim of a bizarre government experiment in Vietnam that has left him haunted by graphic hallucinations. Providing a balance of good to these malevolent visions is Jacob's chiropractor, Louis, who is alluded to more than once as a "guardian angel." The film raises many questions: Is Jacob alive or dead? Which is the real Jacob? Which of his lives are real or imagined? As the film concludes, the answers are provided, though not with absolute clarity nor complete certainty.

Rubin told Huffines that "with *Jacob's Ladder* I wanted people to understand my belief that there is a journey into death, that the spirit freeing itself from the body experiences a battle between the forces of heaven and hell and that the liberation came from the ability to stop struggling, to let go." The film attracted a sizable audience, many drawn by the strong visual style of the film and its graphic depictions of Jacob's hallucinations or visions. Others were attracted to the film's puzzle-like narrative and its challenging, overlapping structure. While many critics found the film confounding and frustrating, few could deny its dark attraction. Describing the film as the polar opposite, the "dark undersurface," of the themes Rubin examined in *Ghost, Globe and Mail* critic Rick Groen said of *Jacob's Ladder:* "It's baffling, it's frustrating, and it's mesmerizing." Janet Maslin, writing in the *New York Times,* appraised it as "a slick, riveting, viscerally scary film." Maslin continued by stating that "there is much to admire in the way the pieces of this elaborate puzzle come together." And the *MPG* called the film a "profoundly moving drama written with great skill by Bruce Joel Rubin." *MPG* also commented on the script's status as a best unproduced film: "All of the praise and hype surrounding the script is absolutely deserved. *Jacob's Ladder* is a complexly structured and intelligently written film, rich with ideas and potent horror."

"There seems to be a deep spiritual hunger many people aren't aware of," Rubin told *People.* "People ask me why I'm so interested in death. What I am really writing about is life. Death is the key—you cannot know the poignancy of life unless you accept its finality." Critics have noted that a large part of society seems to relate to Rubin's sentiments on life and death. "Bruce writes from the heart," stated *Ghost* director Zucker in the *Detroit Free Press.* "The idea that we all have a soul and the idea of the afterlife are very real to him. And I think that's why 'Ghost' struck a chord like it did and struck deep." The entry on *Jacob's Ladder* in the *MPG* also echoed this sentiment, stating that "there is a feeling of such genuine concern for the characters, and such an overwhelmingly sure sense of the unearthly, that the most bizarre things in the film become believable." Rubin agrees that his success comes from his belief in his material and his ability to convey universal emotions to his films' viewers. "I think it might be that audiences care . . . because my real feelings come through. And an audience really does know whether there's a heart in a movie."

BIOGRAPHICAL/CRITICAL SOURCES:

BOOKS

Motion Picture Guide 1987 Annual, Cinebooks, 1987, p. 65; *1991 Annual,* Baseline, 1991, p. 92.

PERIODICALS

Chicago Tribune, November 2, 1990.
Detroit Free Press, November 11, 1990, pp. 1P, 4P.
Globe and Mail (Toronto), November 3, 1990.
Los Angeles Times, July 13, 1990, pp. F1, F12-F13; February 20, 1991, p. F2.
Nation, December 10, 1990, p. 744.
New York Times, July 13, 1990; November 2, 1990.
People, April 15, 1991, pp. 57-58.
Time, October 17, 1983, p. 90.
Washington Post, July 13, 1990, pp. C1, C7; November 2, 1990, pp. C1, C7.*

—*Sketch by David M. Galens*

* * *

RUDE, George F(rederick) E(lliot) 1910-1993

OBITUARY NOTICE—See index for *CA* sketch: Born February 8, 1910, in Oslo, Norway; died January 8, 1993, in Rye, England. Historian, educator, and author. Focusing on individual rioters involved in eighteenth- and nineteenth-century European revolutions, Rude examined the often neglected role of common people in social upheaval. A teacher of modern languages at preparatory schools in England from the 1930s through the 1950s, Rude used information found in French police archives to compose his 1959 work, *The Crowd in the French Revolution.* His "history from below" approach was not readily accepted in British academic circles and in 1960 he accepted a position as senior lecturer at the University of Adelaide in South Australia. Rude later established the bilingual Inter-University Centre for European studies at Concordia University in Montreal, Quebec, where he was a professor of history beginning in 1970. In 1985, Rude's colleagues, including Christopher Hill and E. J. Hobsbawm, composed a *Festschrift* in his honor, titled *History from Below: Studies in Popular Protest and Popular Ideology.* Rude was the author of *Paris and London in the Eighteenth Century: Studies in Popular Protest, Criminal and Victim: Crime and Society in Early Nineteenth-Century England,* and *The French Revolution after Two Hundred Years.*

OBITUARIES AND OTHER SOURCES:

BOOKS

The International Who's Who, fifty-third edition, Europa, 1989.
Who's Who, Marquis, 1993.

PERIODICALS

New York Times, January 30, 1993, p. 11.
Times (London), January 27, 1993, p. 19.

RYAN, Kathryn Morgan   1925-1993

OBITUARY NOTICE—See index for *CA* sketch: Born August 3, 1925, in Oskaloosa, IA; died of emphysema, February 16, 1993, in Vero Beach, FL. Editor and author. After the death of her husband, World War II historian Cornelius Ryan, Kathryn Morgan Ryan used his journal and tapes to describe his struggle with cancer in her 1979 work, *A Private Battle*. After obtaining a degree in journalism from the University of Missouri, Ryan began her career in the 1940s as an associate editor at Conde Nast Publications, where she edited *House and Garden* magazine. In the late 1950s, Ryan was an associate editor for *House and Home* magazine. She served as editor and researcher for her husband's *The Longest Day* and *A Bridge Too Far*, acting as technical adviser for the screen adaptation of the latter. Ryan's 1972 novel is titled *The Betty Tree*.

OBITUARIES AND OTHER SOURCES:

PERIODICALS

Chicago Tribune, February 20, 1993, section 2, p. 19; February 21, 1993, section 2, p. 7.
Los Angeles Times, February 20, 1993.
New York Times, February 19, 1993, p. A19.

S

SAARI, Carolyn 1939-

PERSONAL: Born October 30, 1939, in Jersey City, NJ; daughter of John W. and Ina M. (Bain) Saari. *Education:* Vassar College, A.B., 1961; Simmons College, S.M., 1964; Smith College School for Social Work, Ph.D., 1973. *Politics:* Democrat. *Religion:* Protestant.

ADDRESSES: Home—6042 North Campbell Ave., Chicago, IL 60659. *Office*—School of Social Work, Loyola University of Chicago, 820 North Michigan Ave., Chicago, IL 60611.

CAREER: American National Red Cross, Alexandria, VA, social worker, 1961-65; Bryn Mawr College, Bryn Mawr, PA, field instructor, 1967-68; Family Service of Philadelphia, Philadelphia, PA, caseworker I, II, and III, and acting district director, 1965-69; Smith College, Northampton, MA, field instructor, 1968-71 and 1973-77, research advisor of master's program, 1973-77, research advisor of doctoral program, 1977-82, coordinator of field advisor of master's and doctoral programs, 1977-79, professor, 1977-91; Yale Psychiatric Institute, New Haven, CT, Yale Station, instructor and assistant chief social worker, 1969-71, School of Medicine, instructor and codirector of social work, 1974-77; Child Study Center, Albany, NY, social worker, 1973-74; State University of New York at Albany, Albany, instructor, 1973-74; Institute of Continuing Education, Connecticut Society for Clinical Social Work, New Haven, 1976-77; Loyola University of Chicago, Chicago, IL, professor, 1980—; Institute for Clinical Social Work, Chicago, professor of social work, 1984-92; social worker in private practice, Chicago, 1985—. Conductor of presentations and workshops, 1976—; Smith College, School for Social Work, associate dean, 1977-78, clinical coordinator of doctoral program and director of field work, 1977-79; Loyola University of Chicago, School of Social Work, chair of doctoral planning committee, 1980-86, director of doctoral program, 1986-87; Group for Advancement of Doctoral Education, Loyola representative, 1980-87, member of steering committee, 1980-81, secretary, 1986-87; Illinois Society for Clinical Social Work, member of referral service committee, 1982-85; Psychodynamic Educators Group in Social Work, convener, 1985-90; Far Northwest Counseling Center, case consultant, 1985-90; Children's Memorial Hospital, Department of Social Work, case consultant, 1987-91; case consultant for private group, 1990-92; Council on Social Work Education, Symposium on Clinical Practice, steering committee member, 1990—.

MEMBER: National Association of Social Work (chair of Estelle Gabrial Award Committee, 1986-90), American Orthopsychiatric Association fellow, Council on Social Work Education, Illinois Society for Clinical Social Work, Smith College School for Social Work Alumnae Association (Chicago chapter).

AWARDS, HONORS: Distinguished practitioner, National Academy of Practice in Social Work, 1986; Alpha Sigma Nu Award, 1991, for *The Creation of Meaning in Clinical Social Work.*

WRITINGS:

Clinical Social Work Treatment: How Does it Work?, Gardner, 1986.
The Creation of Meaning in Clinical Social Work, Guilford, 1991.

Contributor of book reviews and articles to periodicals, including *Child and Adolescent Social Work Journal, Journal of Teaching in Social Work, Clinical Social Work Journal, Clinical Supervisor, Social Thought,* and *Social Casework.*

SIDELIGHTS: Carolyn Saari told *CA:* "My choice of social work as a profession was undoubtedly determined by a number of factors. I was greatly influenced by the experience of being a child of liberal New England parents living in Montgomery, Alabama, and by graduating from Robert E. Lee High School during the bus strike led by Dr. Martin Luther King. In addition, the fact that my mother was an educator who became a social worker had a significant effect on my being a social worker who became an educator.

"I have long believed that social workers—who are primarily female and therefore are frequently conditioned and educated to be doers but not theorists—have had the most effective and soundly based approaches to psychotherapy and social interventions in the health and family care professions, but they have not very well articulated theoretical foundation for these activities. I have seen my work as an attempt to draw on what I have been taught about social work practice and to develop a theoretical framework that is compatible with traditional social work and current knowledge. Prominent figures in my understanding of social work practice have been teachers—Mrs. Berenice Cohen of Simmons College School of Social Work and Dr. Roger R. Miller of the Smith College School for Social Work. Major influences in the area of theoretical/practice interaction have been Dr. Charles Gardner of the Yale Psychiatric Institute for his humanitarian insight and practice wisdom, and the writings of Dr. Hans Loewald."

*   *   *

SAFIR, Leonard   1921-1992

OBITUARY NOTICE—See index for *CA* sketch: Born June 5, 1921, in New York, NY; died of lung cancer, December 13, 1992, in New York, NY. Producer, public relations executive, and author. Safir collaborated with his brother William Safire, a *New York Times* columnist, on four quotations anthologies. Safir began his career as a writer for the *Daily Mirror* in 1941. After serving in the United States Army during World War II, he joined the National Broadcasting Corporation (NBC) as the producer of the *Tex and Jinx* radio program. He moved into television in 1948, coediting *We, the People,* and in 1952 became the original associate producer of the NBC morning program *Today.* Safir produced many of television's early live programs during the 1950s and early 1960s, including the *Tonight* show. He moved into the realm of public relations and corporate communications in the 1960s and 1970s, and in the 1980s coauthored books, including *Words of Wisdom—More Good Advice* in 1989 and *Good Advice for Writers* in 1992.

OBITUARIES AND OTHER SOURCES:

PERIODICALS

New York Times, December 14, 1992, p. B10.

*   *   *

SAKS, Mike   1952-

PERSONAL: Born July 30, 1952, in Brighton, England. *Education:* University of Lancaster, B.A. (honors), 1973; University of Kent, M.A., 1975; University of London, Ph.D., 1985.

ADDRESSES: Office—De Montfort University, Scraptoft Campus, Leicester LE7 9SU, England.

CAREER: Leicester Polytechnic (now De Montfort University), Leicester, England, lecturer in sociology, then senior lecturer, 1978-88, head of department of health and community studies, 1989—. Also worked in various consultancy, advisory, and lecturing roles in the health and educational sector; involved in various health and nursing committees at local, regional, and national levels.

MEMBER: British Sociological Association, Society for the Social History of Medicine.

WRITINGS:

(Editor) *Alternative Medicine in Britain,* Clarendon, 1992. *Professions and the Public Interest,* Routledge & Kegan Paul, 1993.

Contributor to *Challenging Medicine,* edited by J. Gabe and others, Routledge & Kegan Paul, 1993. Also contributor to a number of mainstream journals and academic texts in the fields of social sciences and health.

WORK IN PROGRESS: Researching alternative medicine, comparative health care, nursing education, and professions.

*   *   *

SALE, Richard (Bernard)   1911(?)-1993

OBITUARY NOTICE—See index for *CA* sketch: Born December 17, c. 1911, in New York, NY; died of complications from two strokes, March 4, 1993. Director and author. Sale was the author of suspense and comedy films such as *Suddenly,* a 1954 picture starring Frank Sinatra and Sterling Hayden. Sale began his career as a free-lance writer for magazines in the 1930s and in the 1940s and 1950s wrote and directed films for Republic Pictures, Twentieth Century-Fox, United Artists, and British Lion. He frequently composed music for films as well. Among the screenplays Sale wrote or cowrote with his ex-wife, Mary Anita Loos, are *Strange Cargo* in 1940, *Mr. Belvedere Goes to College* in 1949, and *Torpedo Run* in 1958. He cowrote and directed the 1950 feature *I'll Get By* and the 1955 film *Gentlemen Marry Brunettes.* Sale also composed novels, adapting several, including *The Oscar* and *The White Buffalo,* as screenplays that were made into films. In the late 1950s Sale joined the Columbia Broadcasting System (CBS), writing for the television series *Yancy Derringer* with Loos.

OBITUARIES AND OTHER SOURCES:

BOOKS

Encyclopedia of American Film Comedy, Garland, 1987.
Halliwell's Filmgoer's Companion, ninth edition, Scribner, 1988.
International Motion Picture Almanac, Quigley, 1992.
Writers Directory: 1990-1992, St. James Press, 1990.

PERIODICALS

Los Angeles Times, March 8, 1993, p. A16.

*   *   *

SANDSTROEM, Yvonne L. 1933-

PERSONAL: Born August 10, 1933, in Vaesteraas, Sweden; daughter of Sten (an electrical engineer) and Margit (Windahl) Luttropp; married Dag C. G. Sandstroem, August 29, 1954 (died January 31, 1981); children: Anneli E., Helena Sandstroem Robinson. *Education:* University of Lund, B.A., 1954; Brown University, A.M., 1966, Ph.D., 1970.

ADDRESSES: Home—29 Creighton St., Providence, RI 02906. *Office*—Department of English, University of Massachusetts, Dartmouth, MA 02747.

CAREER: University of Massachusetts, Dartmouth, began as instructor in 1969, professor of English, 1979—; translator.

MEMBER: International P.E.N., Modern Language Association of America, Milton Society, Society for the Advancement of Scandinavian Studies, American Literary Translators Association.

WRITINGS:

TRANSLATOR

Lars Gustafsson, *The Tennis Players,* New Directions, 1983.
(With John Weinstock) Lars Gustafsson, *Stories of Happy People,* New Directions, 1986.
Lars Gustafsson, *Funeral Music for Free Masons,* New Directions, 1987.

Lars Gustafsson, *Bernard Foy's Third Castling,* New Directions, 1989.
C. J. L. Almqvist, *The Queen's Diadem,* Camden House, 1992.

WORK IN PROGRESS: Translating August Strindberg's novella *Tschandala.*

*   *   *

SAYRES, William C(ortlandt) 1927-1993

OBITUARY NOTICE—See index for *CA* sketch: Born April 5, 1927, in Detroit, MI; died while flying from Cairo, Egypt, to Geneva, Switzerland, to obtain medical treatment after suffering a heart attack, February 1, 1993. Anthropologist, educator, and author. Sayres spent fifteen years as coordinator of the Columbia University Teachers College program in international educational development, designing curriculum and textbooks to be used in developing countries. He was an instructor at Yale University and the State University of New York at Albany before joining the Columbia University faculty in 1963. Sayres became a professor emeritus at Columbia's Teachers College and acted as consultant to the ministries of education in Lima, Peru; and Kabul, Afghanistan. Sayres was the author of *Sammy Louis: The Life History of a Young Micmac* and *Social Aspects of Education,* as well as two novels, *Sonotaw* and *Do Good.*

OBITUARIES AND OTHER SOURCES:

BOOKS

Fifth International Directory of Anthropologists, University of Chicago Press, 1975.
Leaders in Education, fifth edition, Bowker, 1974.
Who's Who in America, Marquis, 1992.

PERIODICALS

New York Times, February 3, 1993, p. A21.

*   *   *

SCALES, Barbara 1926-

PERSONAL: Born December 8, 1926; daughter of Albert Milton (a machinist) and Myrtle Olive (a homemaker) Hadsall; married Emmet Thomas Scales (divorced, 1976); children: Michael Jon, Jeffrey Charles, Frederick Milton. *Education:* San Francisco State University, B.A., 1963; graduate study at San Francisco Art Institute, 1969-70; University of California, Berkeley, M.A., 1975, Ed.D., 1984. *Politics:* Democrat. *Religion:* Protestant. *Avocational interests:* Painting, children's art and drama.

ADDRESSES: Home—Berkeley, CA. *Office*—Harold E. Jones Child Study Center, Institute of Human Development, University of California, 2425 Atherton, Berkeley, CA 94705.

CAREER: Schoolteacher in Berkeley, CA, 1970-75; University of California, Berkeley, instructor in education and head teacher at Harold E. Jones Child Study Center, 1975-90, administrator, 1991—. San Francisco State University, part-time faculty member, 1989. Venus Gallery, organizing member, 1964; Allston Way Mural Arts Project, designer and coordinator, 1974; Uriarte Project, co-founder and member of board of directors, 1985; consultant to Children's Media Laboratory; artist, with solo and group shows.

MEMBER: International Pragmatics Association, National Association for the Education of Young Children, American Educational Research Association, Jean Piaget Society, Society for Research in Child Development, Amnesty International, California Professors of Early Childhood Education, Berkeley Linguistics Association, Stanford Child Language Association, Phi Delta Kappa, Sierra Club, Museum of Modern Art (San Francisco), Oakland Museum.

AWARDS, HONORS: Grants from Berkeley Civic Arts Commission and Berkeley Schools, 1974, and Skaggs Foundation, 1988.

WRITINGS:

(With P. Monighan, J. Van Hoorn, and Millie Almy) *Research on Play: The Bridge between Theory and Practice,* Teachers College Press, 1987.

(Editor with Millie Almy, A. Nicolopoulou, and S. Ervin-Tripp) *Play and the Social Context of Development in Early Care and Education,* Teachers College Press, 1991.

(Editor with P. Monighan-Nourot, J. Van Hoorn, and K. A. Alward) *Play at the Center of the Curriculum,* C. E. Merrill, 1992.

Work represented in anthologies, including *Current Topics in Early Childhood Education,* Volume 4, edited by L. Katz, [Urbana, IL], 1985; and *The Encyclopedia of Early Childhood Education,* edited by L. R. Williams and D. P. Fromberg, Garland Publishing, 1991.

WORK IN PROGRESS: Chapters for two books; presentations on gender in children's narratives and play.

SIDELIGHTS: Barbara Scales told *CA:* "I began writing about things that I had discovered in my research on children's play. I had long been enchanted by and curious about play as a phenomenon of both childhood and adult life. This interest stemmed from what I initially saw as a similarity to the creative activity experienced in painting and other art work. My curiosity about this has not been satisfied, but writing about the subject of play has nar-

rowed and clarified my thinking. It has also provided me with a number of other topics, such as the kind of language and interactive behavior that goes on in children's play; for example, gender-related selectivity or the influence of context on play.

"Most of my work has been collaborative, with the exception of a few articles or chapters. My vision is primarily that of an artist, so writing is like a kind of translation. I am really great at metaphor, but it is hard work to create links between metaphors. My work with children provides me with a great deal of wonderful material along this line.

"Vivian Paley has been a major influence, as has Anne Haas Dyson, both in my teaching and writing and in my approach to research. Other influences have been University of California professors John Gumperz, in anthropology, and his wife Jenny Cook-Gumperz, in educational sociology. William Corsaro from Indiana University was a powerful inspiration in the early seventies with respect to a methodological and philosophical orientation to research on children. University of California professor Millie Almy profoundly influenced me and helped me discipline myself with respect to writing and thinking about research."

*   *   *

SCHAEFFER, Frank   1952-

PERSONAL: Born August 3, 1952, in Champery, Switzerland; immigrated to United States, 1980; son of Francis (a theologian) and Edith (a writer; maiden name, Seville) Schaeffer; married Regina Walsh, 1970; children: Jessica, Francis, John. *Politics:* "Republican (most of the time!)" *Religion:* Greek Orthodox.

ADDRESSES: Home—Salisbury, MA. *Agent*—Curtis Lundgren, Curtis Bruce Agency, 3015 Evergreen Dr., Suite A, Plover, WI 54467.

CAREER: Schaeffer Productions, Los Gatos, CA, president, 1976-85; director of feature motion pictures, including *Wired to Kill,* 1986; *Headhunter,* 1988; *Rebel Storm,* 1989; *Baby on Board,* 1992; director of the documentary series *Whatever Happened to the Human Race?;* writer.

AWARDS, HONORS: Critics Award, 1979, for *Whatever Happened to the Human Race?;* awards for best director and best film from Academy of Science Fiction and Horror Films, 1986, for *Wired to Kill.*

WRITINGS:

Whatever Happened to the Human Race? (documentary series), Dutch National Television, 1978.
Addicted to Mediocrity (nonfiction), Crossway, 1980.
A Time for Anger (nonfiction), Crossway, 1984.

Wired to Kill (screenplay), American Distribution Group, 1986.
Portofino (novel), Macmillan, 1992.

WORK IN PROGRESS: Kindred Spirit, a sequel to *Portofino; Dancing Alone,* nonfiction about "the quest for authentic faith in the age of false religion"; *The Call,* a novel about not "making it" in Hollywood.

SIDELIGHTS: Frank Schaeffer is a movie maker who has also won praise as a novelist. His *Portofino* is the first-person story of Calvin, an adolescent who accompanies his Presbyterian fundamentalist parents and his two sisters on annual excursions to the Italian Mediterranean, where the parents hope to convert the Roman Catholics from what they perceive as paganism. While the father settles on the sunny beach and surrounds himself with religious literature, the mother roams the shore to proclaim her religious conviction to the hapless sunbathers and swimmers. Calvin, meanwhile, wanders about and meets an odd and enchanting assortment of people, including beach attendants, and old homosexual painter, and an upper-class English girl, Jennifer, who firmly holds her own views on religion as a member of the Church of England. Calvin also experiences a rather curious range of adventures, including an encounter with a dangerous octopus. Richard Eder, in his review for the *Los Angeles Times,* proclaimed *Portofino* "a rich brew of cross-cultural comedy." He added that Schaeffer "makes [the novel's] utterly unpredictable family . . . both painful and appealing." *Portofino,* Eder affirmed, is "sentimental, celebratory, evocative and very funny."

Schaeffer told *CA:* "My pet, wife, and children are a good deal more important to me than my writing. Writing is a way of paying the bills and making life more interesting. Real life is the point, however. My writing is descriptive, not perscriptive. *I* do my living in the real world, not only on the page."

BIOGRAPHICAL/CRITICAL SOURCES:

PERIODICALS

Los Angeles Times, September 17, 1992, p. E10.

*   *   *

SCHAEFFER, Mark   1956-

PERSONAL: Born November 21, 1956, in New York, NY; son of Aaron J. (an educational administrator) and Frances (a Spanish teacher; maiden name, Buchholtz) Schaeffer; married Debra Goldentyer (a writer and producer), October 10, 1987. *Education:* Princeton University, A.B., 1978. *Avocational interests:* Theatre (as play-

wright and actor), music (as listener and performer), computers (as user and consultant).

ADDRESSES: Home and office—933 Rose Ave., Oakland, CA 94611.

CAREER: Visual Education Corp., Princeton, NJ, associate producer, 1978-79, project director, 1979-84; free-lance writer and audiovisual producer, 1984-89; free-lance writer and audiovisual producer in partnership with wife, Debra Goldentyer, 1989—. Founder, Princeton Mime Company; actor in local stage productions, including *White Nights and Golden Sleigh Rides,* 1986-87, and *Under the Golden Dome,* 1987-88.

AWARDS, HONORS: Golden Apple, National Educational Film and Video Festival, 1986, for the educational filmstrip *Becoming an Entreprenuer;* Gold Award, Houston International Film Festival, 1987, for the educational filmstrip *Eating Disorders;* National Award of Excellence, National Office of the Arthritis Foundation, 1987, for writing and producing the slide program *People with Arthritis . . . and People Who Help.*

WRITINGS:

NONFICTION

(And illustrator) *Library Displays Handbook,* H. W. Wilson, 1990.

PLAYS; FOR CHILDREN

(Writer and composer with Barbara Ackerman) *Halleyballoo,* produced at the New Jersey State Museum, 1986.
(And composer and director) *White Nights and Golden Sleigh Rides,* produced at the Creative Theatre of Princeton, 1986-87.
Under the Golden Dome, songs by Rita Asch, produced at the New Jersey State Museum, 1987-88.
Digging the Whole, songs by Asch, produced at the Creative Theatre of Princeton, 1988.
Where Snow Falls Up, songs by Asch, produced at the Creative Theatre of Princeton, 1989.

OTHER

Also author of educational filmstrips, such as *Becoming an Entreprenuer* and *Eating Disorders;* slide shows, such as *People with Arthritis . . . and People Who Help;* videotapes; audiotapes; and print materials for various organizations, including the American Correctional Association, Public Service Electric & Gas Co., Prentice Hall, TDM/ McGraw-Hill and Educational Testing Service.

WORK IN PROGRESS: Celebrities' Feet, a stage play.

SIDELIGHTS: Mark Schaeffer told *CA:* "I'm not really an 'author' in the usual sense of the word—I'm more of a contractor in that all of my writing is done under contract to various clients. Though much of my writing has been published, very little of it appears under my name. The *Library Displays Handbook* is the only exception so far.

"The *Library Displays Handbook* was initiated in 1988 by Richard Lidz, president of Visual Educational Corporation (VEC, my former employer, from whom I'd amicably parted company in 1984). He originally intended to sell it as a videotape idea to H. W. Wilson, for whom VEC had produced several videotapes in the past. I was called in to write and direct the videotape, as I'd done for *Basic Book Repair* the year before. As Dick and I talked, however, we realized that library displays was much too big a subject for a single videotape—that it was much more suited to a series of tapes, or better yet, a book. When Dick sold the idea to Bruce Carrick at H. W. Wilson, my name remained attached to the project as writer.

"Originally, I was hired only as a writer for the project—the matter of who was going to produce the illustrations and sample displays was left unresolved. It wasn't until after the book was completely written that I was asked to handle the art program as well. In a very short amount of time (about six weeks), I produced the line drawings on my computer and (with the help of some hired artist friends) built the display elements.

"For the most part, I know nothing about the subjects I write about—I generally do research, interview experts in the field, and organize information into a clear and (presumably) interesting presentation. In library displays, however, I could in some sense be considered an authority: graphic arts has been a hobby of mine since childhood, and I'd often contributed designs and illustrations to the audiovisual programs I'd produced. Though I reviewed existing literature and interviewed librarians to find out what they'd like to see in such a book, most of the techniques described in the book are my own."

*   *   *

SCHAUB, Mary H(unter)   1943-

PERSONAL: Born June 28, 1943, in Raleigh, NC; daughter of Carter Stuart (founder and president of Apex Motor Lines, Inc.) and Deane (a teacher; maiden name, Russell) Schaub. *Education:* North Carolina State University, B.S. (with honors), 1966. *Politics:* "Conservative Republican." *Religion:* "Member, Apex Baptist Church." *Avocational interests:* Reading.

ADDRESSES: Home and office—306 West Chatham St., Apex, NC 27502-1410.

CAREER: Private math tutor, Apex, NC, 1966-71; Apex Motor Lines, Inc., Apex, bookkeeper, 1966-71; home health care provider for parents, Apex, 1971—; writer, 1972—.

MEMBER: World Wildlife Fund, Science Fiction Writers of America, Nature Conservancy, American Bible Society, Public Service Research Council, Heritage Foundation, United Service Organizations.

WRITINGS:

(With Andre Norton and P. M. Griffin) *Flight of Vengeance,* Tor, 1992.

Works represented in anthologies, including *Survival from Infinity,* edited by Elwood, 1974; *Magic in Ithkar II,* edited by Andre Norton and Adams, Tor, 1985; *Tales of the Witch World,* edited by Norton, Tor, Volume 1, 1987, Volume 3, 1990; *Catfantastic,* edited by Norton and Martin Greenberg, DAW, Volume 2, 1991, Volume 3, 1993. Contributor of a short story to *Analog* magazine, and of a novella to *Galileo* magazine.

WORK IN PROGRESS: "Always thinking. . . ."

SIDELIGHTS: Mary H. Schaub told *CA:* "I began writing in 1972—like Agatha Christie, to see if I couldn't at least equal what was selling. I answered an ad for a science fiction anthology, and although that first try was rejected, I sold the story to the second editor I tried. I then encountered a blizzard of rejections until Ben Bova accepted a story for *Analog,* and I placed a novella with the now lamentably gone quarterly *Galileo.* Meanwhile, I had written a letter of reader's appreciation in the 1960s to Andre Norton, a favorite author, and to my joyous surprise, it grew into regular correspondence. I have been beset by health problems for many years, and am of necessity a homebound hermit. I must express my lasting gratitude to Miss Norton for her encouragement (and bravery) in persisting to invite me to contribute to her various anthologies and to venture into a book-length work. No writer could ask for a better mentor and friend."

*   *   *

SCHEIMANN, Eugene   1897-1993

OBITUARY NOTICE—See index for *CA* sketch: Born February 19, 1897, in Hungary; died February 24, 1993. Physician and author. Scheimann was the writer of a nationally syndicated column, "Let's Stay Well." He received his medical degree from the University of Budapest and came to the United States in the mid-1920s, where he practiced medicine on the Near North Side of Chicago for sixty-five years. Scheimann specialized in problems related to alcoholism, loneliness, and sex. He was a contributing editor of *Forum* magazine and the author of several books concerning health issues, including *A Doctor's Approach to Alcohol and Alcoholism* and *Sex Can Save Your Heart and Life.*

OBITUARIES AND OTHER SOURCES:

PERIODICALS

Chicago Tribune, February 25, 1993, section 3, p. 11.

*   *   *

SCHILLER, JoAnn 1949-

PERSONAL: Born November 26, 1949, in Philadelphia, PA; daughter of Leonard S. and Betty Lou (Sall) Malmud; married Berle Schiller (an attorney), October 7, 1983; children: Jon, Joseph, Abbe, Maggie. *Education:* University of Bridgeport, B.S., 1971; Temple University, M.Ed., 1991. *Avocational interests:* Tennis, reading.

ADDRESSES: Home—331 Cherry Bend, Merion, PA 19066. *Office*—Harcum College, Bryn Mawr, PA 19010.

CAREER: Colonial Penn Insurance Co., Philadelphia, PA, in corporate training, 1978-85; Harcum College, Bryn Mawr, PA, assistant to the president, 1991—. Management training consultant.

WRITINGS:

(With Merry Jones) *Stepmothers: Keeping It Together with Your Husband and His Kids,* Birch Lane Press, 1992.

*   *   *

SCHNUR, Steven 1952-

PERSONAL: Born April 8, 1952. *Education:* Sarah Lawrence College, B.A., 1974; Hunter College of City University of New York, M.A., 1980.

ADDRESSES: Home—19 Montrose Rd., Scarsdale, NY 10583.

CAREER: Bernard M. Baruch College of City University of New York, NY, instructor, 1977; Union of American Hebrew Congregations, editor, 1981-92; Writing Institute, Sarah Lawrence College, 1990—; writer. Mercy College, adjunct professor, 1991-92.

WRITINGS:

FOR CHILDREN

The Narrowest Bar Mitzvah, Union of American Hebrew Congregations, 1986.
The Return of Morris Schumsky, Union of American Hebrew Congregations, 1987.

Hannah and Cyclops, Bantam, 1990.

ESSAYS

Daddy's Home! Reflections of a Family Man, Crown, 1990, published in paperback as *Father's Day,* Avon, 1991.
This Thing Called Love: Thoughts of an Out-of-Step Romantic, Morrow, 1992.

OTHER

Contributor to periodicals, including *New York Times, Reform Judaism, Woman's Day, New Woman, Moxie, First for Women, Twins, Denver Quarterly, Commentary,* and *Real People.*

*   *   *

SCHOR, Juliet B. 1955-

PERSONAL: Born November 9, 1955. *Education:* Wesleyan University, B.A. (magna cum laude), 1975; University of Massachusetts, Ph.D., 1982.

ADDRESSES: Office—Women's Studies, 34 Kirkland St., Harvard University, Cambridge, MA 02138.

CAREER: Williams College, Williamstown, MA, assistant professor of economics, 1981-83; Columbia University, New York City, assistant professor of economics at Barnard College, 1983-84; Harvard University, Cambridge, MA, assistant professor of economics, 1984-89, associate professor of economics, 1989-92, senior lecturer in economics, 1992—, head tutor of committee on degrees in women's studies, 1991-92, director of studies for women's studies program, 1992—. Center for Popular Economics, founder and staff economist, 1978-90; United Nations, World Institute for Development Economics Research (WIDER), research adviser for Project on Global Macropolicy, 1985-91. Wesleyan University, member of board of trustees, 1988-91; Harvard University, research affiliate for center for European studies, 1986—; Economic Policy Institute, member of research advisory council, 1986—. South End Press, founder and editor, 1977-79.

AWARDS, HONORS: Teaching fellowship from University of Massachusetts, 1976-79; Distinguished Teacher Award, University of Massachusetts, 1978; Research fellowship from Brookings Institution, 1980-81.

WRITINGS:

(With Daniel Cantor) *Tunnel Vision: Labor, the World Economy, and Central America,* South End Press, 1987.

(With Gerald A. Epstein) *Macropolicy in the Rise and Fall of the Golden Age,* World Institute for Development Economics Research, 1988.

(Editor, with Stephen A. Marglin) *The Golden Age of Capitalism: Reinterpreting the Postwar Experience,* Oxford University Press, 1989.

(Editor, with Tariq Banuri) *Financial Openness and National Policy Autonomy: Opportunities and Constraints,* Oxford University Press, 1992.

The Overworked American: The Unexpected Decline of Leisure, Basic Books, 1992.

Economic columnist, *Z* (magazine), 1987—. Contributor of articles to periodicals. Member of editorial board, *International Journal of Applied Economics,* 1992—.

WORK IN PROGRESS: Post-Consumerism, for Basic Books; editing *Changing Production Relations: A Global Perspective,* for World Institute for Development Economics Research; research on the environment and on leisure, working hours, and consumption.

SIDELIGHTS: In *The Overworked American: The Unexpected Decline of Leisure,* Juliet B. Schor chronicles the tendency of United States citizens to spend increasing amounts of time working at the expense of involving themselves in such nonprofessional activities as volunteer service, rest, and self-improvement. According to Schor, the trend to work longer hours began in the 1970s after the length of the average workweek fell to 39 hours. Since that point, Americans have been increasing the amount of time that they devote to work. At the time of the book's publication in the early 1990s, Americans were working an average of 47 hours a week. If the pattern were to hold over the next 20 years, according to Schor, "the average person would be on the job 60 hours a week—for an annual 3,000 hours a year."

The tendency to overwork has contributed to a number of problems in American society. Schor notes that overworked employees are sleeping less and experiencing higher levels of stress. She also documents the effect that overworking has on families: parents no longer have the time to provide their children with proper attention and care. Additionally, the author contends that Americans are less willing to involve themselves in learning new skills—such as training to play a musical instrument or acting in local theater troupes—because such nonprofessional activities take time and effort that employees are reluctant to spend after a hard day in the office. People, therefore, devote their free time to such activities as shopping at the mall or watching television, which require minimal energy.

Schor offers various reasons for the tendency to spend more time working. The advance of technology has created higher standards for Americans who work, whether it be in the home or in the office. Schor acknowledges that such efficient labor-saving devices as washing machines and vacuum cleaners have created higher expectations for homemakers who are spending more time in maintaining a pleasant living environment. She also remarks that, with the invention of portable computers and communications equipment, employers presume that their workers are no longer confined by the normal office hours or environment.

In *The Overworked American* Schor also notes that the capitalist system, in which the economy is primarily determined by private parties rather than controlled by the government, has also played a major role in increasing the amount of time spent in professional capacities. The author remarks that it is less expensive to have fewer people work more hours—even if the employees are compensated for overtime—than it is to hire more people. Extra employees require corporations to pay for costly medical benefits. Additionally, Schor asserts that by keeping the number of workers low, employers contribute to high unemployment which, in turn, gives businesses the justification to keep wages down.

Schor also analyzes trends that have contributed to the fluctuation of the American workweek throughout history. During the 1930s economists and members of trade unions led the push for shorter working hours. In the years that followed World War II, some argued that the normal 40 hour workweek should be reduced to 35 hours. At the time industries were realizing substantial financial growth, according to Schor. In the 1950s economic experts began to worry that Americans would eventually be spending too much time in nonprofessional pursuits. But as economic growth began to stagnate in the early 1970s, Schor notes that workers found themselves in a position where they had to work harder in order to maintain the same standards of living that they had come to know. Relatedly, Schor charges that since the mid-twentieth century, Americans have become increasingly fixed on buying material goods in order to provide themselves with a measure of happiness in life. The focus on consumption has resulted, in the author's opinion, in negative patterns of working harder in order to have more money to spend on manufactured products.

To remedy the situation, Schor suggests that all salaried white-collar workers should only be responsible for spending a set number of hours in the office. (One of her contentions is that management takes advantage of salaried employees by paying them a fixed income, while coercing them to work extra hours.) Those who work overtime, in Schor's opinion, should then be provided with additional compensation. Rather than providing overtime employees with more money in all cases, however, companies should consider offering compensatory time to employees who work more than the required number of hours. After a person has worked enough overtime, they should be allowed time away from the office based on the number of hours that they have banked.

While Schor realizes that many employers will be reluctant to take her advice, she cites numerous examples of situations in which shortening the workweek has resulted in no drop-off—and in some cases a rise—in productivity. In an interview with *Newsweek* she pointed out that both Medtronic, Inc., in Minneapolis, and the Kellogg Company in Battle Creek, Michigan, discovered that reducing the number of hours in the workplace boosted the efficiency of their workers. In *The Overworked American* the author also provides examples of numerous countries—predominantly in Western Europe—that have preserved their working and living standards without compromising the length of the workweek.

Several reviewers were impressed with Schor's scholarship. Troy Segal of *Business Week* acknowledged that "solid reasoning and thorough numbers-crunching mark her work." And though he felt that readers might be overwhelmed by the statistics presented in the beginning of the book, he encouraged those unfamiliar with the subject to "bear with it: *The Overworked American* becomes a fascinating blend of social observation and economic theory as it discusses the causes of the work crunch." In the *New York Times Book Review*, Robert Kuttner also commended Schor's work, remarking that "her training as an economist, happily, has alerted her to this widely overlooked pocketbook issue, but without deadening either her ear for the English language or her social conscience. Her book is systematic enough to satisfy the scholar, yet it is witty and engaging for the lay reader."

BIOGRAPHICAL/CRITICAL SOURCES:

BOOKS

Schor, Juliet B., *The Overworked American: The Unexpected Decline of Leisure,* Basic Books, 1992.

PERIODICALS

Business Week, February 17, 1992, p. 18.
Newsweek, February 17, 1992, pp. 42-43.
New York Times Book Review, February 2, 1992, p. 1.

—*Sketch by Mark F. Mikula*

*   *   *

SCHREIBER, Le Anne   1945-

PERSONAL: Born August 4, 1945, in Evanston, IL; daughter of Newton Bartholomew and Beatrice (Meyer) Schreiber; divorced. *Education:* Rice University, B.A.,

1967; Stanford University, M.A., 1968; postgraduate work at Harvard University, 1969-74.

ADDRESSES: Office—229 West 43rd St., New York, NY 10023. *Agent*—Carol Sheedy, Sheedy Agency, 41 King St., New York, NY 10014.

CAREER: Harvard University, Cambridge, MA, teaching fellow, 1971-74; *Time,* New York City, staff writer, 1974-76; *womenSports* (magazine), New York City, editor in chief, 1976-78; *New York Times,* New York City, assistant editor of sports department, 1978, sports editor, 1978-80, assistant book review editor, 1980-82, deputy book review editor, 1982-84; writer.

MEMBER: National Book Critics Circle (member of board of directors).

AWARDS, HONORS: Woodrow Wilson fellow, 1967; Harvard Prize fellow, 1969; Helen Rogers Reid Award, New York League of Business and Professional Women, 1979.

WRITINGS:

Midstream: The Story of a Mother's Death and a Daughter's Renewal, Viking, 1989.

SIDELIGHTS: At the age of thirty-three Le Anne Schreiber, a highly successful journalist, became the first female sports editor for the *New York Times.* But as she approached the age of forty, after ten years of extremely competitive, high-pressure magazine and newspaper work, Schreiber was ready to leave Manhattan for a life of writing and fishing in the country. "After such a decade," she wrote in the preface to her best-selling book, *Midstream: The Story of a Mother's Death and a Daughter's Renewal,* "I was ready for a life of my own invention, a life more contemplative, more pastoral. Above all I wanted a life under my control." In August of 1985, after a first satisfying year of life in the country, her brother telephoned to inform her that her mother was terminally ill with pancreatic cancer. Throughout the next fifteen months, Schreiber commuted between a new home she was restoring in upstate New York and her mother's deathbed in Minnesota, keeping a journal all the while of her experiences in both places. Her resulting book, *Midstream,* is, according to Nina Burleigh in her *Chicago Tribune* review, "a balanced tale of the end of one life and the renewal of another in middle age."

Many reviewers praised the empathy and compassion, as well as the courage and realism, with which Schreiber reports her mother's suffering. "My mother died toothless, blind, her limbs blue and swollen with edema, an oxygen feed strapped to her face," Schreiber wrote in the preface to *Midstream.* "My trial was to keep seeing her, to find her amid the grotesque distortions of the disease. It was the hardest thing I've ever done." Experiencing her mother's pain bodily, as if it were her own, Schreiber found that she needed to distance herself from the process her mother was enduring, if only in order to remain strong enough to assist her through it. Writing in a journal helped Schreiber to achieve this strength. "During the last month of my mother's life, this journal was my means of survival. In part it gave me a saving distance, reminded me that I was a witness to dying, not the one dying. The journal was also my weapon against denial, my way of looking in the presence of so many averted eyes, my way of remembering in the face of so much forgetting." Nancy Mairs wrote in the *Los Angeles Times Book Review* that *Midstream* "comes alive, paradoxically, when Schreiber faces her mother's death. . . . Pain . . . is something both must endure in their separate ways, and she depicts it in its various forms unflinchingly but without either melodrama or ghoulishness."

Midstream is also about the author's renewal at mid-life. "As the shelter that was her mother deteriorates," Christopher Lehmann-Haupt commented in the *New York Times,* "an old house the author is renovating comes to life for her. As the well of mother love drains away, she has a new well dug deep to supply her renovated house with water." Much of the book is devoted to descriptions of a newly discovered natural world around Schreiber's home in New York. In fact, the author's original purpose for the journal was to record her fishing experiences. The combination in Schreiber's journal of two themes—of starting over in a rural life at age forty and of tending her mother's protracted illness and death—did not make sense to her until later. "In the pages of the notebooks I recorded the beginnings of my new life and the ending of my mother's, never imagining that, placed side by side, they might come to coexist with less painful discordance. I wrote in this journal the day I found the old house that I would restore as my new home. And I wrote in it minutes before my mother died, knowing that she was going to die in minutes. The juxtapositions of beginnings and endings were shattering as I recorded them, but ultimately, it was through them that I found points of contact between my living and her dying." Hilma Wolitzer observed in her *Washington Post Book World* review that "*Midstream* charts the dying of one woman and its tragic, rippling effect on an entire family; at the same time it is a chronicle of survival and acceptance."

Critics generally applauded the grace and craftsmanship with which Schreiber wove an engrossing story from her experience. "Her prose is pure, brimming with poetic turns," Ruth Pollack Coughlin wrote of Schreiber in the *Detroit News.* A *Publishers Weekly* reviewer summarized, "Despite the inevitability of the outcome and the universal nature of the experiences described, these closely focused journal entries—potent distillations of sorrow, frustration and exhaustion—develop a powerful narrative impetus." Nancy Mairs applauded the book for an immediacy of approach that allows the reader "to share in a welter of responses such a loss arouses," but she found the descriptions of the natural world and the constant juxtaposition of death and renewal somewhat forced. *Time* reviewer R. Z. Sheppard, however, asserted that Schreiber's connection of her own renewal and her mother's death are ultimately very effective: "She achieves this satisfying parity with emotional integrity and literary tact that suggest a depth of experience the author only hints at. Wisely. The results are clear and lasting observations rather than self-justifying trendy confessions."

BIOGRAPHICAL/CRITICAL SOURCES:

BOOKS

Bestsellers 1990, Issue 2, Gale, 1990, pp. 68-69.
Schreiber, Le Anne, *Midstream: The Story of a Mother's Death and a Daughter's Renewal,* Viking, 1989.

PERIODICALS

Chicago Tribune, January 29, 1990, p. 3.
Detroit News, January 24, 1990.
Los Angeles Times Book Review, January 21, 1990, p. 3.
New York Times, January 11, 1990.
Publishers Weekly, November 10, 1989, p. 54; February 16, 1990, p. 56.
Time, January 22, 1990, p. 68.
Washington Post Book World, January 21, 1990.*

*   *   *

SCREECH, M(ichael) A(ndrew)   1926-

PERSONAL: Born May 2, 1926, in Plymouth, Devon, England; son of Richard John (a policeman) and Nellie (Maunder) Screech; married Anne Reeve (a researcher), April 5, 1956; children: Matthew Erasmus John, Timothy Benjamin Mark, Toby Daniel Luke. *Education:* University of London, B.A. (with first class honors), 1950; attended University of Montpellier; University of Birmingham, D.Litt., 1959. *Religion:* Church of England. *Avocational interests:* Walking.

ADDRESSES: Home—5 Swanston-field, Whitchurch-on-Thames RG8 7HP, England. *Office*—All Souls College, Oxford University, Oxford OX1 4AL, England.

CAREER: University of Birmingham, Birmingham, England, lecturer, 1951-58, senior lecturer, 1959-61; University of London, London, England, reader, 1961-66, held personal chair of French, 1966-71, Fielden Professor of French Language and Literature, 1971-84; Oxford University, Oxford, England, visiting fellow, 1981, senior research fellow of All Souls College, 1984—, Zaharoff Lecturer, 1988. University of Western Ontario, visiting professor, 1964-65; State University of New York at Albany, visiting professor, 1968-69; University of Wisconsin—Madison, Johnson Professor at Institute for Research in the Humanities, 1978-79; University of Regina, Edmund Campion Lecturer, 1985; University of North Carolina at Chapel Hill, Wiley Visiting Professor, 1986; College de France, professor, 1989; Sorbonne, University of Paris IV, associate professor, 1990. Warburg Institute, member of governing committee, 1970-84; Comite d'Humanisme et Renaissance, member, 1971—; Comite de parrainage des Classiques de l'Humanisme, member, 1988—. *Military service:* British Army, Intelligence Corps, 1944-48, served in the Far East; became staff sergeant.

MEMBER: British Academy (fellow), Royal Society of Literature (fellow), Societe Historique de Geneve (corresponding member), Athenaeum Club.

AWARDS, HONORS: D.Litt. from University of London, 1982, and Oxford University, 1990; Chevalier, Ordre National du Merite, 1983; Medaille de la Ville de Tours, 1984; Chevalier, Legion d'Honneur, 1992.

WRITINGS:

(Editor) Francois Rabelais, *Le Tiers Livre,* French and European Publications, Inc., 1964.

(Editor with R. M. Calder) Rabelais, *Gargantua,* French and European Publications, Inc., 1970.

Erasmus: Ecstasy and the "Praise of Folly," Duckworth, 1980, Viking Penguin, 1989, revised edition in French, 1991.

Rabelais, Duckworth, 1982, revised edition in French, 1991.

Montaigne and Melancholy: The Wisdom of the "Essays," Duckworth, 1983, Susquehanna University Press, 1984, revised edition in French, 1991.

(Editor and translator from French) Michel de Montaigne, *An Apology for Raymond Sebond,* Penguin, 1987, Viking Penguin, 1988.

Looking at Rabelais, Oxford University Press, 1988.

(Editor with wife, Anne Reeve) *Erasmus' Annotations on the New Testament: Acts, Romans, First and Second Corinthians—Facsimile of the Final Latin Text, with All Earlier Variants,* E. J. Brill, 1989.

(Translator) *Michel de Montaigne: The Complete Essays,* Viking Penguin, 1992.

Other books include *The Rabelaisian Marriage,* 1958, revised edition published in French, 1991; *L'Evangelisme de Rabelais,* 1959, revised edition published in English, 1991; *Tiers Livre de Pantagruel,* 1964; *Les epistres et evangiles de Lefevre d'Etaples,* 1964; (with John Jollife) *Les Regrets et autres oeuvres poetiques,* 1966; *Marot evangelique,* 1967;

La Pantagrueline Prognostication, 1975; and (with Stephen Rawles and others) *A New Rabelais Bibliography: Editions before 1626,* 1987. Editor of reprints of *Le Nouveau Testament de Lefevre d'Etaples,* 1970; F. de Billon's *Le Fort inexpugnable de l'Honneur de Sexe Femenin,* 1970; *Opuscules d'Amour par Heroet et autres divins poetes,* 1970; and *Amyot: Les oeuvres morales et meslees de Plutarque,* 1971. Work represented in anthologies. Contributor to journals in the humanities.

WORK IN PROGRESS: Research on Renaissance literature, particularly on authors who wrote in Latin and French; research on the history of ideas; research on "Christian laughter."

SIDELIGHTS: M. A. Screech told *CA:* "My main interests lie within the history of ideas, and with authors studied and understood in their historical contexts. The Renaissance particularly interests me; an understanding of the contexts of authors such as Erasmus, Rabelais, Marot, Joachim Du Bellay, and Montaigne requires a study of theology, law, medicine, philosophy, linguistics, aesthetics, and so on, all within the context of the continuity of the Graeco-Roman-Judaeo-Christian traditions."

*   *   *

SEINFELD, Jerry 1954-

PERSONAL: Born April 29, 1954, in Brooklyn, NY; son of Kalman (in business) and Betty Seinfeld. *Education:* Queens College, graduated with degree in communications and theater, 1976. *Avocational interests:* Baseball, sports cars.

ADDRESSES: Home—Los Angeles, CA; and New York, NY. *Office*—c/o Lori Jonas, Jonas Public Relations, Inc., 417 South Beverly Dr., Suite 201, Beverly Hills, CA 90212.

CAREER: Stand-up comedian, actor, and screenwriter. Worked variously as a light bulb salesman, a waiter, and a jewelry street vendor. Creator, with Larry David, and producer and star of *Seinfeld,* National Broadcasting Company, Inc. (NBC-TV), 1989—. Tours frequently as a stand-up comic. Made regular appearances on *The Tonight Show* and *Late Night with David Letterman.* Appeared briefly as the Governor's joke writer, *Benson,* American Broadcasting Companies, Inc. (ABC-TV), 1980. Appeared in numerous television specials, including *The Tonight Show Starring Johnny Carson 19th Anniversary Special,* NBC-TV, 1981; "Rodney Dangerfield—It's Not Easy Bein' Me," *On Location,* HBO, 1986; "Jerry Seinfeld—Stand-Up Confidential," *On Location,* HBO, 1987; *Late Night with David Letterman Seventh Anniver-*

sary Show, NBC-TV, 1989; and *Today at 40,* NBC-TV, 1992.

AWARDS, HONORS: American Comedy Award, funniest male comedy club stand-up, 1988; Clio Award, best announcer radio commercial, 1988; Emmy Award nominations for outstanding writing in a comedy series, 1991, and for best actor in a comedy series, 1992, and American Comedy Award, funniest actor in a television series, 1992 and 1993, all for *Seinfeld.*

WRITINGS:

"Jerry Seinfeld—Stand-Up Confidential," *On Location* (television special), HBO, 1987.
(With others) *Seinfeld* (television series), NBC-TV, 1989—.

Also author of stand-up routines.

ADAPTATIONS: Seinfeld greeting cards, T-shirts, mugs, buttons, and wall calendars.

SIDELIGHTS: Jerry Seinfeld is a well-known stand-up comedian, he is also the creator, producer, and star of *Seinfeld,* a popular NBC sitcom that many feel views the world a little differently than most programs. The show centers on the days and nights of a stand-up comedian, Jerry Seinfeld, and the events of his everyday life. He works his experiences and conversations into his routines, which are shown at the beginning and the end of each episode. Basically, Seinfeld plays Seinfeld. "*Seinfeld* defines itself best by what it doesn't do," maintained Richard Panek in *Mirabella.* "The dialogue doesn't follow the typical setup-and-punchline formula of the typical sitcom. The acting doesn't follow the broad-gesture-and-bombast technique of the typical sitcom. And the sensibility doesn't follow any sitcom, period." Chris Smith, writing in *New York,* pointed out that "the cast of *Seinfeld* is getting the cranky rhythms of New York just right. . . . Most TV shows would try to conjure New York atmosphere by using zany dese-and-dose accents. *Seinfeld,* set in a gray prewar apartment on West 81st Street, has got the *attitude* down: Jerry and his pals obsess comically over the tiny annoyances and dramas of urban life, circa [1993]—stuff like standing in bank lines or hassling with the dry cleaner." Smith also observed that "*Seinfeld* doesn't feel like sitcom television; it feels more like a conversation with your funniest friends."

It is Seinfeld's background as a stand-up comedian, as well as that of the show's cocreator, Larry David, that sets *Seinfeld* apart from other sitcoms, which tend to be more formula driven. Growing up in Massapequa, Long Island, however, Seinfeld was not the family member who earned the most laughs—it was his father. "My dad was very funny," recalled Seinfeld in an interview with Mark Goodman and Lorenzo Benet for *People.* "He turned me on that

it's fun to be funny. That's really why I do it." As far as childhoods are concerned, Seinfeld's was a pretty mild one. "His was a Long Island life, a quiet suburban existence with happy parents and happy children," described Stephen Randall in *Playboy.* "The only unusual aspect of it was the fact that both parents had been raised without parents of their own, which gave them an independence they passed on to their two kids."

This independence was evident in Seinfeld at an early age; he got things the way he wanted them, or he wouldn't take them at all. "As family lore has it," related Jerry Lazar in *Us,* "on Seinfeld's third birthday, he wanted not just a slice of birthday cake but the whole thing. When he was refused, he opted to eat no cake at all rather than back down on his demand." Seinfeld's older sister, Carolyn Liebling, similarly observed in a *GQ* interview with Alan Richman: "He had a very ordinary childhood, but he was very driven. If he wanted a toy, he'd sit at the table crying or arguing or carrying on. He'd obsess about things like that." Seinfeld's main obsession as a child, however, was television. "Jerry was *chained* to the television," complained his mother, Betty, in her interview with Randall. "At one point, I had to get rid of it. I couldn't stand it." This didn't solve the addiction, though. Seinfeld "simply went next door to the neighbors' to get his fix," explained Randall. "Looking back, one realizes that it wasn't wasted time. He talks in TV metaphors, makes jokes about both old and new TV shows and commercials and still harbors a desire to grow up to be Bud on *Flipper.*" Seinfeld told Randall: "I swear to God, I've learned most of what I know about life from TV."

Around the age of thirteen or fourteen, Seinfeld started taping interviews that he conducted with his pet parakeet. This experience, along with watching comedians on television, prompted Seinfeld to choose his career at an early age. As a teenager, though, he was not very sociable or overly popular. "When you retreat from contact with other kids, your only playground left is your own mind," Seinfeld explained in his interview with Richman. "You start exploring your own ability to entertain yourself." So Seinfeld became the type of kid who fell somewhere between obnoxious and funny. He wouldn't hang out and smoke with the other guys in school, but he would pass notes in class just to get a laugh.

Graduating from Queens College in 1976 with a double major in theater and communication arts, Seinfeld immediately began his quest for a career as a stand-up comedian; his first night out was not very promising, however. "July 1976. Jerry Seinfeld takes the stage at Catch A Rising Star, the storied New York comedy club," described Steven Rea in *Entertainment Weekly.* "He clears his throat, mumbles hello, and launches into a carefully honed 15-minute act. The launch is aborted. He freezes."

Recalling his first performance, Seinfeld told Rea, "I was only able to remember the subjects I wanted to talk about. So I stood up there and went, 'The beach . . . Driving . . . Your Parents. . . .' I did that for about a minute and a half and then just left." The performance went over better than expected. "They thought that was what I meant to do," added Seinfeld.

This rocky beginning didn't discourage Seinfeld. In fact, he revealed in his interview with Barbara Walters for *The Barbara Walters Special* that the anxiety and uncertainty of stand-up fascinate him. "I'm really attracted to tension, you know. Maybe that's one of the reasons I became a stand-up comedian. When you walk on that stage there is a palpable tension, and if you can diffuse it that's a wonderful release." Seinfeld soon learned to do just that through tireless hard work and eventually became a regular at Catch A Rising Star, the Improv, and the Comic Strip. "There was no work anywhere else," remarked Seinfeld in an interview with Glenn Collins for the *New York Times*. "So we saw everyone, every night. We did a lot of hanging out—from, say, 9 to 1 or 2 A.M. at the clubs, and then in the coffee shop till 3 or 4. . . . I took no more than a day off. Four years of pretty much working for free, picking up $30 and $50 dollar gigs to support yourself. I think it takes five years just to learn how to express yourself, to know what to say."

In order to support himself while he was learning and perfecting the craft of stand-up, Seinfeld worked at a variety of part-time jobs. He sold light bulbs over the telephone, recounting in his interview with Richman that it was a "tough job. There's not many people sitting home in the dark going, 'I can't hold out much longer.' " Seinfeld also worked the streets, selling costume jewelry in front of Bloomingdales—his cart even had wheels for quick escapes from the police. "Running from the police on the streets of Manhattan—this is a parents' dream come true," he assured Richman. After putting in four years on the New York circuit, Seinfeld had twenty-five minutes of solid material and decided to make the big move to Los Angeles.

Although he moved to Los Angeles to make a name for himself as a stand-up comedian, Seinfeld's career took a brief detour into the world of television sitcoms shortly after his arrival. Cast as the governor's joke writer on the ABC comedy *Benson* in 1980, his part ended up lasting for only a few episodes. "The day the show was supposed to start shooting again after the break, I flew in from New York and showed up at the studio," explained Seinfeld in an interview with Stewart Weiner for *TV Guide*. "I sat down at the table to read the script, but there was no script and no chair for me. Then the assistant director called me aside to tell me that they forgot to tell me I wasn't on the show anymore." The whole experience left Seinfeld feeling annoyed, mostly because he'd wasted his time on television shows when he should have stuck to his stand-up work. "Honing his mind with new comic routines and his body with yoga, he set out to become the consummate comic," related Richman. "I wanted to wind up like George Burns, but with a little more spinal flexibility," Seinfeld explained to Richman.

Seinfeld's big break as a stand-up comedian came about a year after his *Benson* experience—he appeared on *The Tonight Show*. "I remember the date, May 7, 1981," Seinfeld recalled in his *New York Times* interview. "Every comedian knows that date—their own, I mean. So, here I had five years of going out every night and developing my act, and I was going to take all the chips I'd developed and put them into the center of the table on one five-minute bit." His act was a success: "Suddenly I was lifted from the pack, in L.A." Since then, Seinfeld has appeared on the show over twenty times, as well as being a regular on *Late Night with David Letterman*. Throughout the early 1980s, stand-up was all Seinfeld did—he was interested in neither television nor movies. "He traveled across America with his yellow legal pad and his No. 2 pencils, always writing, picking up nothing in the way of residuals except jet lag," related Richman. "He believed that he was suffering for his craft, until one day in the late Eighties, in Boston's Logan Airport, when he had what might be called a financial epiphany." Seinfeld recounted the revelation: "I had this job in Boston at a college. I landed, they didn't pick me up, and I'm waiting at the airport, like, three hours. I'm really getting pissed off, and I'm thinking, The hell with it, I'm getting on a plane, going back to New York, screw them, I'm not doing the show. What do they expect me to do, get a rental car, pay for it? Then I looked in my book and I realized I was making, like, $17,000 for this. I had gone from a $1,500 comic to a $15,000 comic without noticing. I go, Wait a minute. I can afford a rental car."

By the time 1989 rolled around, Seinfeld was up to over three hundred appearances a year; television seemed like the last thing he would do, so he did it. NBC and Castle Rock Entertainment approached him about doing a special, and Seinfeld went to his friend and fellow stand-up comedian Larry David for help. The two spent an evening at the Westway Diner on Ninth Avenue coming up with and discussing ideas. Seinfeld recollected the conversation in his interview with Smith. "The No. 1 question when you're a stand up comedian, is where do you get your material." David replied with: "That's what the show should be. How comedians come up with their material." Seinfeld's answer: "They do this. They hang around with their friends." NBC liked the idea so much that they wanted *Seinfeld* as a series.

"Seinfeld and David structured the show to take advantage of Seinfeld's talent for conversational humor—and not stretch his meager abilities as an actor," asserted Smith. "Seinfeld would play himself, a 37-year-old stand-up comic whose emotional age is holding steady at 25, endearingly immature yet smart. You know the type: the kind of guy who pulls his turtleneck up over his nose, turns around, and says slyly, 'Bazooka Joe.' . . . Most of the time, TV Jerry would hang out in a Greek coffee shop or in his living room yapping with his buddies." Jerry's main buddy would be George, played by Jason Alexander. Modeled after Larry David, George would be a balding, brooding, neurotic nerd who couldn't keep a girlfriend or a job. "My relationship with George is the glue of the show," Seinfeld pointed out in his *New York* interview. "Our conversation is basically the conversation between me and Larry. Two idiots trying to figure out the world."

Two more characters were added to round out the main cast of *Seinfeld*. Michael Richards, a comedian with vertically extreme hair who slides in and out of rooms as if he's on skates, plays Jerry's goofball neighbor Kramer. And finally, former *Saturday Night Live* player Julia Louis-Dreyfus was cast as Elaine, Jerry's hip ex-girlfriend. "We needed some estrogen," Seinfeld explained in his *New York* interview. "It was getting to be too much of a guy show." During *Seinfeld*'s initial run, NBC moved the show around frequently, yet it was still able to build up a cult audience. Since 1990 this audience has grown considerably, consisting of the advertising world's most coveted demographic group—the middle to upper class educated eighteen to thirty-four-year-olds.

Seinfeld is "micro-concept TV," observed Seinfeld in his interview with Weiner, who added: "It's long bank lines, subway muggings, missing rent-a-car reservations, rude waiters. Sneezing is good. No cute kids, no morals tacked onto the end." The most important aspect of *Seinfeld* is the conversation: "It was conceived as a show about conversation," Seinfeld pointed out in his interview with Rea. "The stories are incidental to us. We're more interested in the interplay of the dialogue." Consequently, many *Seinfeld* episodes appear to have no plot. One show has Jerry, George, Elaine, and Kramer looking for their car in a shopping mall parking garage. Another begins with the first three waiting for a table in a Chinese restaurant and ends with them still waiting. More recent episodes incorporate elements of satire. In an hour-long show, Jerry meets New York Met player Keith Hernandez, who subsequently starts dating Elaine. Kramer, and his pal Newman, hold a grudge against Hernandez because they think he spit at them after one of the baseball games they attended. In a classic scene, Jerry reenacts the spitting incident, mirroring a sequence in the popular movie *JFK*.

A series of episodes run during the 1992-93 season continue along the same vein, blurring the line between reality and fiction even further. Jerry is approached after one of his stand-up performances by a couple of NBC executives, who ask him if he's interested in doing a show for them. He and George then come up with the idea for the show—it will be about "nothing," with characters modeled after Jerry, George, Elaine, and Kramer. The executives don't go for the idea, though, and the show ends up being about a guy sentenced to be a butler because he was in a car accident and had no insurance—typical sitcom fare, and everything that *Seinfeld* is not.

"*Seinfeld* episodes are loosely structured, with the anecdotal, stream-of-consciousness style of monologue material," described Richard Zoglin in *Time*, adding: "Seinfeld seems totally at ease as a sitcom leading man, all gawky insouciance and whiny sarcasm." Mike Duffy, writing in the *Detroit Free Press*, had only praise for the show: "Taking ordinary, everyday situations and embarrassing moments of modern life, *Seinfeld* routinely turns them inside out—and then transforms them into sublimely inventive, nontraditional TV comedy." And John J. O'Connor asserts in the *New York Times* that *Seinfeld* is "a brilliant riff on contemporary anxieties and foibles of the unmistakably urban persuasion. Nothing never had it so good."

One of the main things that sets *Seinfeld* apart from other sitcoms is that its star is not really acting—that's the "real" Seinfeld up there. "That's me up there every week," revealed Seinfeld in his *New York* interview. "I just do what I'd do in real life." Many of the conversations on the show are actual conversations between Seinfeld and David, and everything that happens to the "real" Seinfeld, such as getting a television series at NBC, also happens to the "TV" Seinfeld. "I'm the guy. I am the guy," he asserted when Walters asks him the differences between himself and the character he "plays" on television. "First of all, I would say we look a lot alike. . . . It's a strange thing to be that public, I mean, people really know me now. I can't act. That's it, you know."

Seinfeld never expected the show to be as successful as it is. "We figured we'd do six shows and that would be it," he related in his interview with Smith. "We wanted to be a legend, the show they *should* have left on. People would say, 'Boy, did you guys get screwed.'" Despite his television achievements, however, Seinfeld will always consider himself a stand-up comedian. Back in 1990, before he achieved "star" status, Seinfeld revealed his thoughts on this subject in his interview with Randall: "I really feel the key to having a successful career in comedy is never taking the bait of stardom per se. If you think you're a star, you're not a comedian anymore, because a comedian is one of us. Anyway, being a stand-up is a grimy gig. A big star—well, short of an Eddie Murphy—you get up there and the audience will give you a free ride for five, maybe ten minutes. That's it. If you're not funny that night, I don't care how famous you are. It doesn't matter. As long as I'm doing my stand-up, the audience will keep me in my place. It keeps me from being a show-business asshole. Stardom can exist on its own, but laughs do not."

Still holding true to this belief, Seinfeld seeks out comedy venues to try out his new ideas for the show or for a routine. "Two or three times a week I'll go around to a local club and I'll just go on stage and work on some things," he explained to Walters. "I'm having an affair with these people and it's very intimate, and it's not like anything else. They tell me things about myself, [like] if I'm getting a little too big a head. If I'm too confident the audience picks it up and I can feel it in the laughs." Seinfeld went on to reveal in his *TV Guide* interview that "being on TV is not my first love. I'm a stand-up comedian, first and foremost. I'm obsessed with the mechanism of comedy; it's unconquerable, dark, and mystical. A sitcom could never give me that."

What *Seinfeld* has given its star is fame, and with the fame comes a loss of privacy. Stories of Seinfeld's neatness and need for control and perfection run rampant. He owns over twenty pairs of Nike Air sneakers, giving them away to charity as soon as they get a smudge on them. If someone moves something in his apartment or his house and puts it back exactly where it was, he can still tell it's been moved. And as soon as he finishes eating something, he flosses. "Seinfeld's spotless Porsche Carrera 4 is a four-wheel-drive vehicle capable of doing 150 mph on wet pavement in a city where it never rains," describes Richman. "His spotless Manhattan apartment, which he likens to Superman's Arctic lair, is gray and chrome, filled with highly polished German and Italian fixtures, the latest in post-Axis decor. The kitchen cabinets seem constructed of titanium. The minute he walks in, having been away for a few months, he adjusts the clock. This is only a sampling. He insists that everything in his life be spotless, including himself."

Seinfeld views his sudden and overwhelming fame as being really "out of hand. People are interested in me now way beyond what's appropriate," he contended on *The Barbara Walters Special.* "It's very odd, very curious to me, very interesting. And I can feel it, boy. It's like being on a ferris wheel and this is the top of the wheel. I am right now at the top of the ferris wheel, and I know what's coming." When the show's popularity does finally abate, and Seinfeld finds himself at the "bottom" of the ferris wheel, he'll continue to do what he's always done—travel the world as a stand-up comic. "When men are growing up, reading about Batman, Spiderman, Superman, these aren't fantasies, these are career options," Seinfeld maintained in his *New York* interview. "Superman is my role model. I have this very romantic image of the stand-up comic, the solitary challenge of being out there on your own, using whatever you have on you. Every man thinks of himself as a low-level superhero. And it came true for me. I got to do what I wanted to do in life. To me, that's being Superman."

BIOGRAPHICAL/CRITICAL SOURCES:

PERIODICALS

Detroit Free Press, November 20, 1992, Section F, p. 4; December 22, 1992, Section B, p. 6; February 11, 1993, Section D, p. 6.
Entertainment Weekly, March 1, 1991, pp. 29-30; September 11, 1992, p. 35.
GQ, May, 1992, pp. 136-41, 202, 204-05.
Mirabella, October, 1991, pp. 48, 50.
New York, February 3, 1992, pp. 32-37.
New York Times, September 29, 1991, Section H, pp. 33-34; September 16, 1992, Section C, p. 20.
People, June 4, 1990, p. 14; December 2, 1991, pp. 87-88.
Playboy, August, 1990, pp. 104-06, 132, 142-43.
Time, August 24, 1992, p. 63.
TV Guide, May 23, 1992, pp. 11-15.
Us, April 4, 1991, pp. 16-19.
USA Today, October 2, 1991, Section D, p. 1.

TELEVISION PROGRAMS

The Barbara Walters Special, ABC-TV, November 24, 1992.
Seinfeld, NBC-TV, February 11, 1993.

—*Sketch by Susan M. Reicha*

*   *   *

SERLING, Carol   1929-

PERSONAL: Born February 3, 1929, in Columbus, OH; married Rod Serling (deceased). *Education:* Antioch College, B.A., 1950; postgraduate work at University of California, Los Angeles.

ADDRESSES: Office—1940 Palisades Dr., Pacific Palisades, CA 90272. *Agent*—Renee Golden, Esq., 8983 Norma Pl., West Hollywood, CA 90069.

WRITINGS:

(Editor and author of introduction) *Rod Serling's Night Gallery Reader,* Barricade Books, 1987.
(Editor) *Journeys to the Twilight Zone,* DAW Books, 1993.

Also contributor of afterword to *Visions from the Twilight Zone,* written by Arlen Schumer, Chronicle Books, 1990.

WORK IN PROGRESS: Travels to the Twilight Zone, completion expected in 1994.

SERVICE, Robert W(illiam)   1874(?)-1958

PERSONAL: Born January 16, 1874 (some sources list 1876), in Preston, England; died September 11, 1958, in Lancieux, France; buried in Brittany, France; son of Robert (a banker) and Emily (Parker) Service; married Germaine Bourgoin, June 12, 1913; children: Iris. *Education:* Attended Glasgow University.

CAREER: Novelist, poet, and ballad writer. Apprentice and later clerk for Commercial Bank of Scotland, 1889-96; worked variously as a farm laborer, tunnel builder, handyman, singer, and ranch worker, 1896-1903; bank clerk for the Canadian Bank of Commerce, in Victoria, New Brunswick, Canada, 1903-04, Kamloops, British Columbia, Canada, 1904, Whitehorse, Yukon Territory, Canada, beginning in 1904, and Dawson, Yukon Territory, until 1912; *Toronto Star,* foreign correspondent, 1912-14, war correspondent, 1914-16. *Military service:* Served as an ambulance driver and as an intelligence officer for the Canadian Army during World War I.

WRITINGS:

VERSE

Songs of a Sourdough, Briggs, 1907, Unwin, 1908; republished as *The Spell of the Yukon, and Other Verses,* Barse & Hopkins, 1907.

Ballads of a Cheechako, Barse & Hopkins, 1909, Unwin, 1910.

Rhymes of a Rolling Stone, Dodd, Mead, 1912, Unwin, 1913.

Rhymes of a Red Cross Man, Barse & Hopkins, 1916.

Selected Poems, Unwin, 1917.

Ballads of a Bohemian, Barse & Hopkins, 1921.

Complete Poetical Works, Barse, 1921; published in England as *Collected Verse,* Benn, 1930; republished in America as *The Complete Poems,* Dodd, Mead, 1933, enlarged edition, 1938, another enlarged edition, 1942.

The House of Fear, Dodd, Mead, 1927.

Why Not Grow Young?; or, Living for Longevity, Barse, 1928.

Twenty Bath-Tub Ballads, Francis, Day & Hunter, 1939.

Bar-Room Ballads, Dodd, Mead, 1940.

Collected Poems, Dodd, Mead, 1940.

Songs of a Sun-Lover, Dodd, Mead, 1949.

Rhymes of a Roughneck, Dodd, Mead, 1950.

Lyrics of a Lowbrow, Dodd, Mead, 1951.

Rhymes of a Rebel, Dodd, Mead, 1952.

Songs for My Supper, Dodd, Mead, 1953.

Carols of an Old Codger, Dodd, Mead, 1954.

More Collected Verse, Dodd, Mead, 1955.

Rhymes for My Rags, Dodd, Mead, 1956.

Songs of the High North, Benn, 1958, Ryerson, 1964.

Later Collected Verse, Dodd, Mead, 1965.

Contributor of verses and serials to Scottish periodicals, including *Herald, Scottish Nights,* and *People's Friend.*

NOVELS

The Trail of Ninety-eight: A Northland Romance, Dodd, Mead, 1910, Stevens & Brown, 1911.

The Pretender: A Story of the Latin Quarter, Dodd, Mead, 1914, Unwin, 1915.

The Poisoned Paradise: A Romance of Monte Carlo, Dodd, Mead, 1922.

The Roughneck, Barse & Hopkins, 1923; published in England as *The Roughneck: A Tale of Tahiti,* Unwin, 1923.

The Master of the Microbe: A Fantastic Romance, Barse & Hopkins, 1926.

OTHER

Ploughman of the Moon: An Adventure in Memory (autobiography), Dodd, Mead, 1945, Benn, 1946.

Harper of Heaven: A Record of Radiant Living (autobiography), Dodd, Mead, 1948.

ADAPTATIONS:

MOVIES

The Shooting of Dan McGrew (based on Service's ballad), Metro, 1924.

The Roughneck (based on Service's novel), Twentieth Century-Fox, 1924.

The Trail of Ninety-eight (based on Service's novel), Metro-Goldwyn-Mayer, 1928.

Other film adaptations include *Poisoned Paradise,* 1924.

SIDELIGHTS: Robert Service is a poet known to most readers for his Yukon verses that were popular in the early twentieth century. Though relatively free of critical support, Service nevertheless established a substantial readership for his straightforward, rhymed renditions of the wilderness life. Witter Byner noted the somewhat peculiar nature of Service's stature by writing in a 1916 *Dial* that "Service has been a poetic phenomenon" and added that the poet, though "more or less ignored by critics . . . has won a vast following." Edward Hirsch noted likewise in an appraisal for *Southern Folklore Quarterly* that "Service's poems have been essentially neglected by literary scholars" but have nonetheless become "extraordinarily popular." Martin Bucco, in an *Alaska Review* essay, explained Service's popularity by noting that the poet developed "an inspired myth of Northern glory" that instilled northerners with "a sense of tradition." Service's folk poetry, Bucco added, is itself "a signal part of that tradition."

Though Service would eventually develop a reputation as a loner roaming the northern wilds, his life was not an entirely arduous one. Reports vary, but most sources agree that he was born in 1874 in Lancashire, England, where his father worked in a bank. When Service's mother inherited a substantial sum from her late father, a cotton mill owner, the Service family moved to Glasgow, Scotland, the home of his paternal ancestors and his father's birthplace. Among Service's relatives in Scotland was a great-grandfather who claimed to be a friend—and distant relation—to the celebrated Scottish bard Robert Burns, who was revered by Service's family. "To my folks anything that rhymed was poetry," Service later wrote in his autobiographical *Ploughman of the Moon*, "and Robbie Burns was their idol."

Spurred by this connection to great writing, Service explored the arts. During his school years he delved into literature, showing a particular preference for the writings of Lord Tennyson and Edgar Allan Poe. But though his parents were themselves fond of poetry, they marked Service for a more conventional career, and at age fifteen, on his own volition, he began a banking apprenticeship in Glasgow. He maintained his interest in poetry, however, developing an interest in the works of Robert Browning.

In the early 1890s, not long after he began his apprenticeship, Service began publishing his own work in various Glasgow newspapers. These poems, like the verse of writers such as Thomas Hood and the aforementioned Poe, are marked by distinctive—often facile—rhymes. For Service, rhyme was what he enjoyed reading and, thus, what he enjoyed writing. "If two lines could be made to clink it seemed to me to go a long way to justify them," he wrote in *Ploughman of the Moon*. "Perhaps it was because I had such facility in that direction."

Although Service was a published poet by the time he reached his late teens, he abruptly abandoned versification to become a rugby player. Although he showed impressive skill and savvy once on a team, Service grew dissatisfied with his position, and in the season's final contest he broke from his midfield position and dared to score a touchdown. The incident was not viewed with pleasure by the team's captain. Threatened with suspension, Service decided against further rugby play. He switched to cricket and soon proved himself highly skilled in that sport as well. He became bored with this activity as well, however, and eventually abandoned it. "I was saturated with sport to the point of nausea and I jettisoned my experience with never a qualm," he recalled in *Ploughman of the Moon*. "It was as if I had been possessed by a fire that burned itself out by its own intensity."

Service next turned to the theatre, determined to become an actor. Proving himself a worthy elocutionist, he managed to obtain a small role in a production of the play *Rob Roy*. But on opening night he indulged in alcohol before making his first appearance, and when he finally arrived on stage his kilt was backward. In trying to adjust his costume Service only managed to aggravate an already desperate situation, and he eventually dropped the kilt to his ankles, whereupon the actress playing his mother shielded him from the audience's view while simultaneously whispering threats.

After this opening night debacle, Service's theatrical aspirations abruptly ceased. He returned to literature and became absorbed in the works of writers such as Rudyard Kipling, Robert Louis Stevenson, and Jack London. Attracted to the possibility of words, Service decided to pursue a university education. Once again, however, Service's individuality and strong opinions set him apart from convention. After offending a professor with his speculation that Ophelia—the innocent and purportedly pure heroine of *Hamlet*—was probably promiscuous, Service decided that he was not entirely suited for the academic life.

Service explored these various career options while still working at the bank in Glasgow. He also began living in the slums and soon adopted a socialist ideology. Next came a stint in a band of musicians and performers, and after that Service became preoccupied with life as a farmer. He had developed a keen appreciation for the North American western lands' vast spaces and rugged mountains that were populated by cattle herders, miners, and hunters. In 1896 he decided that the outdoor life was for him, quit the bank, and boarded a ship bound for Montreal, Canada.

Once in Canada, Service travelled to the West Coast, where he actually worked, briefly, as a farm laborer. In the fall of 1897, though, he left Canada for California, and in the ensuing few years he drifted throughout western America and Canada and held a range of jobs. In Oakland, for instance, he helped dig a tunnel, and in San Diego he worked as a jack-of-all-trades at a bordello. He returned to the banking profession in 1903, working as a clerk in British Columbia. A series of transfers eventually landed him in the Yukon Territory of northern Canada, where he became a teller in the city of Dawson in 1906.

Service found solace in the rugged landscape of the Yukon, and in the equally rugged people—miners, trappers, and outlaws—he found others who respected his love of freedom and individuality. Inspired by his new surroundings, he once again turned to writing poetry. During the next months he produced several poems on life in the Yukon wilds. After writing each poem, however, he consigned it to a bureau drawer. When inspiration abandoned him, Service came to dislike the poems he had written and so ignored them. He came across the poems again only while cleaning out his bureau. After a re-reading, Service decided that they were at least suitable for private printing and distribution among family and friends. With these intentions in mind he collected the manuscript and sent it to his father, who had moved to Toronto with the rest of the Service family. Service's father then forwarded the poems to a Toronto publisher, William Briggs, who immediately accepted them for publication.

In 1907 Service's collection was published in Canada as *Songs of a Sourdough,* and the volume achieved instant popularity. Before the year ended, the book had been reprinted fifteen times and had been produced in the United States, where—as *The Spell of the Yukon*—it found further favor. Critics, though, failed to share the general public's enthusiasm for the rhymes of rough-and-ready life in the Canadian wilds. In the *Sewanee Review,* for instance, a critic claimed that Service's success "is rather that of the new matter, than of its artistic treatment." But the same reviewer conceded that the poems, at least as testaments to Yukon life, "exhibit considerable skill and are well worth reading."

Among the more notable poems in Service's debut collection is "The Shooting of Dan McGrew," a rhymed narrative that came to typify Service's style. The poem is about desperate men in an unyielding environment. Here a card game culminates in deadly gunplay: "Then I ducked my head, and the lights went out, and two guns blazed in the dark / And a woman screamed, and the lights went up, and two men lay stiff and stark. / Pitched on his head, and pumped full of lead, was Dangerous Dan McGrew, / While the man from the creeks lay clutched to the breast of the lady that's known as Lou." In another celebrated verse narration, "The Cremation of Sam McGee," a rider grants a dead companion his last request in the icy North: "Some planks I tore from the cabin floor, and I lit the boiler fire; / Some coal I found that was lying around, and I heaped the fuel higher; / The flames just soared, and the furnace roared—such a blaze you seldom see; / And I burrowed a hole in the glowing coal, and I stuffed in Sam McGee." Before riding away, the narrator returns for one last look in the furnace, only to have the supposedly cremated McGee exhort him to close the door before the heat escapes. Martin Bucco, writing in the *Alaska Review,* declared, "Of Service's tall tales, none surpasses 'The Cremation of Sam McGee.'"

Buoyed by the success of his Yukon poems, Service vacationed briefly in Vancouver, then returned North to assume another bank teller position in Dawson. He culled records and newspapers to obtain source material for his next collection, *Ballads of a Cheechako,* which appeared in 1909. In this volume, Service again focused on the rugged North and its craggy inhabitants. Lengthy monologues about questionable characters provide the narrative structures for many of these poems, which bear titles such as "The Ballad of Blasphemous Bill" and "The Ballad of

Hard-Luck Henry." The characters in these dramatic poems are predominantly rough, reckless, and restless. As W. A. Whatley observed in *Texas Review:* "Service . . . looks upon the North as the last stronghold of the hostile forces of Nature, into which man penetrates only as a rash and audacious intruder, but in which he has no legitimate place or standing."

In 1910, shortly after resigning from the Dawson bank, Service published a novel, *The Trail of Ninety-eight: A Northland Romance,* a realist account of Scottish roamer Athol Meldrum's experiences in the North American wilds—including the Klondike during the time of the gold rush. After a series of adventures, Meldrum eventually finds himself opposed by Jack Locasto, a vulgar lout who desires Meldrum's wife as his own mistress. Locasto's schemes are effected while Meldrum is away mining for gold. Upon returning to town, Meldrum discovers that his wife has, indeed, become Locasto's mistress and that, furthermore, she is working in a dance hall. Meldrum then commences his own stint of debauchery before regaining happiness with his wife. Much like his previous publications, Service's first novel was warmly embraced by a public eager for ribald tales of the northern frontier. In a *Canadian Literature* essay, Stanley S. Atherton deemed *The Trail of Ninety-eight* "a contrived pot-boiler," but he added that it is "nevertheless a significant contribution to literature about the Canadian North."

Service spent the winter of 1910-11 at a farm that his mother managed in northern Alberta. He then undertook an arduous two-thousand-mile trek back to Dawson. This journey, his last to the Yukon, provided him with material for his next verse collection, *Rhymes of a Rolling Stone.* Prominent among the poems in this volume is "Barb-Wire Bill," in which two adventurers become trapped on an ice flow: "And in the night he gripped me tight as I lay fast asleep: / 'The river's kicking like a steer . . . run out the forward sweep!' / That's Hell-gate Canyon right ahead; I know of old its roar, / And . . . I'll be damned! *the ice is jammed!* We've *got* to make the shore."

In 1912 Service departed Dawson to become a foreign correspondent for the *Toronto Star* in Paris. He never returned to the Yukon. In *Ploughman of the Moon* he recalled his thoughts as he left Dawson: "I felt I was not only quitting Dawson but the North itself. Nine years of my life I had given it and it was in my blood. It had inspired and sustained me, brought me fortune and a meed of fame. . . . 'I will come back,' I said again. 'I will be true to the North.' But . . . I have not returned."

In Paris, Service settled in the Latin Quarter and forwarded weekly pieces to the *Toronto Star.* He also produced a second novel, *The Pretender: A Story of the Latin Quarter,* in which a prominent New York writer finds happiness and further success while dodging sexually reckless women and self-inflated critics in Bohemian Paris. The novel's hero, James Madden, becomes bored with fame and success, and so he determines to commence a new literary career by writing under a pseudonym. While this endeavor proves to be as fruitful as the previous one, Madden must maintain his honor in a world where success, rather than integrity, is prized and coveted. A *Spectator* reviewer described *The Pretender* as "a gay, high-spirited audacious book" and added that it is told "with great gusto and abundant humour."

Service was still in France when World War I began in 1914. By this time he had married and settled in Brittany. But when the war broke out he tried to enlist in a Highlanders regiment. He was rejected for physical reasons, whereupon he continued with the *Toronto Star* as a war correspondent. In addition he served with an ambulance corps. His experiences in these capacities provided material for his verse collection *Rhymes of a Red Cross Man*, which realized immense success upon publication in America in 1916. As in Service's earlier collections, *Rhymes of a Red Cross Man* is comprised of obvious effects and simple rhymes, but the imagery here is often of a more gruesome and unsettling nature. In "My Mate," for example, the horror of war is vividly rendered when a soldier contemplates his dead friend: "Jim as lies there in the dug-out wiv 's blanket round 'is 'ead, / To keep 'is brains from mixin' wiv the mud; / And 'is face as white as putty, and 'is overcoat all red, / Like 'e's spilt a bloomin' paint-pot—but it's blood." In the *Texas Review*, Whatley described such verse as "sincere and vital."

After the war ended, Service returned to Paris with his wife and daughter. He remained there throughout the 1920s, a decade in which he concentrated on the writing of romance novels, including *The Poisoned Paradise: A Romance of Monte Carlo*, *The Rough-Neck: A Tale of Tahiti*, and *The Master of the Microbe: A Fantastic Romance*. None of these novels apparently enhanced his literary reputation in the ensuing years. Neither did *Ballads of a Bohemian*, a verse collection he produced in 1921. *New Republic* reviewer Donald Ogden Stewart, who clearly did not favor Service's work, speculated that the volume "must seem a little flat even to those . . . who felt so strongly moved" by Service's earlier books.

In 1930 Service revived his waning reputation by publishing his *Collected Verse*. This volume, though, would remain his last significant achievement until 1945, when he published *Ploughman of the Moon*, which recounts his life up to his final departure from Dawson in 1912. In 1948 he published a second autobiographical volume, *Harper of Heaven*. More verse collections followed in the 1950s: *Rhymes of a Roughneck*, *Lyrics of a Lowbrow*, *Rhymes of a Rebel*, and *Songs for My Supper* all came from Service

at this time. Carl F. Klinck, writing in *Robert Service*, noted that in these volumes the poet "was surveying his past in terms of the present in which he found himself." In them, Klinck observed, "one may sense Service's growing tendency to stress the lamentable in human existence and to moralize about it; at the same time there is no retreat from the policy of illustrating nearly everything by means of vignettes and suggestive images."

Service, who had lived in Monte Carlo since 1946, died of a heart attack in 1958 and was buried in Brittany. In the years since his death, Service has remained prized for his accessible, vivid verse, particularly as it depicts life in the Yukon. Clare McCarthy wrote in *Contemporary Review*: "The easy style of Robert Service makes him a most readable poet. He described himself as a happy man, because his talent was in proportion to his ambition, and he was able to write the kind of verse that he liked to read."

BIOGRAPHICAL/CRITICAL SOURCES:

BOOKS

Klinck, Carl F., *Robert Service: A Biography*, Dodd, Mead, 1976.
Service, Robert, *The Spell of the Yukon, and Other Verses*, Barse & Hopkins, 1907.
Service, *Rhymes of a Rolling Stone*, Unwin, 1913.
Service, *Rhymes of a Red Cross Man*, Barse & Hopkins, 1916.
Service, *Ploughman of the Moon: An Adventure in Memory*, Dodd, Mead, 1945, Benn, 1946.
Service, *Harper of Heaven: A Record of Radiant Living*, Dodd, Mead, 1948.

PERIODICALS

Alaska Review, fall, 1965, pp. 16-26.
Bookman, January, 1922, pp. 481-84.
Canadian Literature, winter, 1971, pp. 67-72.
Dial, December 14, 1916, pp. 531-32.
Southern Folklore Quarterly, March-June, 1976, pp. 125-40.
Texas Review, July, 1921, pp. 299-308.*

—Sketch by Les Stone

* * *

SHAW, Carlos M. Fernandez
See FERNANDEZ-SHAW, Carlos M(anuel)

* * *

SHAW, Joseph M(inard) 1925-

PERSONAL: Born April 21, 1925, in Estherville, IA; son of Carl E. (a building contractor) and Martha Elizabeth (a homemaker; maiden name, Sunde) Shaw; married Mary Virginia St. John (a registrar), June 8, 1955; children: Nancy Joy, Elizabeth Ann, Margaret Jean, Mary Martha. *Education:* St. Olaf College, B.A., 1949; attended University of Oslo, 1951-52 and 1955-56; Luther Theological Seminary, B.Th., 1953; Princeton Theological Seminary, Ph.D., 1958; also attended Harvard University, 1962-63, and Mansfield College, Oxford, 1975. *Politics:* Democrat. *Religion:* Evangelical Lutheran.

ADDRESSES: Home—910 Highland Ave., Northfield, MN 55057. *Office*—St. Olaf College, Northfield, MN 55057-1098.

CAREER: St. Olaf College, Northfield, MN, instructor, 1957-59, assistant professor, 1959-62, associate professor, 1962-68, professor of religion, 1968-91, professor emeritus, 1991—, chairperson of department, 1985-88. *Military service:* U.S. Naval Reserve, active duty, 1944-46.

MEMBER: Norwegian-American Historical Association, Northfield Historical Society (member, board of directors, 1987-89), Phi Beta Kappa.

AWARDS, HONORS: Colonel Koch Martin Luther Award, Concordia Historical Institute, 1974, for *A History of St. Olaf College, 1874-1974;* Fulbright fellow in Norway.

WRITINGS:

Pulpit under the Sky: A Life of Hans Nielsen Hauge, Augsburg, 1955.

(Translator) Carl F. Wisloeff, *The Gift of Communion,* Augsburg, 1964.

If God Be for Us: A Study in the Meaning of Justification, Augsburg, 1966.

Our New Testament Heritage, Augsburg, Volume I, 1968, Volume II, 1969.

A History of St. Olaf College, 1874-1974, St. Olaf College Press, 1974.

(Translator) Andreas Aarflot, *Hans Nielsen Hauge: His Life and Message,* Augsburg, 1979.

(Editor with R. W. Franklin, Harris Kaaza, and Charles W. Buzicky) *Readings in Christian Humanism,* Augsburg, 1982.

The Pilgrim People of God, Augsburg Fortress, 1990.

(With Franklin) *The Case for Christian Humanism,* Eerdmans, 1991.

Dear Old Hill: The Story of Manitou Heights, the Campus of St. Olaf College, St. Olaf College Press, 1992.

Work represented in anthologies, including *The New Community in Christ,* edited by James Burtness and John Kildahl, Augsburg, 1963. Contributor to periodicals, including *Dialog: A Journal of Theology.*

WORK IN PROGRESS: A biography of Bernt Julius Muus, the founder of St. Olaf College; a book on the life and letters of Th. N. Mohn, the first president of St. Olaf College; compiling his family history.

SIDELIGHTS: Joseph M. Shaw told *CA:* "As a second-year student at Luther Theological Seminary, I wanted to do a term paper in church history on Hans Nielsen Hauge, a prominent lay leader and preacher in late eighteenth- and early nineteenth-century Norway. The library yielded only two dated, somewhat idolizing books about this man. The need for a more up-to-date biography was evident, so I applied for and received a Fulbright scholarship to study in Norway, learned some more Norwegian, gathered material on Hauge, and wrote a biography of the man.

"My teaching career at St. Olaf College gave me ample opportunity to teach and write in two primary areas, Bible and church history. My training is in New Testament studies, but I continued to be interested in such areas as the history of St. Olaf College and the nature and mission of the church colleges, as well as Norwegian-American matters and the use of the Norwegian language. St. Olaf College, founded by Norwegian immigrants and visibly related to the church, has been an ideal place to explore these interests.

"I consider my book *The Pilgrim People of God* my most important statement on the nature and importance of the church, both as it relates to Israel and with respect to the church's mission today."

*   *   *

SHAWN, William   1907-1992

OBITUARY NOTICE—See index for *CA* sketch: Born August 31, 1907, in Chicago, IL; died of a heart attack, December 8, 1992, in New York, NY. Editor and writer. Shawn was the editor of the *New Yorker* from 1952 to 1987, enhancing the reputation of the well-known magazine by emphasizing serious social and literary subjects. He began his career as a reporter for the *Las Vegas Optic* and the *International News* in the late 1920s and early 1930s. Shawn became affiliated with the *New Yorker* as a reporter for the "Talk of the Town" section in 1933. Promoted to managing two years later, he was named editor in 1952. Shawn oversaw every word that was published throughout his thirty-five-year tenure and essentially controlled editorial policy. His encouragement of articles on controversial topics such as the environment, racial strife, nuclear disarmament, and the Vietnam War brought the publication added esteem. New literary figures introduced in the *New Yorker* during this period included James Baldwin, Rachel Carson, and John Updike. In the mid-1980s the magazine was sold to Advance Publications, who forced the eighty-year-old editor to resign. Shawn joined book publishers Farrar, Straus & Giroux in 1987, serving as a consulting editor until his death.

OBITUARIES AND OTHER SOURCES:

BOOKS

Encyclopedia of Twentieth-Century Journalists, Garland Publishing, 1986.
International Who's Who, Europa Publications, 1989.
Who's Who in America, Marquis, 1992.
World Almanac Biographical Dictionary, World Almanac, 1990.

PERIODICALS

Chicago Tribune, December 9, 1992.
Los Angeles Times, December 9, 1992, p. A26.
New York Times, December 9, 1992, p. A1.
Times (London), December 10, 1992, p. 21.
Washington Post, December 9, 1992.

*   *   *

SHEPARD, Neil   1951-

PERSONAL: Born January 29, 1951; son of Stanley (a plastics salesman) and Reba (a homemaker; maiden name, Miller) Shepard; married Mary Spagnol, 1982 (divorced, 1986); married Kate Riley (an anthropologist and writer), September 15, 1990. *Education:* Attended St. Peter's College, Oxford, 1972; University of Vermont, B.A., 1973; Colorado State University, M.A., 1976; Ohio University, Ph.D., 1980. *Politics:* Liberal. *Avocational interests:* Hiking, birding, travel.

ADDRESSES: Home—R.D.2, Box 455, Johnson, VT 05656. *Office*—Department of Writing and Literature, Johnson State College, Johnson, VT 05656.

CAREER: Louisiana State University, Baton Rouge, instructor in English, 1980-82; Rider College, Lawrenceville, NJ, assistant professor of English, 1982-85; Johnson State College, Johnson, VT, associate professor of creative writing and literature, 1985—. Vermont Studio Center, writing coordinator, 1989—; presenter of community writing workshops, 1985-87. Member of Johnson Town Planning Commission, 1989-90.

MEMBER: Associated Writing Programs.

WRITINGS:

Scavenging the Country for a Heartbeat, Mid-List Press, 1992.

Contributor of poems, articles, and reviews to periodicals, including *Southern Review, Denver Quarterly, Poetry East,*

Antioch Review, Poetry Now, and *Poetry Northwest.* General editor and poetry editor, *Green Mountains Review,* 1986—.

WORK IN PROGRESS: The Seven Wonders, a book of poems and essays about the author's travels to China, Southeast Asia, Indonesia, Polynesia, New Zealand, Russia, Czechoslovakia, France, and Ireland.

SIDELIGHTS: Neil Shepard told *CA:* "I grew up in Leominster, a small mill town in central Massachusetts, advertised on highway billboards as the 'Pioneer Plastics City.' In the summers, I escaped to a family home on the Maine coast where the salt air, amusement park lights, and polyglot of languages on the boardwalk first enlarged my notion of the world and whetted my appetite for travel.

"I attended colleges in Vermont, Colorado, Ohio, and Oxford, England, and traveled widely in the United States and abroad, hitchhiking throughout the American West and much of Europe. An avid hiker and amateur naturalist, I trekked through the American and Canadian Rockies, the Cascades, Smokies, Blue Ridge, most of the ranges in the Northeast, and mountains in Switzerland, Austria, Germany, Greece, Norway, New Zealand, Tahiti, and China. I am also a musician. I enjoy playing jazz and blues piano and guitar, and I attribute much of the lyricism in my poems to my early musical training.

"I came late to literature, enrolling in my freshman year at the University of Vermont as a pre-medical student. In my sophomore year, I had a 'spontaneous conversion' experience in chemistry class where, while fixating on the twenty-foot chart of the periodic table, I suddenly began daydreaming the lines of poems. By the end of class, I had determined to change my major.

"My interest in the sciences continues, however, mostly as an amateur birder and stargazer. My interests in music and modern dance have led me into the realm of multi-disciplinary performance pieces; my poems have been set to classical music and choreographed to modern dance."

*   *   *

SHERWOOD, Valerie
See HINES, Jeanne

*   *   *

SILARD, Bela (A.)   1900-

PERSONAL: Born September 6, 1900, in Budapest, Hungary; son of Szilard (an engineer) and Vidor (a homemaker) Silard; married June 4, 1927; wife's name, Fejer (a music teacher); children: John, Andrew. *Education:* Attended school in Berlin, Germany. *Politics:* Democrat.

ADDRESSES: Home and office—300 Washington Ave., Pleasantville, NY 10570.

CAREER: Photovolt Corp., New York City, engineer and president, 1959-67.

WRITINGS:

(With William Lanouette) *Genius in the Shadows: A Biography of Leo Szilard, the Man behind the Bomb,* edited by Robert Stewart, Scribner, 1993.

Also author of a book concerning the cement gun published by Springer-Verlag (Heidelberg, Germany), 1920.

WORK IN PROGRESS: An autobiography.

*   *   *

SILBER, Nina   1959-

PERSONAL: Born June 12, 1959, in New York City; daughter of Irwin (a writer) and Sylvia (a teacher) Silber; married Louis P. Hutchins (a historian), June 17, 1989; children: Benjamin S. *Education:* University of California, Berkeley, B.A., 1981, M.A., 1985, Ph.D., 1989.

ADDRESSES: Home—Needham, MA. *Office*—Department of History, Boston University, 226 Bay State Rd., Boston, MA 02215.

CAREER: Boston University, Boston, MA, assistant professor of history, 1990—. Consultant to Valentine Museum.

MEMBER: American Historical Association, Organization of American Historians, Southern Historical Association.

AWARDS, HONORS: Smithsonian fellow, 1987-89.

WRITINGS:

(Editor with Catherine Clinton) *Divided Houses: Gender and the Civil War,* Oxford University Press, 1992.
The Romance of Reunion: Northerners and the South, University of North Carolina Press, 1993.

Contributor to *American Quarterly.*

WORK IN PROGRESS: Research on ideas of patriotism in late nineteenth-century northern women during the Civil War.

SIMPSON, John (Cody Fidler)   1944-

PERSONAL: Born August 9, 1944, in Cleveleys, England; son of Roy Fidler (a genealogist) and Joyce Cody Simpson; married Diane Petteys, 1965 (divorced, 1984); companion of Tira Shubart (a journalist); children: (first marriage) Julia, Eleanor. *Education:* Attended St. Paul's School, London, 1957-63; Magdalene College, Cambridge, M.A., 1966.

ADDRESSES: Home—London, England. *Office*—BBC Foreign Affairs Unit, TV Centre, Wood Lane, London W12, England. *Agent*—Jacintha Alexander, 46 Emperor's Gate, London SW7, England.

CAREER: Broadcast journalist and author. British Broadcasting Corporation (BBC), radio news sub-editor, producer, and reporter, 1966-72, foreign correspondent based in Dublin, Ireland, 1972-75, Brussels, Belgium, 1975-77, Johannesburg, South Africa, 1977-78; BBC Television News, diplomatic correspondent, 1978-80, political editor, presenter of Nine O'Clock News, 1980-82, diplomatic editor, 1982-88, foreign affairs editor, 1988, reporter in Afghanistan, China, Germany, Czechoslovakia, Rumania, Iraq, Russia, Brazil, and Bosnia, 1989—. Contributing editor to *Spectator.*

MEMBER: Royal Geographical Society (fellow, 1990); Athenaeum; Chelsea Arts Club.

AWARDS, HONORS: Nymphe d'or, Cannes International Film Festival, 1980; James Cameron Award, 1990, for reports on revolutions in Eastern Europe; CBE in Gulf War Honors, 1991, for reporting during the Gulf War; Journalist of the Year, Royal Television Society, 1991; British Academy of Film and Television Arts Special Award, 1992; Columnist of the Year, Magazine Publishing Awards, 1992.

WRITINGS:

(Editor, with others) *The Best of Granta,* Secker & Warburg, 1966.
Moscow Requiem (novel), St. Martin's, 1981.
A Fine and Private Place (novel), St. Martin's, 1983.
(With Jana Bennett) *The Disappeared and the Mothers of the Plaza: The Story of the 11,000 Argentinians Who Vanished,* St. Martin's, 1985, published in England as *The Disappeared: Voices from a Secret War,* Robson Books, 1985.
Inside Iran: Life under Khomeini's Regime, St. Martin's, 1988.
Despatches from the Barricades: An Eye-Witness Account of the Revolutions That Shook the World, 1989-1990, Hutchinson, 1990.
From the House of War: John Simpson in the Gulf, Hutchinson, 1991.

In the Forests of the Night: Encounters with Drug Runners, Terrorists, and Oppressors in Peru, Hutchinson/Random House, 1993.

Editor of the Cambridge literary magazine *Granta,* while in college.

SIDELIGHTS: If it was of international interest and happened during the 1970s, 1980s, and early 1990s, chances are that British Broadcasting Corporation (BBC) television correspondent John Simpson was on the scene reporting the event. He covered the Ayatollah Khomeini's triumphant return to Iran and the taking of fifty-two American hostages that soon followed, the unsuccessful uprising in China's Tiananmen Square, the fall of the Berlin Wall, the Persian Gulf War, and the revolutions in Rumania, Czechoslovakia, and the Soviet Union. Simpson has turned many of the stories he has covered into full-length books, including *The Disappeared and the Mothers of the Plaza: The Story of the 11,000 Argentinians Who Vanished, Inside Iran: Life Under Khomeini's Regime,* and *From the House of War: John Simpson in the Gulf.* Simpson has also written two novels of intrigue: *Moscow Requiem* and *A Fine and Private Place.*

In *The Disappeared and the Mothers of the Plaza,* Simpson and Jana Bennett relate to readers "the apparatus of terror and corruption built by the Argentine military during its rule, and the effects of military repression, through firsthand stories of specific victims and their families," according to Cesar A. Chelala in the *New York Times Book Review.* More than eight thousand protesters against the military regime in Argentina simply "disappeared"—allegedly killed and disposed of by the government. A group of mothers of the missing individuals began demonstrating, carrying placards bearing pictures of their missing loved ones and demanding to know their fates. Some of the mothers eventually "disappeared" as well, but the group is credited with helping bring down the military government. Chelala concluded that Simpson and Bennett's book "is an important reminder of why and how such tragedy ever took place in Argentina."

Simpson's 1988 work, *Inside Iran: Life Under Khomeini's Regime,* "takes readers through an Islamic divorce court and Teheran's southern slums, on tours of Caspian beaches and 11th-century mountain fortresses of the original Assassins sect, and for close-up views of the Iran-Iraq war and of the backroom politicking among the ruling mullahs," noted reviewer Robin Wright in the *Christian Science Monitor.* In the book, Simpson debunks many stereotypes Westerners have held about the country's culture and attempts to explain Iran's religious fervor. The author also points out the flaws of the reign of the Ayatollah Khomeini, Iran's religious and political leader during the

1980s. Wright concluded that Simpson had written "one of the best books to date on a complex and vital subject."

Simpson delineates the Gulf War and its effects on the country of Iraq in his 1991 *From the House of War: John Simpson in the Gulf.* He also examines what Phillip Knightley in the *New Statesman* called "the double standards of the allies and their quick switches of allegiance, from supporting Saddam Hussein in his war against Iran to the almost overnight decision that he was a tyrant worse than Hitler." Simpson declares, according to Knightley, that Iraq "did not suffer as seriously" in the war "as most people in the west assumed." He also tells of five British officers who resigned their commissions after seeing what cluster bombs and fuel-air explosives had done to the Iraqi soldiers, and praises Palestine Liberation Organization (PLO) leader Yasser Arafat's attempts to make peace. Above all, Knightley praised Simpson for "manag[ing] to convey his sympathy for ordinary Iraqis," and concluded that *From the House of War* is "a very readable book by an interesting man."

John Simpson told *CA:* "My work for BBC television news provides most of the material for my writing. I spend seven or eight months each year traveling with a camera team, and have been fortunate enough to report on most of the recent events which shape our world, from the revolution in Iran to the massacre in Tiananmen Square, the breaching of the Berlin Wall, and the revolutions in Czechoslovakia and Rumania. I spent six months in Baghdad before, during, and after the Gulf War. The issue of human rights is of particular importance to me, and my first non-fiction book, *The Disappeared,* dealt with the dirty war in Argentina. I spend as much time as possible in Iran and Central Asia, and have written widely about them both."

BIOGRAPHICAL/CRITICAL SOURCES:

PERIODICALS

Christian Science Monitor, July 11, 1988, p. 20.
New Statesman, August 23, 1991, pp. 34-35.
New Yorker, April 14, 1986, p. 110.
New York Times Book Review, February 5, 1984, p. 18; April 6, 1986, p. 18.

*   *   *

SIMPSON, John E(dwin) 1951-

PERSONAL: Born June 18, 1951, in Mt. Holly, NJ; son of John Edwin (a mechanic) and Betty Lou (a secretary; maiden name, Foster) Simpson. *Education:* Attended Wake Forest University, 1969-70; Gloucester County College, A.A., 1971; Glassboro State College, B.A. (cum laude), 1973. *Politics:* Democrat. *Religion:* United Methodist.

ADDRESSES: Home and office—Thomasville, GA.

CAREER: Stratford Taxi, Inc., Stratford, NJ, cab driver, full-time, 1973, summers, 1974-77; Cherry Hill Board of Education, Cherry Hill, NJ, high school teacher of English and journalism, 1974-77; Macmillan Publishing Company, Riverside, NJ, shipping-materials handler, 1977-79; American Telephone & Telegraph Co. (AT&T), Piscataway, NJ, computer programmer and systems analyst, 1979-92; writer, 1992—.

MEMBER: Mystery Writers of America, National Writers Union.

WRITINGS:

Crossed Wires (mystery), Carroll & Graf, 1992.

Short story titled "The Shot" was published in the *Worcester Review* in 1992.

WORK IN PROGRESS: Grail, a mainstream novel retelling of the Arthurian quest legend in which questers are retirees, completion expected in 1993; *Trapdoor,* a sequel to *Crossed Wires,* completion expected in 1993; research on computer viruses, electronic communication, Welsh-language literature, metalworking, and beer and ale brewing.

SIDELIGHTS: John E. Simpson told *CA:* "My writing schedule is basically this: Tuesday through Saturday mornings, from seven till about noon. Some mornings start earlier; some become afternoons and evenings; and of course there's the rare but glorious middle-of-the-night vision that 'inspires' me to get out of bed and stumble to the office. On the average, I write about a thousand words a day, steeped in about a gallon of hot tea (plain old tea, thank you, none of this designer stuff in pastel boxes). Sundays and Mondays—my 'days off'—are reserved for business matters and recreation.

"I nearly always do first drafts in longhand. I'm very comfortable with a computer but am also very easily sidetracked by the temptation to fool around with fonts, word processor macros, and so on. Working in longhand first forces me to think things through; there's a rhythm to language produced by pencil and paper that I cannot duplicate at the computer keyboard.

"You hear a lot of talk about whether the electronic age will spell (ha ha) the death of literacy. The jury's still out on television's effects—it seems as though every time we turn around, some new pundit is declaring TV itself already dead (by now it's been resurrected enough to put one in mind of the biblical Book of Revelation). But computers are a different story; in my opinion there's great po-

tential in those boxes (frustrating though they can be) for bringing people back to reading and writing again. This is true not just because of the ease of creating text with word processors but because of the explosion of participation in the 'electronic salon' phenomenon—bulletin board systems (BBSs) and on-line services such as CompuServe, America Online, and Prodigy. Every day millions of people are constructing millions of electronic missives for millions of other people (many of them strangers); this must be the first period of history in a *long* time (if ever) that so many are corresponding so regularly with so many others.

"That's part of the reason that I wrote *Crossed Wires,* a mystery that centers around the proliferation of BBSs. Another ulterior motive was this: The protagonist is hearing-impaired (as I am myself), and that of course gave me the opportunity to get my licks in about being hearing-impaired in a hearing society.

"People ask me how I can afford to write full time; the short answer is 'I can't.' For the last several years, I've been living on savings from a variety of sources. What I've made from my sale of *Crossed Wires*—my only 'sold book' so far—was good for only three or four months' living expenses. Maybe that's what will really kill literacy: when all the writers die of starvation."

*   *   *

SINGER, Ray (Eleazer)   1916-1992

OBITUARY NOTICE—See index for *CA* sketch: Born October 24, 1916, in New York, NY; died November 16, 1992. Producer, educator, and author. As a young man in the 1930s, Singer moved from New York to Hollywood, California, where he wrote comedy for the "Milton Berle Radio Show" as well as radio personalities Fred Allen, Kate Smith, and Henny Youngman. In the late 1940s, Singer began selling screenplays, including *Neptune's Daughter* and *A Woman of Distinction.* From the 1950s through the 1970s he was a writer and producer for television, receiving an Emmy Award nomination in 1968. His credits include *The Frank Sinatra Show, The Donna Reed Show, My Three Sons, Family Affair, Here's Lucy, Love American Style,* and *All in the Family.* Singer was an instructor in film and television writing at the University of California at Los Angeles from 1975 to 1988.

OBITUARIES AND OTHER SOURCES:

BOOKS

Who's Who in Entertainment, Marquis, 1992.

PERIODICALS

New York Times, November 19, 1992.

SKELTON, William B(arott) 1939-

PERSONAL: Born May 14, 1939, in Syracuse, NY; son of Edward M. (a railroad supervisor) and Anna B. Skelton; married Gail J. (a college teacher), July 28, 1968; children: Rebecca Anne. *Education:* Bowdoin College, B.A., 1961; Northwestern University, Ph.D., 1968. *Politics:* Democrat.

ADDRESSES: Home—2409 Simonis St., Stevens Point, WI 54481. *Office*—Department of History, University of Wisconsin—Stevens Point, Stevens Point, WI 54481.

CAREER: University of Wisconsin—Stevens Point, professor of history, 1969—.

MEMBER: American Historical Association, Organization of American Historians, Society of Military Historians.

WRITINGS:

An American Profession of Arms: The Army Officer Corps, 1784-1861, University Press of Kansas, 1992.

*   *   *

SKEMP, Joseph Bright 1910-1992

OBITUARY NOTICE—See index for *CA* sketch: Born May 10, 1910, in Bilston, Staffordshire, England; died October 10, 1992, in Weston-super-Mare, Avon, England. Philosopher, educator, editor, and author. Skemp's 1952 translation of Plato's *Statesman,* which was revised in 1987, has become a standard classroom text. Skemp was a Cambridge University fellow beginning in 1939 and had a three-year teaching stint at Victoria University of Manchester before joining the University of Durham staff as a professor of Greek in 1950. He was named a professor emeritus in 1973. Skemp was also coeditor of *Phronesis,* a philosophy periodical, from 1955 to 1964. His writings include *The Theory of Motion in Plato's Later Dialogues* and *The Greeks and the Gospel.*

OBITUARIES AND OTHER SOURCES:

BOOKS

International Authors and Writers Who's Who, tenth edition, International Biographical Centre, 1986.
Who's Who, Marquis, 1993.
Writers Directory: 1990-1992, St. James Press, 1990.

PERIODICALS

Times (London), November 23, 1992, p. 19.

SKIPPER, James K(inley), Jr. 1934-1993

OBITUARY NOTICE—See index for *CA* sketch: Born September 14, 1934, in Columbus, OH; died of cancer, February 15, 1993, in Burtonsville. Sociologist, educator, editor, and author. Skipper, a sociologist, spent most of his career teaching at various colleges and universities. Following the receipt of his doctorate from Northwestern University, he joined the staff at Case Western Reserve University, where he remained for six years. He also taught throughout his career at such institutions as Bowling Green State University, Virginia Polytechnic Institute and State University, and Yale University. He wrote and edited numerous books and articles on sociology, including *In Their Own Behalf: Voices from the Margin,* edited with Mark Lefton and Charles McCaghy; *Approaches to Deviance: Theories, Concepts and Research Findings,* edited with Lefton and McCaghy; and *Deviance: Voices from the Margin,* written with others.

OBITUARIES AND OTHER SOURCES:

PERIODICALS

Washington Post, February 19, 1993, p. D4.

*   *   *

SLADE, Afton J. 1919-1993

OBITUARY NOTICE—See index for *CA* sketch: Born March 2, 1919 in Salt Lake City, UT; died of complications from cancer, January 10, 1993, in La Jolla, CA. Environmental activist and writer. Slade was nationally recognized in 1967 by President Lyndon B. Johnson for her efforts in fighting against air pollution. As cofounder and president of Stamp Out Smog, she received national coverage and recognition for her unique protests, including one in which a group of children wore gas masks. Her books include *Stages: Understanding How You Make Moral Decisions.*

OBITUARIES AND OTHER SOURCES:

PERIODICALS

Los Angeles Times, January, 15, 1993, p. A30.

*   *   *

SLATER, Thomas J. 1955-

PERSONAL: Born December 16, 1955, in Kalamazoo, MI; son of Garrett and Bertha Slater; married Mary Ann Saur (a journalist), May 23, 1981; children: Gretchen Anna, Allison Kimberly. *Education:* Michigan State University, B.A., 1978; University of Maryland at College

Park, M.A., 1981; Oklahoma State University, Ph.D., 1985.

ADDRESSES: Home—110 College Lodge Rd., Indiana, PA 15701. *Office*—Department of English, 110 Leonard Hall, Indiana University of Pennsylvania, Indiana, PA 15705-1094.

CAREER: Northwest Missouri State University, Maryville, lecturer in English, 1985-86; University of Missouri—Kansas City, lecturer in English, 1986-87; Missouri Western State College, St. Joseph, lecturer in English, 1986-87; Illinois State University, Normal, assistant professor of English, 1987-90; Indiana University of Pennsylvania, Indiana, assistant professor of English, 1990—.

MEMBER: Modern Language Association of America, Society for Cinema Studies, National Council of Teachers of English (Assembly on Media Arts), University Film and Video Association.

AWARDS, HONORS: Best Video Documentary Award, Oklahoma University Student Film and Video Competition, 1985, for *Need a Little Shelter;* grant from National Endowment for the Humanities, 1992, for research on silent film screenwriter/producer June Mathis.

WRITINGS:

Milos Forman: A Bio-Bibliography, Greenwood Press, 1987.
(Editor in chief and contributor) *A Handbook of Soviet and East European Film and Filmmakers,* Greenwood Press, 1991.

Other writings include *Need a Little Shelter,* a video documentary, 1985. Work represented in anthologies, including *Dictionary of Literary Biography: American Screenwriters; Second Series,* Gale, 1986; *Film and Literature: A Comparative Approach to Adaptation,* Texas Tech University Press, 1988; and *Inventing Vietnam: The War in Film and Television,* edited by Michael Anderegg, Temple University Press, 1991. Contributor to scholarly journals. Co-editor, *Bravo! A Journal of Freshman Writing,* 1988-90.

SIDELIGHTS: Thomas J. Slater told *CA:* "My books on Milos Forman and Soviet and Eastern European film and filmmakers have been valuable experiences in more ways than one, and I hope they are proving to be valuable to other scholars as well. The books grew out of my work for a dissertation on Forman while I was at Oklahoma State University. The second volume, in particular, was designed to meet what I perceived as a specific need while researching the first.

"My essay in Michael Anderegg's volume on teaching Vietnam documentaries has also been rewarding; it gained far more attention than I ever expected. I strongly believe that students must understand how film communicates. I

also feel that our country never has, and probably never will have, the debate that it needs about Vietnam. Therefore I simply wrote honestly about my experiences, and these ideas came through. I am currently taking the same approach to an essay about Ken Kesey that I am writing.

"My concerns with showing students and others how to understand film and history have also led to my current writing and research interests. For the past few years, my efforts have centered on the life and career of June Mathis, screenwriter and producer, who was the most powerful woman in the silent film industry. Yet she has been almost totally forgotten. Thus far, I have published a few pieces about her, but I hope to obtain a contract for a book. This work may focus just on Mathis, or possibly on several women who helped shape silent film. Their accomplishments have been so thoroughly removed from history that the past two decades of feminist scholarship have not yet been able to reinsert them. An entirely new history of silent film is needed."

*   *   *

SLETHAUG, Gordon E.   1940-

PERSONAL: Born September 22, 1940, in Kalispell, MT; son of Olander (a tree farmer) and Florence (a teacher; maiden name, Dunham) Slethaug; married Mary Manske (an education developer), June 21, 1964; children: Kris, Gavin, Darin. *Education:* Pacific Lutheran University, B.A., 1962; University of Nebraska, M.A., 1964, Ph.D., 1968. *Politics:* Liberal. *Religion:* Lutheran.

ADDRESSES: Home—55 Academy Crescent, Waterloo, Ontario N2L 5H8, Canada. *Office*—Department of English, University of Waterloo, Waterloo, Ontario N2L 3G1, Canada.

CAREER: University of Waterloo, Waterloo, Ontario, assistant professor, 1968-74, associate professor, 1974-93, professor of English, 1993—, chair of Department of English, beginning in 1985. Writer and lecturer.

MEMBER: Modern Language Association, Canadian Association of American Studies, Association of Canadian University Teachers of English.

WRITINGS:

(With Stan Fogel) *Understanding John Barth,* University of South Carolina Press, 1990.
The Play of the Double in Postmodern American Fiction, University of Southern Illinois Press, 1993.

Also author, with Michael Larer, of "Doubles and Doubling in the Contemporary Arts," *Journal of the Fantastic in the Arts* (special edition), 1993. Contributor to books, including *Critical Essays on John Updike,* edited by W. R. Macnaughton, G. K. Hall, 1982; and *The Scope of the Fantastic: Culture, Biography, Themes, Children's Literature,* edited by Robert A. Collins and Howard Pearce, Greenwood Press, 1985. Contributor of articles and reviews to periodicals, including *Canadian Drama, Canadian Review of American Studies, Critique, Early American Literature, English Record, English Studies in Canada, Extrapolation, Melville Society Extracts, Modern Fiction Studies, Queen's Quarterly, Renascence,* and *Southern Humanities Review.*

WORK IN PROGRESS: Complex systems, chaotics, and postmodern American fiction.

SIDELIGHTS: Educator and writer Gordon E. Slethaug told *CA:* "I am interested in various kinds of artistic and literary movements such as transcendentalism, modernism, and postmodernism. I am also interested in the intersection of critical theory and literary practice. It is that which prompted me to write about John Barth, John Knowles, and the various treatments of the double in *The Play of the Double in Postmodern American Fiction.*"

*   *   *

SLOAN, Tod (Stratton) 1952-

PERSONAL: Born July 6, 1952, in Washington, DC; son of Lindley (in international development) and Lois (Petersen) Sloan; children: Daniel K. *Education:* University of Michigan, Ph.D., 1982. *Politics:* "Democratic socialist."

ADDRESSES: Home—1543 South Florence Ave., Tulsa, OK 74104. *Office*—Department of Psychology, University of Tulsa, 600 South College, Tulsa, OK 74104-3189.

CAREER: University of Tulsa, Tulsa, OK, began as assistant professor, became associate professor of psychology, 1982—.

WRITINGS:

Deciding, Methuen, 1987.
(Editor) *Rafaga,* University of Oklahoma Press, 1992.

Contributor to *Journal of Social Issues.*

WORK IN PROGRESS: Modernity and the Psyche.

*   *   *

SLOCUM, Milton Jonathan 1905-1993

OBITUARY NOTICE—See index for *CA* sketch: Surname originally Rosenberg; legally changed, c. 1929; born November 7, 1905, in Clifton Forge, VA; died of conges-

tive heart failure, January 15, 1993, in Santa Monica, CA. Physician, educator, journalist, and author. After beginning his career as a journalist, Slocum went on to practice medicine for more than thirty years in a run-down section of Manhattan known as Hell's Kitchen; among the patients he tended to were bootleggers, pimps, prostitutes, and mobsters. In addition to his medical practice, Slocum also taught part-time for most of his career at New York Medical College-Flower Fifth Avenue Hospital. He published his memoirs, the *Manhattan Country Doctor,* in 1986.

OBITUARIES AND OTHER SOURCES:

BOOKS

International Authors and Writers Who's Who, 12th edition, International Biographical Centre, 1991, p. 789.

PERIODICALS

New York Times, January, 18, 1993, p. D8.

*   *   *

SMITH, Johnston
See CRANE, Stephen (Townley)

*   *   *

SMITH, R(eginald) D(onald) 1914-1985
(Martin Manning, Oliver Martin)

OBITUARY NOTICE—See index for *CA* sketch: Born July 31, 1914, in Birmingham, England; died in 1985. Radio and television producer and director, educator, and writer. After completing studies at the University of Birmingham in the mid-1930s, Smith taught for five years, then embarked on his twenty-seven year affiliation with the British Broadcasting Corporation (BBC). For the British network Smith wrote, directed, and produced numerous radio plays and television films. Among his published works are *New Minds for Old* and *Shakespeare Studies,* as well as *The Writings of Anna Wickham: Free Woman and Poet,* which he edited. He also contributed to periodicals under the pseudonyms Martin Manning and Oliver Martin.

OBITUARIES AND OTHER SOURCES:

Date of death provided by wife, Diana M. Hogarth.

*   *   *

SMITH, Sally Bedell 1948-
PERSONAL: Born in 1948.

CAREER: Journalist and author. Reported for several publications, including coverage of television networks for the *New York Times* and *TV Guide.*

AWARDS, HONORS: Sigma Delta Chi Award for magazine reporting, Society of Professional Journalists, 1982.

WRITINGS:

In All His Glory: The Life of William S. Paley, the Legendary Tycoon and His Brilliant Circle, Simon & Schuster, 1990, reissued as *In All His Glory: The Life and Times of William S. Paley and the Birth of Modern Broadcasting,* 1991.

Also wrote *Up the Tube: Prime Time TV and the Silverman Years.* Contributor to numerous periodicals.

SIDELIGHTS: Journalist Sally Bedell Smith had reported on the television networks for the *New York Times* and for *TV Guide* for several years and had written one book, *Up the Tube: Prime Time TV and the Silverman Years,* before penning her widely reviewed biography, *In All His Glory: The Life of William S. Paley, the Legendary Tycoon and His Brilliant Circle.* Published in 1990 by Simon & Schuster, *In All His Glory* chronicles the life of Paley, who owned and managed the Columbia Broadcasting System, Inc. (CBS) network for many years. Smith gives a detailed account of both Paley's business dealings and his lavish personal life; as Christopher Buckley surmised it in his critique of the biography in the *New York Times Book Review,* "her superb and thorough reporting uncovered all the unpleasantness along with the greatness."

In All His Glory narrates how Paley became involved with CBS as a young man, while it was still a struggling radio network centered in Philadelphia, Pennsylvania. He produced a half-hour program called "The La Palina Smoker" that featured a husky-voiced woman—the show proved so popular that the sales of the sponsor, La Palina cigars, skyrocketed. It was the first of many successes in which Paley demonstrated that programming was the key to becoming tops among the networks. Under his direction, CBS became a major network and made a smooth transition to television, though Paley initially resisted the new invention.

While not minimizing Paley's true triumphs, however, Smith suggests in her book that Paley sometimes took credit for the creative ideas of others, such as longtime CBS president Frank Stanton. She also discusses Paley's two marriages, his numerous affairs, and his extravagant lifestyle which would, on occasion, necessitate flying in freshly killed game birds from Europe. Smith also includes commentary on many of Paley's friends and acquaintances in the biography, such as pioneer news reporter Edward R. Murrow and writer Truman Capote. Reviewer

Leah Rozen in *People* concluded that Smith's work "is thoroughly researched and crammed with telling details, killer quotes and rousing anecdotes."

BIOGRAPHICAL/CRITICAL SOURCES:

PERIODICALS

Business Week, December 10, 1990, p. 10.
Newsweek, December 10, 1990, p. 88.
New Yorker, February 18, 1991, pp. 79-84.
New York Times Book Review, November 4, 1990, pp. 1, 40-41.
People, January 14, 1991, pp. 31-32.*

*   *   *

SNELL, Michael   1945-

PERSONAL: Born August 16, 1945, in Denver, CO; son of H. J. and Theda M. Snell; married September 13, 1986; wife's name, Patricia Ann (an artist); children: (previous marriage) Cameron Sue, Stephan William. *Education:* DePauw University, B.A., 1967. *Politics:* Liberal independent. *Religion:* None. *Avocational interests:* Tennis, flyfishing, shellfishing.

ADDRESSES: Home and office—P.O. Box 655, Truro, MA 02666. *Agent*—Michael Snell Literary Agency, P.O. Box 655, Truro, MA 02666.

CAREER: Wadsworth Publishing Co., Belmont, CA, editor, 1967-78; Addison-Wesley Publishing Co., Reading, MA, executive editor, 1978-79; Michael Snell Literary Agency, Truro, MA, president, 1979—.

MEMBER: Phi Beta Kappa.

WRITINGS:

(With Steve Bennett) *Executive Chess,* Viking, 1987.
(With Emmett Murphy) *The Genius of Sitting Bull: Thirteen Heroic Strategies for Today's Business Leaders,* Prentice-Hall, 1992.
(With Craig Hickman) *The Strategy Game,* McGraw, 1993.
(With Tom Connor and Roger Smith) *The Oz Principle,* Prentice-Hall, 1993.
(With Michael Silva) *Crisis Management,* Wiley, 1993.
(With Murphy) *The Heroic Organization,* Simon & Schuster, in press.

Also ghostwriter for numerous works.

SIDELIGHTS: Michael Snell told *CA:* "I have worked continuously in book publishing for twenty-five years, beginning as an editor with Wadsworth Publishing Company immediately after graduation from DePauw University in 1967. In 1979 I formed the Michael Snell Literary

Agency, a book development company currently located in the National Seashore at the tip of Cape Cod. I have edited, agented, collaborated on, or ghostwritten more than five hundred books on everything from astrophysics to zoology. I specialize in business books of all kinds, from sophisticated technical reference volumes in international trade and finance to low-level beginners' guides on the starting and running of small businesses. My current bestseller, *The Genius of Sitting Bull,* reflects a career-long interest in leadership, business ethics, and corporate social responsibility.

"I represent more than a hundred writers from virtually every state, with the heaviest concentration in New England and the Northwest. Though I handle occasional fiction, such as David James Duncan's *The Brothers K,* most of my projects fall into the adult nonfiction category. In addition to business, I emphasize practical self-help and how-to books in computing, psychology, fitness, and parenting.

"Every year I collaborate on or ghostwrite an average of three books, mostly with prominent business executives and consultants. In addition, I match content experts with professional writers to produce collaborations.

"The only literary agent in *Literary Marketplace* who expressly welcomes new writers, I arrange for the first book publication of over a dozen writers each year. I take special delight in developing talented young writers, navigating them through project development, style improvement, marketing and promotion, book production, and financial management."

*   *   *

SOLOMON, Andrew 1963-

PERSONAL: Born October 30, 1963, in New York, NY; son of Howard (president of a laboratory research firm) and Carolyn (Bower) Solomon. *Education:* Yale University, B.A., 1985; Jesus College, Cambridge University, B.A., 1987, M.A., 1992. *Politics:* Democrat.

ADDRESSES: Home—64 West Fifteenth St., No. 5E, New York, NY 10011. *Agent*—Wylie, Aitken, and Stone, 250 West Fifty-seventh St., Suite 2106, New York, NY 10107.

CAREER: Writer.

WRITINGS:

The Irony Tower: Soviet Artists in a Time of Glasnost, Knopf, 1991.
Art in Embassies, U.S. Department of State, 1993.

Contributing editor to *HG,* 1989—. Contributor to periodicals, including *New York Times Magazine* and *Artform.*

WORK IN PROGRESS: A novel; research on African art.

*   *   *

SOMMER, Mark 1945-

PERSONAL: Born September 30, 1945; son of Adolph and Muriel (Ehrlich) Sommer; married Sandi Schultz (a farmer and landscape designer), October, 1972. *Education:* Cornell University, B.A. (with distinction), 1967. *Avocational interests:* Wilderness exploration, swimming, gardening, reading, adventure, travel, contemplation, and time with friends.

ADDRESSES: Home—P.O. Box 650, Miranda, CA 95553. *Office*—Peace and Conflict Studies Program, University of California, Berkeley, CA 94720.

CAREER: Teacher at experimental elementary and secondary schools in and around San Francisco, CA, 1969-71; organic farmer, 1971—; researcher and writer, 1978—. Inter Press Service, columnist, 1992—. Institute for Policy Studies, associate fellow, 1983-88; University of California, Berkeley, research associate in Peace and Conflict Studies Program, 1988—; Institute for Peace and International Security, research fellow, 1990—; Earthview Foundation, research director, 1990-91; Exploratory Project on the Conditions of Peace (ExPro), cofounder, 1983. Guest on radio and television programs; consultant to foundations. *Military service:* Performed alternative service as conscientious objector to military service, 1969-71.

MEMBER: Phi Beta Kappa.

WRITINGS:

Beyond the Bomb: Living without Nuclear Weapons: A Field Guide to Alternative Strategies for Building a Stable Peace, Exploratory Project on the Conditions of Peace, 1986.
(With Harry B. Hollins and Averill L. Powers) *The Conquest of War: Alternative Strategies for Global Security,* Westview, 1989.
Living in Freedom: The Exhilaration and Anguish of Prague's Second Spring, Mercury House, 1992, second edition, in press.
Pathfinders: Human-Scale Solutions to Global-Scale Problems, Mercury House, in press.

Work represented in anthologies, including *Securing Our Planet,* edited by Don Carlson and Craig Comstock, St. Martin's, 1986; and *Citizen Summitry: Keeping the Peace When It Matters Too Much to Be Left to Politicians,* edited by Carlson and Comstock, J. P. Tarcher, 1986. Columnist for periodicals, including *Christian Science Monitor, Atlanta Constitution, Chicago Tribune, San Francisco Chronicle,* and *Newsday.* Contributor to periodicals, including *Bulletin of the Atomic Scientists, Environmental Action, Intervention, Nuclear Times, Whole Earth Review,* and *New Dimensions.*

WORK IN PROGRESS: Gathering "stories of 'extraordinary ordinary' people who are doing promising work to hear the planet, each other, and ourselves."

SIDELIGHTS: Mark Sommer told *CA:* "My writing reflects the double life I live, divided between the deep woods and the wider world. Having spent most of my adulthood not just in the country but in an ancient forest wilderness, I have nevertheless been strongly drawn to the urgent issues of our time and equally strongly persuaded of the need for a fundamental transformation of human beliefs and behavior to meet the exigencies of this era. After writing two books and dozens of articles describing blueprints for global change, I am now turning the telescope around to examine what is already being done on a small scale by individuals and groups to bring that change about. Describing these extraordinary ordinary people through 'nonfiction storytelling' (using techniques of fiction to describe actual persons and events), I hope to persuade readers that they, too, are capable of doing effective and meaningful work to help heal our wounded world."

*　　*　　*

SOPER, Alexander Coburn   1904-1993

OBITUARY NOTICE—See index for *CA* sketch: Born February 18, 1904, in Chicago, IL; died of heart failure, January 13, 1993, in Rosemont, PA. Educator, editor, translator, and author. An Asian-art historian, Soper spent more than five decades as a faculty member at various universities and colleges, including the Institute of Fine Arts in New York City. In addition, he edited the periodical *Artibus Asiae* for more than thirty years. Focusing on Asian-art scholarship, Soper's numerous books include *The Evolution of Buddhist Architecture in Japan* and *Literary Evidence for Early Buddhist Art in China.* He also translated the works of other authors, including Ch'eng-shih Tuan's *A Vacation Glimpse of the T'ang Temples of Ch'ang-an.*

OBITUARIES AND OTHER SOURCES:

BOOKS

Who's Who in America, 47th edition, Marquis, 1992, p. 3176.

PERIODICALS

New York Times, January 14, 1993, p. D23.

*　　*　　*

SPIKE, John T(homas)   1951-

PERSONAL: Born November 8, 1951, in New York, NY; son of Robert Warren Spike (a theologian) and Alice (Coffman) Spike (a teacher); married Michele Kahn (an attorney), May 26, 1973; children: Nicholas Nathan. *Education:* Wesleyan University, B.A. (cum laude), 1973; Harvard University, A.M., 1974, Ph.D., 1979. *Politics:* "Protestant." *Religion:* Christian.

ADDRESSES: Home—5 via Giramontino, 50125 Firenze, Italy. *Office*—Abaris Books Inc., 45 Memorial Plaza, Pleasantville, NY 10570.

CAREER: Burlington Magazine, London, England, New York correspondent, 1978-83; National Academy of Design, New York City, guest curator, 1981-83, treasurer of Old Masters Exhibition Society, 1984—; independent art historian in Florence, Italy, 1988—. Guest curator for numerous museums, including Art Museum, Princeton University, 1979-80, John and Mable Ringling Museum of Art, 1982-85, Kimbell Art Museum, 1983-86, and Cincinnati Art Museum, 1985-90; consultant for and organizer of numerous exhibitions for museums, including National Gallery of Art, Solomon R. Guggenheim Museum, Fortezza da Basso (Florence, Italy), and Pinacoteca Nazionale (Bologna, Italy). Visiting assistant professor at Queens College of City University of New York, 1988-89; fellow of Pierpont Morgan Library.

MEMBER: International Association of Art Critics, American Association of Museums, College Art Association, Drawing Society, Touring Club Italiano.

AWARDS, HONORS: Kingsbury fellowship for research travel, Harvard University, 1976-77 and 1977-78; grants from the National Endowment for the Humanities, 1980-82 and 1987-90, for travel and research.

WRITINGS:

Italian Baroque Paintings from New York Private Collections, Princeton University Press, 1980.
(Editor) *The Illustrated Bartsch,* Abaris Books, Volume 41: *Italian Masters of the Seventeenth Century,* 1981, Volume 42: *Italian Masters of the Seventeenth Century,* 1981, Volume 43: *Italian Masters of the Seventeenth Century,* 1981, Volume 30: *Enea Vico: Italian Master of the Sixteenth Century,* 1985, Volume 28 (coeditor), 1985, Volume 29 (coeditor), 1986, Volume

31: *Italian Masters of the Sixteenth Century* (with Susan Boorsch), 1986.

Italian Still Life Paintings from Three Centuries, Centro Di, 1983.

Baroque Portraiture in Italy: Works from North American Collections, John and Mable Ringling Museum of Art, 1984.

Aspects of Sculpture: The Paul Magriel Collection, Centro Di, 1985.

Giuseppe Maria Crespi and the Emergence of Genre Painting in Italy, Kimbell Art Museum, 1986.

(With Paul Magriel) *A Connoisseur's Guide to the Met: The Best of the Metropolitan Museum in Four One-Hour Tours,* Vintage Books, 1987.

Harry Nadler 1930-1990: A Retrospective, edited by Peter Walch, University of New Mexico, Art Museum, 1991.

Fairfield Porter: An American Classic, Abrams, 1992.

Catalogue of Italian Paintings in the Cincinnati Art Museum, [Cincinnati], 1993.

Contributor to books, including *The Age of Monarchy,* Metropolitan Museum of Art, 1987; *A Taste for Angels: Neapolitan Painting in North American Collections, 1650-1750,* Yale University Art Gallery/Yale University Press, 1987; *Mattia Preti,* edited by E. Corace, [Rome], 1989; *International Dictionary of Art and Artists,* St. James Press, 1990. General editor, "Illustrated Bartsch" series, Abaris Books, 1989—. Contributor of reviews and articles to journals, including *Burlington Magazine, New York Times, Storia dell'Arte,* and, in Italian, *Atti e memorie dell'Accademia Clementina.*

WORK IN PROGRESS: Velazquez and Italy, a catalogue raisonne of paintings by Mattia Preti.

SIDELIGHTS: John T. Spike told *CA:* "I have dedicated and shall continue to dedicate my life to the study of Italian art from its classical origins until the modern era, circa 1800. The history of Rome, Roman baroque painting, sculpture, and architecture interest me particularly, but I have also published extensively on Neapolitan and Bolognese paintings and drawings of the seventeenth and eighteenth centuries.

"I have always been self-employed, accepting assignments from museums and art galleries to consult on exhibitions and publications. Following the awarding of my Harvard Ph.D. I did not embark upon the traditional tenure-track or provincial museum career routes because I was never willing to distance myself from a major research library or, naturally, from Europe. I therefore moved to New York City with my wife and son. In the summer of 1989 we packed up fourteen suitcases and moved to Italy. This occurred roughly a month after I realized that my reputation had progressed to the point where I could support my family in a foreign country. In fact, I had not fully realized that my knowledge of Italian paintings would be much more generously rewarded in Italy, which in retrospect seems only logical.

"Before relocating to Florence I had contracted with Abrams Inc. to write an illustrated biography of the American painter Fairfield Porter. This project had come to me from Mrs. Fairfield Porter, the artist's widow, who knew of my writings on old masters. I undertook the Porter book because I saw it as perhaps the only opportunity in my career to write a book on an artist that would be a primary source for historians of future generations. I researched Porter's life as thoroughly as I would one of my ancient Italians and attempted to sketch the events, books, and ideas that shaped his life. I did not attempt to read his mind, recognizing the truth of Mark Twain's dictum 'Biography is only the clothes and buttons of a man.' But this at least is a start."

BIOGRAPHICAL/CRITICAL SOURCES:

PERIODICALS

Humanities, May/June 1988, pp. 11-13.

*   *   *

SQUIRES, (James) Radcliffe   1917-1993

OBITUARY NOTICE—See index for *CA* sketch: Born May 23, 1917, in Salt Lake City, UT; died of an abdominal aneurysm, February 14, 1993, in Ann Arbor, MI. Educator, editor, poet, and author. Squires, an English professor at the University of Michigan for several years, wrote poetry about his home state of Utah and authored several critical studies. His numerous collections of poetry include *Where the Compass Spins, Fingers of Hermes, The Light under Islands,* and *Journeys.* His literary criticism includes *Allen Tate: A Literary Biography* and *The Major Themes of Robert Frost.* Squires also edited books and magazines, including the *Michigan Quarterly Review* from 1971 to 1976.

OBITUARIES AND OTHER SOURCES:

BOOKS

The Writers Directory: 1992-1994, St. James Press, 1992, p. 932.

PERIODICALS

New York Times, February 18, 1993, p. B12.

STADLER, Matthew 1959-

PERSONAL: Born January 19, 1959, in Seattle, WA; son of David Stadler (a professor) and Anne (Morgan) Stadler (a consultant). *Education:* Attended London School of Economics and Political Science, London, 1979-80; Oberlin College, B.A., 1981; attended University of Washington, 1986; Columbia University, M.F.A., 1987.

ADDRESSES: Home and office—1020 E. Denny Way, No. 36, Seattle, WA 98122. *Agent*—Gloria Loomis, 133 E. 35th St., New York, NY 10016.

CAREER: New York Native, national news editor, 1983-84, music, book, and film critic, 1984-85; Ballantine Books, New York City, editorial assistant, 1984-85; Anglo-American International School, New York City, instructor in philosophy, political theory, and history, 1985-88; Extension Project, Seattle, WA, cofounder, codirector, and instructor, 1990—. *Antaeus,* New York City, fiction reader, 1986-87; codirector of the Rendezvous Room Reading Series, 1991—.

AWARDS, HONORS: Nomination for best gay or lesbian book, American Librarian's Association, 1990; Lambda Literary Award nomination for best first novel by a gay writer, 1990, for *Landscape: Memory;* Guggenheim fellowship, 1992, for fiction writing.

WRITINGS:

Landscape: Memory (novel), Scribner, 1990.
The Dissolution of Nicholas Dee (novel), Scribner, 1993.

Contributor to books, including *The Working Book,* Delft International Conference on Architecture and Critical Theory, 1990; *Men on Men 4,* Dutton, 1992. Contributor to periodicals, including *New York Times Book Review, Village Voice, Rocket, Seattle Times,* and *Mirage.*

WORK IN PROGRESS: Allan Stein; A History of Sleep.

SIDELIGHTS: Matthew Stadler's first book, *Landscape: Memory,* was nominated for the Lambda Literary Award for best first novel by a gay writer in 1990. The book is narrated by its 16-year-old protagonist, Maxwell Kosegarten, and is set in early twentieth-century San Francisco. *Los Angeles Times Book Review* contributor Merle Rubin called it "a novel about adolescence, a diary of a young man on the verge of forging his erotic and artistic identity." Rubin expressed concern about the novel's "lack of historical texture" but admitted that its strengths "are finally more basic than its flaws." The same critic concluded, "There's something rather breathtaking, as well as uneasy-making, about the ambition and naivete of a novel like this one." *Wall Street Journal's* Bruce Bawer lauded Stadler for providing *Landscape: Memory* "with a level of artistry and assurance rarely seen in so unseasoned a writer."

BIOGRAPHICAL/CRITICAL SOURCES:

PERIODICALS

Los Angeles Times Book Review, December 23, 1990, p. 8.
Wall Street Journal, August 29, 1990.

*   *   *

STAGGENBORG, Suzanne 1955-

PERSONAL: Born April 26, 1955, in Cincinnati, OH; daughter of Robert (an accountant) and Rosalie Albanese (a homemaker) Staggenborg; married Rodney Nelson (a sociologist), September 8, 1980; children: Charlie, Laura. *Education:* Miami University, B.A., 1977; Washington University, M.A., 1979; Northwestern University, Ph.D., 1985.

ADDRESSES: Home—2519 East Seventh St., Bloomington, IN 47408. *Office*—Indiana University, Department of Sociology, Ballantine Hall, Bloomington, IN 47405.

CAREER: University College of Washington University, St. Louis, MO, instructor in sociology, 1979; Northwestern University, Chicago, IL, research fellow at the Center for Urban Affairs and Policy Research, 1981-84, instructor in sociology, 1982-83; Northwestern University Medical School and Northwestern Memorial Hospital, faculty associate and project director for alcohol and crime study, 1985-86; Indiana University, Bloomington, assistant professor, 1986-92, associate professor of sociology, 1992—; writer.

MEMBER: American Sociological Association, Phi Beta Kappa.

AWARDS, HONORS: Northwestern University fellowship, 1980-81, dissertation year fellowship, 1984-85; National Science Foundation dissertation grant, 1984-85; Indiana University summer faculty fellowship, 1988; research grant, Project on Governance of Nonprofit Organizations, Center on Philanthropy, Indiana University, 1991-92.

WRITINGS:

The Pro-Choice Movement: Organization and Activism in the Abortion Conflict, Oxford University Press, 1991.

Contributor to books, including *Community Organizations: Studies in Resource Mobilization and Exchange,* edited by Carl Milofsky, Oxford University Press, 1988. Contributor of articles and reviews to periodicals, including *Social Forces, American Sociologist, Social Science Quarterly,* and *American Journal of Sociology.* Member of editorial board, *Social Problems,* 1990—, and *Qualitative Sociology,* 1992—.

WORK IN PROGRESS: "Women's Culture and Social Change," with Donna Eder and Lori Sudderth; research on the development of the contemporary women's movement, and on movement/countermovement dynamics with David Meyer.

* * *

STARK, Stephen (Edward) 1958-

PERSONAL: Born July 17, 1958, in Washington, DC; son of Theo R. (a bureaucrat) and Elizabeth (a bank official; maiden name, McChesney) Stark; married Rachael Isobel Nadel (a teacher), November 23, 1984; children: Julia Brenna McChesney. *Education:* George Mason University, B.A., 1982; Hollins College, M.A., 1984. *Politics:* "Very liberal Democrat." *Avocational interests:* Beer brewing, running.

ADDRESSES: Home—801 Country Place Drive, No. 109, Houston, TX 77079. *Agent*—Lisa Ross, Spieler Agency, 154 West 57th St., New York, NY 10019.

CAREER: Berkley Publishing, New York City, publisher's assistant, 1986-88; Ellen Levine Literary Agency, New York City, in contract negotiations, 1988-89; Viking/Penguin, New York City, in publicity and sales, 1989-90; Nadel & Philips, New York City, in word processing, 1990-92; University of Houston, Houston, TX, teacher of creative writing, 1992—.

MEMBER: American Home Brewers Association.

AWARDS, HONORS: Shane Stevens Fellowship in Fiction from Bread Loaf Writers' Conference, 1991; fellowship from National Endowment for the Arts, 1993-94.

WRITINGS:

The Outskirts (novel), Algonquin Books, 1988.
Second Son (novel), Holt, 1992.

Work represented in anthologies, including *Elvis in Oz: New Stories and Poems from the Hollins Creative Writing Program,* edited by Mary C. Flinn and George Garrett, University of Virginia Press, 1992. Contributor to periodicals, including *Journal* and *New Yorker.*

WORK IN PROGRESS: A novel "on the dissolution of a contemporary marriage, with rape as a subtext"; a novel about a powerful philanthropist "with a dark past."

SIDELIGHTS: Stephen Stark told *CA:* "If I have a religion, it's literature. Literature is the only place I've ever had what is commonly referred to as a religious experience. For me, literature is the highest form of art—no other form comes close to the bright and vivid and eternal life that exists from the page. The fabulous thing about literature is that there is not an 'original' in the sense that there is an original Jackson Pollock or an original Vincent van Gogh, and we must refer to the original in order to experience the intent (if you will) of the artist. Every faithful copy of a literary text is as perfect and powerful as the original. As difficult as I would find it to live without other forms of art, literature is the one that engages me most thoroughly, the one I find most indispensable.

"Over the last few years, through my literary adolescence and young adulthood, I've been trying to come up with a kind of visceral present tense narrative that puts the reader *in medias res,* not in its sense as a literary device that begins a narrative in the middle of the action, but in the sense that all stories happen within the larger action of ongoing life and that the narrative syllogism is something that's imposed upon crises points in the lives of characters. This plunging of the reader into the middle of things is an attempt to recreate the emotional and tactile world with as sure a verisimilitude as possible. It all goes back to that old creative writing class bromide of 'show, don't tell.' I try to render my fictive world so that the reader experiences it in much the same fashion as the character.

"Finally, I am interested in language. I love the coincidence of words flung against one another. I love the way they can sound—from someone like William Shakespeare or John Keats or William Faulkner—almost as though they were created, like some vast organic puzzle, to fit together in a particular way."

BIOGRAPHICAL/CRITICAL SOURCES:

PERIODICALS

Virginia Quarterly Review, spring, 1989.

* * *

STARR, June (O.)

PERSONAL: Born in Cincinnati, OH; daughter of M. Herbert and Jane (Rauh) Oettinger; married George A. Starr (divorced, March, 1968); children: Stephen Z. *Education:* Smith College, B.A., 1956; Columbia University, M.A., 1961; University of California, Berkeley, Ph.D., 1970; Yale University, M.S.L., 1990; Stanford University, J.D., 1992. *Avocational interests:* Swimming, sailing, yoga, biking, walking, travel to exotic places.

ADDRESSES: Home—7 Arbutus Lane, Stony Brook, NY 11790. *Office*—Department of Anthropology, State University of New York at Stony Brook, Stony Brook, NY 11794.

CAREER: State University of New York at Stony Brook, assistant professor, 1970-75, associate professor of anthropology, c. 1975—. Nature Conservancy, member of Western Pacific Division legal department, 1991; National Academy of Sciences, member of Committee for Research on Law Enforcement and the Administration of Justice.

MEMBER: American Anthropological Association, Law and Society Association, Turkish Studies Association, Middle East Studies Association.

WRITINGS:

Dispute and Settlement in Rural Turkey: An Ethnography of Law, E. J. Brill, 1978.
Adliye: An Ethnography of a Rural Turkish Law Court (documentary film, with teacher's guide), privately printed, 1985.
(Editor with Jane Collier, and contributor) *History and Power in the Study of Law: New Directions in Legal Anthropology,* Cornell University Press, 1989.
Law as Metaphor: From Islamic Courts to the Palace of Justice, State University of New York Press, 1992.

Work represented in anthologies, including *Women and Property: Women as Property,* edited by Renee Hirschon, Croom Helm, 1984; *People's Law and State Law: The Bellagio Papers,* Foris Publications (Dordrecht), 1985; and *Contested States: Law, Hegemony, and Resistance,* edited by M. Lazarus-Black and S. F. Hirsch, Routledge & Kegan Paul, 1993. Contributor of numerous articles to law and anthropology journals.

WORK IN PROGRESS: When Empires Meet: Trade and Markets in the Ottoman Empire, completion expected in 1994; research on the Biodiversity Treaty and third-world ecosystems; research on conservatorships in California and the social organization of losing adult status.

SIDELIGHTS: June Starr told *CA:* "I'm a cultural anthropologist whose field of study is law and conflict resolution. What interests me is the endless cycle of power by which law is created and then subverted by various groups in society. The research method I use is as follows. First a present-day legal institution is studied empirically and contextualized in its social world. Once comprehended as a modern legal phenomenon, the institution can be traced backward to understand the historical moment of its creation, and then traced forward to understand its guises in different political moments. This method allows the researcher to resonate with history. I eschew the interpretist-turn the social sciences have taken, which allows authors to juxtapose any occurrences and institutions, taking them out of historical sequence and placing them in a flotsam and jetsam of an unhistorical theory. The most important influence on my work is that of the historical sociologists (Barrington Moore and his students), who use historical texts and history to reconstruct the social forces

and institutions which, at particular historic times, create social change.

"My early work on the new nation of Turkey asked and answered the questions, 'What dispute-resolving mechanisms existed in the late 1960s in Turkish villages located far from cities and the centers of power? When did villagers turn to law and the legal arm of the state, represented by police, gendarmes, and courts, to resolve conflict?' By the late 1960s there was widespread acceptance of a secular legal system in Islamic Turkey.

"Later I began to wonder how the Islamic Ottoman Empire came to accept secular law and secular courts. Thus my second book on Turkey explored the question of the development of secular law in the Ottoman Empire which, in earlier centuries, had been *the* staunch defender of Islam. I argue that the development of Turkish courts resulted from a power struggle between proponents of an Islamic legal system and proponents of a more secularized, European-oriented elite.

"I am also interested in the present as history. By studying results of compromises between the political elites holding power and challenges by groups seeking control, a researcher can learn how compromises and negotiations among these groups shape the law and, in turn, are changed by the encounter. Frequently the law, any law, has a life of its own, rushing in to intrude on all kinds of relationships, and interacting with them in ways that change both the law and the relationships.

"Currently, I am exploring these ideas through an examination of the new market in biodiversity systems in the United States and abroad. Here one can see law created, reshaped, and subverted in those moments when groups collide. Research also reveals how such encounters reshape a group through the experiences of its members. This new research continues, albeit with very different data, my study of power relations among competing groups and the ways in which this competition leads to the creation of law."

BIOGRAPHICAL/CRITICAL SOURCES:

PERIODICALS

Law and Politics Book Review, October, 1992, pp. 129-30.

*   *   *

STARZL, Thomas E(arl) 1926-

PERSONAL: Born March 11, 1926, in LeMars, IA; son of Rome (a newspaper publisher) and Anna Laura (a nurse; maiden name, Fitzgerald) Starzl; married Barbara June Brothers, November 27, 1954 (divorced August 1,

1976); married Joy Conger (a technologist), August 1, 1981; children: Timothy Wakefield, Rebecca Ann, Thomas Fitzgerald. *Education:* Northwestern University, Ph.D., 1950, M.D., 1952. *Politics:* Independent. *Religion:* Roman Catholic.

ADDRESSES: Home—4320 Centre Ave., Pittsburgh, PA 15213. *Office*—Falk Clinic, 3601 Fifth Ave., Pittsburgh, PA 15213.

CAREER: Northwestern University, Evanston, IL, instructor, 1958-59, associate in surgery, 1959-61, assistant professor of surgery, 1961-62; University of Colorado at Boulder, associate professor, 1962-64, professor of surgery, 1964-80, chairman of surgery, 1972-80; University of Pittsburgh, Pittsburgh, PA, professor of surgery, Distinguished Service Professor of Health Sciences, 1986, director of Transplantation Institute, 1990—. Associated with Presbyterian-University Hospital of Pittsburgh, Children's Hospital of Pittsburgh, and Veterans Administration Hospital of Pittsburgh, 1981—. University of the Witwatersrand, Jane and Michael Miller Visiting Professor, 1966; Royal College of Physicians (Vancouver, British Columbia), special lecturer, 1969; State University of New York at Buffalo, lifetime honorary member of professional staff of Witebsky Center for Immunology, 1983—; University of Madrid, honorary professor, 1989. Fondazione Giovanni Lorenzini, lecturer, 1985; Renal Disease Foundation, member of board of medical directors of Denver chapter, 1963-65; Sandoz Research Institute, member of scientific advisory board.

MEMBER: International Transplantation Society (vice president, 1968-70; president, 1990), International College of Surgeons (fellow), International Cardiovascular Society, Transplant Recipients International Organization (founding president, 1987; permanent honorary chairman, 1987—), International Association for the Study of the Liver, Internationale de Chirurgie, American Medical Association, Transplantation Society, Society of Clinical Surgery, American Association of University Professors, American Geriatric Society (fellow), American Society of Contemporary Medicine and Surgery, American Society of Transplant Surgeons (founding president, 1975), Society of Vascular Surgery (senior member), American College of Surgeons (fellow), American Surgical Association, American Association for the Study of Liver Diseases, Society of Surgical Chairmen, American Association of Medical Colleges, American Heart Association (member of Council on Cardiovascular Surgery), Phlebology Society of America, American Society for Artificial Internal Organs, American Association for the Advancement of Science, American Thoracic Society, Society of University Surgeons, American Academy of Arts and Sciences (fellow), Society of Critical Care Medicine (member of board of directors), Cell Transplantation Society (honorary pres-

ident, 1991), Society for Organ Sharing (honorary president, 1991), American Pediatric Surgical Association (honorary member), Halsted Society, Carroll F. Reynolds Historical Society, Italian Society of Surgery (corresponding member), Italian Surgical Research Society (corresponding member), Deutsche Gesellschaft fuer Chirurgie (corresponding member), Royal Society of Medicine (affiliate member), Royal College of Surgeons (honorary fellow), Royal College of Surgeons (Ireland; fellow), Royal College of Surgeons (Glasgow; fellow), La Societe de Chirurgie de Lyon (honorary foreign member), Asian Surgical Association (honorary member), Academie Nationale de Medecine (France; foreign member), Japanese Surgical Society (honorary member), Surgical Research Society of Southern Africa, Austrian Society of Surgery (honorary member), Central Surgical Association, Peruvian Academy of Surgery (honorary member), Western Surgical Association, Pennsylvania Medical Society, Colorado Trudeau Society, Colorado Heart Association, Santa Clara County Surgical Society (honorary member), Pittsburgh Surgical Society, Pittsburgh Academy of Medicine, Denver Academy of Surgery, Denver Clinical and Pathological Society, Chicago Surgical Society (honorary member), Cleveland Surgical Society (honorary member), Reno Surgical Society (honorary member), Ochsner Surgical Society (honorary member), Johns Hopkins Medical and Surgical Society, Johns Hopkins Society of Scholars, Minute Men of the Medical School of the University of Pittsburgh (affiliate member), Animal Rescue League of Western Pennsylvania (member of advisory board), Sigma Xi, Alpha Omega Alpha.

AWARDS, HONORS: Markle scholar in medical science, 1959; Alumni Achievement Award, Westminster College, Fulton, MO, 1965; achievement awards from University of Lund and Malmo Surgical Society, 1965; Prix de la Societe International de Chirurgie, 1965; named Colorado Man of the Year, 1967; William S. Middleton Award for outstanding research in the Veterans Administration System, 1968; Merit Award from Northwestern University, 1969; Modern Medicine Distinguished Achievement Award, 1969; Eppinger Prize of Freiburg, Germany, 1970; award from Deutsche Gesellschaft fuer Chirurgie, 1970; McGraw Medical Award from Detroit Surgical Association, 1971; Annual Achievement Award from Association of Veterans Administration Surgeons, 1972; Brookdale Award from American Medical Association, 1974; Faculty Scholar Award from Josiah Macy, Jr. Foundation, 1975; Robert L. Stearns Award from Colorado Alumni Association, 1976; David M. Hume Memorial Award from National Kidney Disease Foundation, 1978; named Pittsburgh Man of the Year by Pittsburgh Academy of Medicine, 1981, 1984, 1986; Sheen Award from American College of Surgeons, 1982; Golden Plate Award from American Academy of Achievement, 1983;

Super Surgeon Award from Children Who Have Had Liver Transplants, 1983; First Uremia Award from International Uremia Society, 1983; Myrtle Wreath Award from Pittsburgh chapter of Hadassah, 1983; Heath Award from Pittsburgh Variety Club, 1983; Distinguished Service Award from Pennsylvania Medical Society, 1985; Biannual Prize from Italian Hepatology Society, 1986; awarded keys of the cities of Milan, 1986, and Venice, 1987; Friend of Israel Award from Jewish National Fund, 1987; Hepatology Achievement Award from Sammy Davis, Jr. National Liver Institute, 1987; Distinguished Achievement Award in Organ Transplantation from American Society of Contemporary Medicine and Surgery, 1988; Silver Medal from University of Bologna, 1988; Bigelow Medal from Boston Surgical Society, 1989; Special Recognition Award from Howard University Hospital Transplant Center and National Institutes of Health, 1989; City of Medicine Award, Durham, NC, 1989; Jacob Markowitz Award from Academy of Surgical Research, 1989; Medallion for Scientific Achievement from American Surgical Association, 1990; Excellence in Government Award from Pittsburgh Federal Executive Board, 1990; Distinguished Service Award from American Liver Foundation, 1991; American Gastroenterological Association, William Beaumont Prize in Gastroenterology, 1991, and Hugh R. Butt Award, 1991; Distinguished Achievement Award from American Association for the Study of Liver Disease, 1991; Thomas E. Starzl Surgical Ward was dedicated by Denver Veterans Administration Hospital, 1991; Fondazione Basile Prize from World Association of Hepato-Pancreato-Biliary Surgery, 1991; Medical Gift of Life Award from National Kidney Foundation of Western Pennsylvania, 1992; Medawar Prize from Transplantation Society, 1992; Henry Dunant Humanitarian Award from American Red Cross, 1993; William Ladd Medal, 1993; honorary doctorates include D.Sc. from Westminster College, 1968, New York Medical College, 1970, Westmar College, 1974, Medical College of Wisconsin, 1981, Northwestern University, 1982, Bucknell University and Muhlenberg College, 1985, Mount Sinai School of Medicine of the City University of New York, 1988, and University of Pittsburgh, 1993, LL.D. from University of Wyoming, 1971, D.Med. from University of Louvain, 1985, University of Rennes, 1988, University of Bologna, 1988, and University of Padua, 1992, and D.H.L. from LaRoche College, 1988.

WRITINGS:

Experience in Renal Transplantation, Saunders, 1964.
Experience in Hepatic Transplantation, Saunders, 1969.
(With A. J. Demetris) *Liver Transplantation,* Year Book Medical Publishers, 1990.
The Puzzle People: Memoirs of a Transplant Surgeon, University of Pittsburgh Press, 1992.

Work represented in nearly two hundred collections. Contributor of more than fifteen-hundred articles to professional journals. Member of editorial boards of more than twenty-five journals.

SIDELIGHTS: Thomas E. Starzl told *CA:* "I am a surgeon with a long-standing interest in organ transplantation. The only book that I have written for lay consumption is *The Puzzle People.* This book does not have detailed scientific information, but does explain the principles of transplantation biology in greatly simplified terms. Somewhat surprisingly, the book has been extensively reviewed in the major professional journals and in the literary sections of most major newspapers."

BIOGRAPHICAL/CRITICAL SOURCES:

PERIODICALS

Archives of Surgery, September, 1992, p. 1009.
Boston Globe, September 20, 1992, p. B44.
Hepatology, March, 1993, p. 523.
New York Times, July 7, 1992.
Washington Post Book World, January 19, 1993, p. C9.

*　　*　　*

STERNGOLD, James (S.) 1954-

PERSONAL: Born October 3, 1954, in Detroit, MI; son of Henry (a civil engineer) and Levona (a schoolteacher) Sterngold; married Ellen J. Rudolph (a photographer and film producer), February 1, 1981; children: Marina S. *Education:* Middlebury College, B.A. (with highest honors and cum laude), 1977; Columbia University, M.S.J., 1980; graduate study at Bread Loaf School of English and in Oxford, England.

ADDRESSES: Home—5-2-4 Denen-chofu, Ota-ku, Tokyo, Japan. *Office*—*New York Times,* 229 West 43rd St., New York, NY 10036.

CAREER: Associated Press, New York City, Hong Kong correspondent, 1981-84; *New York Times,* New York City, Wall Street reporter, 1984-89, correspondent in Tokyo, Japan, 1989—.

WRITINGS:

Burning Down the House: How Greed, Deceit and Bitter Revenge Destroyed E. F. Hutton, Simon & Schuster, 1990.

Also contributor of cover stories to *New York Times Magazine. Burning Down the House* was released on audiocassette, Simon & Schuster Audio, 1990.

SIDELIGHTS: Journalist James Sterngold brought a fresh perspective to the well-reported demise of an investment firm in his book *Burning Down the House: How Greed, Deceit and Bitter Revenge Destroyed E. F. Hutton.* As Tessa DeCarlo acknowledged in the *San Francisco Chronicle,* "Several versions of Hutton's decline and fall have already appeared," but she and other critics agreed that Sterngold's was "the best so far." Discussing the wrongdoing and arrogance that felled the once-respected company, Sterngold focuses on the key figures and their personal vices, not on a faceless corporation. In the process, mused DeCarlo, the author "offers several morals worth pondering." Sterngold grounds his analysis firmly in the actual events; as *New York Times Book Review* contributor John Train noted, "Sterngold has an authoritative grasp of the facts." Although the critic found the book marred by journalistic cliches, he felt certain that it would become "the definitive account of this grim affair." For Sallie Gaines, assessing Sterngold's work in the *Chicago Tribune, Burning Down the House* was "a page-turner that grabs more attention than most novels." She called it "a finely written, well-organized, colorful book that makes business issues come alive." Applauding Sterngold's sense of perspective and clear explanations of issues difficult for laymen to understand, she declared that "nobody who wants to understand American management should skip it."

BIOGRAPHICAL/CRITICAL SOURCES:

PERIODICALS

Chicago Tribune, October 28, 1990.
Newsweek, November 19, 1990, p. 68.
New York Times Book Review, October 21, 1990, p. 13.
San Francisco Chronicle, October 14, 1990.

* * *

STIRLING, S(tephen) M(ichael) 1953-

PERSONAL: Born September 30, 1953, in Metz, France; son of Alfred Bruce Stirling (wing commander in the Royal Canadian Air Force) and Marjorie (Totterdale) Stirling; married Janet Cathryn Moore (a homemaker), in April 1988. *Education:* Received B.A. (with honors) from Carleton University and LL.B. from Osgoode Hall. *Politics:* "Conservative/feminist." *Religion:* "Anglican (agnostic)." *Avocational interests:* History, literature, anthropology, karate.

ADDRESSES: Home—50 Cornwall St., Apt. 803, Toronto, Ontario, Canada M5A 4K5.

CAREER: Full-time writer, 1988—. Worked variously as a farm hand, secretary, and bouncer in a recreational establishment.

MEMBER: Science Fiction Writers of America.

WRITINGS:

"DRAKA" SERIES; FOR BAEN BOOKS

Marching through Georgia, 1988.
Under the Yoke, 1989.
The Stone Dogs, 1990.

"FIFTH MILLENNIUM" SERIES; FOR BAEN BOOKS

(With Shirley Meier) *The Cage,* 1989.
(With Meier and Karen Wehrstein) *Shadow's Son,* 1990.
Snowbrother, 1992.
(With Meier) *Saber and Shadow,* 1992.

"GENERAL" SERIES; FOR BAEN BOOKS

(With David Drake) *The Forge,* 1991.
(With Drake) *The Hammer,* 1992.
(With Drake) *The Anvil,* 1993.

"SPARTAN" SERIES; FOR BAEN BOOKS

(With Jerry Pournelle) *Go Tell The Spartans,* 1991.
(With Pournelle) *Prince of Sparta,* 1993.

OTHER

(With Meier) *The Sharpest Edge,* New American Library, 1986.
(Editor) *Power,* Baen Books, 1991.
(With Pournelle) *The Children's Hour,* Baen Books, 1991.
(With Anne McCaffrey) *The Ship Who Fought,* Baen Books, 1993.
(With Susan Shwartz, Judith Tarr, and Harry Turtledove) *Blood Feuds,* Baen Books, 1993.

Contributor to books, including *The Fantastic Civil War, The Fantastic World War Two,* Larry Niven's "Man-Kzin Wars" series, *War World I,* and *War World III.*

WORK IN PROGRESS: Conquistador, for Baen Books; *The Steel,* with David Drake, for the "General" series, Baen Books; *Heavy Iron,* for the "Draka" series, Baen Books.

* * *

STIRT, Joseph A. 1948-

PERSONAL: Born June 8, 1948, in Milwaukee, WI; son of Irving J. (a tool and die maker) and Sarah (a legal secretary; maiden name, Kramer) Stirt; married Judith M. (a nurse), June 12, 1982 (divorced September 20, 1991); children: Caroline Anne. *Education:* Degree from University of California, Los Angeles, 1970, M.D., 1974. *Politics:* "Indescribable." *Religion:* "Mystery." *Avocational interests:* Food, design, art, sports (especially distance running), technology.

ADDRESSES: Home—2809 Magnolia Dr., Charlottesville, VA 22901. *Office*—Department of Anesthesiology, Box 238, University of Virginia Medical Center, Charlottesville, VA 22908.

CAREER: Worked variously as a newspaper deliverer, gas station attendant, truck loader, mail deliverer, and librarian, 1962-71; University of California, Los Angeles, Medical School, assistant professor of anesthesiology, 1980-83; University of Virginia Medical School, Charlottesville, VA, assistant professor of anesthesiology, 1983-88, associate professor of anesthesiology and neurosurgery, 1988—. Expert witness in medical malpractice cases.

MEMBER: International Anesthesia Research Society, American Society of Anesthesiologists, Society of Neurosurgical Anesthesia and Critical Care, Virginia Society of Anesthesiologists, Albemarle County Medical Society, Phi Eta Sigma.

WRITINGS:

(With Richard J. Sperry and David J. Stone) *Manual of Neuroanesthesia,* B. C. Decker, 1989.
Baby, New Horizon Press, 1992.

Also author of play *Cheek to Cheek.*

WORK IN PROGRESS: Quad, a medical thriller about central nervous system regeneration; a medical-legal thriller novel.

SIDELIGHTS: Anesthesiologist Joseph A. Stirt is the author of *Baby,* the true story of his daughter Caroline, who within days of her premature birth in 1984 contracted necrotizing enterocolitis, a life-threatening disease of the intestine. In the work Stirt chronicles her medical treatment—the surgeries, painful tests, and twenty-seven blood transfusions—that she endured for more than two months. Structuring his book like a journal, Stirt includes day-to-day reports on Caroline's condition as well as his frustrating inability to voice a professional opinion about her treatments and his fears for the long-term consequences of her care. As expressed by a critic in *Kirkus Reviews, Baby* is "a touching human drama presented with scientific expertise that makes frighteningly clear the helplessness of patients—as well as their families—once the power of modern medicine is unleashed." Likewise, a *Publishers Weekly* reviewer concluded, *Baby* has a "powerful emotional impact."

Stirt told *CA:* "I was born in Milwaukee, Wisconsin, and left at age eighteen to go to college in California, which was as far away as I could get. At the time, I believed that if I could get physically far enough away from the things I dreaded, the distance would serve as a barrier to their reappearance. Alas, it doesn't work that way.

"My writing career began with a journalism course in my senior year of high school, which caused much gnashing of teeth among my teachers because I had to abandon advanced physics in order to fit in the writing class. One summer in college I wrote a weekly column for the University of California, Los Angeles, *Daily Bruin;* I composed an essay on whatever struck my fancy. That was my first published work.

"After medical school and my internship, I wrote a play for three characters entitled *Cheek to Cheek,* which was accepted for presentation by a small theater in Hollywood, California. Unfortunately, the theater soon suffered financial difficulties and closed. Dismayed, I returned to medicine and completed a residency in anesthesiology, which led to a series of scientific papers. All went swimmingly well until I tired of cranking out research papers, at which time my daughter was born.

"She proceeded to get morbidly ill on her second day of life, and the journal I kept during her ten-week stay in the hospital formed the basis of my first published trade book (I'd coauthored a text on neurosurgical anesthesia in 1989). *Baby,* released in 1992, provides a unique look at the medical profession from the point of view of insiders (my ex-wife is an intensive care unit nurse) who know all too well the downside of what goes on in hospitals, especially with critically ill babies. As my agent at the time said, 'It reads like fiction, but it isn't.'

"As a writer, I'm a combination of a lazy, distracted—easily and purposely—person and a strict disciplinarian. For *Baby,* I worked two hours a day, seven days a week, for six months to produce the first draft. Many of those sessions followed ten- to twelve-hour days in the operating room. Yet when I read my output, I find such work indistinguishable from that which I produced when I was well rested and fresh on weekend mornings. It simply seems harder and more labored when I'm tired, but the output is seamless.

"My current project is a novel, a medical thriller with the working title of *Quad.* I think fiction is where I want to go in the future. If I can succeed in getting my admittedly quirky slant on life down on paper, I think I have a reasonable chance of success, but it's that difficult translation of personality into style that vexes me so."

BIOGRAPHICAL/CRITICAL SOURCES:

PERIODICALS

Kirkus Reviews, September 1, 1992, p. 1119.
Publishers Weekly, October 5, 1992.

STOCKLEY, Grif 1944-

PERSONAL: Born October 9, 1944, in Memphis, TN; son of Griffin J. (a farmer and in business) and Temple (Wall) Stockley; children: one daughter. *Education:* Southwestern at Memphis, B.A., 1965; University of Arkansas, J.D., 1972.

ADDRESSES: Office—Central Arkansas Legal Services, 209 West Capitol, Little Rock, AR 72201. *Agent*—Charlotte Gordon, 235 East 22nd St., New York, NY 10010.

CAREER: Peace Corps, rural community development organizer in Colombia, 1965-67; Central Arkansas Legal Services, Little Rock, AR, attorney, 1972—; writer. University of Arkansas at Little Rock, adjunct professor, c. 1987-92, and visiting professor of law. *Military service:* Served in U.S. Army for two years during late 1960s.

WRITINGS:

Expert Testimony, Summit Books, 1991.
Probable Cause, Simon & Schuster, 1992.

WORK IN PROGRESS: A third mystery.

SIDELIGHTS: Grif Stockley told *CA:* "Thus far, the fiction that I have been able to get published is derived from much of my own personal experience. The protagonist of both novels, Gideon Page, is a middle-aged attorney in a southern city, which all local readers identify correctly as Little Rock. The core of Gideon's personal relationships revolves around his teenaged daughter Sarah. Though my daughter is now about to leave her teens, Sarah is very much modeled on that relationship. Similarly, in *Expert Testimony* much of the action takes place at the Arkansas State Hospital. For many years I routinely represented clients at that facility. In *Probable Cause,* Gideon represents a psychologist who works at an institution for persons with developmental disabilities. I have had some legal experience in that venue as well. My main impetus for writing mysteries comes from writer Scott Turow's success. After reading *Presumed Innocent,* I felt I was capable of writing a mystery with a southern flavor."

*   *   *

STONE, Rodney 1932-
(Matthew Hunter)

PERSONAL: Born September 9, 1932; married, 1970; wife's name, Mavis Anne (a social worker); children: two sons. *Education:* Received M.A. from Cambridge University.

ADDRESSES: Home and office—75 Maze Hill, Greenwich, London SE10 8XQ, England. *Agent*—Blake Friedmann, 37-41 Gower St., London WC1E 6HH, England.

CAREER: Worked for His Majesty's Government (HMG), London, England, as deputy head of the Office of Arts and Libraries, and in Ministry of Agriculture, Treasury Department, and Education Department; full-time writer. *Military service:* Royal Air Force (RAF).

AWARDS, HONORS: Nuffield fellowship.

WRITINGS:

Cries in the Night, HarperCollins, 1991.
The Dark Side of the Hill, HarperCollins, 1992.

UNDER PSEUDONYM MATTHEW HUNTER

Schiller, Heinemann, 1989.
Comrades, Warner Books, 1990.
The Kremlin Armoury, Walker & Co., 1992.
The Gibraltar Factor, Walker & Co., 1993.

WORK IN PROGRESS: A mystery; a thriller (under pseudonym Matthew Hunter).

SIDELIGHTS: Rodney Stone told *CA:* "After service in the Royal Air Force and His Majesty's Government, I decided to do my own thing and draw on my experience. I had always written part-time, but I've now turned professional. I'm interested in most aspects of the novel, and enjoy working with thrillers and chillers, but I have other books up my sleeve that I'd like to try out once I can find a market."

*   *   *

STONE, Todd 1957-

PERSONAL: Born May 1, 1957, in Bloomington, IN; stepson of Thomas J. and son of Anne Hennessy; married Kathryn W. Manson (divorced, June, 1988); married Terri V. M. Stone, January 1, 1992; children: Nicholas, Sarah Gwendolyn, Sarah Ann. *Education:* Indiana University—Bloomington, B.S., 1979; Northwestern University, M.A., 1989.

ADDRESSES: Home and office—1009 Iroquois Ave., Naperville, IL 60563. *Agent*—John Flaherty, 816 Lynda Court, St. Louis, MO 63122.

CAREER: U.S. Army, career officer, including service in Germany, 1979-92, retiring as major; writer, 1992—. Joliet Junior College, instructor; consultant to Argonne National Laboratory and U.S. Army Corps of Engineers.

WRITINGS:

Kriegspiel: A Novel of Tomorrow's Europe, Presidio Press, 1992.

WORK IN PROGRESS: A sequel to *Kriegspiel.*

SIDELIGHTS: Todd Stone told *CA:* "Give an airborne/ Ranger/infantryman army officer a degree in English literature, and what do you get? An author who writes about soldiering. I wanted to get away from the many books that had pieces of equipment as their main characters, and to tell about the small wars that go on in the hearts and minds of the soldiers who use those machines. I wrote *Kriegspiel* for very human, personal reasons, and I wanted to tell a human, personal story. I am moved by the thought of ordinary people—with all their imperfections—caught up in the swell of extraordinary events. Combat and the instability of the 'new world order' offer great potential for this; they provide an ideal crucible for a writer who wants to put people under pressure and reveal some eternal truths about the human condition."

* * *

STOPFORD, John M(orton) 1939-

PERSONAL: Born September 16, 1939, in Kandy, Ceylon (now Sri Lanka); son of Robert Wright (a minister) and Winifred Sophie (a missionary; maiden name, Morton) Stopford; married Sarah Jean Woodman (a teacher), June 11, 1966; children: Robert Woodman, Nicholas John. *Education:* Oxford University, B.A. (first class honors), 1961; Massachusetts Institute of Technology, S.M., 1962; Harvard University, D.B.A., 1968. *Religion:* Church of England. *Avocational interests:* Hill walking, theater, travel, skiing.

ADDRESSES: Home—6 Chalcot Sq., London NW1 8YB, England. *Office*—London Business School, Sussex Place, Regent's Park, London NW1 4SA, England.

CAREER: Baker Perkins Ltd., Peterborough, England, apprentice and skilled fitter, 1957-58; Shell Chemicals (UK) Ltd., London, England, engineer, 1962-64, non-executive director, 1973-77; Guyana Stockfeeds Ltd., Georgetown, acting managing director, 1965; Manchester Business School, Manchester, England, senior lecturer in business administration, 1968-70; Harvard University, Business School, Boston, MA, visiting assistant professor of business administration, 1971-72; London Business School, London, England, professor of business administration, 1972—, academic dean, 1979-84. Orbit S.A. (Geneva, Switzerland), member of advisory board, 1971-75; Bracken Kelner and Associates, director, 1974-79; Webtec Industrial Technology Ltd., director, 1975-90; Centre on Business Responsibility, chairman, 1976-77; United Nations, senior staff member at Centre on Transnational Corporations, 1977-78; London and International Publishers Ltd., director, 1983-89; Vickers, adviser to board of directors, 1987—; InterMatrix Group S.A. (Switzerland), member of advisory board. British Foreign Office,

member of Burrett Review Committee, 1986; Brathay Exploration Group, trustee, 1990—.

MEMBER: European International Business Association (president, 1979-80), Royal Society of Arts (fellow).

AWARDS, HONORS: Fulbright scholar in the United States, 1962; Ford Foundation fellow in the United States, 1968; George R. Terry Book Award from American Academy of Management, 1992, for *Rival States, Rival Firms.*

WRITINGS:

(With L. T. Wells, Jr.) *Managing the Multinational Enterprise,* Basic Books, 1972.
(With Derek F. Channon and D. Norburn) *British Business Policy,* Macmillan, 1976.
(General editor) *Transnational Corporations in World Development: A Re-Examination,* United Nations, 1978.
(With Bob Garratt) *Breaking Down Barriers: Practice and Priorities for International Management Education,* Gower, 1980.
(With Derek F. Channon and John Constable) *Cases in Strategic Management,* Wiley, 1980.
Growth and Organizational Change in the Multinational Firm, Arno, 1980.
(With John H. Dunning and Klaus O. Haberich) *The World Directory of Multinational Enterprises,* Macmillan, 1980, 2nd edition (as sole author), 1982.
(With John H. Dunning) *Multinationals: Company Performance and Global Trends,* Macmillan, 1983.
(With Louis Turner) *Britain and the Multinationals,* Wiley, 1985.
(With Susan Strange) *Rival States, Rival Firms,* Cambridge University Press, 1991.
(With C. W. F. Baden-Fuller) *Rejuvenating the Mature Business,* Routledge & Kegan Paul, 1992.
The Directory of Multinationals, Macmillan, 1992.

Work represented in anthologies, including *Implementing Strategic Processes: Change, Learning, and Cooperation,* edited by P. Lorange, B. Chakravarthy, and others, Basil Blackwell, 1993; *The External Implications of European Integration,* edited by David Mayes, Simon & Schuster, 1993; and *A New Diplomacy in the Post-Cold War World,* edited by R. Morgan, S. Guzzini, and others, Macmillan, 1993. Contributor of articles and reviews to professional journals. Member of editorial advisory board, *Journal of General Management, Journal of International Business Studies, Strategic Management Journal, Management International Review,* and *Journal of Management Studies.*

WORK IN PROGRESS: Research on corporate renewal and relationships between business and government.

SIDELIGHTS: John M. Stopford told *CA:* "My writing is necessarily a part-time activity, most frequently squeezed in at the end of the day. Though I sometimes wish I had the luxury of less teaching, less business, I am not convinced I could use the extra time productively. My books and articles are essentially the product of the crunch between the turmoil of daily life and the search for patterns in the turmoil that can help us all understand, even a little, more clearly what is going on. I need to be actively engaged in the chaos of the market to be spurred to write about what might cause some things to happen and not others. I am not really a theorist, though some have called me that. Rather, I think of myself as an empiricist in search of theory.

"Quite some years ago, I realized that I could not hope to explain much of what was happening in international business if I worked within a single discipline. Instead, I took the gamble of trying to cross boundaries. Many of my friends thought I was mad, for it is much easier to publish academically respected, even acclaimed, work if one sticks within the narrow confines of a well trodden path. They were, and remain, quite right, but that raises a question about the whole apparatus of scholarship in applied social science and, in my case, management studies. Rigor and narrowness versus breadth and loose ends is one form of an endless debate I cannot resolve. I merely chose my own position.

"I suppose I have always been interested in making connections across boundaries, some geographical, some disciplinary. Perhaps this is the product of rapid moves when I was a young boy during the war, or climbing in the Himalayas when still a teenager and suddenly discovering new vistas, or feeling the constrictions of being a very junior engineer in a giant multinational corporation and resigning to try out my own wings without corporate support, or merely being born with insatiable curiosity. In any event, my written work has darted from one topic to another, much to the delight of my critics. There has been a serious purpose behind all this seemingly random motion, however. I have been exploring ideas and alternative perspectives, trying them on like new shoes for size. These are experiments that allow me now to speculate about events with new eyes. Somewhere in all the mess of competing theorizing there must be a way to combine the insights of economics with those of psychology, of business with international relations. Even if my books don't provide answers to the complex issues of today's society, they may make some people stop and rethink their own prejudices."

STOREY, Gail Donohue 1947-
(Gail Donohue)

PERSONAL: Born July 15, 1947, in Cambridge, MA; daughter of Francis D. (in elderly services) and Dorothy (a librarian; maiden name, Gustus) Donohue; married Porter Storey (a physician), October 11, 1987; children: (stepson) Philip. *Education:* Rosary College, B.A., 1969; University of Illinois, M.S. (library science), 1973; St. John's College, M.A. (liberal education), 1982; University of Houston, M.A. (English and creative writing), 1982. *Religion:* "Eclectic contemplative." *Avocational interests:* Yoga, meditation, vegetarian cuisine.

ADDRESSES: Home—3907 Swarthmore, Houston, TX 77005. *Agent*—Ellen Levine Literary Agency, 15 East Twenty-sixth St., Suite 1801, New York, NY 10010.

CAREER: Writer. Maclean-Hunter Publishing Corp., Chicago, IL, assistant editor of *Inland Printer/American Lithographer,* 1969; Idea Communications, Chicago, assistant film producer, 1970; Peer Enterprises, Chicago, publishing production coordinator, 1971; Newberry Library, Chicago, assistant in the Office of the Director, research secretary for *Atlas of Early American History,* and bibliographic assistant to curator of maps, 1971-72; Champaign Public Library and Information Center, Champaign, IL, adult services librarian, 1974-77; Public Library of Annapolis and Anne Arundel County, Annapolis, MD, project director of service to homebound and individuals confined in institutions, 1977-80; University of Houston, Houston, TX, teacher of basic writing, 1980-81, teacher of freshman composition, 1981, administrative director of creative writing program, 1982-86, and teacher of fiction workshops, 1984-86; New Orleans Center for Creative Arts, New Orleans, LA, guest writer, 1987 and 1992. Visiting faculty member at St. John's College, 1983. Volunteer at Houston Area Women's Center's Shelter for Abused Women and Children, 1984-85, and as a literacy tutor, Volunteers in Continuing Education Program, Houston Community College, 1990-91.

MEMBER: Authors Guild, Authors League of America, PEN—West, Poets and Writers.

AWARDS, HONORS: Second honorable mention, Elliott Coleman Award, 1980; first honorable mention for new poetic drama, Dragon's Teeth Press, 1981; Houston Festival Prose Award, 1983; PEN Southwest Discovery Prize, first runner-up for fiction, 1983, finalist, 1984, finalist, 1988, and second honorable mention, 1989; first prize for fiction, Houston Orange Show, 1985; Texas Fiction Contest runner-up, Houston *Chronicle* and Houston Area Booksellers Association, 1985; Virginia Center for the Creative Arts fellow, 1985; Yaddo fellow, 1987; honorable mention, Creative Artist Program Literary Competition, Cultural Arts Council of Houston, 1987.

WRITINGS:

(Under name Gail Donohue) *First Poems of Gail Donohue,* Pine Street Press, 1974.
The Lord's Motel (novel), Persea Books, 1992.

Author of stories, including "Totally Nude Live Girls" and "Geometry Hotline." Contributor of stories, poems, essays, and articles to periodicals, including *North American Review, Chicago Review, Fiction, Mississippi Valley Review, Houston City,* and *Houston Metropolitan.*

WORK IN PROGRESS: A sequel to *The Lord's Motel.*

SIDELIGHTS: Gail Donohue Storey caught the attention of critics with her first novel, *The Lord's Motel,* which "is not the transparently autobiographical effort of many debuting authors," according to a *Library Journal* reviewer. Storey's book focuses on Houston librarian Colleen Sweeny, a thirty-one-year-old Boston native. Colleen lives in an apartment building dubbed the Lord's Motel by its New Age manager, St. Francis. Among the building's other residents is Gigi, a wisecracking computer software salesperson; Barbara, who is single and pregnant; and Mrs. Fritz, a senior citizen prone to fainting spells. Through her Service-to-the-Unserved library program, Colleen becomes friends with Dolores, who is imprisoned for killing her abusive husband. Dolores helps Colleen comprehend her affair with Web Desiderio, a sexually manipulative cruise ship social director who preys on Colleen's lack of self-esteem. According to Lauren Picker in the *Voice Literary Supplement,* "Colleen is the sort of woman that would make [feminist] Gloria Steinem weep; low self-esteem is something she could only aim for." Colleen eventually forges a healthy relationship with Gabriel Benedict, a handsome doctor.

Critics praised *The Lord's Motel* as a humorous, insightful novel. *Dallas Morning News* contributor C. W. Smith noted "the breezy, witty lightness of it all, the nimble flitting from scene to scene, and Colleen's very engaging voice. Colleen's self-deprecating irony and honesty and her shrewdly observant eye unerringly tack bits of reality to the narrative wall." Susan Fromberg Schaeffer, writing in the *Chicago Sun-Times,* commented that "Storey makes things new by writing a novel in which her characters are so alive, so engaging, so *lovable,* that it becomes impossible to ignore them, much less grow used to them." Schaeffer added that "*The Lord's Motel* is a work of art, succeeding on so many fronts—as comedy, as character study, as a study of character *in* society—that it truly dazzles."

"*The Lord's Motel* explores matters of eros and soul in this sexually and spiritually discomfited time," Storey told *CA.* "It deals with serious issues of domestic violence and sexual manipulation but tries to make the pain bearable through wit and knowing humor. I wanted to tell a good story, not simply about getting away from Mr. Wrong and with Mr. Right, but about the inner transformation one must go through to be ready for an intimate relationship.

"I find certain preoccupations in my writing, both linear and non-linear, having to do with the conflicting mysteries of the erotic and the soul. I'm interested in how we create the myth of the divided self and play it out in contemporary life. My characters try to resolve their confusion of soul through their relationships with their lovers and families and through their work, which often has to do with pressing social problems.

"I began my writing career as a poet; Richard Wilbur said that my collection of poems had to do with 'the conflicting claims of order and feeling.' Later, as a student of Donald Barthelme at the University of Houston, I turned to writing short fictions as pure states of feeling, at once sublimated and erotically charged. In 'Totally Nude Live Girls' and other stories, I tried to convey intense love and desire unmediated by conventional expectations. 'Geometry Hotline' used a mathematical proof with diagrams to 'prove' the existence of angels."

Storey gave advice to aspiring writers in *The World and I:* "I would say not to lose heart. To just keep going, whatever it takes. Nobody is going to ask how long did it take? They're going to ask if it's a good book or not. Each writer needs to be true to his own artistic vision and to keep going, to persevere, and to develop as a human being as well as a writer."

BIOGRAPHICAL/CRITICAL SOURCES:

PERIODICALS

Chicago Sun-Times, September 27, 1992.
Dallas Morning News, October 4, 1992, p. 10J.
Library Journal, September 1, 1992; October 1, 1992, p. 45.
New York Times Book Review, August 30, 1992.
Voice Literary Supplement, December, 1992.
The World and I, January, 1993, pp. 273, 289-303.

* * *

STROUHAL, Eugen 1931-

PERSONAL: Born January 24, 1931, in Prague, Czechoslovakia; son of Eugen (a doctor) Strouhal and Antonie (a homemaker; maiden name, Ipoltova) Strouhalova; married Martina Piplova (a systemic engineer), May 8, 1965; children: David, Dita. *Education:* Charles University, M.D., 1956, Ph.D., 1959; Comenius University, C.Sc., 1968. *Politics:* "Never a member of any party; I've three times refused the offered membership in the Communist Party." *Religion:* Roman Catholic.

ADDRESSES: Home—Na Truhlarce 24, 18000 Praha 8-Liben, Czechoslovakia. *Office*—Institute for the History of Medicine, Charles University, Katerinska 32, 121 08 Praha 2, Czechoslovakia. *Agent*—OPUS Publishing, Ltd., 36 Camden Sq., London NW1 9XA, England.

CAREER: Charles University, Plzen, Czechoslovakia, assistant in medical faculty at Institute of Biology, 1957-60; Charles University, Prague, member of science staff at Czechoslovak Institute of Egyptology, 1961-68; National Museum, Prague, curator and member of science staff at Naprstek Museum, 1969-92. Institute for the History of Medicine, Charles University, Prague, assistant professor and director, 1990—. Prague Civic Committee, referee for the environment, 1977-80.

MEMBER: European Anthropological Association (council member, 1981—), Czech Anthropological Society (vice president, 1989—), Czech Orientalists Society (council member, 1985—), Paleopathology Association (founder and council member, 1973—).

AWARDS, HONORS: Award for scientific achievement, Smithsonian Institution, 1973; Hrdlicka Memorial Medal, 1981; Michalowski Medal (Warsaw, Poland), 1986; National Museum Decree of Merit (Prague), 1988; Julian J. Rothbaum Prize, University of Oklahoma Press, 1992.

WRITINGS:

Do srdce maretanske Sahary (title means "Into the Heart of the Mauritanian Sahara"), Vysehrad (Prague), 1974.

Egyptian Mummies in the Czechoslovak Collection, National Museum (Prague), 1979.

Setkani s Aljaskou (title means "Meeting with Alaska"), Vysehrad, 1981.

Die anthropologische Untersuchung der C-Gruppen und Pan-Graeber-Skelette aus Sayala, Agyptisch-Nubien (title means "The Anthropological Examination of the C-group and Pan-Grave Skeletons from Sayala, Egyptian Nubia"), Oesterreichischen Akademie der Wissenschaften (Vienna), 1984.

Wadi Qitna and Kalabsha-South: Late Roman-Early Byzantine Tumuli Cemeteries in Egypt, Volume I: *Nubia,* Charles University (Prague), 1984.

Zivot starych Egyptanu (title means "Life of the Ancient Egyptians"), Panorama (Prague), 1989.

Sedmkrat do Nubie, (title means "Seven Times into Nubia"), Vysehrad, 1989.

Begegnungen mit Alaska (title means "Meetings with Alaska"), Brockhaus (Leipzig), 1990.

Life in Ancient Egypt, Cambridge University Press, 1992.

Life of the Ancient Egyptians, Oklahoma University Press, 1992.

Vivre au temps des pharaons (title means "Living in the Time of the Pharaohs"), Editions Atlas (Paris), 1992.

Contributor to books, including *Dejiny Afriky* ("History of Africa"), Svoboda (Prague), 1966; and *Rassengeschichte der menschheit,* ("Racial History of Mankind"), 1975.

WORK IN PROGRESS: Secondary Cemetery in the Mastabe of Ptahshepses at Abusir; Human Skeletal Remains from the Memphite Tomb of Horemheb; research and a monograph on ancient Egyptian medicine and paleopathology.

SIDELIGHTS: Eugen Strouhal told *CA:* "My personal career is the result of both my personal preferences and external circumstances. I never wanted to study medicine—but I loved history, art history, and archaeology. My parents, in line with the medical and natural history tradition of our family, persuaded me to try it. I did and became interested in theoretical medicine—not in its practical application. Once I graduated and became a doctor, I had to do some practical training in hospitals, but as soon as I got the occasion, I accepted a post teaching medical biology as an assistant at the medical faculty in Plzen. Here I was back in theory. From here I could also realize my interest in history. I had started studying archaeology during my medical studies, and I finished a degree in it three years later.

"With my two rather deviating fields of interest, I was chosen to be a member of the Czechoslovak Institute of Egyptology, beginning January 1, 1961. Taking part in several expeditions to Egypt and the remote area of Nubia, I served as medical doctor for our staff and the local population, at the same time working as a field archaeologist. I became a specialist in excavating and studying human skeletal remains. For this reason I chose physical anthropology as my postgraduate field; I received my Ph.D. in 1968.

"Beginning January 1, 1969, I was entrusted to build up a new Department for Prehistory and Antiquity at the Naprstek Museum section of the National Museum in Prague. During my twenty-four years of service there, its collection grew from 600 to 12,000 objects. I was the author of several large and many small exhibitions showing different aspects of the ancient Egyptian culture—a permanent display was not possible due to lack of space. I continued working with Austrian and English expeditions to Egypt and visited several museums and institutions in Europe, Africa, and North America. My pedagogic activity and scientific career was, however, stopped by the regime for ideological reasons. After the Velvet Revolution, I was invited by the medical faculty of Charles University, Prague, to read paleopathology—the science of the history of diseases—for which I had much material gathered during my twenty years of excavations in Egypt. In 1990 I became head of the Institute for the History of Medicine. I included teaching on the history of medicine in antiquity in my program.

"Writing has been my hobby since my school years. I was editor of a few school journals. I dreamed of becoming a novelist. Later, as my studies progressed, I began to appreciate facts more than imagination and started writing scientific articles and books. I also presented scientific concepts in a 'lighter' version for the general public—mostly journal articles and nonfiction literature. Usually, I start writing a popular book after years of studies, when I have reached a certain overview of the whole problem or topic. I try to be as objective as possible in choosing and interpreting facts, but sometimes I also include my personal views."

*　　*　　*

STUCKY, Solomon 1923-1988

OBITUARY NOTICE—See index for *CA* sketch: Born February 2, 1923, in Moundridge, KS; died July 13, 1988. Minister, farmer, and author. Ordained a Protestant Evangelical minister in 1947, Solomon preached both in Kansas and Michigan until the late 1950s. He also worked as a farmer for fourteen years in Michigan as well as Ontario. Solomon's books include *For Conscience' Sake* and *The Heritage of the Swiss Volhynian Mennonites.*

OBITUARIES AND OTHER SOURCES:

Date of death provided by wife, Naomi R. K. Stucky.

*　　*　　*

SUETONIUS
See MORRIS, Roger

*　　*　　*

SWINBURNE, Algernon Charles 1837-1909

PERSONAL: Born April 5, 1837, in London, England; died of pneumonia, April 10, 1909, in Putney, England; buried in Bonchurch, Isle of Wight; son of Charles Henry (an admiral) and Jane (Hamilton) Swinburne. *Education:* Attended Eton School, 1849-c. 1853; privately tutored by Reverend John Wilkinson and Reverend Russell Woodford, c. 1853-56; attended Balliol College, Oxford, 1856-1860. *Religion:* Raised as an Anglo-Catholic, but became an atheist while attending Oxford.

CAREER: British poet, dramatist, and critic.

AWARDS, HONORS: Honorary degree, Oxford University, 1908.

WRITINGS:

The Queen-Mother, Rosamond: Two Plays, Pickering, 1860, Ticknor & Fields (Boston), 1866.

Atalanta in Calydon, Moxon (London), 1865, Ticknor & Fields, 1866.

Chastelard, Moxon, 1865, Hurd & Houghton (New York), 1866.

Poems and Ballads (includes "Dolores," "Anactoria," "The Leper," and "The Hymn to Prosperine"), Moxon, 1866, published as *Laus Veneris, and Other Poems and Ballads,* Carleton (New York), 1866.

A Song of Italy (includes "Ode on the Insurrection in Candia"), Ticknor & Fields, 1867.

William Blake: A Critical Essay, Hotten (London), 1868, Dutton, 1906.

(With William Michael Rossetti) *Notes on the Royal Academy Exhibition, 1868,* Hotten, 1868.

Songs Before Sunrise, Roberts Brothers (Boston), 1871.

Under the Microscope, White (London), 1872, Mosher (Portland, ME), 1899.

Bothwell, Chatto & Windus, 1874.

George Chapman: A Critical Essay, Chatto & Windus, 1875.

Song of Two Nations, Chatto & Windus, 1875.

Essays and Studies, Chatto & Windus, 1875.

Erechtheus: A Tragedy, Chatto & Windus, 1876.

Note of an English Republican on the Muscovite Crusade, Chatto & Windus, 1876.

A Note on Charlotte Bronte, Chatto & Windus, 1877.

Poems and Ballads, Second Series, Chatto & Windus, 1878, Crowell (New York), c. 1885.

A Study of Shakespeare, Worthington (New York), 1880.

Specimens of Modern Poets: The Heptalogia or The Seven Against Sense, Chatto & Windus, 1880.

Mary Stuart, Worthington, 1881.

Tristam of Lyonesse and Other Poems, Chatto & Windus, 1882, Mosher, 1904.

A Century of Roundels, Worthington, 1883.

A Midsummer Holiday and Other Poems, Chatto & Windus, 1884.

Marino Faliero, Chatto & Windus, 1885.

Miscellanies, Worthington, 1886.

A Study of Victor Hugo, Chatto & Windus, 1886.

Locrine: A Tragedy, Alden (New York), 1887.

A Study of Ben Johnson, Worthington, 1889.

Poems and Ballads, Third Series, Chatto & Windus, 1889.

The Sisters, United States Book Company (New York), 1892.

Astrophel and Other Poems, Chatto & Windus/Scribner, 1894.

Studies in Prose and Poetry, Chatto & Windus/Scribner, 1894.

Robert Burns: A Poem, Burns Centenary Club (Edinburgh), 1896.

The Tale of Balen, Scribner, 1896.

Rosamund, Queen of the Lombards: A Tragedy, Dodd, 1899.

Love's Cross-Currents: A Year's Letters, Mosher, 1901.

Poems & Ballads, Second & Third Series, Mosher, 1902.

Percy Bysshe Shelley, Lippincott, 1903.

A Channel Passage and Other Poems, Chatto & Windus, 1904.

The Poems of Algernon Swinburne, 6 volumes, Harper, 1904.

The Duke of Gandia, Harper, 1908.

The Age of Shakespeare, Harper, 1908.

The Marriage of Monna Lisa, privately printed (London), 1909.

In the Twilight, privately printed (London), 1909.

The Portrait, privately printed (London), 1909.

The Chronicle of Queen Fredegond, privately printed (London), 1909.

Of Liberty and Loyalty, privately printed (London), 1909.

Ode to Mazzini, privately printed (London), 1909.

Shakespeare, Henry Frowde, 1909.

The Ballade of Truthful Charles and Other Poems, privately printed (London), 1910.

A Criminal Case, privately printed (London), 1910.

The Ballade of Villon and Fat Madge, privately printed (London), 1910.

The Cannibal Catechism, privately printed (London), 1910.

Les Fleurs du Mal and Other Stories, privately printed (London), 1913.

Charles Dickens, Chatto & Windus, 1913.

A Study of Victor Hugo's "Les Miserables," privately printed (London), 1914.

Pericles and Other Studies, privately printed (London), 1914.

Thomas Nabbes: A Critical Monograph, privately printed (London), 1914.

Christopher Marlowe in Relation to Greene, Peele and Lodge, privately printed (London), 1915.

Lady Maisie's Bairn and Other Poems, privately printed (London), 1915.

Theophile, privately printed (London), 1915.

Ernest Clouet, privately printed (London), 1916.

A Vision of Bags, privately printed (London), 1916.

The Death of Sir John Franklin, privately printed (London), 1916.

Poems From "Villon" and Other Fragments, privately printed (London), 1916.

Poetical Fragments, privately printed (London), 1916.

Posthumous Poems, edited by Edmund Gosse and Thomas James Wise, Heinemann, 1917.

Rondeaux Parisiens, privately printed (London), 1917.

The Italian Mother and Other Poems, privately printed (London), 1918.

The Ride from Milan and Other Poems, privately printed (London), 1918.

A Lay of Lilies and Other Poems, privately printed (London), 1918.

Queen Yseult: A Poem in Six Cantos, privately printed (London), 1918.

Lancelot, The Death of Rudel and Other Poems, privately printed (London), 1918.

Undergraduate Sonnets, privately printed (London), 1918.

The Character and Opinions of Dr. Johnson, privately printed (London), 1918.

The Queen's Tragedy, privately printed (London), 1919.

French Lyrics, privately printed (London), 1919.

Contemporaries of Shakespeare, Heinemann, 1919.

Ballads of the English Border, edited by William A. MacInnes, Heinemann, 1925.

The Complete Works of Algernon Charles Swinburne, twenty volumes, edited by Edmund Gosse and Thomas J. Wise, Heinemann/Wells, 1925-27.

Lesbia Brandon, edited by Randolph Hughes, Falcon Press (London), 1952, republished in *The Novels of A. C. Swinburne,* Farrar, Straus & Cudahy, 1962.

The Swinburne Letters, six volumes, edited by Cecil Y. Lang, Yale University Press, 1962.

New Writings by Swinburne, edited by Cecil Y. Lang, Syracuse University Press, 1964.

Also author of several unpublished works, including the play "The Unhappy Revenge."

SIDELIGHTS: Algernon Charles Swinburne was one of the foremost English poets of the Victorian period, though serious recognition in his own time often eluded him due to the controversial sexual, religious, and political matter of his poetry. He was known almost as much for his dissipated lifestyle—fraught with alcoholism and a penchant for flagellation—as for his literary work, though he was noted as a fine critic as well as poet, and also wrote novels. When his *Atalanta in Calydon,* a verse play in the Greek tragic style, was published in 1865, critics hailed Swinburne as a poetical genius, acknowledging his ease with lyricism but oddly not recognizing the atheistic and nihilistic themes of the work. But when the author published *Poems and Ballads* in 1866, he was denounced as obscene and immoral. Swinburne also demonstrated his fervid hatred for monarchical government in collections such as *A Song of Italy* and *Songs Before Sunrise,* a sentiment that did not further endear him to most of Victorian England. Toward the end of his life, Swinburne created less controversial works, and critics argue over their relative merit, though most admit the worth of such later writings such as *Tristram of Lyonesse and Other Poems* and *The Tale of Balen.*

Swinburne was born April 5, 1837, in London, England, to a noble and somewhat inbred family—his mother and father were second cousins. His mother, Lady Jane Hamilton Swinburne, was the daughter of an earl; his father, Admiral Charles Henry Swinburne, was the descendant of an extinct peerage. Swinburne's family was Catholic, and had participated in Stuart rebellions against the British throne since the days of Mary Stuart, Queen of Scotland—a fact that helps explain the poet's later fascination with the subject of Mary. Though small as a child—and later as an adult—Swinburne enjoyed vigorous outdoor sports such as swimming and riding. He demonstrated his creative bent early, writing and acting in plays with his siblings and cousins, and he enjoyed reading the works of William Shakespeare by the time he was six years old. He also liked the novels of Charles Dickens.

When he was approximately twelve, Swinburne entered the famed English boys' school, Eton. There he became influenced by other Elizabethan and Jacobean dramatists besides Shakespeare, and developed an admiration for French author Victor Hugo. "It must have been at Eton also," declared David G. Riede in his article for the *Concise Dictionary of British Literary Biography,* "that he developed the flagellation mania that was to remain with him to a greater or lesser degree for the rest of his life. He later wrote numerous letters recounting in gory detail the floggings that had left him bloody but unbowed. He no doubt was flogged, as was the custom, but his later accounts of a tutor preparing the flogging-room with 'burnt scents' or choosing a '*sweet* place out of doors with smell of firwood' or allowing him to 'saturate my face with eau-de-Cologne' before a beating have the ring of the fictional accounts of floggings that he enjoyed writing and reading." While at Eton, Swinburne also sharpened his writing skills, penning several verse tragedies in the Jacobean style. As Riede noted, "one of these plays, '*The Unhappy Revenge,*' survives in manuscript to exhibit a precocious talent for imitative verse and a foretaste of Swinburne's later analysis of the coupling of pain with sensuality."

Due to discipline problems, Swinburne left Eton early, and at the age of sixteen was privately tutored in Northumberland for a time by the Reverend John Wilkinson. He tried to leave this educational situation to become an officer in the British cavalry, but his parents prevented this, fearing he would easily come to harm because of his small size. Eventually Swinburne matriculated at Balliol College, Oxford University, after further studies with the Reverend Russell Woodford in Gloucestershire.

At Oxford, Swinburne became fast friends with a classmate, John Nichol, who introduced him to both republican politics and atheism. Under Nichol's influence, the young poet began writing verse in praise of regicide and made a hero of Felice Orsini, who had attempted to assassinate Napoleon III. Swinburne also met and was influenced by the Pre-Raphaelite artists and writers Dante Gabriel Rossetti, William Morris, and Ned Jones. Some of Swinburne's earliest published poetry can be categorized as Pre-Raphaelite, but for the bulk of his work he did not follow the movement's principles.

Though Swinburne studied hard at Oxford, he eventually failed to take his examinations, and left without graduating. Though he did not greatly approve of his son's choice of career, Swinburne's father supported him in setting up as a writer in London, providing him with a four-hundred-pound annuity and helping him publish his first plays, *The Queen-Mother* and *Rosamond,* in 1860. The former play is set in the court of the French King Charles IX and concerns the slaughter of the French Protestants, or Huguenots. The latter concerns the conflict between Rosamond, the mistress of English King Henry II, and Henry's wife, Queen Eleanor of Aquitane. Though both works contain fine verse, they suffer from the common affliction of verse plays of the Romantic and Victorian periods—lack of dramatic action. Neither play attracted much attention; nevertheless, Swinburne was becoming known in London's literary circles. He became acquainted with literary and artistic notables of the time, including poets Robert Browning and Alfred Tennyson, adventurer-translator Sir Richard Burton, and painter James McNeill Whistler. Indeed, it is Burton who is credited with introducing Swinburne to brandy, for which he developed an alcoholic fondness. He remained friends with Rossetti and Jones, and declared to them and others his admiration for the writings and philosophy of the Marquis de Sade.

After the publication of his first plays, Swinburne completed some of his other works in the early 1860s, such as the epistolary novel *Love's Cross-Currents, Chastelard*—the first tragedy in his trilogy about Mary Stuart, and many of the pieces that would appear in his first volume of *Poems and Ballads.* But these would not see publication until later in Swinburne's career. In 1863 Swinburne left his London friends to be with his favorite sister Edith, who was dying. After her death, he went to visit a nearby cousin, Mary Gordon, who had been one of his favorite companions while he was growing up. Scholars believe if Swinburne had not been in love with her all along, he fell in love with her at this time. He never managed to tell her of his passion, however, and he became violently disappointed and depressed when Mary announced her engagement to Colonel R. W. Disney-Leith. Yet Swinburne remained on good terms with her and occasionally dedicated his works to her.

While still visiting Mary, before her engagement, Swinburne began work on his verse play following the classics Greek style, *Atalanta in Calydon.* Based on the Meleager myth, it was published in 1865 and brought Swinburne a great deal of favorable critical attention. Reviewers were entranced with what Riede described as "Swinburne's great lyrical power and mastery of language," and immediately declared him comparable to Victorian greats Browning and Tennyson. But, as Riede pointed out, *Atalanta in Calydon* "reject[s] all belief in a beneficent scheme of things and even in the possibility of joy" and "is Swinburne's most pessimistic major work." Yet, in Riede's words, "surprisingly, the moral tone, the savage antitheism of the play went almost unnoticed" by the critics who praised Swinburne's art. Swinburne also published *Chastelard* the same year, and reviews of the verse play were generally favorable—some critics saying that it surpassed *Atalanta in Calydon*. But some commentators objected to what they felt was an unsympathetic portrayal of Mary Stuart.

The following year, 1866, Swinburne published his first volume of *Poems and Ballads*. The result was an immediate sensation, producing what Riede labeled "one of the most savage critical barrages in literary history." Individual pieces in *Poems and Ballads* include the nihilistic, sado-masochistic "Dolores," which became a popular chant among Oxford students; "Anactoria," which contains lesbian themes; "The Leper," which endorses necrophilia; and "The Hymn to Proserpine," which shocked Victorian audiences with its attack on Christianity: "Thou hast conquered, O Pale Galilean; the world has grown grey from thy breath." But, as Riede declared, "none of the poems" of *Poems and Ballads* "were designed merely to shock," but rather they "analyze and pay tribute to a part of human nature that may not be genteel but is at least genuine. The volume links frank and fierce eroticism, moreover, with Swinburne's violent but philosophically acute antitheism, for the pleasures of the flesh are consistently viewed as a response to the moral repression of Christianity."

Swinburne turned to themes of republicanism in his 1867 work *A Song of Italy*. One of the poems, "Ode on the Insurrection in Candia," led to his meeting with Italian republican revolutionary Giuseppe Mazzini, a man he had long admired. Mazzini admonished Swinburne to give up writing about love and sex in favor of celebrating the republican cause; the result was two more volumes of republican poetry, 1871's *Songs Before Sunrise* and 1875's *Song of Two Nations*. Rather than being grateful that Swinburne had abandoned his sexually shocking subject matter, many reviewers of these volumes were equally put out by his politics—most of Victorian England being strongly committed to the monarchical system of government. Some of the more liberal journals, however, praised the works, and even some who were hostile to Swinburne's content recognized the power of his verse.

Though Swinburne continued to produce sublime lyrics during the late 1860s and 1870s, his decadent lifestyle began taking its toll. He sometimes frequented a brothel called the Verbena Lodge that specialized in punishing its clients; he stopped his patronage after an argument over price in 1869. But Riede quoted author Oscar Wilde—another of Swinburne's acquaintances—as saying that the poet's exploits were self-exaggerated; Swinburne was "a braggart in matters of vice, who had done everything he could to convince his fellow citizens of his homosexuality and bestiality, without being in the slightest degree a homosexual or a bestializer." Swinburne did experience problems with drink, and had increasing bouts with alcoholic dysentery. By 1879 his condition was so bad that one of his friends, Theodore Watts-Dunton, decided to intervene. He brought Swinburne to live at his home in Putney (outside of London), and slowly weaned the author from excessive amounts of brandy to an occasional glass of ale. Watts-Dunton put the poet on a strict regimen of healthy walks, and generally kept Swinburne from his usual unwise acts, such as going out in bad weather. Most of Swinburne's biographers credit Watts-Dunton with saving the poet's life.

Some, however, also blame Watts-Dunton for cutting Swinburne off from the lifestyle that inspired his best poetry. Previous to moving in with Watts-Dunton, Swinburne had published two of his finest works—the Greek-style tragedy *Erechtheus* and *Poems and Ballads, Second Series*. After, he became terribly fond of Watts-Dunton's young nephew—he had always liked babies and children—and wrote a series of baby poems. While this verse did much to redeem Swinburne's scandalous reputation among Victorian women, most critics agree that the poems are maudlin and devoid of much literary merit. Exposed to few opinions except those of Watts-Dunton, Swinburne gave up his enthusiasm for republicanism in favor of British Imperialism, and the former advocate of regicide was a happy celebrant of Queen Victoria's Diamond Jubilee. But while Riede asserts that Swinburne's work became more and more often needlessly wordy, the poet did produce some noteworthy literature during the latter period of his life. A semi-autobiographical verse play, *The Sisters,* published in 1892 and dedicated to Mary Disney-Leith, broke new ground by giving a verse play a modern setting. Individual poems, including "On the Cliffs," "Thalassius," "By the North Sea," and "Tristram of Lyonesse" are also considered by most critics to be up to Swinburne's earlier standards.

Even Watts-Dunton's care could not succeed in protecting Swinburne from himself forever, though, and one day in 1909 while his caretaker was himself sick in bed, Swinburne went out for a walk on a chilly, rainy day. He caught a cold that eventually became double pneumonia. Swinburne became delirious for a time, reciting verses in Greek; then, on April 10, he died. Since Swinburne had never abandoned his atheism, the Anglican Burial Service was not read over his grave on the Isle of Wight.

BIOGRAPHICAL/CRITICAL SOURCES:

BOOKS

Chew, Samuel C., *Swinburne,* Little, Brown, 1929.

Concise Dictionary of British Literary Biography, Volume 4: *Victorian Writers, 1832-1890,* Gale, 1991, pp. 382-406.

Gosse, Edmund, *The Life of Algernon Charles Swinburne,* Macmillan, 1917.

Grierson, H. J. C., *Swinburne,* Longmans, 1953.

Hyder, Clyde K., *Swinburne's Literary Career and Fame,* Duke University Press, 1933.

Hyder, editor, *Swinburne: The Critical Heritage,* Routledge & Kegan Paul, 1970.

Lafourcade, Georges, *Swinburne: A Literary Biography,* Bell, 1932.

Louis, Margot K., *Swinburne and His Gods: The Roots and Growth of an Agnostic Poetry,* McGill-Queen's University Press, 1990.

McSweeny, Kerry, *Tennyson and Swinburne as Romantic Naturalists,* University of Toronto Press, 1980.

Raymond, Meredith B., *Swinburne's Poetics: Theory and Practice,* Mouton, 1971.

Riede, David G., *Swinburne: A Study of Romantic Myth-making,* University Press of Virginia, 1978.

Swinburne, Algernon Charles, *Poems and Ballads,* Moxon, 1866.

Thomas, Donald, *Swinburne: The Poet in His World,* Oxford University Press, 1979.*

—Sidelights by Elizabeth Wenning

*   *   *

SZANTON, Andrew (Emlew) 1963-

PERSONAL: Surname is pronounced "*zan*-ton"; born January 11, 1963, in Washington, DC; son of Peter Loeb (a consultant and writer) and Eleanor (an executive; maiden name, Stokes) Szanton; married Barbara Cannon (a physician), September 7, 1991. *Education:* Princeton University, A.B., 1985. *Politics:* Independent. *Religion:* Quaker. *Avocational interests:* "Watching noir movies, playing basketball."

ADDRESSES: Home and office—162 Powderhouse Blvd., Somerville, MA 02144.

CAREER: Smithsonian Institution, Washington, DC, oral historian in video history, 1986-88; free-lance writer, 1988—.

WRITINGS:

(With Eugene P. Wigner) *The Recollections of Eugene P. Wigner as Told to Andrew Szanton,* Plenum, 1992.

WORK IN PROGRESS: Collaborative memoir with civil rights leader Charles Evers, publication expected in 1995.

SIDELIGHTS: Andrew Szanton told *CA:* "I have always loved writing and wanted to be a writer. For years I thought that fiction was far more important than nonfiction. Since nonfiction was where I felt most comfortable, this primacy of fiction was vaguely hurtful. As an undergraduate at Princeton, I took a course with playwright and journalist John McPhee that elevated my view of factual writing and of my own ability.

"I joined an oral history program at the Smithsonian after college, not sure what books I wanted to write, but drawn to the talk, the sense of history. We were interviewing creators of the first atomic bomb. As a history major, a Quaker, a pacifist, and a storyteller, I was stimulated on many levels. One bomb creator in particular interested me: Eugene Wigner. He was courtly and modest, an eighty-five-year-old Hungarian gentleman who had known personally most of the great physicists of the century, had been in Berlin when Nazi leader Adolf Hitler came to power, had been close to Albert Einstein.

"I urged Eugene Wigner to write a memoir, knowing that no major book had been written about his life. I heard him say that the desire for celebrity was American; as a European, he wanted nothing more than respect among his peers, which he already had. Thus, he would never write a memoir. Nine months later, he asked me when I could come to Princeton to help him write his memoirs. I came almost immediately and began a three-year search for the facts of Dr. Wigner's life and the voice of Dr. Wigner, as he might have written his own memoir.

"Other memoirs that inspired me included *Exiles* by Michael J. Arlen, *Second Wind* by Bill Russell and Taylor Branch, and *This Boy's Life* by Tobias Wolff. Other writers I admire include John McPhee, James M. Cain, Somerset Maugham, Robertson Davies, Walker Percy, Leo Tolstoy, and Ivan Turgenev. Maugham's book *The Razor's Edge,* Davies's *Fifth Business,* Percy's *Moviegoer,* and Turgenev's *Fathers and Sons* are books I read every year.

"I hope to write at least a few more memoir collaborations. I don't require that my subjects be gentlemen or ladies. I need them to have lived full, unexpected lives, to have the skill and patience to remember, to be generous with their lives, and to give me room to interpret them. I am drawn to people who have experienced American life as earnest outsiders; perhaps that is what connects the Hungarian physicist Eugene Wigner with a civil rights leader from Mississippi, Charles Evers. Both men are tough and courageous, with a strong sense of humor. I find spending time with such people not only interesting but relaxing. I'm still learning.''

* * *

SZWAJGER, Adina Blady 1917-

PERSONAL: Born in 1917; daughter of Icchak Blady and Stefania (Hertzberg) Szwajger; married Stefan Szpigielman, July 27, 1939 (died, c. 1944); married Wladyslaw Swidowski. *Education:* Attended University of Warsaw, 1933-39. *Religion:* Jewish.

CAREER: Instructor at summer camp in Kazimierz, 1939; Bersohn and Bauman Children's Hospital, Warsaw, Poland, 1940-43; worker with Main Committee of Polish Jews, 1945; worked in sanatorium, 1945; pediatrician, beginning in 1945; writer. *Military service:* Member of Jewish-Polish resistance group ZOB during World War II.

WRITINGS:

I Remember Nothing More: The Warsaw Children's Hospital and the Jewish Resistance (memoir), translated by Tasja Darowska and Danusia Stok, Collins Harvill, 1990, Pantheon, 1991.

SIDELIGHTS: Adina Blady Szwajger is author of *I Remember Nothing More: The Warsaw Children's Hospital and the Jewish Resistance,* in which she recounts her harrowing experiences in Warsaw, Poland, during World War II. She was still a student at the University of Warsaw when Germany invaded Poland in early September, 1939. Within only a few days of the invasion, her formal studies came to an abrupt end. Warsaw entered a state of siege, and the citizens held out only briefly before Germans occupied the city. Despite the increasing presence of Nazis in the area, Szwajger managed to flee to a Soviet zone where she intended to resume her medical studies.

By October, the Jewish area of Warsaw was enclosed with barbed wire. Those who remained within the area, known as the Jewish ghetto, were forced to wear armbands signifying that they were Jews. Towards the end of 1939 Szwajger learned that she was scheduled for deportation to the Soviet Gulag, a system of gruesome work camps. She then fled back to Warsaw. By the spring of 1940, the ghetto's Jewish inhabitants were restricted to activity within the area and were often enlisted to do forced labor. Under these increasingly arduous circumstances, Szwajger began working at the Bersohn and Bauman Children's Hospital tending tuberculosis victims. In 1941 conditions in the Warsaw ghetto grew even more grim. Citizens faced execution if they were found outside the area. As food sup-

plies depleted, Szwajger found her own health diminishing. In early summer she fell ill with typhus after visiting a detainment camp, and she was slow to recover. Meanwhile, the Germans imposed further restrictions on food supplies. Consequently, thousands of Jews perished from starvation and disease.

During the summer of 1942 the Germans began deporting Jews from the Warsaw ghetto to concentration camps. Szwajger, despondent over the fate of her family and friends, attempted suicide. After recovering somewhat, she joined the newly formed ZOB, the armed Jewish resistance movement. Szwajger eventually managed to leave the ghetto, whereupon she found residence close by and served as a courier for the ZOB. In the spring of 1943 the Germans undertook the final vanquishing of remaining Jews in the Warsaw Ghetto. But the ZOB mounted considerable opposition, and for three weeks the ghetto was a war zone. More than seven thousand Jews perished in this conflict, and fifty-six thousand survivors were consigned to the concentration camp at Treblinka.

Szwajger found more hospital work during the winter of 1943-44. The following autumn the ZOB launched the Warsaw Uprising, in which approximately two hundred thousand citizens died. During this conflict Szwajger helped Jews escape the ghetto by guiding them through the sewers and into downtown Warsaw. Later she united once again with surviving ZOB fighters. After the Soviets liberated Warsaw in early 1945, the ZOB joined in repelling the Germans from the remainder of Poland.

After the war ended, Szwajger worked briefly for an organization concerned with locating Jewish children displaced during the Holocaust in Poland. She then began a career as a pediatrician. In her introduction to *I Remember Nothing More,* Szwajger commented on why so much time passed between her experiences during World War II and the writing of her memoir: "I have myself to blame that only now am I writing when so many years have passed and so many things have faded from my memory. But immediately after the war I decided not to write any more. Never. What had happened wasn't something to be written about, or read; at least, that's what I thought. And to write about other, everyday, prewar matters didn't make sense. So—better nothing. And maybe I thought—had a faint hope—that if I remained silent, I'd manage to forget at least some of it and be able to live like everybody else.''

I Remember Nothing More has been recognized as a gripping, unflinching account of Szwajger's experiences. Jonathan Yardley, in his *Washington Post* review, described Szwajger's story as "at once terrible and exalting,'' and he affirmed that "it shows us . . . the true nature of the heroic.'' And Kati Marton, writing in the *New York Times*

Book Review, deemed *I Remember Nothing More* an "unsentimental, almost matter-of-fact memoir." She added that Szwajger's book constituted "the most damning and most uplifting of the many accounts of the Holocaust that I have read."

BIOGRAPHICAL/CRITICAL SOURCES:

BOOKS

Szwajger, Adina Blady, *I Remember Nothing More: The Warsaw Children's Hospital and the Jewish Resistance,* Pantheon, 1991.

PERIODICALS

Atlantic Monthly, April, 1991, p. 108.
New York Times Book Review, April 7, 1991, p. 11.
Washington Post, March 27, 1991, p. B2.*

—*Sketch by Les Stone*

T

TATE, Ellalice
See HIBBERT, Eleanor Alice Burford

*   *   *

TAYLOR, Anne 1934-

PERSONAL: Born April 2, 1934, in West Bromwich, England; daughter of Vincent (a municipal engineer) and Hilda (Prescott) Overfield; married Desmond Taylor (a news editor). *Education:* London University, B.A. (honors), 1954.

CAREER: Writer. Worked as a research assistant and writer for *Observer* (a newspaper) in London, England, in the 1960s. Parish councillor in North Yorkshire, 1991—.

MEMBER: Royal Geographic Society (fellow).

WRITINGS:

Laurence Oliphant (biography), Oxford University Press, 1982.
Visions of Harmony, Clarendon, 1987.
Annie Besant (biography), Oxford University Press, 1992.

Editor of *Ryedale Historian,* 1992.

WORK IN PROGRESS: A biography of Scottish writer Robert Cunninghame Graham, who lived from 1852 to 1936.

SIDELIGHTS: Anne Taylor is a writer whose works include *Annie Besant,* a biography of the British spiritualist of the late nineteenth and early twentieth centuries. As Victoria Glendinning wrote in her London *Times* review of Taylor's book, "Annie Besant was among the many western seekers after truth who began to shop around in the beguiling arcade of the unorthodox, the esoteric and the occult." Glendinning praised the biography, noting:

"It is hard to expose people without diminishing them, but that is what Anne Taylor has done for Annie Besant."

Taylor told *CA:* "My lifelong desire to write was encouraged when I went to work for the late William Clark on the *Observer* newspaper in the 1960s as a research assistant for the review of the news of the week. When Clark left to found the Overseas Development Institute, Edward Crankshaw encouraged me to write the pieces for the back page every week. After I left the *Observer* I started to work on an account of the Pilgrimage of Grace (which has not been published).

"I am restoring an old kitchen garden in the intervals of research and writing."

BIOGRAPHICAL/CRITICAL SOURCES:

PERIODICALS

Times (London), April 2, 1992.

*   *   *

TAYLOR, Harold 1914-1993

OBITUARY NOTICE—See index for CA sketch: Born September 28, 1914, in Toronto, Ontario, Canada; immigrated to the United States, 1939, naturalized citizen, 1947; died February 9, 1993, in Manhattan, NY. Educator, administrator, editor, and author. President of Sarah Lawrence College by the age of thirty, Taylor supported and fostered the progressive curriculum established at the school. He was an advocate for changing traditional methods of education, which he considered tedious. Under his direction, students at Sarah Lawrence developed their own curriculum with the guidance of professors and received detailed feedback from instructors rather than grades. Taylor's early experience as a professor of philosophy influenced his writing, which covers educational philosophy, social change, and the philosophy of art. His books include *On Education and Freedom, Students without Teachers: The Crisis in the University, How to Change Colleges: Notes on Radical Reform, Art and the Intellect,* and, as editor and contributor, *The Humanities in the Schools.*

OBITUARIES AND OTHER SOURCES:

BOOKS

Who's Who in America, 47th edition, Marquis, 1992, p. 3314.

PERIODICALS

New York Times, February 10, 1993, p. D23.
Times (London), February 20, 1993, p. 19.

* * *

TAYLOR, Liza Pennywitt 1955-

PERSONAL: Born June 2, 1955, in Washington, DC; daughter of William A. (a journalist) and Mary (a painter, illustrator, writer, and homemaker; maiden name, Bourquin) Korns; married Jeremy M. G. Taylor (a statistician), December 27, 1986; children: Evan George, Graham Patrick. *Education:* Attended University of Oregon, 1973-74; New England Conservatory of Music, B.Mus., 1978; graduate study in contemporary music at California Institute of the Arts, 1978-79; graduate study in biology at University of California, Los Angeles, 1982-84. *Politics:* Liberal Democrat.

ADDRESSES: Home and office—13025 Bloomfield St., Studio City, CA 91604. *Agent*—Sandra Dijkstra, 1155 Camino del Mar, Del Mar, CA 92014.

CAREER: Professional flutist and flute instructor in Eugene, OR, Boston, MA, New York City, and Los Angeles, CA, 1970-81; research associate specializing in AIDS research with the Department of Immunology and Microbiology, University of California, Los Angeles, 1983-90; writer, 1990—. Worked variously as a cook, receptionist, translator, nanny, model, and in musical instrument repair.

AWARDS, HONORS: Ruin, Wing, Dance was nominated for the Pushcart Prize, 1990; *The Drummer Was the First to Die* was named a Book-of-the-Month Club selection, 1992.

WRITINGS:

The Drummer Was the First to Die, St. Martin's, 1992.

Contributor of short story cycle *Ruin, Wing, Dance* in *Santa Monica Review.*

Coauthor of various articles on the clinical immunology of AIDS in various scientific journals, including *Mount Sinai Journal of Medicine, Blood,* and the *Journal of Clinical Immunology.*

WORK IN PROGRESS: The Inland Sea, "a contemporary novel of medical suspense, exploring the genetic and emotional aspects of musical brilliance;" a collection of abstract and experimental fairy tales; *Pink and Blue Shadows,* an essay on post-partum depression; *Writer with Children,* a guide to writing while raising children.

SIDELIGHTS: Liza Pennywitt Taylor is the author of *The Drummer Was the First to Die,* a novel that incorporates historical events and people. A former research biologist, Taylor combined a love of history with her background in science to produce this work, her first novel. The story begins in the India of 1854, with the death of a native musician. By the day's end nearly all of the musician's village has died. The wave of death extends even to India's aristocracy, the British ruling class. The governor and most of his staff and family succumb to what has now been identified as cholera, a disease that attacks the intestine. Hoping to escape the outbreak that has left her an heiress, the governor's daughter, Lillian, returns to London, England. Upon her arrival, she learns that the cholera has travelled ahead of her and now afflicts her homeland as well as India.

Once back in London, Lillian meets Dr. John Snow, the real-life doctor credited with discovering the means by which cholera was spread. The pair fall in love, and Lillian is soon assisting Dr. Snow with his medical investigations into the epidemic—events based Snow's actual probe of the disease. The couple eventually discover that cholera is caused, and spread, by an organism that travels through a population's water supply. As Betty Ann Kevles appraised in the *Los Angeles Times:* "The story is filled with nuggets of scientifically accurate medical history." In addition to her admiration for the author's grasp of technical information, Kevles was impressed with the historical content of the book as well. She continued in her review, "Taylor brings to life the sounds, sights and especially the smells (e.g., the tell-tale 'cholera stink') of a vanished era." While crediting Taylor's use of hard fact and credible research, *Booklist* contributor Donna Seaman characterized *The Drummer the Was First to Die* as "bracing and provocative" and a "thoroughly entertaining tale."

Taylor told *CA:* "I chose cholera as the subject of *The Drummer Was the First to Die* after working in AIDS (Acquired Immunodeficiency Syndrome) research for five years. The deadly power of epidemic disease has always fascinated me. The true story of 19th century cholera researcher Dr. John Snow, on whom the book is based, served as the core for my exploration of the effects that disease can have on relationships, society, ambition, and morality.

"During my years as a musician, the frequent frustrations of that profession sent me into the escapist worlds of Dickens, Trollope, Thackeray, Gaskell, and Eliot. When I attempted my first writing of fiction, it was only natural that I would use a Victorian form as a foundation for a novel whose structure would pay tribute to those authors and simultaneously poke a little fun at them.

"Although most of my reading—and all of my writing—is now contemporary, I still favor writers who are similar to the Victorians in their profluence: Vladimir Nabokov, Margaret Drabble, Edna O'Brien, and William Styron. I also like those authors who succeed in creating a vivid and three-dimensional world in their fiction—much as I try to do in my own writing.

"When answering the frequent question of how I approached the vast body of research called for in a historical novel, I can only say that it was a joy to have an excuse to spend time in a dozen libraries and museums in Los Angeles, California, and London, England. My sources for the medical and social details were primarily periodicals such as the *London Times, Lancet,* and *Punch,* and hundreds of Victorian Realist paintings in London's Tate Gallery and other museums.

"Although I often miss the music which used to be in my life, I think that it has reappeared in my writing. Sometimes phrases of Mozart wrap the rhythms of my sentences. I replay certain Schubert cadences in my mind when I am searching for the right ending to a scene, and the interweavings of fugues sound in the background when multiple story lines flow through and around each other. Writing fiction, however, is much more an expression of my personal voice than music ever was, and I feel lucky to be doing it."

BIOGRAPHICAL/CRITICAL SOURCES:

PERIODICALS

Booklist, July, 1992.
Los Angeles Times, August 4, 1992.

*   *   *

TEARLE, John L.   1917-

PERSONAL: Born January 15, 1917, in Lancashire, England; son of John Laurence and Florence (Edwards) Tearle; married Dorothy Whittle, April 5, 1942 (died May 23, 1992); children: Jane Tearle Shelvey, David, Richard. *Education:* Attended University of Nottingham, 1935-39; University of London, B.Sc., 1938, Ph.D., 1944.

ADDRESSES: Home—Frithsden Copse, Berkhamsted, Hertfordshire HP4 1RQ, England.

CAREER: Kodak Ltd., Harrow, England, research physicist, 1939-47, manufacturing manager, 1947-69, director, 1969-76.

WRITINGS:

Mrs. Piozzi's Tall Young Beau: William Augustus Conway, Fairleigh Dickinson University Press, 1991.

Contributor to magazines, including *Theatre Notebook* and *Private Eye.*

WORK IN PROGRESS: An Acting Dynasty: The Conways and the Tearles; A Bedfordshire Family: The Tearles of Stanbridge.

SIDELIGHTS: John L. Tearle told *CA:* "My career provides an unlikely background for an author whose first full-length book was published when he was seventy-five years old. If my writing merits commendation, credit must be given to the early schooling which gave me a grounding in language, and which taught me to write clear, readable English.

"Retirement gave me time to develop my interest in the acting branch of my family, who toured extensively in Britain and the United States in the latter part of the nineteenth century. Much painstaking and sometimes tedious searching of newspapers and other periodicals was needed to trace their engagements and repertoires, but the effort was rewarded by the picture I was able to build of these actor-managers in their heyday.

"In the course of that research, I discovered that a corrupt version of the death speech of Brutus had survived in performances in England throughout the century and was even declaimed by Godfrey Tearle, the last of the dynasty, at a rehearsal of *Julius Caesar* at His Majesty's Theatre in 1932. My unraveling of this mystery in stage history was my first publication since my scientific papers in the 1940s.

"I was then diverted by a completely unrelated subject. I had been suspicious of the authenticity of *The Diary of a Farmer's Wife, 1796-1797* when it was first published in 1964. I was able to trace its first appearance, in serial form, in 1937, and to expose it as a work of fiction.

"Thus encouraged by the publication of two disparate detective stories in the same year, I was urged to extend my studies to the ostensible founder of the acting dynasty, the enigmatic William Augustus Conway, who made his debut in 1808. It was a stroke of fortune to find that he had been befriended by the elderly Hester Piozzi, the former Mrs. Thrale and the controversial friend of Samuel Johnson. Even more exciting was the discovery that Mrs.

Piozzi was a 'hot property' and that the relationship between Mrs. Piozzi and Conway had puzzled the academic world for 150 years.

"Here at last was the prospect of a story of great importance. This required much more research in foreign fields, both literally and figuratively, as most of the relevant letters were housed in manuscript collections in the United States, and were being studied by professors of English who were steeped in their subject. My only claim to invade their territory was my better acquaintance with Conway so, without the benefit of educational grants or academic supervision, I uncovered the story that had evaded the literary establishment.

"Research, in one discipline or another, has been the mainspring of my literary efforts. There is more to come, if I live to tell the story of my ancestors, who were yeoman farmers in Bedfordshire as long ago as the fifteenth century, and who farmed the same fields for centuries only ten miles from where I write."

*   *   *

TEIWES, Helga 1930-

PERSONAL: Born January 19, 1930, in Meerbusch/Duesseldorf, Germany; daughter of Reinhold and Gertrud (Zaepke) Kulbe; married, 1954 (marriage ended); married, 1972 (divorced, 1976). *Education:* Abitur, 1950; received M.A. in 1957; University of Arizona, B.A., 1978.

ADDRESSES: Home—2611 North Teresa Ln., Tucson, AZ 85745. *Office*—Arizona State Museum, University of Arizona, Tucson, AZ 85721.

CAREER: Hehmke-Winterer Studio, commercial, portrait, and industrial photographer, 1950-57, teacher of photography, 1955-57; Bagel Printing Co., Duesseldorf, Germany, staff photographer, 1957-60; Brodatz Custom Lab, New York City, photographer, 1960-61; Cartier's, New York City, staff photographer, 1961-62; CCF Color Lab, New York City, retoucher, 1962-64; archaeological field photographer in Snaketown, AZ, 1964-65; University of Arizona, Tucson, photographer for Arizona State Museum, 1965-93. Photographs included in permanent collection at Arizona State Museum; work exhibited in solo and group shows throughout the Southwest.

AWARDS, HONORS: Grand Prize, World Photography Society, 1983.

WRITINGS:

(And photographer) *Kachina Dolls: The Art of Hopi Carvers,* University of Arizona Press, 1991.

Contributor to periodicals, including *American Indian Art.*

PHOTOGRAPHER

Bernard Fontana, *Mission San Xavier del Bac: A Photographic Essay on the Desert People and Their Church,* University of Arizona Press, 1973.

Thomas Weaver, *Indians of Arizona,* University of Arizona Press, 1974.

R. E. Ahlborn, *Saints of San Xavier,* Southwest Mission Research Center, 1974.

R. C. Goss, *The San Xavier Altarpiece,* University of Arizona Press, 1974.

Emil W. Haury, *The Hohokam: Desert Farmers and Craftsmen: Excavations at Snaketown, 1964-1965,* University of Arizona Press, 1976.

C. L. Tanner, *Prehistoric Southwestern Craft Arts,* University of Arizona Press, 1976.

Fontana, *The Material Culture of the Tarahumara Indians,* Northland Press, 1979.

Wolfgang Linding, *Navajo,* U. Baer Verlag (Zurich), 1991.

Contributor of photographs to periodicals, including *National Geographic, American Antiquity,* and *Science.*

WORK IN PROGRESS: Writing about Hopi basket weavers, publication expected in 1994; documenting the work of Hopi potters; research on other Native American Indian groups of the Southwest.

*   *   *

TELLER, Walter (Magnes) 1910-1993

OBITUARY NOTICE—See index for *CA* sketch: Born October 10, 1910, in New Orleans, LA; died of cancer, February 17, 1993, in Princeton, NJ. Educator, editor, publisher, and author. As an author and editor, Teller dealt with such topics as instructions on farming, narratives about New England and Middle Atlantic states, and biographies of sailors; he also revived the works of forgotten or neglected writers. He cofounded, coedited, and copublished the weekly *Bucks County Gazette* for four years, and taught his craft at schools and conferences, later becoming a member of Princeton University's advisory council to the English department beginning in 1975. His books include *Roots in the Earth,* written with P. Alston Waring; *The Search for Captain Slocum: A Biography; Cape Cod and the Offshore Islands; Consider Poor I: The Life and Works of Nancy Luce;* and, as editor, *On the River.*

OBITUARIES AND OTHER SOURCES:

BOOKS

The Writers Directory: 1992-1994, St. James Press, 1992.

PERIODICALS

Chicago Tribune, February 21, 1993, section 2, p. 6.

New York Times, February 18, 1993, p. B11.

*　　*　　*

TESTER, S. J(im)   1924-1986

PERSONAL: Born April 8, 1924, in London, England; died of cancer, 1986; son of John Henry (in sales) and Elizabeth (a homemaker; maiden name, Brooks) Tester; married Phyllida Richards (a college lecturer), April 15, 1950; children: Phyllida Ruth, Deborah Mary, Joanna. *Education:* Attended University College, London, 1947-50. *Religion:* Roman Catholic.

CAREER: University of Bristol, Bristol, England, assistant lecturer, 1950-53, lecturer, 1953-68, senior lecturer in classics, history, and theology, 1968-83, member of university senate; writer. Member of Civil Service Commission senior appointments board. *Military service:* Royal Navy Reserve, 1942-47, served in submarines; became lieutenant.

MEMBER: Classical Association.

WRITINGS:

(Translator with H. F. Stewart and E. K. Rand) *The Theological Tractates,* by Boethius, bound with Tester's translation of *The Consolation of Philosophy,* by Boethius, Harvard University Press, 1973.
A History of Western Astrology, Boydell & Brewer, 1987.

Contributor to journals.

SIDELIGHTS: S. J. Tester's *A History of Western Astrology* has been heralded by critics as a long-overdue analysis of astrological practices and their influence on Western society. As Tester's study illustrates, astrology—the study of stars and planets to determine their influence on earthly events—was a respected practice prior to its decline in the late 1600s. Despite its prominence in European civilization, critics have cited a lack of scholarly sources which examine the subject. Anthony Grafton, writing in *New York Times Book Review,* noted that "most readers—and, in fact, most scholars—have a far feebler grasp of astrology than of any other discipline so central to Western culture." For this reason, Grafton writes, *A History of Western Astrology* "fills a large and rather surprising gap," relating a "coherent story that until now had to be pieced together from primary and secondary sources of diverse age, aim, and value."

Tester traces the origin of astrology to Greece in the second century B.C., dispelling popular notions that the practice stemmed from Egypt or another Eastern source. And it is in Europe, according to Tester, that astrology had profound effects. The books details the many prominent figures who relied on astrologers, including Frederick II, Duke of Austria; and Florentine ruler Lorenzo de'Medici. For these individuals, as well as a multitude of other citizens, astrology served a number of functions. It was a factor in medical treatments, a means of explaining historical occurrences, and, as it is most commonly known to contemporary society, a way of predicting the future. As Grafton notes, "astrology allayed fears in a premodern world where fire, disease, bandits outside the walls and disloyal servants within them always threatened social position, wealth and life itself." The practice also proved durable in Tester's estimation, influencing two-thousand years of Western history before the scholarly interest and popular appeal of the subject waned in the seventeenth century.

Many critics were impressed by Tester's chronicle. J. M. Balcer, writing in *Choice,* maintained that "this is not a 'how to do it' book, but rather an outstanding academic study of 'how it was done.' " *Times Literary Supplement* reviewer John Henry likewise found *A History of Western Astrology* to be "a superb general account," but he did perceive several gaps in the work. "There is virtually no discussion of astrology as a practice, as a skilled craft," Henry complained, noting that "we do not learn what astrologers actually did." Despite this shortcoming, the critic declared that "the book is a delight to read and an excellent guide through so complex and wide-ranging a subject."

A History of Western Astrology proved to be one of Tester's final efforts; he succumbed to cancer shortly after completing the manuscript and never lived to see his book in print. The author's widow, Phyllida Tester, told *CA* that her husband's book "was the product of over twenty years of research into the sources and thought and debate. The last chapters were written under pressure of time—as he knew he was dying—so the vast resources of knowledge accumulated were perforce crystallized succinctly into a short space." Grafton found that the circumstances surrounding the book's completion gave the work an added poignancy. "The work of a man who was losing a battle with cancer as he wrote," Grafton noted, "*A History of Western Astrology* stimulates thought and commands respect." Balcer also expressed his appreciation that the book was completed, declaring that "Tester's study marks the first significant academic treatise on astrology. This book will stand as *the* study for generations to come."

BIOGRAPHICAL/CRITICAL SOURCES:

PERIODICALS

Choice, May, 1988.
New York Times Book Review, January 31, 1988, p. 13.
Times Literary Supplement, November 27, 1987, p. 1316.

THERON, Johan   1924-

PERSONAL: Born February 15, 1924, in Pretoria, South Africa; immigrated to United States, 1952; son of Jan Malan (a teacher) and Pietertje (Groeneweg) Theron. *Education:* University of Pretoria, B.A., 1941, LL.B., 1945. *Avocational interests:* Art, music, theater, gardening, travel, reading.

ADDRESSES: Home—37 West Twelfth St., New York, NY 10011.

CAREER: Affiliated with South African Diplomatic Service, 1946-57, member of permanent mission to United Nations, 1952-57; United Nations Secretariat, New York City, served successively as deputy director of budget and chief editor, 1957-85; translator.

WRITINGS:

(Translator) A.J. Dunning, *Extremes: Reflections on Human Behavior,* Harcourt, 1992.

SIDELIGHTS: Johan Theron told *CA:* "I was born and raised in South Africa, although I have resided permanently in the United States since 1952. I grew up speaking Dutch to my mother and her family (they had emigrated from the Netherlands in 1914), Afrikaans to my father (the descendant of a French Huguenot refugee who arrived in South Africa in 1688) and all my Afrikaans-speaking compatriots, and English to those with that mother tongue. Although literature and language have been my main interests in life, I studied law, briefly became a diplomat, and then spent the rest of my career helping to administer the United Nations Secretariat and, ultimately, to edit its official documentation and publications.

"After retiring in 1985, I was at last able to try to follow a family tradition. My Dutch grandfather was a noted scholar and writer; his work was published both in the Netherlands in Dutch and in South Africa in translation. So far, my creative urge has found an outlet in reading and writing book reports for a publishing house, and also in the publication of my first translation from Dutch into English, which turned out to be a Book-of-the-Month Club selection. I consider translation to be the next best thing to authorship, a creative activity which, in my opinion, deserves commensurate recognition."

*   *   *

THIERING, Barbara (Elizabeth)   1930-

PERSONAL: Born November 15, 1930, in Sydney, Australia; daughter of H. J. K. Houlsby and R. J. Hanney; married, 1953 (marriage ended, 1980); children: Nerida,

Paul, David. *Education:* University of Sydney, B.A. (with first-class honors), 1951, Ph.D., 1973; University of London, B.D., 1955, Th.M., 1961.

ADDRESSES: Home—16 Wyong Rd., Mosman, New South Wales 2088, Australia. *Office*—School of Studies in Religion, University of Sydney, Sydney 2006, Australia.

CAREER: High school modern language teacher, 1953-61; University of Sydney, Sydney, Australia, lecturer in Old Testament studies, Hebrew, and feminist theology, 1967—, member of board of studies in divinity, 1973—, and lecturer in continuing education. Equal Opportunity Tribunal of New South Wales, member, 1981—. Public speaker; guest on radio programs.

WRITINGS:

Redating the Teacher of Righteousness, Theological Explorations (Sydney), 1979.
The Gospels and Qumran: A New Hypothesis, Theological Explorations, 1981.
The Qumran Origins of the Christian Church, Theological Explorations, 1983.
Jesus and the Riddle of the Dead Sea Scrolls (also see below), HarperCollins, 1992, published in England as *Jesus the Man: A New Interpretation from the Dead Sea Scrolls,* Doubleday, 1992.

Contributor to books, including *Against the Odds,* edited by Madge Dawson and Heather Radi, Hale & Ironmonger, 1984; and *Temple Scroll Studies,* edited by G. Brooke, Sheffield Academic Press, 1989. Contributor to religious studies journals and newspapers.

Jesus and the Riddle of the Dead Sea Scrolls has been translated into seven other languages.

WORK IN PROGRESS: A book on the research involved in writing *Jesus and the Riddle of the Dead Sea Scrolls.*

SIDELIGHTS: Barbara Thiering told *CA:* "A documentary film *The Riddle of the Dead Sea Scrolls,* based on my research on Christian origins, was made by Beyond International and broadcast by the Australian Broadcasting Corporation on Palm Sunday, 1990. It created nationwide controversy, the effects of which continue. The film has been shown twice, in 1991 and 1992, on the Discovery Channel in the United States."

BIOGRAPHICAL/CRITICAL SOURCES:

BOOKS

Star, Leonie, *The Dead Sea Scrolls: The Riddle Debated,* Australian Broadcasting Corp., 1991.

PERIODICALS

Times (London), September 19, 1992, p. 36.

THIRKELL, Angela (Margaret)   1890-1961
(Leslie Parker)

PERSONAL: Born January 30, 1890, in London, England; died January 30, 1961, in Bramley, England; daughter of John W. Mackail (a professor of poetry); married James Campbell McInnes (a singer), 1911 (divorced, 1917); married George Thirkell (in the military), 1918 (divorced, 1929); children: (first marriage) Graham, Colin, and one daughter (deceased); (second marriage) Lance. *Education:* Educated privately.

CAREER: Novelist and short story writer.

WRITINGS:

NOVELS; EXCEPT AS NOTED

Three Houses (memoirs), Oxford University Press, 1931, Robin Clark, 1986.
Ankle Deep, Hamish Hamilton, 1933.
High Rising, Hamish Hamilton, 1933.
Wild Strawberries, Hamish Hamilton, 1933.
The Demon in the House, Hamish Hamilton, 1934.
(Under pseudonym Leslie Parker) *Trooper to the Southern Cross,* Hamish Hamilton, 1934, republished under the name Angela Thirkell, Virago, 1985.
O These Men, These Men, Hamish Hamilton, 1935.
The Grateful Sparrow, Hamish Hamilton, 1935.
August Folly, Hamish Hamilton, 1936.
Coronation Summer, Oxford University Press, 1937.
Summer Half, Hamish Hamilton, 1937.
Pomfret Towers, Hamish Hamilton, 1938.
The Brandons, Hamish Hamilton, 1939.
Before Lunch, Hamish Hamilton, 1939.
Cheerfulness Breaks In, Hamish Hamilton, 1940.
Marling Hall, Hamish Hamilton, 1942.
The Headmistress, Hamish Hamilton, 1944.
Northbridge Rectory, Hamish Hamilton, 1944.
Miss Bunting, Hamish Hamilton, 1945.
Peace Breaks Out, Hamish Hamilton, 1947.
Private Enterprise, Hamish Hamilton, 1947.
Love among Ruins, Hamish Hamilton, 1948.
The Old Bank House, Hamish Hamilton, 1949.
County Chronicle, Hamish Hamilton, 1950.
The Duke's Daughter, Hamish Hamilton, 1951.
Happy Returns, Hamish Hamilton, 1952.
Jutland Cottage, Hamish Hamilton, 1953.
What Did It Mean?, Hamish Hamilton, 1954.
Enter Sir Robert, Hamish Hamilton, 1955.
Never Too Late, Hamish Hamilton, 1956.
A Double Affair, Hamish Hamilton, 1957.
Close Quarters, Hamish Hamilton, 1958.
Love at All Ages, Hamish Hamilton, 1959.
Three Score and Ten, Hamish Hamilton, 1961.
An Angela Thirkell Omnibus, Hamish Hamilton, 1966.
A Second Angela Thirkell Omnibus, Hamish Hamilton, 1967.
The Brandons, and Others, Hamish Hamilton, 1968.

Also author of *The Fortunes of Harriette: The Surprising Career of Harriette Wilson,* 1936. Contributor of short stories to periodicals in Australia and Great Britain.

SIDELIGHTS: British author Angela Thirkell was a prolific novelist whose career spanned some three decades. Between the 1930s and 1950s, her books were popular with audiences in both Great Britain and the United States. For her settings Thirkell borrowed eighteenth-century novelist Anthony Trollope's fictional Bartsetshire, but she wrote predominantly about characters in modern times. Nevertheless, critics often compared her gentle, humorous tone to that of another eighteenth-century novelist, Jane Austen. Some of Thirkell's better-known novels include *Pomfret Towers, The Brandons,* and *Marling Hall,* and several of her books remain in print. She is also well-known for the memoir of her childhood, *Three Houses.*

Angela Thirkell was born Angela Margaret Mackail on January 30, 1890, in London, England. The daughter of a poetry professor, she was also the granddaughter of Pre-Raphaelite artist Edward Burne-Jones, who would draw pictures for her at her request during her childhood. Thirkell was also related to famed British writer Rudyard Kipling, and spent a great deal of time with his daughter Josephine; the two girls were the trial audience for Kipling's *Just So Stories.* Thirkell recalls these and other experiences in detail in *Three Houses,* first published in 1931.

Thirkell married a famed singer, James Campbell McInnes, in 1911. Though the couple had three children—one of which died in infancy—they were divorced in 1917. She married again the following year, this time to George Thirkell, an Australian military man. The Thirkells travelled to Australia in a troopship in 1920, an experience upon which Angela Thirkell would later base her 1934 novel *Trooper to the Southern Cross.* The couple lived for a while in Tasmania before settling in Melbourne, where Angela Thirkell became a member of the higher social circles, friend to such Australian notables as Dame Nellie Melba, Sir John Monash, and Thea Parker.

Partly because of a desire to write and partly because of a need to earn money, Thirkell began writing short stories while living in Melbourne. She managed to get some of her works published in periodicals in both Australia and England. Thirkell gave birth to another son in 1921, although her marriage was troubled. When her husband's business failed because of the Great Depression, she left him and returned to England in 1929.

Shortly after coming back to England, Thirkell published her book of memoirs, *Three Houses,* which Dennis Drabelle later praised in the *Washington Post Book World* as "a genial exercise in nostalgia for a time when houses were enormous, children scampered through them in disregard of nannies and art popped up everywhere." In 1933 readers saw a virtual explosion of novels from Thirkell—*Ankle Deep, High Rising,* and *Wild Strawberries,* all published by Hamish Hamilton. Thirkell continued to publish one or more novels each year, with few exceptions, until her death in 1961. She took time off from her busy writing schedule in 1949, however, to travel to the United States and give lectures at Yale and Columbia Universities.

BIOGRAPHICAL/CRITICAL SOURCES:

BOOKS

McInnes, Graham, *The Road to Gundagai,* Hamish Hamilton, 1965.
Strickland, Margot, *Angela Thirkell, Portrait of a Lady Novelist,* Duckworth, 1977.

PERIODICALS

Washington Post Book World, February 8, 1987, p. 8.*

* * *

THOMPSON, Donald 1928-

PERSONAL: Born February 28, 1928, in Columbus, OH; son of John Thompson (in livestock feeds research) and Margaret (Prosser) Thompson (a teacher); married Lois Eschenberg, 1952 (divorced, 1972); married Annie Figueroa (a university teacher), January 23, 1972; children: (first marriage) John Christopher, Leslie Ann; (second marriage) John Anthony Donald. *Education:* University of Missouri, A.B., B.S., 1952, M.A., 1954; attended University of Vienna, 1960-61, and Vienna Academy of Music and Theater, 1960-61; University of Iowa, Ph.D., 1970. *Religion:* Protestant.

ADDRESSES: Home and office—N-64 Acadia St., Park Gardens, Rio Piedras, Puerto Rico.

CAREER: Stephens College, Columbia, MO, instructor in music, 1952-54; Christian College, Columbia, instructor in music, 1953-54; University of Puerto Rico, Mayaguez, instructor in general studies, 1954-56; University of Puerto Rico, Rio Piedras, began as assistant professor, became professor of music, 1956-86, chair of department, 1981-86. *San Juan Star,* music critic, 1957-60 and 1975-92; free-lance music director, 1960—; member, Puerto Rico Symphony Orchestra, 1963-73; occasional consultant in arts administration and music in higher education for Musical Arts Corporation and Council of

Higher Education, 1987—. *Military service:* U.S. Army, 1947-49; became private first class.

MEMBER: Puerto Rico Musical Society (president, 1973-77), Music Library Association, College Music Society, Phi Beta Kappa.

AWARDS, HONORS: "Columns" award, Overseas Press Club of Puerto Rico, 1979; essay prize, Puerto Rico Commission for the Fifth Centennial of the Discovery of Puerto Rico, 1992, for "The Contributions of 'Americanos' to Puerto Rican Culture: Education and the Arts."

WRITINGS:

(With wife, Annie Figueroa Thompson) *Manual para monografias musicales,* Editorial Universitaria, 1980.
(Compiler with A. F. Thompson) *Music and Dance in Puerto Rico from the Age of Columbus to Modern Times: An Annotated Bibliography,* Scarecrow Press, 1991.
(Editor and translator) *Music in Puerto Rico: An Anthology of Writings in Translation,* Scarecrow Press, 1993.

Also author of *An Island's Music: A Quarter-Century of Music Reviews in the "San Juan Star,"* in press. Contributor to books, including *Ensayos en honor de Domingo Santa Cruz,* edited by Luis Merino, Universidad de Chile, 1986; *New Grove Dictionary of Opera,* edited by Stanley Sadie, Macmillan, 1992; *Composers of Latin America: A Biographical Dictionary,* edited by Enrique Arias, Greenwood Press, in press. Contributor to periodicals, including *Que Pasa, Revista musical de Venezuela, Revista musical chilena,* and *Inter-American Music Review.* Editorial board member of *Yearbook for Interamerican Music Research,* 1971-75, and *College Music Symposium,* 1979-86; editor, *Music Library Association Bibliography and Index Series,* 1975-79; guest coeditor, *Revista/Review Interamericana,* 1979-80; editorial coordinator for Puerto Rico, *Diccionario de musica espanola e hispanoamericana,* 1989—, and *Bibliografia musicologica latinoamericana,* 1990—.

WORK IN PROGRESS: Research on various aspects of the history of music in Puerto Rico.

SIDELIGHTS: Donald Thompson told *CA:* "In the main, my research and writing have been guided by two factors. One has been my curiosity regarding the history of music in Puerto Rico as a part of the Spanish Empire in the Caribbean until 1898, coupled with the existing general lack of completely reliable information on that subject. The other factor has been the interest of colleagues abroad in learning about the island's music. In addition, it has been perfectly natural to combine research and publication with my main work as a university teacher. This rather systematic approach also characterized my work as a music critic in the island's daily press, where I always attempted to place the event of the moment (concert, opera, or premiere performance of a new work) within some broader context, usually historical. To paraphrase, you can take the teacher out of the classroom, but you can't take the classroom out of the teacher!"

*　　　*　　　*

THOMPSON, James Myers
See THOMPSON, Jim (Myers)

*　　　*　　　*

THOMPSON, Jim (Myers)　1906-1977(?)
(James Myers Thompson)

PERSONAL: Born in 1906 in Anadarko, OK; died April 7, 1977 (some sources say 1976); married, 1931; wife's name, Alberta; children: three. *Education:* Received B.A. from University of Nebraska.

CAREER: Writer. Journalist for the New York *Daily News* and Los Angeles *Times Mirror*. Associated with Federal Writers Project in 1930s. Worked variously as an oil pipeline worker, steeplejack, burlesque actor, and professional gambler.

AWARDS, HONORS: Screen Award nomination, Writers Guild of America, West, Inc., for *Paths of Glory*.

WRITINGS:

NOVELS, EXCEPT AS NOTED

Now and on Earth, Modern Age, 1942.
Heed the Thunder, Greenberg Publishing, 1946.
Nothing More Than Murder, Harper, 1949.
Cropper's Cabin, Lion Books, 1952.
The Killer inside Me, Lion Books, 1953.
The Alcoholics, Lion Books, 1953.
Bad Boy (fictionalized memoir; also see below), Lion Books, 1953.
The Criminal, Lion Books, 1953.
Recoil, Lion Books, 1953.
Savage Night, Lion Books, 1953.
A Swell-Looking Babe, Lion Books, 1954.
The Golden Gizmo (also see below), Lion Books, 1954.
A Hell of a Woman, Lion Books, 1954.
The Nothing Man (also see below), Dell, 1954.
Roughneck (also see below), Lion Books, 1954.
After Dark, My Sweet, Popular Library, 1955.
(With Stanley Kubrick) *The Killing* (screenplay; adapted from the novel *Clean Break* by Lionel White), United Artists (UA), 1956.
(With Stanley Kubrick and Calder Willingham) *Paths of Glory* (screenplay; adapted from the novel by Humphrey Cobb), Bryna Productions/UA, 1957.

The Kill-Off (also see below), Lion Books, 1957.
Wild Town, New American Library, 1957.
The Getaway, New American Library, 1959.
The Transgressors, New American Library, 1961.
The Grifters, Regency, 1963.
Pop. 1280, Fawcett, 1964.
Texas by the Tail, Fawcett, 1965.
Ironside (novelization of television series), Popular Library, 1967.
South of Heaven, Fawcett, 1967.
The Undefeated (novelization of screenplay), Popular Library, 1969.
Nothing but a Man (novelization of screenplay), Popular Library, 1970.
Child of Rage, Lancer Militaria, 1972.
King Blood, Sphere, 1973.
Hard Core (omnibus; contains *Bad Boy*, *The Nothing Man*, and *The Kill-Off*), Fine, 1986.
More Hardcore (omnibus; contains *The Golden Gizmo*, *Roughneck*, and *The Ripoff*), Fine, 1987.
Fireworks: The Lost Writings of Jim Thompson (anthology; includes "The End of the Book," "The Slave Girl in the Cellar," and "This World, Then the Fireworks"), Fine, 1988.

Also wrote under name variation James Myers Thompson. Author of screenplay *Killer at Large*. Work has also appeared in *Jim Thompson: The Killers inside Him*, by Max Allan Collins and Ed Gorman, Fedora Press, 1983. Contributor to television series *Dr. Kildare*.

ADAPTATIONS: The Getaway was adapted for film by Walter Hill and released by National General, 1972; *The Killer inside Me* was adapted for film by Edward Mann and Robert Chamblee and released by Warner Bros., 1976; *Pop. 1280* was adapted for film under the title *Coup de Torchon* by Bertrand Tavernier and Jean Aurenche and released by Par-Afrance, 1981; *After Dark, My Sweet* was adapted for film by James Foley and Robert Redlin and released by Avenue, 1990; *The Kill-Off* was adapted for film by Maggie Greenwald and released by Cabriolet, 1990; *The Grifters* was adapted for film by Donald E. Westlake and released by Miramax, 1990.

SIDELIGHTS: Jim Thompson, an American writer, was best known for his mystery and suspense paperback books that are fraught with immorality and explorations into the criminal mind. His books typically feature depraved protagonists who are involved in theft, sadomasochism, or murder. "Thompson at his best casts the coldest possible eye on life and death and offers us an unsparing view of the human condition," assessed *New York Times Book Review* contributor Lawrence Block. Thompson's disturbing character studies, composed primarily in the 1950s and 1960s, are classified as pulp fiction—sensationalized writing bound in flashy, soft covers. At the time of his death in 1977, Thompson had received diminutive notice from critics, and all of his books were out of print. But more than a decade later, some of his volumes were republished in hardcover omnibus editions and adapted for film, finally bringing Thompson's work under critical review. Meredith Brody, writing in *Film Comment,* suggested, "His body of work may be the most disturbing and the most darkly sadistic of the tough-guy writers." And *New Republic*'s David Thomson called him "one of the finest American writers and the most frightening, the one on best terms with the devil."

Thompson began writing as a teenager, but it wasn't until he was thirty-six years old that he published his first novel. In the following years, he wrote hurriedly, producing ten books in the span of one year alone. Lion Books editor Arnold Hano told *Tough Guy Writers of the Thirties* essayist R. V. Cassill that Thompson wrote the novel *The Killer inside Me* in only two weeks. This 1953 book, considered Thompson's best work by many critics, was inspired by a real-life experience with a West Texas deputy sheriff. Thompson described the encounter in his memoir *Bad Boy.* He notes that as a young man, he was caught eluding a drunk and disorderly fine by the deputy. The law officer approached him and threatened, "Everyone knows me. No one knows you. And we're all alone. What do you make o' that, a smart fella like you? . . . What do you think an ol' stupid country boy might do in a case like this?" This discourse left him wondering if he could have been killed by the agitated officer.

From this occurrence, Thompson developed the main character, Lou Ford, for *The Killer inside Me.* Ford is presented as the well-liked deputy sheriff of a small city in Oklahoma. However, residents are unaware that a schizophrenic, sadistic, and murderous personality lurks beneath the surface of the laughing and jovial lawman. Ford, the narrator, reveals the inner workings of his sinister mind and provides gory details of his murderous attacks. To keep suspicions away from himself, he kills anyone who doubts his innocence in the homicides. When he suspects that his lover is becoming aware of his second self, he plots to marry and later kill her. During their marriage, Ford hits his wife regularly—an act that sexually arouses her—eventually beating her to death. Finally, the community has misgivings about the deputy sheriff's involvement in the murders, and citizens begin to investigate. The novel culminates in a harrowing confrontation between the people of the city and the crazed deputy. In his *New York Times Book Review* article, Block described Ford as Thompson's "single most memorable character." *New Republic*'s Thomson declared of the author's protagonists, "They talk to us in a way we *know* after we have read the books that real-life mass murderers must talk to themselves." Writer and film director Stanley Kubrick as-

sessed *The Killer inside Me* as "probably the most chilling and believable first-person story of a criminally warped mind I have ever encountered" in Thomson's *New Republic* review.

In 1955 Thompson published *After Dark, My Sweet,* another novel featuring a deranged narrator. In the story, the dull-witted protagonist, Collie, collaborates with Fay Anderson, an alcoholic widow, and Uncle Bud, a crooked ex-cop, to kidnap a young boy for financial gain. They accomplish the task, and Collie and Fay become the boy's parental figures. Climactically, Collie kills himself to protect Fay and the boy. *After Dark, My Sweet* differs from other Thompson books because its narrator attempts to resist his violent tendencies. Also this volume provides "that rare animal in Thompson: a wholly coherent, satisfying ending," according to Max Allen Collins in his essay for *Murder off the Rack: Critical Studies of Ten Paperback Masters.* And the same reviewer lauded the book as being "the most accessible, best-crafted of Thompson's psychopath-as-narrator novels."

Following *After Dark, My Sweet,* Thompson was requested by Kubrick to contribute to his film adaptation of Lionel White's *Clean Break.* Released in 1956 as *The Killing,* the motion picture depicts dubious characters involved in an intricate plan to rob a racetrack of two million dollars. Following the heist, a murderous plot leads to the deaths of each thief, except for one. When the last criminal attempts to flee the country, an airport worker accidentally drops the suitcase, emptying the valuable contents. "*The Killing,* a fast-moving, tense, crime story, has been made with art and skill," judged *Saturday Review* contributor Hollis Alpert. He also concluded that "the dialogue is often pointed and refreshing."

Thompson again teamed with Kubrick on a 1957 film adaptation of Humphrey Cobb's novel *Paths of Glory.* He received a Screen Award nomination from the Writers Guild of America West for his contribution. The story details a World War I scandal set in 1916. General Mireau of the French Army, seeking to benefit his personal career, orders his division to attack a secured German post called "The Ant Hill." The mission results in defeat and heavy French casualties. Mireau, who perceives the loss as a result of cowardice, orders three soldiers to be chosen for execution. Colonel Dax defends each of the accused, but finds himself up against an unethical court. The soldiers are found guilty and condemned to death. Dax is offered a promotion soon after the incident, but he refuses to take it due to his disgust over the senseless decisions made by the French Army. In an appraisal of *Paths of Glory* for *The Motion Picture Guide,* a reviewer judged, "Beyond all doubt this is one of the greatest anti-war films ever made." Hollis Alpert, in an article for *Saturday Review,* described the movie as "the finest American film of the year. It is so searing in its intensity that it will probably take its place, in years to come, as one of the screen's most extraordinary achievements."

After assisting Kubrick with screenwriting, Thompson continued writing novels. In 1959 he published *The Getaway*—the portrait of a ring of bank robbers who deceive each other following a theft. In a series of events, all of the criminals are slain except for a husband and wife team who retreats to Mexico with the money. After crossing the border, they find themselves in hell, unable to leave. To stay alive, they must betray one another. "*The Getaway* is Thompson's finest third-person novel and may be his finest hour as a craftsman," remarked Collins. Although Thompson had adapted this book for film, his version was never produced. In 1972 Walter Hill's screenplay of *The Getaway* was made into a motion picture. The film curtailed the hell scene, which Thomson of *New Republic* stated "is the only part of the book that's unmistakable Jim Thompson." It was reported that Thompson was unhappy with Hill's screenplay. However, Stanley Kauffman, a *New Republic* writer, commented: "Outside of the (immense) flaw [Ali MacGraw's lead performance], the picture was smashing."

Among Thompson's other notable work is *The Grifters*. This book delves into the lives of and relationships between three con artists—a mother, a son, and his lover. Through their crooked scheming and greed, the characters contribute to their own demises. The novel, published in 1963, received greater recognition after the release of a critically acclaimed film of the same name nearly three decades later. A writer for *The Motion Picture Guide* pointed out that in the film version of *The Grifters*, "The characters speak in a faintly disconcerting 1950s argot right out of the book, adding an authentic flavor to the simmeringly suggestive stew."

Another of Thompson's successful novels is *Pop. 1280*, a black comedy focusing on sheriff Nick Corey whose personality greatly resembles Lou Ford of *The Killer inside Me*. Like Ford, this lawman is deranged enough to follow a neighboring town sheriff's unscrupulous advice: To kill the pimps who have been harassing him. Corey believes his actions are the will of God. An ironic twist occurs when Corey frames the other sheriff for the murders. During the course of the deadly machinations, the killer must also fend off rumors that his wife is having an affair with her slow brother. Comparing *Pop. 1280* to *The Killer inside Me*, Collins stated that the later volume, "a reworking of his most famous book, may be his best book." *New Republic*'s Thomson called *Pop. 1280* "Thompson's comic masterpiece," and later described it as "a gentle rustic comedy, with cracker-barrel jokes and a lunacy that rises like warm dough." *Newsweek* reviewer Peter S. Prescott

praised the book as "one of Thompson's best tales, and one of the most ingeniously designed."

Overall Thompson's works have met with praise from critics. "They are awesome books that look head-on into the abyss, even when their lazy killers are resting up and telling us how tiring everything is," lauded Thomson in his *New Republic* review. Prescott stated, "He may have written the kind of stories your parents wouldn't let you bring in the house, but he wrote them exceedingly well."

BIOGRAPHICAL/CRITICAL SOURCES:

BOOKS

Tough Guy Writers of the Thirties, edited by David Madden, Southern Illinois University Press, 1968, pp. 230-38.
Murder off the Rack: Critical Studies of Ten Paperback Masters, edited by Jon L. Breen and Martin Harry Greenberg, Scarecrow, 1989, pp. 35-54.
Collins, Max Allen, and Ed Gorman, *Jim Thompson: The Killers inside Him,* Fedora Press, 1983.
The Motion Picture Guide: 1927-1983, Volume VI, Cinebooks, 1986, p. 2356.
The Motion Picture Guide: 1991 Annual, Baseline, 1991, p. 70.

PERIODICALS

Film Comment, September-October, 1984, pp. 46-47.
New Republic, February 10, 1973, pp. 35, 41; April 15, 1985, pp. 37-41.
New Statesman, February 12, 1988, p. 32.
Newsweek, November 17, 1986, p. 90; February 4, 1991, p. 71.
New York Times Book Review, October 14, 1990, pp. 37-38.
New Yorker, January 4, 1958, p. 70.
Publishers Weekly, July 27, 1984, p. 141.
Rolling Stone, November 1, 1990.
Saturday Review, August 4, 1956, p. 32; December 21, 1957, pp. 31-32.
Village Voice Literary Supplement, February, 1982, p. 19.*

—*Sketch by Jane M. Kelly*

*   *   *

TIERNEY, Ronald   1944-

PERSONAL: Born December 12, 1944, in Indianapolis, IN; son of J. Gregory (in restaurant business) and Frances Ruth (in restaurant business; maiden name, Laughner) Tierney. *Education:* Attended Indiana University, 1963-76.

ADDRESSES: Home—North Kenwood Ave., Indianapolis, IN 46208.

CAREER: Worked in family restaurants in Indiana; worked in construction in Fort Wayne, IN; foreman on factory assembly line in South Bend, IN; worked for a bank in Indianapolis, IN, became officer, 1969-76; co-owner of a frame shop in Bloomington, IN, 1977-78; affiliated with Levi Strauss & Co., 1978-82; Ernest Players, San Francisco, CA, cofounder and playwright, 1978-82; *Nob Hill Gazette,* San Francisco, editor, 1982-83; worked as copywriter and advertising manager in Indianapolis, 1984-89; founding editor of *NUVO Newsweekly* (an alternative weekly newspaper) in Indianapolis, 1989-90; writer. *Military service:* U.S. Army, 1966-68, served in Vietnam; became specialist 5 in information; received Army Commendation Medal.

MEMBER: Mystery Writers of America, Private Eye Writers of America.

AWARDS, HONORS: Shamus Award nomination, best first novel, Private Eye Writers of America, 1990.

WRITINGS:

The Stone Veil, St. Martin's, 1990.
The Steel Web, St. Martin's, 1991.
The Iron Glove, St. Martin's, 1992.
Eclipse of the Heart, St. Martin's, 1993.

Author of plays, including *Death in Bloom.*

WORK IN PROGRESS: The Concrete Pillow.

SIDELIGHTS: Ronald Tierney told *CA:* "I am most comfortable writing about ordinary people caught in extraordinary circumstances. My 'Shanahan' private eye series is about a sixty-nine-year-old, semi-retired detective living in Indianapolis. It's not a glamorous setting, and 'Deets' is not a glamorous guy. His wife left him thirty years earlier, taking with her Shanahan's then ten-year-old son. Since that time, he has contented himself with Cubs games, his backyard garden, the camaraderie of his Army buddy, Harry, and the generally small-time investigations nobody else wants.

"What I wanted to do was show that even nearing seventy, a person's life need not be over. So while each Shanahan book is a complete whodunit, the main character evolves as he would in a conventional novel. As the series progresses, Shanahan—through more elaborate and dangerous cases—is increasingly thrust into life. At the same time a more human story unfolds as he begins to confront his past and construct a future. There are common threads that run through this series. One is that life is never over until the last breath is taken. The other is abuse of power—physical, financial, and political—because it is the feeling of powerlessness that defeats us.

"My own career could be described at best as 'checkered.' As far as education goes, I didn't complete college. I never could make up my mind. I switched majors from theatre to journalism to religion and back again. I'd like to think I've made up for my less-than-stunning academic credentials by living a kind of itinerant life. Many jobs, many places—from busing dishes and working a construction site to banking and editing a society newspaper. If a writer's fiction is molded by the life he or she has lived, then I can write with at least some degree of realism about pretty much everybody.

"My first few attempts at a novel were pretty bad. My biggest problem was structure. In the past my writing had tended to meander—the story was merely a series of tangents. By 1990 I had completed three worthless novels and several unpublishable short stories. I noticed a contest asking for entries in St. Martin's annual private eye competition. Mysteries? Was there a better way to learn the craft of writing and to reign in a wandering plot? They also provided a minimum word count and a real deadline.

"The result was *The Stone Veil,* a finalist in St. Martin's competition and a Shamus nomination for best first novel by the Private Eye Writers of America. The book was syndicated in a Hungarian magazine and briefly optioned for movie rights. This introduced Shanahan, and I discovered there was a whole lot more I wanted to say about this man. And while the book didn't shatter any sales records, the reviews were encouraging. The second book, *The Steel Web,* also met with good reviews from the critics, and St. Martin's Press decided they would publish another.

"After *The Iron Glove,* the third modestly successful book in the Shanahan series, I am venturing beyond the sixty-nine-year-old detective as subject. *Eclipse of the Heart* is about a middle-aged San Franciscan caught in circumstances that force him from his comfortable life and bring him face to face with what it means to be alive. The main character, a rather passionless man who makes his living writing cookbooks, is asked during the idle chatter of a dinner party what he would kill for. The answer the reclusive gay author gives his host is not the same answer he discovers during what was supposed to be a harmless holiday in Mexico.

"Though I will continue the St. Martin's detective series, I am working on another San Francisco-based novel. If it has to be categorized, the current work is probably more suspense than mystery, but I hope it is more novel than either. Power and powerlessness play the key roles as several lives converge because of a tragic series of brutal murders. It has as much to do with the effect of the brutal slayings on the characters' lives as it has with who committed them.

"I believe I am an Indiana writer, no matter where I set my stories. Though I'll always be a midwesterner, there is a constant sense of wanting to do something else and of wanting to be somewhere else. If all goes well, the Shanahan series will continue to be my link to Indiana and to the mystery genre. But I need to move on too—writing other types of books and living in other places. What I suspect won't change is what I want my work to do. In all my writing, my goal is to create characters with as much dimension as possible. None are perfectly evil or perfectly good. I want the lives and the situations to be easily understood and believable. I want the story to yield insight. And in the end, I hope there is for the reader—after the humor and the tragedy—some value for having read it beyond a few hours of escape."

BIOGRAPHICAL/CRITICAL SOURCES:

PERIODICALS

Armchair Detective, winter, 1991, p. 32.
Kirkus Reviews, February 15, 1990, p. 227; September 15, 1991, p. 1186.
New York Times Book Review, April 8, 1990, p. 26.
Publishers Weekly, January 26, 1990, p. 406; September 27, 1991, p. 46.

*   *   *

TOBIAS, Michael (Charles) 1951-

PERSONAL: Born June 27, 1951, in San Francisco, CA; son of William and Betty Tobias; married Jane Gray Morrison (a television producer and opera singer). *Education:* University of Colorado, B.A., 1972; attended University of Tel Aviv, Israel; University of California, Santa Cruz, Ph.D., 1977. *Politics:* "Green Party and Democratic Party." *Religion:* "Russian Jew and Indian Jain." *Avocational interests:* "Mountain climbing, all music, zoosemiotics, ethnology, Antarctic microbial ecology, Himalayan lichen studies, all matters pertaining to birds, rocks, gardens, ants, primates, snow leopards, children, and other mammals."

ADDRESSES: Agent—Julie Castiglia Literary Agency, 1155 Camino Del Mar, Suite 510, Del Mar, CA 92014.

CAREER: Dartmouth College, Hanover, NH, assistant professor of ecology and humanities and adjunct professor of English, 1978-80; California State University, Northridge, visiting associate professor of humanities, 1983-85; KQED-PBS, San Francisco, CA, science and current affairs producer, 1985-87; Maryland Public Broadcasting, Owings Mills, MD, executive producer for national and international productions, 1987-89; JMT Productions, president, director, writer, producer, and executive producer, 1989—; director and producer of television programs, including *Mini-Dragons,* Maryland Public Television, 1988, *Sea Power,* Maryland Public Television,

1988, and *The Sixth Annual Genesis Awards,* Discovery Channel, 1992.

MEMBER: People for the Ethical Treatment of Animals, The University of Non-violence—Siddhachalam, Greenpeace, World Wildlife Fund, Population Education Committee.

AWARDS, HONORS: Best of the West Award for best documentary, 1984, for *Kazantzakis;* best mountain film, Banff International Film Festival, 1985, for *Cloudwalker;* Emmy Award nomination, best national news series, 1986 and 1987, both for *Science Notes;* Genesis Award for outstanding network news documentary, 1987, for *Animal Rights;* Cindy Award, Humboldt State University Film Festival Winner, and National Film and Video Winner, all 1987, all for *Ahimsa;* Genesis Award for outstanding network docudrama, 1990, for *Voice of the Planet;* Cine Golden Eagle Award, National Film & Television Golden Apple Award, and Grand Jury Prize, Houston International Film Festival, all 1990, all for *Black Tide;* Emmy Award nomination and two Awards for Cablecasting Excellence (ACE) nominations, all 1991, all for *Black Tide.*

WRITINGS:

NONFICTION

Tsa, IMAJ Institute, 1972.
Dhaulagirideon, Antioch Journal Press, 1973.
Biography of Self-Consciousness, Ann Arbor Microfilms, 1977.
The Mountain Spirit, Viking, 1979.
Deep Ecology, Avant Books, 1984.
After Eden: History, Ecology, & Conscience, Slawson Communications, 1984.
Mountain People (also see below), University of Oklahoma Press, 1986.
One Earth, HarperCollins, 1990.
Life Force: The World of Jainism, Asian Humanities Press, 1991.
Environmental Meditation, Crossing Press, 1993.
A Vision of Nature: Traces of the Original World, Kent State University Press, in press.

FICTION

Deva, Avant Books, 1982.
Ice Bird, Avant Books, 1984.
Voice of the Planet (also see below), Bantam, 1990.
Fatal Exposure, Pocket Books, 1991.
Believe, Berkeley Books, 1992.
Mahavira, Asian Humanities Press, 1993.
Felham's War, Rupa & Co. (New Delhi), 1993.

Also author of *Rage and Reason,* 1993.

FOR TELEVISION

The Tracker, National Broadcasting Co., Inc. (NBC-TV), 1982.

The Lost Tribe, American Broadcasting Co., Inc. (ABC-TV), 1983.

Kazantzakis, Public Broadcasting Service (PBS-TV), 1984.

House for All Seasons, PBS-TV, 1984.

Cloudwalker, Goldcrest Films, 1985.

Science Notes (series), PBS-TV, 1985-87.

Sand and Lightning, PBS-TV, 1986.

Space Futures, PBS-TV, 1986.

The Gift, PBS-TV, 1986.

Destined for Greatness, PBS-TV, 1986.

Animal Rights, PBS-TV, 1986.

Ozone Crisis, PBS-TV, 1987.

The Future of Antarctica, PBS-TV, 1987.

Antarctica: The Last Continent, PBS-TV, 1987.

Ahimsa: Non-violence, PBS-TV, 1987.

Black Tide, Discovery Channel, 1990.

The Making of "Voice of the Planet," Turner Broadcasting System, Inc. (TBS-TV), 1990.

Voice of the Planet (series; adapted from author's book of same title), TBS-TV, 1991.

A Day in the Life of Ireland, PBS-TV, 1992.

OTHER

Harry and Arthur (two-act play), produced in Hollywood, CA, 1991.

Contributor of essays and reviews to periodicals including *Discovery, Bloomsbury Review, Kenyon Review, New Scientist, San Francisco Review of Books, Sciences,* and *Greenpeace.*

ADAPTATIONS: Mountain People was adapted into a pilot episode for a television series, Maryland Public Television, 1988.

WORK IN PROGRESS: Fiction titles including *Vermeer* and *The Immortals: Three Novellas;* nonfiction works including *A Paradox of Souls: Human Population at the End of the Millennium, A History of Idealism,* and *True Conscience,* a treatise concerning animal ethics; feature films, documentary specials, and television series, including *Fatal Exposure, Believe, Freedom: The Life of Susan B. Anthony,* and *Cezanne and Pissarro; Marcus Aurelius Antoninus,* a play.

SIDELIGHTS: Michael Tobias told *CA:* "I am driven by my love of the inaccessible, which compels me in my books and films, my music and mountain climbing, to contradict the motionless moment of insight; to stem the chasm separating tranquility and chaos, to live here and now in spite of the immortality which is assured all things of the earth.

"It is easy to achieve heaven, since we were born there. It is far more difficult to believe that humanity can ease the pain which everywhere assails life, but this has been the guiding path in my work—to imagine, to convey, to feel my way towards some hoped for nexus of physical, biological, and emotional amelioration that is at once joyous and aesthetic.

"In this regard, I have been especially influenced by a number of locales, movements, and visionaries. These include the regions of Bhutan, southwestern Alaska, Bora Bora, and the western peninsula of Antarctica; it includes the philosophy of Jainism, the works of Vermeer, Giorgione, Jan Van Eyck and George Inness; the poetry of Shelley, the fantasias of Purcell; the writing of Kazantzakis, Sannazaro, Cervantes, and Aurelius; the fancies of Hugh Lofting, and the explorations of Kingdon-Ward. Much of my attachment to these aesthetic parts of the puzzle have been explored in my book *A Vision of Nature: Traces of the Original World,* but they in fact inform all of my efforts.

"I would like to see a constitutional amendment mandating vegetarianism, eliminating any and all exploitation of animals—for any purposes. And by animals, naturally, I include homo sapiens. I am also as indebted to plants—congruent with Jainism. I acknowledge that no plant wants to be eaten, and have frequently felt the agitation and neurological unhappiness which consumption must cause plants. Nevertheless, in an imperfect evolutionary schema such as we find ourselves, our goal should be to *minimize* violence. I therefore uphold the philosophy of Jainism which believes that people have certain, profound responsibilities; in order to sustain these responsibilities, to do good in this world, they should prevent themselves from starving to death unnecessarily. And thus, that will inevitably mean the limited consumption of certain fruits, vegetables, and grains. This ascetic discipline is in fact a social blueprint most appropriate to our age, I feel, given the enormous pain that wracks the biosphere. Art, for myself, grows out of that pain, and is in turn bolstered by the myriad joy which I perceive in saying "no" to pain; in fostering peace, in helping all other life forms to the best of my limited ability.

"For in the end, if the pleasures and imaginings of the artist and the appreciator are not sufficient to engender happiness in others, then such passions are tragically useless. The solipsism of all art need not perpetuate isolationism. In a world stricken with ecological collapse, the only hope for human beings—and all kindred life forms—is that the artist take some responsibility for engendering ideals, and ideal joys, beyond his immediate self-satisfaction."

TONKIN, Elizabeth 1934-

PERSONAL: Born February 11, 1934, in Richmond, Surrey, England. *Education:* Oxford University, M.A., D.Phil., 1971.

ADDRESSES: Office—Department of Social Anthropology, Queen's University of Belfast, Belfast BT7 1NN, Northern Ireland.

CAREER: British Civil Service, worked as English teacher in Kenya; Ahmadu Bello University, Zaria, Nigeria, lecturer in English, 1963-66; University of Birmingham, Center of West African Studies, Edgbaston, England, worked as lecturer and senior lecturer in social anthropology, 1970-91; Queen's University of Belfast, Belfast, Northern Ireland, professor, 1991—; social anthropologist.

MEMBER: Anthropological Association of the Commonwealth, Royal Anthropological Institute (fellow), African Studies Association of the United Kingdom.

WRITINGS:

(Editor with Maryon McDonald and Malcolm Chapman) *History and Ethnicity,* Routledge, 1989.
Narrating Our Pasts: Social Construction of Oral History, Cambridge University Press, 1992.

WORK IN PROGRESS: Research on social construction of selves through memory.

SIDELIGHTS: Elizabeth Tonkin told *CA:* "After teaching in Kenya and Nigeria I went back to Oxford for a year's 'conversion' to social anthropology and stayed on to take a doctorate in the subject. During my years as a lecturer in social anthropology at the University of Birmingham I also did fieldwork in Liberia. The people's interest in their past led me to discuss it with them and to record it. This experience stimulated my thinking about the role of 'representations of pastness' in everyone's life and hence in the construction of social life. Present sad conditions in Liberia make work there virtually impossible, but I hope to research differences in remembering in Northern Ireland and the culture of missionary families. I remain very interested in the relation between anthropology and history."

*   *   *

TORY, Avraham 1909-

PERSONAL: Name originally Avraham Golub; name changed, 1950; born December 10, 1909, in Lazdijai, Lithuania; immigrated to Israel, 1947, naturalized citizen, 1947; son of Zoruch Golub and Sara Prusak; married Pnina Ushpitz (an economist), August 10, 1944; children: Shulamith Karby, Alina Tory, Zila Magdasi. *Education:* Attended Hebrew University, Berclay University, and Tel-Aviv University. *Politics:* "Independent Liberal." *Religion:* Jewish.

ADDRESSES: Home—17 Neardea St., Tel-Aviv, Israel. *Office*—Ramahl St., P.O. Box 37795, Tel-Aviv 61376, Israel.

CAREER: Called to the Israeli bar, 1952; attorney in private practice in Tel-Aviv, Israel, 1952—; writer. Maccabi World Jewish Sports Movement Council, executive member; Holocaust Museum and Study, "MASUA," executive member; Beth Hatefutzoth—Diaspora Museum, executive member. *Military service:* Served with Israeli Army.

MEMBER: International Association of Jewish Lawyers and Jurists (member of presidency), Israeli Bar Association, World Zionist Organization Action Committee, National Council for Soviet Jewry, Lithuanian Jewish Academicians (chair of the union).

AWARDS, HONORS: Award from Israel Ministry of Defense.

WRITINGS:

Teruma: Yehudim mi-lita le-vinyan ha-arets u-Medinat Yisra'el (nonfiction; title means "Almanach: Lithuanian Jews in the Upbuilding of the Promised Land"), Ihud Akadaema'im Yots'e Lita, 1988.
Geto yom-yom: Yoman u-mismakhim mi-Geto Kovnah (nonfiction) Universitat Tel-Aviv, 1988, translation by Jerzy Michalowicz published as *Surviving the Holocaust: The Kovno Ghetto Diary,* edited by Martin Gilbert, Harvard University Press, 1990.

Also author of *Habrycha meafort hatshii* (title means "The Legendary Escape from the IX Fortress"), 1945; *Bishviley Habricha Vehazala* (title means "Paths of Rescue and Daring"), 1954; *Hagimnasion Haivri be Marijampole* (title means "The Hebrew Gymnasia Marijampole"), 1983; and *Alyha bilti legalit le Palestine* (nonfiction; title means "Clandestine Immigration to Palestine, 1944-1948"). Contributor of articles and reviews to legal journals.

WORK IN PROGRESS: A history of the Maccabi World movement; a personal account of forty-year law practice in Israel; study on the Holocaust and its aftermath in Lithuania.

SIDELIGHTS: More than forty years after World War II, Jewish nonfiction writer Avraham Tory drew upon his carefully documented records of that time to produce *Surviving the Holocaust: The Kovno Ghetto Diary.* In this work, Tory recounts how German troops rolled into his hometown of Kovno, Lithuania, in June of 1941, killed five thousand of the Jewish residents and herded thirty-five thousand others into a ghetto. This tactic, the author recalls, met with no opposition from his fellow countrymen. In *Surviving the Holocaust,* Tory wrote, "The Lithuanians did not conceal their joy at the outbreak of the war: they saw their place on the side of the swastika and expressed this sentiment openly." Some Lithuanians carried out executions for the Nazis; on October 20, these co-conspirators shot ten thousand prisoners.

Under order of the Nazis, an Elders Council was formed in the ghetto to handle day-to-day details. Already a lawyer, Tory became the secretary of the Kovno council. Almost immediately he began keeping a diary, recording the transformation of the once bustling town into a prison. The author also adds that the ghetto inmates tried to maintain a semblance of a normal community even in the shadow of Nazi atrocity. Tory tells of the doubts within the council that actual compliance with Nazi orders would avert annihilation. They decided to make themselves indispensable to the German war effort by offering manufacturing services such as shoe repair, linen mending and brush production.

Tory kept Nazi decrees and council reports with his diary. Because he would have been killed if these writing had been discovered, the author hid these documents. Before he escaped from Kovno in March of 1944, he buried his records in the foundation of a building, returning several months later to retrieve them. By then, the remaining eight thousand Jewish residents had been shipped to concentration camps in Germany.

Surviving the Holocaust is recognized as a distinguished entry in the canon of Holocaust writings. Because of his record keeping and ownership of official Nazi documents, the information in *Surviving the Holocaust* has served as an exhibit in several Nazi war crime trials at which Tory has testified. According to Robert S. Wistrich in the *Times Literary Supplement,* "the diary lucidly records the heroic will to survive and to preserve of minimum of decency and morality while subjected to indescribable degradation." Louise Erdrich, writing in Chicago *Tribune Books,* concluded: "Tory's careful collection of Nazi edicts shows exactly how evil can be accomplished." Erdrich added, "The power of this book lies precisely in its lack of poetry, in its refusal to generalize. . . . The very understatement of the day to day entries becomes a slow, grinding wail."

BIOGRAPHICAL/CRITICAL SOURCES:

BOOKS

Tory, Avraham, *Surviving the Holocaust: The Kovno Ghetto Diary,* translation by Jerzy Michalowicz, edited by Martin Gilbert, Harvard University Press, 1990.

PERIODICALS

New York Review of Books, November 8, 1990, pp, 52-57.
Times Literary Supplement, November 23-29, 1990, pp. 1261-1262.
Tribune Books (Chicago), May 20, 1990, pp. 1, 4.

* * *

TOWNSEND, Richard (Fraser) 1938-

PERSONAL: Born November 18, 1938, in Asheville, NC; son of Charles (a photographer) and Ellis (a writer and illustrator of children's books; maiden name, Credle) Townsend; married; wife's name, Pala Jacqueline (a painter and teacher of art). *Education:* Attended Mexico City College, 1957-58; University of New Mexico, B.A., 1964; Universidad de las Americas, M.A. (magna cum laude), 1966; Harvard University, Ph.D., 1975.

ADDRESSES: Office—Department of Africa, Oceania, and the Americas, Art Institute of Chicago, Michigan Ave. at Adams St., Chicago, IL 60603.

CAREER: University of Nebraska, Lincoln, instructor in art history, 1967-69; University of Texas at Austin, assistant professor of art, 1974-79; Art Institute of Chicago, Chicago, IL, curator of Department of Africa, Oceania, and the Americas, 1982—. Coproducer of the documentary film *Mexican Ceramics,* released by Bailey Films. *Military service:* U.S. Army, 1958-60; served in Germany.

AWARDS, HONORS: Fulbright scholar in Peru, 1965-66; senior fellow, Pre-Columbian Center, Dumbarton Oaks, 1978-79; grants from National Geographic Society, 1979 and 1980-81, Social Science Research Council, 1980-81, National Endowment for the Arts, 1983-85 and 1987, Center for Pre-Columbian Studies, Dumbarton Oaks, 1989—, Getty Foundation, 1992, National Endowment for the Humanities, and Rockefeller Foundation.

WRITINGS:

State and Cosmos in the Art of Tenochtitlan, Center for Pre-Columbian Studies, Dumbarton Oaks, 1979.
The Art of Tribes and Early Kingdoms: Selections from Chicago Collections, Art Institute of Chicago, 1984.
The Aztecs, Thames & Hudson, 1991.
(Editor and contributor) *The Ancient Americas: Art from Sacred Landscapes,* Art Institute of Chicago, 1992.

Work represented in anthologies, including *The Art and Iconography of Late Post-Classic Central Mexico,* edited by Elizabeth Benson and Elizabeth Boone, Center for Pre-Columbian Studies, Dumbarton Oaks, 1982; *Ethnoastronomy and Archaeoastronomy in the American Tropics,* edited by Anthony Aveni and Gary Urton, New

York Academy of Sciences, 1982; and *The Aztec Templo Mayor,* edited by Elizabeth Boone, Center for Pre-Columbian Studies, Dumbarton Oaks, 1986. Contributor to periodicals, including *Museum Studies.*

*   *   *

TREHUB, Arnold 1923-

PERSONAL: Born October 19, 1923, in Malden, MA; son of Clarence and Rose (Issner) Trehub; married Elaine Epstein (an archives librarian), August 12, 1950; children: Craig, Aaron, Lorna. *Education:* Northeastern University, B.A., 1949; Boston University, Ph.D., 1954.

ADDRESSES: Home—145 Farview Way, Amherst, MA 01002. *Office*—Department of Psychology, University of Massachusetts at Amherst, Amherst, MA 01003.

CAREER: Massachusetts General Hospital, Boston, research psychologist, 1953-54; Northampton Veterans Administration Medical Center, Northampton, MA, coordinator of research and director of Psychology Research Laboratory, 1954-82; University of Massachusetts at Amherst, adjunct professor of psychology, 1972—. *Military service:* U.S. Army Air Forces, 1943-46.

WRITINGS:

The Cognitive Brain, MIT Press, 1991.

Contributor to professional journals.

WORK IN PROGRESS: Continuing research on brain mechanisms of cognition.

*   *   *

TRIFFIN, Robert 1911-1993

OBITUARY NOTICE—See index for *CA* sketch: Born October 5, 1911, in Flobecq, Belgium; immigrated to United States, during 1930s, naturalized citizen, 1942; died February 23, 1993, in Ostend, Belgium. Economist, educator, and author. Triffin was a Belgium-born economist who, in the late 1950s, correctly predicted the downfall of the Bretton Woods Agreement, which was formulated to control exchange rates. A proponent of reform of the world monetary structure, Triffin also counseled European governments on the establishment of the European monetary system. In addition to advising various governments on economic issues, Triffin was an instructor at several universities and taught for more than three decades. He wrote numerous articles and books on international monetary reform, including *Europe and the Money Muddle, The Evolution of the International Monetary System: Historical Reappraisal and Future Perspectives, Gold and the Dollar Crisis,* and *The Fate of the Pound.*

OBITUARIES AND OTHER SOURCES:

BOOKS

Who's Who in America, 47th edition, Marquis, 1992.

PERIODICALS

New York Times, February 27, 1993, p. 27.
Times (London), March 5, 1993, p. 19.

*   *   *

TRINKAUS, Erik 1948-

PERSONAL: Born December 24, 1948, in New Haven, CT. *Education:* University of Wisconsin—Madison, B.A., 1970; University of Pennsylvania, M.A., 1973, Ph.D., 1975. *Avocational interests:* Equitation, skiing, carpentry.

ADDRESSES: Office—Department of Anthropology, University of New Mexico, Albuquerque, NM 87131. *Agent*—John Brockman Associates, Inc., 2307 Broadway, New York, NY 10024.

CAREER: Harvard University, Cambridge, MA, instructor, 1974-75, assistant professor, 1975-78, associate professor of anthropology, 1978-83, curator of Peabody Museum of Archaeology and Ethnology, 1975-83; University of New Mexico, Albuquerque, associate professor, 1983-87, professor of anthropology, 1987—. Universite de Bordeaux I, research associate, 1985—.

MEMBER: American Association of Physical Anthropologists, Societe d'Anthropologie de Paris, Anthropological Society of Nippon.

AWARDS, HONORS: Fulbright scholar, 1991.

WRITINGS:

The Shanidar Neandertals, Academic Press, 1983.
(With J. Radovcic, F. H. Smith, and M. H. Wolpoff) *The Krapina Hominids,* Mladost Publishing, 1988.
(Editor) *The Emergence of Modern Humans,* Cambridge University Press, 1989.
(With P. Shipman) *The Neandertals,* Knopf, 1993.

Work represented in anthologies. Contributor of numerous articles to scientific journals.

WORK IN PROGRESS: Continuing research on the biology and behavior of fossil humans in order "to understand the evolutionary processes leading to ourselves."

*   *   *

TRUMP, Ivana M. 1949-

PERSONAL: Born February 20, 1949, in Zlin, Czechoslovakia; immigrated to Canada, 1972; immigrated to United

States, 1977, naturalized U.S. citizen, 1988; daughter of Milos (an engineer) and Maria (a homemaker; maiden name, Francova) Zelnicek; married Alfred Winklmayr, 1972 (divorced, 1972); married Donald Trump (in real estate), April 9, 1977 (divorced December 7, 1990); children: (second marriage) Donald, Ivanka, Eric. *Education:* Charles University, Prague, Czechoslovakia, M.S., 1972.

ADDRESSES: Home—New York City. *Office*—721 Fifth Ave., New York, NY 10022. *Agent*—William Morris Agency, 1350 Avenue of the Americas, New York, NY 10019; (publicist) Lisa M. Calandra, 40 West 57th St., New York, NY 10019.

CAREER: Entrepreneur, lecturer, and writer. Trump Organization, New York City, vice-president in charge of design, 1979-81, senior executive vice-president, 1982-84; Trump's Castle Hotel and Casino, Atlantic City, NJ, president, 1985-88; Plaza Hotel, New York City, president, 1988-91; Ivana, Inc., New York City, president, 1991—. Also worked variously as a fashion model for Audrey Morris Agency and as a ski instructor. Member of Czechoslovakian Women's Olympic Ski Team, 1972. Member of support organizations for United Cerebral Palsy, March of Dimes, Fund for Arts and Culture in Central and Eastern Europe, The Boys' Town of Italy, School of American Ballet, American Cancer Society, New York Philharmonic, New York City Ballet, City-meals-on-Wheels.

AWARDS, HONORS: Hotelier of the Year award, *Where* magazine, 1989; also recipient of awards for excellence, shared with the Plaza Hotel, from *Conde Nast Traveler, Prestige,* and *Successful Meetings* magazines.

WRITINGS:

For Love Alone (novel), Pocket, 1992.
Free to Love (novel; sequel to *For Love Alone*), Pocket, 1993.
On My Own, (nonfiction), Pocket, in press.

ADAPTATIONS: For Love Alone was adapted for television as a four-hour mini-series, CBS, 1993.

SIDELIGHTS: The daughter of a homemaker and an engineer, Ivana M. Trump rose to prominence as a member of the Czechoslovakian Olympic ski team, a fashion model, and an entrepreneur in her own right. She has served as senior executive vice president of the Trump Organization and has headed the prestigious Trump's Castle Hotel and Casino in New Jersey and the Plaza Hotel in New York City. In 1990, a year before her much-publicized divorce from multimillionaire Donald Trump became final, she founded her own firm, Ivana, Inc. She has also begun work on a new cosmetics line and has become a best-selling author.

Trump found success as a writer after the publication of her first novel, entitled *For Love Alone.* The story centers on the life of Czechoslovakian immigrant Katrinka Kovar Graham, who meets and eventually weds an American aristocrat. Charting the heroine's glamorous social and business activities, the tale describes the betrayal of one of her best girlfriends and the protagonist's divorce from her unfaithful husband as well as her professional achievements. Popular with readers, *For Love Alone* received some kudos from critics. In an article for the *New York Times Book Review,* Barbara Raskin praised the delineations of Eastern Europe found in the first few chapters of Trump's novel and judged the heroine "intelligent and quite decent."

BIOGRAPHICAL/CRITICAL SOURCES:

PERIODICALS

New York Times Book Review, May 31, 1992, p. 39.
Time, April 20, 1992, p. 103.

*   *   *

TRYPANIS, C(onstantine) A(thanasius)   1909-1993

OBITUARY NOTICE—See index for *CA* sketch: Born January 22, 1909, in Chios, Greece; died January 18, 1993, in Athens, Greece. Government minister, scholar, and poet. Trypanis, a Greek native, was an accomplished poet in English, as well as the Greek language. After studying in Greece, Germany, and England, Trypanis received an appointment from Oxford University to the Bywater and Sotheby Chair, which he held for more than two decades. He then taught classics at the University of Chicago for six years. In 1974 he was appointed as the Minister of Culture and Science to the Greek government. His numerous books of poetry include *Stones of Troy, Pompeian Dog, Skias Onar,* and *Katalepton.* His scholarly writings include *The Influence of Hesiod upon the Homeric Hymn on Apollo, The Homeric Epics,* and *Greek Poetry: From Homer to Seferis.*

OBITUARIES AND OTHER SOURCES:

BOOKS

Who's Who, 145th edition, St. Martin's, 1993, p. 1903.

PERIODICALS

Times (London), January 22, 1993, p. 17.

TYLER, David B(udlong) 1899-1993

OBITUARY NOTICE—See index for *CA* sketch: Born October 15, 1899, in Brooklyn, NY; died of heart failure after a long illness, March 5, 1993, in Riverhead, NY. Historian, educator, and author. A naval historian, Tyler embarked on his lengthy career in the early 1920s as a clerk, and a few years later began teaching history. His longest affiliation was with Staten Island's Wagner College, which he served for more than four decades. One of his most well known works about maritime history is his 1939 *Steam Conquers the Atlantic,* which the U.S. Naval Academy utilized in its curriculum. Among the several other titles he penned are *The American Clyde, The Wilkes Expedition,* and *The Bay and River Delaware: A Pictorial History.*

OBITUARIES AND OTHER SOURCES:

BOOKS

Directory of American Scholars, Volume 1: *History,* 8th edition, Bowker, 1982, p. 783.

PERIODICALS

New York Times, March 7, 1993, p. 46.

U-V

ULACK, Richard 1942-

PERSONAL: Born July 4, 1942, in Mineola, NY; son of Gerhard and Martha (Fruehwirth) Ulack; married; wife's name, Karen M., June, 1975; children: Jessica M., Christopher J. *Education:* Stetson University, B.A., 1964; Pennsylvania State University, M.S., 1969, Ph.D., 1972.

ADDRESSES: Home—1088 Chinoe Rd., Lexington, KY 40502. *Office*—Department of Geography, University of Kentucky, Lexington, KY 40506-0027.

CAREER: Indiana State University, Terre Haute, assistant professor of geography, 1971-74; University of Kentucky, Lexington, assistant professor, 1974-78, associate professor, 1978-86, professor of geography, 1986—, chair of department, 1988—. Visiting Fulbright professor at University of the Philippines, 1982-83, and University of the South Pacific, 1991. *Military service:* U.S. Army, Signal Corps, 1964-67; served in West Germany.

AWARDS, HONORS: Grants from Ford Foundation, 1974-75, East-West Center, 1975, National Geographic Society, 1982-83, and National Science Foundation, 1982-83.

WRITINGS:

(With Karl B. Raitz) *Appalachia: A Regional Geography,* Westview, 1984.
(With Michael A. Costello and Thomas R. Leinbach) *Mobility and Employment in Urban Southeast Asia: Examples from Indonesia and the Philippines,* Westview, 1987.
(With Gyula Pauer) *Atlas of Southeast Asia,* Macmillan, 1989.
(Editor with William Skinner) *AIDS and the Social Sciences: Common Threads,* University Press of Kentucky, 1991.

Work represented in anthologies, including *Cities of the World: World Regional Urban Development,* edited by Stanley D. Brunn and Jack Williams, Harper, 1983; and *World Regional Geography: A Global Perspective,* edited by George F. Hepner and Jesse O. McKee, West Publishing, 1992. Contributor of numerous articles to geography journals.

WORK IN PROGRESS: Research on population and development issues in Southeast Asia and the Pacific, especially the Philippines and Melanesia; research on demographic characteristics in the third world, including internal migration and fertility; research on the role of intermediate-sized cities in third world development; research on third world urbanization; project coordinator for *Atlas of Kentucky.*

*   *   *

UNDERWOOD, Michael
See EVELYN, (John) Michael

*   *   *

URAKAMI, Hiroko 1937-

PERSONAL: Born October 13, 1937, in Tokyo, Japan; daughter of Yoshitada (a singer of Noh drama) and Toyoko (a homemaker) Shimizu; married Hiromichi Urakami (a professor), March 23, 1970; children: Tsuyoshi Chiba. *Education:* Japan Cooking School, Certified Cooking Instructor.

ADDRESSES: Home and office—307 4-30-24 Tokumaru, Itabashi-ku, Tokyo 175, Japan.

CAREER: Tsuji Cooking School, Tokyo, Japan, instructor and editor of a cooking publication, 1970-73; Teahouse

Management School, Tokyo, cooking instructor, 1973-78; Yomiuri Culture Center, Tokyo, cooking instructor, 1979—. University of California, Riverside, instructor, 1991-92. NHK (Japanese national television and radio network) Culture Center, cooking instructor, 1988-91; Radio Pacific Japan (Los Angeles, CA), cooking instructor, 1991-92; consultant to Japan Milk Association.

WRITINGS:

Japanese Family-Style Recipes, Kodansha, 1992.

WRITINGS IN JAPANESE

Speed Lunchbox, Bunkashuppan, 1985.
Microwave Cooking, Seishunshuppan, 1991.
Dried Foods Cooking, Gurafusha, 1991.
Speed Cooking, Bunkashuppan, 1993.

Contributor to Japanese newspapers.

* * *

URBANEK, Zdenek 1917-

PERSONAL: Born October 12, 1917; son of Vaclav (a farmer and partner of cooperative enterprises) and Ruzena (Mikulaskova) Urbanek; married Vera Muhlwaldova (a dance teacher), 1940 (died, 1972); children: Jindra (daughter), Michael. *Education:* Attended Charles University, Prague, until 1939. *Politics:* "Never a member of any party, but left of center all the time." *Religion:* "Unbeliever."

ADDRESSES: Home—Stresovicka 64 162 00 Praha 6, Czechoslovakia. *Agent*—Aura Pont, Truhlarska 13, 110 00 Praha 1, Czechoslovakia.

CAREER: Sfinx Publishing House, Prague, Czechoslovakia, editor, until c. 1942; *Narodni Osvobozeni* (title means "National Liberation"), Prague, member of editorial staff, 1945-48; free-lance translator; head of Academy of Performing Arts, Prague, for two years; free-lance writer. Also worked during World War II as a horse driver at father's farm.

MEMBER: P.E.N. (Czech section), Czech Writers' Society, Lidove noviny Society (chair, until 1991), Franz Kafka Society (chair).

AWARDS, HONORS: Order of Thomas G. Masaryk, awarded by Czechoslovakian president Vaclav Havel, 1991; Doctor of Humane Letters, Spertus College of Judaica, Chicago, 1992; Medal of the "Righteous among Nations," Yad Vashem Museum, Jerusalem, 1993.

WRITINGS:

The Dawn of Sadness (short stories), Vaclav Petr (Prague), 1939.

A Dark Stroke (short stories), Vaclav Petr, 1940.
The Story of the Pale Dominic (novel), Novina Publishing House, 1940.
Lives and Consciences (short stories), Vaclav Petr, 1944.
Following Don Quixote (novel), Frantisek Borovy (Prague), 1949.
The Makers of the World, Sixty-Eight Publishers (Toronto), 1988.
On the Sky's Clayey Bottom: Sketches and Happenings from the Years of Silence, translated from the Czech by William Harkins, introduced by Vaclav Havel, Four Walls Eight Windows, 1992.
The Lost Country (short stories), Franz Kafka Publishers (Prague), 1992.
Uncommon Cases (essays), Arkyr (Prague), 1993.

Contributor of Shakespearean and Joycean essays to *Divadlo,* (title means "The Theatre"), 1963-68. Many of the works Urbanek wrote between 1948 and 1989 were published as samizdat (clandestinely printed and distributed).

WORK IN PROGRESS: The Makers of the World Go On.

SIDELIGHTS: Zdenek Urbanek told *CA:* "I started to write all too early. My first short stories were all too lyrical. Later I tried to be more factual. It was said many decades after I wrote my novel *Following Don Quixote* that it is a work that uncovers the moral nerve of the present time and the substantial theme of it. During the half century of totalitarian regimes in our country, I tried to survive, together with my family, on the basis of translating the works of authors from English into Czech. At first it was only British novelist Charles Dickens, but later I persuaded the editors of one or two publishing houses to publish the American poet Walt Whitman or, later again, even American writer and biographer Edgar Lee Masters, or British poet T. S. Eliot. During all my translating I was continuing to write my own essays and short stories. Now both kinds of my writings are published. A thick book of my short stories plus a novella was published in 1992 with the title *The Lost Country.* It contains my stories from 1947 until 1970. But what seems to me as the most important parts of my writing, *The Makers of the World* and *The Makers of the World Go On,* are still in progress. My friends prefer to call the works my memoirs, but I refuse to call them that. They are the stories of individuals, or of groups of individuals, who, by their mere presence or by their activities, formed the world around me from my childhood until now. One of the most important among the creators of my world has been English dramatist and poet William Shakespeare. I studied his writings as a student, but the study became much more intensive when I was asked in the early 1960s to translate his tragedy *Hamlet* for a production in the Prague National Theatre. After a time of hesitation I recognized that *Hamlet,* directly understood by contemporaries of the play, could not be translated into Czech in 1960 in any other way than the one which could and would be understood by the audiences in the same direct way, if possible. After several years of conflict, the new way of translating Shakespeare was generally recognized as the right one."

* * *

VAN DEN BERGH, Nan 1947-

PERSONAL: Born October 15, 1947, in Rochester, NY; daughter of Robert (an employee benefits manager) and Shirley Jane (a homemaker; maiden name, Fishbaugh) Bennett. *Education:* Received bachelor's degree from State University of New York, State University College at Cortland, 1969; Syracuse University, M.S.W., 1977; University of Pittsburgh, Ph.D., 1981. *Politics:* Democrat. *Religion:* Protestant. *Avocational interests:* Running, golf, tennis, skiing, camping, jazz and rhythm and blues, art and art museums.

ADDRESSES: Home—1018 Hilldale, West Hollywood, CA 90069. *Office*—1033 Grayley, Suite 204, Los Angeles, CA 90024.

CAREER: California State University, Fresno, CA, professor, 1981-87; University of California, Los Angeles, CA, director of employee assistance program, 1988—. Psychotherapist, organizational training consultant, speaker, and member of West Hollywood women's issues task force.

MEMBER: National Association of Social Workers, Employee Assistance Society of North America, Society for Clinical Social Work, Council on Social Work Education, Employee Assistance Professionals Associations.

WRITINGS:

(Editor with Lynn B. Cooper) *Feminist Visions for Social Work,* National Association of Social Workers, 1986.
(Editor) *Feminist Perspectives on Addictions,* Springer, 1991.
Feminist Practice in the Twenty-First Century, National Association of Social Workers, 1993.
Employee Assistance Practice in the Twenty-First Century, Sage, in press.

Contributor of articles to periodicals.

SIDELIGHTS: Nan Van Den Bergh told *CA:* "The sociocultural events that have impacted my life, world view, career, and publications include: having been born a World War II aftermath baby boomer; being at the midpoint (chronologically) of *American Graffiti* and Haight-Ashbury; identifying as a 1960s person, former hippie, and

anti-war activist; and growing into adulthood with the women's movement. Hence, I am an activist, shaped by changing American values from 1950s conformity to 1970s activism.

"The feminist movement has been the most significant influence on my life. It is impossible for me to see reality other than through that philosophical and ideological perspective. Feminism is much broader than the 'add women and stir' perspective. Rather it is a world view that challenges traditional patriarchal and capitalist values of conformity and acquisitiveness. It is a force that can bring the world to partnership, interconnectedness, and worldwide concern for each other's welfare."

* * *

Van EWIJK, Casper 1953-

PERSONAL: Born December 9, 1953, in Puttershoek, Netherlands; son of Egbert Van Ewijk (a physician) and Elisabeth (Van Dongen) Torman; married Emma de Zeeuw (a physician), August 25, 1979; children: Roelof, Arend, Sven. *Education:* University of Amsterdam, degree in economics, 1979; University of Tilburg, Ph.D., 1989. *Religion:* None.

ADDRESSES: Home—Pelikaanstraat 5, 1171 DG Badhoevedorp, Netherlands.

CAREER: University of Amsterdam, Amsterdam, Netherlands, associate professor, 1979-92; Netherlands Graduate School of Economics, professor, 1992—.

WRITINGS:

On the Dynamics of Growth and Debt, Oxford University Press, 1991.

* * *

Van SICKLE, Emily 1910-

PERSONAL: Born October 23, 1910, in Vicksburg, MS; daughter of Myron C. (judge advocate general of United States Army) and Esther (Durham) Cramer; married Charles Earle Van Sickle (affiliated with International Harvester Export Co.), December 19, 1937 (deceased). *Education:* Goucher College, B.A., 1931.

ADDRESSES: Home—4201 Massachusetts Ave. N.W., Washington, DC 20016.

CAREER: National Recovery Administration, Washington, DC, clerk and typist, 1933-35, assigned to Manila, Philippines, 1935-36; Office of the Governor, Baguio, Philippines, secretary, 1936-37; American University,

Washington, DC, business administrator, 1966-70, part-time secretary, 1972-75; Postal Rate Commission, Washington, DC, secretary, 1970-72.

WRITINGS:

The Iron Gates of Santo Tomas, Academy Chicago, 1992.

Author of children's stories and poems; contributor to periodicals, including *Washington Post.*

SIDELIGHTS: Emily Van Sickle told *CA:* "I have always enjoyed writing, but the only book I have written is about our imprisonment by the Japanese in Santo Tomas during World War II."

*   *   *

VAUSE, L(aurence) Mikel   1952-

PERSONAL: Born October 4, 1952, in Ogden, UT; son of Laurence F. and Stella (Bowen) Vause; married Janis Barker (a public school development director), April 30, 1975; children: Kelly, Emily, Sarah, Jared. *Education:* Received B.S. from Weber State University, and M.A. and Ph.D. from Bowling Green State University. *Religion:* Church of Jesus Christ of Latter-day Saints (Mormons). *Avocational interests:* Exploration, mountaineering (rock and ice climbing), mountain running, mountain cycling.

ADDRESSES: Home—1670 Twenty-seventh St., Ogden, UT 84401. *Office*—Department of English, Weber State University, Ogden, UT 84408-1201.

CAREER: Weber State University, Ogden, UT, associate professor of English, 1983—, Honors Cortez Professor, 1989, founder and director of National Undergraduate Literature Conference, 1984—, and North American Interdisciplinary Wilderness Conference, 1988—. Peregrine Smith Books, assistant fiction editor, 1983-91. National Western Film Festival, moderator, 1985; Writers at Work Conference, member of executive committee, 1986-89. Ogden City Trails Committee, chairman, 1990—. Public speaker.

MEMBER: Modern Language Association of America, Association for the Study of Literature and the Environment (member of national advisory board, 1993—), College English Association, Western Literature Association, Rocky Mountain Modern Language Association, Western States Social Science Association, Institute for Evolutionary Psychology, Northern Pacific Popular Culture Association, Far West American Culture Association, American Alpine Club.

AWARDS, HONORS: Professor of the Year, Division of Continuing Education, 1986; Crystal Crest Master Teacher finalist, Weber State University, 1987-1992.

WRITINGS:

(Editor with Samuel I. Zeveloff and William H. McVaugh) *A Wilderness Tapestry: An Eclectic Approach to Preservation,* University of Nevada Press, 1992.
On Mountains and Mountaineers: A Critique of Mountaineering Literature, Mountain n' Air Books, 1993.

Also editor of *Rock and Roses: Essays by Women on Mountaineering,* Mountain n' Air Books. Contributor of articles, poems, stories, and reviews to periodicals, including *Environment Review, Climbing Art, Western American Literature, Popular Culture Review,* and *Comment.*

WORK IN PROGRESS: Forty-One Degrees North: A Collection of Short Fiction; editing *The Climbing Life: An Anthology of Mountain Literature,* for Peregrine Smith, and *Rock and Roses II: An International Collection of Essays by Women Mountaineers,* for Mountain n' Air Books.

*   *   *

VERNEY, John   1913-1993

OBITUARY NOTICE—See index for *CA* sketch: Born September 30, 1913; died February 2, 1993. Artist and author. Verney was perhaps best known for his World War II text, *Going to the Wars,* a chronicle of his experiences in the British Army. A noted painter in oils and watercolor, Verney also worked with pottery, painted furniture, and created illustrations. Some of his drawings adorned his own books, including the children's story *Friday's Tunnel.* Verney also produced travel books such as *Verney Abroad,* children's literature, and other books on the topic of war. His works include the memoir, *A Dinner of Herbs,* the juvenile mystery novels *February's World* and *Seven Sunflower Seeds,* the novels *Every Advantage* and *Fine Day for a Picnic,* and the volume, *A John Verney Collection.*

OBITUARIES AND OTHER SOURCES:

BOOKS

The Writers Directory: 1992-1994, St. James Press, 1992.

PERIODICALS

Times (London), February 5, 1993, p. 17.

*   *   *

VICTOR, Daniel D(avid)   1944-

PERSONAL: Born June 1, 1944, in Los Angeles, CA; son of Alfred (a sales representative) and Ruth (a teacher; maiden name, Tofield) Victor; married Norma K. Silverman (a teacher), March 22, 1981; children: Seth Herschel.

Education: University of California, Berkeley, A.B., 1966; California State University, Los Angeles, M.A., 1969; Claremont Graduate School, Ph.D., 1976. *Politics:* "Spiritual muckraker." *Religion:* Jewish. *Avocational interests:* Reading, travel, collecting stamps and postcards.

ADDRESSES: Home—Los Angeles, CA. *Office*—Fairfax High School, 7850 Melrose Ave., Los Angeles, CA 90046. *Agent*—Jane Cushman, JCA Literary Agency, Inc., 27 West 20th St., Suite 1103, New York, NY 10011.

CAREER: Los Angeles Unified School District, Los Angeles, CA, junior high school English teacher, 1966-80, high school English teacher, 1980—.

MEMBER: International Association of Crime Writers, Modern Language Association of America, National Council of Teachers of English, English Council of Los Angeles.

AWARDS, HONORS: Two fellowships and one study grant from National Endowment for the Humanities, 1984, 1986, and 1988.

WRITINGS:

The Seventh Bullet (mystery novel), St. Martin's, 1992.

Contributor to *Scholarly Adventures;* coeditor, *Scholarly Adventures,* 1989-91.

WORK IN PROGRESS: Not a Drop to Drink, a mystery novel, completion expected in 1994.

SIDELIGHTS: Daniel D. Victor told *CA:* "I've enjoyed writing ever since I first began keeping a diary when I was ten, a habit which lasted, on and off, until I was twenty-three. My interests are eclectic. I was attracted to the wonders of fantasy at an early age by the 1950s television series *Space Patrol,* and I was intrigued by the world of conspiracy represented by the assassination of John F. Kennedy. I'm not surprised that I wrote a fictional murder mystery based on historical fact.

"My wife and I share a great interest in mystery stories, and we like to travel, having visited England, in particular, on numerous occasions. In November, 1988, a stray white cat walked in our front door and adopted us, and our home belonged to Snowpuff for four years, until the birth of our son Seth who reigns as the current landlord."

*　　*　　*

VILLELLA, Edward 1936-

PERSONAL: Born October 1, 1936, in Bayside, New York; son of Joseph and Mildred (DeGiovanni) Villella; married Janet Greschler (divorced November, 1980); married Linda Carbonetta (a figure skater), April, 1981;

children: (first marriage) Roddy, (second marriage) Lauren, Crista Francesca. *Education:* Attended School of American Ballet, 1946-52 and 1955-57; New York Maritime Academy, B.S., 1957.

ADDRESSES: Home— Miami Beach, FL. *Office*— Artistic Director, Miami City Ballet, 905 Lincoln Rd., Miami Beach, FL 33139-9880; c/o Publicity Director, Simon & Schuster, Inc., Simon & Schuster Bldg., 1230 Avenue of the Americas, New York, NY 10020.

CAREER: New York City Ballet, New York City, dancer, 1957-58, soloist, 1958-60, principal dancer, 1960-76; Eglevsky Ballet Company (now AndreEglevsky State Ballet of New York), New York City, artistic coordinator, 1979-84, choreographer, 1980-84; New Jersey Ballet, artistic advisor, 1980-82; Ballet Oklahoma, Oklahoma City, and Madison Festival of the Lakes, artistic director, 1983-86; Miami City Ballet, Miami, FL, founding artistic director, 1986—. North Carolina School for the Arts, board member; New York City's Commission for Cultural Affairs, chair, 1978; University of Iowa, Ida Beam Visiting Professor of dance, 1981; United States Military Academy, visiting artist, 1981-82; University of California, regents lecturer, Irvine, 1985. Guest dancer with Royal Ballet (London), 1962 and 1971, Royal Danish Ballet Company, 1963, Boston Ballet, 1968 and 1969, Miami Ballet, 1968-69, and New York City Opera, 1969; guest dancer on television, including *The Ed Sullivan Show, The Bell Telephone Hour,* and *The Mike Douglas Show.* Danced for President John F. Kennedy's inaugural and performed for other presidents, including Lyndon Johnson, Richard Nixon, and Gerald Ford; producer and director of television series *Dance in America,* 1975-77; producer of television special *Harlequin,* 1975.

MEMBER: National Council on Arts, Wolf Trap (member of board of trustees and executive committee).

AWARDS, HONORS: Dance Annual Award, *Dance,* 1964: Emmy Award, Academy of Television Arts and Sciences, 1975, for television production of *Harlequin;* Capezio Dance Award, Capezio Ballet Makers Dance Foundation, 1989; Frances Holleman Breathitt Award for Excellence, for outstanding contribution to the arts and the education of young people; Lifetime Achievement Award, National Society of Arts and Letters; honorary degrees from Boston Conservatory, Union College, Siena College, Fordham University, Skidmore College, and Nazareth College.

WRITINGS:

(With Larry Kaplan) *Prodigal Son: Dancing for Balanchine in a World of Pain and Magic,* Simon & Schuster, 1992.

SIDELIGHTS: Edward Villella has been described by *Interview* contributor Robert Gottlieb as "the greatest male classical dancer America has produced." Best known for performances in the ballets *Tarantella, Jewels, Midsummer Night's Dream,* and *Prodigal Son,* this highly regarded entertainer published his memoirs in 1992. *Prodigal Son: Dancing for Balanchine in a World of Pain and Magic,* written with Larry Kaplan, describes the struggles Villella encountered during his career as a principal performer in George Balanchine's New York City Ballet. In his book, Villella describes his childhood, growing up in a working-class neighborhood in New York City. To keep him out of trouble, his parents enrolled him in ballet classes. Finding a natural affinity for the art, Villella began to imagine himself as a professional performer. But his parents did not have the same vision for their son; they forced him to quit dancing to attend college. Later Villella decided to return to ballet, and he found himself working strenuously to make up for the four-year interruption in his training. In 1957, only a year after his return, he was accepted into the New York City Ballet.

Villella notes in his book that Balanchine's guidance, which stressed high speed and jumping, and his own accelerated training proved detrimental to his body. Eventually his legs would spasm following the first stretch of the day. He writes: "I got to the point where I could barely move, and I couldn't even tell if my feet were pointing or not. My legs were numb between my lower calves and ankles, and because my metatarsals [bones in the feet] had sustained contusions and some of the bones were broken, I lost the ability to grip the floor with my feet." He ascribes most of his physical problems to Balanchine's training regiment. The author maintains: "Balanchine's was not a class to make your body respond as a performer's must respond, to actually help you do his choreography." Villella chose to abandon Balanchine's leadership and study under Denmark's Stanley Williams, whose techniques helped rehabilitate the dancer's abused muscles. Although leaving Balanchine's company allowed Villella to regain strength in his legs, the move hurt his relationship with his former director. He recalls in his book, "All I wanted to do was please him. But I was not willing to destroy myself in order to do so."

Training with Williams, however, did not alleviate all of Villella's physical difficulties. A damaged hip caused him to retire from dancing in 1975. Subsequently, he launched himself into various artistic roles in ballet companies, including positions as choreographer, coordinator, advisor, and director. In 1986 Villella became founding artistic director of the Miami City Ballet, filling a fundamental void in the city's cultural programming. He trains his dancers in the Balanchine technique despite his personal troubles with the method. "Indeed, in some measure he has *become*

Balanchine," proclaimed *New York Times Book Review* contributor Joan Acocella. Writing in *New Republic,* Mindy Aloff suggested that Villella's renewed support of his former mentor's style resembles the plot of Balanchine's ballet *Prodigal Son.* In this stage performance, like the Biblical parable, a son returns to his father. Similarly, Acocella surmised, "He also sees the ballet [*Prodigal Son*] as the story of his own life, above all his life with Balanchine."

After reviewing Villella's documented life story, Aloff assessed: "The goal of Villella's book is selfless, to document a moment, a 'golden age' that Villella experienced intimately." She also noted that he does not fully achieve this goal in his writing. And Acocella concluded, "In the history of the rise of American ballet—as it branched off from its Russian and European roots to become a distinctly American art, more tough-minded, more energized, more democratic—no life is more exemplary than that of Edward Villella."

BIOGRAPHICAL/CRITICAL SOURCES:

BOOKS

Villella, Edward, and Larry Kaplan, *Prodigal Son: Dancing for Balanchine in a World of Pain and Magic,* Simon & Schuster, 1992.

PERIODICALS

Interview, February, 1993, pp. 62-63, 155.
New Republic, June 29, 1992, pp. 36-41.
New York Times Book Review, March 8, 1992, pp. 3, 31.

*   *   *

VIVION, Michael J.   1944-

PERSONAL: Born May 21, 1944, in Wichita, KS; son of Joe Hart Vivion (in the military) and June Laverne (Martin) Hargrove; married Catherine Rubinelli, December, 1977 (divorced, 1981); married Sarah Morgan (a professor), September, 1982; children: Chris, Liz, Molly, Nick. *Education:* Arizona State University, B.A., 1966; Wichita State University, M.A., 1972; Marquette University, Ph.D., 1982. *Politics:* Independent.

ADDRESSES: Home—3614 Harrison, Kansas City, MO 64109. *Office*—c/o Department of English, University of Missouri at Kansas City, 5100 Rockhill Road, Kansas City, MO 64110.

CAREER: Western High School, Anaheim, CA, teacher, 1966-69; Southwest Texas University, San Marcos, assistant professor, 1979-82; University of Missouri at Kansas City, associate professor, then director of composition, then professor of English, 1982—. Member of district task force, Foreign Language Magnets, 1986-87; appointed to Missouri governor-elect's Educational Transition team, 1992; Kansas City School Board, 1992—.

MEMBER: National Council of Teachers of English, Modern Language Association, National Writing Project (regional director), Writing Program Administrators (member of editorial board, 1988—).

AWARDS, HONORS: Fulbright study grant, Free University of Berlin, 1972-73; nominated for University of Missouri Presidential Teaching Award.

WRITINGS:

(With wife Sarah Morgan) *The Writer's Circle: Reading, Thinking, Writing,* St. Martin's, 1987.
(Coauthor) *Houghton-Mifflin English,* Houghton, 1990.
(Coeditor) *Cultural Studies in the English Classroom,* Boynton Cook, 1993.

Contributor to *Contemporary Authors New Revisions,* Volume 40, Gale, 1993; contributor of articles on teaching composition and literature to professional journals.

WORK IN PROGRESS: A post-World War II spy novel.

* * *

VOLK, Patricia (Gay) 1943-

PERSONAL: Born July 16, 1943, in New York, NY; daughter of Cecil Sussman (a restaurateur and sculptor) and Audrey Elaine (a family therapist; maiden name, Morgen) Volk; married Andrew Blitzer (a surgeon), December 21, 1969; children: Peter Morgen, Polly Volk. *Education:* Syracuse University, B.F.A. (cum laude), 1964; attended Academie de la Grande Chaumiere, 1965, School of Visual Arts, 1969, New School, 1975, and Columbia University, 1977-88.

ADDRESSES: Agent—Theron Raines, 71 Park Ave., New York, NY 10016.

CAREER: Appelbaum and Curtis, New York City, art director, 1964-65; *Seventeen* magazine, New York City, art director, 1967-68; *Harper's Bazaar,* New York City, art director, 1969; Doyle, Dane, Bernbach, Inc., New York City, copywriter, 1969-88, senior vice president/creative manager, 1969-87, senior vice president/associate creative director, 1987-88; writer, 1988—. Yeshiva College, adjunct instructor in fiction, 1991.

MEMBER: Authors Guild, PEN.

AWARDS, HONORS: Numerous Andy, Clio, EFFIE, and One Show awards for excellence in advertising; Stephen E. Kelly award, 1983, for "Weight Watchers" advertising campaign; Yaddo fellow, 1983; Word Beat Press

Fiction Book award, 1984, for *The Yellow Banana;* MacDowell fellow, 1984; recipient of the Pushcart Prize.

WRITINGS:

The Yellow Banana (short stories), Word Beat Press, 1985.
White Light (novel), Atheneum, 1987.
All It Takes (short stories), Atheneum, 1990.

Work represented in anthologies, including *Stories about How Things Fall Apart and What's Left When They Do,* edited by Allen Woodman, Word Beat Press, 1985; *A Reader for Developing Writers,* edited by Santo Buscemi, McGraw-Hill, 1990; *Exploring Language,* edited by Gary Goshgarian, HarperCollins, 1992; *Magazine and Feature Writing,* edited by Donna Hickey, Mayfield Publishing, 1992; and *Hers,* Bungeishunju Publishing (Japan), 1993. Contributor of articles and short stories to periodicals, including *New York Times Magazine, New York Newsday, Atlantic, Playboy, New York Times Book Review, New Yorker, Family Circle, Cosmopolitan, Present Tense, Apalachee Quarterly,* and *GQ.*

WORK IN PROGRESS: A novel.

SIDELIGHTS: Patricia Volk's portraits of urban women searching for truth serve as frameworks for her comic novel *White Light* and short story collection *All It Takes.* Volk's characters often possess a wry sense of humor, a trait that helps them survive the emotional upheavals they face. Although some reviewers have cited gratuitous humor and underdeveloped characters in some of Volk's stories, others have noted that, as her work has progressed, Volk has refined her skills to produce what *New York Times Book Review* contributor Gary Krist called "a more powerful kind of comedy—the kind that pierces the ribs and wounds the heart."

White Light concerns troubled advertising executive May Graves who, at thirty-five, thinks she has lost her instincts from living in the city too long. Leaving her husband Roy, May flees to a resort hotel in the Adirondacks to consider her future. The sole guest of the dilapidated hotel, May encounters an odd assortment of characters during her stay, including the hotel's eerie caretaker (who still searches a lake for the body of his father drowned twenty years earlier), a tattooed young man living in a nearby cabin, and a group of Orthodox Jewish dwarfs. An unexpected reunion with her husband and a phone call to her mother for what turns out to be their final conversation add to May's adventure.

The humorous aspects of *White Light* captured several critics' attention, though the novel received only mixed reviews. Nancy Ramsey of the *New York Times Book Review* found *White Light* an "inventive if flawed" work, adding that most characters "are either not well developed or too outlandish, and fail to elicit much sympathy." *Publishers Weekly* reviewer Sybil Steinberg agreed, describing *White Light* as "sassy but forced" and judging the characters to be "mock human beings, from whom both reader and author remain distanced." Offering a more positive assessment was Sheila Paulos of the *Philadelphia Inquirer,* who declared that Volk tells her tale "with a delightful urban sensibility, a quirky sense of humor and a light touch that enable her to circumvent most of the cliches implicit in the subject matter. That's enough to put this book in the winner's circle."

Volk's next work, *All It Takes,* examines the difficulties of establishing and maintaining relationships. Set primarily in New York, the fifteen stories that comprise *All It Takes* involve characters like *White Light*'s May—sophisticated, yet unsettled and unhappy with their lives. The women's attempts to find love and happiness often prove disappointing, but they persevere with spirit and wit.

Several critics remarked that *All It Takes* offers evidence of Volk's maturation as a writer. Judith Freeman of the *Los Angeles Times Book Review* noted that the stories demonstrate "Volk's talent for irony and wit," and she commended the author's decision to vary her style for a few of the narratives, stating that "the more serious stories . . . and those that employ a past tense that seems to give them depth missing in others, are ultimately the most successful." In his review of *All It Takes,* Krist commented that Volk's finely-drawn characters add a powerful dimension to the work. "Volk's women have vulnerabilities the size of barn doors," he wrote, "and they can register with touching accuracy Big Verities like the passage of time, the inevitability of loss, and the fickleness of human affection." Finally, in his defining statement of the author's work, Krist declared that the "comic constellations of character, situation and event are Ms. Volk's specialty."

BIOGRAPHICAL/CRITICAL SOURCES:

PERIODICALS

Boston Globe, September 25, 1987, p. 35.
Los Angeles Times, August 31, 1987.
Los Angeles Times Book Review, February 18, 1990, p. 5.
New York Times Book Review, November 29, 1987, pp. 20-21; February 11, 1990, p. 17.
Philadelphia Inquirer, December 6, 1987; February 18, 1990.
Publishers Weekly, November 10, 1989, p. 49.
San Diego Tribune, April 27, 1990.
Tribune Books (Chicago), January 28, 1990, p. 7.

von MOLTKE, Helmuth James   1907-1945

PERSONAL: Born in 1907; executed by hanging, January 23, 1945; married Freya Deichmann, 1931; children: sons. *Education:* Educated at Oxford University; also studied in Breslau, Berlin, and Vienna.

CAREER: Attorney. Served as legal adviser during World War II in the Foreign Division of the Military Intelligence Service of Nazi Germany.

WRITINGS:

Letters to Freya: 1939-1945, edited and translated by Beate Ruhm von Oppen, Knopf, 1990.

SIDELIGHTS: Helmuth James von Moltke served as a legal adviser in the Foreign Division of Nazi Germany's Military Intelligence Service during World War II, but he did not agree with the policies of the fuehrer, Adolph Hitler. Instead, he used his legal expertise to save many from death at the hands of the Nazi regime. And with like-minded friends, he made plans at his estate, Kreisau—then a part of Germany, now contained within Poland's borders—for the reconstruction of Germany after the downfall of Hitler. He was arrested by the Nazis for treason in 1944, and was executed the following year. Von Moltke expressed many of his hopes and fears during the war in letters to his wife, Freya, which were translated into English and published in the United States in 1990 as *Letters to Freya: 1939-1945.*

In *Letters to Freya,* von Moltke chronicles his increasing disgust for Hitler's regime. V.R. Berghahn quoted him in a *New York Times Book Review* piece on the volume: "A woman . . . saw a Jew collapse on the street; when she wanted to help him up, a policeman stepped in, stopped her, and kicked the body on the ground so that it rolled in the gutter; then he turned to the lady with a vestige of shame and said: 'Those are our orders.' " Von Moltke went on to ask his wife, "How can anyone know these things and still walk around free? With what right? Is it not inevitable that his turn will come too one day, and that he too will be rolled into the gutter?"

Von Moltke also discusses in *Letters to Freya* his horror and disbelief when he learns of the Nazi concentration camps. As Paul West revealed in a *Washington Post Book World* review, "his soul writhes in the presence of psychotic Nazi technocrats and nerdy Nazi families buying up dry goods in Paris. Hitler's showcased Olympic games sicken him no less than mental homes for SS men with nervous breakdowns from executing women and children." Von Moltke's letters continue even after his arrest, almost to the day of his execution. West concluded from *Letters to Freya* that von Moltke was "surely one of the most articulate martyrs of our time."

BIOGRAPHICAL/CRITICAL SOURCES:

BOOKS

Von Moltke, Helmuth James, *Letters to Freya: 1939-1945,* edited and translated by Beate Ruhm von Oppen, Knopf, 1990.

PERIODICALS

Los Angeles Times, June 13, 1990.
New York Times Book Review, July 1, 1990, p. 10.
Washington Post Book World, July 29, 1990, p. 1.*

*　　*　　*

VOZENILEK, Helen S. 1958-

PERSONAL: Born May 24, 1958, in Washington, DC; daughter of Zavis Joseph (a doctor) and Miroslava (a doctor; maiden name, Smrckova) Vozenilek. *Education:* Attended University of Oregon, 1976-78.

ADDRESSES: Home—716 Douglass St., San Francisco, CA 94114.

CAREER: Electrician, San Francisco, CA, 1981—. Women's Cancer Resource Center in Oakland, CA, women's health activist; Tradeswomen, women's equal opportunity activist.

WRITINGS:

(Editor) *Loss of the Groundnote: Women Writing about the Loss of Their Mothers,* Clothespin Fever Press, 1992.

Contributor to periodicals, including *Northwest Passage* and *Peace Center News.* Former editor of *Sisterlode* and *Tradeswoman;* editor, *Women's Cancer Resource Center Newsletter.*

WORK IN PROGRESS: I Can't Believe They Did That! (tentative title), an anthology of "horror stories" experienced by authors in dealings with their publishers; research on mother-daughter relationships and loss, both physical and psychological.

SIDELIGHTS: Helen S. Vozenilek told *CA:* "Born and raised in Tacoma, Washington, I never did learn to appreciate the rain, as some other northwestern writers swear they do. After twenty drenched years, I moved to New Mexico. Under those impossibly huge skies and that enchanted landscape, my writing blossomed. While always trying to devote more attention to fiction, I found much of my time spent on political writing and editing. In addition to my 'gainful employment' as an electrician, I worked in the women's and anti-nuclear/militarism movements, a Herculean task in a military colony like New Mexico.

"After my mother died in 1986 and I could find very little writing about the subject of loss, I decided to publish a collection of women's stories about the loss of a mother. The three-year effort was both difficult and rewarding. The anthology *Loss of the Groundnote* has received a warm welcome from readers hungry for such stories. In the future, however, I would like to concentrate more on writing and leave the editing to someone else.

"I love to read, and I believe this makes me a harsh critic, of both my own writings and those of others. Above all other writing forms, I admire poetry that catches and stirs with its paucity of words. My Rainer Maria Rilke phase is now in its fourth year, with no signs of letting up. Adrienne Rich's works, both poetry and prose, count among the works that influence me most. I currently live in the Bay Area where one could spend every evening going to a reading and never do any writing oneself. I believe in the power of words to sway, mobilize, and incite, and I consider my love affair with words an eternal relationship."

W

WAGNER, Bruce 1954-

PERSONAL: Born in 1954, in Madison, WI.

ADDRESSES: Home—Los Angeles, CA. *Agent*—Miriam Altshuler, Russell & Volkening Inc., 50 West Twenty-ninth St., New York, NY 10001.

CAREER: Writer. Worked as ambulance driver and limousine chauffeur.

WRITINGS:

Force Majeure (novel), Random, 1991.

Author of *Wild Palms* comic strip in *Details* magazine. Contributor to periodicals, including *Esquire.*

SCREENPLAYS

(With Wes Craven) *A Nightmare on Elm Street 3: Dream Warriors,* New Line, 1987.
Scenes from the Class Struggle in Beverly Hills (based on a story by Wagner and Paul Bartel), Cinecom, 1989.

FOR TELEVISION

(And executive director with Oliver Stone) *Wild Palms* (six-hour limited series; based on the comic strip by Wagner), ABC-TV, 1993.

WORK IN PROGRESS: Writing and directing a film version of *Force Majeure.*

SIDELIGHTS: Bruce Wagner has enjoyed prominence with both his fiction and his screenplays. His work often reflects the hectic lifestyles and idiosyncracies of those that live in the fast lane. Powerful moguls, unemployed authors, and egotistical actors populate much of his writing. Both his screenplay for *Scenes from the Class Struggle in Beverly Hills* and his novel, *Force Majeure,* center on the interaction of the privileged and not-so-privileged and

have been praised for their incisive wit and informed satire.

Born in 1954, Wagner was eight when his family moved to Los Angeles, California. From an early age Wagner felt an attraction to writing and dramatic creation. In a conversation with actor Wallace Shawn (*My Dinner with Andre, The Princess Bride*) in *Interview* magazine, the writer recalled that, as a child, he put on self-composed plays for Joe Papp, the respected Shakespearean producer. When he reached adulthood, Wagner pursued writing as a career. As a writer torn between staying true to his art and going for the big money of shamelessly commercial scripts, Wagner often found himself in the same moral dilemmas that confronted his *Force Majeure* protagonist. As he told Shawn: "I made a lot of money doing that, and that was a kind of death. . . . I became a hack." Despite causing anxiety, Wagner's years as a struggling screenwriter provided him with inside information on an often unseen facet of the movie industry. Using that information, Wagner wrote *Force Majeure.*

Force Majeure is a novel about wayward screenwriter Bud Wiggins, who is reduced to working as a chauffeur in Hollywood, the very film capital he hoped to conquer. For Wiggins, whose only produced film was never released, Hollywood is an unending land of schemers and posers who are motivated, inevitably, by either greed or the pursuit of fame. Wiggins, though streetwise and often witty, sometimes perceives his predicament as a tragedy, and, in the final pages, he finds himself in truly crushing circumstances.

Upon publication in 1991, *Force Majeure* readily received recognition as an unflinching depiction of Hollywood. David Finkle, noting that Wagner himself has worked as a screenwriter, declared in the *New York Times Book Review* that *Force Majeure* constituted "the revenge of a cynical Hollywood scribe." Charlie Paikert reported in *Nation* that Wagner's book "mercilessly skewers Hollywood's insular rituals."

Although Wagner won significant acclaim with *Force Majeure,* he has also received attention for his screenplays. In 1987 he collaborated with Wes Craven on director Chuck Russell's *A Nightmare on Elm Street 3: Dream Warriors,* which chronicles the further atrocities of Freddy Krueger, a gruesome, fire-scarred murderer sporting razor-sharp claws on his right hand. As in the original *A Nightmare on Elm Street,* which Craven directed, Krueger plagues teens by stalking them in their dreams. In the *Dream Warriors* installment, Krueger terrorizes a band of youths hospitalized in a psychiatric ward. For obvious reasons, these teens, descendants of the adults who originally burned Krueger to death, are overwhelmingly afraid of sleeping. But Krueger's plans to avenge himself on his killers' offspring is jeopardized when the youths steel themselves to the task at hand and willingly enter their dreams to combat the unnerving villain. In his *Los Angeles Times* review, Kevin Thomas reported that *A Nightmare on Elm Street 3: Dream Warriors* regularly complemented its more straightforward gore sequences with humor and impressive visual sequences. He noted that "the morbid tone of the original has given way to horror comedy set off by quite spectacular and imaginative fantasy sequences." Thomas credited Wagner, among others, with creating the "throwaway humor" that "makes [*Dream Warriors*] really work."

Wagner also wrote the script for director Paul Bartel's *Scenes from the Class Struggle in Beverly Hills,* which Sheila Benson described in the *Los Angeles Times* as "a farce turning on the pan-sexual lust of a collection of high- and low-rent characters in and around the manicured hills of Beverly." Benson also wrote that "Wagner's script has individually hilarious characters." Among the various eccentrics and buffoons in the film are two neighbors vying to bed each other's wives, a housekeeper who worships before the Aztec gods of revenge, and a former grade-B actress who plots the revival of her show-business career even as she mourns her late husband.

While considered a "sleeper"—a film that is well-received but not widely attended—*Scenes from the Class Struggle in Beverly Hills* gained Wagner significant respect and praise from several influential critics. *New York Times* reviewer Vincent Canby pronounced the film "one long smile with an occasional belly laugh," concluding that "there is a crazy kind of sweetness in [the filmmaker's] comedy." Richard Corliss, appreciating Wagner's dark humor, wrote in *Time* that "*Scenes* is an original. And if you are in the right black mood, you could easily laugh till your nose bleeds." The *Nation* reviewer Stuart Klawans also applauded the film, calling it a "brilliantly exe-

cuted new farce" and proclaiming that "no one with a decent respect for bad taste will want to miss this movie."

While *Scenes from the Class Struggle in Beverly Hills* brought Wagner to the attention of an influential group of filmgoers, it also raised new worries for the writer. Where he had previously been concerned with sacrificing quality writing for easy money, Wagner now found himself operating within a new frame of reference. As a relatively unknown writer, Wagner enjoyed an almost unrestrained freedom in the subjects he wrote about and ridiculed. Now, with a semi-hit film to his credit, Wagner saw potential trouble in the expectations of producers, directors, and the filmgoing public. As he told Shawn in *Interview,* "I have this paranoid feeling that if they can censor me now, before I've really done anything at all, if all those steps can be skipped and I can be censored right now for the kind of jokes I write—well, from there I could be censored for the way that I set the table when I eat. Or for the way I walk."

In addition to books and films, Wagner is also the author, with artist Julian Allen, of the comic strip *Wild Palms.* The strip appears every month in *Details* magazine. It is a surreal and disjointed look at life in Hollywood from an ex-insider's point of view. Prone to passages of near-nonsense, the comic's narrator is a formerly successful film executive who is down on his luck and out of his mind. The ongoing story follows his hapless course through the fringes of Hollywood's elite circles. In his strained mind, the people and situations he encounters evoke images from famous films, in one instance he refers to a nanny as looking "like Meryl Streep did in that movie where the dingo stole her baby." In association with noted director, writer, and producer Oliver Stone (*Platoon, Born on the Fourth of July* and *JFK*), Wagner has written scripts for a 1993 television adaptation of *Wild Palms* for ABC-TV.

BIOGRAPHICAL/CRITICAL SOURCES:

PERIODICALS

Details, December, 1992, pp. 197-98.
Interview, March, 1989.
Los Angeles Magazine, August, 1991.
Los Angeles Times, February 27, 1987; June 7, 1989.
Nation, June 19, 1986, p. 860-62; December 23, 1991, p. 825-26.
New Republic, July 10, 1989, p. 26-28.
New York Times, February 27, 1987; June 9, 1989.
New York Times Book Review, September 29, 1991, p. 22.
Premiere, June, 1991, p. 110.
Time, June 12, 1989, p. 73.
Vogue, October, 1991.
Washington Post, March 2, 1987; June 17, 1989.

WAINWRIGHT, A(lfred) 1907-1991

PERSONAL: Born January 17, 1907, in Blackburn, Lancashire, England; died January, 1991; *Education:* Attended Newcastle University.

CAREER: Municipal treasurer and author; appeared on television in Great Britain.

WRITINGS:

TRAVEL; PUBLISHED BY WESTMORLAND GAZETTE,
EXCEPT WHERE NOTED

A Pictorial Guide to the Lakeland Fells: Being an Illustrated Account of a Study and Exploration of the Mountains in the English Lake District (seven books), H. Marshall, 1955-66.
Fellwanderer: The Story behind the Guidebooks, 1966.
A Lakeland Sketchbook, 1969.
A Second Lakeland Sketchbook, 1970.
Walks in Limestone Country, 1970.
A Third Lakeland Sketchbook, 1971.
A Fourth Lakeland Sketchbook, 1972.
Walks on the Howgill Fells and Adjoining Fells, 1972.
A Fifth Lakeland Sketchbook, 1973.
A Coast to Coast Walk: St. Bees Head to Robin Hood's Bay, 1973.
Scottish Mountain Drawings: The Northern Highlands, 1974.
Pennine Way Companion: A Pictorial Guide, 1976.
Scottish Mountain Drawings: The Western Highlands, 1976.
Scottish Mountain Drawings: The Central Highlands, c. 1977.
Scottish Mountain Drawings: The North-Western Highlands, 1977.
A Dales Sketchbook, 1977.
Kendall in the Nineteenth Century: A Book of Drawings, research by John Marsh, 1977.
A Second Dales Sketchbook, 1978.
Scottish Mountain Drawings: The Eastern Highlands, 1978.
A Furness Sketchbook, 1978.
A Second Furness Sketchbook, 1979.
A Ritole Sketchbook, 1980.
An Eden Sketchbook, 1980.
A Lune Sketchbook, 1980.
Lakeland Mountain Drawings, Volume 1, 1980.
A Bowland Sketchbook, 1981.
Welsh Mountain Drawings, 1981.
Lakeland Mountain Drawings, Volume 2, 1981.
A North Wales Sketchbook, 1982.
A Wyre Sketchbook, 1982.
Lakeland Mountain Drawings, Volume 3, 1982.
A South Wales Sketchbook, 1983.
Wainwright in Lakeland, Governors of Abbot Hall Art Gallery, 1983.
Lakeland Mountain Drawings, Volume 4, 1983.
Lakeland Mountain Drawings, Volume 5, 1984.
A Peak District Sketchbook, 1984.
Firewalking with Wainwright: Eighteen of the Author's Favourite Walks in Lakeland, with photographs by Derry Brabbs, Joseph, 1984.
Wainwright on the Pennine Way, with photographs by Brabbs, Joseph, 1985.
A Pennine Journey: A Story of a Long Walk in 1938, Joseph, 1986.
Ex-Fellwanderer: A Thanksgiving, 1987.
Wainwright's Coast to Coast Walk, with photographs by Brabbs, Joseph, 1987.
Wainwright in Scotland, with photographs by Brabbs, Joseph, c. 1988.
Fellwalking with a Camera, 1988.
Westmorland Heritage, 1988.
Wainwright on the Lakeland Mountain Passes, with photographs by Brabbs, Joseph, 1989.
Wainwright's Favourite Lakeland Mountains, with photographs by Brabbs, Joseph, 1991.
Wainwright in the Limestone Dales, Joseph, 1991.

SIDELIGHTS: A. Wainwright enjoyed a career as a municipal treasurer before writing books about walking tours of his beloved Great Britain. He is especially remembered for his work on England's Lake District, made famous in literature by romantic poets such as William Wordsworth and Samuel Taylor Coleridge. Wainwright began a seven-volume series entitled *A Pictorial Guide to the Lakeland Fells* in 1955, completing the work in 1966. After this, he penned most of his books—which were filled with maps, drawings, and later, photographs—for the small publishing company of Westmorland Gazette. According to Christopher Bray in the *Spectator,* Wainwright "never received a penny from their sales. Instead, all the profits have gone to a Kendall [England] animal sanctuary."

Later in his writing career, Wainwright teamed with photographer Derry Brabbs to do a series of books for the publisher Michael Joseph. One of these, *Wainwright on the Pennine Way,* was described by a *Publishers Weekly* reviewer as "not a guidebook but a 'souvenir' "; the critic also enjoyed Wainwright's "wry commentary." Another book Wainwright undertook for Joseph—this time without Brabbs—is *A Pennine Journey: The Story of a Long Walk in 1938.* It caused Deborah Singmaster to comment on its anti-feminist language in the *Times Literary Supplement,* but she also noted that "Wainwright is chiefly interested in the business of putting one foot in front of the other and reaching his goal." Wainwright continued writing until his death in 1991; two of his last books were

Wainwright's Favourite Lakeland Mountains and *Wainwright in the Limestone Dales.*

BIOGRAPHICAL/CRITICAL SOURCES:

PERIODICALS

Publishers Weekly, October 18, 1985, p. 55.
Spectator, July 20, 1991, pp. 33-34.
Times Literary Supplement, February 19, 1988, p. 201.*

*   *   *

WAJCMAN, Judy   1950-

PERSONAL: Born December 12, 1950, in Australia. *Education:* Monash University, B.A. (honors), 1972; Sussex University, M.A., 1974; Cambridge University, Ph.D., 1980.

ADDRESSES: *Office*—Department of Sociology, University of New South Wales, P.O. Box 1, Kensington, New South Wales 2033, Australia.

CAREER: Cambridge University, Cambridge, England, instructor in sociology and women in society, 1975-80, visiting scholar in the department of applied economics, 1988-89; University of Edinburgh, Edinburgh, Scotland, lecturer in sociology and work and technology, 1980-83; University of New South Wales, Kensington, Australia, worked as senior lecturer, became associate professor, 1983—. University of Sydney, lecturer, 1983-85; Industrial Relations Research Unit, University of Warwick, principal research fellow, 1992-94.

AWARDS, HONORS: Research grant, Darwin College, Cambridge, 1977-78; Norman Laski Senior Studentship, St. John's College, Cambridge, 1978-80; research grants from Federal Bureau of Labour Market Research, University of New South Wales, Australian Research Grants Scheme, and Monash University, all 1986 and 1987.

WRITINGS:

(Coauthor) *Women in Society: Interdisciplinary Essays,* Virago, 1981.
Women in Control: Dilemmas of a Workers' Co-operative, St. Martin's, 1983.
(Editor with Donald Mackenzie) *The Social Shaping of Technology,* Open University Press, 1985.
Feminism Confronts Technology, Pennsylvania State University Press, 1991.

Contributor to books, including *Technology and the Labour Process,* edited by E. Willis, Allen & Unwin, 1988; *Women, Work and Computerization,* edited by K. Tijdens and others, North Holland, 1988. Contributor of articles to periodicals, including *Capital and Class, Social Studies of Science, Australian Society, Australian Feminist Studies, Current Affairs Bulletin,* and *Journal of Industrial Relations.*

WORK IN PROGRESS: "Patriarchy, Technology and Conceptions of Skill," an article for *Work and Occupations.*

SIDELIGHTS: Judy Wajcman told *CA:* "My research interests in recent years have centered on employment, technological change, and gender divisions. My research on technological change developed while I was a lecturer at the University of Edinburgh, and I developed a theoretical framework for the analysis of technology and social change in my book with Donald Mackenzie, *The Social Shaping of Technology.* When I took up my present position at the University of New South Wales, I set up a major research project on 'The Future of Work,' which was more empirically based and was concerned with the employment implications of new technology. The project on the future of work is now complete. Several articles based on this research have already been published. My last main project resulted in a book, entitled *Feminism Confronts Technology,* which is both a development from this empirical research and the logical follow-up to my previous book. Drawing on established work in the history of technology, *The Social Shaping of Technology* looked in a general way at how technologies are affected by the social and economic context in which they develop. The aim of *Feminism Confronts Technology* is to bring together sociological debates over the nature of work and technology with recent feminist work on the gendered nature of science and technology. While the approach is necessarily sociological, this project has an interdisciplinary character, drawing on material in economics, history, philosophy of science, and education."

*   *   *

WALKER, Betty A.

PERSONAL: *Education:* Received B.A. and M.S. from Hunter College of the City University of New York, and Ph.D. from the University of Southern California.

ADDRESSES: *Home*—Los Angeles, CA. *Office*—Division of Counseling and Educational Psychology, University of Southern California School of Education, Los Angeles, CA 90089-0031.

CAREER: English teacher, counselor, and director of minority programs at a public junior high school in New York City, 1954-63; high school counselor in Arcadia, CA, 1963-65; Citrus College, Azusa, CA, assistant director of Counseling Center, 1965-67; school psychologist and coordinator of family counseling and group counseling programs for the public schools of Santa Monica, CA, 1967-69; El Camino College, Torrance, CA, psychological counselor, coordinator of minority students' enrichment program, and adviser to Women's Studies Center, 1969-72; Gateways Hospital and Community Mental Health Center, Los Angeles, CA, research psychologist and family group therapy facilitator, 1974-76; University of Southern California, Los Angeles, associate professor of counseling and educational psychology, 1974—, behavioral science consultant and program evaluator, 1978-81, member of executive council of Peace Studies Center, 1984-89. Licensed psychologist and marriage, family, and child therapist; credentialed in pupil personnel services, community college teaching, and school counseling; private practice of clinical psychology and marriage, family, and child therapy, 1969—; University of Southern California, behavioral science consultant and organizational specialist with Family Practice Center, 1981-89. Women's Action for Nuclear Disarmament, member of advisory board, 1984-88; Hiroshima and Nagasaki Commemoration Peace and Arts Festival, member of coordinating council, 1985.

MEMBER: American Psychological Association, National Register of Health Service Providers, Society of Teachers of Family Medicine, Western Psychological Association, California State Psychological Association, Group Psychotherapy Association of Southern California.

WRITINGS:

(With Marilyn Mehr) *The Courage to Achieve: Why America's Brightest Women Struggle to Fulfill Their Promise,* Simon & Schuster, 1992.

Work represented in anthologies, including *Crisis Intervention Handbook,* Wadsworth, 1989. Contributor of about twenty articles to professional journals.

WORK IN PROGRESS: Ongoing research on women's issues.

*   *   *

WALL, Stephen D. 1948-

PERSONAL: Born July 1, 1948, in Fayetteville, NC; son of W. A. (in business) and Rebecca D. Wall; married Kathleen Borger (a registered nurse), April 4, 1988; children: Elsie Kathleen. *Education:* North Carolina State University, B.S., 1970; University of Rochester, M.S., 1972.

ADDRESSES: Office—c/o Taylor & Francis, Inc., 1900 Frost Rd., Suite 101, Bristol, PA 19007-1598.

CAREER: Jet Propulsion Laboratory, Pasadena, CA, staff member, 1978—.

WRITINGS:

(With Kenneth W. Ledbetter) *Design of Mission Operations Systems for Scientific Remote Sensing,* Taylor & Francis, 1992.

Contributor to scientific journals.

*   *   *

WALTHER, Eric H(arry) 1960-

PERSONAL: Born September 23, 1960, in Los Angeles, CA; son of Ralph and Harriett (Bauman) Walther; married Helen Warwick (a librarian), May 31, 1987. *Education:* California State University, Fullerton, B.A., 1982; Louisiana State University, M.A., Ph.D., 1988. *Avocational interests:* Baseball, playing with dog.

ADDRESSES: Home—Houston, TX. *Office*—Department of History, University of Houston, Houston, TX 77204.

CAREER: Rice University, Houston, TX, editorial assistant for *The Papers of Jefferson Davis,* 1988-89; Texas A & M University, College Station, lecturer in history, 1989-91; University of Houston, Houston, TX, lecturer in history, 1991—. *Virginia Magazine of History and Biography,* editorial advisor, 1989-92.

MEMBER: Southern Historical Association.

AWARDS, HONORS: Andrew W. Mellon fellow, Virginia Historical Society, 1989.

WRITINGS:

The Fire-Eaters, Louisiana State University Press, 1992.

WORK IN PROGRESS: Editor and author of introduction to a new edition of Nathaniel Beverley Tucker's *Series of Lectures on the Science of Government,* originally published in 1845; a biography of William Lowndes Yancey.

*   *   *

WARFIELD, (A.) Gallatin 1946-

PERSONAL: Born August 25, 1946, in Baltimore, MD; son of Albert (an investment broker and manager) and Caroline (an artist; maiden name, Kirwan) Warfield; married second wife, Diana Mariella Ugarte (a model), May 7, 1988; children: A. Gallatin IV, Erin Smith. *Education:* Princeton University, A.B., 1968; University of Maryland, J.D., 1973.

ADDRESSES: Home—2598 Route 94, Woodbine, MD 21797. *Office*—3440 Ellicott Center Dr., No. 103, P.O.

Box 2112, Ellicott City, MD 21041. *Agent*—Arthur Pine, 250 West 57th St., New York, NY 10019.

CAREER: Maryland Attorney General's Office, assistant attorney general, 1974-76; Howard County States Attorney's Office, Howard County, MD, chief of Felony Division, 1976-89; criminal defense attorney in private practice, 1990—. Columbia Bank, member of advisory board; Glenelg Country School, member of board of trustees. *Military service:* Maryland Air National Guard, fighter pilot, 1969-77; became captain.

WRITINGS:

State versus Justice (novel), Warner Books, 1992.

WORK IN PROGRESS: A legal suspense novel, for Warner Books.

*   *   *

WAYANS, Keenen Ivory 1958(?)-

PERSONAL: Born c. 1958, in New York, NY; son of Howell (in sales) and Elvira (a homemaker) Wayans. *Education:* Attended Tuskegee Institute.

ADDRESSES: Home—Los Angeles, CA. *Office*—Ivory Way Productions, 5746 Sunset Blvd., Hollywood, CA 90028.

CAREER: Comedian, actor, director, producer, and screenwriter. Began career as a stand-up comedian at various comedy clubs in New York City and Los Angeles, CA. Television work includes: actor in *Irene* (pilot), 1981, and *For Love and Honor* (series), 1983-84; coproducer and cowriter of *Robert Townsend and His Partners in Crime* (comedy special), 1987; executive producer and writer of *Hammer, Slammer, and Slade* (comedy pilot), 1990; creator, executive producer, actor, and head writer, *In Living Color* (series), 1990-92; guest on specials, including *Motown Thirty: What's Goin' On!*, 1990, *MTV's 1990 Video Music Awards,* 1990, *Comic Relief V,* 1991, *The Fifth Annual American Comedy Awards,* 1991, and *The American Music Awards,* 1991; guest on series *A Different World, Benson,* and *Cheers.* Film work includes: actor, *Star 80,* 1983; actor and cowriter, *Hollywood Shuffle,* 1987; actor, coproducer, and cowriter, *Eddie Murphy Raw,* 1987; director, actor, and writer, *I'm Gonna Git You Sucka,* 1988; cowriter, *The Five Heartbeats,* 1991.

MEMBER: Screen Actors Guild, Directors Guild of America, Screen Writers Guild.

AWARDS, HONORS: Emmy Award for outstanding variety, music, or comedy program, American Academy of Television Arts and Sciences, 1990, for *In Living Color;* Emmy Award nominations for outstanding writing in a

variety or music program, 1990 and 1991, and outstanding individual performance in a variety or music program, 1991, all for *In Living Color.*

WRITINGS:

SCRIPTS FOR TELEVISION

(With Robert Townsend) *Robert Townsend and His Partners in Crime* (special), HBO, 1987.
Hammer, Slammer, and Slade (pilot), ABC, 1990.
In Living Color (series), Fox, 1990-92.

SCREENPLAYS

(With Townsend) *Hollywood Shuffle,* Samuel Goldwyn, 1987.
(With Eddie Murphy and Townsend) *Eddie Murphy Raw* (sketch portions), Paramount, 1987.
(And director) *I'm Gonna Git You Sucka,* Metro-Goldwyn-Mayer/United Artists, 1988.
(With Townsend) *The Five Heartbeats,* Twentieth Century-Fox, 1991.

WORK IN PROGRESS: Writing comedy film with brother.

SIDELIGHTS: The second oldest of ten children, Keenen Ivory Wayans grew up in a household where suppertime was filled with humor and laughter. His ready-made audience afforded him the opportunity to develop his unique brand of comedy and to practice for a career in the entertainment business. After his beginnings as a stand-up comedian, Wayans successfully ventured into acting, directing, and writing for film and television. His work, which often pokes fun at the stereotyping of blacks and their culture, has earned him a devoted public following. From his involvement in films like *Hollywood Shuffle* and *I'm Gonna Git You Sucka* to his creation of the prime-time television comedy series *In Living Color,* Wayans has presented controversial, cutting-edge humor that often catches viewers off guard and finds a mixed critical reception. "I want to be an entity," Wayans told *New York's* Dinitia Smith, adding "a source of product, people."

Wayans was born and raised in New York City. Early in his life he experienced racism firsthand. For example, on occasion one local white police officer would prompt Wayans and his brother to race each other and then trip them. Even though Wayans and his family were victims of prejudice at times, he told *People* contributors Charles E. Cohen and Vicki Sheff that his mother and father "always built up our self-esteem." Wayans's father had a career in sales, and his mother was a homemaker. The family lived in a tenement in Harlem until Wayans was six years old and then moved into a predominantly white housing project where Wayans was frequently harassed by white teenagers. The children shared three rooms, and for privacy Wayans would retreat into a bedroom closet and dream about his future as an entertainer.

The same year they moved, Wayans realized he wanted to become a comedian after he saw actor and comic Richard Pryor delivering a stand-up performance on television. "He was doing routines about being poor, about looking for money, about being beaten up by the school bully. It was all happening to me at the time," explained Wayans to Smith. His penchant for humor was also fueled by his family, who would practice making each other laugh at dinnertime. Wayans recalled for Smith, "All of us sitting around the table, the food would just fly out of our mouths! We'd love it when someone would get mad. That's where we get the edge to our comedy."

Because of his flare for comedy, Wayans stood out in a crowd at his high school. "I was a tall, gangly, Afro-wearing teen-ager who figured his best shot at attracting girls was by making them laugh," he confessed to *Hollywood Reporter* writer Christopher Vaughn. Wayans and his younger brother Damon were inseparable, rattling off jokes as a team; they would make up characters and act them out for their friends and family. (Some of these characters later appeared on Wayans's show *In Living Color,* which also starred Damon.) Wayans told Smith that he stayed away from drugs and alcohol in high school, and he worked long hours as a McDonald's manager to help support his family.

After graduation, Wayans attended Alabama's Tuskegee Institute under a scholarship to study engineering. "I had such culture shock down there. . . . [Y]ou'd get downtown and it wasn't nothing but a pharmacy and a Goodwill store," recalled Wayans to *Interview* contributor Kevin Sessums. Wayans continued to liberate his comedy in college, and before his senior year began he decided to quit school and follow his dream of becoming a comedian. He began his career in New York City's prominent comedy club, The Improv, where he met then sixteen-year-old actor and comedian Eddie Murphy. Wayans told Smith that he remembers the young Murphy stating, "'I thought I was the only funny black guy in New York. Now I see there are two.'" Later Wayans would help write Murphy's concert film, *Eddie Murphy Raw,* which became the most lucrative concert film made to that date. Wayans also met Robert Townsend, another aspiring young black entertainer, at the Improv. In 1980 Wayans moved to Los Angeles where he continued his stand-up comedy and tried out for parts in motion pictures and television.

Landing only an occasional television role in Los Angeles, Wayans decided to venture into filmmaking, which he believed was also more conducive to his outlandish form of comedy. He told Vaughn that the scarcity of quality act-ing roles for African Americans in the early 1980s also motivated him to make and act in his own films. Wayans rectified this inequity with Townsend, who had also moved to Los Angeles from New York, in their collaborative 1987 motion picture *Hollywood Shuffle.* Townsend explained the objective for *Hollywood Shuffle* to *Ebony* reporter Marilyn Marshall: "The majority of jobs [acting roles for African Americans] are bogus, [focusing on] stereotypes. Yet people fight for them, and in *Hollywood Shuffle,* I spoke up and said, 'That's not right.' And I tried to do it in a funny way."

A satire, *Hollywood Shuffle* revolves around struggling actor Bobby Taylor, played by Townsend, who must work at a hot dog stand to make enough money to support himself. Taylor perceives that because he is an African American his chances of finding a respectable part in a film are practically nonexistent. Therefore, he auditions and receives the lead role as a pimp in a blaxploitation film—a genre capitalizing on the portrayal of dubious black stereotypes, including pimps, drug dealers, murderers, and thieves. The movie, *Jivetime Jimmy's Revenge,* is being written, produced, and directed by white people. The black actors are trained and coached by whites to act more "black." Disheartened by his role, Taylor imagines himself in satirical situations. For example, he envisions an acting school where black people are taught "black" characteristics by white people; becomes Superman; defeats a bully named Jerry Curl (played by Wayans) by confiscating his curl activator; reviews blaxploitation films in a spin-off of Gene Siskel and Roger Ebert's movie review television show, *At the Movies;* stars in a blaxploitation film called *Rambro: First Youngblood;* and becomes a victim of ridicule by the National Association for the Advancement of Colored People (NAACP) for acting in blaxploitation films. Following his dream sequences, Taylor realizes he has doubts about his involvement in *Jivetime Jimmy's Revenge* and quits. He also pleas for the other minority cast members to leave the production. Later he auditions for a more tolerable acting role as a mailman in a commercial.

Although *Hollywood Shuffle* was written by both Townsend and Wayans, the latter received meager recognition from the critics for his contributions. Wayans told Smith, however, that he felt Townsend deserved the greater publicity. Critics were generally positive about the production. In *New Republic* Stanley Kauffmann called *Hollywood Shuffle* a "lively, knowledgeable film." Armond White, a *Film Comment* contributor, found that the movie "offers a shrewd look at Hollywood's benighted attitudes and nonthinking." "*Hollywood Shuffle* is an exhilarating blast of anger and disgust. Much of it is wildly funny," wrote David Denby in his review for *New York.* And a

Motion Picture Guide writer found Townsend and Wayans's film to be "downright hilarious."

Following his success with *Hollywood Shuffle,* Wayans began work on a parody of his own. A satire of blaxploitation films, the movie was released as *I'm Gonna Git You Sucka.* Wayans, who wrote, directed, and acted in the film, also cast two family members, Damon and Kim. Like the earlier movie, Wayans's solo comedy pokes fun at Hollywood stereotyping. He admits to receiving inspiration from the 1980 slapstick film *Airplane!* when creating *I'm Gonna Git You Sucka.* Wayans told Sessums that the movie is not intended to "satiriz[e] black people but bad moviemaking." In the film, Jack Slade, played by Wayans, takes leave from the U.S. Army to return to his hometown of "Any Ghetto, U.S.A." He wants to investigate his brother Junebug's death, which was caused by wearing too many gold chains. When Slade learns of a gold-chain pusher named Mr. Big, he vows to attack the malefactor's operations to avenge his brother's death. He solicits help from former stars of 1970s blaxploitation films, including *Slaughter*'s Jim Brown and *Truck Turner*'s Isaac Hayes. However, the heroes have lost their abilities to battle the bad guys, creating havoc as they trip and set off a number of loaded guns and detonate dynamite before breaking through the window of Mr. Big's offices. Eventually Slade finds himself fighting alone, but with help from his mother his mission succeeds.

In *People* Wayans expounded on his aspirations for his film: "I wanted to do something that was true to its ethnicity but not restricted to it. That's important to me as a black filmmaker because I feel that our society is painted to be more racist than it is." In the eyes of some white critics, his film was regarded as being degrading to blacks. "There is no racial issue," responded Wayans to Vaughn. "*Sucka* is a parody of a genre film." He concluded, "these are white guys trying to tell me, a black man, what is funny to black audiences." When asked by *Rolling Stone* contributor Jill Feldman if his movie was just another blaxploitation film, Wayans reflected: "There's really no such thing as blacksploitation. Blacksploitation is just an action-adventure movie with black men in the lead." Other critics gave *I'm Gonna Git You Sucka* rave reviews. A reviewer for *The Motion Picture Guide* stated that "Wayans keeps the jokes coming fast and thick, never giving the audience time to stop laughing." The critic concluded, "*I'm Gonna Git You Sucka* is on target often enough to make Wayans a talent worth watching." And Stuart Klawans stated in his article for *Nation,* "No joke is too dumb, no pose too embarrassing, in this amiably slapdash and utterly engaging story."

Wayans's film received a favorable reception despite some marketing problems. He told *American Film* contributor Betsy Sharkey that United Artists (UA) "never got be-

yond the fact that [the movie] was black." Sharkey confirmed Hollywood's bias toward black films through a studio marketing executive who told her: "Historically, there is a belief that black films don't do as well" as white films. She also quoted producer Dale Pollock as saying, "Black films do have an extra burden. They have to be better." Wayans believes such negative attitudes prevailed at UA when it was time to market *I'm Gonna Git You Sucka.* Forecasting that the film would not do well in white areas, UA only promoted the film in predominantly black neighborhoods. Wayans was upset over the UA decision, thinking that the movie should be advertised to white audiences as well. Wayans told Sharkey, "I could have set myself on fire, and it wouldn't have changed their minds." Yet Wayans's film proved successful, grossing nearly seven times its production costs. In Sharkey's article Wayans also commented on how he deals with negative reactions from the film industry. "There are times when you ask yourself, 'What does a black man have to do?' " he related. "But you have to channel those feelings into something productive. Bitterness will kill you." In 1990 when Wayans talked to Cohen and Sheff, he maintained that "this town still has not embraced the black creator."

After attending a screening for *I'm Gonna Git You Sucka,* Fox television network executives enticed Wayans to produce a television program telling him he could have creative reign over the series. Taking the offer, in 1990 Wayans developed a skit format program titled *In Living Color* that has been compared to veteran sketch show *Saturday Night Live.* The show consists of bawdy comedy skits parodying television shows and commercials, motion pictures, black stereotypes and culture, and celebrities, especially prominent black figures. Fox executive Harris Katleman talked about the show's cutting-edge nature to Andrew Feinberg of *TV Guide.* "Two years ago, no one would have aired *In Living Color,*" Katleman opined. "It's too different, too ethnic, and brings up too many issues that standards and practices [censors have] never had to deal with before." "There's nothing subtle about the humor. It's extremely visceral, in-your-face stuff," said *In Living Color* writer John Bowman in Jeffrey Ressner's feature for *Rolling Stone.* Ressner himself concluded his article assessing that "*In Living Color* is about raunch and being raunchy."

In Living Color also features dancing by a group called The Fly Girls and performances by guest musicians. Wayans explained to Smith that "*In Living Color* shows people different sides of black life and black culture. It's important that I do it honestly. I don't just show the black bourgeoisie or professionals—or criminals. I try to show every side of black life." The cast mainly consists of black actors. Four of Wayans's nine siblings have appeared on the show—Damon, Kim, and Marlon acted, and Shawn, who was at first the D.J. for The Fly Girls, became a member of the acting team in 1991. Kim Wayans told Cohen and Sheff, "We're a very tight family, almost like the Osmonds"—a family of popular entertainers who had a variety show in the 1970s. According to Cohen and Sheff, "critics tripped over their adjectives with praise" for Wayans's show.

While In Living Color has received generally favorable reviews, it has been criticized by some viewers for emphasizing stereotypes. One of the skits that received such concern is "The Homeboy Shopping Network." This sketch, which plays on the stereotype that blacks are hoods, features two young black men who sell stolen goods on a home shopping program. Another skit, "The Equity Express Card: Helping the Right Sort of People," presents a wealthy black man having problems using a credit card. Also, certain skits have proved unsettling to some feminists, including sketches wielding jokes about women's breasts, shaving, and tampon use. In particular, one segment featured a woman's talk show ending with women clawing at each other. Members of the gay community have also voiced complaints, citing the characterizations in the "Men on Film" skit, in which two gay black men review movies. Some viewers feel that these depictions, in which the actors speak with feminine voices and rave about leading men in movies, are supplying a dubious representation of gay people to the public. Wayans responded to the reproaching comments in Harry F. Waters and Lynda Wright's Newsweek article: "If the show picked on only one group, I could understand people being uptight. But we get everybody."

In light of In Living Color's controversial nature, Fox network censors actively oversee the writing. Tamara Rawitt, the show's former producer, told Smith: "Usually they jump in the car and come right over during taping." In one instance Wayans shot two versions of a sketch, one racier than the other. The sketch in question was a parody on 2 Live Crew singer Luther Campbell, whose album was banned in several states for being overly sexual. Wayans had hoped the more suggestive version would be chosen, but was disappointed. Wayans did admit to Ressner, however, that he does have certain standards for his comedy. He said that the show would never feature sketches on Nazi skinheads, the Ku Klux Klan, crack cocaine, or AIDS.

Despite these criticisms from viewers and censors, In Living Color has been described as a "groundbreaking comedy show" by Entertainment Weekly contributors Alan Carter and Juliann Garey. Smith called it "a surprise hit" and also emphasized that the program frequently ranked as one of the top-twenty shows in the Nielsen ratings. Ressner lauded In Living Color as being "TV's hottest new comedy show."

After almost three years of producing In Living Color, Wayans and Fox officials became entangled in a dispute over the rerun syndication of the show. The program's copyright was scheduled to revert to Wayans during 1993, but in December 1992, Fox declared that they would air the reruns first. Given no time to challenge Fox before they announced their plans, Wayans ultimately decided to leave In Living Color. "It was absolutely the most difficult thing I've ever had to do," said Wayans to Carter and Garey. "But I had to. I couldn't condone what they did, and how they did it. No one wanted me to leave, but I couldn't continue in good conscience. I couldn't give them a show that was a certain quality and not have them return that quality." Because of Fox's decision, the other Wayans cast members wanted to leave. Having no obligations to the show, Damon and Marlon left immediately, but Kim and Shawn were required by contract to stay. After departing from In Living Color, Wayans revealed he would try to create another comedy show on a different network.

During his career, Wayans has made waves in Hollywood, helping to bring African Americans to the forefront of the entertainment industry. He has not been alone in his efforts, however. Other prominent black males are also working to increase African American participation in quality productions. They include Townsend, Murphy, actor and talk-show host Arsenio Hall, and actor and filmmaker Spike Lee. Calling themselves the "black pack," these five entertainers are best friends and provide support to each other in business. Yet each has made his own name in Hollywood. "I've had to be my own big brother in this business," Wayans related to Cohen and Sheff. "I never talk to people about things. I work them out for myself."

BIOGRAPHICAL/CRITICAL SOURCES:

BOOKS

The Motion Picture Guide: 1989 Annual, Cinebooks, 1988, pp. 119-120, and 1989, p. 84.
Newsmakers 91, Cumulation, Gale, 1991, pp. 455-457.

PERIODICALS

American Film, July/August, 1989, pp. 22-27, 53-54.
Ebony, July, 1987, pp. 54, 56, 58.
Entertainment Weekly, January 15, 1993, pp. 6-7.
Film Comment, March/April, 1987, pp. 11-14.
Hollywood Reporter, January 25, 1989, p. 13.
Interview, December, 1988, p. 56.
Los Angeles Times, April 15, 1990.
Nation, February 13, 1989.
New Republic, May 4, 1987, pp. 26-27.
Newsweek, May 21, 1990.
New York, April 6, 1987, pp. 90-91; October 8, 1990, pp. 29-35.

People, December 12, 1988, p. 185; June 11, 1990, pp. 75-76.
Rolling Stone, November 3, 1988; April 23, 1992.
Time, April 27, 1987, p. 79.
TV Guide, June 2, 1990.*

—*Sketch by Jane M. Kelly*

* * *

WEBSTER, Sally 1938-

PERSONAL: Born May 24, 1938, in Hammond, IN; daughter of James E. (in business) and Robin (a homemaker; maiden name, Wright) Beyer; married Albert K. Webster (a symphony manager), 1961; children: Albert U. B., Katherine. *Education:* Barnard College, B.A., 1959; University of Cincinnati, M.A., 1974; Graduate Center of the City University of New York, Ph.D., 1985. *Politics:* Democrat. *Religion:* Unitarian-Universalist.

ADDRESSES: Home—158 West 94th St., New York, NY 10025. *Office*—Department of Art, Herbert H. Lehman College of the City University of New York, Bronx, NY 10468.

CAREER: Herbert H. Lehman College of the City University of New York, Bronx, NY, associate professor of art, 1985—.

WRITINGS:

William Morris Hunt, 1824-1879 (monograph), Cambridge University Press, 1991.
(Editor with Harriet Senie) *Critical Issues in Public Art: Content, Context, and Controversy,* HarperCollins, 1992.

WORK IN PROGRESS: "*Modern Woman*": *A Mural by Mary Cassatt; Modern Art in America: New Perspectives,* completion expected in 1995.

* * *

WEISS, Winfried (Ferdinand) 1937-1991

OBITUARY NOTICE—See index for *CA* sketch: Born November 10, 1937, in Pfarrweisach, Germany; immigrated to the United States, 1956, naturalized citizen, 1963; died November 21, 1991. Educator and author. Weiss joined the staff at California State University in 1966, where he rose through the ranks to become a professor of foreign languages eleven years later. Among his works is his autobiography, *A Nazi Childhood,* which was released in 1983. Weiss also contributed to literary journals.

OBITUARIES AND OTHER SOURCES:

Date of death provided by Foreign Languages department of California State University.

* * *

WERCKMEISTER, O(tto) K(arl) 1934-

PERSONAL: Born April 26, 1934, in Berlin, Germany; son of Karl Werckmeister (an art dealer) and Rose (Petzold) Werckmeister (an artist); married Maria Eugenia Lacarra, 1965 (divorced, 1983); children: Christina, Robert, Veronica. *Education:* Freie Universitaet Berlin, Ph.D., 1958.

ADDRESSES: Home—2214 Payne St., Evanston, IL 60201. *Office*—Department of Art History, Northwestern University, Evanston, IL 60208.

CAREER: University of California, Los Angeles, professor of art history, 1971-84; Northwestern University, Evanston, IL, Mary Jane Crowe Distinguished Professor of Art History, 1984—. John Simon Guggenheim Memorial fellow, 1981-82; fellow at Wissenschaftskolleg, Berlin, 1986-87; held research fellowships at University of London and German Archaeological Institute, Madrid; visiting appointments at University of Marburg, University of Texas at Austin, and Hamburg University.

MEMBER: College Art Association of America (now College Art Association; founding member of Caucus for Marxism and Art, 1976).

WRITINGS:

Der Deckel des Codex aureus von St. Emmeram: Ein Goldschmiedewerk des 9. Jahrhunderts, Verlag Heitz, 1963.
Die Bilder der drei Propheten in der Biblia Hispalense, F. H. Kerle Verlag, 1963.
Three Problems of Tradition in Pre-Carolingian Figure Style: From Visigothic to Insular Illumination, Hodges Figgis, 1963.
Irisch-northumbrische Buchmalerei des 8. Jahrhunderts und monastische Spiritualitaet, de Gruyter, 1967.
Ende der Aesthetik, S. Fischer, 1971.
Ideologie und Kunst bei Marx und andere Essays, S. Fischer, 1974.
The Political Ideology of the Bayeux Tapestry, Centro italiano di Studi sull'Alto Medioevo, 1976.
The Making of Paul Klee's Career, 1914-1920, University of Chicago Press, 1989.
(Editor with Rainer Rumold) *The Ideological Crisis of Expressionism: The Literary and Artistic German War Colony in Belgium, 1914-1918,* Camden House, 1990.
Zitadellenkultur, C. Hanser, 1989, published in English as *Citadel Culture,* University of Chicago Press, 1991.

Also author of *Versuche ueber Paul Klee,* 1981, and *Bildwende,* 1993. Contributor to books, including *The Villa as Hegemonic Architecture,* by Reinhard Bentmann, Humanities Press International, 1992.

WORK IN PROGRESS: The Political Confrontation of the Arts: From the Great Depression to the Second World War, 1929-1939; research on Romanesque art, political history of art of the twentieth century, and theory and historiography of art history.

SIDELIGHTS: O. K. Werckmeister is the author of *The Making of Paul Klee's Career, 1914-1920,* a chronicle of events in Swiss artist Paul Klee's life between the First World War and the beginnings of the Weimar Republic in Germany. Peter Vergo, in a *Times Literary Supplement* review, wrote that the book has an "intellectual sophistication for once equal to the extraordinary complexities of Klee's mind and work." Vergo further said that Werckmeister paints a very "remarkable and fascinating" picture of Klee as an artist orchestrating his own career. Werckmeister evokes wartime Germany vividly, and this, according to Vergo, gives the reader insight into "Klee's motives and impulses . . . [and] the workings of his mind." Vergo predicted that the book would be controversial and could not be ignored by those seriously interested in Klee's life and artistic development.

BIOGRAPHICAL/CRITICAL SOURCES:

PERIODICALS

Times Literary Supplement, January 12-18, 1990, p. 38.

* * *

WHITE, F(rederick) Clifton   1918-1993

OBITUARY NOTICE—See index for *CA* sketch: Born June 13, 1918, in Leonardsville, NY; died of cancer, January 9, 1993, in Greenwich, CT. Educator, public affairs consultant, and author. After teaching social and political science for eleven years, White founded his own public affairs consulting firm in 1961 and assisted corporations and politicians with political and organizational strategies. He was the mastermind behind the Republican party's 1964 nomination of Barry Goldwater as presidential candidate, and served on many presidential campaigns in the United States as well as overseas. White's books include *You Should Be a Politician,* with Joseph Eley, and *Suite 3505: The Story of the Draft Goldwater Movement* and *Why Reagan Won,* both with William J. Gill.

OBITUARIES AND OTHER SOURCES:

BOOKS

Who's Who in the East, 23rd edition, Marquis, 1990, p. 906.

PERIODICALS

New York Times, January 10, 1993, p. 34.

* * *

WILBER, Cynthia J.   1951-

PERSONAL: Born August 17, 1951; daughter of Del (a baseball player) and Taffy (in public relations) Wilber; married William H. Clopton III (an artist), November, 1973; children: Matthew Carey, Simon J. *Education:* Attended Georgetown University and University of Santa Clara.

ADDRESSES: Home and office—Palo Alto, CA. *Agent*—Kathi Paton, 19 West 55th St., New York, NY 10019-4914.

CAREER: Free-lance writer, specializing in the computer industry. Elementary-level Spanish teacher, 1983-91.

WRITINGS:

Medical Spanish, Butterworth-Heinemann, 1982.
For the Love of the Game, Morrow, 1992.

WORK IN PROGRESS: A work of fiction set in Mexico; biological research.

* * *

WILCOX, Laird (M.)   1942-

PERSONAL: Born November 28, 1942, in San Francisco, CA; son of Laird (a construction accountant) and AuDeene (Stromer) Wilcox; children: Laird A., Elizabeth, Carrie. *Education:* Attended Washburn University, 1961-62, and University of Kansas, 1963-66. *Politics:* Independent. *Religion:* "Non-denominational."

ADDRESSES: Home—P.O. Box 2047, Olathe, KS 66061.

CAREER: Editorial Research Service, Olathe, KS, writer, editor, and public speaker. University of Kansas, Lawrence, founder of Wilcox Collection on Contemporary Political Movements, Kenneth Spencer Research Library, 1965. Also worked as a carpenter.

MEMBER: Amnesty International, American Civil Liberties Union (past member of board of directors; chairman of Civil Liberties Special Interest Group).

WRITINGS:

(Editor) *Guide to the American Left: Directory and Bibliography,* Editorial Research Service, 1978, 15th annual edition, 1992.
(Editor) *Guide to the American Right: Directory and Bibliography,* Editorial Research Service, 1978, 15th annual edition, 1992.

(With John George) *Nazis, Communists, Klansmen, and Others on the Fringe,* Prometheus Books, 1992.

Editor of the annual publication *Guide to the American Occult,* Editorial Research Service. Editor of the newsletters *The Wilcox Report* and *Civil Liberties Review.*

WORK IN PROGRESS: Selected Quotations for the Ideological Skeptic.

BIOGRAPHICAL/CRITICAL SOURCES:

PERIODICALS

Kansas City Star, May 31, 1990, p. C3.
New York Times, August 12, 1992.

*   *   *

WILLIS, Ted   1918-1992
(George Dixon)

OBITUARY NOTICE—See index for *CA* sketch: Full name, Edward Henry Willis; born January 13, 1918, in Tottenham, Middlesex, England; died of a heart attack, December 22, 1992, in Chislehurst, Kent, England. Playwright, novelist, and screenwriter. Hailed by the *Guinness Book of World Records* as the world's most prolific television scriptwriter, Willis created *Dixon of Dock Green,* an immensely popular television series about a friendly, ordinary London police officer. The series aired on the British Broadcasting Corporation from 1955 to 1976. Willis began his television career as a documentary filmmaker, eventually changing his vocation to writing. He went on to write and create forty-one television serials, including *Patterns of Marriage, Flower of Evil,* and *Black Beauty.* He also wrote thirty-nine film scripts, including *The Blue Lamp* with Jan Read, which first introduced the character of Dixon of Dock Green in 1950. In 1960, Willis used the pseudonym George Dixon in publishing the book, *Dixon of Dock Green: My Life,* which was written with Charles Hatton. Among Willis's numerous plays for television and the stage are *Buster, Dead on Saturday* and *Woman in a Dressing Gown, and Other Television Plays,* which was the winner of both the Berlin Festival Award and the London Picture-Goer Award. Willis published other works of fiction, including the suspense thrillers *Death May Surprise Us* and *The Buckingham Palace Connection,* and a juvenile novel, *A Problem for Mother Christmas.* He also wrote two autobiographies, *Whatever Happened to Tom Mix?: The Story of One of My Lives* and *Evening All: Fifty Years over a Hot Typewriter.* In 1963, Willis was accepted to the House of Lords and dubbed Lord Willis of Chislehurst.

OBITUARIES AND OTHER SOURCES:

BOOKS

Writer's Directory: 1992-94, St. James Press, 1992.

PERIODICALS

Los Angeles Times, December 24, 1992, p. A14.
New York Times, December 24, 1992, p. B6.
Times (London), December, 23, 1992, p. 15.

*   *   *

WILLNER, Dorothy   1927-1993

OBITUARY NOTICE—See index for *CA* sketch: Born August 26, 1927, in New York, NY; died of cancer of the small intestine, February 13, 1993, in Manhattan, NY. Anthropologist, sociologist, educator, and author. As a representative of the International Organization of Consumers Unions at the United Nations, Willner convinced the United Nations to adopt consumer rights guidelines. Willner received her doctorate in sociology from the University of Chicago and led a lengthy career as an instructor at such institutions as the University of North Carolina at Chapel Hill, the University of Kansas, and the University of Iowa. In addition, she worked as an anthropologist in Israel and assisted with community development for the United Nations in Mexico. Her books include *Community Leadership* and *Nation-Building and Community in Israel;* she also contributed to *The Sociology of Revolution.*

OBITUARIES AND OTHER SOURCES:

BOOKS

Who's Who in America, 47th edition, Marquis, 1992, p. 3591.

PERIODICALS

New York Times, February 18, 1993, p. B12.

*   *   *

WILSFORD, David   1956-

PERSONAL: Born April 4, 1956, in Nashville, TN; son of James (an educational consultant) and Helen (a school administrator; maiden name, Richardson) Wilsford; married Pascale Canlorbe (a teacher), March 26, 1983; children: Caroline, Christopher. *Education:* University of South Carolina, B.A. (cum laude), 1977; Ecole des Hautes Etudes en Sciences Sociales, Paris, Diplome d'Etudes Approfondies (D.E.A.), 1982; University of California, San Diego, M.A., 1984, Ph.D., 1987. *Politics:* Democrat. *Religion:* Church of Christ.

ADDRESSES: Home—6605 Cherry Tree Lane, Atlanta, GA 30328. *Office*—School of International Affairs, Georgia Institute of Technology, Atlanta, GA 30332-0610.

CAREER: Legislative intern to U.S. Senator Ernest F. Hollings, Washington, DC, 1977; legislative assistant to

U.S. Representative James R. Mann, Washington, DC, 1977-78; University of California, Irvine, instructor in social sciences, 1978-80; Universite de Paris VII, Paris, France, lecturer in politics and history at Institute d'Anglais, 1981-82, lecturer in politics and economics at U.F.R. de Lettres et de Sciences Humaines, 1984-85; Universite de Paris III, lecturer in politics and history at U.E.R. des Etudes Anglophones, 1981-82; University of Oklahoma, Norman, assistant professor of political science, 1987-90; Georgia Institute of Technology, Atlanta, assistant professor, 1990-92, associate professor of international affairs, 1992—. Atlantic Council, academic associate, 1988—; Commission of the European Communities, member of Team 1992 Liaison Group, 1989—; Inter-University Consortium for Social Research on France, member, 1990—; consultant to organizations, including Radio France and Decision Insights, Inc.

MEMBER: International Studies Association, American Political Science Association, Phi Beta Kappa.

AWARDS, HONORS: Samuel C. May Award, Western Governmental Research Association, 1984, for "Exit and Voice: Strategies for Change in Bureaucratic-Legislative Policymaking"; Chateaubriand fellow, Government of France, 1985-86; grants from Atlantic Council and German Marshall Fund, 1989, International Studies Association, 1989-90, and North Atlantic Treaty Organization, 1990; research fellow, Center for International Strategy, Technology, and Policy, 1990—; Lilly teaching fellow, Lilly Endowment, 1991-92; resident research fellow, Max Planck Institut fuer Gesellschaftsforschung, 1992; Pew faculty fellow in international affairs, Pew Charitable Trusts, 1992-93; appointed Distinguished Visiting Scientist, Government of France, 1993.

WRITINGS:

Doctors and the State: The Politics of Health Care in France and the United States, Duke University Press, 1991.
(Editor) *Political Leaders of Contemporary Western Europe,* Greenwood Press, 1993.

Work represented in anthologies, including *Handbook of Comparative and Development Administration,* edited by Ali Farazmand, Marcel Dekker, 1991; *The French Welfare State,* edited by John Ambler, New York University Press, 1991; and *Changing to National Health Care: Ethical and Policy Issues,* edited by Robert Huefner and Margaret Battin, University of Utah Press, 1992. Contributor of articles and reviews to journals in the social and political sciences. Coeditor of special issue, *French Politics and Society,* July, 1990.

WORK IN PROGRESS: The Fiscal Imperative in Health Care, completion expected in 1994; "Political Parties and l'Etat-Providence in France," a chapter to be included in *Political Parties and the Welfare State,* edited by M. Donald Hancock, Marina Arbetman, and Joe Adams.

SIDELIGHTS: David Wilsford told *CA:* "Originally, I intended to become a lawyer and enter politics. As an undergraduate at the University of South Carolina, I was active in student political life and was elected student body president. After a stint on the staff of a congressman in the U.S. House of Representatives, however, I became more and more interested in a scholarly understanding of the 'why' in politics. I returned to graduate school to study political science, where I began the long process of investigating how groups mobilize for politics and how governments make political decisions. My interests quickly broadened beyond the United States. Now my research focuses on political questions across all the advanced industrial democracies."

*   *   *

WILTSHIRE, Susan Ford 1941-

PERSONAL: Born October 13, 1941, in Amarillo, TX; daughter of Jesse Frank (a farmer and rancher) and Lucile (a homemaker; maiden name, Davis) Ford; married Ashley T. Wiltshire (a legal aid attorney), June 7, 1969; children: Matthew Ashley, Carrie Chappell. *Education:* University of Texas, B.A., 1963; Columbia University, M.A., 1964, Ph.D., 1967. *Politics:* "Lifelong Democrat." *Religion:* "Lifelong United Methodist." *Avocational interests:* Farming, theology.

ADDRESSES: Home—1900 Blair Blvd., Nashville, TN 37212. *Office*—Department of Classics, Vanderbilt University, Box 6153, Station B, Nashville, TN 37235. *Agent*—John A. Ware Literary Agency, 392 Central Park W., New York, NY 10025.

CAREER: University of Illinois at Urbana-Champaign, assistant professor of classics, 1967-69; Fisk University, Nashville, TN, director of Honors Program, 1969-71; Vanderbilt University, Nashville, assistant professor, 1971-75, associate professor, 1975-89, professor of classics and head of department, 1989—, Phi Beta Kappa Associates Lecturer, 1991-93. Nashville Family and Children's Service, member of board of directors, 1978-84; Young Women's Christian Association, member of board of directors, 1985-88; member of Vanderbilt AIDS Project, 1987-89, and Vanderbilt AIDS Vaccine Advisory Council, 1992.

MEMBER: International Bonhoeffer Society, American Philological Association (member of board of directors, 1985-88), Vergilian Society of America (president,

1988-90), United Nations Association (member of advisory board, 1986-88).

AWARDS, HONORS: Woodrow Wilson fellow, 1963; grants from National Endowment for the Humanities, 1980-82 and 1987; Best Paper Award, Southern Humanities Conference, 1987.

WRITINGS:

Public and Private in Vergil's Aeneid, University of Massachusetts Press, 1989.
Greece, Rome, and the Bill of Rights, University of Oklahoma Press, 1992.

Series editor, "Oklahoma Series in Classical Culture." Contributor to classical periodicals.

WORK IN PROGRESS: Time for Giving: When a Sibling Has AIDS; First Drama: Siblings in Greek and Latin Poetry, completion expected in 1994.

SIDELIGHTS: Susan Ford Wiltshire told *CA:* "My enormous respect for words came from my father, who was a cowboy storyteller, and from my mother, who has read three or four books a week all her life and who spent the darkest year of the Dust Bowl reading every word Shakespeare wrote. I grew used to taking the long view of things as a child in the Texas Panhandle, where there was lots to think about because there was nothing to see except the horizon twenty-five miles away. Substance and grit came from reading the Bible, then taking up the study of Latin and Greek.

"I like the long view of things, but I also hate to bore people. Writing is the solution to my dilemma. If I write an argument as far back as I can take it and as far forward as it will go, then others can read it or close the book as they please. I think of writing as an act of hospitality to strangers, some of whom I will never meet.

"Writing also bridges my dilemma that I am an activist by conviction but contemplative by nature. Even my scholarly books grow out of my civic concerns. *Public and Private in Vergil's Aeneid* addresses the conflict between public and private life that is a feminist, but more broadly, a human predicament. *Greece, Rome, and the Bill of Rights* is a conscious counter-argument to the right-wing contention that America is a Christian nation. *Time for Giving* also speaks to a vast social crisis.

"I was in my forties before I realized that I love the work of writing. I gained my voice, suited best for the writing of nonfiction essays and stories and scholarly books, when I realized that the word 'authority' has the word 'author' as its root. Both mean to make the stories more spacious."

WIND, Barry 1942-

PERSONAL: Born May 29, 1942, in New York City; son of Fred and Minnie (Unger) Wind; married Geraldine Dunphy (a professor); children: James, Clifford. *Education:* City College of the City University of New York, B.A., 1962; New York University, M.A., 1964, Ph.D., 1972.

ADDRESSES: Home—5844 North Shoreland, Whitefish Bay, WI 53217. *Office*—Department of Art History, University of Wisconsin—Milwaukee, Milwaukee, WI 53201.

CAREER: University of Georgia, Athens, assistant professor of art history, 1967-71; University of Wisconsin—Milwaukee, began as assistant professor, became professor of art history, 1971—. Newberry Library, visiting associate professor, 1984.

AWARDS, HONORS: Fellow of National Endowment for the Humanities at Yale University, 1984, and Brown University, 1992.

WRITINGS:

Velazquez's Bodegones: A Study in Seventeenth-Century Spanish Genre Painting, George Mason University Press, 1987.
Genre in the Age of the Baroque: A Resource Guide, Garland Publishing, 1991.

Contributor to art and art history journals.

WORK IN PROGRESS: Research on clowns and dwarfs in the seventeenth century.

*   *   *

WING, Betsy 1936-

PERSONAL: Full name, Elizabeth Nelson Wing; born April 19, 1936, in Richmond, VA; daughter of Charles Morris (a surgeon) and Charlotte Mercer (a homemaker; maiden name, Purcell) Nelson; married Nathaniel Wing (a university professor), June 16, 1959; children: Eliza Wing Henke, Alexander Kinloch, Susanna Denholm. *Education:* Bryn Mawr College, B.A. (cum laude), 1958; Louisiana State University, M.F.A., 1991. *Politics:* Democrat.

ADDRESSES: Home and office—665 Ursuline Dr., Baton Rouge, LA 70808. *Agent*—Faith Childs Literary Agency, 275 West 96th St., New York, NY 10025.

CAREER: Free-lance translator (from French to English) and writer. Oberlin College, visiting instructor, spring, 1989.

MEMBER: American Literary Translators Association, Amnesty International (group coordinator for Baton Rouge).

AWARDS, HONORS: Grants from National Endowment for the Humanities, 1983, Maison des Sciences del'Homme (Paris), 1983, and National Endowment for the Arts, 1993.

WRITINGS:

Look Out for Hydrophobia (novella and stories), Birch Lane Press, 1990.

Contributor of stories and poems to periodicals, including *Southern Review* and *Boundary 2.*

TRANSLATOR

Catherine Clement and Helene Cixous, *The Newly Born Woman,* University of Minnesota Press, 1986.
Edward Quinn and Pierre Daix, *The Private Picasso,* Little, Brown, 1987.
Denis Hollier, editor, *The College of Sociology,* University of Minnesota Press, 1988.
Catherine Clement, *Opera; or, The Undoing of Women,* University of Minnesota Press, 1988.
Denis Hollier, *Against Architecture,* MIT Press, 1989.
(And author of introduction) Helene Cixous, *The Book of Promethea,* University of Nebraska Press, 1991.
Didier Eribon, *Michel Foucault* (bibliography), Harvard University Press, 1991.
(With Konrad Bieber) Lucie Aubrac, *Outwitting the Gestapo,* University of Nebraska Press, 1993.
George Sand, *Letters to Marcie,* Academy Chicago, in press.

Contributor of translations to periodicals, including *Rolling Stone.*

WORK IN PROGRESS: A long novel about the World War II years "at home" in the United States; translating *Black Salt,* a collection of poems, and *Poetique de la relation,* both by Edouard Glissant.

SIDELIGHTS: Betsy Wing told *CA:* "I grew up in a warm, extended family in Richmond, Virginia, but by the time I was ready for college, I had developed all kinds of ideological reasons why I did not wish to live in the South, among them Virginia's reaction to Brown vs. the Board of Education the year I graduated from secondary school. College further reinforced these ideas and, by the time I was married, I was ready for the semi-nomadic life of academics.

"During the early 1960s, I was able to alternate years in France with years in New York City. After my husband completed his doctoral work in French literature at Columbia University, we moved to Pennsylvania, and then to a farm in Oxford, Ohio, that we worked and managed with the help of children and neighbors. We left Ohio for a city life in Louisiana when our youngest child went to college. I went back to, and even deeper into, the South, which by then seemed to me to have many merits, and certainly not to be responsible for all the social injustice in the world.

"Louisiana is a land that understands the pleasures of living. It is a watery place, and I feel great need for water in my life, satisfying this with weekends sailing on Lake Pontchartrain and summers sailing in the islands off the coast of Maine.

"My fiction deals with the unsafety of the safest of lives, how the dark and light are intertwined, issues of family life, aging, death. The translations I enjoy working on are almost entirely contemporary, though living in the verbose persona of George Sand can be a treat. Translations deal, preferably, with issues of cultural and social change that are evident in the writing of the authors, and that I hope to make evident in the translation."

*   *   *

WING, Elizabeth Nelson
See WING, Betsy

*   *   *

WINGFIELD, Paul   1961-

PERSONAL: Born December 24, 1961, in Durham, England; son of John (a teacher) and Anne Elizabeth (a teacher; maiden name, Rodgers) Wingfield; married Elizabeth Margaret Rosemary Scott (a botanist), July 25, 1987. *Education:* Attended Chetham's School of Music, 1972-80; King's College, Cambridge, B.A. (honors), 1983, M.Phil., 1984, M.A., 1987, Ph.D., 1989. *Religion:* Church of England. *Avocational interests:* "The turf, nineteenth-century art and literature, wildlife conservation (especially parrots), wine and food."

ADDRESSES: Home—12 Benson St., Cambridge CB4 3QJ, England. *Office*—Trinity College, Cambridge CB2 1TQ, England.

CAREER: University of Sydney, Sydney, New South Wales, Australia, research fellow in music, 1987-88; Cambridge University, Cambridge, England, research fellow in music at Gonville and Caius College, 1988-90, fellow and director of studies in music at Trinity College, 1990—.

MEMBER: Royal Musical Association.

WRITINGS:

Leos Janacek: Glagolitic Mass, Cambridge University Press, 1992.

WORK IN PROGRESS: Editions of Janacek's works, including *The Glagolitic Mass* and his two string quartets; research on Janacek's operas, East-European late-nineteenth-century opera, and octatonicism.

*   *   *

WINNINGTON-INGRAM, R(eginald) P(epys) 1904-1993

OBITUARY NOTICE—See index for *CA* sketch: Born January 22, 1904, in Sherborne, Dorset, England; died January 3, 1993. Educator and author. Known for his study of Greek dramatists, Winnington-Ingram spent over four decades as an educator, including almost twenty years as professor of Greek language and literature at the University of London. His books, which focus on Greek drama, include *Euripides and Dionysus, Sophocles: An Interpretation,* and *Studies in Aeschylus.*

OBITUARIES AND OTHER SOURCES:

BOOKS

Who's Who, 144th edition, St. Martin's, 1992.

PERIODICALS

Times (London), January 12, 1993, p. 19.

*   *   *

WITTING, Amy 1918-

PERSONAL: Born in 1918.

ADDRESSES: Office—c/o Viking Penguin Inc., 40 West Twenty-third St., New York, NY 10010.

CAREER: Writer.

WRITINGS:

The Visit (novel), Thomas Nelson [Australia], 1977.
I for Isobel (novel), Penguin, 1990.
Marriages (short stories), Penguin, 1991.
Beauty Is the Straw (poems), Angus & Robertson, 1991.

SIDELIGHTS: Amy Witting is an Australian poet and author who has gained recognition for her fiction. She published her first novel, *The Visit,* in 1977, but it was not until she produced a second work, *I for Isobel,* that she attracted the attention of reviewers. In *I for Isobel,* Witting charts the development of an Australian girl during the crucial years from pre-adolescence to early adulthood. Life for the novel's heroine, Isobel Callaghan, is an unhappy series of admonitions and repressions. Her mother is cruel and vindictive; on the occasion of Isobel's ninth birthday, her mother forbids her to receive any gifts—or to even mention that it is her birthday.

Isobel strives to improve her life after her mother's death, but she finds fitting in a difficult task. She begins a life of wanton promiscuity, but eventually finds this pattern of behavior unfulfilling. A voracious reader, Isobel comes to realize that she is destined for a literary career. She eventually finds an uneasy niche for herself among a group of young intellectuals and writers. Cheri Fein, writing in the *New York Times Book Review,* described *I for Isobel* as the "beautifully told story of a young girl's pain," and she added that it is "written with the surety of someone who knows the territory well."

Witting also won attention for *Marriages,* a collection of six tales on a common theme, one described by Barbara Quick, in her *New York Times Book Review* assessment, as "the ways in which marriage fails to bind the tangled threads of two disparate lives." Among the stories in this volume are "Goodbye, Ady, Goodbye, Joe," in which an elderly farmer recalls the initially awkward sexuality of his marriage, and "The Survivors," in which a farm girl, impregnated by an aloof, hardbitten lover, finds the courage to strike out on her own. Quick described the tales in *Marriages* as "brilliant distillations" and added that the volume proves Witting a perceptive writer about "longings that make us ache to be released from life even as we remain fiercely tied to it."

Aside from writing fiction, Witting has published a poetry collection, *Beauty Is the Straw,* which appeared in 1991.

BIOGRAPHICAL/CRITICAL SOURCES:

PERIODICALS

New Yorker, July 23, 1990, p. 88; April 15, 1991, p. 103.
New York Times Book Review, September 16, 1990, p. 35; January 6, 1991, p. 24.
Washington Post Book World, November 18, 1990, p. 12.*

*   *   *

WOLPE, David J. 1958-

PERSONAL: Born September 19, 1958, in Harrisburg, PA; son of Gerald I. (a rabbi) and Elaine (an administrator) Wolpe; married Eileen Ansel, December 27, 1992. *Education:* University of Pennsylvania, B.A.; University of Judaism, B.H.L.; Jewish Theological Seminary of America, M.A.; also attended Hebrew University (Jerusalem) and Edinburgh University. *Religion:* Jewish.

ADDRESSES: Office—University of Judaism, 15600 Mulholland Dr., Los Angeles, CA 90077. *Agent*—Sam Mitnick, 91 Henry St., San Francisco, CA 94114.

CAREER: Ordained rabbi, 1987. Hunter College of the City University of New York, New York City, instructor in philosophy, 1986-87; University of Judaism, Los Angeles, CA, instructor in modern Jewish thought and director of Ostrow Library, 1987. Lecturer at universities, synagogues, and institutes. Guest on television programs, including CNN and *CBS This Morning.*

WRITINGS:

The Healer of Shattered Hearts: A Jewish View of God, Henry Holt, 1990.

In Speech and in Silence: The Jewish Quest for God, Henry Holt, 1992.

Contributor to periodicals, including *U.S. News and World Report, Washington Post, Los Angeles Times, International Herald Tribune, Logos,* and *Newsweek.* Member of editorial board for the Conservative movement's Torah commentary.

WORK IN PROGRESS: Teaching Your Children About God.

BIOGRAPHICAL/CRITICAL SOURCES:

PERIODICALS

Kirkus Reviews, February 15, 1990, p. 255; July 15, 1992, p. 912.
Library Journal, April 1, 1990, p. 118.
Publishers Weekly, February 2, 1990, p. 71; September 14, 1992, p. 94.

*   *   *

WRIGHT, Larry   1940-

PERSONAL: Born February 2, 1940, in Youngstown, OH; son of Orrin Benett (a journalist) and Dorothy (a homemaker; maiden name, Marquette) Wright; married Naoko Yogi (a homemaker), April 20, 1962; children: Sheryl Lynn, Robert Orrin. *Politics:* Conservative independent. *Religion:* Protestant. *Avocational interests:* Golf, scale-model railroading.

ADDRESSES: Home—14965 Morris Ave., Allen Park, MI 48101. *Office*—*Detroit News,* 615 West Lafayette, Detroit, MI 48226. *Agent*—United Media Enterprises, 200 Park Ave., New York, NY 10166.

CAREER: Okinawa Morning Star, Okinawa, Japan, night news editor, 1961-65; *Detroit Free Press,* Detroit, MI, assistant news editor and cartoonist, 1965-76; *Detroit News,* Detroit, cartoonist, 1976—. *Military service:* U.S. Army Security Agency, 1958-61, became sergeant E-5.

MEMBER: Association of American Editorial Cartoonists, National Cartoonists Society.

AWARDS, HONORS: National Cartoonists Society Award, best editorial cartoon, 1980.

WRITINGS:

Celebrity Cats (cartoon collection), Holt, 1982.
Kit 'n' Carlyle (cartoon collection), Simon & Schuster, 1983.
Motley the Cat from "Wright Angles": Round up the Usual Cat Suspects (cartoon collection), introduction by Mike Peters, Stabur Press, 1988.

Author of the syndicated comic strip "Wright Angles," United Feature Syndicate, 1976-90; and of the syndicated daily panel "Kit 'n' Carlyle," Newspaper Enterprise Association, 1980—. Also author of the comic strips "Uncle Milton," *Okinawa Morning Star,* 1960-65 and *Detroit Daily Express,* 1967; and "Needlescope," *Scope,* 1968.

SIDELIGHTS: The popular comics of cartoonist Larry Wright feature conventional characters who are given an acerbic twist by the manner in which they are drawn and written. A staff cartoonist for the *Detroit News,* Wright contributes award-winning editorial cartoons to the newspaper as well as working on his syndicated feature, "Kit 'n' Carlyle." He has published collections of his work, primarily focusing on cats, in books such as *Celebrity Cats* and *Motley the Cat from "Wright Angles": Round up the Usual Cat Suspects.*

A midwestern native, Wright began his artistic career in Okinawa, Japan, after serving three years as an Army interpreter there in the late 1950s. He worked for four years at the *Okinawa Morning Star,* drawing political cartoons and a strip titled "Uncle Milton." After returning to the United States, Wright began work on "Uncle Milton" again, this time for the *Detroit Free Press,* where he also worked as a copyreader. In 1968, he began a new weekly strip with no recurring characters. Titled "Wright Angles," the cartoon developed a regular cast by 1974 and was syndicated by United Feature in 1976, when Wright moved to the *Detroit News.*

"Wright Angles" focused on the Kane family: parents Tom and Nancy, children Joey and Sharon, and their cynical cat, Motley. While the family rarely strayed from typical suburban dilemmas, some characters were expressed in a sharper comic and political tone: Tom Kane's employer, Mayor Orwell Twit, was portrayed with merciless irony; a friend of the family didn't get a job with the sanitation department when he failed to make the grade at the garbage academy; and door-to-door lawyer Mortimer

Tort had the impressive record of finishing in the top seventy percent of his class. Throughout it all was perhaps the strip's most popular character, Motley, who confirmed every cat-owner's suspicions with his self-centered view of the world; upon his arrival at the Kane household in 1977, his first concern was where the family kept their rats. From that point forward, Motley's interests varied little; among other things, he pondered the benefits of low-calorie mice to reduce his girth and dreamed of being able to use the telephone to place an order for pizza and mice. Motley was featured in Wright's 1988 collection, *Motley the Cat from "Wright Angles": Round up the Usual Cat Suspects.*

Wright is also the creator of the daily panel "Kit 'n' Carlyle," which appears in approximately four hundred newspapers across the United States. Focusing on a woman, Kit, and her kitten, the comic offers a milder form of humor than "Wright Angles." Carlyle's appeal is based more on innocence than the worldliness of Motley, and the drawing of the cats reflects this difference; where Motley is a sharply drawn Siamese, Carlyle has a less pedigreed look and is drawn with a looser line. The kitten is constantly exploring his world, encountering mishaps along the way, but able to redeem himself with cuteness. A selection of these panels was published in the book *Kit 'n' Carlyle* in 1983. With the "Kit 'n' Carlyle" comic, Wright established himself as a cat cartoonist, a reputation that was strengthened with his publication of a collection of cat caricatures, *Celebrity Cats,* in 1982.

BIOGRAPHICAL/CRITICAL SOURCES:

BOOKS

Contemporary Graphic Artists, Volume I, Gale, 1986, pp. 263-66.
Encyclopedia of American Comics, Facts on File, 1990, p. 394.

* * *

WU, David Y(en) H(o)   1940-

PERSONAL: Born April 13, 1940, in Beijing, China; son of Kunhuang Wu (a poet) and Ruokui Chang (a teacher); married Wei-Lan Wang (an anthropologist), August, 1966. *Education:* National Taiwan University, B.A., 1963; University of Hawaii, M.A., 1970; Australian National University, Ph.D., 1974. *Avocational interests:* Chinese calligraphy, portrait drawing.

ADDRESSES: Home—1441 Victoria St., No. 903, Honolulu, HI 96822. *Office*— CUL, East-West Center, 1777 East-West Rd., Honolulu, HI 96848.

CAREER: Academia Sinica Institute of Ethnology, Taipei, Taiwan, technician, 1958-59, research assistant,

1963-66; University of Hawaii, Honolulu, anthropology instructor, 1969, member of graduate school faculty, 1980—; Australian National University, Canberra, research scholar, 1970-74; East-West Center, Honolulu, research associate, 1974—. Academia Sinica, adjunct fellow, 1976—; Chiang Ching-Ko Foundation for International Scholarly Exchange, consultant, 1989-93.

MEMBER: American Anthropological Association, Society for Applied Anthropology, Asian Studies Association, Pacific Science Association (life member).

AWARDS, HONORS: American Anthropological Association fellow, 1969—; Outstanding Research Paper Award, Comparative and International Education Society, 1987.

WRITINGS:

The Chinese in Papua, New Guinea: 1880-1980, Chinese University Press, 1982.
(Editor) *Ethnicity and Interpersonal Interaction: A Cross Cultural Study,* Maruzen Asia [Singapore], 1982.
(Editor with W. S. Tseng) *Chinese Culture and Mental Health,* Academic Press, 1985.
(With Joseph J. Tobin and Dana H. Davidson) *Preschool in Three Cultures: Japan, China, and the United States,* Yale University Press, 1989.

Also author of three monographs; contributor of research papers in English, Chinese, and Japanese to books and journals.

The Chinese in Papua, New Guinea: 1880-1980 has been translated into Chinese.

WORK IN PROGRESS: Early Childhood Socialization in Chinese Societies, a current comparative study of China, Taiwan, Singapore, and the U.S., completion expected in 1994.

SIDELIGHTS: David Y. H. Wu, a cultural anthropologist, is the coauthor of *Preschool in Three Cultures: Japan, China and the United States.* The book was the result of the authors' comparative study of preschools in these countries. The authors, Wu, Joseph J. Tobin, and Dana H. Davidson, observed and videotaped Japanese, Chinese, and American preschool classes in session, then returned to each community to play edited versions of each tape for educators, administrators, and parents. The participants' reactions to the tapes of their own preschools and those of the other countries indicated that the differences in teaching styles both contributed to and developed out of different perceptions of the needs of young children and the purpose of education at this level.

All three cultural communities stressed the importance of imparting language and communication skills to preschoolers, but they disagreed on the reasons for and ideal method of achieving this. While the American teachers stressed students' self-expression, the Chinese relied on recitation, viewing conversation between students as a distraction from the material being covered. In Japan, on the other hand, language was perceived as a means of building group solidarity among the children, and the students were left to talk on their own without adult supervision.

The study revealed a close link between the teaching of verbal skills and issues of behavior and student bonding. The Chinese participants, who focused on prevention of bad behavior, rather than punishment, viewed quarrels among preschoolers as a sign of an inept teacher. While American teachers interfered in children's squabbles, helping them to express their feelings and settle disagreements, the Japanese, stressing the importance of developing group relations, left students to work out their own problems. In the Japanese classes, the teacher allowed the group to determine when an individual's actions were intolerable and then helped them to change or accept this behavior. While American participants perceived the Chinese methods as overly severe and the Japanese philosophy as overly permissive, the Japanese viewers were uncomfortable with the amount of individual attention American teachers provided, believing that the teacher should relate to the class as a whole. Both the Japanese and the Chinese observers were outraged by the American technique of temporarily isolating a child who is worked up or causing trouble.

Reviewers appreciated both the complexity of the study and the accessibility of the resulting work. Carole C. Kemmerer, writing in the *Los Angeles Times Book Review,* commented that *Preschool in Three Cultures* "invites reading. Its style is clear, its methodology fascinating." *New York Times Book Review* contributor Penelope Leach noted, "The book should be required reading for professionals in early education and makes thought-provoking reading for anyone aware of his or her own cultural blinkers and interested in glimpsing the world outside them."

David Y. H. Wu told *CA:* "I have been a productive writer since the age of eighteen. My first article about a Formosan [early name for Taiwan] aboriginal tribe was published in the leading academic journal of anthropology in Taiwan when I was still an undergraduate student.

"When I first arrived in the United States in 1966, I could hardly write in English. It would take me three days to a week to write one page in English. I have by now published four books and three monographs in English and some of them are issued by leading academic publishers in this country. It is gratifying to find my last book, *Preschool in Three Cultures,* reviewed by the *New York Times* and the *Los Angeles Times.* The book was praised on *CBS This Morning* in September, 1990.

"I write almost every day during business hours. I often find it enjoyable to write on the airplane during a long [flight]. Without a pressing deadline, I write very [slowly], but under pressure to meet deadlines, I write fast and well. I am motivated to write my anthropological work because I have a most supportive wife who is also my research partner and critic of my manuscripts. We have been in love since the publication of my very first article, when we were classmates in college."

BIOGRAPHICAL/CRITICAL SOURCES:

PERIODICALS

Los Angeles Times Book Review, June 18, 1989, p. 8.
New York Times Book Review, June 25, 1989, pp. 26-28.

*   *   *

WUNDERLI, Richard (M.) 1940-

PERSONAL: Born November 15, 1940, in Salt Lake City, UT; married Georgiana Burton, December 8, 1967; children: Thomas C. *Education:* University of Utah, B.A. (with honors), 1964, M.A., 1966; University of California, Berkeley, Ph.D., 1975.

ADDRESSES: Home—906 West Cheyenne Rd., Colorado Springs, CO 80906. *Office*—Department of History, University of Colorado, P.O. Box 7150, Colorado Springs, CO 80933-7150.

CAREER: University of Utah, Salt Lake City, instructor, 1965-66; University of Maryland, European Division, instructor, 1968-69; University of California, Berkeley, instructor, 1975-76; University of Colorado, Colorado Springs, assistant professor, 1976-82, associate professor, 1982-91, professor of history, 1991—, chairperson of department, 1984-89. Learning Unlimited (lecture series for senior citizens and retirement homes), education director, 1991.

WRITINGS:

London Church Courts and Society on the Eve of the Reformation, Speculum Anniversary Monographs, 1981.
Peasant Fires: The Drummer of Niklashausen, Indiana University Press, 1992.

Work represented in anthologies, including *A Catalogue of Medieval Legal Manuscripts in the Vatican Library,* Volume I, Institute of Medieval Canon Law, University of California, Berkeley, 1986. Contributor of articles and reviews to history journals.

SIDELIGHTS: Richard Wunderli told *CA:* "I have tried in *Peasant Fires* to write sophisticated history with the stylistic freedom of serious fiction, in order to appeal to the reading public. Those writers whose style has had a great influence on me have been Maxine Hong Kingston, Jonathan Spence, Milan Kundera, and Robert Brentano. For example, I have tried to include the voice of the narrator (the historian) as the shaper of the historical narrative. History, in other words, is not just about the past, but also about how we think of it today and how we construct it for future generations. Consequently, like my aforesaid models, I tend to be introspective about the past. Not surprisingly, my hero in life is Michel Eyquem de Montaigne."

* * *

WYMAN, Max 1939-

PERSONAL: Born May 14, 1939, in Wellingborough, England; son of Frederick and Emily Irene (Bigley) Wyman. *Education:* Attended University of Nottingham.

ADDRESSES: Home—Box 245, Lions Bay, British Columbia, Canada V0N 2E0. *Agent*—Denise Bukowski, Bukowski Agency, 182 Avenue Rd., Suite 3, Toronto, Ontario, Canada M5R 2J1.

CAREER: Journalist in England, until 1967; *Vancouver Sun,* Vancouver, British Columbia, music, dance, and theater critic, 1967-79; *Province,* Vancouver, arts columnist, dance and theater critic, and books editor, 1980-91; *Vancouver Sun,* editor of "Saturday Review," 1991—. Lecturer at universities; host of television series; CBC-Radio, commentator and interviewer, 1975—.

MEMBER: International Food, Wine, and Travel Writers Association, Association of Canadian Cinema, Television, and Radio Artists, Newspaper Guild.

AWARDS, HONORS: Canada Council grants, 1972, 1976, 1981-82, 1988, and 1991; Queen's Jubilee Medal, 1977; Man of the Year Award, Vancouver Community Arts Council, 1986; first prize, series category, British Columbia Newspaper Awards, 1990, for a fourteen-part series on life in the U.S.S.R.

WRITINGS:

The Royal Winnipeg Ballet: The First Forty Years, Doubleday, 1978.
Dance Canada: An Illustrated History, Douglas & McIntyre, 1989.
Evelyn Hart: An Intimate Portrait, McClelland & Stewart, 1991.
(Editor) *Vancouver Forum: Old Powers, New Forces,* Douglas & McIntyre, 1992.

Work represented in anthologies, including *Visions of the Promised Land,* Flight Press, 1986; *The Expo Story,* Harbour Press, 1986; and *The Pacific Rim Handbook,* Harper, 1991. Contributor to magazines and newspapers, including *Maclean's, Western Living, Ballet News, Performing Arts in Canada, Dance,* and *L.A. Weekly.*

WORK IN PROGRESS: A biography of Oleg Vinogradov, artistic director of the Kirov Ballet of St. Petersburg, Russia.

BIOGRAPHICAL/CRITICAL SOURCES:

PERIODICALS

Globe and Mail (Toronto), September 21, 1991, p. C7.

* * *

WYMELENBERG, Suzanne 1929-

PERSONAL: Born September 2, 1929, in Milwaukee, WI; daughter of Clement (in technical advertising) and Gertrude (a homemaker; maiden name, Laur) van den Wymelenberg; married K. Richard Kaffenberger (a health care administrator), September 24, 1977. *Education:* Received B.S. from Marquette University. *Politics:* Independent. *Religion:* None. *Avocational interests:* Gardening.

ADDRESSES: Home and office—9 Rockingham St., Cambridge, MA 02139.

CAREER: Free-lance medical writer. *Time,* stringer, 1965-89.

MEMBER: National Writers Union.

AWARDS, HONORS: Distinction in Medical Communication Award, American Medical Writers Association, 1990-91, for *Science and Babies.*

WRITINGS:

Secondhand Is Better, Arbor House, 1975.
Research at the New England Medical Center, New England Medical Center, 1987.
Science and Babies, National Academy Press, 1990.
(With Beverly Winikoff) *The Contraceptive Handbook: A Guide to Safe and Effective Choices for Men and Women,* Consumer Reports Books, 1992.

SIDELIGHTS: Suzanne Wymelenberg told *CA:* "What keeps me at my word processor, and gets me out of bed in the morning, is the challenge of translating medical and scientific jargon into prose that can be understood by the layperson."

Y-Z

YALOM, Irvin D(avid) 1931-

PERSONAL: Born June 13, 1931, in Washington, DC; married; wife's name, Marilyn (director of the Center for Research on Women at Stanford University); children: Eve, Reed, Victor, Benjamin. *Education:* George Washington University, B.A., 1952; Boston University School of Medicine, M.D., 1956.

ADDRESSES: Home—951 Matadero, Palo Alto, CA 94306. *Office*—Department of Psychiatry, Stanford University Medical Center, Stanford, CA 94305.

CAREER: Mount Sinai Hospital, New York City, intern, 1956-57; Henry Phipps Psychiatric Clinic, Johns Hopkins University, Baltimore, MD, resident, 1957-60; Patuxent Institution, Jessup, MD, consultant, 1959-60; Stanford University School of Medicine, Palo Alto, CA, instructor, 1962-63, assistant professor, 1963-68, associate professor, 1968-73, professor of psychiatry, 1973—, assistant director of Adult Psychiatric Clinic, 1973—, medical director of Psychiatry Inpatient Unit, Stanford University Hospital, 1981—; Center for Advanced Study in Behavioral Sciences, Palo Alto, fellow, 1977-78; psychotherapist; writer. *Military service:* U.S. Army, 1960-62; became captain.

MEMBER: Phi Beta Kappa.

AWARDS, HONORS: Edward Strecker Award, Institute of Pennsylvania Hospital, 1974, for significant contribution to the field of psychiatric patient care; Foundation's Fund Award, American Psychiatric Association, 1976, for research in psychiatry.

WRITINGS:

The Theory and Practice of Group Psychotherapy, Basic Books, 1970, third edition, 1985.

(With M. A. Lieberman and M. B. Miles) *Encounter Groups: First Facts,* Basic Books, 1973.

(With Ginny Elkin) *Every Day Gets a Little Closer: A Twice Told Therapy,* Basic Books, 1974.

Existential Psychotherapy, Basic Books, 1980.

Impatient Group Psychotherapy, Basic Books, 1983.

(Editor with Sophia Vinogradov) *Concise Guide to Group Psychotherapy,* American Psychiatric, 1989.

Love's Executioner and Other Tales of Psychotherapy, Basic Books, 1989.

When Nietzsche Wept: A Novel of Obsession, Basic Books, 1992.

Editor of *American Psychiatric Association Update on Group Therapy,* Volume 5, 1985. Contributor to books, including *Current Psychotherapies,* edited by Raymond Corsini, F. E. Peacock, third edition. Contributor to periodicals, including *Journal of Nervous and Mental Disease.* Member of editorial board of *Psychiatry, International Journal of Group Psychotherapy,* and *American Journal of Psychiatry.*

WORK IN PROGRESS: A novel.

SIDELIGHTS: Irvin D. Yalom is a widely respected psychotherapist, educator, and author whose first writings—textbooks and clinical literature aimed at an academic, professional audience—described his existential approach to psychotherapy: Yalom believes that the anxieties and phobias neurotic people experience can be linked to basic human fears of death, freedom, isolation, and meaninglessness. Yalom first reached a broad audience with his 1989 best-seller *Love's Executioner and Other Tales of Psychotherapy,* a collection of ten case histories told in a manner that emphasizes Yalom's personal feelings about each patient, a technique not found in other clinical literature that typically characterizes the therapist as a distant figure carefully guiding his or her patients toward mental stability. Yalom's approach stems from his belief that the doctor and patient must develop an intimate relationship before therapy can be beneficial. Yalom told an interviewer in *Bestsellers 90:* "If you adopt an attitude of naivete so that you're in wonder at what the person can teach you, you're discovering things together with the person, generally that's the best kind of relationship to have. Those are almost always people I can help."

The title story of *Love's Executioner* relates the case history of a seventy- year-old woman, Thelma, trapped in her memories of an affair she had nearly a decade before seeing Yalom. Her lover, her previous therapist, refused to speak with her afterward, and the recollections of their affair were driving her to suicide. Her obsessive fantasy was simply to talk with her former lover. After futile months of therapy, Yalom arranged for the man to come to a session, hoping to break Thelma's dependance on the past by enacting the role of "love's executioner." But after the session, though Yalom protested, Thelma decided to stop attending therapy: those few moments with the man who obsessed her were enough for her to continue living. Yalom remained unsure if the experience really improved Thelma's situation or merely allowed her to remain alive and haunted, however. In "I Never Thought It Would Happen to Me," Elva, whose husband's recent death had already depressed and isolated her, has her sense of security further destroyed by a purse snatcher. Yalom was able to help Elva by studying the contents of her large purse with her. Each item held special meaning for Elva, and explaining those meanings intimately linked her to Yalom and made her realize that, though she was alone, her solitude was something that could be shared.

Another case history, "In Search of the Dreamer," details the impotence and subsequent headaches from which an accountant, Marvin, suffers. He ultimately learns, once Yalom hears the contents of his nightly dreams, that he is obsessed with caring for his agoraphobic wife and is also afraid to die. A story that many reviewers cited because of the surprising honesty of Yalom's telling, "Fat Lady," narrates the plight of an obese woman, Betty. Yalom's irrational, derogatory attitude toward overweight women stifles his ability to help his patient. In an excerpt from the book printed in *Bestsellers,* Yalom wrote: "I could scarcely think of a single person with whom I less wished to be intimate. But this was *my* problem, not Betty's. It was time, after twenty-five years of practice, for me to change. Betty represented the ultimate counter-transference challenge—and, for that very reason, I offered then and there to be her therapist." As the sessions continue, the woman slowly loses weight and changes, and at the same time Yalom is able to alter his own prejudices by confronting them.

Yalom related his reasons for writing *Love's Executioner* in *WB:* "I feel that the field of psychiatry had become so mechanistic and so biologically driven that therapists are not seeing the whole person and they're losing sight of the story in each person. I wanted to tell the story of what happens in psychotherapy in a way that brings the human dimension of it back to the center stage. And I hope my book will show people that therapy is not mysterious, that we're dealing with issues that are present in the very process of being human and that at times we all need help in our lives. Therapists are troubled individuals too, struggling all the time."

In addition to its popularity among readers, *Love's Executioner* received attention from critics, many of whom cited Yalom's abilities as a writer. "In his case histories, Dr. Yalom makes us feel the three-dimensionality of his patients' personalities: the poignancy of their suffering, the drama of their struggle and their capacity for utterly unexpected revelation," wrote *New York Times* reviewer Eva Hoffman. "What he gives us are vivid portraits of people caught in an almost tragic paradox of both knowing and unknowing; and in examining their conditions with such sympathy and dignity, he convinces us that therapy can take an honorable place among the endeavors to shed delusion, and gain truer knowledge of the human condition." Patrick Reardon, writing in *Tribune Books,* also commended Yalom's depiction of his patients: "In his willingness to reveal his own feelings and experiences, Yalom has established a context in which his 'patients' can also be seen as complex human beings and be highlighted as the heroes of his book." "Yalom's aims are to understand what other therapists might label as psychopathology as varieties of existence pain; to help his patients to experience the givens, the truths, about life and their lives, that will set them free; and to relate to them as whole and yet ultimately mysterious and unknowable human beings," explained James S. Gordon in the *Washington Post Book World.* He concluded: "*Love's Executioner,* with its detailed discussions of the process of therapy and its dozens of valuable asides on clinical practice, is enormously valuable for any psychotherapist. For the general reader, it is a lovely introduction to the riches of the existential approach and a fine and absorbing collection of stories."

Yalom made his fiction debut with his next book, 1992's *When Nietzsche Wept: A Novel of Obsession.* The novel is set in Vienna in 1882, and the main conceit is a number of fictional meetings between Freidrich Nietzsche, the German philosopher who wrote *Also sprach Zarathustra* and forwarded the theory of the superman, and Josef Breuer, an Austrian physician who was psychoanalyst Sigmund Freud's mentor. Nietzsche is ill and depressed, and Breuer is anguished over his unsatisfying domestic life, his inability to find his life's meaning, and his obsession with a former patient, Bertha Pappenheim. Known as "Anna O.," Pappenheim was an actual patient of Breuer's, and in his treatment of her he made the revolutionary discovery that her neurotic symptoms vanished when thought processes hidden in the unconscious mind were made conscious through hypnotism. At the request of the intellectual Lou Andreas Salome, Breuer admits Nietzsche to the sanitarium in order, Nietzsche believes, to treat his physical ailments—migraine headaches, insomnia, nausea, dizziness—but actually to cure his mental despair, made more acute by Salome, who had recently ended her relationship with the philosopher. In return for Breuer's care, Nietzsche uses the philosophy he is cultivating to care for Breuer's own despondency. Breuer turns to the young Freud for help in establishing a way to help Nietzsche, but the sessions go slowly at first because Nietzsche is convinced that his philosophic ability is derived from his pain. The novel relates the struggle each of the men experiences and the help each eventually receives. In *Publishers Weekly,* Yalom explained to an interviewer, "In the Nietzsche book I suggest that real healing doesn't happen until there's true rapprochement, until the duplicity ends and the two can reveal themselves, one to the other."

"*When Nietzsche Wept* is fascinating for its friendly portrait of the chess match that is psychoanalysis at work, but there is a further attraction in its harvest of Freidrich Nietzsche's ideas on the four great dilemmas of human existence: death, freedom, loneliness, and the problem of finding meaning in life," commented Ron Hansen in the *Los Angles Times Book Review.* "Yalom's own shrewd intellectual thriller succeeds because of his informed insights into existential thought and the birth of psychoanalysis, and because he had the good novelist's instinct to let his brilliant characters be who they are, and talk." The *Chicago Tribune* critic Joseph Coates, despite his criticisms of Yalom's novelistic skills and patches of ineffective dialogue, wrote, "*When Nietzsche Wept* is the best dramatization of a great thinker's thought since [Jean-Paul] Sartre's *The Freud Scenario,*" and concluded that readers will finish the book because they will "[realize] that Nietzsche's thought is what all of us live, whether we want to or not."

BIOGRAPHICAL/CRITICAL SOURCES:

BOOKS

Bestsellers 90, Issue 1, Gale, 1990, pp. 80-83.

PERIODICALS

Globe and Mail (Toronto), September 9, 1989.
Los Angeles Times Book Review, December 28, 1980; September 9, 1990, p. 14; August 23, 1992, pp. 3, 7.
New York Times, September 6, 1989, p. C19.
New York Times Book Review, September 3, 1989, p. 5; September 30, 1990, p. 46; August 9, 1992, p. 21.
Publishers Weekly, August 17, 1992, pp. 397-98.
Times Educational Supplement, March 8, 1991, p. 30.

Tribune Books (Chicago), August 20, 1989; July 26, 1992, p. 4.
Washington Post Book World, August 13, 1989, p. 3; July 26, 1992, p. 2.
WB, September/October, 1989, pp. 17, 24.*

—*Sketch by Roger M. Valade III*

*   *   *

YELTSIN, Boris (Nikolayevich)   1931-

PERSONAL: Born February 1, 1931, in Sverdlovsk, U.S.S.R. (now Russia). *Education:* Graduated from the Urals M. Kirov Polytechnic Institute with a degree in engineering, 1955.

ADDRESSES: Office—The Kremlin, Moscow, Russia.

CAREER: Joined the Communist party in 1961. Worked in various positions for the party, 1968-76. Appointed first secretary of the Sverdlovsk District Central Committee, 1976; secretary of the national Central Committee for Construction, 1985; first secretary of the Moscow City Party Committee (mayor of Moscow), 1985; named as non-voting member of the Politburo, 1986; resigned Politburo seat, October, 1987, and fired by Mikhail Gorbachev from post as mayor, November, 1987; elected to Congress of People's Deputies of the Soviet Union, 1989; quit Communist Party, July, 1990; elected president of the Russian Federation, November, 1990.

WRITINGS:

Against the Grain (autobiography), Summit Books, 1990.
(Author of introduction) Ron McKay, editor, *Letters to Gorbachev: Life in Russia Through the Postbag of Argumenty I Fakty,* Viking, 1991.

SIDELIGHTS: Russian President Boris Yeltsin has been one of the most instrumental figures in the changes that have turned the Soviet Union into a group of independent nations. First rising through the ranks of the Communist Party, then repudiating it under the new openness fostered by Mikhail Gorbachev, Yeltsin protested against Party officials' abuse of power and privilege, thus making him a favorite of the Russian people. When free elections were introduced in the Soviet Union, Yeltsin was elected first to the new Soviet Parliament, the Congress of People's Deputies, in 1989, and then president of the Russian Federation in 1990. In this capacity, he led the resistance against a coup attempt by Communist hard-liners in 1991 and helped obtain the release of Prime Minister Gorbachev, who was held prisoner during the coup. Once the coup was put down, Yeltsin pressured Gorbachev to resign his post and dissolve the Soviet Union. When this had been accomplished, Yeltsin, as leader of the Russian Federation, the most powerful country in the former Soviet Union, became, in some ways, Gorbachev's successor on the international scene. *Against the Grain,* Yeltsin's autobiography, recounts the obstacles he encountered in his rise to prominence, as well as detailing other major events in his life.

Yeltsin was born in Sverdlovsk, in the Ural Mountains of the Soviet Union, on February 1, 1931. From the beginning, Yeltsin was inclined to go against authority. When he was eleven years old, he and a friend stole hand grenades from a nearby weapons warehouse. One of them exploded, causing Yeltsin to lose the thumb and forefinger of his left hand. A few years later, upon the occasion of his eighth-grade graduation, he grabbed the microphone during the ceremony and denounced the head teacher, calling for his dismissal. Though Yeltsin was supposed to be barred from continuing his education as punishment for this action, he managed to get reinstated.

Yeltsin went on to study engineering at a polytechnic institute in the Urals. After his graduation, he worked as a construction engineer, directing building projects from the mid-1950s to the late-1960s. In 1961, inspired by the reforms being instituted by then-Soviet Premiere Nikita Khrushchev, Yeltsin joined the Communist Party. By 1968 he was doing work for the party, serving as deputy head and then secretary of the Sverdlovsk District Central Committee. Yeltsin eventually rose to First Secretary of that committee—a position similar to being the mayor of Sverdlovsk—and at this post he first gained a reputation as a reformer.

In 1985 Yeltsin's reputation gained the attention of then-newly named general secretary of the Communist Party, Gorbachev. Impressed, Gorbachev brought Yeltsin to Moscow as secretary of the national Central Committee for Construction, then quickly promoted him to secretary of the Moscow City Party Committee. This was, again, a position similar to mayor, but this time Yeltsin was mayor of the capital of the Soviet Union, Moscow. By the following year, Yeltsin had been named as a non-voting member of the Politburo, the decision-making arm of the Communist Party, where he promptly aligned himself with Gorbachev's reformers.

In the meantime, he had also begun cleaning up Moscow's local political bureaucracy, firing many corrupt officials. Yeltsin encouraged a freer press as well, and promoted the adoption of private markets to replace the U.S.S.R.'s state-controlled economy. He tried to ensure better food supplies for the city's population, and he spoke out against the special privileges—such as limousines, elegant vacation homes, and exotic delicacies—given to the Party elite. Yeltsin later revealed in his autobiography, *Against the Grain,* that when he was offered the use of Gorbachev's

old country vacation home, or *dacha,* he was deeply shocked and refused the offer. "As long as no one can build or buy his own dacha, as long as we continue to live in such relative poverty, I refuse to eat caviar followed by sturgeon," he declared. "I will not race through the streets in a car that can ignore traffic lights. I cannot swallow excellent imported medicine knowing that my neighbor's wife can't get an aspirin for her child. Because to do so is shameful."

It soon became clear to most observers that Gorbachev's reforms were not coming fast enough for Yeltsin. He began publicly criticizing Gorbachev and other party leaders, particularly conservative Yegor Ligachev, for the inactivity of their bureaucracy. Most notably, he made a speech in October, 1987, to the Communist Central Committee, in which he took its leadership to task. Yeltsin's remarks angered Gorbachev, and the Soviet leader forced Yeltsin to resign from his Moscow position and threw him out of the Politburo. The following month, while Yeltsin was hospitalized for a heart condition, he was forced from his bed to apologize for the speech before the Moscow party organization. Friends and foes alike thought that this was the end of Yeltsin's political career.

Perhaps because of Yeltsin's popularity with the people, however, Gorbachev offered him the face-saving but relatively powerless position of deputy chairman of the State Construction Committee. Though he was barred from politics by Gorbachev, the Soviet people protested on his behalf. And when the Soviet Union began to allow free elections in 1989, Yeltsin ran for and won a seat on the Soviet Congress of People's Deputies. In this position, in addition to providing continuing opposition to Gorbachev and other mainline Communist Party members, Yeltsin toured the United States, gaining attention for his views in the West.

At about this time, Yeltsin was also busy composing his autobiography, *Against the Grain.* The volume alternates between a diary of his 1989 campaign for the Congress of People's Deputies and an account of his earlier life, including his childhood battles with his father, skipping school to hike in Siberia for two months, and his conflicts within the Communist Party. Critic Christopher Lehmann-Haupt of the *New York Times* declared *Against the Grain* a "rambunctious, free-swinging and altogether absorbing book," and John Cruickshank, reviewing the work in the Toronto *Globe and Mail,* explained that "what Yeltsin provides" in *Against the Grain* "is not an articulated program of reform or a convincing ideological critique of the present Soviet government. He offers instead a promise of strength, boldness, and a heroic approach to politics. And he tars virtually all other members of the Soviet ruling class—his potential rivals—with accusations of corruption and elitism."

The "promise" Cruickshank wrote of would seem to have been fulfilled. In 1990 Yeltsin was elected President of the Russian Federation, and a short time later, left the Communist Party. The following year found him bravely leading efforts to stop a coup by communist hard-liners to overthrow Gorbachev's government; millions of viewers around the world saw news footage of Yeltsin standing on top of a tank, facing the military forces of the coup and turning them away from the Russian Republic's headquarters. Once Gorbachev was restored to power and the government stabilized, Yeltsin was instrumental in the changes that led to the dissolution of the Communist Party and the breakup of the Soviet Union into independent republics. These efforts forced Gorbachev from power, increasing Yeltsin's influence. As Russia grappled with further economic and social reforms in the 1990s, Boris Yeltsin continued to be an important player in the country's ongoing transition from totalitarian superpower to democratic republic.

BIOGRAPHICAL/CRITICAL SOURCES:

BOOKS

Newsmakers: The People Behind Today's Headlines, 1991 Cumulation, Gale, 1992.
Yeltsin, Boris, *Against the Grain,* Summit Books, 1990.

PERIODICALS

Globe and Mail (Toronto), April 21, 1990.
Los Angeles Times Book Review, April 8, 1990, pp. 1, 11.
New York Times, March 15, 1990.
New York Times Book Review, March 25, 1990, p. 3.
Times (London), March 10, 1990.
Times Literary Supplement, May 4, 1990, p. 466.
Washington Post Book World, May 13, 1990, pp. 1, 4.*

—*Sketch by Elizabeth Wenning*

*　　*　　*

YUDELMAN, David 1944-

PERSONAL: Born September 20, 1944, in Johannesburg, South Africa; son of Jack (a retailer) and Anne (a bookkeeper; maiden name, Fisher) Yudelman; married, wife's name Pamela Jill (a teacher), December 13, 1977; children: Jonathan, Adam. *Education:* University of the Witwatersrand, B.A., 1964, B.A. (with honors), 1965; London School of Economics and Political Science, London, M.Sc., 1969; Yale University, Ph.D., 1977.

ADDRESSES: Home—153 Wolfrey Ave., Toronto, Ontario, Canada M4K 1L4. *Office*—Ontario Hydro, H19B1, 700 University Ave., Toronto, Ontario, Canada M5G 1X6.

CAREER: Rand Daily Mail, Johannesburg, South Africa, political and financial journalist, 1964-67; *Times,* London, England, political and financial journalist, 1967-70; *Financial Mail,* Johannesburg, political and financial journalist, 1970-72 and 1975-76; University of the Witwatersrand, Johannesburg, political scientist, beginning in 1979; Queen's University, Kingston, Ontario, senior research associate at Centre for Resource Studies, 1982-86, adjunct professor of political studies, 1985-86; Bank of Montreal, Montreal, Quebec, adviser on legislation and government, manager of policy analysis, and manager of information and analysis, 1986-89; Ontario Hydro, Toronto, planning officer, senior strategic projects officer, and section head of executive writing projects, 1989—. Frost & Sullivan (political risk analysts), associate, 1983-87; speechwriter. African Night School, teacher, 1962-67.

AWARDS, HONORS: Grant from Social Sciences and Humanities Research Council of Canada.

WRITINGS:

The Emergence of Modern South Africa, David Philip (Cape Town), 1982, Greenwood Press, 1983.
(Editor and contributor) *Financing Canadian Mining in the 1980s,* Centre for Resource Studies, Queen's University, Kingston, Ontario, 1984.
Political Risk in Extractive Industries, Volume II, Frost & Sullivan, 1985.
Canadian Mineral Policy, Past and Present, Centre for Resource Studies, Queen's University, Kingston, Ontario, 1985.
(With J. Crush and A. Jeeves) *South Africa's Labor Empire,* Westview, 1991.

WORK IN PROGRESS: The Great South African Erotic Novel, completion expected in 1994; *Forty Ways to Drive Your Parents Crazy,* with sons Jonathan and Adam Yudelman, 1994; *The Perverse in the Ivy League,* 1995.

SIDELIGHTS: David Yudelman told *CA:* "I found out early in life that I could rarely understand anything complex until I had written about it. Since I need to understand, I need to write. The two things I most urgently need to understand have always been, though it took a while before I could frame them in terms of grand abstraction, power and the perverse.

"Thus, I have written extensively about South Africa, my country of birth, where the issue of power is particularly problematic. The focus of this writing, essentially, has been the symbiotic relationship of political and economic power. There has been a consensus among reviewers that the major achievement of this body of work is that it provides a new way of looking at and analyzing South Africa. It tries to steer an independent path from the disputes raging from the 1970s to the 1990s between various schools of nationalist, Marxist, and liberal thought, and rejects the theory that South Africa is *sui generis* and not, therefore, susceptible to comparative analysis. Reviewers have said that my work has had a major impact, not only in its own subject area, but also in the conceptual approach it has opened to others in entirely different areas. I think that's the reason I still get invited to present papers on historical and contemporary topics, in South Africa and elsewhere, even though I have been devoting less and less time to original research on those topics since the late 1980s.

"I have also written fairly extensively and somewhat less passionately about the relationship of political and economic power in Canada, especially the relationship of natural resource industries to government.

"My fascination with the role of power extends to individual relationships as well. In fact, though I have little to show for it as a writer, I probably have a deeper interest in this, and in the perverse, than in the topics on which I have published. To understand them I have begun to write about them, but I am still searching for the right genre. I believe I will write far more significant fiction than academic analysis, journalism, or rhetoric; but I know that writing fiction as a profession will require far more self-discipline than I've had to display in any of the many and varied salaried jobs I've had to date. I've done my best writing during all-nighters, never stayed too long in one job, and rarely returned to the same type of job, but I have almost always worked in the protective confines of some external deadline or discipline.

"Many convicts fear freedom as much as they yearn for it. I hate to admit it, but I share their ambivalence."

*   *   *

YUILL, Nicola M. 1965-

PERSONAL: Born June 28, 1965, in Sheffield, Yorkshire, England; children: William. *Education:* University of Sussex, B.A., 1980, D.Phil., 1984.

ADDRESSES: Office—School of Cognitive and Computing Sciences, University of Sussex, Falmer, Brighton BN1 9QH, England.

CAREER: University of Sussex, Falmer, Brighton, England, research fellow in experimental psychology, 1983-86, lecturer in psychology, 1988—; Cambridge University, Cambridge, England, research fellow in Unit on the Development and Integration of Behaviour, 1986-88.

MEMBER: British Psychology Society (associate fellow), Experimental Psychology Society.

WRITINGS:

(With Jane Oakhill) *Children's Problems in Text Comprehension: An Experimental Investigation,* Cambridge University Press, 1991.

Contributor to books, including *Handbook of Educational Ideas and Practices,* edited by N. Entwistle, Routledge & Kegan Paul, 1990; *Dyslexia: Integrating Theory and Practice,* edited by M. Snowling and M. Thomson, Whurr, 1991; and *The Child as Psychologist,* edited by M. Bennett, Harvester, 1993. Contributor to periodicals, including *British Journal of Developmental Psychology* and *International Journal of Behavioural Development.*

WORK IN PROGRESS: Research on children's conceptions of desires, dispositions, and personality; research on methods for improving children's text comprehension; research on the effect of studying psychology on "naive theories of personality."

SIDELIGHTS: Nicola M. Yuill told *CA:* "My main current research activity concerns children's developing understanding of the concept of a personality disposition. The research involves the analysis of adults' use of such terms and empirical study of children's explanations of individual differences and the time course of traits. I am focusing on two issues: the concept of a trait as explanatory and the coherence of explanations couched in terms of traits. I am also studying children's understanding of desire and disposition.

"A further interest is children's judgements of emotion and morality, investigating the different bases on which such judgments are made. For example, some work suggests that young children judge emotions on an apparently selfish basis: a person is pleased to get what he or she desires, regardless of whether it hurts someone else. Older children appear to consider social emotions such as guilt in judging emotions; however, my current research suggests that young children are able to adopt different stances in flexible ways. I am using such results in an attempt to describe young children's conception of desire, and to account for the ways children's judgments change with age.

"I will shortly be doing further experimental work on children's text comprehension, in particular the relation between comprehension skill and working memory. I also have an interest in methods of improving text comprehension, and have developed and tested a program to develop skills in comprehension monitoring and awareness of linguistic inference, which I hope to extend at some future date.

"My passive research interests are in the general areas of social cognitive development and psycholinguistics/reading, and include cross-cultural developmental psychology, language and the attribution of responsibility, and moral development."

* * *

ZEVELOFF, Samuel I. 1950-

PERSONAL: Born May 2, 1950, in New York, NY; son of Harold and Muriel (Rubins) Zeveloff; married Linda Kass, August 19, 1973; children: Abigail, Naomi, Susannah. *Education:* State University of New York at Binghamton, B.A., 1972; City College of the City University of New York, M.S.Ed., 1973; North Carolina State University, M.S., 1976; University of Wyoming, Ph.D., 1982.

ADDRESSES: Office—Department of Zoology, Weber State University, Ogden, UT 84408-2505.

CAREER: Science teacher at intermediate and secondary schools in New York City, 1972-74; North Carolina State University, Raleigh, instructor in zoology, 1976-78; University of Wyoming, Laramie, instructor in zoology, 1982; North Carolina State University, visiting assistant professor of zoology, 1982-84; Weber State University, Ogden, UT, assistant professor, 1984-86, associate professor, 1986-87, professor of zoology and chairperson of department, 1987—, coordinator of North American Interdisciplinary Wilderness Conference, 1989-91, representative at Oxford Polytechnic, Oxford, England, 1991. Cambridge University, invited visiting scholar, 1991.

MEMBER: American Society of Mammalogists, Council on Undergraduate Research, Sigma Xi, Phi Kappa Phi.

AWARDS, HONORS: Grant from National Science Foundation, 1985.

WRITINGS:

Mammals of the Intermountain West, University of Utah Press, 1988.
(Senior editor with C. M. McKell, and contributor) *Wilderness Issues in the Arid Lands of the Western United States,* University of New Mexico Press, 1992.
(Senior editor with L. M. Vause and W. H. McVaugh, and contributor) *Wilderness Tapestry: An Eclectic Approach to Preservation,* University of Nevada Press, 1992.

Work represented in anthologies, including *Evolution of Life Histories of Mammals: Theory and Pattern,* edited by M. S. Boyce, Yale University Press, 1988; and *Great Debates and Ethical Issues,* edited by R. Holt and R. Conover, Weber State College Press, 1989. Contributor to professional journals and popular magazines, including *American Naturalist, Colorado Outdoors,* and *Nature.*

WORK IN PROGRESS: "The Evolution of Altriciality" in *Trends in Ecology and Evolution.*

ZWEIG, David 1950-

PERSONAL: Born November 30, 1950, in Toronto, Ontario, Canada; son of Robert Isaac (a manufacturer) and Belma Speigal (a manufacturer; maiden name, Jacobson) Zweig; married Joy Poretzky (a merchandiser), May 4, 1992; children: Rachel Ilana. *Education:* York University, B.A. (with honors), 1972, M.A., 1974; Beijing Languages Institute, degree, 1975; Beijing University, degree, 1976; University of Michigan, Ph.D., 1983.

ADDRESSES: Home—139-3 Cushing St., Cambridge, MA 02138. *Office*—Fletcher School of Law and Diplomacy, Tufts University, Medford, MA 02155.

CAREER: Florida International University, Miami, FL, lecturer, 1982-83, assistant professor, 1983-84; University of Waterloo, Waterloo, Ontario, Canada, assistant professor, 1985-86; Tufts University Fletcher School of Law and Diplomacy, Medford, MA, assistant professor, 1986-90, associate professor of international politics, 1990—. Nanjing University, visiting research scholar, 1986 and 1991-92; Harvard University Fairbank Center for East Asian Research, associate in research, 1986—, member of executive committee, 1990-91; University of International Business, visiting research scholar, 1992. Conference coordinator and conductor of seminars; commentator for radio and television.

MEMBER: Canadian Institute for International Affairs, American Political Science Association, Association for Asian Studies.

AWARDS, HONORS: Sino-Canadian student exchange fellow, Association of Universities and Colleges of Canada and Department of External Affairs, 1974-76; doctoral fellow, Social Sciences and Humanities Research Council of Canada, 1981-82; postdoctoral fellow, Harvard University Fairbank Center for East Asian Research, 1984-85; research grants from Social Sciences and Humanities Research Council of Canada, 1985-86 and 1992-95; Henry Luce Foundation, 1989-91; and Ford Foundation, 1992-93; Advanced Scholars Program for Study in the People's Republic of China fellow, Committee on Scholarly Communication with the People's Republic of China, 1991-92.

WRITINGS:

Agrarian Radicalism in China, 1968-1981, Harvard University Press, 1989.
(Editor with William A. Joseph and Christine Wong) *New Perspectives on China's Cultural Revolution,* Harvard University Press, 1991.
(Editor with Suzanne Ogden, Kathleen Hartford, and Lawrence Sullivan) *China's Search for Democracy: The Student and Mass Movement of 1989,* M. E. Sharpe, 1992.

Contributor to books, including *Chinese Rural Development: The Great Transformation,* edited by William L. Parish, M. E. Sharpe, 1985; *Everyday Forms of Peasant Resistance,* edited by Forrest Colburn, M. E. Sharpe, 1990; *Building Sino-American Relations: An Agenda for the 1990s,* edited by William Tow, Paragon Press, 1991; and *China Briefing 1991,* edited by William A. Joseph, Westview Press, 1992. Contributor of articles and essays to periodicals, including *China Quarterly, Peasant Studies, Journal of Northeast Asian Studies, China Business Review, Harvard International Review, Boston Globe, New York Times,* and *Asian Wall Street Journal.*

WORK IN PROGRESS: Internationalizing China: The Domestic Political Economy of China's Open Policy; researching "China's Brain Drain in the U.S. and Canada."

SIDELIGHTS: David Zweig told *CA:* "When I was twenty-one I had two choices in front of me: become a lawyer or go to graduate school and study China. In envisioning the first, I saw myself ten years later, married, with two kids, and living in the suburbs of Toronto. The second option seemed much more exciting. I have never regretted the choice. I lived in China for four years, which enabled me to watch the emergence of China from the radical, Maoist insanity to a more open, more personal society. I am currently writing my second book about China. I follow the lives of my urban and rural friends as they grow wealthier and their lives grow more comfortable. Yet even in this current open and rapidly developing period, there is a frenzy that is all China's. The country's deeply entrenched desire to grow rapidly will make it a model for others to study, but it will also bring new competition and crises that are uniquely Chinese. The future is worth watching."